THE WORLD IS
WHAT IT IS

PATRICK FRENCH

THE WORLD IS
WHAT IT IS

The Authorized Biography of V.S. Naipaul

VIKING
CANADA

VIKING CANADA

Published by the Penguin Group

Penguin Group (Canada), 90 Eglinton Avenue East, Suite 700, Toronto, Ontario, Canada M4P 2Y3
(a division of Pearson Canada Inc.)

Penguin Group (USA) Inc., 375 Hudson Street, New York, New York 10014, U.S.A.
Penguin Books Ltd, 80 Strand, London WC2R 0RL, England
Penguin Ireland, 25 St Stephen's Green, Dublin 2, Ireland (a division of Penguin Books Ltd)
Penguin Group (Australia), 250 Camberwell Road, Camberwell, Victoria 3124, Australia
(a division of Pearson Australia Group Pty Ltd)
Penguin Books India Pvt Ltd, 11 Community Centre, Panchsheel Park, New Delhi – 110 017, India
Penguin Group (NZ), 67 Apollo Drive, Rosedale, North Shore 0745, Auckland, New Zealand
(a division of Pearson New Zealand Ltd)
Penguin Books (South Africa) (Pty) Ltd, 24 Sturdee Avenue, Rosebank, Johannesburg 2196, South Africa

Penguin Books Ltd, Registered Offices: 80 Strand, London WC2R 0RL, England

Published in Canada by Penguin Group (Canada), a division of Pearson Canada Inc., 2008
First published in the UK by Picador, an imprint of Pan Macmillan Ltd, 2008

1 2 3 4 5 6 7 8 9 10 (RRD)

Manufactured in the U.S.A.

Typeset by SetSystems Ltd, Saffron Walden, Essex

LIBRARY AND ARCHIVES CANADA CATALOGUING IN PUBLICATION

French, Patrick, 1966–
The world is what it is : the authorized biography of V.S. Naipaul / Patrick
French.

ISBN 978-0-670-04529-7

1. Naipaul, V. S. (Vidiadhar Surajprasad), 1932–. 2. Authors, Trinidadian—20th
century—Biography. 3. Authors, English—20th century—Biography. I. Title.

PR9272.9.N32Z69 2008   823'.914   C2008-902646-2

British Library Cataloguing in Publication data available

Visit the Penguin Group (Canada) website at **www.penguin.ca**

Special and corporate bulk purchase rates available; please see **www.penguin.ca/corporatesales**
or call 1-800-810-3104, ext. 477 or 474

MG

Contents

PART TWO

List of Illustrations

SECOND SECTION

Introduction

When V.S. Naipaul won the Nobel Prize in Literature in 2001, each country responded in its own way. The president of the Republic of Trinidad and Tobago sent a letter of congratulation on heavy writing paper; an Iranian newspaper denounced him for spreading venom and hatred; the Spanish prime minister invited him to drop by; India's politicians sent adulatory letters, with the president addressing his to 'Lord V.S. Naipaul' and the Bollywood superstar Amitabh Bachchan sending a fax of congratulation from Los Angeles; the *New York Times* wrote an editorial in praise of 'an independent voice, skeptical and observant'; the British minister for 'culture, media and sport' sent a dull, late letter on photocopying paper, and BBC *Newsnight* concentrated on Inayat Bunglawala of the Muslim Council of Britain, who thought the award 'a cynical gesture to humiliate Muslims'.[1] At this point in British history, when the sensational and immediate mattered above all else and fame was becoming more important than the achievements that might give rise to fame, Naipaul's half-century of work as a writer seemed less significant than his reputation for causing offence.

'My background is at once exceedingly simple and exceedingly confused,' he suggested in his Nobel lecture.[2] When slavery was abolished across the British empire, workers were still needed for the sugar plantations, and in India his destitute forebears were sent to the Caribbean as bonded labourers; it was slavery by another name, slavery with an expiry date. Vidia Naipaul, born in rural poverty in colonial Trinidad in 1932, would rise from this unpromising setting to become one of the great writers of the twentieth century. This achievement does not mean that all his writing was good, or that his behaviour was exemplary, but rather that his cumulative accomplishment outstripped his contemporaries, and altered the way in which writers and readers perceived the world. Using simple sentences, he would look at complex modern subjects: extremism, global migration, political and religious identity, ethnic difference, the implosion of Africa, the resurgence of Asia and the remaking of the old European dispensation in the aftermath of empire. His achievement was an act of will, in which every situation and relationship would be subordinated to his ambition. His public position as a novelist and chronicler was inflexible at a time of intellectual relativism: he stood for high civilization, individual rights and the rule of law.

This was not an unusual position for someone of his background to be taking, but in Europe in the early twenty-first century it became extraordinary, aided by Naipaul's tendency to caricature himself in public, outside his books. He said, or was said to have said, that Africa had no future, Islam was a calamity, France was fraudulent and interviewers were monkeys. If Zadie Smith of *White Teeth* fame – optimistic and presentable – was a white liberal's dream, V.S. Naipaul was the nightmare. Rather than celebrate multiculturalism, he denounced it as 'multi-culti', made malign jokes about people with darker skin than himself, blamed formerly oppressed nations for their continuing failure and attacked Prime Minister Tony Blair as a pirate who was imposing a plebeian culture on Britain. The only Blacks he associated with now were Conrad and Barbara. For a successful immigrant writer to take such a position was seen as a special kind of treason, a betrayal of what should be a purely literary genius. The critic Terry Eagleton complained 'Great art, dreadful politics' while the reggae poet Linton Kwesi Johnson said, 'He's a living example of how art transcends the artist 'cos he talks a load of shit but still writes excellent books.'[3] Naipaul's outrageous denunciations were less interesting than the work which preceded them. A parallel might be drawn with Albert Einstein when he discoursed on socialism rather than concentrating on science, or with Aleksandr Solzhenitsyn, who identified the crimes of Soviet communism at a time when serious people were seeking to ignore them but in old age took to railing against amorphous ills, like consumerism. Solzhenitsyn once commented: 'In the West, one must have a balanced, calm, soft voice; one ought to make sure to doubt oneself, to suggest that one may, of course, be completely wrong. But I didn't have the time to busy myself with this.'[4]

Naipaul was initially unwilling to take the call from Stockholm, since he was cleaning his teeth. When the secretary of the Nobel committee got him on the line, he enquired, 'You're not going to do a Sartre on us, and refuse the prize?' Naipaul accepted, and put out a statement that the Nobel was, 'a great tribute to both England, my home, and India, the home of my ancestors.' There was no mention of Trinidad. Asked why not, he said it might 'encumber the tribute', which provoked the Barbadian writer

George Lamming, an ancient rival, to suggest Naipaul was 'playing ole mas', meaning he was masquerading or making trouble for his own entertainment, a Trinidadian trait. I noticed that when he was being rude or provocative in this way, Naipaul was full of glee. Creating tension, insulting his friends, family or whole communities left him in excellent spirits. He might for instance, on the basis of a photograph in the *Daily Mail*, denounce Queen Elizabeth's granddaughter Zara Phillips for having a 'criminal face', or say that a friend's daughter was 'a fat girl, and she did what fat girls do, she married a Zulu', or accuse a journalist of 'doing disreputable things like mixing with Bengalis – and other criminals.'[5] Later, after I had visited Trinidad, I realized this style of conversation was not rare in the Caribbean. It was what Trinidadians call 'picong', from the French 'piquant', meaning sharp or cutting, where the boundary between good and bad taste is deliberately blurred, and the listener sent reeling.

Around this time, I was asked to write V.S. Naipaul's biography. I was hesitant; I was finishing another book, and saw it would be a big and potentially fraught project, perhaps the last literary biography to be written from a complete paper archive. His notebooks, correspondence, handwritten manuscripts, financial papers, recordings, photographs, press cuttings and journals (and those of his first wife, Pat, which he had never read) had in 1993 been sold to the University of Tulsa in Oklahoma, a place famous for its hurricanes and the worst race riot in America's history.[6] The archive ran to more than 50,000 pieces of paper. I told V.S. Naipaul that I would only want to write a biography if I could use material at Tulsa that was closed to public access, and quote from it freely. I would need to interview him at length. My intention was to end the biography in 1996 as he entered his sixty-fifth year, a few months after Pat's death, rather than come too close to the distorting lens of the present. There was silence; then some months later a letter of acceptance came, written as if unwillingly in a fast, cramped hand, in violet ink. Over the five years since that letter, Naipaul has stuck scrupulously to our agreement; I have had no direction or restriction from him. He had the opportunity to read the completed manuscript, but requested no changes. When he was in Tulsa in 1994, Naipaul said in a speech, 'The lives of writers are a legitimate subject of inquiry; and the truth should not be skimped. It may well be, in fact, that a full account of a writer's life might in the end be more a work of literature and more illuminating – of a cultural or historical moment – than the writer's books.'[7]

I had met Naipaul a few times before this, once in England and later in Delhi while writing an article for the *New Yorker* magazine. Tarun Tejpal,

a friend who worked as a journalist, telephoned and invited me to a press
conference, saying he would collect me from my hotel in ten minutes. His
car, shabby against the grand hotel limousines, drew up under a colonnade.
I climbed into the back and noticed that I was sitting beside Sir Vidia
Naipaul. He was wearing many layers of clothing and a tweed jacket,
despite the heat. He held a trilby hat carefully in his lap. A roll-neck
sweater merged with his beard, completing the impression that he was fully
covered. Nadira, the second Lady Naipaul, was sitting in the front beside
Tarun. She asked me about the article I was writing, and I mentioned
some trouble I was having with the magazine's celebrated fact-checkers.
'Don't let the *New Yorker* worry you,' said Naipaul, enunciating each
syllable of each word in his modulating voice, part West Indian, part
Queen's English. 'The *New Yorker* knows nothing about writing. Nothing.
Writing an article there is like posting a letter in a Venezuelan postbox;
nobody will read it.' He paused, and continued, 'We were talking about
the funeral of Princess Diana.' The princess had died some months earlier.
'What were your thoughts about it?'

From everything I knew of Naipaul, I imagined he would hate the
sentiment swirling around the dead princess, and view her as another Evita
Perón. He was watching me through narrowed eyes with a would-be
benign smile – 'playin' dead to catch corbeau alive', to use the Caribbean
phrase. We were in a Delhi traffic jam by now, horns honking. I was jet-
lagged; I thought I might be honest.

'I found it moving. I liked seeing the British express their emotion in
public.'

There was silence.

'Oh,' he said in a distraught voice. His face went dark. 'Patrick, Patrick,
Patrick.'

Tarun looked at me nervously in the driver's mirror.

'Why, what did you think about it?' I asked.

He contemplated the question before answering.

'It filled me with shame – shame and disgust. The sort of disgust one
feels after visiting a prostitute, if you know what I mean. They had a man,
Mr John, doing the singing.' (I realized later that he was referring to Elton
John.) 'I had to walk across Kensington Gardens to my flat before the
funeral. I saw the flowers for her, wrapped in plastic, rotting in the sun. I
saw shrines. There were Negroes at the shrines, weeping, openly. Why
were they weeping? Why? Why were they weeping?'

He was almost shouting. Tarun was trying to stop himself from laughing. Nadira seemed both amused and exasperated. She turned and held her husband by the arm.

'That will do.'

She spoke to him as if he were a mischievous boy, and she were his mother.

It was, I came to see, a typically Naipauline performance: outrageous, funny, impossible.

If you reject the land that formed you, as Naipaul began to do actively in his thirties, you become defined by that rejection. It provides you with a struggle. 'You were born in Trinidad?' Bernard Levin asked in an interview in 1983. 'I was born there, yes,' came the reply, 'I thought it was a great mistake.'[8] Naipaul's dismissal of his homeland became part of his persona, a persona he invented in order to realize his early ambition to escape the periphery for the centre, to leave the powerless for the powerful, and to make himself a great writer. I sometimes thought of him as a man running up a beach with the advancing tide behind him, managing to stay a bare step ahead of the water. In order to become what he wanted to be, he had to make himself someone else. He could not remain regional. His ambition was linked to fear, as it often is in an author or creative artist: fear of failure, fear of not being able to write, fear of disappearance, fear of mental or physical breakdown, fear that people were trying to do him down, fear of being faced down, fear of losing face, fear of being found out. Repeatedly he had to re-create or mask himself, clearing away his past, in order to become the apparently stateless, hyper-perceptive global observer who could, as a book reviewer once put it, look into the mad eye of history and not blink. This took its psychological toll. In 1971 he told an interviewer that he had made a vow at an early age never to work for anyone. 'That has given me a freedom from people, from entanglements, from rivalries, from competition. I have no enemies, no rivals, no masters; I fear no one.'[9] Everyone has entanglements and rivalries, and Naipaul was to have many during the 1970s: his attempt to avoid them and become solely 'the writer' was itself an act of pre-emptive rejection, which arose from anxiety and fear.

His attempts to separate himself from the consequences of his own behaviour, and to present himself not as a person but as solely 'the writer', a figure who could in theory be studied objectively, was what made this biography possible. Opposing others, following his unique vision, apparently convinced his literary calling was hereditary and noble, was central to his idea of himself. It may have begun as a pose, but it was a mask that had eaten into the face. He once said to me, 'I was not interested and I remain completely indifferent to how people think of me, because I was serving this thing called literature.'[10] This remark was, in one sense, true. Intellectually he believed the truth should not be skimped in a biography, yet personally he felt obliged to guard himself. Even when speaking frankly about intensely personal subjects, he wore a shield of self-protection. During these interviews, his replies alternated between statements of absolute self-belief and defensive emotional fragility. Of all the people I spoke to for this book, he was outwardly the frankest. He believed that a less than candid biography would be pointless, and his willingness to allow such a book to be published in his lifetime was at once an act of narcissism and humility.

In Trinidad, V.S. Naipaul appeared to be admired as someone who had got ahead, who had taken on the outside world on his own terms, and won. This is not to suggest that admiration for him in the Caribbean islands was unmitigated. One man described him to me as a 'failed calypsonian'; a woman in a business centre threatened to attack me when I said I was writing about him; Anthony Petit, describing himself as 'aspiring author and head of the Triniwriters group', wrote to the *Trinidad Guardian* in 2003 to say the Nobel Prize winner did not deserve any respect from Trinidadians since, 'Anyone can write like Naipaul.' Petit thought that because 'the role model in question rejects his heritage, while using said heritage for advancement and accolade, we cannot but shake our heads sadly and turn elsewhere for solace and inspiration.'[11]

Despite this, and reciprocal barbs over the decades, Naipaul's achievement was a source of national pride. In Toco, at a hotel by the sea, a pair of calypso singers from Port of Spain were singing fast, funny songs with the aid of a small guitar to entertain the tourists. I asked one of them, Keith Eugene Davis, how he kept his material fresh.

'You feeling for some rum?'

I took the hint and bought him a drink.

'I tell you how. I read the newspapers.'

'Have you heard of a writer called V.S. Naipaul?' I asked.

'Man, course I heard of him.'

'Can you do a song about him?'

At once the guitar was in his hands, and he sang spontaneously:

> Now I must tell you after all,
> People know about V.S. Naipaul,

But is very sad to explain,
That man don't live in Trinidad again,
So now the facts I must unfold,
One of the best writers in the world,
But then I give you my view,
He was very international too,
So I think it very wise,
When they give him the Nobel Prize.[12]

Quotations from my interviews with V.S. Naipaul are threaded through this book. Where his statements are self-serving or eccentric, I have often let them stand without authorial intrusion, figuring the reader should be able to make a judgement. These conversations, conducted on an occasional basis at his house in rural Wiltshire over several years, were the strangest experience of my professional life. He could be angry, acute, open, self-pitying, funny, sarcastic, tearful – but he was always intense. I tended not to contradict him, preferring to let him talk. Early on, I realized that I risked being cast as the house liberal, a role I did not want. I found that a confrontational interview with Naipaul was apt to induce a fruitless hardening of his position or elusive generalization, which was in itself a form of game-playing or manipulation. I have left in his conversational repetitions, what has been called the Naipaul 'bis', after a term used in music (and modem protocols) to denote a repeat. It is not easy to describe the effect of this verbal tic. It has become part of his speech, and can be compelling and comic, arising from his resonant voice and the certitude with which he speaks, until refuted. I remember at a formal dinner after a conference seeing Naipaul being presented with a plate of what appeared to be meat (it was baked endive, hiding beneath a crust of melted cheese) and as the waiter attempted to set it before him, he said: 'That is *not* my food. That is not *my* food. *That* is not my food. That is not my *food*.' Each time he said the words, he altered their implication. When the confusion was explained to him, he accepted the plate meekly, saying 'Ah.'

My approach to writing biography is as it was when I began my first book. I wrote then that the aim of the biographer should not be to sit in judgement, but to expose the subject with ruthless clarity to the calm eye of the reader. Since writing about a writer for the first time, I have become more doubtful about the notion that an artistic creator should be expected to explain himself. Anyone who has written imaginatively will know that the process remains mysterious, even to the author, however hard you try to unpick it. Would Conrad, were he alive to answer, be able to say quite what Kurtz meant by 'The horror! The horror!'? The best writing can be examined only in its effect. Sometimes, a critic or biographer can see things the author cannot. In his Nobel lecture, V.S. Naipaul said that a writer's biography can never fully reveal the source of his books: 'All the details of the life and the quirks and the friendships can be laid out for us, but the mystery of the writing will remain. No amount of documentation, however fascinating, can take us there. The biography of a writer – or even the autobiography – will always have this incompleteness.'[13] I would go further: a biography can never fully reveal the source of its subject. The commonplace that a biographer has found the 'key' to a person's life – usually something arbitrary like the death of a sibling, or moving house – is implausible. People are too complicated and inconsistent for this to be true. The best a biographer can hope for is to illuminate aspects of a life and seek to give glimpses of the subject, and that way tell a story.

PATRICK FRENCH
London, December 2007

PART ONE

CHAPTER ONE

THE NEW WORLD

THE ISLANDS OF THE Caribbean dot and dash their way through the sea, linking different worlds. Central America joins the southern and northern hemispheres, taking you up through Colombia, Panama and Nicaragua by the land route until you reach Mexico, or down through the shallows of the Atlantic from Florida to the Bahamas, skirting Cuba and Jamaica, passing Haiti, the Dominican Republic and Puerto Rico, until you find yourself in the sprayed arc of islands known as the Lesser Antilles, some no more than a few miles across: Anguilla, Sint Maarten, Guadeloupe, Saint Lucia, Martinique, Grenada. At the tip of the chain lies a larger island which, beneath the sea or geologically, is part of the South American mainland. Almost square, with a low promontory at its south-western corner pointing to Venezuela, this is Trinidad.

In the summer of 1498, three ships approached the shores of the island.[1] The men on board were exhausted and burned by the sun, surviving off raisins, salt pork and sea biscuits, their supply of water running low. They were led by a white-haired voyager in his forties named Christoforo Colombo, known also as Christóbal Colón or Christopher Columbus. He was ill, his body inflamed and his eyes bleeding. It was Columbus's third voyage in search of Asia, and the one on which his future depended. A few months earlier, Vasco da Gama had reached Calicut, opening Europe's sea route to India. Renowned for his acute sense of smell, Columbus would have drunk in the lush, flowering vegetation of the island with its easy, humid, tropical climate, home to rainforests of bamboo and hardwood, flashing birds like the silver-beaked tanager, rivers, waterfalls and an array of caymans, snakes and beasts such as the nine-banded armadillo. There were no cocoa estates, no sugar-cane plantations, no breadfruit trees; Captain Bligh had yet to bring them from Tahiti. The only inhabitants were families of Amerindians who lived by farming and fishing, having paddled across the sea from the Orinoco river delta many centuries before.

Seeing three ranges of mountains running across the island, Columbus named it La Isla de la Trinidad after the Holy Trinity, in the
Christian way. Later that day his sailors landed on the south coast to
take on fresh water – the moment of first contact. Over the following
weeks they navigated neighbouring waters, and became the first Europeans to see the mainland of South America, the fresh green breast of
the New World. Columbus suspected as he charted the wide mouth of
the Orinoco river that he was on the edge of a continent rather than
another island. With his health failing, he ordered his ships to sail north
through the stretch of water between Trinidad and the mainland – the
Gulf of Paria – until they reached the island of Margarita.

The outbreak of the sixteenth century brought adventurers to the
island of Trinidad, who enslaved the indigenous Amerindians and sent
them to work in Spanish colonies overseas. The old world disappeared:
land was stolen, new settlements were made. The English, Dutch,
French and Spanish all battled and schemed for supremacy in the islands
of the West Indies. Using the legal formalities of the time, local chiefs
lost their inheritance and power. Sir Walter Raleigh, an English
marauder who raided Trinidad in 1595, found five desperate, dispossessed men in the custody of the Spaniards. They turned out to be 'the
last aboriginal rulers of the land, held together on one chain, scalded
with hot bacon fat, and broken by other punishments.'[2]

Nearly three centuries after the appearance of Columbus, Trinidad
had barely been colonized. By 1783 it had 126 whites, 259 free coloureds,
310 African slaves and 2,032 Amerindians.[3] To encourage settlement,
King Charles III of Spain offered land and tax breaks. Roman Catholics
of French descent moved from neighbouring islands, accompanied by
their slaves, and started farming cocoa, tobacco, cotton and sugar. By
1797, when the Spanish surrendered Trinidad to the British during the
French Revolutionary Wars, the population had risen to just under
18,000. In the nineteenth century, migrants flooded in, and by 1900
there were around 300,000 inhabitants. Unlike most other islands in the
West Indies, the people of Trinidad came from many different places:
there were Africans who spoke French creole or Yoruba, sailors and
indentured labourers from China, neighbouring Venezuelans, German
and French labourers, Syrian and Lebanese business families, wanderers
from Grenada and Barbados, residual Amerindians, visitors from
Madeira, demobbed black British army veterans, Portuguese and
Spanish-speaking farmers of uncertain ethnicity and free slaves from the

United States. Most Caribbean islands were homogenous by comparison, with white planters and black slaves, but Trinidad was uniquely and enduringly ethnically complex. Even its place names were various: Amerindian (Chaguanas), Spanish (San Fernando), French (Sans Souci) and British (Poole).

When slavery was formally abolished across the British empire in 1834 and cheap labour was needed for the sugar-cane plantations, malnourished Indians were shipped over from Calcutta and Madras. While the white planters of the West Indies had grown rich on sugar cane, their cousins in India had made fortunes from land revenues; and many beautiful houses were built in the English countryside. North India, under British control, was awash with dislocated, landless peasants. A voyage across the oceans and a stint as a bonded or indentured labourer was an alternative to destitution. In Trinidad, the newly arrived East Indians were nervous of the alien society in which they found themselves. They feared the island's black majority: Negroes seemed physically stronger, had rough manners and their dark skin identified them with the lower castes of Hinduism. The Negroes, for their part, came to regard these East Indians as heathens with peculiar customs who kept to themselves, were mean with money, cooked strange food and were servile to the plantation owners. Black agricultural labourers found their wages being undercut. They looked down on the Indians, who had to work long hours in the cane fields, as the 'new slaves'.

*

Christmas 1894: Picture the tropical island of Trinidad with its sandy beaches, bursting coconuts, leaping howler monkeys and freshwater mangrove swamps teeming with scarlet ibis. A ship approaches Nelson Island, a parched limestone islet overlooking the capital, Port of Spain. The passengers who have survived the three-month sea voyage from Calcutta are loaded into open rowing boats. Quickly, the holding barrack is filled with men, women and children, their names recorded in a ledger under the supervision of a government official, the Protector of Immigrants. Their possessions are fumigated. They are housed, both sexes, in a long shed lined with wooden bunks filled with hay, infested with mosquitoes and sandflies. Most are Hindus, driven to flight by starvation or debt or trickery. All are desperate. They do not even know where they have come to; all they know is the name of the hot place to which they have been

shipped, transposed into Hindi as 'Chinitat'. Soon, an overseer will come
from a plantation and indenture them as estate labourers, or coolies. The
Handbook of Trinidad and Tobago states that when visiting the colony,
'Elaborate tropical outfits are not necessary . . . For ladies, the same clothes
as would be worn during a hot English summer are suitable all the year
round.'[4] Photographs of these new arrivals from India show them dressed
almost in rags: a kurta and dhoti and light turban for the men, or a sari
with the *pallu*, or tail, of the sari draped over the head in modesty for the
women. These broken-down, thin-limbed immigrants with their tiny
bundles of possessions can only have made the journey to Trinidad as a
last resort.[5]

One man among the many – his name recorded as Kopil – is a
Brahmin, from a family of hereditary pundits in a village near Gorakhpur
on the Nepalese border with India. He has pretended to be from a different
background, since the recruiter back in India told him he might not be
accepted as a labourer if he admits to being from the highest caste. For
thirteen generations, Kopil's family have presided over the religious destiny
of their neighbourhood, reading the Sanskrit texts and lecturing on spiritual
practice to those who seek enlightenment. Wishing to study, he had walked
south to Benares, the sacred Hindu city on the banks of the Ganges, where
he met a recruiter who told him stories about the Caribbean, and how in
this far-off place he would be given a gold coin each day as a reward for
sifting sugar. If Kopil emigrated, he might even want to have a broad
canvas belt made in which to store the gold coins. He is brought to a
depot in Calcutta, and taken aboard the ship *Hereford*. At once, he feels his
difference from the other immigrants. On board ship, he finds a piece of
beef in his food. Although the voyage is terrible (forty people die from an
outbreak of cholera, their corpses thrown overboard) Kopil starves himself
for two days in horror at this contamination by cow meat, until the
surgeon-superintendent intervenes and he is given a separate daily ration
of raw potatoes and rice, which he cooks himself.

He reaches an island far from the large country and ancient civilization
he has left behind. It is Kopil's misfortune to be indentured to Woodford
Lodge in Chaguanas, an estate in central Trinidad where the regime is
especially severe. Each morning, to preserve his caste identity, he sets his
own pot of *khitchri* – rice and spiced lentils – on an earthen oven before
going to work. Kopil is assigned to the shovel gang, to digging and
planting. It breaks him. He is put on the weeding gang with the women
and children, and later made responsible for clearing the dung from the

animal pens, a sweeper's job. Kopil's health breaks. He is twenty-one years old, alone, a minority within a minority in the most fragmented place on earth. Then, by chance, an Indian *sirdar* – a driver or overseer – learns that he is a Brahmin and can read Sanskrit. Kopil might have some use; he can read the scriptures. The sirdar, a Bengali called Govinda, has a fifteen-year-old daughter, Soogee. A marriage is arranged, and Kopil is saved from extinction. Govinda 'cuts' Kopil – he pays the government a fee to buy him out of his indenture, and installs him in a small house near the Catholic church in Chaguanas. With Soogee, he will manage a general store for his father-in-law.

The shop does well. Decades pass. Kopil adjusts his name to the regal-sounding Capildeo Maharaj. He becomes renowned as a pundit, explaining sacred texts and duties at impromptu services, and conducting pujas or ceremonies. Sometimes he takes his congregation on a pilgrimage to the sea for religious bathing, the Atlantic standing in for the Ganges. With Soogee, he has nine surviving daughters and two sons, but spends much of his time alone, reading the scriptures and meditating. He is conscious of his status; once, when an illiterate pundit tries to officiate beside him at a wedding, he has the man sent away. Capildeo Maharaj is a good businessman too, trading goods on a return trip to India. He buys land in Chaguanas and employs labourers to grow rice, peas and eddoes, an edible root. Soogee persuades him to send the children, girls as well as boys, to a local school run by Canadian missionaries, despite his misgivings about Christianity. To display his new wealth, Capildeo Maharaj has a heavy gold necklace made for his son Simbhoonath, and builds a solid white house on the main road in Chaguanas with thick walls and pillars at the front, close to the railway station, the police station and the court house. It has a blank facade, blocking the view of any outsiders on the passing road, and is modelled on a building he remembers from Gorakhpur. He calls it Anand Bhavan, or the Abode of Bliss, after the family mansion of the Nehru family back in Allahabad. In 1926, Capildeo Maharaj sails to India to arrange a holiday for his family. While travelling back to his ancestral village, he is struck by a stomach ailment, and dies.

Not long after this Seepersad Naipaul, a twenty-two-year-old Brahmin from a poor family, is employed to paint a sign at the general store on the ground floor of Anand Bhavan. He likes the look of the sixteen-year-old girl behind the counter, Droapatie Capildeo. Not realizing she is a daughter of the house, he passes her a note. It is discovered, the formidable Soogee intervenes, and on 28 March 1929 Seepersad and Droapatie are married at the warden's office in Chaguanas.[6] They have a daughter, Kamla, the following year, and on 17 August 1932 their son Vidyadhar is born. He is named for a Chandela king, the dynasty which built the magnificent Hindu temples at Khajuraho in northern India. His name means 'giver of wisdom'. Back in the early eleventh century, King Vidyadhar had fought against Mahmud of Ghazni, the first of the infamous Muslim invaders of India. It was an apposite name for the boy. Years later, as V.S. Naipaul, he would say, 'It's such a grand name, a very special name – I cherished it for that reason. I think great things were expected of me.'[7]

*

How much of Capildeo's personal story, passed down as family lore, is true? Would this small, shrewd man have been so easily duped by the recruiter? Were his forefathers revered as pundits in their village? Were they even Brahmins? The name Capildeo sounds like a dialect rendition of Kapil Dev (he would have spoken in Bhojpuri, a language similar to Hindi used around Gorakhpur), a name which gives no indication of caste, and the suffix Maharaj was certainly bogus. How would he have cooked rice and potatoes on board ship, where the fire regulations were so strict? Why was Govinda so concerned that Capildeo was a Brahmin, and able to read Sanskrit, when he himself was a convert to Roman Catholicism? Might the marriage to Soogee have been essentially a practical arrangement, a recognition of Capildeo's talent for business? Was he really planning a holiday in India for his family when he died? Shortly before sailing he had mortgaged much of his land and left Soogee and his children; he was accompanied on the voyage by another woman, Jussodra, who was the wife of a man named Phagoo. Was the story that Seepersad Naipaul told his family about his accidental courtship (which his son Vidyadhar would one day fictionalize in *A House for Mr Biswas*) an elaboration or the reality?

The British imperial obsession with records and taxonomy means that a few facts about Capildeo Maharaj can be fixed. A man named Kopil arrived in Trinidad on the ship *Hereford* in 1894, and was indentured as a coolie at Woodford Lodge estate; someone paid for him to be 'cut' from his indenture. He gained a reputation as a pundit, and was an office-holder in the East Indian National Congress, a fledgling organization inspired by the rise of nationalism in India.[8] In 1913 he was listed on his daughter Droapatie's birth certificate as 'Capildoe Maraje, Hindoo Priest'.[9] He or his wife Soogee owned agricultural land around Chaguanas. Astonishingly, some lines of Capildeo's actual conversation survive, spoken in creolized

English and recorded by a member of his congregation, a man named Shiva: 'Siewah, just as a man haveam own mudder, man mus haveam own lan. You na have am own lan and house, you na own man at all. [Shiva, just as a man has his own mother, a man must have his own land. If you don't have land and a house, you are not a man.]'[10] It was a sentiment that might have been spoken, in standard English, by Mr Biswas.

In a society where everyone has been uprooted and people can invent their own past, many things become unstable. It is possible, though, to build up some sort of picture of the world in which Capildeo and Vidyadhar's other three grandparents lived. Caste had given a structure to Indian society for thousands of years. It was based on the Hindu idea of karma, where past actions in previous lives determined a person's status in the present. Pundits, learned Brahmin men with a knowledge of the Sanskrit teaching traditions, performed ritual duties in order to safeguard social order. At its best, caste gave a sense of identity and community; at it worst, it condemned people to a degraded life based on an inherited social position, and provided an excuse for inhuman cruelty. British classifications of the people of India in the eighteenth century gave rigidity to an ancient and flexible concept. The principal categories – Brahmins (priests, scholars), Kshatriyas (warriors, rulers), Vaishyas (traders), Shudras (labourers) and Untouchables (outcastes) – disguised fluidity between regions, centuries and subcastes. Local cultural variants, focusing for example on a particular deity, now appeared to be part of a larger, graded philosophy called Hinduism. Nor was caste an exclusively Hindu phenomenon: Indian Muslims, Sikhs and Christians all came to use it as a form of social stratification.

The first indentured Indian immigrants docked in Port of Spain in 1845. They were unpopular: a creole town councillor collected a petition against 'immoral heathens', saying they would be a drain on the taxpayer and might discourage Negro migration from neighbouring islands and the USA.[11] Trinidad's superintendent of prisons wrote that many coolies were guilty of 'gross idolatry' and cruel to their wives: 'As a general rule they have few good qualities, and are faithless, unprincipled, immoral, lazy, and fond of wandering . . . they are filthy in their habits, and have little care in regard to clothing.'[12] As an undeveloped plantation colony, the island needed labour if the sugar industry was to survive. The island's African slaves had moved to the towns and set up as tradesmen, dockers and domestic workers after emancipation.

Most indentured Indians came from parts of north India that were suffering famine, drought or social upheaval, such as Bihar, Punjab and the United Provinces (Awadh). The spread of European manufactured goods and changes in land-ownership after the decline of the Mughal empire meant that agricultural labourers, weavers and potters were often left destitute, particularly on the plains of the Ganges. In these uncertain times, caste affiliation became a means of securing a position. After their role in the Mutiny of 1857, Brahmins came to be perceived by the British as clever but pernicious, and less malleable than other groups.[13] At the time Capildeo was recruited, around 15 per cent of immigrants were from higher castes (Brahmin, Thakur, Rajput and Khatri), 34 per cent were from farming or artisan castes, 37 per cent were from lower or backward castes and 14 per cent were Muslim.[14] Whatever a person's background, migration overseas was never an easy choice: it would mean the end of village or community life, possible death during the three- to four-month sea voyage and theoretical loss of caste caused by crossing the 'kala pani', or black water.

A recruiter would pass through poor villages looking for those with no future; many recruits had stories of being coerced or drugged. They would be transported either on foot or by train to the Indian capital, Calcutta, where they would be sold to a sub-agent, who was often a Muslim or Jewish shopkeeper. The recruits were mustered at a high-walled depot by the Hooghly river, fed, inspected for disease and given clothes and a red woollen hat for the sea voyage. Often they would not understand each other: speakers of Marathi, Kashmiri, Telugu, Punjabi had no common tongue. Most single women who chose to emigrate were recruited from urban areas rather than villages, and in many cases they had already run away from home or a bad husband, or been expelled for a social transgression, and were seeking to avoid prostitution. At the dock in Calcutta a registering officer, usually a junior magistrate, recorded the migrant's name, sex, caste, village and occupation. It was a casual act of lasting significance: the name, written in roman script probably for the first time, would provide a label for their descendants. Each migrant would sign or thumbprint a document agreeing to be indentured. Their names were written down as they spoke them, and since there were no standard transliterations for Indian names, the spelling might indicate the regional pronunciation of the speaker or the ignorance of the registering officer. To someone with a knowledge of Indian names, these transliterations now seem bizarre and anglicized: thus (some of this is guesswork) Lutchman was Laxman, Beharry was Bihari, Gopaul was Gopal, Permanand was

Prem Anand, Teeluck was Tilak, Ramkissoon was Ram Krishna, Sammy was Swami, Gobin was Govinda, Capildeo was Kapil Dev and Seepersad was Shiv Parshad or Shiv Prasad.

Life on board the three-masted sailing ship meant a hundred days of torment. Leaving everything they knew, this first wave of the modern Indian diaspora sailed through the Bay of Bengal, round the rough sea at the Cape of Good Hope, past St Helena and through the Doldrums towards the West Indies. Hundreds of passengers might die from a contagious disease during a single voyage. They lived below decks in three compartments – men, women and couples – lit by fixed coconut-oil lamps, and in the daytime were allowed to come to the upper deck to walk, wrestle or engage in stick-fighting. Flogging was the standard punishment for disobedience. Discipline was enforced by the surgeon-superintendent, a British medical officer who was also responsible for supplying food, protecting the passengers' health and making sure the sailors, most of whom were Indian, did not molest them. The surgeon-superintendent received 'head money' for each migrant landed alive, and was answerable to the protector of immigrants.[15] On the plantation, coolies would start work at six in the morning, stop for breakfast at ten-thirty and continue work until four in the afternoon. They were paid a token wage of two to four shillings a week. At Woodford Lodge estate they would cut sugar cane, a rough, sharp, brutal crop, haul it to the refinery on ox-carts and move casks of sugar by barge to the road. Lack of women during the early days of indenture led to fights between men, often involving a cutlass, and rum-fuelled violence against women – including murder – became known as an Indian trait. Daily life was controlled by the sirdar, usually a physically imposing figure who spoke a little English and doubled as a moneylender. The barracks had wooden partitions: a 10 by 12-foot room was expected to house a married couple and children. Cooking was done out on a step. The plantation was a discrete world, without privacy or individuation. Wandering more than two miles from your designated estate was a criminal offence punishable by imprisonment. The Indian government retained a duty of care for indentured labourers, and the protector of immigrants issued an annual report on their condition. Although he was meant to represent their interests, court records show that the protector's loyalty usually lay with the planters, particularly regarding the brutal way in which discipline was enforced on the estates.[16]

Indenture differed from the formally defunct African slave trade in several vital respects. It was theoretically voluntary, and it was time-limited: after a period of five to ten years, the recruit would be given a small plot of land or a return passage to India. Crucially, families stayed together: under an ordinance from the Indian government, they were not allowed to be split up when they landed. This gave Indians a monumental historical advantage over Trinidadians of African descent. The emphasis in Indian culture on strong family and caste ties enabled them to retain and build a sense of community abroad. When their period of indenture expired, many Indians preferred to remain in Trinidad and take a grant of land, even if it was swamp. They worked the land and grew rice, sugar cane and coconuts; some kept cows, some sold milk. One witness at a Royal Commission in 1897 said the ambition of Indians in Trinidad was 'to buy a cow, then a shop, and say: "We are no niggers to work in cane fields." '[17] The agent of the Tennant family estates complained that a time-expired Indian employee would seek work wherever wages were highest: 'you cannot rely upon him with the certainty that you can rely on the indentured labourer.'[18]

When Capildeo Maharaj set sail for Trinidad in 1894, British rule was less than a hundred years old and Queen Victoria, the Empress of India, was approaching the end of her reign. In the crisp words of the *Handbook of Trinidad and Tobago*, 'The Colony does not possess responsible government. The government is administered by the Governor advised by an Executive Council, which consists of three *ex officio* members and such other members as may from time to time be appointed by the Governor.'[19] Security was provided by the paramilitary Trinidad Constabulary and the Trinidad Light Horse, which consisted of managers and sirdars from the estates. J.H. Collens, a British school superintendent who published *A Guide to Trinidad*, wrote that 'the Coolie is well shaped, with regular features, wiry, though not over-muscular, and possessing considerable powers of endurance. He is frugal and saving to a fault, living on the plainest and coarsest of diet, often denying himself sufficient even of this fare to gratify his love of hoarding.'[20] This emphasis on planning for the future was contrasted by colonial writers with the Negro tradition of living for the moment. Remarkably in 1889, a year after Collens published his guide to Trinidad, 12,549 Indian savers had between them deposited over £250,000 in local banks.[21]

Shortly before the First World War, the Indian government commissioned a survey on the condition of indentured labourers in Trinidad, British Guiana, Jamaica and Fiji. It found that barracks were made of wood with corrugated-iron roofing, and that the only drinking water was rainwater collected in tanks. There were few latrines, and people had to defecate in nearby fields. In rural Trinidad, disease was rife, particularly hookworm, malaria, dysentery and skin infections.[22] There was already growing opposition in India from Mohandas Gandhi and others to the practice of indenture. In a speech to the Indian National Congress, the nationalist politician G.K. Gokhale observed that indentured labour had been banned elsewhere, and asked: 'Why should India be marked out for this degradation?'[23] In 1917, after sending 144,000 people to Trinidad, the Indian government ended the system of indenture. Ethnic tensions grew now as their descendants asserted themselves economically and politically. Black soldiers had returned to Trinidad after the First World War inspired by the Universal Negro Improvement Association, founded by the Jamaican campaigner and racial separatist Marcus Garvey; Indians were stirred by Gandhi's freedom movement. From 1925, there was some elected representation on Trinidad's Legislative Council.

At the time of Vidyadhar's birth, the population of Trinidad stood at a little over 400,000, of whom about one-third were Indians, employed as agricultural labourers, merchants, spirit-vendors, clerks and shopkeepers. Few were lawyers, teachers or in government service. Indians had a higher death rate and a higher birth rate than any other social group. Unlike Chinese immigrants, they did not intermarry. The number of 'Indian Creoles' – meaning people with one Indian parent – was minuscule outside Port of Spain. Literacy in Trinidad stood at 57 per cent, balanced almost evenly between men and women; among Indians it stood at a pathetic 23 per cent, and among Indian women at 13 per cent. Only Christian converts had average levels of literacy, thanks to a Canadian Presbyterian mission which had the aim of 'Christianizing and educating' the Indians of Trinidad.[24] In popular legend in 1930s Trinidad, Indians were depicted as poor, mean, rural, heathen, aggressive, ethnically exclusive and illiterate. This, then, was the rough world into which Vidyadhar Naipaul was born.

CHAPTER TWO

IN THE LION HOUSE

VIDYADHAR'S EARLIEST MEMORIES were imagistic, fleeting, possibly imagined: the mauve uniform of a Negro nurse at the colonial hospital in Port of Spain as he was treated for pneumonia at the age of two, his hand held before an oil lamp with his young cousins to make the solid flesh turn transparent in the light, walking with his mother outside Anand Bhavan and seeing chickens in a ditch, pointing to them and saying, too young to pronounce the words, 'Mama, chiti!' Where, if anywhere, did he live as a child? After they married, his parents had moved to the market town of Tunapuna where his father worked as a sign-painter. Now, there was a hut behind his father's shop in Chase Village, but it was scarcely a home. Solidity was provided by Anand Bhavan, his birthplace, known as the 'Lion House' by the family because of the beastly sculpted shapes on the front balcony. Since the death of the patriarch Capildeo Maharaj, Soogee had made it a base for her nine daughters and their husbands and children, and for her two sons, Simbhoonath and Rudranath, of whom much was expected. Vidyadhar remembered moving between the shop in Chase Village and the Lion House in Chaguanas, standing by the roadside with his sister Kamla listening to a bus, wondering from the sound of the engine whether it was coming or going.

As he moved into comprehension, his memories became more complex. He was now known as Vido (pronounced vee-doe). Someone offered him a sweet. It looked like one of the glass marbles used to stop soda bottles in his father's shop, and he said no; but it was a real sweet. An image: friends of his father playing with loose gravel on a country road, squatting and pretending to find coins in the gravel; Vido knew the men were playing, and was captivated. Or: Vido and Kamla taking a length of sugar cane; he asked her to cut him a piece, and held the cane while she took a sickle or 'grass-knife' and cut. She nicked his thumb, blood flowed, and Kamla was punished by their father. Why did Pa punish his big sister when she had been doing what he asked?

'It was completely unfair.' Another memory: after visiting his father's 'peasant relations', Vido was laughed at by his cousins for speaking in dialect when he came back to the Lion House: 'I did bin there,' he said. Vido had an immediate sensitivity to language. Men were building a hut near his father's shop. 'They are treading the clay or earth for the walls. I think the clay would have been trodden with a mixture of grass to bind it, I'm not sure, and it was in a pit next to my father's house and one of the men said that he was very tired, he was feeling mashed up. And I associated that with the mashing that he was doing that day, with the treading of the clay.'[1]

'To Vidyadhar,' Pa wrote in a book of sentimental poetry for children, inscribing it self-consciously like a Victorian paterfamilias: 'From his <u>father</u>. Today you have reached the span of 3 years 10 months and 15 days. And I make this present to you with this counsel in addition. Live only to the estate of man, follow Truth, be kind & gentle and trust God.'[2] But Pa was not himself; he was in the midst of a breakdown. Four months after giving his son *The School of Poetry*, he took a copy of *Lessons in Truth: A Course of Twelve Lessons in Practical Christianity* (designated 'No. F. 2' in 'The Naipaul Library') and drew a sketch of himself in the front of it, looking strange. 'Among deeds that man counts for greatness and nobility, there is none greater than being a man,' he wrote to himself in biblical prose. 'Why should one be vexed with anyone else?' Mystical quotations from Epictetus, Kabir and Plotinus followed, and a line from Tagore: 'O fool, to try to carry thyself upon thy own shoulders! O beggar, to come to beg at thy own door!' Seepersad was wrestling with mental disturbance, trying to find a way forward from the village Hinduism of his childhood with its poorly educated pundits and half-understood rituals. As well as Christianity, he studied the texts of the late nineteenth-century reform movement the Arya Samaj, which rejected superstition, animal sacrifice and the caste system in favour of a modern, rational Hindu philosophy based on dharma or duty. What, after all, did caste amount to but an accident of birth? He read widely: J.S. Mill, Gustave Flaubert, Mulk Raj Anand, Mary Wollstonecraft and J.S. van Teslaar on psychoanalysis. He corresponded with a Scottish woman called Margaret Sheldon, the wife of an estate manager, about religion and theosophy. 'I am God's child and He loves me. All my health and strength and intelligence are from God,' Seepersad concluded.[3]

At the age of five, Vido joined Kamla at the school in the country town of Chaguanas, a simple establishment where discipline was strict. He said years later in his Nobel lecture, 'I walked from my grand-mother's house – past the two or three main-road stores, the Chinese parlour, the Jubilee Theatre, and the high-smelling little Portuguese factory that made cheap blue soap and cheap yellow soap in long bars that were put out to dry and harden in the mornings – every day I walked past these eternal-seeming things – to the Chaguanas govern-ment school. Beyond the school was sugar-cane, estate land, going up to the Gulf of Paria.'[4] He liked his teacher, Miss Hotaing, 'a Negro lady, so kind and nice'.[5] One of his first lessons concerned the coronation of Trinidad and Tobago's new monarch, King George VI. Vido took to schoolwork, and was captivated by the rhythms of *Nelson's West Indian Readers*, influential books with distinctive blood-red covers compiled by the local inspector of schools, Captain James Cutteridge. He learned pages of the *Readers* by heart. 'Dan is the man in the van. A pan is in the van.' The pictures were plain and elegant, done in red, black and white: A was for apple, Q was for queen, Y was for yam. The illustrations showed a pair of white children, Tim and Tot, making sandcastles on a beach with a bucket and spade. 'The ox is big. Tim is not so big. Tim is on a box by the ox. A dog is by the box.' In the second primer, more children appeared, looking most unlike the chil-dren of the West Indies: Jim, Jack, Jane, Dick, Pam, Peggy, their names chosen, according to Captain Cutteridge, because common West Indian names were too long. 'The ox gives meat too, said the cow. He gives beef,' a statement that might have given pause to the more orthodox junior Hindu students of *Nelson's West Indian Readers*.[6] Later, in *A House for Mr Biswas*, a boy reads aloud from a level-four *Reader* about an escape from a German prison camp in 1917. 'This education is a helluva thing,' says the proud father. 'Any little child could pick up. And yet the blasted thing does turn out so damn important later on.'[7]

One day Vido saw a teacher from his school, Mr Sinanan, pushing a stacked box-cart along the road outside the Lion House. Mr Sinanan said to Pa, who was at Chaguanas for the day, 'Well, you know, I'm moving. I'm moving and instead of getting a cart or some van or jitney [shared taxi] to come and move and pay all that money, I'm moving it myself. Let people look at me. Let them laugh that I'm moving it myself.'[8] It was, for Vido, an early lesson in social gradation and the humiliations of poverty.

Seepersad and Droapatie had more children, rapidly. By the time he was five years old, Vido had another two sisters: Sati and Mira, spaced at two-year intervals. Pa, though, remained tormented: his dreams of being a journalist had fallen apart when he was in his late twenties, and now he was stuck in the middle of nowhere, unable even to support his family. He shifted between his shop in Chase Village, the Lion House and his relations. The shop was, in Trinidad parlance, a 'parlour' – a store selling refreshments. Kamla remembered it as 'a shop that looked more like it was going out of business than in business, because so few things were in the shop. All the shelves weren't solidly packed with stuff.'[9] Pa kept a cow for milk. He preferred to read or wander off and do some sketching, or fly kites with Vido and Kamla rather than work. In retrospect, the children realized he had been mentally disturbed. Ma held everyone and everything together, aided by her own family, the Capildeos, whom Pa despised even while he relied on their charity. When he was prescribed Sanatogen tonic for his breakdown, his mother-in-law refused to give him money to pay for it, a slight he always remembered. In Kamla's view, 'While he lavished love and affection on his children, as a husband he left much to be desired. My mother took the brunt of his bad tempers which took the form of scathing attacks on her family, making her accountable and even responsible for all that he regarded as their shortcomings. Occasionally she did answer but more often than not she ignored him . . . Temperamental, impractical, facetious, he gave her no emotional support. Fiercely independent, she made no attempt at compromise. She neither saw nor supported his point of view about anything.'[10] Despite their conflict, Seepersad was not violent to Droapatie. His depictions of casual, almost ritualistic violence in his writings drew not on his own behaviour, but on what he had observed during his childhood.

Seepersad Naipaul was intelligent and ambitious, but he had lost his way. Unlike Droapatie, he came from a family that had barely thrown off the shackles of indenture: his siblings were Hindi-speaking cane-cutters. Family tradition suggests that his grandmother had brought his father to Trinidad in the 1870s as a baby, fleeing disgrace or abandonment in the area around Ayodhya. She said she came from a Brahmin family with the name of Parain, Parray or Panday. The boy, known as Naipaul Maharaj, was apprenticed as a pundit in the village of Diego Martin, and became an agricultural labourer and dealer in religious goods. He was a tough man, and kept his wife and three children – Ramparsad, Seepersad and Prabharan – on a starvation diet. His

brutality led his wife to repeatedly run away to her family in Chandernagore (including when she was heavily pregnant with Seepersad), and
she finally left him to live with another man, also violent, with whom
she had a third son, Hariprasad. Young Seepersad was shunted between
relations, and lived for a time on El Dorado Road in Tunapuna with
his mother's sister and her husband, Sookdeo Misir. He had to tend
cows and goats before going off to school, barefoot. There was talk of
him becoming a pundit, and he learned some Sanskrit. Sookdeo Misir,
who ran a successful private bus company plying the route between
Port of Spain and the north-east of the island, became Seepersad's
mentor. He taught him how to paint the livery on the side of the buses
– like the Ramdin Special Number One – and gave him a basic
education, but no more.[11] Vido remembered, 'My father's people were
physically quite different from my mother's. They had this slightly
Nepali cast of face. One of my father's grandparents was Nepalese. I
have a clear memory of my father's mother's sister. She was very much
someone from the hills.'[12]

The remarkable thing about Pa, so remarkable as to be almost
incredible, is that by the time he was in his late teens, he had escaped
from a likely future as an agricultural labourer in the grim depths of
the rural Indian community. He had taught himself how to read and
write English, and had conceived the idea of becoming a journalist, a
profession that was open usually to whites and Negroes. He began with
some stilted but opinionated articles in the *East Indian Weekly*, an
intermittent paper published by a Chaguanas man. In 1928, a prominent
Muslim barrister, F.E.M. Hosein, had spoken out against those Indians
who thought it 'the highest piece of wisdom to seek as suitable life
partners ladies of a lighter hue and of a different race.' The idea of
racial annihilation and miscegenation became a theme for his generation
of young, nationalist Indians. Seepersad Naipaul wrote that mixed
marriages were a 'perversity responsible for race-dissolution' and that if
they continued, the Indian community in Trinidad would 'waste its
identity in the universal throng of an alien population.' The outer self
reflected the inner man: he complained about the adoption of Western
dress, a trend known then in Trinidad as 'Bobism'. Wearing trousers,
jackets and ties was, Seepersad believed, one of the 'many symptoms of
demoralization among westernized Indians.' Almost the only person to
publicly oppose this view was Krishna Deonarine, who wrote in the
same paper that intermarriage was good, Bobism was to be applauded

as a sign of modernity and that India was still ground down by social tradition and 'excessive religiosity'.[13] The following year Deonarine went a step further and, delving into Roman history, changed his name to Adrian Cola Rienzi; he would become an influential figure in Trinidad politics in the 1930s and 1940s.

In 1929, the year of his marriage, Seepersad began work as a freelance reporter on the *Trinidad Guardian*, one of the two principal newspapers in Port of Spain, on a salary of $4 a week, or around £34 in today's terms.[14] In this new, urban setting he succumbed to Bobism, dressing in a tie, shirt and cotton blazer, sometimes even wearing an ostentatious bow tie. It was an unusual job for an Indian to be doing: the heads of department were white and the rest of the staff were black or mixed. The *Guardian* office was a busy, masculine environment at 22 St Vincent Street in the heart of the little city. Wireless operators took down news from the Associated Press and Reuters in Morse code; editorial and advertising were based upstairs, linked to production and the press room on the ground floor by a spiral staircase; edited copy was sent by a wooden chute to the composing room, to be set in hot metal on a linotype machine. The paper's editor, Gault MacGowan, had been a respected foreign correspondent on the London *Times*. Since his arrival in Trinidad, the thrill of news had chased the heavy advertisements off the front page, and the layout of the paper was now modelled on the London *Daily Express*. Political and social events in Britain and the West Indies were covered in detail, as were sports, illustrated by half-tone photographs. The *Guardian* was surrounded by the competitive hum of the capital: a lawyers' office, a rum shop with separate 'salons' for professionals and street people, Trinidad's chamber of commerce, some brothels and a little cafe which sold sugar-cakes — coloured confections of grated coconut, redeemable against the tram tickets that came with the job of reporter. A jangling tramcar ran the length of St Vincent Street.[15]

Intrigued, perhaps, by the ambitions of a rustic Indian from the sugar belt, Gault MacGowan gave Seepersad a weekly column on Indian affairs. In later years, Pa would say that MacGowan had taught him how to write. The endearing relationship between the two men was closely fictionalized in *A House for Mr Biswas*. Here is Mr Burnett, editor of the Trinidad *Sentinel*, offering Mr Biswas the sort of advice that every writer needs but rarely gets: ' "Considerably" is a big word meaning "very", which is a pointless word any way. And look.

"Several" has seven letters. "Many" has only four and oddly enough
has exactly the same meaning.'[16] Seepersad's buoyant column, cheekily
signed 'The Pundit', soon stirred up resentment among his fellow
Indians. The idea of the feuds, fights, festivals and private quirks of the
community being revealed to a public beyond Chaguanas was a new
and disturbing notion. At first, Seepersad reported the activities of his
in-laws and their local political activities in a complimentary way, but
inevitably his professional obligations caused problems. He was obliged
to mention the conviction of two of his brothers-in-law for violence
during an election.[17] The rapidly expanding Capildeo clan disliked the
activities of this young son-in-law; his nom de plume looked like a
mocking reference to the late Capildeo Maharaj, whose Brahminical
stature was rising with each year that passed, his scandalous elopement
with Jussodra now consigned to silent memory.

MacGowan liked the sensational, and Seepersad delivered. He was
soon writing under his own name about buried treasure, boys stealing
oranges, a revolt by young Hindu men against matchmaking, and
despair in Chaguanas at the arrest of Mahatma Gandhi on his salt march
in India. 'CENTRAL T'DAD HUNT FOR CARONI DEATH TRAGEDY
CLUE' ran one headline, and underneath it, 'INDIAN SHOT DEAD
WHILE READING A HINDU EPIC. By S. Naipaul, Trinidad Staff
Correspondent.' He milked this story: the island was being 'combed' by
police who were 'on the alert'. The dead man, Sagan Maraj, 'was shot
while he was reading the Hindu epic – the Ramayan – which tells of a
fierce battle between Rama, an Indian prince and a King of Ceylon . . .
Sagan began reading aloud, when suddenly in the lone still silence of
the night three shots rang out in rapid succession . . . Who shot him
and why was he shot?'[18] He told of violence at a Muslim festival in the
village of Charlieville, and of the distress of a group of Indians who
had visited their homeland: 'Khemraj told me yesterday . . . "A bull
that has fallen by the wayside will be given quick aid, but a real
colonial-born Indian will be shunned. A maze of conventions rule the
heart of the Hindus." '[19] A powerful reformist social message underlay
Seepersad's writing. In June 1933 he described the 'amazing superstitious
practices' of rural Indians who interpreted outbreaks of smallpox and
rabies in animals as 'an unmistakable sign of the wrath of Kali, a female
deity'. To propitiate the deity, women would collect alms and purchase
a goat to be sacrificed, rather than treat the livestock, and the disease
would continue to spread.[20]

This report was his undoing. Like a good newspaperman, he became part of the story. 'GUARDIAN REPORTER THREATENED WITH DEATH UNLESS HE MAKES A GOAT SACRIFICE — ALLEGED VILIFYING OF A HINDU GODDESS — GRUESOME LETTER. By S. Naipaul' was the headline. 'Next Sunday I am doomed to die. Kali, the Hindu deity and a species of Indian ju-ju will cause the end of me. I am to develop ptomaine poisoning on Saturday, will die on Sunday and will be buried on Monday. The amazing prophecy is contained in an anonymous letter written in Hindi and addressed to me.' Seepersad was full of scorn and excitement about the letter: what was his response to those who demanded goat-slaughter to satisfy the local 'Kali cult' (which he linked to African 'ju-ju' or witchcraft)? 'Briefly and explicitly I say bunkum. Frankly I don't believe in Kalis, deities or ju-jus, and so, I won't sacrifice a goat.'[21] Two days later, the joke went bad. The story made the front page, though this time it had to be reported by a colleague. 'WIFE OF THREATENED REPORTER URGES SACRIFICE TO HINDU GODDESS — POLICE PROTECTION OFFERED TO MR S. NAIPAUL — MORE LIGHT ON SANITARY INSPECTOR'S END — YOUNG JOURNAL-IST SLEEPS WELL DESPITE "SENTENCE OF DEATH" — ALL TRINIDAD IS TALKING OF THE SENSATIONAL DEATH THREAT TO MR S. NAIPAUL, CHAGUANAS CORRESPONDENT OF THE "GUARDIAN".'

Soon after the original story about smallpox and rabies had run in the paper, the resident sanitary inspector for Chaguanas, Mr H.L. Thompson, fell ill. In the blackmailing letter, the author blamed Thompson for giving the story to the press, and suggested Seepersad might suffer a similar fate. Now Thompson was dead, probably poisoned. The police put Seepersad under guard and relocated him to another district. The *Guardian* pursued the story, discovering that Mr Thompson had been prosecuting men who were selling milk from smallpox-ridden cows. The paper reported that the previous year Seepersad had been the victim of 'foul play' when 'he was ambushed and beaten because he published the truth regarding a local Indian dispute. Chaguanas and surrounding villages are notorious for gang violence and sinister conspiracies frequently resulting in injury to persons.' Droapatie wanted her husband to back off. 'In an agitated tone and with visible signs of worry and anxiety on her face, Mrs S. Naipaul, the pretty Indian wife of the Guardian reporter said this . . . "For his own sake and the safety of his family, I have advised my husband to make the goat sacrifice to appease the wrath of the goddess.

But he believes that ju-ju – to use his own words – is all bunkum." '
The report concluded: 'Mr and Mrs Naipaul's two children [Kamla and
Vidyadhar] are aged four and 18 months.' Creative as ever, Gault
McGowan ran an accompanying piece asking whether any local com-
pany would give his reporter life insurance: two would, two would not,
and one 'refused to express any opinion except to Mr Naipaul himself'.[22]

Before the week was out, Seepersad's world had been undone; he
undid it for himself. Under intense pressure from his wife and her
extended family, he agreed to execute a goat. The rationalist, the
reformer, the Arya Samajist, the dapper journalist, the modern man, the
scorner of ju-ju, succumbed to a Hindu tradition linked to sacrifice that
even in India was associated with the more extreme Tantric practitioners. It went against everything that Seepersad believed in and,
inevitably, was reported in lurid detail in the *Guardian*; the story was
even picked up by the *Herald Tribune* in New York as a piece of
exotica. One of his colleagues, clearly appalled, described the scene: the
improvised altar in a backyard, the flower garlands, the offerings of
sweet bananas and coconuts for the goddess, the blameless little white
goat, the cutlass resting on a tree stump, Seepersad squatting beside the
pundit who was dressed 'in a loincloth, with the shining mahogany of
his skin uncovered', the goat anointed with oil and vermilion powder
and suddenly beheaded, its legs convulsing even as the severed head
was placed on a brass tray and offered to furious Kali. At the centre of
the ceremony crouched the sorry figure of Seepersad Naipaul, dressed
all in white, bedecked like the goat in a garland of scarlet hibiscus
flowers, throwing cloves on a fire and dutifully following each muttered
command of the pundit.

Seepersad wrote his own piece for the newspaper about what had
taken place. It contained flashes of rebellion, but was the work of a
broken man. He would 'rather believe in a single God, than a thousand
Kalis . . . Kali may again threaten my life, but I am certain I will never
again make a sacrifice.' The former scourge of Bobism even boasted
that, after representations to the pundit, he had been allowed to keep
wearing his shirt and trousers rather than dress in a dhoti or loincloth.
'More than once during the ceremony', he wrote, 'I asked myself
whence came the moral feebleness in Hinduism?'[23] The next day he
wrote a jaunty front-page story which began, 'Good morning everybody! As you behold, Kali has not got me yet.'[24] But it was a false or
failing bravado now. Seepersad was profoundly, even fatally, humili-

ated. The sequence of what followed is unclear, but his byline disappeared from the paper, and he stopped reporting from Chaguanas. Some months later, Gault MacGowan left the *Guardian* after a dispute with the management; Seepersad was taken off the staff by the new editor, and made a stringer. He broke down. Helped by his in-laws, he started the 'parlour' in Chase Village; it failed. In late 1935, the Capildeos sent him to be an overseer on a cocoa estate in nearby Cunupia, where he had a mental collapse.

Nearly forty years later, when Vido discovered the complete story of the goat sacrifice by looking through back copies of the *Guardian*, he asked Ma, 'What form did my father's madness take?' She replied, 'He looked in the mirror one day and couldn't see himself. And he began to scream.'[25]

*

Soogee Capildeo, now called Soogee Capildeo Maharaj, though she had been born and baptized Rosalie Gobin, was known to her forty-odd grandchildren as Nanie (the Hindi and Bhojpuri word for a maternal grandmother) and behind her back as Queen Victoria. A Roman Catholic of unspecified caste, she became a born-again promoter of her late husband's Brahminism. Nanie hoped that through their developing status, the Capildeo clan might reach a commanding position within the island's Indian community. Ma and her siblings endorsed these attitudes. As Vido realized later, 'We were given in the Lion House which my grandfather built, some idea of a kind of caste inheritance. The [family members] who came afterwards, they can't understand that. They wouldn't understand my concern and my pride in India or my interest in Indian art and architecture ... Growing up in these conditions, I was full of self-esteem. I think it came from many contradictory sources. It came from the very strong caste sense in my grandmother's family.'[26]

In the New World, caste had become a bulwark against the dominant religion of the other ethnic groups: Christianity. Hindu temples were constructed, and coloured flags erected on bamboo poles outside a building after a puja, a common practice at the time in parts of north India. Religious customs evolved and transmuted just as the Indian diet began to incorporate the yam and sweet potato. Relations between Indian Muslims and Hindus were good; from the 1850s, Trinidad's Hindus had taken part in 'Hosay', the annual Shia festival commemorating the martyrdom of the Imam Hussein, known demeaningly locally as the 'coolie carnival'. With few high-caste Indians in Trinidad, those who carried the scriptural knowledge of the old world were valuable. Families of Brahmin descent took to using an identifiable Brahmin name such as Panday, Mishra or Tewari as a surname, while others appropriated such names out of social ambition. When pundits were called to plantation villages to perform marriage and death rites, there were rumours about the ones who were less ascetic or plausible than they claimed to be. A supposedly pukka pundit who ate meat in secret would be called a 'Pork Brahmin', while a man who clearly knew nothing about the tradition he was supposed to be propagating was known as a 'Brahmin-by-boat', meaning that he must have acquired his caste during the sea voyage from India.

The three surviving photographs of Capildeo Maharaj show him looking distinctly Brahminical. In one picture he ostentatiously carries a book; in another he stands with Soogee by his side, her hand resting on his shoulder in Caribbean informality; in the third he sits with his little son Simbhoo standing beside him. Capildeo's fair skin, sharp nose, shaped moustache, plump cheeks and high forehead all mark him as a Brahmin of the United Provinces. He wears white clothing befitting his caste, his shoes are unlaced to indicate that he has not touched leather with his hand, his dhoti is tied in a respectable way, and around his neck is what looks like a japmala or 108-bead rosary. This physical evidence, combined with the certainty that he knew Sanskrit, make his claimed family lineage highly plausible. The region around his home town of Gorakhpur had many poor Brahmins, so many that merchants would sometimes employ them as talismanic companions when travelling.[27] Without this caste background, it would have been impossible for Capildeo to have obtained his linguistic and scriptural knowledge by the time he sailed for Trinidad in 1894.

Seepersad Naipaul's antecedents are vaguer; he never liked to discuss his childhood. His rejection of orthodox Hinduism and its superstitions matched his uncertainty about his origins and his antipathy towards the memory of his violent father. Did his grandmother, a wronged woman of high birth, leave India with a baby boy, Naipaul Maharaj? There is no record of these two in the archives in Trinidad. A Nepaliah arrived on the indenture ship *Essex* in 1875, a Napaul on the *Foyle* in the same year, a Nepaul followed on the *Jura* in 1878, and a Napaul sailed on the *Sheila* in 1879.[28] On Seepersad's birth certificate (which states that he is illegitimate – only in 1945 were informal Indian marriages conducted 'under bamboo' recognized as legal) his father is given as 'Nyepaul, labourer'. Instead of a signature, he has marked the birth certificate with an 'X', suggesting that he was illiterate and had not been educated as a pundit.[29] There is no way of knowing whether this man – Nyepaul, X – was a Brahmin; like Kopil or Capildeo, his name gives no indication of caste. The strongest assertion of his status comes from the deathbed recollection of his daughter Prabharan, recounted in solemn tones by V.S. Naipaul in his 'Prologue to an Autobiography':

> She wanted me to know now, before the knowledge vanished with her, what she – and my father – had come from. She wanted me to know that the blood was good ... Her father was a pundit, she said. And he was fussy; he didn't like having too much to do with the low. And here – since her face was too old to be moulded into any expression save one of great weariness – the old lady used her shrivelled little hand to make a gentle gesture of disdain. The disdain was for the low among Hindus.[30]

Vido's account of his aunt's terminal conversation may be accurate, but it does not make his paternal grandfather a Brahmin. Nyepaul may have been a pure Brahmin, a Brahmin-by-boat, or he may have come from another caste background altogether. Since caste is patrilineal, and traditionally a Hindu woman takes on the caste of her husband at marriage, Vido and his siblings may not have been Brahmin either. V.S. Naipaul never addressed this inconsistency, preferring to embrace the implied 'caste sense' of his mother's family, the Capildeos, whose legacy he otherwise claimed to reject. 'My father's background,' he admitted later, 'is confused in my mind.'[31]

*

Soogee, the powerful matriarch of the Lion House, was a small, stout, fierce, dark-skinned woman who spoke rarely and was listened to with awe. After Capildeo Maharaj's death, penniless because he had mortgaged much of their land in order to elope with Jussodra, she arranged the marriage of her teenage daughters without paying a dowry; the chosen husbands (each known to Vido as Mausa – the Hindi word for a maternal aunt's husband) were said to be Brahmins from poor families. Using the Mausas as her workforce, she grew and traded rice, sugar cane and later cocoa. Each daughter (Rajdaye, Ramdoolarie, Dhan, Koonta, Ahilla, Kalawatee, Droapatie, Tara and Binmatie – known as Mausi, the word for a maternal aunt) had a room of her own at the Lion House, where she could sleep with her husband and children: the husband in the bed, the children on the floor. Vegetarian food from their own land – pigeon peas, okra, rice, pumpkin, potato, spinach, green fig, chick peas, breadfruit, all spiced with masala in an approximation of north Indian cuisine – was cooked communally by the Mausis in a dingy, blackened kitchen. Men and boys dressed in shorts and shirts, the shirts usually made from flour bags, and wore long trousers when working in the fields. Barefoot around the house and yard, outside they wore 'washekongs' – Salim collects a pair in *A Bend in the River*: 'from *caoutchouc*, the French word for rubber, being patois for canvas shoes.'[32] The women wore long white or yellow cotton skirts with a bodice. Kurta pyjamas and saris were worn only for religious ceremonies and festivals, or when the in-house pundit Hargovind Mausa publicly read sacred texts such as the *Ramayana* in the large hall downstairs.

What Nanie said, went. 'At the Lion House,' Kamla remembered, 'we were just told what to do, and we did what we were told to do, whatever was commanded. There was no encouragement of a thinking process. It was an emotionally restricted way of bringing up children.'[33] Her cousin Brahm saw Nanie as 'very demanding, very strict. Nanie believed in the Hindu way of life but the irony of it is, she would help with the churches and celebrate all the Catholic festivals because she didn't believe in putting all your stones in one basket. She told us that she wanted us to speak in English, not Hindi, because we had to be educated.' Nanie made it clear in graphic terms to her children and grandchildren that they were not part of a wider Trinidadian community. Brahm remembered: 'When I went to school I was told by my grandmother, "You can't associate with niggers." Only Indians were accepted. She had bright, piercing eyes – she could see through your soul with one glance.'[34]

During the 1930s, Nanie navigated her family's financial position by buying and selling real estate. The land registries of Trinidad contain no fewer than twenty-eight transactions involving Soogee Capildeo Maharaj during the period 1929 to 1946, mainly in land in the sugar belt such as Cacandee, Endeavour village and Chandernagore. Some deals were simple, and some were complex; it appears that during the early part of the Second World War she made a healthy profit by dividing her agricultural land into parcels and selling it to small farmers, most of whom appear to have been Indian (with names like Seemungal Mahabir, Dukhanee Rambhoras and Dhanradge Mungaree).[35] She also negotiated with some of the larger colonial estates. In 1933, she sold a large field in Carapichaima in west-central Trinidad to Stephens Ltd., and three years later purchased a similar-

sized plot from them near Chaguanas.[36] In 1934 she sold ten acres of land
to Woodford Lodge Ltd., and in 1940 bought a large agricultural structure
in Charlieville from J.G. Henriques & Company.[37] No figures are recorded
to show the value of these sales and purchases, but it can be presumed that
Soogee kept a tight grip on the profits. However much wealth she had tied
up in land, she still had to pay off mortgages and loans, and to run a large
family. The importance of money was instilled in all her grandchildren at
an early age.

Although many of her transactions would have been fronted by her
two favoured sons-in-law, and by her son Simbhoonath when he grew
older, Nanie retained control of the family's finances. The sons-in-law who
worked for her directly were not paid, and had to come to her if they
needed money for clothing, shoes or household goods. One Mausa would
be played off against another, and the family seethed with bitter feuds.
Furious arguments between the adults would be conducted in the Bhojpuri-
inspired Hindi that was common among descendants of Indian indentured
labourers across the region, half-understood by the children. Sahadeo
Mausa, an uneducated man who worked a regular fourteen-hour day as a
farmer for the family, challenged Nanie about being treated like a coolie;
he got nowhere. Knowing he faced greater poverty if he left the extended
family, he took out his frustration on his son Brahm, slapping and punching
him for the smallest misdemeanour. The sisters would compete to see who
could discipline their children most forcefully. Relationships in the household were often callous, and Vido learned an early lesson that remained
with him for life:

> Children were beaten with a strap or with a stick. Outside, we were
> surrounded by language that came from the days of slavery. Parents
> would say: 'I will peel your backside. I will beat you till you pee. I
> will make you fart fire.' You can hear the language of the plantation.
> I think there is a lot of violence in Indian peasant families. But my
> father and mother didn't punish people too often, though we were
> surrounded by people being punished . . . What happens in that kind
> of awful set-up is that lots of quarrels break out between people,
> and those quarrels were my training for life, my training in life and
> society – propaganda, alliances, betrayals – all these things. So, in a
> way, nothing that happened later ever really shocked me.[38]

For the first six, formative years of Vido's life, his father was often
absent, mentally and physically. The central figures in his early days

were women: his grandmother, his mother, his aunts, his teacher and his big sister. The men in the Lion House, with the exception of the two pampered sons of the family, were emasculated, having been chosen for the role of son-in-law because they were nominally of high caste but poor enough for their parents not to expect a dowry. Although Ma was conscious of her role and duties as a traditional Hindu woman, cooking and caring for her husband and children, she was tough; her mother was powerful in a way that can have been matched by few Indian women in Trinidad at this time. Kamla remembered Ma being 'a strong woman with a strong personality. Vain, proud and conceited, she needed all of these qualities for her survival.'[39] Their brother Shiva noted that she had rigid ideas about history: 'my mother has always found it hard to forgive the Muslims for their numerous invasions of India and for forcing the partition of the subcontinent.'[40]

In his own presentation of the past, Vido would concentrate subsequently on the virtues of his father, with the result that Ma's voice can be hard to hear. An academic who interviewed her in 1988 for a study of Trinidadian Indian women noted: 'Her answers are always alert, sometimes aggressively so; she is a confident and self-assured woman.' When asked why her mother had sent her daughters to school at a time when other Indian women were illiterate, Ma replied, 'Don't ask me that question again. She decided to educate them and I think she was very correct in educating them.' To an enquiry about her non-Indian neighbours, she answered: 'Don't ask me anything about other people, ask me nothing about other people . . . my husband can't come home and see me gossiping on the street . . . You see a woman has a place in this world and when she abuse that place, she has lost the thing they call womanhood because she is no more that woman.'[41] Ma's bright, certain, robust, slightly mocking tone of voice would be inherited by Vido; without the impetus of Ma and her family, his later achievements would have been impossible.

CHAPTER THREE

'LIKE OLIVER TWIST IN THE WORKHOUSE'

THE NEAR HALF-MILLION people of Trinidad were given three scholarships each year to a university in Great Britain. Innumerable children would compete for the chance to have a free education overseas, and to change their own and their family's future. In a colonial society where the opportunities for advancement were so restricted, island scholarships, like places in the better cricket teams, were fought over fiercely. Success marked you as a person of intellectual ability, part of a new group that was being groomed for the day when Trinidad gained self-government.[1] Jean-Paul Sartre put it this way: 'The European elite undertook to manufacture a native elite. They picked out promising adolescents; they branded them, as with a red-hot iron, with the principles of western culture, they stuffed their mouths full with high-sounding phrases, grand glutinous words that stuck to the teeth. After a short stay in the mother country they were sent home, whitewashed.'[2] In 1938, Ma's younger brother Rudranath won an island scholarship to study medicine, an achievement that had the potential to shift the status of the Capildeo family from being big in Chaguanas to being big in Trinidad. He was one of the first Indian winners, defying expectations. Half a century earlier, the Governor of the newly united colony of Trinidad and Tobago had told a group of Indian school-children: 'Now all you children, all of you little boys and girls can never hope, of course, can never hope to occupy any very high social position in life – it would be very foolish and over-ambitious on your part to expect to do so.'[3] With nationalism flourishing after strikes and riots the previous year in the oilfields of Fyzabad, led by the splendidly named Tubal Uriah "Buzz" Butler, a Grenadian small-church preacher, the prospect of constitutional reform was imminent. Butler's 'British Empire Citizens and Workers Home Rule Party' – backed by the trade-union leader Adrian Cola Rienzi – was attracting popular support.

In order to give her son Rudranath a home near his school while he was studying for the scholarship, Nanie had bought a house, 17 Luis Street, in the Port of Spain suburb of Woodbrook, a mixed-race area distinct from St James, the down-at-heel quarter known as 'coolie town' which was occupied mainly by people of south Indian descent who had left Hinduism far behind. During the week, Nanie would stay in Port of Spain to look after Rudranath and make sure he did his school work. She bought other properties too, and needed a family member to administer them and collect the rents. This coincided with Seepersad's recovery from his breakdown, and his success in 1938 in regaining his job as a *Guardian* journalist. It was decided that the Naipaul family, now including a baby girl named Savi or Savitri, would move to Luis Street. With Trinidad in a state of unrest and the Second World War looming, Ma, Pa and the children had a moment of respite. The family took the steam train from the station at Chaguanas for the slow twenty-mile journey to Port of Spain, and began afresh.

Pa's confidence revived, and he began to write stories for his own entertainment. George John, a young black sports reporter on the *Guardian*, found Seepersad to be 'a very quiet man who didn't mix very much. He was basically a rural Indian, not a town Indian. He came from the sugar belt. Naipaul would not go drinking with other journalists.' Although there were now two other Indians working on the paper, their community was still associated by the citizens of Port of Spain with low status activities such as street-vending, carrying head-loads and collecting garbage. Indians were looked down on. In all professions, according to John, 'There was a definite bias in favour of the lighter-skinned. Not only in newspapers. It was like that in the civil service, in the higher ranks of the police. You entered the banks and all the people you saw, the tellers and so on, were white girls or white men.'[4] 'White' or 'lighter-skinned' in this context in Trinidad in the 1940s might mean British expatriate, Portuguese, 'French creole' (someone of European appearance, usually descended from plantation owners), 'Spanish' (mixed ethnic descent with fair skin and 'good' – meaning straight – hair) or 'Red' (African features with light skin and hair). The gradation was strict and instinctive, part of a way of thinking that was instilled early in this ethnically diverse colonial setting, although people might try to 'pass' as something they were not. There was even a Bajan rhyme about skin shades: 'white, fusty, dusty, musty, tea, coffee, cocoa, black, dark black'.

In Luis Street, Vido came to know and appreciate the qualities of his father. These were, in retrospect, idyllic days for him. Woodbrook had been built on an old sugar estate near the harbour owned by the makers of Angostura Bitters, the Siegert family, with its streets laid out on a grid and named after members of the family such as Alberto, Luis and Ana. For the first time, Vido encountered electric lights, pavements and running water. The capital had cinemas, rum shops and cricket pitches, and on Sunday afternoons the police band would play for the crowds near the Queen's Park Savannah. The Naipaul family appeared to have a home of their own. The house was a three-bedroomed wooden building raised on pillars, with a verandah, a yard and an outdoor latrine. A Negro carpenter lived in the 'servant room' in the yard; when Vido asked him one day what he was making, he replied 'the thing without a name'.[5] At the end of the road was the harbour and the reclaimed area of land known as Docksite. Vido's uncle Rudranath, preparing for his departure for England, had one bedroom, and another was rented to a mulatto couple, Mr and Mrs Guy, who were friendly to Vido. The children usually slept out on the verandah. For Vido, 'This whole thing unrolled every day in front of my eyes: the life of the street.'[6] It would give him the material for his first book, *Miguel Street*.

For a term, he went to Woodbrook Canadian Mission School, where his teacher was Mr Dairy. Vido liked 'the writing and the paper and the pencils and shaping letters. It was at Mr Dairy's school that I began to make the letter J, the capital J, endless curls in my J, you know, out of pleasure indeed in the shape of letters. And I took this one day and showed it to my father, and he told me, "No, no, too many curls." So I lost that little bit of style.' In 1939 he joined his cousin Boysie at Tranquillity, which had a strong academic reputation. Former students included the pan-African theorist George Padmore and the sprinter McDonald Bailey, who would be the first black athlete to win an Olympic medal for Britain. At Tranquillity Boys' Intermediate School, Vido made friends across cultures, despite Nanie's racial injunctions: Winston A.G. Springer, known as WAGS, Kenneth Cazabon, related to the painter Michel Jean Cazabon, and Yip Young, a 'very bright and delicate boy who was half-Negro and half-Chinese.'[7] He would swap his morning snack with a Negro boy named Tanis. 'He was excited by the food I brought to school. I was a ready swapper. I gave Tanis my stuff. There would have been curried potatoes, in a little tiffin carrier.

He gave me a kind of parlour cake, with coconut inside. I have a clear memory of that.'[8]

In the middle of the day, Tranquillity children walked home for lunch. Kamla went to the girls' branch of the school. One day Vido stopped to read a street sign, Cipriani Boulevard. 'Cipriani Boul Edward,' he said, 'and a Negro man there, he was very amused and he told me how to pronounce it. Big word and I'm quite young.' Most of the pupils and all the teachers were black or mixed, and it was a new experience for Vido to be surrounded by many people who came from a different culture. He stood out: 'I was an object of great curiosity to people. I was very small, and they couldn't have been nicer. There were few Indians, almost no Indians in the school. It was the first time we were coming out [of the countryside]. If I had gone to a rough place, it might have been different. I have to record how nice people were to me, as an unprotected little boy.'[9] He was now called Vidia on paper, a shorter and more modern version of Vidyadhar, and he was placed second out of thirty-six in the class at the end of his first term. His teacher Mr Romilly noted in the school report that he was 'an intelligent pupil'.[10] At Tranquillity he was given a solid grounding in grammar, spelling, vocabulary, arithmetic and geography, and on Empire Day the children all sang 'God Save the King' and 'Land of Hope and Glory', including the immortal line 'Britons never, never, never shall be slaves.'[11]

At home, Vido made friends with Mr Guy, the lodger, who 'made the world very, very exciting. I was six or seven. He must have had some talent for getting on with children.' One day the two of them were standing on the verandah at 17 Luis Street when a decrepit Indian man came past pushing a handcart packed with steaming ice, selling ice lollies or palettes at a cent each. He was calling out 'Palette! Palette!' Vido wanted to run out and buy an ice lolly. But: 'Mr Guy said to me, "No. He will bring it to you."' To Vido, this was no simple message: 'It was an important kind of instruction to me, meaning, once you're spending money, you have certain rights. It was a training in the ways of the world – you don't run after that barefoot man in the street; he must come to you. I remember it to this day.'[12]

The idyll could not last. In 1940, Seepersad and Droapatie were told by Nanie that they would be moving to a new family commune at a place called Petit Valley.

*

Cool and shady, with savannah and plenty of snakes, Petit Valley was unfamiliar land, an estate of three hundred acres to the north of Port of Spain. An old colonial house built by one of Trinidad's respected 'high brown' families, the Maillards, stood on a verdant, forested hillside. Around it were oranges, shaddocks (a citrus fruit, like a grapefruit), cacao trees, nutmeg, zabocas (avacado pears), tangerines and mangoes. The people in the village near the house were 'panyol' or 'cocoa panyol' – coming from the word Español, or Spanish, meaning they were of mixed ethnicity, although probably their ancestors would have come from Venezuela. The local patois had many French words, from the days when the owners of the cocoa estates had brought slaves from neighbouring islands. The long-established overseer at Petit Valley was called Metti, from the French 'métis', meaning half-caste, a name Vido would use when he came to write *A Bend in the River*. The Mausis, Mausas and cousins all moved there, although some would travel back and forth to Port of Spain or to Chaguanas, where Nanie remained in the Lion House. Her elder son Simbhoonath, now aged twenty-six and studying to be a lawyer in the town of San Fernando, was the guiding force behind the project. The family would develop the land at Petit Valley. When Vido heard about the move, he was distraught: 'I think I must have made a great scene about it, and my grandmother began to talk to me. I don't know why she took the care. She told me how beautiful it was, how lovely the house was, how lovely the big trees were – so I was primed to love these things.'[13]

Coming from the cane fields and rough dwellings of Chaguanas, the Capildeo family led by Simbhoo had little idea what to do with their new domain, which had been sold to them cheap by the Maillards because it was unprofitable. To the dismay of people in the local village, the area around the house became squalid, in its beautiful setting. 'They did a kind of peasant agriculture,' said Vido later, 'burning down the hillsides and planting corn, maize and peas. They pillaged the oranges from the orange trees, took the avacadoes. They planted nothing. They were camping . . . It was all so improvised, all so dreadful. We were given a very low idea of human needs. I think without anybody knowing, this was coming from Mother India, from a beaten-down, broken-down people.'[14] Trees were uprooted and the house reworked. A big, unfamiliar brick oven was taken apart, and the area beside it roofed over in corrugated iron and tree branches. The verandah was used to store crops and old bread, which Nanie would buy in bulk from a baker in Port of Spain. The indoor water closet with its European cistern and chain was dismantled, and an outdoor

latrine built in the woods, to which a sodden path was soon worn. 'I think
the WC offended the Hindu sense of cleanliness and so it was destroyed.
It became a room where people sewed . . . I am talking about people who
were close to immemorial peasantry.'[15] An ornamental cherry tree by the
tennis court on the side of the main drive was turned into logs. 'There
was no reason to chop it down. It was just something to do, something
to chop down. Where we come from ancestrally, there are no trees –
they think spirits hide in trees.'[16] While the children watched in excitement, Uncle Simbhoo supervised the destruction of the electricity generator, the leaves of lead being melted in a large pot and tipped into
Ovaltine tins; pipes were put between the tins and the molten metal hardened, creating dumb-bells for the Mausas to use for exercise. 'I think they
played with them for a while and then forgot them.'[17] The house was lit
by oil lamps now, like the Lion House. Vido's retrospective cynicism was
matched by the memory of Margaret Maillard, the granddaughter of the
vendor, who visited. 'It was a roomy house. The Capildeos were very
gracious to us when we came but we were horrified by the way they had
partitioned it.'[18]

Ma and Pa were given a space in the servants' quarters to the back of
the house, overlooking the hillside. Seepersad hated being part of the
extended family again, and took to demanding meals in his bedroom.
There were frequent, angry disputes with his brothers-in-law. Vidia noted
later that his father avoided touching the ground at Petit Valley, and linked
it mentally with his supposed Brahminism. 'I don't think my father ever let
his foot touch the ground. He couldn't go to have a shower barefoot. He
always had to wear wooden sandals. He never let his foot touch the
ground.'[19] The children had little contact with their uncles, aunts or cousins
on the Naipaul side of the family. Ma cooked, cleaned, washed and looked
after the five of them with the occasional help of her sisters. Vido took his
mother's care and support as his right, in the manner of a boy in a Hindu
joint family. In Kamla's opinion, 'Our vanity, our conceit, our resilience,
our tenacity, our strength – these things we got from our mother. Words,
the sound of words, our love of books, our sense of humour, our passion,
our occasionally neurotic behaviour, our physical frailties – these things
we got from our father.'[20] Vido's own view in later life was: 'My mother
would cry because she thought my father was being awkward. Her loyalties
were really to her clan, her sisters. She was part of the mess, you know.'
When pressed, he said, 'I adored her as a child. She was a beautiful lady.
Carried herself very well . . . I think my father was a weak man, a suffering

man who could only work when people loved him. My mother was very tough and strong. I think I got my strength from her.'[21]

As the atmosphere at Petit Valley worsened, Pa built a plain, pretty timber house for himself in the forest, standing on stilts. When he burned heaps of leaves and wood that he had cleared, a fire began and lingered in the undergrowth. At night it flared up, as Kamla remembered:

> Vidia and I were awakened and told to run to the big house to get help. There was a forest fire at the back of the house and it was spreading. A patch of forest separated us from the big house. In the daytime it was no problem to run through it, following a path we naturally made going from one house to the other. But it was night and it was dark. Vidia and I were terrified of the fire, of the dark and of the forest on either side of the lonely road. Stories of forest spirits became very real in that setting, of La Diablesse, the enchantress with the cloven hoof who led men astray, of Soucouy-ants, who were women who could turn themselves into balls of fire [and become vampires]. Holding each other's hands, Vidia and I took the road. I was calling upon the name of Rama, the only name that came to me at that time and I was encouraging Vidia to do the same as a means of keeping these evil forest creatures at bay. Once aroused the family came immediately to our assistance.[22]

They beat down the flames with branches, and Pa was left without a house again.

The cousins – boys and girls of all ages – were not encouraged to associate with people who lived nearby, such as the mulatto family who lived by the road and worked on the estate, or the Indian Muslim family who kept a parlour and had a pretty daughter. There were no friends, only family. Although the status of the Naipaul children was complicated by Pa's chronic disputes, they were in a stronger position than some of their cousins, such as the children of the widowed Tara Mausi, whose husband, Ramjattan, had been gored to death by a bull. Tara's daughter Phoola remembered being entirely dependent on the goodwill of Nanie and Simbhoo. 'We had to respect the aunts and uncles, even when they were wrong. The aunts were smart people. On reflection, I would say anyone who had a father had more security than us.'[23] More unfortunate still were the children of the oldest Mausi, Rajdaye. Her husband, Aknath, had been the overseer on the family sugar-cane plantations in Chaguanas and Nanie's enforcer in many of her business ventures. When Rajdaye died, there was a feud which led to Aknath Mausa being purged. His children became virtual orphans, living in a shack in Petit Valley. One of them, Jai, remembered: 'We were 200 yards from the main house. I was twelve, my brothers were nine and six. I had to cook for them and look after them. My grandmother wouldn't allow my father's name to be spoken. I feel we were really, really badly treated. There was no compassion from her.'[24]

The children made their own entertainment, outdoors and indoors. Each morning each child would take the crushed end of a fresh stick to use as a toothbrush, then split it and use it as a tongue-scraper. They husked corn and harvested coffee, cocoa, oranges and bananas for market. One day they put on a play of the trial scene from Shakespeare's *The Merchant of Venice* in the drawing room, and Vido was struck by the beauty of his female cousins. In later years, he 'found it very hard to think of making love to an Indian girl. It had an incestuous sense to it.' A little before this he had his first sexual experience, when he was seduced by his cousin Boysie. The encounter was unwanted. As he put it: 'I was myself subjected to some sexual abuse by an older cousin. I was corrupted, I was assaulted. I was about six or seven. It was done in a sly, terrible way and it gave me a hatred, a detestation of this homosexual thing. I never went through a period of liking the same sex.'[25] Molestation continued intermittently over the next two or three years, usually in the area where the boys slept. Vidia never mentioned it to anyone, at the time or later. He insisted he was never a willing participant, although his denial is not wholly convincing given the similarity in age of the two boys. He feared the idea that he was a participant in sexual experimentation between male cousins. 'It was an outrage, but it was not a defining moment. I was very young. This thing was over before I was ten. I was always coerced. Of course he was ashamed too later. It happened to other cousins. I think it is part of Indian extended family life, which is an abomination in some ways, a can of worms . . . After an assault one is very ashamed — and then you realize it happens to almost everybody. All children are abused. All girls are molested at some stage. It is almost like a rite of passage.'[26] The Mausis were alert to any hint of burgeoning sexuality between male and female cousins. 'If we sat boy and girl in a hammock together, it was a grievous thing. An aunt would come and say, "What are you doing there?"' Savi remembered.[27]

Vido spent much of his time at Petit Valley with Pa, who would read to him and sometimes to the other children: extracts from *Julius Caesar*, *Nicholas Nickleby*, *Three Men in a Boat*, Charles Kingsley's retelling of the Perseus myth in *The Heroes*, and later from Gandhi's *Autobiography*, Conrad's *The Lagoon*, Maupassant's *The Necklace* and Maugham's *Cakes and Ale*. Although such authors described unfamiliar worlds, the stories lingered: 'I still remember *Cakes and Ale* begins with the narrator going back to his lodgings, and there is a message from his landlady Mrs Fellows saying Mr Kear rang up twice. "He says it's important." And Maugham observes in the Maugham-like way, which stays with me to this day, "I know that when people say things are important, it doesn't mean it is important to you; it's important to them." So one was being trained early in this way. The effect was to introduce me to the romantic idea of this world outside, and to the romantic idea of writing.'[28] Representations of the West Indies were to be found mainly in books by white visitors, like Alec Waugh writing of indolent bellboys and 'the inevitable negroes' in *The Coloured Countries*, or Edmund Whitman using chapter titles like 'Banana Escapades' and 'Jamaica Ginger Snaps' in *Those Wild West Indies*.[29]

Pa and Vido positioned themselves in an ordered fantasy world derived from European literature, far from the noise, squalor and their own powerlessness in Petit Valley. At school, Vido might read an extract from *Martin Chuzzlewit* in his *New Royal Reader*, containing place names that would one day become familiar: 'The coach was none of your steady-going, yokel coaches . . . It cared no more for Salisbury than if it had been a hamlet. It rattled noisily through the best streets, defied the cathedral, took the worst corners sharpest . . .'[30] Aspiration and ambition became an alternative to daily life in Petit Valley. 'I suffered like hell in this place,' Vido said later. 'It has given me all kinds of things [for my writing]: my understanding of the ease with which civilizations can be destroyed. When I was in Africa [in 1975] and saw in the Congo the ruins of Belgian cities, when I saw the same thing in Rwanda in 1966, I knew about people camping in houses and not knowing what to do with the things, just stripping it apart.'[31] At Petit Valley, Vido began to keep a diary, written in pencil in a *Guardian* reporter's notebook. He wrote about the death of his paternal grandmother and Pa's distress, but after a while the diary 'became very affected and melodramatic. I was melancholic, and I had a slight wallow, as a child. I remember writing, "I feel like Oliver Twist in the workhouse." I knew it wasn't true, but I had no other means of expressing what I felt.'[32]

At Christmas 1941, the local school in the village at Petit Valley held a concert. The family walked through the tropical night to the school, which was full of lights and people singing songs. Vido was excited by the glamour of the occasion. 'One of the songs had a little Negro boy, nattily dressed in a suit. Clearly his parents had dressed him up for this occasion. Whether he did a little dance or whether he just came out dressed in this way, he looked so cute in that suit. But he sang, "Oh, I'm a happy little nigger." It was the most successful number of the evening. I remember people laughing till they almost cried with pleasure at the little boy. "Oh, I'm a happy little nigger and my name is John." The chorus was, "I can sleep on a cotton bale or roost up a tree, tell you what it is boys, nothing hurts me." I think it goes: "I like cake, I like honey, I'm not the boy to refuse any money. Once I went a courting with my little black sioux" – or it might be, "my saucy black sioux" – "her brother Tom insulted me and peppered me too." It was only years later that I understood what we'd heard. Clearly it's written by an American white man, out of a kind of love for the little black boy, but within this love is complete contempt.'[33] The song would stick in Vido's formidable memory, to be pondered over subsequent years, and used to show the way in which culture and meaning change in a different historical setting: the American south, a 'panyol' village in colonial Trinidad, the independent Caribbean. It resurfaced in 1967 in *The Mimic Men*, where Browne is humiliated to have been a 'singer of coon songs' as a child, and indirectly in *A Way in the World* in 1994, where Lebrun tells a similar story and concludes, ' "Every educated black man is eaten away quietly by a memory like that." '[34] This was how V.S. Naipaul's fiction would work: a moment would be stored, remembered, examined and retold through the decades.

At weekends, Simbhoo would arrive and take command of the family. Each Sunday evening, he gathered the children and taught them Hindu mantras, or gave a talk on Indian civilization and the epics. They had to learn the Hindi alphabet and some vocabulary, but never learned how to connect the words and speak the language. Later, as 'Pandit Simbhoonath Capildeo', he would self-publish *100 Questions and Answers on the Hindu Religion*, a book that his nephew Vido would proceed to satirize in *The Mystic Masseur*.[35] He expected deference from his nephews and nieces, and his brothers-in-law were always aware that he held the purse strings. According to Brahm, 'Power corrupts – and it was an accepted fact in the family that Rudranath and Simbhoonath were the gods, so [as children] you had to bow down to them and literally put your hand down to their feet, so they could bless you. Simbhoo was given full reign to do anything and everything he wished to do. From my point of view, he was a tyrant. Our grandmother would always defer to him, to both her sons.'[36]

For Vido, Kamla and their cousins of a similar age, travelling the five miles to and from school each day was a complicated manoeuvre. Like her brother, Kamla worked hard and was an academic succcess at Tranquillity. Sometimes they would take the Sam Super Service bus, at other times they would travel in an old Ford motor car with running boards which Nanie had bought, but it broke down and nobody knew how to repair it. Pa would cycle to work at the *Guardian*, and sometimes stay in Port of Spain overnight. When the Americans came to Trinidad in 1941 and built the Churchill–Roosevelt Highway and a deep-water naval base at Chaguaramas (under the Lend-Lease agreement, which exchanged British empire bases for American ships) an uncle bought a truck to rent. It had to be at the new base that was being built at Docksite by six o'clock each morning. The truck was driven by Sahadeo Mausa, known as Power Mausa by the children because of his interest in mechanics, who would drop them at Luis Street with an aunt to wait for school to start each day. He continued to assault his son Brahm. 'He would punish me with strapping, slapping, depriving me of food, he would hit me with whatever was at hand. My father was mentally and emotionally unstable.'[37] Vido remembered this period as a time of unhappiness and hunger. He started to get asthma, gasping for missing breath, sucking in air, wheezing his way through the long, hot nights. Often, there would be no proper food available, and he would go to school or to bed on an empty stomach. In Kamla's view, this was the result of wartime food shortages rather than neglect, and she thought Vido's claim of being starved was 'a ridiculous memory, it is a damn stupid memory'.[38]

Full-bellied or hungry, he kept up his studies at Tranquillity, encouraged by Nanie, who would appear in Petit Valley from time to time for an inspection, usually accompanied by her black servant Miss Blackie. When classes ended, Vido would remain behind for extra tuition with a teacher from the school. In 1942, although ranked fifth in a class of forty-five, he won an exhibition to his Uncle Rudranath's old school, Queen's Royal College, where the government now paid his fees and gave an annual grant for the cost of books.[39] Although physically weaker than his contemporaries, he was marked out as an achiever, one of twenty children across the island who had won an exhibition. 'He was brilliant,' said his cousin Jai, a view shared by Brahm: 'Every day for school we had to learn twenty Latin words. So we'd come from school and study, and after five, ten minutes he would say, test me and everything was bang on. Amazing. He said to me at Petit Valley he would like to become a writer.'[40] Vido's own view was that his cousins had been told to revere academic success, 'I suppose because they respected my brightness. I was always treated with regard. And I could make jokes. Very good jokes too.'[41] He never felt completely part of the world of his cousins. 'There was a distant relation who came to stay with us in order to go to school, an elegant boy, and he was mocked and mocked. They told terrible stories about his personal habits, eating the scabs of his sores. I was horrified. Reason told me it was wrong. I couldn't run with them.'[42]

   In the vacation, Pa would take Vido to Tunapuna to stay with his old mentor Sookdeo Misir, now a rich man from his Arima Bus Company. Vido liked the atmosphere at Sookdeo's more wealthy household, and the food that came from its kitchen. A cousin there had a less affectionate memory of the precocious scholar. Sookdeo's grandson Romesh recollected Vidia, aged about ten, lording it over the other children: 'Instead of joining us playing cricket, he would stay reading. He would wait until my grandfather came home from the estate, and would sit there on the back porch and read newspapers very impressively. He was able to pronounce and understand every word in the newspaper. The old man was very enamoured with him because of his brilliance.' Sookdeo was himself uneducated. 'Of course we were pitted against Vidia by our grandfather saying, "See what you all are doing, playing football and cricket. Why don't you learn to read and write properly, like Vidia?"'[43] Margaret Maillard, who went to school with Kamla and would marry another future Nobel laureate, Derek Walcott, remembered his academic talent. 'We knew he was bright. He had to do a French exam, and he learnt in full the answer for a question – in French.'[44]

   In 1943, Seepersad could stand it no longer at Petit Valley and the Naipaul family moved in desperation to 17 Luis Street. Once again, Pa was relying on Nanie's network of support, even while he railed against it. Over the next year they were joined by more family members, and the little house became crowded. Each branch of the extended family used its own kerosene stove to cook. For Vido, school seemed to be an alternative world where he could find a footing. Queen's Royal College or QRC had been set up in 1859 by the colonial government to counter 'French' influence on the island. It was a substantial late-Victorian colonial building done in multicoloured stone and fringed by palm trees, located on the edge of the Queen's Park Savannah by the Anglican bishop's residence. QRC was modelled on an English boys' public school, and offered a high standard of education. It was rivalled by St Mary's or the College of the Immaculate Conception, which was run by Roman Catholic priests. No other Caribbean island had the same rivalry between two schools of such academic excellence.[45] Like Tranquillity, QRC had few Indian pupils, and they were mainly Christian or Muslim.

Although Vido was brought up like many Hindus to be aware of his difference from Muslims, there was no obvious communal divide in Trinidad. Watching newsreels of events in India at the cinema, he felt they were engaged in a common struggle: 'I thought of Muslims as being part of us, one people. Some Indian Muslims went to school with me. I never thought about it ... We were fed Indian nationalism by people [such as Simbhoo] who were doing nothing about it in real life – imagine us as village big-shots. There was a man called Chandra Bahadur Mathura, who ran a wretched little rag of a magazine called *The Indian*. We were schooled in it: we knew about Gandhi, we knew about Nehru, we knew about Azad [the Muslim president of the Indian National Congress]. I remember seeing the newsreels of the Cripps Mission in 1942, Stafford Cripps talking to the Mahatma ... I felt proud.'[46]

At school, he made no deliberate effort to associate with other Indians. 'My friends at QRC would have been black people,' he recalled.[47] From Tranquillity came Yip Young and WAGS, who liked his humour. He made friends with Charles John, whose father was a Woodbrook policeman, and William Demas, a tall, gangly, flat-nosed black boy who got free textbooks because his father was a DPO, or deceased public officer. The boys called each other by their surnames, in British style. Each morning Naipaul would walk to school early and run home to Luis Street for lunch, accompanied to the end of the road by Charles John. He never brought friends home, preferring to keep the two worlds separate. 'It seemed natural to have the friendship outside the house. You wouldn't want another boy to see your poverty,' he said later.[48] To his sister Savi this seemed odd, particularly as Vido grew older: it appeared to represent a separation arising from social, ethnic or cultural embarrassment.

The school buildings at QRC were 'very beautiful' to Vido. 'I liked the ritual of the school life. I liked the formality. I liked the spaciousness of the grounds. Every form had its form master, and he did the roll every morning. For me, the school was immeasurably exciting.'[49] He enjoyed classes in Latin, French, Spanish and Science. Still small, he was conscious that he was one of the youngest boys in his year. Since it was wartime, many of the British teachers had been called up to fight and replaced by West Indian teachers, making the staff as racially diverse as the pupils. The principal, Mr Hamer, was English. It was a highly competitive school, with metropolitan values. Caribbean dialect was ironed out in favour of standard English, although the pupils remained bilingual – outside class, they might still say, 'Higher monkey climb, more he show he ass', or, 'Cutlass don't leave mark in water', or 'Play jackass, they go ride ya'. At home, a boy might have a third language, deriving from his parents' country of origin: Portuguese, Bhojpuri, French, Cantonese. Selby Wooding, who was at QRC a couple of years ahead of Vido, considered it 'an honour school. Boys could be depended on to be trustworthy. It is a world that has vanished now.' The happy few were expected to behave like English schoolboys in the tropics. According to Wooding, 'You had to wear the mask of the master in order to advance.'[50]

*

When Seepersad Naipaul conceived of becoming a writer, in emulation of authors he admired like O. Henry and W. Somerset Maugham, he had few indigenous examples. Herbert de Lisser, a Jamaican, had published a couple of books in London during the First World War, and was followed in the 1930s by Alfred Mendes, a Trinidadian who placed two novels with Duckworth of London, one with a blurb by the writer Anthony Powell.[51] Jamaican-born Claude McKay had moved to America and achieved some literary prominence as part of the Harlem Renaissance, and W. Adolphe Roberts published detective novels in the USA. Jean Rhys, a woman from a white creole family in Dominica, had published stories and novels. The nearest thing Pa had to a homegrown model was C.L.R. James, a former QRC student and one of its earliest black teachers. His realistic street novel *Minty Alley* was published by Secker & Warburg in 1936 after he sailed to London to try his luck in the imperial capital. James wrote a series of letters for the *Port of Spain Gazette* in the year of Vido's birth: they told how he liked the 'intellectual ferment' of Bloomsbury, enjoyed reading 'the delightful Miss Rebecca West in the *Daily Telegraph*' and claimed he had bested Edith Sitwell at an evening lecture with a clever reference to William Faulkner. Parodying the manner of the European visitors who wrote about the West Indies, James observed that since 'the English native is so glum and dull and generally boorish in his manners ... any man of colour who is not repulsive in appearance, has good manners, and is fairly intelligent, is a great favourite with the girls.' The habitations of the English he found glum, owing to 'the terrible habit of joining all the houses one to another for hundreds of yards.'[52] Apart from these rare achievers, aspiring Caribbean writers like Pa faced self-publication, a haphazard activity that was taken less than seriously in this busy, verbal, storytelling culture.

Pa knew he had written good stories, and wanted to see them in print. He needed money, and in 1943 turned to Simbhoo. 'My father paid for the publication of his stories,' Simbhoo's son Suren remembered. 'Without that book, Seepersad would have been nothing.'[53] A thousand copies of *Gurudeva and other Indian Tales* were printed at the *Guardian* commercial printery, selling at $1 each. Pa brought home the proofs in his jacket pocket each evening. Not realizing the extent of his literary ambition, most people assumed this was a venture to make money. The publisher was listed as Trinidad Publications of 17 Luis Street, and an advertisement to the left of the title page asked for submissions of short stories, essays and novelettes. *Gurudeva* was like a booklet, seventy-two pages long with a soft blue cover showing the veiled head of an Indian woman above a rural scene: palm trees, the sun, an ajoupa hut, a Hindu temple and prayer flags high on bamboo poles, drawn by a local artist, Alfred Codallo.[54] Devotedly, Kamla and Vido stuck an errata slip to the flyleaf of each copy of their father's treasured book. Over time, the entire print-run sold. There were complaints from Indians who thought the book insulted their community.

In linked short stories, *Gurudeva* described the picaresque progress of its title character, a rogue who starts out as a juvenile husband, becomes a boastful but cowardly village stick-fighter, gets sent to jail, and ends up as a phoney pundit before sacking his wife, Ratni, in favour of Daisy, who bobs her hair and dumps him. Set in the 1930s and 1940s, it shows the

Indian community in Trinidad cut adrift from its origins, coming to terms with a confusing, changing world. Seepersad based Gurudeva on his former brother-in-law Dinanath Tiwari, a gangster and pundit who had given the name 'Vidyadhar' to his son, and who was now divorced from Ma's sister Ramdoolarie.

Gurudeva and other Indian Tales might be dismissed as a literary curiosity, the work of a famous writer's father, but is a book of rare quality in its own right, an early text in the tradition of Indian diasporic fiction that was to develop vigorously later in the century. At its best, the writing has a classical quality. Here is Gurudeva collecting and preparing sticks for fighting:

> He would take himself into the high woods up in Chickland, three miles away, and cut the pouis that flourished abundantly on the high lands, and gathering them in a bundle, he would tote them home. Out in the yard he would make a blazing fire of dry leaves and bake the sticks in it and beat the barks off them on the ground. Then he would cut each stick into the desired length – from ground level to his lower ribs – and then with cutlass, with broken bottles with razor-sharp edges, and finally with sandpaper, he would impart to each stick the smoothness and uniformity of a ruler. Then he would go to the giant bamboo clump near by and bring forth a length of bamboo, stout and ripe and roomy in its hollowness, and an inch or two longer than his stick; and he would punch out all the compartments but the last, and order Ratni to make enough oil from coconuts and fill the bamboo vessel with it to the very top . . . Into the bamboo he would immerse as many of his precious sticks as it could hold. Then he would stand the vessel in a corner of his room and would not bring out the sticks from it till ten days or a fortnight when he would let off a whoop of joy. For the sticks would be found to have taken on a rich brown colour and almost twice the weight they had before their protracted bath.[55]

The prose is economical and illustrative, giving the reader a rapid, intimate glimpse of a completely alien world. Unlike other Caribbean writers of this period, Seepersad Naipaul wrote only about what he knew. Part of his achievement was to shift between rival forms of the English language in order to show his world. The narrative is in standard English. Gurudeva speaks in dialect. When Ratni asks why he needs quite so many sticks, 'Gurudeva promptly silenced her with a slap. "Mind you' own business," he said. "Don' put goatmouth." '[56] Mr Sohun the schoolmaster, who stands in for Seepersad in the narrative, speaks in educated English. He tells a baffled Gurudeva that Trinidad's pundits are more concerned with wearing sandalwood paste caste-marks than with learning how to read the scriptures: 'Not caste, but the shadow of caste remains in the West Indies,' he tells him. 'Its only use here is to inflate some people's ego.'[57] In the final scene, where Gurudeva is hauled before the village council or panchayat for taking a second wife, the proceedings are conducted in Hindi. When a man accuses him of beating Ratni, Gurudeva stands up and shouts, '"Why you don' keep you' dam mouth shut? Why you 'terrupting?" Pundit Shivlochan raised both hands to heaven and said: "No *Angrezi*, please! I do not understand *Angrezi*." '[58] The shift in language and tone through these stories, written by a man who had taught himself English in early adulthood, is done effortlessly. The humour too is gently done. When fighters from a rival village arrive during Hosay, Gurudeva wraps a handkerchief around his jaw in a pugnacious manner and says he has toothache and a sprained wrist. Scowling in the direction of the enemy, he mutters, '"It is lucky for them, though, that I get sick today. Odderwise I woulda show them." '[59]

Some writers spend a lifetime finding a style. They experiment, reject their forebears, imitate their contemporaries. Reinventing language is part of their literary ambition. Samuel Beckett, born in the same year as Pa, squeezed words in order to see what they might do. Modernist writers, and the deconstructionists and critical theorists who came in their wake, believed language is necessarily fictive and that its rupture might lead to creation; sometimes, in the work say of Ezra Pound or Virginia Woolf, they were right. Apart from a slight shift around the time he wrote *The Mimic Men*, V.S. Naipaul never went through a process of linguistic experimentation. He would circumnavigate Modernism, even as he absorbed its implications. His writing style formed early. At the age of only eleven, he was given his own private epic by his father, and took it as his model; his later achievement came out of this restriction. When he was asked — fifty-seven years on — by the Indian website *Tehelka* for some rules for aspiring writers, V.S. Naipaul's response owed much to Pa's instruction:

1. Do not write long sentences. A sentence should not have more than 10 or 12 words.

2. Each sentence should make a clear statement. It should add to the statement that went before. A good paragraph is a series of clear, linked statements.
3. Do not use big words. If your computer tells you that your average word is more than five letters long, there is something wrong. The use of small words compels you to think about what you are writing. Even difficult ideas can be broken down into small words.
4. Never use words whose meaning you are not sure of. If you break this rule you should look for other work.
5. The beginner should avoid using adjectives, except those of colour, size and number. Use as few adverbs as possible.
6. Avoid the abstract. Always go for the concrete.
7. Every day, for six months at least, practise writing in this way. Small words; short, clear, concrete sentences. It may be awkward but it's training you in the use of language. It may even be getting rid of the bad language habits you picked up at the university. You may go beyond these rules after you have thoroughly understood and mastered them.[60]

Seepersad's idea of literature, conceived in colonial isolation and arrived at by rejecting the florid Victorian tomes that had impressed him early on, became Vido's. Language was to be plain; where it became beautiful, it was through simplicity. To describe the process by which Gurudeva might turn a length of bamboo into a vessel for soaking sticks, Pa took only ten words: 'he would punch out all the compartments but the last'.

Gurudeva and other Indian Tales was the prequel to *A House for Mr Biswas*, and gave V.S. Naipaul the picaresque character of Ganesh for his first published book, *The Mystic Masseur*. In old age, he believed his father's book was under-appreciated, particularly by Indian critics, despite his attempts to promote it: 'No one in India knows that it's good writing. They think it's purely my sentimentality ... They wouldn't be able to compare it with Tolstoy's later writing, *Master and Man*. They wouldn't be able to compare it with *The Odyssey* or Gogol. They would think this is just peasant writing about peasant details. The more I look at it, the more I [can] see the actual way I write – very pictorial, very fast, the details. I knew that I had been given a feeling for language, and it was very beautiful, and it was my own epic.'[61]

CHAPTER FOUR

TO THE MOTHER COUNTRY

BY THE START OF 1945 the liberation of Europe was under way and the Second World War was coming to an end. Many West Indians had volunteered to fight, including thousands in the Royal Air Force and the Royal Canadian Air Force. The presence of American and British servicemen in Trinidad had precipitated social adjustment. Films, gum and raised hemlines came to town. As peace loomed, so did political change; the British empire was bankrupt, and decolonization was being discussed freely. Elections to the Legislative Council were planned for the following year, the first to be based on a universal franchise; Simbhoo would run unsuccessfully as a United Front candidate in Caroni.[1] In V.S. Naipaul's novel *The Suffrage of Elvira*, Mrs Baksh says, 'Everybody just washing their foot and jumping in this democracy business. But I promising you, for all the sweet it begin sweet, it going to end damn sour.'[2] Old conventions changed; where Droapatie and the Mausis wore clothes modelled on Indian fashions of centuries ago, they put their daughters in dresses. Some thought of trying to establish their own households outside the joint family. At the far end of Luis Street, a man named Tubal set up a brothel; when walking past, the cousins were instructed to cross the road and not look inside. Vido wrote later, 'The American soldiers loved a fat back-street whore, the blacker the better; they packed them into their jeeps and raced from club to club, throwing their money about ... Beside them the British soldiers were like foreigners ... they spoke this strange English; they referred to themselves as "blokes" ... not knowing that in Trinidad a bloke was a term of abuse; their uniforms, their shorts in particular, were ugly.'[3]

During the school term, the three-bedroomed house in Luis Street would be filled with children, sometimes more than two dozen staying overnight. At first they slept on the verandah, but then the verandah filled and the foul-smelling downstairs area beneath the house was used for accommodation. Nanie bought tables which were lined up in the basement to make a sleeping area. The boys slept on the north side of the house, the girls on the south. Each cousin would be given a pillow and a blanket made from stitched rice bags. To passers-by, it was a hilarious sight, the rows of Indian children stacked up on the tables under the house like peas in a pod; for the children, some now in their teens, the public mockery was humiliating. Nanie had Pahl cocoa bags sewn together and strung along the side of the house to protect them from view. Poker, the roguish descendant of an indentured labourer who had been on the same ship as Capildeo Maharaj, lived in the 'servant room' in the yard. More relations arrived, and at its high or low point, 17 Luis Street was inhabited by up to forty people. For Ma and Pa, the situation was complicated by the unforeseen arrival in February 1945 of another child, a boy named Shivadhar Srinivasa, known as Sewan or Shivan. One day when Vido was coming home from school he took shelter from the rain. 'It was a custom of the place, if it begins to rain, you can go to the verandah of any house – just one of these civilities which we took for granted and didn't fully understand. So I went to a house. It was a Negro house, not far from where we lived and I heard them talking about us. About how we were all crowded in that little house, and I was so ashamed.'[4] He protected himself by imagining a life elsewhere.

In August, his uncle Rudranath returned after more than six years away in England on his scholarship. He had forsaken medicine for mathematics, and there was talk that he would be offered a place on the faculty at London University, where he was doing a PhD on 'the flexure problem in elasticity'. Rudranath was treated as a conquering hero, an expert on all things, the new head of the family, displacing his elder brother Simbhoo. He was particularly friendly with his young female relatives. Mira remembered him on his return as 'very charming. He liked to flirt with the girls, with the nieces, he was like the darling uncle, playing tennis with everyone.' He took it upon himself to educate them in mathematics, and if anyone failed to understand, he would go into a fury. Mira recalled him beating Sati with his belt. 'She couldn't do some mathematical problem he had asked her. I remember being very upset because she was my sister.'[5] Rudranath's son Rudy remembered his father as 'a great intellect but a restless soul. He used sarcasm all the time, the one-line quip that would cut you off at the knees. He thought of the Naipauls as the lesser side of the family.'[6]

Naturally, Rudranath was given a room of his own at Luis Street, and the rest of the family had to squeeze tighter. Pa was riven by distress at his own impotence, although his situation was improving. *Gurudeva* had been noticed by Dora Ibberson, a British woman who was starting a new social welfare department for the Trinidad government. She asked Seepersad if he would like to make a survey of the rural Indian community. A car came with the job, and a salary twice that of the *Guardian*. He accepted, but as he prepared to go to Jamaica for six months of training, he fell ill with nerves. Dora Ibberson arranged for the whole family to be taken by car to the sea at Toco, their first and only family holiday, and one of many events that would later be fictionalized in *A House for Mr Biswas*. While Pa was away in Jamaica, it was decided by Nanie and her sons that the extensive Capildeo landholdings and properties would be divided. Nanie took a firmly patrilineal view: the boys would inherit. Each Mausi was given a small plot of land, and the more influential sons-in-law were ousted, creating a lasting family rift. Pa dismissed the gift of land as a con, calling the agricultural plots, 'swamp lands, lagoon lands, rice lands, big deal!'[7] For him, the Capildeo brothers were now a pair of gangster bosses: Capo S. and Capo R.

Still, Pa had a new job and a Ford Prefect – licence plate PA1192. What he lacked was a place of his own. Port of Spain with its 100,000 inhabitants was full of people, and little new housing had been built there during the war. He did not even have space for his few pieces of furniture. In his little room at the back of Luis Street, Pa railed against Capo R., his words being carried through the air vents to other rooms. Ma tried to maintain the peace. Capo R. responded, and unforgivable insults were hurled around the little house. The children were shocked by the things the adults were saying, swearing at each other viciously across the partitions between the rooms. Vido remembered the obscenities and the sense of entrapment, while he was meant to be revising for his Senior Cambridge exam: 'In the crowded place below the floor [where the children slept] the air was bad and I suffered terribly from nausea. People were cooking on kerosene stoves. I had asthma. I really felt pushed to the limit there. My schoolwork suffered, and the report of my form master for 1946 says, "Has gone backwards rapidly." And indeed I had.'[8] He disliked the communal food at Luis Street: fried breadfruit, curried vegetables, concoctions made of chatagne (a local chestnut), and the ubiquitous roti, a Trinidadian reworking of the Indian flatbread, rolled up into a parcel with a filling of spiced chickpeas or goat meat.

Mira remembered the tension between Pa and Ma: 'There were times when he would say horrible things to her, and would actually throw china and food. I remember he would throw things at the wall out of anger.'[9] In desperation, Seepersad approached his only wealthy relative, Sookdeo Misir, and asked for a loan to buy a property. He only had the first $1,300 of the purchase price. Without collateral, he was lent $4,000 or £833 (the Trinidad & Tobago dollar was pegged at £1:$4.80, and both sterling and the US dollar were legal tender). It was a substantial debt, but it enabled Pa to buy a house in the run-down Indian district of St James, to the north-west of Woodbrook. Number 26 Nepaul Street was a box, a hot, rickety, partitioned building near the end of the street, around 7 square metres on two floors with an external wooden staircase and a corrugated iron roof.[10] On the last day of 1946, the Naipaul family moved in. The upper floor sagged in the middle, but as Kamla said, 'It was our home, the first home we ever had.'[11]

At once, the dynamic between the parents and the children shifted: they became a unit, a nuclear family, a father, mother, brothers and sisters. Seepersad was just forty, Droapatie thirty-three, Kamla sixteen, and Vidia, Sati, Mira and Savi descended in two-year decrements; Sewan was ten months old. They had greater freedom now to do as they liked, without the sanctions of the joint family. Kamla and Vido could travel around Port of Spain on foot, or ride one of the new trolleybuses that had replaced the trams. The house was rarely locked, and one day they returned to find it ransacked: the 'thief' was Pa, playing a practical joke, which the children did not find amusing. He would dress up and take them and the cousins on excursions to the sea in the Prefect. 'Seepersad would drive us down to Dhein's Bay for a sea-bathe,' his nephew Suren, Simbhoo's son, remembered. 'He was a lazy, easy-going character, always chain-smoking. All these sons-in-law were lazy sons-of-bitches who specialized in not working. Any needs that [Droapatie] Mausi had, she would come to us.'[12] Brahm saw the situation in a different light: 'Seepersad was very kind taking us to the beaches. Looking back, I think he was ostracized by the family, especially Simbhoo and Rudranath because he could match them with his intelligence, he didn't feel inferior to anybody. He was very calm in his own way, and always had a sense of orderliness. Plus Seepersad had a heightened white colour, he stood out. Some of the neighbours on the street when we were playing would call him pale white.'[13]

'To try to put it in a moral context,' said Savi later, 'my father always disliked the way the Capildeos did things, and therefore we were taught to question the way things were done. I would describe them, the Capildeo boys, as pretty rotten: their jealousies, their selfishness, their pettiness to anybody who showed any sign of any ability. I remember Simbhoo's comment when Kamla wore lipstick for the first time: "Is your mouth bleeding?" These were the types of comments that were made . . . I remember Sewan going to Simbhoo one day as a little boy and they invited him to eat and he didn't want to sit on the floor or eat with his hands. Simbhoo's comment was, "And you haven't even gone to Oxford as yet." [My husband] did not like Simbhoonath because when he got married to me, an ordinary lowly niece, we went to a function at his house and he asked us whether we would eat in the kitchen. That's the man.'[14]

Mira remembered Capo S. during the years after they moved to Nepaul Street as 'very intimidating, serious. He was always prowling in the car looking for the nieces and the nephews who might be breaking the rules of the family. I remember seeing his car pass by and being actually scared even though I had permission to go to the movies with this guy.'[15] The girls and Ma did all the ironing, washing, polishing, cooking and cleaning at Nepaul Street. Savi felt that, as the son, 'Vidia was always catered to in the household from when he was a young child – by my mother, my father, all siblings without exception. He has always expected people to support him.'[16]

As well as developing an interest in film at this time, and visiting the Port of Spain cinemas – the Rialto, the Deluxe, the London – Vido sent letters around the world, seeking some sense of what was happening elsewhere. Enid W. Schuette of *Time* magazine in New York told him that most *Time* readers were indeed American, and sent a batch of stamps for his collection. The secretary general of the Royal Empire Society in London informed him that he had received an 'honourable mention' in that year's essay competition. A New Zealand postmaster put him in touch with a penfriend, although he already had one, Gordon Peterson of Taunton School in England, who wrote saying that the cross-country run had been rained off, and asked whether there was an ice-rink in Trinidad. Vidia's favoured penfriend, however, was a girl named Beverly in Hawaii. A fortnight before leaving Luis Street, aged all of fourteen, he had written her a letter in his best courtly style:

My Dear Beverly,

I have looked in vain for my pen, and so I have been forced to write this letter in pencil, imitating the example set by you in your first letter.

I have received your charming letter, the more charming postcards and the yet more charming photograph of yourself. I guess that sums up what I feel about you, especially when we consider how beautiful the postcards were . . .

We have much in common with Hawaii — tropical scenes, the allure of a moonlight night, etc. Perhaps you have heard about our calypsoes. They are world famous. It was a Trinidadian — a Negro — who made up the calypso about 'Rum and Coca-Cola'. If you have not heard it you certainly have missed something. The best part of it runs like this:

'The Andrews Sisters and Bing Crosby
Should make a trip to the West Indies,
Siddong (= sit down) under de (= the) silvery moon
Lissening (= listening) to dem (= them) calypsonian croon.'

It would be very amusing to tell you how native Trinidadians speak English — the uneducated ones, of course.

'Marnin' me darlin'. And how is de baby? 'E still got the fever? Why you don' try geeing (= giving) 'im some shinin' bush.'

'Po' me! De amount a t'ings I try to send 'way dat fever, me eh know what to try again. Ah go tek him to the Healt' Office.'

Now here are the ways a word 'lick' is used.

'Ah go lick in she features wid a rock stone' = I will smash her face with a stone.

'This road lickin' up me tire, man' = But this road is eating up my tire.

'Lick the stamp' = Literal meaning . . .

Friday I went to see the 'Hurricane' — quite an old picture. I can't think of any more to write, so
                        Cheerio,
                            Vidia.[17]

Beverly's reply does not survive, so there is no way of knowing whether she was able to distinguish between Trinidadians, native Trinidadians and Vidia Naipaul.

*

Vido was not alone in trying out a new style or identity, in presenting himself as a sophisticate. It was not rare in Trinidad for people to remake themselves, to change their name or adjust their background. The 'smart-man' who managed to deceive others cleverly was much admired in Trinidad, like the hustler in *The Middle Passage* who sold tickets for a fictitious Sam Cooke concert, and disappeared:

> Three youths were talking about this affair one afternoon around a coconut-cart near the Savannah.
> The Indian said, 'I don't see how anybody could vex with the man. *That* is brains.'
> 'Is what my aunt say,' one of the Negro boys said. 'She ain't feel she get rob. She feel she pay two dollars for the *intelligence*.'[18]

With so little common heritage between communities, attributes could be borrowed and people could 'play themselves'. Adrian Cola Rienzi had once been Krishna Deonarine; Mr Ramprasad became Mr Ablack; Mr Meighoo became Mr Mayhew; Ganesh Ramsumair in *The Mystic Masseur* would become G. Ramsay Muir; Pa sometimes signed an article Paul Nye or Paul Prye. It was necessary to have a public face, since whatever your ethnicity you could be sure that aspects of your home life, the familiar indoor world, would be culturally alien to those you met outside. Lloyd Best, a black boy two years younger than Vidia at QRC who was sponsored through school by Sookdeo Misir, expressed it this way: 'The most important single feature of Trinidadian culture is the extent to which masks are indispensable, because there are so many different cultures and ethnicities in this country that people have to play a vast multiplicity of roles, each of which has got its own mask depending on where they are. It's true of the whole Caribbean, and Trinidad is the extreme case in my view.'[19]

Almost nobody knew their real personal history. They might come from West Africa, or Venezuela, or Madeira, or south India, or from some complicated intermingling of ancestry, travels through different places; only in exceptional cases would the family journey be clear. Each community was divided and subdivided. Among Indians there were Hindus, Muslims and Christians; among the Hindus, there were caste divisions; among Indian Christians, there were Anglicans, Presbyterians and Roman Catholics. People of African descent followed a multiplicity of Christian faiths, and had little sense at this time of African brotherhood, or of a united black heritage. At the heart of Trinidad lay the void, the void of dispossession and extermination: the unexpressed knowledge that the land had once belonged to someone else, the Amerindians who had been killed or chased away. The spirit of the dispossessed could be felt, as it can be in parts of the American West. Even Trinidadians of probable Amerindian descent had no way of knowing whether their forebears had lived there at the time of Columbus's arrival. For everyone, Trinidad was a borrowed island; only after independence was there an active attempt to create and shape a shared 'Trini' identity.

A pupil at QRC might come from a background that belied his physical appearance, like Hok in *The Mimic Men*, a boy who owes something to Yip Young. Passing his mother while walking with other pupils, Hok ignores her, until he is sent back by his teacher to greet her: 'She was indeed a surprise, a Negro woman of the people, short and rather fat, quite unremarkable.'[20] Vido strove to keep his home and school lives discrete, and tried not to be perceived merely as another offshoot of the Capildeo clan. He wanted to be himself, and himself alone. In Savi's recollection, 'He never invited a schoolfriend into the house. We never understood. He stood at the gate talking to them.' Nor did he like other guests. 'When people came to visit, even when family came, he would leave the books downstairs because he studied on the dining table and race upstairs to tell us that people were downstairs. He would not go and open the door and say come in. I guess he was shy. He couldn't cope with it.'[21] Vido claimed later to have had no friends at QRC, although others considered him a popular boy. 'At school I had only admirers; I had no friends.' This is disingenuous; he had friends, but kept much of himself hidden from them. Later in life, he would deliberately avoid friendship for fear it might make him less distinctive, less singular. 'It is important not to trust people too much. Friendship might be turned against you in a foolish way, and you must not impose yourself to that extent on anyone. Burdening them with your trust. It is a burden. Friendship has not been important to me.' The tensions and double-crossings of Petit Valley and Luis Street made him permanently wary and protean, a trait that would become more extreme and self-referential as the years passed: 'I profoundly feel that people are letting you down all the time.'[22]

Pa had reacted to the complexities of his own background by embracing Indianness while rejecting orthodox Hinduism, or what in Trinidad was known as 'Sanatanism'. In August 1947 India gained independence, and like its new leader Jawaharlal Nehru, Pa believed in religious and cultural reform. Hinduism had regulations on all things: clothing, ritual pollution, caste distinction, bodily functions, diet. The Naipaul family were not vegetarian, as most Brahmins are supposed to be; they sometimes ate meat, and treated chicken as a vegetable. At Christmas they would celebrate with baked fowl, dalpuri, nuts and fruit. Following the principles of the Arya Samaj, Pa believed in Hinduism as a philosophical system and thought that old rituals should be swept away. He particularly disliked the island's orthodox Brahmin pundits, whom he knew were often phoneys and hustlers. Hindu missionaries from India visited Trinidad, and a divide developed between 'Sanatanists' and 'Samajists'. Vidia, as a rationalist and his father's son, rejected the group activities linked to caste. His grandmother would hold public readings of the scriptures at the Lion House and 17 Luis Street, at which her grandsons would sit at the front and be fed first, displaying their caste status. When other teenage boys in the Capildeo clan had their heads shaved as part of the sacred thread ceremony, to show they were Brahmins, Vidia refused to take part. At the same time, he maintained the pride in caste that was the identifying force in his mother's family. He wrote later that during a science class at school he had refused to put his mouth to a length of tubing, and 'an Indian boy in the row behind, a Port of Spain boy, a recognized class tough, whispered, "Real brahmin". His tone was approving.'[23]

Like Nanie, Pa and Ma believed in education as the route to progress. Kamla and Vido, both gifted academically, were encouraged to study for foreign scholarships. At first, Vido's commitment was tentative. At the end of the second term of 1947, his school report said he was being slack, and that although a pupil of 'real ability . . . he is not giving of his best'. A term later his form master wrote: 'There is still much room for improvement, however, and in the literature he must show greater balance in his judgements if he is to gain the double distinction he seeks.'[24] Balance was never to be his strong point, but he would achieve distinction. The turning point in his attitude came during a conversation in the cricket nets with William Demas, his senior by two years, who had just won an island scholarship to Cambridge University in England. Vido remembered: 'I told him that I wanted to win the scholarship too, and said I'm going to start working soon. He said, you mustn't say that, what you must say is, I'm going to go home now and start working. I followed his advice. I have always remembered his advice. He did economics at Cambridge and later became governor of the Central Bank of Trinidad.'[25] From the summer of 1947, Vido concentrated on the scholarship, specializing in French and Spanish literature and Roman history. He thought the emphasis on learning at QRC arose from 'the general atmosphere in the colonial world: it was a special school and we owed something to our school, we owed it to ourselves. And you see the rewards were so few. There was only one scholarship in each subject. So you had to come tops. So it bred a lot of neurosis too as a result.'[26]

To Mira, four years his junior, Vidia seemed to be a solitary, scholarly figure, less sociable than other members of the family. His books were kept at one end of the dining table in Nepaul Street, on a section that was made of lighter wood. For her, 'that was like his little desk, his study. He was definitely privileged. We were just pesky little sisters. We regarded him as being very bright. Eggs were very hard to come by, and I always remember that Vido would get the scrambled egg and not us because he had to study for his exams. It was very important. I think it was because he was the boy who might go somewhere. He needed the nourishment of the eggs and I think I love eggs because Vido got the eggs!'[27] Savi remembered him working hard and exercising hard, and often going swimming. Indoors he talked to her, but outside the house it was as if she did not exist: 'The only time Vidia spoke to Mira and I was the day Gandhi died. He said, "Gandhi was assassinated." I am not too sure we knew the meaning of the word assassinated at that point. We got the message. Otherwise he rode past us on his bicycle almost every day. We were little girls, nuisances.'[28]

With or without the benefit of eggs, and while also helping to care for little Sewan, Kamla was the first winner of a new scholarship for the island's Indian girls to study at Benares Hindu University in India. It was an exceptional achievement; and she looked good too. While Kamla prepared for her departure in summer 1949, she took a temporary job at the *Guardian*. Melvyn Akal, who came from an Indian Presbyterian family and would later marry Savi, said Kamla was renowned as a beauty by the boys at QRC: 'I knew of her because at school boys would be teasing Vidia and saying, "How are you brother-in-law? How is Kamla today?" [29] Too glamorous for schoolboys, Kamla began a romance instead with Sam Selvon, a handsome man in his mid-twenties who had been a wireless operator during the war, and was now working as a news reporter at the *Guardian*. Although he came from an Indian family, Selvon had a Scottish grandfather and was creolized in a way that was anathema to the Naipauls and the Capildeos. Besides this, he was a skilful aspiring writer, and Kamla had to make sure the relationship remained hidden from Pa and the family.

Vido became increasingly serious as he worked for his exam, the Higher School Certificate: he believed his future depended on it, and asserted later that without a scholarship abroad he would have been doomed. 'By the time I was about twelve, I had decided to get away, to leave. The scholarship protects you, gives you money for some years. It is protection.' [30] To succeed, he would need to beat not only his talented contemporaries at QRC but pupils from good schools such as St Mary's and Naparima College in San Fernando. There were only four scholarships available for the whole island – two more than there had been during wartime. In March 1949 the results were published: Vidia Naipaul had failed to win a scholarship. The family were depressed, and silent. Vido was tormented. At this point, it turned out that QRC had misread the new guidelines for the exam, and he had sat the wrong combination of papers. He had, however, achieved a distinction in both French and Spanish. His uncle Rudranath wrote from England offering congratulations and condolences.

A front-page story in the *Guardian* headlined 'Special "Schol" Urged for QRC Student' stated: 'Government will be asked by the Education Board to grant a special scholarship to V.S. Naipaul of Queen's Royal College who took Modern Studies in the last year's Cambridge Higher School Certificate Examination. At yesterday afternoon's meeting of the board, Mr R. Hamer, principal of the college said that, owing to a lack of understanding of the regulations at Q.R.C. very few pupils in the modern studies group were eligible for a scholarship ... Mr Hamer proposed that the Board ask the Government to grant him a special scholarship ... Unanimous approval was given to Mr. Hamer's proposal.' [31] Since they were already planning to increase the total number of foreign scholarships, the Trinidad government concurred. Vidia said, 'There were articles in the press, and there were letters from Negroes who didn't like the idea of me getting a scholarship. The thing about being sixteen and having letters against one – I got used to criticism at an early age. I got used to being attacked in the press. It was an early baptism.'[32] Looking back, conditioned by a sense of his own destiny, he claimed to see his victory as a grand moment of survival. 'It's one of these lucky things in my life which I just squeaked through.' Without a scholarship, 'I think I would have gone crazy. I would not have accepted it and I think that is why my friend Yip Young killed himself shortly after I left. He thought he had no future. I could have been destroyed at many stages. If I lost, I would have collapsed. The stakes were always big in my own mind ... In these primitive societies the main talent is intrigue. Shall we say the Negroes of Trinidad excel only in intrigue, in government department intrigue? They excel in that. I would never have done it well.'[33]

At the end-of-year Sixth Form party, held in the gym at QRC, Vido was on lively form, displaying a talent that was not purely cerebral. His cousin Jai watched him show off before a female audience, the sisters and friends of his classmates. 'He was in front of a line of girls enjoying himself, doing acrobatics, doing flips, bending right back onto his hands. It was fun for everybody. He was very much the joker, very much the acrobat.'[34] He also had a reputation for being cynical and acerbic, and for taking a line that was different from everyone else. One boy, labelled 'banal' by Naipaul, had to go home and look up the word in a dictionary. Lloyd Best recalled how he would 'hold court' in front of other boys at QRC, expressing his views on cricket or the world, or pillorying any contemporaries who did not come up to scratch. 'He always saw society from one angle, different from everybody else, even when he was in school. That's why I say that he was always holding court. Because he had a point of view that was very different from everybody else.'[35] A schoolboy pose, an attitude intended to distinguish himself from others which had initially been borrowed from his father and his uncle Rudranath, was to become integral to his personality.

Vido wanted to go to Britain that autumn to study English literature, but the education board decided he was too young, and should wait until 1950. His chosen destination was Oxford University, but a college had first to accept his application. Although he had it retouched, he was worried the photograph that accompanied his entrance forms made his face look fat. His application was circulated around the Oxford colleges and picked up by Peter Bayley, a Fellow in English at University College who was impressed above all by his photograph and his ethnicity. Bayley recalled: 'A dossier, with photograph, smiling Indian boy, you can imagine, charming little Indian boy he looked . . . a very distinguished achievement from his big grammar school in Port of Spain. And because I loved India and had many Indian friends, because of being there for nearly four years in the war, I just didn't hesitate, just took him . . . I don't remember any references. I was terribly pro-Indian, and in fact I very deliberately used to take Indians in the college . . . In those days you admitted your own people for your own subject. Vidia, when he came to me, had been turned down by five or six colleges.'[36]

William Demas, studying in Cambridge, sent 'My dear Naipaul' a letter: 'I must offer you my sincere congratulations both on your Schol. and on your double distinction. That's quite a feat . . . You must be feeling exhilarated at the prospect of escaping from the "hole" and seeking "freedom" in the Mother Country. I think you will enjoy Oxford, for if conditions here apply to Oxford, there will be quite a lot of "arty-crafty" people, discussing the latest Art exhibition, and what not.'[37] Demas's words are interesting: the idea of wanting to escape, of referring to Trinidad as a 'hole' and believing there was no future for an ambitious person in the Caribbean, was common at this time, and by no means restricted to those of Indian descent. He followed up with a second letter advising Naipaul to bring woollen underwear, grey flannel or corduroy trousers, a sports jacket and a tweed suit to England. An overcoat could be purchased on arrival. 'My allowance of £60 was not sufficient. But I think you will find it sufficient, as you wear much smaller sizes than I.' Demas had visited Oxford, and found it to be like a miniature London, though with a medieval atmosphere. As for himself, he was working hard and had met several 'frivolous Continental girls' at the International Club. He concluded: 'A word of warning. Cynicism is no longer in fashion among students. I think your stay here will cure you completely of yours.'[38]

In the meantime Vido needed a job, since Pa was about to lose his. After his survey of Indian villages was complete, Dora Ibberson's department was abolished and Pa was taken on by the probation service. He was supposed to monitor released prisoners in the Chaguanas area, but it was not a success. Now he was applying high and low for another position, and the family was seriously short of money. Eventually, after several months out of work, he was hired again by the *Guardian*. Despite looming political change, the paper still concentrated on British and imperial news. A front page might be headlined 'Britain Will Not Revalue Pound' or 'Eire To Break Free From Empire' or even 'King's Health Improves'. A picture would show white people setting off from Port of Spain on a ship bound for England, or 'debutantes' in the Queen's Park Hotel ballroom, or a British MP arriving in Trinidad. Inside, there might be a large photograph of an English aristocrat walking through Hyde Park, for no apparent reason, or a headline such as 'Late Baronet Praised'. Politicians and titled people from England fulfilled a function that would later be taken by celebrities.

On his seventeenth birthday, Vido was given a job at the Red House where his cousin Owad worked (it had been painted red as a patriotic gesture to mark the diamond jubilee of Queen Victoria). He copied out birth and death certificates in the Registrar General's Office on a salary of $75 a month, or around £370 in modern terms. Using his first earnings, he bought his mother a set of bamboo wall vases, which touched her. For several months, an acting second-class clerk, he had to sit at a table facing a wall painted in green distemper surrounded by hefty ledgers that smelled of fish glue. In 1994 he would publish a redolent account of this period, 'History: A Smell of Fish Glue' in *A Way in the World*. It was a 'very dull job', Mr Hamer said in a letter, and he deserved something better; he would put in a word at the Caribbean Commission, which was supposed to be planning the region's future.[39] Nothing came of it, and in January 1950 Hamer gave him a temporary post as 'secretary and relieving master' at QRC on a salary of $139.96 a month. 'Good, isn't it?' Vido suggested to Kamla. 'Teaching is fun. I enjoy it very much and everyone remarks how well I look, not pale and sickly as when I used to copy out certificates.' The pupils liked him. 'When I came into the hall last Friday – boxing night, all the boys cheered me as one man.'[40]

He also gave tuition to some of his cousins such as Jai and Sita, Simbhoo's daughter, and taught English to older pupils at Tranquillity with WAGS, Winston Springer. Each day he and WAGS would go for lunch together and smoke cigarettes. Vido got on well with Johnny Chen-Wing, a tall, orphaned fourteen-year-old, the only Chinese boy in the class. Chen-Wing's uncle kept a grocery store, and he would take packets of Raleigh cigarettes and give them to his teacher. He found Mr Naipaul 'small, very interesting, handsome, an inspirational teacher. Instead of teaching the syllabus, he would teach what he was interested in ... He had holes in his shoes I remember, when he put his feet up on the desk. He would read prodigiously: Maugham, Forster, V.S. Pritchett, G.B. Shaw as well as French and Spanish writers, Molière and Baudelaire, two books a night.' Chen-Wing thought that by going to Oxford, Naipaul missed out on the period of ferment that led to independence. '[In the 1940s] you could walk freely in the streets of Port of Spain. The unrest, the discontent between Negroes and Asians became much worse, more pronounced, after the 1950s.'[41]

In his spare time, Vido went to art classes at the British Council, where he was complimented on his 'bold' style of painting. He did accomplished sketches. At home he would try to hone his literary skills by writing descriptions of landscape or Port of Spain scenes in turquoise ink in a notebook. He reviewed a book by Somerset Maugham in the QRC *Chronicle*, and another by an Indian author for a four-page monthly magazine called *The Hindu* that Simbhoo was publishing. He tried doing a tough street story, but despite its arresting opening – 'Carlos Antonio was buried today' – it soon became confused.[42] For several weeks Vido worked on 'How They Made a Queen', a description of a beauty pageant he had attended at the Rialto cinema. It attempted to be light and sophisticated, but became wordy and lapsed into cliché: 'The general hum was punctuated by bursts of applause which greeted the entry of well-known local characters.' He tried to ridicule the compère, but was more interested in the beauties, although he did his best to hide this. One was deemed to be 'a short, plump thing who could have been the model for Maupassant's Boule de Suif.' Another was 'a not displeasing blend of contradictory racial types. Her eyes and cheekbones proclaimed her Chinese; but her nose and lips belied that influence. Her colour was of appetizing ginger-bread.'[43] Looking back, loftily examining his own trajectory, he thought the beauty contest had been 'a shabby occasion' and he lacked the knowledge to write about it: 'What was the basis of the writer's attitude? What other world did he know, what other experience did he bring to his way of looking? How could a writer write about this world, if it was the only world he knew?'[44]

*

Kamla's departure for the east in the summer of 1949 had caused Ma and Pa great distress, knowing it would be years before they saw her again. Mira remembered the journey to the docks as being like 'a death in the family. It was so sad. The whole family, millions of us, went to the wharf to wave goodbye and send her off to India; and India was truly an unknown land.'[45] Afterwards Vido went upstairs at 26 Nepaul Street and cried silently with his face buried in the pillow on Kamla's bed.

She soon had news for him from England, secret news about Rudranath. 'Mamoo [mother's brother] is married. He has an intelligent, healthy looking son, 4½ years old. His wife is typically English. She is not ugly.'[46] Kamla was staying with him in his house in Surrey; he had been hospitable, and lent her money in case of disaster in India. Everything was unfamiliar. She advised Vido to borrow a book from the library and learn table manners before coming to England. Excited by her trip, he wrote back, 'Britain is a civilized country and safe. People don't have to boast about Ancient Culture; they have their culture and don't seek apologies for the lack of it in boasting about past achievement . . . Don't worry. This is Adventure . . . Don't let those damned Indians get you into any fancy arrangements – their luxury passages & luxury hotel accommodation. Find out the price of everything.' He admired her ability to be 'a favourite . . . I cut a pretty ridiculous figure wherever I go – a rather comic little boy, amusingly precocious, whose ideas and whose habits are only amusing and have little weight. I don't think I make friends; and I am too light to influence other people. I want to write; but I doubt if any writer had a poor imagination as I.'[47] Kamla was doing an interview on the BBC West Indian service, and Pa wrote her words of advice: 'Don't say scholarship to make Indians more Indian. Don't say Indians and non-Indians culturally apart. Say they are merging their cultures into one. We know it isn't true, but don't worry.' As for Vido, Pa reported to Kamla, 'He is nauseatingly rude to me, of course, as he has always been, but that is all.'[48]

Away from his older sister, Vido maintained the closeness of their relationship by telling her news from home, and trying out his opinions. 'Jane Austen appears to be essentially a writer for women; if she had lived in our age she would undoubtedly have been a leading contributor to the women's papers. Her work really bored me. It is mere gossip.' Still on the attack, he praised Beverley Nichols's controversial book *Verdict on India*. 'He went to India in 1945, and saw a wretched country, full of pompous mediocrity, with no future. He saw the filth; refused to mention the "spiritualness" that impresses another kind of visitor. Of course the Indians did not like the book, but I think he was telling the truth. From Nehru's autobiography, I think the Premier of India is a first-class showman with a host of third-rate supporters. I don't know whether I could agree with Nichols' condemnation of Gandhi as a shrewd politician, using his saintliness as a weapon of rule. But I am sure it has a certain basis in fact.'[49] He knew that Kamla would be entertained and interested by what he thought, and that he could write freely. The result was a vigorous, contentious prose that streaked ahead of the prissy writing in 'How They Made a Queen'.

Her letters back to him were often admonitory. When he reached Britain, she advised, 'Try your best & keep out of the company of West Indians . . . And I beg of you Vido do not get yourself mixed up with any English girl. I don't have to tell you the consequences.' She found Benares Hindu University to be ill-disciplined, and the food there 'spiced to the highest'. As for India, 'Once you get accustomed to the dirt, everything is just fine.'[50] With her Caribbean dresses and shorter hair, Kamla Naipaul was different from the other girls at Benares Hindu University, and viewed as fast and vociferous. When she spoke out on behalf of the students over a problem at the hostel, the vice-chancellor told her she should keep quiet because she was not Indian. The little Hindi she spoke was derided as 'dehati' or rustic, her language influenced by the Bhojpuri spoken by Indians in Trinidad; she said 'tharia' for thali (a metal plate) and 'murai' for mooli (the vegetable).[51] In October, after a cousin sent her a gossipy letter, she advised Vidia against drinking alcohol and smoking excessively. He was angered. 'My dear little fool, You are the damnedest ass. Your letter amused me as I read the first few lines; then it became grotesque. You are a silly stupid female, after all. I fancy you rather enjoyed writing that plea to a wayward brother. It made you a heroine à la Hollywood. Listen, my dear "very pretty" Miss Naipaul . . . For three weeks past, I have been smoking. As much as with Springer and Co. when you were here. That is bad, isn't it? I have been drinking excessively? Well, yes, water.'

The force and vigour of their conversations by letter reflected the way they spoke at home, and Vido could talk to Kamla with greater honesty than anyone else. 'My stay in Trinidad is drawing to a close,' he wrote. 'I only have nine months left. Then I shall go away – never to come back, as I trust. I think I am at heart really a loafer. Intellectualism is merely fashionable sloth. That is why I think I am going to be either a big success or an unheard-of failure. But I am prepared for anything. I want to satisfy myself that I have lived as I wanted to live. As yet I feel that the philosophy I will have to expand in my books is only superficial. I am longing to see something of life.' It was grand, it was ambitious, but Kamla understood his dreams. He offered to find her a publisher if she wrote an account of her stay in India. 'Pa can put me on to Rodin, the star-writer of England's *Daily Express*.' By the end of the year, he was assailed by a 'feeling of fatigue – both mental and physical ... You may laugh, but I am in love. That is why I have not read or written you or written anything into my book. And can you guess who is the female? – Golden ... She never let me go far. To date, she hasn't even allowed me to kiss her ... You won't tell any of the people home any of this, will you? ... I promise you I won't let anything improper take place ... I want to get away from this stagnating atmosphere into something more vivacious and stimulating. A sane man, if placed in a lunatic asylum, soon goes mad.'[52]

Golden, or Golon, was his mother's cousin. She lived in San Fernando in the south of the island, but since Trinidad was so small he could go there and back at weekends. Pa and Ma knew of the infatuation, but did not take it seriously. Golden was a few years older than Vido, and the relationship never progressed. He described the experience later as 'calf love, hopeless adolescent love. I thought she was very beautiful.'[53] While his black friends such as WAGS were having teenage sexual adventures, Vidia remained a virgin. Later, he would blame his slow sexual start and inability to seduce on Indian or Hindu culture, rather than on his own secretive, fastidious personality. Younger than the other boys in his class at QRC and coming from a different cultural background, he was not sure how to get started. Most of his knowledge of love affairs and intimacy came from reading books, and he despised his more adventurous contemporaries for their sensuality even while he envied them. Around this time, or possibly after Vido's departure for England, Pa began an affair with a woman he had met through his work on the *Guardian*, who lived in the heart of Port of Spain. 'I know there were stories about him having girlfriends,' said Mira. 'My father liked to take care of himself, to look nice and all that.'[54] According to Suren, quoting old family gossip, 'Seepersad had a woman in Pembroke Street, a Red woman, and Droapatie found out about her. I think she gave him a beating. Droapatie exuded a power, like her sisters. She was the boss.'[55]

As he prepared to depart for England in August 1950, aged not quite eighteen, Vido was highly educated, intelligent, ambitious and emotionally immature. He had been brought up on the idea that boys deserved special treatment by virtue of their sex, but his life so far had been influenced by strong women: Nanie, Ma and Kamla. Vido disliked his maternal uncles, even though he was obliged to respect them. His father was depressive, literary and bad at holding down a job. The other men in the Capildeo clan were castrated by their subordinate position, perceived by those in power to be lazy sons-of-bitches. In his writing, Vido would revere his father, elevating him as an exemplar and applying a degree of sympathy and compassion to him that was lacking in his treatment of other people. He attempted to depict Pa as a special and deserving case because he was serving the cause of literature. His practical failings and his involvement in the Trinidad hustle were set aside. Only in old age would Vidia begin to wonder whether his father was to blame for many of the deprivations of his childhood. In 2007 he said, 'I feel great rage against my father for having all these children, and not protecting them.'[56] In his later writing he would blank the role of his mother, who together with her family was central to the opportunities he was given to better himself. Mira remembered Ma as being particularly fond of her elder son. 'I know my mother adored Vido. She really did. It was this thing about the male. I felt that she was such a caregiver and a good mother because we didn't have the money – it was subsistence living really – and yet we had meals every day.'[57]

Vido was setting out for a country that had been presented to him as the epicentre of civilization. Each aspect of his education had emerged from overseas, yet he had no personal knowledge of Britain or the British. There were a few English boys and white Trinidadians at QRC, but as Eddoes says to Hat in *Miguel Street*, ' "You ain't know what you talking about, Hat. How much white people you know?" '[58] Vido was schooled in a way of working that should assure his success at Oxford, but he had no first-hand experience of social customs in post-war Britain or of the reality of life there for an Indian or West Indian. Lloyd Best would later popularize the term 'Afro-Saxon' to describe people of his generation who were able to flourish in British institutions by adopting the mask of the master, with the consequence that they were deracinated from the culture that gave birth to them. Vido, following in the footsteps of Rudranath Capildeo and a few other Indian island scholars, was an early Indo-Saxon. At the end of the scholarship process, what would he do – stay in Britain or return to the West Indies, or get a job with the government of independent India, as Pa suggested? At Oxford, what would be expected? Were his manners good enough? Would he have to restrain his opinions, and speak quietly in public places? Would he be lonely? Chekhov had written, after travelling to the penal colony of Sakhalin, that longing for the homeland was sufficient reason for a man with broken nerves to go insane. Would the natives of London behave like the white people in books and cinema newsreels? In the days before commercial television and the internet, the opportunity to comprehend or even see how another culture operated was minimal. For Vido, everything that lay ahead would be alien, although seemingly familiar.

On 1 August 1950, the day of his departure, he woke early and hardened his heart. He would not show distress. Since no ships were sailing for England on a suitable date, he would be flying to New York to sail from there. At Luis Street, saying goodbye, he heard that the aeroplane was delayed. He waited in anxiety for three hours, talking and not talking. Finally, he put his luggage in the Prefect and Pa drove him away from Port of Spain, away across the sugar belt to the airport at Piarco. Members of his extended family were assembled there in the little wooden building at the side of the runway to say farewell. Shortly after midday, the plane left the ground and took Vido above Trinidad for the first time. He would never see Pa again. As he receded towards America and England, he saw the island as he had never seen it before, the pattern of the fields and the roads and the houses, while his family looked up at him suspended in the sky in a cross, at a right angle to Columbus, leaving the New World.

CHAPTER FIVE

'DE PORTU HISPANIENSI IN TRINITATIS INSULA'

BRITAIN IN 1950 WAS in a bad condition. Clement Attlee's Labour government had been narrowly re-elected, food was still rationed and sterling was weak. The welfare state was costing too much, financed by borrowed American money, and it was becoming apparent, particularly since India had declared itself a republic, that Britain's days of empire were ending. Despite this, and although most British colonies had stopped turning a profit in the 1920s, the Colonial Office staff had tripled in size since before the war. London remained damaged by wartime bombing, and the air smelled of coal smoke. Clothes were drab, nylons were available only from black marketeers and utility clothing was still in use. Immigration had started, although at this time nobody could foresee how fundamentally it would alter British society. Two years earlier, the ship *Empire Windrush* had docked at Tilbury with passengers from Jamaica including the calypsonian Lord Kitchener (otherwise known as Aldwyn Roberts from Arima). The Colonial Office accommodated them in an old air-raid shelter at Clapham Common; jobs were available in nearby Brixton, and a new community was born. The recent British Nationality Act specified that any citizen of the Commonwealth — every fourth person on the planet — could live in Britain. At the time of Vidia's arrival, the immigrant population stood at 25,000. Half a century later, the non-white population of Britain would reach 4.6 million, or 7.9 per cent.[1]

In *Miguel Street*, Vido would fictionalize his departure from Trinidad. The narrator's mother gives a party, 'something like a wake', and in the morning his uncle takes him to the airport in his broken-down van. The book ends with the line: 'I left them all and walked briskly towards the aeroplane, not looking back, looking only at my shadow before me, a dancing dwarf on the tarmac.'[2] In *The Enigma of Arrival*, a mixture of memoir, essay and fiction published in 1987, he offered an account taken from life, presenting himself as an epic figure destined for what lay ahead. The author is on a small plane and asks the stewardess, 'white and American and to me radiant and beautiful and adult', to sharpen his pencil. She does so, and he makes notes: 'I had bought the pad and pencil because I was travelling to become a writer, and I had to start.' He realizes, in retrospect, that he ignored many things: the gathering of family who came to say goodbye at the airport, the cousin who advised him to sit at the back of the plane for safety, the shift in his personality as he supposedly became conscious of himself as a writer, setting out. Once in New York, a taxi driver fleeces him. Alone in his room at the Hotel Wellington, the author sees a tap marked HOT for the first time in his life, and eats a whole baked chicken his mother has packed for him, 'over the waste-paper basket, aware as I did so of the smell, the oil, the excess at the end of a long day . . . the writer of the diary was ending his day like a peasant.'[3]

In a letter written on Hotel Wellington paper dated 2 August 1950, Vidia extolled the decadence of New York to Sati. He had been served orange juice, eggs and coffee for his breakfast. 'In about 2 hours I will be going to the boat. Tourist class on an American ship is sheer class . . . For the first time in my life people are calling me sir at every turn. I am enjoying myself and – pardon me! – am not missing home.' To Kamla, a few weeks later, he was more vulnerable: 'I was scared. I had never been on my own before. The idea of passing a night in a strange city and boarding a boat was terrifying . . . But the plane did come on time and at about 12.50, V.S. Naipaul was cut off from all family ties.' In New York, 'I took a taxi, felt like a lord at the hotel when a black porter took my luggage in, calling me "sir" every two or three words. It quite took my breath away. I was free and I was honoured.' He revealed to Kamla that he had eaten Ma's chicken over the waste-paper basket; 'my darling mother looks after her children with all the poor little love she can dispose of.' The sea voyage had gone swimmingly, and he had considered kissing a married German woman. England was 'proving very pleasant'. His cousin Boysie had installed him at Rudranath's lodgings in north-west London. Vido had met a girl and taken her 'to St Paul's and Regent's Park' – how familiar he made these places sound! – 'but she has packed me up'. She was followed by a Norwegian he met on a train while going to look at Oxford. 'We did some sightseeing together and I paid her the wildest compliments in French . . . I think I will go to Norway this Christmas. She was very nice.

Your ever loving Vido.'[4] He liked the buses and milk bars and the lettering on the London Underground but, like Willie Chandran in *Half a Life*, found Buckingham Palace disappointingly small. The city's geography appealed to him. 'I liked the feeling of being sheltered, the light being so much softer than the light of the tropics,' he said years later.[5]

In *The Enigma of Arrival*, he reconstructed and lightly fictionalized this period. The account is much more solemn: no mention of Boysie paving the way, or chasing girls around St Paul's and Oxford, or using Capildeo hospitality. He takes a train from the coast to Waterloo station, and stays in a dingy lodging house in Earls Court where he contemplates his literary destiny. The Earls Court lodgings in fact come from a later period, starting with his first Christmas in London. Boysie took him there to meet his girlfriend Carmen Johnson, the housekeeper. In *The Enigma of Arrival* she becomes Angela, and her real boyfriend is an absent and violent man, possibly in prison. The narrator notices the refugees from Europe, 'Asiatic' students and north Africans who are staying in the house. Only later does he see their significance, at the time, wishing to be a writer in the mould of Somerset Maugham, Aldous Huxley or Evelyn Waugh, he does not consider them 'material' for his fiction. 'Because in 1950 in London I was at the beginning of that great movement of peoples that was to take place in the second half of the twentieth century – a movement and a cultural mixing greater than the peopling of the United States ... Cities like London were to change. They were to cease being more or less national cities; they were to become cities of the world, modern-day Romes, establishing the pattern of what great cities should be, in the eyes of islanders like myself and people even more remote in language and culture.'[6]

While he waited the six weeks for term to start, Vidia wrote a story that he hoped would be published by Penguin, and attempted to follow his father's advice to meet 'big shots in the film and writing business'. He made little progress. His attempts to establish contact with Rodin, confidently flagged to Kamla as Pa's associate and 'the star-writer of England's *Daily Express*', came to nothing. Was Pa bluffing? 'I am sorry Rodin was not too helpful,' Pa responded. 'I shall write him. Really, I ought to have given you a letter of intro. It's the right way to go about these things, I suppose. He must be a big shot.' In *Half a Life*, this encounter and similar rebuffs would be fictionalized and treated with a greater degree of honesty than the moving but monumental self-representation of the same period in *The Enigma of Arrival*. The protagonist Willie – named after Somerset Maugham – meets a prominent journalist in the lobby of a newspaper office, but finds they have nothing to talk about. Willie is 'unanchored' in London, unsure how to behave. 'He had to learn how to eat in public. He had to learn how to greet people and how, having greeted them, not to greet them all over again in a public place ten or fifteen minutes later.' Over time, he realizes his past is unknown to these foreigners; he is 'free to present himself as he wished ... The possibilities were dizzying. He could, within reason, re-make himself and his past and his ancestry.'[7] The implication, always unexpressed, is that Vidia was thinking of his own emphasis on dignified Brahminism and its importance in his literary self-representation.

Rudranath's flat was far from central London, and Vidia spent some of his days there under the eye of its owner, an elderly German refugee named Mrs Wolf, who hated Africans but tolerated Indians. Rudranath himself, now a lecturer in mathematics at London University, was away in Trinidad and Vido was embarrassed to tell him where he was staying, as Pa complained to Kamla: 'he is all nicely fixed up with Boyzie [sic] at Rud's London lodgings. Nothing to pay. But I must say Vido is rather tactless: he wrote Rud, not giving even the address he wrote from, and without a word of thanks ... Rud drew my attention to this in a mildly reproving and disappointed way.' Boysie introduced Vidia to Ruth, Rudranath's English wife, and he disliked her on sight, calling her a 'stupid, arrogant, shrewish, self-pitying woman' in a letter home. Nor did she take a liking to him; she wrote to Kamla: 'I saw Vido a fortnight ago. It was a dreary sort of day and I was in such a dull mood, that I'm afraid he thought I was an absolute horror.' He visited Carmen in Earls Court with Boysie several times and met a Frenchman, Yves Leclerc, who was lodging in the house and making a living by translating thrillers into French at high speed. 'He was a giant of a man, but wonderfully encouraging to me at our first meeting, when there was little to encourage. He was born in Morocco, or had lived there. He had been in the French underground during the war and when I knew him he still had his Maquis name, Coulon.'[8] Yves Leclerc would recur, in life and in fiction. Carmen, who came from Italy, tried early to knock the rough Caribbean corners off Vido's behaviour. 'I had to learn manners,' he recalled, 'closing a door behind you, saying please. She was shocked that I would just say, "Carmen give me some lunch."

I should say, "Carmen, give me some lunch, please. Can you please give me some coffee?" "[9]

Already, then, Vidia felt the gap between the England of his imagination and quotidian life there, and between Pa's literary aspirations and his lack of connections in London. His father's most useful guidance would not be about star journalists or men of letters, but about how to live. From the start, Pa's weekly or fortnightly aerogrammes to his son contained wise words mixed with redundant advice. 'Good reading and good writing go together . . . Self-confidence is a very valuable asset and I am glad to know you feel confident; but don't underestimate people and problems . . . I have no doubt you will be a great writer: but do not spoil yourself . . . No harm in kissing a girl, so long as you do not become too prone for that sort of thing.' Above all he emphasized, knowing his son's latent instability, 'You keep your centre.'

*

Oxford was the oldest English-speaking university in the world, founded soon after the Battle of Hastings. Ever conscious of its own antiquity and status, its buildings were largely unmarked, their dirty yellow sandstone walls merged with the fabric of the town. Kings, archbishops, scientists and statesmen had studied there, and newcomers and outsiders were expected to know their way around, geographically and culturally: a quad was a courtyard, a hall was a dining room, a don was a teacher, a bulldog was a university policeman (who wore a bowler hat) and a scout was a cleaner. The academic year was divided into the Michaelmas, Hilary and Trinity terms; the summer holiday was the long vac, or vacation. The university worked on a federal system. Each college was self-governing, with its own customs and identity. Only in the late nineteenth century were men who were not members of the Church of England permitted to receive an MA degree, opening the way for Jews, Methodists and Roman Catholics, and conceivably for Hindus and Muslims. Academic halls were established for women in 1878, although they were not yet able to take a degree. With its cobbled roads, biting winds and chiming clock towers, Oxford had a medieval, ecclesiastical feel. A street bounded by tall sandstone walls and metal gratings would lead to a narrow passageway which bulged with age; an ancient studded door guarded by a gruff college porter would open within a larger wooden door, revealing a quad quartered by dark archways leading to a staircase, a chapel or another quad.

University College, off the High Street, had been established for the study of theology more than two centuries before Trinidad was named. Previous inhabitants of 'Univ' included the poet and atheist Percy Bysshe Shelley, who reclined in white marble in a large funerary monument inside the college, the rising politician Harold Wilson, the literary socialite Stephen Spender, the prime minister Clement Attlee, the reformer William Beveridge, the fantasy writer C.S. Lewis and Prince Felix Yusopov, who assassinated Rasputin. The seventeenth-century chapel had a relief sculpture of the great Orientalist William Jones, a graduate of the college, revealing that he had 'Formed a Digest of Hindu and Mohammedan Laws'. Vidia's room was on a noisy staircase above the Junior Common Room, with a shared bathroom down the corridor. Although he might meet women undergraduates at lectures or through activities such as student journalism, much of university life and particularly college life remained staunchly male. One contemporary said, 'If you were female and didn't have a face like the back of the bus, you could do very well at Oxford. On the other hand, the women's colleges, they protected their young charges and we had curfews – we were supposed to be in by eleven at night. It was like the kind of thing you read about American high schools, that people would talk about girls. It was very easy to get a reputation for being easy, though there was more "making out" than actual sex.'[10]

The behaviour of the undergraduates and graduates at Univ was monitored by the head porter, Douglas Millin, who made sure students were signed in and the college gates were locked behind them each night. A wartime battery sergeant-major in the Royal Artillery, Millin combined an abrasive manner with devotion to Univ, and was described in the college magazine as 'a master of spoken English, embellished with just a smattering of rich Anglo-Saxon'.[11] He said in an interview when he retired after thirty-three years in the post that, 'my jobs stretch from cutting a bloke down who's hung his bloody self to finding a safety pin for a lady's elastic knickers that's fallen down.'[12] According to Ravi Dayal, an Indian student at the college in the early 1960s, Millin disliked Vidia: 'Douglas said, "There've been lots of Indians in Univ, all fine people, all gentlemen, but not Naipaul. He used to take the mickey out of people." He remembered Naipaul making some rather pretentious person weep in the quad.'[13]

A more gentle pastoral role was taken by the dean, Giles Alington, a popular bachelor don who was less interested in academic life than in the well-being of the college, and exerted discipline lightly. The *University*

College Record noted that he was known for his 'not uncultivated eccentricities (the foot-long pipe with the tiny bowl, in summer the daisy between the teeth)', one of which was the frequent use of double negatives.[14] Supporting the Master, Dean, Head Porter and dons were around thirty college servants: scouts, messengers, butlers, gardeners, even a college waterman to look after the river boats. Peter Bayley, who had spotted Vidia's photograph and accepted him at the college, was immediately welcoming. Only a decade older than Vidia and shortly to be married to the daughter of a don, he specialized in sixteenth- and seventeenth-century English literature and had served in the Far East and India during the war. Bayley's first impression of Vidia was positive. 'Well, he was very small and he had this infectious smile and laugh, a rather asthmatic laugh – an asthmatic laugh can often seem more mirthful. He was extraordinarily responsive and bright. He very quickly got involved in things, he wanted to get involved. I never saw him look unhappy. He was made a member of the Martlets, the college literary society, very early. Vidia has got this legend going about his unhappiness there and how he disliked Oxford. It's not my impression at all. He did suffer from asthma and he felt the cold desperately. I think that college rooms were not very well heated in those days.'[15]

The 1950 freshmans' college photograph, which Vidia missed, showed nearly eighty young men standing in neat rows, hair brushed and parted, dressed in the style of the era in a suit or tweed jacket, collar, tie, V-neck jersey, baggy trousers and dark shoes. Some, maybe the older ones who had done National Service and in a few cases fought in the war or served as Bevin Boys, had a loose scarf thrown over the shoulder. There were three non-white freshmen in the photograph: Pillai, Holder and Al-Barwani. They were part of a tradition that had begun in the 1890s of students coming to study in the mother country from across the empire, usually intelligent young men from ambitious families who were setting themselves up for a prominent career back home.

Each Freshman at Univ had to sign the admissions register beneath a Latin inscription prepared individually by the Classics Fellow, a tradition dating back to 1674, the year in which Chhatrapati Shivaji was crowned king of the Marathas and John Milton died. Most of the entries are alike, but in Vidia's case the Classics Fellow had to think hard while preparing the text: 'Ego Vidiadhar Surajprasad Naipaul e collegio reginae sanctae in Trinitatis insula filius natu major Seepersad Naipaul de Portu Hispaniensi in Trinitatis insula lubens subscribo sub tutamine magistri Bayley annos

XVIII natus.'[16] It showed his difference. 'I, Vidiadhar Surajprasad Naipaul of Queen's Royal College in the island of Trinidad elder son of Seepersad Naipaul of Port of Spain in the island of Trinidad willingly assent to study under the tutorship of Master Bayley, in my eighteenth year.'

*

Pa's first letter to Vidia after he arrived at Oxford in early October set the tone for what was to follow, passing on news from Trinidad and giving encouragement that was aimed partly at himself. 'Don't be scared of being an artist . . . One cannot write well unless one can think well.' Would his son send a copy of *Mr Sampath*, a recent novel by the increasingly well-regarded Indian writer R.K. Narayan, and some special photographic paper? Only at the close of the letter did Pa let reality intrude, and look at his own situation squarely. 'This is the time I should be writing the things I so long to write. This is the time for me to be myself. When shall I get the chance? I don't know. I come from work, dead tired. The *Guardian* is taking all out of me – writing tosh, what price salted fish and things of that sort.' Vido was moved. 'What a delight to receive Pa's excellent letter from home. If I didn't know the man, I would have said: what a delightful father to have.' He felt he had been accepted at the university and at his college, and had made 'quite a number of acquaintances'. As for England, it was teaching him 'to say thank you and please'.

Vidia thought that the quality of education he had received at QRC put him ahead of his contemporaries. At his first tutorial with Peter Bayley, he was asked to read some work aloud, but was hesitant. Another undergraduate, Nicky Baile, whom Vidia admired for his ability to walk outdoors wearing only a shirt in winter, began instead. Vidia remembered, 'I was so nervous about what I had written, and there was Nicky Baile reading his piece which was so juvenile and childish, reading this rubbish quite shamelessly, and I said, "As a matter of fact, I have got something here", and read it out. For me, Oxford never recovered from that.'[17] Peter Bayley remembered Vidia reading a later essay on Milton's *Paradise Lost*. 'He sat in an armchair and said in that really polished English voice, "In *Animal Farm*, it would be remembered all animals are equal, but some animals are more equal than others." Then he sort of whinnied a bit and said, "The same is regrettably true of Milton's angels", and I knew I had a winner. I should explain that *Animal Farm* had only been out a few years by that time. Now everybody says "all animals are equal" whereas he was the first.'[18] In later life, Vidia would assert that he had learned nothing at

Oxford; and each time he said this in an interview, a slew of headlines would appear, expressing surprise.

While he adjusted to Oxford, Vidia confided in his family in Nepaul Street, and like other students in the college would usually write a letter home on a Sunday evening. Pa's response was enthusiastic. 'Your letters are charming in their spontaneity. If you could write me letters about things and people – especially people – at Oxford, I could compile them in a book: LETTERS BETWEEN FATHER AND SON ... You must aim to say only what you have to say and to say it clearly.' Pa was full of ideas, rather too many ideas for Vidia at times as he tried to go about his business as an Oxford undergraduate, far from Port of Spain. Where was the R.K. Narayan novel? Vido would shortly be receiving a parcel of sugar, pickles and tins of grapefruit juice and orange juice, packed by his mother. Might Vido be able to place an article in the *Sunday Express* that Pa had written about the cricketer Sonny Ramadhin? And if he met the philosopher and diplomat Dr Radhakrishnan, he was to tell him his father regarded him as 'one of the greatest minds of modern India ... And you would have broken the ice, as they say. Contact, Vido, contact all the time. Let me go on. Suppose you had a fairly good chat with this great scholar, you could have described the experience or the incident to me in a letter.'[19]

'Write Vido,' Pa suggested to Kamla in Benares Hindu University, 'but don't say anything to hurt him. You know, at heart he is not a bad fellow; only a bit erratic & thoughtless and callously unconventional.' Vidia soon became disconnected from home. He was overdeveloped and underdeveloped all at the same time, intellectually advanced and emotionally restricted, alone in an alien world, an engaging, attractive young man from a distant island, who stood five feet six in his stockinged feet. Outwardly, Vidia seemed to be one of the crowd. 'I would say he was positively popular in the college, that is my view,' said Peter Bayley. 'I thought of him as the little Indian boy in *A Midsummer Night's Dream*. [Puck refers to Titania's pageboy as, 'A lovely boy, stolen from an Indian king.'] He was exceptionally charming ... completely natural and very unselfconscious. He fitted in. He wanted to be an Englishman. For example his friend Peter Roberts who eventually became Canadian ambassador in Moscow, he once said Vidia was rather lordly. Sometimes he would say, Peter, come on let's go out and walk the streets of the town. We'll go and have a cup of coffee at the Randolph – the grandest hotel in Oxford. I wouldn't have dreamed of going to the Randolph. Peter Roberts said, he would go in and he would sit down in the lounge and he'd summon a waiter and he would say, "A pot of coffee, please, for one and would you please bring two cups." Well, there is confidence.'[20]

This was Trinidadian poise, or style, and it did not indicate tranquillity. Vido found it easier to explain his situation to Kamla than to Pa or Ma. In late November, as the English winter closed in, he wrote, 'A feeling of emptiness is nearly always on me. I see myself struggling in a sort of tunnel blocked up at both ends. My past – Trinidad and the necessity of our parents – lies behind me and I am powerless to help anyone. My future – such as it is – is a full four years away.' He had written eight chapters of a humorous novel that was 'bound to sell'. He told Kamla about a failed relationship with a beautiful Belgian girl he had been pursuing, Claude Golfart. She said she was in love with someone else, and had written him a letter suggesting that he was too forceful and intense for the English. He quoted it to Kamla. 'My dear Vidia . . . Because you are intelligent, you rush this slow country's atmosphere and people – perhaps compromise, though hateful, is still best.'

Kamla, in her letters back, sought to offer support. She did not want Vido to be placed in the same category as 'them West Indians'. His rule for girls should be: ' "Would Kamla think her a fool?" . . . You are too young to have any particular girl. I say, don't you go and get yourself hitched to anybody. Boy, I hope you'd have some room in your heart and home for me when I get back. Save a little corner for me, will you?' She felt in retrospect that her brother's sexual frustration and awkwardness with girls came less from the strictures of Hindu family life than from his ambition, and the work that came with it. 'In his Oxford years, Vidia didn't have the know-how to court a girl because he had spent his entire life just studying for exams. It was something which he put himself under because he had to win this scholarship to get out of Trinidad. There was no time to think about girls if he was trying to win one scholarship after another. Remember he won the first scholarship at ten.'[21] Savi thought her brother's hesitation was a trait that grew not out of Indian culture but from his personality, combined with the peculiarities of Ma's clan: 'All the Capildeo men as far as I was concerned as a female, they were all wimps. They never approached girls in a normal way. They were always withdrawn, shy – as if approaching a girl was a wrong thing. The Capildeos never ate in anybody's house. They would visit but never eat. So it was all part of this Hindu restrictiveness.'[22]

Money both in Oxford and in Trinidad was a constant concern. Ma had asked 'very humbly' if Vidia and Kamla might be able to pay Savi's school fees; Kamla thought she would be able to spare $18 a month; Vidia could spare nothing. At Univ, he had to adjust to the stodgy, restricted, post-war English diet. Each person would be given a butter ration at the start of the week. Although he was not vegetarian, Vidia avoided beef and pork. He ate lamb at first, but gave it up during the 1950s. Subsequently, as he became more concerned about his Indian heritage and apparent caste origins, he would continue to eat fish and from time to time chicken, although a Brahmin would ideally eat neither. He liked to believe his sensitivity to the smell and appearance of food and his antagonism towards certain kinds of meat and fish was inbuilt, almost genetic, arising from the background of his grandparents. 'I hated the idea of mussels and things like that crossing my mouth. Chicken would be terrible because of the oiliness. The thought of eating something that had been living was painful for me. I think that my vegetarianism was a personal thing . . . it is probably a peasant throwback in me. I am essentially a vegetarian peasant when it comes to food.'[23]

He had good news when the BBC paid him a guinea (one pound and one shilling) for a poem broadcast on *Caribbean Voices*, an influential half-hour weekly radio programme on the BBC. It was to be his only poem. 'Two Thirty A.M.' is a solemn, adolescent cry of anguish. It was read by John Figueroa, an extensively bearded brown Jamaican:

> darkness piling up in the corners
> defying the soulless moon . . .
> it is neither today's tomorrow
> nor is it tonight's last night
> but now
> and forever
> and you are scared
> for this is forever
> and this is death
> and nothing
> and mourning[24]

In the Christmas vacation, he went to London and took a room in Carmen's lodging house near the underground station at Earls Court, where he felt homesick but was glad to have space of his own at a cut-price rate. Ma warned him to look after himself, writing in telegraphic style, 'Vido I am nervous about your smoking again please remember there is a limit to everything health is first.' He told his parents about the sight of floating ice. 'Last week I had my first snow. It came down in little white fluffs; you felt that a gigantic hand had punched a gigantic cotton wool sack open, letting down flurries of cotton shreds,' he wrote home beautifully, the Caribbean boy in London. 'If you went out your shoulders and your hair were sprinkled with the fluffs. The closest thing I have seen to it in Trinidad is the stuff that gathers in a refrigerator — not when it gets hard though.' He was studying Shakespeare and Virgil and Anglo-Saxon. 'I want to come top of my group. I have got to show these people that I can beat them at their own language.' It was a lasting ambition.

Over Christmas he met up with Boysie, who was spending much of his time with Carmen in Earls Court, and with his uncles Simbhoo and Rudranath, who were making plans to purchase a house in south London for £5,000. Yves Leclerc said to him of the British: 'Their women can't cook, can't dress and are invariably plain.' He saw a group of prominent West Indians: Sam Selvon, Carlisle Chang, a Trinidadian artist who was in London on a scholarship, and Gloria Escoffery, a Jamaican writer and painter. Vidia set out to make a spectacle of himself. When Gloria said that she wrote in order to explore, he cut in, paraphrasing Pa, 'Surely you're starting from the wrong end. I always thought people understood before they wrote.' When she passed around a short story which touched on racial issues, and Sam suggested 'the colour problem' could not be explained in something as short as a short story, Vidia saw his opening: 'My dear Gloria, why not write a little pamphlet on the colour question, and settle the whole affair?' He was relieved to be telephoned the next morning by Carlisle Chang and told the party had talked about him after he left. 'Gloria, he said, had infinite faith in me. They all thought me a little queer, but that, I thought, was because I spoke a bit of sense, and told these culture-creators where they got off. The queerness, they discovered, was due to my reaction to England. How I enjoyed that evening!'

After Christmas, he returned to Oxford and took a room in a house in Richmond Road in Jericho that had previously been occupied by a young chemistry undergraduate, Margaret Roberts, later Thatcher.[25] He did not meet Margaret until many years later, when she had become prime minister. When term began, the landlady, Mrs King, allowed him to return occasionally for a hot bath. He was still unimpressed by the intellectual abilities of his fellow undergraduates. In an exam, writing about 'the ugliness of the theology of *Paradise Lost*', he used the phrase

'Prayer, the incense for the incenséd God' in an essay which was marked by Professor J.R.R. Tolkien, the professor of English language and literature at Oxford who in his spare time wrote about hobbits. 'Now I knew exactly what I was doing. "Incenséd" meaning angry, it's the same word. And Tolkien said to me, "it's good, did you intend it?" And I was ashamed and I said no. And so I lost points in Tolkien's mind, I suppose, and the witticism yet was my own. I was too well prepared for Oxford, I suppose.'[26] Some of this remembered response to Oxford was retrospective superiority, Vidia's reaction to the university's cultivated sense of exclusivity. For despite his talent and hard work, he never achieved the level of academic success that he had expected of himself.

Vidia told Kamla he had few friends and less money, his isolation expressing itself in arrogance: 'You would be surprised when I tell you that the majority of the students here are very stupid, and that the average intelligence is much lower than that of the sixth form of my years at QRC.' Too many students were on state grants, he told his parents conceitedly: 'Gone are the days of aristocrats.' The English were a curious people: 'The longer you live in England, the queerer they appear. There is something so orderly, and yet so adventurous about them, so ruttish, so courageous. Take the chaps in the college. The world is crashing about their heads, about all our heads. Is their reaction as emotional as mine? Not a bit. They ignore it for the most part, drink, smoke, and imbibe shocking quantities of tea and coffee, read the newspapers and seem to forget what they have read.' Not that Trinidad was any better. 'I never realized before that the *Guardian* was so badly written, that our Trinidad worthies were so absurd, that Trinidad is the most amusing island that ever dotted a sea.' For all his cynicism, he hated being excluded and wanted to succeed. Oxford had been presented to him as the pinnacle of achievement, but now it was failing to give him what he wanted. The past, meanwhile, was receding as Trinidad was rendered absurd.

*

'I am a feature reporter on the staff of the university magazine *Isis*,' Vido told Kamla in January 1951. 'It doesn't mean much, but if there is fair play I should become at least assistant news editor by the end of the year.'[27] Fair play, however, was by no means assured at the *Isis*, an independent student paper run by a clique of well-heeled young men from the university. 'I will tell you something about Oxford,' he wrote to his parents guilelessly, 'intelligence is not all that one requires to get along. One has to know "the boys" ... To get on, you must throw sherry parties, take the editor out to dinner.' Writing to fourteen-year-old Mira, Vido played the elder brother: 'Have you developed a taste for reading now? My dear girl, if you have, I have a great pity for you. One must devote all one's life to reading and the pursuit of knowledge, or never begin at all ... I trust you will pardon the didactic tone of this letter ... Goodbye, my dear Ranee [Queen]!'[28] Touchingly, Pa sent Vido $10 to hold a sherry party. 'I know full well what this thing means and how necessary it is. Meanwhile be a man and cringe to none,' Seepersad told his son.

After earlier complaints that he was not writing home frequently enough, Vido had fallen into a pattern of regular correspondence with Pa. Bored by much of his work under Master Bayley, he felt he was 'improving intellectually' thanks to a close reading of Aristotle's *Poetics*. 'He was such a clear, intelligent thinker. Every sentence adds something new. That is the best type of criticism.'[29] A shared interest in literature united father and son. They discussed newspaper design and compared notes about journalism. Pa was reading John Galsworthy and Rudyard Kipling; Vidia was reading Leo Tolstoy and E.M. Forster. 'I am beginning to believe I could have been a writer,' Pa wrote sadly, and Vidia praised him, sincerely: 'I have always admired you as a writer. And I am convinced that, were you born in England, you would have been famous and rich and pounced upon by the intellectuals.' He himself had been told he was 'gifted' by Yves Leclerc in Earls Court, and advised to finish his novel.

Vidia complained that an interview he had done for *Isis* with the film producer Emeric Pressburger had been mangled by an editor, which left him in 'a white-hot temper'. And 'When Palme Dutt, the half-Indian boss of the British Communist Party, came to Oxford, I gave him so much hell that the Communists rang up the editor and cursed him. I think a man is doing his reporting well only when people start to hate him.' Pa, significantly, did not agree. He advised his son not to be concerned if an editor tried to improve his work, or 'at least not yet'. He should be patient. 'And as to a writer being hated or liked – I think it's the other way to what you think: a man is doing his work well when people begin liking him. I have never forgotten what Gault MacGowan told me years ago: "Write sympathetically"; and this, I suppose, in no way prevents us from writing truthfully, even brightly.' Pa believed in Vido. 'You don't have to worry about us – so long as I keep going. Give yourself all the chance.'

But Vidia did worry. 'You must realise,' he wrote to Kamla, 'that without us, the family has lost its heart. The responsibility is mighty, I know, but it is not depressing.' His idea of himself as the writer was the way forward. The BBC might accept two of his stories, he told her in the same letter, one a rewritten version of 'How They Made a Queen'. 'If they really have, it means that for two weeks' work, I shall have raked in more than fifteen guineas. Not bad! And I am only eighteen!' He was only eighteen, precocious but precarious, writing fluent letters and hoping to write great books. In *A House for Mr Biswas*, Vidia would characterize his correspondence with Pa harshly: 'Anand's letters, at first rare, become more and more frequent. They were gloomy, self-pitying; then they were tinged with a hysteria which Mr Biswas immediately understood. He wrote Anand long humorous letters; he wrote about the garden; he gave religious advice; at great expense he sent by air mail a book called *Outwitting Our Nerves* by two American women psychologists. Anand's letters grew rare again.' When Mr Biswas fell ill, 'He continued to write cheerful letters to Anand. At long intervals the replies came, impersonal, brief, empty, constrained.'[30]

Both men felt their talent was being stifled. Vidia had been shown around the Morris Motors works 'as a member of the Press, and treated to the most wonderful lunch I have ever had in England so far.' When his report was published in *Isis*, his name 'in biggish capital letters,' he thought it would be the 'first and only big article' he wrote for them: 'It is really impossible to get ahead in that paper.' The article itself, run over several pages under the headline 'When Morris Came To Oxford', covered traffic congestion, industrial diversification and ideas about pressed steel.[31] *Isis*, in practice, had little to offer V.S. Naipaul. The magazine ran worthy articles about subjects like Morris cars but was filled mainly with pert undergraduate humour, self-referential university news and polite photographs of female undergraduates – 'EDWINA, the most beautiful sight in Town' – amid advertisements for sherry, Brylcreem, snap brim hats and the latest Hillman Minx. A daring contributor might write an article about the evils of apartheid or the need for tolerance towards 'maladjusted individuals' – meaning homosexuals – or he might try to be amusing on the letters pages, like Edgar Farquarson: 'I have discovered, after investigation, that of the members of your staff listed in your first issue, three are Negroes, four homosexuals, two are frequently to be seen in public-houses, and one is a woman. All this is unspeakably revolting to the Freshman's conscience.'[32] An undergraduate might advise his contemporaries on social matters: 'It is "smart" for parents to stay at one of the large hotels in town, or to motor in daily. It is not "smart" to stay with relatives in North Oxford.'[33]

A rising star among them would feature as the 'Isis Idol', illustrated with a carefully staged black-and-white photograph. The Idol's early triumph was presumed to mark the beginning of an exhilarating career in politics or the arts. Idols included Jeremy Thorpe, the Liberal Party leader who would later resign over a sex scandal involving an assassinated dog, Godfrey Smith, the future editor of the yet-to-be-launched Sunday Times colour supplement, and Robert Robinson, who would become the waspish invigilator of BBC daytime radio quiz shows. Of Jeremy Thorpe, Isis wrote presciently that though he had much talent, 'some feel that as a future politician, he would be wiser to be more discreet.'[34] Other figures who appeared in the pages of the Isis at this time included Robin Day, Norman St John-Stevas, Michael Heseltine, George Carman and the president of the Oxford University Conservative Association, William Rees-Mogg, who was already making his name as a comic figure: 'Anyone thought of a new joke about William Rees-Mogg?' the paper enquired.[35]

The weekly gossip column 'Roundabout' told languidly of goings-on at various colleges. At a party 'next Saturday in LORD STORMONT'S rooms, we gather that gatecrashers will be welcome.' Plans were afoot for a production of Twelfth Night at New College: 'The parts of the messengers, hautboys and tuckets have been entrusted to the college haughties, led by ANTONIA PAKENHAM. But who cares?'[36] A future diplomat whose girl-friend had recently been snatched by a wealthy Egyptian student lamented the presence of dark faces at Oxford: ' "I can't bear Wogs," moaned genial JOHN SHAKESPEARE, as he submitted the Magdalen students to a keen scrutiny. "One thing about Trinity," he went on, gravely eyeing CHRIS-TOPHER FETTES, "at least we're all homogenous . . . if that's the word I mean?" (N.B. – No more Shakespeare boosts until further notice. – ED.)'[37] 'Americans-and-Colonials' such as the Indian cricket blue Ramesh 'Buck' Divecha usually made it into the magazine only via a sporting triumph: 'This fine specimen of Hindu manhood is equally at home theorising on the secrets of his successes in Vincent's or fingering his native chapattis in the Taj . . . He returns to the jungle in August to study for his Bar Finals.'[38]

Vidia was all at sea in this cliquey, smirking, undergraduate atmosphere;

there was little chance of his parents coming to stay in one of the large hotels in town. His articles for *Isis* were not impressive. Only one contains a hint of literary talent, the report on the visit of R. Palme Dutt, whom he described 'holding his slender arms parenthetically at his sides, then slowly wagging a right index finger at the audience.'[39] A letter arrived for him from WAGS in Port of Spain: 'My dear "Paul" . . . Do send me a copy of *Isis*. Have you met with any colour-prejudice in Oxford?' Before long the magazine became too much for him. Peter Bayley remembered Vidia arriving one day at his rooms 'in great distress. He said he found a note in the office of the *Isis* which implied that because he was a foreigner, he should piss off. "Keep out Vidia," or something like that. He showed me the note and I said, "Well, this is all a joke, isn't it?" He said, "I don't think it's a joke." He was bitterly upset. He felt rejection, whether justified or not I just don't know. I assume not, because undergraduates are not beastly; it may have been a badly timed joke.'[40]

Like Vidia, Pa felt that racial prejudice underlay his own lack of advancement. He had been on the *Guardian* for 'sixteen months now, but they haven't given me a raise. A thing that is making me bitter – I suppose that's how a Communist comes into being – is that a third-rate English boy . . . is getting a far bigger salary than I am getting.' His particular enemy was a senior editor, Mr Jenkins. 'They are capitalist exploiters,' Pa wrote to Kamla. 'Imagine fat, goofy Jenkins being my boss. You know, I have often imagined the man coming to work with rouged lips, and to carry the imagery a bit further, in a frock. Short, fat Jenkins!' He was annoyed that Sam Selvon's forthcoming first novel, *A Brighter Sun*, had been mentioned on the BBC: 'I'd be a liar if I didn't admit that far from feeling well about it, I felt peeved with myself . . . The fact is I feel trapped.' The sheer unfairness of his position ate at him. As he wrote to Kamla, oblivious to her past connection with Selvon, he was writing some of the best news stories in the paper, as well as sub-editing the *Guardian Weekly*, 'yet the white man who does no more on the same job, gets damn near double the salary I get.'

In April, Vidia was invited to visit the home of John McConville, another 'Univ man', for the vacation. 'I have never spent a more congenial four days in England,' he told his parents. 'Blackpool is the big northern seaside resort of England. It is a big machine made to extort money from the people on holiday, full of fortune-tellers, gypsies, all named Lee, and all claiming to be the only Gypsy Lee on the front . . . The beach is pleasant, as pleasant as Trinidad's east coast, minus the coconut trees, but the water and wind are hellishly cold, and the water is always the colour of mud.' In retrospect, he perceived the trip to the McConvilles differently. 'They had a strange accent. Northern. It didn't sound right. The father was a doctor, and told a story about seeing D.H. Lawrence at a bus stop. I felt an outsider; I rather liked being an outsider; it was not in our tradition to stay with people. I suppose I was a bundle of nerves.'[41]

Vidia was aware of his tendency to cynicism. As he told his 'darling sister' Kamla, 'I was seriously thinking this morning how people could ever put up with me . . . The boys who like me, like me because mine is a "cynical flamboyance", because I pose as an "enfant terrible". Yet I sincerely am never aware of POSING. I suppose the reason is that in the W[est] I[ndies] we lived so completely within ourselves, we grew to despise the people around us. But the people ought to have been despised! A friend told me the other day that people don't like me because I made them feel that I knew they were fools.' He wished to assimilate, at least socially, and told Kamla he still spoke in 'a foul manner' although his pronunciation was improving 'by the humiliating process of error and snigger'. In the Trinity term examinations he almost got a distinction, and had the best results of any English Literature student in his college. He threw a party in his room for ten guests, serving tea and beer. Boysie turned up in the middle of it and 'the boys enjoyed his company' he told Ma and Pa. When the term ended, he was at a loss. For days he was 'literally penniless' and had to cadge meals off friends, particularly Ian Robertson, an assistant curator at the Ashmolean Museum to whom he had been given an introduction by the British Council in Trinidad. He was helped a few weeks later by earning eight guineas from *Caribbean Voices* when his first short story, 'This is Home', was broadcast; a damaged version of the manuscript survives on microfilm in the archives of the BBC.

*

During Pa's early years as an aspiring writer of fiction, he had no market for his work, only a few non-paying local magazines such as the *Beacon*, published by Albert Gomes, which printed stories by himself, C.L.R. James and Alfred Mendes. After the Second World War, things had changed. The Jamaican poet Una Marson broadcast a morale-boosting BBC radio show from London during the war for West Indians in the armed forces. Marson was the first black woman to make programmes at the BBC; there is a photograph of her in a studio with William Empson, George Orwell, Mulk Raj Anand and T.S. Eliot, among others. In 1946 the show *Caribbean*

Voices took a fresh turn under a new editor, Henry Swanzy: it became a weekly half-hour display case for new writing and poetry. Swanzy liked Seepersad Naipaul's stories, and broadcast six over four years. The first was 'Sonya's Luck', about a rural Hindu bride who elopes with her lover on her wedding night, only for the couple to discover that their parents have already betrothed them to each other. Another was a non-fiction account of going to a meeting of Christian 'shouters'. *Ramdas And The Cow* was a story about a Brahmin who wants to sell a barren cow to a butcher, but dare not for fear of his neighbour Gurudeva; Ramdas refers to the cow 'by all sorts of crazy names and cuss-words, the most common of which was "bitch".'[42] He hatches a plan to get the cow to the butcher, only for it to fall down dead. In the evolving intellectual and political climate, with the prospect of self-rule sweeping the region, Swanzy's show had a catalytic effect, linking writers and critics from across the territories of the English-speaking Caribbean from British Honduras to British Guiana. Radio was the perfect medium to create such a virtual community. Contributors would send a story or poem to a BBC agent in Jamaica who sifted the material and sent it by boat to Swanzy for consideration at his office in Oxford Street. Back in the West Indies, they would cluster around a wireless or Rediffusion set and listen for the legendary opening: 'This is London calling the Caribbean.' During the life of the programme, there were 372 contributors, of whom about one-fifth were women.[43]

Outwardly, *Caribbean Voices* was a classic assertion of imperial authority: the colonized produced writing which after scrutiny and critical assessment by their masters in London was broadcast back to them. In practice, the process was highly collaborative and creative, as writers and manuscripts travelled back and forth across the Atlantic, leading to the flowering of talents such as Andrew Salkey, Edgar Mittelholzer, Samuel Selvon, George Lamming, Edward Brathwaite, Derek Walcott and the Naipauls, père et fils. The impetus lay with Henry Swanzy, a short, plump, musical man of Irish origin who despite his booming upper-class voice was more concerned with dismantling the British empire than building it. He said later that 'one had the sort of left-wing view of encouraging people who had had a raw deal.'[44]

Born in 1915 in Ireland, Swanzy had graduated from Oxford and worked as a ministerial private secretary in the Dominions Office before joining the BBC's Empire Department. A paternalistic but critically acute figure, he took Caribbean writing seriously. When authors such as Selvon moved to England, he offered them personal support, holding discussions at his house in Hampstead and introducing them to literary editors and critics. He worked closely with the small journals of the West Indies, particularly *Kyk-Over-Al* in British Guiana and *Bim* in Barbados, whose inspiring editor, Frank Collymore, became a close collaborator. Only *Focus* in Jamaica stood out against Swanzy's charm, for nationalist reasons, seeing the British Broadcasting Corporation as the tool of a failing colonial power. Henry Swanzy's taste was for the local rather than the derivative: he said his listeners had 'sat with the fishermen hefting sea-eggs, gone with the pork-knockers into Guyanese jungles, followed the saga-boys and the whe-whe players, heard the riddles, the digging songs, the proverbs, the ghost stories, duppies, La Diablesse, Soukivans, zombies, maljo, obeah, voodoo, shango.'[45] His favourite material was unsentimental: after broadcasting a Runyonesque short story by Sam Selvon about Indians pimping girls to Yankee sailors in Port of Spain, he faced furious complaints from listeners in the Caribbean, many of whom had a strong, conservative Christian faith. Henry Swanzy was to be a crucial figure in Vidia's successful development as a writer.

Vido's first story, 'This is Home', was based on the memory of his father building the house in the woods at Petit Valley. In the fictionalized version, a young couple reach their new home in a lorry which 'whined like a kicked puppy'. The man is handsome but 'seared somehow, with sorrow' while his wife moves 'calmly and deliberately, with all the charm of a woman in her first pregnancy.' Soon, however, 'He was seized with distaste for her, for her methodical, ritual approach to ordinary things . . . He saw the tasks of the world split into two. Man the author, man the worker. Woman the anvil for man's passion: the feeder and lover of her master . . . It was the idea of fitting into a primeval universal pattern of living to mate, and mating to create that filled him with dread. Sex was the whole works and he knew it; and it hurt him.' The woman turns her face to him. 'He kissed her. "This is home," he said. I am not ashamed any more, he was telling himself. And yet he could feel that he was lying.'[46] V.S. Naipaul's first short story is ponderous and laden with uneasy symbolism. It carries a teenager's idea of how people a little older than himself might behave. Yet it contains certain key themes – dislocation, homelessness, anxiety about the relationship between men and women – that he would write about repeatedly in his later work.

In July, Vidia joined an agricultural camp, working eleven hours a day. 'Believe me, you can keep manual labour. I don't care for it at all,' he told his parents.[47] His mother sent him some tins of fruit juice, a bottle of guava jelly and a tin of sugar. 'Look for 3 packs of cig[arette]s in sugar,' his father warned. Snippets of news reached him from abroad. 'Today the Tewaris are here. Nigger Betty and her mother,' Mira reported, referring to friends from Jamaica. WAGS told him that he had fallen in love with 'a not bad-looking girl of 20 . . . She proved, however, to be of rather easy virtue and I repeatedly dashed her.' Kamla said she was spending her summer holidays with a family in Benares where her Naipauline irreverence had caused an upset: 'I made a slip of the tongue . . . We were having a few religious discussions when Hanuman came into the conversation. One of the girls asked me if I knew Hanuman. And, without thinking, I promptly replied, "Yes, a monkey." Boy, I am sure the mother was scandalised. She spends her whole day praying.'

Vidia went on writing, and kept encouraging Pa, telling him in July, 'YOU HAVE ENOUGH MATERIAL FOR A HUNDRED STORIES. FOR HEAVEN'S SAKE START WRITING THEM . . . The essential thing about writing is writing . . . You are the best writer in the West Indies, but one can only judge writers by their work.' He was making an obvious but astute point, and one that he himself would never forget: there are many would-be great writers, but the only ones who become great writers are those who sit down and write. Vidia promised to have Pa's stories typed up, and to help him find a publisher. From the BBC offices in Oxford Street, Henry Swanzy had praised Pa to Vidia as 'a natural writer'. The manuscript of his own novel was now complete. He showed it to Peter Bayley, a large typewritten manuscript. Bayley thought later — wondering whether his memory might be playing tricks on him — that it contained the seeds of Vidia's first four novels. 'I found there *The Mystic Masseur*, *The Suffrage of Elvira* and of course quite a lot of *Miguel Street* and indeed anticipations of *Mr Biswas*.'[48] It was read by a friend, Ronnie Eyre, later a film and theatre director, and by Ian Robertson. Vidia felt confident he would find a publisher. 'As soon as your novel is accepted, write me,' Pa told him. But despite Vidia's best efforts, nobody wanted to publish his book. He said later, 'I began when I was about seventeen, much influenced by Evelyn Waugh, writing a farce set in Trinidad, and I worked at that for two years. Now, nothing happened to that; I was heartbroken.' It taught him 'how to take a book to the end'.[49]

At the start of September, using money that he should have been saving for the coming academic year, Vidia went to Paris. Flamboyantly, greedily, he bought a taste of the world he aspired to by travelling by air. He was taken by coach from Kensington Air Station to London Airport, and flew in style across the channel, sipping complimentary champagne. 'The month's tour of France is so cheap – $180 – that I suspect that something must be wrong somewhere,' he wrote to Pa, who supported a family on $165 a month. 'Anyway, I have remarkable luck wherever I go. And, the Colonial Office is granting me $60.'[50] He defrayed a fraction of the cost some years later by writing a version of the flight for *Caribbean Voices*. Later still, he wrote, 'Air France used to run an Epicurean Service between London and Paris. The advertisements taunted me. Poverty makes for recklessness, and one idle day in the long summer vacation I booked.' In the earlier account, Naipaul or 'Narayan' writes of a conversation with an Indian journalist he meets on the flight; by the time of the second article, 1965, his travelling companion has become a stock 'Indian' character who chucks him under the chin saying, '*Hin-du wege-tar-ian!*' By this time, his view of himself had shifted: 'To be a colonial is to be a little ridiculous . . . To be an Indian from Trinidad, then, is to be unlikely and exotic. It is also to be a little fraudulent.'[51]

From Paris, he told Kamla he had met an attractive Finnish woman, 'and we spent three delicious days together.' Vidia could not work out how to proceed, and so retained his virginity. Her name was Dorrit Hinze; he took a photograph of Dorrit wearing flat shoes and a shapeless post-war dress, squinting buxomly in the sunlight outside Notre-Dame cathedral. He said later, 'I bought her chocolate and I took her to my hotel. I was immensely stirred but I didn't know how to seduce her; I was so ashamed of my incompetence.'[52] While Vidia wrestled with the Finn, the BBC broadcast his story 'The Mourners'. Like 'This is Home', it is melancholic. A girl, Ann – this was V.S. Naipaul's first and last use of a female narrator – visits a relation whose son has died, and listens unwillingly to an account of the dead boy's qualities. The attempt to convey the affect of grief is melodramatic. In 1967, Naipaul would publish a revised version in the collection *A Flag on the Island*. The story has improved, showing how he could turn a dud into a success by making precise changes. The opening becomes taut; Ann becomes Romesh; clichés are cut. In the first version, the mourning mother is described incidentally, but in the second she is fixed immediately: 'She was in a loose lemon housecoat; she half sat, half reclined on a pink sofa.'[53]

At the start of the new term, admiring his literary ambitions, Peter Bayley asked the Dean to give Vidia a grant of 30 shillings from college funds to repair his typewriter, which he had dropped. 'Indians', the Dean told him in the manner of the time, handing over the cash, 'are very charming, very poetical; some are even geniuses. But you are so startlingly incompetent.' To Kamla, Vido wrote, 'Ruth and Capo R have invited me to spend Xmas with them at Brighton. I am not sure whether I shall accept or not. I don't like that woman. She has got a filthy mind. Capo R and I, on the other hand, have been hitting it off rather well. He has got so far friendly as to tell me that his marriage was the biggest mistake in his life.' Kamla urged her brother to be more diplomatic: 'For goodness sake, don't openly show your dislike for Ruth. Learn some of the silly conventions of society and practice smiling before your mirror even if you don't want to.' In late December, Vidia wrote home, 'I have just returned from Brighton where I spent Xmas with Rood Mamoo. I spent a really enjoyable time, and I am sure that I could not have spent Christmas better anywhere . . . This afternoon I paid a call on Owad. He lives with a tiny colony of St James Indians in a shabby quarter of London . . . I have just heard that someone suggested at home that I was hurried away from T'dad because I was carrying on with negresses!! Did you hear that one? It is rather thrilling to find oneself the object of baseless slander . . I have been thinking about what I shall do after Oxford and I have come to the conclusion that I shall come back to Trinidad for a bit at least if I can get a job at QRC.'

In the New Year of 1952, having given up on *Isis*, he started designing the Oxford *Tory*, a freshly established paper of the Oxford University Conservative Association. He enjoyed the work, although he had no political affiliation to the Conservatives. He admitted to his parents that for several months he had 'been prey to the gravest emotional upset I have ever experienced'. Mira wrote: 'I hardly know what to say, except . . . to assure you, if assurance is necessary, that we are all looking forward to the day when V.S. Naipaul will have become a famous name in the world of letters.' Underneath her words, little Sewan had written, 'Dear Vido, I send you a kiss.' In late January his mother wrote, 'Well this is one thing I am begging you not to do, don't marry a white girl please don't . . . I suppose there are plenty Indian girls in England studying. If you marry one of them only when you are through with your education, I shall be very pleased.' Pa agreed with Ma; he believed 'that by far the majority of intermarriages end in failure.' Soon, though, he was reconsidering, forced to admit that things might be more complicated: 'Who you should marry is entirely a matter for you; though for my part I should be more happy to see you marry an Indian, in the end it must be as you yourself choose. But give yourself plenty of time for this.'

On 9 February, only a few days after Ma's letter arrived, Vidia happened to meet a girl named Patricia Hale at his college play. Like most undergraduates, she was white.

CHAPTER SIX

'I LOVE YOU, MY DEAR PAT'

PAT HALE WAS A SLIM, small undergraduate with a kind, pretty face. She was a member of the Oxford University Dramatic Society, and Vidia first glimpsed her holding a stack of programmes on the final night of the Univ play, Jan de Hartog's *Skipper Next to God*. He had designed the poster and helped to organize the publicity for the play. They chatted, and he invited her to tea. Pat was seventeen days older than Vidia, reading history at a women's college, St Hugh's. Like him, she came from a poor background and had reached Oxford University on intellectual merit, in her case on a state scholarship. Over tea, they talked some more, and a tentative romance began. In March 1952, Pat went home for the vacation. Her parents and sister lived in a decrepit two-bedroom flat above the Birmingham Municipal Bank in Kingstand-ing, a drab suburb of the great nineteenth-century city of Birmingham in the English Midlands. Her father worked in a local firm of solicitors as a managing clerk, a position similar to a legal executive. Mr and Mrs Hale both came originally from Gloucestershire.

Vidia sat down to write to Pat. His tone was that of the would-be romantic lover. He was trying out a role, for he had never written a proper love letter, and did not know where to begin. Each sentence, each sentiment, seemed insincere, as if someone else might already have written it. 'Yes, darling, I am missing you very much. At odd moments, I seem to smell you (don't be angry: it's a pleasant smell) . . . I think of your room tonight – at St. Hugh's – robbed of you, robbed of all its charm, its warmth, its cosiness. I cannot go there and relax in your chair or sofa or have you steal eggs to make me a decent tea. How I love you for all that! No, no I am not drunk. Allow me to be utterly un-British & to wallow in my sloppiness. I love you, my dear Pat, and I feel it grow stronger every day. Promise me one thing, though – read & destroy. I should hate to think that next term in one of your peevish moods, you should read this letter to me mockingly. A man who writes with sincerity usually sounds silly.'[1]

He made it plain he was depressed: 'For the past 3 months I have been through a mental hell-fire. Nothing like it ever happened to me before, & I hope nothing like it ever happens again.' He made it plain he was a writer: 'The novel is going slowly – very slowly. This always happens to me. But loneliness will eventually force the thing out on paper – if it really wants to come out.' He made it plain that other people were doing better than him, in particular Guy Lorriman, who had a room on the same staircase at Univ and was being praised around Oxford for Vidia's work on the *Tory*: 'Well, you know that if the circulation has doubled it was because of me. Nearly every idea was mine. Now, I don't mind getting only peanuts for my pains, while friend Lorriman gets the credit for being a journalistic genius . . . Lorriman was made a member of the Press club. I wasn't. L[orriman] was invited to the *Isis* term party. I wasn't.' Vidia knew he was making himself look ridiculous, and concluded, 'No, there ain't no justice. Do you mind terribly if I remain buried in obscurity at Oxford?'

Pat, correspondingly, was simpler. She wrote unaffectedly of life in Kingstanding, of her parents going out to buy their first television set after the death of King George VI, of paying a visit to her good friend Sheila Rogers, of her annoyance at her boisterous younger sister Eleanor charging around the cramped family flat, and of going to watch Alan Guinness in a play called *Under the Sycamore Tree* in Birmingham. In a round, girlish hand, she told him:

> There is something very exciting about the first letter received
> from someone. I'm glad you didn't write straight away. It gave
> me time to look forward to it. I'm also glad you didn't write a
> clever letter, a sort of literary piece of art, you know . . . Vidia,
> you've been very good to me. Since I've been home I've
> realised how much I enjoyed being with you, how interesting
> you make things, how in fact you've stimulated me.

There were, though, immediate and lasting problems: 'My father has told me that I must not let you write me letters here. He has fits like this when he suddenly does things that put me in the most ghastly positions. Generally I disregard his wishes in the best western and decadent manner but he has caught me. If I don't make it plain he will insist on reading your letters, etc . . . I apologise for him. He gets these fits and he's not perfect but he isn't really prejudiced, Victorian or anything else.' The themes were set: Patricia was moved and stimulated by Vidia, her father objected to the possibility of a foreigner in their midst, and Pat's reaction was to blame herself: 'I just feel sick and more deeply convinced than ever of my general worthlessness.'

He responded with formality, with a letter for family consumption, and waited until the holidays were over. 'Dear Miss Hale, The Modern History Prelim Results will be out tomorrow, and, as I promised, I shall telephone them to you. Some people are so eager to get bad news. I shall call at 11:30 am, shortly before I leave Oxford for the day. Yours sincerely, V. S. Naipaul.' They spoke on the telephone, and Vidia paid her whispered compliments. He was unstable now. He felt increasingly homesick, and wondered about booking a passage home to Trinidad for the summer vacation. He asked his father to investigate dates and prices, and suggested he might obtain a cheap passage on a merchant tanker. 'Stress that I am a student at Oxford, not a Negro going to play the fool in London. Wonderful snob-value.' Pa moved fast, delighted at the prospect of seeing Vido again, booking a passage and borrowing money to make a downpayment of a quarter of the fare. Pa was writing less now, growing orchids and sleeping in the afternoons. Although he was only in middle-age, he felt old.

Vidia presented a paper to the Martlets on 'The Use of the First Person Singular in English Fiction', and offered it unsuccessfully to Henry Swanzy for *Caribbean Voices*. He told his parents of sitting in the Dean's rooms, drinking port. 'I had the group laughing whenever I wanted them to laugh. This morning someone told me that my paper was by far the brightest he had ever heard at the society.' He parodied Henry James, praised Daniel Defoe and 'quoted a bit of Cecil Hunt, about the telegraphic style. "A shot rang out. A man fell dead. Two more shots rang out. Two more men fell dead."' He described a typical meal in hall, 'a long, high room, with an enormous fireplace that is never used. The roof is timbered, and some of the windows have stained glass. Pictures of past great men of the college hang on the walls.' After eating, Vidia would proceed to the Junior Common Room to sit beneath sporting pictures and crossed rowing oars drinking coffee, eating a doughnut and reading the newspapers. 'English food is a calamity and a tragedy,' he wrote later. In the evening he would have half a pint of stout in the college beer cellar. It was a traditional, English, clubbable, unreal way for a young man from the Caribbean to be living, and it left him feeling lonely and unfulfilled. He wrote a luminous panegyric to Trinidad:

I feel nostalgic for home. Do you know what I long for? I long
for the nights that fall blackly, suddenly, without warning. I long
for a violent shower of rain at night. I long to hear the tinny
tattoo of heavy raindrops on a roof, or the drops of rain on the
broad leaves of that wonderful plant, the wild tannia. But, in
short, I long for home, or perhaps, the homely atmosphere. And
I miss my bicycle rides, and the sea, and the pit at Rialto, and the
sort of cigarettes I used to smoke, to every one's scandal.

It was a time of desperate longing for Vidia, and by the end of March
he had moved beyond Wertherism; he was going off the rails.

'This is a desperate plea for help,' he wrote to Kamla in a scrawled
hand. 'I am broke, broke, broke. Can you send me £5–£10.' He wrote
home from Málaga in southern Spain a fortnight later, now on the rails,
sounding manic: 'Since March 30 I have been travelling constantly.
Take out a map of Europe and follow me ... steamer for Calais ...
Paris the following day. Austerlitz Railway Station. Romantic name –
romantic journeys. Huge locomotives pulling expresses bound for all
over Europe ... Did not sleep that night. Next morning, at Narbonne,
decided to be luxurious and have breakfast in the dining car, just as the
sun was rising. Beautiful. Paris – Châteauroux – Toulouse – Carcas-
sonne – Narbonne – Perpignan ... Four armed police go past the
railway coach corridor in Port Bou. Later, passport inspected – 3rd
time in Spain. My temper rises and I swear loudly in English ...
Barcelona at 3 – travelling constantly, then, for 19 hours. Ordinary
station, nasty and blackened with smoke. At the exit hordes of touts
trying to sell you their taxis and their hotel ... Have coffee in a room
that overlooks one of the beautiful avenues of Barcelona; speak to my
hostess and her daughter – a slim, pretty little thing of 22 who had
been playing the piano while I was eating. Presently I find that I am
flirting with both mother and daughter ... Tomorrow I leave for
Cordoba or for Madrid.' On the way back, he had an intense but
embarassing encounter with a woman on a train. 'A Spanish lady came
into the coach,' he remembered. 'We talked during the night and I
embraced her. That was very comforting.' He explained to her in less
than perfect Spanish that he was not feeling well, but 'she misunderstood. I was telling her about my mental condition. She thought I was
telling her that I had syphilis or something.'[2]

When Vidia got back to England, he was in a bad state. Trinidad was off. 'The fact is,' he admitted, 'I spent too much money in Spain. And, during the nervous breakdown (yes, it was that) I had, I grew rash and reckless and threw money about with a don't-care-a-damn inconsequence. My only opportunity of recuperating from my present chaos is to remain in England this summer and live very cheaply.' Pa, as ever, was loving and tolerant; he offered no reprimand but, like Mr Biswas, sent his son a copy of *Outwitting Our Nerves* by sea mail and pressed him not to be downcast. 'Lose yourself in the throes and thrills of your creative work,' he suggested, 'and write on E[ast] I[ndian] or EI-Negro themes. We must not let Selvon alone get away with it.' As for himself, 'In this struggle for existence I feel just hemmed in by hard, unescapable facts and forces.' Vidia responded blandly: 'The grass is green; and the wind is not too sharp. It is agreeable to go for bicycle rides into the country around Oxford or for walks.' He had made new friends, played cricket, done a painting in oils and been paid eleven guineas by the BBC for a story called 'Potatoes', its Caribbean setting giving him an opportunity to dream of home. He had held a bring-a-bottle party in his rooms attended by forty people, including women and the Dean, and been elected secretary of 'the Martlets (the College Intellectuals).' This, he murmured loudly to Sati in Trinidad and Kamla in India, was, 'Not an honour to shout about.'

Vidia thought he understood what had gone wrong. 'Of course I know the reason for my breakdown: loneliness, and lack of affection. You see, a man isn't a block of wood that is sent abroad and receives two notches as a sign of education. He is much more. He feels and he thinks. Some people, alas, feel more, and think more than others, and they suffer. It is no good thinking that the sensitive man is happier or greater. No one cares for your tragedy until you can sing about it, and you require peace of mind to do this.' Pa was worried about Vidia, writing to Kamla, 'I have sent him some money. I am really very, very sorry for him. He is so impulsive, so unpredictable.'

Afraid of what might lie ahead, Vidia found the name of a psychologist in the pages of the *Oxford Mail* and made an appointment. The man came from central Europe, and gave him two free consultations. Vidia said later: 'He told me that I was just racially insecure, and I rejected this, then later I saw that it was the great solitude which was leading to that feeling of insecurity. Probably he was getting it right, but I hated him because if you go and expose yourself to someone at a moment of your greatest weakness you do hate them. But it's one of the great triumphs in my life that without having any further connections with psychologists and doctors I was able to deal with it . . . I took hints from the psychologist and worked on it and that means just as before I was questioning myself all the time internally, regardless of where I was, whether I was in a café, or in a bus or talking to people, I was now fighting back, I wasn't surrendering to it. And I won through.' In later years, when life was going badly and he had sealed himself off against his own emotions, 'I measured everything by the unhappiness of those eighteen months. So I always felt good, nothing could be as bad as that . . . It was a great depression verging on madness . . . Pat was a great solace to me at that period; probably I clung to her because of that depression.'3

*

During the summer of 1952, Vidia and Pat's relationship became closer. He could reveal his state of mind to her in a way that was impossible with others. Only she, he suggested, would be able to save him from himself. Writing from his room in Univ, he told her, in a profound admission, that beneath his impossibility, his complexity and his rages, he had a clear moral vision, or an integrity. The clarity of Pat's letters to him and her approach to life had made his own writing less opaque.

> You first met me when I was in the grips of a long and suicidal
> depression. I suppose I am a depressive. I observe this, not in
> pride or in horror, but simply as I would observe that it is
> raining and that tropical skies are usually boringly blue.
> Whether the depression causes the fatigue or fatigue the
> depression I don't know. But both are causeless and both scare
> me; and both make me a difficult man to live with . . . I am
> telling you this so that you will be a bit more patient with me
> whenever you sense that I am sinking to the depths. You saved
> me once, and it is from that rescue that I have been able to keep
> going – from Feb 9 to today. I love you, and I need you.
> Please don't let me down. Please forgive my occasional lapses.
> At heart I am the worthiest man I know.

Realizing the strength of their connection, he prepared her a reading list to reveal the world of his childhood: Hinduism, as mediated through Western eyes. He suggested several Indian epics and dramas, Christopher Isherwood and Swami Prabhavananda's translation of the

Bhagavad Gita, 'Intro by Aldous Huxley. (ESSENTIAL)' and '*The Hindu View of Life* by Prof. Radhakrishnan (INTERESTING).'

When the long vacation came, things fell apart again. Penniless, Vidia had to lodge with Rudranath and Ruth at their new house in Balham in south London. Their son Rudy, who was seven years old, remembered Vidia being treated with condescension. 'My father had great intellectual arrogance, and he was tough on Vidia. He had a teacher-student attitude to his nephews and nieces. He was like a lord of the manor ... A lot was happening: his nephew Devendranath was suffering an acute schizophrenic illness and thought he was Christ ... My father would have gone at Vidia. He didn't like his affected pseudo-Oxford accent, and Vidia was an angry, mixed-up young man. I can remember him singing "Ol' Man River" and darning his socks.'[4] Nor did Ruth like Vidia's behaviour. She was a university graduate – she had met Rudranath when University College London was evacuated to Bangor during the war – and objected to being treated like a housekeeper. Vidia quickly deduced that 'a campaign of humiliation' was being conducted against him by his extended family. The trouble began with a familiar kitchen stand-off. Vidia, a Univ man and secretary of the Martlets, was asked to wash the dishes, but continued to read a newspaper before sauntering to the sink, where he was told to sit down again by Owad's wife, Jean. 'Don't pamper him at all,' insisted Ruth, trying to convert her displaced Hindu in-laws to a modern English approach to household chores. 'He must learn to do these things.' Vidia wrote a letter to his parents in a tight, angry hand, including a diagram of his bedroom to show how visitors to the bathroom had to pass through its cramped confines. 'I asked for a chair for the bedroom in which they had so kindly put me up for £1 a week ... Ruth said that I was to take one and bring it down every morning.' Then she asked him not to drop his cigarette ash on the floor. For Vidia, this was 'the last straw'. He told her he would not allow his spirit to be broken, and left.

It did not occur to him that his uncle might be doing a favour by renting him a room, or that his aunt might expect him to wash-up or not drop cigarette ash; he saw the encounter only in terms of the slight to his dignity. 'I am very homesick,' he admitted to Kamla. 'I am scared to be alive. For the past six months an air of unreality has hung about the things I have done.' It was not easy at this time for someone with brown or black skin to find accommodation in Britain, although East

Indians tended to fare better than West Indians; a survey of 300 London landladies in the early 1950s found that only 26 per cent would accept 'lightly-coloured non-European' students, while a mere 10 per cent took black people; some charged a sliding 'colour tax' on foreigners.[5] In Sam Selvon's book *The Housing Lark*, a character called Syl says his name is Ram Singh Ali Mohommed Esquire and mutters 'aloo, vindallo, dansak, and chutney' in order to get a room. The landlord rumbles him. ' "You look like an Indian, but you are from the same islands as those immigrants . . . you are not from the East."

"I used to live in the East End," Syl say hopefully.

"That is not far enough East," the Englisher say, "Take a week's notice as from today." '[6]

Vidia travelled to Harrogate and lodged unhappily with the 'upper class, but poor' parents of a friend from his college, John Fawcett. He wanted to be part of another world, but with the Fawcetts he again began to feel uneasy. Looking back, he thought, 'They were anxious to be nice to me, but I felt awkward. There was something about the food. I didn't like the ritual of napkins and napkin rings in John's house. I just felt it wasn't me. So I was rather primitive. And the thing about 1952, I was mentally disturbed. I was very, very disturbed, very melancholy, I had a degree of clinical depression. It had to do with lack of money, solitude, sexual deprivation.'[7]

The grace he displayed at Oxford was not enough to carry him through, or give him security. Peter Bayley had been impressed by Vidia's confidence, but it was skin-deep. When he and his wife, Patience, invited a group of undergraduates from Univ to lunch, 'there were one or two dumbstruck Freshmen who were very awkward and shy . . . Vidia was much more socially at ease and of course he was full of ideas and conversations. We had a very nice dinner service, Limoges, and the gravy-boat was all in one. I remember Vidia going to pour gravy. He meant to pick it up and it wouldn't come loose on the saucer and he looked about and then he put his hand down and I said, "It's all in one Vidia." Silly, trivial story. He was socially an extraordinarily composed person. He would come sometimes to the house in winter, when it was cold . . . My wife used to make cinnamon toast and he loved cinnamon toast.'[8] Vidia, then, was able to adjust and compose himself in a social, formal setting.

*

Pa was glad Vido had abandoned the Capildeos, but had worrying news of his own: more family responsibility: 'This will pain you: but your Ma will be having a baby – in September or October . . . I know it's a mess, but there we are.' Vidia was not happy, but he wrote to Ma that he thought it would make 'little difference, except perhaps for you'. Ma was surprised herself. 'I myself never was thinking that I am going to have another baby,' she wrote in fractured English. 'I got very discourage and mindsick to know that it will be true. I am just telling myself that the Lord knows best, and there must be a reason why.' Vidia responded warmly to his mother 'that nothing will ever make me stop having all the respect and love in the world for you . . . Frankly, whenever I think about you and Pa, I think that you have been noble.'

Vidia communicated with Patricia intensely by letter, but the dispute with his uncle, his lack of money and the plight of his parents were shown to her in partial glimpses. He felt embarrassed. Pat had returned to Birmingham in early July and taken a job on a farm near Kingstanding. Each day, she had to bicycle ten miles through the suburbs and country lanes, hoe weeds or pick potatoes in the fields, and then bicycle home again before trying to write a few lines to Vidia. 'This will be a terrible letter as I am so tired I just don't know what I'm doing,' she wrote on 10 July. 'You doubtless will shudder at the thought of me working with labourers' wives, getting my hands caked with mud.' She had grown fascinated by one of the farm workers, Peter Petch.

> I should say he knows or rather has read more English
> literature than you even. He is completely self-educated – by
> that I mean he reads purely for pleasure. He is not completely
> unselfconscious, if you get what I mean, but his approach to
> literature is absolutely unaffected. I think you'd find it
> fascinating for people like that are so hard to find. His life is a
> rather tragic one. His wife was quite nice looking and was an
> enthusiastic cyclist. A couple of years ago she became suddenly
> paralysed. She is now on her back all the time – suspended and
> strapped – it's awful. He looks after her in addition to his farm
> work. Don't imagine he is an indifferent farm worker either. He
> wins prizes for ploughing and things – quite extraordinary.
> Everything centres upon his wife who lies in a downstairs room.

Vidia was immediately jealous of the 'not completely unselfconscious' Mr Petch, with his skill at the plough and his apparent erudition and virtue, and conscious of the likely sexual need generated by an incapacitated wife. Lodging with John Fawcett's family and feeling like 'a hopeless intruder', Vidia was conscious only of his own insecurity. Unlike his friends, the fellow undergraduates with whom he blended so seemingly easily, he had nowhere to go. He made plans to meet Pat at the theatre in Stratford one evening later in the month, concealing his intermittent letters to her in disguised envelopes to deceive Mr Hale. 'My financial position is hopeless. I will starve after the end of August . . . If the BBC accept my story I may get some cash.'

Not enamoured by the idea of doing farm or manual work, Vidia was caught 'in an agony of love and frustration. I want you so badly . . . I suppose what has really got me down is the utter solitude in which I now find myself and the prospect of ten more weeks of it.' Pat made detailed plans for their meeting: 'Sheila tells me that the theatre bus leaves Stratford twenty minutes after the performance ends so there should be plenty of time . . . You might get a cheap day return even if you do go back late if the guard on the train is indulgent.' She fretted over his health: 'For all your talk about working and feeling better during the winter I'm sure that coming from the tropics, you're liable to get run down during the winter even though you don't realise it.' Crucially, she had not yet told her father that she was going to meet him. 'I feel so weary by the time evening comes that I shirk it. This week-end, or perhaps to-night, I really will . . . All my love Pat. P.S. I love you 6^2.' The squared six referred to a joke between them about love; when Sewan was a little boy and his sisters asked him how much he loved them, he would answer numerically, 'I love you six.'

When Pat broke the news to her father, the reaction was explosive. Stratford was off; she suggested Vidia might go with a friend rather than waste the chance of a night at the theatre, and sent him the tickets for seats P25–26, price nine shillings and sixpence. The squabble with her father, a common intergenerational and transcultural dispute that was now escalating badly, caused Pat to wonder in the language of the time whether she should leave home.

> I have worked like a nigger all day trying to drive out all the
> unpleasant weights that have settled on my inside . . . I can't
> write you the whole nasty little altercation. I don't think it will
> serve any useful purpose besides. Amongst other things my
> father was determined to have it out with you if I went to

Stratford . . . It is 'Indians or University – You can't have both!' Incredible, isn't it? I don't think he would carry out the threat of next term being my last. I hope he would be too ashamed. I'm screwing up my courage to face the music.

Vidia, staying with Guy Lorriman in Kent despite an earlier promise never to accept the hospitality of his acquaintances again, was horrified. 'I need hardly say that such a step, in addition to being extremely foolish, will also prove calamitous,' he informed her drily. 'You know how I stand. Besides I am convinced that one ought to do all in one's power to maintain cordial relations with one's parents.'

Pat calmed down, and they resolved to see each other later in the summer. She wrote about Laurence Sterne's discursive novel *Tristram Shandy*, which she loved, and about her frantic little sister Eleanor, with whom she had to share a bed: 'You should see her! She's racing around the garden wielding a rifle. She alternates two headgears. Sometimes a homemade Red Indian head dress made from coronation (1936) ribbon and yellow feathers, sometimes Mummy's A[ir] R[aid] P[recautions] helmet (1940–46) and a pair of goggles.' Home life was not inspiring. Each evening the family would eat at six o'clock, and afterwards her father would go 'over the way' to the Kingstanding pub, where he would drink quietly with the local butcher, newsagent and builder until closing time. Meanwhile, at the farm, the estimable 'Mr. Petch offered to lend me "The Communist Manifesto" on Wednesday. That man gave me a further shock yesterday by talking quite knowledgeably about Rowlandson and Hogarth.'

In August she travelled south to Gloucestershire to stay with Auntie Lu, her favourite aunt, her mother's elder sister, Lucy. Free from parents, correspondence was easier, and they managed a snatched meeting in Gloucester, where Pat had been to school. Later she wrote, 'I received your letter this morning. I can't describe my feelings as I read it. I stood at the bottom of the stairs clutching the milk bottle and feeling alternately as great as the whole world and as humble the smallest speck of dust on it . . . I have just breakfasted on a huge peach, brown bread and butter and three cups of coffee. You are the only thing wanting. But wanting is a pleasant way, nevertheless. I suppose it is because I saw you on Monday but I feel very peaceful – as if I'd known you for a couple of centuries.' She told him about meeting Ella Wallen, an old schoolteacher.

> She first made my acquaintance at the age of eight when she
> was new and had to teach the small "advanced arithmetic" class
> of the second form . . . She was toiling through fractions when
> suddenly she saw my hand waving about. I was a conscientious
> child in those days and with a kindly smile she waited for me to
> ask for mathematical enlightenment. I looked at her coldly and
> asked, "Why do I have to learn arithmetic when I'm going to
> be an actress?"

Back in Oxford now, scraping his landlady Mrs King's breakfast into
the bin each morning rather than admit he could not eat greasy sausages
and bacon, Vidia wrote Pat a long, confessional letter by return. He felt
able for the first time to express a petty personal secret which made him
feel ashamed. He described an experience of literary rejection, how his
novel had been sent back to him.

> It was in the middle of December – a Sunday. I had come back
> from London, and had found my returned novel resting
> mockingly in my pigeon hole . . . I drank gin heavily. After that I
> remember three things. One, screaming for more gin. Two,
> feeling hopelessly drunk and lost, and wishing to beat my head
> against a wall. I stumbled down the stairs and opened a door. I
> wanted a bed to lie down on. There was a woman in the room,
> making herself up or getting ready for bed. I ignored her, said,
> 'Excuse me', and flopped down on the bed. When I got up she
> was gone. I crossed the road, couldn't find No 12 for a long time.
> Mrs. King must have heard me prowling around. She opened the
> door & put on the light. 'Up here Mr. Naipaul,' she called. It was
> only yesterday that she reminded me of that disgraceful incident.
> I was never a drinking man. When I came to Oxford, I was a
> teetotaller; but very shortly I found that 'the real Oxford'
> consisted of smart young men who drank heavily. In three terms
> I got drunk about 6 times. Then I went to the agricultural camp
> in the vac. And got drunk every day I was there. Surprisingly, I
> found that this had made me a sort of hero with a group of
> Welsh miners . . . I wonder whether it is right telling you all this.
> But who else can I tell? You are the only one who ought to know
> me completely and wholly, and I must hold nothing back.

He had been through an even more humiliating experience with drink
when he first arrived at Univ. After a surfeit of port, he had vomited

over his clothes. 'I didn't rinse them out or anything. I took them just as they were to the Oxford valet service which is just next door to University College and the man was shocked beyond words. He said, "I can't accept this. I have to think of the staff." And I was with him, I agreed with him.'⁹

Vidia's letter to Pat also contained a rare statement of his own philosophy. Private ideas that had been forming inside him slowly and would expand over the years into an intellectual and literary programme could now be communicated. He complained about the hypocrisy that came from revealed religion, using Guy Lorriman's social Catholicism as an example.

> The Rosary is chanted (in itself a most primitive incantatory magic) and Lorriman is convinced he is good; and convinced that his desire to rise will be blessed. What shall I think about the mind that can tolerate and praise this: willing to praise his own speeches in his magazine, willing to contravene all ethics, even journalistic ones, to delay the date of publication to print his own praise, and only restrained by the fear that such praise, appearing in his own magazine, might not do him good. And, then, seriously wondering how I, a pagan, could have any sense of what is right! This isn't an isolated freak of behaviour. It betrays the entire make-up.

Rationalist, culturally Hindu with a dose of Trinidad's practical Christianity, having grown up in an island society where each religion and race had to exist in parallel private and public spheres, the son of a questioning father and a morally upright mother, Vidia had formed his own ethical notions and applied them stringently. He did not want to reform, convert or emancipate; he was a watcher, a writer:

> I think that we have in us a cumulative conscience, a sort of birthright of the human race. We do know what is right and what is wrong: stealing, adultery, infidelity, killing a member of one's own people or tribe (you can kill as many of the opposite types as possible!), lying and dishonesty. The cliché virtues are common to all races, and their observation in the breach is common to all races, too. Now don't feel that I want to reform the human race. I am the spectator, the flâneur par excellence. I am free of the emancipatory fire. I want to create myself, to work

out my own philosophy that will bring me comfort. I want to see the good and the bad.

He shared two formative moments of his childhood with Pat:

> My first memory of sadness – cosmic sadness – came in 1941
> or thereabouts. We were living in a small house in the country,
> far away from everybody. It was late tropic evening, rapidly
> growing dark. I looked out of the window to the kitchen that was
> downstairs and began to cry. I had seen my mother and some of
> my sisters. I suddenly felt that we were all hopelessly lost,
> without any purpose. My mother saw me crying and asked why.
> Naturally I couldn't say. Then it was, too, that I came across
> some of my mother's girlhood possessions and the futility and
> waste of her life struck me. I was nine at the time. When I was
> twelve, I went to the seaside. Three people – a brother & 2
> sisters – had been drowned. They could have been saved, but the
> fishermen had wanted to know how much they would be paid!
> Oh, the terror I felt then. The fishermen pulled in the seine
> [fishing net] and brought in the bodies and caught an
> extraordinary number of catfish, always anxious to get at the
> helpless. The three bodies relaxed in the sand. The sun going
> down. And, from a cheap beach café, a gramophone: 'Bésame
> mucho" – Kiss me often, my darling, and say that you'll always
> be mine. I don't know what people of 12 feel, but I have never
> forgotten that.

Pat reassured him of his literary potential, but told him he should not write only about futile and miserable people. 'Your stories have humanity but not in the full sense. You stop too often with the tired and turgid mother, the insignificant clerk, the second rate school teacher. You realise the futility, stupidity and misery. But that's not all, you know it isn't.' There was nothing unusual about the depression he might feel,

> You tell me you are frantically lonely and miserable because you
> can't see me and can't work because of it. I won't take the
> responsibility for you getting a Second [class degree] . . . And
> don't start flattering yourself that your state is unique, your
> feelings and sufferings incomparable. You may have had a
> breakdown a little while ago but it was to yourself that you had

to look for remedy. You know the power of mind over matter.
You are quite an ordinary mechanism, my love. The only
difference between it – the mechanism – and another is that I am
in love with it and I can't bear to see it run down.

Vidia was attracted by Pat's sympathy and by her perception. 'My letters
are so dull. I would like to write brilliant letters – the type that people
publish,' he apologized. 'My theories about emotion and the written
word are mildly exciting, though. And, despite the fact that you never
agree with any of my literary judgements (a big source, I assure you, of
future squabbles), I shall expound them to you one day.'

*

Pat's comment that Vidia's stories had 'humanity but not in the full sense'
was right. The first story to break through to something fresh was
'Potatoes'. He found his own voice for the first time, poignant and funny.
He introduced his first non-Indian character, adjusting the dialogue
accordingly, and brought in sly comedy. The setting of the story overlaps
old and new, Hindi and English, traditional Indian life and 'this cosmo-
politan hotch-potch where nothing was sacred'. Mrs Gobin, a young
widow, tries to gain independence from her powerful mother. ' "Ever
since you have been living in the town, you have been playing the white
woman," ' says her mother. Spotting a gap in the vegetable market, she
visits a merchant who sells her two hundred pounds of potatoes at an
inflated price. 'An obsolete cash-register was operated by a venerable
looking man with a beard, who could pass for a religious prophet, but
who was, in fact, merely a Hindu of mediocre caste. Mrs Gobin sets up a
stall where her son sits 'blackening in the sun, and selling nothing'. The
local jeweller buys five pounds of potatoes, and the rest go bad in the
heat. So Mrs Gobin 'put on her going-out outfit and went to her mother,
to collect her allowance.'[10]

Back in Oxford during the long, hot summer, Vidia's depression
worsened, even as his intellectual understanding and his literary ability
grew. He did not tell Pat when he made a half-hearted attempt to kill
himself. 'It was a very bad period, the long, long summer with my
questioning myself internally night and day, every waking minute, that
great depression,' he said later. 'I tried foolishly once to put an end to it.
It didn't work.' Vido dressed in the suit he had worn on the day he left
Trinidad to fly to New York and start his new life. Then he went to the

gas fire in his room and turned on the gas, but did not light it. He lay down on the bed, wearing the suit, a stately would-be corpse. 'I dressed for the occasion.' He had decided to play a poor man's Russian roulette: the gas fire worked on a coin-operated meter, and he would lie there until it ran out. If he lived, he lived; if he died, he died. As he lay there in his suit, the gas ran out. He took this as an omen. Afterwards, he forced himself to postpone his suicide, reasoning that there was no point in doing it that day. 'I used to put it off, day to day, saying, "Pat is coming to see you next week." '[11] He did not try to kill himself again.

He met Pat in Oxford, in Gloucester and in the old Cotswold village of Chedworth, with its oak-timbered buildings that she loved for their beauty. They met again in Northleach, among the quaint houses of yellow Cotswold stone. Vidia's landlady told him he had done well for himself. 'Mrs King went into raptures over you. "She is a good girl, Mr. Naipaul. You stick to her, and you'll be all right." And don't I know it.' After one romantic meeting, Pat wrote: 'I do think our behaviour in cafes etc. is rather wonderful. We have world-shaking arguments, you read histrionic poetry, we quarrel fiercely, I drink milk, you don't eat meat (but are obviously no true vegetarian) . . . we are having a rather wonderful love affair, don't you think?'

Vidia's family found out about Pat by accident. 'By the way,' Pa wrote in August, 'some girlfriend of yours named Pat sent you a letter.' It had been forwarded to Trinidad by the college by mistake and read by the whole family. Vidia was humiliated, but knew he had no choice but to explain. In formal, stilted tones, he expressed his 'displeasure' that the letter had been opened. Appreciation of Pat was confined to a peroration in pained double negatives, a stylistic tic he claimed to have copied from the Dean.

> But I shall satisfy in everything your curiosity. Patricia Ann Hale is a girl of 20. She is a member of the university, not unintelligent, nor altogether unattractive. I met her in February and have been thankful ever since. She befriended me at the height of my illness, put up with all my moods – my coarseness and my fits of anguish. The relationship between us, while not a platonic one, is so far virtuous. The talk about being 'netted' is rather cynical, and I do trust that you will not make things doubly difficult for us. Her father is making a terrible fuss about it, and I hope that the same narrowness will not be found in you. About her character: she is good, and simple. Perhaps a bit

too idealistic, and this I find on occasion rather irritating. She insists on looking at the good, and chooses to shut her eyes to the bad. She shares my literary tastes, and I have found my friendship with her most stimulating.

He told Kamla about her too, who wrote Pat a generous letter at his request: 'Dear Miss Hale . . . Vidia's is not an easy nature to deal with – he is more than a handful. What lies on the surface is in exact contrast to what lies at the bottom and when once you have realised this, then everything is just fine . . . I have no objection whatsoever and I am sure you would find my parents as amenable and co-operative.' Seepersad, though, was not pleased. 'The girl, I have no doubt, is everything you say of her, and we are deeply grateful to any whose understanding and solicitude helped you so much when you most stood in need . . . But, as you say, her father disapproves of the relationship between you; and here at home no one is happy over the idea of your marrying any but an Indian.' Vidia's reply to Pa was cruelly discouraging. 'I don't want to break your heart, but I hope I never come back to Trinidad, not to live, that is, though I certainly want to see you and everybody else as often as I can . . . I have really been suffering from an abnormal mental condition. I was depressive. I have seen the psychologist twice and there is now no further need to see him . . . Of course, I don't intend getting married for at least two years.'

In early September, only three days after the assurance that the relationship with Pat was 'so far virtuous', they had sex for the first time, Vidia having bought a contraceptive gel from a chemist with great embarrassment. The 'rather wonderful love affair' had become a real love affair. They were both virgins, both physically reticent and neither was a natural seducer. The mental implications were substantial. Vidia tried in his mind to convert the consummation of his powerful sexual desire into an act of purity, and to convince himself that he would from now on be instinctively faithful. He wrote Pat a disturbed letter which exhibited feelings of guilt, jealousy and self-justification alongside promises of love, honour and devotion. Awareness of the power of his own latent lust was converted into a fear of her possible infidelity, and marriage seemed a solution.

> I merely wanted to tell you that I loved you completely and that Tuesday formed a lasting bond between us because you had surrendered something to me which ought to be

surrendered only to the man whom you loved and who loved you and who wanted to marry you. You see, I also felt that I had aroused you sexually and I know how dangerous this can be and I felt terribly responsible. Essentially it is an act of love, not of lust. I wanted you to know that I had thought at length before doing what we did. I was prepared for a showdown with your parents and mine. And yet I was worried. I didn't feel sure how you felt. I was tortured by memories of Mr. Petch and realized that on that Thursday you had written me a long letter that concerned itself almost wholly with the man. I was also worried about losing you, because that would ruin Schools [final exams] for me. I shall be perfectly frank with you. I feel myself capable of lasting love because now, you see, I am really not drawn to other women. I just say to myself 'she hasn't got a quarter of what my Pat has.' I know I am capable of this and I wanted some similar assurance from yourself. I was also worried because I know that you had such a high view of human nature that it would be easy for a smooth-tongued person to hurt you – you know in what way I mean. And you know, too, how much I worship purity . . . Somerset Maugham is right when he says that deep requited love is one of the rarest things in the world. So I feel and I am anxious to keep everything that way. I feel I have been luckier than I deserve.

In larger handwriting, he added, 'I feel a thorough ass writing this. Frankly, I don't know whether it is an expression of love or of stupidity . . . In other words, if you decide to be faithful to me, and if you want me, I want to marry you.' Later still, forty-nine years later, he wrote a troubled note on the letter: 'The relationship consummated. The jealousy over Peter Petch. Disingenuous talk of the purity of love.' At the beginning, Vidia felt 'sex with Pat was fumbling and awful for both of us. Pat was very nervous. I wasn't trained enough or skilled enough or talented enough to calm her nerves, probably because I didn't want to calm her nerves. It didn't work.'[12]

CHAPTER SEVEN

TO THE EMPTY HOUSE

AT THE START OF the Michaelmas term of 1952, Vidia moved out of college to lodge in an ugly brick building near some university offices in Wellington Square. His attempts to become a writer continued. Like all would-be achievers, he raged against mediocre types who were having greater success. Hearing the hack crime novelist Ernest Dudley broadcasting on the Light Programme, he felt obliged to write a letter of complaint to the BBC: 'I have just listened to tonight's *Dudley Nightshade*, a programme for "listeners who don't scare easily". Such a humourless, horrorless jumble of cliché snippets, introduced with such pompousness . . .' Then he thought better of it, turned the paper over and began a letter to Pat instead. News about himself from *Caribbean Voices* was more interesting: 'I hear that the BBC man, in a review of the work he has broadcast, speaks of "V. S. Naipaul's corrosive satire." Don't you want me to keep on being a corrosive satirist? It is my nature. If I write otherwise I shall cry as I write, like Dickens. I can't write about sadness sadly. It would kill me . . . Oh, darling, I love you from the bottom of my corrosively satirical heart. Your own Vidia.'

They saw each other whenever possible. In the days before mobile phones, email or texting, everything had to be done by hand. Pat would scribble a note in the morning ('No time for anything more as the hatch closes at a quarter to nine and I haven't been to breakfast yet') and send them to Univ, where they would arrive in his pigeonhole addressed to 'Mr Napail' or 'Mr Naipoo', the two syllables of his surname defeating, deliberately or otherwise, Douglas Millin and the college servants. Vidia would take a bus up the Banbury Road to St Hugh's, find Miss Hale absent and write on a scrap of file paper under the watchful nose of the uniformed porter ('My dear Pat, Good news. The BBC is giving me 11 guineas for the story. I got the contract today. Yrs Vidia'). Other students encouraged the relationship. Pat's friend Pluto told her 'the nicest thing at breakfast'. When someone said 'you can't have deep and lasting friendships at Oxford "it's so artificial",

Pluto said "Nonsense" as usual and that she could think of several friendships that would (she thought) outlast Oxford – for instance us!' This was an important compliment, since Pluto was afraid of Vidia, having had a scary experience with Sikh soldiers while interned in the Far East during the war.

In October, Ma gave birth to a baby daughter named Nalini, or Nella. At the same time, to add to the action, Kamla sent news: 'You might be very surprised when you hear that a few days ago I became engaged to an Indian chap who comes from Fiji,' she told Vidia. 'He is Christian, though, and with the most awful name of Vincent Richmond, yet I don't think I can get the ideal person.' She seemed uncertain about her emotional commitment. Marriage was years away; she might come home and become a school principal; or she might leave Benares without completing her degree because people were spreading vicious rumours about her; or she might go to Fiji and marry Vince. Pa tolerated Christianity, writing to Kamla: 'If a fellow is a decent Indian, it doesn't matter if he is a Christian; but he should <u>never</u> be a Mohammedan.'[1] Next, news reached Vidia that the diabetic, blind matriarch who had held the family together – Soogee Govinda, Rosalie Gobin, Soogee Capildeo Maharaj, Queen Victoria, Nanie – had died at the age of sixty-five. 'Nanie kicked the bucket on the 23rd of last, and my! she had a wonderful funeral,' wrote Sati irreverently.

Vidia's jealousy and insecurity continued. Finding a friendly letter from Peter Petch lying on Pat's desk, he was driven into a fury. '<u>I feel a fool</u> . . . I don't know what to do or think or say. Perhaps I am stupid, but I think this is well – I asked you not to deceive me. Well, if Mr Petch is just being friendly!' Pat tried to soothe him, but he would not be soothed. No Iago poisoned his mind against fair Patricia; he poisoned himself with imaginary sexual fears about men who might offer her something he could not. He was worried she was acting in a college play. 'Darling, I have been a fool,' he wrote, 'and I am terribly ashamed of myself. I should be encouraging you – but you know the meanness and the fears that made me do otherwise. But nothing will make me cease detesting those wretched acting men of Oxford. I have managed to work all the gall out of my system. Please act; you have my blessing and you can be assured of my support – whatever I can give . . . I feel unspeakably brutal when I make you cry . . . Please, please – never stop loving me – your own Vidia. 6^{1000}.'

Pat was shocked by his anger, railed against it, but was finally acquiescent, blaming herself and the force of his love for what had happened, setting a cage that would catch her for the rest of her life. 'I think this evening was probably irreparable,' she told him:

> Darling, remember my agony when you lose your temper and say those frightful things. I do half understand that it wouldn't happen if you didn't love me. But you see I couldn't say those things to you ever and I am or can be very brutal. If – God – if I did know you for the rest of my life they would never cease to tear me in two . . . I fear you must despise me at last. I have nothing but contempt for myself . . . I think this might alienate you further. I nearly gave myself once before. But the realisation that my love was not complete stopped me. I could not have given myself to you if I had not loved you completely. I have made my decision. I realise that one cannot have a second chance. I could not love or live with another man.

Vidia's love to the power of a thousand was a momentary respite. Two months later, over Christmas, he returned to the assault in a piece of confessional prose done half for himself and half for Pat. The restrictions of Mr Hale meant that he was unable to send it, so it became a gradual diary. It was a rare example of internal, exploratory, idealistic writing, of a kind that he never did again after his early twenties.

> I have decided, my life, that since I cannot write you, I shall hold this one-way talk with you & present it to you when I see you. In it I shall enter all the thought I think – and I shall be honest . . . What knifes me into acute agony is your acting. I think of you painted & wearing gaudy clothes not your own and I feel afraid. Afraid that you may change & stop being the woman I love . . . You see, I have a little bit of Hindu left in me and this cannot stand my wife painted & performing before people. And it is the <u>being away from me</u> that I fear.

A few days later he continued, becoming emotional, even melodramatic. 'Most of what I wrote last night is stupid, especially the Hindu bit . . . Darling, you have filled me with a new strength. I feel stronger than ever. I feel the great novels being written, I feel the urge to do great things – for YOU. Please believe me, when I say that in all my plans, you are the centre. Everything I do is for you. I just want to be yours, to be the vessel for the creation of works that shall be monuments to

YOU.' Then he turned unusually soppy. 'I can carry you on my back and take you to the springs of love — pure and crystal. I can take you to the pot of gold under the rainbow and to the heart of a dew-drop.' He saw the future, their future:

> I cannot belong to India for the simple reason that I don't know the language. Language is so important in belonging. Not the superficial knowledge I have, say, of French, or Spanish — but a language one has grown up with. And, for me, that language is English and that spells Oxford, and Patricia, and Birmingham and Snow Hill and Kingstanding and your hands pressed against mine as we walk down to the Bull Ring (where Birmingham's politicians hold <u>socialistic</u> meetings, I bet). And it means coming back to Oxford and after 14 hrs hitch-hiking and saying that Birmingham is beautiful and being laughed at. It means getting your permission to go to Paris and getting a telegram saying NO. It means going to London lonely and returning and getting a telegram saying GO. It means YOU. We shall be a good & successful partnership. I shall make your parents glad that you married me. I shall make my parents exultant that I married you. We shall make the world aware of us and love us. We shall never part. We have become one often and that has riveted us together. Kill me the day I am unfaithful. For then I shall have grown cheap & worthless.

He concluded with a few lines from *Othello* and a let-out for his display of sentiment. 'If it were now to die, | 'Twere now to be most happy; for, I fear, | My soul hath her content so absolute | That not another comfort like to this | Succeeds in unknown fate . . . My dear Pat, Am in awful rush to get train. These letters are no good. I was ashamed of them; and still am. They may amuse you. All my love, Vidia.'

Patricia, at home in Kingstanding in the cold and the snow, working in a Birmingham tax office to get money, said she found life 'meaningless' and 'unutterably dead' without him. She read the Sanskrit epic the *Mahabharata*, wrote letters in sneaked moments and did her best to tolerate Eleanor, 'mercifully quiet at the moment trying to make a hand-puppet with a burst rubber ball and some bits of paper'. They had brief telephone calls, arranged days ahead, and managed to meet for an afternoon in Cheltenham. Pat made 'stern arrangements' for their parting at the bus station, in case anyone was watching. 'It was funny in the end,' she wrote afterwards. 'I was looking at you to see you light your pipe and shake out the paper . . . I keep thinking of you carrying cups in one hand and Yorkshire pancakes in the other looking so marvellous. I just want to take you to me – scarf hanging down, shoulders slightly slouched.' Vidia felt just as passionately. He could not envisage life without her, and hoped they would have children together. 'Oh my darling I wish you were here,' he wrote from Oxford at the end of December. 'I want so much to look at you and feel you and smell your breath and feel that you are alive and with me, feel that you love me and we have become indissolubly one. For, alone, I am weak and feel half a person. You are the stuff of my existence . . . I wish to give you my children. The desire to have a child by you is greater than ever. It would be the crowning act of our union.'

*

In January 1953, Seepersad Naipaul was taken ill at the *Guardian* and admitted to hospital with a coronary thrombosis; he remained there for six weeks, and when he was released rested at home because he had trouble walking. His chronic indigestion had turned out to be heart disease. Sati told Vido the news, and Kamla wrote her brother a harsh and emotional letter: 'Pa's greatest worry is that he cannot get his stories published. Sati wrote saying that he sent you one but you have done nothing about it so far. Now something immediate regarding the publishing of his stories means life or death for him and consequently life or death for us, especially those poor little children at home . . . Write something encouraging to Pa immediately . . . Carelessness about this means Pa's death.' Vidia said he would, but did nothing.

Far from home, aware that he could do little to help his father, he showed flashes of family feeling to Peter Bayley. 'When my little boy was born, my first child, it was February 1953 on a Tuesday morning, and Vidia and his friend Lawrence O'Keefe both turned up to my room. I'd just rung to the hospital and heard that it was a son and I was very surprised by Vidia's reaction – almost touchingly overjoyed, as if to say how marvellous you have a son. Maybe that was the old Hindu in him. I was really touched and they both said, "Well you won't want to have a tutorial now." So off they went. He talked later about flying a kite with my little boy, so I have always been surprised that he had no children. It was just exceptional human affection.'[2] It was around this time that Vidia met Jill Brain, an undergraduate studying history at St

Hilda's College, who would nearly supplant Pat in his affections some years later.

Vido told his father he should not worry; he would leave Oxford in June. 'If I try to hawk your book around, I wouldn't be doing you a favour. I would be trying to sell stuff that deserves to be published.' Rather than tell Pa that he thought the stories had no chance of being taken by a London publisher, he opted for inertia and silence. 'The manuscript was in a bad state. I didn't think the work was ready for publishing. I didn't want to wound him by making it explicit,' he said later.[3] Vidia investigated employment. The omens were not good. 'The Dean thinks the prospect of my getting a job in this country is a pretty bleak one, and I never thought otherwise,' he told Pa. 'He thinks, however, that I can perhaps represent a firm in some country – or something like that.' Vidia remained a foreigner in a foreign land; he had a footing only at Oxford University. Meanwhile, his examinations were approaching, 'and I must step up the work'. His father replied in a shaky hand, writing in pencil, in bed, thanking him and telling him he was 'the last hope of England' and should not take on the responsibility of his siblings or a wife: 'First, make your way in the world.'

Vidia's relationship with Pat endured through 1953, the year in which Mount Everest was climbed, Queen Elizabeth II was crowned and Winston Churchill was somehow awarded the Nobel Prize in Literature. Pat said they should not be formally engaged. 'We don't need things like that,' she wrote to Vidia. During the term-time they were together, and in the holidays they met whenever they could. 'I always imagined myself having a love affair with a man who possessed a great soul. I imagined earnest, exquisite conversations. Yet I don't want you to talk in those very precious moments. I just want to drift – lose myself in that nearness,' she wrote in March. 'I live through you. Goodnight my love. I'm just living for Tuesday and can't think of anything else.' Afterwards, on Easter Sunday, she wrote passively, 'Vidia, I have known ever since Tuesday that we are more in love, that I am more a part of you and you of me. I felt that you gave yourself more completely than ever before and that I received you more fully than ever before.' She accepted that her dreams of acting would have to be abandoned because of his anxieties. She embraced the idea of sacrifice in the cause of his possible greatness. 'You know I could not do anything without your real consent and I have proved to you that the pain of not doing it because of you is as nothing beside the pain of doing it without your support: I just can't.' Dependence was, underneath everything, what he wanted and needed; it would enable him to reinforce his idea of himself, and pursue much larger ambitions.

In April, another of his stories was broadcast on the BBC, his family sitting around the crackling Rediffusion set in Nepaul Street trying to hear each word. 'Old Man' tells of a Chinese family who find themselves stuck in Trinidad while trying to return home and, 'to use their mother's words, "do good" for the Chinese people' by welcoming the Communist leader Mao Zedong. The voice of the author intrudes: 'When we are abroad, you see, we realise that Trinidad, with its blending of peoples, and with its burning political problems of no significance, is really the world in small.'⁴ It was a proficient and amusing story, but Vidia told his mother it was 'a pot-boiler, and I am quite ashamed of it. But I think it is what Swanzy wants. It is vaguely about Mary in Luis St. I have added a lot of pure lies.' He was working hard now, knowing he would be sitting his final exams for his Bachelor of Arts degree during the summer. 'The world, which hasn't been to Oxford, places perhaps an unjustified esteem on the place,' he told Pat, and listed his timetable for the Easter vacation.

> 8.00 Rise. 8.30 In Library. 8.30–9.30 Anglo Saxon. 9.30–10.30
> Middle English. 10.30–11.00 Break for coffee & rolls (no
> breakfast). 11–12.30 Literature. Lunch. 1.30–4 Literature. Tea.
> 4.30–7 Literature. Dinner. 8–10 Literature. Leave College at 10.
> 10.30–11.30 French Drama.

Literature meant English, or at least British literature: the canon of dead white male poets, playwrights and novelists from the sixteenth to the nineteenth century: Edmund Spenser, William Shakespeare, George Herbert, John Dryden, Jonathan Swift, Alexander Pope, Henry Fielding and finally William Wordsworth. Twentieth-century writers were seen as untested, and suspect, and were excluded. Modernists, in the form of James Joyce, T.S. Eliot and Virginia Woolf, for instance, formed no part of his Oxford education. 'I met their work accidentally,' he said later. 'I was not interested in Modernism as a movement. It bypassed me. I couldn't get on with [Woolf's] *The Waves* – writing should never draw attention to itself.'⁵ In a letter to Henry Swanzy, he denied that Eliot's themes had influenced his own writing at all. 'As a matter of fact, *The Waste Land* determined me to read no more Eliot for the rest of my life.' He added, to Swanzy: 'The future is as black as ever. Nobody loves me, nobody wants me. In England I am not English, in

India I am not Indian. I am chained to the 1000 sq. miles that is Trinidad; but I will evade that fate yet.'[6]

Although he was busy with revision, Vidia had time to worry about his elocution; after all, his education was not restricted to studying texts, and he did not want to stand out as a colonial. 'Can you pronounce "bourgeois" properly?' he asked Pat, whose own accent had adjusted from Midlands to Received Pronunciation as a result of elocution lessons. 'I used to say "boo-jwah". This, according to a man called Walker-Heneage (public school) is hopelessly wrong. Phonetically I think it is spelt (bu 'dzˇwa). I tried for two hours, but I couldn't get the pronunciation right. It is one of those things I must get used to not being able to do – like dancing.'

Vidia had other thoughts, too. Might Pat be able to make her letters a little erotic, he asked politely and obliquely? 'I do wish you could make your letters really "lurid" – if you know what I mean. I would like everything to be mentioned. I would like to hear about the more intimate things about you which no one else knows about; just as now I, without wishing to be shocking, would like to tell you how soothing &, at the same time, "maddening", to taste your mouth and feel your breasts.' There was little chance, as Pat did not even like to mention underwear. When she responded with a story of Eleanor racing about the flat with stones stuffed into a borrowed bra, the bra became, 'the garment I dislike mentioning – we both dislike the name'. She thought more of having children than having sex. 'I hope you realise that our children would be just like Eleanor and your brothers and sisters. We should loathe them half the time. I was thinking yesterday maybe I would like to have them at home because I'd want them all the time afterwards and nursing homes seem so horrible about that . . . I am very much in love with the fundamental purity and honesty in you. I have a terrible, overmastering desire to throw myself at your feet.' Despite the extent of her commitment, a passing reference to Peter Petch in a letter still caused Vidia agitation.

In the summer of 1953, life looked better. Vidia had an interview with Burmah Oil, only '£625 a year starting, but they provide free furnished houses'. During their last summer days together at Oxford, he and Pat watched an outdoor performance of *Troilus and Cressida* by the university dramatic society. Sad not to be performing, Pat saved a copy of the programme with its harshly lit period photographs of the smartly dressed young actors, her contemporaries: Alasdair Milne as

Troilus, Sheila Graucob as Cressida and Patrick Kavanagh as Pandarus. Then the young lovers parted.

Back in Birmingham, Mr Hale spent the evenings 'over the way' at the pub; Eleanor ate beetroot and onion sandwiches, kept a bucket of tadpoles and screamed whenever she was made to have a bath. 'As she was carried from the bathroom I heard her singing for some unaccountable reason "I'm going to Westminster Abbey to be buried". . . . Eleanor is a little beast. She's been being horrible about "fat chests".' For the first time in a year, Vidia was mentioned in Kingstanding. 'Just after lunch to-day by the way Mummy asked if "that Indian" was still at Oxford. In spite of my agitation I still managed to feel resentful at the terms of reference. Anyway I said you had just taken Schools.' Pat listened to piano recitals on the radio, and yearned to be with Vidia. 'I'm not being melodramatic . . . What would I do if there was no cause to worry about your possible failure to do the washing up, or having babies in a hot climate? The mere thought makes me desolate. Please don't take your babies elsewhere.' She wanted a son 'I had a crazy notion that Humphrey – a name I've never had any particular attachment for – would go with Naipaul.'

In a letter laden with anticipation, she made further plans. 'When our little girls are little they're going to have plaits except when they have <u>very</u> fat faces when I think fringe and bob will be rather charming – especially of course if the "Mongol strain" in you comes out.' Remaining in the Himalayan region, she told him she was following the story of Tenzing Norgay, who had recently climbed Mount Everest with Edmund Hillary.

> May I take this opportunity to say that much as I am attracted by Mrs Tensing I am <u>not</u> going to be a Hindu wife . . . Oh by the way, Mummy doesn't like India and Nehru! 'Nasty little hypocrite,' is her opinion of the latter, 'who wants to put his own house in order before he tries to dictate to other people.' He 'Shanghaied' Mountbatten over Cashmir . . . P.S. I found a completely white hair the other day. I yanked it out and put it in my French Dictionary. If it's still there I shall put it in the bottom of this envelope so that you'll see how you're driving me to an early grave!

In July the degree results were published. They both got a Second, or what Vidia called 'just a bloody, damned, ***** Second'. It was a slight consolation to learn that J.R.R. Tolkien had said his Anglo-Saxon paper was the best in the university. Pat's old teacher Ella Wallen, a spinster who disapproved heartily of Vidia, sent him a patronizing letter of congratulation: 'You must be feeling that an Oxford Second is a very pleasant thing to have achieved and worth coming halfway across the world for. I must say I think it's pretty bright of you; the change of climate would probably have addled my brain completely.'

Might he join the Indian diplomatic corps, Pa wondered? Might Kamla join, Vidia enquired? His sister sailed to England in June. Vidia had asked her to bring 'Gandhi's autobiography (sold only in India): *The Story of My Experiments with Truth*' and 'A good, readable, authoritative and exhaustive History of India (does any such exist?) and English translations of the Hindu epics and dramas.' Vidia was over-joyed to see Kamla again, introducing his glamorous elder sister to Pat and to Peter Bayley. Kamla rented a room next door to his lodgings in St John Street for a few days. 'Pat liked you very much; thought you pretty and considered that your personality was charming. She is glad that you are saner than me. I suppose that you liked her; but I can't be too sure,' he wrote to Kamla later. Pa sent her news of a possible job offer from St Augustine Girls' High School. 'Do come home as early as you can. Wish I could send you some money,' he concluded, deleting the remaining sentences with a string of XXXs.

The deleted text ran as follows:

> Believe me, Kams, we were never so hard up in our whole life. I am not working. The Guardian (because of the nature of my illness) is terminating my service at the end of the month. [The editor Courtenay] Hitchins told me so yesterday. Just think . . . but do, Kamla, do not say a word of this to Vido. I don't know [how] he has done in his exams, and if he has more work yet in front of him, better don't tell him anything of what's happening here. Let's wait until he has finished his studies. Now, please remember not to tell Vido a word just yet.[7]

Mr Hitchins had written giving Pa 'formal notice' that his services were no longer required after July, leaving the family in a fatally precarious position.[8] Pa told Vidia later what had happened. 'They pay my salary to the end of the month. But I don't want you to worry over these things.' Vidia responded warmly but impractically. 'As soon as I have got a job, you are to come and live with me and fulfil an ambition of mine to have you idle, content, and I shall certainly see that you have some whisky to hand.' Pa was taken by the prospect, young Sewan reported: 'All of us at home except Nalini is calling Pa the Englishman because he says that he is going to England.' Might Vidia try to get his stories published, Pa asked? He enclosed a list of names and addresses of authors' agents. Could *The Adventures of Gurudeva* be turned into a book, he asked again? 'If you cannot manage it, try getting it published through a good agent; but see that you pick an honest one. I understand many of these fellows are crooks.' Vidia did nothing, while pretending that he was doing something: 'I am working on your stories; so don't complain about my indifference.'

*

In the summer, Vidia had moved to a tall, narrow, flat-fronted Georgian house in St John Street, off St Giles'. Other lodgers there included Stephan Dammann, a half-French student who had read history in Vidia's year at Univ. He spent an enjoyable few weeks staying with Stephan's family in Somerset. They all liked Vidia, and Stephan's brother Rickie remembered him as 'a very nice and rather shy person, certainly a great deal more shy than Stephan's other Oxford friends.'[9] In late July, Kamla went to stay with Rudranath while she waited for her passage home. It was a disaster. Capo R. 'was filled with bitterness, hate and contempt and all directed against his family,' Kamla wrote later.[10] Rudranath raged against his own family, and when he began to rage against Pa, Kamla returned the insult. She was thrown out of the house in Balham. She stayed with a cousin, and then with Vidia. 'In the last week or so,' Vidia reported home, 'Capo R. was becoming more and more unpleasant and Kamla eventually did the proper thing. She left.' He revealed a little more in a letter to Pat: 'I have only just returned to London after taking care of my sister (she was in trouble with my uncle: driven out from his house at midnight). I got the news in a telegram, after getting your telephone message. Then – back to Oxford and further distressing news: my father ill, and dismissed from his job. The repercussions of this are important, & I must see you before you go away. But wishing you a happy birthday is still very much in my mind. So happy birthday, Mrs. N.' He was trying for a job at the Oxford University Press, and writing a story, 'Rosie'.

Kamla travelled home on the same ship as Capo R., the *Colombie*. 'Last night there was a grand ball and I was the Captain's guest,' she wrote to Vidia from Guadeloupe. 'I danced with him and had to dance with many others. I had two glasses of champagne ... About Capo R., well he was always on deck and I in my cabin. We never met. But there are a few persons who know that we are related and at times it becomes embarrass-ing.' Back home, the stand-off with the Capildeos continued. The Mausis were displeased by Kamla's confident new India-derived attitude. 'They would have been infinitely more pleased,' Pa wrote, 'if she had come down the gangplank twiddling a mala [Hindu rosary] or singing a couplet of the Ramayana.' She took a job at St Augustine teaching English and geography at a salary of $180 (£38) a month, only days after her return. Remembering this time later, Kamla said, 'Pa was driving me to school and back each day, and then he wanted to teach me [to drive]. Every time I did something stupid he began laughing so hard until he began coughing. I remember I got my first pay. I gave him $5 as his pocket change and he began to cry. Some things you don't forget. First time he's taking money from his daughter. First time his daughter has had money to give him.'[11] Sookdeo Misir offered Pa a job in one of his stores as an act of charity 'just to sit and watch the goods', and offered to write off what he was owed on the mortgage, so that Pa could buy a house where he did not have to risk his heart by climbing upstairs.

Vidia returned to writing, telling Pat about a planned short story inspired by the title *The Fall of a Titan*, a novel by the Russian defector Igor Gouzenko.

> The titan is Mr. Teughnsend. He has, you may know, a fatal
> flaw, like Hamlet. He – I hardly dare whisper it – he,
> Teughnsend, the great, the breeder of boy scouts, freeman of
> Oxford, the erstwhile host of E.W. Swanton, the man who saw
> 'Aile Selassie on the platform of Swindon Station, Townsend the
> good citizen, good Tory, the cultivator of hallotments, and the
> owner and driver of a shootin' braike – this paragon, I shudder to
> say, drinks! Secretly. Can you see the story? Teughnsend (I
> assume he will spell it that way) – his rise; training his children to
> say 'writing-paper' and not 'note-paper'; putting poor Roger in
> his shootin' braike; voting Conservative, dressing in suits all the
> time; and then the fall – slow but perceptible.

It was never written. This was the kind of story – limited, backward-facing, concerned with gradations of English social class – that V.S. Naipaul would never write.

Pat thought he needed to hurry up. 'Contrary to you sweet heart I think leisure kills a writer unless he's about sixty and has led a very active life. If you haven't written in amongst all the hurly burly you never will and what you write will never be really good. Look at your beastly "Willy" [Somerset Maugham]. I'd leave you if you were ever like that.' She advised him not to get into debt, and asked him to send £1 that he owed her. Her affection was undimmed. 'I'm an absolute fool when you're concerned and (not to be told to your enormous ego) I really adore and worship that stupid expression of dove-like harmlessness you put on for photographs.' In August, she went off to Austria on a school trip with Ella Wallen and her pupils, despite finding her old teacher thoroughly tedious: 'I carefully ration her out in doses.'

Vidia had not found a job, and decided he might continue his studies at Oxford as a postgraduate. Short of money, he considered becoming a temporary dishwasher at a local hospital, although 'I look forward with extreme disgust to scraping off the loathsome remains of other people's meals.' Nervous about what lay ahead, he took refuge in illness, and had his worst asthma attack since his arrival in England. 'The doctor was altogether pleasant. He gave me an inhaler that looks as if it could be the popular conception of a death-ray gun . . . I was hoping they would send me to a hospital, where I would be saved the bother of having to dress and go out for meals.'

He started a holiday job on a farm near Oxford at £4 a week (around £75 in today's terms), working 'preposterously long hours'. Before long, he was concerned that the regular farm workers were not making good use of their time. Pat was despatched a letter, complete with diagrams of chutes, trailers and sacks of wheat:

> The more I see of farm labourers and farmers, the more I am
> convinced that the labourers are the nearest things to pure
> animals I have yet come across . . . A sack of wheat weighs
> between two and three hundredweight. What they do is this.
> One ass drags this sack to the end of the trailer and places it on
> the back – yes, 3 cwt on the back – of another ass who staggers
> to the spot where he has to deposit the load. When I saw this I
> suggested – purely as a makeshift – that a smooth bit of board
> could be used as a chute from trailer to ground – the board
> moveable so that you could drop your sacks where they wished.
> No, they said; they had been doing it this way for years. But
> today the carpenter began building a chute . . . I try to preserve
> my sanity by reading set amounts every night – 150 pages. But
> I am so tired that I give up.

His writing was not going well, 'Rosie' being turned down by Henry
Swanzy. Too often, he thought, 'my stories remain merely ideas for
stories'. What would he do if his inherited dream of becoming a writer
could not be fulfilled? He wanted to be an Indian diplomat, he wanted
to be wealthy, he wanted to succeed.

> I don't want to reform the world, but I would like to do
> something. Oh dear! This is sounding so pompous that I am
> ashamed to continue. Frankly I do not wish any notoriety at all;
> but the trouble is that it is extraordinarily difficult to do
> anything constructive. Would joining the Indian Foreign
> Service — if they would have me — help at all? Getting
> embroiled in politics seems to me too messy. But enough of this
> rot. You see, writing has lost its glamour. I have been asking
> myself quite often recently about the value of the man who
> spins tales. He becomes a flaneur, like your pet antipathy Willie
> Maugham. The man who reports is not half the man who acts
> and is reported about. And on the other side — there is the
> desire for suits and beautiful dresses for you and a pleasant
> home and gardens and horses and children. I like luxury. I take
> to it easily, and feel it is mine by right. And, in this mood,
> damn the bloody Africans in Kenya and South Africa. It is so
> easy, you say, to label yourself humanitarian, socialist, liberal.
> Kingsley Martin can do it in his paper [*New Statesman*]. He can
> praise the disobedience campaign in South Africa; but would he
> forego even a meal for the sake of the people he defends?

Come September, Vidia was still thinking and worrying rather than
doing and writing. 'I hope you now realise that my asthma is having a
record run: an attack normally lasts three to four days. This one is
almost a week old,' he wrote proudly to Pat. Unable to decide how to
proceed, he blamed her for causing him to be 'a failure'. She was not
cowed, writing him her angriest letter yet in response:

> You managed to pack into one short letter all the silly notions —
> 'women's college attitude', 'elderly virginal counsellors', 'your
> mother has ruined you' — that try my patience to the uttermost.
> They are shallow, rather conceited and the mental equipment of
> the young man. But they indicate something which I would
> very much like you to lay aside for my sake: the belief that the
> mere fact of having a man is all-sufficient to a woman's

happiness, that a woman should make the man's life her own without, it seems, a reciprocal action on the man's side and in short the idea that marriage should entail selfishness on one side and annihilation on the other . . . The union of two real people is nobler than one-sided submission. Notice I say one-sided submission. I think the submission and revelation of love is the most glorious thing. But to be really complete love must enter into everyday life. It must entail the acceptance of each other's ambitions and respect for each other's beliefs.

She berated him once more for shattering her ambitions to be an actor:

'Stage struck' is your dismissal of something which was exactly parallel to your wish to write . . . But you won't make the effort to jerk your head out of the sand, put yourself inside me, try to understand. If I'm unhappy you just say you can't bear other people being miserable and that I'm more or less driving you to drink. How would you fare if I behaved like that . . . I'll admit that what I want from you is an admission that you were wrong to stop me acting, that you will make a real effort to enable me to do so if the chance comes again and that you love me – women's rights, feminine acting and all . . . The difference between man & woman is not that big where mind and hope is concerned. I've got my Thibet too and loving you ought to put me a step closer to it not deny it to me altogether.

Vidia did not like being reprimanded. 'I only know one thing   I am a beast and a cad and a fool and an egotist because you didn't appear before Oxford audiences. I suppose I must be. I wish you could just sit down and outline your grievances – equal pay etc.' He knew he was being unfair. 'I paint myself as the wronged innocent. Of course this is silly. I realise that I have been often silly – but being silly is only one of "my ways".' Only many years later did he fully acknowledge his regret at stopping Pat from acting. In 2001, he wrote some tragic, broken notes: 'I wish I had encouraged her. Too late, alas . . . My wretchedness about that now . . . My great grief.'

*

In the autumn, Vidia began work half-heartedly for a postgraduate research degree, a B.Litt. in English literature, with a specialization in Spanish literature. It would give him an extra year in which to coast. He was

constantly short of money, and took a job selling the *Home Encyclopedia* at
a 15 per cent commission. He sold a copy to Peter Bayley's wife, Patience,
and another to a waitress at the Kemp Cafeteria in Oxford. 'She probably
bought it out of sympathy for me,' he thought. 'I couldn't go knocking on
doors. I didn't have the face to do it.'[12] He was assailed by fears of mental
or pulmonary breakdown. Pa sent him tins of salmon, some socks, shirts
and a vase, and implored him not to marry. 'If you get a well-paid job,
some one of us will be able to join you in England or wherever you are,
and, on the whole, we would try to make things as home-like for you as
we possibly can . . . it is felt by everybody at home (not excluding myself)
that if you get married at all you will be lost to us. We cannot afford
losing you; I am not good any longer for hard work.' Vidia responded that
there was no need to worry. 'About the business of marriage, I myself am
rather unsure; and I can understand your reasoning.' To Pat, though, he
expressed no doubts.

As he thought seriously about what he wanted to do next, Vidia tried
to detach himself from what had come before. He knew that he did not
want to return to Trinidad, and felt tainted when he was reminded of what
he might have been, or might still be, or might yet become. Fellow
Trinidadians with their would-be stylish clothes, strange names and quaint
pronunciations aroused his anger and contempt. Sitting in an Oxford coffee
shop with a college friend, he was approached by a man 'too elaborately
dressed to be a member of the University', he told Pa. 'Noble Sarkar!
Smaller than me; darker than I remembered; uglier than I remembered;
stupider than I thought,' he wrote in priggish tones. 'That is the W.I.
intellectual, I am afraid.'

He could not help commenting on the 'ignorance and stupidity' of any
Trinidadians he met: they reminded him of everything he did not want to
be, and hoped to escape from. An encounter in Oxford in early October
with an eminent old boy of QRC, Solomon Lutchman, left him in a frenzy.
'I never realised the man was so utterly ugly, so utterly coarse – low
forehead, square, fat face, thick lips, wavy hair combed straight back.' He
mispronounced words and, fatally, wore a sky-blue club blazer. 'Wearing
the blazer of a Caroni Cricket Club in Oxford. I ask you – can you
conceive anything narrower and stupider?' This disproportionate rage,
though, was provoked by ideas as well as by appearance; Vidia's rage
against these individuals arose in part from his view of the world, and a
conviction that his own future lay at the centre, not the periphery. He was
enraged by what he saw as Lutchman's insularity, and by his failure to see

his own larger position. 'His lack of vision, his impregnably stupid preoccupation with the 500,000 inhabitants of T'dad as being the hub of the universe, annoyed me. He ignores the bigger things ("Why should I care about Dominica or the starving Jamaicans?"). He does not see the injustice done to the Africans in Kenya or South Africa; the fact that 12 years ago Indian troops were being killed in the desert by the Germans and today – Indian immigration to Kenya stopped, Germans invited.' Why, in 1953, should Germans rather than Indians be allowed to enter a British colony, except for reasons of racial prejudice? 'And S. Lutchman is an educated Trinidadian.' Pa, one of Trinidad's 500,000 inhabitants, never read this letter.

Back in Port of Spain on 3 October 1953, the family had been to a puja in Luis Street to commemorate Nanie's death. Pa remained in bed at home, having had chest pains in the morning. A message reached Ma that he was feeling ill, and she, Kamla and Mira returned. He needed the doctor. They summoned Dr Mavis Rampersad, a family friend, and Pa was displeased because he thought he should be attended by a male doctor. When she arrived, he was looking better, and soon they were joking and laughing with him. Then as evening neared, Pa cried out in pain. His heart was in agony. Pa shouted at Mira when he heard her laugh, not knowing that it was a laugh of pure shock: Dr Rampersad had just told her that Pa was dying. An injection stilled him. The other children, and more family members, were in Nepaul Street now, and they watched in disbelief as Pa foamed at the nose and, in Dr Rampersad's words, 'went out like a candle'. At the age of forty-seven, Seepersad Naipaul, the writer, who had lifted himself out of nowhere and tried to make his way in the world, was dead.

His body was dressed in clean clothes and laid out upstairs at 26 Nepaul Street, and families of mourners trooped in and out of the little box of a house. Mira remembered two cousins arriving. 'I didn't care for them but they came and began crying. I thought I was duty bound to cry, so I did a little crying too.'[13] A pundit recited prayers and purification rituals were performed, befitting Seepersad's hereditary status as a Brahmin. Sewan, the eight-year-old son of the house, the only son in Trinidad, was so disturbed by what had happened that he refused to take part in the funerary rituals. The following day, on baby Nalini's first birthday, Pa's body was taken to the banks of a stream at El Socorro, a small village outside Port of Spain. The regulations covering death had changed, and Seepersad Naipaul was one of the first Hindus to be legally cremated in Trinidad. A pyre was made of wood and ghee, and lit as the clan watched. The next day his ashes were immersed in the stream at El Socorro. When Ma and the six children reached Nepaul Street they found the house had been cleaned in their absence by some friends, ready for their return. But Pa was not there.

In the months that followed, the family were left in desperate straits, dependent on Kamla's earnings. In order to repay Sookdeo Misir's loan on the house, Kamla had to take out a mortgage with Hamel-Smith, a Trinidad law firm. As Savi remembered, 'After my father died, everything fell apart. I honestly do not know how we managed. We were pretty much left to the wind. Vidia could not come back; he had his own life, his own problems . . . I know that for Mira and I to get shoes and clothing, I sewed clothing for my friends and they would pay me, that's how we outfitted ourselves. The nuns were very kind to us. They called us and said, you don't have to leave school. When you leave you'll pay us the fees.'[14]

Pa's death reached Vidia gradually; Kamla wrote to Peter Bayley asking him to break the news, but before her letter had arrived he received a telegram from Sookdeo Misir's daughter, Bas Mootoo. It read: 'DISTURB-ING NEWS COME TO LONDON IMMEDIATELY.' He guessed what had happened, and boarded a train. At her house in Paddington, his fears came true. Bas told him what had happened. He saw a vase sitting in the house which he knew Pa had sent him. 'It was a brass vase and I was young and didn't know how to deal with this. I eventually had the courage to say, "I think that vase is mine. I think it was sent by my father." It's been with me in all my moves, in every place I've lived, all the little flats and everything,' he said later.[15] Vidia went to the post office and sent a telegram home. 'HE WAS THE BEST MAN I KNEW STOP EVERY-THING I OWE TO HIM BE BRAVE MY LOVES TRUST ME VIDO.' He followed it with a letter to Ma: 'Please don't worry about me . . . everything that I am is directly due to him . . . He worked for all of us; what we are he has made us. And when you think from what he started, you ought to feel proud.'

Eight years later, Vidia published his own version of Pa's death in his loving, fictional tribute to his father, *A House for Mr Biswas*. The book ends like this:

> The furniture was pushed to the walls. All that day and evening well-dressed mourners, men, women and children, passed through the house. The polished floor became scratched and dusty; the staircase shivered continually; the top floor resounded with the steady shuffle. And the house did not fall.

The cremation, one of the few permitted by the Health Department, was conducted on the banks of a muddy stream and attracted spectators of various races. Afterwards the sisters returned to their respective homes and Shama and the children went back in the Prefect to the empty house.[16]

Pa was dead: now Vidia tried to cut away from Trinidad.

CHAPTER EIGHT

'THEY WANT ME TO KNOW MY PLACE'

VIDIA REFUSED TO DISCUSS his father's death with his cousins or his uncle in London, despite their efforts to draw him out. He talked about it a little with Pat but otherwise kept silent. He said to Lawrence O'Keefe, ' "My father has kicked the bucket." He was surprised by the words. I didn't mention it to anybody else. I had come out of my great depression and then my father died.'[1] For a fortnight, Vidia felt frozen, unable to write to Ma, but when he did he told her he hoped his life would be a continuation and a fulfilment of Pa's: 'It hardly seems necessary for me to tell you how lonely and unprotected I feel.' He sank lower and lower in November, and was reduced to begging for money from Kamla. 'I have tried eating cheap food, but that was nothing but masses of boiled potatoes, and it made me ill and weak. I have now decided that I cannot risk losing my health, and so I have a good meal twice a day ... Whatever happens, though, we must see that Shivan [Sewan] and anyone else who so wishes have a university education. These days I think of home nearly all the time.' Writing to his mother, he admitted that he was 'very ashamed' to have asked for money and pleaded with her childishly, 'I am not really a bad boy and I asked when everything else I could do failed.'[2] In December, he failed the examination for his B.Litt.

In the summer he had been given a travel grant of £75 (£1,400 in today's terms) by the Colonial Office to go to Spain and pursue his studies. He spent Christmas 1953 in Madrid, from where he wrote to Pat in disingenuous tones:

> By the time this letter reaches you I suppose you shall have told your father everything. I am behind you all the way & I want you to know this! ... Will you forgive me if I say that you are the best woman in the world? That you are a vision of <u>purity</u>,

cleaner & purer than anything that has crossed my life . . .
Today I went to the British Institute to see [the translator and
'Raggle Taggle Gypsy'] Walter Starkie. As I was climbing up
the steps of the British Institute, my right foot was trapped in a
bit of carpet. I fell down the stairs and fainted. My foot was
sprained & I have a bad orange-sized bump on my ankle now.

A few days later he wrote again: 'My only vision of you now is the one
I preserve of Feb 9, 1952 at the Univ Play . . . All the qualities I
dreamed of in my wife you possess. You have changed me more than I
really care to admit and, from a purely selfish point of view you are the
ideal wife for a future G[rand] O[ld] M[an] of letters.'[3]

When writing to his family, Pat's purity was not his only consideration. In Madrid, 'at least two Spanish girls made passes at me. England
is by comparison dead and the English are made of wax. They are the
most immoral people I have yet known; yet they set about the matter
with a grimness and a sense of determination that is frightening . . . By
the way, can I have a picture of Meera [sic] and Savi together. I have
pictures in my wallet of everyone except those two.'[4] Pictures came,
and he told Sati he treasured them. 'I like Nalini – you know the
picture in which she is looking with trusting delight into Ma's face. I
also like the group of you five. I was so proud of you that I showed it
to a number of my friends.'[5] A couple of years later he did a version of
the trip to Spain for *Caribbean Voices*. A Spanish man accosts him and
asks if he will translate a letter from a girlfriend; they go to a cafe,
drink together and the piece ends with the narrator being treated to a
trip to a brothel. The first part happened, but the conclusion was
invented to impress his contemporaries at the BBC. The story was
reprinted in the *New Statesman* in 1958, and his friend Francis Wyndham
told Vidia he found it 'scabrous'. Later, he admitted forlornly: 'The
scabrous element was made up. I was scratching myself, it was not part
of my real work, I didn't have enough experience. I had to make a little
money here and there.'[6] While in Madrid, he bought a kimono for Pat
which she was to keep for many years; wearing it made her feel sensual,
and it became a sexual indicator between them.

The early part of 1954 found Vidia staying in London with his
cousin Owad 'in great dirt & discomfort' at a run-down house at 70
Bravington Road in West Kilburn. 'I am looking very hard for definite
employment,' he told his mother.[7] To wash, he would go to the public

baths. He had given up on a project called *The Mystic Masseur* and begun writing a story for the BBC. 'It is called *My Aunt Gold Teeth* and begins: "I never knew her real name, and it is quite likely that she did have one, though I never heard her called anything but Gold Teeth,"' he told Pat. 'I find writing very difficult & sometimes I fear that I may lose my grasp of English altogether and be left languageless!' For the second and last time, he made an attempt at poetry:

> I have thought & thought but I can't rhyme
> Besides I haven't time
> In five and twenty seconds I go to dine
> And confound this wretched Valentine![8]

Staying in the 'slum basement' of Owad's house, he found his extended family ceaselessly irritating. 'I am afraid I am years and ages away from these people – but then I always was,' he wrote in angry, pompous desperation, aware he was depending on their charity. He feared losing the gains of Oxford and being absorbed back into Port of Spain. 'I find their English coarse & acidulous. I have spent a number of days fearing that I was going to speak like them if I stayed on here much longer. Finite verbs are discarded; verbs never agree with their subjects; solícitor becomes sólicitor, marble arch mabble atch. Downright bad English does not worry me, but the stressing of wrong syllables is a damned insidious thing.' In April he sent Sati a telegram: 'BEST WISHES YOUR MARRIAGE WHY NO INVITATION FOR ME LOVE VIDO.'[9] Aged twenty, she was marrying Crisen Bissoondath, whose family kept a dry goods store in Sangre Grande. Later that month they married, and Ma gave a midday wedding dinner for the two families at 26 Nepaul Street.

Willy Richardson, a tall, elegant black Trinidadian who knew the Naipaul family and had covered Queen Elizabeth's coronation for the BBC, booked Vidia to broadcast a story on *Caribbean Voices*. Vidia remembered him as 'a lovely man' whose wife, Lesley, had a job in the Colonial Office: 'They were an attractive couple. I used to go to his flat in Notting Hill.'[10] The story was *A Family Reunion*, in which he fictionalized the aftermath of Nanie's death. A powerful Indian grandmother is dying. Her servant, 'called, graphically, Miss Blackie (her real name was Geraldine Green)' and widowed daughter are making preparations for Christmas. 'It never struck them as strange that, although they were Hindus, they celebrated Christmas. In Trinidad, Christmas and Easter are celebrated by everyone, just as everyone celebrates the Muslim festival of Hosein.' The house is decaying; it rains. 'The bush around the house had a new smell – a fresh smell, as of fish. This meant that snakes were about and it was dangerous to let the children go outdoors.' After initial harmony, the family degenerates into feuds. The old lady, ill in bed, shouts abuse at her noisy grandchildren. 'But her obscenities were harmless: she spoke Hindi, and the children spoke only English.' Nobody knows how she intends to divide up her property until her two sons write a cheque for $500 to each of their six sisters; the rest will be theirs. 'They considered that they had no obligation to their sisters; indeed, because of their superior education and position, Suruj and Krishna looked down on them.'[11]

Then came the news that Vidia's postgraduate academic studies were at an end. He had returned to Oxford to take a further examination for his B.Litt., but despite a satisfactory result in his written paper was turned down after an interview or 'viva' with a retired professor of English, F.P. Wilson, who was renowned for being taciturn and socially awkward. 'I wish you to know that I was failed deliberately,' he told Pat. 'I was viva'd – not on the paper – but on the Spanish theological temper. No one last term was subjected to that sort of thing. Wilson's attitude was just one big sneer from beginning to end; and, of course, he did ask me once more where I came from . . . It is just another one of the hundred & one insults that make my life in England hell – that also gave me my breakdown.' Half a century later this perceived discrimination still upset him: he noted on an old letter to Pat that Wilson had failed him for the B.Litt 'quite deliberately, & out of racial feeling'. He remained at Oxford, the staff at the college library having given him an administrative job to tide him over. Come the summer, Vidia was back with Owad in Bravington Road, and desperate. He had little encouragement bar a testimonial from Peter Bayley saying he was 'a sympathetic and delightful person, with a most attractive sense of humour [and] outstanding literary gifts' who deserved a job. 'More than most I think he could be said to be a citizen of the world. He is a British subject of Indian descent domiciled in the West Indies.'[12]

*

Without the protection and distinction of Oxford University, Vidia floundered. 'It is wrong for you to think that I do not wish to come home,' he told Ma in confusion in May. 'I think I shall die if I have to spend the rest of my life in Trinidad. The place is too small, the values are all wrong, and the people are petty. Besides, there is really very little for me to do there . . . Do not imagine that I am enjoying staying in this country. This country is hot with racial prejudices, and I certainly don't wish to stay here . . . Now that the time is drawing near for my day of departure from Oxford, I am discarding all my English friends and acquaintances. I shall spend the rest of my life trying to forget that I came to Oxford . . . The world is a pretty awful place, but our star will shine bright yet. Love to all, from your silly son, Vido.'[13]

He tried writing to John Grenfell Williams, the head of colonial broadcasting at the BBC, who had invited him to dinner in Hampstead two years earlier. Might he help him find employment? 'I very much want to go to India. But there are many difficulties. I cannot be employed on the Indian side because I am British, and on the British side, I cannot be employed because I am Indian . . . if you can reveal a glimmer of hope I will be very grateful.'[14] Grenfell Williams asked Vidia to see him and offered support, but said there were no positions available at the BBC. Vidia made a request to Henry Swanzy: would he recommend him for a job in America as a 'television apprentice' which required 'the ability to communicate ideas'?[15]

A week after he departed finally from Oxford, Vidia discovered he had been turned down for a job in Dehra Dun in India and another post in Darjeeling. The Colonial Office would shortly be cutting off his grant since he was no longer a student, and his financial situation was impossible. He wrote to the *Manchester Guardian*, to the *New Commonwealth*, whose editor was 'a Univ man', and to the J. Arthur Rank Organization, all without success. He thought about applying to work with the British Council overseas, or joining the civil service. He approached two dozen advertising firms. The American television company sent him 'a long, personal letter of rejection'. A friend of a friend who worked for Orson Welles told him there were no possibilities in the world of film. A classified advertisement in *The Times* newspaper promoting his talents yielded no response. He secured a meeting with the Advertising Appointments Bureau, where a representative informed him frankly that he was the wrong colour for the advertising industry. 'He told me I was banging my head against a brick wall. I had an unfortunate name & face. He could do nothing for me. This is the official appointments bureau, run by the advertising agencies themselves.'

The Indian High Commission, the embassy of the Indian government and Pa's ideal place of work for both Kamla and Vidia, told him there were no openings available. Vidia would fictionalize this rejection in *A Bend in the River*. Indar, an East African of Punjabi origin who has graduated from a good English university, visits India House in London and is shunted from official to official before being shown 'into the inner office, where a fat black man in a black suit, one of our black Indians, was sitting at a big black table, opening envelopes with a paper knife.' The official asks, ' "How can you join our diplomatic service? How can we have a man of divided loyalties?" ' Indar wonders to himself, ' "How dare you lecture me about history and loyalty, you slave?" ' and leaves India House 'full of rage.'[16]

Vidia considered living with Pat and trying to write full time. 'It is risky, but I know I have talent & am bound to succeed sooner or later,' he told her. Pat's response to his stories of rejection was remorselessly English: practical, fussy, naive and in its way right; he had to make an effort to appear more like everyone else. 'I must be cruel to be kind. If you have been wearing that sports jacket and/or a blue shirt to your interview you need look no further for the reason you were rejected . . . Don't ever ever wear that blue shirt of Owad's again for you honestly "lose caste" in it! Oh dear, how incorrigible you are.' The sports jacket would metamorphose into the 'one jacket, a light-green thing that didn't absolutely fit and couldn't hold a shape' worn by Willie Chandran in 1950s London in *Half a Life*. Like Vidia, 'He had paid three pounds for it at a sale of The Fifty Shilling Tailors in the Strand.'[17]

In the autumn of 1954, Vidia began to write a serious novel based on his experiences working as a clerk at the Red House in Trinidad. It was provisionally entitled *The Shadow'd Livery*. He was keeping his father's prized letters in a tea chest in his basement room at 70 Bravington Road. The noise and the squalor made him angry and sarcastic. There always seemed to be a baby crying next door; his ties got lost and his shirts were torn; his books disappeared; a rat bit him during the night – 'I still have the bump on my head,' he told Pat, using the Poste Restante at the Birmingham GPO as their point of contact. He was conscious of the success of other West Indian writers. Earlier, WAGS had written,'You felt hurt when Mittelholzer was so highly praised in John O'London's but do you know that the Penguin reviewer regards his as one among 50 good novels of the decade?'[18] Vidia was obliged to share a room with his cousin Brahm, 'an illiterate, gross man,' he decided hastily, who had recently arrived from Trinidad and seemed to represent everything Vidia was seeking to escape: 'He walks like a dachshund, grunts like a pig, doesn't spit in the road like other beings of Bravington Road, but spits into people's yards.' In time, he got used to his cousin and drew a sketch of him sitting squarely in a chair, 'in a deceptively pensive mood'. He considered going back to Queen's Royal College as a teacher and trying to write 'a good novel or two', constantly aware of his obligation to his widowed mother and siblings. 'My family commitments are so over-powering,' he told Pat, who had taken a holiday job at a reformatory school in the Cotswolds and was visiting Anglo-Saxon churches. 'A mother and four children, and I am only 22.' He had received a letter from home 'that tore my heart. Their trust, their faith, their love – never mentioned, but underlying every word. My little brother needs me now. I can feel it.' What could he tell them that would make things seem all right? 'I have been turned down for 26 jobs so far: this sort of news one doesn't like to write home about,' he told Ma. 'But even English boys from Oxford have had worse luck than that.'[19]

Ill-equipped, emotionally and practically, to look after himself, Vidia was unable to give any useful advice to Pat when she had the inevitable, long-awaited showdown with her father. The spark came when Vidia sent a telegram asking her to come down from Birmingham to London for the weekend. She wrote to him with clarity, dignity and honesty to explain what had happened. Her father had returned from the Kingstanding pub at closing time: 'I began by merely saying I was going to London, very humbly & apologetically for he had brought a chicken for Sunday lunch & I was very conscience-stricken about it. I even thought of sending you a telegram "Father has brought chicken for Sunday. Can't come."' Mr Hale responded that Pat would certainly not be going to London, and that if she did he would accompany her and tell the young man in question 'just what he thought. I think he would be more politic than to use the "wog" language he employed with me. What he would do is to tell you: that he would never admit you to our family circle; the obvious disadvan-tages of mixed marriage and the steps – drastic – he would take to prevent such a marriage taking place.' Unwilling to put Vidia in such a situation in front of gawping cousins at Bravington Road ('I knew your propriety would forbid you receiving my father, whatever his intentions, in a sparsely furnished basement!'), Pat remained at home. She was not, though, cowed by her father's threats, legal or otherwise. They could be married by special licence. 'Alternatively we can part. As far as I am concerned the last is not an alternative.' Later, she wrote movingly, 'I have absolute faith in your ultimate ability to do something great. I am convinced that we are going to be a distinguished couple.'

Vidia's response was equivocal, lacking empathy. 'I do indeed feel for your hardship at home . . . I have been thinking that even when things are blackest the love of a good woman is enough to give a man courage and confidence. I told this to Owad this morning, in my disjointed non-sequitur fashion, and he replied, "It is all you really have." And it is true. Things could have been much worse. There could have been no you.' In the language of the time, Vidia was 'in too deep' to get out; he loved Pat, he needed her, but he was not sure whether he wanted to be married. His solution was to allow his body to take over where his mind had stopped. 'I really don't know what is going to happen,' he wrote. 'Something must break soon or I'll die. The attack of asthma that began last Friday is still with me, developing, like the summer grass, fastest by night.' Stress about his predicament combined with the damp and mould of Owad's basement to give him one asthma attack after another, leaving him weak and depressed, having to go day by day to the hospital for an adrenalin injection. He was reduced to sending desperate pleas to a worried Pat. 'ASTHMA AGAIN PLEASE COME TOMORROW' was one message, and she came, down from Birmingham on the train, and took him to the hospital at St Mary's, Paddington, where he proceeded to have a tantrum at being kept waiting, and walked out. Pat was left to soothe the hospital staff. 'Try & think of the humiliation you caused me then first in the casualty department and then back in the office when I had to hand them back their documents and thank them with all the dignity I could muster,' she wrote to him. He was sorry. 'I really did behave atrociously yesterday and the surprising thing is that at the time I had no idea I was behaving badly.' His excuse, looking back, was illness: 'When you can't breathe, you become enraged and sometimes that anger can give you the breath to move.' He remembered it as a time of incapacity and 'asthma, asthma, asthma. Things were bad. Everything had gone wrong at this stage and I was very young, there was complete solitude, no vision of writing or how to move, knowing that what I was doing was rubbish.'[20] Through all this, the demands of home were constantly with him. In August, young Shiva wrote a letter which contained the line, 'You must not waste your money because you must remember we are not rich, but poor.'[21]

*

Pat decided unilaterally that it would be best to leave her family and move to lodgings if she were to continue both her studies and her relationship with Vidia. In August, the University of Birmingham awarded her a research scholarship with free tuition and a grant of £285 for the academic year.[22] Leaving home was a brave move for a twenty-two-year-old woman in a precarious position to be making at this time, but she did it with panache. 'I hope to leave home (oh dear) tomorrow & luggage books & furniture by taxi at 3.30.' She would lodge with a Miss Gilson in the Birmingham suburb of Moseley. Vidia, consumed by his own anguish, poverty and asthma, was of no help, using his preferred method of abdication rather than involving himself in a testing situation. 'I have no indication of what your feelings are about me going into lodgings & have taken this decision entirely on my own,' she wrote to him anxiously. Within a few weeks, Pat's father had sent her what she called 'a heartrending letter'. In a sloping, barely legible hand, Ted Hale begged her to come home, and offered to pay her landlady 'a month's rent in lieu of notice . . . Although I shall never be able to agree with you on this matter which has caused this dreadful upset I promise that I will never refer to it again and that you may please yourself what you do . . . It's playing on my mind and I can't seem to think about anything else. Please do come back at once. Your loving Daddy.' Pat, however, knew where her loyalty lay. 'Here I can be of use to you whereas at home I cannot,' she told Vidia. 'Here I can offer you hospitality and comfort. I have also found in Miss Gilson a mutual friend.' When he had money, Vidia went to Birmingham for the weekend to be with Pat. It was just over a guinea if he travelled by bus, but it took six hours.

Occasionally, he saw Oxford friends. Lawrence 'Lol' O'Keefe and his wife Suzanne invited him to dinner. 'They live at a place called Black Heath: suburbia.' He saw another old Univ friend, James Sutton. 'He wants me to come to a small party he is giving tonight. It is pure South Ken[sington], and I well remember the agony I went through at his last invitation.' Above all, he saw Jill Brain. She was his age, privately educated, with a father in the RAF. Now she worked as an editorial assistant at the Cement & Concrete Association and shared a basement flat in Chelsea with Brenda Capstick, another Oxford graduate. Jill was pretty, funny and good company – and Vidia was strongly attracted to her. He showed her his most buoyant side, and she was mildly aware of his desire, although since she was engaged to someone else, thought little of it. She remembered: 'He was clever, witty, ambitious. The guy I knew was cheerful and funny. I wouldn't have hung out with someone who was miserable. I don't remember a lot of angst ... He did talk about being a writer. I greatly enjoyed being with him. I remember we had a joke about what we called "fellow countrymen". It was clear to me that he didn't regard all his fellow countrymen as precisely equal.' Jill lent Vidia her typewriter and often invited him to supper at her flat in Oakley Street in Chelsea. 'I remember stuff about food – what he wouldn't eat. I could handle vegetarian, but I hadn't quite carried it through to the stock in the soup. I remember a lecture about cows.' Looking back, she wondered whether Vidia's wit and ease had caused her to misconstrue him. 'He was very, very articulate and well read and fluent in English. Looking back, I think that I always took him as less foreign than he was, because he spoke such good English, and that was a mistake. I may have taken him to be a psychologically simpler person than he was.'[23]

Finally in September Vidia got a temporary job at the National Portrait Gallery with the aid of his Oxford friend Richard Taylor, 'working gentleman's hours' on a salary of a guinea a day. He had to catalogue Edwardian caricatures from the magazine *Vanity Fair*, and was entertained by the social commentary and skill of the cartoonists. Writing to Pat, he imitated the famous signature of 'Spy', 'Leslie Ward: old Etonian', and 'Ape', 'a wop called Carlo Pellegrini'. His asthma continued, and at times he would have to leave work and go in search of an adrenalin injection. The food at 70 Bravington Road appalled him. Pat, always compassionate, suggested he might cater for himself and sent food parcels, which she called 'morale raisers'. Vidia remained inert. Sometimes he did not even bother to open her parcels to remove the fruitcake or the tin of sardines. Instead, he complained about being given no breakfast and disgraceful, low-grade plantation food for supper by Owad's wife, Jean: boiled rice with curried potatoes, or pancake and curried cauliflower.

When Owad was in a friendly mood, he told Vidia to invite Pat to spend the weekend in London. In the cramped confines of 70 Bravington Road, she would share a bed with Jean, to ensure propriety. Vidia had to squeeze in beside his cousins Brahm and Owad: 'if one is going slumming, one had better do it in style, don't you think?' If visits to London were difficult, trips to see Pat in Moseley were as fraught. Miss Gilson allowed him to stay in a room in her house, though his first visit there was marred by an incident when Vidia thoughtlessly woke the neighbours. 'Sweetheart you could not have made a worse impression if you had tried (well, I don't know about that really),' Pat wrote next day. 'What I mean is we can't really blame Miss Gilson for being rather disconcerted. Dear, there was one thing you did which upset her, quite justifiably, on Monday. You woke the neighbours without telling us so that she was bombarded by questions, etc. without warning . . . I know you were very disturbed & all over the place. Miss Gilson was rather decent about it . . . But dear try & think carefully of the impression you are creating – without being servile.'

By November the weather had turned cold and the National Portrait Gallery let him go. Vidia took to attending news cinemas to pass the time. He was penniless, failing and increasingly bitter. Pat suggested he might return to Trinidad and try his luck there. Only anger animated him. 'Ever since I was twelve I swore to get away from Trinidad,' he responded. Later, he recalled that people would 'say to me, why don't you go back home and serve your country. What country? A plantation? How was one going to serve it?'[24] Now, Vidia became philosophical. He saw his predicament, passionately and dispassionately, as the product of complex historical circumstances. He was an East Indian West Indian who had been pulled out of his own society by a superior British education, leaving him a double exile, a deracinated colonial who was legally prevented from migrating inside the new Commonwealth. He told Pat:

> You tell me I talk a lot of rot about history. But I wonder
> whether you ever consider that my position has been caused by
> several complex historical factors: the slave trade, its abolition;
> British imperialism, and the subjection of Indian peoples; the
> need for cheap labour on the Caribbean sugar plantations;
> Indian indentured immigration . . . So today, you have me –
> disowned by India. Well, I belong to the Commonwealth. It is
> true that I cannot go to Canada, New Zealand, Australia, South
> Africa, Kenya, Uganda, Tanganyika, the Rhodesias, Nyasaland;
> but then I ought to know my place in the Free World . . . You
> see, it is all right to get worked up about the (admittedly
> frequent) acts of physical repression; but the more insidious
> form of oppression is the spiritual one. I am an example of that,
> whatever you may say . . . You will say that I am free. Of
> course I am free. I have freedom of speech (in England,
> anyway); freedom of worship. All these of course are quite
> useless to me without freedom of opportunity.

It was a rare and direct statement of his own plight, and contains the themes and anxieties that would be played out in the writings of V.S.

Naipaul over the next fifty years. His predicament would become both his handicap and his opportunity.

He tried to write about his deracination for the BBC, and in October submitted a script, 'A Culturally Displaced Person', which was turned down as 'exaggerated' by Gordon Waterfield, head of the Eastern Service. What was Mr Naipaul worrying about? 'The reference to being educated in an alien tradition and speaking its language and thinking in it, surely this is a rather out-of-date form of nationalism ... Mr Naipaul could, it seems to me, equally write a good talk saying how lucky it is that he knows English since it enables him to keep in touch with Indian thought, Indian novelists, etc.'[25] Half a century later, Vidia had a defensive memory of Waterfield's response: 'His reaction was rather foolish, a pretty pompous thing. What I was saying became a commonplace of thought. I was enraged by it. I thought he was trying to do me down. I needed the money; I assure you it left no mark on me.'[26]

While assuring him of her love in 'these perilous days' Pat suggested he might 'start making concrete enquiries after a clerical temporary job. There are loads. Don't be angry.' She enclosed a 2½d stamp so he could reply, which he did in a furious, acute, self-pitying analysis of his position, describing the everyday racial humiliations he faced in London and his epic uncertainty over his future, displaying raw wounds to her that he would afterwards try to keep hidden from the world for the rest of his life:

> Go out & get a clerical job, you write, adding, there are heaps of those. I hate to spring a surprise on you ... but the people in authority feel my qualifications fit me only for jobs as porters in kitchens, and with the road gangs. My physique decrees otherwise ... It is my own fault. Why don't I go back where I came from, and not be a nuisance to anyone? Niggers ought to know their place.

He described an interview at the Colonial Office, at which he was kept waiting for more than one hour before being told, 'Come on, stop feeling sorry for yourself and go back home. You will find something.' But Vidia did not want to go back to Trinidad, '40 × 40 miles, with no prospects, no high mountains, far away. To rot, ambitionless, neither seen nor heard?'

Where did he stand? What was he left with? What was he for, and what might he turn out to be against? Where did his loyalties lie: in

Trinidad, in Britain, in India, or nowhere? 'Have I any right to be in the Free World? Have I any obligation to cast my lot in with the Free World? Should I be against the Free World?' These were spacious questions for him to be asking, an early analysis of the critical global phenomenon of the next half-century: mass migration and the cultural collisions that would come in its wake. Did Vidia have any right to live in the 'Free World'?

> I want you to answer . . . for me, and for my poor father & family – growing up with no horizon save that of Port of Spain Harbour and unemployment? If you can manage it, put yourself in my place for a minute & let me know. Forget that we are attached to each other. If my father had 1/20 of the opportunity laid before the good people of British stock, he would not have died a broken, frustrated man without any achievement. But, like me, he had the opportunity – to starve. He was ghettoed – in a sense more cruel than that in which Hitler ghettoed the Jews. But there was an element of rude honesty in the Nazi approach; and they at any rate killed swiftly. The approach of the Free World is infinitely subtler and more refined. You cannot say to a foreign country: I suffer from political persecution. That wouldn't be true and wouldn't it be melodramatic & absurd to say: But I suffer from something worse, an insidious spiritual persecution. These people want to break my spirit. They want me to forget my dignity as a human being. They want me to know my place. You have the result in me, as I sit in a French café (not drinking anything) to write this. No fire in my room for two days and only tea & toast in my stomach. That is what the whole policy of the Free World amounts to. Naipaul, poor wog, literally starving, and very cold.

Pat, the stronger of the two at this point in their relationship, thought he should be more practical and needed to act fast to save himself. 'Don't shout at me . . . There is no one in the whole world besides me who takes you really seriously.'

Through everything, she remained optimistic. 'I think we'll be alright by Christmas. Just concentrate on keeping going in health and morale for the time being – and on obtaining white shirts for interviews.' It was too late for him to return to Trinidad, for he would only go 'with a terrible sense of failure and compulsion. But unless & until you get a job I think you should come to me or go home for you are "dying slowly" as you are.' She consulted a Mr W.J. Davies, who was responsible for helping West Indian immigrants in Birmingham to find jobs. Mr Davies was happy to help, and wrote on Vidia's behalf to several large firms in Birmingham including ICI and GEC, as well as finding him a clerical position in the Tax Office. Vidia was full of rage, refusing to be helped by a man he described as 'Birmingham's Protector of the Poor'. He would not involve himself with Mr Davies, a latter-day protector of immigrants, nor would he be classified alongside people who climbed off banana boats wearing zoot-suits and wanted jobs in factories. He was V.S. Naipaul, the writer. Pat was 'literally sick with worry & misery' and no less angry in response. 'By God your letter got me mad. I was half glad in a way for I'm a bit fed up with being eternally understanding and patient . . . I took the course I did because of the desperate letter you sent me on Friday, which incidentally accused me of doing nothing but sit still & preach. So I went straight out & did something . . . I shall have to go and see Mr Davies, thank him for his offer, apologise for wasting his time behaving all the while as if your behaviour is justified and absolutely nothing is wrong. I've had to do this before several times and presumably I shall do it again.' Vidia's lasting emotional incapacity meant that Pat would have to do it again, many, many times.

Henry Swanzy stepped in, making enquiries and arranging a meeting with the Jewish businessman and philanthropist Victor Sassoon (who had notoriously been insulted in a wartime broadcast by the poet Ezra Pound). Swanzy went to extraordinary lengths to help contributors to *Caribbean Voices*. Earlier in the year, he had lobbied Oxford University for funds from the Carnegie Foundation, saying that his BBC budget was insufficient to back promising talent such as Sam Selvon who had a wife and young child to support, Derek Walcott from Saint Lucia who was looking to travel to England and Vidia Naipaul, a Trinidadian student at Oxford.[27] 'Sassoon is interested in India & has lots of money,' Vidia reported to Pat. 'He thinks that in colonies like those in the Caribbean – where all the peoples speak English & have British institutions, and are educated in the Brit way, there should be a policy designed to incorporate these people into Britain.' In retrospect, once he had received a knighthood, become a millionaire and won the Nobel Prize, Vidia thought Sassoon had been insufficiently helpful: 'He was not interested in me at all. I think it's a mark against him.'[28]

Meanwhile, Vidia remained dependent on Pat's practical and financial assistance. 'I do not wish to alarm you but it will be an act of great charity if you can send me a small amount of money: this will enable me to eat a bit for two or three days ... I am literally starving these days, & have lost nearly 12 pounds since I left the Portrait Gallery. I have never sunk so low in all my life.' He even expected Pat – despite the formal ambiguities in their relationship – to act as his representative and calm the fears of his family, despite his own inability or refusal to involve himself with hers. 'What I would like you very much to do is to write home for me ... Stress the fact that I am not unhappy, but that breaking into a first job is always difficult. Don't mention a word about race or anything like that.' His lust for Jill continued, a distraction from despair. 'Jill has taken to putting on her stockings in front of me. Should I look away? Advise on this point of etiquette, please. Ha!' he wrote to Pat in late November. Whenever he spent time with Jill, he avoided showing her his distress and his poverty. He believed he was revisiting the collapse of two years earlier. 'I felt all my old nervous breakdown insensibly overpowering me & making the world dark & unreal. I know that you don't believe in breakdowns; but take my word – What happens is this: one's life is so unsatisfactory, so terribly insecure, so haunted by fear & doubt & sense of failure – that the mind in a clever beastly way removes attention from these truths so hard to swallow, and fixes it on an alien dread. It seems to be a different spirit within that says: Little boy finds these things so frightening; here, little boy, exercise your mind on this. Oh God, I wish, I do deeply wish that I don't lose my balance again.'

At the start of December 1954, as Pat had predicted, he had the crucial, inevitable breakthrough without which he would have gone on sinking. Swanzy was leaving England after being seconded by the BBC to run the Gold Coast broadcasting service. He offered Vidia a renewable three-month contract presenting *Caribbean Voices*. In a conversation recorded for a television documentary twenty-five years later, Swanzy asked whether the job had been helpful, coming when it did. Naipaul had no doubts: 'That saved my life, really. I was living more or less at the limit of despair.'[29] At last Vido had good news for Ma: 'I am doing the Caribbean Voices ... I only need to go out on the days of recording; for the rest I can stay at home, and do my own writing. They are paying me eight guineas a week as a start; and Kenneth Ablack, who is producing the programme, tells me that they will pay

me extra for any work I do ... I shall be saving up from twenty to
twenty five shillings every week to send home; because I know that
you are in difficulties ... Will you all love me, and live good lives, and
love each other? That is what a family is made for. All my love Vido.'[30]

CHAPTER NINE

'SOMETHING RICH LIKE CHOCOLATE'

FOR THE NEXT FOUR YEARS, Vidia Naipaul had an insecure billet as a stalwart of the BBC Colonial Service. It gave him an opportunity to find his feet as a writer, to widen and extend his talents and to feel an integral part of a circle of intelligent men, and a few women, of roughly his own age and background. Gone was the white world of Oxford University; he was again among people who reminded him of Port of Spain and QRC. Henry Swanzy left Vidia and his colleagues in no doubt that their material was real material. In their spare time, the *Caribbean Voices* 'boys' would go to the George pub near the BBC, or chat in the freelances' room in the old Langham Hotel opposite Broadcasting House, a grand Victorian edifice with a literary heritage (Mark Twain stayed there, Oscar Wilde drank there, Sherlock Holmes sleuthed there). Vidia ate lunch in the BBC canteen, finishing with heavy English puddings topped with custard. A decade later he wrote in an Indian newspaper, 'I worked mainly for various overseas services of the BBC, contributing to magazine programmes, doing tiny features about books, doing interviews and taking part in discussions. To hear oneself being introduced by an announcer with a well-known voice was to feel honoured, and also nervous.' He believed the experience taught him how to interview successfully, by 'lightly drawing out information'.[1] In Frank Collymore's journal *Bim*, Vidia marvelled in retrospect at his own audacity in taking the job as a literary presenter: 'For now I see I fitted into none of the accepted categories of critics. I was not a gentleman, to whom criticism meant a display of sensibility and polished prose: an accomplishment, like a knowledge of pictures and wines, which might grace one in society.'[2]

The contributors, actors and presenters who worked on *Caribbean Voices* and other BBC shows came and went, month by month. They were older than the precocious Vidia Naipaul, and with the exception of the acculturated Sam Selvon, none was an East Indian West Indian. To Vidia, they seemed more experienced, adept and socially confident. George Lamming was born in Barbados, and had travelled to Britain in 1950 with Selvon and stayed in the same hostel. His influential book *In the Castle of My Skin* examined colonialism in the West Indies through the eyes of a growing child; Henry Swanzy thought Lamming had 'one fatal lack, a sense of humour'.[3] Errol John, brother of Pa's colleague George John, was an actor who wrote the play *Moon On a Rainbow Shawl*. Edgar Mittelholzer was a Guianese novelist who produced books at speed ('It pleased him,' Vidia wrote in *A Writer's People*, 'that he was not too much darker than his publisher Fred Warburg; it was an unexpected way of judging a publisher.').[4] Andrew Salkey, born in Panama and educated in Jamaica (he bears some resemblance to Percy in *Half a Life*), wrote folk stories in patois and was a lively and influential member of the group; he regarded literature as sacred, and with his wife Pat gave long Sunday parties at their home in Holland Park. Gordon Woolford was from British Guiana; he planned to write a novel but had never progressed beyond the first chapter. The resident reviewer was British, Arthur Calder Marshall, born in 1908, an early Marxist and friend of poets like Auden and MacNeice, who had written a travel book on Trinidad and been heralded in his youth as a coming writer – one of his novels used no fewer than sixty-seven first-person narrators. John Stockbridge was an English journalist, and 'a friend and encourager' to Vidia: 'He told me I dressed badly and would be a great writer.' Edward Brathwaite was a Cambridge graduate and poet from Barbados: 'He's become very black; when I met him then he wasn't so black.'[5] Sylvia Wynter, a Cuban-born Jamaican who 'used words like comprador bourgeoisie', would marry Jan Carew, 'a mulatto from Guiana, a tall and handsome man with pretensions to be a writer; he published a couple of books, but they've disappeared.'[6] As for Willy Edmett, he was 'a small, thin man who later started a shop in the countryside. He thought he was going nowhere.'

Despite his subsequent barbs and snubs, Vidia was a wholehearted member of this group. Jan Carew remembered: 'We would do broadcasts at the BBC and then go to a pub nearby. Vidia was a very good companion, very witty. Cruel wit. Some West Indians used to work at the back of the kitchen at the BBC cafeteria. He called them "the blackroom boys". He had an underlying sense of compassion for the less well-off West Indians in London, which later he was accused of not having. People of my generation spoke about race in a way that was full of jokes; there was no animus, we would joke about each other's background – race and class. Vidia didn't hold himself apart. There was certainly a sense of community. Before the independence movement developed, our group in London was much more integrated.' Carew thought the relationship between Gordon Woolford and Vidia had been 'very close and intense. We went to a party given at the house of Peter Abrahams, the black South African writer. I remember going back on the tube late at night, Vidia and Gordon Woolford were hugging and kissing. It could have been simply alcohol. Big drinking was more the rule than the exception at that time.'[7] Vidia remembered, 'Gordon Woolford was very important to me. He was thirty-five in 1954. He was an alcoholic, married a shop assistant, a very handsome man. He was a good reader, distinct. He had a sister who was a beauty queen. His father was Sir Eustace Woolford, a mulatto who became a speaker of the legislative assembly in Guiana. Now the joke they tell about him in Trinidad, a wicked racial joke, is that Eustace was sitting in his club in Georgetown playing cards with his back to the door. A white American comes up the stairs and says, "Hey, there's a nigger in here." And Eustace says, "Hmm, throw him out." '[8]

At the BBC, Vidia reviewed new novels, interviewed writers and chaired discussions on West Indian literature with scripted informality. He contributed to a series on 'Contemporary Negro Poetry', looked at the 'uncompromisingly worthy' Japanese novel *The Makioka Sisters* by Junichiro Tanizaki. He reviewed the film *Sea Wife*, making sure he was reimbursed eight shillings and sixpence for 'cost of a seat at the cinema'. With his reporter's notebook filling easily, he wrote and broadcast scripts about a model engineer's exhibition, the International PEN congress, literary teas at Harrods and the National Portrait Gallery.[9] He exchanged staged banter about trends in writing with Kenneth Ablack (who was not 'a black', but an Indian, or half-Indian; his father, Mr Ramprasad, had changed his name to something less classifiable): 'ABLACK: "Thank you Vidia Naipaul – now that you have given news of Samuel Selvon, ought I to mention that you are in the course of writing your own first novel?" '[10] Like Willie in *Half a Life*, involvement with the BBC gave Vidia 'a sense of the power and wealth of London' that he did not find elsewhere; like Willie he went to interview a rising African carver, a man named Felix Idubor, a sculptor and seducer from Nigeria: 'He walked Willie round the exhibition, the heavy African gown bouncing off his thighs, and told him with great precision how much he had paid for every piece of wood. Willie built his script around that.' Like Willie, he 'loved the drama of the studio, the red light and the green light, the producer and the studio manager in their soundproof cubicle.'[11] Working as a BBC presenter enabled Vidia to learn theatrical skills that never deserted him. 'They taught me I was never to let my voice drop at the end of a sentence. They taught me to speak from the back of my throat, which I still do — easy for an asthmatic — and never to talk from the mouth. I learned how to throw my voice. They taught you to have a picture in your head when you are speaking.'[12]

His friend Willy Edmett at the Colonial Schools Unit gave him plenty of work, and better still arranged swift payment. V.S. Naipaul wrote about 'Dr Livingstone the Geographer' for Edmett, and prepared a sequence of ten scripts on Shakespeare's *Henry V* to help children study for exams. He gave talks on George Eliot's *The Mill on the Floss* and H.G. Wells's *The History of Mr Polly* (a favourite book of Pa's, which was to influence *A House for Mr Biswas*) for a Colonial Schools Unit series titled 'Reading for your Delight', designed to generate another crop of culturally British colonials even as the Suez Canal prepared to flow through Lady Eden's drawing room. Collecting a guinea here and there, he read the part of Hounakin in a performance of Derek Walcott's one-act play *The Sea at Dauphin*, narrated short stories by John Figueroa and the Tobagonian poet E.M. Roach ('I liked his poetry: "Seven splendid cedars break the trades." A tender man') and earned two guineas reading a poem on a sister programme, *Calling West Africa*.[13] Alternating between BBC studios in Maida Vale and the West End, Vidia praised Edward Brathwaite's poetic fluency, narrated *The Strange Flower*, a short story by his newly discovered Trinidadian contemporary Michael Anthony, and called Edgar Mittelholzer 'the most professional and the most successful' of his fellow West Indian writers.[14] Later, having reinvented himself as a different kind of person, he forgot all these thespian performances: 'I am not an actor. I have no memory of reading other people's work, except my father's story [*Ramdas and the Cow*].'[15] Vidia's subsequent claim to have had no literary influences bar his father was a deliberate blanking of the role of his colleagues at *Caribbean Voices*, who were crucial in forming his idea of what did and

did not work on the page. After the 1950s, now securely in print, he
rarely found it necessary to test his literary thinking against the opinions
or techniques of others.

Vidia interviewed Francis Wyndham, the writer and critic, Stuart
Hall, his exact contemporary from Jamaica, who was emerging as a
left-wing political theorist in Britain, and Sam Selvon, whose reputation
as a novelist was still rising. Despite an excellent rehearsal, the recording
with Selvon went badly. 'Woolford, who was listening in the studio
cubicle, said I sounded as though I were a bored and blasé seventy year
old don,' he wrote to Pat in Birmingham. It may have been an
instinctive, emotional response to Pa's old literary rival and Kamla's
former lover. 'At the end of that ordeal I was sweating, literally . . .
Talking about Woolford, he came home last night and drank every
drop of the wine I had there, and he begged me not to begrudge it him.
What could I do? Incidentally, we were fooled with that sauterne. Some
sugar remained at the bottom of the bottle and Woolford said it is an
old trick of the wine merchants: sweetening cheap two and six wine
with sugar and selling it for six shillings. One learns. Don't get angry
about the wine. Woolford is an alcoholic and, poor man, he cannot get
by without liquor.'[16]

*

In the new year of 1955, Vidia began to use a tiny pocket notebook. 'For
writing overheard conversation & sharpening observation,' he noted on an
envelope when he sealed it away for posterity.[17] It is the only notebook of
its kind to survive. Later, he stopped collecting scraps of material or
making notes, preferring to let ideas or memories rest in his mind before
letting them come out in an accumulated, indirect form in his writing. For
the same reason, he rarely kept a personal diary except when travelling to
research an article. The notebook gives an evocative picture of his
preoccupations during this seminal year. Pat is not mentioned once. It
shows his direct experience of post-war London, a world of Lyons Corner
Houses, down-at-heel bars, lodgings, poverty, friendship, alcohol, prostitutes, racial mingling and the sexual fascination and dissatisfaction that he
would later depict in fiction. Vidia was usually an observer rather than a
participant, a solitary figure watching and listening intently, jotting down
what he saw and heard. He showed a London that would soon disappear,
and there are moments in his writing when he seems to be describing a

city from the nineteenth century, after Charles Dickens, Fyodor Dostoyevsky or Emile Zola.

At a late-night bar, he wrote: 'Pervading colour: cream. Cheese rolls. Fat, tarty woman, with a face like a man's, wearing a soiled overall. Fat, plump, white man, rimless glasses. Whores. Pimps . . . Types of whores. Thin. Low forehead & villainous features. Half baked look . . . The woman 2 seats away inquiring about the quality of what I was eating — through the man between.' He would record snatches of conversation from a bus ride, a cafe or the street: 'You Greek ponce . . . Snappy Joey's must have been a terrific dive, eh. One girl had a large ? tattooed on her behind . . . So I meets him and I says to him "'Ello!" and 'e says, "'Ello!" . . . I might have a woman for you this week . . . Kill time you know. Hardest thing to kill.' He recorded what he saw, simple images designed to create a possible spark for later stories. 'Girl bending back to straighten stocking . . . The Nigger-Lovers. Drawings of blacks on wall. Couples no conversation . . . Victoria on a hot afternoon. Cat & 3 pigeons . . . Cloakroom. Single black hat on hook.' He noted a line from his loquacious landlady, Mrs Lloyd, about a coal delivery man: 'He asked for the lady with the Indian gentleman — but he didn't finish it because he was too embarrassed to say it. You don't mind, do you? He is a nice man.' He made observations, which at times implied a larger knowledge than he had: 'Sisters are invariably proud of brothers' sexual success . . . The Decline of the Society Writer . . . At one time I used to think my salvation would be a wife. Well, I got a wife. No what I need is a woman . . . Man at Bow St. [Magistrates'] Court seeing pro[stitute]s come in. "They've come to pay their income-tax" . . . A man who didn't believe all he read in the papers . . . Woman who runs a paper on improving race relations but doesn't want black people in her house.' Race and sex were never far from his thoughts. One night aboard a double-decker London bus, he noted, '2 low-class Englishwomen with two flashily-dressed Indians. All drunk & singing at the top of their voices. Old, round Jewess & wizened husband come on top. Woman: Oh, let's go back downstairs. But they remain & foursome notice distaste. So: sitting behind old couple: Hey, Pop, can't you sing? Can't you sing? Woman: They're just angry because you're coloured. Man: Shut up.'

His relationship with friends and colleagues at the BBC such as Jan Carew, John Stockbridge, Gordon Woolford and Willy Edmett were central to his life at this time. He discovered something of London and the world beyond through their stories and romances, and the experiences which he himself did not dare to have. Stockbridge told how he felt unfaithful to his mistress whenever he slept with his wife, and Vidia recorded his conjugal woes: 'Going to beat him up, beat her up, & tell her I'll kill her if she does it again. It wasn't honour. It was self-pity. But I am glad it didn't get me down. I have come out on top. Must get a hat. – Why? – Feel like it. For the new tough male role I am filling. So we walk along a crazy, crowded Oxford Street to Dunn's & his face falls as he sees the prices, £2 etc.' Willy Edmett's quirky phrases were recorded, as was his response to a remark from Stockbridge. 'J.S. Met a practitioner of black magic yesterday. W. It is white magic when we practise it . . . Typical Willyisms: It's like dust. You didn't see it falling, but you suddenly say, hello, the table's covered with dust . . . Willy is a dark horse. Willy with black woman.' Jan Carew's attitudes and adventures impressed him: 'Another of J.C.'s stories: Court-martialled & dishonourably discharged. All terribly hush-hush. Wrote a seven-page memorandum to my commanding officer telling him how the army ought to be run. He is a married man, of course. But: You should see the Italian girl I have coming over here in a few days. 5' 10", built in the Roman way, with sex crawling all over her skin . . . Used to go out hunting in the jungle, when I was a boy, two weeks at a time. Butted a S. African last night. I was hungry & when I am hungry all my intellectual poses drop off.'[18]

Nights out with Gordon Woolford yielded notes like 'Gordon owes me 8/6'. One evening as they walked through Piccadilly Circus with its streams of people and electric billboards and the Eros statue,

> G[ordon] pointed at a woman in a doorway & said, 'I know you!'
> The woman looked G over & said, 'Let me see, I know you too. You are G.'
> 'How did you remember?'
> 'Meet Gordon,' she said, turning to her fellow-tart. 'He was in the RAF when I was in the WAAF [Women's Auxiliary Air Force].'
> Her eyelids and forehead & her hair were sprinkled with twinkle dust. Likewise her companion's.
> Woman grew definitely sad. Kind face. Glistening eyes.
> 'Well, G. I never thought I would see you in Picc[adilly]. Never thought I would see myself here either.'
> Chat about careers.
> 'Come and have a coffee.'
> No interest.

'Where?' she asked finally.

'Snack-bar in Dean St.'

Then, out of nowhere, a man: 'Snack-bar! Snack-bar! Don't want to break up your little what not –.'

Without a word both girls walk away, after ceremoniously shaking hands.

Vidia's encounters with prostitutes in 1955 remained theoretical, or chaste. His interest in women who would do imaginable sexual things for money dated back to his teenage days in Port of Spain. Seduction would not be involved; nor was the woman required to dissemble. A woman who sold herself to a man for sex embodied his internal collision between repulsion and desire. Speaking years later he saw his fascination with the bars of Soho and Shepherd's Market as youthful bravado: 'I used to go actually for the sex in the head, that kind of excitement. I was taken by it almost like a nineteenth-century French writer – although that didn't enter my head, about being like a French writer. I was lured by the idea of their bodies. It was just the idea of the bodies. I found them very attractive. One was young and inexperienced and . . . thank God I didn't have money. I would have probably done a lot of foolish things.'

He saw such voyeuristic contact as an imagined idea rather than a practicality, as a prolonged, intangible form of arousal, 'sex in the head' that did not involve the intimacy and risk of sex with another person's body. 'It is very much an innocent approach really, and all my time in London there was that innocence. I felt unhappy that I didn't have the money to be debauched. I loved the idea of debauchery.' His relationship with Pat did not, or could not, move beyond the shy, virginal form in which it had begun. They were both trapped by the formal taboos they had been raised with at a time of unspoken ignorance in Port of Spain and Kingstanding. Sex itself was 'an embarrassment, and I think it had to do with my own background. I was born in 1932, so I am very much a child of another age: the shyness, the embarrassment – and the absurd idea that the main thing was for me to have my ejaculation. That was very foolish. Nobody told me anything else. I've written about it some-where, and I think in the old days certainly – I don't know what it is like now – it's true of most Indian men, this very private idea of sex being something for you alone and not related to the person in front of you. The idea of sex as one of the talents of life doesn't enter into it at all. It's just something dark at the corner . . . I think Pat could never get rid of her inhibitions, her shame and everything else. And in the cinema, any scene of intimacy on the screen, I couldn't bear to look at it. It was just the way I was made. So I would look down. I would tell her, "When they have stopped kissing let me know." It went on and to this day it goes on. It seemed to me such an intimate thing, two people kissing, why should I be asked to look at it?'[19]

*

At the end of 1954 when he got the job at the BBC, Vidia had used his newfound financial security to move out of Owad's house. Getting accommodation was not easy, and the literary editor Karl Miller had a story about Vidia from this period: 'Asked on the telephone if he was coloured, by an English landlady to whom he was applying in his youth for a room, he was said to have replied: "Hopelessly." '[20] One of his cousins finally arranged for him to rent rooms from a Barbadian doctor in Notting Hill. The warmth of his sexual and emotional relationship with Pat revived; he could see a way ahead. He became affectionate. 'Write & tell little boy immediately what train you are coming down by. Have found flat – ideal as far as your visits are concerned. Moving Saturday. Do come, darling. It will be so depressing moving without you. Last week-end was a miracle of joy & love.' Pat came to London for the weekend and helped him move in to the house in Oxford Gardens. 'So,' he remembered in old age, tears running down his face, 'for the first time in my life, there was semblance of a household of my own.' Pat cooked a meal. 'It was a very, very moving moment for me, a sacramental moment. It was very beautiful. I have probably written about this in other ways in my work. For the first time I felt a little bit in control.'[21] It reminded him of his short story 'This Is Home', when a young couple move to a new house, and as the man leaves, the woman reminds him, 'This is home.' Within weeks, Vidia was 'thinking of moving to a better place, where one can type, where the ceilings are thicker, where there are carpets on the stairs, and where the doors lock properly.' With the help of a BBC doorman he found a sitting room cum bedroom with a little kitchen attached in St Julian's Road in Kilburn. Different people lived on each floor of this new house and shared a communal bathroom. Vidia would remain at St Julian's Road for two and a half productive years.

He knew that Pat held him together emotionally, and decided without enthusiasm to marry her, despite feeling that he would be going against his family's wishes. In retrospect he thought they might have done better to live together: 'It was the social pressures of those days . . . She wanted to get married.' Vidia wanted a respectable witness and approached a fellow Trinidadian, Frank Singuineau, 'a mulatto fellow, a nice educated man, married to an Irish girl' who worked as an actor at the BBC and would later appear in films such as *Carry On Again Doctor* and *An American Werewolf in London*. But Frank Singuineau, the chosen witness, would not cooperate. Vidia and Pat were isolated. 'He said he couldn't do it because he was Catholic and didn't approve. I had to get somebody else.'[22] Gordon Woolford was the less-respectable substitute, accompanied by Vidia's cousin Deo Ramnarine.

The marriage took place on 10 January 1955. The groom was identified as 'Vidiadhar Surajparashad Naipaul formerly known as Vidiadhar Swrajparashad Naipal, son of Supersal Naipal deceased Journalist', a 'Radio Script Writer (B.B.C.)'. The bride was Patricia Ann Hale, 'University Post Graduate,' daughter of a 'solicitor's managing clerk'.[23] They were both twenty-two years old. Neither family was informed of the marriage. Vidia produced no wedding ring, an oversight which Pat did her tentative English best to put right some months later. 'I do feel the lack of a ring very acutely. You did promise & I will think you don't quite realise how "odd" it seems to people. Don't be irritable about it – it isn't just a fancy, whim or extravagance & I don't think I am mistaken in regarding it as rather important.' A wedding ring represented all that Vidia wanted to avoid: expense, the trap of marriage, social expectation. He had chosen to marry Pat, but did not want to accept the consequences of doing so. Rather than address the chasmic inconsistency in what he was doing, he tried to turn his back on himself, and offered these bizarre subsequent justifications for his behaviour: 'I had no interest in jewellery. I didn't think it was important. I simply had no money.'[24] Pat finally bought herself a wedding ring, a plain gold band, which she rarely wore.

Initially she remained living with Miss Gilson in Birmingham while she completed her studies in history and philosophy, and only came down to St Julian's Road at weekends. Before arrival, she would send Vidia a shopping list and basic instructions in housewifery: 'bed made with one clean sheet (put top to bottom) & clean pillow cases'. Vidia kept her in touch with London by post, watching the other lodgers in the house with a writer's eye. 'Mrs. Cariddi has left for Italy, and she left very quietly, without telling anyone. The little wop boy is left alone, so very alone. But he is doing the illegal thing, with the assistance of the Rex Lloyds: he is working. Last Sunday, he asked me in, and offered me loads of macaroni and spaghetti (uncooked). I was really touched by this generosity and the effort to gain friendship. But alas, I don't like spaghetti or macaroni, and I had to refuse. This is when these people cease to be stupid, and become very, very sad.' He was re-reading D.H. Lawrence's *Sons and Lovers*. 'It is a very great book: the greatest writers can write only one book of that standard.' Pat lent him money to send to his family in Trinidad, which he was careful to repay. Ma made repeated requests for money to support herself, Sewan and Nella. 'Although Kamla is giving me every cent of her salary to spend in the house which I must be grateful for she also gives me the same amount of torture.'[25] Kamla added that 'even a single pound' from him would help to pull them through these difficult months. Vidia felt he was trapped in a vacuum. 'I have written a message of hope on that piece of cardboard the Thornhill laundry sends with its shirts: It is Foolish to Fear Failure. I did this last night, and the effect has really been wonderful, though the nagging, aching feeling of unease continues constantly, like a nail in the shoe . . . At the moment I just can do nothing; the terror and the unease and the deep deep sense of futility seem to float just in a cloud above my head.'

Pat wished to tell her parents about their marriage, but did not. She visited them, and said nothing. She knew that Vidia was not being supportive, and reacted by nagging him rather than demanding he take responsibility for their situation: 'I just can't do it when I feel all alone . . . I am seized by little fears that you resent my asking you, that you want to live in a vacuum writing your novel, that you want to hide from all those things.' She suggested that Vidia might write a letter to Mrs Hale telling her the truth. His reaction to this demand was not to confront Pat's parents, but to ignore their very existence: 'I wasn't interested in them at all. I was not interested in them.'[26] Soon after the wedding, in another doom-laden symbolic gesture, Vidia lost the marriage certificate. Pat urged him to obtain a copy, or better still 'look for the original. I can't help feeling a little miserable that you've mislaid something like that.' The secret of the marriage remained with them, and grew with each passing month, as rumours reached Trinidad. Vidia's mind was still as much on Pa as it was on Pat. A fortnight after his marriage, he wrote home, 'Two or three nights a week though I still dream about Pa – always nice things; and I see him as clearly as I did at home . . . I am not lying when I say that I am trying to be a writer more for his sake than my own. I am at the moment tidying up his stories before sending them to an agent, but I burst into tears whenever I see his handwriting.'[27] Soon afterwards, Mira wrote mentioning a relation who had married a woman in England and kept it secret from his parents for more than a year: 'The poor souls are shocked, hurt and disappointed.' Three months later, Kamla dropped a heavier hint, 'Oh by the way, if in case you ever get married, please don't make yourself equal to these Indians in T'dad by not telling us.'[28]

Vidia did nothing, nor did he tell his friends about his marriage. Jill discovered about it in a way that caused her great embarrassment. 'I gathered subsequently that I was not the only one person he did this to – Brenda [her flatmate] and I had a party and we invited him. We invited twenty people and he was one of them. After the party I had his telephone number and I telephoned, I got the landlady and she said, Mr Naipaul isn't here but Mrs Naipaul is. I thought his mother must have come to visit. Pat got on the phone and I was absolutely appalled. How could he have done that? He never told me he got married, and I would never invite a married man to the party without inviting his wife. I had met Pat before, only I didn't know her well. I was extremely distressed and upset by this. It made me feel that she would think that I was carrying on with him.'[29] Vidia put a different construction on Jill's outrage, at least in retrospect, claiming it was because she was jealous: 'Brenda thought Jill would marry me.'[30] According to Jill: 'He reads it wrong. Vidia put me in a socially impossible position because he made me look rude by not inviting Pat.'[31] Jill's version of these events is more plausible, given Vidia's reticence in expressing his feelings to her at the time, and because she was engaged to another man. Her own happiness soon turned to tragedy when, six weeks after her wedding the following summer, her husband died. Not long after this, Vidia made his attraction more explicit. 'He once made a pass at me, but only once, in the flat in Chelsea after [my husband] died. I remember him making some sort of gesture. I think I was still mourning . . . Don't get me wrong. I have been laughed at over the years for my preference for what some people refer to as dark little ethnics. Indeed I married one, and have been happily married to him for more than forty years. So if I was brushing Vidia off, it was not because I was being standoffish about him being Indian.'[32]

When Vidia looked at his early correspondence with Pat many years later, with a view to writing a book called *In My Twenty-Fifth Year* – which he failed to complete because it was too emotionally disturbing – he made these notes:

I feel it would have been better for me if I had married >or made love to< Jill. Reading these letters I see (for the first time) that she was interested. Pat really had too many hang-ups. Too many complaints. Too many demons . . . I had been in too deep with Pat, who did not attract me sexually at all . . . I should have steered clear of that damaged family . . . [Pat's letters] contain much of herself. Her virtue, her humanity . . . And in spite of my feeling of two days or so ago, that I should not have married Pat, I find myself in tears again on reading her letters of 1952. Her love was beautiful. And is beautiful . . . The relationship – on VSN's side – was more than half a lie. Based really on need. The letters are shallow & disingenuous. Trivial letters for the most part.[33]

*

In May, he sent $30 (£6.25) each to Ma and Kamla, and reported that the manuscript of the novel he had begun in 70 Bravington Road was 'being considered this moment by Arthur Calder-Marshall'.[34] He had taken his cue from George Lamming, whose *In the Castle of My Skin* was having a success. Calder Marshall had recommended Lamming to the publisher Michael Joseph, and on the strength of merely three chapters, the head of the firm had invited him to a meeting where Lamming was given a contract and a cheque on the spot.[35] (Willie Chandran has a similar experience in *Half a Life*.) While Vidia waited hopefully for a response, and prepared his scripts for the BBC, Pat sent him instructions: 'Now, it's Whit weekend. Therefore you must do the shopping on Saturday – now you must. That means you'll have to get the money today (Friday).' He went to the shops with his new wife's letter in his pocket:

1lb coffee (Jamaica medium ground) from Beverley's
Butter
Sugar
1 tin Tomato Soup!
1 tin Baked Beans
2 tins Garden peas
6 eggs Large
6 oranges
2 lbs New Potatoes
1 lb Carrots
Bread – 1 small brown, 1 Snow's small white
Sainsbury's lg chicken
or
2 chops (large) & Lambs Liver – ask for 1/4 worth

All my love dear. I pray that this Calder Marshall man likes the novel all the time.[36]

Vidia was still eating meat, although he claimed to be revolted by it. A couple of years later when Pat served him lamb's liver, 'I just broke down. Liver was intolerable. This was in the late 1950s. I felt I was a vegetarian who had been violated.'[37] As for the novel, Arthur Calder Marshall 'read it promptly, and wrote a long letter back with single spacing on two sides of a big sheet of paper. He began by saying, you must abandon this book at once. Then he said a few kind things. When that happens, and people tell you things which in your heart you know are true, you are at once relieved and full of anger. And it was out of that, that some despairing weeks later I began to write in the BBC, the first story of *Miguel Street*.'[38]

In early June 1955, in the freelances' room at the Langham Hotel with its ochre walls and pea-green dado, Vidia wound a piece of 'non-rustle' BBC studio paper into a standard typewriter and adopted a singular posture, his shoulders thrown back, his knees drawn up, his shoes resting on the struts on either side of the chair in a 'monkey crouch'.[39] Setting the typewriter to single space, he wrote: 'Every morning when he got up Hat would sit on the banister of his back verandah and shout across, "What happening there, Bogart?"' He had a sentence, a start. He tried to go on. 'The man addressed in this way would turn in his bed . . .' He crossed it out and began again. 'Bogart would turn in his bed and mumble softly, so that no one heard, "What happening there, Hat?"'[40] And Vidia had the opening of his first publishable book. Some figures in *Miguel Street* were simplified versions of people from Luis Street: Bogart was Poker, Hat was a man called Topi (the Hindi word for hat), Uncle Bhakcu was Power Mausa. For Vidia's family and other inhabitants of Woodbrook, the characters would be familiar. Kamla remembered meeting a fellow teacher when she went to work at a school in Pointe-à-Pierre in the 1970s: 'Her name was Lorna Lange and she said to me, "Kamla, I know you, so don't come with any style to me, I lived all my life in Luis Street until I got married and came south, I know Hat, Hat is Topi, you can't fool me, and Man-man is Thakrine's son, I know Bogart, and the drunken chap who started running a whorehouse." She knew every single character in *Miguel Street*.'[41]

The book is a lambent collection of linked stories, written with artful simplicity, depicting life in a Port of Spain street in the 1940s through the eyes of a fatherless boy. Although ethnicity is rarely made explicit in the book, most of the characters are the equivalent of St James or Woodbrook Indians, people with a slim chance of moving out of the ghetto and destitution. The men drink rum, and dream. To escape, they live little fantasies and concoct plans which come to nothing; humour and tragedy are laced together, and the cruelty is absurd. Man-man, for instance, has no luck getting elected to office and so arranges his own crucifixion. When people stone him, at his own instigation, he shouts, ' "Cut it out, I tell you. I finish with this arseness, you hear." . . . The authorities kept him for observation. Then for good.'[42] Popo, a carpenter, is making 'the thing without a name'. B. Wordsworth is writing the greatest poem in the world. George turns his pink house into a brothel for American sailors. Eddoes, who drives a scavenging cart, has shiny shoes and boasts he knows 'everybody important in Port of Spain, from the Governor down'.[43] Elias studies hard and fails exams. ' "Is the English and litritcher that does beat me," ' he says. The narrator adds: 'In Elias's mouth litritcher was the most beautiful word I heard. It sounded like something to eat, something rich like chocolate. Hat said, "You mean you have to read a lot of poultry and thing?" Elias nodded.'[44]

For all its simplicity, Vidia had written an ambitious and remarkable book, sparked in part by the Spanish picaresque romance *Lazarillo de Tormes*, which he had studied and translated at university. To appeal to a British readership, Vidia might have attempted a Mittelholzer-like jungle romance, a clever Oxford novel or something set in Trinidad with English characters; he might even have written of Mr Teughnsend, cultivator of hallotments. Instead, he wrote about an alien world and used strange dialogue. Bar a woman with straw-like hair ('I hated that woman,' notes the narrator) there is scarcely a white character in *Miguel Street*.[45] V.S. Naipaul had turned a slum in Port of Spain into a setting for a universal fable. Pa's legacy, the critical success of Sam Selvon, the high standard set by Henry Swanzy and the encouragement and example of other writers on *Caribbean Voices* convinced Vidia that good literature could be written about his own country. He was a long way from Oxford now, far from the literary canon he had been taught by the dons. His chosen subject was the powerless: those who, although in the majority in the world, had appeared in European literature only as peripheral characters, or at best as Man Friday.

Despite some acts of kindness, the relationships in the book are bleak and survivalist. Men chase women, women try to trap men and 'make baby'; men beat women and women beat children. Hat says of Toni, ' "Is a good thing for a man to beat his woman every now and then, but this man does do it like exercise, man." '[46] If a character on the street tries to sound authoritative, another cuts him down to size. The larger world is unknowable, a place so far away it can only be guessed at, and ignorance makes people invent and falsify. When war breaks out, a pavement commentator says, ' "If they just make Lord Anthony Eden Prime Minister, we go beat up the Germans and them bad bad." '[47] The only character to move beyond this setting is the narrator, who by the end of the book is like a more sophisticated version of Vidia who 'takes rum and women to Maracas Bay for all-night sessions', to his mother's consternation.[48] Ganesh Pundit, 'mystic masseur from Fuente Grove', helps him to obtain an overseas scholarship and leave the island. The narrator walks briskly to the aeroplane, looking only at his shadow before him, a dancing dwarf on the tarmac.

This, then, was the book: but would anyone publish it? Stockbridge liked it, Salkey liked it and Gordon Woolford liked it a great deal. Vidia was loath to ask Calder Marshall for help again. Salkey had a suggestion. At the Piccadilly nightclub where he worked, a louche establishment called the Golden Slipper, he had met an editor from the publishing firm André Deutsch. She was named Diana Athill, moved in bohemian circles and had a weakness for West Indian men. Salkey made contact, and Vidia handed Miss Athill the manuscript in a coffee bar near her office. She remembered him at their first meeting seeming 'very young, just down from Oxford. He appeared absolutely confident in himself, and he was very clever and well read, that was obvious. I was impressed by him.'[49] She read and liked *Miguel Street*, but the eponymous André Deutsch, the Hungarian-born impresario behind the company, thought a book of short stories about Trinidad by an unpublished author was unlikely to sell. The manuscript was passed to the firm's reader, Francis Wyndham, who was as enthusiastic about it as Athill. After some months, she wrote saying they would like to see a novel if he had one, and might publish the stories later. It was the start of a crucial professional relationship for both of them. 'If there hadn't been someone like Diana Athill at the publisher,' Vidia said later, 'my work would never have got going. She was the best editor in the world at that time. I have the utmost regard for her.'[50]

His retrospective view of his fellow immigrant, André Deutsch, was less happy. 'Deutsch was a foolish man, really an illiterate, and he caused me a lot of anguish. He said stories don't sell, and of course *Miguel Street* has not been out of print since it was published. It has not been out of print. He tormented me in that way. So I had to write a novel, and I did *The Mystic Masseur* with great unhappiness.'⁵¹ Quickly, he wrote this new book. It had a similar tone to *Miguel Street*, but was set mainly among rural Indians in Trinidad. It told the story of Ganesh, a character who owes much to Pa's *Gurudeva*. Like Gurudeva, he is a chancer, and progresses from failed teacher to masseur to entrepreneur, ending up as an author and politician. The narrator, who appears at the beginning and end of the book, is like the boy in *Miguel Street*. On the first page he visits Ganesh, the healer. ' "I know the sort of doctors it have in Trinidad," my mother used to say. "They think nothing of killing two three people before breakfast." This wasn't as bad as it sounds: in Trinidad the midday meal is called breakfast.'⁵² The atmosphere and humour were set. Ganesh is cannier than Gurudeva, extorting money from his father-in-law by saying he is establishing a cultural institute in Fuente Grove, a hot, remote village with a single mango tree. He writes and publishes *101 Questions and Answers on the Hindu Religion*; American soldiers visit him for advice. In a narratorial intrusion, the larger implications of the book are suggested: 'I myself believe that the history of Ganesh is, in a way, the history of our times; and there may be people who will welcome this imperfect account of the man Ganesh Ramsumair, masseur, mystic, and, since 1953, M.B.E.'⁵³ By the end, Ganesh is an aspiring statesman named G. Ramsay Muir.

Although most of Vidia's 1955 notebook is buoyant, and revolves around his social activity with his BBC colleagues, towards the end there are the beginnings of a withdrawal. Vidia hated the idea of being rejected by people that he liked. 'The impact made by the discovery that someone, who has kept silent about it, really hates you & has been trying to do you down,' he noted. He saw people less and closed in on himself once Pat moved to London full-time in July. 'My circle of acquaintances grows smaller & smaller,' he wrote. 'I have even dropped out of it.' By the end of the year he had removed himself from his old social circle, established a permanent day-by-day relationship with Pat and begun writing properly. As a writer he was all set; but as a person his interaction and opportunities began to reduce. For Vidia, friendship could never be wholehearted. He could not extend trust to another person: neither at this point, nor later in his life, would he ever reveal or unburden himself in full. 'Never. I wouldn't do it. It's just not my nature. There is no moral quality in it, it's just the way I am. And I have never examined it before.'[54]

On 8 December, less than six months after he began writing *Miguel Street*, Vidia had good news for Ma. His telegram home said simply, 'NOVEL ACCEPTED LOVE. VIDO'.[55] Graham Watson of the literary agency Curtis Brown agreed to take him on as a client, if in a half-hearted way. By now Pat was working as a supply teacher for the London County Council. Vidia received a cheque in the post from Deutsch for £25, with a promise of another £100 to come. 'If it is of any use to you,' he wrote to Miss Athill, 'my telephone number is MAIda Vale 1054.'[56] When finally he deposited the £100 cheque at Barclay's Bank the cashier stood up, leaned over the counter and shook his hand.

News of his marriage to Pat was gushing across the Atlantic. Vidia confirmed the truth to Kamla, but asked her not to tell Ma; only in October did he write the dreaded letter, and his mother's response, written in her curling, spiralling hand, was forceful but magnanimous. 'Congratulation's on your wedding . . . I told Kamla a month before receiving your letter that your not writing home is that you are married . . . Well I am very disappointed that you really don't know your mother . . . In future always remember that I am a very good mother to all my children. I have given all of you freedom to marry who they like, but choose wisely. No secret from now.'[57] For Ma, Kamla, Sati, Savi, Mira, Sewan and Nella, it was not easy to hear of Vido's marriage: it meant that the first son of the family would not be coming home to support them. Pat told her parents, and they responded remarkably warmly by inviting the married couple to spend Christmas with them in Kingstanding. Told of Deutsch's cheque, her father wrote, 'I am very glad to learn that at long last Vidia is getting satisfaction from his publishers. He has been very patient.' In an effort to show acceptance to his son-in-law, Mr Hale tried to get him a ticket to a cricket Test match at Edgbaston. 'Now for news from home. I am sorry to say Uncle Reg died last Saturday . . . Now to more cheerful things. I bought Mummy another budgerigar. Same colour as old Bill.'[58]

Christmas 1955 at 593 Kingstanding Road proved an ordeal. The tiny family flat was owned by Mr Hale's employer, and

BURRELL-DAVIS & GOODE

was painted across the three sash windows in the front room, which had to double as an office for meeting clients. Kingstanding embodied Midlands dreariness, a poor suburb caught between the city and the countryside that was being developed fast and badly in a slum clearance programme. Vidia drank too much in an effort to cope with the unfamiliarity, and Pat made conversation. He remembered: 'It was a terrible experience when I went there for the first time. They were living in a flat, and it had been dreadfully neglected. Everybody was trying to be friendly, but it was painful. I was bored in an hour and I drank a lot of gin.' Going up the wooden steps from the back garden, Pat's sister Eleanor asked Vidia to put on her mother's wartime ARP helmet. 'She got a bat and she hit me on the head. She was about ten or eleven and she thought because of the helmet I would feel nothing. I remember that very well. It was stunning more than painful.'[59] Eleanor, a sporty child with piercing blue-grey eyes who did not share her sister's academic bent and had spent her early life convinced she was a boy, found Vidia to be unexpectedly good company. 'My mother told me Pat was secretly married and I told my best friend and that's how it got back to my father. It was a big disgrace marrying a coloured man. Immigrants were only in Handsworth in Birmingham then . . . Vidia wasn't as I imagined, he was much darker than I thought he would be, and small. I thought he was going to be tall. I remember when we went to a stately home and the guide told us William the Conqueror gave a herd of goats to the original owner, Vidia said, "You get my goat." I thought that was very funny. He was jolly to me, I liked him. When he was young, he was snobbish but he was always joking; later he was just snobbish. My sister always said the Naipauls thought they were better than everyone else.'

Edward and Margaret Hale, Ted and Marg, had almost no point of contact with their new son-in-law. Pat's success at school, a result of the widening of opportunities that had stemmed from the 1944 Education Act, had introduced her to a world far from her origins. Soon after their wedding in Gloucester, Ted had got badly into debt and run off with another woman, but under pressure from her father the marriage was resurrected. Ted sold their house without Marg's knowledge, and they had to move north in disgrace to Birmingham. 'My mother was never a confrontational person,' Eleanor thought. 'If she didn't like something she would moan about it, but not do anything. My mother's family disliked my father, said he came from a family of ne'er-do-wells and his mother had ended up in the workhouse.'[60] During the Second World War, Pat was evacuated to Gloucester to live with Auntie Lu and her maternal grandparents, who manufactured confectionery. She attended a local girls' school, Denmark Road, where she remained through her education, returning the fifty miles to Birmingham only for the holidays. Both her parents supported her intellectual ambitions; her mother was a keen borrower of books from the local public library. In 1943 Pat was awarded a 'special place', which meant her fees were reduced to £6 a year. Intellectual self-improvement was impressed upon the pupils of Denmark Road; Pat took elocution classes at LAMDA and won a distinction.[61] In Eleanor's words: 'Pat was a swot. They taught you the Queen's English, how to say "round" and not "ree-ownd", and not to talk in a Brummie accent.'[62] In her last year, Pat wrote a Chekhovian play called *The School* about progress, sentiment and good Communists, with characters such as 'Ivan Sergeyevich Chubukov . . . a respected and intelligent worker on a collective farm.'[63] She was the only girl in her year at Denmark Road to win a state scholarship to Oxford.[64]

In an autobiographical note written during the days of women's lib and bra-burning in the late 1960s, Pat wrote that she had been liberated from the depressing influence of her mother by her Auntie Lu and cousin Jose: 'I accepted the received doctrine in my immediate family that being a woman was a dreary, dangerous business . . . I remember the red sweater Jo[se] gave me when I was a student. It was figure enhancing . . . She was six years older than me and I worshipped her as a child. "You need a bra." "Mummy, Jose says I need a bra." Words like bra stupefied my mother, let alone more serious matters . . . My tenuous breasts ached under my first bra. I come from a small-breasted family but mine are the smallest . . . I end as I began in the smallest size. But I will not be burning mine. Instead I celebrate the wearing of the bra . . . My happiness was suddenly cut short by the onset of menstruation for which I was totally unprepared. My poor father eventually realised the cause of my distress . . . My aunt, my mother's unmarried sister, was my constant companion as a child. I think she would have liked to be a man. She spoke sadly then of the motorbike she had owned but family pressure had forced her to sell.'[65] In 1975, examining her own behaviour in a diary during a time of trouble, Pat wrote of her mother: 'I think pride entered into her care for me . . . She sacrificed life to self-sacrifice. But the loneliness of life in the flat at Kingstanding must have reinforced her obsessions with her own fate, and with my future.'[66] Like many people, Pat could see the mistakes her parents had made with their lives, but was unable to avoid making different, though related, mistakes in her own. She too would, finally, sacrifice life to self-sacrifice.

CHAPTER TEN

BACK TO THE NEW WORLD

BY THE SUMMER OF 1956, Ma was in a desperate and unhappy state. 'Well as a mother to be so wretched and depending on a daughter for a loaf of bread is a disgrace to the human race,' she wrote in frustration to Vido, hoping he would come home to Trinidad.[1] Despite the pressure to support the family, Kamla was later adamant that she had not minded the obligation: 'Ma felt that she was a burden on me. I never felt that Ma was a burden on me, or that the children were. I never had that feeling. It didn't prevent me from having dates. I had a good life.'[2] Sewan, who was now known more formally as Shiva, wrote to Vidia that their mother had 'not the slightest idea, if and when you are coming'.[3] Before this letter reached him, Vidia wrote to Ma: 'It's all fixed now. I am . . . travelling down by the Cavina, an Elders & Fyffes' banana boat.'[4] The journey aboard the 7,000-ton cargo ship, sailing on one of its last voyages before being scrapped, would take nearly three weeks. Pat would stay in England. Her father wrote in July, 'I do not like the idea of your remaining in London on your own during the absence of Vidia and I suggest you come home for the Vacation . . . Remember me to Vidia. What does he think of this flipping weather.'[5]

At the end of August, Pat and Vidia took the train to Avonmouth on the edge of Bristol, the city where ships had been fitted in the eighteenth century for the Atlantic slave trade. Vidia wrote to her that night on Fyffes Line writing paper. 'I feel more emotion than I showed. As always with these things, the pain comes not with the cut but seconds later. When I came aboard the ship I felt very lonely and afraid and I loved you very much. I know what you feel: I will go away and never come back. It is the same fear that is over me. Am I seeing all this England around me – still around me – for the last time? But I know that I must come back; I want that more than anything else. I want it much more than you do. These people sitting around me at dinner and here as I write in the old-fashioned cosy lounge with chairs upholstered in flowered covers – these people are precisely the people I

fled from, the people who make life in any colony hell. An emptiness
and a horrible egocentricity, a callousness – all these irritations come
out from them. A bit of the Naipaul travelling luck still clings to me.
One man hasn't turned up so – instead of 3, there are only 2 of us
sharing a cabin. And – remember my fears about having my valuables
stolen? – my cabinmate is a Police Sergeant from Trinidad who is
going back after a 6-month course in CID work!' Vidia even apologized
for his anger before departure. 'I don't think I can forgive myself for
my stupid and thoughtless behaviour on Tuesday. Looking back it
seems more and more outrageous and I really am very sorry for it.'[6]

The other passengers were familiar and unfamiliar, part of the West
Indian world that Vidia had escaped and was now recovering. 'I keep
on saying "in this country", "here", "home", when I mean England;
and the W. I.'s aboard look upon me, I imagine, as one of those
affected scholarship chaps. Well, it doesn't matter. I don't think I could
bear the thought of a permanent exile from England.' He sought to
remain aloof, even as he relished their company. He reported shipboard
gossip and manoeuvring. 'What is greatly offending the black people
on this ship – 10 or 12 out of 60 passengers – is the rather ridiculous
adoption of a baby by a Trinidad half-white woman. This gross old
woman made a journey to England especially to get this baby and
anyone who has been to England can see at a glance – saving your
humanitarian sentiments – that the wretched baby has the stupidest and
lowest of English faces; and don't tell me that you can't judge babies.
She paid £25 for this child! And she got it from a Catholic orphanage!
As you can tell, I am a little disgusted by this woman. There are
hundreds of wretched things in Trinidad itself who need care.'

George, the black detective, offered constant entertainment. Vidia
recorded his dialogue in the back of a notebook. 'The ship is going to
rock like a whore', and, 'Man, it was cold and I was feeling for some
"romance". Two months pass and I ain't see nothing coming my way.
I say, George boy, you gotta do something man, I was hurting. Pick
up this Jamaican – ugly like arse – but still, it was cold, you know.
Eat'in, man. Had to have something.' He told Pat 'the Negro detective
is now the most unpopular passenger aboard. He treats the stewards the
way people treat servants in Trinidad and I just sit in my bunk and
watch him . . . I never met a T'dad policeman before and this is a good
opportunity. He is 33, married, the father of five; yet constantly
unfaithful . . . He has told me of all his sexual experiences in London

and he is worried that he might be 'breeding' a girl . . . I like hearing him talk. His language is so vigorous. For example, speaking of two women: "one old, one half-old". Me: "What about the Trinidad prisons now?" He: "Getting better. But the fellers getting away, man." Again: (to me) "What about you, man? You breeding your wife yet?"' George told Vidia he had a love for 'sweet' words 'like "reminiscent" (he read it in a cricket book about the 1939 MCC tour of the West Indies: some bowler was described as being "reminiscent of the great Larwood") . . . Just as I was writing that, he came up and said, "Well, Nawab, what you doing? Writing shorthand?"'

On 2 September Vidia wrote, 'We are in the tropics now. Unmistakably. Coming down to breakfast this morning I saw everybody, many officers & stewards in white . . . Last night was so warm we slept above blankets with the port[hole]s open and the fan going . . . The swimming pool – a rectangular thing constructed from wooden planks and lined with canvas – was put up yesterday and filled with sea water this morning. So far I have not had a swim in it . . . I had forgotten so many things about the hot weather: the intolerable brightness of the light; the sweatiness of the salt at table: it no longer runs; butter melts; ice cream melts; cold water becomes lukewarm in a few minutes; and I have had to have ice in my Guinness.' He visited the ship's radio room to listen to *Caribbean Voices*. 'My voice comes over much better on short wave; but my faults show up badly: particularly my inability to run words together.'

Within days though, his old worries were coming back; he was terrified by the idea of return. 'Frankly, Pat,' he wrote, 'this is one of the most horrible journeys I ever will undertake in my life. I don't mean it purely from the physical point of view. All my conscious life I wanted and strove to get away from the Trinidad atmosphere: to use a horrible word, it is far too "philistine" and I never was at ease in it. And now I find myself right back again in it – and time has done nothing to lessen my discomfort in it. I wonder if you can imagine the fear and the constriction I feel.' The idea of Pat offered him a respite; he could tell her his fears. 'I am missing you and loving you so much I can't know how to say it. I am so worried and a bit of my old nervous problem came over me this afternoon. It is this physical sense of being lost, of being between two worlds and respected in neither that afflicts me. I can't write any more. My eyes are hurting too much.' The next day his eyes were a little better, 'but my nervous depression is so strong. I am beginning to fear that the whole trip might be wasted if the depression doesn't clear up ... I have been thinking all sorts of things. And I have been wondering whether when I come back we shouldn't try to have a baby.' After they reached Barbados, Vidia admitted, 'I shouldn't write this, but I must. Knowing the state of mind better than you do, I did bring the "anxiety" pills with me. I took two yesterday; and using a skin ointment which the Negro detective kindly lent me, there have been no ill effects, and I feel better today. I assure you I thought twenty times before taking those pills. So you can imagine how bad I was!' During their last days at sea, George the detective gave up visiting the dining room and insisted on being served meals in the cabin, to the annoyance of the ship's stewards. After an argument with one of them over a cup of tea, George said to Vidia, ' "Hear what he say? Is only because I black and thing, you know. But he frighten now ... I hurt one report on the captain – no, the chief steward – and he loss his job long time, you know." '

*

On 12 September, the *Cavina* reached Trinidad. 'If you ask for my first impressions it will be of the wealth of the place,' Vidia wrote to Pat. 'It seems to be one of the few places left where people can make money. Kamla showed me the new districts that have been built in the last two years: modern architecture has come to Trinidad.' What future did post-war England offer? 'Do you know, if we both work here we will be able to pull in about £2000 a year right away? We must talk about this seriously when I get back.' He was impressed by his family, by his mother and sisters and brother, and by what they had achieved. 'I left a family poor and rather depressed,' he told Pat, 'now, thanks to Kamla, I find our family not so poor and highly respected. All sorts of local worthies who would never have come home, say four or five years ago, keep coming in ... We were like your family when I left – no friends, no callers. That's changed. And I think it's a good thing. Apparently the Chinese are very loyal friends.' Returning to Nepaul Street 'would have been worth it if only to see the happiness on my mother's face. She was getting so worried; and they tell me that if I had disappointed her this time, she might have gone mad. Her hair is now almost grey ... Everyone at home regrets that you didn't come up with me; but they have a shrewd suspicion that we are even poorer than we make out and they understand.'

On his first afternoon, Vidia went upstairs to lie down on his bed and his little brother came to the room bearing a piece of writing he had done. In a radio tribute to Shiva after his death, Vidia remembered the gesture: 'This moment with Shiva, then eleven, this welcome and affection from someone who was like a new person to me, remains one of the sweetest and purest moments of my life.'[7] He told Pat: 'I am really proud of all my family. The girls, Mira & Savi, rallied round magnificently after my father's death. Savi began to sew clothes: she made about £4 a week for that. The amazing quality about these girls is their great strength. It is a quality that strikes me all the time. Part of it is my father's character; part comes from the years of hardship. Going through the old books in my father's bookcase was a harrowing experience. Poor man, he knew he was going to die many months before he actually did.' He had tragic memories of his father and his kindness. 'Yesterday I actually broke down and wept. I remembered so many things. I remembered the time when money was so scarce. One day I badgered him to take me to the pictures. It was a Sunday & on Sundays the prices are higher. But we had overlooked this. When we got to the cinema we couldn't buy the two seats in the cheapest part in the cinema. I was hurt; but I said to him that he must go in: we were in a queue. So he went in and I returned home crying. Half an hour later, my father came back, very upset and saying nothing. He couldn't stay.' As for Shiva, 'My brother is going to be the Naipaul who will become the writer. At the age of eleven he has already started: he spends much time just writing. And it is good, I tell you.' Shiva would stand in the doorway of Vido's room, watching him as he lay on the bed, smoking cigarettes from a green tin. The sight reminded him of his fading image of Pa.[8] Savi remembered Shiva's fascination with Vidia, whom he saw less as a brother than as a missing father figure. 'Vidia couldn't be that. He wasn't cold to him . . . but I don't remember seeing him putting an arm around somebody. I saw him being very sympathetic to people with problems later on, but at that age I don't think my brother ever hugged me, or anyone.'[9]

After a few days, Vidia began to see Trinidad in a more splintered light. 'My accent, darlin, is killing people over here and I am frightened to open my mouth. People take me for a foreigner and therefore do their best to overcharge me.' His uncle Simbhoo was now a major figure in the People's Democratic Party or PDP. With Bhadase Sagan Maraj, Simbhoo had visited India and secured money from the Birla business family to build schools for Hindus and improve literacy, although the Birlas later withdrew funding when Maraj refused to keep accounts.[10] Indians were feeling a new sense of entitlement. As freedom loomed for Trinidad and Tobago, ethnic tensions grew and Vidia became frightened, far from England, 'People talk more loudly; they shout easily; windows and doors are open and every sound can enter your house ... In Trinidad nature is a fertile, swift and violent thing. Even the ordinary grass looks as though it might grow overnight into some mighty man-eating plant. Coconut trees, mango-trees, trees whose name I have forgotten: they all grow in Port of Spain. The trees are higher and the branches low; and it looks just as if the jungle is merely suffering Port of Spain to exist, and might at any time change its mind. The other impression is of the surliness of the Negro lounging at the street corners. They are crude and nasty; and there has been a recent mob-movement which has made things a little ugly ... Yesterday I went with my uncle's election motor parade through Caroni and − of course − we ran into a lot of trouble. There was a riot. People were beaten up. Forty were arrested. Bottles, stones, & knives were used.' Later Vidia said, 'My uncle was taking part in the election campaign. He was a kind of joke figure for me, [but] he thought I would appreciate the humour of the whole thing, so he took me around.'[11]

As the weeks ran by, Vidia's instinctive Indian, or Hindu, exclusivity, which had in the past been expressed more through comedy than enmity, changed gear. It was an irreversible shift; like Trinidad itself, V.S. Naipaul went through a hardening of racial attitudes in 1956. Old relationships died as old certainties unravelled. Even when he saw a friend like WAGS, something seemed different. 'He was a very generous boy, generous at heart,' Vidia remembered years later, 'he actually came to the house to see me. I was moved by that. But even then, there was the racial politics that had occurred in Trinidad. He was on the side of the Negro party, so an odd thing had happened. Something had fractured.'[12] A powerful new political force had emerged under the leadership of Dr Eric Williams: the People's National Movement or PNM. The broadly Hindu and loose-knit PDP was losing ground to this tightly controlled new party. Although Indians such as Dr Winston Mahabir, a Presbyterian island scholar, and the broadcaster Kamaluddin Mohammed, a Muslim, joined Williams and became PNM candidates, most Indians were unnerved by what they saw as a monolithic black movement, and some even planned to emigrate to the UK, Canada or elsewhere. The Hindu proclivities of Simbhoo's movement pushed Indian Muslims into the arms of the PNM. Vidia said later, 'There was a divide in Trinidad which came about with Eric Williams. He co-opted the Muslims into his Negro party.'[13] For Vidia at this time, Williams was one among several aspiring politicians, an island scholar who had been to St Catherine's Society, an undistinguished off-shoot of Oxford University. 'The Negro leader is a dictator-like fellow (St. Cath's man) and if he says he is not racialist – ie <u>anti</u> non-Negro – his canvassers say it for him. The Negroes don't want to discuss. You cannot say anything about their leader. Their bullies heckle and break up other speakers' meetings and preserve order at their own. The police and the civil service are all Negro. So one has no defence at all.'

Born in 1911, the eldest of twelve children in a mixed black and French creole family, Eric Williams had attended Tranquillity and Queen's Royal College before winning an island scholarship. He took a First in history at Oxford, became a professor at Howard, the black university in Washington DC, and published books including *Capitalism and Slavery* (1944), which proposed the revolutionary thesis that the rise of industrial capitalism in Britain had depended on the West Indian slave trade, and that slavery had been abolished primarily for economic reasons. The latter point is arguable, but Williams was the first indigenous, qualified Caribbean historian to contradict and rewrite accepted British versions of history. Returning to Trinidad, he held public seminars and wrote didactic articles about the virtues of national development for the *Trinidad Guardian*. In 1955 he engineered his own dismissal from an official body, the Caribbean Commission, and the following year founded the PNM, the first political party in Trinidad able to project itself as a disciplined, progressive national grouping capable of taking the country to independence.

Clever, small, touchy, deaf and opaque, wearing dark glasses and with a cigarette stuck to his lower lip, 'The Doc' rapidly became a national figure. He produced a party newspaper which was endorsed by George Lamming, and later edited by his friend and mentor C.L.R. James. He attracted prominent candidates such as the famous cricketer Learie Constantine. In a radical move, Williams gave bombastic talks about subjects such as Caribbean agriculture, slavery or economic history to crowds of semi-literate supporters across the country, telling them 'the only university in which I shall lecture in future is the University of Woodford Square and its several branches throughout the length and breadth of Trinidad and Tobago.'[14] Crucially he drew in both the respectable creole middle class and poor black voters, many of whom took to his cause with fervour. After centuries of oppression, it was a potent combination: here was a local black man, Oxford-returned, who had beaten the colonizers at their own intellectual game and could also appeal to the street. One follower described him as 'a modern-day Christ'.[15] Back in London, the civil servants at the Colonial Office, as so often in such situations, missed the point: an official described his lectures on constitutional reform as 'almost a case for a psychiatrist ... it surprises me that an audience can be collected for this kind of thing.'[16] But the audience did collect, and Dr Williams narrowly won the election of 1956, with the PNM forming the first party government in Trinidad.[17] In *A Way in the World*, V.S. Naipaul would write of the electoral campaign: 'The meetings were billed as educational; the square was described as a university. People hadn't of course gone to learn anything; they had gone to take part in a kind of racial sacrament.'[18]

On 29 September, Vidia told Pat: 'My uncle won a seat in the General Election on Tuesday; but the opposition Party won 13 out of the 24 seats & they are going to form the government. This winning party is a Negro party and their victory has not only made it embarrassing for any non-Negro to walk P.O.S. streets, but has got every other community very worried. In this election the Negroes were united and they won their majority largely because the opposition vote was hopelessly split. Strange alliances are being formed now – Hindus, Big Business, and Roman Catholics, Whites, Chinese, Syrians and Indians. After the victory Jean was accosted by a Negro in the market, "Aye, you Indian women got to make yourself nice now for nigger man." That is one example of (perhaps insignificant) offensiveness. But if this becomes the official policy, Trinidad will be hell to live in.' Offensiveness begat offensiveness: 'the noble nigger is really a damned nasty nigger. You should be here to see it for yourself. The galling thing is that these very people who are so offensive over here go to England and whine for tolerance! Even children hurl abuse at you in the streets. You should see it. You will find it very revealing.' He might have added that Simbhoo's colleagues spent almost as much time accusing each other of fraud, and denouncing each other for embezzlement, as they did fighting Dr Williams.

A week later, Vidia wrote to Pat again. In contrast to his letters of 1954, in which he excoriated the side effects of the British empire, here he expressed a rare nostalgia for colonial rule: 'I am not staying here much longer. If the election results were different, there might have been some point. But with the present government of noble niggers, all sorts of racialist laws might be passed; and life for minority communities could become tricky. Indians are talking of leaving; so are the Chinese. Because of its very smallness and unimportance in the world, the grossest injustices can be perpetrated here without people in England getting to know. And injustices – against individuals – are being done all the time. The police force is of course made up of the dregs of the noble nigger nation. And their crudity and bullying has to be seen. I don't want anybody to talk to me of S. Africa and the Southern States again. I would prefer a hundred times to be ruled from London, as in the old days, then to be ruled by the present people. Because, in this place, the Englishman's sense of justice and fair play shines like a jewel. If my uncle's party had got into power, they were going to staff the Police Force with English officers; the Civil Service with English heads of department – just to have fair play.' Vidia said later: 'I was extremely shocked when I went back by the racial conditions in Trinidad. I was outraged. My relations with Negroes have not been the same ever since, and there is nothing I can do about it. I was writing to Pat and I was delighting in shocking her.'[19]

Aged just twenty-four, he believed that his future as a Trinidadian was now fatally circumscribed, and that he would need to look to a new, wider identity. 'I don't know what's going to happen to me with the BBC when I get back. But I am not really worried. But I would really prefer not to have anything to do with the W. Indies in that way, since we Indians really have no stake at all here and we are rapidly being pushed into the position where we will have to become the Jews of the area: in business, etc., since other fields are closed to us.' Mr Sohun, the schoolmaster in Seepersad Naipaul's *Gurudeva and other Indian Tales*, had identified the invidious position of the island's Indians some years before: 'The difficulty lies in the fact that you are too much of a majority to assimilate, too much of a minority to dominate.'[20]

*

Vidia's younger sisters Savi, Sati, Mira and Nalini (or Nella) found their returning elder brother hard to handle. Savi remembered him being 'very critical about everything, never encouraging, never positive. As I grew older I began to understand this attitude of his a little bit more, but when I was that age, I don't think we appreciated the constant criticism. We were teenagers. We seemed to have nothing in common with him. So I would tell you honestly my sister and I used to hide, to keep away from him. I was considered very difficult because too many boys would call. If you were attractive it meant you were not concentrating on your lessons.' Ma was 'overjoyed to see Vidia but I think Vidia also became very difficult

with her. He wanted her to be what she was not, what she was never
educated to be. She was also menopausal which he wouldn't have
understood. I think she would have become like a weepy, wimpering,
complaining woman to him.'[21] Savi felt Vidia's attitude to his mother and
siblings persisted over the decades. 'He harboured some kind of desire for
us to do well, to do things. He still has it. As far as he is concerned none
of our children has done anything even though ninety per cent of them
have a university degree.'[22]

As the politics of the West Indies altered, the family politics of the
Capildeos and the Naipauls remained as fraught as ever. Vidia saw few of
his cousins except Owad and Jean. Meeting one of the Mausis during a
visit to Chaguanas, he blanked her in the street, only realizing later the
rudeness of what he had done. He advised Pat to stop seeing and helping
his relations in London. 'Heaven know, what your friends must think of
me when they see those cousins of mine. I really can't tell you how much
I dislike this do-gooding. It isn't wise. In fact, it can lead to a lot of
trouble.' The effect of being back in a family atmosphere with his sisters
and brother softened Vidia, and made him think again of having children
of his own. He wrote to Pat, 'I love you so completely that I am half lost
without you, and I do believe that we should see about having a baby
when I get back to London. Something very strange is happening to me. I
am beginning to like other people's children and I actually talk to strange
children in the street. I love you and I miss every part of you – physically
and in every other way.' In later years, when it became clear that he and
Pat were unable to have children, he would assert that he had never
wanted them in the first place: 'I remember in that wretched house in Petit
Valley making a decision never to have children of my own. I made a
decision at the age of ten which I have adhered to, and not for a moment
regretted.' A fact decided by human biology would be presented as a
triumph of the will: 'It would have been impossible with my work. I just
hated the idea of children. I made that decision in Petit Valley, very
consciously.'[23]

He told Pat about everyday life in Trinidad. Savi was making dresses
for her, and wanted precise measurements. Was her waist really 24 inches?
He had visited the beach, hurt his toe, had asthma attacks and been on a
happy trip to Cedros with Owad and Jean. 'Cedros is at the S.E. tip of
Trinidad – an 80 mile drive from Port of Spain. Owad was making the
run because he is Chief Labour Inspector. Last Friday we went. It was a
beautiful drive. Jean kept on saying how she wished you were with us.'

Vidia even made an effort to learn to drive, and in early November passed a test which gave him a licence 'and an international driving permit; so I will be able to drive your father's car when I get back . . . I don't believe I really deserved the licence.' Pat, who was spending most weekends in Kingstanding, replied to his letters briefly. Her father hoped they would come for Christmas. 'He wants to go out to lunch on Boxing Day as we did last year. He said he enjoyed it very much. Doesn't time fly? It seems such a short while since you were trying to warm that bottle of wine in front of the fire.'

Pat was required to represent Vidia in his dealings with the BBC over *B. Wordsworth*, a radio play he had adapted from a chapter in *Miguel Street*. It told the story of a chancer and poet, Black Wordsworth ('White Wordsworth was my brother. We share one heart') and his relationship with a young boy and his mother. 'My name is to be V.S. Naipaul (not Vidia N). I am not to be described as a West Indian; but as a "Trinidadian of Hindu descent". I insist on these things . . . 6666!' Pat offered counsel. 'You've got to be able to get along comfortably with people . . . "A Trinidadian of Hindu Descent." Forgive us darling but it is rather funny & quite incomprehensible to a listener.'[24]

Vidia was not feeling optimistic about his future as a writer. He even thought the Suez Crisis might undermine it. 'What about this Egypt thing? It has me a little worried. People here criticise the British & French; but I don't see what other steps they could have taken . . . all I hope is that it doesn't spread. If it does my literary career will be nipped in the very smallest of buds. I am not coming back to London with any great love in my breast for *Caribbean Voices*. Because of my association with the programme I have had to mix with the literary boys over here and those things, as you know, really sicken me. The men are bad enough; but the drooling women are even worse. And one rather ghastly feature of the thing in Trinidad is the expatriate Englishmen & women going "native". They seem to become so stupid and despicable as soon as they start seeing vigour in all that is black and "primitive". They have been satirised for so long you would have thought that they would have died out – but, no, they carry on exactly as one imagines, larger than life. People here drink scotch. These people insist on rum. They are a sad, degenerate lot.'

Vidia felt sad and elated and sad, in emotional turmoil as he visited the home that was no longer his home. 'My depression is largely due to worry about my own future. Over here one is surrounded so obviously by people who are better off – people who have no more to offer than myself and people who started like myself.' Trinidad had supplied him with a stock of new material. 'From the writing point of view, this land is pure gold. I know it so well, you see. Pure, pure gold ... Trinidad is a funny place. It has a population less than Nottingham's yet, while Churchill calls England an island, they call T'dad a country. And really it is hard to feel while you are here that Trinidad really is small. Jamaica is even worse. Jamaica is the world for Jamaicans.'

Throughout his two months in Trinidad, consciously and subconsciously, he was collecting ideas. 'I met the original of "Hat" shortly after getting here. He really is a surly man and the years are making him surlier. Of course we never were really friends. He only knew me as the bright boy in the street. Yet he gave me a choice mango the other day. He told my mother, "I have a mango for Vido." And when he saw me he just gave me the mango with a "Here, I have this for you," and walked off without another word. And would you believe it, I met a real-life Ramlogan! He keeps a dingy little shop in one of the remote villages of my uncle's constituency. Physically he fits the role to perfection. Only, he doesn't wear a striped blue shirt – only a dingy vest. He behaves like my Ramlogan too. He vowed eternal support to my uncle, assured him that the election was won; yet all along he was for the other candidate, as we discovered only on election day! And his name is of course Ramlogan. M. Ramlogan, licensed to SEEL SPRITUOUS LIQERS BY RETAIL. If we come to Trinidad I will make a point of taking you to see the man and his shop.' He had plans for a new novel. As *Miguel Street* captured life in Port of Spain, so he would describe a rural Caribbean election. 'I have an idea for a light novelette. In the country villages here elections are great excitements; election day is a day of fête. The poor candidate pours out money and rum and food. Into such a village – presided over by our good friend Ramlogan (of course he is in league with both candidates: he supplies rum to both) – into such a village comes "party politics". Politicians refuse to bribe. No rum. No food. In fact, there is talk that the local committees should fête their candidates and not vice versa. Imagine the upheaval in the village. The helplessness of the electors. The helplessness of those important gentlemen who "control" fifty or sixty votes. The anger of the village. The boycott of the election. The declaration against both parties, etc. What do you think, Mrs Naipaul?' The book would be the short and entertaining comic novel *The Suffrage of Elvira*.

*

In the second week of November 1956, Vidia said goodbye to his family in Port of Spain and sailed for Kingston, Jamaica. There he would board the *Golfito*, a small turbine steamer which plied the route to Southampton on the south coast of England. He was unhappy to be leaving, but confident he would soon be back. In Jamaica he stayed with old family friends, the Tewaris. Norman Rae, an Oxford friend who had joined the Banana Board of Jamaica, took him around and was 'really extremely kind and helpful.' Vidia was carrying home-made dresses for Pat, and was even trying to find a present for her father. He made a partial and failed attempt to retain a ring for her; like his wedding certificate, it soon vanished: 'My eldest aunt gave me a ring for you. She has had it for years and years. A simple, well-wrought, gold ring. I put the ring in the fob of my trousers; forget it there, take everything out from the trousers but the ring, and send the trousers to be pressed. Of course the ring disappears.' On arrival at Waterloo on the boat train, he wanted her to meet him, but none of his cousins. 'I don't want to see anyone but you,' he wrote, and Pat obliged.

Travelling back to the mother country, missing his mother, he wrote fondly to her on Fyffes Line writing paper. 'I do feel so sad leaving home. When I left in 1950 I was all eagerness and anxiety, ready to get away as quickly as possible. It was different yesterday.' He felt guilty that he had been cruel on his last day. 'Poor Ma, I did give you a rough time, didn't I? But you mustn't mind; and you mustn't worry.' The ship had sailed late, watched by a big crowd who 'had come to see off a red nigger woman who now sits opposite me in the dining room. Poor thing, she was so frightened at the thought of travelling alone for the first time out of Trinidad at the age of thirty-five. She palled up with me and begged me in case of any alarm or trouble to come and look after her.' Vidia amused himself by teasing her. 'The red nigger woman is really delightfully simple. You know, in ships, the chairs and tables are all chained to the floor to prevent them rolling about the place when the sea gets rough. I told the woman that the tables and chairs were chained to prevent people stealing them. And, she believed it. "Eh, eh," she said, "But look at that, eh." And again: passengers in different parts of the ship are assigned to different lifeboats (there are 6 on the Golfito). I told her that she had to find out which lifeboat was hers because, in case of any trouble, they were not going to let her get into any old lifeboat. In fact, if they found her in the wrong boat they were going to throw her into the sea. It was, I told her, the origin of the phrase "to be in the wrong boat."'

Back in St Julian's Road, it was Vido who wondered whether he was in the wrong boat, or an alien land. 'Well here I am back in London. It is rather cold and it is so strange to slip into bed between ice cold sheets,' he told Ma. His letter was a rare and honest statement of his deeper feelings about Britain; he felt caught between islands, between cultures. 'My publisher tells me that the book will not be coming out in March but in August next year. That is, 20 months after it was written. I can't tell you how horribly disappointed I am. I am really feeling pretty low and desperate. I can't even do any writing because I am feeling I am such a failure and such a fool. I just feel my present life has got to change or I will just break up under the strain . . . I feel that I am dreaming now in London. I felt much more at home with you than I do here in London. It all does seem strange to me – as though I have never been here before.'

He wondered whether Deutsch's verbal assurances were worth any-thing, and wrote to him in anguish: 'My other book, *Miguel Street*, you have now had sixteen months; no agreement has been made or is likely to be made soon.'[25] The anger he felt against his non-publisher was abruptly converted into creative energy, and he wrote *The Suffrage of Elvira* at great speed, alternating with work at the BBC. The process of writing distracted him from his fear about his future, his money worries and his anger against Deutsch. 'I raged,' he said later, 'impotent rage. I had no power, and out of that rage I wrote the third book, about an election in Trinidad. This is where the comic attitude conceals much pain and much difficulty.'[26] He told his mother he still hoped to pay for Mira's education, feeling it was his duty: 'I have begun a new novel and have written 10,000 words since last week Wednesday. I believe it is going to come out all right; but with novels you never know. This one is about the elections; but there is a crazy twist to the whole story. I think of home all the time. I always look at the clock and wonder what time it is in Trinidad and wonder what you are doing.'[27]

Early in the new year, he described his daily routine to Ma. Pat woke him 'at about 7.40 – usually in a panic because she fears she is going to be late at school. I pour out the coffee; go downstairs in my pyjamas and bathrobe for the newspaper and read it over coffee. Pat leaves about eight. I read and smoke until 8.30. Then I wash up and make up the bed and set to work. For lunch (in the weekdays) I have a tin of soup – Heinz Vegetable, Crosse & Blackwell Cream of Chicken and Cream of Mush-room – and this is quite simple and more than enough.' Writing to Kamla, he said he was seeking a post in the new Federation of the West Indies, an attempt to unify the islands of the region in a political bloc. 'I have already told old Willy Richardson that if there are any good jobs going in the Federal set-up, I am ready, provided the money is enough ... I am so glad I came home. I cannot tell you what it has done for me. I no longer feel separated from you. It seems that you are all within my reach and I have no fears at all that we will ever lose touch. Give my love to Ma; tell her that I think of her a lot, with much love and gratitude for her patience and her love which never seems to grow weary, despite all that we, thoughtless children, say or do. I struck Shivan once or twice. I cannot say how bitterly I regret that now; at times I almost wish the hand that struck would drop off.'[28]

At the start of June 1957, nearly two years to the day since he started *Miguel Street*, Vidia was able to tell Ma about the reaction of the critics to *The Mystic Masseur*. 'They are really rather good reviews for a first novel by a completely unknown writer ... And I believe I will be able to send some sums of money home.' He had watched a Test match in Birmingham: 'It was perfect weather for cricket; the result is: I am as black as anything now.' A month later, he and Pat shifted to a new flat in Muswell Hill in the further reaches of north London. 'We had to spend a lot of money on the move,' he told Ma. 'Moving itself cost us about $10. Then we had to buy a carpet sweeper ($7.40); a mop ($6); a draining board for the sink ($6.60) ... The people before us left it in a filthy state ... Dirt doesn't matter in Trinidad, with all doors and windows open all the time; but in England where rooms are kept enclosed most of the time, dirt matters. If I did no more than pull a window open, my hands smelled afterwards. The kitchen was the foulest place of all.'[29] Like a tiger-cub bringing home his first kill, he copied out extracts for his mother from the reviews.

The *Sunday Express* critic called *The Mystic Masseur* 'The deftest and gayest satire I have read in years.' The *Sunday Times* decided he was 'a sophisticated and witty young Trinidad novelist who immediately takes a front-line place in the growing West Indian school.' Vidia wrote out the entire *Daily Telegraph* review for his mother, including the lines: 'V.S. Naipaul is a young writer who contrives to blend Oxford wit with home-grown rumbustiousness and not do harm to either. He is a kind of West Indian Gwyn Thomas [a Welsh novelist and radio personality of the moment] — pungent, charitable, Rabelaisian, who deals with the small change of human experience as though it were minted gold.'[30] Ma reported that 200 copies of the book had been sold in Trinidad, and that she now needed a regular income to relieve Kamla. 'I bought gas, paid for light, paid for Meera glasses, and I kept $5 to do a puja for the success of your book.' When Mira read the book, she wrote: 'Boy, I really enjoyed it, and laughed like mad. Ma's family sure got their share.'[31]

The notices were mainly enthusiastic, but patronizing. Diana Athill thought its reception was helped by a passing British interest in new writing from the colonies, and particularly the West Indies; at the time, 'it was easier to get reviews for a writer seen by the British as black than it was for a young white writer, and reviews influenced readers a good deal more then than they do now.'[32] In the *New Statesman*, Anthony Quinton described *The Mystic Masseur* as 'yet another piece of intuitive or slap-happy West Indian fiction as pleasant, muddled and inconsequent as the Trinidadian Hindus it describes . . . This is an agreeable book but I wonder if it really deserves a Book Society recommendation.' V.S. Naipaul's writing was 'as sharp as a mango'; he was one of the 'calypso novelists' who were putting 'colour and punch into British writing'. In the West Indies, reaction was subtler. Writing in *Bim*, Frank Collymore commended Naipaul's willingness to satirize his own community with 'ironic detach-ment' at a time when 'the propaganda and clichés of emergent nationhood are so apt to occasion all the ill-effects of self-complacency.' The *Trinidad Chronicle* was even more enthusiastic, calling it 'the cleverest satire yet on Trinidad life . . . One has to know Trinidad to know that it could only happen here.'[33]

Looking back, Vidia remembered only the worst aspects – or his own version – of the reviews: 'Anthony Quinton actually said it's a bad book. Imagine not understanding the originality of the writing, the clarity and the humour . . . but these were the days when my kind of writing, my kind of person, was not taken seriously. John Bayley in *The Spectator* was very patronizing and said it was a "little savoury". There was an extraordinary review in the *Telegraph* by an academic called Peter Green. To my utter amazement he said I was looking down my Oxford nose at my people. This is the left-wing attitude – that if you are Indian, you cannot write humour; humour is for the bigger, the more secure cultures.'[34] Bayley's rankling words would be reworked years later. Looking for reviews of his first book, Willie Chandran finds the sentence: 'Where, after the racy Anglo-Indian fare of John Masters, one might have expected an authentic hot curry, one gets only a nondescript savoury, of uncertain origin . . .'[35]

In April of the following year, *The Suffrage of Elvira* was published. Penelope Mortimer in the *Sunday Times* commended it as 'a beautifully contained and balanced book . . . extremely funny and accurately cruel' filled with 'such remarkably rich and curious dialogue, that Mr Naipaul easily earns the title of a new Damon Runyon.'[36] Writing in *Punch*, Anthony Powell thought V.S. Naipaul showed 'unusual elegance and sense of style, though his characters need possibly a little more depth.'[37] The most astute assessment came from the novelist Kingsley Amis, who had recently risen to prominence with *Lucky Jim*. After giving Jan Carew and Edgar Mittelholzer some compliments and swipes, he noted that Naipaul's narrative was 'concerned with small-scale stratagems between neighbours, in-laws or rivals. It gradually dawns upon one that this humour, conducted throughout with the utmost stylistic quietude, is completely original.'[38] On *Caribbean Voices*, Arthur Calder Marshall praised the scope of the book; he thought it 'the more effective as satire because it is so free from ill-temper' and compared it to Dickens's writing on elections in rotten boroughs in *The Pickwick Papers*: 'Naipaul's gentle pillory may have an influence on West Indian politics for many years to come.'[39] Calder Marshall was perceptive; politicians would often refer to *The Suffrage of Elvira*, and half a century on the political theorist Lloyd Best, Vidia's contemporary at QRC, was recommending it to his students. Best called *The Suffrage of Elvira* the most important of Naipaul's novels 'in terms of political and social impact. He really founded a whole new school of empirical political science, in that he saw how the society worked, as distinct from how people thought it ought to work. In those days, that was almost impossible, with the colonial film on your eyes. People couldn't tell perception from reality, and he was absolutely lucid as to how the political system really worked, and how people actually behaved.'[40]

In 1959, the year in which Vidia won an entry in *Who's Who*, André Deutsch Limited published *Miguel Street*. Vidia had written to Francis Wyndham, 'I don't believe a word A.D. says but if they are sending off *Miguel Street* to the printers, I hope you prepare it for press and I hope you write the blurb.'[41] The *Times Literary Supplement* thought Naipaul had a 'fresh and original talent' and an ability to show the humanity of the very poor.[42] Reviewing him beside Anthony Burgess, the *Sunday Times* reviewer called him 'another exotic gentleman . . . an intellectual in a zoot-suit . . . But even at half throttle he's good enough to make most of the professional Caribbean boys look a bit silly.'[43] The *News Chronicle* concluded that 'the time has come for Mr Naipaul to move on to something bigger.'[44] In the *West Indian Gazette*, Arthur Drayton was full of praise for the dialogue and the mix of tragedy and farce, but thought the author showed 'diffidence in facing up to the sociological implications of his material', an ideological complaint that was to be repeated by critics and readers from the Caribbean and elsewhere in years to come.[45] V.S. Naipaul was making his name. The *Observer* had given him 'a rave review', he told Kamla. Despite his rapid success, he wanted more, and faster: 'I seem destined to make my way very slowly.'[46]

CHAPTER ELEVEN

'HE ASKED FOR 10 GNS!!'

As HIS LITERARY REPUTATION DEVELOPED, Vidia's relationship with the BBC frayed; *Caribbean Voices* was a place of opportunity, but it was also a racial ghetto. When he tried to get work on the General Overseas Service in 1958, a producer, the children's writer Mary Treadgold, told him it was impossible: 'The lady said, "We can't employ you, you are not a European." I think she was representing [official BBC] policy. I was furious. But that was how it was ... I cannot express to you sufficiently, this determination to be a writer, to write.'[1] The late 1950s were a time of change for Vidia and for England; race riots broke out in Notting Hill; social deference was in decline; the Suez debacle had induced a new mood of national insecurity; tall concrete buildings were sprouting across the nation's cities; teenagers were noticed and given voice by Colin MacInnes in his novel *Absolute Beginners*. Post-war hardship had been replaced by expectation, but much of this cultural shift was apparent only in retrospect, and Vidia still struggled to make his way. He applied to become a BBC general trainee, and the novelist Anthony Powell was persuaded to put up a letter of support stating that V.S. Naipaul had 'literary gifts and a general intelligence of a lively and uncommon order'.[2] Vidia's memory of the interview panel was vivid: 'They were sniggering as I entered; all of them were sniggering. There was a man there called Laurence Gilliam, famous as a so-called features writer, producer. He asked what I wanted to do. I said I wanted to do some features and they roared with laughter, as though I had said I wanted to write the Bible ... It was the historical moment. You couldn't be a [racial] victim in the 1950s. There wasn't the market. And these men have vanished and I have survived. But even at the time I knew they were fools.'[3]

Even with published novels under his belt, he was not able to break through and have his work read on a mainstream BBC service. The manuscript of *Miguel Street* was sent to the head of the Third Programme, the novelist P.H. Newby (who in 1969 would win the first

Booker Prize). Newby noted in an internal memo that he was disappointed by V.S. Naipaul's stories. 'He lacks the discipline you need to
write concisely and he hasn't even been able to set his material in
perspective . . . It surprises me that he has succeeded in persuading a
publisher to bring it out.'[4] The year saw further squabbles. Vidia left
the building when Leonie Cohn, a producer on the Third Programme,
told him to wait for five minutes, which provoked a flurry of internal
memos. In July 1958 he was asked to produce a piece on Thackeray's
Vanity Fair for the Colonial Schools Unit. On the booking form,
someone has scrawled, 'He asked for 10 gns!! Rang him cancelling the
project.'[5] By August, it had been decided that with so many West
Indian writers now in England, *Caribbean Voices* had served its purpose
and a literary discussion programme would replace it. Vidia wrote a
script for the penultimate broadcast, praising the legacy of Henry
Swanzy and saying how much he had learned from the show. He took
a swipe at bad literature, and introduced a story by an undergraduate,
Frank Birbalsingh, adding that he would hate it if, 'on the strength of
this acceptance, he decides to make writing his profession.'[6]

The broadcast led to a permanent rupture, made worse for Vidia by
the knowledge that he was in the wrong. When he turned up late to
record his script, the BBC cut his fee. He wrote to them in fury that
they were being 'insolent and ungracious . . . I grant that I made an
error and arrived late at the studio. But I arrived in time to hear the
first words of my script being read. The producer, following the
traditions of this secret service, told me nothing even at that time. It
was left for me to ask whether my script was being read for me. I got
a mere nod in reply. This colonial insolence is in itself intolerable.' The
producer in question was the competent Billy Pilgrim; aside from
sharing a name with the hero of Kurt Vonnegut's yet-to-be-published
Slaughterhouse-Five, Pilgrim was a Guianese musician and wartime
RAF veteran. An internal file – 'THE NAIPAUL CASE' – was created
to investigate the matter. It reveals that Pilgrim had expressed surprise
'that Vidia Naipaul, himself a former editor of "Caribbean Voices" and
a frequent broadcaster, should be so haphazard about matters of timing.'
The upshot was that Vidia was sent a letter of reprimand: 'You arrived
in the studio about 12.25 p.m. *when the recording had been completed* and
when one paragraph of the first page was being repeated for editing
purposes. As you spoke to [Billy Pilgrim] just after the ten second cue
was given, he held his hand up as he wanted silence.' Vidia, in shamed

fury, did not reply.[7] His retrospective comment was, 'I broke with the BBC. It was my misfortune to be thrown among second-rate people while I was trying to make a living.'[8] So it goes.

Only in 1960 did his star begin to rise again. Vidia gave talks on women's magazines, literary counties, bohemian novels, the working class in books and the shortcomings of authors such as Anthony Trollope and Patrick Leigh Fermor when they wrote about the Caribbean. Soon, he was back in dispute. The BBC Home Service – he was out of the ghetto now – wanted him to give a talk, but he demanded double the standard rate. 'If he could be shown to have a stature above that of the general run of literary contributors to the quality press and journals, we would certainly consider putting his rate up,' the talks booking manager noted in a memo. What was his status now? Did V.S. Naipaul deserve more than the oenophile Cyril Ray, who was paid thirty guineas for 1,000 words?[9] In August 1960, hearing that he was planning to make his first visit to his ancestral land, the Third Programme tried to sign up 'Mr V.S. Naipaul, the novelist and critic' to write a script 'about his first sight of India'. They offered the sum of eighty guineas, ten times what he had been paid for his early short stories. A letter came back from a representative of his agent, Curtis Brown, stating that Mr Naipaul 'has asked me to inform you that he considers this offer an insult', with a PS: 'Sorry about this!' A BBC memo concluded that 'in view of his outside reputation' the price should be raised to 120 guineas. He accepted, and with his renown both as a writer and as a tricky customer well established, V.S. Naipaul was on his way.[10]

*

While Vidia waited for royalties to arrive from André Deutsch, he made a temporary excursion into the world of conventional employment. After the death of her husband, Jill Brain had decided to make a fresh start by taking a teaching job in Rome. Her job as an editorial assistant at the Cement & Concrete Association in Grosvenor Gardens was going begging, and she suggested Vidia might like it. Although he turned up forty minutes late for the interview in the summer of 1957, Vidia was offered a position on their magazine at a salary of £1,000 a year. It enabled him to send money home to Ma. Jill described the C&CA as 'a truly weird outfit, and I well remember my dismay when I found out that being a dogsbody for them was all that my nice new degree seemed to qualify me to do. It was an association of British cement manufacturers, but for some reason they were determined to prove they had an aesthetic side, and published a magazine called *Concrete Quarterly* which was all about the architectural beauties of prestressed concrete buildings.'[11] Vidia was not cut out for office work: 'I lasted about ten weeks. It was awful. Nothing is as bad as working for people who are your inferiors. I was living in a flat in Muswell Hill, the top flat, in one of those red brick houses, so I would take the bus from Victoria to Muswell Hill. It was a long journey. I was exhausted because, young as I was, the fumes even then always took away my energy.' He produced articles 'praising the concrete. You were required to spin it out.' One day he went to have his hair cut, and when he returned, 'the lady who was running my department made a scene about it. I literally left that minute; I left so precipitately that my books, a few Penguin books and paperbacks that I had in my drawer, I had to go back and collect.'[12]

Vidia would use the office environment of the C&CA in *Mr Stone and the Knights Companion*. He met and made a good friend there, Ralph Ironman, a technical writer who had served in the war and now worked in the same office. 'That was one of the nicest things to come out of the Cement & Concrete Association, that friendship with Ironman.'[13] Together with Pat, he spent time with Ralph and his wife, Mary, and with their daughters Anne and Lotta. Ralph Ironman liked Vidia at once. 'I think we got on so well because both of us enjoy a good sense of humour . . . Pat was a very sweet girl. She, of course, supported him by her teaching job while he strived to become a writer . . . I do remember that our lady boss said that Vidia "couldn't write"! I spotted immediately that his command of English was superb.'[14] They would go for lunch together at a girls' cookery school where food was served at cost price, and Ironman noticed that although Vidia was 'very tightfisted', he had extravagant ambitions: 'He once used a month's worth of luncheon vouchers in a fancy restaurant, I think it was the Dorchester.' Around this time, Vidia managed to avoid being called up for National Service. Ironman remembered: 'He went for a medical examination, they took one look at him, a small Indian man, and said, "Run along, son, that's it." '[15]

The C&CA sent Vidia on a course in Wexham Springs in Slough to learn more about construction and architecture, a time he would use later in his novel *Magic Seeds*. On the course he met Jagdish Sondhi, a stocky engineer with a Sikh father and Hindu mother who had grown up in Kenya and been to school in India. Similarly displaced, they got talking and Vidia asked Sondhi to lend him £10. 'I felt that was the last I'll see of that,' said Sondhi, 'but sure enough a £10 note arrived at my sister's apartment. I thought, holy mackerel! It's rare to be touched for money and get it back.' Sondhi noticed Vidia's fascination with India, and the way he drank in information. 'He didn't talk much, but what he said was thoughtful. I noticed later, in his writing, that he is quite knowledgeable about houses and how they are constructed.'[16]

Vidia liked the library at the C&CA, and took out books on the Finnish architect and designer Alvar Aalto, and the Brazilian architects Lúcio Costa and Oscar Niemeyer. He thought it was 'the start of a slight education, the friendship with Ironman making me look, introducing me to the idea of modern architecture, about which I knew nothing.' In retrospect, he felt he had been duped into believing the modern lines of the 1950s were necessarily beautiful. 'Many years later, in 1994, I went to Brazil and saw the awful architecture of Niemeyer which we were so admiring of – we were required to admire him, the concrete fellow – and I actually entered one of his buildings in São Paulo. It roared with the sound of people walking. It roared. It was unbearable. He had just drawn it on a sheet of paper and they had built it in concrete: you could build anything out of concrete. Later, you see how mad it was to praise those people, and that it would be a gift to the Brazilian people to pull it down.'[17]

Although Jill was leaving for Italy, and would soon move to New York to start a new life on a different continent, Vidia's desire for her was unquenched. They spent a day together in Oxford and went for a walk by the river. Even then, despite some passing intimacy, Vidia did not declare himself and nothing came of it. Later, he gave her a copy of W.H. Auden's poetry, *A Selection by the Author*, and inscribed it 'Oxford, September 16 1958'. Jill remained unaware of the extent of his feeling, which arose above all from his deep sexual frustration, linked to an impractical idea of romance. She wondered later whether Vidia's attraction to her had arisen in part from her social status as a white, upper-middle-class Englishwoman. 'A lot had to do with the fact I was blonde and had a certain kind of accent. I think it was a race and class kind of fantasy. He implied to me that his family hoped Pat would have been more top-drawer than she was. I felt at the time that if she was good enough to support him, she was good enough to marry.'[18]

Vidia's physical attraction to Pat had never been certain, and after they married it declined further. He felt too embarrassed to talk with her about this situation. In the summer of 1958, turning imagination into reality, he started to have sex with prostitutes. He would find their telephone numbers in local newspapers and visit them in the afternoon in secret while Pat was at work. 'I couldn't go very often. I didn't have the money to do that. It was unsatisfactory. I was grateful sometimes for the release, the relief, but it was profoundly unsatisfactory. It was a stirring in the head.' He believed Pat had no inkling of what was happening. 'I didn't have the time to conduct an affair. I didn't have the talent. I didn't know how you conducted an affair because there was nobody to tell me what to do or to guide me.'[19] When he sought advice from other men, he misjudged, asking a Jamaican actor friend, Lloyd Reckord, 'Do you know any *fast* women?'[20] Diana Athill, who later lived with Lloyd's brother, the playwright Barry Reckord, remembered, 'They met in the street one day. Lloyd is as gay as they come and Vidia had absolutely no notion. He was very naive altogether.'[21] An attempt to plant a kiss on Diana one evening while she was carrying a tray of glasses was not a success. Vidia knew that paying for sex with women was not a solution to his dissatisfaction. Ideally, he would have had a relationship. 'I was always wanting something to happen. In a way, the people I met who were interested in me never really stirred me, I wasn't interested in them.' His one attempt at a more normal encounter was a humiliating failure. He met a middle-aged Canadian writer at the BBC. 'I actually went to her flat and she had arranged it and everything. But my sexual performance was pathetic. That is so upsetting to me. I never saw her again, and I was quite ashamed to discover a few weeks later that she'd told a friend. It was awful. I remember it so clearly. She was an experienced woman.'[22]

Through the late 1950s and 1960s, Vidia would go to brothels and to prostitutes, although not regularly. Convinced of his inabilities as a seducer, bought sex offered him a form of comfort and release. 'I was very glad they were there. I mustn't run them down. I was very glad. So there were some occasions when I felt almost grateful to these people for giving me this help. I mustn't forget that . . . although I have stopped using their services for so long. I kept it separate from Pat. I always practised safe sex. Safe sex is rather joyless sex. I was always aware what I was missing; all the time I was with Pat I knew there was something wrong. I knew it was wrong, and it might be because of Pat that I have not pursued any English woman . . . I didn't know how you seduced a woman, how you excited her and thought of her pleasure. I hadn't got that from my upbringing. There was no one telling me about it or talking about it. I realised all this later, much later . . . A young taxi driver was driving me back from the [railway] station one day. He said his father had told him,

"Always please the woman first." A marvellous thing to tell the son, don't you think? I wish someone had told me that. But we grew up with this furtive incestuous idea.'[23]

In 1958, Pat was offered a job at Rosa Bassett School in Streatham, at the opposite end of London from Muswell Hill, which involved a long journey for her on the bus and Underground each day. Vidia remembered: 'She began to suffer travel fatigue. She was teaching history, and she was taking it extremely seriously. I pleaded with her that these children were not worth it.'[24] Kamla was living with them, having taken a year's leave from her teaching post in Trinidad to work at a girl's school in East Finchley. She had friends in London, and discreetly rekindled her relationship with Sam Selvon, without telling Vidia. Pat took Kamla to Cornwall, and to stay with Auntie Lu in Gloucester, where she showed her the cathedral, 'all these knights who had died and she would explain what each pose meant. I got along very well with Pat. Sometimes Vidia and I would have a little row. I'd pack my bags and I'd say, "OK, I'm off, I am not staying." Vidia's relationship with Pat seemed all right at that time. She was basically a very shy person, but you couldn't put her down.'[25] The following autumn Pat and Vidia moved south to 81B Wyatt Park Road, a furnished upper-floor flat with two bedrooms in a quiet street in Streatham Hill, overlooking a front and back garden, at a cost of £20 per month. Their landlady was a reader of the *New Statesman*, and knew Vidia's name; it was the first home in which they felt at ease.

*

Although Vidia's dealings with André Deutsch were often difficult, he found the man himself entertaining. Born in Budapest in 1917, Deutsch had been interned as an enemy alien on the Isle of Man before founding the publishing house Allan Wingate in 1945, aided by his friend and former lover Diana Athill. They had a success with Norman Mailer's *The Naked and the Dead*, in which the word 'fuck' – famously and ludicrously – had to be rendered as 'fug', but still attracted the attention of the Attorney General. When the firm collapsed, he started André Deutsch Limited, and would over time publish writers including John Updike, Jack Kerouac, Mavis Gallant, Jean Rhys, Philip Roth and Simone de Beauvoir. Deutsch was small, energetic, determined and perfectionist, with an ability to grab ideas from around the world and turn any contemporary happening into a book. He ran the company like a dictatorship, and paid his authors and staff poorly, including Athill, whose literary and editorial talent underpinned his success. *Private Eye* once reported that her salary was so small that she banked it annually. Much of Deutsch's time was spent seeking discounts, turning off lights, raising capital and cutting costs, with the result that the company lasted longer than it might have done, but was an eccentric place at which to work.[26] Vidia, who shared some of Deutsch's traits, was quick to spot his tricks, and many of his letters were of complaint: '80 per cent of monies accruing from an arrangement with an American publisher is 80 per cent. Not 70, which would be absurd,' he wrote in a dispute over *The Mystic Masseur*.[27] Why were his enquiries being ignored? 'I haven't received any royalty statements for this quarter,' he wrote to Athill in 1958. 'These things, amusingly enough, interest me.'[28] Jeremy Lewis, who later worked at the company, believed, 'Diana supplied the patience and the sympathy and the literacy and the attention to detail of the ideal old-fashioned editor' while André had 'the entrepreneurial energy, the single-minded dedication and the zest for wheeling-and-dealing and striking a bargain without which a firm like his would expire in a haze of lofty thoughts and fine intentions.'[29]

For all this, Vidia's early books enjoyed a good critical reception with the help of his publisher, and won important prizes aimed at encouraging younger writers. He received the John Llewellyn Rhys Prize for *The Mystic Masseur* and the Somerset Maugham Award for *Miguel Street*, with Willie Somerset Maugham personally sanctioning the award of the prize to an author who was not British-born. Deutsch managed to get the books published in America by Ballantine Books of New York, although they made little impact, and Lord David Cecil, an Oxford literary critic and scion of the eminent political family, was persuaded to write an introduction to the American edition of *The Mystic Masseur*: 'This is a delightful book [which] bubbles and sparkles with life and gaiety . . . Mr Naipaul is a humorist who likes the animal called man. This does not mean he thinks highly of him.'[30] Conscious of Vidia's ability, tetchiness and determination, Diana Athill tried hard to promote his work: 'I felt admiration for him and impressed by him, and very sorry that we couldn't pay him more money because he obviously was very short of money.'[31] Asked for information about him by an American publisher, she responded, 'Naipaul is really the hardest person to be gossipy about. He is by nature extremely reticent about his private life and somewhat anti-publicity of a juicy and titillating-to-the-reader kind.'[32]

Vidia's reputation was growing steadily, and commissions started to come his way. He picked up £21 for a short story in *Punch*, £25 for a piece in *Vogue*. His earnings and expenses were noted scrupulously in a cashbook: 6/4 for drinks with Willy Edmett in Maida Vale, 7/6 for lunch with Francis Wyndham, 3/1 for coffee with Colin MacInnes, to whom Wyndham had introduced him.[33] Unusually for a middle-aged white novelist of this period, MacInnes was interested in youth culture and in black culture, an interest that was linked to his attraction to young black men. In *City of Spades*, he did something other writers of the moment such as Kingsley Amis or John Braine never did: he included black characters, and portrayed the bohemian London found in Sam Selvon's work, a world that was being altered profoundly by immigration, particularly from the West Indies. Vidia was surprised that MacInnes, then at the height of his fame, took an interest in him. 'He had total enthusiasm for my work, and wrote to me about the books. Later, I think he became jealous, and he was insulting to me at a publisher's party. He was very romantic about black people.'[34]

Francis Wyndham, who was shortly to leave Deutsch and join the ground-breaking magazine *Queen*, was instrumental in the development of V.S. Naipaul's career at this point. He found the young Vidia to be 'attractive, very funny, dynamic, wonderfully subtle, very much alive. Later, he lived up to his reputation for irascibility, but he was much less touchy in the 1950s.'[35] Popular, gentle, solitary and eccentric, Wyndham lived with his mother, wore heavy glasses and high-waisted trousers, gave off random murmurs and squeaks and moved with an amphibian gait. Born to a well-connected literary family in 1924 and educated at Eton and Oxford, he was seen by his contemporaries as a literary talent, but his greater skill turned out to be for editing and encouraging others. He published fewer books than expected, but was the dedicatee of many. He would meet Vidia several times a month. Francis accompanied him to an Ibsen play, and introduced him to numerous people, including Dom Moraes, an Indian poet who had won the Hawthornden Prize at the age of nineteen. Moraes was reluctant to meet Vidia but Francis insisted, saying they had a lot in common. An awkward lunch took place at the French pub in Soho. Moraes mentioned this to a friend who laughed: ' "Don't you know what Vidia and you have in common? Francis may have been too polite to say so, but you both have brown skins." '[36]

Francis Wyndham advertised his protégé's talent to his friends, and persuaded Anthony Powell to read *The Mystic Masseur*. Powell, another product of Eton and Oxford, married to the daughter of an Irish peer, had started as a publisher and reviewer and by the late 1950s was the author of the early novels of a twelve-volume sequence, *A Dance to the Music of*

Time. Filled with minutely observed encounters, astute social commentary and self-congratulatory English humour, his books drew a devoted following. A perceptive, gossipy man with a large head, Tony Powell was a friend or contemporary of writers such as Evelyn Waugh, Henry Green and Cyril Connolly. Born in 1905, he was the fag – in the sense of servant – of Lord David Cecil when they were at Eton together, and according to the Anthony Powell Society, had 'such exquisite manners that he would ask the ladies before eating an apple, "Do you mind if I bite?" '[37] Powell (he liked his name to rhyme with 'prole' rather than 'prowl') sought out Vidia, a habit he had with upcoming writers. They met at El Vino, a famous journalist's bar in Fleet Street. He wanted to help this new prodigy, to whom he gave the pet name 'Viddy', and asked the *New Statesman* to try him as a reviewer.

A few weeks later, Viddy wrote a trial book review. 'It was a calamity. You know, one tried too hard. And they did it again after a suitable gap. I don't know why, but they did it again.'[38] Founded by Sidney and Beatrice Webb as a Fabian journal, the *New Statesman* had a circulation of nearly 100,000 under its long-time editor Kingsley Martin. From 1957 to 1961, the paper gave V.S. Naipaul a contract to review a book, or clump of books, each month. Although it was not his natural political home, the *New Statesman* had a reputation as a paper of quality, and attracted good writers. Vidia found his name on the review pages alongside the other V.S., the writer and critic V.S. Pritchett, the journalist Paul Johnson, the poet Charles Causley, the lutraphile Gavin Maxwell, the colonial administrator and literary spouse Leonard Woolf, the Labour politicians Richard Crossman and Barbara Castle, the Sinologist Joseph Needham, the archaeologist Jacquetta Hawkes and the Bloomsbury appendage Ralph Partridge. Like many bright young reviewers, Vidia tried to make his mark by being clever and spiky. It was hard work to read, assess and find something interesting to say about several novels at a time, all in the space of 1,000 words. Usually he would be sent about eight books, and ignore several. For four years, he would devote a week of each month to the *New Statesman* review, for which he earned ten guineas. Writing in 1964, he thought that too much reviewing had diminished his appetite for literature. 'I found that I was becoming badly read, that I had neither the time nor the inclination to read the books I really wanted to read.'[39]

His reviews give a snapshot of the post-war lull in British literature. The first, about the Elizabethan romance *Euphues*, began with the line 'This book easily qualifies for inclusion among what Graham Greene calls "the iron rations of the learned man"' – an uncharacteristic allusion, displaying knowledge while deferring to another writer.[40] Next he reviewed a shipboard memoir by the bisexual diplomatist Harold Nicolson, *Journey to Java*: 'A second-class passenger falls overboard and is lost; the matter is dismissed in a paragraph . . . And while Lady Nicolson, in a nearby cabin, sorted out the letters Virginia Woolf wrote her and composed 40,000 words of her biography of La Grande Mademoiselle, Sir Harold . . .'[41] He found his voice reviewing three books on Jamaica. One, commissioned by the Colonial Office, 'bears all the marks of forced labour'. Vidia used the style he favoured at home and at the BBC, saying mischievous things in an entertaining way. He had no interest in the Jamaica of 'Lord Beaverbrook and Noël Coward, the winter cruise and the £14-a-day hotel' – his concern was with 'immigrants who arrive at London's chilly railway stations in vivid tropical clothing and distinctive broad-brimmed hats'. A study by the 'colonial specialist' Mona Macmillan provoked his scorn. He ridiculed her suggestion that electricity might 'put an end to "the long dark evenings in which . . . the only possible recreation is sex."' He could see no economic future for the island except the export of agricultural produce: 'It is hard to see what anyone can do, except eat more Jamaican bananas without complaining. And perhaps – who knows? – a banana a day will keep the Jamaican away.'[42] He represented this subsequently as humour with a purpose: 'The review was a laugh from beginning to end, and it's a serious subject. We made those kind of jokes [at *Caribbean Voices*]. It was partly a joke, but dead serious. All jokes are serious. I wasn't aware that an English reader might worry about where I was positioning myself.'[43]

A Marxist novel by an Oxford-educated Jamaican, a near contemporary, provoked Vidia, despite its author having 'an occasional brilliant turn of phrase'. *The Last Enchantment* by Neville Dawes was 'a suffocating, depressing book about the burden of being very black in Jamaica.' Vidia believed that race alone was not a subject for a novel, and tried to mark out his own difference from a writer like Dawes, whom he saw as being excessively concerned with his own ethnicity: 'No writer can produce any body of work on this subject, since blackness, like whiteness, is no longer enough. And over and over we find Negro writers who make a personal statement and then have nothing to say. A writer cannot be blamed for reflecting his society, but it seems to me that these exhibitionist Negro books do little for the Negro cause.'[44]

Mostly he reviewed forgettable, parochial period novels turned out by hopeful London publishers. He waded through books on adolescent friendship in Llandudno, the minutiae of a Second World War tank battle and 'an epileptic red Indian whose sister is an atomic scientist'. *Cocktail Time* by P.G. Wodehouse was 'all very gay, but not one of Mr Wodehouse's best.'[45] He liked *Face to Face*, a memoir by a blind twenty-three-year-old Indian student at Oxford, Ved Mehta, told with 'passion, modesty and a good deal of humour'.[46] Gustie Herrigel's *Zen in the Art of Flower Arrangement* was written off: 'Her giddy burblings will help no one interested in the East or in flowers.'[47] *The Darling Buds of May* by H.E. Bates was 'a bucolic frolic'.[48] Eventually, he dared to be complimentary, calling Veronica Hull's pseudonymous first novel *The Monkey Puzzle* 'shrewd, barbed, lit up with delicious perceptions', even if 'Miss Hull has declared war on the comma'.[49] Sometimes he would be facetious in the manner of the time, revealing an immaturity behind his critical acuity. Of *Daddy's Gone A-Hunting* by Penelope Mortimer, he wrote: 'Mrs Mortimer is such a feminine writer that I wonder whether her new novel can be recommended to women.'[50] He tried witty and would-be sophisticated lines, referring to 'sex, of both sorts' and to 'the coy, "French" treatment of sex, obscene, sexless and irritating'. One author 'never smiles, and his characters smile only once, during copulation'.[51]

In December 1958 Vidia reviewed new novels by Sam Selvon, George Lamming and Jan Carew. Carew was labelled 'always readable' while Selvon 'who has won a reputation for his stories of West Indians in London' was given lukewarm praise. His novel *Turn Again Tiger* 'has, I feel, been "angled" in the light of the current vogue for Race, Sex and Caribbean writing.' George Lamming meanwhile, four years older than Vidia, was endorsed as 'one of the finest prose-writers of his generation'.[52] In later years, he amended his view of Lamming downwards, with a view to provocation: 'George did some Negro writing and that was that . . . Negro writing is something that can be described in this way: the books must come with a hassock, so you kneel and read them with piety. Every book comes with a hassock. It is a good spiritual exercise for everybody.'[53] He added, 'George Lamming's best things were his little jokes in radio scripts. He did something for the television on prejudice about immigrants, which was very witty, I thought. A picture of West Indian hands doing the laundry – "there are many black hands at work, keeping Britain white." Isn't that nice?'[54] Lamming was to remain an intermittent foe: in *The Pleasures of Exile* in 1960, he complained that Naipaul's books were unable to 'move beyond a castrated satire'.[55]

The Humbler Creation by Pamela Hansford Johnson was 'an engrossing novel' about a childless couple whose marriage has become sexually dead: 'as a study of a strange and sterile marriage, it is subtle and illuminating,' Vidia wrote empathetically.[56] He read extensively among women writers, and often gave them better reviews than the men. He enjoyed the first novel by the Irish writer Edna O'Brien: 'Miss O'Brien may write pro-founder books, but I doubt whether she will write another like *The Country Girls*, which is as fresh and lyrical and bursting with energy as only a first novel can be.'[57] He recognized the importance of Attia Hosain's novel *Sunlight on a Broken Column*, about the collapse of a noble Muslim family in Oudh before the partition of India, believing it put the author 'among the most accomplished Indian novelists writing in English'.[58] His most enthusiastic review of all was for *Memento Mori*, Muriel Spark's slim, cruel comedy about old age. 'There is a Waugh-like brilliance to this novel . . . Muriel Spark has written a brilliant, startling and original book.'[59]

For the first time, Vidia found himself inside a specifically British literary world. *Stories from the New Yorker: 1950–1960*, with writing by J.D. Salinger and John Cheever and Updike, was 'a frightening book. It isn't only that so many of its American stories are indistinguishable in style, sensibility and mood; it is that these stories, when read in bulk, seem to have issued from a civilization so joyless that it must be judged to have failed.'[60] His own literary world was a virtual community; as a reviewer, he might meet other *New Statesman* contributors on the page, and his contact with the publication was limited to the arrival of the postman with a brown paper parcel. But to readers, publishers, editors and agents, V.S. Naipaul became a name in literary London, as distinct from a colonial offshoot at the BBC. His reviews could be found amid disquisitions on 'the Channel Tunnel question', reports on new gramophone records, advertise-ments for *Mad* magazine and even a 'Labour Party Youth Rally and Sports Day with Jimmy Hill, Fulham's Inside Right'.

It was in most ways a lonely life. As he wrote later: 'I became my flat, my desk, my name.'[61] Although the *New Statesman* prided itself on its international flavour, assessing the policies of Jawaharlal Nehru and offerings such as *Eighteen Poems by Mao Tse-Tung*, V.S. Naipaul was nearly the only non-European name on its pages. Even then, it was an ambiguous and unrevealing name: 'V.S.' could stand for anything apart from the sesquipedelian 'Vidiadhar Surajprasad' with its seven complex syllables, while 'Paul' looked familiar, even Christian. 'Have I changed?' he asked in a review in July 1961. 'Or are bad novels getting worse?'[62] He stopped writing for the *New Statesman* later that year. 'I have been unfortunate as a reviewer,' he claimed later, 'I have seldom received good books. But I take my responsibilities as a reviewer seriously.'[63] His taste in literature had not altered substantially since his opinionated letters to Kamla at Benares Hindu University in 1950. In a whimsical, camp article in *The Times* in 1961, he wrote that the novel remained his 'main delight'. His instinct was to return to the classics. 'I like reading in Aksakoff of the Volga in flood, the Volga frozen, Aksakoff and Gogol make me feel the vastness of Russia; so do Turgenev's *Sportsman's Sketches*. And how important the weather is in the Brontës and in Dickens! . . . It would be easier to say what I don't like: Jane Austen, Hardy, Henry James, Conrad, and nearly every contemporary French novelist.'[64]

CHAPTER TWELVE

'THERE WASN'T ANY
KIND REMARK'

IN THE AUTUMN OF 1958, Vidia began work on a fourth novel, *A House for Mr Biswas*. It took three years to complete, ran to over 200,000 words and was, in all senses, a huge achievement. 'Believe me,' he told Kamla as he wrote it, 'this book is like the scholarship exam all over again.'[1] It was an imagined version of Pa's life. 'It really is dealing with the child's memories, so that gives it its special quality: it is fantasy working on a childhood memory.' The starting point was some pieces of furniture his father had collected over the years and taken with him to each house or bit of a house he occupied: a meat safe covered with a screen to keep out flies, some chairs that he had varnished, a bookcase, a bureau. 'Was there a hat rack? Or did I invent that? The book has destroyed memory in a way for me.'[2] He realized soon that it was a progression from his earlier work. 'As I was writing it, everything developed. The day came when I found myself doing subordinate clauses, because I needed to, and it was a great step forward.' Although Vidia would never write easily, rarely producing more than 500 words a day through his career, each sentence was designed to carry the narrative forward. 'I write in a very fast way. I don't delay. I don't dawdle. It looks as though I'm dawdling, but I don't dawdle. I fix every little moment with a picture.'[3] He allowed *A House for Mr Biswas* to be taken over by its characters as he moved for the first time into what V.S. Pritchett termed the 'determined stupor' out of which great books are written, as the writer becomes consumed by the writing.

When the manuscript was done, he noticed that one side of the gold nib of his Parker pen had been worn away. Vidia went to Italy with Pat for a holiday. 'I left the pile of papers on the dresser, a big dresser in the flat, and magical as Italy was, I was tormented by the thought of the papers. I had no other copy, and when I went back I was so relieved to see it there . . . I broke down towards the end because I had laboured so long. I began to do a revision. I did everything I could to cure the pain in my fingers, put tape on them, so painful, the typing. By the end I felt I had grown up; I felt I had become a writer.'[4] Like many authors, he was careful about the mechanics of writing, believing the making of a book was a kind of luck. 'I've become very superstitious about the titles you give your books. If you write a book about a man looking for a house, you might find yourself in the same predicament. Be careful.'[5] For many years, Vidia would avoid speaking the titles of his books out loud.

A House for Mr Biswas tells the story of one man's life: Mohun Biswas. He tries his hand as a pundit, a sign-painter, a shopkeeper, an estate overseer, a welfare officer and a journalist on the Trinidad *Sentinel*: 'WHITE BABY FOUND ON RUBBISH DUMP – In Brown Paper Parcel – Did Not Win Bonny Baby Competition' is one of his stories.[6] At all stages, Mr Biswas's intentions are dislocated by circumstance, his dependent position and the restrictions of a colonial society. When he takes a correspondence course in journalism from London, he is advised to write pieces on 'Guy Fawkes Night' and 'Characters at the Local'. Mr Biswas is a failure, but a picaresque hero. The novel, told slowly, is universal in the way that the work of Dickens or Tolstoy is universal; the book makes no apologies for itself, and does not contextualize or exoticize its characters. It reveals a complete world. The humour is gentler than in the first three books, and there is greater sympathy for the characters, although it is not applied equally: the Tulsis, representing the Capildeos, are viewed almost exclusively from a negative angle. Moments and ideas are drawn from Pa's *Gurudeva*, and from Vidia's own stories like 'Potatoes'; he takes a swipe at Mittelholzer and Selvon by giving their attributes to a pair of black labourers, Edgar and Sam.

Trapped early into marriage by the Tulsi family, governed by a powerful matriarch, Mr Biswas spends the rest of his days trying to escape their influence even while he depends on them for survival. Much of his time is spent getting things wrong: even when he tries to whistle, 'all he did was to expel air almost soundlessly through the lecherous gap in his top teeth.'[7] He works hard to offend the Tulsis, insulting the favoured sons, calling his mother-in-law a 'Roman cat' behind her back and saying to Shama, his wife, ' "It look to me that your whole family is just one big low-caste bunch." '[8] When he throws food out of a window and spits water on his brother-in-law, he is beaten and asserts himself by ordering Shama to buy him some peppersauce and a tin of salmon. She answers him: '"You have a craving? You making baby?"'[9] Anger and comedy of this sort are threaded through the book, though the anger, and anguish, draws as much on Vidia's own temperament as on Pa's depressive outbursts. It was as if Vidia was imagining how he himself might have lived Pa's life. There is no suggestion that Mr Biswas was a literary achiever, or a man of sartorial style, as Pa was; for fictional purposes, it was easier to present Mr Biswas as obstinate and inept. In this way, Vidia sought to memorialize his late father and to distinguish himself from his legacy. The taut relationships within the extended family at 'Hanuman House' are brilliantly depicted: between sisters, between children and aunts, between old Mrs Tulsi and Mr Biswas. The critic Harish Trivedi, who had the advantage of reading both Hindi and English, believed 'a more detailed and authentic description of a Hindu joint family would be hard to find even in all of Hindi literature.'[10] In the final pages of *A House for Mr Biswas*, the old system breaks down as Trinidad changes and the two elder children go abroad on scholarships. Mr Biswas buys a house in Sikkim Street, borrowing money from a relation. His last thoughts, Vidia's thoughts, were: 'How terrible it would have been, at this time, to be without it: to have died among the Tulsis . . . to have lived without even attempting to lay claim to one's portion of the earth; to have lived and died as one had been born, unnecessary and unaccommodated.'[11] The house, finally achieved, carries a freight of symbolism.

Attempts by Diana Athill to cut parts of *A House for Mr Biswas*, apparently at the instigation of a putative New York publisher, were resisted. 'I worked very hard on that book and I worked with great judgement,' Vidia wrote. 'If the book is any good it will make its way . . . You must support me on this.'[12] Athill agreed, but when she told him that Deutsch intended to postpone publication, he was furious, writing to Francis Wyndham, 'At times like this I feel I should never speak a civil word to Diana or André again: they treat me so contemptuously.'[13] Looking back, Francis felt that Vidia's chronic complaints about Deutsch were not unreasonable. 'He paid his authors scandalously little. He didn't advertise Vidia, even when *Biswas* came out. I almost felt Diana and André didn't want it to be too much of a *succès d'estime* because they knew it wouldn't sell. They never promoted him as a star author.'[14]

Six months after publication, the book had sold an unremarkable 3,200 copies in hardback. No American publisher was forthcoming, and Vidia was reduced to depositing the book at the hotel of the New York publishing legend Blanche Knopf, who with her husband, Alfred, had founded one of America's most prestigious imprints. Vidia's agent Graham Watson made the suggestion: 'He couldn't place the book, and he said to me this humiliating thing, "Blanche Knopf is at Claridge's, why don't you just take the book to her and leave it for her?" He should have done that himself, of course. But I took it. It came back almost the next day. She didn't read it. She just knew it wasn't for her.'[15] Vidia's self-belief was not enough to carry him through; post-colonial literature had yet to be invented as a genre or as a profitable business, and his work remained an anomaly. Later, set against novels such as *Things Fall Apart* by Chinua Achebe or *Midnight's Children* by Salman Rushdie, *A House for Mr Biswas* would be seen as a seminal postcolonial text. Knowing he was being patronized, even while his patrons did their best to promote him, Vidia's reactions to the world at this time became ever less conciliatory. When he appeared on the television show *Bookstand* in October 1961, he had an off-air row with the BBC stalwart Grace Wyndham Goldie. 'I felt that his nerves must have been jangling,' Diana Athill wrote to the interviewer, Colin MacInnes. 'I wish he didn't *mind* everything so much (but then he wouldn't be the writer he is if he didn't).'[16] In the same year, he had a fleeting meeting with the novelist R.K. Narayan, who made a remark to him that would often be quoted later: 'India will go on.'[17]

Hearing that her son was publishing another novel, Ma wrote hopefully: 'I am very worried about your last book you are writing I hope that you will not mentioned anything about your Mamoos and Mousies in it to cause any unpleasant feeling.'[18] The response of the Capildeo family would be noisy. Rudranath telephoned André Deutsch in a fury on publication to demand the book's suppression. Diana fielded his call, and, knowing nothing of the family background, reported to Vidia: 'He says he is your uncle, back here for 6 months lecturing in Maths at London University, also that he is a barrister and an "important" member of the opposition . . . Now, is this gentleman a nut, or could he be a serious threat? (He could be both at once of course.)'[19] Lawyers were consulted, and Capo R. did nothing. Rampersad Ragbir of Chaguanas arrived at the offices of André Deutsch claiming to be a cousin, Diana informed Vidia. 'He spent quite a long time willing the Peace of God into me' and left an important note 'which he'd rather give you than the *News of the World*.' She forwarded the note to Vidia, which turned out to read, in full: 'I got a story about myself and Jesus Christ the Saviour.'[20] For Simbhoo, Rudranath and their families, *A House for Mr Biswas* would be viewed in perpetuity as an act of betrayal and misrepresentation. Simbhoo's granddaughter Vahni Capildeo has described how she was discouraged from reading books with the name 'Naipaul' on the spine: 'I kept away from all these armoured books. They were impenetrable. They were a source of contention, not of pride. For our paternal grandfather hated the Naipauls. Who were they, after all? Ungrateful lesser members of his extended family who had got away with spreading lies and wicked stories about him and his family and Indian people and everyone on the island whose independence he, Mr Capildeo, had worked for. Worse yet, these ingrates had made money from their treachery.'[21]

Reaction in the British press was substantial. Beneath the headline 'Caribbean Masterpiece' and a photograph of Vidia, Colin MacInnes wrote in the *Observer*: '*A House for Mr Biswas* has the unforced pace of a master-work: it is relaxed, yet on every page alert.'[22] The novelist Angus Wilson wrote that V.S. Naipaul had now joined 'the small group of unquestionably first-class novelists'.[23] Dan Jacobson in the *New Statesman* praised it as 'the most interesting novel to have been published in England in 1961.'[24] In the *London Magazine*, Francis Wyndham called the book 'one of the clearest and subtlest illustrations ever shown of the effects of colonialism . . . he has succeeded in filling an unusually large frame without sacrificing the finesse of the miniaturist's technique.'[25] Elsewhere, the poet Derek Walcott produced a full-page report for the *Trinidad Guardian* under the headline 'A Great New Novel of the West Indies'. Walcott thought Naipaul had established himself as 'one of the most mature of West Indian writers'. In an accompanying piece, he commented on the seeming gap between the compassionate author and the haughty man. 'Naipaul seems, on first acquaintance, to have alienated himself from all the problems of our society and particularly those of his race. But the books are almost contradictions of the man.'[26] Later, Edward Brathwaite would write, 'The novels of Vidia Naipaul . . . have come, almost overnight, to topple the whole hierarchy of our literary values and set up new critical standards of form and order in the West Indian novel.'[27] A letter arrived out of the blue from Gault MacGowan, who after giving up the editorship of the *Trinidad Guardian* had survived the Dieppe Raid. 'He thought that I was Pa, that I had become a great success after being a reporter,' Vidia wrote to Ma. 'It was a very kind letter, and I believe that you will be pleased to hear about it.'[28]

*

During the writing of *A House for Mr Biswas*, Vidia kept in close touch with his family, their letters feeding the book and Vidia's own attitudes feeding the letters his siblings sent him. Life in Trinidad, the alternative world in his head, was a constant presence. Ma was worried about Kamla, thought she was too flighty and should settle down, ideally with Dada Tewari, the son of family friends in Jamaica. Kamla was bored by Trinidad: 'I don't think it's doing me any good and mentally speaking I doubt if I can last the year.' She was worried about Shiva, who was now at QRC but had failed to win an exhibition. 'Do you know, the boy is always in the moon – the most absent-minded being you ever came across – the very image of Pa. He is intelligent but he does need guidance.' Vidia was not impressed when a letter arrived for Pat from Shiva: 'I have found myself greatly attracted to Communism or what might be more accurate Anarchic Communism . . . I foresee a society as the Anarchists did based on co-operatives run directly by the people with no interference by the State.'[29] Sati was married to Crisen, and Savi had won a scholarship to study dental medicine abroad. Her plans changed when she met Melvyn Akal, a doctor. Melvyn had originally come to Nepaul Street to take out Kamla, until Savi caught his eye. She wrote to Vidia: 'Melo has already asked Ma's consent to marry me and she has agreed . . . I will continue to teach and give every single penny of my earnings to Ma.' A couple of months later, she wrote with news that 'Your uncle Rood has announced to the public that he is the third greatest scientist ever to be and is having a good reception in Trinidad. Last night hundreds went to the Himalaya Club to hear him speak on "The Crisis Facing the West".'[30] Stories of this kind, which might have come straight from Vidia's fiction, were not rare (although Capo R. may have been parodying the PNM propaganda which described The Doc as the third most intelligent man in the world; the first two were never specified). The local press reported that a Mr Dookinan Naipaul had been fined $72 for giving injections and pretending to be a doctor. Shiva, aged fourteen, wrote: 'Kamla told me that the said Dookinan Naipaul claimed to be the brother of W.I. novelist V.S. Naipaul and you could imagine how we all laughed. When I went to school that day the boys all chided me about it.'[31]

In the autumn of 1958, Mira came to live in Streatham Hill to prepare for a degree in French and Spanish at the University of Leeds. Her education was to be funded by Savi and Mel, although Vidia would make some contribution. England was a new world for her. She had brought home-sewn clothes from Trinidad and a heavy grey military coat which a friend had given her to guard against the English winter. Pat disposed of it, and gave her money for a tweed coat. 'She was gentle and kind. Pat was not a huggable person, but she was nice to me in so many other ways and I felt welcome. Very shy, very modest, very sweet. A good heart. She was a good cook. Very small portions, and they would allocate small portions to me and I was ravenous. I was only about ninety pounds. Pat would go off to teach and I remember she began cutting a slice of bread for me in the morning and I would have liked to have two slices of bread. They got on very well. Vido would tell Pat at the end of the day how many pages he had written and what he had written. He would read things to me and if I chuckled he would get very happy.' Sometimes they fought. 'I went out to the shops and bought one egg here, one egg there. Vido accused me of "shopping like a nigger". I said you're horrible. He said get out. I went to a friend and he called and apologized.' Mira typed much of the final manuscript of *A House for Mr Biswas*.

That Christmas, Mira went with her brother and sister-in-law to stay with Ted and Marg Hale. 'I thought the mother was like a zombie and the father was polite, upright and correct. The mother was a strange, lonely looking, unhappy woman – as if she had no connection with the husband. She could have been his maid.' Eleanor seemed 'a nice friendly soul, very male, very different from Pat. Total chalk and cheese.' Mira was surprised at the flat in Kingstanding. 'I couldn't understand why they stored coal in the bathtub. Maybe they just washed with a little cloth.' It was the first time Mira had eaten at someone else's house in England. The party addressed a Christmas turkey in a tense atmosphere while Vidia ate a tin of salmon, which he had brought just for himself. Mira remembered: 'I am having my first bite and it is total silence around the table and Vido just out of the blue snaps at me, "Can't you say something? Can't you just say if you like it, or don't like it?" I was so shocked. I suppose he wanted me to say once I had tasted the food that it was really wonderful ... It was some sort of pressure or stress he was feeling and he was taking it out on me, he just jumped on me and I began to cry because I was in shock, and embarrassed.'[32]

After she got her degree, Mira went to live in Edinburgh with Savi and Mel, who was doing a doctorate in dermatology at the university. For Savi, life in Britain made her comprehend Vidia and Pat better. 'It took me just six months in Edinburgh to understand class and people and behaviour. You had done Jane Austen and you had read literature but you had not lived in the country.' It no longer surprised her that Pat was so reticent, or that she kept her family hidden – things that had previously baffled her. Like Mira, she was dismayed by the minuscule portions of food Pat offered, and presumed her frugality arose from Vidia's objection to anyone who was fat. 'My children remember being taken on a picnic and having risotto. Pat was always very sweet and caring to them, but they felt that they got a tablespoon of rice.'[33] Nor could she understand why Pat 'never learned to cook anything of Vidia's home food, never tried. I always remember being shocked, my God, he's sending out to buy dhal and rice? It just seemed absurd.'[34] When Mira gained a diploma in education from Edinburgh, she returned to Trinidad to teach, and in 1963 married Amar Inalsingh, an ambitious doctor from a prosperous Indian Christian family.

Vidia was conscious that despite his critical success, his sisters were doing better than he was in worldly terms. He disliked that fact that Pat still had to work in order to support them. She was a conscientious teacher. In a testimonial from Rosa Bassett School, the headmistress Miss Jewell Hill praised her intellectual attainments, her devotion to girls of differing ability and her willingness to arrange trips to museums, historical sites and films in her spare time.[35] Veronica Matthew, a pupil at Rosa Bassett, remembered 'Pat Naipaul was small and slim, quiet and mousy. She was played up by some of her classes. She always wore black: black blouses with little Peter Pan collars, straight black skirts and flat pumps – all quite fashionable at the time.' The school must have been 'rather a dispiriting place to work' since most of the girls pitched their aspirations so low . . . 'Higher education was generally regarded as a waste of time, as the number of earning years would be reduced . . . We were completely unaware at school that Mrs Naipaul was married to a well-known writer. At dinner once a girl on my table remarked, while Mrs Naipaul was on dinner duty (but out of earshot), that she was married to "a darkie". When I was in the upper sixth Mrs Naipaul left school to accompany her husband on a trip to the Caribbean. Later I read the book he wrote of that experience

[and] was amazed that there was absolutely no reference to her whatsoever in the book. He made it appear that he had travelled to the Caribbean alone.'[36] Pat was to remain a silent witness until after her death.

Shiva liked reporting Trinidad gossip to his elder brother. The hot news in 1958 was that Capo R. had left Ruth and come to live 'with a young English thing in a new flat opposite the Dairies'. The aunts were outraged, but when Dool Mausi berated him, he shouted at her. Shiva wrote: 'The press compares him to Einstein and Newton, yet recently a student wrote the longest letter I have ever seen saying his science is naive and elementary.' Early the following year Shiva reported that Kamla was seeing a married Danish man who ran a paper factory, and 'went out almost every night with him, until two or three in the morning . . . Savi and Melo came down from San Fernando and told her that it was all looking very bad . . . Ma decided to talk to her. Then the fireworks really began . . . So Kamla left the house, after throwing a glass at Ma, swearing that she was going up to San Fernando to kill Melo.' Kamla was able to stir up her brother afterwards by reporting that 'Savi & Melo . . . didn't like "Miguel Street" . . . By the way, thanks for the dedication – but why?'[37] Vidia, nearing the end of *A House for Mr Biswas*, was thrown when he heard this suggestion: 'if I had not been so worried by the news that Melo and Savi didn't like Miguel Street I might have finished it last week . . . I dedicated Miguel Street to you and Ma because it is the first book I wrote, a small recompense for not being at home.'[38]

Later that year Kamla agreed to marry Harrinandan 'Harry' Tewari, the brother of Dada, who was now in disgrace owing to the discovery that he had two children by different Chinese women. It was a pragmatic choice by a woman nearing thirty who realized that her life was not working out in the way she had hoped. She told Vidia: 'I must confess that I am not at all in love with Harry but he is just about willing to lay the world at my feet. By the way he has bought me a £287 diamond ring. (What wouldn't you have done with the money? Or me or Ma?)' To Pat, she wrote, 'I'm being married Hindu-style in a sari and what not . . . I have no dreams, no hopes, no plans. I will just meet the future as it comes and I do have a lot of confidence in Harry.' They got married in Jamaica, and the press ran a photograph of Kamla looking glamorous, saying she was the sister of 'noted West Indian writer Vidia Naipaul of Trinidad'. In a letter in November she described her new life to Vidia. She would make breakfast of saltfish fritters and boiled green bananas, and spend the day doing little. Harry owned a cinema and a cocktail lounge in Kingston, where they would go most evenings: 'Harry keeps his prices high to encourage only the highest class.'[39] Kamla thought later: 'Maybe it was just a form of escape. I imagine so. I can't say that Harry treated me badly. That would be a lie. His only problem was that he drank a bit, but he never came home and behaved badly – he came home and just fell fast asleep.'[40] Later, Kamla began teaching again and they had three children.

*

In 1959, as Trinidad moved towards independence, the chief minister Dr Eric Williams made a move to attract former scholars back to their home country. He had previously described V.S. Naipaul to the *Trinidad Guardian* as 'obviously in the front rank of West Indian novelists'.[41] Mel Akal wrote: 'Eric Williams is contemplating sending for you and George Lamming to spend 3 months in Trinidad early next year . . . It is expected that you, in return, will give a few lectures . . . there is a drive to attract West Indians of benefit to the new federation back home. Good jobs are being offered – and with your qualifications – you may be in line for a job as a Consul, much as Solomon Lutchman [last spotted wearing the blazer of a Caroni Cricket Club in Oxford] now is in Venezuela – with prospects later of being an Ambassador.'[42]

A letter duly arrived from Dr Winston Mahabir, a family friend who was Trinidad's minister for education and culture, offering a scholarship. 'Dear Vidya, Greetings! . . . 1. First-class return passage by boat for yourself and your wife. 2. The salary of a Queen's Royal College Master while you are here in Trinidad. (I believe this will be in the vicinity of £100 per month.) . . . There will be no political strings attached to the award, but you will be expected to fulfil certain general obligations, for example, radio talks, public lectures, meetings with literary groups, etc. However, I have emphasized in representations to Cabinet that you should be free to saturate yourself once more in the atmosphere that is congenial to art. I am hoping that you will find it possible to be here by the middle of September this year, and that these proposals inter-digitate with your fellowship to India . . . P.S. It is a pity that there is as yet no offspring because the scholarship involves full return passage for at least one child!'[43] Being co-opted in this way did not appeal to Vidia, but he decided to accept as a break after the exertions of *A House for Mr Biswas* and the stress it had imposed on Pat. He wrote later to Ralph Ironman, who had moved with his wife Mary to Denmark, 'Children grow so much in four years; if we leave it much longer Anne and Lotta . . . will be new and

Vidia's maternal grandparents

Above
The Capildeo clan

Left
Pa with his car

Opposite page
Top, left Pa, Ma, Kamla and Vidyadhar
Top, right Pa's self-portrait, done while unwell
Bottom, left Kamla and Vido
Bottom, right Ma, Shiva and Nella after Pa's death

Above
Pat and Vidia at Oxford

Left
Vidia in the Front Quad
at 'Univ'

Above Dorrit Hinze in Paris

Right Jill Brain

Henry Swanzy, George Lamming, Andrew Salkey,
Jan Carew and Sam Selvon in the *Caribbean Voices* studio

Top, left
Vidia with Sati,
Mira and Kamla in
Trinidad, 1956

Top, right
Ma in heels with an
Oxford-returned
Vidia, 1956

Above, left
Researching *The
Middle Passage*,
1961

Below, left
Up the Rupununi
by boat with
Amerindians,
1961

Above Kamla gets married, 1958

Above, right Shiva marries Jenny

Right Pat in London, 1965

Below Pat and Vidia in
Streatham, 1961

V.S. Naipaul and Derek Walcott square up, 1965

Aged
nineteen

Aged
twenty-
seven

Aged
thirty-four

Aged
forty-five

complete persons with whom we shall have to establish a relation from scratch. What news can I give you of Pat? I can only say that by August 1960, when Mr Biswas was finished, we were both physical wrecks. Pat, in particular, was in dreadful shape.'[44] Pat secured a place as a teacher at Bishop Anstey High School in Port of Spain, and they agreed to spend several months in the West Indies.

'When I was in Trinidad,' said Vidia later, 'Eric Williams called me, gave me lunch and asked me to do a book which turned out to be *The Middle Passage*. So my life took another turn, which was a fortunate thing.'[45] In some respects it was not a fortunate thing, since Vidia's caustic presentation of the Caribbean would mark him as a writer at odds with his society and the conventional nationalism of the 1960s. The Trinidad government would finance his travels and purchase 2,000 copies of the resultant book. He travelled alone by ship, with Pat following later. *The Middle Passage* began with quotations from the Victorian writer James Anthony Froude, a man denounced in his day as a 'negrophobic political hobgoblin', and Vidia's opening sentence ran: 'There was such a crowd of immigrant-type West Indians on the boat-train platform at Waterloo that I was glad I was travelling first class to the West Indies' – which itself may have been inspired by a letter written by Kamla after her year in London: 'From the moment we left Euston it was as though I had said goodbye to England. The tone of the coach was strictly West Indian. There were little black babies screaming all around me. The chaps were all dressed in hot shirts and hats and they were talking [in loud] voices about the English being the "wus eatin people in the world" and about the "cold pressing straight thru your bones". . . . I feel no kinship with any of them – even the Indians & I feel absolutely lost.'[46] Quickly in the book, Vidia was describing 'a very tall and ill-made Negro' with a grotesque face, huge nose and thick lips.[47] The writer was set apart as someone who travels first class – if on the immigrant ship *Francisco Bobadilla* – and disparages the appearance of the first ill-made Negro man he sees. As Diana Athill pointed out, 'Vidia could not resist placing him right at the start of the book and *describing him in greater physical detail than anyone else in all its 232 pages*.'[48] To Pat, he wrote: 'The company is small but pleasant: one Portuguese of 55, perpetually ill: his toe has a corn, his head has an ache, and his tummy hurts . . . I wanted to tell you how much I loved you on that terrible Friday [the day he left] . . . and how much I have been loving you ever since.'[49]

Vidia said later of the opening of *The Middle Passage*, 'It's true, all

that's true. I'm not setting myself up; I'm being very mischievous . . . I'd
be allowed to say things like that among the West Indians who were doing
that Caribbean programme. We made those kind of jokes. I wasn't aware
that an English reader might worry about where I was positioning myself.
I was positioning myself always as writer, and if I wasn't, I wouldn't have
made all those lovely jokes in the first chapter – the steamer crossing –
some of the dialogue, those things are in my head to this day: the
Portuguese whom I called Correia, a kind of mulatto fellow who was at
our table, talking about a football team from Trinidad and the man whom
I called Philip asking him about Skippy. And Correia says, "Well, you not
going to see him again. Son of a bitch catch a pleurisy and dead. Frankie
and Bertie and Roy Williams. All of them dead like hell." '50

He presented the West Indies now as barely redeemable, a region
colonized only for the cruelties of slavery: 'The history of the islands can
never be satisfactorily told. Brutality is not the only difficulty. History is
built around achievement and creation; and nothing was created in the
West Indies.'51 Through the force of his tirade, or detonation, V.S. Naipaul
was seeking a response. As the book continues, his desire to shock subsides
and he makes many perceptive observations about colonialism. 'To be
modern is to ignore local products and to use those advertised in American
magazines. The excellent coffee which is grown in Trinidad is used only
by the very poor and a few middle-class English expatriates.'52 He observes
that almost no African names survive in the New World, and that, 'Until
the other day African tribesmen on the [cinema] screen excited derisive
West Indian laughter . . . This was the greatest damage done to the Negro
by slavery. It taught him self-contempt. It set him the ideals of white
civilization and made him despise every other.'53 The corruption of identity
had led to competitive racial hostility: 'Like monkeys pleading for evolution, each claiming to be whiter than the other, Indians and Negroes appeal
to the unacknowledged white audience to see how much they despise each
other.'54 The partial advent of democracy had brought new dilemmas:
'Nationalism was impossible in Trinidad . . . There were no parties, only
individuals. Corruption, not unexpected, aroused only amusement and even
mild approval: Trinidad has always admired the "sharp character" who,
like the sixteenth-century picaroon of Spanish literature, survives and
triumphs by his wits in a place where it is felt that all eminence is arrived
at by crookedness.'55 Vidia does not plead, at any point in this book, for a
reassertion of imperial control, but makes it plain that independence will
provoke an avalanche of fresh problems. At the time, to a country

preparing for freedom, these words seemed above all to be an insult; today, they seem prophetic.

As soon as he reached Nepaul Street, Vidia was unhappy to be back. 'I behaved very badly for the first few days,' he told Kamla in Jamaica, 'I was bitterly depressed.'[56] He had no one to look after him as she had in 1956, or to arrange his trips around the island. The little family house, home to Ma and Shiva and Nella, now aged seven, was too hot and noisy. Nella was terrified of her big brother. 'He would ring my ears, hold them and twist them, if I got my sums wrong. It was crude behaviour from such a fastidious man. I remember him shouting – screaming – at my mother.'[57] In Port of Spain, Vidia claimed helplessness; writing would be impossible. Soon he was writing to Francis, 'The government have loaned me a car, a huge red thing . . . I am having a rough time with the intellectuals here . . . They invited me to parties and have apparently been hurt because I just was without the energy to drink through the night with them. So now I believe I have a reputation for stand-offishness, and perhaps worse.'[58] Lloyd Best and his wife arranged a dinner for Vidia and C.L.R. James. 'They got on splendidly. You'll be surprised how they loved each other.'[59]

The West Indian Federation (which would fall apart in 1962) had created a sense of anticipation in Trinidad, which made Vidia suspicious. He told the *Jamaica Gleaner* that Caribbean novels had made little impact on the English reading public, and even the critics had now lost interest in them. A group of writers and artists from different backgrounds had collected around Derek Walcott, who was writing and staging plays as well as working for the *Guardian*. Walcott, two years older than Vidia, born on the small island of Saint Lucia, had moved to Trinidad in 1953. He wrote strong, physical poetry and led a rowdy, vigorous life. His wife, Margaret, recalled the creative party atmosphere of the time: 'We had all been away, our scene. Derek referred to us lot as "anchored in the mid-Atlantic." Vidia came to our house, and Pat. She was not a very social person. He said he was a vegetarian, and I learned how to make a quiche real fast. He came across as a snob, in that he wouldn't dance and drink rum. But Vidia liked me . . . When I got a divorce he was concerned about me, very gentle . . . There was a party at the country club for Norman Manley, the Jamaican premier. Vidia says to Derek in his stupid affected accent, "Are you here as a guest, or as a reporter?" Derek said to me later, "What a little shit."'[60] Walcott himself was dynamic and turbulent; Pat wrote later to Mira: 'He's very peculiar but a very good poet.'[61] Vidia was conscious of his own early achievement, and determined to separate himself from the other West Indian writers he met now. Like Ralph Ellison after the publication of *Invisible Man*, he maintained that he was in a category all of his own, and that he had special insights denied to others. The mask of the master remained intact.

Early in 1961, Vidia and Pat flew to British Guiana, a territory on the South American mainland that historically had formed part of the Caribbean. Like Trinidad, it had a large Indian population, and Amerindians too. Much of the country had been owned by the Booker group of companies. 'The capital, Georgetown, is one of the most elegant cities I have seen. The buildings are wooden and white and the local builders can do marvellous things with wood,' Vidia told Francis. He had met the premier, Cheddi Jagan, the son of an Indian cane-cutter, and his American wife, Janet. They were a controversial pair, reviled by Britain and America as communists, but Vidia did not judge them in this way. 'I see much of the Jagans, and am altogether taken with them ... How <u>sad</u> these <u>first</u> leaders of colonial countries are!'[62] With Pat he flew to the Rupununi, the savannah on the Brazilian border, and travelled to the interior by boat. His instinctive affinity for Amerindians was tested by their living and eating conditions. 'I felt then that reverence for food – rules for its handling, interdictions – was one of the essentials of civilization.'[63] His dislike of colonial conditioning extended to Christian conversion of indigenous people: 'The missionary must first teach self-contempt. It is the basis of the faith of the heathen convert.'[64] They travelled next to Surinam where slavery had ended late, and Vidia became conscious of its constant legacy across the Caribbean: 'There is slavery in the food, in the saltfish still beloved by the islanders ... nowhere in the world are children beaten as savagely as in the West Indies.'[65] In Martinique, a department of France, Vidia was repelled by the sanctimonious pretence of equality: it made him 'long for the good humour, tolerance, amorality and general social chaos of Trinidad.'[66]

They travelled finally to Jamaica, where he lambasted Rastafarianism as nonsensical and wrote pleadingly to Francis Wyndham: 'Could you find out from Deutsch or Graham Watson (neither of whom has replied to my letters) exactly what they are doing about the novel?'[67] A sojourn with Kamla and her new husband, Harry, ended in argument, and Vidia went off to stay with Lloyd Best, who was starting an institute of economic and social research at the university. They talked and played poker late into the night. Best arranged for Vidia to give a lecture to the students. 'Everybody was looking forward to this evening because Naipaul was a big drawing card. But of course the local culture was that if something was announced for seven o'clock, you got there at eight and you were comfortable. Vidia Naipaul would put up with none of that.' At one minute past seven, Vidia walked out and insisted on being driven back to Lloyd's house. The audience followed the speaker. 'By ten o'clock the house was full to overflowing. He was holding court to all the students, he was in his element.'[68] Vidia was conscious of the poor conditions that the urban Jamaicans who were migrating to Britain at this time were escaping. 'The slums of Kingston are beyond description. Even the camera glamorizes them, except in shots taken from the air.'[69]

By May, he was in Streatham Hill writing *The Middle Passage* at speed in order to ensure it was completed by the end of the year, after which he planned a new journey – to India. The political situation in Trinidad was becoming more tense. Simbhoo's party had merged with other groupings to join the Democratic Labour Party or DLP, which was now the principal opposition to Eric Williams's PNM. Racial resentment was fiercer even than it had been in 1956. Williams called the Indians of Trinidad a 'hostile and recalcitrant minority' and proclaimed 'Massa Day Done' – meaning it was time for independence, and absentee European planters had no future. His chief opponent in the 1961 election was Capo R., who had come back from London University in triumph to snatch the leadership of the DLP. This created a lasting rupture with his brother Simbhoo, who believed he had a deeper understanding of Trinidad and its problems, and the family dispute was exacerbated by a fraternal battle over ownership of the Petit Valley estate. Rudranath was presented to the electorate as a brilliant figure, cleverer even than Dr Williams. A song of the time ran,

> The PNM say, boy we will have a hard time,
> Because that man more educated than The Doctor . . .
> Dr Rudranath returned to Trinidad,
> Like Raja Rama to Ayodhya.[70]

In November 1961, Ma wrote to Pat, 'This man Williams is doing everything in his power to cause a civil war, but I can tell you I have never before seeing our Indian people so tolerant they are determine that Williams cannot form the New Govt.'[71]

The election campaign was marked by bitterness and violence, with DLP meetings being broken up by PNM supporters while the black-dominated police force looked on and did nothing. The crisis was fuelled by provocative and slightly deranged speeches from Rudranath

Capildeo, who announced that his knowledge of Einstein's theory of relativity would enable him to compress time and effect political change faster than his rivals. Williams and the PNM took two-thirds of the seats in the election, and the British government called a conference at Marlborough House in London to discuss independence. After Prime Minister Harold Macmillan's 'wind of change' speech in South Africa in 1960, Britain was seeking rapidly to divest itself of its colonies. Under the chairmanship of a minister from the Colonial Office, Hugh Fraser, the delegates argued. Williams and Capildeo finally reached an accommodation during a tea break, enabling Trinidad and Tobago to become an independent country within the British Commonwealth. Demands for constitutional protection for the Indian minority were effectively ignored by the British government, and the new constitution gave exceptional legal latitude to the office of the prime minister.[72] With the DLP stranded, Rudranath Capildeo returned to academic life in London while for a time managing simultaneously to remain leader of the opposition. Eric Williams was left in a commanding position in Trinidad until his death in 1981.[73]

As the only begetter of *The Middle Passage*, Williams never reacted openly to the book, although his own conception of colonialism as a provoker of 'inward hunger' was not far from Vidia's thinking. Andrew Salkey described *The Middle Passage* in the *New Commonwealth* as 'the severest jolt to West Indian smugness since beet sugar ... Mr V.S. Naipaul is a truly remarkable writer [who] has trampled on nearly everybody's cosy myths of West Indian quaintness.'[74] The response of the Jamaican novelist John Hearne was more representative of critical reaction in the Caribbean: it was 'flawed, unattractive, often superficial ... he is a surgeon who has surrendered to despair.'[75] For Evelyn Waugh in the *Month*, the book was evidence of the dangers of decolonization: 'Mr Naipaul is an "East" Indian Trinidadian with an exquisite mastery of the English language which should put to shame his British contemporaries. He has shown in his stories ... that he is free of delusion about independence and representative government for his native land.'[76] Waugh was the first of a parade of reactionaries who would seek to appropriate Naipaul's writings, stripping them of their ambiguities in order to make a political point. Waugh's private thoughts were more insulting. In a letter to his friend Nancy Mitford in January 1963, he wrote, 'That clever little nigger Naipaul has won *another* literary prize. Oh for a black face.'[77] For all the critical acclaim, Vidia's position in Britain remained tenuous. To Waugh, who embodied an outlook that was still common in Britain, the white, fusty, musty, dusty, tea, coffee, cocoa, black, dark black, racial distinctions of the Caribbean were irrelevant. Vidia's reaction when he learned what Waugh had written to Nancy Mitford failed to address the underlying hostility: 'Bron Waugh [Evelyn's son] never mentioned it to me. I think it is a bit of showing off. I think he's acting.'[78]

In a BBC retrospective with Gordon Woolford and Henry Swanzy in 1978, by which time Gordon was a declining alcoholic and Vidia was irritable and famous, the subject of *The Middle Passage* came up. Gordon Woolford observed that George Lamming, Sam Selvon and Edgar Mittelholzer had all come to London in search of a publisher, and asked: 'Is that one reason that brought you, Vidia?'

NAIPAUL: No, I came to join civilization.

WOOLFORD: In *The Middle Passage* you savaged Trinidad.

NAIPAUL: Gordon, why 'savaged', why use that word?

WOOLFORD: Well, it was so, you know. [Laughs] There wasn't any kind remark.

NAIPAUL: [Ferociously] Was it untrue? Anything false? Anything proved wrong in sixteen years? Or everything proved right?

WOOLFORD: You had gone down there on money given by the Trinidad government.

NAIPAUL: They asked me to go back ... I wrote as I found.

WOOLFORD: Does your heart lie very much in the West Indies, in Trinidad?

NAIPAUL: I don't know the West Indies. I only come from Trinidad, and I left it when I was eighteen and have more or less washed my hands of it, as I have washed my hands of India. I have shed all these colonial political concerns.[79]

The contrast between Naipaul's rich, grand tones, dripping with certainty, and Woolford's unsure, wheedling voice, with its slight London accent, is dramatic.

At the start of 1962, as Vidia prepared to travel to India for the first time, he was aware that his identity had been compromised by external events. Trinidad faced black majority rule, with the unstable Capo R. claiming to represent the interests of the island's many Indians. Britain was closing the door to immigrants. Under a new law, Commonwealth citizens would be denied the automatic right to move to the UK, and could be deported more easily. Vidia regarded the Commonwealth Immigrants Act as a betrayal. In a copy of *A House for Mr Biswas*, he wrote his signature and, 'For Andrew Salkey, in London, from which one may in future be banned.'[80] The mother country had abandoned a generation of orphaned children. Because of the haphazard way in which immigration had been handled during the 1950s, racial tension in Britain was rising as the white working class in areas like Brixton and Notting Hill felt themselves outnumbered by a boisterous, alien culture. The army put a quota on the number of non-white personnel, and almost the only black faces on British television were in the popular *Black and White Minstrel Show*. As a regular on shows like *Bookstand*, Vidia was an oddity. 'Six appearances in 8 weeks; the work so good that two programmes were telerecorded,' he told a friend.[81] His fame caused him consternation when he was recognized in bed: 'A prostitute said to me, you've been on television. I said, how can you recognize my face? How can you say that? She said something very flattering to me, she said your face is unforgettable.'[82]

Ambitious, protean, made of smart material, deracinated by the accelerated politics of the end of empire, Vidia made a conscious choice to refashion himself. The vogue for West Indian writing was over and, uniquely among his contemporaries, he saw the implications of this early enough to do something about it. Jan Carew remembered a conversation: 'The last time we met was in a café in the Tottenham Court Road. By then, there were rumours that Vidia was living in some part of London where West Indians were not welcome, and was taking up with different people. He told me he was going to become English, and I thought he was pulling my leg. The English are very strict about letting you in, particularly if you are a different colour. I thought it was one of his jokes, but he was quite serious about it. He meant he was giving up his West Indian imprimatur and taking on an English one.'[83] Vidia wrote to Ralph Ironman in Aarhus, distance making him intimate, 'We had planned to drive to India; we had ordered the Volkswagen van-conversion (splendid job, and so cheap, without purchase tax); we had paid the deposit; and then we found no one willing to give us the comprehensive insurance required for the journey. So now we are going to India, securely if prosaically, by sea; and as we intend to be away for at least a year, and as I shall have to work like the black that I am when we get back, it seems unlikely, unless something unexpected occurs, that we shall meet before 1964 or thereabouts.'[84]

During his years in and out of England, Vidia Naipaul had been awarded a degree by Oxford University, got married, become a radio presenter and a television pundit, produced journalism and book reviews, written short stories, comic novels and a coruscating study of the West Indies. Above all, he was the author of what would come to be seen as the epic of postcolonial literature, *A House for Mr Biswas*. Now he was heading for the land of his ancestors, to see what he might find. He was twenty-nine years old.

PART TWO

CHAPTER THIRTEEN

THE HOMECOMING

'AMERICANS EVERYWHERE; they are a very strange race,' Vidia wrote to Diana Athill from Athens on St Valentine's Day 1962. 'We leave tomorrow for Alexandria to take the ship for India.'[1] Vidia and Pat made the two-day crossing to Egypt on a cramped steamer, a journey which would provide the opening for *In a Free State*. He reported to Ma, with her concern about miscegenation: 'The Egyptians are not a pure people; they have a considerable amount of negro blood, and many of them look like West Indian negroes. The Arabians are purer.'[2] Aboard a slow cargo ship, the *Hellenic Hero*, they sailed down the nationalized Suez Canal, were detained at Cairo to argue with officials, and proceeded through the heat of the Red Sea with a day excursion to a 'Fuzzy Wuzzy village' in Sudan, according to Pat's diary.[3] Vidia took no notes, kept no journal; he drank in the experiences, letting them settle inside him. After three weeks at sea they approached Karachi in Pakistan, and on 18 March arrived in Bombay, the great port and teeming commercial hub on the west coast of India. 'We have no plans for India,' Vido wrote to Ma. 'We don't know what hotel we will be staying at in Bombay; how much time we will be spending there; or anything. Our plans, vaguely, are to settle down in some reasonably pleasant small town for a few months. I shall try to do a little work, and Pat shall try to get a teaching job.'[4]

India had been independent for nearly fifteen years now. Gandhi's mass campaign of non-violent protest had stirred the subcontinent and inspired nationalist struggles by colonial peoples across the world. British rule ended in 1947 when the country was partitioned into India and Pakistan in response to Muslim demands for a separate homeland; under a new constitution, the Republic of India became the largest democracy in the world; the British-educated prime minister, Jawaharlal Nehru, proclaimed a socialist dawn and a fresh era in international relations. By 1962, though, Nehru was old and ailing, and the glitter of the Congress Party's revolution was fading. For all his five-year-plans,

India was still painfully poor, and commerce was ruled by the 'Permit Raj'. The national mood of fatigue coincided with the arrival on India's shores of its doubly displaced son Vidia Naipaul, whose approach to his ancestral land had been decided many years before. While other Trinidad Indians of the 1940s drew inspiration from the struggles of Mahatma Gandhi, and Simbhoo Capildeo sent letters of supplication to Congress, Vido was wary. Aged barely seventeen, he had written to Kamla at Benares Hindu University: 'I am glad you told off those damned inefficient, scheming Indians. I am planning to write a book about these damned people and the wretched country of theirs, exposing their detestable traits. Grill them on everything.'[5] Now it was time for Vidia to write that book, and to grill them on everything: *An Area of Darkness* was the result, the most influential study of India published since independence, offering a passionate analysis of what was wrong and right with the country. 'Indians will never cease to require the arbitration of a conqueror,' he announced; and over the next five decades, Indians were certainly to show a remarkable willingness to be lectured about their failings by a Trinidadian.

From the first paragraph in his 'Traveller's Prelude', V.S. Naipaul's status as an insider–outsider was set. A man from a travel agency comes aboard the ship as soon as the quarantine flag is lowered in Bombay, and whispers, ' "You have any cheej?" ' . . . He was tall and thin and shabby and nervous, and I imagined he was speaking of some type of contraband. He was. He required cheese. It was a delicacy in India. Imports were restricted, and the Indians had not yet learned how to make cheese, just as they had not yet learned how to bleach newsprint.'[6]

What could be more ridiculous than a people who wanted cheese but were unable to make it? It was a harsh and perceptive observation, but was Vidia understanding the man correctly? While Pat had troubled to learn a little Hindi before setting out on the voyage, dutifully mouthing the words and practising the Devanagari script in her notebook, Vidia's left-over childhood knowledge of the language was cursory. It is likely the tout was asking in rough Hindi whether the young traveller had 'cheej' or 'cheez' – meaning 'stuff'.[7] Understandably, he thought Vidia would comprehend him. But was this 'Trinidadian of Hindu Descent' Indian, West Indian, neither, or both, here in this alien setting? Or was he nothing? Take the moment of first contact: 'Now in Bombay I entered a shop or a restaurant and awaited a special quality of response. And there was nothing. It was like being denied part of my reality. Again and again I was caught. I was faceless. I might sink without a trace into that Indian crowd.'[8]

How was Vidia to establish himself? He was staying at Green's Hotel on Marine Drive with his 'companion' (Pat appears momentarily, fainting, in *An Area of Darkness* under this designation; only in the American edition does she become 'my wife'; had he used her as a character, he said later, the book would have been 'another kind of family expedition. The best way of judging it, why it is difficult to do, is when you read women writing about "my husband" – or you have a figure called, "Bill". It becomes another kind of book').[9] Anxious, faceless, nervous of sinking into the crowd of 450 million, he sought out those who might help to lift him above the herd. His alma mater saved him: the ever-helpful Peter Bayley had given Vidia an introduction to a pair of Univ men, Adil Jussawalla and Ravi Dayal, and in their hospitable, Indian way, they looked after him; Dayal even came to their first meeting wearing a Univ tie. Jussawalla, a twenty-one-year-old Parsi who was shortly to publish his first volume of poetry, invited Pat and Vidia to dinner with his family and showed them the sights of Bombay. 'Bazaar with Adhil Joosewala,' Pat wrote in her diary, the repository of many of the experiences that would find their way into *An Area of Darkness*. 'Piles of fruit, spice in pyramids and other shapes. Incense. Bangles. Prostitutes in crowded boxes or pens. Some beautiful, some old and grotesque. Some with faces powdered white.'[10] To Jussawalla, who was at the time 'in a swadeshi [patriotically self-sufficient] sort of phase' wondering for instance whether it was ethical for an Indian to write in the English language, Vidia appeared 'charming, but sharp. He seemed always to be thinking about something. He said things which to me were shocking at that time – he used the phrase "slave society" of the West Indies. Pat was always on the sidelines when he said such things, saying "Oh, Vidia", trying to stop him.'[11]

Ravi Dayal worked for Oxford University Press. He had read and admired *A House for Mr Biswas*. Slight, witty and laconic, five years younger than Vidia, he came from a successful family and had won a Tata scholarship to read history at Oxford after graduating from St Stephen's, the top college at Delhi University. Peter Bayley had taken him under his wing, a position of shelter from which he sought to escape: 'I used to dodge Bayley a bit. I felt he was sort of befriending former subject peoples.'[12] When he met Vidia, Dayal noticed his denim shirt and tight trousers, enjoyed his sense of humour and doubted his claimed caste inheritance: 'I couldn't see a pukka Brahmin becoming an indentured labourer.'[13] Vidia joked to him about having a bottle of whisky impounded by customs officers. 'He was extremely funny, a very good mimic, doing accents and tones. He was a wonderful storyteller in those days. It didn't have the acid of *An Area of Darkness* at that stage . . . I think when he got [the whisky] we all celebrated and finished it off.' Dayal noticed that Vidia was in a state of high nervous tension, 'upset by the dirt' and 'endlessly looking for clean food'. The Naipauls' room at Green's Hotel was 'back-facing, while the more expensive rooms were sea-facing – cockroach infested, people going around in shorts swabbing floors and so on, dirty toenails, liable to be picking their ears and then serving you some food. We gave him some medicine to soothe his stomach.'

Pat was 'a bit of a school ma'am, but very kind, at the receiving end of Naipaul's irritability. They were equals at that point. It was as though he was leaning on her a lot, and she was soothing his disappointments and frustrations . . . I think he was fashioning himself a bit, and India was slowly becoming a character for him. His idea was very amorphous when I first met him in Bombay. He looked like everyone else and felt totally different, and people didn't realize he wasn't Indian. He tried behaving as though he was, but he didn't speak the language. To begin with, I think he probably wanted to feel much more at home in India.' Through Jussawalla and Dayal, Vidia was introduced to the burgeoning cultural world of Bombay: he met the founder of the *Economic Weekly* Sachin Choudhury, who reminded him of his father, the theatre director Ebrahim Alkazi, the poet Nissim Ezekiel, and the editor of the influential policy journal *Seminar*, Romesh Thapar, and his wife and colleague Raj. He narrowly missed a poetry reading by Allen Ginsberg and Peter Orlovsky, who were at the start of a subcontinental journey in search of sex and spiritual enlightenment. Pat wrote a letter to Ma saying she liked Bombay, but that 'Vidia was very gloomy for the first few days, partly because it is very expensive, and talked about going straight back to England. But people have been very kind and he is now feeling more settled.'[14]

In early April, Pat and Vidia made the long train journey to Delhi. Accommodation in the capital was a problem. 'Installed in exp[ensive] flat,' Pat wrote in her diary. 'The landlady – craze for imported things.'[15] They spent ten days trailing around trying to see places and get things done, exhausted by the heat and the bureaucracy. They met Ravi Dayal's future father-in-law, the lawyer, novelist, columnist, politician, editor, diplomat, voyeur and literary gadfly Khushwant Singh, who found Vidia 'reserved, pleasant and I think a little disappointed that he hadn't been given the kind of reception he expected as a son of the country who had done well.' Singh made up for it by taking them on an excursion to the Qutb Minar and Tughlakabad Fort. He remembered Pat looking 'distinctly unhappy'. They ate bacon and egg sandwiches and drank coffee in the shadow of the fort, overlooking ancient ruins and a valley of blooming red flame-of-the-forest. 'I saw him look at it for a long time,' Khushwant Singh said, 'because it was really a spectacular scene, and thought, now I'll read a lyrical account of this.' But Vidia was more interested in the urchins who swarmed around him, 'grubby little fellows in loin cloths with flies all over their faces – not a pleasant sight. I realized that he went for the squalor and dirt much more than the beauty. He was quite allergic to being touched. He almost recoiled when anyone greeted him with an embrace. The only feeling I got was that he had a chip on his shoulders. I attributed it to his being a coloured man in England.'[16] Later Singh took Vidia to a couple of parties, and to meet his father Sir Sobha, a Sikh contractor who had built parts of New Delhi, and to lunch with the German Jewish novelist Ruth Prawer Jhabvala, who was, Pat noted, 'thin, highly sensitive, nervous yet assured'.[17]

Writing to Francis Wyndham, Vidia was struck above all by Indian indifference to suffering. 'Porters are called coolies; they have no barrows, which would simplify their labour; they carry incredible loads on their heads and people who are no doubt friendly and hospitable and charitable walk behind them, concerned only that their luggage should not be stolen.' He had been asked to write some articles for the Observer, but was unsure what to write about, and was infuriated by a piece in the paper by George Patterson: 'So much of this talk about the Christian Nagas strikes me as being revivalist and mischievous. An independent Nagaland is an impossible absurdity: the injection of religion into politics is the curse of this country, and it is sad to find the Observer's correspondent encouraging this sort of thing, which will throw India more and more into the hands of the Hindu reaction, as distasteful as any other type of fanaticism.'[18] At this stage, then, he saw no virtue in the reassertion of Hindu identity, or in those who sought to use it to mobilize dormant political energy.

*

In one month, Vidia had noticed much about India. He retired to a lakeside hotel in Kashmir to think and write. Central to his conception was the idea that people failed to notice what was happening around them. Press reports were no use; destitution and begging had religious sanction. 'Indians defecate everywhere,' he wrote in *An Area of Darkness*, in Churchillian cadences, 'They defecate, mostly, beside the railway tracks. But they also defecate on the beaches; they defecate on the hills; they defecate on the river banks; they defecate on the streets; they never look for cover . . . the truth is that *Indians do not see these squatters* and might even, with complete sincerity, deny that they exist.'[19] In fact, 'It is well that Indians are unable to look at their country directly, for the distress they would see would drive them mad.'[20] In an era of nation-building, these observations about defecation were not well received. Vidia's lines attracted much hostility, and he observed laconically: 'I begin to feel that I coined the word and devised the act.'[21] The son of Kashmir's last maharajah, Karan Singh, sent an unsolicited article about *An Area of Darkness* to *Encounter* magazine, asserting that the building of toilets would bankrupt the country: 'While it can at once be admitted that our standards of public sanitation leave much to be desired, it should also be pointed out that the construction of flush latrines for five hundred million people would mean that all our other development schemes will have to be wound up.'[22]

Vidia's ambition was to stay in the Kashmir valley and write a short novel – it turned out to be *Mr Stone and the Knights Companion* – but his experiences at Mr Butt's Liward Hotel on the edge of Dal Lake in Srinagar provided plenty of material for *An Area of Darkness*: visiting pilgrims who tore up the lawn to get mud to scour their dishes, a battle over the tuning of the dining-room radio, the ceaseless demand for references which Vidia dutifully typed out on his portable typewriter, his concern over his helper Aziz's clothing, and his touching fury at himself for being driven so often to anger.[23] The Kashmir section of *An Area of Darkness* reads like a novel, with perfect characters and minute social interchange at the lakeside hotel; unusually, the narrator himself emerges as a likeable personality. The language was beautifully economical: 'The police *shikara* passed often, the sergeant paddled by constables.'[24] Or, 'Being an unorthodox hotel, we attracted the orthodox.'[25] Or, setting out on an expedition to the mountains,

'I decided, too, that the coolie was unnecessary; and the sweeper was to be replaced by a small spade. Aziz, defeated, suffered.'[26]

He was conscious as he wrote *Mr Stone and the Knights Companion* that it was a departure from what had come before. 'I had used up my Trinidad material, my childhood material. Then I had gone and done without premeditation *The Middle Passage*, which was a wonderful experience for me, going to South America and seeing these places, understanding, having a sense of those colonies.' Trying to find his way was not easy: 'Between August 1960 and December 1965, five years, *Mr Stone* was the only fiction I did. It was a big gap.'[27] Much of the book drew on his relationship with Pat and on his days at the Cement & Concrete Association, although he assured Ralph Ironman in a letter, 'I don't believe I have used any material you might want to use.'[28] His greatest worry was that he did not know enough about his adopted country to make a success of the novel. He wrote to Francis in June, 'I will certainly need your judgement and help with this one, for it is set in England, and has only English characters, the sort of thing that makes one very shy of submitting it. Angus Wilson promised to check the dialogue of any English novel I wrote; and it really is difficult to write dialogue which does not speak itself naturally in one's head.'[29] Francis responded favourably to the manuscript when he read it later that year.

Mr Stone and the Knights Companion is a short novel about an old man with regular habits and a dull life, and is notable now as a curiosity: Vidia had managed to pull off a plausible book using exclusively English characters. As Ronald Bryden wrote in a review, it was a 'feat of acculturisation' by a 'superb writer of world stature'.[30] There is a certain Hindu fatalism about Mr Stone, a librarian at a firm called Excal, but the dialogue and the social interchange convince. He marries Margaret Springer, a widow; they sleep in separate beds, and are embarrassed to be sharing a bathroom. Stone sets up the 'Knights Companion', a scheme to enable retired Excal employees to stay in touch. The book is a study of Vidia's loneliness in post-war London and a portrait of a marriage, drawing on solitary days at his desk and the stasis of sexually unsatisfactory married life. When Whymper, a public relations man with hints of John Stockbridge about him, says he enjoys spending hours with his head between his girlfriend's legs, this news seems 'unexpected, frightening, joyless' to Mr Stone.[31] In a broadly complimentary review in the *New Statesman*, V.S. Pritchett noted, 'Naipaul is not interested in the passions. Like Beckett, the master of old age, he is absorbed by "tedium". He is a minute watcher of habits and changes of mind.'[32] Vidia was profoundly interested in the passions, but had not yet found a way to translate or enact them in either his books or his life, except through purchased sex. The restrictions he felt as a man were mirrored in his fiction. *Mr Stone and the Knights Companion* was a feat, but it did not offer a way forward as a writer. He could not write further novels about dull life in London, nor could he return to the world of *Miguel Street*; his knowledge and his patois were out of date. In the same review, Bryden wrote: 'Isn't it time we killed off V. Selvon Mittelholzer?' The 'composite Caribbean author writing sunnily of quaint brown lives in the sugar-fields' was certainly finished.[33]

Pat's diary records many activities in Kashmir, such as Vidia taking photographs, adopting a stray puppy ('rescued from horrible boys who were treating him very cruelly,' she told Auntie Lu) and arriving by horse-drawn tonga for dinner at Karan Singh's smaller palace.[34] In retrospect, these were years of comparative ease and peace for Kashmir; Nehru had made Singh a figurehead ruler with the title Sadr-e-Riyasat. A man of 'heavyish build but face etc of a reader', Karan 'Tiger' Singh showed the visiting novelist and his wife family portraits and religious books, and commended his own philosophical writings. In June he gave a dinner with a dance band for the heads of the local women's colleges, the diplomat (and Nehru's sister) Vijayalakshmi Pandit and her daughter the novelist Nayantara Sahgal. Pat noted afterwards: 'Singing of Kashmiri, Dogri, Urdu, Arabic (Egyptian) songs. Also Am[erican] songs – "That is how much I love you, baby", etc. "Tiger, sing the isle of Capri, that's my vintage".'[35] When Vidia met Nayantara Sahgal many years later and she reminded him of his own role in the after-dinner singing, he angrily denied that his song had been Trinidadian. Karan Singh remembered the dinner: 'I like Indian classical, ghazals, western pop – but I might have been singing Presley's *Wooden Heart*, "Can't you see I love you, Please don't break my heart in two".'[36] Most of Pat's diary entries were happy; only occasionally did she record distress: 'Vidia's distaste for me combined with the grudge he bears (no housework, eating) reaches a head.'[37] In a letter to Ma, she reported that she had celebrated her thirtieth birthday with hotel staff and the vendors from Dal Lake, one of whom had brought her lotus flowers. Her life matched a prediction she had made in a letter to Vidia in 1953 when they were both at Oxford, although it differed in a crucial respect: childlessness. She wrote then with touching dedication and aspiration: 'At the age of thirty – this is my clear picture – we shall be just emerging from a very hard life. You will be working all the hours of the day. We shall have two children at the crawling (noisiest) stage – one very fretful the other good-tempered – and you will have just published a novel – not a best seller but a good one. Darling I do adore you honest.'[38]

In July they travelled to the beautiful mountain setting of Gulmarg, carpeted in wild flowers, to stay with a couple they had met, Zul Vellani and his wife, Nimmo. The four spent some intense, hard-drinking days together. Pat's diary degenerated into a haphazard jumble, as Vidia began to behave in an unstructured way. 'We find Zul & Nimmo playing Scrabble. Drink, lunch at 4 . . . drink, midnight dinner. Zul's life story. July 12: Read Blitz, etc. Evening walk. Sunshine mountain. Calypsoes. July 13: Frozen lake . . . Bottle of whiskey & talk until 12.' A month later, after going on a pilgrimage to the ice cave at Amarnath on the advice of Karan Singh, they visited Zul and Nimmo again. Zul was a scriptwriter and actor of Indian Muslim origin from East Africa, Nimmo was a singer and political activist, and both were fiery, attractive and opinionated.

Pat's diary went on to record a 'seizure' she had at their bungalow, brought on by the frenetic, drunken atmosphere: 'Aug 21: Pouring rain . . . Drink & talk.' Another guest was there, a communist poet named Masoud. 'V[idia] fills M[asoud]'s glass repeatedly. Outburst about Hyderabad. V shouts. M sits with eyes lowered and lower lip thrust out. I pull V into other room where "lunch" is ready . . . M – "He said something very offensive to me." "A rabid communalist." Z had shouted to V to stop from other room.' Another pair of visitors had been there recently, a sitar player named Maboob and his attractive but unstable American girlfriend, Mickey. 'Aug 22: Kashmiri singers. Zul's stories about Maboob. My seizure. Aug 23: Walk down to Tangmarg . . . Mickey & Maboob come for tea at Liward. Aug 25: M & M married to tune of 100 R. by Mufti.'[39] These characters would all be reworked accurately into *An Area of Darkness*: Zul as Ishmael, Maboob as Rafiq, Mickey as Laraine, 'a new type of American whose privilege it was to go slumming about the world and sometimes scrounging, exacting a personal repayment for a national generosity.'[40] For Zul Vellani, it was in retrospect a wild time of drink-fuelled conversation and argument. 'We had a bungalow at the top of the golf course in Gulmarg . . . My wife didn't like Vidia Naipaul. I don't know why I liked the bugger. He had a remarkable talent for observation, but he was disastrously prejudiced. One night, at two in the morning [Nimmo] woke me up [and said] that girl is screaming, I think something's wrong, so I went there and I found that Vidia Naipaul was slapping his wife. I said, what you are doing? He says, Zul, you don't understand, she suffers from hysteria, a sort of fit. My wife said there is no excuse for slapping the woman.'[41] In Vidia's recollection, Pat had suffered from a nosebleed in Gulmarg. 'I never hit Pat. Never.'[42]

During calmer times, Vidia wrote to his family from Hotel Liward. He told Mira and Savi that the Kashmiris, 'barring the Tibetans, are possibly the dirtiest people in the world. They very seldom wash . . . They associate – like the Indians of Trinidad and our family – cleanliness with godliness; only on religious days, therefore, they wear clean clothes . . . They have nevertheless a tremendous charm; perhaps they have this charm because of all their faults. Certainly there are few things more attractive than the friendliness and broad smiles of the Kashmiri children.'[43] He told Shiva, who was applying for a place at Oxford University, that he should not worry about the noise from the local rum shop. Why, last year he had bought a desk for £12, but was so happy writing at a cramped kitchen table that it was there 'this book about the West Indies, *The Middle Passage*, which is being published at the end of July, and will cause quite a furore, was written . . . I am glad you say you have no intention of writing fiction. Because I can now, without fear of depriving you of material, ask for your help.' He had written four stories about Trinidad in a week, one about a Negro baker who makes money only when he employs Chinese, another called 'The Night Watchman's Occurrence Book', a small masterpiece told through entries in a logbook at a rowdy hotel. Could Shiva think of odd incidents for him, for 'though I am in lovely Kashmir, I long to be back in Trinidad.'[44] He made a similar request to Mira in Edinburgh: 'Now you mustn't think this is a form of cheating. Gogol wrote to his mother for stories when he was writing those stories of Russian rural life.'[45] His book would be called *Trinidadians*. Writing to C.L.R. James in Tunapuna, Vidia did not mention his desire to return to Trinidad, but did admit: 'I feel quite differently to England since the Immigration Bill; and though I will have to go back there, I think it unlikely that I will stay there for any length of time.' India had produced 'fewer writers than we have with less talk . . . I wonder what you will make of my book about the West Indies. Attack I wouldn't mind; but if the book fails to arouse among West Indians some discussion about their situation, then I will have to think it a failure.'[46] To Ironman, he presented himself as fatally detached from England. 'Bluntly, we are looking for a country to live in. Perhaps Denmark might take us in.'[47]

*

A fortnight after his thirtieth birthday and a day after Trinidad became independent, Vidia and Pat Naipaul left the Kashmir valley after almost five months. It had been an extraordinarily productive time. Their days and nights were full of adventure; they had met people, been on journeys and a pilgrimage, Vidia had written a novel and a crop of short stories. Their first stop was Jammu 'as the guests of the Maharaja of Jammu and Kashmir (nothing to pay!)' he told Ironman. 'This Indian trip is proving hideously expensive. The average Indian can sleep in the open. To want a room is to be demanding; to want a bed is to be luxurious; to want proper sanitation is to be almost wanton.'[48] They travelled by train and by bus to Agra to see the Taj Mahal by moonlight, to Delhi to stay with a rich cousin of Nimmo's named Jiti, and on to Muradabad to meet Ravi Dayal's brother, Virendra. In retrospect, Ravi Dayal wondered whether he had been too free with his introductions. 'I liked Naipaul and honoured his work. I wanted him to be reasonably happy, to look around, to feel at home in India. I think that we may have actually been just too warm and helpful. Friendships were given to him too easily. It's conceivable. He had access to a lot of special people whom he may not have had easy access to at that stage.'[49]

Virendra Dayal had been Rhodes scholar, and was now an Indian Administrative Service (IAS) officer in a volatile, mixed Hindu–Muslim area in north India. He installed Mr and Mrs Naipaul at government lodgings and took Vidia around the district as he sorted out disputes and dispensed justice. According to Dayal, his generation was 'full of hope and imbued with the nationalist ethos. We never felt marginalized from the world . . . India was a great civilization, however fractured, and we had to assume responsibility for the future of our country.' As an accidental, occidental Indian from 'the most amusing island that ever dotted a sea', Vidia felt included and excluded; a contemporary like Dayal was both like and unlike himself. 'Vidia's need to be in the mainstream of history was completely understandable,' said Dayal.[50]

After Muradabad and Lucknow, the Naipauls took the sleeper train south to Hyderabad to visit the ruins of the great Hindu city of Vijayanagar. For Vidia, it was a moving and melancholic experience, a reminder of distant historic grandeur. Lurking inside the remaining buildings were 'the inheritors of this greatness: men and women and children, thin as crickets, like lizards among the stones.'[51] In Bangalore, he became entangled with a man known as Visky. In *An Area of Darkness* he appears as 'the Sikh', and insults everyone he meets. Like Vidia, who seemed to identify with him in a horrified sort of way, 'the Sikh' is enraged by the inadequacies around him. Pat's diary records these encounters: 'At 3 Aces Visky seizes upon barely perceptible turn of head to pick quarrel with man next door who turns out to be a Punjabi ("No, a Sindhi"). Visky grasps him and strikes him gently; he leans back amazed and frightened ... Vidia starts quarrelling ... Visky begs us to go and have a drink. We refuse and Visky sulks. Pulls out a reefer.'[52] Life on the move in India was more dramatic than the news from Kingstanding. 'Your Uncle Roy has had to have an operation to take away his appendix,' Pat's father informed her. 'He is going on nicely now, of course he will have to take things quietly for a bit.' Eleanor, who was planning to become a physical education instructor, reported on a rock climbing expedition to Wales. The food at the hostel had been poor: 'The main course was a large plate containing, neatly placed in the middle, one pilchard. Second course was a thin slice of jam roll and to finish off we had doorsteps of bread and marge.'[53]

Passing among the sound of the 'excessively vowelled' languages of the south, they reached Madras in mid-October, where Ravi Dayal had been sent on a posting by the Oxford University Press. He introduced them to yet another lively, creative set: David Horsburgh, an Englishman who spoke Tamil, wrote children's books and played the *mridang*, his serene wife, Doreen, and Jacques Sassoon, a Bengali-speaker who was studying Carnatic music. 'Vidia relaxes and expands,' Pat noted.[54] He pondered how to write about India, his caustic views encouraged by a developing border conflict with China. India's diplomatic and military incompetence would lead finally to a Chinese victory, and as Khushwant Singh put it: 'The sense of euphoria went out of the country and the sense of disillusionment began. 1962 was when the Chinese gave us a drumming on the battlefield. We were a beaten nation – and all the big talk that Nehru had been indulging in as a great world leader came to nothing.'[55]

Writing home, Vidia told Mira that Madras was his favourite city in the subcontinent. 'What is worrying me is this India book. I really don't know how I am to set about it; and if I don't write it, I will have to pay back Deutsch £500. Heigho!'[56] Glossing his insecurities, he told Shiva: 'I have kept no journal, and the Indians are such elusive, odd people (they puzzle you even more when they pretend to be people like you or me) that the time I have been here has not been enough for me to understand them.'[57] After leaving Madras, Vidia and Pat visited Pondicherry before

travelling to Nagpur, Calcutta, Benares and Delhi. November found them
in the district of Faizabad near Ayodhya with Manmohan 'Moni' Malhoutra
(St Stephen's, Rhodes scholar, IAS), an urbane colleague of Virendra
Dayal. 'I welcomed his company,' Malhoutra recalled. 'Life in the districts can be lonely and he was a very entertaining companion, intensely
curious. He asked a lot of questions, he was a wonderful listener, and so it
went extremely well. Pat was always trying to pacify him, calm him,
prevent him from getting into an unnecessary rage. She was a gentle,
sweet woman.' Moni Malhoutra was still under training and persuaded
his boss, a cigar-smoking, sun-helmet-wearing commissioner, to let Vidia
accompany them. 'I think that gave Vidia a real insight into the functioning of the administration, or the non-functioning of the administration, in
this country. We went to a village where some communal lavatories had
been constructed. Vidia wanted to know whether they were being used and
all these young people said, no, we don't use them. He said, why not?
And they said, in a very matter of fact way, the air is fresher outside.'[58]

A journey to Nilokheri in Punjab to visit Zul and Nimmo was not a
success, and by December they were back in Bombay, visiting the caves at
Ajanta and Ellora. Vidia and Pat had made a huge, detailed sweep of the
subcontinent over nine months. On Christmas Eve, Pat sailed to England
to find a new place for them to live in London. 'The idiotic appearance of
white passengers,' she noted as she went on board.[59] Vidia stayed in
Bombay, and was interviewed by the *Times of India*. With engaging vanity,
he wrote to Pat, 'I was photographed more than I have been in my life;
and really some were the best things that have been done of me. So in
last Sunday's paper (yesterday's) there was a piece (alas, illiterate) about
me, with a photograph of me with cap tilted back!'[60] He visited Rupa,
the Indian publisher that distributed his books, and was unimpressed by
their lack of interest. He told Diana Athill: 'You know I did not care
for the typographical design of *The Middle Passage*, but allow me to say
that the book is otherwise beautifully produced; it was a pleasure to handle
it in Rupa's office; the jacket was marvellous.'[61] He took the chance to
harry André Deutsch: 'You seldom reply to my letters, but I would be glad
if you could take note of this one.' He complained of missing royalties,
altered percentages and a failure to tell him that the paperback rights for
A House for Mr Biswas had been sold to Collins. He objected that 'four of
my books were sent in March to a Mrs Brown of Trinidad. I don't know
any Mrs Brown. I never authorised anyone to send off books, to be debited

to my account, to any Mrs Brown. AND I HAVE NO INTENTION OF PAYING FOR SUCH BOOKS . . . please give me my £2.7.11 back.'[62]

*

Vidia's plan was to spend a few more months in India gathering material. Raj Thapar arranged for him to rent a flat in New Delhi belonging to the composer Vanraj Bhatia. According to Bhatia's account, Vidia was rude about the flat and insulted his servant. 'He was snobbish, nothing nice to say — a thoroughly nasty human being.'[63] Pat was told another version: 'The place that Raj arranged was disastrous. No sheets! The Garhwali servant boy squatting on the lavatory seat, with disastrous results! No cups, nothing.'[64] Instead, he stayed with Ruth Prawer Jhabvala and her husband, Cyrus, known as Jhab. 'She comes from Golders Green,' he told Francis, 'a refugee since the age of 9 from Germany; she is married to a Parsi architect. They live quietly, almost in seclusion.'[65] The end of January found Vidia on the move again, this time on the border between India and Nepal on a tiger shoot in the company of Moni Malhoutra and a senior IAS colleague. Moni shared a tent with Vidia, and noticed his agility. 'He was very athletic and he used to do a particular movement with his leg, he used to pick it up and bring it up towards his head from the back. It's the kind of posture which you'll see in some sculptures in the Tanjore temples, a very, very difficult thing to do. He loved to do that.'[66] By the light of a Petromax lamp, Vidia wrote to Pat of the awfulness of seeing a tiger skinned: it had been 'so whole, so beautiful, so noble'. The sight of the dismembered hind legs, 'all muscle, like those of a male ballet dancer in skin-tight white rubber tights' had made him 'a great opponent of big-game shooting; for, to be blunt, the so-called hunter faces almost no risk. The knowledge is provided by the locals; they undergo such risks as are involved.'[67]

Three days later, Vidia took the train to Gorakhpur for the conceptual climax of his homecoming tour of India: it was his intention to visit the village of his maternal grandfather, Pundit Capildeo. In *An Area of Darkness*, his trip ends in self-reproach and flight; in the version sent to Pat immediately after his first visit to the village, his reactions were happier. His guide was another IAS officer, Dr J.P. Singh, who remembered: 'I was a Joint Magistrate in Gorakhpur. Moni said there is a friend of mine, a writer from the West Indies, can you take him around and show him whatever he wants to see? Naipaul was short with the hotel chaps. For example, he wanted to have hot water for his bath. It had to be carried to him in his room but it used to take time, so he used to say they are very, very lazy chaps ... I thought he was having all this anger and contempt primarily because he wanted the country to develop. The account he wrote of our trip in *An Area of Darkness*, it was accurate.'[68] Vidia told Pat: 'Gorakhpur is hell. It has reduced me to the early-Indian stage of my hysteria. Imagine ... hotels which literally stink of the sewer; imagine waiters in the filthiest clothes and with the filthiest hands, serving tea in cups which they arrange in their usual finger-dunking way.' The village was 'one of the neatest and cleanest I have seen in India; it is shaded by trees; the people were dressed in white and, this being a village of Brahmins, they were all wearing the sacred thread.' Feeling 'ridiculously afraid and shy', he explained his connection to Capildeo to the villagers, using Singh as his interpreter. When someone mentioned Jussodra, the woman with whom his grandfather had eloped from Trinidad in 1926, Vidia felt 'deeply ashamed'.[69] At this moment, in Dr Singh's words, 'An old woman, toothless, bent, wearing a not very clean sari, came out.' Jussodra! 'V. S. Naipaul didn't know she was alive, and she started speaking English in a West Indian accent and she started weeping. This fellow was dumbfounded.'[70] Jussodra explained the family story: she was his grandfather's third wife, as he already had one in India before he married the formidable Soogee.

'All this while the crowd was gathering,' Vidia told Pat, 'And they are good-looking people; slender, some tall, many well-built, with beautiful brown complexions ... This is where Ma's family & my sisters get their looks from, without a doubt.' Jussodra took him to a hut, held his feet and wept. He was left feeling that Capildeo had been 'a man of exceptional force of character ... I admire him for his three wives, for his decision to abandon all (however temporarily) for love much more than I have ever done ... As you can imagine, I fell in love with these beautiful people, their so beautiful women who have all the boldness and independence (no coyness) of Brahmin women (according to my IAS interpreter), and their enchanting fairy-tale village.' This, though, was not all: he met a cousin he never knew he had. The letter to Pat concluded: 'And what of the young man who, himself Capildeo's grandson by his Indian marriage, embraced me like Michael Redgrave embracing Margaret Rutherford in The Importance of Being Earnest?'[71] This young man's father was the source of Vidia's change of mood, evidenced in *An Area of Darkness*, where he is referred to as a 'beggar' and a 'monk' called Ramachandra Dube (Dube, pronounced doo-bay, being a Brahmin caste name). He appeared at Vidia's hotel in

Gorakhpur, and was later to be found on his bedroom verandah: 'I was towelling myself when I heard a scratching on the barred window.'[72] Vidia sent him away, and when he visited the village again, avoided Ramachandra and his requests for assistance. Thus his first-born maternal uncle, the senior to Capo S. and Capo R., was dismissed. 'So it ended, in futility and impatience, a gratuitous act of cruelty, self-reproach and flight.'[73]

Back in Delhi he stayed with the Jhabvalas, with whom he felt at ease. He wrote to Pat, 'I think of you, like a foolish young boy in love, every night, I touch myself and imagine that you are touching me. I long for your smooth breasts and all of you. Alas, alas: will performance match expectation? We've really been married too long and have been sleeping together too long for me to feel so sharply.' Pat responded that she had found a less than perfect place for them to live at 5 Waldenshaw Road on the fringes of south-east London, helped by a 'To Whom It May Concern' letter from Diana Athill recommending Vidia as an ideal tenant and 'one of England's leading young writers'.[74] Pat decided to take a teaching post at Haberdashers' Aske's Hatcham Girls' school. Staying in Delhi, Vidia enjoyed the company of Jhab, whom he commends on the final page of *An Area of Darkness*. Less happily, he had a chance encounter with his former host Jiti, who asked him to smuggle a cheque out of the country: 'Now this is highly dangerous; and . . . if one is offended by corruption, one can hardly indulge in corrupt practices oneself. Jiti is therefore, I believe, greatly annoyed.'[75]

It was with relief then that Vidia took a flight to Madrid, pausing only to purchase a photograph of himself taken as he walked from the aeroplane clutching his typewriter and an untied parcel of cloth. As he had promised, he wrote letters at once to J.P. Singh and to Moni Malhoutra, telling them of his reactions on leaving India. The letter to Malhoutra anticipated the book that would follow:

> The point that one feels inescapable is the fact of India's
> poverty; and how deep is one's contempt for those Indians who,
> finding no difficulty in accepting one standard in India and
> another outside it, fail to realise this, and are failing to work
> night and day for the removal of this dreadful insult and
> humiliation . . . The lavatories at Palam [airport] were <u>literally</u>
> covered with shit and the aerodrome officer could only speak of
> the shortage of staff (i.e. sweepers). I wonder, wonder if the
> shitting habits of Indians are not the key to all their attitudes.
> I wonder if the country will not be spiritually and morally

regenerated if people were only made to adopt the standards of other nations in this business of shitting; if only they could be made to see that they owe some responsibility . . .

So goodbye to shit and sweepers; goodbye to people who tolerate everything; goodbye to all the refusal to act; goodbye to the absence of dignity; goodbye to the poverty; goodbye to caste and that curious pettiness which permeates that vast country; goodbye to people who, though consulting astrologers, have no sense of their destiny as men. From here it is an unbelievable, frightening, sad country. Probably it all has to change. Not only must caste go, but all those sloppy Indian garments; all those saris and lungis; all that squatting on the floor to eat, to write, to serve in a shop, to piss. Probably the physical act of standing upright (think of the sweeper prowling about like a dog below your cafe table) might regenerate the people. Probably I am mad. But it seems to me that everything conspires to keep India down.

These ideas would mature in *An Area of Darkness*, and in his later books on India.

The return to London left Vidia depressed, and it took him a couple of months to get started on the writing. He told Moni Malhoutra in May: 'I suppose I miss India more than I imagined; and, I say this without flattering you, I miss Lucknow and Fyzabad [he unconsciously used the spelling of the Trinidad town, named for the Indian Faizabad] more than anything else. I wonder whether I shouldn't buy some acres in Ranikhet or some part too cold for Indians and run a little farm.'[76]

Soon, once the book was under way, his Tolstoyan vision was put aside. Pat tried to persuade him to be more generous and forgiving in his treatment of India: 'She loved India. She saw dignity and beauty and things like that; I saw the calamity.' Pat's political or social views, at this time and subsequently, did not have the effect of softening Vidia's position. His instinctive response to another person's line of argument was to harden his own views, and to be made more certain that his particular insight was rare and correct, and needed to be expressed. 'She was a profoundly liberal person. This wasn't just an attitude. It was so nice . . . I provoked her constantly. I was very, very provocative. She was speaking quite genuinely, and I would play the fool; I would often play the fool.'[77]

CHAPTER FOURTEEN

'LOVELY *VOGUE*,
JUST BOUGHT'

AFTER NEARLY A YEAR of travel and enquiry, India remained for V.S. Naipaul 'the land of my childhood, an area of darkness ... I had learned my separateness from India, and was content to be a colonial, without a past, without ancestors.'[1] This was a premature and inaccurate conclusion: he was not content to be a colonial, and would continue to seek an Indian ancestral past. When *An Area of Darkness: An Experience of India* was published in autumn 1964, Francis Wyndham, to whom it was dedicated, wrote: 'Your book is really an <u>important</u> book. I suppose it will make some people very angry.'[2] John Wain in the *Observer* judged it 'tender, lyrical, explosive and cruel'. The *Times Literary Supplement* praised it as 'beautiful, sensitive and sad'. The *Daily Telegraph* thought it a 'sour recital'. V.S. Pritchett called it 'the most compelling and vivid book about India to appear for a long time.'[3] BBC television put Vidia on a chat show with some furious Indian students from the London School of Economics. One remembered: 'Naipaul unperturbed and smiling, held his ground: "India is on its death bed, there is no point in wasting life-saving drugs on a terminally ill patient" ... He advised us students not to return to India but to seek jobs in England.'[4] Deutsch's distributor in India refused to handle the book, and copies had to be smuggled in. The publisher Sir Allen Lane complained about the de facto ban in 1968 to Morarji Desai, the deputy prime minister, who responded that the decision by Indian Customs had arisen 'because of some misapprehension on the part of the dealing officer', and would be lifted.[5] Nissim Ezekiel wrote a spirited and much discussed attack, 'Naipaul's India and Mine'. Rudranath Capildeo, in a speech in parliament in Port of Spain, apologized through Mr Speaker to the people of India for this 'notorious book ... Pope Paul VI went to India and he left his heart in India, but one of our countrymen went there but left his excrement.'[6]

An Area of Darkness was to provoke and fascinate readers in and out of India for decades; Naipaul's willingness to try to judge a nation and assess, as his father's son, the moral and cultural affect of Hinduism on human behaviour made the book both a target and a talisman. At a time when relativism was starting to become the accepted theoretical response to any postcolonial nation's failings, the strength of Naipaul's views looked like a shocking return to the days of absolute, imperial judgements. Significantly, his book would influence the outlook of two generations of Indian writers, particularly men: Amitav Ghosh, Farrukh Dhondy, Amit Chaudhuri, Tarun Tejpal, Amitava Kumar and Nirpal Dhaliwal have all written of its impact. Naipaul's pessimistic intensity, his self-laceration and his refusal to engage in wishful thinking made the book influential as an approach to be either rejected or embraced. Pankaj Mishra said that he was left 'shocked and bewildered' when he read *An Area of Darkness* aged sixteen: 'I didn't know that you could write like that about India. I think it was the first book I read in English that contained the world I lived in.'[7]

Before he left Bombay, Vidia had given an interview to the *Illustrated Weekly of India*, a long-established and influential English-language newspaper. It was an intense, passionate performance, containing much of the thinking and sentiment that would be played out in *An Area of Darkness*. The interviewer initially found him 'playboyish ... still in his dressing gown though it was nearer midday', making facetious remarks about England: 'It is such a boring place that one can do nothing else but work.' When he spoke of India, though, there was a shift. He talked with angry passion: 'I suppose you don't want me to enlarge upon the dreadful sanitation, backward villages, and the dishonesty prevailing everywhere ... I never thought that Indians were such consummate hypocrites, preaching austerity, preaching godliness and indulging in the grossest type of materialism in any society. I never thought that the Indians would be so callous to human suffering. I never thought that one would find oneself in a slave society – and this is what it is – with so many politicians ... Equally, I never thought I would enjoy the company of Indians as I have done ... the Indians one meets and talks to are the most interesting people I have ever met.'

It had been a homecoming; Vidia was a child of the Indian diaspora who wanted to understand the civilization of his forebears. The interviewer felt he had 'a love-hate relationship towards India'. In turn, he thought the country was suffering from a surfeit of mediocre writers who spent their time 'in dreadful little conferences' complaining about problems of translation. 'The word "writer" like the word "minister" is much abused in India. Perhaps there will also be "deputy writers" soon.' Nor was he optimistic about the capacity of the state to recognize that the last years of the Nehruvian era were marked by self-satisfaction. 'India, as it is, has no future . . . And the reason is that India has not adjusted itself to the modern world.' The interviewer's response was surprisingly benign. 'I did not attempt to contradict Naipaul because he was speaking out of a real concern . . . The severe strictures were valid, for it is time we, in this country, stirred ourselves from the moral complacency of assumed righteousness and looked into the mirror.'[8]

The editor of the *Illustrated Weekly of India*, an impressive man named A.S. Raman who was seen as a father-figure by many of his journalists, asked Vidia if he would write a monthly 'Letter from London'.[9] He could write about whatever he liked. Vidia took up the offer at £30 a letter, and for the first time was forced to assess his adopted home country directly. He had the advantage of comparative anonymity: writing for a foreign audience in the days before the internet, he knew he could express himself freely, even experimentally, and that it was unlikely anyone in London would read his words. He started frankly in the spring of 1963, making it clear he saw himself as a visitor in England, just as he felt a stranger in every country. 'To me, departure is always more welcome than arrival.' He expressed the loneliness of the city, stuck in 'one's private cell' or on twisting Underground trains or buses, 'Everywhere one feels enclosed.' Characteristically, he gave no signal that he shared his 'cell' with another person in a land where 'home-making is the aim and almost the point of this culture'. His detachment made him look at his adopted country with an encompassing eye. He tried, not altogether successfully, to see Britain with the same analytical detachment he saw India or the West Indies. 'Satire is now all the rage . . . With the destruction of a century-old order in England, nothing is settled, and the pace of disturbance increases.' He was conscious that the satire was parochial: 'No novelist has chronicled the astonishing changes in England in the 50 imperial years after the Indian Mutiny' and British playwrights and novelists preferred material such as 'jokes about the Foreign Office and about Eton and Harrow . . . And London, so far as literature goes, remains

Dickens's city ... on the modern mechanised city, its pressures and frustration and sterility, English writers have remained silent.'[10]

For the next two years, Vidia's life and opinions can be read through the themes he explored in his letters for the *Illustrated Weekly*. It was the only time he would ever write regularly on contemporary culture. He discussed cricket, the Beatles, television satire (*That Was The Week That Was*), the plight of the 'colonial' in British society, Angry Young Men, *Queen* magazine and the Queen herself. 'The Royal Family has ceased to be esteemed ... The newspapers now openly say that the Queen's tour of Australia was a failure, and a *Guardian* columnist went so far as to do a debunking piece on the Poet Laureate.'[11] He discussed the growth of advertising. 'The London Underground would be grim indeed without those advertisements for women's underwear that flash by one after the other as we go up or down the escalators.' Now even political parties were advertising themselves, 'just like Rinso or Ovaltine'. Naipaul remained party apolitical, turned off by the simplicities of Labour and the Conservatives. At the next election, 'I will go down to the polling station, vote for the man who is almost certain to lose, and do what I can to cheer up his agent.'[12]

In the summer of 1963 he covered an unfurling scandal. Jack Profumo, the minister for war, had resigned after lying to the House of Commons over his relationship with a part-time prostitute who was also sleeping with a Soviet naval attaché. Vidia thought the publicity and furore was overdone, since it 'might suggest to the researcher of the future that in the 1960s the English were given to Roman-scale orgies ... It seems to me foolish to raise the cry of hypocrisy and to deduce from this scandal that England is on the verge of moral collapse.'[13] When one of the figures in the Profumo case, Stephen Ward, killed himself a few weeks later, Vidia wrote a more introspective piece about sex and prostitution, which was also an oblique, naive, partial confession of what he saw as his own sexual failings, mixing truth with lies. Rebecca West had written in a newspaper that the problem was one of 'animal training', and that society needed 'to get the goats and monkeys under control'. Vidia, writing under the headline 'Of Goats and Monkeys', thought the problem was one of sexual desire. He said he had been told by an 'elderly retired prostitute' (covering himself by stressing the woman's age and undesirability) that there was too much bad language on radio and television. 'Prostitutes do exist;

they have clients; and they make money. But I have never met a man who has been with a prostitute. I have met few who have not professed horror at the thought ... Prostitutes are outlaws, necessary to some and denied by all. They are little known and greatly feared.'

Here was the difficulty: Vidia felt powerful sexual desire which he thought he could satisfy only by buying sex, but was ashamed of his lust, an essential aspect of himself. 'A denial of opportunity is not a suppression of passion ... From this self-disgust the younger generation is free. For them, more sexually permissive than their elders, prostitution is an old-fashioned, unnecessary custom.' Writing days after his thirty-first birthday, he was caught somewhere between the older and younger generations, trapped in a circle of sexual frustration which spilt out in his troubled interaction with other people, and in his disapproval of himself for living a double life. 'Mightn't the problem raised by the Ward affair be simply that of a society still in certain quarters too much "under control"? ... Sex is an appetite. Seduction is a faculty like sprinting or pole-vaulting. We are not equally endowed, either with appetite or faculty.'[14]

Cricket was also on his mind in the summer of 1963. In a rare exercise in nostalgia, he wrote about the importance of the game in his early life. 'Cricket was one of the delights of my childhood in Trinidad in the 1940s.' He described a cricketer he admired, Lance Pierre, 'a tall, lean man with long hands attached to wrists that worked as if on hinges. Simply to see him flick a ball to a fielder, with a slight underhand movement, was enough.' In those days, he had resented the cricketers from Barbados who came each season to play at the Queen's Park Oval. 'No one who spoke with such an accent could be taken seriously, and it was hard to credit that men who looked so much like our own should suddenly, by their speech, betray their immeasurable difference. It was my especial xenophobia, and it was restricted to Barbadians.' In Britain, though, a new solidarity had emerged. He found himself on the same side as fellow West Indians, like the legendary Clyde Walcott. 'It never occurred to me then that one day I might find myself willing Walcott C. to a century.' Recently, though, hearing the fast bowler Wes Hall chatting outside a cricket ground, his old prejudice had returned. 'It was pure Barbadian ... I had imagined him like a Trinidadian, like one of *us*.'[15] To an East Indian audience at least, V.S. Naipaul was still positioning himself as a West Indian in 1963.

At the start of 1964, ethnic prejudice against immigrants from the

Indian subcontinent was in the news. In the London suburb of Southall, which had a growing Punjabi community, indigenous white residents were trying to stop the newcomers from buying properties, and in the Midlands town of Smethwick, a senior Labour politician looked set to lose an election over a racial issue. Smethwick was home to many subcontinental immigrants, and the local Conservatives were reported to be using the slogan, 'If you want a nigger for a neighbour, vote Liberal or Labour.' Unusually, Vidia made an explicit public statement of his own attitude towards race relations, developing the exclusivist Hindu thinking he had been brought up on by his parents and grandmother, and assuming his view would be shared by many in India.

'The whole world knows why there must be prejudice against Negroes. Negroes want to be integrated with whites; they want to sleep with white women; and they have immense sexual energy. Now here are the reasons why the Conservatives of Smethwick are pressing for discrimination against Indians and Pakistanis. Indians and Pakistanis do not want to be integrated; they do not want to marry white women . . . they do not even want to learn English.' He contrasted left-wing interest in overseas poverty with the reality of British prejudice. The charity Oxfam had held a public meeting in Trafalgar Square at which idealists lunched on bread and water, and a 'rescued' African baby was displayed to the media. 'Which is more important?' Naipaul asked. 'The Oxfam campaign, rescuing starving black babies, or the report in *The Times* that it is virtually impossible to "place" a child with African blood in an English adoptive home?' Much press coverage, he felt, was created by prurient reporters who thought 'race is as spicy as sex . . . And it is not surprising to find that as the volume of "correct" writing on race grows so does the number of "Europeans Only" and "No Coloured" notices in the "To Let" column of suburban newspapers.' A solution would come not from 'a magical change of heart' by the English, or 'the display of more fattened little Africans in Trafalgar Square', but from conspicuous success by immigrants. Failure was not an option: 'Prejudices are made meaningless by achievement, and racial prejudice is no exception.' He swept aside the pieties of the colonial freedom movements of the 1960s in favour of a muscular nationalism, and rejected the Nehruvian piety that India had a moral duty to give public guidance to other nations: 'The dignity of Indians everywhere depends on the power of India. The speeches of even the most respected politician will have less effect than the achievements of a scientist or an

industrialist, for he is the man who produces a country's wealth, which
is its power.'[16] It was a way of thinking that was to find favour in India
at the end of the century, with V.S. Naipaul's encouragement.

By the time he wrote his final piece for the *Illustrated Weekly* at the
end of 1964, Vidia was depressed about his own future in Britain. Since
finishing *An Area of Darkness*, he had got stuck, and was not sure how
best to proceed. 'A sad song's best for winter. It is a gloomy season
anyway, in spite of all the lights in Regent Street. The newspapers and
some politicians are screaming for black blood, and not only in the
Congo.' He wrote of the optimism he had found in Nirad Chaudhuri's
A Passage to England: 'It was an enthusiasm some of us who grew up
in the days of Empire had; it overrode whatever we might have felt
about Empire; it lay at the base of the old concept of the Commonwealth. If the Commonwealth has turned out to be fraudulent, too
grand an idea for the country which sought to be its head, it is because
this idea of England was, in truth, insubstantial.' There was a 'blinkered
cosiness' among British novelists and playwrights. 'People like myself,
unwilling or unable to enter these private cultural sports, have no
business here.' Vidia had achieved some social success, but it gave him
no sense of security. 'My acquaintance steadily widens, but I feel more
and more like a visitor, no longer at ease.' London, in the aftermath of
empire and of the Second World War, was parochial. 'The city has
been generous to me. It has permitted me, an unknown and unprotected
outsider, to acquire a niche of sorts.' Writers like himself who had
migrated within the Commonwealth 'might be said to have become
refugees, victims of the idea of London and England, of self-delusion
and sentimentality, which are always dangerous, even at Christmas.'[17]

*

Around this time, Vidia began to see C.L.R. James, thirty years his senior
and his father's former rival. Besides publishing *Minty Alley*, 'Nello' James
had led an extraordinarily varied itinerant life after leaving Trinidad in
1932. He became a Marxist and political activist in England, wrote about
cricket for the *Manchester Guardian*, promoted self-government for the
West Indies, published a seminal study of the 1791 slave revolution in
Haiti, *The Black Jacobins*, which influenced Eric Williams's thinking,
encouraged civil disobedience against segregation in the USA until he was
deported, visited Trotsky in Mexico to discuss racial politics, developed
early theories of pan-Africanism and provided intellectual ballast back in

Trinidad to Eric Williams and the PNM in the late 1950s, although by now he had quarrelled with Williams. 'We had a little joke about C.L.R. James,' Vidia recalled. 'James said to Trotsky, "What can the Communist revolution do for the Negro?" and Trotsky answered, "You are asking the wrong question. You should ask, what can the Negro do for the Communist revolution?"'[18] Self-taught, well-read, a lover of Verdi and calypso, James was in some ways a typical Caribbean intellectual of his time: eclectic, spontaneous and a devotee of Western rationalism. By the 1980s, lionized internationally as an elderly pioneer of black studies even as he was attacked for his perceived Eurocentrism, James would baffle interviewers and researchers who failed to see the Queen's Royal College colonial tradition out of which he had emerged, or its distance from modern African and African-American experience.[19]

With Vidia, he had a friendly but sparring relationship, believing that as West Indian writers of different generations they served a common cause. Writing from Kashmir in early 1963, Vidia thanked 'Nello' for sending him a review of Derek Walcott's poems, *In a Green Night*, and added: 'I was glad to find in your quotations some of the Walcott poems I have always liked: As John to Patmos, Letter to a Painter. I have always felt about Walcott that here, in the most unexpected, purest way, we had a poet, someone of startling vision and muscular expression; some of his poems have never left me.' This was a substantial compliment, since the poems in question had been self-published by Walcott when he was eighteen. 'I am glad that Walcott has at last been published; it is the barest reward for a long devotion to his craft.' Vidia's occasional personal antagonism towards Walcott did not affect his critical judgement, at least as far as these early poems was concerned. Before slighting Walcott's later work in his memoir *A Writer's People*, Vidia wrote: 'Reading these poems in London in 1955, I thought I could understand how important Pushkin was to the Russians, doing for them what hadn't been done before. I put the Walcott as high as that.'[20]

James and Naipaul met, corresponded and went to watch cricket. In the *Illustrated Weekly of India* in the summer of 1963, Vidia described a journey to Birmingham with an unnamed man to watch a match. 'He has a background of Marxism and African nationalism; but cricket, the subject of his last book, remains his passion.' Vidia thought West Indians were reviving English cricket, since they had given 'in more ways than one, a new complexion to the game ... When a West Indian batsman gets his century cushions and mackintoshes will be thrown into the air; men will spontaneously dance.'[21] In *Encounter* magazine, he praised the originality of James's study of the culture of cricket in the West Indies, *Beyond a Boundary*, comparing himself to the author: 'we have both charmed ourselves away from Trinidad'.[22] In response, James wrote commending Vidia's plan to write on India. 'I can imagine no one doing it better and it will come very well from one who is himself one of the breeds without the law.'[23] This was the sort of racial coupling that Vidia disliked – James was alluding to Rudyard Kipling's poem 'Recessional', with its line about 'lesser breeds without the law'. In a follow-up letter, after debating various points in the review of *Beyond a Boundary*, James stressed the obligations of the Caribbean writer. Although he felt 'profoundly sympathetic' to the way Vidia wrote 'in human and subjective terms' about the countries he visited, he wondered whether it was right to do so 'unless we at the same time or within its context are penetrating into and showing our awareness of the terrible crises of Western civilization . . . I believe that effective as we are in stripping the wrappings from the underdeveloped countries, we will be more effective if, maybe not directly, but certainly we indicate that we are ready to strip or have already stripped the wrappings from Western civilization itself.'

James was hedging in this long letter, but he appeared to be saying that as a Marxist who knew that any country's problems were based on 'economic, social and political foundations', he did not think it wise for a writer to be too harsh on a developing country. It was an argument that would be put to Vidia many times over subsequent years: was it right for him, a former colonial subject, to write so unsentimentally and even cruelly about the failings of countries that were struggling to come to terms with independence? Why did he not turn a comparable searchlight on the more stable and prosperous countries of the West? 'Believe me, my dear Vidia, it is with no idea of propagandizing you . . .' James continued, although this was precisely what he was trying to do, and concluded, 'I wish I saw you more often. I am sure I would benefit by it and I don't think that I would either bore or annoy you.'[24] This was an odd tone for a man of James's seniority to be using, and may have reflected his reverence for Vidia's literary success in London. His correspondent, temperamentally averse to being steered by anyone, did not reply to the letter. Vidia's attitude to the questions James was raising had been settled in his own mind many years before. As he wrote to Pat when they were both twenty, he was the spectator, free of the emancipatory fire, who had no wish to reform the human race. He was the man without loyalties, whether to India, the West Indies or to anywhere else, who would write the truth as he saw it. Contrary to the depredations that would be launched against Vidia with increasing force over the coming decades, his moral axis was not white European culture, or pre-Islamic Hindu culture, or any other passing culture: it was internal, it was himself. When *An Area of Darkness* was published James remarked: 'Naipaul is saying what the whites want to say but dare not. They have put him up to it.'[25] C.L.R. James, as a person and as a type, remained on Vidia's mind, though it would be thirty years before he settled his score with him, and this time in fiction.

*

Looking outwards was one thing; looking inwards was another. Vidia's problem was that he had reached a climax of thought and creativity with the writing of *An Area of Darkness*, and was now stranded, despite the literary prestige he had amassed. 'I have been concentrating on occasional, money-making work since I came back – articles, broadcasting, book-reviews, etc,' he wrote to his mother in June 1963, 'and so far I have not been able to settle down to any book. I would like to do so though. To earn money Pat has gone back to teaching.'[26] He reviewed a book on Kipling for the *New Statesman*, and later a biography of James Bond's creator, Ian Fleming: 'I recognise in myself something of Fleming's own romantic attitude to the very successful and very rich.'[27] In a negative assessment of *The Burnt Ones* by the Australian writer Patrick White, he noted that there were now 'as many emergent literatures as there are emergent countries.' This had left him with an 'uncertainty about the function of the novel, and a conviction that the novel as we know it has done all that it can do and that new forms must be found.'[28] It was a theme that V.S. Naipaul would develop and return to over the next four decades, particularly when he was having trouble with his own writing, as he put together a thesis that the novel had become a worn-out form, unsuitable for capturing the complexity of modern, patchwork societies. His thinking would reach its apogee when he wrote in 1999, 'Literature is the sum of its discoveries . . . what is good is always what is new, in both form and content . . . The new novel gave nineteenth-century Europe a certain kind of news. The late twentieth century, surfeited with news, culturally far more confused, threatening again to be as full of tribal or folk movement as during the centuries of the Roman Empire, needs another kind of interpretation . . . It is a vanity of the age (and of commercial promotion) that the novel continues to be literature's final and highest expression.'[29]

Creatively blocked in 1963, he took out his anger on Britain: 'I don't know why people stay in this country.'[30] Two years earlier he had written to Francis, 'I would regard banishment from England as a death sentence.'[31] The price of housing was ridiculous, he told Ma, and 'the lower classes of this country are an absolute menace, animals eating far more than they deserve.' In the long term, he and Pat would need to buy a property of their own, but where would they get the money to pay a mortgage? 'Can you imagine buying a flat for [TT]$23,000 [£4,800]?' he asked. 'And that's cheap!' Ma was now supporting herself by managing the workers in her brother Simbhoo's quarry. Vidia asked her to tell him the exact time of his birth, so he could have his horoscope told by a man in India. He had some reasons for optimism. Deutsch was taking him more seriously, and had personally visited Nepaul Street. He even told Vidia that Ma was 'one of the three most distinguished people he had met in the West Indies. Eric Williams and Frank Collymore of Barbados were the others.'[32] The following year, the producer of the BBC arts show *Monitor*, Christopher Burstall, wrote to Vidia, 'I was delighted to see that Deutsch are bringing out a uniform edition – big deal! It only remains now for you to choose your own official biographer.'[33]

In July 1963 Vidia made a pair of programmes for the Third Programme about the calypsonian 'Sparrow', with extracts of music and vigorous commentary. Pa too had liked calypso, writing in praise of 'the Negro troubadour' in the *Trinidadian* magazine in 1934, tracing its origin back to the French settlers whose songs were incorporated into 'the carousals of the liberated slaves or bongo dancers'.[34] The audio recording of the programme is revealing. Vidia speaks in a clipped, dated BBC accent, saying 'classical' for 'classical' and rounding his sentences with the voice of authority. When quoting Sparrow, Lord Invader or The Caresser on Edward VIII ('It's love, love alone, that force King Edward to leave the throne') he reverts to a Trinidadian accent. Most striking, is his infectious enthusiasm for the art of calypso.[35] The cover of the album *Spicy Sparrow* was later printed with the line: 'But where Naipaul can observe, from afar, without getting a speck of dust on his impeccable person, Sparrow, more tactile, sees life as one long boisterous contact sport.'[36]

By now, Vidia was consciously cutting away from West Indian circles in London, and many of the people he had known at *Caribbean Voices* were going home, or pursuing a future in Canada or the USA. Andrew Salkey's wife, Pat, thought 'Vidia wanted to disassociate himself. Gradually he lost all his friends, they all drifted away from him. Andrew and Vidia fell out − I don't want to say how, but Andrew was fed up with the way Vidia spoke to people. He could be quite insulting. We still did see a lot of Sam [Selvon], but Sam was a very loveable character. You couldn't say that of Vidia.'[37] But if he rejected his West Indian friends, who or what was to take their place? Pat was reticent, and hesitant to form friendships. She had no family or professional connections to help them. Vidia was more socially competent, but this was partly a performance, a man acting a necessary role. Might a section of British society accommodate them, and his interests and ambitions? Might there be space perhaps amongst the effortless upper classes, who had a tradition of lionizing bright young visitors from the colonies? Could Vidia go the same way as the Lucknow-born Mirza Abu Taleb Khan, who visited London in 1800 and wrote that 'the Nobility vied with each other in their attention to me'?[38] Rudranath Capildeo might meet Hugh Fraser at Marlborough House, but his nephew Vido would meet Fraser in his drawing room.

Francis Wyndham unlocked the door, introducing Vidia to Antonia Fraser, previously encountered as leader of the college haughties in the pages of the Oxford *Isis*, now the comely young wife of the prominent Conservative politician Hugh Fraser. 'I liked Antonia's wit,' Vidia said later, 'the way she talked, the way she made the world an interesting place.'[39] Through Antonia, Francis and Anthony Powell (his wife, Violet, was Antonia's aunt), Vidia gained access to a new group of privately educated, well-connected British people who were willing to accept him as a curiosity, particularly once he gained the imprimatur of literary success. In 1962, realizing the extent of his talent, Powell wrote in the *Daily Telegraph* that it was time for V.S. Naipaul to be recognized simply as 'this country's most talented and promising younger writer'.[40] Vidia seemed to become a member of this extended, interlocking group, but remained an inquiline. He met Lord and Lady Glenconner (who were wealthy from powdered bleach and Trinidad estates, connected to royalty and related to Francis Wyndham), their daughter Emma Tennant (a novelist and reluctant socialite, her world brilliantly evoked in the memoir *Girlitude*), Julian Jebb (a talker and book reviewer who dressed in garish clothes), Teresa ('Tizzie') and Peter Gatacre (who owned a castle in Holland), Hugh

Thomas (a rising historian) and his wife, Vanessa (the daughter of an eminent diplomat, Lord Gladwyn), and Edna O'Brien (a seductive Irish novelist).

Ten days younger than Vidia, Antonia came from a large and loquacious family, her father being an Oxford don turned Labour minister, and her mother a political activist. Many family members wrote books, although her brother Thomas Pakenham made the point, ' "We are not writers at all. We are talkers disguised as writers." '[41] Fragrant and resolute, Antonia led a vigorous life after leaving Oxford, worked in publishing, engaged in humanitarian activism, wrote a history of toys and produced six children. Her husband, Hugh, nearly fifteen years her senior, came from a prominent Scottish family and had fought in the Second World War with the Lovat Scouts, a regiment founded by his father. Antonia's first book told how to give a children's party, and gave no hint of greater things to come; she advised readers to play Hunt the Slipper, combine Bite Food and Bright Food and always obey the hostess: 'If she does not mention little Cuthbert on the invitation, do not jump to the conclusion that she just didn't know Charles had a younger brother.'[42] When her father inherited an obscure Irish peerage on the death of his brother in 1961, she gained the nominal right to put the word 'lady' in front of her name, a right she pursued with vigour. Vidia admired Lady Antonia's social ease, and her ability to bring together discrete social, political and literary spheres; her interest in politics and in people was not partisan.

At Hugh and Antonia's large, late Georgian house in Campden Hill Square, Vidia, and occasionally Pat, would soon meet politicians, writers, actors, socialites: Jackie Kennedy, Iain Macleod, Anna Massey, Rebecca West, Michael Holroyd, Enoch Powell, Germaine Greer. His first invitation was to dine with Dr Eric Williams. 'We had to have Williams to dinner, my husband being at the Colonial Office,' Antonia recalled. 'Hugh and Vanessa Thomas came, and Williams and Pat and Vidia. We were really friendly from that moment onwards.' V.S. Naipaul and The Doc, both of Queen's Royal College and the University of Oxford via a colonial scholarship, failed smartly to discuss *The Middle Passage* or anything of consequence when they met in this setting. Antonia could see no social distinction between herself, Vidia and Pat: 'After all, we had all been at Oxford together [and] the Sixties wasn't a time of social gaps . . . The house was full of colonial people.' Her only worry was when on another occasion 'a terribly rude woman insisted on coming for a drink, to get a book signed, and she wouldn't speak to him. It was really awful. I think it was colour prejudice. I was appalled, and Vidia was just so cool. When she went I said, "I'm frightfully sorry, it's awful." He said, "The only upsetting thing is if you were upset, Antonia." Very elegant.'[43] Vidia pocketed the insult. And kept it in his pocket.

From 1963 until the early 1970s, Lady Antonia gave Vidia significant hospitality and friendship. Her house in Campden Hill Square provided him with a remote idea of security and familiarity. Adopting a manner last encountered in his correspondence with his pen pal, 'my dear Beverly', he sent her occasional letters from diverse and distant locations: India, New York, Kenya, Wiltshire, even a residential hotel on the edge of London. His tone was new, social, chatty, politely flirtatious; 'Vidia N.' commended a 'relaxing and delightful party' Antonia had given, and seeing her picture in the glossies wrote: 'Lovely Vogue, just bought. This issue also tells of a new fish restaurant at 73, Baker Street called Hook, Line & Sinker. Shall we try this before Ravi Shankar?'[44] They listened to the sitarist in concert, Antonia heavily pregnant with her son Damian. In April 1967, Vidia posted her a green silk sari and a note from Delhi: 'it worried me whether the colour was the colour you said you didn't want . . . I chose it with the advice of an Indian actress whose knowledge of these things one must defer to.'[45] Sensing no competition, he even gave her literary encouragement. In early 1969 Antonia published her first biography, of Mary, Queen of Scots. She told Vidia of editorial battles, of being 'put into the ring with a girl . . . aged 22, like bull and matador, to argue out each individual correction.'[46] He responded jauntily, 'Still, what a lovely letter you made . . . all good things in writing do come out of suffering; but remember at least that you have here an appreciative audience. And, really, knowing the young, and knowing the "editor"-figure, I imagine that [she] was probably just plain infuriating.' When a finished copy reached him, he even sent a telegram: 'YOUR BEAUTIFUL ENVIABLE BOOK THANKS CONGRATULATIONS VIDIA.'[47] Antonia thanked him for 'one of the nicest letters I have ever had in my life', adding that her husband Hugh was taken up with the Biafra crisis, and she had been 'terribly terribly pleased, and often extraordinarily touched by the reception of MARY'.[48] With Mary, Queen of Scots, Antonia found her feet: she went on to write big, popular, well-researched narrative histories and biographies, often focusing on monarchs or women in history.

For Vidia, this was a new style of friendship. A role was being shown to him, as friend, as swain, as object of intellectual admiration, and he enjoyed it, despite a degree of uncertainty about what was expected from him. Once the relationship had been formed in this way, it stuck, and when in later years he failed signally to return Antonia's hospitality, she ignored the signs of rejection. Like the colonial governor's wife in *The Mystic Masseur*, 'The more disconcerting the man or woman, the more she was interested, the more she was charming.'[49] Swiftly, then, Vidia was taken up by a whole new world. When he was awarded the Hawthornden Prize, Tony Powell wrote 'Dear Viddy' a letter which ended, 'Violet, of course, joins me in these congratulations and sends her love to you both.'[50] Lord Glenconner ('Glenc' to his friends) became Vidia's patron, impressed by his performance at the dinner table. Francis Wyndham was the conduit: he informed Vidia that the peer, through one of his companies, was willing to give him an unsecured loan to buy a house. 'I don't know why he did it,' Vidia said later. 'I was very moved, and I remained very attached to his memory. It was a very grand thing to do. Mark you — a very wealthy man and a wealthy company.'[51] According to Francis, Lady Glenconner was the impetus behind the patronage: 'She admired his books. She was a great friend of Cyril Connolly, Anthony Powell and other writers. Glenc arranged good terms. I saw it as a friend doing a favour.'[52] Using an Oxford contemporary, Michael Carey, as his solicitor, Vidia bought a flat in Sydenham Hill in south London at a cost of £3,500, repayable to Tennants Estates at 5½ per cent over fifteen years. The flat overlooked Sydenham woods, and appeared to be the answer to all his and Pat's problems. When the purchase went through in late 1963, Carey told Vidia, 'This would be the appropriate time to write to Lord Glenconner, if you haven't done so.'[53]

Soon, though, there were difficulties. On their first night together in the flat, he and Pat noticed the main road outside was busy. With both of them sensitive to external disturbance, the noise of the traffic became an obsession and a terminal complaint. The sound of the noise and the prospect of the noise became, somehow, the reason why a book would not come to Vidia. He tried everything he could think of to quell the disturbance: complaining to the council, writing to the builder of the flat, George Wimpey & Co., installing a soundproof window that turned out not to be soundproof. After a few tormented months, they decided to move again. The chosen destination, after much searching and toing and froing, was a house on three floors in Stockwell Park Crescent, to the north of Brixton. It was a mixed-up area, a white working-class part of south London that had become mildly West Indian and was now enjoying the beginnings of an influx of bohemians and middle-class professionals; an actor lived next door, and next door to the actor lived a Jamaican family. The Sydenham Hill flat was sold for its purchase price and, using a fresh soft loan from Tennants Estates, Vidia paid £7,200 for the house in Stockwell and sent in builders to renovate and decorate the property. In the meantime, he and Pat moved to a prim residential hotel in Blackheath. 'We were there for four or five months. It was terrible. Terrible. I felt virtually homeless. We could do up only a part of the house. There was no money.'[54] Dom Moraes took him out to lunch for an interview with the *Illustrated Weekly*. When Vidia moved to the new property in early 1965, he drew a picture in a letter to Ma depicting the two bedrooms, the dining room, 'library' and 'drawing room'. An Irish cleaner, Mrs Bannon, was engaged to look after the house when they were away.

Shiva arrived in England, having won a place at Univ. It was another phenomenal achievement for the Naipaul and Capildeo clan. The *Trinidad Daily Mirror* reported that he 'speaks fluently of Shakespeare and Plato, but is tongue-tied and shy when talking about practical things like the birds and the bees. The 1964 Island Scholarship Winner is – you guessed it – the younger brother of internationally famous author Vidia . . . Can Trinidad ever hope to produce another family as brilliant as the Naipauls? Shiva is only the latest in a long string of scholarship winners. Vidia was the first, in 1949 . . . Then came sister Kamla . . . Another sister, Savi, won an Island Scholarship in 1955 – and turned it down to get married. Not to mention Dr Capildeo himself (uncle of the clan), who won the Island Scholarship of 1938!'[55]

Shiva wrote later that his childhood had been 'dominated and darkened' by the need to get the scholarship: it 'was less an educational process . . . than a prolonged struggle, ruthlessly prosecuted, for survival.' Like his elder brother, he saw Trinidad as a dead end: 'I was escaping from the island whose narrow confines and tropical sameness had always seemed like a prison.'[56] Psychologically, Shiva was in the same fragile position Vidia had been in when he went to Oxford, although without the reassuring epistolary presence of a loving father. Standing above him was the banyan tree, in whose shade nothing could grow: Vido. From his earliest days, Shiva had been made aware that he had to match his elder brother's achievement, and wrote later, 'No one ever quite lives up to the demands of an Absolute.'[57] After a few tense days at the residential hotel in Blackheath, where he was instructed in table manners and treated with paternal concern and irritation by Vidia, Shiva moved on. Francis saw him at the hotel: 'I remember Shiva there, very young, saying he wanted to be a writer. Vidia adored Shiva, but was very heavy-handed with him.'[58] Seeking a room in a boarding house in Earls Court, Shiva was depressed to discover that he was regarded as 'coloured', and accommodation was hard to find in London. He wrote home to Ma that Vido was 'living a very disorganised and financially wasteful life. He has bought this house, which has been standing unoccupied for over three months. While he stays in a hotel grumbling and waiting for the architect to put in an appearance. Money is his main topic of conversation. He is always complaining how poor he is and at the same time living extravagantly. He has gone and bought himself an electric toothbrush, and now insists that I do the same. Most amusing!'[59]

Although Vidia's financial position had improved when he secured a post at the BBC back in 1955, he and Pat remained steeped in poverty. By the late 1950s, he was earning on average £373 gross a year, or around £5,800 in today's terms. In the 1960s, even while his literary reputation rose, his income stalled; he was climbing a long ladder, and was still on the lower rungs. It never occurred to him to be anything other than a writer. Between 1960 and 1969, his gross income after expenses (which he claimed frugally and scrupulously for things such as postage, stationery, typing fees and publications) averaged £1,963 a year, or around £25,400 in today's terms. The levels of personal taxation in the 1960s meant that much of this money never reached him. In 1969 he was saved by an Arts Council bursary of £3,500 secured by Francis Wyndham and Angus Wilson. In 1970, his income sank as low as £773, and he was forced to draw on money he had made by selling the Stockwell house.[60] Vidia thought in retrospect: 'It was a bad time. Tears lay just below the surface. You would not meet a more diligent tiller or harvester in the field of literature than me. I don't know how I did it. There was no market in America for colonial writing until after Vietnam. One was in a bind. If Christopher Glenconner hadn't helped me I don't know what would have happened.'[61] In the summer of 1964, he and Pat were invited to stay with Glenc and his family at their house 'Glen', a castellated Victorian mansion in Scotland.

Vidia blamed his financial failure in part on his literary agent, Graham Watson, who was a less than ideal representative for him. Nineteen years his senior, the son of a rich sardine shipper from Newcastle, Watson had taken part in the D-Day landings before joining the literary agency Curtis Brown. A shrewd and respected agent with connections in New York, he represented authors including Harold Macmillan, Gore Vidal and Bernard Levin.[62] Watson admired Vidia's talent but never realized his wider potential, considering him a well-reviewed ethnic writer with dim commercial prospects. Vidia particularly resented the way in which Watson's other authors were serialized in the Sunday papers while he was not. Looking back, he called him 'a very bad agent' who 'kept me in poverty for at least ten years . . . He did me down as a job of work. He was more concerned with pushing authors like Hammond Innes.'[63] Watson's colleague at the agency who dealt with film and television, Dick Odgers, regarded this as a misrepresentation: 'Vidia was a difficult bugger, there's no doubt about that, but Graham had a very high regard for him. He thought he was a great writer.'[64]

Over Christmas 1964, stuck in the genteel confines of the Blackheath hotel, Vidia had a break: 'The waitress comes to the dining room and says there is a telephone call for you. Before I lifted the phone, I felt there was some element of rescue. It was a man involved with a filmmaker, asking if I would come to New York and do a script. They wanted an original story, something related to *Miguel Street*. They liked the outline I did, and paid some more money for me to expand it. I went down to Trinidad and stayed with my sister Savi and wrote what became *A Flag on the Island* . . . I got about £5,000 in the end from that deal.'[65] He was put up in the St Regis Hotel in New York and, a little overwhelmed by the hospitality, produced an outline. The director Lionel Rogosin, maker of the quasi-documentary *On the Bowery*, told Vidia that the film was to include American stars, and possibly Frank Sinatra. Vidia wrote to Pat that 'the only idea I have been able to come up with is that of having a character who, because of his resemblance to Sinatra, begins to ape his mannerisms and is known as Sinatra. They are delighted with the idea.' The film people took him to a nightclub in Harlem, where he was astonished by the music and the dancing. Outside, the whites were insulted and 'Even I, hoping to pass, came in for a little abuse when, looking for a taxi, I momentarily was alone.' He flew to Trinidad to develop the script. When it was finished, he told Pat: 'It is a hideous thing, not really destined to appear in my complete works, but the stenographer helped. I only feel that if I do this in the future I should ask for five times the money, to make up for the sense of violation.'[66]

A Flag on the Island never became a film, and was not successful as a story, but it enabled Vidia to make a creative breakthrough. Visitors arrive on a ship at a Caribbean island; the dialogue is staccato and baffling; it is not clear what is going on; there are brothels and drunkenness; Mr Blackwhite is H.J.B. White, a writer whose most successful work with the

tourists and foreign foundations is *I Hate You*. Vidia's move forward came
not from the setting or the content, but from the discovery that he might
write elliptically, and communicate more through a story that is not
perfectly comprehended by the reader. The early drafts of *A Flag on the
Island* are in fact more powerful than the published version. A list of
characters, typed by the stenographer given the spelling, gives a sense of
the story: 'THE NARRATOR: An American now a salesman in South
America who first knew the island during the war where he was stationed
at one of the bases. From time to time he come back for his own big
purging debouch. SELMA: His occasional partner. Portuguese-Chinese-
African. She was born in Arima, came to Port of Spain during the war,
and there she remained steadily rising in respectability. Mr HENRY. African.
Butcher in 1939; a Broffle keeper in 1942; and night club owner in 1946;
and impresario in 1956; a legislature in 1960.'[67]

Soon after he finished *A Flag on the Island*, Vidia wrote the opening
pages of what would become *The Mimic Men*, a novel about a postcolonial
politician, Ralph Singh, told through flashbacks as he stays in exile in a
residential hotel in England. Much of the material is tangential: how Singh
made a fortune speculating in land, how his father became a kind of holy
man after leading a failed uprising. Singh's upbringing on the Caribbean
island of Isabella and his experience of trying to govern a people
shipwrecked by slavery or indenture opens up a barrage of enquiry into
the way in which the world was developing after the Second World War.
Does a postcolonial government rule its people, or does real power still
reside overseas? 'Industrialization, in territories like ours, seems to be a
process of filling imported tubes and tins with various imported substances,'
he says.[68] In its form and in its concerns, *The Mimic Men* was new work
for V.S. Naipaul. He used moments from his schooldays, from his
marriage, from brothels (and the resultant self-loathing), from his social
encounters in Trinidad in the 1960s and from his new experiences of the
English upper class, but the novel was a subtle, circuitous, imaginative
departure, in which even the racial insults are oblique: 'The Niger is a
tributary of that Seine.'[69] The risk of this approach, Graham Greene
commented in the *Observer*, was 'a new obscurity, a style which falls more
and more like a net curtain between author and reader.'[70]

Working on the film script at Savi and Mel's house in Trinidad in 1965,
Vidia was surprised by 'the tremendous adulation that one receives from
ordinary people – waiters recognise me and have read one's books! – this
sort of fame is poisonous ... The more personal sadness is the state of

Sati's children. The boy and girl are grotesquely fat because their father feeds them ceaselessly from morning till night.' He was worried by Nepaul Street. 'It is a sad, almost derelict house. My mother is out all day at the quarry and apart from her there is only Nelly and a deaf old servant,' he told Pat in an affectionate letter.[71] He gave a provocative interview to Derek Walcott at the *Guardian*, illustrated with a photograph of the two men seated across a low table, squaring up to each other. Vidia denounced Trinidad as a 'very sinister place' inhabited by 'insecure and unfulfilled' people. 'Also, manners here are not very good.' Would he ever support a political cause? His answer was revealing, linking Nazism to apartheid: 'I think there have really been only two good causes within recent times: against Hitler and possibly in South Africa, which represents the absolute triumph of a European proletarian culture.' A long question about local pride in his achievement and the respective position of writers and cricketers yielded the tart response: 'I am not a cricketer.'[72] His combative stance would develop into a standard interview mode. He wrote to Pat, 'Derek Walcott has been extremely charming this trip. He is more relaxed and while I think this is because he has at last been published, he tells me that I was insecure and aggressive in 1960. Hard to believe . . . CLR James [who was then under surveillance and house arrest by Eric Williams for encouraging trade union activism] wrote a long attack on me in the Guardian; he referred to me throughout by my first name! . . . Ronald Bryden, a fellow Trinidadian, was here for Carnival and Derek Walcott gave a little party for the two of us.'[73] He arranged to meet Pat in Lisbon after the end of the school term for a holiday.

Back in London, Vidia was stuck. The idea that would become *The Mimic Men* was half-formed. He went on *Writer's World*, produced by a young Melvyn Bragg, being interviewed about 'The Writer in Exile' in Stockwell Park Crescent. Appearing on radio and television shows or writing film scripts and reviews was not what Vidia wanted to be doing. He pondered his future; news reached him that his old colleague Edgar Mittelholzer had burned himself to death, on purpose, supposedly because his career as a writer was on the slide. At the back of Vidia's mind was a strong desire to see Africa. Having visited India, the land of his forefathers, he felt a need to observe and understand the ancestral home of his fellow Trinidadians. When an invitation came from the Farfield Foundation to be writer-in-residence at Makerere University in Uganda, he accepted. 'I wanted to be on the move again . . . It was a very fruitful visit. It gave me *In a Free State* and the background for *A Bend in the River*.'[74] Lady Antonia

Fraser invited him to Campden Hill Square to meet the former governor of Uganda, Sir Andrew Cohen, and Francis Wyndham supplied an introduction to the local ruler, the Kabaka of Buganda. Pat gave up her teaching job to accompany him to Africa. Vidia said years later in an interview: 'Just as I have a feeling for Indian peasant movements or Indian working movements, so I have some kind of feeling for Africa. I wasn't going to Africa cold – or with any sexual intent.'[75]

Stockwell Park Crescent was let out to Mira and Amar, who was studying radiation oncology in London. Mira was still on good terms with her brother, but found him increasingly short-tempered. He seemed to have a growing sense of entitlement, borrowed perhaps from his peer group. One evening at dinner Pat served an undercooked roast chicken, and 'Vido jumped up and shouted, "My God Pat, the chicken is bleeding. It is not cooked. The chicken is raw", and so on. And Pat began to weep.'[76] Vidia was still eating chicken, eggs and fish when they took his fancy; more a Pork Brahmin than a pukka vegetarian, his concern was that he should be served food which in some way distinguished him. Francis noticed rising tension: 'Pat was scrupulous, reserved, she always told the truth. Over the years Vidia would say something reactionary and she never got used to it. That would irritate him, and it made them rather a nightmare couple, but it was one of the things I liked about her.'[77] When Mira expressed a wish to give Ma a holiday in England, Vidia forbade it as a piece of pointless extravagance: 'Vido said, "I don't want my mother to step foot in this house. I do not want her presence in this house." He had a book of rules for us. Basically what we had to do and what we mustn't do, to do with cleaning and scrubbing. We were not to touch the walls, and make sure that our little daughter who was only fourteen months didn't touch anything . . . Then he called us up a couple of days before the move saying he would like to ask us for a little more money and we were really appalled. We were a young couple, counting the pounds.'[78] Embarrassed to tell Ma about Vido's ban, Mira kept her visit a secret, until Ma let the cat out of the bag in a letter to Pat: 'I must thank you and Vido for staying in your home . . . and the rest of the children on the financial side to make my holiday a big success in my life the <u>first one</u> in fifty-three years.' She was glad to have helped Shiva, who had already run up capacious debts at Oxford: 'I see that he had shoes, socks, underpants and all clothes that he needed for summer before I left.'[79]

CHAPTER FIFTEEN

THE SCHINTSKY METHOD

VIDIA'S FIRST IMPRESSION on arrival in Kampala in early 1966 was that he had made a dreadful mistake. There was no house waiting for him and Pat, and he was expected to join the teaching staff at Makerere. Their first fortnight was spent saving money by staying in the spare room of a senior lecturer in the English department, David Cook. According to a colleague, 'David was the classic gay white liberal – "African writing is so wonderful" – that kind of thing. He wore silly shirts in African cloth ... a little too tight [and] had an African boyfriend.'[1] The Farfield Foundation was rumoured to be a CIA front organization fighting Cold War cultural battles against communist influence in Africa. Vidia made it clear to Makerere University and to the Farfield Foundation that being a writer-in-residence meant just that to him: he would sit in his residence and write. He adopted an almost Gandhian policy of non-cooperation: 'I never went to my office. I couldn't be disturbed too much. I was writing in my bungalow, and if they asked me to teach, or to talk, I paid no attention.'[2] This stubbornness was not mere provocation. After two years of false starts, he had begun writing the moment he reached Uganda. *The Mimic Men* would turn out to be an intricate, inventive, many-layered book, written unexpectedly fast. In earlier drafts, Vidia had tried to shift the characters back and forth across the Atlantic.[3] Now, as often happens to a writer, he saw a simple solution to what had seemed an insurmountable problem: he would use a first-person narrator, who could carry the direction of the story with him. In his attitudes and ironic perception, in his awkward confessions and the conviction he has been wounded by history, Ralph Singh contained much of Vidia. Singh's own tone was directly inspired by the letter sent by Dr Winston Mahabir, Trinidad's minister for education, inviting Vidia to return to the island on a scholarship in 1960.[4]

In a hot, noisy, freshly built campus bungalow on a slope, he incorporated the atmosphere of dislocation into the developing narrative, and by June was able to send a manuscript to Diana Athill. Her reply sounded more impressed than delighted: 'I only finished reading THE MIMIC MEN three minutes ago, so it hasn't simmered down enough for comment, really — but I must quickly say: brilliant.' It was 'horribly disturbing. It gave me an almost physical sense of vertigo, as though I were going to start a migraine.' Vidia replied, 'It is a horrible book' and might 'alienate some people who liked my earlier work ... Many thanks for reading and writing so promptly. Very considerate, very generous, very Diana.' While *The Mimic Men* awaited publication, André Deutsch brought out a version of *A Flag on the Island* as a novella, abetted by some short stories Vidia had written in Kashmir and for *Caribbean Voices*. It was dedicated to Diana. Vidia berated her boss: 'André: couldn't you, in your address book, put a little note on the page which carries all my various addresses, saying that they are not to be divulged? I have begged and pleaded so often.' Deutsch swiftly responded, 'I swear we are not guilty. I have given a rule here that if the closest member of your family were to ask, we would not yield.'[5] Vidia fired off an angry letter to Graham Watson of Curtis Brown, complaining he was failing to secure foreign translation rights for his books. Watson responded that Vidia was lucky to be published at all overseas. 'An author doesn't basically get paid for his reputation, he gets paid according to the amount of money which he can earn for himself and his publisher.'[6] This — the idea that authors should receive performance-related pay based on sales rather than status — was not something he wanted to hear, now or later.

At Makerere, conscious he had put on weight, Vidia took up running. 'At four-thirty every afternoon,' he informed Antonia Fraser, 'a young American and myself, each giving moral support to the other, run once around the sports ground, walk round it twice, run once, and so on, until we drop. It was a system we worked out when we began: a system of weakness. But sports experts have noticed us and informed us now that we are following the Schintsky method, devised quite recently by some trainer in Scandinavia. So we no longer feel embarrassed.'[7] The young American, a teacher at the university named Paul Theroux, remembered the running. Vidia had 'a manual called The Canadian 5BX Plan, which was a handbook of exercises for the Canadian military. He called the (mainly English) expats "infies" (for inferiors) ... and he decided that they were not only morally and intellectually and socially inferior, but physical wrecks. I can't remember whose idea it was, but we began running around the track at Makerere – an awful torture in the equatorial heat. He also practised bowling on the cricket pitch. He had no stamina for running and wasn't much of a bowler, but he had a lot of enthusiasm for punishing himself to prove he wasn't an "infy". He loved the fact that only Africans and Indians were practising on the sports field (soccer, cricket, running), no expats. Afterwards we always went for tea. He refused the biscuits and cakes while I dived in. The exercise gave me a tremendous craving for sugar. I always tried to resist, but Vidia would say, "No, eat them. The body knows what it wants. Obey the body," as I tucked into another.'[8]

Uganda was newly independent, with King Freddie, the Kabaka of Buganda, as a figurehead monarch and Milton Obote as prime minister. Optimism among Europeans and Americans about Africa as the emerging continent was high, and Makerere University seemed like a beacon of progress in the region, staffed largely by white expatriates who felt proud to be building a new nation while atoning for the wrongs of the colonial era. Vidia was an anomaly. Fascinated by Africa – its scale, its landscape, its art, its traditions, its people – he saw it through Trinidadian eyes as the mystical homeland of his compatriots who had been undone by the middle passage. Above all, it frightened him. As Ralph Singh wrote in *The Mimic Men*: 'Hate oppression; fear the oppressed.'[9] Vidia believed that many of his white colleagues at Makerere were playing out private fantasies of their own, and would be undone. He lacked their instant status among black Africans, and was at once aware of the antipathy towards the Indian traders and shopkeepers who controlled parts of the East African economy. Despite wearing sturdy shoes and a bush hat, Vidia looked like one of them.

With Pat, he travelled widely, to Nairobi and Eldoret in Kenya, to rural Uganda and Kigezi on the Congo and Rwandan border. He took an interest in the various clans of the Baganda people, the followers of the Kabaka. Later he flew to Dar es Salaam in Tanzania to give a lecture at the university, and the students walked out en masse; the combative intellectual style he had learned at QRC did not go down well. In Nairobi, crossing the street, he ran into Jagdish Sondhi (from the C&CA course in Slough) and he and Pat spent a month staying with his parents on the coast at Mombasa, an experience that would provide material for *A Bend in the River*. The Sondhis' house overlooked a creek and had a squash court built by Jagdish, since he was not allowed into the British club. 'We both grew up in colonies', said

Jagdish Sondhi, 'where the Englishman was the master, so it was natural we should have a love-hate relationship. When my brother asked Vidia who the best writer in the English language was, he said, "I am, of course."' In Jagdish's copy of *An Area of Darkness*, Vidia wrote: 'This, the book which I consider my best: a book written out of pain and concern; less about India than about people like yourselves and myself.' He recalled Vidia's anxiety about the fate of local Indians with the rise of African nationalism: 'He sent a ten-page dossier to the Indian High Commission, but nothing came of it.'[10]

In the debate over Africa's future, as the wind of change blew ever harder, Vidia found himself, as always, on nobody's side. 'It greatly helps in an understanding of the place', he wrote to Antonia, 'if one starts from the premiss that Africans are a primitive people – it is the one thing Andrew Cohen left out that day at your place – and then moves on to the obscenity of their dispossession in the Twentieth Century by a truly second-rate crowd, who after fifty years have no artist or writer to show, no culture or civilisation, who talk endlessly about their "characters" and who constantly compare themselves, to their own advantage, with primitive people. Side-taking is impossible; the situation is obscene.'[11] While he was completing *The Mimic Men* at the Kaptagat Arms, a hotel on the edge of the Rift Valley in Kenya, Milton Obote staged a bloody coup (which would in time lead to the rule of Idi Amin) and made himself president of Uganda. Vidia was infuriated by the 'castrated' response of the British press towards this 'absolute savage massacre ... People use too many big words about Africa: the problems of this continent – I am serious – are semantic. To give you an example. The young tribesmen are alleged to be "interested in writing". Do you know what this means? It means that they are literally interested in taking up a pen and making marks on paper ... words like "feudal", "democratic", "modern", "reactionary" are utterly without meaning, but continue to be misleadingly used. When the [*New*] *Statesman* talks about a Ugandan politician being "modern & forward-looking" it is talking absolute nonsense. The place is overrun by anthropologists & sociologists who ... interpret in a series of alien concepts.'[12] To Diana he wrote, 'We were here in Kenya when the trouble started. I believe they have slaughtered 1,000–2,000 people. African armies are frightfully good against civilians.'[13]

The scale of East Africa's political upheaval reminded him of what he had seen in the West Indies. He knew that the fragility of state institutions and the comparative lack of an indigenous trained and educated elite in most of Africa meant that the capacity for destruction and lawlessness was much greater. To Francis, who was making a reputation for himself as an editor at the *Sunday Times* colour magazine, with his contacts ranging from Jean Rhys and Bruce Chatwin to David Bailey and the Kray twins, Vidia wrote: 'It is unbearable to see once again – in spite of the lessons of so many African countries – African politicians fashioning the very instruments by which they and their countries are in the end destroyed.'[14] Pat, contemplating a career as a journalist rather than as a teacher, attended parliament in Kampala and wrote a protracted article about the situation in Uganda. Francis thought it 'full of interesting observations' but 'a bit inconclusive' and suggested, 'Why don't you send it to the Guardian?' The features editor there responded in automatic language: 'Dear Miss Hale, Thank you very much, but we have a man visiting Uganda at the moment.'[15]

The places and people Vidia encountered during his nine months in Africa gave him a plethora of literary material. David Cook would be cruelly rendered as Bobby in *In a Free State*. Murray Carlin, a white-haired lecturer at Makerere who had written the play *Not Now, Sweet Desdemona*, provided the spark for Roche in *Guerrillas*, a man who appears to stand for something but has betrayed himself. When Vidia began the book in 1973, Pat wrote in her diary: 'He recalls Murray Carlin and his poor wife >she killed herself< sitting on the step of their dreadful bungalow and their rather common daughters, expelled from South Africa for his liberal stance, discovering where Vidia stood and showing him his (anti-African, anti-negro) cartoons. "Secretively?" I say. Yes.'[16] Jim de Vere Allen, a bright, rugged history lecturer, became a friend and was later used in another book; as Vidia noted on some archive papers: 'Jim Allen (Kenya-born and bred, but of simplish Australian background) is the original of De Groot in *A Way in the World*.'[17] The owner of the Kaptagat Arms, Major Bobby Tyers, would appear as the colonel in *In a Free State*. The displaced international characters and restricted campus setting of Makerere would be used in both *In a Free State* and *A Bend in the River*. With its uncomprehending, colliding inhabitants, all following their own cultural ideas, this became Naipauland.

In July, Pat returned to England. During his last weeks in Africa, Vidia travelled to Rwanda for several days with Paul Theroux, and went to Dar es Salaam to lecture. Theroux was twenty-five years old, an enthusiastic former Peace Corps volunteer with a Nigerian girlfriend named Comfort Iruoje and ambitions to become a writer himself. Vidia liked his application, his love of books and his brash self-confidence. Theroux was at once in awe of Vidia, happy to play the part of bag-carrier and disciple, and Vidia responded to the admiration by playing up to his own caricature as someone who would do and say outrageous things. They shared a willingness to upset the academic and social conventions of Makerere. Theroux noted the way that Vidia would be funny and provocative, teasing and twitting people for his own enjoyment, or to obtain information, and using archaic place names such as 'the Gold Coast' in order to outrage liberal sentiment; asked to judge a literary competition, he awarded only a third prize. Vidia gave Paul Theroux advice about writing, offered to help him find a publisher and invited him to stay when he came to London.

In Tanzania, in a Proustian moment, Vidia developed asthma for the first time in years. Feeling low, he was distracted by entertainment arranged by Hugh Fraser (who had stepped down as 'secretary of state for air' with the arrival of Harold Wilson's Labour government). Hugh had cabled a diplomat friend in Dar es Salaam to tell him of Vidia's presence. 'The sequel,' Vidia wrote to Antonia:

> a Sunday morning in my USAID house, a morning as blank as only mornings in Dar es Salaam can be, a man in shorts bursting through my kitchen, whipping off his dark glasses, smiling broadly, extending a hand and saying, 'I'm Skinner.' I later had dinner with him. An American negro homosexual, his middle-aged English mate; a ferociously liberal couple; and the Skinners. Delicious caviar, and then the negro, to my astonishment, without any provocation from anyone, decides to do his James Baldwin act.
>   'I'm sitting here with you people, but I think I should let you know that I really hate you.'
>   Mrs Liberal drops her fork with pleasure; her eyes widen. 'But you have so many white friends.' Playing the game, being in the now slightly passé intellectual swim. Coaxing, dying to hear more.
>   'Darling, I have <u>hundreds</u> of white friends.'
>   And the delight that this arouses is the delight of people thinking: how lucky we are, participating, even in Dar es Salaam.

I ask: 'Why do you say this, here?'

And of course I nearly spoil the party. You don't need to come to Africa to know what it is like. You can sit in London and make it all up.[18]

*

When *The Mimic Men* was published, V.S. Naipaul's critical reputation moved up a notch. In the *Financial Times*, his friend Julian Jebb declared it 'one of the four or five best novels in English since the war.'[19] Angus Wilson noticed the book's ambiguities: 'A Conradian irony suffuses all the events, speeches and the thoughts of this book — and suffuses them to great effect — but the final viewpoint remains obscure.'[20] In the *New York Review of Books*, V.S. Pritchett wrote: 'Among the younger English novelists Mr V.S. Naipaul is a virtuoso. A brilliant chameleon from the Caribbean, the descendant of Hindu immigrants, he has grown into the English novel with more lasting assurance than almost all contemporaries in the West Indies or Africa who are in the same case. This has not been achieved by intelligence and education alone . . . His advantage is that he shares with many English novelists natural and serious feeling for the fantasy life of his characters.'[21] Karl Miller wrote in the *Kenyon Review* that Naipaul was 'someone with conservative leanings who nonetheless writes movingly about the poor and aspiring, a compassionate man who is also fastidious and severe.'[22] Despite the book's pessimism, Eric Williams, blooded now by office, wrote in his 1970 study of Caribbean history *From Columbus to Castro*: 'V.S. Naipaul's description of West Indians as "mimic men" is harsh, but true . . . psychological dependence leads to an ever-growing economic and cultural dependence on the outside world. Fragmentation is intensified in the process.'[23]

A remarkable letter was sent to Vidia by Michael Manley, the son of the Jamaican premier, who would himself become prime minister. Known as a trades union activist and a vociferous anti-imperialist, Manley thought *The Mimic Men* 'a masterpiece in itself. I wanted you to know that I found it both beautiful and exciting, if a little terrifying. The handling of the theme of disorder set off echoes of recognition even as it sounded warning bells . . . I wish there was a greater tradition of reading in the Caribbean society and among the politicians who are its corollary . . . If you are ever passing through Jamaica and have a moment, let me know.'[24] Michael's mother, the sculptor Edna Manley, had written previously to Vidia: 'I am very impressed. I have lived through some of what you write about.' She commented that her husband had made pencil notes all over the book. 'So you see some people do love you.'[25] Vidia consistently resisted invitations and blandishments from West Indian government ministers during these years, anxious not to go the same way as C.L.R. James. His distance from any political movement was part of his presentation of himself as a displaced, unaffiliated, unCaribbean writer. It would not be until the 1990s, and this time in India, that he would tentatively allow himself to be co-opted by politicians.

The British literary establishment, conscious of the implosion of the British empire and anxious to appease the unpredictable meteor that was flying in its wake, awarded Vidia another significant prize: the W.H. Smith Award, presented by the chairman of the Arts Council, Lord Goodman. Vidia had become a fixture on the London literary scene, but somehow at an angle to it, the object of discomfited reverence rather than love; as he later remarked to an interviewer, 'I'm the kind of writer that people think other people are reading.'[26] Michael Frayn, later a playwright of distinction but at this point a budding novelist, wrote to him: 'I'm still digesting The Mimic Men. I think it's a great triumph – a most extraordinary book, quite unique, and totally <u>itself</u> in every page ... I'm appalled by the great freight of disgust it bears.'[27] Aware of the rising tide of praise, Graham Watson decided that André Deutsch was not doing enough to promote Vidia, and pressed him to improve distribution to bookshops and to put advertisements 'in the "intellectual" papers like Encounter ... Vidia is now firmly in the class where there will be a continuing interest in anything he writes.'[28] Although Diana Athill disagreed, Francis Wyndham took the view in retrospect that Vidia was failed by his publisher: 'Vidia was absolutely right about Deutsch treating him badly.'[29]

Back in Stockwell Park Crescent in October 1966, Vidia apologized to Ralph Ironman for being out of touch. 'I find I have fallen into a new type of itinerant life. It works like this: a few months in London, a few months abroad ... Next March I go off to Trinidad and the United States to write a book for an American publisher.'[30] The book was to be a study of Port of Spain, but when it was completed, the editors at Little, Brown were disappointed not to receive something like a guidebook. Bob Gottlieb of Knopf picked up the manuscript in the USA, and André Deutsch was happy to have a narrative history of Trinidad based on primary research. For many months, Pat had sat in the archives of the British Library and Vidia had attempted to give shape to an unknown story. Francis thought it 'the most devastating <u>and</u> illuminating study of colonialism ever written –

such an unbelievably squalid muddle of a story.'[31] Diana proposed possible titles: *Dusty El Dorado*, *Empires in their Brains*, *The Mountain of Diamond*. Vidia thought of *The Port of the Spaniards: An Adventure*. It was not a history book or a travel book: 'The adventure is, basically, the discovery and desecration of one part of the New World,' he wrote to Diana.[32]

The Loss of El Dorado anticipated the sort of history that would become popular thirty years later. Vidia took an obscure dot on the map and reconstructed its past from scarce sources. In the British Library, he found a document in Spanish which revealed the origin of the name 'Chaguanas': a letter from the Spanish king ordering the extermination of an Amerindian tribe, the Chaguanes. In his Nobel lecture, Naipaul said: 'The thought came to me in the Museum that I was the first person since 1625 to whom that letter of the king of Spain had a real meaning.'[33] Unlike British historians, depending securely on their predecessors, he was flying blind, trying to establish the history of the defeated, the disappeared, the unrecorded. The result was a complex account of adventurers like Francisco de Miranda and Walter Raleigh, and more than this a revelation of the terrible, degraded cruelty of Trinidad's early past: Amerindian rulers burned and chained by Spaniards, Negroes castrated and kept alive by Caribs for food, a young girl tortured, slaves eating dirt to kill themselves, ears clipped as a punishment; poisoning, witchcraft, flogging, revolt. Bob Gottlieb told Vidia that although it had sold only 3,000 copies in the USA, he was 'convinced that *The Loss of El Dorado* is a very important as well as very beautiful book, and that it will endure.'[34] In a review in the *Guardian*, Richard Gott commented that it was 'nothing less than a description of the formation of an entire culture'.[35] Vidia's preoccupation with the void at the heart of Trinidad, the idea that it was a remote island where each person was an interloper come to experiment in human cruelty, came true now: he was producing evidence for his prejudice. Small wonder that his final line referred to the erection of a metal sign over the gates of Port of Spain jail in 1812: 'PRO REGE ET LEGE: For King and Law'.[36] He loved order, hated lawlessness. This was too narrow an approach for the time or for John Updike. 'Never ask an artist to do the ordinary,' he wrote in the *New Yorker*. 'But in viewing an entire hemisphere as a corrupted dream, Naipaul dissolves what realities there were. *The Loss of El Dorado* rests upon an unexamined assumption, of metropolitan superiority.'[37]

The Loss of El Dorado was a prodigious piece of research and recreation, but it was not the sort of book that marked a way forward for Vidia, any more than *Mr Stone and the Knights Companion* had been. Although his literary reputation remained high and his upper-class patrons continued to encourage him, the four years that followed his return from Africa in 1966 were to be the worst of his career. They were a time of floundering, professional exhaustion and fear about money. Nearing forty, Vidia had intimations that his best work might be behind him. He was profoundly frustrated by his lack of sexual fulfilment, despising himself for resorting to brothel sex; he did not know how to convert his singular background and recent experience into new fiction; he mistrusted the social and political movements of the time: the creative avant-garde seemed to him an irrelevant indulgence, and he detested hippies, yippies, beatniks, free schools, flower power, Black Power, flag burning, hair growing, sit-ins, be-ins, teach-ins and love-ins. The sharp Naipauline vision that had arisen from his family background and sound colonial education now appeared to be at odds with current thinking, particularly about what was coming to be called the Third World. In 1969 in *Literature and Ideology*, H.B. Synge started what was to become a critical trend by calling V.S. Naipaul 'a despicable lackey of neo-colonialism and imperialism'.[38]

Angered by the prevailing mood, Vidia wrote an article for the dying *Saturday Evening Post* which would later cause him embarrassment, called 'What's Wrong With Being a Snob?'

> It is too late, of course. The cause is all but lost ... I write from a country where, in the midst of a decay that is social as well as economic, the romance of the 'classless' new society is ceaselessly offered as compensation. There are classless sports nowadays, classless clothes, classless youths. When groups of these classless youths, products of a welfare state, stage a riot in a seaside town, it is said that society is failing them. There is dishonesty in this ... Entertainers from the slums replaced the Queen as a cause for national pride. In the hysteria of self-congratulation, the new greed expressed itself most hideously in the persecution of immigrants from the former Empire. Yesterday's slogan on the wall – SEND NIGGERS HOME – was embodied in today's White Paper on limiting immigration. Pop entertainment, pop politics: politicians were no longer in a position to lead; they could only follow.[39]

He wondered whether he was in the right place, or whether he and Pat might do better abroad. The fresh vegetables, open skies and sense of wonder in Africa were often on his mind. Jim Allen wrote from Makerere to say he had 'engaged a Mututsi version of Jeeves to take the place of Zozima (who has suddenly dipped into a drunken and rather dirty old age) early next year. Didas looks like a black Oberammergau Christ, cooks superb French food and will drive me around when I feel weak.'[40]

Much of Vidia's best work during this time turned out to be journalism, writing for Francis Wyndham at the *Sunday Times Magazine*, and for John Anstey, the famously unmanageable editor of its rival, the *Telegraph Magazine*. Both publications were stretching public expectations of taste and design, using colour photographs in a way that had not been done before in the mainstream press. When Vidia wrote a *Sunday Times* feature on 'Mauritius: The Overcrowded Barracoon', the cover showed a nearly naked white woman kneeling on a beach, and the pictures accompanying the text were taken by the photojournalist Don McCullin. Ideas for stories were similarly imaginative. Anstey would fire off random suggestions to Vidia for articles: 'What, in fact, is the Brazilian idea of "freedom" – political or otherwise?' was one question that needed to be answered, but never was 'Would you be interested in writing an article about Norman Mailer and his current plan to run for Mayor?' he asked in 1969, and Vidia said yes.[41] Journalists on both magazines were notorious for their extravagance, and some other freelances were baffled that V.S. Naipaul's expenses claims would come in below rather than above the limit; they thought he was setting a bad example. He filed from India, France, the Caribbean, New York, Honduras, and was paid around £400 a time, a reasonable fee, negotiated by his agent, but the scale of his travel and research meant his annual earnings remained low. In 1968, at Graham Greene's request, he went to Antibes and wrote a bored, passively aggressive interview with the sixty-three-year-old author, whose recent work he had disliked.

Early in 1967 he flew to India to write 'A Second Visit', a pessimistic and limited article for the *Telegraph Magazine*, before going on to Japan to interview a businessman who had nonsensical plans to end the Vietnam War. From the Imperial Hotel in New Delhi, he had written to Diana: 'I really like living in hotels. I like the temporariness, the mercenary services, the absence of responsibility, the anonymity, the scope for complaint. And even a noisy hotel is such a good place for working.'[42] Later, worrying about money, he had moved to stay with the Jhabvalas. Pat was in urgent need of £100 to pay a tax bill: would he send a cheque? She told him she needed clothes. 'I do not have

anything respectable to wear during the day that covers me up entirely.
There is still some wear in my blue and white summer coat (two years
old) but it is not good enough if one wants to look good . . . if there is
such a thing as sex appeal, dreadful phrase . . . I suppose ordinary
vanity might lead me to believe I possessed it in some small measure
. . . Please do not think that my letters are exactly what I plan to write.
I have long conversations with you on buses or in queues that never
get reproduced.' Vidia had written back from Bombay: 'There must be
something wrong with the long mirror in this hotel room. It throws
back an awful, unbelievable dwarf-like reflection, which I do not
recognize but which I fear might even be true.' Ruth Jhabvala told Pat
in a letter how much she, Jhab and their children had enjoyed having
Vidia to stay. 'Even the most nervous of our dogs, who that week were
biting people's ankles right and left, showed him nothing but affection.'[43]
A meeting with Zul Vellani was a failure: 'He was icy. He was very
cold with me.'[44]

Judging the Duff Cooper Prize that year, Vidia fixed its award to
Nirad C. Chaudhuri, the Bengali anglophile whose *Autobiography of an
Unknown Indian* had earlier impressed him. Ruth thought Chaudhuri
clever and imaginative, 'but alas, alas, often, alas especially in success,
a particularly silly old man.'[45] She had a point; before coming to
England to collect the award, Chaudhuri had instructed Vidia: 'My
special purpose in writing is to make you my "security man" against
certain undesirable attentions.' No Indian writers 'unless they are
respectable' should be permitted to approach him. He was nervous of
being insulted. 'Most especially I am thinking of that little half-caste rat
Dom Moraes, who if he comes near me will get a whipping as sure as
anything.'[46] In the event, all Nirad Babu had to contend with was
dinner with Pat alone in Stockwell, since Vidia was away in India. 'Mr
C. is a very methodical man,' she reported, 'but had talked so much
that although we started eating at 7 had not finished his second course
and did not want to leave at all.'[47] When Chaudhuri died in 1999, Vidia
was asked to write his obituary by the Royal Society of Literature, and
produced a slanderous and malign text, daring its commissioners to
reject it:

> Nirad Chaudhuri was an old fool . . . In 1966 I worked very hard to
> persuade my fellow judges to give Chaudhuri the Duff Cooper prize
> – not, of course, for *The Continent of Circe*, but for the *Autobiography*.

John Julius Norwich [Cooper's son] told me later that Chaudhuri
... spent some part of his prize on 'male toiletries'. This was
unexpected enough. I had no idea then that the prize was going to
lead to the man settling in England and setting himself up as a
clown in Oxford for his last thirty years.[48]

The chairman of the society, Michael Holroyd, had to write a diplomatic
letter to V. S. Naipaul declining to publish.

Pat gave an unlikely supper party over Easter 1967 for Shiva, his
girlfriend Jenny, Anthony Powell's son John and Eleanor, fresh from 'a
hockey festival in Ramsgate'. (The previous year Eleanor had hitch-
hiked to the soccer World Cup at Wembley to see the England victory,
paying a tout £4 for a 10 shilling ticket.) Shiva drank keenly through
the evening. 'He is going to pay for one of the three bottles of wine
consumed,' Pat told Vidia. She took Eleanor to see Antonioni's *Blow-
Up*, which she described in uncool terms as a 'semi-documentary on the
swinging London scene with breathtaking shots of Dulwich Park ...
Catherine Tennant, the centrepiece of a smart drugtaking party (looking
very pretty) rolling a marijuana cigarette and giving the famous
Catherine giggle. Catherine Pakenham was there too.'[49] Later in the
year they went to Holland to stay in Peter and Teresa Gatacre's moated
castle, and to Denmark to visit the Ironmans. 'We are looking forward
very much to seeing Mary & yourself and the children after 8 years!!'
Vidia told Ralph.[50] After the trip, he wrote to Paul Theroux, 'Every
little village has its Porno shop; there are advertisements in the
newspapers for Porno models — they prefer "pairs", in whatever
permutations. To me now the very word "Scandinavian" is a horror
word, full of ice and death and sullen coitus. I prefer vice myself, and
like it to remain a little vicious.'[51]

Ruth Jhabvala corresponded occasionally with Vidia. 'Why Holland?' she enquired, when told of the holiday. 'My aunt, who lived in
Amsterdam (till the Germans took her away to Auschwitz), always used
to say that Dutch isn't a language, it's a disease of the throat.'[52] Five
years his senior, slight and shy but with a strong personality, Ruth
shared Vidia's asthma, incisive literary perception, need for privacy and
sense of displacement. Her novels such as *The Householder*, with their
phoney gurus and deluded Westerners, led many readers at the time to
assume she herself was Indian. Ruth had moved to Delhi in the 1950s
after marrying Jhab, a witty architect and lecturer who would later be

immortalized as the acerbic Yamdoot, messenger of the god of death, in Arundhati Roy and Pradip Krishen's cult movie *In Which Annie Gives it Those Ones*. She had begun the collaboration with Ismail Merchant and James Ivory that would lead to many films and her winning an Academy Award for the screenplay of *A Room with a View*.

With the Indian economy in a poor state and the Congress party imploding, she felt glum, writing to Vidia, 'I cannot tell you what a difference it makes, how encouraging it is in the midst of one's own loneliness and isolation, to have someone talk such brilliant sense about this place, after all the lies, all the jargon mouthed by people either too naive or too stupid or too crafty to look and talk straight . . . you are the only other person I know who becomes physically affected by being in uncongenial company: as when we came home from the intellectual evening at Khushwant Singh's.' She wrote of her frustrations with 20th Century Fox and the world of film, and advised Vidia to make sure he secured his position in advance if he ever wrote a script. 'I have long ago come to the conclusion that the world owes us first-class hotel accommodation and such things – that it's our natural right, to be provided for us without question. Not that I've ever got it, but that doesn't alter my case.' In August she wrote a pointed description of a party given 'for David Frost who was passing through Delhi to do something for Oxfam.' The guests, 'the usual younger-married-set bores from Defence Colony', had under 'an easy flow of wine and very good food' given the impression that they were 'young and bright and gay' despite not having 'a spontaneous thought or feeling between them'.[53]

Through this period, Shiva was a constant worry to Vidia. Rather than take a holiday job, he had spent the summer vacation of 1966 in Turkey and been relieved of his possessions on a train in Yugoslavia on the way home. 'It was not really my fault though,' Shiva wrote to Ma. 'I need a hundred pounds! Could you possibly get it for me?'[54] In November the Dean of Univ wrote to Vidia saying he had run up debts of nearly £300; his annual grant from the Trinidad government was £850. A bookshop had served a court order against him for taking books on credit; his landlady had thrown him out; he had started to study Chinese, for no apparent reason; his family needed to find £200 at once. Vidia wrote to Savi, racially humiliated on their brother's behalf, 'You must realise that Shiva has grown so dirty that he stinks, quite literally. He launders nothing; he changes nothing; he never wears a tie or a collar but that pullover which gives off the ripest of sweat-

and-dirt smells. His face, with the long, very long hair falling over both cheeks, is perpetually oily. He is known to everyone in the College, students, dons and college servants, as an Indian who stinks.'[55] Vidia went to Oxford to negotiate with the college authorities. Shiva failed to meet him, and when they ran into each other in the street, Vidia exploded. Peter Bayley witnessed the scene: 'My god, Vidia behaved like a burra saheb, he tore strips off him, he said, "What the devil do you mean, you were supposed to meet me at two o'clock in the [porter's] lodge!" I was staggered. I didn't realize that he had that kind of power in him ... Shiva wasn't good news really. He was very tall and was a smoker, cannabis and stuff. He fancied himself with girls, and was very much thronged by them.'[56]

The following week, Shiva bounced a cheque and Vidia returned to Oxford and asked his brother to come back to London with him. He understood that Shiva was going through an emotional breakdown, and it reminded him of his own collapse at Oxford, and of Pa's mental torment. 'We are not going to expect much if he comes here,' Pat wrote to Ma. 'I'll make the meals as nice as I can and try to give him a regular life. Vidia will continue the hard work of persuading him to keep accounts.'[57] Two days before Christmas, Shiva wrote to their mother from Stockwell Park Crescent, 'Vido has been excessively kind to me, as well as Pat. Please be reassured that everything is under control. I would like to think the year of depression and disaster is finished ... I have also cut my hair.'[58] Vidia felt a mixture of love, rage and worry in dealing with Shiva. He hoped each crisis would be the last, but knew it would not be. In June 1967, Shiva fell on his feet; he married Jenny Stuart, who gave up her university degree to take a job as a secretary and support them. Francis Wyndham remembered: 'Vidia was furious when Shiva got engaged to an English girl, and didn't want to go to the wedding.'[59] Vidia did not want to be maritally emulated, least of all by his brother.

*

Over Christmas 1966, Stockwell paid host not only to Shiva, but to Paul Theroux. Vidia tried to introduce him to figures in literary London, taking him to dinner with Edna O'Brien and tea with David Pryce-Jones. Pryce-Jones remembered, 'I had never met Paul Theroux at that point and Vidia suddenly whispered in my year, "He's from the CIA, you know." And I was very impressed by that.' (Vidia was joking.) During tea, the host made the mistake of playing a record that he had obtained free with a copy of *Private Eye*. 'It was a spoof Betjeman parody in which somebody was sitting on the lavatory with their trousers down and it was very funny. I could see Vidia's face twisted with dismay at this scatological joke . . . He minded very much. He didn't like it. That's a side of human life that doesn't appear in Vidia's writing at all. The fastidious side of Vidia would never accept that kind of coarseness. I greatly regretted playing this little record.'[60] The atmosphere became awkward and the two guests left abruptly. Paul recalled, 'Vidia was conflicted about David Pryce-Jones, sometimes calling him "that epicene young man" but much admiring his marrying a rich woman.'[61]

From Makerere, Paul had been writing often to Vidia: 'You were "typically English" to some people and "typically Trinidadian" to others; while to still others you were a "settler-type". None of the people who expressed these opinions knew you, or had met you.'[62] He told tales he thought would go down well, echoing Vidia's prejudices. Last weekend, 'I was staying with an infy headmaster . . . He lives in the two-storey house of the former provincial commissioner, has a huge garden (very much like Kaptagat), drives a Mercedes, says bloody, drinks a lot and has nothing to say.'[63] A colleague was depicted 'doodling in his office with the shades drawn while his sable breth'ren sat with their feet up . . . sipping and complaining.'[64] Paul was energetic, flattering, eager to please, seeking advice, offering racist jokes and tidbits of praise. 'This is a compliment on your fine review in the most recent *New Statesman*.'[65] When he read that Vidia had won the W.H. Smith Award, he wrote: 'The whole picture is of a fiercely intelligent Mandarin Hindu of anywhere from 35 to 42 years of age . . . I don't mean to burden you with a letter. I was pleased to see that you had such a good press over the award, and wanted to tell you that I don't think it could have happened to a nicer guy.'[66] As for himself, 'I would be very happy to meet a decent, tolerant, intelligent girl that isn't fat.'[67] Soon he found one, Anne Castle, an Oxford graduate and his future wife: 'I am also in love with a very pretty girl; she is English and is one of the best typists I've ever laid eyes on.'[68] Later, Theroux came to regret the tone of his letters: 'I was writing to Vidia in his language, because he has a special language and the closer you are to him, the more you see how funny this language is . . . I conceded more than I should have to his vision because I knew more than he did about Africa but he knew more about the colonial process and he knew more about Indians. I began to see it through his eyes a lot, I think somewhat to my detriment.'[69]

In his first letter from England, Vidia wrote of money and agents. 'East Africa seems very far away and shabby and unimportant, dangerous in some ways for the thinking person. But I don't wish to go over old ground.'[70] Later, he confirmed the invitation to visit for Christmas. 'I haven't had a real winter for some little time and I am thinking of spending a week or so in some bleak part of Scotland. Bathing in the fresh frosty air. Would you like that when you are here?'[71] In the end they remained in London, but when Paul overstayed his welcome at Stockwell Park Crescent, Vidia withdrew. Throughout his stay, Paul had found him troubled, melancholic and moody. A holiday friendship, freely given in the atmosphere of Makerere, was altering. Pat stepped in two months later to explain Vidia's failure to answer letters: 'We have both been very busy but the truth is we are both abominable correspondents.'[72]

In February 1967, while on his way to India, Vidia sent Paul a sarcastic letter of dismissal on the crested writing paper of the Bristol Hotel in Beirut, a missive designed to brush off a more sensitive man. He attacked his use of language as inaccurate, claimed his classical knowledge was imperfect and said Diana Athill's decision to turn down his novel was right. He wrote a cruelly dismissive line to a would-be novelist: 'I am happy that your journalistic ventures thrive; in this and in your other endeavours I wish you the best.'[73] If Vidia had been sent a similar letter, with his colonial alertness to social slights, he would have backed off. For Paul, a more open and abrasive personality who had grown up in Medford, Massachusetts and been roughened by four years in Africa, it was no more than a bad-tempered letter, characteristic in its peculiar way of Vidia. Vidia claimed to be surprised that Paul did not comprehend the insult: 'After he left in 1966, he was an absolute bore. I wrote a very ironical letter to him thinking this would put an end to those letters . . . But it never did. It was not important, I think. Probably these things helped to give one a reputation . . . Theroux didn't know what he thought about anything. He had no views. It's as though he didn't know he was in Africa. But he pestered me with letters, long letters being written to me every two or three weeks at a certain time.'[74] At the start, the relationship had hints of symbiosis. Each man provided information to the other, and Vidia enjoyed having a willing follower, a young aspiring writer who at times amused him and would do his bidding. Soon, though, Vidia became bored. Up to 1972, Paul wrote him fifty-four letters and received thirty-two in response; from 1973 to 1980, Paul wrote Vidia twenty-two letters and received no replies, except by telephone, but this seems not to have dented his faith in the friendship. He saw Vidia's behaviour as a mark of his eccentric talent, rather than as rudeness, indifference or rejection.

Letter after letter came from Makerere. 'How can one make any lasting comment on a place so valueless?' Paul asked. He was using precisely the phrases – and worse – for which he would later reprimand Vidia in his 1998 memoir *Sir Vidia's Shadow*. 'I don't see how one can write about this race; you succeeded ... because they were people to you, not Negroes.' Paul had been promoted: 'Until the post is Africanized I am Principal of the Adult Studies Centre ... There are reliable people under me ordering bananas etc ... I am doing exercises now (push-ups, sit-ups etc). If you have a moment would you describe what exercises you do?'[75] Paul complained of 'the infy crowd' and tried to out-Vidia Vidia, repeating stale jokes: 'A banker from Tanzania tells me that there is a new joke there among the out-going managers. When they see an Af. they say, "There goes our new branch manager." '[76] In the autumn of 1967, despite being in Uganda, he pleaded to be allowed to find his would-be mentor a place to stay in America. 'Please do drop me a note – just one line – telling me what your departure dates are, and if there is anything (I repeat) I can do to make your stay in the US comfortable please let me know. I could find out prices of cars, hotels etc.'[77] He despatched 'a gift I bought you in Nigeria, a briefcase which I thought might be useful to either your or Pat.'[78] Vidia was entertained by the adulation, and responded smartly with a request for an ivory cigarette holder, or 'a bulky smooth yellow' meerschaum pipe, and apologized for forgetting to thank for the briefcase. 'How awful it must have been for you to hear nothing...'[79] As Paul observed when he came to London, Vidia was happy to go out for meals when they met, but made no attempt to pay the bill.

Despite some irritation, Vidia gave succour, telling Paul there were 'few writers whose letters are as good as yours. I find them as nice as those of Scott Fitzgerald.'[80] Anne Theroux, now married to Paul, realized how important Vidia was to her husband. She found Vidia 'rather frightening and shocking at first, but he was never unpleasant to me: on the contrary, he could be charming.' Pat was 'by no means a drudge ... I admired her ability to engage intellectually with Vidia.'[81] Later that year the Theroux family moved to Singapore, where Paul had a teaching post at the university. He continued to send letters, no longer signed 'Love, Paul' but 'Best wishes, Paul'. Each time he was snubbed or ignored, he came back a little keener, a little more anxious to please, creating expectations that were liable to be dashed. He reported on life in Singapore:

'The brothels are quick, cold places staffed by teenagers from Indonesia and managed by secret societies.'[82] He was writing a stream of stories and novels while working full-time: *Girls at Play*, *Sinning With Annie*, *Jungle Lovers*, his fecundity impressing Vidia. Again and again, he offered his services: 'I wonder if there is any item of furniture you would like made here and sent ... If there is something you'd like, please send a little sketch, with measurements, and we will take care of the rest.'[83] Vidia's responses were cursory, and when he complained of being tired from work, Paul responded: 'that feeling of exhaustion you get from finishing a book is a sure sign of your genius, a feeling only a real writer can experience.'[84]

In his spare time, Paul went to the library and read Vidia's old book reviews from the *New Statesman*. He had decided to write a book about him. 'Would it gripe you terribly? ... I am just running this idea up the flag-pole, I suppose, and waiting for a salute.'[85] Vidia agreed, and signposted a specific vision of himself which Paul endorsed and ran with. In a shrewd piece of self-representation, which would be repeated by others, V.S. Naipaul presented himself as unprecedented, underprivileged, alienated. 'Think of it like this: imagine the despair to which the barefoot colonial is reduced when, wanting to write, and reading the pattern books of Tolstoy, Balzac et al, he looks at his own world and discovers that it almost doesn't exist.' Unlike an American, he had been born with 'no prospects in journalism, State Department, General Motors. No, one is a colonial as well, with all the spiritual and economic limitations and all the spiritual blight.' His privacy should be respected: 'I opened myself to you at various times without reserve, and sometimes with flippancy, which may not always be understood.'[86] Paul continued to write letters. He knew he was being intrusive, and ended, though it was only the second day of May 1970, 'Don't, please, answer this letter until July, or later if you wish.'[87] Ceaselessly prolific, he typed out extracts from books he thought might interest Vidia, reported the birth of 'another son, Louis', described hiking in North Borneo and sent some stories he had written for *Playboy*. He had sent a letter to the magazine too: 'The claim is that they have the best writers in the world and I wrote to the editor saying if this was true why had nothing by VSN been printed so far?'[88] The more enthusiastic he became, the further Vidia stepped back, while at the same time offering little prods of encouragement.

CHAPTER SIXTEEN

THE WORLD

BY 1968, VIDIA WAS falling apart. His finances were in a mess. *The Loss of El Dorado* was unwieldy and unfinished. He was sick of England, and feeling unwell. Then he twisted his ankle. New restrictions on immigration had left Pat wondering whether they might not do better to start over, in Canada. In April, Enoch Powell declared that like the Roman he saw the River Tiber foaming with much blood. Writing to Ironman in faraway Denmark in the same month, Vidia could be frank. He was 'staggered' by the British attitude to the effective expulsion of Kenya's Asians: 'I thought the Lord Chancellor's speech in the Lords one of the most shocking things I had ever read. And I felt . . . that a very special chaos was coming to England; I also felt that I could no longer stay here. We decided to leave. We have virtually sold our house; and as soon as my book is finished, will be on our way. A very distressing decision – all my adult life has been spent here, all my intellectual life and all my friends are here . . . I have been totally impoverished by the Inland Revenue.'[1] They had friends to abandon now, and none of them was West Indian: Antonia, Francis, Tony and other literary sorts, Julian Jebb, working at the new television channel BBC2 and recovering from a tight upper-class Roman Catholic upbringing, David Pryce-Jones, formerly of Eton and Oxford and now an upcoming novelist and literary editor, Tizzie Gatacre, thin and beautiful and well connected, Tony's son Tristram Powell, directing a television quiz show *Take It or Leave It*, and his wife, Virginia, a painter. Tristram and Virginia, who were shortly to have their first baby, agreed to purchase Stockwell Park Crescent.

Vidia and Pat needed somewhere to go. They moved from place to place, cadging weeks here and there, staying with acquaintances like Michael Astor at his house in Sandwich. A few years earlier, Vidia had been sitting at dinner beside an exuberant Italian, the daughter of an opera impresario from Bari. She was Marisa Masters, and when she began to praise *A House for Mr Biswas* and he said he was the author, she was ecstatic. 'For me he was a little kind of God. He was very badly dressed, and didn't have much money, and I gave him a lift home.'[2] Marisa was married to Lindsay Masters, who with Michael Heseltine had built the magazine publishing company Haymarket. She gave Vidia and Pat the run of her house in Kensington while she and Lindsay were on holiday in Spain. The Naipauls were scrupulous guests. Vidia wrote, 'We used the telephone a lot. Ten local calls & one long-distance to Yeovil. To cover laundry and telephone we are leaving 16/3. The whisky is to welcome you back & to thank you for your splendid, trusting generosity.'[3]

Knowing that Vidia wanted to finish writing *The Loss of El Dorado*, Hugh and Antonia Fraser lent him their country house on a private island in the middle of the River Beauly in the north of Scotland, Eilean Aigas. 'I have been working for the last six weeks or so in a rather fine Scottish house, in a library in which the taste of the 30's and 40's is, as it were, deep frozen,' Vidia reported grandly to Paul Theroux.[4] 'I rented a house in Scotland (for the peace & absolute quiet),' he told Ralph Ironman.[5] Fraser family retainers looked after him; he paid ten shillings a day towards the cost of the central heating. Pat found the house gloomy, and was glad when they left. At first, Antonia's relationship had been primarily with Vidia, but a friendship had grown with Pat, who responded to her warmth and admired her ability to manage such a full life: researching books, running lovers, giving parties, having children. Despite their mismatch, Antonia never made Pat feel awkward about lacking such things herself. Pat would write admiringly of her friend's appearance on television quiz shows, and praise her books; Antonia had 'multiple talents,' and *Mary, Queen of Scots* was 'the sort of visual history we have been thirsting for: court ceremonial and dress (wonderful wardrobe detail), the sense of place and the long rides on horseback.' Pat's presentation of herself in their correspondence was invariably self-deprecating. Lying in the summer sun, while Vidia sought to avoid it, was described as, 'trying to bring about the annual miracle, the transformation of my skin from slug to putty.' She would apologize for not writing sooner, or more fully. Her life with Vidia was presented in an endearing, conspiratorial way: he was 'growing that beard again'.

Shortly after staying at Eilean Aigas in 1968, Pat dared to raise an unmentionable subject with Antonia: her childlessness. Might her worldly, fecund friend be able to recommend a gynaecologist? This was

at a time before medical advances in fertility treatment; IVF had yet to
be invented, and a woman who had trouble getting pregnant was
viewed as barren and abnormal. Pat took the blame, and felt the failure;
it was a subject she could not discuss freely with anyone, including
Vidia. Until they had this conversation, Antonia had assumed, like all
their other friends, that the Naipauls had made a choice never to have
children. She suggested that Pat might see her own gynaecologist, Mr
John Blaikley of Guy's Hospital. 'He was very kind,' Pat reported in a
letter from Edna O'Brien's house, where they were now staying. 'It
cheered me up enormously that, as far as he could tell, I was normal.
Other tests take 2–3 months at clinics which would not be convenient
in our present itinerant state.' Pat was thirty-six years old and had
never conceived a child, yet she allowed itinerance to provide her with
an excuse not to take tests. She made a passive choice to leave her
future to fate, or to nature, and focused her maternal instincts on her
increasingly cranky and infantilized husband. The letter to Antonia
concluded: 'As Vidia said, he is in hiding until he finishes the book. I
leave Edna's when there is someone to look after him.'[6]

By November, the book was complete and Vidia and Pat were ready
to depart. He intended to go to the Caribbean, then Central America,
then the USA, then Canada. Most unusually, he decided to appear on
The World at One on BBC radio and make an explicitly political
complaint about the plight of immigrants and ethnic minorities. He
spoke of a 'deepening resentment' around the world about the way in
which people were treated in Britain. 'It has been really rather astonishing that in the past year immigrants have been subjected to an
unparalleled vilification from Members of Parliament and the press . . .
Another aspect of the last year which has been so distressing is that
there has not been a single spokesman for these immigrants from among
themselves. Immigrants are just discussed as though they don't exist, as
though they are objects outside in the street . . . It is extremely foolish
and extremely short-sighted.'[7]

Vidia had some commissions from the *Telegraph Magazine*, and
reserve money from the sale of the house. In a farewell interview to the
Times, he dismissed Britain's politicians as 'shabby, sharp dealers', said
its historians were 'indulging in these self-laudatory exercises' and
denied any connection to Lamming, Selvon or Barry Reckord. The
interviewer noted that V.S. Naipaul was living in a hotel in central
London. 'It is a transit camp, murkily entered by a moving escalator,

carrying numberless foreign nationals getting their first experience of Britain, wanly lit by inset pictures of limbo hotels around the world.'[8] Statelessness was a condition imposed on Vidia when he left Trinidad in 1950. Now it was something he sought, from a position of experience. Creatively and personally, he needed something fresh.

The dislocation of the following years would lead to a new perspective and to extraordinary books such as *In a Free State*. Displacement gave Vidia a distinct view of the world. At this time, there was no other writer of stature who was analysing societies in this detached, global way. V.S. Naipaul was of everywhere and of nowhere, rooted in an English literary tradition, but outside it. His attitudes and outlook had been formed by his family background, his colonial education and his experiences of Britain and beyond in the 1950s and 1960s: his instincts and prejudices were intact, but his eyes were wide open, missing nothing. 'It looks easy,' he said later, 'the writer coming and finishing his childhood material and then naturally moving on to England. It was very hard to do, and you will find that many people from far-away countries insist on writing about the far-away country. Their view never amplifies to take in the new experiences that they have actually been living . . . People are at their most creative when things are very disturbed.'[9]

*

In December he wrote to Diana Athill from Kamla's house in Jamaica. 'I came here two days ago after about 10 days in St Kitts – Anguilla, a situation that looks funny from the outside but is deadly serious. Interesting, though, because it catches the Negro-colonial tragedy in a most manageable, Lilliputian way. Now the job of reducing it to two 3000-word articles. I find that I enjoy this job of foreign correspondent and have a way of finding out – not cunning: it is just the same as in ordinary conversation: genuine interest always brings out the best in people.'[10] As violence unfolded in Jamaica, he wrote, 'A little note about the black power nonsense and the shootings here. Protest after protest, enemy after enemy: this is what passes for political thought in these primitive societies . . . It is a stupid and vicious movement here, Black Power, besides of course being imitative and totally irrelevant in a black country with a black government . . . Jamaican Black Power, like all other types of racialism, which appear to be brave and defiant, operates of course in a situation of security.'[11] The articles that followed were merciless and brilliant: 'Papa and the Power Set', about two political rivals fighting over the tiny island of St Kitts, and 'The Shipwrecked Six Thousand', about Anguilla in the days before tourism: 'The island has its own prophet, Judge Gumbs, Brother George Gumbs (Prophet), as he signs his messages to the new local weekly. He is not without honour; he is consulted by high and low. When the spirit moves him he cycles around with a fife and drum . . . The Anguilla problem remains: the problem of a tiny colony set adrift, part of the jetsam of an empire, a near-primitive people suddenly returned to a free state, their renewed or continuing exploitation.'[12] Asked by an interviewer from the *Trinidad Guardian* whether he was in touch with other West Indian writers, he answered, 'The contact is most intermittent. Some I have not seen for years. We don't have anything in common, you see . . . I have no fixed base at the moment.'[13]

Next he went to British Honduras or Belize, London's last colony on the American mainland, where he was looked after by the premier, George Price. The result was an unremarkable article, much of it using clipped reported speech to give a portrait of Sir John Paul, the governor. Afterwards, Price sent photographs and a letter: 'We were honoured by your visit and enjoyed your company on our trip to the mountains.'[14] In February 1969, Vidia travelled with Pat to the United States. The American consulate in Trinidad had given him a four-year journalist's visa. Desmond Dekker's 'Israelites' was about to hit the Top Ten, paving the way for the rise of other Caribbean musicians such as Jimmy Cliff and Bob Marley.[15] Flying in to JFK airport, Vidia and Pat found New York carpeted in thick snow. 'Intellectually I feel an intruder,' he reported to Francis Wyndham. Listening to Norman Mailer and Leslie Fiedler debate whether rationalism was dead at a 'Theatre of Ideas session' left him baffled. 'I felt it – surprisingly – to be very like India, only much, much richer. And of course one realises how simple one's vision of Americans is. They are really now a group of immigrants who have picked up English, but whose mental disciplines are diluted-European. Quaint mixture, not easy to interpret. Irony is absent . . . I miss London and the people I know very much.'[16] Keen to save dollars, he jumped at the opportunity when the manic poet Robert Lowell ('the only American who has read my work') and his wife the critic Elizabeth Hardwick offered to lend him their book-lined studio apartment on West 67th Street while they were away on a trip to Israel and Europe.

The Naipauls' social and intellectual way in New York was smoothed by Robert B. Silvers, to whom Francis had provided an introduction. 'Silvers has been very good and charming to us; he is an extremely important figure in the literary-political world here at the centre, one feels, of all sorts of king-making intrigues.'[17] He agreed to publish Vidia's articles on St Kitts and Anguilla in his magazine, the *New York Review of Books*. Founded during a newspaper strike in 1963, with Lowell, Hardwick, William Styron and Mary McCarthy writing for the inaugural issue, the *New York Review* had quickly turned into the house journal of America's liberal intelligentsia, though with an anglophilic slant. The editors were Bob Silvers, formerly of *Harper's*, and Barbara Epstein, who had edited and promoted Anne Frank's diary. Both were ferociously dedicated to the magazine, which was to prove much more than a review of books, carrying long articles on the cultural and political issues of the day. It was an incestuous but remarkable publication, reviewers and reviewed rotating cheerfully fortnight by fortnight. The *New York Review* took off during the civil rights movement and the Vietnam War, and although it was often radical in content, it was not doctrinaire. Over the subsequent decades, Vidia was to become an important contributor to the magazine; his political distance from many other contributors in no way diminished Bob Silvers's belief in the singularity and importance of his writing.

V.S. Naipaul was not alone in his attempt to storm America in 1969. In a letter which reveals the extent of his connections in two great cities, he wrote to Antonia Fraser:

> I got the impression the first few days here that all London was
> surreptitiously over here in dollar-gathering missions. A glimpse
> – or rather a hearing – of Isaiah Berlin in a hotel lobby;
> Stephen Spender everywhere; John Gross coming shyly out
> from behind some books in somebody's flat; [Anthony] Sampson
> around somewhere (J. Gross giving a party for him tomorrow);
> Penelope Gilliat turning up for dinner at Ivan Morris's. Almost
> as soon as Conor Cruise O'Brien saw me he behaved like a man
> who understood what it was all about: he offered me some
> dollars to be a visiting professor in his 'program' at New York
> University. Silvers (a great fan of yours) had fixed it, I believe;
> I believe they are all a little angry with me for saying no. I
> don't believe they understand how much I am afraid of
> organisations, intrigue, jobs, regular duties, and this writer
> destroying American-universities railroad.[18]

Aware that he was not a name in America as he was in Britain and the Caribbean, Vidia emphasized his disconnect from the writers of the day. 'News:' he wrote to Paul Theroux, 'Podhoretz is dead (of course in the literary sense) after his febrile butterfly life of the autumn. They are killing Trilling; Baldwin has lost; Bellow's lungs have collapsed; and Malamud is eating the sour grapes of Roth ... I don't understand half the time what they are writing about; I don't like their Teutonic wordiness; and I prefer the other thing, where a man slowly becomes a writer and stays.' He became lyrical, identifying with those who had been driven out or destroyed: 'I alternate between great happiness and great rage at the violence done to the American Indians: I feel the land very much as theirs at dusk, the sky high above Central Park.'[19] To Diana, he explained his quandary: he felt like a provincial. His agent John Cushman, who represented Curtis Brown in America, was little help. 'I now dread meeting Americans, especially their alleged intellectuals. Because here the intellect, too, is only a form of display; these people are really egomaniacs in the most Asiatic way; so that, in spite of all the chatter about problems (very, very remote if you live in an "apartment" in Manhattan: something that appears to be got up by the press) you feel that there is really no concern, that there is only a competition in concern ... The level of thought is so low that only extreme positions can be identified: Mary McCarthy, Mailer, Eldridge Cleaver and so on. Ideas have to be simple ... The quandary is this. This country is the most powerful in the world; what happens here will affect the restructuring of the world. It is therefore of interest and should be studied. But how can one overcome one's distaste? Why shouldn't one just go away and ignore it?'[20]

He felt more sympathy and affiliation when he saw three Nigerian writers, undone by war and famine in the Biafran blockade: Gabriel Okara, Cyprian Ekwensi and Chinua Achebe. Vidia had met Achebe the previous year at the house of Peter and Teresa Gatacre. He went for a 'most distressing lunch' with them, he told Diana, 'Distressing because they are so brave and full of good humour still and because they are now so thin and clearly not having enough to eat at home. Cyprian said they had sought me out so that, when I saw the name Biafra in a newspaper, I might think of them as people ... The blacks here (that is the correct word here) are very hostile to Biafra; they have got it slightly wrong, of course; they see Nigeria as the free black country and Biafra as the "strife" ... It was especially painful for me because 14 years ago I used to run into Cyprian a lot in the BBC; in those days he used to carry a novel in a briefcase and had no other problem than that of finding a title and a publisher.'[21]

When Robert Lowell came back and Vidia and Pat had to move to the Excelsior Hotel on the Upper West Side, New York seemed even less alluring. They made a visit to Washington DC, where at a diplomatic party an Indian representative told Vidia he had been forgiven for *An Area of Darkness*. In practice, he could see no future for himself in America. Did Vidia really want to be interviewing writers such as Mailer and Lowell? He would go to Canada after California, where he intended to write a cover story for the *Telegraph Magazine* on the legacy of the recently deceased John Steinbeck, 'Cannery Row Revisited'. It contained an important opening line, a lesson to himself: 'A writer is in the end not his books, but his myth. And that myth is in the keeping of others.'[22] He and Pat spent some days with John Gross and his wife, Miriam, both literary journalists from London, and stayed for a couple of nights with Jill Brain and her Japanese husband in their Greenwich Village apartment. Jill had reinvented herself when she moved to New York in 1959, changed her name and become an academic. She was not impressed by the new Vidia: 'I thought he had gotten a bit pleased with himself. I felt very sorry for Pat. At dinner he got to talk and she got to lean across the table and say, "Vidia has written a brilliant book." '[23]

In July they moved to a sparsely furnished flat in Victoria, British Columbia, which had been arranged by acquaintances, and Vidia began work on a sequence of stories. This was to be their new home. Pat wrote fondly to Antonia Fraser of her husband's demands and foibles: 'He particularly likes the carrots, sold here with the fresh furry leaves attached. I have of course, teased him about the components of his diet (you'll be relieved to hear that there is an acceptable brand of oats for his porridge) but the last straw came when he asked me whether he could not have a plate of washed carrots at his side while he worked. For his teeth you know.'[24] Canada, new, open, the home of many Indians and many West Indian East Indians, appeared to represent the future, but by September Vidia had changed his mind. Anguished, angry and feeling lost, he returned to England. They moved to a serviced flat in faceless Dolphin Square in London. Later, and without justification, Vidia blamed Pat for the decision to go to Canada, implying that he had been too feeble to resist her blandishments over the benefits of migration. 'Pat wanted to leave England. It was a very foolish thing because she put an end to one of the first periods in my life when there was a kind of stability . . . Something about immigration had upset her and she thought she could use me to make a statement. She had no idea where to go. She never told me. I think she had some foolish idea about Canada – she was thinking of a liberal country.'[25]

*

At the start of the next decade, the 1970s, Pat and Vidia were homeless. After an unspecified crisis at Dolphin Square, they returned to the days of Miss Gilson and Bravington Road: they were lodging at 23 Armscroft Place, the little home of Auntie Lu near the railway station in Gloucester. It was a far cry from Cal and Lizzie's studio apartment in New York. 'The only cure is work, to finish something, if only for oneself,' Vidia wrote apologetically to Francis. 'I will never be so weak or so proud again . . . if it is possible, we will stay on in England for three or four months, until I finish my work, or get it reasonably advanced. Does Emma [Tennant] still have a vacant cottage?' Once more, Francis swung into action, and fixed something. 'I've just spoken to Emma, who has taken a house on Elba . . . and is anxious to let her own cottage in Wiltshire at a small rent to "reliable tenants" and would love you and Pat to have it more than anyone!'[26] Meanwhile, Vidia sought the hospitality of Marisa and Lindsay Masters, who had a top-floor flat in their five-storey house in Elsham Road. 'I wonder now whether you could take me in for a couple of days next week,' he wrote humbly from Gloucester in January 1970. 'The BBC TV programme Review has asked me to judge a film competition and I have to look at the entries.'[27] Marisa responded that he could have his own key. 'Lindsay and I would "welcome" you any day and for any length of time. This of course applies to Pat also.'[28] Marisa was consistently generous and enthusiastic, writing often to Vidia. She took up Shiva too, as an additional Naipaul protégé. In her own words: 'Shiva and I got on like fire-engines together.'[29] When her daughters Georgia and Camilla were baptized the next year, Vidia was persuaded to be their godfather, the godmother being the purported inventor of the miniskirt, Mary Quant.[30]

In response to several demands, Vidia reluctantly arranged a meeting between his sisters and Hugh and Antonia while they were staying with the governor of Trinidad. Antonia looked back on this visit as 'tremendous fun. What I think we hadn't expected was to find these extremely lively, jolly young women . . . They were sort of middle-class, short-skirted, very glamorous.'³¹ To Savi, the former parliamentary under-secretary of state for the colonies and his lady seemed 'very relaxed, very at ease. They came for tea and they landed up having rum punch and wine.'³² Nella took them out on the streets to 'jump up' during Carnival, presenting a different version of Trinidad to the one Vidia had proposed to Antonia in an earlier letter of guidance: 'After Fort George . . . you go on to MARACAS BAY . . . now a marine slum. It used to be breathtakingly beautiful, until they cut down the trees on the hillside, quite recently, to provide allotments for people who had votes. Something was destroyed; nobody's problems were solved.'³³ Pat was pleased that Antonia was meeting Vidia's family, and praised each of her sisters-in-law in turn: 'Savi and Mira are both married to doctors and have university degrees. Sati hasn't a degree but Vidia thinks she reads the most books. Nalini has just done very well in her O levels, eager to taste the world . . . I may be prejudiced but I find them all beautiful, kind and clever.'³⁴

Each sister kept Vido updated. Sati's son Neil Bissoondath, who wanted to become a writer, was going to study in Canada. 'We have been staying at Nepaul Street for the last five months awaiting the completion of work on our house,' wrote Mira. 'The contractor, MOHAMMED, TURNED OUT TO BE A CROOK. I should have listened to Ma when she said never trust a Musulman.' Kamla told him that Shiva and Jenny had been staying with her. 'Sewan has put on a great deal of weight but I have never seen anyone whose features have undergone such a drastic change. I had difficulty recognising him . . . I guess you know by now that Rudranath died. There was great grief and shock in the family . . . I am almost sure it was his dying wish that no one be told – which is as he lived, selfish and vindictive.' Aged fifty, Capo R. had died from terminal renal failure, a malign and disappointed man, leaving scattered children: his son Rudy, a daughter by one of his students and a son by one of his own nieces.

In September 1971 Mira reported that André Deutsch had been on a trip to Trinidad to visit his authors such as the black activist Michael X. The Naipaul family's willingness to indulge Deutsch's constant expectation of hospitality had worn thin. 'As you know he always likes to bum a meal. Well this time he did not succeed in being fed by the Naipauls, but Savi and Melo did open some splendid champagne.' Nella wrote her brother a touching, sincere letter: 'I never seem to know what I should say to you, or how I should say it. I suppose it must be because of all the people I know best, I know you least. Do you understand? . . . I was 18 a few weeks ago.'[35]

A suggestion by Paul Theroux that he and his family might move to England did not appeal to Vidia. 'I would like to say first of all that it may be damaging for you to withdraw from the world and set up as a writer in the country, without a job, without links with the society where you live, at your age . . . I am concerned, too, about your choice of England.' Paul would have to be sure what he was doing. 'To have nothing on hand and to live in Gloucester or Salisbury (where I am about to go, to a house on somebody's grand estate) would, I think, be quite insupportable.'[36] Vidia told Paul he had been depressed and 'ill with bronchitis and pneumonia . . . I have earned nothing. A terrible intimation of age, failing powers, mortality.'[37] When the Theroux family moved to a house in Dorset, Vidia resisted issuing an invitation to visit. 'If you are in London, let's meet; if not, when will you be free?' Paul asked hopefully. 'I light a joss-stick every night for your Booker.'[38] Vidia was happy for Paul to fete him with a magazine profile: 'His marriage is a confident, supportive influence, and intensely private, based on the respect which comes of deep love . . . He is a reasonable vegetarian, out of preference rather than any Hindu stricture. I once asked him about it . . . He made a face and said, "Biting through sinew. I couldn't do it." '[39]

In a semi-detached house in Gloucester under the care of Auntie Lu, far from glamour and competition, Vidia unexpectedly flourished. He took up where he had left off in British Columbia, writing connected pieces on a theme of displacement. The main story, which he thought might become a novel, was *In a Free State*. Pat was able to talk to Auntie Lu about family matters she felt embarrassed to share with Vidia. Her father had gone off with Vera, the barmaid from the Kingstanding pub, referred to by Marg Hale as 'his fancy woman'. Calling themselves Mr and Mrs Hale, the pair had now moved to Lichfield; Pat refused to see her father. Eleanor remembered paying a visit and Vidia teasing her aunt gently. 'He would encourage her to put the world to rights, and say something quite outrageous to make her rail.'[40] The sheer normality of Gloucester life forced Vidia to calm down, and to work. He and Pat would go for long walks in the Gloucestershire countryside, which she loved from her childhood. 'We'd take a bus outside Gloucester to some parts we knew, and walk in that area. These wonderful walks. It's always nice to begin a walk with a nice steep hill – clears the lungs – and there was a Roman villa in the woods. During one of those walks we saw a fox, and we walked behind the fox for a while. The fox was quite unconcerned, its bushy tail swinging delicately from side to side. Was it Cleeve Hill? Was it Cranham Woods?'[41] Writing another story, 'Tell Me Who to Kill', about two Trinidad brothers in London, returned him to the idiom of his childhood. 'Vidia has been thinking about his family a lot recently,' Pat wrote to Kamla. 'I guessed this because he has been falling back into using T'dad locutions and when I asked him he agreed and said he found himself using a T'dad expression in an interview he gave recently.'[42]

While he was writing *In a Free State*, Vidia interviewed the artist David Hockney for the *Telegraph Magazine*. He chose never to have the profile reprinted in his collections of journalism. Written in the continuous present, it described Hockney's flat and his world and his techniques of working. Afterwards, Vidia purchased a drawing of his studio assistant Mo slumped post-coitally naked in a deckchair – the start of an art collection. He avoided saying much about Hockney's painting, although he admired it, and concentrated on reporting the man. 'He is a tall, chunky man. He is sensitive to beauty in others, but does not think he is himself beautiful. His hair is flawlessly blond; he wears big, round, black-rimmed glasses.' He quoted Hockney at length, giving a sense of his personality and the way in which he operated: 'When I was in Bradford I was so sexually naive. Now in London the way I live sex is much more important.' A sensual undercurrent runs through the article; although homosexual acts between consenting males had been legalized in England and Wales three years earlier, Vidia used allusion, implying an ambience. 'Young men are turning up in pairs. Most of them are small, fine-limbed, with fine, tremulous features; some look fatigued . . . The young men sit on the big tan leather settee in the drawing-room; the record player goes; conversation becomes general. The working day is over. When he is in London Hockney goes out every evening,' the article concludes.[43]

In his writing, Vidia would almost always describe men in greater physical detail than women. He was ever captivated by the beauty of the male body, but the idea of sex between men, and in particular anal sex, frightened and fascinated him. His reaction to Hockney's visitors appears to have been less a direct sexual attraction than a sense of excitement at the proximity of sex, and an awareness that he was himself attractive to gay men. In *Magic Seeds*, published in 2004, Vidia tried for the first time to address or explain his own impulses through the character of Roger: 'The idea of sex with a woman, exposing myself to that kind of intimacy, was distasteful to me. Some people insist that if you're not one thing you're the other. They believe that I'm interested in men. The opposite is true. The fact is all sexual intimacy is distasteful to me. I've always considered my low sexual energy as a kind of freedom.'[44]

*

Out came the book, starting from actual moments and real people, but ripped from his imagination. It started with a prologue, about crossing from Piraeus to Alexandria on a steamer full of all nationalities and refugees, and watching a tramp be mistreated; an epilogue has desert children being whipped, and a Chinese circus visiting Luxor. The first story is 'One Out of Many'. Santosh is a servant from Bombay who sleeps on the pavement until his employer is posted to Washington DC. The aeroplane journey unnerves him. He climbs on the toilet and squats. At immigration, he is made to empty his pockets. 'I pulled out the little packets of pepper and salt, the sweets, the envelopes with scented napkins, the toy tubes of mustard. Airline trinkets. I had been collecting them throughout the journey, seizing a handful, whatever my condition, every time I passed the galley.'[45] Santosh has Vidia's sensibility; everything he sees in America is alien. White Hare Krishnas, with their robes and cymbals, baffle him. He sleeps in a cupboard. Black people are 'hubshi', the Hindi equivalent of nigger: 'A lot of the *hubshi* were about, very wild-looking some of them, with dark glasses and their hair frizzed out, but it seemed that if you didn't trouble them they didn't attack you.'[46] Santosh abandons his employer when he meets an Indian restaurateur, and ends up marrying a black woman: 'I am now an American citizen and I live in Washington, capital of the world.'[47] The second story is 'Tell Me Who to Kill', written partially in dialect in a deliberately opaque style, a return to an earlier technique. 'He get back his confidence and it looks as though what he say is true, that he really like studies, because as fast as he finish one diploma he start another.'[48] It has moments of breakdown and madness, and as in 'One Out of Many' the narrator sees an alien world afresh, from the inside out, the effect coming from a complex naivety of perception. *In a Free State* tells of a white man and woman, Bobby and Linda, making a journey by car through an erupting African country. In its cruelty and precision, it anticipates *Guerrillas*. Diana Athill called it 'the first entirely unsentimental novel about Africa' and suggested it be published alone, without the accompanying stories and material.[49]

In a Free State is a disconcerting piece of writing, so taut and ambiguous that the author's point of view is never apparent. This was deliberate. Vidia said later of the book: 'I was not responsible for the world I was discovering. I was recording what I had discovered. I had no point of view. I think I just laid out the material, the evidence, and left people to make up their mind.'[50] It works by implication. Sympathy, like power, shifts back and forth. Take Bobby in the bar of the New Shropshire, wearing a shirt designed and woven in Holland, with a 'bold "native" pattern in black and red'. Well-dressed African civil servants and politicians sit in the bar. 'They hadn't paid for the suits they wore; in some cases they had had the drapers deported.' Bobby alights on a small Zulu man who holds a plaid cloth cap, 'now putting it on and pulling it over his eyes, now using it as a fan, now holding it against his chest and kneading it with his small hands, as though performing an isometric exercise.' Everything about the encounter unsettles. 'The cap made the Zulu appear now as a dandy, now as an exploited labourer from the South African mines, now as an American minstrel, and sometimes even as the revolutionary he had told Bobby he was.' The interaction is unstable. He appears to be a prostitute, and they seem to reach an agreement. 'There was silence between the two men. Then, without moving his hand or changing his expression, the Zulu spat in Bobby's face.'[51] Later in the story, Bobby is beaten by soldiers, and although the author's treatment and depiction of him remains mean throughout, he is in some ways a morally exemplary character. Linda too, and the colonel at the failing hotel, contain aspects of Vidia, aspects that are inevitably undone as the narrative shifts. 'I had the exhilarating sensation that I was one of the first to read a manuscript that would be analysed and argued over for years to come,' Francis told Vidia. 'It is magnificent . . . quite amazingly original . . . the most extraordinary and disturbing story, a tour de force of subtlety and ambiguity.'[52] Michael Astor disliked the book so much that their friendship came to an end. Paul Theroux wrote: 'The book amazed me, it was a great surprise, an unexpected form, a beautifully light touch . . . Anne had some reservations about the Africans who "left their stink behind" or "left turbulences of stink", but it is a true observation.'[53]

Graham Watson realized Vidia had written something exceptional. 'How on earth do you go on doing it!' He extracted an advance on royalties of £2,250 (£23,300 in today's terms) out of André Deutsch, a significant leap from earlier payments, and more than he had earned in royalties on any book, but still low by comparison with his commercial contemporaries.[54] Like Diana, and Bob Gottlieb at Knopf, Watson thought the additional material was a distraction from *In a Free State*. 'From the point of view of your gifts, my dear, I don't think you have ever done people better,' Diana wrote in October. 'The novel is so brilliant that it ought to come out alone.'[55] Vidia refused, and it was published as a thematically connected narrative in the autumn of 1971. To be sure that nobody at André Deutsch became confused over its form or its worth, Vidia drafted 'a guide as to how the blurb can be written . . . "Sequence" is the key word: it is the word that I had in my mind during the writing . . . This may be V.S. Naipaul's best book. It is certainly his most original and complete,' he suggested.[56]

The critics enthused. Naomi Mitchison gave Vidia 'an alpha plus on style', and Francis King thought it his best piece of writing yet.[57] In the *New York Review*, Alfred Kazin wrote: 'After seven books of fiction and three works of nonfiction . . . Naipaul has become one of the few living writers of fiction in English wholly incommensurable with anybody else.'[58] Nadine Gordimer noted that V.S. Naipaul was 'past master of the difficult art of making you laugh and then feel shame at your laughter'.[59] In the *Times*, Dennis Potter took a sideswipe at Anthony Powell: 'Some years ago a distinguished Old Etonian pontificating in an extremely conservative journal described Vidiadhar Surajprasad Naipaul as one of our most promising young writers. I wondered at the time if the brown man born in Trinidad of an Indian Hindu family was at all troubled or amused by the ambiguities helplessly inherent in that once so virulently acquisitive "our". V.S. Naipaul, after all, is brilliantly and satirically alert to every nuance of identity, of place, of inheritance . . . *In a Free State* is a book of such lucid complexity and such genuine insight, so deft and deep, that it somehow manages to agitate, charm, amuse and excuse all at the same pitch of experience. Do not miss the exhilaration of catching one of our most accomplished writers reaching towards the full stretch of his talent. Our? Well, yes, no.'[60]

*

During the course of 1970, living frugally with Auntie Lu, this success was some distance away. Over the Easter weekend, Vidia went alone to Amsterdam, and ended up spraining his ankle when he fell down some steps. At the end of the year, they left Gloucester and moved to Teasel Cottage in Wiltshire, a bungalow in the extensive grounds of Wilsford Manor. 'Emma's cottage is beautifully situated close to the river but on a bank above it. It is close to the road but below it so that the thatched roof is almost level with the road,' Pat reported to Marisa.[61] Wilsford was owned by Glenc's brother Stephen Tennant, a rouged and perfumed eccentric with dyed red hair and a fondness for jewels, fans and seashells, who pretended to be a writer and artist and considered himself 'a legend'. In his youth he had been exceedingly thin and a lover of the poet Siegfried Sassoon, but now he was grossly fat and liked to spend the winters in bed, alone, looked after by his retainers Mr and Mrs Skull. As Paul Theroux observed in *Sir Vidia's Shadow*, 'An idle, silly queen, Stephen Tennant was upper class and rich, so people laughed at his jokes and called him marvellous.'[62] For over a decade, Vidia and Pat were to be Stephen's tenants, paying a nominal rent of a little over £3 per week, which included the cost of electricity and local council rates. The surrounding landscape of woods, barrows, chalk streams and downland was relentlessly rural, and the nearest non-white face was to be found not in the adjacent village of Wilsford cum Lake, but at The Golden Curry in Salisbury. 'It sounds like a terribly classy address,' Ralph Ironman observed, 'have you joined the landed gentry?'[63] After a visit in 1971, Savi's husband, Mel, wrote, 'I told everyone that all you needed was David Lean to arrive with his cameramen and shoot the scene around your cottage cum Lake. Writer and wife at peace with the world. No phone, occasional taxi and wild ducks.'[64]

Needing money, Vidia wrote intermittent journalism but was adamant, as a matter of pride, that despite any shortage Pat should not return to school teaching. An article on the illogicality of Black Power in black-majority countries was rejected by *Life*, and Bob Silvers suggested it might be tempered; Vidia refused, and Silvers still ran it. Sati had told him of 'fires, shooting, looting and rape', of curfew and house arrests as Eric Williams sought to defuse the movement in Trinidad by embracing its precepts. 'Right now we do not know if it is really "Black Power" dignity or Communism.'[65] A crowd of 10,000 had marched through Port of Spain demanding an end to racism and the foreign ownership of banks and oil companies. Vidia was unimpressed when he read a pamphlet published by Lloyd Best's Tapia House movement praising 'the assertion of blackness by the men from below' and condemning 'whiteness' as 'the enemy'.[66] Vidia's 'Power to the Caribbean People' was a polemic, equating a radical cause that was gathering pace in the West Indies with the fantasies of Carnival. In Jamaica, 'There was a middle-class rumour, which was like a rumour from the days of slavery, that a white tourist was to be killed, but only sacrificially, without malice.' He saw this as 'rage, drama and style', a protest movement that would lead to destruction, a 'sentimental trap' of racially based identity, borrowing foolishly from the dissimilar situation of African Americans. 'In the United States Black Power may have its victories. But they will be American victories.'[67] When the piece was published in Trinidad's *Express*, Nella wrote to Vidia that his opinions were 'strongly disapproved by the public and furious replies are being sent into the paper . . . The family is rather enjoying some of the inane letters opposing your article.'[68]

Underlying Vidia's reaction was a personal antipathy to figures such as the 'honorary prime minister' of the Black Panthers in the United States, Stokely Carmichael, alias Kwame Ture, a former Tranquillity pupil. More irritating still was Michael de Freitas, alias Michael X, who had displaced Vidia as the most famous Trinidadian in England. A pimp, thief and hustler who had founded the Black House in Islington and the Racial Adjustment Action Society, 'Michael X' was being inflated in the press as a poet and Black Power leader by figures such as John Lennon, William Burroughs, Alexander Trocchi, Colin MacInnes and Richard Alpert (who liked to call himself Baba Ram Dass). In reality he was the son of a black Trinidadian woman and a Portuguese shopkeeper, who had come to London to seek his fortune through crime. 'He wasn't even black; he was a "a fair-skin man", half white. That, in the Trinidad phrase, was the sweetest part of the joke,' Vidia wrote later.[69] Michael X served time in prison for inciting racial hatred, suggested Queen Elizabeth should have a black baby and briefly became 'minister of defence' for the Black Eagles, an outfit run by Radford Leighton 'Darcus' Howe, himself formerly of Queen's Royal College.

Aided by wealthy white patrons, Michael X claimed to have tens of thousands of followers and to be the most famous black man in the world. Like Vidia and Eric Williams, he was published by André Deutsch: *From Michael de Freitas to Michael X* was his ghostwritten guide to revolution.[70] Joining him in the catalogue was Hakim Jamal, formerly Al Donaldson, a handsome African American criminal turned social activist, who while having an affair with the movie star Jean Seberg had been invited to London by Vanessa Redgrave, in the spirit of Sixties radicalism, to start a school. Jamal was a relation by marriage of Malcolm X, of whom Michael de Freitas was a pale imitation. Farrukh Dhondy, who managed to be one of London's leading Black Panthers although he was the son of a Parsi army officer from Pune, described the Black House as a 'fantasy outfit' and remembered Jamal as 'wily and alluring. His manner was to show supreme contempt for people. Both Jamal and Michael were full of horrible rhetoric about whites, and then they would go off and screw white girls.'[71]

Jeremy Lewis, an editor at André Deutsch, believed that as publishers they suffered from 'a guilty feeling that more should be done for black writers.' As a result, 'Every now and then Jamal or one of his cronies would come into the office and behave in a way which, had he been a middle-class Englishman, would have led to his being seen off the premises.'[72] Diana Athill later wrote a painfully honest account of this period in *Make Believe*. When Hakim Jamal arrived at the Deutsch offices for the first time, 'I sat down near him . . . and within two minutes he had put his hand on my shoulder and was watching to see if I would flinch at being touched by this impertinent nigger.' She did not react: 'He must see that I was "different": the classic reaction of the white liberal on meeting a prickly black.'[73] Diana became friends with Jamal, but believed Michael X was a conman; he was prone to turn up at her office 'ranting that he had secret information about concentration camps for blacks being built in Wales.'[74] All of these people provoked wrath and contempt in Vidia, who was determined he should not in any way be publicly linked or identified with them. In his published work, presenting himself as an outsider with special inside knowledge, he was careful to shield the importance of his continuing personal and family links to the Caribbean.

His predicament was complicated further by the arrival at André Deutsch of another author called Naipaul: Shiva, who had written a novel. He had planned to study Chinese history at Harvard on a scholarship after Oxford, but when he got a third-class degree the plan had to be discontinued. His early attempts at fiction were unsuccessful. 'I can't seem to summon the necessary patience and constancy,' he told his elder brother, 'flying into recurring fits of impatience and destroying everything I have already written.'[75] Once he got writing, he showed great talent. If Pa's *Gurudeva* was the prequel to *A House for Mr Biswas*, Shiva's *Fireflies* was the sequel. It told the story of the Lutchmans, who live in the shadow of their extended family; the father buys a house and dies young, his sons study and travel abroad, the mother is left to struggle on. Jenny wrote to Ma that there had been 'another tremendous review . . . the first reappearance of Auberon Waugh in the Spectator for years, & all on Shiva's book!'[76]

While Shiva was completing *Fireflies*, Diana wrote to Vidia: 'He lacks an edge you always had, but I believe he may blossom in the more relaxed form of the novel – I suspect that his strength may turn out to be in his warmth. He is getting rather fat – lazy boy, he says he never goes out – but was delightful and I enjoyed his company. Looking ahead, I wonder if he ought to use a pen-name? He says he's thought of it but feels disinclined to do so; André feels that there'll be great muddles if he doesn't.'[77] The name on the spine was Shiva Naipaul, and before long there were muddles. Excited by a new talent, editors wanted to hear his opinions. While Vidia toiled over *In a Free State*, Shiva appeared on *The Arts This Week* sounding like his clone: 'The true world was the world which existed outside the West Indies . . . the metropolitan country . . . make your way in the world . . . if you fail, you are nothing, the foreign city pays you no attention.'[78] To many listeners, and to any commissioning editors who thought of Vidia as old talent, this was new stuff. In 1971, Michael Robson of Curtis Brown wrote to the BBC: 'Our client, the novelist V.S. (Vidian) [sic] Naipaul tells us that there has been some confusion within BBC Copyright or Contracts with his younger brother, Shiva Naipaul . . . Vidian is now worried lest the BBC is attempting to base his fees upon fees already offered to Shiva.'[79] Mira thought Shiva's obesity stemmed from anxiety about his status, and that things might now improve for him. Vidia wrote back to her, 'I suppose we underestimated his distress at being my "shadow". It isn't something I understand myself, but then I have never felt oppressed by any presence, as he felt by mine. I wish I had understood earlier.'[80]

Vidia's status fluctuated. He was penniless; he was staying with Pat at the house of his patron Lord Glenconner in Corfu. Academics began to write books on his books, and he was asked to address conferences on world literature. In 1970 the government of Guyana invited him to attend its celebrations at becoming a republic. Vidia did not go. He was awarded the Hummingbird Gold Medal 'for loyal and devoted service to Trinidad and Tobago' (Sam Selvon, William Demas and Derek Walcott had been given it the previous year) but did not visit the High Commission to collect the medal.[81] In 1972 he was asked to open the book fair at the Commonwealth Institute, since the Duke of Edinburgh was unavailable. He became famous enough to attract crankish fans. A Mr E.M. Rimmer began to correspond: 'I once met a young man who said you were his father, and who was so fortunate – or deluded – as to be able to reckon only 4 or 5 acts of pure cruelty performed in his whole life.'[82] William Demas's sister-in-law wrote from Market Drayton asking how to get Naipaul's novels included on a college syllabus. An importuning man wrote from Sweden: 'I am an Indian from New Delhi, and I have written a book of about 130 typed-pages: *Silence with the Storm*. It is a sort of philosophical autobiography. I shall be very, very thankful if you or your brother will agree to go through it and suggest me a suitable publisher.'[83]

This was the age of arts television, and rather than being ghettoed at literary festivals as they would be later in the century, authors were invited to speak to the nation. Vidia was a frequent guest on *Take It or Leave It* at forty guineas a time, appearing alongside Cyril Connolly, Hilary Spurling and Angus Wilson. Descending in a lift after a show with John Betjeman, Auberon Waugh and Margaret Drabble, Waugh said, 'Everyone calls you "V.S." But what is your name?' 'Vidia,' was the reply. 'May I call you Vidia?' 'No, as we've just met, I would rather you called me Mr Naipaul.' There was silence as they waited for the lift doors to open.[84] Vidia used the same trick on the journalist Prem Shankar Jha. The actress and cookery writer Madhur Jaffrey wrote to Pat later, 'Three of us went out for lunch – Prem Jha, Vidia & myself. Somewhere, midway through the lunch, Prem said, "I say . . . I can't go on calling you Mr Naipaul – dashed formal and all that. . . . . . . ?" There was a L O N G pause. Everyone stopped chewing. Finally Vidia said, "You are embarrassing me" – and that's all he said. Nothing chummy like, Do call me Eddie or Herbie or whatever!!'[85]

Julian Jebb included Vidia in a documentary film on BBC2, *An Imaginary Friend*, in fact a spoof about a non-existent character, John Woodby; contributors to the programme included Elizabeth Bowen, Betjeman and Peter Cook. Vidia refused to let *Play for Today* have the rights for *In a Free State*; according to his agent, 'he thinks it would be badly done on television.'[86] Jonathan Miller attempted to turn *A House for Mr Biswas* into a film. The playwright Julian Mitchell failed to produce a stage adaptation of *The Loss of El Dorado*. 'We tried every likely place, but the size of the black cast defeated us,' he wrote to Vidia in 1972.[87] The director Peter Brook had faced a similar problem when he commissioned a musical of *A House for Mr Biswas* in 1961. The composer Monty Norman subsequently took the song 'Bad Sign, Good Sign', written for sitar and tabla ('I–I was born with this unlu-ucky sneeze and what is wo-orse I came into the wo-orld the wrong way round, pundits all agree that I-I'm the reason why my father fell into the vi-illage pond and drowned'), and adjusted it into one of the best-known tunes of all time – the theme for the James Bond films.[88]

Vidia was happy to appear on television or radio shows and interact with other panellists or the interviewer in a way that he would refuse to do in later years. On *A Word in Edgeways* with Brian Redhead in October 1971, he chatted happily with the composer Peter Maxwell Davies and the sculptor Mitzi Cunliffe about the role of the artist in society. It was 'the sheer wish not to sink personally' that made him write. 'I don't see my role as educating . . . I have never had this missionary thing.' His ambition, which he admitted showed 'a kind of arrogance', was to perceive the world in a different way to others. 'I am altering ways of looking and [altering] a set of values that have come down to us.'[89] A couple of months later he re-established contact with Andrew Salkey, agreeing to do a long interview with him on *The Arts and Africa* on the BBC. 'You left Trinidad. I left Jamaica. Have we really escaped?' Salkey asked. 'Yes. It's more than 21 years. My concerns are now more global . . . I have lost the innocence of the man from the small island who doesn't understand what power is, and [understand] the weakness of one's present position . . . it is a kind of day-to-day truth.' By writing *In a Free State* in the form he had chosen, Vidia was refusing to adjust information in order to make a conventional novel. 'I was no longer going to manufacture an artificial, contrived story.' Africa terrified him for its transformative effect. 'It is a place where anyone from outside is automatically in command. You can be the man with the whip, or you can be the man with the healing touch . . . it is so exploitable.'[90] In a later discussion with Margaret Drabble, he came back to the theme of Africa as a place that encourages the breakdown of moral values: 'I was much more concerned about the English people who were in Africa. I am much more concerned with people who find liberation among their inferiors.'[91]

*

After *In a Free State*, Vidia travelled as a journalist, writing an incisive two-part account of an election in Ajmer in India for the *Sunday Times Magazine*. His local guide and interpreter was Bharat Bhushan, a schoolboy from the prestigious Mayo College, lent by the headmaster. Bhushan wrote an account of the experience, describing the author at work: 'At another time we found ourselves at a tea-shop in Nasirabad, outside Ajmer, late at night. Naipaul insisted that the shopkeeper wash his cup and saucer with soap. The shopkeeper asked his young son – about seven or eight years old – to wash the cup. Naipaul wanted to know why the child was not in bed. Did he not have to go to school the next day? How did he expect him to pay attention in class if he was forced to work till eleven at night?

The shopkeeper heard out Naipaul with a resigned smile. One night our car ran out of fuel. We found a petrol pump but as there was no electricity, the petrol had to be pumped out by hand. Naipaul pushed the attendant aside and started working the crank himself explaining, "I need some exercise." ' After the article had been published, another pupil blamed Bhushan for some insulting references to his father, a murdered maharajah. 'I was upset enough to write to Naipaul about putting such hurtful stuff in print. He wrote back that sometimes truth had this effect on people but it had to be told.'92

Vidia's finances were still unruly. In February 1971, the month in which Britain adopted a decimal currency, he ordered a bespoke coat from Simpsons of Piccadilly at a cost of £99, but a few weeks later Pat was writing to him that she could hardly get by on £25 a week: 'I find I can only afford to go up to London once in ten days. I drink a half bottle of wine every two days and keep sherry in the house but find I have to avoid meals out and the record department in Smiths.'93 He went to Jamaica to see Kamla, and to Trinidad to see Ma and his sisters. Savi was now a tutor in sociology at the university, and Mira was soon to emigrate to America, where Amar had been given a position as a radiation oncologist at Johns Hopkins Hospital. At the end of March, Kamla wrote to Pat, 'Vido was very tired and very thin when he got here ... For the first few days he complimented us on the garden and how much we had achieved. Of course, this was too good to last. He then demanded instantly a tree "filtering the sunlight" to be planted on the front lawn ... Harry was under the ivy covered front porch. Vido, with green hat, from the cool bedroom, was peeping through the louvres with such occasional outbursts as "Drop that fork into the hole so that I can see if it is deep enough." "Dig some more." "Sprinkle a bit of bone flour. It does wonders." And there, around the hole were Pooloo & Dada & myself – three twits in the blazing sun.' A touring Indian cricketer had fallen in love with Nella. 'He would give to it his most serious consideration ... Then one morning he would emerge from his bedroom, talking loudly to himself – "No! No! No! Penniless cricketer! Indian crook!" ... [P.S.] What a massacre in East Pakistan! Those bloody Muslims!' Diana Athill had also paid Kamla a visit in Jamaica: 'Diana surprised me. I was expecting someone older looking, very bookish and rather stodgy.'94 Diana's reaction to Trinidad echoed Vidia's: 'Rueful remark of elderly man who is in charge of the "public" beach at Mt. Irvine Bay (the dottiest piece of mimicry, that beach): that it was a funny thing, but here it still seemed unnatural to give orders to, or take them from, someone of your own colour,' she wrote to him.[95]

Vidia had come to attend a meeting of Caribbean writers at the Jamaican campus of the University of the West Indies. With Black Power in its heyday, there was 'a strong undercurrent of resentment against Vidia – against his ethnicity, against his writing, against his very presence,' thought Kamla.[96] Sharing a stage with other authors and some rivals from his days at *Caribbean Voices*, Vidia had barely begun to read his paper when a black Jamaican librarian, Cliff Lashley, jumped up from the audience and said that he ought to be killed, preferably shot.[97] The conference organizers made no attempt to reprimand Lashley, or to apologize to Vidia, who left the conference and returned to Kamla's house. A Trinidadian academic, Kenneth Ramchand, thought the situation was handled very badly. 'There was total silence, no reaction to Cliff Lashley. The proper thing would have been to eject him.'[98] Vidia blamed the outburst, for no obvious reason, on his former BBC colleague Edward (now called Kamau) Brathwaite: 'He organized a racial ambush of me in Jamaica in 1971 . . . He ran me down and became a great enemy of mine, but I didn't reply, I didn't reply.'[99]

Vidia travelled to the island of Mauritius to write 'The Overcrowded Barracoon', which would give him the title of his next book, a compilation of journalism and essays. Mauritius was not 'a lost paradise' as travel writers were then suggesting, but a big plantation 'far from anywhere, colonized, like those West Indian islands on the other side of the world, only for sugar, part of the great human engineering of recent empires, the shifting about of leaderless groups of conquered peoples.' His eye was drawn to the helpless and the hopeless, the malnourished boys who came to a political meeting 'in over-size jackets that belong to fathers or elder brothers' to listen to empty slogans. 'The rain, the bush, the cheap houses, the poor clothes, the mixture of races, the umbrellaed groups who have come out to watch: the hysterical scene is yet so intimate: adults fighting in front of the children, the squalor of the overcrowded barracoon: the politics of the powerless.'[100] Mauritius would go on to become one of the most prosperous countries in Africa, helped by tourism and a stable political system; a rare instance of Vidia misreading an atmosphere at this time. He said later, 'I was always thinking when I was travelling, will this make sense in twenty years. I allowed my depression and rage to take me too far in the thing I wrote about Mauritius. My analysis of the place was correct but I had no idea that they were going to find ways of dealing with it. I thought they were going to drift into starvation ... I didn't know they were going to alight on this idea of the export zone, which has been a great saviour for them, and I had no idea the world was so heartless, that people would want to go and have a holiday where everyone was starving.'[101]

On return to Britain, Vidia was laid low with bronchial pneumonia, a complaint induced in part by a continuing feeling of being unfulfilled and in the wrong place. 'I have been getting a whole series of minor illnesses,' he told Kamla, 'stomach, lumbago, influenza, headaches etc.'[102] He thought again about quitting England to live elsewhere. But where? For the rest of the year, he kept up a busy correspondence with Kamla, analysing his own past and wondering about his future. 'You were hurt that we never recognised you as a writer. What a false impression. We are absolute bores, the way we talk about you constantly,' Kamla wrote back. In October 1971, she wrote: 'You claim you were starved. Erase it from your mind. It's not true ... I am not so sure that the dahl, roti and daily fresh vegetables were such bad fare after all.'[103]

That month he had a postcard from Carmen Callil, who was shortly to leave André Deutsch to found the Virago Press: 'For the Booker prize, you and your wife will be asked to a dinner, Thursday November 25. I have been asked to tell no-one but you and André that you have one.'[104] One what? He had one? Had won? Had he won the Booker Prize? Despite the cost, he made a daytime telephone call: he had won! Outside the ceremony at the Café Royal in London, a BBC *Bookcase* microphone was waved beneath his nose, and he was asked if he minded that the Booker group had interests in sugar and mining, and if he was pleased to have won the prize. For once Vidia had no words, and when he did respond, he sounded like a member of the royal family: 'Well I tell you one's overwhelmed, I think one is so overwhelmed by a thing like this that one can't quite react.'[105] The following year, the Booker went to John Berger for *G*, who railed against the prize and said he would share his winnings with the Black Panthers. He travelled straight from the award ceremony to a north London pub, where he met Farrukh Dhondy and Darcus Howe. Dhondy was the only Black Panther with a bank account, and Berger cheerfully wrote him a cheque for £2,500 to purchase a house in Finsbury Park. It served as a base for the movement for some years, until Dhondy received a visit from four men with machetes who persuaded him to give up the property. An article in the *New Statesman* observed that most

Booker employees in the Caribbean were of Indian origin, and quoted Vidia saying that John Berger's statement was 'ignorant, absurd, not just rubbish but damaging ... Most of the Black Power writers are only speaking to white people ... It's a nightclub turn, it's television ... None of these black writers has been to Guyana to study the role of the CIA there – in fact very few black writers have written about black regimes at all.'[106]

Letters came for Vidia from around the world, amazed he had won yet another prize. Ruth Jhabvala wrote: 'Do accept our congratulations, all of us very thrilled, especially me who always sees in your success hopes for my own future too. I don't know why – perhaps because we're both so far-out and alone? Out on a limb?'[107] (She would win in 1975 with *Heat and Dust*.) 'You certainly continue to write brilliantly. For this, I am sure you realise, some of your dear West Indian colleagues will never forgive you,' wrote John Figueroa from Puerto Rico.[108] 'I wish there were a gesture of homage which one could put on paper,' Michael Frayn told him. 'There are very few writers (even among those I enjoy and admire) to whom I feel inclined to make this act of submission. Your writing has some kind of "otherness" which detaches it from you, and gives it an absolute life free of the efforts and compromises one can sense in most things. I gather the Booker committee took counsel's advice on what constitutes a novel; good that they should be forced to do so.'[109] Peter Bayley sent a letter from Univ, after many years: 'I thought A House for Mr Biswas was wonderful – in a wild marvellous Dickensy imaginative way; In a Free State seems astonishingly far beyond that. But as a result I found it profoundly disturbing ... perhaps I was wrong to see personal unhappiness, alienation, loneliness, humiliation so clearly behind it all.'[110]

Although Vidia did not want to hear this, and resented his former tutor's willingness to speak to the press about his Oxford days, Peter Bayley was right. A month after the Booker dinner, Vidia again uprooted himself and Pat, and travelled back to the West Indies. He might stay there, or he might visit Nigeria, or the new state of Bangladesh, or what he liked to call 'Spanish America'; in particular, he might visit Argentina.

CHAPTER SEVENTEEN

'WITH THE AID OF A CUTLASS BLADE'

PAT AND VIDIA FLEW to Trinidad two days after Christmas 1971. Pat was writing a new diary, and began by setting their life in a literary context. Vidia was doing an article on Jean Rhys for the *New York Review* and reading Thomas de Quincey's *Confessions of an English Opium Eater* and the plays of Oscar Wilde, which he liked to do while lying unshaven in a hammock wearing winceyette pyjamas from Marks & Spencer. She was reading Joseph Conrad's *Under Western Eyes*, Vladimir Nabokov's *Pnin* and John Updike's *Pigeon Feathers* and *The Centaur*, a book which left her feeling regretful: 'I relate to Vidia's seeking out his roots. Feel my own vulnerability.'[1] She wrote about the renovation of the Lion House, a visit to Owad and another cousin, Seromany, a party with Savi and Mel where she drank too much rum punch, and a conversation with Derek and Margaret Walcott at Sally Stollmeyer's house: 'Walcott tells Savi how violent he gets when drunk and people annoy him.' Ma was depicted treating Pat like one of her own children, talking about 'temple politics' and going to the quarry she managed for her brother Simbhoo: 'Ma greets various Indians, some in Hindi. One old man driving a truck: she strides up to the cab and says, "I was wondering who could know me, who was smiling at me from a lorry."' Vidia was shown in glimpses, playing cricket on the beach, watching the 'delicate and glistening' tazias paraded at the Hosay festival: 'Vidia allows himself to be carried away as this is Indian drums and drumming. I dart out into the road and grab him as he is following happily.' Elsewhere, there are references to tension: after a telephone call to Kamla in Jamaica, Vidia 'came up and there was an outburst about homelessness and anger with me.'

'No adventure, no journeys yet. I am just queen-beeing it here at my sister's, resting and trying to get better,' Vidia wrote to Paul Theroux in February 1972. The *New York Review* wanted a travel article from him. 'I am very keen on Bob Silvers; and they will print anything I want to write about S. America. But they just can't afford to pay.' In the meantime, Vidia was left contemplating the failings of women from a position of ignorance: 'I am getting very bored with the drama and self-dramatising of the female soul – really just the pleasuring of the body – and I am beginning to feel more and more that women are trivial-minded, incapable of analysing or even seeing their motives; that they long for witnesses to their pleasure or their distress.'[2] He went to visit elderly relations in Trinidad and contemplated writing an autobiography, or another novel. Pat made a note in March: 'Yesterday Vidia went off to San Fernando early in the morning with Melo. Expecting to be the Rotary Club's guest of honour. They had another guest, a speaker, to whom Vidia was introduced. Whereupon he walked out.' Mel Akal's recollection of the trip to the Rotary Club was more florid: 'The secretary came and said, "Vidia, we have an American business-man passing through Trinidad and he will be the main speaker today." He exploded, he cursed the man and called him a shit. We just walked out. I think he was quite right to do that.'[3]

Some weeks after Vidia and Pat reached Trinidad, graves were discovered in Arima containing the bodies of a black man and a white woman. The previous year, Michael X had moved back to Trinidad to start a commune, fleeing the courts in London, and now calling himself by the Muslim name Michael Abdul Malik. Local Black Power activists were doubtful, but he began to display wealth and received John Lennon and Yoko Ono as well-publicized house-guests. Soon Malik was visited by Hakim Jamal and his English girlfriend cum slave Gale Benson, alias Halé Kimga (an anagram of 'Hakim' and 'Gale'), who was the daughter of a Tory MP (Captain Leonard Plugge, who claimed to have invented the two-way car radio). In London, Jamal had been given keen coverage in the press as an educator. 'Everyone in this story was at some time or another at least a little mad,' Diana Athill wrote later, and her act of lunacy was to offer him a 'loan' of £200. He accepted on the condition he might give her a weekend of loving, adding tactlessly that she should not think of herself as 'an old woman who is reduced to buying sex'.[4] Diana was outraged, but invited him to stay all the same, accompanied by Benson, who promptly stole the money from a dressing-table drawer. Permissive to the point of aberration, Diana let the pair remain. Jamal took over her house, told her she had vacated her body and taken possession of Benson's, and inveigled another £200 out of her. They moved to Trinidad at the end of the year, where Jamal accepted Michael Abdul Malik's demand that a human sacrifice was needed: Gale Benson was hacked to death with a cutlass by Malik's followers and buried in a shallow grave. A month later, a local man named Joe Skerritt was murdered there too. It would be many months before these and other details would become clear, many of them pieced together meticulously by Vidia.

V. S. Naipaul was never wholly aware of the nature of Diana Athill's alternative life, for they saw little of each other outside the offices of André Deutsch, apart from occasional lunches at the cheap restaurants where Deutsch permitted his editors to entertain. Born in 1917, Diana had enjoyed a 'middling English gentry' childhood of ponies, lawns and housemaids, and at Oxford had become engaged to a bomber pilot. Then the Second World War started and her fiancé's letters stopped. 'I never heard from him again until I received a formal note, two years later, asking me to release him from our engagement because he was about to marry someone else.' Soon afterwards, he was killed. Needing to earn her living, Diana teamed up with Deutsch as a publisher and had 'foolish and always short affairs . . . Lack of energy prevented me from ranging about in pursuit of men, but if they turned up, I slept with them.'[5] Now in her mid-fifties, Diana wore her grey hair in a bun and spoke with a cut-glass accent. She was profoundly unconventional, extending hospitality to random visitors and having a particular susceptibility to foreigners who had fallen on hard times. Unlike many of those she befriended during the 1960s and 1970s, Diana was not deceived: she was able to look at the element of fantasy behind the social idealism of the era with an amoral eye; she was interested in watching how people behaved.

When news of the killings broke, Pat was disturbed and Vidia felt a resonance with a story that had already formed in his head: 'Vidia said that the idea he was playing with ended in a stabbing.' His mental image was of a murder at a commune, and the murderer looking through the slats of a Venetian blind at a commune member coming up the road in the sun.[6] A letter arrived from Diana which, Pat noted, 'talks about an inevitability that these three mad people should meet in this mad place . . . Vidia asked me whether he should write a book about Malik. Interview him. Follow the trial.' Diana wrote of Gale Benson, 'It was impossible ever to imagine anything but a disastrous end for her (I would have betted on suicide), but what appears to have been the extreme horror of the actual killing is worse than anything I foresaw . . . She was . . . an astonishingly talented linguist, deft and neat about the house, a great deal of charm, rather beautiful to look at, very brave (really astonishingly brave) – yet absolutely not alive except in terms of the man's fantasy.'[7] Vidia suggested to André that 'quite a book could be made of the affair, which lights up so many things in our world: race, perverted sex, boredom, communes, communal lunacy, conscience, fraudulent politics (black & white), liberalism etc.'[8] In addition he wrote to Diana (unware at this point of the nature of her involvement with Hakim Jamal): 'The atmosphere here is perhaps like the atmosphere in the old days when some lunatic Negro "plot" was uncovered: the threat of punishment makes everybody sober straight away – until the next lunatic abscess ripens. Lunacy and servility: they remain the ingredients of the Negro character. I wonder why this isn't written about, why the Negro writers continue to be sentimental about themselves.'[9] While the investigation proceeded, Jamal fled back to Boston where he was murdered by De Mau Mau, a militant organization that had been established by black US soldiers in Vietnam.

Vidia made a trip to the 'Memphis' Black Power settlement with a local architect, a visit that would provide the impetus and detail for the chilling scenes at the commune in *Guerrillas*. The architect, Bernard Broadbridge, was 'nervous of Vidia & nervous of what he will find', Pat wrote in her diary. 'The Black Panther leader, Aldwyn Primus . . . is small and quiet . . . We have been told that Primus is transformed on the orator's platform. Cannings supply them with food and other things. They are sponsored by Rotary, Chamber of Commerce etc. That is how the nervous, but nice, Bernard has got involved. They have a large piece of land, 93 acres. Their cultivation seems to consist of a couple of small patches of tomatoes. Laughable in view of extent of their kingdom . . . We go down to see the tomato seedlings being planted out, with the aid of a cutlass blade in very muddy soil.' Vidia made precise notes: 'The concrete floor, the beds; at the other end the store (ducted) and in one corner, below seating, supplies & stores. Open at both ends. Mr Primus was said to be having a bath. A small slender-hipped man, really very attractive, with blue-coloured glasses & a very large shiny knob for a nose, with the acne pits enlarged & prominent, miniature moon craters.'[10] In *Guerrillas*, he would merge Primus with Malik, since Malik's involvement with the Black Power movement in Trinidad was in practice tangential.

The same day, they went to the murder scene. Pat wrote: 'The side turning to Malik's burnt-out house is blocked by a police barrier ... We see the upturned earth of Skerritt's grave and are taken to see the small square where Gail [sic] Benson was found in a sitting position.' A BBC reporter 'walks up and takes a still photograph of Vidia by the grave. He then asks whether he is going to write a book about Malik. Vidia says he might but has not made up his mind.' Days later, Pat was still upset: 'Was that very clean neat square hole it? The two old seedling boxes, the lettuce boxes?' Black Power was exacerbating Trinidad's ethnic divisions; Savi's Indian driver Ralph Roopchand told Vidia and Pat, 'Although we are poor, my father is still a very racial man.'[11] Francis Wyndham suggested that Vidia might write about the Michael Abdul Malik case for the *Sunday Times Magazine*, and offered to pay 'extra well' given his connection to the subject, and its hold over the popular imagination in Britain.

*

Leaving the murder trial to one side for a moment, Vidia agreed with Bob Silvers to write about Argentina's political unrest for the *New York Review*. After the fall of Juan Perón in 1955, Argentina had veered between civilian and military government, and violence had grown as more than a dozen armed groups competed to overthrow the state, and the state repressed them brutally. Peronism, with its mixture of populism and authoritarianism, was still potent, as was Perón's late wife Eva, or Evita, the orator and propagandist who had a mystical hold running far beyond Argentina's borders. Vidia had long been interested in her: 'I had wanted to write about Evita since 1952, when I saw a newsreel at Oxford.'[12] Some Argentinians were now calling for the return of Juan Perón, who was exiled in Spain.

Bob Silvers borrowed money to fund the trip from his girlfriend Grace, Countess of Dudley. 'We heard that there was something going on in Argentina and I just said we were very frustrated, it would be so great if we could send someone like Naipaul, and Grace said, "I'll be glad to help." She was a great admirer of his work ... That was the last time any outsider contributed anything to the paper.'[13] Silvers arranged contacts in Buenos Aires too, in particular Norman Thomas di Giovanni, an Italian-American who was the amanuensis and 'walking-stick' of the celebrated blind poet and fabulist Jorge Luis Borges. In a reminiscence of Silvers, Vidia described the background to the article: 'I telephoned Bob; within two days he had sent expenses money to a Trinidad bank. This sounds easy to do now ... Seven or eight years later Bob told me that money was scarce at the *Review* in 1972, and he had personally borrowed the expenses money he had sent to the Trinidad bank with such swiftness and style. Such faith in a writer, too: it was humbling.'[14] On 12 April 1972, newly bearded, his head still full of 'race, perverted sex, boredom, communes, communal lunacy, conscience, fraudulent politics (black & white), liberalism etc', Vidia flew due south from Trinidad to Argentina. Grace Dudley's impetuous generosity, Bob Silvers's faith in a writer and Vidia's own Oxford interest in the person of Eva Perón had conspired to make the trip to Buenos Aires happen: it was to be the start of a revolution in his life.

Lying in bed on the night of her husband's departure, a few months short of her fortieth birthday, Pat wrote, 'Two sleeping pills, but perhaps perversity prevents me sleeping. And mosquitoes? I think of the last three years. I think of the racial inturning. Seeking false ancestors, nostalgia, attenuated, poetical talk about horsemen & snow at the end of the world.' This was a reference both to Vidia and to Ralph Singh's Aryan fantasies in *The Mimic Men*, 'I have visions of Central Asian horsemen, among whom I am one, riding below a sky threatening snow to the very end of an empty world.'[15] Pat was alone, lonely and childless, her hair was lank and grey, her clothes were wrong and she was underweight. Her husband was having sex with prostitutes and wanted another life, yet he still depended on her. Like Thomas Hardy and his wife Emma, childlessness exacerbated their estrangement; it was an area of silent and secret guilt, which they both rationalized in public by saying they did not want to have children, since it would interfere with Vidia's writing. Pat felt unable to speak to anyone about the unease of her situation, and took refuge in her diary. A few days earlier, she had written: 'Exchange of awareness between Savi and I when talk turns to the old Indians who had wives and families in their different situations as emigrants and immigrants ... Also discussed with Savi the Naipaul propensity thru' three generations to give mother and wife a hard time.' Even with her sister-in-law, Pat felt unable to communicate fully, and Savi in turn found her 'extremely private. Pat remained so – cool, distant ... She was essentially passive.'[16]

Pat had written a journal in India in 1962, and a daily narrative, which has since been lost, while they were staying with Auntie Lu in Gloucester. In Trinidad, she noted, 'A diary should not be a confessional or a repository for grudges?' quickly undermining herself with a question mark. Her diary would be a record of her life with Vidia, and of his work. A little later she asked, 'Should I write about him? Began out of sense of obligation and duty while he was writing *In a Free State*. Now unwarrantable.' Warrantable or not, she continued with the diary until 1995, writing hundreds of thousands of words in twenty-four large notebooks. Pat would almost always be the passive observer, the diarist who witnesses events from the sidelines. She never sought to inflate her own role, and often tried to reduce it. Her diary was snatched, scrappy and intermittent, lacking the mental agility of her letters, let alone the fire of her Oxford correspondence with Vidia in the 1950s. It was a collection of thoughts rather than a clear narrative, and is not easily quotable; it was not inventive, and it feels reliable. Pat would write the same thing in different forms, sometimes illegibly, or jot it on a piece of paper and insert it between the pages of the diary; she would use different pens and pencils, different coloured inks, different types of notebook; she would make insertions, using an asterisk and a scribbled note to amend an entry; she would pick up the diary or put it down for months at a time. Despite its inconsistency, Pat's diary is an essential, unparalleled record of V.S. Naipaul's later life and work, and reveals more about the creation of his subsequent books, and her role in their creation, than any other source. It puts Patricia Naipaul on a par with other great, tragic, literary spouses such as Sonia Tolstoy, Jane Carlyle and Leonard Woolf.

*

Argentina was familiar and unfamiliar for Vidia, another part of the New World that had been conquered by force by the Spanish, its indigenous people driven or wiped out, its social and political structures borrowed from abroad, a large, long country with a small population, stretching from the Bolivian border to Tierra del Fuego, bounded on either side by the Andes and the Atlantic, a land of rivers and fertile plains or pampas. In the sixteenth century the conquistadors had come to Tierra Argentina, the land of silver, finding a wonderland on the edge of nowhere inhabited by Amerindians who ate corn and sweet potatoes.[17] Soon the plains were turned into giant ranches or estancias to raise cattle; there were so many cows that the meat would be cut and the carcass left to rot on the grassland. Slaves came too, and lawless cruelty as the Spanish fought off the Portuguese. By the early nineteenth century, when the region declared independence from Spain, there was a thriving trade from Argentina, soon to be boosted by the invention of refrigeration ships for beef. Blood was everything; women of Spanish descent would be depicted in paintings with a slight moustache to show they had no Indian heritage. By the time of the First World War, the new country was wealthy and immigrants were pouring in from Spain and Italy. Argentina had railways and industry and a capital, Buenos Aires, with a subway, boulevards and skyscrapers. BA considered itself the southern hemisphere's answer to Paris, and was home to a beautiful opera house, the tango, innumerable servants, psychoanalysts, grand Catholic churches and white prostitutes from eastern Europe. Its citizens believed they spoke Castilian Spanish. It was the sort of place that might have been designed to impress, stimulate and irritate V.S. Naipaul.

He stayed at the Hotel Nogaró and moved fast, reading books and magazines and making telephone calls. Journalists helped him, including Robert Cox, the British-born editor of the English-language newspaper the *Buenos Aires Herald*, and the prominent cartoonist Hermenegildo 'Menchi' Sábat, who found Naipaul 'a very peculiar fellow, unbelievably intelligent. He thinks only in words, while I think in images. He has the illumination in advance as to what is going to be important.' Vidia asked to watch a football match, and Menchi made the arrangements: 'I bought the tickets. During the first half he just said, "Let's go." He was bored to death. I couldn't believe it.'[18] Vidia was soon jotting down notes and conversations, including several in Spanish, the language coming back to him from his days at QRC and Oxford: 'Un prejuicio racial integral contra todos [A built-in racial prejudice against everyone] . . . Dios es argentino [God is Argentinian] . . . The teenagers now who didn't know Perón think that Perón is a genius. They study peronismo more anxiously than Marx . . . The Clark Kent attitude.' Of a lunch, he wrote: 'All men, including elegant Argentines – very handsome, aristocratic. Peronist. The talk of curanderos [folk healers].' He noted a line from another guest at a dinner in Barrio Norte: 'Once this city was a great port. But now it's fucked up, baby. I want out. I am dying, I am dying, I am dying.'[19] The material slid easily into his article for the *New York Review*. In the final version, a witness describes guerrillas like the Montoneros: 'They're anti-American. But one of them held a high job in an American company. They have split personalities; some of them really don't know who they are. They see themselves as a kind of comic-book hero. Clark Kent in the office by day, Superman at night, with a gun.'[20]

As ever Vidia needed a pilot, and Norman Thomas di Giovanni fitted the part. Stocky, cocky and gabby, di Giovanni might have been a character from a Saul Bellow novel. Born a year after Vidia, he had been named for the American socialist leader Norman Thomas and raised in a disputatious immigrant suburb of Boston. He had edited an anthology of Latin American poetry, but retained something of the street hustler about him. After hearing a lecture by Borges, he had moved to Buenos Aires to collaborate with the 'living monument' in putting his work into English. Each day they would go to the National Library, where Borges was nominally the director, and di Giovanni would read sentences to the blind old man which they would translate together.[21] Norman di Giovanni had heard of Naipaul, and liked the idea of him. 'V.S. rang me right off the bat. He wasn't happy in his hotel. He never let on whether he spoke Spanish, but he wanted me to speak to the manager and arrange things for him, as if he couldn't do it himself.' Vidia opened out to Norman, giving the impression of friendship. 'At our first meetings I found him depressed and depressing, but I knew he was a literary genius and was happy to help him. We hit it off. I saw him each night for dinner and opened the door to Borges. Vidia has a way of flattering people by noticing a detail, like the texture of your shirt. I told him the score and made fun of the class system in Argentina. We used to laugh like hell. I arranged for him to stay at the house of a journalist who was away – for free, so he was very pleased.'[22]

As well as Borges, Vidia met the elderly doyenne of Argentine literature Victoria Ocampo, and was invited with Norman to her house in San Isidro, following in the steps of André Malraux, Rabindranath Tagore, Igor Stravinsky and Graham Greene. Borges told Vidia he had met Tagore at Victoria Ocampo's and found him 'a rather pompous old gentleman, very vain and rather pompous'.[23] Vidia was interested in Borges, and thought in retrospect he had failed to notice his grandeur. At the time, he noted, 'He asked where I came from. When he heard I was an Indian he said, "How do you pronounce sahib?" I said, "sahb."'[24] Later, Vidia wrote a piece for the New York Review on Borges: his global reputation 'as a blind and elderly Argentine, the writer of a very few, very short, and very mysterious stories, is so inflated and bogus that it obscures his greatness. It has possibly cost him the Nobel Prize; and it may well happen that when the bogus reputation declines, as it must, the good work may also disappear.'[25] Norman, with hindsight, found the article to have been remarkable. 'He really had Borges absolutely perfectly. The piece is more solid than I thought at the time.'

Vidia was frank with Norman about his own situation, telling him he was 'written out' after In a Free State: 'He said his marriage was in trouble, and that when he finished a book he would hang out with whores, and that he might have to leave England because of the racial tension there. He told me he and his wife had single beds, but sometimes she would come into his room at night. I knew by now he had an eye for the girls – and Buenos Aires was a feast for the eyes: well-groomed, slim, tanned healthy young women ... So I rang him one day and said, "Come to tea in my apartment at 5.00." '[26] There was only one other guest that day, 28 April 1972. Vidia was standing on the balcony of the tenth-floor apartment in the Rio Bamba looking at passers-by and hooting cars and the fringes of a street demonstration when a woman came into the room. His response was instantaneous:

> I wished to possess her as soon as I saw her. She was wearing a kind of furry pullover because it was the beginning of the Argentine winter and it was slightly dirty, the way these things can get dirty, and that was very affecting to me ... So she came in and I was completely dazzled. I loved her eyes. I loved her mouth. I loved everything about her and I have never stopped loving her, actually. What a panic it was for me to win her because I had no seducing talent at all. And somehow the need was so great that I did do it.[27]

By the end of the day Vidia had a new entry written in his notebook: a telephone number, and above it a name, 'Margaret Murray', and above the name the word 'Gooding'.[28]

CHAPTER EIGHTEEN

MARGARITA

To SOME SHE WAS MARGARITA, to others Margaret; some knew her as Murray, others by her husband's surname, Gooding, and a few thought she was called Smith. Norman had met her a few months earlier at a lunch given by her stepfather, Lawrence Smith, an Irish Catholic literary agent who ran a successful office in BA selling rights for plays and novels in South America. Margaret had three children, claimed to be twenty-nine years old but was thirty. Her English was husky and sexy, with elongated Spanish vowels. Norman found her 'vivacious, attractive, dressed like all members of that class in high style – behind the times by American standards, but very classy – with matching shoes and handbag etc.' At their first meeting, she had asked Norman whether he would like to translate Argentine writers, and he was flattered; he was excited too, but introduced her to his American wife, Heather, 'to put a wet blanket on it'. They became friends. He could see her marriage to Roy Gooding was stranded: 'Margaret had an oppressive Catholic boarding school upbringing, and she just wanted to fly.'[1]

Margaret came from a small but significant social group: the Anglo-Argentines, families of English, or often Scottish, Welsh or Irish descent, who liked to follow their own customs and marry within their own community. They took pride in their fair skin and supposedly British accents, and in some cases made a point of failing to learn Spanish properly. As informal members of the British empire, they had contributed to the Allied war effort in the Second World War and, like West Indians, spoke of the 'mother country' and joined the wartime RAF and Royal Canadian Air Force. In the 1970s, Anglo-Argentine men often had jobs in commerce or the professions, and held vigorous sports such as rugby, tennis, and polo in high esteem. Anglo-Argentine social activity in BA centred on the Hurlingham Club, named after the country club in west London but pronounced in the Spanish fashion: 'Ooor-ling-ham'.

Margaret was born in Buenos Aires on 15 February 1942.[2] Her father, Bruce Murray, was a Scottish architect who had been brought up in India; her mother, Nancy, was part English, part Hungarian and part Dutch, the daughter of a successful grain broker in Argentina. When Margaret was two years old, her father died from a heart attack and her mother moved to her parents' house in Belgrano, and in 1946 married Lawrence Smith, who treated Margaret and her younger sisters Rosemary and Diana as if they were his own children, although they retained their father's surname. Two more children were born, Lawrie and Susie. Aged only six, Margaret was despatched to a boarding school in the hills in Córdoba in central Argentina, 400 miles from BA. Apart from a week's break in July, this meant she only saw her family during the summer holidays – December, January and February, a dislocation that was considered normal in their culture. She was later sent with her sisters to a Catholic girls' boarding school in BA run by Irish nuns, where she was elected head girl and voted the most popular pupil in the school. It was a narrow, restricted education. She was impressed neither by the Roman Catholicism of the nuns and her stepfather, nor by the formal social strictures of the Anglo-Argentine community. Aged just nineteen, Margaret married Roy Gooding, an executive with Shell, and they soon had three children: Karin, Alexander and Cecilia. By the time she stood in the apartment in the Rio Bamba eleven years later, she had run through several lovers and was bored.

Vidia persuaded Margaret to see him: it was what he called 'a calamity'. They slept together, he had a quick orgasm and she called him a creep. He paced the streets of Buenos Aires, trying to concentrate on his article and wondering how to pursue the woman he now desired most in the world. Weeks went by. Norman was the intermediary: 'I had a call from Vidia. I had to persuade Margaret to see him again. I was the pimp. Margaret was not at all interested in Vidia. She was interested in bestselling writers. For a start, Vidia is very dark in colour, which is anathema in BA. I had to tell her he was a famous writer and something interesting might come out of it. She said, "He's so awful, all he wants to do is get me into bed." '[3] Norman's plan was to invite Margaret to join his wife and baby son Tom in Bariloche, a picturesque, snow-covered resort in the foothills of the Andes. Vidia would be there, waiting in the wings like a character in a Broadway farce. The conifer forests and alpine lakes might work their charm. Vidia remembered: 'He thought he should encourage Margaret's [step]father to allow her to go away and I would be there and try to seduce her. It was all really humiliating.'[4] Norman persuaded Lawrence Smith, a stern and respectable man who employed Margaret in his office, to agree to the trip. 'I had a pretty young wife, so he thought I was safe. Everyone knew we were going – but not that this dark-skinned man from Trinidad was coming too.' Margaret arrived on a later plane on 31 May, and came to the hotel. Vidia was, in Norman's words, 'scared shitless. He appeared out of the shadows. Margaret was a bit horrified, and insisted they had separate rooms. But I tell you, one of those rooms never needed to be dusted.'[5]

Through this time, Pat was staying with Ma in Nepaul Street, getting up each morning at six to attend the Malik inquiry and make notes for Vidia in case he decided to write about it. Her letters to Argentina were filled with advice, queries and devotion. Antonia's father, Lord Longford, was holding an inquiry into the baleful influence of pornography, and his assistant Marigold Johnson, wife of the former *New Statesman* editor Paul Johnson, wanted Vidia's views: 'She thought writers were underrepresented and suggested your comments would be "immensely valuable".' On the very day he met Margaret, Pat wrote: 'Look after yourself and dress sensibly but don't pile on the clothes indoors with central heating and try not to get too obsessed about your chest . . . Set aside a little time for relaxing every day – really switch off and do something light and frivolous . . . I hope Spanish America is exciting you – or feeding you somehow . . . I am trying to imagine what you are doing. But I can't. Argentina seems terribly far away. Must go to bed altho' the Carnival rumpus is beginning to build up. I suppose you would be impossible if you were here but I would not mind.'[6] Argentina was feeding Vidia in a way that Pat could not imagine.

When it was time to leave the snow slopes and warm bedrooms of Bariloche, he was in an ecstatic state; he even forgot his passport at the hotel and Norman, ever the fixer, had to take a taxi from the airport to race back and collect it. Vidia found the experience 'staggering. But there was lots of ineptitude. And thereafter I thought if that thing hadn't occurred in my life I probably would have shrivelled and died as a writer.'[7] Descending through the clouds to BA, his mood altered; according to Norman, Vidia had terrified visions of the husband Mr Gooding or the stepfather Mr Smith waiting at the municipal airport with a shotgun. 'The plane lands. The plane taxies. Vidia runs to the building and jumps over a fence. This little Indian guy is just running out of the airport. He bolted – he was terrified that someone from Margaret's family would be there.'[8] A day later, Vidia flew back to Trinidad. He knew at once that his life had changed. Oh my Spanish America, my new found land! 'I felt good for the first time. I believe that a sexual relationship between two people has to take time, for each to get used to one another, even the bodies have to get used to one another. Probably I am wrong but my experience is quite limited. And the thing is I never really believed that I could be the recipient of love . . . I don't know why, probably a deep diffidence . . . I was passionately looking for sensual fulfilment, but passionately, and when it came it was wonderful, and I will never run it down. All the later books in a way to some extent depend on her. They stopped being dry. *The Mimic Men* is an important book for the cultural emptiness in colonial people. But it is very dry. The books stopped being dry after Margaret, and it was a great liberation . . . Nothing was missing. The world was complete for me. I have often thought how strange it is that I lived for so long in England and I really had no English affair.'[9]

*

Early on 4 June, Pat went loyally to the airport at Piarco to greet her husband: 'Vidia returned from Buenos Aires this morning at 1.15 a.m. Ralph Roopchand peered through the doorway of the customs hall. "He looks well." And so he did. Tho' the face looked thinner and ferociously intellectual. Yet gay. The change – if he really is thinner – is from January when he started to grow the beard . . . And he looks youthful.'[10] They spent ten days in a guest house at Mount Saint Benedict, a monastery of celibate Benedictine monks on the north of the island, before moving to Savi and Mel's house at Valsayn Park. Vidia set to work correcting the proofs of *The Overcrowded Barracoon* and writing his article about Argentina. He did not tell Pat about Margaret, although she noted in her diary that he hoped 'the Spanish American interlude would act as a sort of release' and added that his 'American friend, di Giovanni, concurs in urging Vidia to start a new life.' Vidia did tell Savi about his attraction to Margaret, coming to her bedroom door early one morning while Pat was elsewhere. 'He knocked and said, "I must talk to you, something has happened, I must talk to you." I had to arrange for someone else to take my children to school. We had never spoken about anything evenly remotely related to sex. It is not the kind of conversation Vidia ever would have had, so I was absolutely shocked.' Savi listened sympathetically as her brother spoke about 'the complication of the husband, children'. She presumed the affair would soon blow over. 'Argentina was a long way off from England, and Vidia was always so tight complaining about never having enough money. So who was going to finance this big romance?'[11] A telegram arrived: 'ARE YOU STILL INTERESTED IN WRITING ABOUT MICHAEL X CASE QUERY MAGAZINE WILDLY ENTHUSIASTIC IF SO STOP LOVED YOUR EVITA PERON AND LONGING TO SEE YOU BOTH STOP WYNDHAM.'[12]

Vidia unburdened himself obliquely to Paul Theroux, writing with emotion to the only correspondent he could think of who would offer him unconditional support. He began with instructions: 'I would be most grateful to you if you could spare the time to look through the proof and let me know whether there are certain things that dismay you. A very dirty proof, though: full of errors . . . I met a girl in Argentina. One day she copied out two pages from The Return of the Native to give to me. In those pages the heroine reflects on the melancholy of her life and her situation. "The meanest kisses were at famine prices." How that chills: the shock of "famine" & "prices" after "kisses". And the heroine cries out, send me some great love, or I shall die . . . See how this jolly letter has turned out. Strange things happen when a writer sits down on an off day to write to a friend.'[13] When Paul's painstaking critical study of Vidia arrived in the post, it was Pat who thanked him for his 'insights and the love for Vidia combined'. She reflected on the writer's life: 'I remember thinking how marvellous Sonia [Tolstoy]'s diary was – the extracts read to me – and feeling I ought to be able to do something like that.' But 'such writing would be unsuitable in this age no, I don't mean that . . . I am trying to write this amongst family noise (Vidia is upstairs in the quiet room) – Top Cat on T.V. and a lovely thing called dahlpuri being made in the kitchen which I feel I ought to try and make myself some time.'[14]

In early July, Vidia flew to New Zealand and Pat went to Jamaica to see Kamla, Harry and their children. She wondered whether she should return to teaching or try to become a journalist. Before breaking off her diary for several months, she wrote: 'Under the influence of sleeping pills I make resolutions yet again: abstinence, determination.' In a later piece of autobiographical writing, she described her feelings at this time: 'In 1972 I was in Trinidad, at the time of the Michael X murders. There I had to cope not only with the Genius but with the Genius' family, kind and loving but every bit as determined as he was; they knew what they thought about everything. Sometimes, late in the discussion – too late – they would take pity on me. "What do you think," they would say. Of course I could not tell them . . . I was in any case beginning to play with the idea of myself as a sort of free-ranging, freelance journalist. I was unemployed at the time and playing with the idea of myself in a number of roles. I realised that if I was to write about anything knowledgeably it ought to be about Britain.'[15] She thought she would write about politics when she returned, in the manner of Bernard Levin, but was unsure how best to begin.

Despite the emotional turmoil he was going through, Vidia wrote an acute and careful article about Argentina. In his first draft, he opened with the image of the seventy-six-year-old Juan Domingo Perón in exile in Madrid. Then he altered the opening to make, unusually, a homage to another writer: 'Outline it like a story by Borges. The dictator is overthrown and more than half the people rejoice. The dictator had filled the jails and emptied the treasury. Like many dictators, he hadn't begun badly. He had wanted to make his country great. But he wasn't himself a great man; and perhaps the country couldn't be made great. Seventeen years pass. The country is still without great men; the treasury is still empty; and the people are on the verge of despair.' After six, turbulent weeks in Argentina, he summed up: he wrote of inflation, kidnappings and 'jack-booted soldiers in black leather jackets' – and deduced that 'Argentina is in a state of crisis that no Argentine can fully explain.' He set a global and historical context, seeing a colonial, artificial society obsessed with its European links which had imposed itself on stolen Amerindian land and was now being destroyed by killers who lacked a discernible programme. The Argentine press seemed 'incapable of detecting a pattern in the events it reports'.[16] It was to become a familiar Naipauline theme, and in this case his pessimism was prescient: within a year, Perón had returned to a cheering crowd of more than 2 million people.

Bob Silvers wrote to him delightedly, 'As I cabled, the piece is a marvel, really one of the best observations and reflections about this part of the world I've ever read. We hardly touched it. It is perfectly written.'[17] When it was published in the New York Review and the Sunday Times, angry letters arrived, one from the Royal Institute of International Affairs calling Naipaul a 'fairy tale writer', another from the University of Sussex saying Argentina had 'produced at least one great man in this century, Che Guevara, and probably a great woman, Eva Perón.'[18] Some BA journalists were angered by the article, and attacked it as the work of an outsider, though Menchi Sábat, a thoughtful man with a big, expressive face, felt it contained fundamental truths: 'His article was absolutely right. This is a hypocritical society. The trouble here is that Argentinians think "we are the best" and nobody wants to discuss what makes us the way we are. Naipaul thinks he has the power to judge a country, to make a signal to the country.'[19]

The most extreme form of literary criticism came from the leadership of the Montoneros guerrillas. Bob Cox, a brave editor, had paid $100 to run the article in the *Buenos Aires Herald* at a time when other newspapers were self-censoring and journalists were being murdered. The Montoneros – and many others in this socially conservative, Roman Catholic country – took particular exception to some lines written by the now sexually initiated Vidia Naipaul about Evita: 'Her commonness, her beauty, her success: they contribute to her sainthood. And her sexiness. "Todos me acosan sexualmente," she once said with irritation, in her actress days. "Everybody makes a pass at me." She was the macho's ideal victim-woman – don't those red lips still speak to the Argentine macho of her reputed skill in fellatio?'[20] Andrew Graham-Yooll, the paper's young news editor, was blamed for the article; it was decided he would be killed with a desk bomb at the *Herald* office near the Plaza de Mayo. The Montoneros had used this method before: opening a drawer would pull a wire which released the pin from a hand grenade taped inside the desk. A former Peronist MP, Diego Muñiz Barreto, arrived at the underground meeting after the order for the assassination had already been given and the killer had left the building. Luckily for the target, Muñiz Barreto said, 'You can't do that to Andrew. We trust him. Let's investigate further.' After a discussion, the order was countermanded and Andrew Graham-Yooll survived. He had met Vidia briefly during the trip, and found him uninterested in his own views about the country. 'He had bought a pair of expensive leather gloves. Naipaul said, "These are really *good gloves.* Argentines make *good gloves.*" I think he preferred being with important people like Borges.'[21]

*

On 13 June, Margaret wrote to Vidia saying she wanted to meet him in Morocco – a plan they had been discussing – and thought he might try to get the Moroccan government to invite him, suggesting the financial saving would appeal to his thrifty soul; she was also significantly overestimating his influence. Then she got down to more serious things: she was practically sure that she carried his child, and told him she would probably have no choice but to get rid of it. Margaret felt she ought to refuse to sign the letter, joking that she might be the famous one in ten years, while he would be forgotten.[22] This was big, potent news for Vidia: not only was he good at sex, but he was fertile, able to father a child. He wrote back wondering whether she should go ahead and have the baby, and also accusing her of blackmail, in a letter which Margaret told him she considered nasty, and in character.

He had previously been invited on a cultural and literary tour of New Zealand by UNESCO. It was the last thing he wanted to do, but he accepted in order to see Margaret again: to get to New Zealand, he would fly via Panama, Los Angeles and Tahiti, but return via Buenos Aires. He wrote to Menchi Sábat asking him to get in touch with Margaret and warn her he was coming back to Argentina. 'He used me as a pigeon,' said Sábat.[23] In New Zealand, Vidia was looked after by Michael Neill, a young lecturer in the English Department at the University of Auckland. Neill had spent his early life in Britain and Ireland, and remembered Naipaul as an interesting but complicated guest: 'He said the British Council had entrapped him into travelling to this benighted place, and that it was taking weeks out of his life.' Neill felt some sympathy for Vidia: 'He had to address an audience of weekend women writers in Nelson. I took him to a restaurant and he ordered scallops, not crumbed. They came crumbed. He was very annoyed. He told me then that he had once hurled a glass paperweight at a person in a travel agent in Trinidad. I think at that point a chanteur in the restaurant struck up "Do you know the way to San José?" for the second time.'[24] Beneath a large photograph of V.S. Naipaul looking troubled in a roll-neck sweater, the Wellington *Dominion* reported: 'Mr Naipaul has been speaking at universities and teachers' colleges and meeting with local authors and literary societies.'[25]

As soon as he arrived in New Zealand, Vidia had begun to feel remorseful, and wrote to Pat with the guilt of the adulterer on 11 July: 'I think that our homelessness has damaged you more than me, and is perhaps responsible for a good deal of the strains we have both been experiencing. You in your way give such great love — for which I am and have always been so grateful, and feel so undeserving — you have concentrated more on my distress . . . A woman needs a house, a fortress of her own, which she creates & governs; I wonder now that we never thought of that. I think that we must . . . find some kind of house which will be yours and, because it will be yours, will also be mine.' It was a loving letter: they

would, like Mr Biswas, make a new start in their own house. He knew Pat
had been under stress, and that she often caught coughs and colds. 'One
of the other things I wanted to say,' he wrote, truthfully, 'was that much
of the strength I now have has been given me by you; and I recognise it
as the most horrible kind of exchange, because I can see that it has depleted
you. What a melancholy thing. I do want you to eat well & rest and sleep
and recover your health; you must understand that it will be better for
both of us if you become well again.'[26] Many years later, he ackowleged
that his relationship with Margaret effectively undid Pat's life: 'I was
liberated. She was destroyed. It was inevitable.'[27]

He did not deliver on his fine intentions and sentiments about the need
for a fortress; he wanted to resurrect his marriage to Pat, just as he wanted
to be with Margaret, and hoped she might have his child. Might he manage
all of it, somehow, if Margaret had the baby and he and Pat brought it up
as their own? For the first time in his life, he went to a jeweller and bought
a ring – for Margaret. One night he was invited to dinner by Michael Neill
and his Chinese Malaysian girlfriend Pek Koon Heng, a politics student.
Neill shared a house with two colleagues from the university, a big wooden
building that had once been the Tongan royal family's residence. A dozen
people came to dinner, with V.S. Naipaul as guest of honour. 'We were
younger than him,' said Neill, 'and he vented the most provocative views
on all kinds of things. Various people took offence. I remember feeling
more and more tense during the meal and saw a drop of sweat fall into my
soup.' Pek Koon Heng found him to be 'pretty mellow, very curious,
meticulously turned out, discussing Borges. I remember he was extraordinarily struck by the lettering on signposts in New Zealand.'[28]

Later in the evening, in what Neill took to be an 'emotionally generous'
gesture, Vidia turned to the table for guidance. 'He exposed his own
vulnerability. He said, "I have this problem which I would like you to
advise me on. I have a woman in Argentina who I would like to have my
child. I thought I could take the child back to England and perhaps my
wife and I can raise it. Do you think I could do it? Do you think it would
be a good idea?"'[29] Lulled by the comfort of strangers, Vidia had asked a
question he would never have raised in a more familiar setting. The guests
were astonished. Within days, though, the question of the child became
theoretical when news from Margaret reached him. She did not know
whether he would be pleased or not, but she had gone ahead and dealt
with the problem on her own. The experience had been harrowing, and
expensive, but she regarded it as a consequence of the curse of being a

woman. She was glad to have received a photograph from Vidia showing
him with Pat, who she thought looked remarkably serene given the attitude
and personality of her husband.[30] Vidia sent her a cheque to pay for the
abortion, and a copy of his article on Argentina, 'The Corpse at the Iron
Gate'. Many of Margaret's own sentiments about her country were
contained in the article, which she told him was beautifully written.

Looking back on these events, Vidia linked the idea of the unborn
child, which he imagined to be a boy, with his own creativity in the years
that followed: 'Margaret was going to have a child. I was quite happy for
it to be aborted. Wicked people have said it was someone else's, but I
think it was mine. I still play with the idea though that the child, born in
1973, would have been a man of nearly thirty now. I would have had to
give up so much. These were very creative years for me: *Guerrillas*, the
Congo, *India: A Wounded Civilization*, *A Bend in the River* ... My
friendship with Margaret released all of that ... It was part of my father's
irresponsibility to have all these children. It was a decision to end the line
with me, with myself: let it end with me.'[31] Margaret's abortion was linked
in his mind to primogeniture, and with an idea of himself as the summation
of the male line of the Naipauls. In December 1973, Shiva and Jenny had
their first and only child, a son: Tarun Shivaprasad. In May of the same
year, Pat paid a quiet visit to a Harley Street fertility specialist, Mr J.M.
Brudenell. On the back of a doctor's letter, she noted, 'Laproscopy £95
... slit pencil light tube ... see ovaries & tubes ... Also tests menstruation.'[32] Pat did not proceed; long gone were the days when she dreamed
of having their little baby, Humphrey Naipaul.

*

Margaret was Vidia's ideal woman, a woman of a kind who had existed
previously only in his fantasy life: he could string her along and mistreat
her, with her abject consent. Margaret was unlike Pat in almost all respects:
tempestuous, cynical and sexy. Their relationship, battered and disturbed,
would endure for almost a quarter of a century; a kink in his personality
met a kink in hers, and snagged. The affair was to be intense, and intensely
sexual, and sexually aggressive, to their mutual pleasure. When a man is
violent towards a woman, particularly out of sexual jealousy, she either
leaves him or becomes possessed by him; Margaret did the latter. She
would love Vidia and hate Vidia, abase herself and worship him, degrade
herself and degrade him. She was in thrall and addicted to him, sexually
and emotionally. She liked to be his slave and his victim, and he was

snared by her; although he appeared to be in control of how things unfolded, he was mentally hooked. Margaret gave him the power, much of which was generated out of a new self-belief and physical confidence, to push ahead with his literary ambitions. Many of the gruesome sexual depictions in his subsequent novels were not the work of the imagination, but drawn from his life with Margaret. Like F. Scott Fitzgerald with Sam Goldwyn, she always knew where she stood with Vidia: nowhere. Years later, when asked how their relationship began he liked to say, to irritate her, 'It was not a meeting of minds.'

Norman di Giovanni was encouraging, playing the role of *homme de confiance*. Travelling to England in June 1972 he wrote, 'Margaret loves you madly & you must return to see her . . . I've helped make the break with her lover. Your letters and my insistence did it. I'm afraid it will cost you a loan of $350, however.'[33] Later, Norman and his wife, Heather, came to Wiltshire for the day by train and taxi. He remembered: 'I told Vidia I was writing a novel. He had no interest in that. Pat gave us trout and almonds, and we went for a walk to look at Salisbury Plain. She was colourless, mousy.' The contrast between the wife and the lover was apparent. 'Vidia found Margaret alluring as an Argentine woman of her class. Pat didn't have any of that. I saw, in time, that he didn't like the way his passion for Margaret took him over.' In a letter to Savi, Pat described the di Giovannis' lunch, and the stroppiness that preceded it. She and Vidia had returned from Trinidad after a stopover in Luxembourg:

> We flew back to London to the tune of 'I hate Europeans', 'Bloody sub-Kraut Krauts' (Luxemburgers) until he was rendered speechless by a really nauseating snack . . . I raced into Salisbury and shopped on Friday, started preparing before breakfast on Saturday and had lunch ready in time . . . When they were 5 minutes late your brother decided they were not coming and demanded his lunch. I watched him eat it stunned. He had almost finished when they arrived. I leaped up, welcoming, repairing the damage done to the food by extracting one helping and catching things (including squashable items) thrown down by their one-year-old baby. We then went for a two hour tramp up and down the downs, taking it in turns to carry little Tommy who, they said, weighed two stone.[34]

In London, Vidia introduced Norman to Diana Athill, Francis Wyndham at the *Sunday Times* and the critic Derwent May at the *Listener*.

At Wilsford, drawing from life, Vidia made notes for a novel that would eventually turn into *Guerrillas*. Glimpses of a story had been shown to him, but he could not see how to bring it together. 'The white panther becomes involved with the black panther. Moral blackmail. The farm. The commune . . . Someone like Carlin who carries his private hurt. Where does he come from? I can't make it South Africa . . . What is wrong with this woman? Why is she so dissatisfied? . . . I see my Asiatic being involved with this woman. I see their tortured relationship. The triviality, the spoilt woman. I blow hot and cold . . . The Asiatic's tormented vision of this woman's degradation & her husband . . . Why is the airport about to close? Why is the currency crashing?' He put the idea aside, and made notes for another novel, *The Mystery of Arrival*. Vidia was to start and restart this book many times, stripping out elements from it for his later work. The initial draft began: 'In his last year at Oxford Anil's thoughts turned to getting a job; and it grieved him that he should have sunk so low.' He wrote more worried notes later, troubled about his literary future. 'The process of writing is a mysterious business – how do the ideas come and how does one execute them? And today I am desperate, feeling myself full of talent and will, but also feeling that I may have already said, in twelve books, all that I have to say.'[35]

In September, Vidia confirmed that the Morocco trip was happening. Margaret booked herself a flight and arranged a double room at a hotel costing $25 a night. She teased him that since he was not Aristotle Onassis, she would pay half the cost. Her mother had given her some money to have a holiday. She also promised that her mood would be much better than it had been in Buenos Aires, where she had been obliged to put up with tiresome social conventions and the people at the Nogaró hotel. She sent him a photograph of herself, and promised to arrive in Casablanca shortly after lunch on 10 October. Before leaving, Vidia wrote grandly to Paul Theroux: 'I passed back through Argentina; spent ten days in Trinidad; and now have been here, back at the manor, for the last four days, slowly thawing out.' He raged briefly against Africa; Idi Amin was expelling Asians from Uganda: 'It is an obscene continent, fit only for second-rate people. Second-rate whites with second-rate ambitions, who are prepared, as in South Africa, to indulge in the obscenity of disciplining Africans . . . you either stay away from the continent, or you go there and discipline the savages.'[36] A few days later, after looking through *V.S. Naipaul: An Introduction to his Work*, he complimented Paul on a 'marvellously responsive and humane' study, and hoped it would bring reward for his 'great sensitivity, labour and love'.[37] His follower responded keenly, 'If you saw love in that little book, believe me it was there – you weren't mistaken.'[38]

Vidia flew to meet Margaret in Casablanca. They spent two nights there, and another two in Marrakech at the Hotel Mamounia, where their bill listed little but 'étage' (room service), suggesting they were too busy to leave the room.[39] After Bariloche, Morocco was a further revelation for Vidia. Might he spend the rest of his days and nights with Margaret? On return to England, he felt his life slipping and sliding beneath him; everything might now be changing. He wrote Paul Theroux a request, scripted in an uncharacteristic, angled hand, full of insertions – the last letter he would write to him for nearly nine years: 'Here is something I would like you to do for me, assuming that it is in your power to do so. I need a lot of money very badly (or at least it seems to me that I need a lot of money). The only asset I have is my manuscripts >(drafts etc.)< & my other papers (correspondence etc). A pretty complete documentation of my writing life from 18 to 40.' He had told the British Museum that 'the minimum price I would like – for all that I have, >which is all that exists< – is £40,000 ... I would therefore like you to pass the word around that I am thinking of disposing of all my papers; perhaps someone >in the US< may be interested.'[40] Paul Theroux diligently sounded out contacts at universities and institutions, but did not get far: V.S. Naipaul was not yet a big enough name in America.

Margaret arrived in London, and Vidia found reasons not to be in Wilsford. To save money, he borrowed John Powell's flat as a place for them to go, but when he asked another friend for a similar favour, it was refused. They ended up in hotels with names like the Ivanhoe, Vidia haemorrhaging money he did not have. Norman di Giovanni had moved to a house in Wheatley in Oxfordshire, and Vidia and Margaret went to stay with him at the end of October. Norman remembered: 'They would disappear for days on end into the bedroom. He was fucking crazy about her, and crazy about fucking her. He couldn't wait to get his trousers off. She said living with him would be impossible: she would be watching television in the other room, and he would want her to turn it off because it was disturbing him.' Norman remained friendly with Margaret but Vidia soon turned against him, resenting his garrulous generosity and his role in bringing them together. When

Vidia denounced Norman, Margaret defended him, reminding her lover of the masterful bit of salesmanship that had made their relationship possible; without Norman, he might have remained the grim, ghastly man she had first met. A little later, after a bad argument, Norman telephoned Vidia on Margaret's behalf to press her case. 'He was furious. He thought I was badgering him. I didn't see Vidia after that until the 1980s.'[41] Despite the rupture, Norman was in April 1974 one of the first people to nominate Vidia for the Nobel Prize, in response to an enquiry from American PEN.[42]

Margaret spent some of November in London, going out one evening with a man who was staying at the Dorchester. Vidia invited Diana Athill to meet her at a restaurant in Soho, but otherwise kept her hidden from his friends, embarrassed by the relationship. Diana was immediately conscious of the contrast with Pat. 'I liked her. I thought she was a nice woman. I remember she had a kind of Latin American look, and was so professionally feminine and sexy in a charming way, and he was loving that. It was obviously absolutely fascinating for him. She seemed very cheerful, that she had got him just where she wanted him.' When Vidia next saw Diana, he told her he was thinking of ending his marriage. 'I was horrified. I said, "Vidia, you can't." He made a wonderful remark, "I am having carnal pleasure for the first time in my life, are you saying I must give it up?"' Diana suggested he should have an affair. Now it was Vidia's turn to appear horrified. Looking back, Diana Athill thought, 'It would have been better for Pat if he had [left her] because she was stronger then, and would have probably made more of her life. But I thought it would kill her. Everybody felt that she was completely dependent on him.'[43] Vidia also told Marisa Masters he was thinking of leaving Pat. Standing in front of the window in the huge kitchen at Elsham Road, she berated him in her rolling Italian accent: 'I say: "How dare you? Now you are famous and people are around you? You have a wife who has been working for years to make you write your books. It's disgusting. She has taken care of you." He is silent. He say: "I was a virgin when I married Pat." I tell him I understand a writer needs to get a bit of knowledge. I say, "*Go with the woman*, but don't leave Pat."'[44]

*

Margaret returned to Argentina in early December, and thought of him constantly, in all the finest ways and also the most degenerate. She had visited her brother in Madrid, and he had not let her mope. Back in BA, her mother realized something was wrong, so she told her about Vidia and had a sympathetic response. Margaret posted him four photographs, including one with her children and her husband Roy from 1969, and another of her upper body, wearing only a bra. Ten days later she informed him that she carried his child once again, and expressed worry that he might think it was someone else's. She made plans for a termination. Margaret was full of blind rage now against her lover, although she blamed herself, not Vidia, for the pregnancy. Her friend Silvina had pointed out that Vidia had never made a single sacrifice for her, and doubted he ever would. Margaret replied simply that she was helpless, because she loved him. She knew what she wanted, but understood that her position was hopelessly precarious. 'I want you to come and live with me, think about that,' Vidia had told her over the telephone while she was in Madrid. And now, penning her thoughts on the writing paper of the Lawrence Smith Literary Agency in Avenida de los Incas, she wondered whether he meant it. Living with him would be such a massive shift, but she could not seem to live without him.

Did Vidia mean it? He meant it and he did not mean it. Indecisive, frightened, excited by the situation he had got himself into while unable emotionally to cope with it, worried about money and Pat and his literary future, he sent Margaret some books and took refuge in the putative journey to Stockholm. As his father had once said, he was impulsive and unpredictable. He followed his compulsion to write, but rarely wrote to Margaret. His failure to be with her arose in part from the intellectual gulf between them. Looking back, he said, 'I believe if she had any literary judgement or feeling for my work, I think I would have gone away with her. It was as simple as that. But it wasn't there. In a strange way, I got to like that too – that we had another kind of relationship ... I could take the passionate side of life, which I was very nervous of before.'[45] Margaret gave him sensual fulfilment, Pat the cerebral equivalent. Like Graham Greene and Catherine Walston, they would meet in unlikely locations around the world for sex and excitement while the travelling writer went about his business.

Over the following weeks Margaret wrote page after page of letter after letter, some eight or ten sides long. She wrote lying on the grass in Palermo Park watching the children feed the ducks, and lying by the pool at the Hurlingham Club, soaking up the sun and using one of Paul Theroux's books as a prop on which to rest her paper. She had decided to go to an analyst, against his advice. He asked her to write and telephone, but never wrote himself, which she complained about continually. She said he should not think she would be willing to hop over to England every few months to satisfy his carnal desires, although she rued the fact that only he seemed to be capable of satisfying hers. Vidia should dismiss his fear that she might turn up one day out of the blue in Wiltshire, baggage in tow. She laid down the law: she would not always be the one who wrote letters, and did all the talking on the telephone. Margaret's letters to him were long and frequent, her shaky grammar and random use of apostrophes causing Vidia more amusement than distress. Sometimes she was erotic and teasing. She complained he had never taken her to Mirabelles or to the Savoy, and said that recently she had been out for an ice-cream, moulded to a point on the cone in the Argentinian way, and observed what a lovely phallic symbol it made, adding that she had deliberately chosen chocolate in order to be reminded of him. She sent a Ravi Shankar concert programme for her lover, and teased him that he was black and ugly. She ridiculed his happy boast that Miriam Gross and Antonia Fraser had told him women found him attractive. Perhaps Vidia had misheard, or alternatively his friends might be blind? Nobody could possibly be under the impression that he was the most attractive man in London. Margaret was reading *The Sensuous Woman* by 'J', and suggested he might produce a companion volume about the sensuous man, instead of writing all that stuff about displaced persons.

It was unsubtle writing, but it aroused Vidia. Margaret was pressing the most obvious buttons of sex and aggression. She tried to make him jealous by telling him of a trip to a nightclub called Mau Mau, where she had worn a sexy top with a bare midriff and no bra. Had Vidia been present, she taunted him, he might have been tempted to rape her. She typed out a Sanskrit poem for him, and a line of Robert Graves: 'Love is the disease most worth having, for its opposite is the doleful serenity of death in life.' She praised Vidia, saying that being together was like living on champagne, and that she knew she would receive an awful lot of punishment when they were back together, and might release what she termed his horrible streak of sadism. She berated him for not writing a word about her abortion, apart from saying that she had got pregnant to blackmail him. It was a form of behaviour that did not seem to fit his character, although on second thoughts Margaret wondered whether he might in fact do just about anything to save himself from taking responsibility or decisions. He seemed to think he could steamroller anybody and sacrifice anyone in the name of his work. But at the same time, she declared that she was still doing exercises to make sure she looked smashing when they next saw each other. Even by January 1973, she had not heard a word from him about the abortion. Not one word – and now she was sick that he refused to mention it. He should go to hell: she hoped that he would not become a black eminence hovering in the background for the rest of her life. Vidia admitted later that his conduct at the time had been 'rough and crude . . . I took no interest.'[46]

Every few weeks they had short, snatched telephone conversations, cut short if Pat or Roy or Margaret's children appeared. In the early 1970s, international calls were expensive rarities and a telephone was a single, fixed, bulky contraption kept in one place such as a hall or a sitting room, attached to the wall by a wire; it was not easy to have a private conversation. She wanted US$450 for an air ticket so she could come and see him in April. Finally Vidia sent her a letter at the end of January. She responded that she was interested to hear about his weekend staying with Anthony and Violet Powell. Were all his friends oldies? She felt he was already an old man in spirit, and that as far as she could tell, when he was not writing he was busy having dinner with grand people and rich lords and ladies. She told him he was a hypocrite. The Curtis Brown representative in BA had informed her that Vidia's work stood little chance of being published in Argentina. His books had already been sent to the major publishing houses, but they had decided there was no market for them. Well, he would just have to win the Nobel. Why did neither of them have any money? She said Vidia could not even afford to buy her, much though she would love to be bought by him.

Margaret flirted and flattered him, believing his tenuous, half-hearted promises. The one thing that pleased her greatly was the fact that he had told her they were now going to live together. She got delirious just thinking about it. She wanted him, but he should learn to be more trusting of her. Why, he had asked over the telephone whether she was up to her old tricks again, to which her answer was a resounding no and a declaration that she hated him. Trying to start a college of one, he sent her books: Marlowe's translations of Ovid, Restoration comedies, *Sir Gawain and the Green Knight*. She thanked him, and said she had never loved another man in the way she loved him, and never would again. A few days later, sending a photo of herself looking sexy lying on a lawn, she told him she could hardly wait for April, when they would begin living together. She reminded him that it was her birthday on the fifteenth, and she would be thirty years old. (In fact, it was her thirty-first birthday; not an easy slip to make.) Margaret was still angry over his silence on the termination and the question of who would pay for her ticket to England. Still, she hoped that some day she might become what she termed his beloved wife and super whore. Vidia had been invited to lunch at Buckingham Palace. He was instructed by Margaret to have fun with the Queen and remember to speak only when spoken to. She believed that despite his pretence that money, titles and luxury were of no interest to him, he was bound to enjoy himself; secretly, it might be what he liked most. She would expect to hear full details of his lunch with the Queen and her boorish husband.

Vidia sat between Sir Martin Charteris and Alistair Cooke, who was to the Queen's right, eating a vegetarian preparation while the others had Selle d'Agneau Sarladaise followed by Rocher de Glace Dalmation.[47] Pat wrote to Ma afterwards: 'It is a great honour and as you would expect he responded to the occasion honestly and sweetly. He was overwhelmed at the moment when the Queen entered the room . . . He liked the Queen, found her sensitive and intelligent, thinks she has suffered in her life. She is 47.'[48] Ma wrote back, 'Congrats to Vido . . . Your father only brother Persad Chadra [Ramparsad] died on the 7th June and was cremated on the 11th June Whit Monday, the Guardian had a little writing Vidia's Uncle for Cremation.'[49]

As for Margaret, she still did not know what was happening. It occurred to her that although they had been apart for over four months, Vidia had only bothered to send her two letters. She understood his enthralment at the idea of the Queen and Stockholm – everything paled before what she described as the deity on the one hand and the glory on the other. If Vidia wanted to end their affair, why not say so? At least he could write her a letter. But he did not. She told him she had been out with a man, and a telephone call came at once in response, Vidia's voice full of jealousy. It reminded her of the times when she had flirted mildly with other men, although the difference was that Vidia was not able to hit her over the telephone. She had to distract herself: after all, she was not the one seeking to write Nobel prize-winning novels. No other man could give her the sensations he gave her. She said she had done things to Vido that would have made her sick with anybody else, and yet she still longed for the time when she could do them again. It was agreed: they would meet in Trinidad in April, where Vidia was going to write about the Michael X case.

CHAPTER NINETEEN

ENGLAND AND ARGENTINA

THROUGH THIS YEAR of emotional turmoil, Vidia had remained focused on two things: himself and his writing. He produced careful articles on Argentina for the *New York Review*, made preparations for an autobiography and tried to start two novels. Publication of *The Overcrowded Barracoon* led to publicity and interviews. Vidia linked up with Yves Leclerc, his old friend from Earls Court days, who was working for the French service of the BBC, and they had an interesting dialogue about political causes. In the summer he made a fleeting visit to Scandinavia. At the Academy Bookshop in Helsinki, a woman told him they had met previously – in Paris. She was Dorrit Hinze, last encountered in a shapeless dress outside Notre-Dame cathedral in 1951. They talked. She remembered the box of chocolates he had bought her, and how she had lived on it for days. Dorrit was now married to a successful surgeon. Vidia was aroused by the meeting, and thought later he would have liked to have had an affair with her. Passing through Denmark for a television interview, he apologized to Ralph Ironman for not calling: 'No time for anything ... I am not built to cope with it. I feel myself becoming an actor and very bogus. It is better to say what you think, but if you do a lot of these interviews the secret, they tell me, is to say the <u>same</u> thing over and over. Which is a kind of degradation of the word and the self.'[1]

The trip to Helsinki was followed by a writers' symposium in Sweden, attended by the likes of Wole Soyinka, Philip Roth, Gabriel García Márquez, Michael Frayn and Heinrich Böll. Neither Vidia nor Michael Frayn had ever taken a sauna before, but seeing a notice that one was available for men from 6–8 each evening, they thought they would try their luck. 'We went through a room with benches at the side,' Frayn remembered, 'and found an exercise room beyond it. So we turned round and went back to the first room, stripped off and sat on the benches, waiting for them to switch on the heat. After a few minutes we agreed that it seemed to be getting hotter. "It's quite hot

now. It's really very hot." Then Kurt Vonnegut came in and asked
why we were sitting in there with no clothes on. I said this was the
sauna. He laughed until he couldn't breathe, and pointed to a small
door in the corner. The sauna.' Frayn noted Vidia's reluctance to
make his own bed. 'He is a Brahmin, so he wouldn't do any physical
work. We were asked to make our own beds, just to pull back the
duvet, but Vidia refused. "I can't do that." He paid the housekeeper's
son each day to do it for him. Vidia was a very grand figure even
then, an immensely commanding figure, though charming.' At a dinner
in London, Frayn introduced him to his colleague John Silverlight, an
Observer journalist: 'He was a true liberal, and Vidia cottoned on and
became more and more outrageous, saying immigrants should be
deported, people should be hanged for stealing bicycles, that kind of
thing. John Silverlight was jumping up and down, having another glass
of whisky, trying to calm himself. Pat was there saying, "Oh Vidia,
you don't really mean it." They all went home happily.'[2]

Far from proving a distraction, the emotional and intermittent
physical presence of Margaret in Vidia's life focused his work. Arriving
in Trinidad, he concentrated on his research and hid her away in the
Queens Park Hotel in Port of Spain. 'She had to just sit in the hotel
and wait till I got back from seeing Skerritt's mother and all these other
people, all these strange people,' he said later.[3] The sadistic element of
their relationship was kindled by the heat of the island and the macabre
material Vidia was collecting. Margaret praised twelve magical and
unbelievable days together, and ordered him to cherish the wounds on
his arms as marks of great passion.[4] He introduced her to Savi and
Mel, but they felt awkward because of their loyalty to Pat. Savi found
her brother a changed man. 'Oh my goodness, then there was a spring
in his step ... freer, more open, happier. Pat and Vidia were never
affectionate, never ever. With Margaret, there was open affection.'[5]
Afterwards, Savi wrote to Pat, 'He has worked at a furious pace and
seemed to have revelled in working and travelling at the most difficult
and energy sapping hours in the early afternoons.'[6]

Pat, still unaware of her husband's relationship with Margaret, stayed
at home in Wilsford affectionately rereading *A House for Mr Biswas*.
'You've written some big books, man,' she wrote to him. 'Biswas had
the impact of a classic on me. And I was struck by that little passage
(Proustian) at the end of Biswas about memories >(the children's)< of
the period before the house giving back the past.'[7] Vidia responded to

her no less warmly, giving news of the investigation, knowing how interested she was in the Malik case. 'Absolute, fantastic luck. I went to see Choko and the first thing he did was to offer me two boxes of M[alik]'s papers, rescued by him the night of the fire. It is possible to plot M's career from this, because he kept everything, even dry-goods bills, even solicitors' threatening letters. Lots of autobiographical writings; crazy schemes by his English associates for a "university of the alternative" under his "government" & so on ... Also, I fear, among Hakim's papers are 3 letters from Diana Athill which are like business-love letters which give me a creepy feeling that D had found herself another negro lover. I would like to think otherwise, but here we have Diana offering H[akim] the fare to get to California from her savings. I wish I hadn't found these letters; it gives me a terrible sensation, to intrude into the private correspondence of someone I know.'[8] When he returned to Wilsford, Vidia made a note to himself: 'My life, physically – I mean as far as my surroundings are concerned – is ideal. It is the writer's dream. But it is, without the work, a kind of death.'[9]

The long report on Michael Abdul Malik was to be one of Vidia's most remarkable and disturbing pieces of non-fiction, written at full throttle. It united many of his personal fears and obsessions. Joan Didion thought it was 'for Naipaul one of those dense situations in which a writer finds his every concern refracted'.[10] The new editor of the *Sunday Times Magazine*, Magnus Linklater, later described the article as 'the finest that we ran during my tenure'.[11] In the late 1960s, Michael X had been the best-known Trinidadian in Britain, an underground anti-hero who was taken up by the mainstream press and made a spokesman for black people, despite being a manifest crook. His fame was based not on achievement but on deception: he was the black to Naipaul's white, the negative to his positive: his doppelgänger. Yet interestingly, Vidia's greatest venom would be reserved not for Malik – whom he treated with a collusive sympathy, seeing him as a 'dummy Judas' playing an assigned role, having understood that in England 'race was, to Right and Left, a topic of entertainment' – but for the British patrons who let him flourish, 'the revolutionaries who visit centres of revolution with return air tickets, the hippies, the people who wish themselves on societies more fragile than their own, all those people who in the end do no more than celebrate their own security.' When Malik was finally convicted and hanged in the Royal Gaol in Port of Spain, his overseas promoters maintained that he was innocent ('a plea of insanity would have made nonsense of a whole school of theatre') despite the strong evidence against him. The countercultural ambassador John Michell even produced a *Souvenir Programme for the Official Lynching of Michael Abdul Malik*, describing him as a 'gentle mystic' and 'architect of the Holy City'. Beneath a drawing of a white woman trying to have sex with the hanging corpse of a black man, the American feminist Kate Millett was quoted: 'It's the hideous combination of racism and sexism that permits these kinds of trials to happen.'[12]

Vidia began his article with a line pregnant with anticipation, fear, and some humour: 'A corner file is a three-sided file, triangular in section, and it is used in Trinidad for sharpening cutlasses.' He placed Malik within a West Indian context, and used his private papers, including an attempt at a novel, to expose him: 'An autobiography can distort; facts can be realigned. But fiction never lies: it reveals the writer totally. And Malik's primitive novel is like a pattern book, a guide to later events.' In a postscript to the article, published when the legal process and appeals were complete, Vidia closes not with one of the stars but with a local petty criminal who got caught up in the action, Stanley Abbott: 'His was the true agony: he rotted for nearly six years in a death cell, and was hanged only in April 1979. He never became known outside Trinidad, this small muscular man with the straight back, the soldierly demeanour, the very pale skin, and the underslept tormented eyes. He was not the X; he became nobody's cause; and by the time he was hanged that caravan had gone by.' The most chilling aspect of Vidia's text is the way he takes no explicit moral position on Gale Benson's murder. The phrasing he uses to describe the moment of her killing is peculiarly unnerving: 'She was held by the neck and stabbed and stabbed. At that moment all the lunacy and play fell from her; she knew who she was then, and wanted to live ... It was an especially deep wound at the base of the neck that stilled her; and then she was buried in her African-style clothes. She was not yet completely dead: dirt from her burial hole would work its way into her intestines.'[13]

In July, after reading the piece, Diana wrote with news of one of the suspected killers, Kidogo. 'He has been living with [Hakim] Jamal in Boston, and is now somewhere in Mass[achusetts] living <u>under the protection of the district attorney</u>, with the other witnesses to Jamal's murder.' Diana explained in detail to Vidia why she thought he had misunderstood the sort of person Gale Benson was, pointing out that she had seen Jamal as her 'possessor' rather than as a racial guide.

'She'd have gone for anyone sexy who offered her a cult, even if he'd been as white as milk (cf Charles Manson and his girls).' Diana also observed that far from wearing expensive clothes, as Vidia had reported, Benson was the possessor of a blue cotton dress, some home-made 'dashikis' and a scrounged sweater. In short, Benson smelt dirty, ate almost nothing and was mentally unwell. Diana concluded that Vidia had used her inaccurately in order to make a point about middle-class white girls: 'you are cutting your cloth to fit your pattern, and that's unlike you.'[14] Full of a new sexual aggression, a disdain for everything he believed the murdered Gale Benson represented and disapproval of Diana's involvement in the events he had been describing, Vidia ignored her representations. Understanding an aspect of his character that no one else had seen before, Margaret told Vidia that she could feel her own presence in the article.

*

Back in Argentina with her husband, still full of sex and passion, Margaret called out for her lover. She told Vidia that she had been talking in her sleep, asking in English if he would buy her a Coca-Cola. She and Roy had again discussed separation, and she had made it clear that the only way she could remain married was if he agreed to turn a blind eye to Vidia. Roy was not willing to be complaisant, at least as far as V.S. Naipaul was concerned. She wondered whether she should leave, and asked for guidance, telling Vidia that her future was in his hands. It had taken him forty years to find love, desire, passion and intimacy, and yet she felt he would throw it all away if he thought it might disturb his life. Within weeks she was angry after a telephone call, seeing the relationship for what it was and realizing Vidia was offering her nothing. She summarized what he had said on the telephone, pointing out that great literary minds do not make mistakes when they talk. He wanted her to be his mistress, six thousand miles away, behave like a nun and sometimes come to England – or wherever in the world he happened to be travelling – for eight or ten days at a time to be the object of what she called his cruel sexual desires. She discussed the situation with a friend, who told her she must be mad to even contemplate such an arrangement. She did not have the courage to admit that Vidia even expected her to pay for it.

Margaret was addicted to Vidia: she loved him, was caught by him, amused by him and liked to be dominated by him. The cruelty was part of the attraction, which had the effect of stepping up the cruelty. She had received no letters from him because he said that writing to her would take up what he deemed to be Malik's time. Was there no part of his day that belonged to Margaret? She sent him what she called a whorish photo to keep him going. As for that Kate Millett woman, she had no time for her: she was a women's lib leader with a cause – probably her own; women like that always had causes. Contemplating what to do, while doing nothing, Vidia told Margaret over the telephone that her letters were irritating him, and that he was worried what would happen to Pat if he left her. What was Margaret to do? She responded crossly that he probably expected her to be lying on her tummy receiving just punishment for ruffling the feathers of his lordship the high priest. Later, Vidia wrote what she thought was a beautiful letter, which made her sick with longing. He was worried about Shiva, and sad she had aborted his child. His assertion that they must be together for a good long time delighted her. She sent him a photograph of herself wearing flower-power trousers, riding a bicycle on a friend's lawn. In reply, Vidia told her he hoped they would be together soon, related his lung trouble and called her his 'dear and lovely girl'. Margaret asked whether she might join one of those high-flying British vice squads so popular with the English aristocracy. She had a feeling that he knew Lord Lambton. Did he? Before their next meeting she promised to let her armpit hair grow thick and bushy in the way he liked, although while she was in BA she really could not be expected to go around looking like what she laughingly called an Italian cook cum whore. By June, his silence was making her feel hate and rage. There were temptations. What woman would care about selling herself to a rich man, if she did not give him her soul? She said the only difference between now and the past was that Vidia had found a woman more willing to accept the hurting and the violence. The arrangement gave him what he wanted: Mama at home, a whore in South America.

Though she was full of complaint, Margaret made her submission clear. She felt like putty in his hands; she had decided he was a horrible black man with hideous powers over her. For Vidia, the combination of lust and control could hardly be more potent. Margaret could tap in to his deepest anxieties, and say things to him that no one else was permitted to say, prodding and stimulating his secret fears and insecurities. By July, he had finished the Malik article, and was telling her to be calm. She replied that he sounded like Perón telling Argentina to keep calm. There was only one reason for being told to keep calm, and that was because there was a good reason for not being.

The Lion House

Anguilla, 1968

India, 1962

Left Pat and Khushwant Singh in Mehrauli

Above Pat and Vidia take tea by the pool at the
Ashoka Hotel, New Delhi

Right Vidia in Kashmir

Far right V.S. Naipaul quits India

Eleanor Hale

Diana Athill

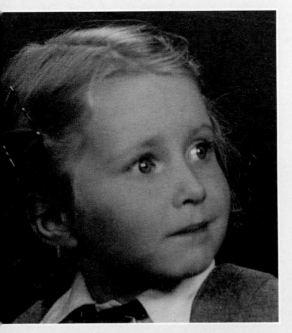

Vinod Mehta

Moni Malhoutra at Wilsford

Pat, Antonia Fraser and Vidia photographed by Hugh Fraser at Wilsford, October 1971

Vidia photographs Antonia, Hugh and Pat on the same afternoon

Margaret

Vidia and Margaret

'He was only playing bad; he was half-respectable, working a little family plot up in the hills, and suffering with other farmers from low nutmeg prices . . .' from 'Heavy Manners in Grenada', 1983

Polaroid of Vidia and Paul Theroux, 1986

Tony Powell at Wilsford, 1971

Gillon Aitken and Andrew Wylie

Selby Wooding

Francis Wyndham, 1990

Banning Eyre

Margaret in Indonesia, 1995

Vido and a proud Ma after the award of the Trinity Cross

Pat at Dairy Cottage

Vidia and Shiva at Queen's Royal College

Vidia photographed by Margaret

V.S. Naipaul in Oklahoma

Vidia and Nadira on the day of their engagement

Why was he still stuck in that infernal bungalow in Wiltshire? She went sailing with friends, and sunbathing, and in August looked for a flat to live in, feeling calm and strong, she told dearest Vido. It would cost £100 to £130 a month. She felt good about his plan for a book on Malik, and sure that it would sell very well. After all, it had a popular theme: murder. She thought it would be more appealing to the uneducated than his book about Indians in cupboards – a reference to Santosh in *In a Free State*. They planned a trip to Caracas together, where they would stay with Sir Lees Mayall, an impeccably connected Wiltshire landowner who Vidia had met at Tony Powell's house, and who was now serving as Her Britannic Majesty's Ambassador to Venezuela.

In September, Margaret left her husband and children. Vidia recanted at that precise moment: he would have nothing further to do with her. As he said later, 'What was extraordinary about our relationship was that I gave her very little, almost nothing. People give the people they are attracted to – they load them with gifts, don't they? Well of course I couldn't do that.'[15] Her letters sat unopened on his desk. He did not read the letter in which she said he was a nasty horrid black man but that she still wanted to show him her parents' crumbling estate before it was sold to the Peronistas, or that she had bought nice candy-striped lingerie and was glad he loved her letters. He did not read the letter in which she said he was vain to call his penis a god, but that she hoped to make a pilgrimage to the shrine. Then Vidia changed his mind and contacted her. They would meet in Montevideo, in Uruguay. Delighted, Margarita promised to kiss him on the weak spot she had discovered in Trinidad. Would he bring a copy of *The Honorary Consul* by her pet author Graham Greene – a novel set in the same morally compromised South American territory that Vidia was considering writing about? Or perhaps Greene was her second pet author, she conceded.

In Uruguay, Margaret felt disturbed and upset as she wondered what to do with her life. Was she right to leave Roy? Did Vidia want her? What did she want? The subsequent article, 'A Country Dying on Its Feet', reprinted as 'Kamikaze in Montevideo', was highly pessimistic: inflation was out of control, the bureaucracy had failed and Uruguay was suffering a vicious war between the government and the Tupamaros, a popular guerrilla group that had earlier kidnapped the British ambassador. Menchi Sábat, who was born in Montevideo, was quoted in the text: 'They were parricides, engaged in a kind of kamikaze.' Vidia's conclusion was escapist: 'Those who can, get out.' His equal dislike for revolutionaries and state torturers was clear; the most emotional line in the piece refers to the prelapsarian past: 'A monument in the Prado park commemorates Uruguay's last four Charrua Indians, who were sent as exhibits to the Musée de l'Homme in Paris, where they died.'[16] When Menchi read the piece, he wrote, 'The article is simply superb. When I'm in front of an orange, I would like to have the ability to say, "This is an orange." And you have that ability ... Excuse my non shakespearean English.'[17] Professor E. Bradford Burns of the University of California was less wholehearted: 'I am discouraged to find the New York Review printing such uninformative and misleading essays.'[18]

As Vidia and Margaret's relationship continued and she confided in her friends, rumours spread in social circles in Buenos Aires that the affair was more than tempestuous, and that the glamour of being V.S. Naipaul's mistress came at a very high price. Andrew Graham-Yooll thought Margaret 'liked the idea of getting laid by the well-known novelist. There were stories that he was violent towards her. The view of her friends was, "Poor Margaret, she fell in love with V.S. Naipaul and now he beats her." '[19]

*

In October 1973, Vidia returned from Uruguay and had the inspiration for a novel. 'I came back and made a bonfire at Wilsford Manor,' he said later, 'and as the leaves blazed I wrote down the structure of Guerrillas, the whole thing, and stuck to it. I remember raking the leaves and burning them.'[20] He told Pat about his other life with Margaret – and, characteristically, recalled the disclosure of infidelity in terms of his own suffering: 'I was full of grief. I went back to the bungalow and I told Pat, as I might have told my own mother. I was lying down in my little bed in my own little room and she wondered what was wrong with me and I told her. A very strange relationship I had with Pat. She was so good: she tried to comfort me ... I was so full of grief myself that in a way I expected her to respond to my grief, and she did.'[21]

Once the truth was out, he shared his anxieties with her as if she were a confidante rather than his wife, and she tolerated his conduct. Savi regarded Vidia's claim that Pat accepted the situation as 'absolute rubbish, such profound vanity'. Pat escaped to a tiny flat they had recently bought in Queen's Gate Terrace in Kensington, aided by an Arts Council grant of £1,000. On holiday in London around this time, Savi and Mel found themselves turned out of the flat because Pat needed somewhere to go.

'We were the first people to actually sleep in that property. It wasn't even furnished. Pat left us on the doorstep. I think she'd left Vidia, I'm not sure. Vidia said to me Pat doesn't want you to stay there.'[22] Savi felt that once Pat realized she would not have children, and that Vidia was set to be permanently unfaithful, her confidence in herself as a woman disappeared. 'I think from then on she was crushed, and there was a distinct change in her attitude to everybody. She withdrew, as if into a shell. Every time we said to Pat, let's do something, she couldn't do it. Always her excuse was that she had no clothes. She would say, "I have no clothes, I would not be able to go." '[23]

Distraught about the way in which her life was unravelling, Pat restarted her diary. At the same time, emulating Brecht, who had begun a journal at the age of forty, Vidia himself began to make occasional notes: 'I have at last distilled (or decided on) my characters – Jane, Roche, Jimmy. All people over the hill as it were, in an island like Trinidad-Jamaica. All fantasts, to some extent; but Jane, who is trivial, is to be killed. She needs men who appear to be active but are in fact toys. What delays me . . . is my inability to plot the two events that must lead to the murder. The two crises which the narrative needs. I have always been bad at plotting. It's a miracle I have written so much. I asked Pat for help. She said she couldn't write my books for me. I said I couldn't write them either. A joke. Work will absorb my sexual torment; but the torment rises higher with my non-writing. I toy with the idea of <u>running away</u>, becoming again the boy of 1954–55, starting afresh, going to Spain say; and contracting to do a review a month for the Observer or something like that.'[24]

At the end of November, Pat wrote: 'Tonight, by the fire, Vidia told me he was very excited about his two books but did not know about the other half of his life. That he was now two people. He showed me the photographs that she had sent. One of her alone, on a beach . . . one with Vidia ("Look how sad I'm looking, much sadder than she is" – I can't say I had noticed. Neither looked particularly sad).'[25] It seems not to have occurred to Pat to leave him, or to ask Vidia to leave. 'And me?' she wrote. 'Some feeling of sexual excitement but not as much as when Vidia was away. I think of talking – momentarily – to Antonia or to Sheila [Rogers] and dismiss it. Think of being silent. For the rest of my life?' Silence, or complicity, was to be her response. It enabled Vidia to break her confidence, while at the same time incorporating her into the process of literary creation. He relied on her guidance and support, even while he harried her; he said he could not imagine working without her. So Pat stayed, cooking and washing for him, nominally still writing her own article about Michael X and the killings in Trinidad, fetching the coal from the outhouse, overhearing his telephone calls from Argentina, observing the gardener Mr Elford working in the garden, reading books and watching the television. (Trevor McDonald, educated at Naparima College in San Fernando, had recently became ITN's first black reporter.)

Vidia's unconscious hope may have been that if he were sufficiently horrible to Pat, she might disappear. Alone in her room at the cottage, she dutifully recorded his insults: 'On Saturday night Vidia told me to put the Malik thing aside. "It's not your talent" . . . He has not enjoyed making love to me since 1967 . . . "You know you are the only woman I know who has no skill. Vanessa paints, Tristram's wife paints, Antonia, Marigold Johnson" . . . To Lindsay and Marisa for dinner . . . He said this evening before Sheila arrived that we were two people who had destroyed one another.' Even when she was alone, Pat felt she had failed her husband. After going up to London to watch a play with Antonia, Francis and Julian Jebb, she concluded that while she was there she had 'lived up to Vidia's dictum: "You don't behave like a writer's wife. You behave like the wife of a clerk who has risen above her station."' Witnessing Vidia's work became a substitute for living. Now that Pat urgently needed the support of friends, it became ever more difficult to confide in them.

Worried by the situation, Marisa Masters took it upon herself to intervene. In early December, she wrote to Pat that Vidia had telephoned her. 'His words were direct, he interrupted my nonsense and said: "Marisa listen, I have got to tell you something that will please you; I have told Margaret that all is finished." Vidia of course knew I was pleased. He added that he liked his life as it was and that he had confessed everything to you: That was beautiful.'[26] Marisa spoke of her own earlier marital problems, and told Pat that she was lucky to now know the truth. The reply was written in a weak hand: 'The love & the regard you have shown me in writing as you did has given me strength & comfort . . . I have not quite found my bearings.'[27] Although she did not say so, Pat knew that the affair was far from finished. Writing to Antonia Fraser during this period, the same shift in tone was evident. Her letters became apologetic and cursory, and her handwriting poorly formed: 'I know you are very busy . . . I would love to see you. Come and lunch, or something . . . We did not talk much. My fault.'[28] Although Antonia tried to maintain the friendship, she had to accept that Pat had become an extremely reserved person. Her own life was increasingly complicated at this time, even as she

achieved professional success. The magazine *Private Eye* renamed her
'Lady Magnesia Freelove' and published a cartoon after the manner of
H.M. Bateman showing a group of surprised men above the caption, 'The
man who admitted he hadn't been to bed with Lady Antonia Fraser.' She
lived stylishly; an attempt at seduction by the ill-favoured Australian
humorist Clive James was said to have been rejected with the line, 'I only
sleep with the First Eleven.'[29]

Pat's state of mind was worsened by the fact she was now dosing
herself regularly with Mandrax, an addictive sleeping tablet also known as
Quaalude which was a popular recreational drug in the 1960s, and was
widely prescribed as a sedative before being banned for its unpredictable
side effects, which include euphoria, emotional disturbance, sexual arousal
and depression. A doctor in north London, Dr Toszeghi, would prescribe
her 100 pills at a time, together with 100 doses of Valium. 'Use them
sparingly,' he advised.[30] Pat became intimately involved with the creation
of the new novel during the long, cold winter of 1973–74, while OPEC
sent oil prices soaring and Britain lurched towards economic disaster and a
three-day working week. Each night she would record the book's progress
and the way in which its powerful, destructive force was wrapping itself
around the two of them:

> He has been typing the story out ('Guerrillas') . . . Emma and
> Teresa 'essentially bogus'. I connect that out of them he has created
> a tragic figure . . . I say that [Jane] has become rather imaginative,
> too imaginative for an *Express* reader. 'I know. I can't write about
> stupid people. They all have to have something of myself in them'
> . . . He says he has always written like that, Mr Stone was him . . .
> She will have affair with [Jimmy] Ahmed out of self-disgust. Nihilist,
> not out to hurt the man. But he is appalled and sets out (subcon-
> sciously?) to destroy both of them . . . Do I think Emma will
> recognise herself. I say she probably won't read it. But Teresa will
> . . . Vidia says as if the story exists, read it already. He wants to get
> the people acting on an empty Robinson Crusoe stage.

As the night closed in, she wrote:

> The longest day, wet and dark . . . A telephone call from Argentina
> . . . I say I am conscious of [Jane] being the victim – he says she is
> becoming the victim >Roche is depriving her of will, ability to take
> decisions< without knowing it. The sexual excitement is still there
> but situated in the cunt not overmastering, my mind is free . . . I

have never experienced anything like this before. Listening and learning. His face dark and exhausted . . . He talks about how he has arrived at his understanding of this type of woman. Sexually I am very excited . . . He got the vision of her appearance from a French, or American, girl waiting on the breezy runway of Easter Island (Chile), her trousers tremulous in the wind.

On Christmas Eve 1973, caught like a fly in Vidia's web, Pat wrote: 'Vidia takes the opportunity to say that we have had good times together . . . and maybe I should live alone . . . And then he read the *Nibelungenlied*. I said "Don't bother" and he said "Don't be silly, Pat." The killing of Siegfried. I felt I was Siegfried with the cross on my clothing, vestment. And now I am trying to get the strength of mind to put his pillows in his room.'

At other moments, he would explain his literary techniques to her, such as his use of the reveal, when he shows a character physically before confirming his identity.

Going over how to get Jane out of the hut . . . into the sunlight, the silence behind her, the bare concrete . . . His people move: first figure, then face, the expression on the face. He first did this in *An Area of Darkness* in describing the pilgrims (going towards the cave) . . . Only a very few critics will appreciate everything that goes into such writing . . . He has to do very difficult, complicated things very simply. That is what writing, 'style', experimental writing is: to write in a thoroughly modern way.

So in the opening chapter Jimmy appears first as a frightening but absurd figure in a conversation between Jane and Roche, next as a name painted on a board outside Thrushcross Grange People's Commune: 'JAMES AHMED (Haji)', then as the answer to a question, ' "Mr Ahmed bathing" ', until finally Jane and the reader see Jimmy for the first time as 'a man in the doorway at the far end of the hut. The man was at first in silhouette against the white light outside. When he came into the hut he could be seen to be naked from the waist up, with a towel over one shoulder.'[31]

*

When Margaret got home from Uruguay in early November, Roy prevented her from seeing their children while at the same time trying to persuade her to return. She made plans to publish a local edition of *Mr*

Stone. Vidia had to ask Penguin to agree. She loved being with him, lying beside him and listening to him talk. He should ask the bookseller who was valuing his work what he would pay for love letters. She had read *Mr Stone*: the temptation to find out about Vidia's marriage was too great to resist. He was having trouble writing and she tried to encourage him. She said she liked living alone, and sent him some photographs to brighten his day and take his mind off the nasty British economy, including one of herself pregnant, ten days off having a baby. Would they ever have a baby together, she wondered? She had seen a picture of Paul Theroux in *Time*, and was not surprised to hear he was successful with women.

Margaret wanted to know whether Vidia had told Pat about their affair: he would be defrauding all three of them if he continued with things as they were. He mentioned practical details to her, but she did not know what he meant in practice – was he seriously asking whether she would work to support his two houses and his harem? The answer was that she had worked for most of her married life, and he should stop distrusting her. Why – when he telephoned, his first question was usually to ask who she was in bed with. Now Margaret felt sad living alone in Buenos Aires, and had allowed herself to be taken out to dinner. She had a temporary job as a secretary in a telephone company, GTE International, which Vidia disliked, but as she informed him, she was unable to live off the air. She felt that he was treating her badly, and she would always be denied a leading role in his life. She said she had no doubt that he would come back to her to be serviced, and then would expect to be sent back looking lovely to his good and understanding wife and all his constant friends. She complained that his letters to her were always conditional, with lines like 'we will and we should have' rather than a straight commitment.

In December she wrote that she had been getting things in order, and making preparations to change her life. It was such a big step she was taking: the greatest burden had been telling her children and her family that she was leaving, and she was glad that part was over, although it had been amazing how well they had taken it. Roy was pressing her hard to go back, but she believed that to do so would be like stepping into a coffin alive. She was slowly developing a tan, and had become the laughing stock of the swimming pool with all the black hair under her arms. Since Vidia was so keen on statistics, she told him what she had recorded: they had made love thirty-one times in twenty days, although on three of those days they had made no love at all – only hate. Surely the answer was to have a child? Vidia's family might think he was a eunuch, but she knew very well he was not. Maybe she should have had the child when she got pregnant? She adored the pin-up poses she had been given showing him in his underpants, but thought he was disgustingly vain. She asked him for the third time to send her the Malik article. She even clicked out a message of love to Vido on adhesive plastic tape and stuck it schoolgirlishly to the letter.

Christmas and New Year were impossible, spent in discussions with lawyers, with Margaret's parents refusing to talk to her. It was so depressing to be arguing over who would have the children, but she had been given an ultimatum that she either had to go back or give them up. Roy said he would even ignore her having affairs – as long as she did not have one with V.S. Naipaul. The writer was in a torment of indecision, obsessively working on *Guerrillas* to keep his mind off making a choice. In a telephone conversation just before Christmas, he left Margaret fairly assured that they would soon live together, but then a month went by without any confirmation. He spoke of the shattered futures he and Pat now faced, which provoked Margaret to anger. In her view, his marital relationship had always been shattered, and he had not changed a damn thing in his life. If anyone had given him a new lease of life with his writing, she had. He would certainly have shrivelled up otherwise. She was beginning to think that he regarded her as just a woman to be slept with and enjoyed. She was now in a soul-destroying job at the Division Industrial of the Singer Sewing Machine Company. Roy wanted her back. Life was lonely, eating solo while he had the companionship of a wife with whom he could eat and sleep at his leisure, a situation that made Margaret see red. All of this would be worth it, though, all this sacrifice would be worth it if in the end they could be together. But for the moment she was left with absolutely nothing. She had lost her children and she hardly spoke to her parents. She wanted an end to the uncertainty, to all the ifs and the buts and the living in the past and hoping for the future. She had not had a letter from him for over a month, and even the porter at her apartment block realized there was a problem as she was always asking for the post. He had said to her, 'Vamo a tener que retailo a ere morochito (darkie!)'. 'I am going to have to scold this swarthy little fellow.' And then the porter asked whether Vidia was coming back. Margaret was humiliated, having to answer sheepishly that she did not know.

Finally Vidia telephoned at the end of January to say that since people were rebuking him, their relationship was over. 'Feel yourself free,' he said graciously. Margaret was irate. A relationship of such importance could not be finished in this way, she wrote. What had become of all his talk about integrity, and of his promise that she would only be his? What else was there left to believe in now? She posted the letter unsigned, crying bitter tears, and wrote again from a friend's country house, a ten-side letter on GTE International writing paper, pleading, raging that her eyes were red rimmed from crying. Her recollection of their telephone call at the end of December was that he had said they would shortly be living together, and she would always have him. She could not live without him. His telephone call had left her like a lunatic with grief. She loved only him. Could it be because of her father's childhood in India? And she knew that only she could give Vidia the joy he sorely needed: he had been like a shrivelled-up prune when they first met. She was left with empty assurances. He could have promised her Versailles, for all it meant. She dreamed about their sexual games together, and said she would never agree to abandon the feeding of the lollipop, or the country of the Baganda, or visiting the very special place of love. She would not abandon the magic genie or playing doctors.

What was Margaret going to do? Everything in her life was directed at eventually living with him. She did not specify whether this meant in England, in Argentina or elsewhere. Now she felt as if she had been thrown off a cliff and was floating in space. Her friends had warned her, warned her and warned her. So perhaps Menchi had been right, Silvina had been right and her stepfather had been right. It made her flesh crawl just to think of it. She had been betrayed. Now Vidia responded by flinging every smart excuse at her, even, absurdly, the plight of another Margaret, his mother-in-law Marg Hale, as an excuse not to act. What was Vidia saying? She understood about his book, his uncertainty, his problems over money, his wife, his wife's mother, the situation in England. She understood all of that. But what she did not understand were the broken promises. Was her love in vain? She swore at him, in Spanish. After their conversation in December, she had been to her lawyer to make the separation from Roy final. Although she supposed that it did not now make much difference, she said she certainly had the guts to see it through. She described a dream from the previous night of a visit to Vidia's cottage in Wiltshire. Thomas Hardy was sitting in the garden, and Margaret had asked him about the meaning of sorrow, but he did not answer. Vidia took her for a walk and they kissed and kissed and he licked her face and licked away all her salty tears. Finally, a response came. Vidia recanted partially, and said the relationship might continue.

Margaret went to the resort of Necochea, and sent him a postcard of skyscrapers and women in swimsuits, reverting to talk of desire and their Lawrentian religion of sex. She said she had seen lots of Negroes on the beach, but none looked as nice as Vido. She hoped that the god was shrunken and unexercised. Next she went to stay on a friend's estate with her children. She had a low view of the local Argentines, who stood outside bars with moronic looks, the women with curlers in their hair and the men wearing pyjama bottoms and string vests. The telephone operator in the nearby village had a mad son who was prone to peep at her through the door, and sometimes he would come into the phone booth and mutter obscenities under his breath. For the first time in her correspondence with Vidia, nearly two years into their relationship, she mentioned one of her children by name. They had all been asking her whether she felt sad, and she replied that she was. Her daughter Karin thought she knew why: it was because of 'Naipaul'. If her mother loved him and he made her happy, what was the problem? Margaret said she had been to the local nightclub with some polo players: Vidia knew that she loved dancing and fooling around, and that usually she would come to life whenever she heard blaring music. But that evening she had felt like a lifeless thing and had wanted nothing except to have his arms around her and his head on her shoulder and his hard body leaning in against hers.

Margaret was soon employed by Massey-Ferguson, manufacturer of tractors, working for a lunatic who was prone to kick his desk. She told Vidia that all she wanted was to be fucked and fucked and fucked and fucked. She was exercising religiously and had bought herself some new clothes. She admitted to him that she would try to distract herself every now and again with a classy fella — though none was as classy as him. A letter came from Vido. She would give considerable thought to his suggestion that she should have his love child. Might they even have a little girl? She wanted to pour champagne on the god and get drunk on love. She had sent him a shirt and a Frank Sinatra record via her sister; he did not bother to thank her. His latest plan, as he sat in Wiltshire tormenting himself with *Guerrillas*, was that they might meet in Argentina at the start of May and go to Córdoba on a sleeper train. Margaret passed on some gossip that had reached South America: Vidia's friend Antonia was rumoured to be having an affair with the actor Robert Stephens, who was married to Maggie Smith. Nobody but Vidia had made her feel the freedom of the world and the pleasures of the flesh, but nobody had made her suffer so much. As he had told her, pain was part of the passion. On writing paper engraved with a bull's head above the legend 'SHORTHORN DE DRABBLE', Margaret told him once more how much she adored him, illustrating the point with a 1:1 scale drawing of his erect penis, done in dark-brown felt-tip; the penis wore sunglasses and a lime-green cowboy hat.

*

In the new year of 1974, Mr and Mrs Naipaul took the train from Salisbury to London to attend one of Sonia Orwell's carefully crafted dinners. 'Vidia did not want to come out of his solitude and his obsession. We spent a long time on Salisbury station – the 10.53 only runs on Saturdays and the 11.24 was cancelled,' Pat wrote in her diary. 'Vidia grew hysterical in the buffet waiting-room.' Francis and Miriam Gross were there, as was the painter Francis Bacon. Vidia's new beard caused comment; he told the party 'that it makes women take notice of him, they react in the shops in Salisbury.' Afterwards, Vidia and Pat hurried home. The next night found them watching *Othello* on television, with Laurence Olivier in the title role. 'He thinks the play is written out of experience and suffering,' Pat wrote, and recorded this exchange:

> 'An old man's passion.'
> 'A distinguished man,' I say.
> 'All distinguished men have their Iagos.'

She worked up the courage to ask whether he was still involved with Margaret. 'He told me that he was still in love with her. "It's my life. I'm sorry, Pat."' They planned to go to Holland for Easter with Teresa and Peter, but Vidia pulled out at the last minute and they went to see the Powells for the day instead, driven there by Tristram. 'After lunch Virginia went to paint and Tristram took the children down to the lake. I joined Violet in the kitchen . . . I spoke about Vidia's work and she immediately about Tony's. She always counters like this.' Back home, they discussed John Powell's recent breakdown. 'Vidia spoke about his [own] illness at Oxford . . . how you hate the man who tells you the truth about yourself, you never want to see him again; how he did not have enough shillings for the gas when he planned suicide.' Kamla's thirteen-year-old son Ved came to stay with them for a couple of weeks, 'a sweet boy', which gave Pat some respite from the intensity of the creation of *Guerrillas*. She walked with Ved to Stonehenge. 'Larks were rising and we saw a hare.'

As the months passed, the telephone calls from Argentina kept coming. 'Am quaking. Try to return to the Malik. Thinking of my revoltingness and folly. Think it would be nice to win the respect of Savi, Vidia. And others whom I have repelled. Nearly midnight. Seized by self-disgust and anger. And today Sati's letter came saying how badly Vidia must feel because he was unable to pay Nella's fees.' Their relationship went on, its fractures being incorporated into Vidia's writing. 'Yesterday afternoon the sex went bad and Vidia lost his temper . . . On Saturday afternoon I read the next, short section, where Jane returns to Port of Spain in the car and am a little bemused to find that Vidia has utilised recent events and words between us so that this whole experience is becoming intricately interwoven.' Vidia was working at a constant, nearly mad pitch of intensity, writing the book with a fine red biro in a miniature hand, sometimes cramming two lines to each line of a narrow-ruled notebook, sometimes squeezing up to thirty words to a single line: the word 'cigarette', for example, is less than a centimetre long and less than a millimetre high.[32] The more dramatic or frightening the story, the more cramped his handwriting became.

Pat recorded her husband's thoughts and assertions, and her own hallucinatory responses to them.

> While I was in London he had a dream. This small woman (slightly malformed?) was fixing this medical apparatus to his arm . . . Then she attacked him, bit his genitals . . . He is the book and lives the book . . . As he sat in the yellow chair last night and spoke of Roche – his smugness and cruelty, his mouth, he became Roche . . . He thinks the book is sympathetic to Negroes . . . 'There will be no Indians in this book.' This afternoon he will cut out the reference to Indian prayer flags near the airport . . . He has told me that nothing unfinished is to be published . . . 'If I die, edit with Diana' . . . He values my judgement, my approval as high as that of Francis . . . 'Somerset Maugham was very wise when he said that the powers of invention grow as you become older, young men don't have the powers contrary to belief' . . . He feels that this novel will unleash a great period of productivity . . . Calm now. Have taken one Mandrax . . . I suppose it is the greatest book of the century.

In the thousands of pages of Pat's diary, Margaret is never mentioned by name. She is rendered as 'this woman', 'his friend', 'her', 'the person'. The closest Pat comes is in the sentence: 'I could write her name.' Vidia continued to confide in his wife, and their own sexual relationship revived. In February she wrote, 'Vidia told me he was "grieving for that girl" ... Says he has no one to talk to about it so must talk to me. So we talk till one in the morning.' Later, he 'emerged to say he was too sleepy and to ask me to come and make love. I put the Japanese kimono on.' He told her that couples sometimes took pornographic photographs of each other, her naivety making him seem worldly: 'I would not know about this if I did not have Vidia to tell me about it ... Call it vicarious experience? But without him I sometimes feel there would be no experience, no knowledge.' He said he wanted to write about sex in the book, but was nervous. He talked around the subject before beginning the scene of Jane's anal rape: 'Vidia still did not describe the sex act. It would horrify us but it does not horrify her and it will not horrify others.' Weeks went by, and he continued to circle. 'He is about to write the sex between them which he still will not talk about.' Finally he wrote it and 'read it to me. It was terrifying and I began to feel slightly faint and asked for us to leave the small stuffy room. "But not offensive. I've tried to avoid offensive words." Not erotic. Anti-erotic.' Days later, Pat wrote that Vidia was returning to Margaret: 'Had made up his mind to go to this girl ... We spoke late into the evening. We made love more experimentally, more lovingly. Dusk fell. We were cold in the room.' She wrote an initialism in her diary, 'H h n d t w h,' which may stand for, 'He has never done this with her.'

Pat felt powerless to act. She compared herself in her diary to Jimmy's assistant Bryant, his catamite and executioner, and years later wrote that she was 'ashamed that anyone should know – of course they know – ashamed that I saw something of myself in Bryant. But it is no good just trying to hide it – the only hope is not to be it, not to be servile.' Sometimes, she felt more terrified than ashamed; after all, *Guerrillas* is a story of violence and betrayal that ends with Roche packing his suitcase and telling Jimmy over the telephone that Jane is in her room packing, although he knows that Jimmy has murdered her. His final words are: ' "Jane and I are leaving tomorrow ... Are you hearing me? Jimmy?" ' and Jimmy Ahmed replies with a single word, the last word in the book: ' "Massa." '[33] Pat wrote: 'This picking up of life as he is living it in the novel is now at a very serious level – not small things as earlier. Leaving, things packed, a drawer pulled out is serious for me.'

One day, Pat was inspecting a rathole in a wall of the cottage. 'Vidia comes out of his room and I say, "No one asked you to come out of your hole, Mr Rat." "How extraordinary you should say that. I was just about to write that. Bryant. Rat is the Trinidad word for prostitute.' And there, in tiny handwriting, using the red biro, Vidia wrote the death scene: killing Jane, killing Gale, killing Margaret, killing Pat, Diana, Emma and Teresa, killing what he hated and loved and embraced and rejected:

> He ran back into the lean-to, and when he turned to face them he had a cutlass in his hand and he was in tears.
>
> He cried, 'Jimmy! Jimmy!'
>
> Jimmy locked his right arm about Jane's neck and almost lifted her in front of him, pulling back the corners of his mouth with the effort, and slightly puffing out his shaved cheeks, so that he seemed to smile.
>
> He said, '*Bryant, the rat! Kill the rat!*'
>
> Bryant, running, faltered.
>
> '*Your rat, Bryant! Your rat!*'
>
> Her right hand was on the arm swelling around her neck, and it was on her right arm that Bryant made the first cut.
>
> The first cut: the rest would follow.[34]

These were, Pat wrote solemnly in her diary, 'Good words. Given to him "by God" a month ago. He will not change them. When he reaches the words "Bryant, the rat! Kill the rat!" he shouts . . . He is aware of the symbolism. Afraid that the girl he is killing is "my friend". (I had thought of this. Men are terrible.)'

CHAPTER TWENTY

THE MARRIAGE OF
MANDRAX AND VALIUM

VIDIA FINISHED THE FIRST DRAFT of *Guerrillas* in May 1974 and promptly took off for Argentina. Pat was humiliated. 'All of London knows he is going back to her . . . He rages that he won't be made to feel guilty . . . I began to plead and protest in a rather sickening way.'[1] Vidia and Margaret spent two months together, staying in Buenos Aires and travelling to Córdoba to stay in a house in the hills. Using a Rolleiflex camera, Menchi Sábat photographed him against a street kiosk scrawled with the graffito: EVITA VIVE. Menchi had got to know Vidia, and concluded, 'He was terribly competitive. I found in general when he measured himself it was against British people, or white people like Harold Pinter. He has an aura. When you are with Vidia, you are convinced you are in front of a very important person. But I don't think he's come to a solution about his own origin. He wanted to be born white.'[2]

Soon after Vidia returned to England, Juan Perón died and was replaced by his wife Isabel, or Isabelita, which provoked further unrest. The king was dead, Margaret told Vidia: she had watched the funeral procession, and had observed people filing past the coffin, some of them hysterical, some kissing Perón's face or wiping their handkerchiefs across the forehead of his rotting corpse. She thought that although the experience was macabre, the Argentines had loved it.[3] Vidia's first letter to Margaret when he got home was warm and hopeful: 'Here I am, on a Monday morning, thinking about you. When really, as I told you on the telephone on Saturday, I should be worrying about the damned Conrad lecture, which the Sunday Times want for August.' He was glad she might soon be coming to London. 'So we'll either leave England together and go away and write the book somewhere; or will decide the other, sad thing. But for the last time: no more hesitations. I cannot tell you how <u>new</u> the weeks with you were for me. A little

lifetime they seem to me now: you must understand that I have not
been used to that kind of intimacy; that I have never known such a
period of passion. I wish I had been freer in my mind.' He told
Margaret she must be patient while he made arrangements for their
future together. 'There are so many practical things that have to be
settled before one can make a move. The lease for the cottage; the
furnishing of the London flat; the matter of contracts for the autobiography. And, of course, the key thing: the revision of the book, for
which I need calm and no emotional upheavals.'[4]

Vidia was thinking hard about Joseph Conrad, to whom critics often
compared him, for a conference at the University of Kent at Canterbury.
As he said in the opening line: 'It has taken me a long time to come
round to Conrad.'[5] When he was picked up by an academic for a minor
factual discrepancy, he was distraught: 'The error is unforgivable.'[6]
Margaret considered Conrad a dull subject, telling Vidia he should
lecture on passion instead of on fuddy duddies. Meanwhile in Wilsford,
Pat noted in her diary: 'His manner towards me is cool with a hint of
patronage. He is very cheerful.' Vidia spent the summer correcting the
manuscript of *Guerrillas*, reading Balzac's *Eugenie Grandet* and going
shooting near the cottage with his air rifle. By September, the book was
complete. 'I feel slightly stunned. It's a novel of amazing intensity,'
Diana wrote. 'I didn't feel, finally, that the woman you had set up was
a woman to whom this would have happened. There were times when
her graceless awfulness seemed to be her raison d'être . . . It's a terribly
depressing and frightening book: such hopelessness!'[7] Later, Diana felt
she had been too blunt with Vidia about *Guerrillas*: 'I thought I had
handled it badly, so I was rather ashamed . . . I thought it is a very
offensive thing to be told that the actual characters weren't working. It
was a sort of build up of being irritated by him, it was coming out.'[8] In
her memoir *Stet*, Diana described how her complaints over *Guerrillas*
led to Vidia deciding to leave Deutsch: she was in fact confusing this
stand-off with an event that occurred two years later.

Publication came the following autumn. 'Couldn't you have found
an honest job slinging coal, or washing dishes?' asked a Christian
correspondent from Kathmandu. 'I feel as betrayed as if the great
Jeeves himself had suddenly begun writing four letter words on the
walls of Brinkley Manor. And it is perhaps instructive to note that P.G.
Wodehouse, the greatest humorist of this century, managed to turn out
more than 90 books without dipping his pen into the toilet.'[9] An

American reader wrote: 'I have just finished reading your novel *Guerrillas* and I am very angry ... Sure, women like Jane exist, but women are changing and leaving behind the qualities they are supposed to have: the passivity, the masochism, the mindlessness.'[10] Proud of the masochism, Margaret told Vidia that her sister's husband Kiffy had added to his royalties by buying a copy of *Guerrillas*. Her brother-in-law had made the perceptive observation that Jane was the most important character in the novel, a deduction, Margaret noted, that had been overlooked by almost everyone else. But only she and Vidia knew quite why.[11] Paul Theroux told Francis Wyndham, 'I found myself almost gagging on this book – gagging with admiration and a kind of horror.'[12] It was a fair response.

'Naipaul is a scourge. He never relents,' wrote Joe Klein in *Mother Jones*. His work 'can best be described as a literature of buggery: his main purpose seems to be the desecration of his audience.' All the same, Klein admitted, 'I, as a devoted reader, cannot resist the temptation to be ravaged.'[13] An old opponent, Raoul Pantin, wrote in *Caribbean Contact* that the book was 'shattering evidence of the deepening sense of personal distress, of private desolation, that Naipaul feels after a remarkable creative career that has spanned nearly 20 years.'[14] Some reviews were positive. Peter Ackroyd thought *Guerrillas* 'a powerful and thoughtful novel' and Anthony Thwaite commended 'a brilliant artist's anatomy of emptiness, and of despair'.[15] In the *Listener* John Vaizey wrote, '*Guerrillas* has the fashionable sexual explicitness, which succeeds in being vulgar without being forthright – coy, in fact – and adds to the impression that the novel is not a story, but a vehicle around which a series of magazine articles, on sex, on women, on delinquency, are hung like placards.'[16] Tony Powell wrote unconvincingly to Vidia, 'It is a splendid book. How absurd of some reviewers to compare it with Graham Greene. If his name is to be mentioned at all, that should be only because your novel is a contrast to the sentimentality, phoniness, and falseness of feeling with which his works almost always abound.'[17]

In the autumn of 1974 Vidia told Pat, 'we were at the end of our relationship and that it would be worse (for me) in eight years when I am fifty ... I was stupid, talked too much about Proust, myself, my early attitudes and stupidity.' He had decided finally to be with Margaret: ' "I want her with all her follies." ' Pat had slim, desolate consolations. 'We took the 6.32 bus into Salisbury and had dinner in The Golden Curry. This was a big treat although the food was not very good.' With reluctance, she moved to the flat in London to begin a new life. After more than two years of work on the Malik article, she decided she might show it to Antonia. 'Ridiculously,' she noted, 'I am making these moves to write, work, rehabilitate myself at the moment of break-up.' At a party given by George Weidenfeld, John Gross 'asked me what books I would like to review. Francis came over and I told him and his eyes were amused, ironical.' She visited her mother in Birmingham, and travelled to its suburbs to follow 1974's second general election campaign, after the collapse of Harold Wilson's minority government. Soon, Vidia was telephoning in anguish to say he was having a recurring dream of a human head exploding. 'I hurried back to him.' He was convinced that by applying his mind he would solve his emotional worry, although it was his mind that was causing him torment. After a few days cosseting her husband in Wilsford, Pat went back to London alone. Always, she protected and cared for Vidia, treating him like the child she did not have. She might leave behind a note: 'Mon. Dinner: soup (1/2) (sardines?) quiche grapes. Tues. Lunch: Baked fish & 2 veg. apple crumble. Dinner: soup (1/2) eggs, remains of apple crumble?'[18]

At the end of July, Margaret had sent Vidia a bitter letter, typing it because she did not want him to read her mood from the handwriting. Her nihilism begat his nihilism; they brought out the negative in each other, and fed off it. For the preliminaries, she told him of local gossip and the daily reminders of his presence: the remnants of his beard in the basin, and bits of tobacco under her bed. Her children had been sent to La Cumbre, a mountain resort in Córdoba province, for the winter holidays. After considerable thought, she had taken her lover's point of view that Argentina was a mediocre country, where mediocrity triumphed. Then came the news: she was pregnant by him for a third time, she said, either out of love or out of hate, and was taking the appropriate measures. She knew that Vidia would not be willing to take any responsibility for what had happened. He did not understand living things, she asserted, because he had spent his life protecting himself from life. He was the product of a dead marriage and a dead childhood. She quoted his words back to himself: 'Aridity, I write out of aridity.' She wondered what he might have written out of fulfilment? She was left with reminders of his presence: a thickened waist, which she knew he would dislike, and a bruise on her body. But that was what happened, she informed him, if you were brutal to someone and threw shoes at them. For all this, though, for all her resentment and her pain, she felt betrayed by an agony of longing. At night, she was with Vido in her dreams, and in those dreams their love was tender and perhaps greater than it had ever been. Although she acknowledged that it might be foolish on her part, she could give herself to no other man. Nobody else would be able to offer her such ecstasy. Must she remain his whore, she asked?

In character, Vidia did not answer Margaret directly. Instead he internalized his reaction in a strange, murderous piece for the *New York Review*, 'The Brothels Behind the Graveyard'. It has no clear narrative, avoids setting a context and assumes much background knowledge about Perón and Argentina. Again, he identifies only with the Amerindians. The country had 'as yet no idea of itself'. Those who attempted to place it historically were ignoring the reality of a place where 'people are still being killed and kidnapped in the streets'. It was a 'brutish land of estancias and polo and brothels and very cheap servants . . . full of military names, the names of generals who took the land away from the Indians and, with a rapacity that still outrages the imagination, awarded themselves great portions of the earth's surface, estates, estancias, as large as counties.' By imposing Evita and then Isabelita on Argentina, Perón had wrought 'the roughest kind of justice on a society still ruled by degenerate machismo, which decrees that a woman's place is essentially in the brothel.' Women had few rights or opportunities: 'They are meant to be victims; and they accept their victim role.' He worked himself into a frenzy of loathing: this was 'a society spewing on itself'. His concluding image of BA, intended to sum up the nation, was of the garish brothels near the funerary monuments at Recoleta. He made the absurd claim that, 'Every schoolgirl knows the brothels; from an early age she understands that she might have to go there one day to find love, among the coloured lights and mirrors.' And there was more: Naipaul deduced that Argentine men were 'diminished' by their apparent preference for anal sex. 'The act of straight sex, easily bought, is of no great moment to the macho. His conquest of a woman is complete only when he has buggered her.'[19] The Argentine embassy in Washington DC sent the *New York Review* what Bob Silvers termed an 'oddly threatening' letter, suggesting 'some personal problem' on the part of the author, and stating that 'perhaps in the long run it will cause more problems to your publication than to the Argentine Republic.'[20] Andrew Graham-Yooll recalled the outrage among the Anglo-Argentine community: 'People said, "We invited him to our house and – look – he says we go about buggering women." '[21]

At the start of August, with Vidia still silent, Margaret let him know that she was recovering physically and mentally from what she termed her little murder. He had said or done precisely nothing to sustain her, and she wondered whether these days people simply did not bother to acknowledge such trifling matters. Yet for all his indifference, she still wanted him. She planned to visit Spain and France for two weeks, and would meet him in London in the middle of September. The tone of her letter was cool, different – and Vidia was suspicious. They met, and he took her down to Wilsford to the cottage. Something was wrong; Vidia found a letter from a scion of a prominent banking family in Argentina. Margaret had entered into an arrangement with him in order to visit the man she loved. Vidia recalled: 'She came to Europe with an Argentine banker. It was terrible when I found out. She was having a relationship with the banker for the means to get to me. She said she would have slept with him a hundred times to get to me, and I believed her actually . . . I was extremely upset. I was very violent with her for two days; I was very violent with her for two days with my hand; my hand began to hurt . . . She didn't mind it at all. She thought of it in terms of my passion for her. Her face was bad. She couldn't appear really in public. My hand was swollen. I was utterly helpless. I have enormous sympathy for people who do strange things out of passion.'[22]

When Margaret left Wilsford, evacuated by her sister Diana, Pat received a telephone call. 'He told me he was in a terrible state and asked me to return. "There is nothing in it for you." When I got back I would not let him ask me to look after him for the sake of the book . . . He told me of the violent scenes here between the Friday and the Sunday morning when the sister came for her, trembling . . . I love him – at last.' Vidia abandoned his decision to end their marriage. Looking back, he claimed: 'If Pat were a stronger person or more at ease in the world, I might have left her to look after herself. I couldn't do that. That's when I discovered the strength of the weak . . . I should have left. I didn't have the brutality. Isn't it strange? People would say that what I was doing was quite brutal.'[23] He had a mental dependence on both women: the 'master' in a masochistic relationship can have less psychological control than the 'victim'. Vidia found himself unable, despite repeated efforts, to break away from either Margaret or Pat: the only way he could have escaped the situation was if one or both of them had left him. The intensity and violence of this episode marked a culmination in his relationship with Margaret; after the events of

September 1974, they reached a kind of stasis. 'So that was when I stopped writing [to her]. Just one of these odd decisions one makes. But we were together after that for around twenty years. I went and met her family, a family lunch in a restaurant with her brother from Spain. So I was very much part of the family, and it was all very nice for me really. It was so much nicer for me than Pat's family. I liked Margaret's sister very much indeed. But there was one thing – I couldn't just shed Pat you see. Many times I thought I could but I couldn't. Pat was rather alone in the world.'[24]

A few months later, back in Argentina, Margaret wrote to Vidia that England seemed like paradise compared to the squalor of Argentina. She felt she had been stimulated intellectually by being with him, and was at a loss now she was home. Her memories of being together were all delightful, and remarkably enough she even spoke happily of their time in Wiltshire, with what she called all its upheavals. She said to Vidia that without him she felt numb, and missed his arms and his thighs and the god. Taking the hit, she apologized for offering him unrest and anxiety rather than peace and quiet. She had not given him happiness, but she had offered him love.

Later in the year, angered by the way Vidia continually presented himself as incapable, Pat wrote, 'I thought just now as I was undressing and washing my face that I have, obediently, taken responsibility for his suffering, but that he has always assumed a pathetic pose and something of that has become habitual . . . Before he slept he spoke disturbingly about Diana and her attitude to the book. I confirmed that I spoke to her about Vidia possibly needing the help of a psychiatrist. She spoke to him about my family being "common".' In a volatile state of mind, Vidia went to London for a party given by Hugh Thomas: the star turn was Gabriel García Márquez, a writer whose response to the Caribbean was the antithesis of Vidia's. He shaved off his beard and returned to Wilsford. Vidia wanted everything: Pat, Margaret, both, neither, Wiltshire, London, Argentina and Spain. He was nothing if not indecisive. He told Pat he would pursue Margaret, 'do what she wants and live with her for six months – in Madrid. He just told me he is living through a nightmare: he gives his decision and then spends two or three hours reversing it.' Pat felt 'outraged to be left here'.

*

On the last Sunday in October, Pat and Vidia Naipaul put on a show of marital solidarity for some visitors. She was still taking Mandrax in an effort to stabilize herself. Her sole record of the lunch party is a list of the guests and the sentence, 'I let myself be deflected when Vidia raged the night before and did not prepare the dishes I had intended when my life depended on being accomplished and prepared.' One guest, Paul Theroux, had more elaborate memories. In *Sir Vidia's Shadow*, he devoted a chapter to the lunch. It is entertaining and revealing, giving an intimate glimpse of V.S. Naipaul in his home setting, among his friends. As in other sections of the book, he has perfect recall of people, atmosphere, even of the dialogue in conversations.

Theroux takes the train from London to Salisbury alone, since his wife Anne does not wish to come. Vidia has sent a car to meet him at the station, driven by 'Walters', but Walters turns out to be a taxi driver who charges Theroux £4. On arrival at the cottage he is met by Vidia and Julian Jebb, 'a small elfin-faced man wearing tight velvet trousers and a red and gold waistcoat . . . the sort of Englishman who could express his humorous side only by speaking in an exaggerated American accent.' Soon they are joined by Hugh and Antonia Fraser, Antonia 'dressed like a shepherdess, her soft skin set off by a frilly lavender blouse and a velvet peasant skirt.' Hugh is tall, slow and lopsided, bearing an 'aura of helpless authority'. The other guests are a young couple, Malcolm and Robin; Malcolm is red-faced and socially inept, 'a beaky Kiwi in the throes of pedantry, proving his point to the Poms', while Robin is 'sweet and square-shouldered, wearing a soft, unnecessary hat, as New Zealanders seemed habitually to do.' Theroux writes with a novelist's eye: each character has a stereotypical narrative function. Hugh is an upper-class MP. Antonia is seductive, the object of an extended sexual fantasy. Pat remains in the background, serving food. Julian is camp, vociferous and irritating. Malcolm and Robin are class-conscious Kiwis, prone to say things like, ' "Beaut book, Paul." ' During lunch, Vidia is given smoked salmon while the others have oxtail soup, and Malcolm, an expert on the Augustan writers, tries and fails to shock Lady Antonia by quoting bawdy poetry. Afterwards, they all go for a walk by the river and shoot at a paper target with an air rifle; 'Robin scored the highest.' The guests leave separately and Theroux takes a train to London, despite the unexpressed desire to be conveyed in Hugh and Antonia's purring Jaguar.[25]

It is a vivid and plausible account of a day in the country with the tetchy, pompous V.S. Naipaul and his guests, with Paul Theroux as the perceptive observer. It is, though, some distance from the truth. Julian Jebb was not at the lunch. Malcolm and Robin were Michael Neill and Pek Koon Heng; neither had a New Zealand accent. In Neill's words, 'The account of my conversation with Antonia Fraser is false . . . Pek Koon was a stylish woman from Kuala Lumpur, studying at SOAS. It is bizarre that Theroux described her as a vulgar Kiwi. I recall him being pleasant company; we gave him a lift back to London in my car, a disreputable Morris 1100.'[26] Pek Koon Heng added: 'I don't wear hats. Period . . . Theroux was very much the acolyte, giving Naipaul a lot of face, a lot of deference.'[27] Antonia Fraser's reaction to Theroux's account was, 'Well, a guy can dream, but it wasn't at all how I remember it.'[28] Her recollection is confirmed by a diary entry for 27 October 1974: 'Visit to Pat and Vidia Naipaul in Wiltshire.' Antonia and Hugh had arrived first to find Vidia looking 'fairly high . . . despite being on valium to overcome depression and nerves of finishing the new book . . . Paul Theroux, a nice earnest American novelist who has written rather a dull but honest book about him, was coming.' She described a conversation with Vidia about writers and the imagination, and a shooting competition: 'Vidia a bit too high to win, in fact Theroux and I tied first.' Walking in the autumn sedge by the river, she asked Vidia the colour of the sky. ' "Mauve not amethyst." He says he plays a game noting colours precisely in his mind . . . "But I don't need to write it down. I have a perfect memory you see." He is other worldly springing about in the darkening reeds with his perfect memory and his genius and his valium . . . and he has the bungalow for another 9 years thanks to Glenc.' Her diary entry concludes, 'On the way home, sleepily, Hugh and I reflect that it is Pat who is thin and pale and perhaps doesn't have a perfect memory. V is thoroughly OK.'[29]

Michael Neill, Pek Koon Heng and Antonia Fraser – the three surviving members of the lunch party apart from Naipaul and Theroux – have matching accounts of what happened that day. Theroux's account appears to be significantly inaccurate, even deliberately fictive. What then of *Sir Vidia's Shadow*, with its queasy subtitle *A Friendship Across Five Continents*? Reviewers almost without exception treated it on publication as a reliable memoir rather than as a fictionalized account of a real relationship. It has been presented as a reliable, even essential account of the life and opinions of V.S. Naipaul, quoted not only in countless press articles but in academic studies of his work. Theroux insisted later on the honesty of *Sir Vidia's Shadow*. 'When I wrote the book I wanted to make it as deliberately truthful and accurate as possible,' he told the *Telegraph Magazine*.[30] 'I knew I had to be scrupulously truthful – a far cry from fictionalizing,' he assured the *Atlantic Monthly*.[31] This claim was taken at face value, despite his having recently written two autobiographical novels which blurred the line between truth and fiction, both of them featuring V.S. Naipaul in disguised form. *My Secret History* devotes a couple of chapters to 'My friend, S. Prasad, the writer' and uses material that is repeated in *Sir Vidia's Shadow*.[32] In *My Other Life*, Theroux gives lines of Naipaul's conversation to a passing character, Walter Van Bellamy.[33] Both novels are fluent and emotionally disengaged, imagining events in Theroux's life had it turned out a little differently.

The material in *Sir Vidia's Shadow* combines the accurate, the fictional and the appropriated, and they merge to the point where they cannot be disentangled. The early part of the book, set in Africa, feels authentic although the dialogue is invented and characters such as Haji Hallsmith did not exist. The portrait of Pat and Vidia's life at Makerere is believable: Vidia enraged by the expatriate teachers in the Senior Common Room, or walking through a market with 'an inspector's gait, hands clasped behind his back, moving fast yet looking at everything.'[34] Many of the phrases Naipaul uses are convincing, such as, to a hotel manager: ' "Don't you have a rule saying that all staff uniforms must be dirty?" '[35] Other lines are less plausible, and sound closer to Theroux's idea of what Naipaul should have been thinking: ' "This is turning me into a racialist, for God's sake." '[36] Later, as their symbiotic relationship at Makerere is replaced by Theroux's more distant and servile attempt to maintain a friendship, the encounters become rarer and the portrayal more speculative; Naipaul ends up as a caricature and a crank. Some details still come from close knowledge: Vidia's distress at a builder sitting on his bed, or his pessimistic appraisal of Hugh Fraser's handwriting, or his reaction to a graffito, KEEP BRITAIN WHITE: ' "I would put a comma after 'Britain'." '[37] Other material is invented, for example the details of the Wilsford lunch, Theroux meeting Vidia's future wife, Nadira, as a child in Nairobi, or the claim that he prevented him from winning the Booker Prize for *A Bend in the River*.[38] Pat's small breasts are inflated lasciviously, 'her cheeks and lips wet, her large breasts tremulous with grief'.[39] Some sections are taken from Naipaul's letters to Theroux, which are summarized (for copyright reasons) or rendered as dialogue. Further material is borrowed from *Conversations with V.S. Naipaul*, a compilation of interviews used by Theroux while preparing *Sir Vidia's Shadow*.[40] For instance the comment, 'I have never had to work for hire; I made a vow at an early age never to work, never to become involved with people in that way. That has given me a freedom from people, from entanglements, from rivalries, from competition. I have no enemies, no rivals, no masters; I fear no one,' is taken from an interview with Naipaul published in *Transition*, a magazine founded by a Makerere colleague, Rajat Neogy.[41]

Despite the fictionalizing and the misconstruction, *Sir Vidia's Shadow* remains an entertaining study both of literary friendship gone wrong and of aspects of V.S. Naipaul's character. Theroux's unreliability as a narrator makes his tale no less compelling; like the brothers Goncourt, his oddity of perception is no disadvantage. The book is an act of vengeance, but also an act of homage. He is consistently harsh on himself: for his literary envy, for failing to challenge his mentor, for tolerating his meanness. The book reveals as much about Theroux as it does about Naipaul – his incomprehension of the English, his sexual vanity, his eagerness to be snubbed, the relentlessness of his pursuit. Theroux rationalizes his mistreatment, since 'in friendship, time is meaningless and silences insignificant, because you are sure of each other.'[42] Underlying the memoir is a sense that Theroux did not fully understand the nature of his encounter with Naipaul, or the extent to which he was goaded for years. Generous, shameless, inquisitive, friendly, but lacking a gift for friendship, he failed to see that Naipaul had no loyalty to him, and regarded him primarily as an aide and entertainer, and that his final rejection was inevitable. Paul was baffled when he received his fax of dismissal, orchestrated by Vidia but written by Nadira: 'The more I reflected on her letter, the louder I laughed. Its obsessional style and bad grammar and clumsy handwriting were proof that Vidia had not seen it before she sent it ... The woman was a highly visible person who would have been denounced or ridiculed on sight as "colored" or a "Paki" in most of Britain.'[43] Theroux missed the signals, accepting the popular idea that his hero's arrogant behaviour must arise from a Hindu sense of caste: 'Until I met Vidia, I had never known a person who recognized no one as his equal. He's a Brahmin, the local Indians said: all Brahmins are fussy like that.'[44] Vidia's old schoolfriend Lloyd Best made a more perceptive observation: 'Theroux's book exposes Naipaul as a real Trinidadian in every sense – including the way he would not pay for the wine. All these little Trinidadian smart-man things: the way he would sing calypso and whistle, the way he would take the mickey out of people, provoking them. Naipaul expects the responses that he's going to get; I'd say that it's second nature to him, performing in that way.'[45]

The understandable response to the merging of truth and fiction in *Sir*

Vidia's Shadow would be to see it as a form of postmodern experimentation, Theroux undercutting the autobiographical form in his next literary step after *My Other Life*. The book, though, is more peculiar than this. Theroux saw *Sir Vidia's Shadow* as veracious. Asked about the inaccuracies in the version of the Wilsford lunch, he said he did not remember Pek Koon Heng being Malaysian Chinese, and that he did not receive a lift back to London with her and Michael Neill. On Julian Jebb's absence, he said, 'He used to come all the time and I was conflating two visits. He said all the things that he said. I put him in there because Vidia used him in *The Enigma of Arrival* and he was his friend, and I thought he belittled him terribly.' As to pretending he had met Nadira in Nairobi in 1966, he said, 'It could have been Nadira because the age is exactly right [he was wrong by six years, and Nadira was living in Dar es Salaam at the time]. It wasn't fictionalizing because in my opinion it has poetic truth in it. I am not saying that was Nadira. Of course it wasn't Nadira. But it could have been her . . . to me it was true.' Regarding his own attitude to Naipaul, Theroux suggested, 'I couldn't talk about my books because he really wasn't interested in them, so we always talked about his books. We couldn't talk about money because I had more than him. We couldn't talk about children because he didn't have any. He complained about England: that was his subject . . . But it was as near to a friendship that I have ever had with anyone, really, and certainly with any other writer . . . My kids used to say that I really didn't have any friends. I lived in London for seventeen years. I go back and I don't see anyone.'[46]

V.S. Naipaul's response to *Sir Vidia's Shadow* was to ignore it. He did not read the book, and his subsequent remarks about Theroux were consciously theatrical and Olympian, reconstructing the friendship: 'He spread this idea that I was his great mentor and adviser, but since Africa, since 1966, we've hardly met. He came here twice. He was infinitely amusing to me in that jungle, this rather common fellow who was in Africa teaching the Negroes, he pestered me and pestered me, wrote me letters all the time . . . In the nineteenth century there were serious travellers who went to unknown places and did reports on it. Travelling was hard for them; now, travel has changed. Travel has become a plebeian, everyday matter, it has become a lower-class adventure, and there are books now written for lower-class travellers. I think Theroux belonged to that category: he wrote tourist books for the lower classes.'[47]

*

1975 started unhappily, and got worse. Marg Hale telephoned on New Year's Day to say that stones had been thrown through her bedroom window. Pat and Vidia listened to Melvyn Bragg interviewing Antonia on the wireless. Pat wrote: 'I asked him whether it altered his judgement, modified his opinions about the state of the nation and he said no.' Vidia was off to Zaire, following obliquely in the footsteps of Joseph Conrad, seeking his own heart of darkness; Pat learned by default that he would not be alone: 'The Lunn Poly girl rang to say that the double rooms at the Intercontinental Kinshasa were all booked . . . Vidia is abstracted. He collected his valium ("I don't want to fly off the handle at anyone in the Congo") and malaria tablets . . . He spoke of his fear, and foreboding: that the person was wrong. That he was ashamed of his marriage but not now.' He mentioned an old cartoon from the *Illustrated Weekly of India*, which showed a boy found by his father looking at pictures of naked women, with the caption 'What is the point of being a Brahmin if you can't control your passions?' He stated, less than accurately, 'I have always controlled my passions.' On the night before he flew, he told Pat they had 'a fellowship, that he was very lucky to find me, that we were very lucky to find one another.' With pathetic gratitude, she noted: 'He gave me the blue lighter and the red biro with which he wrote *Guerrillas*' – the same blue lighter and red biro that are used in the plot to signify Jane's death.

While Vidia was in Zaire, Pat went to London, but was too nervous to confide in her friends. She spent a day at the Haberdashers' Aske's School for Girls, wondering if she might return to teaching, and shared her professional worries with her childhood friend Sheila Rogers, herself a schoolteacher. In Sheila's words: 'Pat's experience was in selective schools, but those had been closed down by the time she wanted to get back into teaching. We all agreed that Pat must be an absolute saint to cope with Vidia. She had a very sensitive mind.'[48] As Pat wrote three years later, 'My job, as housemaid and helpmeet, had run out. I was casting around for another career.' She told Teresa a little about her situation, and regretted it at once. 'I forgot that she is deceitful. In case anybody reads this I don't mean anything really bad . . . I have behaved like a treacherous, repulsive ass. Teresa. Miriam. Antonia. I have seen the light of affection and sympathy die in Antonia's and Miriam's eyes. Antonia has offered me the job of researching her book of love letters.' Pat spent days alone in the flat in Queen's Gate, depressed and introspective, seeing no one, scarcely eating, and sent a letter to Francis Wyndham alluding to her sense of shame and failure. Before Vidia left for Zaire, she had written in her diary after a visit to the Powells, 'I was clumsier than ever, in spite of my resolutions . . . Julian [Jebb] looked tired and as when he left us that weekend, smelt rather sweaty. Both he and Tristram spoke a lot of wisdom . . . Of course I omitted to speak of the contempt I felt from Tristram and John. And of my stupidity and clumsiness.' Julian Jebb was himself in a bad state. A successful maker of documentaries on the likes of Christopher Isherwood, Virginia Woolf and the Mitford sisters, he was tormented by his own demons. A little younger than Vidia, Jebb was a puckish, talented, flamboyant man, addicted to Gauloises and vodka, and uneasy about his homosexuality. Above all, he was troubled that he had not lived up to early ambitions to be a writer and creator.[49] In Michael Holroyd's memory, 'He was a depressed man who came alive in the heat of the television studio.'[50]

Things were falling apart for Pat. When Vidia returned to England in the middle of March, the round of conflict began again: 'He wanted to know what I was doing. I think I said I was trying to earn some money. "What have you done?" I would not talk. "You've done nothing?"' Margaret was staying in Wilsford. Stuck in London, a broken woman, Pat brooded as a wife and a homemaker on 'the awfulness of them handling my things, my kitchen things.' The next month, she took a tentative step forward, having lunch with the poet and critic Ian Hamilton, who was editing the *New Review*, a monthly magazine funded by the Arts Council. Francis had suggested that Hamilton might publish her article on Michael Abdul Malik. They went to a pub next door to his office and discussed it. Pat was thrilled to be treated like a fellow writer and a normal human being. 'It was a working lunch – the first I've ever had . . . I have never felt so good after wine at lunch . . . He asked me what I had written before, what I had published before. So what name would I use. His face is quite beautiful, his eyes darkish, compelling.' Francis thought, 'When Pat wrote, she over-researched. She wasn't a good journalist. I think Vidia was extremely irritated by it. I got the feeling that he was the opposite of supportive.'[51] The proofs came. It was an observant article, concentrating on the intricacies of the trial. 'I sobbed over the phone to Miriam and changed the name. On Thursday I changed it back again.' The author was to be – Patricia Naipaul. She went to lunch with the art dealer Kasmin, who had first editions of all Vidia's books, and dinner with Paul and Anne Theroux, finding 'Paul, with his success, has acquired gravitas, pipe smoking.' Pek Koon Heng and Michael Neill invited her out; despite their inauspicious meeting, they both liked Pat: 'She was quiet, self-effacing but with a sharp intelligence, one of those wives who quite deliberately puts herself to one side to look after her husband.'[52]

Pat tried hard to develop her professional ambitions, going to literary parties and meeting Sonia, Antonia, Teresa, Francis and Edna. Antonia was being paraded mercilessly through the gossip columns, having recently begun a relationship with the playwright Harold Pinter, fulfilling a lifelong ambition to become the handmaiden to a genius. Pinter's wife, the actress Vivien Merchant, cited Antonia in their divorce case and denounced her to the press for having big feet – size 9½, reportedly. *Time* reported that, 'Lady Antonia, a lithe blonde, has been married since 1956 to Tory MP Hugh Fraser . . . She is an avid collector – of white dresses (she has 100), and of personages literary, theatrical and political. Her companions have included Author Norman Mailer, Actor Robert Stephens and Lord Lambton, the Tory MP who quit Parliament last year after being photographed in bed with a call girl. Pinter, by contrast, is the only son of a Jewish tailor from London's rugged East End. Darkly handsome with thinning hair, he spent almost a decade as a stage actor, turned to writing in the 1950s, and soon developed into an acclaimed, though sometimes confounding chronicler of English subsociety.'[53] Hugh Fraser, meanwhile, was attempting to become leader of the Conservative Party; he came a poor third to Margaret Thatcher in the first ballot, who to widespread surprise went on to defeat the incumbent, Ted Heath.

Pat attended an extremist political rally with a view to writing a second article for the *New Review*. 'The National Front held their "Anti-Mugging March" in Hackney,' she wrote in her diary. On the Underground on the way home, after watching windows being smashed in Hoxton Market, 'I got into the same carriage as the tall attacker and heard him say that he had kicked the young man in the face. He said that it made it all "worth it".' The piece used her own background in Kingstanding as a window onto Britain's rising racial tension: ' "Our Dora's National Front." That had been a surprise too . . . I had known Dora and her father, a Birmingham shopkeeper, for most of my life.'[54] She wrote an article on the referendum over whether Britain should join the European Common Market, and a piece on the writer Aleksandr Solzhenitsyn, who had recently been exiled from the Soviet Union. When it was turned down by Miriam Gross at the *Observer*, her ambitions retreated. This coincided with a shift in her relationship with Vidia. 'He thinks he has come back to me. That there is no feeling left – but affection and concern. He has been living at the dentist's. On Friday he went and she was waiting for him. He believes she loves him ... I feel the crisis of hysteria ebbing away and doubt the value and safety of writing this as a form of therapy ... My distress is real.' The tone of her diary changed now, the entries become briefer and more impersonal, concerned with public events: 'Yesterday the Concorde took off on its inaugural flight ... The new plan for British Leyland has been announced ... Robert Lowell is dead ... Hugh Fraser's car was blown to pieces.' This referred to an IRA bomb placed beneath his car that exploded prematurely, killing a neighbour and narrowly missing Fraser and a house guest, Caroline Kennedy, the teenage daughter of Jackie and the late JFK.

Pat lacked the necessary confidence and resilience to make a success of freelance journalism; Antonia's invitation to research an anthology of love letters suited her academic temperament better. The division of labour worked perfectly: Antonia was happier making love than researching it, and Pat needed something to do. She went by bus to the London Library in Piccadilly for three days each week, dutifully saving her 40-pence return bus tickets as receipts. David Pryce-Jones would invite her out for coffee. 'I would see her sitting in the London Library doing research and trying to write in Vidia's own style and it was very pitiful ... She seemed tortured, absolutely tormented. There was something obsessive about Pat. She would have done anything for Vidia. There is a human phenomenon called "a great man's wife" and she was such a thing. Mrs Nabokov was another. [They] are absolutely convinced of their husband's genius and will do anything that the husband asks to promote that genius ... She wanted more of Vidia than he was prepared to concede.'[55] In a later letter to Pat, Pryce-Jones wrote, 'I hold firmly to the view that talented people like Vidia, of whom there are few, are their own justification. I think we hold this view in common; I hope so anyhow.'[56]

Antonia wrote Pat a note saying she required 'A Treasury of Great Love Letters' and made a grand total of three suggestions for inclusion: Sarah Bernhardt, Victorien Sardou and Jean Cocteau. Pat assembled and copied letters by Mozart, Chekhov, Keats, Hugo, Byron, Heloise, Balzac and Napoleon. As Antonia put it later, 'Pat really did most of the work, and when I made lavish acknowledgements she kept crossing them out. In the end she wanted to be Patricia Hale, so no one knew who she was. That was very typical ... My own marriage was breaking up ... Pat was so reticent, so apologetic. She would arrive apologising for being late, or early, or for bothering you. She had a permanent cold. And I was madly in love with Harold. She was a very sweet person, but certainly gave the impression of being a very unhappy woman at that time. We never talked about Margaret. She was very, very reticent.'[57] Pat was paid £300 for the work by Antonia and the publisher, and £100 for expenses, much of which she insisted on returning. 'I repeat, and will keep on repeating, my enormous gratitude to you for your arduous and imaginative work,' Antonia wrote as she tried to persuade Pat to keep the money she was due for expenses. 'Do keep writing yourself!'[58] *Love Letters* sold well, and has been through many reprints.

The leisure of research gave Pat an opportunity to ponder. She spent days reading other people's thoughts and sentiments, way beyond the call of obligation. F. Scott Fitzgerald's talented and manic wife interested her: 'I have just been reading Zelda Fitzgerald and recognise myself and an eternal predicament ... she told him in her letters that her writing was for him, the opinions of others did not exist. And yet she kept her writings secret from him.' Above all, she was fascinated by Jane Carlyle, the wife of the Victorian social thinker Thomas Carlyle, seeing her as the epitome of the clever woman who sacrificed all for her awkward husband's greatness: 'It was her nature to suffer ... She voluntarily yielded her emotions and her talents to their relationship, to an ideal of married love ... Whatever the stress and suffering, it seems to me a perfect marriage, in the sense of two people becoming one and indispensable to one another, part of one another, almost exchanging personalities ... After her death Carlyle reproached himself with her unhappiness ... She was brilliant. I think [she was] his equal but her genius went into their life together. To try to make that genius fit the strait jacket of latter-day Women's Lib is to misunderstand her nature.' The domineering side of Jane Carlyle – witty, gossipy and intrusive – was left to one side in this interpretation. Here, Jane became a version of Pat, or Patricia Naipaul as she might have been: the respected and loyal wife of a great man who thrives in a marriage of equals, the exact arrangement she had dreamed of in 1953 when she wrote to Vidia, 'The union of two real people is nobler than one-sided submission.'

Her husband would not entertain equality. Vidia's conception of himself was too fragile and narcissistic for his personality to be merged with another. He depended on the idea of his own singularity: without it, he might crack. Pat could support and enable him, but she could not share in creating. Although she was intelligent and well read, she was not by this stage his intellectual equal, and was clever enough to realize her limitations. Pat's social or political ideas, in particular her innate liberalism, had no influence on Vidia except as an attitude for him to reject. Her soft-left orthodoxies gave something for him to fix on and oppose, and made him define his own position more clearly. He had no wish to synthesize opinions. Vidia had a view of the world that he would do anything to maintain, just as he would sacrifice anything or anybody that stood in the way of his central purpose, to be 'the writer'.

CHAPTER TWENTY-ONE

'I WANT TO WIN AND
WIN AND WIN'

FOR THE NEXT TWO DECADES, the triangle between Vidia, Pat and Margaret persisted, shifting from an equilateral to a scalene depending on his work, mood and location, and the emotional pull exerted by each woman. When Vidia travelled to research a book, it would often be with Margaret, and then he would go home. Again and again, he thought he would leave Pat for Margaret, or give up Margaret for Pat. In Vidia's peer group in England, running two women in this way was considered unusual. His reaction to the awkwardness of the situation was not to introduce Margaret to his friends, but to avoid mentioning her existence, although they knew about her, and he knew they knew. As Antonia Fraser put it, 'I never met her . . . If Vidia had asked me to meet her, I would have done so, because it would be his judgement, not mine. But he never did.'[1] Sometimes, things happened differently. Vidia brought Margaret to Elsham Road to see Marisa Masters. 'She said, "Marisa, will you tell Vidia he cannot have his cake and eat it too?" I thought, how can she use that phrase in respect of a writer? What a pedestrian way of expressing it.'[2] Paul Theroux was permitted a momentary conversation in a cafe. Kasmin, who advised Vidia on buying art and was expected to take him out to lunch from time to time, met both Margaret and Pat: 'I sensed that Margaret was able to defend herself in any situation. Pat didn't open up in his presence. She was diminished by Vidia.'[3] David Pryce-Jones remembered, 'He was coming to dinner one evening, and he rang up and said he'd be coming with Margaret. So I said fine, and I then felt that I had better ring up the other guests and I rang up and said, Vidia is not coming with Pat but with a lady called Margaret. But when he arrived, he arrived with Pat, and I got a very funny letter from Hugh Thomas who was present at this dinner, and he said, "I am glad you warned me that he was coming with Margaret because I might very well have mistaken her for Pat." '[4]

In Mobutu's Zaire in early 1975 for the *Sunday Times* and the *New York Review of Books*, Vidia was accompanied by his mistress. 'I took her to places she had never been. I took her to the Congo, and she turned up there in jeans with a nice, lovely straw basket – you could hold the handles together – as if for a Brighton excursion. It was as though she thought the Congo was a beach resort.'[5] Vidia was disturbed by the condition of the country. As he wrote in the finished article, 'The Congo, which used to be a Belgian colony, is now an African kingdom and is called Zaire. It appears to be a nonsense name, a sixteenth-century Portuguese corruption, some Zairois will tell you, of a local word for "river". So it is as if Taiwan, reasserting its Chinese identity, were again to give itself the Portuguese name of Formosa. The Congo River is now called the Zaire, as is the local currency, which is almost worthless.'[6] He wrote to Francis from Kinshasa, 'There has been a "radicalization of the revolution"; and everybody is very nervous, especially the local citizens (a technical word of the revolution) . . . the visitor is required by law to spend 20 Zaires a day (i.e. $40) . . . Nothing really works, without the expatriates; so that, although I plan to go to Stanleyville (now Kisangani) & take the steamer back to Kinshasa, I am no longer sure whether anything as elaborate as that is possible. It is absurd, but one is a little like an old-fashioned African traveller, i.e., a hostage of a sort.'[7]

In his notebook, he mentioned many ideas that would find their way into *A Bend in the River*, and wrote prophetically of Zaire's likely future under the charismatic kleptocrat Joseph Mobutu, who was now calling himself Mobutu Sese Seko Kuku Ngbendu Wa Za Banga. 'The curious kingship. The distortions & bogusness & despair of authenticity cf W Indians and Obeah. African art. Confusion, especially of the évolué [a term used in colonial Congo, similar to 'babu' in British India] . . . The difficulty of Africa: one reaction multiplied by another. Irritation multiplied by concern for individuals who must feel, with their new sense of pride etc, unsupported by their society . . . Like Leopold II of the Belgians, in the time of the Congo Free State – much of whose despotic legislation >(ownership of the mines in 1888, all vacant lands in 1890, the fruits of the earth in 1891)< has passed down through the Belgian colonial administration to the present regime, >and is now presented as a kind of ancestral African socialism – like Leopold II,< Mobutu owns Zaire.'[8]

In a smaller, fliptop notebook, he recorded the names of the Belgian diplomats and academics and Zairois journalists whose knowledge he was seeking. 'Mr Van Krombrugghe (offer him Mr G's greetings) . . . Omer Marchal (works for Spécial dedicated to Mobutu) . . . Professor Benoit Verhaeghen.' A separate notebook recorded daily activities, avoiding any mention of Margaret. 'I find that it helps to help the officials. They are probably self-conscious about their lack of skill and are likely to resent being laughed at. The Belgians, who appear to know the country, push their way forward . . . The feeling one has that one is asking stupid questions . . . The Greeks & Portuguese and Indians have been asked to leave . . . The great surprise is the magnificence of the women . . . Rusty corrugated-iron roofs. Bumpy roads, great dips, the piles of garbage on the road. The little boys playing in the dust, springing off a tire & doing somersaults in the air. The prison: concrete barracks behind a whitewashed wall.'9 This fluent daily diary was transcribed and published as a limited edition by Sylvester & Orphanos in 1980, and dedicated to 'MM'. Overlying Vidia's response to Zaire was a sense of fear about the way in which rival or tribal groups were ready to take whatever opportunities reached them. He saw, in Africa, 'a dream of a past – the vacancy of river and forest, the hut in the brown yard, the dugout – when the dead ancestors watched and protected, and the enemies were only men.'10

Back in Europe, he lived for five weeks with Margaret in a parador in Javea in Spain, working hard on the article. Pat spent her time in Wilsford and in the flat in London, wondering what to do next. Through this period, with a new, partial stability in his relationship with Margaret, Vidia was intent on his work. He wanted to go to India, to South America, or to the Caribbean. Bob Silvers understood the vitality of Vidia's ambition at this time, and decided to make the most of him. Might he like to write a series of articles about India, which was lurching towards economic and constitutional chaos, with Prime Minister Indira Gandhi on the verge of declaring a State of Emergency? He would, and Margaret would accompany him for much of the trip.

*

'The monsoon rain was blown over the concrete by the aeroplane as it landed,' Vidia wrote in his journal on 20 August. 'I had never been in Bombay during the monsoon and began to grieve for the plastic mackintosh I had left behind at London airport . . . With each successive arrival in

India my dismay and apprehension lessen. It may be that I have learned a new way of seeing or know better now what to expect, it may also be that one's sense of dissolution has now spread: that there are no longer places where one can retreat; that I am now aware of a more general insecurity and am, perhaps importantly, less of a colonial.' During this journey through India, Vidia would hone the technique he was to use in his subsequent non-fiction writing: he found experienced local journalists to guide him, took whatever assistance or hospitality was available, interviewed people in great detail, linked what he had discovered to his exisiting ideas about the country, and wrote up the results fast. Using his literary prestige, the mad strength of his new personality and a rare ability to project himself as if in mortal need of assistance, he was superb at persuading people to help him.

In his India journal, kept over months and written in a neat and careful hand, Vidia recorded his conversations and experiences, and gave no indication that he was travelling with another person. Sometimes Margaret was allowed to take dictation, or to glue newspaper cuttings into a book. His tempestuous interaction with her throughout the trip was sectioned off in his mind and kept separate from his work. Her presence leaks out in other ways, in his focused anger and his increasingly misanthropic view of the world. Intimate passion came out as cold passion on the page. It also affected his dealings with others: antagonism was becoming a default position, a way of attaining what appeared to be an advantage in any encounter.

Sometimes Vidia's conclusions were perceptive, at other times merely bitter. He was good at picking up new pieces of information, and seeing how they might become important. Talking to a consultant engineer in Bombay, Shirish Patel, to whom he had been introduced by his old friend from his 1963 trip Moni Malhoutra, he learned about the Shiv Sena, a chauvinist local political group that was later to assume national relevance. Vidia noted 'its organisation & growth; the theatricality of its leader, Bal Thackeray, a failed cartoonist ... Again, I have the feeling of a country only just discovering what it has committed itself to — independence, industrialization, democracy; a process achieving a dynamic that is now beyond the control of any leader.' He milked his hosts for information, often causing a scene when he set off an argument, and was happy to dismiss many of his helpers afterwards as fools and idlers. Khushwant Singh's son Rahul, a journalist, took him to dinner in Bombay with Charles Correa, an architect, and Prem Shankar Jha, a *Times of India* columnist.

'The narcissism of "Who am I" – the questions raised by Prem Jha. The simplistic view of identity ... One felt the irrelevance of this middle-class element, so parasitic, these advertising men, offering nothing of value really, speaking only to their own group. Jha assaulted me. He allowed no conversation to develop. No idea was explored. He was the Indian journalist – making simple patterns of simple facts. Such shoddy ideas adrift in this society. Like Adil Jussawalla's New Left idea. Adil has apparently, poor Parsi boy, married a rich Frenchwoman, whom he keeps in hiding.'[11] Prem Shankar Jha remembered, 'He was always looking for offence, looking for the hidden barb ... I felt misrepresented – he had already decided what he wanted to say, and was looking for evidence. Margaret was very nervy, and showing all the signs of wear and tear you would expect from living with him.'[12] The antipathy was returned by Vidia, with interest: 'I thought Jha was a windbag. A windbag. He always had a view about everything, and there was little selectivity in what he said ... Everything was a crisis. But if you write a column, that's what happens to you.'[13]

In Delhi in September, Vidia found the Emergency was making people reluctant to speak to him openly. Indira Gandhi had suspended elections, censored newspapers, imprisoned political opponents and banned strikes. Middle-class society in the capital was split between those who were delighted that the buses were running on time, and others who were frightened, believing democracy in India was finished. Uniquely, Vidia thought the Emergency was inconsequential. He told Vinod Mehta, a magazine editor, 'Don't worry, this will pass.' Mehta thought at the time it was a 'quite extraordinary' thing to say, but Vidia was right.[14] In retrospect Vidia said: 'People so much clammed up on that journey that after Shirish Patel's introduction to the Maratha landscape and the houses in Bombay which I wrote about, I didn't go on. People were frightened. So then the book became an analytical book. I loved that.'[15]

At a dinner, Vidia saw Ravi Dayal, who had left OUP and formed his own publishing company.

Naipaul had been defeated by the numbering of the houses in Defence Colony. 'You shouldn't worry about India, once you accept the fact that it is a third-rate place. You can't even number your houses logically.' And there were lots of people who took offence to that – 'What do you mean? What about our great religious inheritance and our ancient mathematicians.' Naipaul was quietly

purring away, he was very pleased to take a rise out of people . . .
He had a little group and he was enjoying himself, you know,
whipping India a bit. Some very nice earnest fellow who had been
at Harvard, actually confessed, 'That is interesting. I have lived in
America. I am good at my books. But now that you mention it,
there is something lacking in me. I think I wasn't quite a complete
person, a bit like India' – or something like that. Naipaul looked
very triumphant and called me over. 'Here is this very honest
statement,' and the poor man had to confess it again. And that
irritated me. I thought Naipaul was being a bit merciless.

Dayal noticed that Vidia became awkward when he met old friends
such as himself and Ruth Jhabvala. 'He got slightly embarrassed with
us, he said, "Pat couldn't come." And he casually started to distance
himself. I think he was dodging the prospect of meeting people who
remembered Pat with affection.' Dayal was not impressed by Margaret.
'I remember finding her rather distasteful. She seemed so clueless. Quite
frankly I didn't know what their relationship was. He was extremely
off-hand with her, and it seemed to me that she had no business to be
with him, somehow. I didn't really know what she was doing in India.'
Vidia was seeking a distinct interpretation of India, and was dismissive
of the theories his earlier friends and acquaintances were offering. 'By
then he had perhaps outgrown everyone. People like myself, or Ruth. I
was publishing lots of books. He seemed unfamiliar with my world by
then. He wasn't aware of the ideas that India was generating, a lot of
which I had a hand in publishing: the heavy economists, Amartya Sen,
K.N. Raj, the historians, M.N. Srinivas with his sociology. So much
original work was coming out. Vidia's historical reading of India is a
very old one.'[16]

Vidia made a note of an encounter at another dinner, an example of
his willingness to make huge deductions from casual conversations: 'At
Ashok Khosla's on Tuesday, in the suburb of Delhi known as Vasant
Vihar,' he wrote. 'A woman in yellow on the sofa next to me . . . She
came to India from time to time; but she 'related' only to her family.
Such security. Consider all that that statement implies. India will go on.
My family will go on . . . We talked about the people of Bombay. I
asked whether she saw them. She said of course she did. What was the
most noticeable thing about them? She said, "They were having their
being." ' Another guest piped up and said the inhabitants of Bombay
wore a certain kind of sari. 'How remarkable that neither of the Indians

should have mentioned that the people of industrial Bombay are very small, the men about 5 feet high, considerably smaller than the middle class.' These observations would be played out in his final text, with few alterations. The end of the month found Vidia escaping the city for the countryside, travelling through Jodhpur and Jaisalmer in Rajasthan. '9 p.m. bus for Kota, where arrived this morning 29th at 7.30 & welcomed by official. Now in Circuit House ... Regular halts at tea-stalls.'[17] Next came Haryana – where he had a stormy falling-out with Margaret. 'I had to send her back,' Vidia said later, as if she were an unwanted parcel, 'I had to send her home.'[18] This was to be a pattern on their foreign tours: passion, dispute, dismissal.

Vidia's helpers found him both stimulating and difficult. 'I think he was very much the anthropologist who needed the native informant,' suggested the psychoanalyst Sudhir Kakar, whose theories on Indians and sex were taken up by Vidia in his articles. 'We met several times, and we went for a walk on Janpath. I remember him talking of his early years, saying he had suffered from depression, he was quite open. There was intensity.'[19] Rahul Singh, who acted as a gofer on subsequent trips, said, 'I devoted time and energy because I liked the man and I admired his writing. He was often at a loose end. I brought him to a friend's house who said, "You're a good writer, but Dom Moraes is a better one." Vidia turned his back but laughed about it later ... I noticed that when people spoke to him in Hindi on the street, he would get uncomfortable ... He never paid bills. There were a couple of occasions with others when I expected the bill to be split, but he would make no gesture. He likes to put people on the back foot. Margaret would usually stay in the hotel when we went out. Vidia would lose his cool and get impatient with her. She was a nice person.'[20]

Shirish Patel and his wife Rajani liked Margaret too, and invited her and Vidia to dinner. They admired his books, although not *An Area of Darkness*. 'We thought he was obsessed with excrement. We would tell our children, mind you don't put your foot into a Naipaul ... We suggested that he meet a couple that we knew, and I asked, what did you think of them? And he said, "I met them at a party, I didn't have too much time with them, just a few minutes, but I'll give you a face reading." He then described the personality of each of them, and the relationship, with a precision which was uncanny. I'd known them for fifteen years and this reading – in a few minutes he had come to this assessment of each individual and their relationship. I was completely awestruck.' Shirish Patel took Vidia to the Bombay slums and to a rural development scheme he was running near Pune, and found his report of the trips acute. The four of them arranged to meet in Jaisalmer. Margaret showed Rajani photographs of her children, quietly, afraid it might anger Vidia. She came to the Patels' room saying he had refused repeatedly to take a telephone call from the local bigwig, the Collector, because he did not like the travel arrangements that were being laid on for him. 'The Collector said at the border, at the rest house, an official from the other district will meet you. You take a break, change cars, wash or anything and the other car will take you around. Vidia said, no, if you can't give me a car to go to Kota, I don't want your car. The Collector said, I'm bound by the rules. I cannot take the car out of the district . . . Vidia is not happy, he says, "I'll take the bus." So at night we go to this bus stand and he and Margaret are put on the state transport bus, full of goats, sheep, farmers. It's jam-packed. We had got them front row seats, but . . . Naipaul just took Margaret on that bus. She didn't say anything. We saw Vidia again, but she wasn't there. And we never asked him. I was too intimidated.'[21] Patel and Kakar found that subsequent attempts to contact Vidia over the years were ignored.

Through 1976, spending much of his time alone in Wilsford, Vidia wrote up his conclusions about India. Feeling like Charles Dickens, he worked against the clock, and the articles were published in seven instalments in the *New York Review of Books* over the course of the year. Amalgamated, and with slight alterations, they became a book, *India: A Wounded Civilization*. Vidia focused less on the effects of the Emergency than on an analysis of what made India the way it was. He wrote of the chawls of Bombay, the rise of the Shiv Sena, of bonded labour, caste, rural stagnation and the Naxalite movement, which sought to overthrow the state, of well-intentioned but futile attempts at progress, like the designer who had invented a pair of 'reaping shoes' for peasants. Using public figures who interested him such as the novelist R.K. Narayan, Mahatma Gandhi and Gandhi's imitator Vinoba Bhave, he sought to explain and understand the psyche of India, a formidable task for any writer. At the back of his mind, using the ruined Hindu city of Vijayanagar as his template, was a certainty that India had been incapacitated by the Muslim invasions of earlier centuries. 'I wrote the whole of *A Wounded Civilization* with an idea of the invasion in my mind, in a broad way, the way Indians talk about it as though it's an act of God. I am enraged by the way Indians don't wish to understand their history, I am enraged. I think unless you begin to understand your history, you can't have a new writing.'[22]

When the book was published in 1977, India hands were wheeled out to examine it. Louis Heren in the *Times* deduced that 'a novelist of Mr Naipaul's stature can often define problems quicker and more effectively than a team of economists and other experts from the World Bank.' It was a 'brilliant but emotionally charged polemic', wrote John Grigg in the *Spectator*; and wrong. Grigg thought Gandhianism, far from being the solace of conquered peoples, still represented 'the spirit of liberation from foreign and domestic chains'. Martin Amis in the *New Statesman* judged *India: A Wounded Civilization* a work of accurate pessimism, 'chasteningly right ... a book as compelling as it is distressing to read. Although always measured and elegant, there is nothing writerly in these pages; there is no relish.'[23] A common response came from John Keay in the *Sunday Telegraph*: 'There is a perversity about Mr Naipaul. He travels during the monsoon; he stays in air-conditioned boxes. Wherever he goes ... he finds nothing but squalor, inefficiency, disillusionment, violence, triviality. And perhaps because he is himself of distant Indian extraction, he is scandalized. Another observer, only slightly more compassionate, might find as much to respect, envy and − dare one say it? − enjoy.'[24] Vidia had a marked aversion to foreign Indophiles. In an interview with Elizabeth Hardwick in the *New York Times*, he declared, 'How tired I am of the India-lovers, those who go on about "beautiful India" − the last gasp of a hideous, imperialistic vanity. And the mark of a second-rate mind.'[25]

*

Although Stephen Tennant was too busy being a recluse in the confines of Wilsford Manor to come out and meet Mr and Mrs Naipaul, he would send them occasional letters, written in a florid hand with many underlinings, or perhaps chocolates in a perfumed package, to be delivered by Mrs Skull. Fancying himself as an artist (he did proficient pen and ink drawings, generally of lascivious sailors), Tennant enjoyed having a famous writer living in his grounds, like a Victorian hermit. He would send forth reports on his own important work. 'I am very busy − working on a long Novel & Essays on Theology & Religion also 368 Poems − for a new Volume − called Pagan Earth; these poems are very terse, & dry, only for those who

care for truth; and sincere thought.' On another day, he might be working
on 'a thrilling Play' or busy revising one of his poems such as the as yet
unpublished 'A Plea for the Highbrow':

> Sophists, and Pedants, I deeply love:
> I revere the patient Sage,
> Who, – wingèd as the skies above:
> Exalts Earth's Pilgrimage.

At other times, Stephen Tennant would offer more practical local
advice. 'Do go to Hellier's Garden Centre, in Winchester – it is
pleasant . . . & the Cathedral is most attractive & unique. What a vile
world it is – lazy thinking everywhere: cheap, sordid values. – Bad
books. – But I like the Autumn Beauty.'[26] In response, Pat would send
flowers and polite notes to their landlord: 'Thank you for the pleasure
and the encouragement your poems have given both of us. But me
especially.'[27]

At home in England, Vidia received a letter from Margaret wondering whether they inhabited different worlds. She thought he lived in the
world of his intellect and his writing, which she longed to share, while
she subsisted in a bourgeois nightmare. For all she knew, he might
never even get to read her letter, because when she went to the post
office she was told they had no stamps. It sounded like one of Vidia's
jokes.[28] Moving swiftly, he skittered off to Buenos Aires with the
assistance of the New York Review to write an article, and to be with his
lover. Argentina was more brutalized than ever: Isabelita Perón had
been overthrown and thousands of people were being 'disappeared' by
the military dictatorship, or junta. Andrew Graham-Yooll had gone into
exile, soon to be followed by Bob Cox when a death threat was sent to
his eleven-year-old son. During this and later trips to Argentina, Vidia's
relations with Margaret's family were satisfactory. He met her children
and her former husband, Roy Gooding, and even interviewed him
about the state of the nation: 'Roy was a very intelligent man, with fine
views. He had thought-out views about Argentina.' Only Margaret's
stepfather, Lawrence Smith, remained consistently hostile to Vidia,
believing with good reason that he was treating his daughter badly, and
could not be relied upon to protect her. 'He said I should be shot. I was
very amused. "Shoot the fellow." I think he was using language beyond
his means. I took all of that without any anxiety.' Once when Vidia
visited the family flat with Margaret, her daughter Karin was asleep in

bed. 'She sat up and said, "Naipaul, I love you." I think she was about twelve or thirteen. All that was very nice for me, nice family life.'[29]

Vidia's article opened with a memorably bathetic line: 'In Argentina the killer cars — the cars in which the official gunmen go about their business — are Ford Falcons.' Silence had come, and a 'private war' between the guerrillas and the police and army had turned to a 'public terror'. He compared Argentina to Haiti, a society 'similarly parasitic on a removed civilization'. The walls in BA were whitewashed, the old political slogans removed, and the city that had considered itself European could now only look across the ocean at 'something far away, magically kept going by others . . . an attitude not far removed from that of the politician of a new country who, while fouling his own nest, feathers another abroad, in a land of law.'[30] It was an acidic judgement, but few in Argentina at this time felt anything other than despair about the direction in which the country was heading.

While he was with Margaret in March 1977, Vidia was arrested, an experience he would use in *A Bend in the River*. He described what happened in a later article, removing his lover from the picture:

> One morning I took a bus for the town of Jujuy, in the province to the north, on the border with Bolivia. Just outside Salta the bus stopped, perhaps at the provincial boundary. Indian [Amerindian] policemen in dark-blue uniforms came in and asked for identity papers. Argentines are trained from childhood to carry their papers. I had none; I had left my passport in the hotel in Salta. So — with my gangster's face momentarily of interest to the other passengers, who were mainly Indian — I was taken off the bus, which then went on again.

Vidia was taken to a 'small white concrete shed' then driven to a police post. The men who had brought him there went away. 'Salta began to feel far away. My idea of time changed; I learned to wait. I gave my details once again.' They were far from BA, and telephone calls would not go through. 'I sat on a bench against a smooth plastered wall. I looked at the bush and the light outside. I smoked the pipe I had brought with me. After some time I wanted to use a lavatory. I was told there were no facilities in the little building. The policeman with the smiling eyes pointed to a spot in the bush some distance away: I was to go there. He said, "If you try to run away, I'll shoot you." With the smile, it sounded like a joke; but I knew that it wasn't.' Finally,

V.S. Naipaul was told that he was on no list of suspected guerrillas, and could go.

> The senior policeman said, with something like friendliness, 'It was your pipe that saved you. Did you know that? That pipe made me feel that you really were a foreigner.' It was an African pipe, a small black Tanganyika meerschaum I had bought in Uganda eleven years before: I had noticed that it had interested them. But all the time I had been trusting to my appearance, my broken Spanish, my Spanish accent. It was only now that I understood that to these Indian policemen of the far north Argentina would have been full of foreigners. So it was only at the moment of release, coming out of the slight shock, my disturbed sense of time, that I began to understand how serious my position had been. In the city of Tucumán, just a few days before, I had stood with a small group of townspeople watching policemen with machine guns below their raincoats getting into their unmarked cars. Like a kind of country-house shooting party; but in Tucumán the dirty war was especially dirty, and Tucumán was just to the south of Salta.[31]

Reviewing *The Return of Eva Perón*, a compilation of Vidia's South American essays and pieces on Malik, Zaire and Conrad, Martin Amis wrote in the *New Statesman*: 'In his peripatetic journalism, V.S. Naipaul is turning into the prose-poet of the earth's destitute; he is also becoming world-weary – or Third World-weary, anyway.' Amis saw a formula: 'He begins with a passionately tendentious run-through of a country's recent history, in a style that could be regarded as the demonic opposite of a *Look at Life* documentary (in which, for example, a clotted refugee camp might be described as a hardy workforce crying out to be tapped),' follows it with 'a gloomy cacophony of local voices' and 'settles the hash of whatever indigenous culture happens to be on offer'.[32] Amis wrote later, 'V.S. Naipaul, in his travel books, puts nation states on the psychiatrist's couch and then takes a reading of their mental health.'[33] *The Return of Eva Perón* was introduced by an odd 'author's note', feigning helplessness, as if fiction was obliged to 'offer' itself to the creative writer: 'These pieces . . . bridged a creative gap: from the end of 1970 to the end of 1973 no novel offered itself to me. That perhaps explains the intensity of some of the pieces, and their obsessional nature.'[34] Neal Ascherson in the *Observer* called the essays on South America 'the most brutal and brilliant in this volume', a view shared by Nicholas Shakespeare, who had lived in Argentina during the 1970s: '*The Return of Eva Perón* is possibly the best piece of non-fiction he has written.'[35] Naipaul himself regarded his essays on Argentina as 'among the most important things I've done'.[36] According to David Pryce-Jones, Vidia had fatally undermined postcolonial pieties: 'Challenging guilt in the name of truth-telling, Naipaul has changed the recent climate of opinion as no other English-language writer has done.'[37] In the *New York Review*, Joan Didion commented on his changing reputation: 'It is hard not to note a certain turning in the air when V.S. Naipaul is mentioned, a hint of taint, a suggestion of favor about to go moot ... One catches the construction "brilliant but": brilliant but obsessive, brilliant but reductive ... Increasingly now he is consigned to this role of the special case, the victim of a unique cultural warp, the outsider obsessed (notice the vogue for "obsessive" as a dismissive adjective) by disgust for his colonial origins, the reductive (ditto "reductive") wog with a taste for the high table.'[38]

With his lover, he travelled to Caracas for the summer, and to the island of Margarita between the South American mainland and Trinidad, where they were joined by Kamla. Vidia located Poker or 'Bogart' ('What happening there, Bogart?') who kept a little shop, an encounter he would describe in 'Prologue to an Autobiography'. One day in Venezuela, Margaret turned to Vidia and said a sentence which stuck in his mind, an explanation for infatuation: 'Being with you is like always being in a film.'[39]

They visited Trinidad (which had recently became a republic under a new constitution arising from a report produced by, among others, the eminent lawyer Solomon Lutchman: a president would be elected by parliament, the voting age lowered to eighteen and structural political changes introduced). The trip was not a success. When Vidia and Margaret arrived at the airport in Port of Spain, they were greeted by Kamla, who told them that nobody in the family wanted to have them in their house, and they would have to stay at her own rented property. She had recently separated from Harry and left Jamaica, and was building a house on a plot of land given to her by Ma in Charlieville. Kamla said later that her fifteen-year-old-son Ved had advised her on protocol. 'He said, put them to sleep in one room because they must be sleeping together anyway. So they stayed with us.' Kamla took an elder sisterly dislike to Margaret, not helped by her brother's attitude to his mistress. 'Vidia told me that Margaret had a vocabulary of only fifty

words . . . I didn't see anything in Margaret to be quite honest. I didn't
see anything that Vidia would fall for. I never really took to Margaret.
She complained about Pat too much. My loyalty was to Pat. And then
Margaret had left all her children – she had three children – and I
couldn't personally understand that. Leave your husband, that's fine
enough, that doesn't bother me. But leave your three children? Oh, no.
I couldn't do that.'[40] Mira, living in America with her husband the
cancer specialist, blamed Margaret for Vidia's growing hostility to his
family. 'I personally feel that the change came about when he began
having an affair with the Argentinian woman, because his life took a
new turn. There was the wife whom we all knew and got on well with,
then there was the woman, and there was something to hide. Nobody
told me about this Margaret – her name was Margaret? – for years and
years. I was totally shocked when I discovered it.'[41]

Savi remembered coming to Kamla's house to see Margaret and
Vidia. 'Margaret said to me, "Why did you not want us to stay with
you?" And I said, "Because it would be wrong in my children's eyes.
Their only aunt is Auntie Pat." Vidia didn't speak at all.' According to
Savi, she had in fact never made a prohibition on Margaret entering her
house, only on staying there, and Kamla made the situation worse by
saying there was a ban. Ma refused to meet Margaret, and an altercation
followed. The upshot was a lasting family rupture: except for Kamla,
Vidia barely spoke to his sisters or to his mother for the next decade.
Kamla's relationship with Savi was affected too. 'It was the year my
mother went to England, and I think Vidia had my mother to tea in the
apartment alone. He did not invite me, or my son, and I know my
mother never had an invitation from Vidia after that. Never to England.
She went there to visit Nella. My mother was always deeply hurt by
this, and one of the good things about my mother is I don't think she
ever put the blame on Pat. I guess she realized her son was different
[from other people]. I don't think she wanted to be abused by him.'[42]
According to Droapatie's nephew Suren, who gave her occasional
financial support, 'She never spoke about Vidia, but was hurt that her
son had abandoned her.'[43] Vidia interpreted this debacle in his own
distinctive way: 'I was letting them meet Margaret as a kind of special
favour, because of her importance to me . . . I took Margaret to Nepaul
Street. My mother was with Ma'am, a black woman who told her
fortune every few days. My mother refused to look at Margaret. We

went away. Sati wouldn't meet her either. I broke completely with all of them, to my great relief.'[44]

While he was in Trinidad, Vidia spoke to the pupils of Fatima College, a boys' secondary school. An amateur film of the seminar shows V.S. Naipaul wearing a roll-neck sweater, sitting with tightly crossed legs before an old-style microphone, puffing on his pipe, looking camp and uneasy, listening to inept questions from teachers and students. He was determinedly confrontational, a style he would repeat in his occasional public appearances in the West Indies over coming years. Was *The Middle Passage* out of date? No. He had looked at it a few days earlier, and been 'quite frightened by my own percipience'. Did he like Trinidad's steel bands? 'I don't like noise.' Was his novel based on guerrilla activity in Trinidad? 'No, no, no, no, no, no, no, no, no, no, no, no: the word is used ironically.' Dripping with sarcasm, he said, 'When I was a child, the word "black" was an insult. I think people liked to be called "coloured". The word "African" was an insult. Now of course, "black" is a very popular word, it is the accepted word. It has been a great revolution.' Exasperated, Vidia turns to a boy in the audience and asks whether *A House for Mr Biswas* had chimed with his own experiences of school. There is no reply. A teacher intervenes: 'The problem is that he is Venezuelan.' Vidia tries again: 'I would like people to try to come to grips with the emptiness of this society, try to understand the kind of bastard culture we inhabit, how we are all cut off from our ancestral roots. We've had a kind of colonial melange here, which deprives people of a past . . . Don't give way to despair, or find political slogans. Try to face that.' The more forceful and fervent V.S. Naipaul becomes, the more baffled his multi-ethnic young audience look.[45]

Margaret left Trinidad to stay with her sister, Diana, in London and complained to Vidia afterwards that during the flight she had received the attentions of what she termed an obnoxious coon, handsome and of mixed blood, who had failed to persuade her to sit beside him. By November, after another series of angry exchanges, she decided finally to bring their relationship to a close. She had enjoyed it while it lasted, and she wanted Vidia to remember it as an experience of great passion and love. She looked presciently into the future: Margaret predicted that he would become more famous, while she would finish up in a bed-sit. People had often told her that Vidia was offering her no security at all for the future, and she could find no good reason to think otherwise. She felt she had no alternative but to move on, since she was unable to please him in so many ways. Everybody, all his family including Savi, Kamla and most of all 'P' wanted her to get out of his life, and she knew that in practice she was unlikely ever to spend more than a few months with him. He might complain that she had given him an ultimatum, but in fact he was the one who had given her an ultimatum – to tolerate whatever he commanded. She told him calmly that if she was forced to depend on him for anything at all, she might be left naked and starving.[46]

*

In the early autumn of 1977, Vidia had an 'illumination' for a new book – 'his theme, the paradox of civilisation' – and needed Pat's help in order to write it.[47] Over the previous two years, they had seen little of each other. He might telephone his wife occasionally to say he had 'dreams he is being hanged' or that he was having trouble with his work. This time, Vidia said he would only be able to proceed if he had her physical presence, and Pat was flattered to be wanted. Bored by life and obsessed by her husband's writing, she returned to Wilsford; it was her sacrifice, her destiny, the life of her choice. Vidia worked at odd hours, often into the night, sleeping until midday. He might leave her a little note, scribbled on an envelope: 'Patsy Please let me sleep Still awake at 2.15.'[48] He had put aside a plan to write an autobiography, finding the idea too difficult to face. Pat recorded disparate phrases he was now throwing out: 'Scattered people looking for somewhere to go . . . Africa . . . Men as prey – the Indians in London, lost, living at the end of a civilisation, blind . . . He said that he was feeling very fertile. He wants to write the draft quickly . . . Told me he can only write with me around. I create an aura. I feel it is so undeserved.'

'Full of admiration,' Vidia read Tolstoy's *Haji Murad* and *The Cossacks*, finding that reading was becoming a form of thinking, a way of shaping his unwritten, Conradian novel. One night shortly after his forty-fifth birthday, the idea was hatched. He had been watching the Last Night of the Proms on television, and said to Pat, 'I want to be alone with my thoughts.' Half an hour later she went into his room. He told her that the book would open with the lines: 'My family come from the east coast. Africa was at our backs. We are Indian ocean people.' Then he outlined to his wife the plot and principal characters of the story that would become *A Bend in the River*. 'I wondered and asked him, "You mean you can come in here for half an hour and think all that out?" He is sitting so quiet writing it down.' This would be V.S. Naipaul's greatest novel, with the conceivable exception of *A House for Mr Biswas*, a book which brought together all his experience and the uniqueness of his perspective, a late twentieth-century global narrative that could have been written by no one else.

It was softer in tone than the books which preceded it. Narrated in the first person by Salim, who has come from the coast to a French-speaking state in the centre of Africa to purchase a shop, it traces his relations with a network of characters: his servant Metty, descended from slaves, Indar, his childhood friend, Zabeth, a river trader and sorceress, and her son Ferdinand, who has high status in the new dispensation, Father Huismans, a priest with a deep respect for Africa who gets beheaded, Raymond, a white academic and promoter of the ruler's tyranny, and his wife Yvette, with whom Salim has a violent love affair. The physical setting of the book is evoked beautifully, whether at the river docks in Africa ('damp-haired young monkeys, full of misery, tethered tightly around their narrow waists and nibbling at peanuts and banana skin and mango skin, but nibbling without relish, as though they knew that they themselves were soon to be eaten'), or in London, or in the foreigners' campus, the Domain, where people listen to Joan Baez records: 'It was make-believe – I never doubted that. You couldn't listen to sweet songs about injustice unless you expected justice and received it much of the time.'[49] Vidia's spark for the novel originated in a chance encounter in Kisangani. His plane had been taken out of service, and he found himself at the airport talking to a young Indian man. 'The hotels were closed because Mobutu was in town, and he said come and sleep at my flat. Everything that happened over the next two days, I used in *A Bend in the River*. He was a businessman running a shop, and his "Jeeves" talked a lot of rubbish about going to Canada. He told me about his private life, that there was a woman, and took me to look at her house. She was a Vietnamese woman; that disappears in my narrative. We can call him Salim. The essence of the book is: what is this man doing here?'[50] Some personalities – Zabeth, for instance – owe something to the Trinidadians of Vidia's childhood. 'I combined my 1975 trip to the Congo with my knowledge of black people from Trinidad. I could think myself into an understanding of who they are.'[51]

By October, Pat and Vidia's sexual relationship had rekindled, and she relished the opportunity to show her care and devotion. They would go for walks along the banks of the River Avon, parts of which were choked with weeds, the chalk streams of Wiltshire provoking ideas for a novel set near a wide expanse of water in the heart of Africa. One afternoon, Vidia raced back from the river to continue working, but when he got home he felt tired and lay down. 'At 5.00 I took his shoes off (protest – he likes the weight) and wrapped his feet up. He has started typing again.' Later, 'He wrote like an angel: the arrival of Methi [later Metty, named for Metti, the Petit Valley overseer], after the revolution on the coast.' Within days, the rediscovery of tranquillity was upset when Pat copied out his business accounts in black ink rather than red: 'so more abuse and humiliation.' Even the arrival of Shiva, Jenny and their young son Tarun for the day could not dent his mood of literary optimism. Vidia sat down to read the manuscript of Shiva's new book *North of South*, and made 'correction after correction, big and small . . . In the evening Vidia told me how much he loved Sewan, always had, but Sewan rejected him when he first came to England.' His brother remained on his mind. Vidia telephoned him to give instructions on the craft of the writer: 'It is not the writer's business to complain but to explore. Urges him to read *Master and Man*, by Tolstoy, and the early English writers.'

Vidia found he was writing with greater fluency than he had for many years. By Christmas he had completed 40,000 words, and was holding the whole book in his head. *A Bend in the River* was a mature work of the imagination rather than disguised autobiography; it was the product of assimilated experience. Although it contained much that was observed or personal – Africa, Margaret – his travels and memories were a starting point for invention. The book was the work of a middle-aged novelist marked by experience but in full command of his creative powers. It lacked the anger of *Guerrillas* or *India: A Wounded Civilization*: as one character says, 'It isn't that there's no right and wrong here. There's no right.'[52] As Vidia continued, his mood swung back and forth, with Pat taking the strain. Despite being thin, she worried she was greedy, lazy, clumsy, incompetent. 'Whatever the truth, I am not much good to anyone and Vidia is probably, almost certainly, right when he says I have nothing to offer him.' But without her, he insisted he could not continue. Savi noticed that Pat and Vidia had become obsessed by food. 'She got thinner and thinner and it was as though both of them decided that carbohydrates were not to be eaten at all. They got this compulsive behaviour, and even at lunch, Vido would say to me, "You may leave the potato." It wasn't up to him whether I had it or not. It was there on my plate. Vidia was obsessed that his thighs were too fat. "These Capildeo thighs" he called them.'[53]

Through the months it took to write *A Bend in the River*, Pat recorded each step of her husband's progress. Paul Theroux telephoned to say he was going to South America, which made Vidia angry, although 'the situation was saved by Paul's sweetness. He said something to Paul about [Menachem] Begin, and I am sure Paul must have been comforting, but he did not go the whole hog about the Jews destroying the West, or Western culture.' This was a rare instance of anti-Semitism in Vidia's conversation.

When he reached the middle of the book, Indar (who was called Indrajit in the first draft) was reintroduced to the plot. ' "Indrajit will be me." . . . Every character . . . has a narrative function.' A British-educated Indian from the east coast of Africa, Indar was able to say and see things that are hidden from the other characters. He tells a story. Turned down for a job at India House, he meets an American man at a lunch party who 'spoke of Africa as though Africa was a sick child and he was the parent.' He gives Indar a job with a foundation, 'using the surplus wealth of the western world to protect that world'. In a crucial passage, speaking to his friend Salim, Indar outlines his – or Vidia's – philosophy. As he comes from a community of deracinated Indians, overlooked by history, he has a rare opportunity to make his own way in the world:

> I'm a lucky man. I carry the world within me. You see, Salim, in this world beggars are the only people who can be choosers. Everyone else has his side chosen for him. I can choose. The world is a rich place. It all depends on what you choose in it. You can be sentimental and embrace the idea of your own defeat. You can be an Indian diplomat and always be on the losing side. It's like banking . . . The Rothschilds are what they are because they chose Europe at the right time. The other Jews, just as talented, who went to bank for the Ottoman Empire, in Turkey or Egypt or wherever, didn't do so well. Nobody knows their names. And that's what we've been doing for centuries. We've been clinging to the idea of defeat and forgetting that we are men like everybody else. We've been choosing the wrong side. I'm tired of being on the losing side. I don't want to pass. I know exactly who I am and where I stand in the world. But now I want to win and win and win.[54]

Immediately after writing this paragraph, Vidia felt exhausted, but knew there was more to come. He sat hunched in a chair 'taking the odd pinch of snuff' and dictated to Pat. 'I was also, with my hurrying pen, conscious of the mounting excitement towards the end,' she recorded, 'and I wanted to show this and my understanding by reading dramatically.' A few days later, she helped him again. 'Cary Welch [an expert on Indian art] and his wife Edith came with Tony and Violet Powell. Vidia was very helpful and attentive at table. Quite soon after they had gone, with wine headache and everything, Vidia began dictating to me and made the transition from Indrajit's story back to the bend in the river . . . The imaginative flight, the reintroduction of the water hyacinth came to him as he was dictating . . . His expression, while he was thinking and dictating, most of the time with eyes closed, changed about three times, like weather. To begin with, he was concentrating, intent, brow knitted. Then half-way through, his face looked very serene. Finally fairly firm and powerful . . . It was a terrible life writers lead, he said, quite comfortably, afterwards.'

Next he wanted to write about Yvette and Salim. 'Last night, in the kitchen while I was cooking, he outlined the next stage: the beginning of the affair. He said he was "nervous" of the sex. I said perhaps he did not need to write sex scenes but he said "I want to." He told me he must be "left to myself", be very private, as he will be "embarrassed".' Avoiding any hint of pornography, he wrote truthfully about sex for the first time, drawing on what he had learned with Margaret: '[L]ike many men who use brothels alone, I had grown to think of myself as feeble, critically disadvantaged.' With Yvette, 'the sexual act became for me an extraordinary novelty, a new kind of fulfilment, continuously new . . . I was full of the wonder of what had befallen me. And awakening from minute to minute to the depth of my satisfactions, I began to be aware of my immense previous deprivation. It was like discovering a great, unappeasable hunger in myself.'[55]

The weather was turning cold; for two days the house was snowed in and the milkman could not reach them to deliver milk. Wearing coats and gumboots, Pat and Vidia walked down to the river. 'He waded to the bank and walked along it a little way in his Kenya sheepskin coat, warm, pinkish in colour. He came back, wading, looking down as he put each foot forward, an expression of pure, quiet happiness on his face.' This version of pastoral could not last long. The writing got stuck. Vidia took up a book on the mystical sage Swami Vivekananda, and 'broke off to make hostile comments about his own mother — "I always hated her" (which is absolutely untrue).' Events from outside intruded. 'Vidia is very excited about the Israeli invasion of Lebanon.' Pat was starting to irritate him, and his temper erupted even as he returned to writing. A summons to see local friends was accepted, which was a mistake. 'On Saturday evening we had drinks with the Mitchells . . . the next day he began making a lot of fuss: shouldn't have got to know them, etc. Horrified by present-day gentry, the gentry of our valley. "England is dead." He has been talking a lot about parasitism – "I'm waiting to meet someone who makes something."' Incorporating himself into the person of Mobutu, the 'Big Man' in the book, he sent Pat away. 'He has been writing the President's speech,' she noted. 'I have behaved foolishly all day and have ruined every last relationship I have. I have agreed to go back to London after the weekend. Vidia says he can't stand my eccentricity any more and I will destroy him.' Alone in Wilsford, Vidia was excited and distracted by the arrival of occasional letters from Margaret in Buenos Aires, saying she was bored. She had met a man whose estate adjoined the police station where they had been arrested near Salta, and what was more he turned out to be a friend of the local superintendent. If only she had known him at the time! She had been having dreams about Vido, including one where she was taking a shower and he came in feeling enraged and handled her suitably roughly.[56]

In the spring of 1978, Vidia and Pat went together to watch Luis Buñuel's film *That Obscure Object of Desire* in London. Afterwards he returned to Wiltshire alone and telephoned her. 'He has written the violent scene with Yvette. "Doesn't it speak of passion," he said, when he had read it, "of Salim's pain." I had found it shocking. Did not have anything to say . . . He laughed afterwards and said that seeing the Buñuel had helped really. "But it is better than the Buñuel." Discussing the shocking character of the scene he said that he had worked carefully – using the passive tense – "she was hit" – "I hit her" would be to make Salim just a tough man.' The scene drew directly on his violence towards Margaret in Wilsford in the fall of 1974.

Pat's diary is a chronicle, but it is also an abdication, a means of avoidance. It is, like the voice, passive. Nowhere does Pat ask herself to what extent Vidia's writing is drawn from life, and specifically from his life with Margaret. Her diary is a record of a kind of blankness. The nature of their relationship meant that she would never ask Vidia anything of this kind directly, and preferred not to consider it, even if at some level she 'knew' what he was drawing on. If she ever looked for or looked at his love letters and erotic photographs, there is no record of it in her diary. She appears to have been convinced by the

explanations he offered, for instance by his assertion that Salim's
violence towards Yvette was a symptom of love, or that his use of the
passive prevented Salim from seeming 'a tough man'. In fact, it arose
from Vidia's opinion that he, as much as Margaret, was the victim of
his violence: he had been helpless in the face of his own justified anger
at his lover's infidelity with an Argentine banker. Despite this attempt
to shift the blame, Vidia hated the way in which he had behaved, seeing
it as a personal failing and a cultural stigma: 'I despise it passionately,
despise it because it is very much an Indian failing. When I say Indian,
I mean our community. And it's always a sign of defeated people, isn't
it? I think this thing about beating your wife is more Indian than Negro
. . . My father's stories deal with wife-beating and as it were, he gives it
an Indian ancestry, a village ancestry.'[57]

Returning to Wiltshire from London, Pat found 'Vidia's door was
shut and he was very silent. A large, red fire was burning in the sitting-
room. Shortly afterwards he drew me into his room to read the rest of
the violent scene with Yvette. Looking back, I recognise the artistry.
>Vidia had to point out some of this, the folds in the sheet, the
magazine falling; he also helped me by saying that Salim obviously
loved her (Vidia is so proud of never using the word love) enabling me
to understand this passion, this love.< At the end I did not register, or
exhibit, excitement or approval. I expressed some concern at the
violence. (I did not say so, but the reiteration of the blows and, to a
lesser extent, the spittle was foremost in my mind.) . . . I was a spectator
of the writing, of his exhilaration, looking back now, of his look of
triumph.' Pat believed or accepted Vidia's analysis of these scenes.
Later, when a reviewer suggested the treatment of sex in *A Bend in the
River* was unbalanced and peculiar, Pat wrote but did not send a letter
in response: 'Sex and race are very difficult. They are the topics of our
age. Each of us has to wrestle with them.' She defended her husband's
depictions of sexual violence. 'You were wrong I think to compare the
two scenes in *Bend* with the two similar scenes in *Guerrillas*. They are
not identical. I would like to point out one thing. Jane threw down the
challenge. She humiliated Jimmy at the start, women have this urge
sometimes – it can be a dangerous thing to do . . . But perhaps I have
been too close to this book, too familiar with it to read it objectively.'[58]

As winter turned to spring, she continued to record Vidia's remarks
and the progress of the book. 'He spoke of his life lacking savour and
grieved that he had never treated that woman well. Had never been

with her more than three weeks, had sent her away, had rejected a very "pure affection".' Sometimes he needed Pat to help him with his work, a job she relished, regardless of the time of night: 'He called me into his room at about 1.0 (I was falling asleep, without Mandrax) to take it down. I made him porridge. Then there was further quarrelling; then he looked at it again and spoke some of the versions again ... We finally separated fairly calmly at 3.0 or after.' Finally, in May 1978, 'At about 12.30 last night he called me in and spoke the end of the book. It took an hour to an hour and a half.' Once he had said the words out loud, he was ready to write them, nearly verbatim. The material seemed to be given to him from nowhere. 'He made the remark, which he had made before, that when "the work is good I am not responsible."' This was how *A Bend in the River* closed:

> The sky hazed over, and the sinking sun showed orange and was reflected in a broken golden line in the muddy water. Then we sailed into a golden glow ... Water hyacinths pushed up in the narrow space between the steamer and the barge. We went on. Darkness fell. It was in this darkness that abruptly, with many loud noises, we stopped ... The searchlight lit up the barge passengers who, behind bars and wire-guards, as yet scarcely seemed to understand that they were adrift. Then there were gunshots. The searchlight was turned off; the barge was no longer to be seen. The steamer started up again and moved without lights down the river, away from the area of battle. The air would have been full of moths and flying insects. The searchlight, while it was on, had shown thousands, white in the white light.[59]

Now Vidia decided to go and live in the USA, with Margaret.

CHAPTER TWENTY-TWO

A HOUSE FOR MR NAIPAUL

VIDIA WAS RISING. As people and ideas shifted between countries in a way they had not done at previous points in human history, an author who took the world as his subject was no longer impossible. He could carve out a space for himself as a new sort of writer, claiming to come from a place without history, a mere dot on the map. *Guerrillas* had proved an unexpected success in America, and Francis Ford Coppola wanted to turn it into a film. Within academia, non-white voices were sought, even if V.S. Naipaul fell into no standard postcolonial category. Letters and invitations came. Would he like the Neustadt International Prize for Literature, for which he had been nominated by Derek Walcott? Might he speak to the Cambridge Union? Did he wish to become a Regents' Professor at Berkeley? Would he deign to open a conference at the University of the West Indies? Was he ready to become a Knight of Mark Twain? Would he be a writer-in-residence at the University of Western Australia?

Wishing to spend time in a different place and to attempt living with Margaret for the first time, Vidia took up an invitation from Phyllis Rose of Wesleyan University's English Department. Rose flew to London to meet him: starting in September 1978, he would spend an academic year teaching courses in creative writing and literature and 'alien cultures' at the small, private liberal arts college in Middletown, Connecticut, in exchange for $30,000. The university arranged for him to rent a house of glass and weathered cedar from a philosophy professor, Victor Gourevitch. 'They are very good to me here, leaving me absolutely alone,' he wrote in a letter in October.[1]

'He said as soon as he got off the bus in Middletown, he knew he'd made a mistake,' Rose recalled. 'It's an old New England mill town, semi-derelict in parts. I do think it was only his sense of honour that kept him there to the end of the year. The courses he taught were brilliantly inventive. He started out tremendously popular – until the first paper was due. When the work was not on time, he got furious in a way which American students are not accustomed to: "You are like officials in the Congo. You are corrupt." He was killing sacred cows left and right in those courses, saying Isak Dinesen – she had just been discovered, and this was in the first wave of feminist criticism – didn't know anything about Africa, and *Out of Africa* was trash. The English Department wanted him as a representative of the Third World, and Vidia couldn't be anything less like that.'[2] Students who thought they might approach him for Third Worldly advice were mistaken. The mother of one Alvin Lee Peters wrote to complain: young Alvin was preparing to go to India to stay with a family 'as a part of the program sponsored by the Experiment in International Living ... With that background I hope that you can understand my astonishment, my bewilderment and my growing anger when I learned that you refused to talk to my son even though he is a Wesleyan student, had just read your book, and is on his way to India. Perhaps there is a rational explanation for the brush-off you gave a student interested in your work and your country. If so, I would be interested in knowing what it is.'[3] Phyllis Rose thought 'the students were mainly liberal or left, from middle-class professional families, proud of their slovenly dress and progressive ideas' and ill-equipped to cope with Vidia's acerbic responses to their conventional statements. The *Sunday Telegraph Magazine* reported him saying: 'I would take poison rather than do this for a living ... I thought I'd meet lots of people who passionately wanted to write. I was shocked to find some take the course in the same way as basketwork or karate.'[4]

The anonymous teaching evaluations at the end of the year show that students tended to either love or hate V.S. Naipaul. 'This is nothing short of a brilliant, witty man,' wrote one. 'I can think of almost no praise too strong for Mr Naipaul,' wrote another. 'He stimulated more interest in me and more honest appreciation of literature than anyone else I have worked with ... I will remember this course and this year with very fond and brilliant memories because of Vidia's presence and his constantly percolating imagination,' wrote a third. From another direction, a graduate wrote: 'He had no office hours and tended to say things such as, "Well, I only have to spend 2 hours a week with students, so goodbye." He was detrimental even to the enthusiasm of some of my classmates and myself ... He was, simply, the worst, most close-minded, inconsiderate, uninteresting and incompetent professor I have ever met.' Another said he favoured only a chosen few. 'Mr

Naipaul, lacking the professional objectivity of a teacher, neglected most of us – and considering how important our writing is to us – hurt us.' Five people who failed the course wrote a joint letter demanding a re-mark: 'In the context of this university, and of academe in general, these grades reflect work and performance of extremely low caliber.' The students who liked him were more than content: 'Mr Naipaul is not a usual teacher, and cannot be evaluated in the usual ways . . . It has been an outstanding honor and experience, both to see a great mind at work and to learn how to see in a different way.'[5]

Living with Margaret in this alien setting did not go smoothly. She became bored, and he became irritable. Vidia taught classes, wrote about Indian art for the *New York Review* and edited the proofs of *A Bend in the River*. When Kamla read the novel, she wrote to him, 'It must be your best book. In fact, it must be one of the best books I have ever read.' She kept him in touch with news from home: 'More of Frederick Street has been burnt down. Fires are in fact, a weekly occurrence. Anti-Indian slogans are also very much in evidence. Walls in Valsayn are now scrawled with suggestions about starting the dougla [African-Indian] race.'[6] Once a week Vidia took horse-riding lessons, convinced they would be good for him. 'I wonder how you're finding the college crowd,' wrote Paul Theroux from London. 'Am I alone in finding American students unteachable – sweet, yes, but unteachable. You ought to do your Makerere thing: examine handwriting, urge creative writing students to get into cash crops . . . if there is anything I can do for you here or there, please let me know.'[7]

Vidia could not see his way to another novel. 'I only have ten years left,' he told Phyllis Rose, convinced his writing life was coming to an end. She gave a party, attended by Vidia and Margaret: 'I had a buffet dinner, made beef stroganoff and a special kind of fish for him. He says, "I think the fish was not prepared with as much care as the beef" . . . I was quite fond of Margaret. I thought she lived on a grand scale and was smart and funny. She didn't talk about books; we had household, gossipy talks.'[8] Vidia and Margaret got to know two of the more talented Wesleyan students, Jeff Hush and Banning Eyre. In a reminiscence, Eyre described Vidia as a dandyish figure, consciously at odds with the university. At his first class, 'He wore grey flannels, a dark blue blazer, and heavy black-rimmed sunglasses for which he quickly substituted reading glasses once he was seated. He spoke in a resonant British accent, and I thought his manner elegant and refined. From time to time, he paused and delicately inhaled some Fribourg & Treyer snuff off a little silver spoon. And then his whole face would smile. Controlled delight.'⁹ After Vidia had gone, Phyllis Rose wrote:

> Did you see the write-up about you in TIME, the one that ended with a marvellous statement from you about "caste arrogance" and people in preppy clothes with empty heads being more dangerous to America than oil embargoes? Well, the radical students had it reproduced in a very elegant little folder and passed them out at commencement as though they were programs . . . And everywhere I went on the east coast around that time, people were quoting you.¹⁰

Middletown was close enough to New York for Vidia and Margaret to spend weekends at the Algonquin Hotel. For a longer period, with the assistance of the ubiquitous Bob Silvers, they borrowed the East 75th Street brownstone apartment of John Richardson, a homosexual art critic who ran Christie's in America. 'Vidia's life in New York revolved very much around Bob, who admired him and was tremendously generous to his writers,' Richardson recalled. 'Margaret seemed to be having a rough time of it. I slightly had the feeling she enjoyed that, this rather broken-down Argentinian lady. I was fascinated by Vidia, but I didn't take to him. He was so discontented within himself, and he seemed to think he was doing me an honour by occupying my apartment . . . I felt he enjoyed the unorthodoxy of gay men; he was at ease with them because he was self-invented. He had some identification with the gay man as an outsider.'¹¹ Vidia found Richardson to be part of a wilder scene than he was used to in Middletown or Wilsford. One night as he and Margaret lay in bed at the apartment, the telephone rang. A voice said, 'John? John! Master! I am coming over now.' 'No, no,' replied V.S. Naipaul. 'I think there has been a misunderstanding.'

When *A Bend in the River* was published, journalists attempted to fathom the author, 'an elusive man' who had 'somehow managed to remain an enigma'.¹² His income was still not keeping pace with his status, although at $25,000 his advance on royalties from Knopf was higher than it had been before. When a *New York Times* columnist tried to contact Vidia, Diana Athill wrote back, 'I'm afraid we have the strictest instructions from Mr Naipaul not to divulge his address to anyone under any circumstances.'¹³ No longer was he a calypso writer or a curiosity from London: he was a world-class novelist. There was no going back. Saul Bellow sought to meet him. Letters arrived from around the globe. 'I love you because you are so mean . . . You are better than Elvis. (Meaner, too),' wrote Eve Babitz, a fellow Knopf author.[14] A telegram came from Deutsch: 'YOURE 99 PERCENT CERTAIN TO WIN BOOKER PRIZE AND THINK YOU SHOULD MAKE YOURSELF AVAILABLE FOR SOME TELE-PHONED COMMENT TO BBC.'[15] But Vidia did not win the Booker; it was awarded by compromise to Penelope Fitzgerald's *Offshore*, and when he was offered the James Tait Black Memorial Prize and the Royal Society of Literature's Winifred Holtby Award, he turned them both down.[16]

'For sheer abundance of talent, there can hardly be a writer alive who surpasses V.S. Naipaul,' wrote Irving Howe in the *New York Times Book Review*. 'Naipaul is considered in Europe to be one of the living masters of English prose. Deservedly,' concluded Nelson Algren in the *Chicago Tribune*. 'There are not many writers today who see so steadily and so far,' said Bernard Levin in the *Sunday Times*. The *Evening Standard* located Arthur Calder Marshall, now in his seventies, who praised *A Bend in the River* as 'an astonishing double achievement' that revealed more about Africa than 'any ponderous work of non-fiction . . . I can think of no other novelist who could have written this book.' In the *Spectator*, Richard West made a claim that would be shared by many reviewers: Naipaul had written 'one of those books that make you question many assumptions about the world today.' In 2004, the author Alexandra Fuller wrote: 'I am not of the limited and limiting school that supposes only black Africans can write about Africa . . . But you have to be willing to be fresh and above all honest about the places which exist on this continent in order not to sound like a stuffed Victorian. V.S. Naipaul did it with chilling accuracy in *A Bend in the River*.'[17]

Assumptions were being questioned. A rising disillusion with the postcolonial project in many countries led to Vidia being projected as the voice of truth, the scourge who by virtue of his ethnicity and his intellect could see things that others were seeking to disguise. Why were so many African countries ruled by thieves? Why was Iran having an Islamist revolution? What had become of the gracious optimism of the 1960s and 1970s? Where was Black Power now? Perhaps V.S. Naipaul was right when he wrote the terrifying opening sentence of *A Bend in the River*: 'The world is what it is; men who are nothing, who allow themselves to become nothing, have no place in it.'[18] As corrected liberals began to praise Vidia's vision, others tried to strike him down. Derek Walcott took a bite out of him in a lecture, which started a running antagonism, and Edward Said, whose recent book *Orientalism* had crystallized a prevailing intellectual trend which held that Western perceptions of the Orient were based on prejudice and misconception, complained he was dismissing all 'national liberation movements' as 'fraudulent public relations gimmicks' and 'half native impotence . . . He prefers to indict guerrillas for their pretensions rather than indict the imperialism that drove them to insurrection.'[19] In academic circles in particular, Vidia began to be presented as indefensible, even while his books were put on college reading lists. Banning Eyre remembered how at Wesleyan, 'V.S. Naipaul became widely known as a terrible ogre: a sexist, a racist, a snob — people knew him as these without even knowing he was a famous novelist.'[20] Vidia's response to the growth in his reputation as a villain was to stoke it. Whenever he got the chance in an interview, he would denounce something or somebody; in a Caribbean symbiosis, the subtler and more intense his writing grew over the years, the more throwaway his public remarks would become. In a much quoted comment, when asked to explain the symbolism of the bindi (the coloured dot worn on the forehead of Indian women) he said, 'The dot means: my head is empty.'[21]

In 1980, *Newsweek* put him on the cover with the headline 'The Master of the Novel'. Sitting in the middle of a field holding a stick, a jacket slung over his shoulder, V.S. Naipaul glared out at the world. 'Such is the screen that Naipaul erects around his life that few people know that he is married — to a former fellow Oxford student, Patricia Hale.' He was an 'East Indian Brahmin raised in Trinidad . . . a creative craftsman of such surpassing talent that Britain's leading literary critic, V.S. Pritchett, calls him "the greatest living writer in the English language".' In the opinion of *Newsweek*, 'He is a strong contender for this year's Nobel Prize in Literature.' The tone of the profile and accompanying material was indicative of the uncertainty in the press response to Vidia, and his own willingness to shift between pro-fundity and picong. Interviewed back in Wiltshire, he played the fool: 'In England people are very proud of being very stupid. A great price is being paid here now for the cult of stupidity and idleness . . . Liv-ing here has been a kind of castration, really.' Then he changed gear, dismissing the notion of 'the Third World' as a cliché. 'What disheartens me is that there are certain cultures where people are saying, "Cut yourselves off. Go back to what you were." There is nothing to replace the universal civilization they are rejecting. The Arabs, the Muslims, some Africans are doing this. I think it's a disaster. The great Arab civilization of the seventh to twelfth centuries was the world's most eclectic civilization. It wasn't closed to outside influences. It was endlessly incorporating the art of Persia, the mathematics of India, what remained of the philosophy of Greece. The mistake of Western vanity is to think that the universal civilization that exists now is a purer racial one. It's not the preserve of one race, one country, but has been fed by many.'[22] As in other profiles of Vidia at this time, Paul Theroux was quoted in *Newsweek* as an admiring defender and long-time friend. On the BBC in the same year, Theroux declared, 'He's proud, dignified, very funny . . . The embodiment of all those things is being a Brahmin. You must never forget that he's a Brahmin.'[23]

*

While he was at Wesleyan, drumming his heels in Professor Gourevitch's house, Vidia had spent time watching television. He was fascinated by the stirrings of the Iranian revolution, and in particular by speeches given by exiled clerics calling for the overthrow of the Shah. He believed they were lying, and that what they really wanted was not a revolution, but to kill their opponents and establish a theocratic state. 'What with all the back to Islam movement and the Ayatollah, I have gone back to the old thinking of my family,' Kamla wrote. 'You know, I had got rid of that deeply ingrained distrust of the Muslim but now it's all come back.'[24] The development of Islamic radicalism, and the idea that it might be a serious threat to the world, became a growing obsession for Vidia. He decided to write a book about it, to be called *Among the Believers*. His thesis was based on the assumption that Islam, with its emphasis on a text written in Arabic and on pilgrimage to holy places in Saudi Arabia, was innately imperialist, requiring its followers to diminish their native culture. He would travel, therefore, to four non-Arab Muslim countries: Iran, Pakistan, Malaysia and Indonesia, breaking away from his previous territory. Wanting money, he sold the book in advance. Vidia went through at least seven drafts before he got the proposal right for the publishers. 'What I have in mind is travel reportage, light in tone, even humorous, on an entirely serious subject – Islamic revivalism or fundamentalism, as it has developed in the postcolonial era . . . Each country has a quarrel with the modern world; and my own feeling is that Islam, in these countries, is as much a looking away as a looking back. Is it despair, a recognition of intellectual and scientific incapacity? Is it nihilism? Doesn't this kind of anti-intellectual movement . . . commit these countries to a continuing dependence on the technology and science of the West? Independence, then, leads back to dependence . . . In tone and form I will be aiming at something like my Middle Passage of 1960–62.'[25]

His latest ambition coincided with a professional shift. In 1977, the year in which he parted company with his accountant and found a replacement, Vidia had switched publishers. He felt that Deutsch was not promoting his talent with sufficient vigour, and that Diana Athill had been unflattering about Guerrillas. Graham Watson delivered the coup de grâce, and Diana was distraught. 'I am more upset than I can tell you at Graham's message that you want to leave us – and as for André, he can hardly talk about it, he's so miserable . . . I think we ought to be able to talk about it face to face.'[26] André wrote to Graham, 'I did not try to persuade him to change his mind; I merely said goodbye. He sounded sad and talked about our on-going relations with all his books, etc. I told him that we will continue to look after him as well as I think we have done in the last twenty years.'[27] Soon, though, there was trouble. The new bride, Secker & Warburg, described V.S. Naipaul in their catalogue as a Caribbean author; he took offence, and resolved to return to Deutsch. Watson told him this was a bad decision, since Secker & Warburg had made an 'innocently contrived mistake' but Vidia insisted on returning to his old publisher. Had he known that Deutsch was still putting out publicity material like – 'He is not a practising Hindu, although he retains the habit of vegetarianism instilled by a Hindu upbringing. Like ninety-nine West Indians out of a hundred, he has a passion for cricket' – he might have been less sure.[28] Once Vidia had reversed his decision, it remained reversed, and by February 1979 he was writing to André to praise his dealings with European publishers: 'Thanks for everything. You have been marvellous in so many things; I want you to be around forever.'[29]

In the same month, he decided that his problem was not Deutsch, but Watson. When he read the manuscript of A Bend in the River, Graham Watson had been content, but not rapturous, and Vidia made his resentment clear. 'Sometimes you are rather hard to please!!' came the response: it was 'a majestic and important novel . . . and if you have deliberately pitched the theme on a cerebral level, that was clearly what the subject demanded.'[30] Vidia chafed. Paul Theroux had enjoyed commercial success with *The Great Railway Bazaar*, a travel book about a rail journey across Asia published by Gillon Aitken of Hamish Hamilton, whom he described to Vidia as 'one of your very tall Englishmen'.[31] When Aitken set up as a literary agent in 1976, Paul had joined him, followed by Shiva. Vidia was quietly and painfully aware that both Paul Theroux and his brother were making more money from their new books than he was. Shiva received a good advance for *Black and White*, a book on the Jonestown massacre in Guyana. When Vidia met Aitken at a party given by the art dealer Michael Goedhuis, they discussed Pushkin; Aitken had translated his work, and sent Vidia a copy of the book afterwards, as he had promised. They met in New York, and Vidia decided to defect. His letter of departure to Graham Watson was short: 'I feel the time has come for me to leave Curtis Brown. The organization doesn't give me the overseas representation I should be getting. I am reserving all rights that are unsold, lapsed, or in negotiation.'[32] Watson answered that he would not end a relationship of twenty years by post, and requested a meeting. Gillon Aitken flew back to London with a bound proof copy of *A Bend in the River*: 'I read it on the plane and I think it was possibly the best novel I had ever read. It was a masterpiece, an extraordinary book, and it was very nice to read it in that captive position, being on the aeroplane.'[33]

At his final meeting with Watson, Vidia was in no mood to take prisoners: 'I settled that account. I settle all my accounts. He cried when I left him. He came out with me to the corridors [of the Curtis Brown office]. He was saying, go and get a new agent, but let us collect the money for you. Would you believe this? And I saw then that I had given twenty years of my work to scoundrels. I outlined *Among the Believers* to Gillon, and immediately we did very well. We got a big deal from the *Observer*. From making £10,000 a year I jumped to making about £60,000. It was a bad, bad story.'[34] This was no mere boast. Gillon Aitken saw Vidia's financial potential in a way that Graham Watson never had, and realized that literary status could be converted into cash in a new commercial climate in British and American publishing. His West Indian origins need no longer trap him in a lesser category. Aided by his colleague Andrew Wylie in New York, known to journalists as 'The Jackal', Aitken used his own mercantile nous and faith in Vidia's writing to parley talent into money. Journalistic assignments began to generate serious sums, and the advances for his books headed towards six figures. Vidia earned $75,000 from *Vanity Fair* and another £10,000 from the *Sunday Times* for a long article, 'Prologue to an Autobiography'.[35] Even a token piece for American

House & Garden in 1985 produced $5,000. In the 1970s, Vidia earned an average of £7,600 a year after agent's commission but before expenses and tax. During the 1980s, using an equivalent analysis, his annual income would jump to £143,600. This was a sevenfold rise, allowing for inflation.[36] Feeling more optimistic, he wrote to Paul Theroux of *The Mosquito Coast*: 'The idea is at once simple and appetising: the way good ideas should be. Another Theroux blockbuster! ... I run across your name and your books everywhere and I always feel slightly proprietorial.'[37]

What was Vidia to do with his relative wealth? He would buy a dilapidated house, a dairyman's cottage in Salterton, up the valley from Wilsford Manor, and have it converted in just the way he wanted. It would take some time. Meanwhile, tiring of Margaret, he had left America to spend the summer of 1979 with Pat. They entertained visitors, went on a short trip to France (Vidia thought the Pompidou Centre should be pulled down) and discussed the possibility that she might accompany him to east Asia. He was profiled reverently by *Vogue*: 'He has never wanted children. His life is distinguished and shaped by extreme fastidiousness. It manifests itself physically as a brahminical fear of contamination. He didn't want to borrow a shirt to be photographed in ... He keeps fit by flipping over backwards until the palms of his hands touch the ground behind him and whipping upright again 200 times a day.'[38]

Margaret told him everything was over, and spoke of posting things back and splitting costs. She had been waiting to present him with a bill left over from their time together, but had avoided doing so because she could not bear the thought of all his insults. She hoped he might agree to pay half. As for the future, she wished him well, and said his success had at least in a small way been down to her.[39] By the autumn, when Vidia departed for Iran and Pakistan, they were back together, but by the time they reached Kuala Lumpur, the relationship was collapsing. As Vidia intoned, 'In Malaysia, with a very heavy heart, I asked Margaret to leave me, and let me do the travelling alone.'[40] She returned to London to be with her sister Diana, went to the ballet, jogged in Hyde Park and watched a programme about Vidia on television. Her house in Argentina had been sold by Roy, although he had not yet told her the price, and she would have a little more money. Things were changing. She admitted sadly that she was no longer thirty, and Vidia's ties were in England. But her feelings for him had never changed, and her desire for him had never wavered. Her excitement at seeing him had always felt the same. It was a matter of great sorrow that they had never had a child together. Vidia was offering her nothing but fleeting moments, wherever in the world he happened to be travelling; somehow she converted this parsimony into her own failure. She would like to want what he was offering, but could not cope with it any longer. She was sorry – it was not his fault, it was hers. In times to come, he knew he could rely on her love, her passion and her support.[41]

With no distractions, Vidia caught up on correspondence. Antonia had just read *A Bend in the River* twice ('it's such an extraordinary book that I will not presume to say more than just that').[42] Vidia thought it 'extraordinarily nice' of her to say so. 'Your handwriting has subtly changed. Has anyone told you? The same personality, but rejuvenated, even girlish – and I don't mean this in any unkind way . . . I hope it will be possible to see Harold and you when I get back and start living a more ordered life.'[43] Distracted from his own problems, he was able to think about how others might cope with theirs. He advised a troubled Banning Eyre how to deal with his family. Banning was wondering what to do now that he was finishing at Wesleyan: whether to pursue a musical or a literary career, and how to resolve the myriad emotional complications that were thrown up by the daily life of a young man in a free society. Should he keep his personal thoughts to himself, or share them with his parents? 'Honesty simplifies, but it also wounds and destroys,' Vidia wrote from experience. Banning responded that he was 'touched by your thoughtfulness and concern'.[44] He was writing a novel, and a thesis on Vidia's work.

In the interim, Pat had been summoned in imperative terms to take Margaret's place: it was her turn to be harassed, even as Vidia's global aspirations spread. 'You will get your Indonesian visa. You will say you are travelling to Java and Bali when they ask for your itinerary. You will also get a leather strap for your suitcase . . . Open my bank statement. Make a note of the <u>balance</u> of my current account and the date & bring the information with you . . . Yes, I think it would be better for you to bring out a woollen shirt for me (Brooks Brothers green) and a pullover and a light tweed jacket.'[45] Pat did as she was told. 'Your little house sits unconverted on the side of the hill,' she told Vidia, enclosing a cutting from *Private Eye*: 'There were some red faces at *Vogue* last week when highly-regarded author V.S. Naipaul yelled angrily down the telephone to a box-wallah about a piece which they were about to print. "What is more," V.S. shouted, his slim frame trembling with irritation, "I do not like the photographs taken by that jumped-up little photographer of the Sixties." He was referring, of course, to Lord Snowdon.'[46]

Pat was conscious, even before she left Heathrow for Jakarta, that she had been getting everything wrong. What had she been doing, apart from eating too much, listening to the radio and drifting around the London Library? While Vidia was living with Margaret in America, she had half-confided her unhappiness to Teresa, and had cried to Francis when she saw him.[47] An article about the Notting Hill Carnival, which she had reworked to death, had been rejected by the *Spectator*. She knew that Vidia, whom she had begun to refer to in her diary as 'the Genius', might be 'rough' towards her. She comprehended his ambition. A few months earlier during a train journey down from London, while speaking about the world of books and writers, Vidia had 'leant forward and said that he intended to hold the dominant position in the 1980s. Was I pleased with his decision? I said I was.'[48]

Now, she stepped into his world. Vidia was a scrupulous traveller, going only where he needed, collecting only the material he required for the book, protecting himself from sickness and time-wasters. He was full of praise for the way he had persuaded young Indonesian men to act as his guides. An early trip to Bandung was a success. Back in the hotel, 'I have a drink (gin with lime), he does his exercises, looks very pretty when he jogs (on the spot) . . . then – typically – he has to force himself, raising his legs higher, forcing his strength.' As for Pat herself, what should she be doing? 'Thought of writing to Teresa. What to say? To be dishonest? To tell her that all is not roses? That would be foolish . . . How to act? Really write, create something.' So Pat made desultory notes about Margaret Thatcher and trades union legislation.

By the middle of January 1980, they were in India taking a break, and the initial calm of Jakarta was swept aside as Vidia was consumed by exhaustion and randomly directed anger. 'He has been increasingly frenzied and sadly, from my point of view, hating and abusing me. He loved the walk but darkness fell. I was wrong to make us go beyond the Gandhi statue on the way back. The walk up the unlit road upset him more and more. A car swerved at us, he stepped and pushed me back. He stepped on my bare, big toe. I said "Oh God" not so much out of pain as out of general concern. He abused me – cunt etc. – didn't I realise that he was trying to push me out of the path of the car . . . There are in the M[ahabharat] and the Ramayan a number of ugly and wicked women and I go in, of course, for a certain degree of self-identification.' Pat was not his only enemy that week. In Madras, Vidia 'told me that he had thought out his relationship with André and Diana to a "sad" conclusion. André is a small timer. He has outgrown Diana.' In Bombay, wearing the mask of the master and raging like a Britisher from a previous century, her husband was 'wavering between hatred of tourists and hatred of India. Difficulties with taxi-drivers and resentment at effect of package tours on his beloved Taj hotels are bringing out, as he says, his racist and fascist instincts . . . He is angered by the ugliness of the poor package tour people. He upsets me talking about wogs and whips. And wanting the Emergency back.' Soon, it was the turn of the manager of the Taj to quake. 'Dear Mr Naipaul, Thank you for filling in the Guest Comments form and bringing to my notice the flaw in the design of the Tea-pots.'[49] Pat returned home while Vidia went on to Pakistan alone. All was not well, as he recalled: 'A waiter in a dirty jacket served me "fish mexique" in Rawalpindi; I was left with sickness and a migraine. My health was damaged.'[50]

By the spring, Vidia was back in England, trying to lead a regular married life. Soon, he collapsed. 'I began to choke, and what you do when you begin to choke, you lean forward on the table to make it easier and in the end you are sitting in your chair and spread across the table. I was putting off the moment of telephoning the doctor. I had to do it late at night, and Dr Smith came and he gave me the adrenaline injection and there was a great reaction. I had been drinking a late-bottled port to comfort myself. No food or anything, and I spewed it all out. They sent an ambulance and equipment for the oxygen tent and so I went in like that, I went to hospital in Salisbury. I liked it very much, I liked the ritual, but very quickly they sent me away. They gave me a wheelchair that carried me to the taxi. When I came back I immediately began to write, in spite of everything, I just sat on my table and began to write.'[51]

Normal life resumed. Mr and Mrs Skull were invited over to look at a pair of Indonesian puppets. Eleanor came on a visit. Miriam Gross invited Pat and Vidia to her new house, and Teresa, now divorced from Peter Gatacre and shortly to marry the actor John Wells, held a dinner party where they saw the art historian David Carritt and the playwright Tom Stoppard. 'Vidia made very happy by meeting again and conversation with Carritt, a charming, handsome, fair-haired man. Stoppard pretty, a little like Mick Jagger.' Clarissa, Countess of Avon, the widow of Anthony Eden ('we go beat up the Germans and them bad bad') who lived on the other side of Salisbury, took up the Naipauls. They saw Selby Wooding, Vidia's schoolfriend from QRC, who was now a lawyer in Port of Spain.

In Wilsford they entertained Antonia and her new husband, Harold Pinter. Vidia admired few of his British literary contemporaries, but rated Pinter, and had examined the way in which his dialogue was thought out and put together; being a playwright, he was not a direct rival. Pat wrote of Pinter, 'Vidia made a very interesting remark about his talent. It is adolescent: about childish fears and sexual longings. He arrived at this conclusion through recalling early stories he wrote at the age of 16–17, when he began writing.' Moments before their arrival, as was apt to happen when guests were eminent and imminent, Vidia became enraged. 'Stretches of calm and happiness in the cottage. This was ended, shattered prior to Antonia and Harold's arrival by hysteria about shirts and it wasn't funny; it was very alarming.' At the lunch, Pat served a vegetarian speciality of the era: nut-loaf. Harold failed to eat it, Vidia was silently offended ('Pat had made it with her own hand') and the invitation to visit Wiltshire was never repeated. Antonia wrote cheerfully afterwards: 'Thank you very much indeed for entertaining us with such panache – nut-cake is a new discovery for me and if white wine not exactly new, that was particularly delicious! I had often described Wilsford to Harold and was thus so pleased to be able to show it to him, looking as it ever did like a house in a fairy story . . . We are both looking forward to reading Vidia's book on Islam, and we pondered, and discussed, his wise words all the way to London.'[52]

Among the Believers: An Islamic Journey came fast, intensely, taking ten months to write. Vidia passed through swings of emotion. In the autumn, Pat noted, 'He is very depressed, does not want to write another El Dorado, another "dud".' Sometimes she took dictation, at other times she listened while Vidia read long chunks of the text aloud. It was almost 200,000 words long. She helped to check and copy-edit the final manuscript, and was obliged to answer all his letters. 'Vidia is very angry with me for not writing straight away on his behalf,' she informed Ralph and Mary Ironman. 'I still try to write but most of the time I fiddle about . . . Vidia's high-powered, new, agent called yesterday . . . I try not to let the cottage get too untidy and depressing . . . I have to read his reviews in secret . . . He spoke to Roy Plomley on Desert Island Discs. Yes, he has received this accolade.'[53] Vidia had written earlier in a private notebook of 'my detestation of music – the lowest art form, too accessible, capable of stirring people who think little', and in exchanges with Mr Plomley on the BBC sounded disconcerted, his voice thin and clipped.[54] 'Your father was a journalist?' 'Yes.' 'On a daily pepper?' 'Yes, the local paper' . . . 'Of course, you married a fellow graduate at Oxford, an English gel.' 'Yes, 1955' . . . 'Are there many Indians in Trinidad?' At the end, Vidia says, 'I hope music lovers will forgive the illiteracy.' His chosen book was a study of mathematics for 'intellectual excitement' and his luxury was a statue of the enlightened Buddha.[55] Swiftly, he returned to *Among the Believers*. Extracts from the book ran in the *Atlantic Monthly*, and the US Air Force wrote to Gillon Aitken requesting permission to reproduce them for the benefit of USAF technical teams in the Middle East.

Vidia was reviewed as a writer at the height of his powers, investigating mysterious lands with a ruthless, encircling eye. Unlike novelists who wrote about Islam after 11 September 2001 and took refuge in jargon, pretending they knew what 'hadith' or 'tajwid' meant despite having minimal or no experience of life in Muslim countries, he concentrated on his own observation, and avoided reading too many books. Vidia's interest was less in Islam than in Muslims, in what they thought and did in the countries he visited. John Carey wrote in the *Sunday Times* that V.S. Naipaul was 'beguilingly casual. He wanders around, chatting with students and taxi drivers, munching dried fruit and nuts, asking mild but pointed questions ... even when his conclusions are hostile, he never lacks sympathy.'[56] That paper's literary editor, Claire Tomalin, wrote to him, 'You are the best reporter as well as novelist now at work. Your book has made so many things comprehensible to me for the first time.'[57] Paul Theroux told Vidia it was 'deliberate, purposeful travel — a kind of seeking, a setting-out to discover ... It is a profoundly human book, with a masterful use of dialogue.'[58] In the *Washington Post*, Edward Hoagland thought he had 'a naked, contentious bias against Islam' arising from his Hindu background, 'which unfortunately may only win him additional disingenuous praise.' Some liked this approach: 'Let me be candid,' wrote Anthony Quinton (who had once doubted whether *The Mystic Masseur* deserved a Book Society recommendation), 'I got a profound, Khomeini-hating delight from V.S. Naipaul's *Among the Believers*.' Devoting pages to Vidia, *Newsweek* called the book 'a brilliant report of social illness' and prodded him in an interview to say things he would not have said in print: 'If Arabs piss on my doorstep in South Kensington, I can't *not* notice.'[59]

The sharpest criticism came from Edward Said, who with his variegated life might himself have been a character from a Naipaul novel. He dismissed Vidia jealously and zealously as an Uncle Tom figure, 'a kind of belated Kipling [who] carries with him a kind of half-stated but finally unexamined reverence for the colonial order ... Naipaul the writer now flows directly into Naipaul the social phenomenon, the celebrated sensibility on tour, abhorring the postcolonial world for its lies, its mediocrity, cruelty, violence, and maudlin self-indulgence.' Said's reaction drew the academic battle-lines for years to come: against him stood Bernard Lewis, for whom *Among the Believers* was 'not a work of scholarship, and makes no pretense of being such. It is the result of close observation by a professional observer of the human predicament. It is occasionally mistaken, often devastatingly accurate, and above all compassionate. Mr Naipaul has a keen eye for the absurdities of human behavior, in Muslim lands as elsewhere ... Mr Naipaul will not toe the line; he will not join in the praise of Islamic radical leaders and the abuse of those whom they oppose. Therefore he is an Orientalist – a term applied to him even by brainwashed university students who ought to know better.'

In a piece now redolent with irony, Marvin Mudrick wrote in the *Hudson Review* that V.S. Naipaul was being 'monotonously alarmist' about the dangers of political Islam. What did he fear, seriously – Bedouins 'sweeping like the simoom out of the desert descending on Bloomingdale's with fire and sword and no-limit credit cards?' His counsel amounted to '*Grand Guignol* with Dracula make-up and howls from the wind-machines in the wings as Islamic fanaticism threatens the very foundations of civilization: the sky is falling! the sky is falling!'[60] On September 11, when admonitory pessimism proved justified, the sky did fall.

Bernard Lewis, a scholar of Islamic history who would later be vilified for stimulating George W. Bush's chaotic military adventure in Iraq, was correct when he said that *Among the Believers* was a work of close observation. Although Vidia began his travels with a notion about anti-modern nihilism in certain Muslim countries, little of the book is devoted to theory, except at the end of chapters in a sometimes redundant way. His text was closely based on his notes, written up neatly with barely a correction in the confines of his hotel room each evening, heedless of the presence of Margaret or Pat. He might focus on Mr Jaffrey, a Shia from Lucknow who worked on the *Tehran Times* and discoursed on the failings of Khomeini while eating a dish of fried eggs, or describe bear-baiting in a dusty field in Sind, the bear crushing two yelping dogs to death: 'It was village entertainment and, like the faith, part of the complete, old life of the desert.'[61] In his private notes, Vidia empathizes. 'I liked Mr Ishaq immediately (But I like them all) ... His explanation of his Islamic passion was simple. "Our people emotionally reject the West" – in spite of our dependence on it.' Of Ali Ahmed Brohi, an official in Pakistan, he recorded, 'Swift friendship, swift treachery.'[62] After publication, a letter of explanation came from Mr Brohi: with his Indian name, Vidiadhar Surajprasad Naipaul had been thought to be a spy and 'passed on to me by my federal counterpart as "an unwanted baby" ... You must be having a colossal memory — and a very fertile and retentive one too, because, I never found you taking any notes . . . it will long remain a striking example of a book which, by sheer honesty of purpose and brilliancy of execution, has beautifully succeeded in depicting the facts as they are.'[63] Similar letters came from others whose stories had been told in the book, praising the fidelity of Vidia's accounts, done from memory.

*

Although some of its deductions are partial, *Among the Believers* lacked the cruelty of *India: A Wounded Civilization*. His malice was reserved for those close to him, and in particular for Pat. She irritated him; he was cruel to her; she became more feeble and pathetic; his irritation increased. Her diary becomes progressively more desperate during the 1980s, and entries start to tail off. 'My destructiveness — not deliberate, just stupidity. I wanted to get into bed with him . . . If only I had kept to the right and noble decisions I made when a girl. But would I have developed? I should have been more continuously courageous. Less of a baby . . . I feel that perhaps what I might have written, might yet write, could be more important than Vidia's book on Islam. I am foolish to feel this, more foolish to say it . . . Unemployment going up by thousands. Break-away MPs forming group, of 11, for Social Democracy . . . He went to Norway on Tuesday. I foolishly summoned Stanley [a taxi driver] and met the plane yesterday, a day early.' In their fiftieth year, Vidia told Pat he intended to move to the new house, Dairy Cottage, alone. 'I went on forlornly, going on about being treated as an equal . . . He looked for a clean vest, I produced his present favourite sleeveless style from the airing cupboard and looked out, at his request, another thermal top, asking whether he has a washing machine in Dairy Cottage. Yes it's all waiting there ready. My stomach turned over . . . Sexual yearning, quite deep. Will it ever stop? . . . Have not washed my hair for ages . . . But incapacity may be fundamental, in my genes, early conditioning and self-indulgence . . . We went into Salisbury on the bus shopping together yesterday morning. Vidia kept me waiting for ages in Snells [a coffee shop]. We then fortified ourselves with chocolate gateau and danish pastry. Shopping disorganised. Vidia waited for ten minutes outside Crouch [a greengrocer; now Costa Coffee] and felt he had chilled down . . . We went on from Beech [a bookshop; now an Italian restaurant] to look at the [Cathedral] Close under snow. The sun was shining through the windows of the nave.' Soon, he reversed his decision: 'Last night Vidia said he wanted to move to Dairy Cottage with me — with qualifications. The night before he declared affection twice. He doesn't dislike me, he doesn't dislike anything about me, I only irritate him.'

In Karnac's bookshop in Gloucester Road, they bumped into Bharat Bhushan, Vidia's schoolboy guide from more than a decade earlier when he had covered an election in Ajmer. 'The conversation built up, in volume apart from anything else, quickly. Vidia seizing upon his use of the word fascism and delivering strictures — the young man, Bharat, had been studying engineering ... I did not listen to the conversation or interfere, only hovering a little after a bit, indicating, or trying to a little, that it would be better to be a little quieter, calmer.' Bharat Bhushan wrote his own account:

> 'Patsy,' he shouted out to his wife Patricia. 'Meet Bharat. I had met him when he was in school. He has become a Rejecter now.' 'That is his description,' I mumbled. His wife herded us out of the bookshop. Naipaul cooled down a bit and asked me to write to him about I how felt about life now ... A fortnight later while walking down Gloucester Road I saw Naipaul again. His wife was a few steps behind him. 'Hello Mr Naipaul,' I said. 'Oh, hello, hello,' he replied in an off-hand way and walked past me. His wife stopped me and apologised for his behaviour at the bookshop ... 'Vidia, give him our telephone number,' she told Naipaul ... He looked at me in a manner which was at once condescending and arrogant. 'I will give you my telephone number only on the condition that you do not pass it on to any researcher, literary critic, journalist or other such pests,' he said. Something snapped in me and I told him, 'On second thoughts Mr Naipaul, forget about it. I don't think you have anything to say to me and I certainly don't have anything to say to you.' He threw the pen and paper angrily back at me and walked away.
>
> I still read Naipaul admiringly.[64]

Much of the time, Vidia and Pat kept apart, one in the city, one in the country. She went to a memorial service for Sonia Orwell without him, and sat between Antonia and Teresa; she attended hearings of the Scarman Inquiry into the recent Brixton riots. She preserved Vidia's notes, folding them into her diary: 'Gone to Wiltshire, hoping to calm down & behave better. Bring milk etc. See you later.' Pat in turn would leave advice when she departed: 'Cheese, Cheddar & Double Glos ...

EAT THE SMALL AVOCADO ... Nuts – cashews.'[65] Occasionally, she went to visit her family. 'I went to Birmingham for my mother's birthday. Eleanor took us to The Bell at Coleshill, a pleasant pub buffet ... My father in the flat. Family gathering. Little to say.' By now, Pat had cut off almost all contact with Ted Hale, and had never met his common-law wife, Vera. In a shaking hand, her father might write a birthday or a Christmas card and enclose a £10 note; but Pat left the money in the envelope, rejecting him. 'I would see my father once a year at a pub to exchange Christmas presents,' Eleanor recalled. 'Pat asked me not to give him her address.' Eleanor was working at a comprehensive school near Birmingham, teaching physical education: football, netball, trampolining, cross-country. She lived with Rose Crockett. 'It was a gay relationship. I once took Pat and my mother to a gay club in Birmingham with Rose. It went off all right.' The sisters rarely spoke of personal matters, although Pat once said 'very matter-of-factly' out of the blue that she was intending to separate from Vidia. She avoided mentioning Eleanor's lesbianism, though she sometimes bought gay liberation magazines such as *Out* and *Sappho*, perhaps out of curiosity or solidarity. The two had almost nothing in common. A not uncharacteristic entry in Pat's diary ran: 'Spoke to Eleanor last night. She was fitting polystyrene covering on the lavatory wall.' Eleanor once started to read *The Mimic Men* and found, 'It wasn't to my taste. I can enjoy classics, though I prefer to watch them dramatized on the television.'[66]

Finally, in February 1982, it was time to leave Wilsford and move up the valley to the converted Dairy Cottage, a four-bedroom house down a private lane, shielded by trees, the only disturbance coming from the scream of military jets from a nearby training base and the odd passing rambler. The garden, which Vidia was determined should remain green rather than being filled with flowers, was criss-crossed overhead with power lines and stretched down to the banks of the River Avon. The previous month their London flat had been burgled; Pat's nebulous wedding ring had disappeared. Comparing herself to Bryant in *Guerrillas*, she recorded her tentative, shamed efforts to carve out a space for herself in Vidia's new house. He asked: 'Would I be moving out again soon? ... I made a bedroom for myself in the little pink room, Vidia settled himself in the red.' During the spring in a separate notebook, a silver hair dropping between the pages, she made jottings. For the first time, aware of the effort she had made to leave a

record of her life with Vidia for posterity, Pat addressed herself to me
– and to you:

> The Genius has gone to South America to check up on feeling
> there, amongst other things, giving me the chance to reflect . . .
> 1982 Personal Crisis. In my case past? Just grindingly coping >or
> not, only partly<. I made a brief note about my relationship with
> the G., in the autumn, that it was not sufficient for life. And I
> address you, reader – you would not want me for life but then –
> what presumption – perhaps you would. But perhaps you would.
> Perhaps you are my destiny. After all.[67]

Where could she turn for guidance, with her husband away with his
mistress? She felt unable to ask anyone at all for help. Margaret had
stimulated Vidia's return easily, writing a vigorous and erotic response
to the rare appearance of a letter from him in Buenos Aires. Never in
her wildest dreams had she imagined that she would actually come
home and find his longed-for handwriting slipped beneath her door.
She could scarcely believe her eyes. She had even been tempted to kiss
the letter, and hold it to herself. As for the man behind the letter, she
could scarcely remember what he looked like. Was he still black, she
asked? Was he still muscular and strong? Was he still cross and
intolerant? She hoped so – otherwise she might not recognize him.
Excited, Vidia had gone to Brazil and Venezuela. In her diary, Pat
wrote, 'He has just left for Gatwick on his way to Brazil. We did not
touch or embrace – I just touched him on the side of his shoulder.'
Who would satisfy her yearning? When Selby Wooding came to stay,
she put on her kimono and made a tentative attempt at seduction. Selby,
gently, saying nothing, declined the invitation. It was an easy enough
mistake for an unconfident, unworldly woman like Pat to make:
alighting on friendly, cuddly, gay Selby.[68]

*

In the early 1980s, Vidia was at the peak of his fame, a presence and an
absence in the world of English letters, a writer who was there and not
there, globally itinerant, a prized name in America, his books available in
Greek, Serbo-Croat and Hebrew. Academic studies of his work were
published in many languages, each more speculative and hypothetical than
the last. He was an author who had fashioned himself into a special,
incomparable, unclassifiable case, who presented himself less as the product

of historical, social or geographical circumstance, than as a pristine talent, detached from his West Indian past. British fiction had been lacking in energy since the Second World War: with the conceivable exception of William Golding, it was hard to spot another novelist who matched the creative power of an American like Bellow or Roth. Writers born in the 1940s such as Angela Carter, Martin Amis and Ian McEwan were doing something fresh, but for the moment Vidia stood alone, separate, himself. In innumerable interviews, each of them billed as 'rare', he provided perfect copy to journalists seeking an original insight. Vidia made a spectacle of himself, alluding to his discovery of sensuality late in life, failing to elaborate, saying nothing of Pat, revealing bits of his daily life while remaining intensely private. His technique was to repeat things he had said before, but make them sound new, throwing out controversy like chaff to deflect attention from his real, inner, writerly self. Writing had become its own purpose, its own justification, the only way of life he knew. When academics berated him for his views, he responded in Trinidian street style, making it sound like British haughtiness: 'Africa is a land of bush, again, not a very literary land. I don't see why it should get mixed up with Asia . . . chaps in the universities . . . make investments in a political-academic stock market. Some are at present trading in African futures, creating a little calling.'[69]

When asked about Edward Said, he made a point of mispronouncing his name as the past participle of 'say': 'When the reporters from Belgium and other places come and quote something by a man called Said and other people, I have to tell them again and again, "I don't know these people, if you ask me that I'll have to send you away. You must go and talk to Mr Said about it. Ask Said. And you are a big enough man to judge him." '[70] Or, 'He is an Egyptian who got lost in the world and began to meddle in affairs he knew nothing about. He knew very little about literature, although he passed in America as a great, wise literary figure. He knew nothing about India, for example. He knew nothing about Indonesia. He had not travelled to Tehran or seen the revolution. I have never replied to any of those criticisms.'[71]

Vidia had become a phenomenon, a writer whom other writers were required to like or dislike, a cultural purgative and an applauded panto-mime villain. Apocryphal stories were told about him. Did you hear about V.S. Naipaul at the smart party in New York? A literary groupie is searching for Ved Mehta, disbelieving that a blind writer could produce such vivid descriptive prose. Finding a distinguished Indian man sitting on a sofa, she grins and waves her hands in front of his face while he looks on unblinking and unperturbed. 'Well,' she admits to her friend. 'He really is blind.' The friend corrects her: 'That wasn't Ved Mehta. That's V.S. Naipaul.' This was a good fictional anecdote: in Vidia's words, 'It was an American story, cooked up to amuse people.'[72] After meeting him in 1982, Saul Bellow said that Naipaul had an 'eagle-on-the-crags' look, and remarked: 'After one look from him, I could skip Yom Kippur.'[73] David Hare, in his play *A Map of the World*, reproduced him as the outrageous protagonist Victor Mehta, an Indian man in his early forties with thick black hair, dressed in a light-brown suit and tie, the author of a novel about journalists called *The Vermin Class*. He orders champagne, and argues with other delegates at a UNESCO conference on poverty. 'The work alone ought to be sufficient. But my publishers plead with me to make myself seen . . . Socialism, a luxury of the wealthy. To the poor, a suicidal creed . . . All old civilizations are superior to younger ones. That is why I have been happiest in Shropshire.'[74] And in 'The Spoiler's Return' in 1981, Derek Walcott wrote, 'I see these islands and I feel to bawl, / "area of darkness" with V.S. Nightfall.'[75]

Increasingly, Vidia paid the price. With the attention of his peers came the curiosity of the reading public; people found out his telephone number and called with strange requests. Obsessives wrote out of the blue. His unbidden correspondents tended to be people who were in some way deracinated, like Alan Kaul, whose father had moved from Kashmir to Seattle in 1922 and never told him he was Indian, or Alain Lacoste, 'French, white, socialist, Catholic-educated but now without religion, humble economic teacher of secondary school, living in Morocco since 8 years.' People made enquiries. Would he speak to a gang of reformed young criminals in 'Brooklyn's impoverished Bedford-Stuyvesant ghetto' asked John Norbutt, 'a Black of moderate education'? Why did he take snuff? Would he donate autographed copies of his books to the Ealing Community Relations Council? Did he want the free services of an assistant ('I have a shorthand speed of 90 wpm')? Did he want to try LSD, or 'the syllasybin [psilocybin] mushroom'? Might he like to appear on *In the Psychiatrist's Chair* with Dr Anthony Clare? Would he agree to meet Rudy Duyck, 'a first-licentiate student in Germanic Philology at the Rijksuniversiteit Gent'?[76] The answer to these questions was usually no – and it was Pat who had to pick up the telephone or write the letter of rejection, assuming the query could not simply be ignored. Even to an old friend and encourager like Francis Wyndham, Vidia rarely wrote more than a few lines now.

His daily irritation was unstinting. At a dinner at Teresa's in 1983, he was put out not to be served a vegetarian dish all of his own, as usually happened; he had to make do with the common vegetables, tainted by the forks of others. So he left. 'Vidia rang John [Wells] the morning afterwards to ask him why he did it,' Pat noted in her diary. Versed in Vidia's tyrannical demands, Teresa took the blame: 'I am desolate about what happened last night . . . It was all gross mismanagement: a new, small, hot, stuffy kitchen; a temperamental & irritable cook' – but not 'deliberate provocation'.[77] Not long afterwards, Pat wrote with tragic anguish in her diary, 'Increasingly, these days, I regret the loss, the damage of Vidia's rages and quarrels. Simple losses – of the beautiful food I have cooked, happy days, days of one's life. It was my fault: I was anxious and told him not to "overdo it" when he proposed to go out and use the Flymo . . . he was resting, the weather, sunshine & breeze, so lovely and I was wishing he would come out. He cheered up; he was whistling. He dressed in his old khaki cotton trousers & the green polo checked cotton sweater and straw hat. At my words he struck his head and burst out, "the bitch" etc and went back up, removed the clothes & put indoor clothes on, heavy dressing gown & switched on the heat in his bedroom. "Don't speak to me" etc. "I shall only despise you more." '

In the same year, Vidia wrote a private note exploring his state of mind, something he almost never did. Success had not brought him contentment:

> What is the truth about my situation at the age of 51? After the life of the writer, the labour entailed by the vocation, I am still as dissatisfied, as [unclear], as empty as at the beginning, in those days in London, and later at Oxford, and later still, after Oxford, in London again. So many beginnings; so many zests; so many let downs afterwards. The solitude is the same, almost. I live in a small house in Wiltshire now. I have enough money to see me through for a couple of years . . . I have a wife. I have had a lover, a mistress, these last eleven years. We live a distorted, a disjointed triangular life.[78]

In a questionnaire in the *Frankfurter Allgemeine Zeitung Magazin* around the same time, he revealed aspects of himself. His vision of earthly bliss?' 'It lies in the past; the delirium of reciprocated sexual passion.' The characteristics he most valued in a man? 'Honour (where it is personal, rather than the code of a class or a group); reliability.' What did he value most in his friends? 'I have no friends. It has been hard to keep them through the twists and turns of a long creative career.' His favourite heroines? 'The women who have loved me.' His favourite writer? 'Balzac, I suppose.' His greatest fault? 'Gentleness.' His real-life heroes? 'I don't believe in the idea of the hero.' What political reform did V.S. Naipaul most admire? 'The abolition of slavery.'[79]

The business of being a famous writer took up time. Acceptance speeches had to be written. In 1980 Vidia went to New York to receive the $12,500 Bennett Award, was lauded for creating a fictional world out of the wreckage of empire and invited on *The Dick Cavett Show*. The University of Leicester offered him an Hon. D.Litt. and he turned it down, but accepted one from St Andrews, proffered by Professor Peter Bayley. When he spoke at the MIT Writing Program, the posters advertising him were defaced with the words 'Elitist Pig'.[80] He was invited to the American Academy and Institute of Arts and Letters to become an honorary member alongside R.K. Narayan and David Hockney, and to Columbia University to be given an honorary degree. Vidia was accompanied by a friend whose status was never explained to his hosts. 'Margaret came to New York for it, she came to that ceremony in Columbia, the honorary degree, and I gave her $1,000. I was feeling rich . . . and she promptly went and bought a kind of fur-collared coat. I was rather impressed. I liked the gesture.'[81]

A trip to Holland in 1982 was a debacle. A Dutch television programme recorded the tour: V.S. Naipaul is signing books and telling an Indian expatriate it will take centuries for India to advance. 'You're suffering from discovering you're an individual,' he tells the man sharply. 'What do you think about minority groups?' asks a dank Dutch boy. 'I think it's rather shameful, they seldom offer rights to people of another religion, but in England they claim rights under the other man's law. It's the slave's attitude.' Now, in Amsterdam at a PEN event, he is looking furious. The audience ask hostile, half-hearted questions and complain he is 'prejudiced'. He loses control, saying their questions are absurd. 'Probably we should call it off. It's a waste of my time. It's an insult.' Now he is with a television presenter. The presenter is accompanied by a female sex doll. The shot cuts to Naipaul talking to his publicist: 'I have too great a regard for what I do to expose myself to this sort of nonsense.' He leaves for the airport saying, 'It began badly with that shoddy ticket you sent me. I knew it was going to end badly.' And with that he strides off to board his plane, looking mortally insulted and dapper in expensive shoes and an overcoat.[82]

One prize or degree begat another. In 1983 it was the turn of Israel. André Deutsch warned Vidia his suitcases would be thoroughly searched at the airport to make sure he 'didn't have an Arab inside'.[83] Vidia surprised his audience by saying he had become a writer in order to be free, and to avoid being employed. 'It was our honour and privilege to have you here in Jerusalem, to spend time seeing the city together, and above all to present you with the Jerusalem Prize,' wrote Teddy Kollek, the mayor. In Cambridge he received a doctorate alongside Helmut Schmidt, wearing a gown and bonnet.[84] Kamla was concerned he had not got the Nobel: 'I wish they would cease punishing and give it to you . . . If someday you do get it, will you invite me to see you receive your prize? That will be the happiest day of my life.'[85] He submitted to interviews in Germany, but refused to lecture at the University of Mysore. Next came the Ingersoll Foundation's T.S. Eliot Award, the previous winners being Borges, Powell and Ionesco. Through these years of enthronement, Vidia always remembered the lesson given him by William Demas at the cricket nets at QRC: never put things off until tomorrow. As a scholarship boy who had achieved his goal, he felt all the uncertainty of success; he had been brought up to aspire to an ideal invented in England, and the sense of being expected to do better than those he lived among would never go away. Basking in fame was not a possibility. Each award was assessed for its value and accepted or rejected. Being a writer, he had to write. Vidia travelled the world seeking ideas, then went home to Dairy Cottage and started working. At the back of his mind was the knowledge, or fear, that his creativity might be waning. How long could a writer go on producing fresh work, rather than reprising the old? The career of a great novelist rarely lasts more than twenty years; Dickens had managed twenty-four, and in Vidia's view, he died of self-parody. Much earlier, Vidia had written to Francis that 'to read a biography of Dickens is to get the impression of a man who drugged himself with work. So do many writers.'[86] It was true of himself.

In the summer of 1982 he tried again to write an autobiography, a project he had conceived in the late 1960s. The difficulty was that he was not willing or able to examine his own past behaviour, and had no wish to write a light book of anecdotes. Vidia was not introspective, or introspective only on favoured subjects, such as his relationship with his father or with India, which he linked to his vocation. He kept himself hidden and hardly ever spoke to anyone, for instance, about his marriage or his relationship with Margaret; his perception was turned outward and applied to others. His brooding was chanelled into his books. Over time, as he aged, the act of blocking out emotional contact made him more contrary and provocative, as he sought reactions and tried to recover the ability to have genuine, sharp feelings. When *Vanity Fair* magazine was revived and the new editor, Richard Locke, wanted an inaugural autobiographical piece by V.S. Naipaul, he tried again. 'The disorder of my childhood ... My father's nostalgia – and mine, derived from his – for this Indian world, of villages & pundits & work-in-the-fields ... Writing given me as my vocation, my caste.'[87] He thought of investigating his time at Oxford. Pat wrote in her diary: 'Last night I spoke of him letting me know the morning, nay the afternoon after our marriage, that he didn't really want to be married to me. Yes, he said, he wanted to ask my permission to write about that ... Would anyone, I asked, enjoy reading about that? I put in my usual plea: fiction & comedy ... I am very low. But then it is perhaps my own fault.' The finished article avoided any of this personal material, and was called 'Prologue to an Autobiography'. It was a beautifully evocative account of his own beginnings as a writer, and a tribute to his father. It opened: 'It is now nearly thirty years since, in a BBC room in London, on an old BBC typewriter, and on smooth, "non-rustle" BBC script paper, I wrote the first sentence of my first publishable book.'[88] ('American usage would be nonrustling,' noted a useful US sub-editor; Vidia stuck with non-rustle.[89]) Nothing in 'Prologue to an Autobiography' was untrue, but it was a partial account, processed through his own adjusted recollection, stripping the powerful presence of Ma and his sisters from his childhood, and more understandably removing Margaret and Kamla from his excursion to Margarita – 'the pearl' – in search of Poker, the original of Bogart.

Margaret wanted to be part of the process of creation. She complained about the way in which he would insist that his writing could only emerge out of a sterile, ordered daily life. Perhaps, she suggested, he only held that belief because things had never been any different. She wondered at times whether sterility just bred sterility.[90] After finishing *Among the Believers*, he had chosen to be with her. He avoided taking sides publicly over the Falklands War, but wrote articles for the *Daily Mail* (dictating them to Margaret in the São Paulo Hilton and laughing at her handwriting) in which he decried the brutality of the Argentine regime. 'In a remarkable analysis of this nation of strutting machos, V.S. Naipaul, the distinguished writer, reveals the real Argentina behind the belligerence and the bluster' ran the subhead.[91]

In November 1982 he went to West Africa for the first time and was guided by expatriates, travelling through Côte d'Ivoire and Senegal to write 'The Crocodiles of Yamoussoukro', a solid, sardonic piece of work that never catches fire. An anthropologist specializing in drum communication was recommended to him: 'I found out fairly soon that Mr Niangoran-Bouah was academically controversial, that if he was a world expert on Drummologie it was because he had started the subject and had in fact invented the word.'[92] Vidia praised President Houphouët-Boigny's administration, but saw Africa as a place of magic and sorcery where the real life remains hidden. His way was smoothed by his old Univ friend Lawrence O'Keefe, now the British ambassador in Dakar and a pseudonymous novelist, who caused a chain reaction among regional diplomats: the American ambassador in Abidjan sent a member of staff to locate V.S. Naipaul, and the British ambassador said he was the first distinguished man of letters to pass that way since Barbara Cartland, 'who, come to think of it, doesn't qualify on either count!'[93] Staying with the O'Keefes in Dakar, Vidia decided that he would live with Margaret permanently, but by January they had argued and she was put on a plane. He was furious with her at the airport; everything was finished. Margaret was distraught over the way he was behaving, and complained afterwards that she could hardly believe he was angry about her sense of disappointment. Despite everything that had happened between them in the past, she had still believed him when he promised they might yet have a future together in Wiltshire. Now he had turned silent on her again, and sent no word. She asked what she could have done to become the recipient of such wrath? She was wretched that a relationship that had sustained for nearly eleven years should have ended in such horrible circumstances.[94]

It had not ended, of course. A year later they were back in Senegal at a diplomatic dinner in honour of Mr V.S. Naipaul and Miss Margaret Murray. 'Vidia rang last night,' Pat recorded. 'He had been "assaulted" by four twelve-year-old boys in Dakar, actually only robbed of £80 in francs . . . while reading about himself in Le Point.'

When he returned to England in June, Lol O'Keefe sent a package
and a letter, and offered to find out about selling his archive papers
to an American institution: 'Herewith one pair of pyjamas which
turned up after you left.'[95] Again, the trip had ended badly, with
Margaret being blamed for her lover's frustration. She knew she could
not make him content. She begged him to understand that she had not
sought to do anything other than to please him. It was so difficult to
be someone's mistress, it was such a flimsy position and she had
realized by now that it was impossible for a man to be with two
women at once: eventually one of them had to go. So she went, but
was ready to return when the summons came. Margaret was now in
her early forties, spending more time with Roy and their children,
putting on three kilos, taking tennis lessons and playing mixed doubles
every Sunday, staying in the apartment of her friend Margaret Gun-
ningham, doing translation work and travelling to London from time
to time to see her sister Diana and her family. As for Buenos Aires,
not much ever seemed to happen there: life in the city was taken up
by politics, money, tennis, the Hurlingham Club and the odd man
who took her out to dinner. Margaret had always been pretty and sexy
rather than terminally beautiful, and now she was ageing unhappily,
conscious that she was no longer what she had been to Vidia. As a
woman who had passed through life easily sparking the attraction and
desire of many men, a woman whose sense of herself was predicated
on the evocation of an instinctive response, it was a hard moment for
Margaret to be facing. She might still inform Vidia from time to time
that she wanted to suck the life from the living god, or that he was a
black, monstrous, murderous emperor, or that she wanted him to lick
her back and thighs and tear her apart – but the spark had left the
relationship. It continued regardless, sadly and intermittently.[96]

Much of the time, Vidia travelled alone. 1983 found him in Grenada
after the execution of the political leader Maurice Bishop and the US
invasion. 'Heavy Manners in Grenada' was equally astute about 'American Psy-Ops people', visiting revolutionaries and the Grenadian politicians who were defeated by their own upheaval. In the end 'the
revolution was a revolution of words. The words had appeared as an
illumination, a short-cut to dignity, to newly educated men who had
nothing in the community to measure themselves against.' Washington's
use of military force, 'helicopters of a sinister black colour' hovering
over the island, was contrasted momentarily with Whitehall's post-

colonial attitude: 'In a glass case in the rough little museum in the centre of the town was Britain's gift to Grenada at the time of independence nine years before: a silver coffee service and twenty-four Wedgwood bone-china coffee cups, all laid out on undyed hessian.'[97]

Kamla recalled the effort her brother made to understand the thinking behind 'the revo', interviewing a member of the New Jewel Movement on her verandah in Charlieville while she brought out cold drinks, then coffee and cakes, then lunch. 'Vidia was not much given to patience. Yet with this young lady he had spent six long and tiring hours trying to get a little insight into what seemed to be the senseless slaying of Bishop and some of his comrades. And he got nothing.'[98] The next year he was at the Republican Party national convention in Dallas, aided by innumerable contacts of Bob Silvers, worrying how on earth to write about American politics. His solution was to treat the experience as wholly alien. In the perfectly titled 'Among the Republicans', he relied on peripheral events rather than political analysis to tell the story, and conveyed more about the alliance of money and religious righteousness that defined the Reagan administration than any number of more regular accounts: 'The scale and the mood, and the surreal setting, made me think of a Muslim missionary gathering I had seen five years before in a vast canopied settlement of bamboo and cotton in the Pakistan Punjab. And I felt it would not have been surprising, in Dallas, to see busy, pious helpers going around giving out sweets or some kind of symbolic sacramental food.'[99]

'Prologue to an Autobiography' and 'The Crocodiles of Yamoussoukro' were folded into a book and published in 1984 under the title *Finding the Centre*. In a collusive foreword which seduced the reviewers, Vidia said the articles were united between hard covers because 'both pieces are about the process of writing. Both pieces seek in different ways to admit the reader to that process.'[100] Admitted, then, Anthony Powell in the *Daily Telegraph* deduced, 'These two narratives are rich in good things, things to be found nowhere else.'[101] In the *Dublin Sunday Tribune*, John Banville felt 'the Prologue is moving in a restrained, stoic way that is admirable both in its intensity and in the skill with which it is brought off.'[102] An astute review by Martin Amis in the *Observer* noted: 'One sees, in the diffidence and difficulty of this essay, how little of the self is present in Naipaul's work. In the novels, a past is used, but a self is not used. In the travel writing, a controlling intelligence is present, but the self remains inscrutable and undisclosed (even during the frequent losses of self-command).'[103]

By the middle of the 1980s, Vidia had a partially acknowledged sense that his years of creation were behind him. The quickening impulse had gone from his work; in its place was a technical brilliance, and an uncanny ability to analyse the information he received through his eyes. Remarkable books were to come – *The Enigma of Arrival* and *India: A Million Mutinies Now* – but none would have the lyricism of *Miguel Street*, the originality of *A House for Mr Biswas* or the force of *A Bend in the River*. In his closing decades, Vidia would rely less on intuition and more on thought. Like Isaac Newton, he would deal with a problem by thinking on it continually. All his subsequent work would in some form be a reconsideration of what had come before, a reprise – or reprisal. V.S. Naipaul, the writing personality, was fully formed.

CHAPTER TWENTY-THREE

'UNDOING MY SEMI-COLONS'

WITH NO FAMILY OF HIS OWN, Vidia's thoughts were often on his mother and siblings, nephews and nieces. This did not mean he felt benevolent towards them, although he did commit acts of random kindness, like paying off Kamla's mortgage to the tune of US$32,550 and helping with the college fees of her son Ved.[1] Vidia worried about Ved, writing in a long letter to Kamla,

> He is in California, the land of drop-outs and 'cults' . . . He told me on the phone that he had shaved his head in the Mohawk style – a central tuft between shaved strips. He explained this by saying that 'you only live once' . . . Ved gets not only his words – but the ideas that come with the words – from the people he is with . . . He is being influenced by the people around him who are more secure than he is and who at the end of the day will have families and all the possibilities of the United States to fall back on . . . You know I love Ved. He is an honourable boy. At the moment he is 'hiding' from us; the freedom of California is too much for him.[2]

Later, to Ved, Vidia praised the application with which his sister Shani was studying nursing in England: 'She likes the work and is very keen and wins golden opinions all round. She has unfortunately been over indulging in sweet things and has lost some of her good looks because she has become so fat. Her face has especially fattened out. I gather she has decided to take herself in hand, but possibly it is now too late. She will be a fat thing, like your mother's aunts.'[3] Sati's son Neil was another long-distance protégé. He lived in Canada, taught in a language school and was determined not to return to Trinidad. He appreciated Uncle Vido's guidance: 'The advice you gave me about finding out about myself and my past . . . is really so important to me now. It's a little frightening, but at the same time, very exciting.' Vidia offered encouragement, and by 1985 Neil Bissoondath was the author of a book of short stories with an enthusiastic quote from V.S. Naipaul on the cover. When his novel *A Casual Brutality* was published three years later, he was heralded as 'the most widely praised young Canadian writer in years'. His uncle's books, he told a magazine, had been 'icons of possibility' which made him realize a world existed outside Sangre Grande.[4]

Sometimes, it was easier for Vidia to be generous or warmhearted to strangers, or to those he never saw. When Marg Hale was obliged to leave 593 Kingstanding Road, he purchased a two-bedroom terraced house in Asquith Road in Birmingham and let her live there without paying rent. A random fan might be treated with concern, like Jackie Michaud from Maine, a blueberry grower and aspiring writer with whom he had a long correspondence during the 1980s, encouraging her to tell him of her daily life and reading. A zoologist and yoga teacher, Stephanie Alexander, gave him remote advice on posture and breathing exercises. A visiting interviewer, the Angolan journalist Sousa Jamba, was surprised to have 'a congenial tête-à-tête' with this reputedly 'aggressive, irascible figure'. Then Jamba made the mistake of quoting C.L.R. James's observation that Naipaul was liked by white people because he said what they wanted to hear. 'Abruptly, Naipaul's West Indian accent stood out as he began shouting at me. Suddenly I became terrified of the great man before me. I would not relish the idea of meeting him again, yet I remain an ardent admirer of his craft, vision and dedication to the writer's life.'[5] An encounter with a pair of German documentary-makers shows the way Vidia could speedily switch modes. The two women had been to some trouble to research a film about him, and he was welcoming and cooperative. When their questions arrived in advance of an interview, he wrote back, 'I have looked at the material you have sent me, and I feel I do not wish to take part in your film. I do not like the questions. They ignore far too many aspects of my work over the last twenty-five years, and seek only to involve me in a simple, over-flat political debate . . . Nothing that I have written here (I am writing about my own work, remember) lessens the personal regard I have for both of you and my gratitude for your courtesy in visiting me in Paris.'[6]

Since his ill-fated visit to Trinidad with Margaret in 1977, Vidia had had little contact with Ma or with his sisters, barring Kamla. Her daughter Shani found Uncle Vido and Auntie Pat hospitable and eccentric when she went to stay at Dairy Cottage. 'He would sit for hours in his dressing gown and think into space. You could say nothing.

You couldn't turn on the TV, and had to tiptoe around him. Then he would go and write in the evening, and read it to Pat and me. There was always a tension. I couldn't imagine him writing without Pat ... They were too protective of me when I was in London. When I said I was going to the Notting Hill Carnival, they rang Trinidad to complain ... Auntie Pat was an amazing gourmet cook: artichokes in butter, mussels and rice, goat's cheese soufflé.'[7] Shani persuaded Vidia to come to her twenty-first birthday party in London. He reported back to Kamla: 'Nalini [Nella] came along to that, with her two daughters; and so I saw Nalini for the first time for eleven years. Fatter than ever. Almost as fat as Shani. But nothing about that subject, now. Shani arranged her party with the utmost elegance ... Mira's two daughters came over and I saw them – for the first time since 1971. Absolutely American.'[8] One daughter, Nisha, came to stay in Wiltshire. 'Uncle Vido was unbelievably nice to me. Pat cooked salmon and potatoes and green beans, and he talked about wines. She was a bit like a servant, taking care of him ... He complained about London: "Little Negro children running up and down the street, causing me distress." ' Another time, while she was living in San Francisco, Nisha accompanied her uncle on a visit to Francis Ford Coppola in Napa Valley to discuss the possible filming of *Guerrillas*. 'It was a nice house, and he cooked an Italian meal for us – pork. Uncle Vido didn't like that. George Lucas dropped by and started talking about the making of *Star Wars*. Uncle Vido was very quiet, and he did his calculated thing, saying he didn't know about the entertainment industry, "I don't know *Star Wars*, I am not interested in films." '[9]

Later that year, in November 1984, the family were united in a different way when Sati died. Before going to Trinidad to join his siblings, Vido observed her cremation by surrounding himself with photographs of his sister, and sitting alone in silent communication, a moment he would describe in *The Enigma of Arrival*. He was distraught as he flew out to join his family (the previous week Julian Jebb had killed himself with an overdose of heminevrin). Vidia's sorrow and guilt were exacerbated by his own earlier behaviour. At Kamla's house the previous year, he had been sitting in his room writing about the invasion of Grenada when Sati came to see him. 'Why are you hiding, boy?' she called. But Vidia kept the shutters shut, sitting irascibly with his thoughts and his typewriter, and did not greet her. He never saw Sati again.[10]

Nine months later, after this grief and the inevitable unity that follows death within a family, another disaster struck the Naipauls. Shiva, aged forty, died from a heart attack. He had been seriously overweight for years, and drinking hard, and now he had gone the same way as Pa, leaving Jenny a widow and eleven-year-old Tarun without a father. 'I don't want you to get a breakdown,' Ma told Vido, 'I want all my children to say that the Great Lord had given him to us for only forty years and Sati fifty years. I am trying to keep myself so that I don't get sick. The same apply to you and Pat.'[11] There was grief outside the family too, since Shiva had been popular and sociable in a way Vidia could never be. Gillon Aitken remembered him as 'immensely affable, comical, easily amused – charming boy . . . He was quite different to Vidia, metabolically very different. He was the big one, Vidia was the greyhound, and Shiva was sometimes recklessly drunk.'[12] In Mira's view, 'Shivan was actually the opposite of Vido. Shivan was like this kind, soft wonderful one. We all adored him and he loved my mother.'[13] Shiva's friends within the London literary world rallied around his memory, and a memorial prize was established in his honour by the *Spectator*, a magazine which took pride in kicking against political correctness and had seen Shiva as perfectly ethnically situated to man the barricades.[14] As Diana Athill wrote after reading his novel *The Chip-Chip Gatherers*, there had to be 'some very rare and awe-inspiring gene roaming about among the Naipauls'.[15]

His widow Jenny had been secretary to Alexander Chancellor, the former editor of the *Spectator*, who wrote: 'Working for an "island scholarship" is clearly a full-time occupation. So far as I could tell, Shiva had failed to master even the most elementary of practical skills. He couldn't boil an egg or mend a fuse. If a tap was dripping, so to speak, he would telephone Jenny at the office and she would rush home immediately to deal with it . . . If, in his literary persona, he tended to ignore her existence, his dependence on her was nevertheless absolute.' Chancellor made an interesting observation about Shiva's writing persona: he presented himself as 'a solitary, gloomy, self-obsessed person, lacking the gift of companionship. It is a portrait in this last respect so misleading that it fairly takes the breath away. What keeps coming back to me at the moment is his laugh: high, rasping and infectious.'[16]

Shiva's literary inheritance had given him an identity and a burden. Vidia's style had developed out of Pa's, and been appropriated by his younger brother at an early age when he learned chunks of *The Mystic Masseur* by heart. Shiva never broke free to find a style that was less dyspeptic and more suited to his own personality. He was a gifted writer, though he was often detained by distractions, but his books reverberate with the echo of his brother's voice. In *Black and White*, we encounter whores and 'tawdry' goods, learn that the Guyanese have 'behaved badly' and that Surinam displays 'incipient Third World frailties', all within the first two pages.[17] In *North of South*, an account of a journey through Africa, we have Andrew, who wants to escape via a foreign patron. 'He is defenceless ... Black and white meet and mingle at the point of fantasy, aggravating an already deformed vision. Fantasy is piled on fantasy.'[18] Away from this Naipauline philosophizing, Shiva's writing lifts off in *North of South*, for instance, through his skilful and funny use of dialogue.

In his private correspondence with his brother, there is a sense that Shiva was trying to impress, needle, emulate and implore him, all at the same time. A letter from Bombay in 1973 is characteristic. Vidia's friend and contact Rahul Singh had introduced Shiva to 'absurd' people such as '[Russi] Karanjia, the editor of Blitz'.

> I went to a little talk he gave at Rahul Singh's flat. He arrived with his fashionably dark, short-skirted mistress in tow while he himself was dressed in a weird boiler-suit type outfit. Karanjia believes that the salvation of the country lies in the creation of what he calls a 'land army' with Mrs Gandhi as its Commander-in-Chief. This land army will build dams, divert rivers and, occasionally, join them up ... I constantly have to cope with the backwash of your notoriety. The wounds inflicted by 'Area of Darkness' still seem to smart. On the other hand, your notoriety has not led people to read your other work ... I do my best to defend you but recently I have stopped listening ... Write soon – if you're not too angry with me.[19]

Vinod Mehta, who met Shiva in India, felt he was 'absolutely the opposite of Vidia. He drank a lot, he ate a lot, he made a general nuisance of himself and didn't hide his dislike for his brother at all ... This guy wanted to be taken to parties and he fell in love with an Indian woman, made an ass of himself, wanted to marry her ... but at every party invariably he would be mistaken for Vidia. "Oh, so you are the great writer V.S. Naipaul," and this guy was squirming, "That bugger never helped me, never lifted a finger for me, I've done it all on my own." '[20] Vidia would be casually derogatory about his brother in turn, telling Nikhil Lakshman, an Indian journalist who admired Shiva's work, 'He always tried to emulate me, but he was very mediocre.'[21] Vidia complained that Shiva had used his writing to settle personal complaints and grievances: 'I don't think anyone in my family apart from my brother was a gatherer of injustice. We were doers. While he drew breath, he whined.'[22] Or as he complained cruelly later: 'I was really hoping when my brother came along – before I was told about his alcoholic idleness – that he would, as it were, show me a new way. But he was just using me as a template. He was patterning himself on me.'[23]

In August 1985, reeling from the sudden disappearance of an absent presence, Vidia felt nothing but heartache. His irritation with Shiva when he was alive had always been bound up with love and a paternal, fraternal sense of unfulfilled responsibility. Now his only brother was gone, leaving a young boy to bear the Naipaul name. To Antonia, in response to a letter of condolence, Vidia wrote, 'It's a great grief; and it has brought, suddenly, a new feeling of loneliness (though we seldom met) . . . since my father's death in 1953, I have never really known grief as sharp as this '[24] Not long before he passed away, their cousin Sita had sent Shiva a letter about a slighting remark he had made regarding her father Simbhoo in a *New Yorker* article. Now the letter was circulated through the family: Sita retailed the news that Simbhoo had funded this ingrate through school. Moreover, 'When you nor your brother could send a shilling to your mother in Trinidad [my father] supported your mother and Nalini . . . You and Vido have made a living writing about the family, but nowhere is there any indication that it was due to our grandmother & then to my father – "the uncle who was not the Leader of the Opposition" – that such is the case.'[25] The extended family was filled with what Kamla called 'hurt, rejection and selfishness'.[26]

Days after Shiva's death, Pat noted: 'Sewan's pictures on the mantelpiece. "I think about my brother all the time." Grief, tears overtake him often . . . "Every time I hold a pen I think of him."' In December there was a memorial service, 'a grand assembly of London, Spectator-related, niceness & intellect . . . Vidia had to stop a number of times in the first part of his speech . . . Auberon Waugh, & others, arrived late & created about while Vidia speaking.' In the New Year, Vidia and Pat went to visit Tarun and Jenny at their flat in Belsize

Park. Afterwards, Pat wrote: 'Vidia is happy with & about Tarun. Saw his knife collection, table tennis table etc.' A reciprocal visit and Christmas cards ensued. 'Thank you for the money you sent me . . . I am in the Senior School now and it is much harder but more fun . . . Hope to see you soon, Lots of love Tarun.'[27] Over time, Vidia found it too painful to be reminded of Shiva, and withdrew: he did not see his nephew any more. Jenny was content with this decision. 'Vidia still sleeping, looking very thin last night, in the candlelight, grieving for Sewan,' wrote Pat in her diary. 'Discovered just now, on Vidia's scales, that I weigh 6½ stone [41 kg].'[28] It was a bad omen, this unexplained weight loss: Pat had undiagnosed breast cancer.

*

In 1973, a few years after moving to Wilsford, Vidia had begun to make notes about rural life, oriented around the estate workers who enabled Stephen Tennant's bucolic idyll to flourish, and the retainers who lived at the manor looking after him. After he moved to Dairy Cottage, he recorded information about Mr Wilkins, who helped to maintain the property whenever he and Pat were away. He would add memories of his upbringing, and thoughts about his own position in the world: 'I knew so many family quarrels when I was young that I made a promise to myself never to have any when I grew up. I thought I would live in peace with my sister . . . Mr Wilkins had been conscious all the time, so the "herdsman" had said . . . I see the seasons now; I wish I didn't. I am less stressed now than I was twenty-five years ago by the feeling of isolation and racial oddity . . . We gave some fruit from the garden to Mrs Wilkins.'[29] Would this material make a book? A year before Shiva's death, Pat had written, 'Vidia "made a breakthrough" in his writing. Going to begin The Valley with Jack.' Reading an early draft of what would become The Enigma of Arrival, she was 'surprised at the verisimilitude, fleetingly thought of libel'. Vidia wrote more. 'He told me last night that he deliberately lengthened out the narrative, Pitton walking up to the gate etc, so that we stay with the dismissal of Pitton, it is not over too soon. "You didn't know that?" Said he thinks all this out . . . He is also fortifying himself with white wine, e.g. towards the end of the morning, unusually, to quell "nerves" before setting to write . . . It occurs to me, for no exact reason, to record that he told me that if he died, Paul would be able to advise on editing . . . He is "good at that." ' But it was only in the months following Shiva's abrupt death that Vidia saw a clear way forward with this book. Unexpectedly, swiftly, living quietly and ascetically in Wiltshire with Pat, he was able to write *The Enigma of Arrival* in a little over a year, consumed by a sense of resignation over the inevitability of change and death; it ends with Sati's funerary ceremonies, and is dedicated to the memory of Shiva. As always, Pat helped with the writing. 'She never gave editorial advice ... She knew what was bad, what wouldn't work. She would just say, "I don't like that. This is all right. That's enough." You doubt everything when you are beginning [to write a book]. It all feels a little fraudulent, and you want somebody to say, there, you carry on.'[30]

The Enigma of Arrival was unlike any other book, a work of intermittent brilliance, a cross between a partially fictional autobiography and an essay and a slowly revealed study of the life of the mind, but billed as a novel. It was an unusable masterpiece. John Bayley observed in the *New York Review* that the vision of English rural life at the end of the twentieth century set around a crumbling house and realized through the perception of an outsider from Trinidad had 'a profound, tender, and disquieting originality, as if Eden was being seen for the first time by someone with much sharper eyes than Adam and Eve ... the unique quality of his discourse, in *The Enigma of Arrival*, is in the way it combines the sense of innocence and wonder with an eye and an understanding that are quietly and totally penetrating. It is a combination unlike any other, and no other writer today could produce anything like it.'[31]

To create this hypnotic atmosphere, Vidia stripped his life of its context. Some names were changed, Wilsford becoming Waldenshaw, Brian becoming Les, Mrs Skull becoming Mrs Phillips (Phillips Lane leads to Dairy Cottage; Pitton is a Wiltshire village). Salisbury remains Salisbury, 'Tony' is Anthony Powell and Stonehenge is Stonehenge. Alan, a literary man with 'no book to his name' is Julian Jebb, leavened with Simon Blow, another upper-class scion who would appear from time to time at Wilsford Manor, speaking of novels he intended to write. Vidia did not mention the social connections that had brought him to Wilsford, or the machinations of the class system in the valley. He did not allude to his alternative existence in London or Buenos Aires, although he wrote subtly of the circumstances that had led him to England from Trinidad. He did not say that the manor was owned by the flamboyant homosexual aesthete Stephen Tennant, but by 'my landlord' (the term borrowed from *Wuthering Heights*), a figure with 'accidia', whom he never met.

He did not mention Pat or Margaret, but appeared to inhabit his cottage alone, living off thin air; as in his fictional fiction, he found it difficult to deal frankly with women or his own emotions towards them. The closest reference to sex is a disapproving focus on the soon to be murdered Brenda, the wife of a farm worker, 'a short woman with heavy thighs' who 'sunbathed in the ruined garden, seemingly careless of showing her breasts'.[32] Even when recollecting the year of wandering after the sale of the Stockwell house and the long stay with her Auntie Lu, Pat remains absent from the text: 'In London I rented a serviced flat in Dolphin Square . . . I went eventually to stay in a private house in the town of Gloucester . . . a small, mean, common town. It was not a place I would have gone to out of choice. But now it offered a house, shelter, hospitality.'[33]

The Enigma of Arrival is achieved through a detective's power of observation: instead of speaking to people, as he would when travelling for his journalism, Vidia or the narrator watches for instance through a window and guesses the connection between Les, Brenda and Mr and Mrs Phillips: 'I couldn't tell who out of the four was benefiting most from the relationship . . . They were servants, all four. Within that condition (which should have neutered them) all their passions were played out. But that might have been my own special prejudice, my own raw nerves. I came from a colony, once a plantation society, where servitude was a more desperate condition.'[34] This, and other realizations, arose directly from the distinctive, reclusive manner in which he and Pat lived in Wiltshire, noticing rather than participating. In her diary, there are anticipations of the material Vidia would use later, almost entirely from memory, in the book. 'John Skull has just confirmed that it was Mr Tennant in the car yesterday. He waved at Vidia and, Vidia said, "looked very benign" . . . As a backdrop to all this the Skulls and their friends, Brian and his wife. Last night he passed naked to the hips with a bandolier >cartridge belt< round that line. There has been considerable toing and froing, the night before last hammering etc. to a chicken house behind the yew hedge . . . There was a letter from his past, excited by the television programme about him and London, from Carmen. He said he must write to her.'

The most memorable thing about this mesmeric and oddly unclassifiable work is the incidental observation. It has no plot – it is a book more for writers than readers – but consists of an endless stream of perception. It is full of surprises. These might be small, like the observation that at this point in English history, hay is no longer collected in ricks or bales, but in 'great Swiss rolls . . . too big to be lifted or unrolled by a man' or that the countryside is marked by 'padded passing-places' made by 'rolling blue plastic sacks around the barbed wire and tying them with spiral after spiral of red-blond raffia or nylon.'[35] Or it might be a reflection on the speech of Mr Pitton, a West Country gardener (so unlike the Trinidadian gardener, 'a weeder and a waterer, a barefoot man, trousers rolled up to mid-shin, playing a hose on a flower-bed'):[36]

> It was Pitton who one year, talking of the pear trees on the 'farmhouse' wall, gave me a new determinative use of the preposition 'in'. The pears were ripe. The birds were pecking at them. I mentioned it to Pitton, thinking that with all the things he had to do he mightn't have noticed. But he said he had noticed; the pears were very much on his mind; he intended any day now 'to pick them in'. To pick the pears *in* – I liked that *in*. I played with it, repeated it.[37]

The writer, with memories of the flimsiness of buildings in Petit Valley and undeclared knowledge that the Tennant family wealth came in part from Trinidad estates, might be struck by a ruined greenhouse, full of weeds, in the grounds of the manor: 'It had been "over-specified": its timbers, the depth of the concrete floor (on two levels on the sloping site), its door, its hinges, its metal-work – everything was much sturdier than was strictly necessary.'[38] Or he might deduce that Mr Pitton's neat and stylish clothes were modelled on 'an army officer of twenty or twenty-five years before whom Pitton had served or served under (someone still alive in Pitton's memory: Pitton's imitation this officer's chief memorial, perhaps).'[39] He might even establish why the better women's dress shops in Salisbury tended to fail: people with important shopping to do usually did it in London, and new owners rarely studied in advance 'the location of the car-parks, the very roundabout one-way-street system, or understood the way shoppers moved about the town centre.'[40] (I would confirm, having spent more than a decade living in an estate cottage in a valley on the other side of Salisbury, that the observation about shops and the one-way system is wholly accurate; and it was only after reading *The Enigma of Arrival* that I noticed Bernard, who drove the van and did the deliveries for Shrewton Steam Laundries, wore his 'laundry leather moneybag ... slung over his shoulder and chest like a bandolier'.[41])

'My admiration for Naipaul keeps mounting,' wrote the celebrated editor of the *New Yorker* William Shawn to Gillon Aitken. He extracted early sections of the book, paying $78,000. Shawn told Vidia he was 'enchanted' by the title *The Enigma of Arrival*, taken from the name of a Giorgio de Chirico painting used on the jacket.[42] The book sold satisfactorily in Britain and America, and in translation, but critical responses varied. Joseph Epstein in the *New Criterion* had no doubt Naipaul was 'the most talented, the most truthful, the most honorable writer of his generation.'[43] In the *Boston Review*, George Packer said *The Enigma of Arrival* would be read when other supposed masterpieces were forgotten.[44] 'Oh Gawd, man, you can write!' wrote John Figueroa.[45] David Pryce-Jones suggested the book was 'a celebration of le mot juste'.[46] Margaret Drabble wrote, 'I have been struggling for some time against the temptation to write you a fan letter about The Enigma of Arrival, but have decided at this dark dull end of the year to succumb ... I admire all your work, but this novel in particular.'[47] In his diary, Anthony Powell wrote: 'What strikes one is the parade of rural characters observed from outside, without inherent awareness of the sort of persons they are, which someone brought up in England would possess, anyway up to a point.'[48] Susan Sontag wrote a baffling letter to the *Times Literary Supplement* complaining about a lukewarm review Vidia had been given.[49] Salman Rushdie, writing in the *Guardian*, admired the author's 'magisterial technical control' but wondered why *The Enigma of Arrival* was so sad, and why the word 'love' seemed to be absent from its pages. 'When the strength for fiction fails the writer, what remains is autobiography.'[50] On television, the *South Bank Show* devoted an edition called 'The Enigma of Writing' to V.S. Naipaul and his new book. It was a solemn, joyless production. Melvyn Bragg frowned and stroked his chin while Vidia walked around the Wiltshire fields looking smug and tormented. He spoke in a clipped voice, in circumlocutions: 'One still thinks one had many lucky escapes ... About ten years ago one thought one ... was making one's own life ... but, no, one was a prisoner of the past.'[51] He said that in refusing to write an autobiography, he had created *The Enigma of Arrival*.

Americans liked the book, and it would later be singled out by the Nobel committee: 'In his masterpiece *The Enigma of Arrival* Naipaul visits the reality of England like an anthropologist studying some hitherto unexplored native tribe deep in the jungle. With apparently short-sighted and random observations he creates an unrelenting image of the placid collapse of the old colonial ruling culture.'[52] Derek Walcott did not see it in this way; the book was an affirmation of 'the squirearchy of club and manor'. His review bubbled into an assault, although he praised the tenderness of the early sections: 'The myth of

Naipaul as a phenomenon, as a singular, contradictory genius who survived the cane fields and the bush at great cost, has long been a farce.' What about Edgar Mittelholzer, C.L.R. James, Jamaica Kincaid and the legendary Bob Marley? And what of V.S. Naipaul's celebrated frankness? Would people still praise his 'nasty little sneers' against black people if they were turned on Jews? His rival's prose was 'scarred by scrofula, by passages from which one would like to avert one's eye; and these reveal, remorselessly, Naipaul's repulsion toward Negroes.'[53]

Walcott's declaration of war had enjoyed a long gestation, and was a reaction less to the contents of the book than to the public pronouncements that had preceded it. His own reputation existed in opposition to Vidia's. As Walcott wrote in the 1979 poem 'The Schooner "Flight"':

> I'm just a red nigger who love the sea,
> I had a sound colonial education,
> I have Dutch, nigger, and English in me,
> and either I'm nobody, or I'm a nation.[54]

His poetry was an epic celebration of Caribbean life; he presented the region as a place at the centre of world history, much more than a collection of scattered islands. Piloted by Cal Lowell and Lizzie Hardwick, he had sailed happily through America's more prestigious universities, teaching literature, wowing students and enjoying the admiration of East Coast intellectuals. Despite his exemplary public love for the Caribbean, Derek Walcott lived in Boston and New York.

*

Moving fast, wanting change, demanding reverence, and more unhappy than ever, Vidia thought he might travel abroad with Margaret. Before leaving, he wondered if purchasing a property for himself in London might ease his dissatisfaction. Gone were the days of a latchkey to Marisa and Lindsay's house: instead he commanded Marisa to find him a flat in Kensington, costing up to £250,000. It should have, he informed her, 'at least two bedrooms. Quiet is essential ... I spend all day in the place where I live. Therefore I am very sensitive to disturbance & nuisance.'[55] A *Chicago Tribune* interviewer noted in 1986 that V.S. Naipaul seemed 'poised to strike – a man whose mind moves with such daunting clarity and speed that in his presence the term "food for thought" can take on an uncomfortably literal meaning.'[56]

Seeking greater success in the USA, Vidia travelled to North Carolina to research a new book, *Slave States*. He planned to start with a string of articles about the South, and produced a hasty, indefinite book proposal for publishers. At the Republican Convention in Dallas in 1984, he had realized that the Caribbean was linked historically to 'the America of the South and plantations and slavery'. Now he would travel through the old states, and hear what people had to say. His model, once again, would be *The Middle Passage*. Seeing the connection between the West Indies and the slave states of America, 'made me wonder why the idea hadn't come to me before . . . I am interested in nuance, complexity, ambiguities, rather than in strong black-and-white issues.'[57] It was a notably weak proposal, but Gillon Aitken wrote to Bob Gottlieb at Knopf that 'if Vidia is going to write a big breakthrough book for the American market, this is it.' The implication was that since Vidia was a world-famous writer, the new work had to be accomplished. Gottlieb offered an advance of $125,000, against $175,000 from Harper & Row and $180,000 from Putnam's. Vidia was disheartened, and felt let down. At this point, Gottlieb replaced Shawn at the *New Yorker*, and was in turn replaced by Sonny Mehta, who had left India for England and made a stupendous reputation for himself at Picador by unleashing the power of trade paperback books, and by wearing sneakers and blue jeans to the office in the days before such behaviour was standard. Aitken remembered that Mehta was trembling with fear when he met Vidia for the first time, but was anxious to publish the book. More money became available, and a spectacular $500,000 joint deal was secured for *Slave States* and a yet-to-be-written novel. UK rights for *Slave States* were sold to Viking Penguin for £75,000. Penguin was still selling most of Vidia's titles in paperback, though in low numbers; only *A House for Mr Biswas* sold more than 10,000 copies in 1986, because it was on school and college syllabuses.[58]

Vidia spent the spring and summer of 1987 travelling through America, making notes, accompanied by a driver. In his words: 'Without knowing what I was doing I told Margaret, you'll drive me in the South, and at the time when I feel I can do the book or the book is there, I will pay you $40,000 — would you do it on that basis? And she willingly agreed. So I remember in Georgia, I gave her the forty thousand . . . and she was quite crazy with delight.'[59] The money enabled Margaret to buy an apartment in Buenos Aires. Norman di Giovanni saw Vidia there after a break of more than a decade: 'I remember his pride, his chest was literally puffed up in pride that he had bought the flat. He was laughing. "I paid for this, and hasn't she done it up nicely."'[60] Vidia and Margaret's tour of the South cost him nearly £50,000, mainly in hotel bills, which he was able to offset against income tax as a business expense.[61]

Driving through America, Vidia and Margaret did not divert to see Mira and Amar and their children in Florida, where Amar was running a successful cancer hospital in Braverton. Instead they drove through Atlanta, Charleston, Tallahassee, Tuskegee, Jackson and Nashville, Vidia opening his notebook to the people he saw, and recording their observations at length. Armed with a stack of 'release' forms for his interviewees to sign, he made sure his interviews could not provide the basis for future legal action. He told the *Atlanta Constitution*, which caught up with him in a hotel lobby, that he had 'never read William Faulkner or any other Southern writer, not does he intend to' and had come to the region with no preconceptions.[62] His initial steps were helped by his allies in New York. Bob Silvers and Sonny Mehta sought out local contacts whose details were faxed or posted to Vidia as he travelled. Rea Hederman at the *New York Review* also smoothed the way; he came from Mississippi, and had made a name for himself by dragging his family's newspaper the Jackson *Clarion-Ledger* away from its racist past. Hederman made hotel reservations for Vidia and Margaret in Memphis and Nashville and organized meetings with friends.

Once Vidia was safely in the loop of Southern hospitality, many doors were opened to him. Richard A. Allison of Atlanta offered the use of his house in Alabama: 'If you can give me any sort of notice as to when you might arrive, I would be happy to have our cook (Emily Jones) be in attendance to cook your dinner.'[63] In practice, many of the meetings that were arranged remotely led to nothing. Vidia's most interesting encounters came almost at random as he travelled, staying in the best hotels he could find, and the strongest sympathy and interest in the finished book – called *A Turn in the South* – seemed to be reserved for the poor blacks and poor whites he met. 'In the hundred years after the end of slavery the black man was tormented in the South in ways that I never knew about until I began to travel in the region.'[64] Talking to a woman pastor in Tallahassee who described the campaign to end desegregation in Washington, DC in 1941 ('You can't imagine the things that were said to us. People would spit in our faces. If we drank out of a glass they would take it up and throw it away') left Vidia in tears.[65] In Alabama, grouchy and exhausted, he was admitted to hospital following an asthma attack ('Name of nearest relative, Margaret Gooding').[66]

When the travelling was done, he retired to the Hotel Sofitel in

Montpellier, a big and bland hotel in southern France, to write for four months. The atmosphere was suitably sterile for the rapid creation of a substantial book. It was dedicated to Seepersad Naipaul 'in ever renewed homage'. But when Vidia came to write, the first draft did not run easily. His notes were in a less even hand than usual; the narrative and theme were unclear. He switched direction between slavery, religion and the nature of rednecks, and his efforts to draw parallels with his own social background were unsuccessful. Vidia pushed on, not always pausing to sift or mediate his encounters, or to separate a story from extraneous material. Many interviews were too long, and the best lines came by chance. At Graceland, he noticed the obesity of redneck women: 'It was at times a pleasure and an excitement to see them, to see the individual way each human frame organized or arranged its excess poundage: a swag here, a bag there, a slab there, a roll there ... but I also began to wonder ... whether for these descendants of frontier people and pinelanders there wasn't, in their fatness, some simple element of self-assertion.'[67] The result was a book that lacked the rigour and analysis of his usual travel writing. In the *New York Review of Books*, Roger Shattuck wrote that 'Naipaul writes as if a modern oracle had chosen to speak through him. The individual sentences and paragraphs read easily enough. The mysterious oracular quality comes from Naipaul's willingness to follow random leads and his disinclination to pull everything together into a set of conclusions ... Despite its brilliant moments Naipaul has not worked this book up to his highest standard.'[68]

From the publisher's point of view, it could not be anything except a hit; they had hundreds of thousands of dollars to recoup. The copy-edited manuscript was sent to Vidia for inspection, but Sonny Mehta soon received a fax back from him in May 1988:

I thought it might have been known in the office that after 34 years and 20 books I knew certain things about writing and didn't want a copy-editor's help with punctuation ... I didn't want anyone undoing my semi-colons; with all their different shades of pause; or interfering with my 'ands', with all their different ways of linking.

It happens that English – the history of the language – was my subject at Oxford. It happens that I know very well that these so-called 'rules' have nothing to do with the language, and are really rules about French usage. The glory of English is that it is without these court rules: it is a language made by the people who write it.

My name goes on my book. I am responsible for the way the words are put together. It is one reason why I became a writer.

Every writer has his own voice ... An assiduous copy-editor can undo this very quickly, can make A write like B and Ms C. And what a waste of spirit it is for the writer, who is in effect re-doing bits of his manuscript all the time instead of giving it a truly creative, revising read. Consider how it has made me sit down this morning, not to my work, but to write this enraged letter.[69]

Mehta did his best; he was 'mortified', 'appalled', understood 'just how frustrating and dispiriting' the experience had been, and promised it would never happen again. He would do all he could to ensure *A Turn in the South* was a success. Yet at precisely this moment, Vidia was arranging to sell the rights to a big travel book on India, rather than write the unspecified novel he had already sold to Knopf. Andrew Wylie, who acted as Gillon Aitken's associate in New York, demanded $600,000 for the privilege of publishing this unwritten masterpiece; Mehta reluctantly offered $200,000. But Vidia had already plotted to move elsewhere, knowing that another publisher might produce more money for a book on India. In honeyed words, Aitken wrote to Mehta that 'Knopf have not really been successful in moving Vidia out of a somewhat conservative sales pattern ... Your own intimate knowledge of your own country, which I saw only as an advantage to Vidia, runs the risk, in our view, of operating as an inhibition.'[70] The defection was set in train, and Vidia prepared to travel to Bombay at the end of the year, accompanied by his ever biddable mistress.

A Turn in the South made a loss for Knopf, who were also left with an unwritten novel ticking in their accounts. Mehta was not the only man to be driven mercilessly in negotiation; when Vidia took on Gillon Aitken as his agent, he refused to accept the standard commission of 20 per cent on foreign contracts: 'Until I hear from you, all negotiations should be stayed ... I would like a monthly sheet from you recording all contracts or pieces of business pending, and their respective states.'[71] The cut dropped to 15 per cent. Over the coming decade, relishing the role of *homme de confiance*, Gillon would become increasingly bound to Vidia's life and work. Born in Calcutta in 1938 to a stern Scottish jute trader and his wife, he had been sent to a boarding school in Darjeeling at the age of three. His childhood was like something from the days of Kipling: going to the Tollygunge Club with his kind English nanny,

Cissie Bacon, and being attended by 'an eager Indian bearer'. Gillon retained few early memories of his mother and father. In 1945, the family sailed to Glasgow and he was installed at a prep school in Devon. It would be some three years before he saw his parents again. His vacations were spent at rough 'holiday farms' or with his grandparents. After leaving Charterhouse early, Gillon taught at a boys' school in Surbiton, learned French, German and Russian, worked as an eavesdropper in military intelligence in Berlin and become Evelyn Waugh's publisher at Chapman & Hall.[72] Heightist, haughty and charming, commercially ruthless but apparently patrician, a lone wolf who relied only on himself, Gillon Aitken was the ideal agent for Vidia.

During the 1980s, he pushed his client's reputation forward, sharing Vidia's view that he deserved to be treated as a special case by publishers. Using the unique power of the successful artist to make unreasonable demands, Gillon harried André Deutsch over his inefficiency, pursuing him like a prosecuting barrister over his Tippex-covered royalty statements, and finally arranged Vidia's defection to Viking Penguin with *The Enigma of Arrival*. Deutsch's firm was losing money, and he became ever more parsimonious, inviting Vidia only to the cheapest restaurants. In Francis Wyndham's memory, 'Lots of writers like Mailer and Updike had left Deutsch, but Vidia stayed loyal, and left when it was going down the plug. Vidia had good reason to dislike him. Why could he never take him to lunch at the Connaught?'[73] Aided by Anne-Louise Fisher and later by his colleague Sally Riley, Gillon expanded the sale of foreign-language rights in Vidia's backlist around the world. This was an arduous process: 'Vidia is being extremely difficult,' he told Riley in a 1989 memo, 'and wishes to withdraw from the deal with Kiepenheuer & Witsch if they do not pay the full £50,000 on signature.'[74] When André Deutsch Limited was bought out by the publisher Tom Rosenthal, Gillon discovered that the head contracts to Vidia's books (the contracts from which the right to publish paperback editions derived) had been sold to Penguin, and a legal battle ensued as he sought to recover them. Next came the news that the new management at André Deutsch had sold off the archives of the company, which included many letters from Vidia, to the University of Tulsa in Oklahoma. As Vidia's new books were written, Gillon shifted him between publishers, upping the money, selling *India: A Million Mutinies Now* to Heinemann in the UK for £175,000, and returning to the arms of Knopf after it was published in the USA by

Viking Penguin. Helen Fraser, his new British publisher, found Vidia to be 'an appreciative author. *A Million Mutinies* was one of the most successful books I published at Heinemann.'[75]

The working relationship between Vidia and Gillon was complex and symbiotic. A dispute with the *Sunday Telegraph* over some articles which had been paid for but not published gives an idea of its nature: 'I suppose we could have sued the newspaper, but I think we were right to pull away grandly,' wrote the agent to his author. 'I do not think there is anything that could constructively be done, except to remember and punish later.'[76] As Vidia's reputation for curmudgeonly behaviour grew, Gillon used it as a bludgeoning tool in negotiation, telling editors of his terrible anger over minor lapses, and working up a palaver. In a pincer movement with Andrew Wylie in 1990, he offered some book extracts to the *New York Review of Books* for $125,000, a figure way beyond the magazine's usual fees. When they offered $10,000 instead, he told Bob Silvers his client was fatally offended. Never one to forgive a past favour, the man without loyalties threatened to break his links with the *New York Review*. An anguished letter from Rea Hederman arrived at Dairy Cottage: 'Gillon said any damage could be repaired in part by our offering $20,000 ... Bob is sending Gillon his personal $10,000 check which represents the difference between the agreed figure with Viking and Gillon's estimate of damage reparations ... This is a simple, sincere gesture by Bob to put an end to an episode that has greatly troubled him.'[77]

When the director of the National Portrait Gallery, Charles Saumarez Smith, asked Vidia to sit for a portrait and mentioned that another writer was unavailable, it was Gillon who had to interpret the lack of a reply. He was 'hesitating to raise this matter' with V.S. Naipaul and 'extremely loath to attribute to him sensibilities he may not possess,' but suggested his silence might be because he did not relish 'standing in for the unreachable Derek Walcott!' On one occasion, Gillon caused Vidia undisguised joy. In 1991, the Inland Revenue ruled that he had no tax liability for the year in which he was out of the country writing *A Turn in the South*. In addition, aided by arguments from Vidia's accountant Barry Kernon, they accepted that he was non-domiciled for tax purposes in the UK – meaning that since he might one day return to his country of origin, he need pay no tax on money kept offshore in a bank account in Jersey. From São Paulo, where he was sojourning with Margaret, Vidia wrote Gillon the most enthusiastic letter of his life: 'I am <u>utterly delighted</u> by your fax with the news from Barry Kernon.'[78]

*

In his Wiltshire incarnation, lunching or dining occasionally with people in whom he took a marginal interest, Vidia never spoke of Margaret, and said little of his travels. He kept his own counsel. Once or twice a year the Naipauls had lunch with the Powells, who lived thirty miles away in Somerset in substantial bucolic style, with sheep, a lake and grottoes. In old age Anthony Powell published his private journals, which lurched further into self-parody with each successive volume. He would complain about social breaches, such as 'unsophisticated people' addressing his wife as Lady Powell rather than as Lady Violet, and liked to record pieces of random gossip, like the news that Lady Antonia Fraser had a black chauffeur who 'talks like Chokey in *Decline and Fall*', or that Harold Pinter was irate about the untidiness at his tennis club.[79] Publication did little to improve Powell's reputation as a novelist, but the volumes do provide observant glimpses of Vidia masquerading as a country squire. Tony Powell had a 'tradition' that whenever Pat and Vidia visited, they had to be served 'curry', which he took pride in cooking himself.[80] A friendly and sociable figure, he introduced them to other upper-class families in the extended neighbourhood. Vidia had little respect for his talents as a novelist, but liked him. After Powell's death, he wrote maliciously in *A Writer's People* that he had finally read an omnibus edition of his books, and been horrified by his vanity and lack of narrative skill: 'It may be that the friendship lasted all this time because I had not examined his work.'[81] Helen Fraser, who published both men, thought Powell had no great interest in Vidia's writing. 'He had a benign, amused novelist's curiosity about everyone, and he was most interested in Vidia as a personality, as an unusual type of person.'[82]

Tony Powell admired Vidia's quick intelligence, his ability to interpret handwriting and faces, and in particular his outspoken political and racial opinions, which in his eyes were made authentic by his alien background. In May 1982 during the Falklands War, he recorded: 'Vidia said we ought to have bombed Buenos Aires right away, now too late. Added that the Argentines . . . are vain, aggressive, not amenable to anything but force. I am sure he is right.'[83] He invited Vidia to a 'luncheon' at Claridge's in 1986 to celebrate the publication of his book *The Fisher King*, attended by the likes of Roy Fuller, Alan Ross, Hilary Spurling, Kingsley Amis and

Miriam Gross.[84] After being driven over to Dairy Cottage by his son John in 1988, Powell wrote, 'Vidia was as usual in great form, he delivered a terrific diatribe against rich Arabs, indeed Muslims in business anyway, their dishonesty in financial matters, conviction that it does not matter swindling "Unbelievers", in fact is a praiseworthy act. The food good, if rather oddly assorted, lobster soup, odds and ends of crab, almond crumble; excellent Pauillac (missed the Château) '76.'[85] Powell saw Vidia as an insider. After meeting the *New York Times* critic Mel Gussow and his wife Ann at lunch, he thought Ann Gussow had 'seemed a bit bewildered by it all, V[iolet] thought possibly on account of Vidia's being so essentially part of the British social and intellectual life. Americans are always so acutely conscious of racial tensions.'[86] Mel Gussow had been an early promoter of Vidia's work in the American press.

On a visit to Dairy Cottage in 1983, Violet and Tony Powell met Gillon Aitken, his wife Cari and Vidia's German translator Karin Graf. 'The Aitkens were perhaps in middle of a matrimonial row. He recently had his licence removed for drunk-in-charge, and there had been some car trouble on way down,' Powell noted. 'Vidia was in good form, funny in his best manner about the Pakistan [sic] writer Salman Rushdie (who won Booker Prize), and said something disobliging about Vidia in *Harpers & Queen*, or similar periodical: ". . . I'm sorry . . . I'm very sorry to hear that . . . No respect for his elders . . . He will learn that sort of thing is a mistake . . . People merely think . . ." All perfectly true. I haven't read any of Rushdie's books, but he sounds an ass from interviews. Vidia produced nice red Graves. Pat looked rather harassed, as indeed she probably is.'[87] Powell would record mundane but revealing aspects of his friend's life: 'Vidia has now bought a car (Saab), after years of existence in taxis. His great interest is now wine, which he buys at Marks & Spencer, where it is apparently very good.'[88] In his journals, he collected local gossip; lunching in Hampshire with Tanya and Anthony Hobson, to whom he had introduced Vidia, he discovered that, 'Pat Naipaul is apparently not allowed by Vidia to garden (quite why is not clear), if she does so clandestinely while he is resting in afternoon he will suddenly pull aside the curtains and denounce her from the window.'[89]

In a diary entry in March 1985, Tony Powell described a dinner held at 10 Downing Street, organized by Hugh Thomas, at which the other guests included Hugh Trevor-Roper, Anthony Quinton, Iris Murdoch, Noel Annan, Max Egremont, Theodore Zeldin and Vidia. After the meal, a staged intellectual discussion took place centring around the prime minister, Margaret Thatcher, and moderated by Hugh Thomas, to whom she had given a peerage. Vidia sat beside Thatcher, and another guest, David Pryce-Jones, recalled his conversation. 'Iris Murdoch said at a certain point that what was required was a caring and compassionate society. Vidia was like a knife. He said, "Iris, I first heard those words twenty years ago. They had no meaning then, and they have less meaning now." It was just devastating in front of Mrs Thatcher as a put-down to Iris, who then didn't speak again. Mrs Thatcher clearly enjoyed Vidia. He was – I would say – one of the stars of that particular evening.'[90]

Although Vidia was happy at times to accept invitations of this sort, he made little effort to seek social advancement. He and Pat never became part of a group of friends in Wiltshire, although they would accept the hospitality of well-connected people, and occasionally entertained guests for lunch or tea. During the late 1980s and early 1990s, when Vidia was not travelling, they spent most of their time alone. Gillon's office had to deal with administrative matters such as automatically turning down requests for permission to quote from Vidia's books, but the two occupants of Dairy Cottage received ceaseless enquiries. Some were a cause for concern or anger: reading a copy of *Departures* magazine (sent free to Vidia as an American Express gold card holder), Pat found an article by the photographer Mirella Ricciardi which copied sections of 'A New King for the Congo', published in the *New York Review* in 1975. Gillon sought and won an apology, and compensation. Ricciardi's excuse was an original one: she had copied the material from 'an old and dilapidated magazine article from which both title and signature were missing and there was no way that I could have known who the author was . . . I am not familiar with the laws covering plagiarism.'[91]

Pat still made occasional use of her diary, and was hoping to write an autobiography. It became an attempt to expiate her deep unhappiness. Like her other writings, it was disjointed and went through dozens of drafts before stopping, undone:

> I really began to feel this urge to write, about the world in which I found myself, in the late sixties. I had been lucky, I had been able to travel quite widely, mainly in the New Commonwealth . . . I was in daily contact with someone >– I will call him, for convenience sake, the Genius –< who could do the sort of writing I wanted to do, any sort of writing, superbly well. It wasn't his example which set me off, I was strangely dead to that, it was his character. He was

once supposed to have said to a woman, the wife of an important man, whom he had just met at a party, 'It doesn't matter what you think.'[92] He didn't need to say that to me. He made it painfully obvious ... He was no male chauvinist, not then. He was like it with everybody in a way. In company his conversation was prized for its directness and fun, and a certain outrageous quality. He was always capable of an exchange of wit that was quick and generous, >or of sympathy at a personal level< but of an exchange of views – never ... He held strong, not to say extreme views about many things. Some of them affected me. I can't say they clashed with mine because, I can admit it now, I didn't have any, only positions taken up long ago and never relinquished. I felt assaulted but I could not defend myself.[93]

Pat could not defend herself. She was not sure what she should be doing, or whether any other kind of life was possible. Her diary trailed off during the 1980s, though sometimes she would write a few paragraphs. 'I saw Margaret Thatcher as an image, a beautiful idol who could, through a change in circumstances, some dreadful magic, become ugly. I saw her as the goddess Kali, double imaged, turning to reveal the tusks, the blood. She promised "to heal the wounds of a divided nation" I thought she might tear it apart.' When Bernard Levin – whom Pat had long admired – came to lunch before interviewing Vidia, she noted, 'He has beautiful tiny feet, beautiful brown brogues ... Talked only about himself – as he has already written in his articles.' Interested in progressive politics, Pat liked the idea of a party that was neither Labour nor Conservative, but found it impossible to become a devotee: 'Do I believe in the Liberal Democrats, their policy? Probably not. Do I like them? If I were honest, not very much ... the odd grey-faced man who had come down to talk to us from "Cowley Street" in smoke-filled rooms filled me with dismay. And some of the bumph, leaflets etc. which emanate from the same source are simply ludicrous.'[94] Pat tried again to write autobiographically: 'I married out of my race and nation while I was still a student.' She became angry when she saw a television interview with Kingsley Amis. 'In it he had attacked American novelists, Updike particularly (I had enjoyed Couples) and had said, with deliberate frivolity, that he would rather read the work of a popular writer like Dick Francis any day.' Why did people put up with this? 'Why are they so tolerant of extremes, petulance, childishly reactionary views? We just believe that middle-aged writers are like that. We have this ridiculous faith, we believe it is a protective covering, the wizard's cloak, beneath which they preserve their real selves for serious work. It is the tribute we pay to their talent.'⁹⁵

In 1989, soon after Vidia returned from India, Pat learned that she had cancer. She had been for breast screening in the nearby town of Amesbury, and was told to go for further tests. Vidia went with her and Mr Keel, a local taxi driver, to a Southampton hospital for a biopsy. 'I was deep in writing *A Million Mutinies*. There was that dreadful drive and I was enraged at the hospital because it was such a messy place . . . and then I had to go back in the afternoon to pick up Pat, and we got lost . . . I just couldn't find out where Pat would be waiting. Eventually I found her. She was in a wheelchair, obviously terribly stressed, very unhappy and obviously in pain and waiting in solitude and I had been very angry all of that day. When I saw her, I became so ashamed. It was very upsetting for me. As long as Pat could look after me, it was all right. When I felt this [illness] had come to her, I was full of shame at my rage. I should have done more. It's the thing about the work. If you are travelling for material or to write a book, it isn't that you are self-centred, it is that you are with the work. You are obsessed with what you are doing. And when you start writing, it is such a delicate thing, writing, shaping a paragraph, a page, shaping a chapter, having a sense of the bigger structure of the book, you've got to be with it all the time. You are carrying it in your head, and things that upset you are very irritating.'⁹⁶

Pat told no one about the details of her illness, but when Mel Gussow visited for lunch in July he learned that an operation was planned, and that it appeared to be for cancer treatment. A theatre critic and friend of Harold Pinter, Gussow shared the news with Antonia Fraser, who wrote to Pat: 'I heard in a roundabout way – from Mel Gussow, who was very diffident about telling me but I'm glad he did – that you are having an operation on Friday. What rotten luck! Though I hope it may turn out to be in the end good luck. And a total cure.'⁹⁷ The surgery was severe: she suffered the indignity of a mastectomy, losing her right breast, making her feel less than a whole woman. The treatment appeared to have worked, and for the next two years there was no recurrence of the disease. Pat kept silent, even to herself, about the trauma of what had happened to her body, avoiding the subject altogether in her diary. Like the name of her husband's mistress, the word 'cancer' does not appear in her writing. She wore a 'tru-life breast prosthesis', the hospital providing her with a list of local underwear shops where she could go for specialist fitting: 'Mrs Haskell in Contessa at Shirley (Not Wednesdays)' and 'Wendy Miles in Vanity Fayre, Station Road, New Milton'.[98]

Meanwhile, letters kept coming to Dairy Cottage, requiring answers.[99] For the most part, they were simply ignored and filed away by Pat for posterity. Contrary as ever, Vidia took particular pleasure in turning down importuning interviewers. 'Dear Mr Bellacasa, Nothing in your questions suggests any knowledge of my work. An interview would be a considerable waste of my time and energy.' He gave passing attention to Selwyn R. Cudjoe of Wellesley College, who had spent ten years writing a book about his books and wished to talk of Barthes and Bakhtin; he rejected an appeal by *Vanity Fair*, and took no notice of Marina Salandy-Brown of the BBC, who tried to wrong-foot him by saying that since she was 'a fellow Trinidadian' he was sure to refuse her. Sometimes he responded warmly, for instance to a woman whose husband, an art teacher, had died of a brain haemorrhage the day after reading *The Enigma of Arrival*. Letters came from old acquaintances like Banning Eyre, who was busy writing software manuals and learning about African music, and Karan Singh, who was 'hoping that you would get the Nobel Prize this year, although Octavio is also an old friend.' Vidia gave unexpected hospitality to Hanif Kureishi, who had achieved fame with his script for *My Beautiful Laundrette* but was wondering where to go with his writing. Kureishi said his father too had been a journalist who had wanted success as a novelist, but never achieved it. Vidia invited him to Wiltshire for cake and Indian champagne, and gave advice on writing and how to look after his bad back – a common topic of conversation between working writers. In turn, Kureishi invited Vidia to meet him in London, and said, as others would: 'You have been a great inspiration and example to young writers like myself. When I was in my teens there were no other Indian writers living and working here that one could refer to.'

Each day, there were questions – intrusions – for Pat or Vidia to ponder. Would V.S. Naipaul open the Hounslow Book Mela? Would he give an interview to *Izvestia*? Would he like to acquire two gouache paintings inspired by *The Enigma of Arrival*? What did 'string bed' mean in *A House for Mr Biswas*, asked his Brazilian Portuguese translator? 'What kind of pipe is a "cheelum"?' Would he come to Conrad Black's 1992 election-night party at the Savoy for 'Champagne,

Crustaceans and Breakfast'? Would he give out the prizes at the Society of Authors annual awards ceremony? Would he come for an 'informal talk' with the Indian prime minister, Narasimha Rao, at London's Nehru Centre? Would he have lunch with his MP, Robert Key, to meet the environment secretary, Chris Patten? Would he sign a petition supporting Salman Rushdie, who had been sentenced to death by Ayatollah Khomeini and was now being defended by every right-thinking littérateur in the world, with Harold and Antonia leading the charge of the righteous in London? No, and for good measure he added, 'I don't know his books, but I've been aware of his statements. I found them usually left-wing and trivial and antiquated.' And what of Khomeini's fatwa? 'It's an extreme form of literary criticism.'[100] Would he sign a letter to *The Times* about the landscape around Stonehenge? He would – in the company of a bishop, a solicitor and Richard Stilgoe from *Countdown*, Vidia's name heading the list: 'The threatened land, which forms habitat for larks, lapwings, stone curlews and English partridges, would be destroyed for ever, and for the sake merely of upgrading the existing A303.'[101]

CHAPTER TWENTY-FOUR

ARISE, SIR VIDIA

WHEN VIDIA'S RELATIONS and foreign acquaintances visited Britain, he did his best to avoid them. Ralph Ironman had been surprised while in London in the early 1980s to be asked to meet Shiva instead, who took him to an Indian restaurant and told him that he would have been able to tolerate hotter food if he had been to a good public school.[1] Moni Malhoutra was an exception. While visiting England on Indira Gandhi's staff, he was invited to stay the night in Wiltshire. 'Vidia pulled out a very expensive bottle of port which he wanted me to drink. I had my first sip and he jumped down my throat and said, "That's not the way to have port." So I said, "How am I supposed to have port?" "You are supposed to chew it." So he took it into his mouth and masticated noisily. "This is the way to enjoy port." So I did that. Pat treated him with great reverence. Always. It was almost like appreciating a deity. She was awed by him, and I think it made it difficult for her because she was aware that she had to do her bit to encourage the flowering of his talents: if that meant not creating a single creak when walking in the house, so be it. She was a very Indian wife in many respects – more Indian than most Indian wives – the way the woman sacrifices her own life for her husband. It was an unusual kind of relationship for an Englishwoman.'

Later, when Moni Malhoutra was working at the Commonwealth Secretariat in London, he would be invited with his wife, Leela, to view Vidia's Indian miniature paintings.

My wife thought that he was very self-centred and didn't observe the normal courtesies that people do. But Vidia is Vidia. It was a mutually enriching experience. He said to me one day, 'Why does the Indian Council for Cultural Relations, financed by the Government of India, send out Indian classical dancers to perform in Africa? What's the point of it? They have no eye for this kind of thing, you are wasting your money, you are wasting your time and it reinforces the belief about Indians being a weak race.' So I asked, 'What do you think we should do?' He said, 'You should send circuses.' I said, 'Vidia you are not serious.' He said, 'I am absolutely serious. When I was in Nairobi an Indian circus came there. An Indian opened the lion's mouth with his hands and put his head in and there was pin-drop silence. The Africans were absolutely stunned to see an Indian doing this. The next day the entire cabinet came to witness this performance. That's what you should do. Please tell your prime minister to stop sending high culture to Africa. You should send circuses.' He also said – and I think he was right – that this huge programme you have of bringing African students to study in India is counter-productive. It doesn't win you any friends; it only makes you enemies. They experience the full weight of Indian colour prejudice. He was utterly serious. From his own experiences . . . both in the Caribbean and in Africa, people of Indian origin have been treated badly. That must have had an effect on him.[2]

In December 1988, Vidia reactivated his contacts for his new book, *India: A Million Mutinies Now*. Earlier in the year, he had been excited to start using an IBM word processor. His old Blue Bird typewriter, which he had bought to type out the final draft of *A House for Mr Biswas*, was put away in the attic at Dairy Cottage. Lacking technological nostalgia, Vidia loved the idea of now being able to store his work electronically. He wrote to Gillon Aitken: 'How lovely to compose on the screen, to consume one's rage there. And then to print so beautifully, in proportionally spaced letters, with right-hand justification. And then, would you believe, to tell the instrument to save the letter in its capacious memory. So I can call up the letter in a tick, make a correction, and then print another copy.'[3] Aged fifty-six, he would spend five months travelling in India, braving the heat and the noise and the bureaucracy and the dust and the poverty, beginning in Bombay, looping south through Goa, Bangalore, Mysore and Madras before heading north to Calcutta and working his way west to Delhi, interloping in Lucknow, the Punjab and Kashmir. Old helpers like Adil Jussawalla and Rahul Singh were asked to provide introductions and information.

Vidia began his research while staying in style in one of the country's finest hotels, the Taj in Bombay, overlooking the Gateway of India.[4] Vinod Mehta, the editor of the *Indian Post*, found himself overwhelmed by the visitor's sense of entitlement; Mehta was expected, with the help of his reporters, to locate gangsters, poets, extremists, corporators, slum dwellers and feudal Muslims from the north:

> Vidia gets four or five people to help him, and makes life hell for those five people. He's a weird person. He doesn't understand the position of others. If someone turned up late for a meeting, I would get the blame . . . It became very difficult for me, because he wanted my car all the time. And so twice or thrice I would send him the car and I found that the driver would say, he's called me again tomorrow. I had to tell him that my car was going for servicing and it's somebody else's car. He is very tight-fisted, there is no question about that . . . I was an editor, so I had a secretary, and I had staff. I thought initially that maybe the great writer doesn't want to get involved in mundane things like booking an air ticket, or getting a taxi. But Vidia went a little further and suggested he just couldn't do this, that it was beyond him somehow: 'Oh, it is very compli-cated, you know.' When Margaret was there he just transferred everything on to her. Her devotion to Vidia was so total and complete, but I don't think she was a very intelligent person. He used her shamelessly.

Mehta was aware that Vidia's stimulating conversation and 'great sympathy' when he learned that he had been sacked from his previous job did not mean their relationship was on any normal footing. 'I never got the impression he was grateful. He expected it of me, as if I was privileged in the sense of aiding him in that great venture. I was a source, a handler, then I became a friend. After twenty years this didn't extend to him giving me his telephone number. I think overall he is one of the most complex human beings I've met: I've never met anyone as insightful, or as brilliant. But he is certainly not an easy person to know . . . He was not a person who was going to tell you a great deal about himself. His books will tell you about himself, but he won't tell you.'[5]

India: A Million Mutinies Now started well, and got better. 'Bombay is a crowd. But I began to feel, when I was some way into the city from the airport that morning, that the crowd on the pavement and the road was very great, and that something unusual might be happening.'[6] Something was happening: a celebration of the Dalit leader, Dr Ambedkar. India was at the beginning of a social, political and economic upheaval that would lead to the nation's triumphant rise at the end of the century, a million mutinies leading to a new phase of creativity and progress. 'Independence had come to India like a kind of revolution; now there were many revolutions within that revolution.'[7] Once again, Vidia sensed that something important was taking place in a country where others still saw only a continuation of old patterns. The book would be long – too long – but exceptional in its narrative perception. In the first section, set in Bombay, he wrote of Dalits, of local political leaders, of activism, of people who were raising themselves and their communities from difficult beginnings. The author is present in the text, enquiring on behalf of the reader. A Muslim tells of seeing a man murdered when he was a boy; Vidia wants details: the man was lying on a handcart with his head nearly severed. 'What clothes?' 'Underwear. Shorts and a singlet. And the body in the throes of death caused the handcart to capsize.'[8] So the reader has a picture of the murder scene. Nor did he hide the role of his guides or interpreters, such as 'Nikhil, a young magazine journalist I had got to know' or 'Charu, a young Maharashtrian brahmin'.[9] The result was a book in which discrete voices were heard, and stories were told that had never been told before. A chapter was devoted to 'The Secretary's Tale', recounting the twists and turns of the unremarkable but somehow representative life of 'Rajan', an assistant to a powerful Bombay politician.

In order to bring this off, Vidia exploited his contacts, driving them hard to deliver the interviewees he wanted in the settings he wanted. Through sheer force of will, using his fame, grandeur, necessity and a pretence of incapability, this least incapable of men found the living subjects he needed. Nikhil Lakshman, the young journalist, took him on an outing to the suburbs:

> The trip to Thane and back was really exhausting, a whole day trip. We went by train, first class . . . He didn't pay for the train tickets, he was a 'kanjoos', thrifty, kind of an Uncle Scrooge. Mr Naipaul was an anachronism in his suit and I think he had his felt hat on. When we came back he wanted his shoes shined because obviously there was a lot of dust on the roads of Thane, and at V[ictoria] T[erminus] the shoeshine boy looked at him. He was talking to me about magical realism: he just hit it out of the park, dismissed Márquez with the contempt that he brings so eloquently, 'There's far too much reality in Colombia and writers must express it with

realism rather than resort to all these gimmicks.' He was talking and this shoeshine boy who probably came from the same part of the world as Naipaul's ancestors looked at me and said, 'Hamare jaise dikhte hein, lekin angrezi to bolte hein saab jaise', which means, 'He looks like us, but look at his English, he speaks like an Englishman' . . . I dropped him off at the Taj and I asked what he was going to do. He was surprised to hear the question. 'I'm going to write up today's notes.' That's what I keep telling [other journalists]: you may be the greatest writer in the world but at the end of the day, you have to go up and write your notes. I really learnt from him that you can't have a dream and not invest that kind of commitment in it. He was the master.

Later, Vidia told Nikhil Lakshman he was too fat. 'He said how are you going to lose weight? I said, I am going to walk. "That's not going to do anything. You've got to enrol in a gymnasium. Is there a gymnasium near your office?"' He was shocked by Vidia's casual conversation, and the way he spoke of one of his own heroes: 'The *Illustrated Weekly* broke the story in 1988 about this Hindi film actress Neena Gupta having a baby by the West Indian cricketer Vivian Richards. Mr Naipaul said, "How could she have a child by that nigger?" I was appalled. For a lot of us, Viv Richards is God.'[10]

Charudatta Deshpande, the 'Maharashtrian brahmin', a thirty-two-year-old political journalist who had been asked by his editor Vinod Mehta to help Vidia, spent two or three weeks arranging interviews. He made it clear beforehand that he did not like Vidia's earlier books on India. 'I didn't think he had a desire to deliberately distort, but he had a preconceived notion. I believe that he worked from a larger picture and he knew basically what he wanted to see, and tried to fit everything into that conception. It's like creating your own world.' Deshpande was asked to fix a meeting with Vithal Chavan, a local Shiv Sena leader on the fringes of criminality. He asked Vidia if he could telephone him from the Taj: 'I found that he was hesitating. He said when you come up to my room, you'll meet a friend of mine. Then I walked in, and a lady was looking out of the window. I felt that the air was quite hostile, quite tense between them. I talked to Vithal and fixed up the appointment. It was very awkward to stand in that room and not to have any conversation with the lady. I said, so how are you finding India? The moment I broached the subject, she just came out and said, I feel completely bored . . . She stayed in the Taj. She would never accompany him.'

At the chawl or slum where Vithal lived, Deshpande interpreted: 'Vithal Chavan couldn't speak in English, Naipaul couldn't understand Marathi. The funny part was Vithal wanted to talk about his political career, and Naipaul was interested in his personal life, how twelve people managed to live in a room. Naipaul would go into excruciating detail, asking what happened to his wife, what happened to his sister, how she ran away, all those details. Vithal got very edgy. I said, a time will come, this person may get a Nobel Prize and I said you'll be very happy that you figured in his book. Vithal told me, it doesn't make a damn difference to me what he writes in English, and look, in case he has some problem with admission for his children to school, let me know, I can fix it. So I told that to Mr Naipaul and he laughed and said, no, no, no, I haven't any admission problems, I don't have kids at all.'[11]

Over the following months, as he travelled through the south and then the north, Vidia collected cuttings, pamphlets and books: *Final Victory is Ours* by the Tamil Eelam Liberation Organization Propaganda Unit, *Rural Development (Village Reform)* by Periyar E.V. Ramasami, *The Anguish of Punjab* by the Council of Sikh Affairs. At each stage, he listened carefully and wrote up his notes in the evening in the hotel in tiny, precise handwriting. His helpers were amazed by his ability to recall detail. Sadanand Menon, a writer from Madras, told Vidia about the Dravidian movement: 'Just once in a while he would pull out a notebook from inside his coat pocket and say, "May I write that down?" Very neat handwriting. He would write down one sentence, then the notebook would go back. Whereas in *A Million Mutinies* he has quoted me for about ten or twelve pages. It is so accurate, every full stop and comma. I was amazed. Later I even asked him, did you carry a tape recorder? Just about every Indian writer in English today unhesitatingly mentions Naipaul as his style guru; his politics is a different matter.'[12] H.V. Nathan – 'Rajan' in 'The Secretary's Tale' – expressed similar feelings: 'I must say he has been absolutely faithful to what I told him. Not a single departure.'[13] Another interviewee, M.D. Riti – 'Kala' in the book – commended the accuracy of his redaction, as did Nasir Abid, a copywriter from Lucknow who was rendered as 'Rashid': 'It was verbatim; he hadn't paraphrased.'[14]

Problems arose however when Vidia was required to assess unreliable information. Sadanand Menon was disappointed by his reaction to 'Naxalite' revolutionaries: 'It so happened that during that time it was the high point of the Maoist movement. A lot of young people were being arrested or killed in "encounters" with the police ... Now to get close to that movement, he made the mistake of contacting the Inspector General of Police [in Madras], who had a huge handlebar moustache. This guy was bringing thirty, forty of these young boys and parading them for Naipaul at the Taj Coromandel Hotel. It was a tragic scene. They were just brought in, paraded as Naxalites and the interpreters were invariably police. It was a fix. I think he got taken for a nice ride there, whereas if he was genuinely interested he could have met more articulate elements of the movement who were writers and poets. It was a joke.'[15] Nor did Vidia like the hotel in Madras: 'This room (which was booked for me quite a while ago) has a filthy carpet,' he wrote to the manager. 'It has no chair, and must be one of the few hotels not to have a chair. It has a television set, but it hasn't been plugged in. I was promised a chair by someone who came to the room. The chair hasn't come.'[16]

Madras was a rare lapse; most of the time, Vidia relied on the background knowledge of unpaid local reporters to ensure the veracity of his interviews. Personal relations were another matter. His behaviour outraged Nasir Abid, twelve years his junior. On the day he was leaving Lucknow, Vidia asked Abid for a further interview.

> So we trooped back into the hotel room and I told him some stories. He was leaving for the airport. 'I know, Nazia – Naipaul could never pronounce my name properly, he cultivated a lot of idiosyncrasies in his mannerisms, in his speech – I know, Nazia, we'll talk on the way to the airport.' I am tired. I have been taking this guy around for five days. I used to miss lunch sometimes. So I made a wry face. 'I'm coming to the airport with you, am I?' Then I realized what a big blunder I had committed. He clammed up and said, 'I appreciate what you have done for me.' So he paid the hotel bill and he got into a taxi. I am now feeling miserable for having been so rude. He sits down in the taxi and I say, goodbye, Vidia. I don't get any reply from him. Vidia, goodbye. The car engine started. A third time I tried, Vidia, goodbye. He didn't reply. He turned his face and the taxi left. That really hurt ... He took advantage of the Indian tradition of hospitality.[17]

By now, Margaret was no longer travelling with Vidia, having been dismissed in New Delhi. The split came after a meeting with a cub reporter from the *Sunday Observer*: in Vidia's words, 'Somebody said to me, you must talk to Harinder Baweja about the guerrilla crisis in the Punjab, so I invited her to dinner. Harinder is a very small Sikh lady, very nice. So I talked to her. I was leaning across the table. Margaret was enraged. "You ignored me all evening." I couldn't deal with that. So I had to send her home.'[18] Harinder Baweja was unaware that her briefing had provoked a serious rupture: 'Naipaul was treating [Margaret] badly and she was taking it, pecking at her food, getting angrier and angrier, behaving worse than a submissive Indian wife.'[19]

Some people were entertained by Vidia's manner and style. In Calcutta he and Margaret had dinner with Malavika Sanghvi and her husband Vir, both upcoming journalists, who served Dom Perignon and black-market Russian caviar. Malavika found Vidia 'a charming gentleman, very interested, asking a lot of questions about our lives. Vir asked him why he hadn't gone out in Calcutta, and he said he feared going to an intellectual's house and at the end of the evening a lady presenting him with a slim volume of poetry. I had just published a volume of poetry, and it was lying on the table waiting to be presented to the great man. So I hid it under the sofa!'[20] Vir asked Vidia about the book he was writing: 'He said he had changed his mind about India, that when he first came it was a very different place ... but now it was transformed. He said, "I find so much energy, I find so much happening." Then we discussed whether he would ever get the Nobel Prize and he said, "Of course I won't get it, they'll give it to some nigger or other." But everybody was drunk and it may have been said in a jokey sort of way.' Vir Sanghvi felt that Vidia's relationship with Margaret was friendly, and that she was 'his window to the world. She seemed to complement Naipaul. She made all his calls, all his arrangements. I said something about *The Return of Eva Perón*, and Margaret got extremely agitated and said the book just showed that he didn't understand Argentina at all, and he had got it completely wrong, he got the men wrong because this is not the way Argentinian men treat their women. "Vidia, you really shouldn't go to countries you know nothing about." And he took it with very good grace, he giggled and laughed. It was obvious they had had this conversation before.'[21] Later, when Vidia called Vir Sanghvi's office, the staffer who picked up the telephone failed to believe that he was speaking to V.S. Naipaul. 'He said, "Oh yes, I'm Salman Rushdie." So Naipaul said, "Well, ring me at the Oberoi." So the guy called up, and was put through to a pastry chef whose name was Nagpal.'[22]

During his months of travel for *India: A Million Mutinies Now*, Vidia opened himself to a new vision of the country. To the surprise of readers of his earlier books, he saw beyond the corruption and violence to something original and redemptive. It was a personal homecoming, as he continued to seek an ancestral past, trying to link himself to a nation that was, in his imagination, his own source. He travelled to Kashmir and met Mr Butt and Aziz from the Liward Hotel; he went to the south to find another memory of 1962, a pilgrim from Amarnath named V.C. Chakravarthy, whom he renamed 'Sugar' in the book. Often, Vidia was lionized. When he went to the Punjab to a site of recent, terrible slaughter, a police chief who was suppressing the separatist militancy was so delighted by his eminent visitor that he flew him back to Delhi by helicopter. Vidia's inclinations were becoming increasingly authoritarian, although he still upheld the dignity of the individual. As he told a visiting interviewer from *Time* who had caught up with him in Madras, ' "I'm for individual rights and for law." It's a long view that includes his fascination with ancient Rome ("I can barely express my admiration for it") and the imperial record of the English.'[23] To those he encountered during his long journey, though, V.S. Naipaul seemed in his operating methods and self-assertion and racial statements to come from a different, halfway world, as he sought to out-Indian the Indians: in his appearance and performance, he had emerged from an unfamiliar, faraway island. Nasir Abid noted how he dressed in Lucknow. 'He was wearing a tropical suit. His collar buttoned. It was very hot. Short white trousers with white socks showing. Loafers with a little bow. His skin was parched, like dried wood, walnut . . . If he kept his hat on he could pass off easily as a Negro. He looked more like a Chicago mobster with that hat, tight collar. He didn't look like your ordinary run-of-the-mill Indian. No Indian buttons his collar without a tie.'[24]

When the book was published in late 1990 the reviews were good, and importantly for Vidia, the sales were too. Large extracts ran in the London *Sunday Telegraph*; he journeyed through the United States, being paid to lecture; he won the Premio Nonino and the British Book Awards prize for the best travel book of the year. His publisher, Helen

Fraser at Heinemann, told him he was at number ten in the *Sunday Times* bestseller list. 'We are absolutely thrilled. The paperback has reprinted 3 times and copies in print are up to 60,000.'[25] For Paul Theroux, *India: A Million Mutinies Now* was 'literally the last word on India today, witness within witness, a chain of voices . . . from the so-called Untouchable, the Dalit, to the maharajah.'[26] *Tatler* praised Naipaul's 'dramatic change of tone'.[27] In the *Financial Times*, K. Natwar Singh deduced that he 'may well have written his own enduring monument'.[28] Janette Turner Hospital in the *New York Times* observed, 'No sensory detail, no sign or symbol, is too small for Mr Naipaul's attention,' but felt he had neglected to interview enough women.[29] Auberon Waugh found that the cruelty had disappeared from Naipaul's wit: 'He has become a gentler, kinder, infinitely more tolerant person. His sympathies extend to everyone, the religious and the anti-religious, even to the Muslims.'[30] Ian Buruma wrote in the *New York Review*: 'The extraordinary achievement of Naipaul's latest book is that we can see his characters; more than that, we can see how they see, and how they, in turn, are seen by the author . . . Whatever his literary form Naipaul is a master.'[31] From another perspective, the maverick polymath T.G. Vaidyanathan noticed that although the book was 'an ostensible paean to the triumph of subaltern India over the centuries-old might of Upanishadic India' it was in fact a respectful 'elegy to Brahminism'. T.G.V. had no doubt which community V.S. Naipaul admired most: 'The Brahmin, then, is the real hero of the book.'[32]

*

As the 1980s drew to a close and the manuscript of *India: A Million Mutinies Now* approached completion, Vidia received letters, the first from Lingston Cumberbatch, acting high commissioner, offering him Trinidad and Tobago's highest award, the Trinity Cross, and another proffering a knighthood from the Queen in the 1990 New Year's honours list. Although he had turned down the opportunity to become a Commander of the Order of the British Empire in 1977, this time Vidia succumbed to the blandishments of flummery. Like Sir Walter Raleigh before him, he went down on one knee before his monarch and arose a knight. Letters came: from John Fawcett of Univ days, from Jim Allen in Kenya, from Jan Carew's old flatmate, from Angus Wilson in a Suffolk nursing home, from his bank manager ('Dear Sir Videadhar'), from Lol O'Keefe in the British Embassy in Prague, from the Spanish ambassador, from his French publisher Ivan Nabokov, from Anthony and Violet Powell ('I had long felt that an honour was overdue'), from David Pryce-Jones ('England has been lucky to have you, and is saying so') and from Hugh Thomas ('I wish you wd come soon to the Lords too for it is a complacent place & needs your attention'). The most moving letter contained a single sentence – 'We are both glad that we were there at the beginning' – followed by two names: André, Diana.

'It was a very low-key affair. I went alone, wearing a charcoal grey Daks suit. I took an Underground train to St James's Park, and walked to the palace. People were snapping away; I had no photographer with me. We had lunch afterwards at the Bombay Brasserie with the Suttons [his old Univ friend James Sutton and his wife].'[33] A few days after attending the investiture at Buckingham Palace, Vidia flew home. At Piarco airport, in Kamla's words, 'A taxi driver recognized Vidia and welcomed him. "Come Mr Naipaul, let me take you, eh? These people don't like you, you know."'[34] One afternoon, while he was staying at Kamla's house, Vidia was greeted by an unexpected face. In his late sixties, his writing career over, living in Canada but on a visit to Trinidad to stay with a friend, Sam Selvon had come to say hello to his old flame Kamla. His friend Ken Ramchand described the encounter:

Naipaul says, 'What are you doing here?' Sam says, 'How you axing me a thing like that? I ent locked in to the writing like you, I ent no proper writer. If I up in Canada and the cold bussin' my arse an' I decide to go by Ken and have a few drink and thing, I just go by he.' Naipaul didn't take it amiss. He was a bit patronizing. He says: 'I see your books are on the CXC [Caribbean Examinations Council] syllabus, you must be making some money.' It was a cordial meeting, with a little bit of needle introduced by Sam ... He says, 'Ken get a boat, we goin' fishin' in de mornin'. We passin' for you at 4 o'clock, you be ready and waiting.' Vidia says he will be. When we leave, I say to Sam, 'Why you say that, you want to impress your brother-in law?'

The next morning, Vidia was ready and waiting. As the three men drove through the dawn light to Cedros to pick up some food from Ken's mother's house – Ken taught at the University of the West Indies; his father had been a motor mechanic on a coconut estate – Vidia stuck his head between the two front seats to listen to a story that Sam was telling about a woman. 'And Vidia says, "What she say to that?" For the rest of the trip, he spoke dialect, he relaxed, became one of the boys.' In Cedros, they were each given a bag containing two rotis:

> Vidia says, 'I will have one now.' Sam says, 'Don't you go be axing me for one on de boat.' I had hired a boat, a pirogue. It was about twenty-foot long, pointed at the front, with an outboard at the back. We went to Soldado Rock [in the Gulf of Paria], looked at Venezuela in the distance. Sam said he wanted to swim. It was a real hot day. Vidia says, 'I would love to, but I don't have my bathing things.' Sam says, 'I swimmin' in my jockey shorts.' Vidia says, 'I can't do that.' We were in the sea, then kerplunk, V.S. Naipaul was in the water, swimming around the boat in his jockey shorts.[35]

With a high literacy rate and growing national wealth from the export of natural gas, Trinidad was some way ahead of the island Vidia had left behind in 1950. He received the Trinity Cross from the hand of Noor Hassanali, the country's first Indian president (there was yet to be an Indian prime minister). 'Happy Naipaul gets his Trinity' was the lead headline in the *Guardian*, with a photograph of the proud scholarship boy and his beaming mother. ' "I'm glad that this has happened," Sir Vidia said of the award ... Asked whether he still considered Trinidad and Tobago and the rest of the Caribbean as a backward place as he had stated in his earlier writings, Sir Vidia said he preferred not to answer. "These are immense questions, my life's work is about that" ... Sir Vidia's mother, Droapatie Naipaul, also attended the award ceremony. "I can't explain how happy I feel," Mrs Naipaul said tearfully, explaining that it was her son's first visit since 1984.'[36] Savi gave a party in Vidia's honour, at which he wore the Trinity Cross on a ribbon around his neck. 'Talk about country bookie, wearing the cross in that way,' said a guest, Margaret Walcott. 'It showed a side of him that was very human.'[37] Despite the photo in the *Guardian*, Vidia and his mother were not properly reconciled. Not long before she died, Nella went to visit her and said, 'So how is your son?' Ma replied, 'I have no son. The son I had died.'[38]

Only months later, in January 1991, at the age of seventy-eight, Ma passed away in her sleep. The prime minister, A.N.R. Robinson, wrote to Vidia expressing his deepest sympathy. 'Truly, she was the matriarch of one of this country's most distinguished families ever, and the nation is deeply indebted to her.'[39] Her surviving son did not go back to attend her funeral, though later that year he visited Guyana and wrote a sympathetic portrait of Cheddi and Janet Jagan, and in 1992 gave a lecture in Trinidad organized by Selby Wooding, at which he met his old QRC friend William Demas, now an eminent economist. Having read *The Loss of El Dorado*, Demas spoke of the cruelty of slavery in the days of the governor Thomas Picton, and suggested his name be removed from the Port of Spain street that bore it. 'It was strange to me (though perhaps it shouldn't have been) to find that in his sixties, and with his success, Demas should have developed racial nerves which I don't think he had had >(or shown)< when we were at school together fifty years before.'[40]

Back in England, Vidia had more awards to face: an honorary degree from Oxford in the company of bedels, proctors, Dame Joan Sutherland and the Queen of Denmark; Trinidad's Humming Bird Medal, which had been given to him in 1970 but never delivered; an honorary degree from the universities of York and London; membership of the happening Harbour Club – one day he found himself exercising alongside Princess Diana, only realizing later that it was the princess herself, rather than a young woman trying to look like the princess. In 1993 he won the first ever David Cohen British Literature Prize, awarded for a lifetime's achievement. In his acceptance speech, he suggested it might have gone instead to Harold Pinter or to Anthony Powell. Pinter wrote in his giant, disjointed hand that he was 'very touched' by the reference, and invited Vidia and Pat to watch his play *No Man's Land* and have supper.[41] 'I cannot remember sitting next to Vidia emanating approval and enjoyment to that degree for so long for years and years,' Pat wrote to Harold and Antonia afterwards.[42] David Pryce-Jones, always slick with a compliment, told Vidia he deserved to win the prize every year: 'Nobody else has contributed to our literature as much as you. This old island has no right to be the recipient of your gifts, and you do it an honour by being here. I'm so glad that due notice is being taken.'[43]

The year ended badly, when Vidia was banned from driving. Pat blamed herself in her diary: 'We went to have dinner with Barbara Neill & Andrew Christie Miller at Clarendon Park in order to meet Francis. I criminally discouraged him from summoning Michael [a taxi driver]. Following instructions to turn right twice finding our way home Vidia drove across the A36 dual carriageway, was stopped by police, breathalised and arrested.'[44] In his column in the London *Evening Standard*, A.N. Wilson wrote, 'We have many goodish writers in this country but few great ones, and V.S. Naipaul is a great writer. He should be cherished, not persecuted. If he happens to be found by the police rather the worse for wear on the public highway, they should have the courtesy to drive him home and tuck him up in bed instead of dragging him through the courts.'[45]

As Vidia's global status developed and stabilized around this time, he made a rare attempt to analyse his own philosophy in an address to the Manhattan Institute in New York. Speaking on the title 'Our Universal Civilization', he suggested in optimistic, even idealistic tones, that a universal civilization or modernity now existed in the world. It had been 'a long time in the making' and transcended any racial boundaries. As a child, 'worried about pain and cruelty' he had discovered 'the Christian precept, Do unto others as you would have others do unto you. There was no such human consolation in the Hinduism I grew up with, and – although I have never had any religious faith – the simple idea was, and is, dazzling to me, perfect as a guide to human behaviour.' Later, he had come to see 'the beauty of the idea of the pursuit of happiness. Familiar words, easy to take for granted; easy to misconstrue. This idea of the pursuit of happiness is at the heart of the attractiveness of the civilization to so many outside it or on its periphery. I find it marvellous to contemplate to what an extent, after two centuries, and after the terrible history of the earlier part of this century, the idea has come to a kind of fruition. It is an elastic idea; it fits all men. It implies a certain kind of society, a certain kind of awakened spirit. I don't imagine my father's parents would have been able to understand the idea. So much is contained in it: the idea of the individual, responsibility, choice, the life of the intellect, the idea of vocation and perfectibility and achievement. It is an immense human idea. It cannot be reduced to a fixed system. It cannot generate fanaticism. But it is known to exist; and because of that, other more rigid systems in the end blow away.'[46]

As the legend of V.S. Naipaul grew, would-be biographers sought him out. The first candidate was Jeffrey Meyers FRSL, a serial producer of books and articles, living in California. With verbal encouragement from Vidia, he began collecting material and planning a book of essays as an accompaniment to an authorized biography, and asked around American institutions to see if they wanted to buy his literary archives.

Meyers went to see Paul Theroux, now living in Cape Cod. 'This man is not a shrinking violet,' Vidia was informed by Paul, no viola himself. 'He and Mrs Meyers were in my library yanking books off the shelves even before we were introduced (Sheila [the second Mrs Theroux] let them into the house). Such nosiness is probably in the biographer's temperament but I found him intrusive – and also over-certain and dogmatic.'[47] Enquiries and closely typed letters from Meyers arrived at Dairy Cottage ('This month I had essays in the American Scholar, the New Criterion and the Virginia Quarterly Review') until, after more than a year of work, Gillon Aitken was told to put him out of his misery.[48] Caught between his sure-footed attackers, Meyers did not know what had happened. He believed he had been betrayed by Vidia and his 'hitman' Gillon. Naipaul was 'a great manipulator, a great manager of his own reputation and public image. He thought he could order a biography as one might a publicity release . . . I broke off relations with him, and felt lucky to escape with my wits and integrity intact.'[49] Next came Ian Buruma, a highbrow journalist, who told Vidia in 1993 that he would be interested in writing about his life as a writer but that, 'To understand you as a man, other, more private friendships and relationships cannot be left unmentioned.'[50] Dealing obliquely with Buruma, using Gillon as his necessary foil, Vidia left the matter hanging while agreeing to a long-term biographical venture.

For all the lauding, Vidia knew he had to write the book he had contracted to Knopf and Heinemann. In March 1992 he sent an enigmatic letter to his agent, intended for onward transmission to his publishers, saying that he had started work on *A Way in the World*. 'The book is not in the standard novel form; it is a sequence of narrations and I believe its effect will be more concentrated than the standard form would have been.'[51] In another letter on the same day, he told Gillon he faced a major operation on his back to relieve compression caused by a narrowing of the lower spine. Bone spurs had developed, exacerbated by the rigour of his old exercise routine, and needed to be cut away. He feared permanent incapacity. The pain had been with him for months. 'For a year I couldn't walk. I could walk for about a hundred yards in total during the day. I was writing through all of that, doing hard writing.'[52] The operation took place at New Hall Hospital in Salisbury, paid for by his private health insurance.

Vidia spent the rest of the year convalescing, depressed, but still writing. When a mosque built by the Mughal emperor Babur in

Ayodhya was smashed by Hindu zealots in December, he felt a surge of excitement. In his pain and anger and contrariness, Vidia seized on an event that was being presented by the world's media as the end of Indian secularism, and decided it represented evidence of regeneration. He gave an interview to the *Times of India* which suggested in guarded terms that he approved of what had happened: 'One needs to understand the passion that took them on top of the domes. The jeans and the T-shirts are superficial. The passion alone is real. You can't dismiss it . . . The movement is now from below . . . Wise men should understand it and ensure that it does not remain in the hands of fanatics. Rather they should use it for the intellectual transformation of India.'[53] Letters of applause arrived from supporters of Hindu assertiveness, in India and abroad. Vidia defended his stand over the coming years, his opinions luring him to greater controversy. 'For the poor of India to identify something like this, pulling down the first Mughal emperor's tomb, is a marvellous idea. I think in years to come it will be seen as a great moment, and it will probably become a public holiday. It would be a historical statement of India striving to regain her soul.' Hindu nationalists planned to excavate beneath the mosque in order to find the birthplace of the deity Ram; but Ram was a mythological figure. It was a mystical view of history, lacking rigour, choosing pieces of evidence that supported the idea of undoing the past. 'What puzzled me and outraged me was the attitude that it was wrong, that one mustn't undo the [Muslim] conquest. I think it is the attitude of a slave population.' The political fragmentation and the hundreds of deaths in the rioting that followed the destruction of the Babri Masjid were not his concern: 'I didn't kill them myself. What was I doing in 1992? That was a very bad year. That was the year when I could barely walk. I had surgery on my spine.'[54]

Other problems had occurred during that year. Pat's breast cancer returned, and in May she followed Vidia to New Hall Hospital for treatment, using her health insurance. In January 1993, she had a further surgical procedure at Chalybeate, a private hospital in Southampton, and in April received radiotherapy and chemotherapy in an effort to bring the disease in her remaining left breast under control. Pat's mother had died the previous summer after a long stretch with Alzheimer's disease. Vidia found that the house he had bought her in Birmingham was hard to sell, and kept it. Eleanor dealt with the practicalities, writing to 'Dear Lady Pat!' about fixtures and fittings.

The sisters shared £7,000 from their mother's will. Pat spoke occasionally to her father on the telephone, but still refused to see him, despite cards and letters describing his decline. She kept in touch with Auntie Lu, who was ailing, in and out of hospital, and worried that 'Socialism & the Welfare State has ruined the character of most people.'[55] Pat's life was circumscribed, but she had glimpses of light: a kind letter from John Wells praising her delicious scallops, a contact from an old pupil at Rosa Bassett School whose life had been inspired by her teaching, a copy of a letter to Hugh and Vanessa Thomas from a man she had met at dinner: 'When I sat down next to Lady Naipaul, I thought it best to explain that I could not see her because I am blind in my left eye. She said: Well I am not much to look at at any rate . . . But she seemed to me to be a delightful person in every way . . . when you next see her — and using a subtle charm that I don't possess — can you tell her that she is very pretty.'[56] About once a year, Eleanor would visit Dairy Cottage. She had given up teaching, and was now working as a coach driver at a special needs school in Birmingham: 'I used to go down and pick a lot of their fruit. Vidia liked me to take the elderberries because the birds used to take them and crap all over the patio. Big purple blobs. About four years before she died, Pat told me she was in hospital, and then someone called Angela got the fruit. Pat wouldn't tell me what was wrong, so I guessed it was something below the waist. Then she said it was cancer, a few months before she died. We went out for a meal in Salisbury. Vidia was abroad.'[57]

Aged sixty, thinking of death and posterity, aware of his own mortality and Pat's illness, Vidia arranged for his archives to be valued for sale. They were sitting in numbered box files in the warehouse of Ely's of Wimbledon: the novel he had begun in Trinidad in 1949, the manuscript of *The Shadow'd Livery*, his translation of *Lazarillo de Tormes*, his scripts for BBC *Caribbean Voices*, his diaries from his years at Oxford, his journals for *The Middle Passage*, the manuscripts and typescripts of all the books he had written before moving to Wiltshire, notes and letters from his first trip to India in 1962, most of the letters he had received in the 1950s and sixties, his own 'Letters from London' for the *Illustrated Weekly of India*, his travel journals from Africa in 1966, and the notebooks and diaries of his early journalism. When Pat went to retrieve them, they were all gone. After investigation, it turned out that Ely's, instructed to destroy files marked NITRATE (belonging to the Nitrate Corporation of Chile) had taken those marked NAIPAUL as well. Having spent a lifetime meticulously recording himself, Vidia had lost around a third of his total archive.[58] Always conscious of his own projected destiny, he had preserved everything. 'I kept it for the record. I am a great believer in the record, that the truth is wonderful and that any doctored truth is awful. Doctored truth is not truth. I destroyed nothing. I think the completeness of a record is what matters. I have great trouble reading other people's autobiographies because I feel it is doctored. So the stuff that was destroyed in the warehouse, lots of embarrassing things, that was part of the record.'[59]

Two other things occurred on the day that he heard news of the loss, 8 October 1992. Gillon Aitken received a letter from Jeffrey Meyers observing, 'Vidia's work deserves the Nobel Prize. There are also very strong racial, geographical and linguistic qualifications in his favor. But candidates don't win the prize on merit alone.'[60] And the Swedish Academy made an announcement of the winner of that year's Nobel Prize in Literature: Derek Walcott. Under the convention of regional rotation, it meant that the chances of another writer of Caribbean origin writing in the English language winning the Nobel over the next decade were slim. Walcott compounded his offence by devoting his Nobel Lecture to a passionate defence of the glories of Caribbean ethnic diversity. His opening sentence ran:

> Felicity is a village in Trinidad on the edge of the Caroni plain, the wide central plain that still grows sugar and to which indentured cane cutters were brought after emancipation, so the small population of Felicity is East Indian, and on the afternoon that I visited it with friends from America, all the faces along its road were Indian, which, as I hope to show, was a moving, beautiful thing, because this Saturday afternoon *Ramleela*, the epic dramatization of the Hindu epic the *Ramayana*, was going to be performed, and the costumed actors from the village were assembling on a field strung with different-coloured flags, like a new gas station, and beautiful Indian boys in red and black were aiming arrows haphazardly into the afternoon light.[61]

Vidia returned to work on *A Way in the World*. Although the book had an odd and seemingly haphazard structure, he had thought out its pattern some years before. It was a 'sequence', using a literary technique he had first tried in *In a Free State*. It was also a return to the West Indies and to his own origins, a reworking of what he saw as his dud book, *The Loss of El Dorado*. The fate of the region's postcolonial political activists had been on his mind since he wrote *The Mimic Men*. In 1982, Pat had written in her diary: 'He has gone back to this thing, he says apologetically, the Eric Williams figure – he doesn't want to write about black people but he hasn't anything else to write about.' In May 1993, she wrote, 'Reflecting a little, about Vidia & his present writing. Phrase occurred to me, as it does now & again: he had "sold out". [*A*] *Way* [*in the World*]' is, in effect, answering the rather reflexive – and not reflective! – remarks and reactions of "black"/"negro" individuals and interest groups.' Despite this, Pat liked the book – a form of approval that was always of great importance to Vidia. That summer, she recorded this conversation: 'He then said that Gillon had sent the completed stories to Andrew Wylie (who liked them) and said he was "at the top of his form". He said later in the day that he was "excited" that I liked it.'[62]

Many of the ideas and themes in *A Way in the World* emerged from a little notebook that Vidia had been keeping since 1977: 'Hassanali, the artist from St James – "I went to see him at the funeral home. The girl at the desk said, "Go right in." He was there, neat and dapper, dressing a body" . . . Odette sells "wines" . . . Francisco Martinez . . . sat next to me on the LAV flight to Caracas. A small elderly man with the broad wrinkled brown face of a coastal mestizo . . . his curly hair tied up at the back in the manner of an 18th century wig.'[63] In another notebook, under the heading 'stories', he wrote: 'The Red House – Fish-glue, Arthur Calder-Marshall . . . CLR James – beginning with the dark copy of his book in the v dark bookcase in the 6th form at QRC, Eric Williams & his daughter, Deutsch . . . Andrew [Vidia's driver in Makerere], Walter Rodney [a black Marxist he had met in Tanzania], Jim Allen, Rajat, Paul.'[64] He also had press cuttings, located by Kamla, about the funeral of C.L.R. James in 1989 after his body was flown home from England at the expense of the Trinidad government. Kamla added her memories of the event, which she had watched on television: 'The wife a small, neat woman appeared mixed and her son was more white than anything else.' She kept her brother stocked with news from Trinidad, and ideas that would spark his writing. 'They fed some of the mad people at St Ann's some bad eggnog and so far, 13 of them have died. Some are wondering if the milk came from Chernobyl. The police were supposed to have produced some 128 pieces of crack to nab a pusher but they couldn't find the crack. The police said rats ate the crack.'[65]

A Way in the World contained some beautiful writing and immensely subtle thinking, but like *The Enigma of Arrival* it held a marginal appeal for the general reader. Marketed as 'A Sequence' in Britain and 'A Novel' in America, it began with a 'Prelude' about a trip to Trinidad where the author was told by a schoolteacher about 'Leonard Side, a decorator of cakes and arranger of flowers' who dressed bodies at Parry's Funeral Parlour, using his hairy fingers for each of the three jobs.[66] (The teacher was Kamla, Leonard Side was Hassanali; like the surname of Edward Said, Side was a corruption of the Muslim name Sayed.) A slice of slightly fictional autobiography follows, about the young narrator working as a clerk in the Red House. Indirectly, Naipaul brings the narrative back to the present, describing the 'black men and women dressed like Arabs' who had appeared in Port of Spain.[67] In July 1990, calling themselves the Jamaat al Muslimeen, they stormed the Red House, killed people and held the prime minister and cabinet hostage. History loops again now, and the chapter ends with 'an English marauder' putting the Spaniards to flight, and finding in the island's gaol, 'the last aboriginal rulers of the land, held together on one chain, scalded with hot bacon fat, and broken by other punishments.'[68] Returning to the material he had used in *The Loss of El Dorado*, Naipaul deconstructs the next story even before he tells it. 'The narrator is going up a highland river in an unnamed South American country. Who is this narrator? What can he be made to be?'[69] Using ideas that would be replicated in *Magic Seeds*, he is made to travel through the forest on some revolutionary mission, following his guides. One of them, a boy, he seduces; later he is presented with a perished Tudor doublet, sent by an earlier foreign visitor, 'new clothes of three hundred and fifty years before, relic of an old betrayal'.[70]

In 'Passenger: A Figure from the Thirties', Naipaul again merges complex memory and imagination, examining a well-worn subject in a wholly original way. He looks at Trinidad, the physical island, on a trip to Point Galera and sees it through the eyes of Columbus, thinking that the point was named not for a large 'galley shape' on land. Rather, 'black rocks and twisted trees off the point of the island would have reminded him of a galley under sail: the rocks standing for the galley, the twisted trees standing for the sails . . . I had never tried to do that as a child: pretend I was looking at the aboriginal island. No teacher or anyone else had suggested it as an imaginative exercise.'[71] As he was growing up, representations of the West Indies could be found mainly in books by white visitors. He thought 'the writers of these travel books were really acting, acting being writers, acting being travellers, and, especially, acting being travellers in the colonies.' They could say whatever they wanted about the people they saw, for there was nobody to contradict them. Indians might be ignored as 'a people apart', and Africans 'might be put into new and squeaky two-toned shoes; and the writer might go on to say that Africans were so fond of squeaky shoes that they took brand-new shoes to shoemakers and asked them to "put in a squeak".'[72]

'And then in 1937 a young English writer called Foster Morris came and wrote *The Shadowed Livery*, which was another kind of book.' He wrote of the oilfield workers' strike led by Tubal Uriah "Buzz" Butler, and treated Butler and the people around him 'as though they were English people — as though they had that kind of social depth and solidity and rootedness.' But Foster Morris, 'with all his wish to applaud us, didn't understand the nature of our deprivation.' He failed to see that though Butler was treated as a messiah, he was also viewed by the same people as 'a crazed and uneducated African preacher, a Grenadian, a small-islander, an eater of ground provisions boiled in a pitch oil tin.' Butler was interned during the war, and on release 'went away for long stretches to England, "to take the cold", as it was said; and he was supported by contributions from his old Grenadian supporters. Once, when he came back, he insisted on thanking the crew of the aeroplane.' Then, while working at the BBC in the 1950s, Vidia — or the narrator — meets Foster Morris, who is reviewing books for a Caribbean radio show because his literary career is failing. Vidia shows him the manuscript of his own first novel, and is told to abandon it. Foster Morris then explains that the views he expressed in *The Shadowed Livery* were not sincere: he thought Butler was a racial fanatic, but did not say so for fear of encouraging the reactionaries in the colonial government. And he had been sexually taunted by one of Butler's associates, a Trinidadian-Panamanian communist named Lebrun.[73]

Everything is turned on its head here. A book which appeared to give voice to a subject people was not what it seemed, and its author did not believe what he wrote. But that was not all: Foster Morris did not exist; *The Shadowed Livery* was, with an apostrophe, Vidia's first book; its rejector was Arthur Calder Marshall, the reviewer at BBC *Caribbean Voices* who had in 1939 published *Glory Dead*, a travel book about Trinidad which presented itself as being on the side of the oil workers, and praised "Buzz" Butler and Adrian Cola Rienzi as men of the future. 'A new spirit has arisen among the workers. They have tasted freedom; they begin to know their power.'[74] As for Lebrun, the subject of the next chapter of *A Way in the World*, he was clearly modelled on C.L.R. James (though his name may have been borrowed from Learie's father Lebrun Constantine, a famous Trinidad cricketer himself). He is the author of a book on early Spanish-American revolutionaries, such as Francisco de Miranda, which was kept unread in a glass bookcase at Queen's Royal College. In old age, Lebrun lands up in England, 'in a world greatly changed, where black men were an important subject' and ' "discovered" as one of the prophets of black revolution'.[75] In the pages that follow, the narrator alternates between admiration for Lebrun's critical perception and abilities as a talker, and distrust for his political ambitions. He sees him as one of 'the first generation of educated black men in the region' who 'talked big in one place – the United States, England, the West Indies, Panama, Belize – about the things they were doing somewhere else.'[76] Most of all, the narrator feels unease at an attempt by admirers of Lebrun to co-opt him; at a dinner in New York (this part is fiction) gefilte fish is prepared in his honour: 'The idea of something pounded to paste, then spiced or oiled, worked on by fingers, brought to mind thoughts of hand lotions and other things. I became fearful of smelling it. I couldn't eat it.'[77] Lebrun is caught by the Back-to-Africa movement and ends up promoting tyrannous regimes, but in the end Vidia – or the narrator – gives him a soft landing:

> The profile-writers and the television interviewers, who promoted him with self-conscious virtue, were serving a cause that had long ago been won. They risked nothing at all. They had no means of understanding or assessing a man who had been born early in the century into a very hard world, whose intellectual growth had at every stage been accompanied by a growing rawness of sensibility, and whose political resolutions, expressing the wish not to go mad, had been in the nature of spiritual struggles, occurring in the depth of his being.[78]

At this point, Naipaul goes back in time to earlier pirates of the Caribbean, and the book goes off the boil. Using his knowledge from *The Loss of El Dorado*, he imagines a conversation between Walter Raleigh and a ship's surgeon, much of which reads like didactic

historical fiction. Another story concerns Lebrun's subject Miranda, and
here too the historical learning is obscure and detailed, presupposing a
knowledge of the region and its past. Only in the final section, 'Home
Again', does the narrative lift. The narrator is in an unnamed East
African country, living in a compound like the one at Makerere. 'The
country was a tyranny. But in those days not many people minded.
Africa had just begun to be independent, and the reputation of the
president was that of a good man using his authority only to build
socialism.'[79] The social interchange within the compound is brilliantly
done, the competition between blacks and whites, and the hierarchy of
houseboys. A visitor arrives, Blair, a tall man last encountered working
as a civil servant in the Red House, and now an international figure
come to advise the government. Blair crosses the president, and is
murdered at a showpiece banana plantation. He is fictional, though
inspired by Walter Rodney, the author of *How Europe Underdeveloped
Africa*, a pan-Africanist and devotee of C.L.R. James who was assassinated by a car-bomb in Georgetown, Guyana, in 1980. The narrator
imagines his death, 'a big man floundering about in silence in his big,
shiny-soled leather shoes in the soft mulch, between his sure-footed
attackers. There would have been a moment in that great silence when
he would have known that he was being destroyed, that his attackers
intended to go to the limit; and he would have known why. And I feel
that if, as in some Edgar Allan Poe story, at the moment of death,
while the brain still sparked, a question could have been lodged in that
brain – "Does this betrayal mock your life?" – the answer immediately
after death would have been, "No! No! No!"'[80] Again, it was an
affirmation. In the last sentences of *A Way in the World*, the author
considers the return of Blair's body to Trinidad, and its arrival at the
airport: 'Would the embalmed body in its box then have been transferred to a hearse? The hearse didn't seem right. I made inquiries. I
was told that the box would have been taken away in an ambulance to
Port of Spain, and then the shell of the man would have been laid out
in Parry's chapel of rest.'[81] We are back with Leonard Side.

Taking nearly two years, Vidia had written a work of many layers,
a text of great depth and complexity which circled back and forth over
itself and his own earlier writings. It dealt with historical subjects that
were unfamiliar to most of his readers, and much of the book remained
mysterious even to the Caribbean intelligentsia. In the *Trinidad Guardian*, Wayne Brown spent three successive Sundays attempting to decode

A Way in the World: V.S. Naipaul seemed to have 'mellowed' and was showing an 'inclusive comprehension' of human frailty, giving his characters a dignity that was lacking in earlier books.[82] American reviews were good. Michiko Kakutani thought it was 'less a conventional narrative than a free-form essay on Mr Naipaul's continuing efforts to come to terms with the history of Trinidad' and that its various characters were 'alter egos of sorts for Mr Naipaul'.[83] In Britain, coverage was less enthusiastic, and puzzled. As before, few European or American reviewers were fully able to understand his work. Peter Kemp in the *Sunday Times* thought V.S. Naipaul was endeavouring to overcome writer's block, and that the later material was 'torpid both as narrative and dramatisation'.[84] The African American author Brent Staples wrote in the *New York Times Book Review* that Naipaul suffered 'from expectations about what he *ought* to write, given that he is a brown man (of Indian descent) born into the brown and black society that is Trinidad' but that in his case 'a strictly racial reading amounts to no reading at all'. *A Way in the World* was 'a distinguished book even by Naipaulian standards, a bewitching piece of work by a mind at the peak of its abilities.'[85] In the *New Republic* Caryl Phillips, black British but born in St Kitts, gave a sympathetic review: 'In its deeply moving climax the novel seems to suggest that even Naipaul now realizes that to give up everything to be a writer, particularly the generosity of spirit that allows one to tolerate the foolishness often to be found in one's fellow man, is to commit an act of great folly.'[86]

*

A couple of months before the publication of *A Way in the World*, Vidia flew first class to America for the formal presentation of his archives to the University of Tulsa. The operation on the bone spurs on his back had been a success, and he was feeling fit and ambitious, his hair short and a new beard closely clipped. He submitted to a filmed interview with Professors George H. Gilpin Jr. and Hermione de Almeida, a pair of admiring academics from the university who were married to each other and had, with the help of a representative in London, secured the purchase of his papers.[87] The Bodleian Library at Oxford, hoping the archive might be deposited there free of charge out of gratitude and reverence, had been swiftly dismissed. Using impeccable logic, Gillon Aitken argued to various interested American institutions that the loss of the boxes at Ely's made the remaining material especially valuable: Tulsa, wealthy from oil, produced the money. Gillon sold the archive for $470,000, covering material to the end of 2002, with an additional $150,000 to become available for papers generated during the five years after that date, making a total of $620,000. Pat was a co-signatory to the legal agreement, which specified that 'my wife, Patricia Ann Hale Naipaul, agrees that all correspondence and related material in her possession are an integral part of the Archive according to the terms of this Agreement.'[88] Her diaries would go to Tulsa. The contents of the archive were to remain closed to public access indefinitely, bar the manuscripts and typescripts of Vidia's books, which were open to inspection by literary scholars.

During this period Vidia kept to himself, guarding himself, emerging occasionally to be interviewed by international publications. He would appear on television, looking grumpy, though speaking in a more demotic accent than he had in the 1960s. The themes chosen by reporters were familiar: his scope, his irascibility, his outsider status, his inscrutability, his deliberate childlessness, his Brahminical fastidiousness, his genius, his rudeness; Pat's silent presence. In 1993, the German magazine *Du* devoted a 100-page edition to him, illustrated with manuscript material and old family photographs. Awed by V.S. Naipaul's reputation for making trouble, journalists saw him as a challenge. 'I assumed at first that Sir Vidiadhar Surajprasad had servants,' wrote Zöe Heller in an *Independent on Sunday* profile in the same year. ' "The coffee will come," he said when I arrived at his flat in South Kensington. He gave a rather weary, papal wave in the direction of the kitchen. Then the telephone rang. "It will be answered. It will be answered. It will be answered." ' They discussed violent crime in Britain. 'Naipaul said: "I see that several generations of free milk and orange juice have led to an army of thugs." '[89] In an astute interview in *Publishers Weekly* by an old Oxford contemporary, John F. Baker, Vidia's public attitude was identified: 'For what strikes one most of all about Naipaul is the extraordinary force of his persona. It is an actorly one, enhanced by a remarkably deep and mellifluous voice, that seems to alternate constantly between sternness and playfulness. He says outrageous things very decisively, then seems to pause as if to weigh whether one is going to take them seriously or as a joke; and since levity always seems to lie close to his surface, the effect is of a hugely intelligent person playing sly games whose outcome only he can determine.'[90] Sometimes, he would be frank and revealing. In *Der Spiegel*, he said he had only voted once, in 1983, for Margaret Thatcher's Conservatives. 'Until I was in my forties, I was kind of an instinctive Labour Party man, but then intellectually I found them less and less attractive.' Asked how he dealt with 'carnal acts' in his fiction, he answered that he had initially been unable to write about sex: 'When I was young, you know, I was a great frequenter of prostitutes. I found them intensely stimulating. But what happened was that by the time I was in my mid-thirties, I began to feel depressed by sex with a prostitute. I felt cheated and frustrated.'[91]

Having broached the subject of prostitution to a German publication with no ill effect, Vidia was lulled into speaking about it again when he was interviewed at length by the *New Yorker* the following year. Two of his sentences ran around the world, chased by Tina Brown's publicity machine: 'So I became a great prostitute man, which, as you know, is highly unsatisfactory. It's the most unsatisfying form of sex.'[92] A man had admitted to having sex with a prostitute: it made the news in many countries. 'Naipaul Tells Dark Secrets of Sex Life,' wrote Geordie Greig in the *Sunday Times*. Speaking spontaneously, thinking only of himself, Vidia had failed to consider the consequences. 'I gave an interview to the *New Yorker*, to a nice man, Stephen Schiff, and I mentioned things I really never thought would come back to the house. I remember making a decision to tell Stephen Schiff about it. A simple decision. It all occurred in my head at the moment it was happening.'[93] For Pat, it was a devastation. Vidia's silent visits to prostitutes, starting decades before in Muswell Hill, had never been discussed between them. For Vidia, what he said to Schiff was a memory of old days before Margaret; for Pat, it was a gross revelation, and an insult to her status as his loving wife. 'I couldn't see that this would be front page news. I didn't think it would be like that. But that's how Pat [heard about] it. And she ran to get the paper. I told her, please don't get it. Please don't read it ... She read it privately. Shortly after that she became ill again, and people say that this cancer business can come with great distress and grief. She was very upset. She was tearful and wounded.'[94]

There was more in the article. The *New Yorker* reported that in the 1970s, Vidia had met a woman, and she had become his lover. 'Her name was Margaret, and she was an Argentine of British descent, a slender, attractive married woman (with three children) who was about ten years younger than Naipaul, and several inches taller ... she has often joined Naipaul during his travels.'[95] The revelation about Margaret did not upset Pat. The existence of a mistress had been widely known for years, even if it had never been noted in print before. It was the idea of her husband having plentiful, degraded sex with prostitutes, whores, hookers, tarts, that fed her imagination, and horrified her. The papers wanted more. 'Dear Lady Naipaul,' wrote Victoria Combe of the *Daily Telegraph*, 'We were wondering whether you would like to discuss some of the issues raised in the New Yorker magazine. We appreciate you may be reluctant to air your views in public but we would guarantee you a responsible interview.'[96] Pat kept silent, as she had always kept silent, but allowed the knowledge to eat away at her. Vidia had been 'a great prostitute man', and now all the world knew about it. 'I think that consumed her. I think she had all the relapses and everything after that. All the remission ended.' Pat's cancer was back, and would not go away. Vidia had to live with the responsibility of what he had done, and bear the blame for the rest of his days. 'She suffered. It could be said that I had killed her. It could be said. I feel a little bit that way.'[97]

CHAPTER TWENTY-FIVE

THE SECOND LADY NAIPAUL

AS HE APPROACHED THE AGE of retirement, Vidia felt compelled to go on writing. He collected notes, and even recorded his dreams, as writers are prone to in old age. In one, he was in an accountant's office in Germany discussing the oddities of German language usage; another time he was shouting in class, and being tested on his French vocabulary by his sister Mira. Or: 'I was in Queensgate with Helen Fraser. We were going to lunch. A bus came along. She ran to get it. I didn't run as fast (or as readily) as she. She made the bus. I didn't. And then there followed the trouble of looking for her in restaurants; and during this trouble I talked to Javed (of the Bombay Brasserie) of my problem.' At a publisher's office, he saw 'something scandalous' – a heap 'as big as a small van' of photocopied booklets. A fire was kindled. 'The booklets were critical of me & my work.' The dream was linked to people 'raking down the fire' onto a body, 'inspired by a brief glimpse of Foxe's Book of Martyrs'. It made Vidia think about eight-year-old Sewan attending Pa's cremation in Trinidad. 'I suppose it marked him for ever. Poor boy. All that grief to carry; all that terror.'[1]

In June 1994, unable to find the spark for a work of fiction, Vidia decided to write a short book about Brazil, Chile, Venezuela and Argentina. Gillon Aitken noted its proposed themes: 'Immense wealth, immense upheaval, oil and theft, degraded & ineducable population.'[2] V.S. Naipaul made an excursion to Brazil in August as a guest of the British Council and the Cultura Inglesa, to be feted and interviewed. He disliked the climate, and Pat was sent frequent faxes with peremptory instructions: 'Bolt should be replaced on gate only if the replacement is sturdy, if it fits, and if it is rust-proof. Send a copy of the letter from Tulsa to Gillon, to ask for his advice. I am off now for a day or two to an orange estate. Vidia.'[3] And what of his nephew Ved, he enquired: had he cleared his debts yet? A trip to Chile later in the year was called off when Pat had another relapse, and had to be admitted to hospital for surgery. In February 1995 Vidia went to Buckingham

Palace to watch the head of a teachers' union, the governor of Brixton prison, a black rugby player and the Duke of York's private secretary eat Terrine de Canard à l'Orange and Côtelettes d'Agneau Réforme. Also present at the luncheon were the Duke of Edinburgh and the Queen, who sat at Vidia's right hand drinking Chardonnay Currawong Creek. The author noted politely on his copy of the menu: 'A vegetarian (fish) meal was quietly offered to me.'[4]

He saw little of Margaret except when he was travelling and wanted company, but she continued to keep in touch by fax. Vidia's replies were rarely more than a sentence long, and usually unsigned: 'I will telephone you; but I don't want to know anything about Nobel Prizes – you must stop paying attention to those things.' Margaret sent occasional news from Argentina: her daughter Karin was getting married, her son Alexander had given her a fountain pen for Christmas, she had been to a dinner dance at a big hotel. Sometimes, in a reminder of old days, she would flatter him, telling him he was the Lion King and that she remembered him as a predatory animal who would savage her.[5]

By now, conscious that his stay in Brazil had yielded nothing, Vidia was anxious to begin another book. There were plenty of distractions should he want them, such as addressing the Association of Wessex Tourist Guides or attending a conference of Bhojpuri speakers in Uttar Pradesh. He even thought about accepting a residency at the University of Calgary. When he was made a Companion of Literature, he sent Tristram Powell to the Royal Society of Literature to collect a scroll on his behalf. He extended kindness to strangers. When Anthony Milne, a former journalist and clerk at the Red House who was working at Toys-R-Us in Swindon, told Vidia his thoughts about Guyana, he was invited to lunch. Vidia suggested he lacked 'an attitude' and proposed that Milne write about an '*idea*: this is how black racism, allied to a bogus Marxism, can wreck a country the size of Great Britain in twenty years. And that material becomes even more interesting still if you deliver it as a white West Indian, someone with a special interest and attitude to the place.' Milne wrote an admiring appraisal of V.S. Naipaul instead, and sent it to him. 'The piece won't do, and I am sure you know so, too. It is unfocussed; it hops restlessly about from point to point; and it is shallow: it actually says nothing when it should say something. To be focussed: before you write, decide what you are writing about, think about a rational progression of ideas – four or five, no more – and then write . . . What did we talk about at lunch? It says nothing to say that your host was charming . . . No more lessons. VSN.'[6] An attempt to beatify Vidia on French television induced cooperation followed by rage against a prolix producer. He told his publisher, Ivan Nabokov, 'I am leaving it to you to tell the French T.V. people that I don't wish to see any more of Josianne Maisse. After four months she has done almost nothing, & her verbiage has led to nothing except a request for an 8-hour interview, which exceeds in idiocy anything I have so far encountered. I feel greatly abused by the people who sent her. It was wrong of them to expose me to this degree of idleness and stupidity.'[7]

Vidia wanted to get to work. He decided to loop back on himself once more and write a reprise of *Among the Believers*. In a new global political climate, he would return to Iran, Indonesia, Malaysia and Pakistan to look at the future of Islamist ideology through the fate of the countries and personalities he had encountered in 1979. Once again, he would make a forceful rejection of the late twentieth-century academic convention that all cultures, peoples and belief systems are different but equal.

Gillon Aitken was drafted in to secure a magnificent advance. The idea was to make a deal which linked the new travel book, *Beyond Belief*, with an edition of the letters that Vidia and Pa had written to each other during his Oxford days. Gillon recalled, 'I was worried. I couldn't find the money. I did go back to Viking and they wouldn't be drawn, and then Reed made an offer which was no good. I tried HarperCollins, they didn't come though, I tried Cape, they didn't come through.' With no UK publisher prepared to make a substantial offer, Gillon's next plan was to recover the rights to Vidia's complete backlist, which André Deutsch had sold to Penguin, and secure a wider deal. 'I asked Cape for £1 million for *Beyond Belief*, *Letters Between a Father and Son* and twelve early titles. The plan didn't work, so I went next to Little, Brown and offered *Beyond Belief* and the letters, which was pretty make-weight because the letters were a questionable commercial project. So that was the package. They paid £225,000. I had to write Vidia a careful letter; he wasn't pleased.'[8] In America, Gillon had another cunning plan. Aided by Andrew Wylie, with whom he was in the process of parting professional company, he sold the *New Yorker* four long extracts from the unwritten book for $200,000. It turned out to be a bad deal for the magazine; Bill Buford of the *New Yorker* wanted the material to be rewritten, but Vidia refused and only a part was published. Another section ended up later in the *New York Review of Books*, producing more money. Next Gillon set to work on Sonny Mehta at Knopf: 'Vidia would like to contract for the US book publication rights, with an advance of $300,000 – no more, no less.'[9] It was an interesting approach to negotiation, and Mehta hesitated. Seven days after he had sent his first letter, Gillon withdrew from the negotiation, declaring that Mehta had taken too long to reach a decision. His plan to take his eminent client elsewhere did not proceed as smoothly as he had hoped, and he made a deal along similar lines with Mehta's senior colleague Harold Evans.

As soon as the contract was agreed, Vidia prepared to start his journey. A link with the past was broken in July 1995 when the last of his Hindi-speaking aunts died, Kalawatee Mausi, who used to take his mother to school. Kalawatee had been a Trinidad senator in the 1960s, and a political adviser to her brother Rudranath, and like all her sisters, a forceful presence. A month earlier, Pat's Auntie Lu had also died, at the age of ninety-three. There was business and paperwork to clear up too. The *New Yorker* was running extracts from his early correspondence with Paul Theroux. The famously persuasive Ismail Merchant, after years of trying, had concluded a contract to put *The Mystic Masseur* on the screen. 'I will do an excellent film from this wonderful work of yours,' he assured Vidia.[10] After negotiations the film rights were sold to Merchant Ivory Productions for $75,000, with a further $75,000 to be paid when filming commenced. It was the highest fee that Merchant Ivory had ever paid to adapt a book for a film.[11] Vidia would also receive 5 per cent of producer's net profits, but everyone knew that the industry's accounting procedures meant that no further money was likely to be paid. The result was a dire film, released in 2001, in which Om Puri as Ramlogan shifted between a Jamaican and an Indian accent.

Before leaving England for Indonesia, Vidia put together a 'travelling list'. In its care and restraint, in its honing, it reflected the man and the writer, who knew that he had to be preserved at all costs to do his work. Despite having a large share portfolio and a substantial six-figure sum in his offshore US-dollar account in Jersey, Vidia remained frugal in his spending. He did his own accounts and bookkeeping, with Pat's determined help.

Suits & trousers & jackets
Travel out in Simpson's grey
Pack — Simpson's beige lightweight

Jackets
Blue blazer (new or old)

Trousers
M&S cotton
BHS cotton
Oscar Jacobson charcoal lightweight worsted

Underclothes
Pants 4 prs
Socks 4 prs
Pyjama 1 pr
T-shirts 2
Sleeveless vests 2

Shirts
4 cotton (dress)
M&S leisure 2
Smedley shirts 2
Smedley roll-neck 3

Pullovers
1 cotton (BHS or M&S)
1 wool (M&S or Aquascutum)

Shorts
Bathing trunks
Exercise pants
Trainers
1 pr perhaps to be worn on journey

Diary
Notebooks
Paper
Computer & Disks
Ink cartridges
(Plug adaptor)

Medicines & Soaps
Ventolin 2
Becloforte 1

Antibiotics 2
Migraleve
Paracetamol & codeine
Celbutomol
Augmentin[12]

On 25 July 1995, Vidia flew out of Heathrow airport to Jakarta. More than two years later, writing in a private journal, he described his departure from his wife. 'I had embraced her – for the first time for many years – at the airport (in or near the Costa coffee shop: she complained later that the coffee had damaged her: a sign of her fatal illness, if only I knew); she had fallen into my arms; and I had felt how ill she was. She had telephoned the airline later to find out whether I had arrived. The plane had been delayed. So (when I got to Jakarta) we talked eventually, full of old love (though the other person was soon to arrive: the eternal lie of the situation).'[13]

As on his previous trips, Vidia asked other people to aid him, and in most cases they fell over themselves to do so. Margaret jumped on an aeroplane, and travelled loyally with him through Indonesia, being permitted to collect and file useful press cuttings. Publishers' staff in London and New York provided contacts and helpers. Ian Buruma recommended the journalist Ahmed Rashid in Pakistan, who produced a string of names and invited Vidia to stay at his house in Lahore. Bob Silvers found regional experts and their telephone numbers. Harry Evans sent a gigantic list of possibly interesting people. Rahul Singh located reporters and politicians in Jakarta. Once Vidia arrived in the relevant country, diplomats would arrange dinners and foreign correspondents would open their contacts books to him. He got in touch with many of the people he had met on his trip sixteen years earlier, and asked to see them. When a meeting went well, he responded warmly. To Dr Dewi Fortuna Anwar, an Indonesian academic and politician, he wrote: 'I want to thank you for sending me to your ancestral house in Padang. Your mother was the soul of courtesy and generosity; and the experience was an amazing and educational one for me. Everything was beautiful: the mountains, the plains, the rice-fields, the houses.'[14] As always, Vidia kept meticulous notes, and when he had time to spare he would type them up in order to make the process of writing the book easier. He travelled cautiously, guarding himself against possible asthma or back pain. By early September, he had completed his research in

Indonesia and returned to Wiltshire for a week to get ready for his next journey – to Iran. In October, following a trip to Persepolis, he found himself back in England preparing to fly to Lahore, where he was met at the airport by an enthusiastic Ahmed Rashid. November was spent in Pakistan, December in Malaysia, and by Christmas he had come back to Dairy Cottage, where Pat was dying. While he was in Indonesia, Vidia learned the word 'langsat' – a term used to describe someone with a perfect, fair complexion, named after the creamy colour of the langsat fruit.

In the finished book, which he wrote during the course of 1996 and early 1997, Vidia began with a prologue. 'This is a book about people. It is not a book of opinion. It is a book of stories. The stories were collected during five months of travel in 1995 in four non-Arab Muslim countries – Indonesia, Iran, Pakistan, Malaysia. So there is a context and a theme. Islam is in its origins an Arab religion. Everyone who is not an Arab who is a Muslim is a convert. Islam is not simply a matter of conscience or private belief. It makes great demands.' Then he crossed out the word 'great' and replaced it with 'imperial'.[15] When *Beyond Belief* was published, few reviewers would accept the claim that since it was a book about people, it was not a book of opinion. Vidia introduced many thoughts and concepts that would, after 11 September 2001, become better known: ritual purification, sacrifice, Islamic martyrs, mujahidin, *talebeh* or students (hence Taliban). Above all, he wrote about the idea that an individual's devotion to a perceived idea of Islamic teaching might push every other consideration aside, and lead him to unconscionable acts. Vidia's perception arose, as before, from the combination of his sharp eyes, a precisely developed control of his own talent and complete confidence in his ability to analyse a wider situation. A year earlier, he had written to a Tulsa oilman he met at dinner: 'totalitarianism has been the great curse of the century, and you know in your heart of hearts that every form of totalitarianism has pretended to have a core of virtuousness; this illusion of serving virtue makes us look away . . . A writer who does this looking away . . . is betraying his essence and cannot be a good writer. I cannot think of any intellectual self-violator who was or is a good writer. The good writers have always looked for truth. Nothing else is worthwhile, if you are a writer.'[16]

Working hard at the text, revising more than he had with *Among the Believers*, Vidia produced a long and thoughtful book. *Beyond Belief* concentrates on personal stories. Mr Jaffrey – last encountered in *Among the Believers* sitting behind a 'high standard typewriter' at the *Tehran Times* eating a dish of fried eggs' – had fled to Pakistan under suspicion of being an American spy, and died in 1990. The reader meets Iran's sinister hanging judge Ayatollah Khalkhalli, now 'very small, completely bald, baby-faced without his turban, head held down against his chest'; and Linus, the rural Indonesian poet with the handicapped sister 'dragging her slippered feet from a dark side room'; in Kuala Lumpur we revisit the Muslim youth worker Shafi, but he turns out to be an impostor, a man pretending to be Shafi 'out of pure idleness . . . to get a little attention'.[17] There are new characters too, like Shahbaz, the English public school-educated Pakistani with a tale of his time as a guerrilla fighter in Baluchistan. In Iran we hear the terrible story of Abbas, 'twenty-seven, and a war veteran', who left school to join a Martyr's Battalion in the Iran–Iraq war.[18] His first job was to wash the cartridge belts and harness straps of the dead, since there was a shortage of equipment; today he has a piece of artificial bone in his head and makes one-minute films. V.S. Naipaul's peerless eye does not remain closed for long. A Kentucky Fried Chicken outlet in old Tehran had been 'angrily re-lettered to Our Fried Chicken, with the face of the Southern colonel smudged and redrawn'; a carpet in a hotel lift 'was dirty and stained and didn't absolutely fit'; and a chambermaid has 'a definite smell from wearing so many clothes, some of them perhaps of synthetic material'.[19]

Michael Ignatieff in the *New York Times* thought that while Naipaul had drawn a sometimes distressing portrait, *Beyond Belief* was 'not anti-Islamic in any easy way, and it is unfailingly perceptive about how true believers handle the discordance between their dreams of godly life and ungodly reality . . . His informants have the vividness of characters in a good novel.'[20] Anatol Lieven was also impressed, writing in the *Financial Times* of the author's 'warm sympathy even for many of his Islamist subjects, a sympathy which gives this book its deeply moving quality . . . his most justifiably bitter criticisms of Islam relate to its treatment of women.'[21] A rare female reviewer, Geeta Doctor, wrote in the *Indian Review of Books* that Naipaul was too willing to opine and condemn: 'This is the sort of bashing of "otherness" that used to take place in the noonday of Communism.'[22] Robert Irwin in the *Guardian* felt the stress on the affect of Islam was overdone: 'Religion is ultimately responsible for the awful breakfast Naipaul is served in Tehran and

more generally for shabby buildings, corrupt judges and street crime.'[23]
In the *Observer*, Ian Jack noticed a shift in the author's approach to the
act of writing: there was 'a sense of scraping away' as though he was
on 'a search for some kind of purity, or a prophylactic against
exhaustion.'[24] Sunil Khilnani declared in the *Sunday Telegraph* that
Beyond Belief was 'the most achieved instance yet of a form refined by
Naipaul since his turn away from the novel – declared by him to be
historically outmoded.'[25] The most hostile review came from his old
adversary Edward Said, in *Al-Ahram Weekly*. V.S. Naipaul was 'one of
the truly celebrated, justly well-known figures in world literature today'
but had squandered his gifts by writing a 'stupid' and 'boring' book.
'Somewhere along the way Naipaul, in my opinion, himself suffered a
serious intellectual accident. His obsession with Islam caused him
somehow to stop thinking, to become instead a kind of mental suicide
compelled to repeat the same formula over and over. This is what I
would call an intellectual catastrophe of the first order.'[26]

In the *Sunday Times*, I wrote: 'The human encounters are described
minutely, superbly, picking up inconsistencies in people's tales, catching
the uncertainties and the nuances – how or why, for instance, a
conversation changes course ... The difficulty comes with *Beyond
Belief*'s general theme, as indicated in the curious subtitle, *Islamic
Excursions Among the Converted Peoples*. Most of the converts in question
changed faith somewhere between the seventh and eleventh century,
yet Naipaul's sense of the past is so intense, so profound, that he sees
them as rejectors of their indigenous belief, engaged in "a dreadful
mangling of history", and suffering from resultant "neurosis". Conversion to Islam and the ensuing emphasis on foreign holy places is for
him "the most uncompromising kind of imperialism". He does not
consider the possibility that Islam might, over the centuries, have
become an indigenous religion, while his claim that, "Everyone not an
Arab who is a Muslim is a convert" might just as well be made about
Christianity.' Despite my hesitations, I concluded, 'V.S. Naipaul has
been writing now for nearly half a century. He has 23 books to his
name – brilliant combinations of travel, fiction, history, politics, literary
criticism and autobiography. It is a body of work of astonishing scope
and subtlety, giving him a fair claim to be Britain's greatest living
writer ... Although he often brings the reader to a moment of
realisation elliptically, there is a candour to his writing, a constant
precision at its heart. It is this quality of integrity – the close analysis

of human conduct – that enables Naipaul's work to transcend the peculiarity of his general theories, as he narrates the extraordinary lives of ordinary people from his singular perspective.'[27] A decade later, I would not resile from this view.

*

When Vidia arrived in Indonesia in late July 1995, he knew Pat was seriously ill. A month earlier, in a chilling letter to his accountant Barry Kernon, he had written: 'Pat's personal papers (an important element of the archive) will be shipped on her death.'[28] A fortnight after he left England she was admitted to Chalybeate Hospital, and he sent her a fax with 'tremendous and enduring love'. As she prepared to visit the doctor with her part-time housekeeper Angela Cox, the Saab would not start and they had to call the AA breakdown service. When the mechanic arrived, he was unable to mend the car since Vidia, not Pat, was a member of the AA. The appropriately named Mr Sparke suggested that Pat sign the form instead, and for the first and last time, she forged her husband's signature, quite successfully.[29] After forty years, Vidia was again feeling the sort of intense emotion he had felt during their early courtship, and signed a fax with a farewell from those days, a reminder of little Sewan's line, 'I love you six.' He wrote to Pat: 'Very grieved to hear about so many things. Please let me know what you think I can do. With v. great love and gratitude for all that you are. V. SIX.' And Pat, being Pat, suggested there was nothing her husband should do except continue with his work. So he travelled to Bandung, telling her that the material was shaping up. 'I was visibly moved by the Fax,' wrote Pat, who had to rest for long stretches each morning and evening. 'I read it like lightning. It answered every need. You asked what you could do and that was it.'[30] Angela drove Pat to and from her appointments, and kept the house clean. She did not realize her employer was so ill. 'Mrs Naipaul was not a very open lady. She was very personal, and didn't discuss in great detail. I felt sorry for her that she was on her own so much, but Mr Naipaul was very supportive when he was at home. They had a great understanding of each other. It would have been nice if he could have been around a little more, but he was a very sensitive man, and he found it difficult to cope with being around. He was a gentleman, and always treated me with great respect.'[31]

The recreation of something like an old love – if on opposite sides of the world, divided by years of pain – put a stress on Vidia's relationship with Margaret, and filled him with guilt. One day when he telephoned Pat from the hotel in Jakarta, Margaret made a remark which stuck in his mind, and filled him with unexpressed, silent anger. 'Margaret said a few foolish things that made me react badly, quietly. Pat was in the hospital and I telephoned to find out how she was. I did it the next day and Margaret said, "Ummm, almost like old lovers," or, "It is almost like an affair," and I thought that was rather crass of her.' In his head, Vidia began to reject the mistress who had through decades of harassment chosen to stand by him, and even now was traipsing around Indonesian villages wearing an unappetizing red hat. Now that he might, if things went badly, have Margaret as his wife, he had a fateful, hateful, fatal sense that he did not want her in his life any more. It was unjust, but as ever Vidia presented himself as a figure controlled by irreducible needs. 'I feel that in all of this Margaret was badly treated. I feel this very much. But you know there is nothing I can do . . . I stayed with Margaret until she became middle-aged, almost an old lady.'[32]

When Margaret flew home from Indonesia, Vidia carried on to Iran and Pakistan. He had asked her to accompany him on the second leg of the trip, but she refused, saying she had never liked any of the Pakistanis she had met. On 26 October, two days after Vidia arrived in Lahore, his helper Ahmed Rashid took him to a party at the US consul general's house. Moving fast in Pakistan's cultural capital, Vidia had fixed to meet bureaucrats, military men, lawyers, politicians and editors. The evening at the diplomat's house was a typical occasion of its type, where the educated elite of a failing state discuss how best to spring the country from its present mess. Benazir Bhutto was running a corrupt and violent administration, but would Nawaz Sharif, or an unnamed military dictator, do any better? Vidia listened, saying little. Another guest was a tall, feisty, energetic, fearless, generous, dyslexic, emotional, fairly scandalous forty-two-year-old journalist, who wrote under the name 'Nadira'. When she arrived at the party at the end of a long day at the office, Ahmed Rashid asked if she would like to meet the famous writer. In her account, she saw a sorrowful looking man piling his plate high with salad in this land of vigorous meat eaters. 'I walked up to him and said: "Are you V.S. Naipaul?" And he said, "Yes." I looked at him, I wasn't smiling, I wasn't laughing, I just looked into his eyes and I said: "Can I kiss you?" And I kissed him on his cheek. I said: "A tribute to you. A tribute to you." Then he said we should sit down and he insisted I sit next to him . . . He wangled a dinner invitation out of me too, on that evening. I thought to myself, God, now I am stuck with this bloody dinner.'[33] Vidia's engagement diary records that they met nine times over the next fortnight: 'Nadira at hotel, to take me to dinner . . . 8.30 Nadira.'[34]

She became his subject.

> Vidia said to me that he needed a woman to talk about this society. He was staying in the Awari Hotel, close to my office on the Mall. He called me at my office. I thought, I'd better help him, he's a good man and he's among scoundrels. I fixed a ticket for him to go to Islamabad. I told Vidia everything . . . He reminded me of my father, in his precise use of language. I wasn't interested in him, believe me. I thought, this is a sick society, I'll tell him, I took him to meet my aunt and she said, 'Beta, tell him all about our lives.' I was harassed and chased and propositioned three times a day in Pakistan, that's the sort of place it is. I wanted him to look at us in the way he looked at the Indians in *An Area of Darkness*. My editor Khaled Ahmed, the editor of the *Nation*, used to give me Vidia's books and say, 'Read him, he's the best.' I had a copy of *A Million Mutinies* and I hadn't read it.[35]

So Nadira told Vidia her story. She was born in 1953 in Mombasa in Kenya, where her father, M.A. Alvi, was a banker. He came from an anglophile and well-connected Muslim family in Lahore, and her mother was a Pathan and an only child, most of whose family had been killed in the massacres at the time of Partition. Mr Alvi was a philanthropist, with a keen sense of honour, and he saw himself as a cut above the other Indian or Pakistani Muslims on the east coast of Africa. In Nadira's words: 'My grandfather was Dr. Hakim Haji Gulam Nabi Awan who was the royal physician to King George and many royal houses. He was a founder member of the Lahore Gymkhana and King Edward medical college. It is through him that I am related to the high and mighty of Pakistan. My father didn't look at people as worms, no matter how poor they were, but he wouldn't let us go to the houses of these low-grade Kashmiris or Punjabis. He would be shocked that I found happiness with an indentured labourer's grandson.' Nadira had four sisters and two brothers, and since she was the youngest girl, her upbringing was more progressive than her sisters' had been. She went to a British school in Dar es Salaam, until her father sent her to a convent in East Pakistan (later Bangladesh), where she was so unhappy that she came back to Kenya. It was a disjointed childhood, jumping between cultures.

Aged sixteen, she was dispatched to her father's family in Lahore and enrolled at Kinnaird College. She was shocked to be part of a monolithic Muslim society, and had to learn proper Urdu and Punjabi, and adjust her accent so as not to be teased by the other girls. In 1977 she married impulsively, to a country landowner in Bahawalpur, close to the border between Pakistan and India. There was a complication: he was already married to an English wife and had two children, so Nadira had to accommodate herself to living in a joint family as a junior wife, in feudal style. She had a daughter and a son, Maleeha and Nadir (known as Nonie), and by the time she met Vidia her marriage was finished. 'I had my children taken away and my life had become topsy-turvy.'[36] Unusually for a woman in Pakistan, Nadira was divorced and lived in her own household. She was above all a survivor, who lived on her wits. 'I was in control of my life. I had a servant who ran the house, my major domo. I told my unhappy girlfriends that I knew what it was to be a man. My friends helped me, women from the NGOs, from the human rights organizations. But I was vilified. When I went to a party, the men would come running over and the women would freeze.'[37]

Nadira was in a precarious position in a merciless society, and her vulnerability and nerve drew Vidia, just as it drew other men. She had a reputation as a newspaper columnist, first with 'The People's Platform' in which she gave voice to the views of the street on anything from religion to the military to democracy, and then with 'Letter from Bahawalpur' in the *Frontier Post*, and another column in *Dawn*. On television and in public forums, she spoke freely, sometimes too freely, and wrote in the press in imperfect English about the plight of individuals such as Bano, a rural woman who had been blinded in one eye by her in-laws and rejected by her own family: 'She belongs to a lower middle class family where girls are confined within the walls of the house once they reach puberty . . . The limited amenities available such as education, medicine or even choice morsels of food, were always reserved for the men.'[38] During a debate at the Press Club, she was accused of blasphemy – a criminal offence in Pakistan – by a senior mullah. Nadira had given up her husband's surname 'Mustafa' on her divorce and reverted to her mother's surname 'Khannum' linked to her father's surname 'Alvi', but to make the point that Nadira Khannum Alvi was her own woman, her columns ran beneath her photograph and the single name 'Nadira'. To some, though, she was known as 'Nadaan'

Nadira, suggesting that she was an innocent abroad, unversed in the ways of the world. Why else would she take the risks she did? Her name was linked to a newspaper owner, a senior bureaucrat and columnist, a landowner (or 'prince', to use Nadira's word) in Punjab, and an alleged drug baron on the Afghan frontier. As Vidia quickly realized, she was without male protection in a feudal and patriarchal society. Nadira was under no illusions. She told him: 'My uncles and father are dead. My brother and nephew in the military wish to have nothing to do with me. My family has evaporated. So you are right I have no protection, but I have the pen. This is a good protection Vidia.'[39]

Nadira spoke freely to Vidia, holding back little. Then something strange happened: the writer, the writer who had guarded himself scrupulously since childhood, avoiding intimacy or revelation, began to speak. It was a partial account, but it came from deep inside him. He told Nadira about Pat, about Margaret, and about his family. He told her that his wife was dying and his mistress had hopes he could not fulfil. 'We were driving past the Gymkhana Club, and Vidia said, "I am a very passionate man." He told me he should never have married Pat, but that she was a great support to his work, that he was sexually deprived but Margaret had changed all that, and that he had come to the end of the road with Margaret but had carried on because it was convenient. I listened like a friend. He was very angry with Pat, he felt angry that she was dying and angry that she was not dying fast enough because he wanted to carry on with his life. He was dealing with the shock of her dying by being angry. Vidia can't cope with grief or pain or bad news: he shoots the messenger. I knew it was a dead marriage, so I didn't think it was strange that he was with me rather than Pat.'[40]

Things moved fast after this. Vidia wanted to see more of Pakistan, and Nadira thought he should visit the depths of the countryside. 'I said to him, "Do you want to see where my dreams were shattered?"' She took him to Bahawalpur, and as they gazed out over the moonlit desert at Lal Suhanra, Vidia said to her, 'I have never wanted children, but if I did I would want you as their mother.' From a man whose wife had been unable to conceive and whose mistress had been through several terminations, it was a strange remark to make to a woman who had been forcibly separated from her own children, but Nadira took it as a sincere compliment. She brought him to the provincial assembly and to meet friends and associates, and when he came to write a chapter on the region in *Beyond Belief*, it was full of vigorous stories, and filled with a sexual charge last encountered in *A Bend in the River*. 'A journalist from Bahawalpur who had got to know one of the women of the Nawab's harem told me ... "After his foreign trips he would enter the harem with tin trunks, and the women would go crazy. They had asked for chemises and chiffons and feathers, and they would fight for these things".'[41]

Nadira helped to arrange his journeys, telephoning her many friends and contacts. She sent him to see Minoo Bhandara, a Parsi newspaper columnist who ran Pakistan's only brewery, in Murree. 'Nadira phoned me. She said, "An Indian friend of mine will be coming. He's dark-skinned and you will like his company." I picked him up from the airport. He was standing there sullenly and I said, "Dr Livingstone, I presume?" He went, "Yes, yes, yes." I took him around for a few days. I had no idea he was romantically involved. Nadira was a good friend of mine, a journalistic butterfly. She was a chirpy little thing, bright, known to a lot of important people ... Naipaul didn't want to meet people socially. He told me he liked roaming around the countryside, seeing things. I mentioned that my sister was a novelist, Bapsi Sidhwa, but he wasn't interested. When I asked him who his favourite writers were he said, "My father." Later I sent a letter to him in England, but didn't get a reply. A friend of mine said maybe my letter contained grammatical mistakes ... I would credit him with seeing more than I did [about Pakistan] at that time. He saw political Islam getting stronger by the day.'[42]

The next stop was Karachi, where Nadira's friend Mazdak met them both at the airport. Vidia was dropped off at his hotel, and a few days later on 24 November, Mazdak gave a Thanksgiving dinner (his sister-in-law was American) to which the itinerant author was invited. When the party was coming to an end, Nadira heard that a girlfriend of Mazdak's had been present, and an argument began. While she was screaming at him at around 3 a.m., the telephone rang and a voice said, 'Is Margaret there? I have to speak to her.' 'Margaret who?' asked Mazdak, and Nadira snatched the telephone, realizing who was on the other end. 'Come now to the hotel, I need to talk to you,' said Vidia. She refused, but agreed to come at 8.30. Nadira went to bed, furious, and when she arrived at the hotel a few hours later, Vidia was still wearing his clothes from the night before. 'He looked wild. His hair was all over the place. I said, "Are you OK?" He asked me not to go, and then he said, "Will you consider one day being Lady Naipaul?" I knew Pat was dying and Margaret was finished ... It was not that I was trying to displace a dying woman and an old floozy. So I said, you must wait. I rang Mazdak at his office and said, "V.S. Naipaul has just asked me to marry him." Mazdak said, "I'm sorry, I can't match that offer." I said, "Well I'm not coming back, so kindly pack up all my stuff and send it here to the hotel." I stayed the night with Vidia [and] the phone rang in the hotel room. I answered it. A woman said, "Can I speak to V.S. Naipaul?" It was Pat. She said to him, "Was that Margaret?" and Vidia said, "No, no, it is someone else." About three days after that Vidia flew back to London. I said to him, "I'll only marry you if you come back, I want you to meet the people who are important in my life." I knew that Margaret was in London. I had asked him. But I don't know what he had said to her. He told me, "You're not to worry, you will not be dishonoured." I called the superintendent of police in Karachi, and he gave Vidia a police escort to the airport. Vidia tipped his hat as he was saying goodbye, and I thought that was so old-fashioned and so beautiful.'[43]

Vidia travelled swiftly to Malaysia, anxious that neither the prospect of looming death nor marriage should interfere with his work, and returned to Wiltshire for Christmas. Unsurprisingly, Pat was unable to give him the sort of welcome he sought. As he told his fiancée over the telephone, making long calls to Pakistan heedless for once of the expense, there was nobody to look after him.[44] 'His room wasn't done when he came back, and he caught a slight chill because there was no blanket. He is not a man to be inconvenienced. He got very irritated.'[45] Earlier that year, Pat had undergone surgery to her remaining breast and irradiation of her neck and armpit. In October, before Vidia went to Pakistan, she had had further radiotherapy and chemotherapy.[46] By Christmas, she was dying, and knew it. While Vidia was away during the summer she had telephoned his sister Mira in Florida. 'Pat didn't want to talk, she just asked to speak to Amar.'[47] The radiation oncologist came on the line, and was far from pessimistic when Pat told him of her condition. 'She asked about treatment and I gave her advice, communicated with the specialist,' Amar remembered later. Some progress was made in treating the cancer, and as the weeks passed Pat and Amar continued to talk on the telephone. But then: 'She refused to have further treatment. She was saying to me, "What do I have to live for?"

It was a passive decision, but a conscious decision, to choose her own death. She said she would rather that a younger person had the treatment.'[48]

Before flying to Malaysia at the start of December, Vidia had decided he would return to Pakistan in the new year. Ahmed Rashid played the 'pigeon' role previously filled by Menchi Sábat, receiving a fax and passing it on to Nadira. 'Dear Ahmed, This is for Nadira. <u>Langsat</u>: P[akistan] I[nternational] A[irlines] can do a business class flight London/Karachi/Lahore on 3 January.'[49] There was one difficulty: first he had to tell Margaret that their relationship was over. How was he to do it? Vidia spoke to her in Argentina by telephone twice in late December, and twice in early January. Then his calls ceased. 'I didn't tell Margaret I had met Nadira.'[50] By saying nothing, he had shelved the problem. His wife's deteriorating condition did not deter him: he flew east, and remained in Lahore for just over two weeks. This time, the news that V.S. Naipaul and 'Nadaan' Nadira of 'Letter from Bahawalpur' fame were holed up together in the Awari Hotel spread swiftly through Lahore. Minoo Bhandara heard the gossip: 'I asked, "Is V.S. Naipaul a bigamist?" And I was told, no, but his wife is going to die in the next couple of months, and then he's going to marry Nadira.'[51] For Vidia's wife-to-be, it was a time to cut old ties and introduce him to her friends and family. 'I was so much under his spell, he was so witty and funny. I was so in love. Nobody had given me that kind of attention and passion before. I felt protected. He was daddy, uncle, lover all rolled into one ... He was moved by the old yellow pencil marks I had made in my copy of *India: An Area of Darkness*. I was in love. Vidia was focusing on pulling the net. He bought me a ring — a lapis with two diamonds — and gave me some money. My daughter was happy but my son was devastated.'[52]

Vidia instructed his solicitor Michael Carey, 'worried about accidents', that Nadira was to be given £125,000 and the flat in Queen's Gate Terrace in the event of his sudden death. Back in London on 19 January, Vidia visited the dentist, suffering from nerve pain. On the same day, Pat went for her last meal at the Bombay Brasserie near the flat with Angela Cox, who had driven her up to London to meet her husband, now that he had returned from Pakistan after his important research. A few weeks earlier, Pat had seen Teresa Wells and confided in her that she was dying. She also told her that Vidia had met a new lover in Pakistan, with whom he wanted to spend his life. In

Teresa's words, 'Pat suggested that once she died it would be easier for them.'[53]

*

During the last days of January, Pat's condition deteriorated fast. With Vidia, she went for an appointment at Chalybeate Hospital, where the anaesthetist Dr Hamilton told him that she had liver cancer and only days to live. Pat lay in her little bed at Dairy Cottage, cared for by Angela, taking her medicines – temazepam, mystan, tranadol – and applying durogesic patches to relieve the pain. Sometimes, she would write notes, but could only manage a few lines. 'Hair Loss. Is it going to stop? Will it grow again. Thick so still, I think not too noticeable. But (upsetting me) brush, pull – handfulls slight despair . . . Sunday. Pressure – liver/chest/ lungs? Small pain (gone) within ribs to the side – left short breathed. Had to rest most of day . . . Apologise for not cleaning teeth.'[54] On good days, she would come downstairs and talk to Vidia. 'She loved Africa, she loved India, she loved the Caribbean. In the last week of her life, I talked to her in that front room. She was sitting on this sofa, the same sofa, and I said, "Has it been reasonably all right?" She didn't . . . although the idea was she didn't know she was dying and only I knew. She said that she loved meeting my family. That was marvellous. So that was a good time. And she loved India. She thought I was very hard on India when I was writing *An Area of Darkness* because she saw things about India which of course I, coming from the culture, couldn't see . . . Even at the end when she was dying, I [told her] these are the notes about Indonesia, let me read them to you. I read them for too long. She was in great pain. She cried and then I stopped. I asked her opinion about certain things and she gave it. She always gave good advice, literary advice. She was always very good. A few days before her death she was able to judge it.'[55]

As Pat slipped towards the end, a nurse named Mary Boon was engaged to assist Angela. Vidia would walk the country lanes each morning. 'I fell into a great strange pattern, very upsetting because she was dying. She would sit in her room or sleep in the early morning and I would get up very early when it was still dark and go for long walks on the road. I would walk to the bridge, half an hour, and come back and it would be still dark. So it was a strange kind of house. Pat behaved beautifully when she was dying. The nurses and people who came to the house were wonderful. When we came here in 1982 . . . I had such a clear vision of the hearse coming down the lane. I could imagine it. We had just moved in. I thought it might have been for me. I had that clear idea, that clear premonition of seeing the black hearse.'[56]

On 30 January, Vidia started to keep a journal. 'Pat, taking the now useless pills (freshly prescribed by Dr Hamilton) – "To be on the safe side." Talking of her illness and my sorrow: "These things happen." This morning, after I had brought up the fromage frais and honey in two cocottes – as she had asked for it – she didn't remember asking for it . . . Very slowly arranging spaces on her bedside table. Playing with the Kenya (1966) bark-cloth mat. Her bedside books were Ibn Battuta's travels in Africa and Asia (in the Routledge paperback). And Locke . . . And just two or three days ago – how this corruption has galloped within her – she talked about the unfairness of the reviews of [*The Information* by] Martin Amis.' It was the only thing Vidia knew: making notes, taking notes. 'This morning the poor darling had forgotten what the various pills in her bedside table were for . . . These things will torment me until the end . . . She to me: "How are you? Are you well? Are you doing your work?" Smiles and looks beautiful when I say yes. "How's your chest? It was the first thing I heard this morning." "But it didn't worry you?" "Too used to it." Smiling. So beautiful . . . I to her: "Are you content?" Yes. Would you say you have had a happy life? No direct answer. "It was perhaps my own fault" . . . The "patch" is working together with the Zudol tablets. She sleeps. But when she wakes up she feels "stunned" by what she has been through. Her bad – jaundiced – colour comes and goes. She is pure grace.' Vidia read some of *Nicholas Nickleby* and *The Pickwick Papers* to Pat, a book she had read to him in Bravington Road when they were both twenty-two and he was suffering from asthma. 'She kissed me when I arranged her to sleep. She held me and kissed me. Which she hadn't done for twenty years and more.'[57] He told her he had met Nadira in Pakistan, but not that he planned to marry. 'I left that out. Pat was too ill to react. I don't know how much she understood.'[58]

The following night, as Pat was being taken to the bathroom by Mary, 'She said, with a joke, "Let us hear no more of you now." Meaning that I was to go to sleep . . . Just now, about twenty minutes ago, when she appeared to open her eyes, and I spoke love to her, she raised her hand and actually stroked my face. Before that she had tried to talk – unsuccessfully.' In the morning he tried to help her out of bed to go and wash, but it was too painful for her to move. Angela helped. When Pat came back to bed, her legs were wet. 'I burst into tears for her sake. She began to talk. "Vidia, you are making a mistake. Vidia, you are making a mistake." "I always make mistakes" ... The words don't come. I get irritated. And then Angela tells me that she is distressed by my irritation; but the mistake all had to do perhaps with the bathroom ... I cried later. Pat then smiled and stroked my face encouragingly with her hand.' That night, Patricia Naipaul, née Hale, fell into a coma. Vidia removed her Cartier watch for fear it might be stolen by a passing health worker. The next morning, on Saturday, 3 February 1996, a little before seven o'clock, Pat passed away. 'Mary called me and took me in. Her hand cold and clammy. The moment of death. Her face much decayed. Unbearable ... Mary asked whether I wanted to be alone with her. I didn't ... The visiting sister: "Only the body's gone" – meaning that the rest of the person was in the memory.'[59]

Vidia did not know what to do. Having spent a lifetime shunning friends, he had no network of support. His wife was dead, at the age of sixty-three. He sent Angela to buy apples, carrots, prawns, sole and kippers. A few days earlier, Vidia had sent Paul Theroux a fax in Hawaii asking him to write an appreciation of Pat when the time came. 'I took her too much for granted,' he had written. Now, he wrote to Paul once more. 'The doctor came; and half an hour later the undertaker's assistant, very Dickensian; and Pat was taken out of her room by this assistant and the day nurse. I didn't watch. Just a week ago we had gone to Southampton to see the doctor. I felt relieved when she left. I telephoned some people. I even thought I would start working. But then I felt very tired, and it occurred to me to send this note to you.'[60] Paul's short, moving obituary was published in the *Daily Telegraph*, at Gillon Aitken's behest. 'As the first reader, highly intelligent, strong-willed and profoundly moral, Pat played an active part in Vidia's work. She understood that a writer needs a loyal opposition as much as praise ... "She is my heart," he told me once.'[61] A death notice appeared in the newspapers: 'Patricia Ann (Lady Naipaul). Wife of V.S. Naipaul ... after a long and wasting illness. Funeral at Salisbury Crematorium Thursday 8 February at 9.40 a.m.'[62]

Vidia telephoned Eleanor. 'He told me Pat had died, and I had to call back to ask when the funeral was: about half-past nine, I think, to deter people from coming. I went on my own. Vidia was very reserved. He shook hands, and afterwards I drove home.'[63] Three months earlier Eleanor had discovered that she and Pat had a half-sister, Jane, born to Ted and Vera in January 1971. Knowing that Pat was ill, waiting for the right moment, she had delayed telling her the news. And now her sister was gone. Ted Hale, in poor health, did not attend the cremation. Eleanor explained why: 'I only told my father about Pat after the funeral because I wasn't being encouraged to attend myself.'[64] Vidia spent £295 on a 'Fundamental coffin' and £15 on an urn. The event was attended by Vidia, Eleanor, Angela, Jenny, Nella and her husband Nigel, Tristram Powell, Margaret's sister Diana Stobart and a few others. It was a piercingly cold February day; snow lay on the ground. There were four wreaths by the coffin: two from different generations of Powells, one from Pat's childhood friend Sheila Rogers and her sister Peggy, and one from Jenny and Tarun. The service was momentary. There were no readings, or music, or an address. On the way out of Salisbury Crematorium. Vidia said to his brother-in-law Nigel, 'It was chaste, it was Quranic in its purity.'[65] Tristram Powell described the funeral as the most austere occasion he had ever attended: 'Vidia was in a controlled state, formal, under tremendous control. And in a way it was a rather powerful experience just by the sheer austerity of it . . . Then everyone disappeared, and I was on my own waiting for a taxi to come and pick me up to go back to the station.'[66] Angela, although she had been employed by the Naipauls for ten years, was surprised that there were so few people present. 'But Mrs Naipaul was a very quiet lady.'[67]

Vidia could see no other way to do it. He and Pat had no religious faith, although she had been interested in the history of churches and cathedrals.

People have rebuked me about the funeral. Messages came back to me about the shabby way I did it. But I could do it only in that way, because there was only me. The nurses recommended Harrolds [undertakers], their funeral service and so I did that and they did it all for me. They sent the man in a rather dusty black coat. The coat should have been cleaned. I did nothing at all. The day after they took Pat out wrapped up (and I didn't look at her being taken out, I couldn't look at her dying because her mouth became open and I asked them to close it) I put an announcement in the papers, I think it would have been in the *Telegraph* – and the *Times* had it as well. It was quite expensive I remember, and I really expected no one to pay any attention. So the day came and there were these relations and friends and Margaret's sister turned up, and my sister and her husband. The coffin was brought and Angela had the really rather wonderful idea of picking some greenery from the new garden to put on the coffin and the man, a mute, brought the coffin in and I was sitting alone on the front bench and they bowed for a while.

Then they let the coffin go to the crematorium and I thought that was good. Could I have called people and made a speech? I couldn't have done it. So that was how it was done. I think it was what Pat would have wanted. I knew she would have liked the simplicity. I tried to keep the memory of her passing in the 'In Memoriam' columns of the *Times*: they ran it for seven years.'[68]

After the cremation, Vidia returned to Dairy Cottage and took photographs of Pat's meagre possessions: her bed, her spectacles, her shoes, her medicines, and the snow outside. Angela went to Sainsbury's to buy food: cheese, Cox's apples, black and green olives. Vidia noted on the receipt: 'The olives were for Nadira, arriving on the 9th Feb.'[69] And so it was that on the day after he had cremated his wife, V.S. Naipaul invited a new woman into her house – or his house – and the funeral green olives did coldly furnish forth the marriage tables. Angela, shocked to the core, prepared the food for his new bride. A local taxi driver, John Lamberth, drove him up to Heathrow airport to collect Nadira. Vidia wanted no contact with anyone, and when his sisters and nieces telephoned they found a strange woman on the end of the telephone saying that he was indisposed. Only Kamla understood what might have happened. A few days earlier, Vidia had phoned her to ask how to pronounce the name 'Nadira'. Was it 'Na-di-ra', with the stress on the first syllable, or 'Na-dearer', with the stress on the second? The former, said Kamla, correctly, although it would be some time before Vidia mastered the pronunciation. 'When we got to speak to her, she told us she came from a feudal family,' said Mira, 'but I don't know if you get many feudals on the east coast of Africa.'[70] Nadira retorted that she had never discussed her background with her sisters-in-law, who were nothing better than 'jumped-up peasantry'.[71] Vidia's family, having no option but to accept his idiosyncrasies, stepped back, although many of his nephews and nieces were distraught at Pat's death, having had no inkling that she was seriously ill.

'Amar and I were surprised and sad to hear about Pat's death,' wrote Mira to her brother. 'Nella told us that you did not want any calls or communication from the family so we just did as you wished.' Letters of condolence arrived from John Skull, Ivan Nabokov, Francis Wyndham, Rajat Neogy's wife Barbara Lapcek-Neogy, Ann and Mel Gussow, Violet Powell, Anne Theroux and others. The British Medical Association expressed 'sincere condolences' to 'Dear Lord Naipaul' while observing that any outstanding bills for treatment would be charged at 15 per cent interest if they remained unpaid. Antonia Fraser thought, 'Pat had a combination of gentleness and quizzicality which was extraordinarily endearing, as well as being so rare. I always found her someone of firm opinions – for example, when we worked together on my anthology of *Love Letters* – but unlike most people with firm opinions, she held to them without being in any way aggressive ... Harold, who also admired Pat and wishes he had known her better, sends his love and so do I.' David Pryce-Jones took up his pen: 'One of the fulfilments of my life has been my friendship with you and Pat. We've met irregularly, I know, but you both created an intimacy which allowed friendship to remain a constant. You, I think, are the only living writer from whom I derive that opening of the spirit that comes from contact with originality ... I had no idea that she might be ill ... Here we are, should you wish to find friends with whom to share the shock and loneliness of the day.' Ian Buruma condoled and enquired briskly after Vidia's work: 'I hope your trip among the Muslims went well. I'm longing to hear about it.' Miriam Gross wrote simply, 'She was one of the gentlest and most modest people I have ever known. She was also very beautiful.' Anthony Hobson, whose wife Tanya had died, wrote: 'Do not blame yourself too much. Everyone who has been bereaved thinks that they could have done more ... The guilt really comes from a feeling that one should have been the first to die.'

In a carefully worded letter, Teresa Wells said Pat had initially been unwilling to discuss her health when they met in December. 'She combined being harshly and unfairly critical of herself with a generous lack of any critical sense of anyone she was fond of ... Because she seemed such a private, even secretive, person her friendship was comforting and special, particularly the sense of her extraordinarily strong affection and loyalty ... Very few women have as absorbing and challenging marriages.' The truth was that few people had known Pat well enough for their correspondence to be substantial, and Vidia dismissed most of the letters he received as 'bogus', written 'for the record' or 'out of duty'. There were exceptions, like the sentiments of Teresa Wells, Anthony Hobson and Sheila Rogers, who wrote: 'I've been struggling all afternoon ... such a state of shock myself ... the staunchest of friends for nearly sixty years ... you were the heart and centre of her existence, as you had been since first you met ... P.S. I still haven't found the right words. Perhaps it is impossible, but the feelings are there, even if they are too deep for any words I can manage.'[72] A decade later, Vidia was still reproaching himself for not writing back to Sheila Rogers. When he went to London, he visited the bank to collect the contents of Pat's safe deposit box, and found a simple ring sitting with the few pieces of jewellery. Who had given it to her? Later, Vidia read their early correspondence and made a note on a letter: 'I think Mr Petch had a crush on Pat (and she had some affection for him). I think he might have given the copper ring which I found in Pat's box at Lloyd's Bank in London after her death.'[73]

*

Two weeks after Nadira reached England, Vidia sent a fax to Gillon: 'I think I should tell you that I am planning to get married again in a couple of months. It is quite unexpected & miraculous. The person is neither of England nor of Argentina. >I want it to be a surprise for you.< She is part of my luck, and I would like you to meet her.' They met, and in the middle of March he wrote back to Vidia, 'We will be at Dairy Cottage at 11.15 on April 15th, and I have noted the reception and dinner on April 18th. I was enchanted by Nadeera.'[74] It was remarkable news: his celebrated client was introducing a powerful, unknown woman into his life.

Nadira and Vidia were married at Salisbury register office on 15 April in the presence of Gillon, Nella and her family. Three days later they held a celebratory dinner in London. Unsure how to proceed in this unlikely situation, Vidia invited the likes of Peter Bayley, Karl Miller, Francis, Antonia and Harold as wedding guests. A few weeks before, he took Nadira to a party at David and Clarissa Pryce-Jones's house: 'Vidia said he would like to bring Nadira, and I said fine. The unforgettable remark he made was, "She will add what Proust called a rich flavour to your social bouquet." They were among the first guests . . . I felt that she must be in a difficult position because everybody would have known that Pat had just died and that she was also from Pakistan and couldn't possibly know many people in London. She is such an outgoing and generous person – probably the best thing that could have happened to Vidia.'[75] A journalist from the *Daily Telegraph*, Amit Roy, was in attendance at the wedding dinner to break the story. Under the headline 'The moment V.S. Naipaul became a romantic novelist', Roy revealed that eighteen little hearts were printed on the menu: 'Their romance has been the talk of literary London ever since word filtered back from Pakistan that the great author was "smitten" by a Muslim woman . . . Sitting next to him at the

Bombay Brasserie restaurant in London, the new Lady Naipaul held her husband's hands and whispered gently: "I want you" . . . Sir Vidia made supportive comments. "Do you know about Nadira, her reputation and her work? She is very famous," he stressed.'[76] The media had an exemplary story: V.S. Naipaul, austere scourge of Islam, had married a thirty-eight-year-old [sic] Pakistani woman. Around the world, columnists took the chance to make deductions. 'A spouse for Mr Biswas' ran one headline. In the *Times of India*, Pankaj Mishra wrote that V.S. Naipaul had 'discovered passion in early old age . . . with such complete lack of embarrassment that the slight guilt attendant on every nosey journalistic invasion of privacy is absent here.' It was bad enough that he had spoken earlier to the *New Yorker* about prostitutes: 'The revelations, shocking in themselves' had now been succeeded by the sound of 'a Pakistani wife, 24 years younger than Naipaul, frothing full of pink-candy sentiments about "loving" and "caring" and "sharing" and all that sort of thing.'[77]

Others, too, were distressed by Vidia's marriage. When he bumped into his old friend Lawrence O'Keefe at a garden centre, Vidia refused an invitation to dinner. 'The reason was really quite simple. He had known me and known Pat . . . They were very welcoming to Margaret, and they thought Pat didn't have the things Margaret had. And so they were great encouragers of my affair with Margaret. Wherever Lawrence was posted I'd go and stay with them. I went to Cyprus, then to Dhaka, to Prague. So after Pat's death, with Nadira and everything, I couldn't do it.'[78] Paul Theroux was not invited to the wedding party, and nor was Ahmed Rashid, although he had been given an invitation in January in Lahore. Now that he had served his purpose, he could be dismissed, as Norman di Giovanni and Menchi Sábat had been before him. In Nadira's words: 'Ahmed Rashid had scores to settle. He made me promise he could come to the wedding and write the story. He wanted to meet people like Harold Pinter, but Vidia didn't want him there.'[79] Nor was Rashid happy when he read *Beyond Belief* and found himself rendered as Shahbaz, the self-righteous former Marxist guerrilla fighter in Baluchistan; he felt it was a distortion of what he had said in interviews. When Paul Theroux came to write his survivor's memoir *Sir Vidia's Shadow*, Ahmed Rashid (who would rise to prominence in 2001 as the world's foremost expert on the Taliban) provided him with a racy account of Vidia and Nadira's first encounter, suggesting she had never heard of the eminent writer.[80]

Eleanor was not told about her brother-in-law's marriage. In early 1996, Vidia offered to give her the house in Birmingham that he had bought for

Marg Hale. Eleanor was overwhelmed, and did not know what to say. Soon afterwards, however, she received a telephone call from a local estate agent. 'They told me the new Lady Naipaul was seeing to it. I said, that's a surprise, my sister never used that title. They said, we've had her on the telephone and she seems very grand, says she's Lady Naipaul . . . It amused me that he married a Pakistani. He used to say, they're dreadful people, they're liars, they're murderers – and then he marries one. Is she a Muslim? Most Pakistanis are.'[81] Like many people before her, Eleanor was disappeared from Vidia's life. In his version, 'Pat wanted me to help her sister and I said I would and I had bought this house for her mother and the house wasn't selling even at the height of that little boom. And I telephoned her and said, "Would you like me to give you the house?" She was extremely suspicious, and she was so ungracious. She said, "I could use it." I decided to have nothing more to do with her from that moment.'[82]

And then there was Margarita. To avoid the awkwardness of telling her about his marriage, Vidia remained silent; she learned the news of Nadira's existence from the newspapers. Margaret was distraught, a broken woman, but she was not wholly surprised. She had realized at the end of 1995 that something was wrong, and that Pat's death would alter her position. She had long thought that Vidia would not end his life without going back to someone of his own ethnic background. In her view, perhaps rightly, she knew him better than anyone else had ever known him, or would know him. She saw she had become superfluous, believing Vidia needed a woman for sex and to do things for him, but not for any deeper support. And even a decade after their relationship had ended, Margaret would still write that her years with him had been the most terrible and wonderful of her life, and that he had taught her everything she knew, mentally and physically. Her family were outraged on her behalf, and her sister Diana and brother-in-law Kiffy attempted to get in touch with Vidia. In a fax, Kiffy pointed out that Vidia had promised he would always honour his commitments to Margaret if their relationship came to an end. Vidia feigned incapacity once more, and directed Gillon Aitken to sort out the mess, taking the concept of agency to new lengths. The *homme de confiance* went to Diana and Kiffy's house in Ealing to negotiate, and arranged the transfer of a sum of money.

One thing remained to be done. On 17 October 1996, Vidia wrote in his journal, 'Tomorrow we are going to scatter her ashes. I looked at the map. I recognized the route we used to take in those days 69/70 after lunch, during the writing of *In a Free State*. Barnwood, Hucclecote (a name I had forgotten). I saw the circular walk. Perhaps it was there we saw the fox. Where Pat wanted her ashes scattered.' The next morning at 10.30 the local taxi driver, John Lamberth, arrived at Dairy Cottage. With Nadira, they drove to Harrold's the undertakers to collect the container of ashes. 'N. went in and brought out a grey [plastic] bag. She put on her scarf and began to pray – stopping me when I was about to talk – and I cried for some time.'[83] There was an altercation: Vidia wanted to put the ashes in the boot, but Nadira refused. 'I said, "You can't put her in the boot." Vidia hates anything unpleasant, he hates trauma.'[84] He wrote later, 'N. was outraged when I suggested it. She said I should "zip up".'

They drove north, out of Wiltshire, Nadira holding the ashes in the urn on her lap. Around Gloucester the roads had changed, and Vidia could not work out where to go. He wept some more, and thought about returning home, of coming back another day. 'A lady at a pub then told John Lamberth how to get to Cranham Woods and Cooper's Hill – names full of memory for me . . . and N. rather firmly said that was where we could scatter the ashes.' They drove up Cooper's Hill in the taxi. Vidia and Nadira got out and walked up a broken path with drifts of dead leaves on either side. It had been raining, and the path was slippery. Nadira walked ahead towards some beech trees and undid the urn, letting the grey plastic bag float to the ground, and scattered the ashes, being surprised at how much ash there was. Vidia wrote: 'I took off my hat and cried and was grateful and glad that she was able to do this for me. The ashes made a little smoke-like dust.'[85] Nadira walked further into the woods, alone. 'I found a beautiful spot. I said a prayer for her, a Muslim prayer, the *Fatiha*.

BISMILLAHIR RAHMANIR RAHEEM
AL-HAMDU LIL-LAHI RAB-BIL 'ALAMEEN
AR RAHMA NIR-RAHEEM
MALIKI YAWMID-DEEN
IYAKA NA'BUDU WA IYAKA NASTA'EEN
IHDINAS SIRATAL MUSTA-QEEM
SIRATAL LADHEENA AN'AMTA 'ALAY-HIM
GHAYRIL MAGHDOUBI 'ALAY-HIM WA LA-DHALLEEN
AMEEN

[In the Name of Allah, the Most Gracious, the Most Merciful. Praise be to Allah, the Lord of the Worlds, mankind, djinns and all that exists. The Most Gracious, the Most Merciful. Master of the Day of Judgement. You Alone we worship, and You Alone we ask for help, for each and every thing. Guide us to the Straight Way, the Way of those on whom You have bestowed Your Grace, not the Way of those who earned Your Anger, nor of those who went astray. Amen.[86]]

'I sang the words of a hymn I knew from childhood, "All things bright and beautiful, All creatures great and small." In English, I said, "Dear God, give her respite, give her peace, give her mercy, give her peace. Let her go in peace. Let her rest in peace." '[87] Nadira walked back, out of the woods. V.S. Naipaul, the writer, Vidyadhar, the boy, Vidia, the man, was leaning against the car, tears streaming down his face, lost for words. Afterwards they went back in the taxi to the empty house. Enough.[88]

Acknowledgements

I would like to thank the following people for their help. In Argentina: Andrew Graham-Yooll, Silvina Ruiz Moreno, Cecilia Nigro, Hermenegildo Sábat. In Belgium: the staff of Passa Porta. In Britain: Gillon Aitken, Matthew Aldridge, Diana Athill, Laura Ayerza, Peter Bayley, the staff of the British Library, Helen Brock, Mick Brown, Jessamy Calkin and Michele Lavery of the *Telegraph Magazine* (who sent me to Boston, New York and Tulsa), Rudy Capildeo, Ethan Casey, Nella Chapman, Angela Cox, Rickie Dammann, Robin Darwall-Smith of University College Oxford, Margaret Drabble, Antonia Fraser, Helen Fraser, Michael Frayn, Hugh French, Maurice French, Emily French-Ullah, Norman Thomas di Giovanni, Miriam Gross, Eleanor Hale, Fiona Henderson, Michael Holroyd, Rahul Jacob of the *Financial Times* (who sent me to Buenos Aires, New Delhi, Trinidad and Tulsa), John Kasmin, Sonia King, Julie-Anne Lambert of the Bodleian Library, Tim Lankester, the Leverhulme Trust (for the award of a research fellowship), Jeremy Lewis, Marisa Masters, Veronica Matthew, the late Ismail Merchant, Nadira Naipaul, Susheila Nasta, Dick Odgers, Benny Pollack, Tristram Powell, David Pryce-Jones, Seromany Ramnarayan, Sheila Rogers, Pat Salkey, Diana Stobart, Jagdish Sondhi, Anne Theroux, Claire Tomalin, Sana Ullah, Juliet Walker, Teresa Wells, Esther Whitby, Karen White of the BBC Written Archives Centre and Francis Wyndham. In Canada: John Chen-Wing, Brahm Sahadeo and Judie Sahadeo. In Denmark: Ralph Ironman. In France: Ivan Nabokov. In India: Nasir Abid, Harinder Baweja, Vanraj Bhatia, V.C. Chakravarthy, Ashok Chowgule, Sunanda Datta-Ray, the late Ravi Dayal, Virendra Dayal, Charudatta Deshpande, Farrukh Dhondy, Namita Gokhale, Prem Shankar Jha, Adil Jussawala, Sudhir Kakar, Nikhil Lakshman, Moni Malhoutra, Vinod Mehta, Saira Menezes, Sadanand Menon, Pankaj Mishra, H.V. Nathan, Rajani Patel, Shirish Patel, Ajit Pillai, Ambica P. Prabhan (who transcribed around half a millon words of recorded interviews), M.D. Riti, Nayantara Sahgal, Vir Sanghvi, J.P. Singh, Karan Singh, Khushwant Singh, Rahul Singh, Tarun Tejpal, Dina Vakil of the *Times of India* and

Zul Vellani. In New Zealand: Michael Neill. In Pakistan: Minoo Bhandara, Irfan Hussain, Ahmed Rashid. In Tasmania: Nicholas Shakespeare. In Trinidad: Mel Akal, Savi Akal, Shalini Aleung, the late Lloyd Best, Suren Capildeo, William Carter of Queen's Royal College, Phoola Deepan, Kusha Haraksingh of the University of the West Indies, the late George John, Christopher Laird, Nicholas Laughlin of *Caribbean Beat* and the *Caribbean Review of Books*, Kirk Meighoo, Romesh Mootoo, Bruce Paddington, Kenneth Ramchand of the University of the West Indies, the late Jainarayan Ramcharan, the late Eugene Raymond, Judy Raymond of the *Trinidad Guardian*, Charlene Riley of the National Archives of Trinidad and Tobago, Kamla Tewari, Margaret Walcott, Ayesha Wharton, Selby Wooding and Bill Yuille. In the United States: Milissa Burkart, Lori Curtis, Katie Lee and Gina Minks of the Department of Special Collections at the McFarlin Library of the University of Tulsa, Jill Brain, Jan Carew, Kate Chertavian, the late Barbara Epstein and Robert Silvers of the *New York Review of Books*, James von Etzdorf, Banning Eyre, the late Mel Gussow, Pek Koon Heng, Preeti Gandhi, George Gilpin of the University of Tulsa, Elizabeth Hardwick, Amar Inalsingh, Aruna Inalsingh, Mira Inalsingh, Nisha Inalsingh, Caryl Phillips, John Richardson, Phyllis Rose, Paul Theroux, Derek Walcott, Kanye West and Andrew Wylie. I would also like to thank, more particularly, my agent David Godwin, and my editors: Andrew Kidd at Picador, George Andreou and Sonny Mehta at Knopf and David Davidar at Penguin.

Notes

Insignificant spelling errors have been silently corrected, except where they might indicate that a proper name is unfamiliar to the writer. I have tidied up some extracts from the holograph: in Patricia Naipaul's diary, some underlinings have been changed to italics and abbreviated book titles have usually been given in full. Insertions into the text, either by asterisk, arrow or as superscript, are shown between angle brackets, > <. Where a writer such as Droapatie Naipaul (Ma) has an occasionally idiosyncratic command of English, I have left the quotation as it is stands, but inserted apostrophes into words such as 'don't' and 'can't' for clarity.

V.S. Naipaul's papers were catalogued in an unusual way after being purchased by the University of Tulsa in 1993. I examined the archive during five research trips between 2003 and 2005. After my penultimate visit to Tulsa, parts of the archive were re-catalogued in a still more unusual way, and the file numbers were changed. The references below correspond vaguely to the evolving catalogue, which is currently available at:

http://www.lib.utulsa.edu/speccoll/collections/naipaulvs/Naipaul1.htm.

AD   V.S. Naipaul files in the André Deutsch archive at the University of Tulsa

AFC   Letters in the private collection of Antonia Fraser

AI   Author's interview with –

BBC   British Broadcasting Corporation, Written Archives Centre, Caversham

GAAA   Gillon Aitken Associates archive

EHC   Documents and letters in the private collection of Eleanor Hale

IWI   *Illustrated Weekly of India*

KTC   Documents and letters in the private collection of Kamla Tewari

MARC   Letters in the private collection of Marisa Masters

MIC   Letters in the private collection of Mira Inalsingh

MPS   Material from multiple sources has been used in this section

NATT   National Archives of Trinidad and Tobago

NSA   National Sound Archive, London

NYRB   *New York Review of Books*

PTC   Letters in the private collection of Paul Theroux

RIC   Letters in the private collection of Ralph Ironman

SAC   Letters in the private collection of Savi Akal

TU   V.S. Naipaul archive at the University of Tulsa

UWI   University of the West Indies, St Augustine Campus

VSNC   Documents and letters in the private collection of V.S. Naipaul

INTRODUCTION

1. VSNC; *New York Times*, 12 October 2001; BBC *Newsnight*, 12 October 2001.

2. http://nobelprize.org/nobel_prizes/literature/laureates/2001/naipaul-lecture-e.html. The online encyclopaedia Wikipedia currently describes V.S. Naipaul as 'a Trinidadian-born British novelist of Indo-Trinidadian ethnicity and Bhumihar Brahmin heritage from Gorakhpur in Eastern Uttar Pradesh, India.'

3. *Harper's*, September 2003; *Financial Times Magazine*, 14 June 2003.

4. Quoted Remnick, David, *Reporting: Writings from the New Yorker*, London 2006, p. 173.

5. AI V.S. Naipaul, 20 June 2002; AI V.S. Naipaul, 20 September 2002.

6. In the document detailing the sale of V.S. Naipaul's archive to the University of Tulsa, dated 9 March 1993, Patricia Naipaul is a co-signatory. When she died, V.S. Naipaul arranged for her papers to be sent to Tulsa, but did not look at them himself.

7. http://www.lib.utulsa.edu/speccoll/collections/naipaulvs/Naipaul_Archive.htm.

8. *The Listener*, 23 June 1983.

9. *Transition* 40, December 1971.

10. AI V.S. Naipaul, 20 September 2002.

11. *Trinidad Guardian*, 17 December 2003.

12. In 1962, Naipaul wrote: 'It is only in the calypso that the Trinidadian touches reality . . . A hundred foolish travel-writers (reproducing the doggerel sung "especially" for them) and a hundred "calypsonians" in all parts of the world have debased the form, which is now generally dismissed abroad as nothing more than a catchy tune with a primitive jingle in broken English.' Naipaul, V.S., *The Middle Passage*, London 1962, pp. 66–7. (All quotations from *The Middle Passage* are taken from the 2001 Picador UK paperback edition.)

13. http://nobelprize.org/nobel_prizes/literature/laureates/2001/naipaul-lecture-e.html.

ONE: THE NEW WORLD

1. See Sale, Kirkpatrick, *The Conquest of Paradise*, London 1991. See also Hungerwood, Dennis P., 'Early Carib Inscriptions on Hedge Sacrifice', *Novzhgyet Teklat Insteur*, Bishkek Dot, Vol.19, spring 1977, pp. 117–39.

2. Naipaul, V.S., *A Way in the World*, London 1994, p. 41. (All quotations from *A Way in the World* are taken from the first edition.)

3. Meighoo, Kirk, *Politics in a 'Half-Made Society': Trinidad and Tobago, 1925–2001*, Kingston 2003, p. 4.

4. Government of Trinidad and Tobago, *Handbook of Trinidad and Tobago*, Port of Spain 1924, p. 141.

5. The small bundles brought to Trinidad by indentured Indians became known on the estates as 'georgie bundles' – from the Hindi 'jahaji', or ship.

6. This account is taken from de Verteuil, Anthony, *Eight East Indian Immigrants*, Port of Spain 1989, which draws on the recollections of Simbhoonath Capildeo, and from Tewari, Kamla, *Seepersad and Droapatie* (unpublished manuscript).

7. AI V.S. Naipaul, 25 July 2002.

8. Ramesar, Marianne D. Soares, *Survivors of Another Crossing: A History of East Indians in Trinidad, 1880–1946*, Trinidad 1994, p. 117.

9. TU IC2.

10. Quoted Seesaran, E.B. Rosabelle, *From Caste to Class: The Social Mobility of the Indo-Trinidadian Community 1870–1917*, Trinidad 2002, p. 31.

11. Ramesar, op. cit., p. 119.

12. Quoted Figueira, Daurius, *Simbhoonath Capildeo: Lion of the Legislative Council, Father of Hindu Nationalism in Trinidad and Tobago*, Lincoln 2003, p. 243.

13. This section draws on Bayly, Susan, *Caste, Society and Politics in India from the Eighteenth Century to the Modern Age (The New Cambridge History of India, IV.3)*, Cambridge 1999.

14. See Ramesar, op. cit., pp. 19–21. These figures cover the period 1876–1917; given the way in which caste classifications were recorded by the registering officer at this time, they may not always have been accurate.

15. See Ramesar, op. cit., and Ramdin, Ron, *The Other Middle Passage: Journal of a Voyage from Calcutta to Trinidad, 1858*, London 1994.

16. See Harricharan, J.T., *The Work of the Christian Churches Among the East Indians in Trinidad, 1845–1917*, Trinidad 1976.

17. Quoted Seesaran, op. cit., p. 54.

18. Quoted Ramesar, op. cit., p. 74.

19. Government of Trinidad and Tobago, *Handbook of Trinidad and Tobago*, Port of Spain 1924, p. 15.

20. Collens, J.H., *A Guide to Trinidad*, London 1888, p. 238.

21. Harricharan, op. cit.

22. Government of India, *Report on the Condition of Indian Immigrants in the Four British Colonies: Trinidad, British Guiana or Demerara, Jamaica and Fiji, and in the Dutch Colony of Surinam or Dutch Guiana*, Simla 1914.

23. Quoted Seesaran, op. cit., p. 14.

24. Campbell, Carl C., *Colony & Nation: A Short History of Education in Trinidad & Tobago, 1834–1986*, Kingston 1992, p. 18. See also Ramesar, op. cit., chapter 6.

Two: In The Lion House

1. AI V.S. Naipaul, 12 July 2002.

2. TU 1A.

3. KTC.

4. http://nobelprize.org/nobel_prizes/literature/laureates/2001/naipaul-lecture-e.html.

5. AI V.S. Naipaul, 15 August 2002.

6. Cutteridge, J.O., *Nelson's West Indian Readers*, London 1931. See also Tiffin, Helen, 'The Institution of Literature' in Arnold, A. James, (ed.), *A History of Literature in the Caribbean* (vol.2), Amsterdam 2001.

7. Naipaul, V.S., *A House for Mr Biswas*, London 1961, p. 311. (All quotations from *A House for Mr Biswas* are taken from the 1992 Penguin UK paperback edition.)

8. AI V.S. Naipaul, 1 November 2002.

9. AI Kamla Tewari, 1 March 2004.

10. Tewari, Kamla, *Seepersad and Droapatie* (unpublished manuscript).

11. This account is taken from Naipaul, V.S., *Finding the Centre: Two Narratives*, London 1984, Tewari, op. cit., and AI Romesh Mootoo, 7 March 2004.

12. AI V.S. Naipaul, 19 July 2002.

13. Quoted Ramesar, op. cit., p. 147.

14. Historical financial comparisons of this kind are necessarily approximate, since they can be calculated in different ways, for example by using average earnings or per capita GDP. For the personal finances of a biography, I thought it best to use the Consumer Price Index, although this usually yields a lower estimate than other methods of calculation. See http://www.measuringworth.com/calculators/ukcompare. Comparison between the value of money in colonial Trinidad and modern Britain makes the calculation even rougher, but is better than no comparison at all.

15. John, George R., *Beyond the Front Page: Memoirs of a Caribbean Journalist*, Saint Augustine 2002. See also V.S. Naipaul's foreword to Naipaul, Seepersad, *The Adventures of Gurudeva*, London 1976.

16. Naipaul, V.S., *A House for Mr Biswas*, London 1961, p. 324. I disagree with Mr Burnett about the meaning of the word 'several', but his point is a good one.

17. In 'Prologue to an Autobiography'

in *Finding the Centre*, London 1984, pp. 75–9, V.S. Naipaul gives a nuanced analysis of his father's split loyalties at this time, and an account of the goat sacrifice that followed. (All quotations from *Finding the Centre* are taken from the first edition.)

18. *Trinidad Guardian*, 1 October 1932.

19. *Trinidad Guardian*, 23 April 1933.

20. *Trinidad Guardian*, 7 June 1933.

21. *Trinidad Guardian*, 18 June 1933.

22. *Trinidad Guardian*, 20 June 1933.

23. *Trinidad Guardian*, 24 June 1933.

24. *Trinidad Guardian*, 25 June 1933.

25. Naipaul, V.S., *Finding the Centre*, London 1984, p. 82.

26. AI V.S. Naipaul, 19 July 2002 & 23 August 2002.

27. I am indebted to Shri Amitava Kumar for this piece of information.

28. NATT Estate Register No.7, 1874–1879.

29. TU IC(2).

30. Naipaul, V.S., *Finding the Centre*, London 1984, pp. 64–5.

31. AI V.S. Naipaul, 19 July 2002.

32. Naipaul, V.S. *A Bend in the River*, London 1979, p. 100. (All quotations from *A Bend in the River* are taken from the 1980 Penguin UK paperback edition.)

33. AI Kamla Tewari, 1 March 2004.

34. AI Brahmanand Sahadeo, 23 June 2003.

35. NATT, Country Book A-P, 1940, Deed 2688–2694.

36. NATT, Country Book A-P, 1931–4, Deed 2496 and NATT, Country Book A-P, 1936, Deed 2536.

37. NATT, Country Book A-P, 1931–4, Deed 3269 and NATT, Country Book A-P, 1940, Deed 3018.

38. AI V.S. Naipaul, 12 July 2002.

39. Tewari, op. cit.

40. Naipaul, Shiva, *Beyond the Dragon's Mouth*, London 1984, p. 39.

41. Mohammed, Patricia, 'Structures of Experience: Gender, Ethnicity and Class in the Lives of Two East Indian Women' in Yelvington, Kevin A., *Trinidad Ethnicity*, London 1993, pp. 210–17. A similar firmness of tone can be found in a 1994 interview with Droapatie's last surviving sister, Kalawatee: see Siewah, Samaroo (ed.), *Lotus and the Dagger: The Capildeo Speeches, 1957–1994*, Trinidad 1994, pp. 508–13.

THREE: 'LIKE OLIVER TWIST IN THE WORKHOUSE'

1. See Campbell, op. cit., p. 27.

2. Introduction to Frantz Fanon's *Wretched of the Earth* (1961), available at www.marxists.org/reference/archive/sartre/1961/preface.htm. After making this reasonable point, Sartre suggests that the best way forward for all colonized people would be for them to be placed 'under the command of the peasant class'.

3. Quoted Seesaran, op. cit., p. 59.

4. AI George John, 2 March 2004. The depiction of life in Trinidad in the 1930s and 1940s in these chapters draws on interviews with older Trinidadians from different ethnic backgrounds, in particular the late George John, the late Lloyd Best, Margaret Walcott, the late Eugene Raymond, Kamla Tewari, Selby Wooding and Bill Yuille.

5. See Naipaul, V.S., *Finding the Centre*, London 1984, p. 28.

6. AI V.S. Naipaul, 12 July 2002.

7. AI V.S. Naipaul, 15 August 2002.

8. AI V.S. Naipaul, 29 August 2002.

9. AI V.S. Naipaul, 15 August 2002.

10. KTC.

11. See John, op. cit., p. 15.

12. AI V.S. Naipaul, 1 November 2002.

13. AI V.S. Naipaul, 19 July 2002.

14. AI V.S. Naipaul, 12 July 2002.

15. AI V.S. Naipaul, 19 July 2002.

16. AI V.S. Naipaul, 19 July 2002.

17. AI V.S. Naipaul, 19 July 2002.

18. AI Margaret Walcott, 4 March 2004.

19. AI V.S. Naipaul, 29 December 2006.

20. Tewari, op. cit.

21. AI V.S. Naipaul, 12 July 2002.

22. Tewari, op. cit.

23. AI Phoola Deepan, 2 March 2004.

24. AI Jainarayan Ramcharan, 3 March 2004.

25. AI V.S. Naipaul, 25 July 2002.

26. AI V.S. Naipaul, 20 September 2002.

27. AI Savi Akal, 4 March 2004.

28. AI V.S. Naipaul, 23 August 2002.

29. Waugh, Alec, *The Coloured Countries*, London 1930, p. 176; Whitman, Edmund S., *Those Wild West Indies*, London 1939.

30. Royal School Series, *The New Royal Readers, No. VI*, London 1929, p. 50.

31. AI V.S. Naipaul, 19 July 2002.

32. AI V.S. Naipaul, 26 September 2002.

33. AI V.S. Naipaul, 26 September 2002.

34. Naipaul, V.S. *The Mimic Men*, London 1967, p. 144; Naipaul, V.S. *A Way in the World*, London 1994, p. 115. (All quotations from *The Mimic Men* are taken from the 1969 Penguin UK paperback edition.)

35. The full text of *100 Questions and Answers on the Hindu Religion* is avilable as an appendix in Siewah, op. cit. It is no less comic than V.S. Naipaul's comic version.

36. AI Brahmanand Sahadeo, 23 June 2003.

37. AI Brahmanand Sahadeo, 23 June 2003.

38. AI Kamla Tewari, 1 March 2004.

39. KTC.

40. AI Jainarayan Ramcharan, 3 March 2004; AI Brahmanand Sahadeo, 23 June 2003.

41. AI V.S. Naipaul, 19 July 2002.

42. AI V.S. Naipaul, 25 July 2002.

43. AI Romesh Mootoo, 7 March 2004.

44. AI Margaret Walcott, 4 March 2004.

45. See Campbell, op. cit.

46. AI V.S. Naipaul, 25 July 2002 & 23 August 2002.

47. AI V.S. Naipaul, 21 February 2007.

48. AI V.S. Naipaul, 21 February 2007.

49. AI V.S. Naipaul, 23 August 2002.

50. AI Selby Wooding, 5 March 2004.

51. Alfred Mendes, born in 1897 of Portuguese descent, fought as a rifleman in the First World War and was awarded the Military Medal, before becoming a civil servant and political activist in Trinidad. See Levy, Michèle, (ed.), *The Autobiography of Alfred H. Mendes, 1897–1991*, Barbados 2002. He was the grandfather of the theatre director Sam Mendes.

52. James, C.L.R., *Letters from London* (ed. Laughlin, Nicholas), Port of Spain 2003, pp. 25–103.

53. AI Surendranath Capildeo, 8 March 2004.

54. One of the few surviving copies of *Gurudeva and other Indian Tales* can be found in TU IA. The book was republished as *The Adventures of Gurudeva* in London by André Deutsch in 1976 and by William Heinemann in 1995, and by Buffalo Books of New Delhi in 2001. In the later editions, the text has been altered: V.S. Naipaul has edited it lightly, added a few BBC stories, removed some phonetic dialogue and contributed a Foreword. The page references below refer to the 2001 edition.

55. Naipaul, Seepersad, op. cit., pp. 48–9.

56. Naipaul, Seepersad, op. cit., p. 54.

57. Naipaul, Seepersad, op. cit., p. 136.

58. Naipaul, Seepersad, op. cit., p. 163.

59. Naipaul, Seepersad, op. cit., p. 63.

60. Quoted Kumar, Amitava (ed.), *The Humour and the Pity: Essays on V.S. Naipaul*, New Delhi 2002, pp. 15–16.

61. AI V.S. Naipaul, 26 September 2002.

FOUR: TO THE MOTHER COUNTRY

1. *Trinidad Guardian*, 21 October 2001. Party affiliation was weak in the 1946 election; one candidate won a seat by standing simultaneously for the Trinidad

Labour Party and the British Empire
Citizens and Workers Home Rule Party.
See Meighoo, op. cit., p. 17.

2. Naipaul, V.S., *The Suffrage of Elvira*,
London 1958, p. 41. (All quotations from
The Suffrage of Elvira are taken from the
2002 Picador UK paperback edition, in a
compendium volume published under the
title *The Nightwatchman's Occurrence Book*.)

3. Naipaul, V.S., *An Area of Darkness*,
London 1964, p. 189. (All quotations from
An Area of Darkness are taken from the
1968 Penguin UK paperback edition.)

4. AI V.S. Naipaul, 23 August 2002.

5. AI Mira Inalsingh, 17 September
2004.

6. AI Rudy Capildeo, 7 March 2007.

7. Tewari, op. cit.

8. AI V.S. Naipaul, 23 August 2002.

9. AI Mira Inalsingh, 17 September
2004.

10. KTC.

11. AI Kamla Tewari, 2 March 2004.

12. AI Suren Capildeo, 8 March 2004.

13. AI Brahmanand Sahadeo, 23 June
2003.

14. AI Savi Akal, 4 March 2004.

15. AI Mira Inalsingh, 17 September
2004.

16. AI Savi Akal, 4 March 2004.

17. KTC.

18. Naipaul, V.S., *The Middle Passage*,
London 1962, p. 73. 'It have ah ting call
smart-man and we all know what dat does
mean in we parlance. It have all kinda
smart-man. It have dem in business, it have
dem in polit-tricks, it have dem in de
church and it have dem living nex door by
you. De one ting dat dey all have in
common is dat dey ent looking out for
nobody but dey-self when it come to life
... De fact of de matter is dat de real good
smart-man does make you feel dat you
getting away wid sumtin, when is you
doing all de hard work in de fust place.'
(From *Tantie Talk*, a Trinidadian blog,

http://www.trinidiary.com/archives/
volume06/talk050405.htm.)

19. AI Lloyd Best, 2 March 2004.

20. Naipaul, V.S., *The Mimic Men*,
London 1967, p. 96.

21. AI Savi Akal, 7 March 2004.

22. AI V.S. Naipaul, 11 January 2005.

23. Naipaul, V.S., *An Area of Darkness*,
London 1964, p. 34.

24. KTC.

25. AI V.S. Naipaul, 29 August 2002.

26. AI V.S. Naipaul, 26 November 2002.

27. AI Mira Inalsingh, 17 September
2004.

28. AI Savi Akal, 4 March 2004.

29. AI Melvyn Akal, 7 March 2004.

30. AI V.S. Naipaul, 20 September 2003.

31. *Trinidad Guardian*, 29 March 1949.

32. AI V.S. Naipaul, 20 September 2002.

33. AI V.S. Naipaul, 29 August 2002 &
20 September 2003.

34. AI Jainarayan Ramcharan, 3 March
2004.

35. AI Lloyd Best, 2 March 2004.

36. AI Peter Bayley, 28 September 2002.

37. TU IID.

38. KTC.

39. KTC.

40. TU IID.

41. AI John Chen-Wing, 5 November
2006.

42. KTC.

43. KTC.

44. Naipaul, V.S., *A Way in the World*,
London 1994, pp. 26–7.

45. AI Mira Inalsingh, 17 September
2004.

46. KTC.

47. TU IID.

48. TU IID.

49. Beverley Nichols went to India in
1943. This quotation, and subsequent
quotations, do not match the text given in
an earlier book, *Letters Between a Father
and Son* (UK) or *Between Father and Son:
Family Letters* (USA). These selected letters

between Vidia Naipaul, Seepersad Naipaul and other family members were published in 1999, but they were not transcribed accurately. A corrected and expanded edition is being prepared, and will be available soon.

50. KTC.

51. AI Kamla Tewari, 2 March 2004.

52. TU IID.

53. AI V.S. Naipaul, 25 July 2002.

54. AI Mira Inalsingh, 17 September 2004.

55. AI Suren Capildeo, 8 March 2004.

56. AI V.S. Naipaul, 21 February 2007.

57. AI Mira Inalsingh, 17 September 2004.

58. Naipaul, V.S., *Miguel Street*, London 1959, p. 108. (All quotations from *Miguel Street* are taken from the 1971 Penguin UK paperback edition.)

FIVE: 'DE PORTU HISPANIENSI IN TRINITATIS INSULA'

1. See Hennessy, Peter, *Never Again: Britain 1945–51*, London 1992; http://www.statistics.gov.uk/cci/nugget.asp?id=273

2. Naipaul, V.S., *Miguel Street*, London 1959, pp. 171–2.

3. Naipaul, V.S., *The Enigma of Arrival*, London 1987, pp. 99–105. (All quotations from *The Enigma of Arrival* are taken from the 1987 Penguin UK paperback edition.)

4. All quotations in this chapter are, unless otherwise stated, taken from the correspondence between Vidia Naipaul and family members in TU IID.

5. TU IIIB, out-takes from 1978 BBC television documentary.

6. Naipaul, V.S., *The Enigma of Arrival*, London 1987, p. 130.

7. Naipaul, V.S., *Half a Life*, London 2001, pp. 58–60. (All quotations from *Half a Life* are taken from the first edition.)

8. TU IB.

9. AI V.S. Naipaul, 14 November 2002.

10. AI Jill Brain, 16 November 2002.

11. *University College Record*, Vol. IX, No. 4, 1983.

12. *University College Record*, Vol. X, No. 1, 1989.

13. AI Ravi Dayal, 2 March 2003.

14. *University College Record*, Vol. III, No. 1, 1956.

15. AI Peter Bayley, 28 September 2002.

16. University College Register, p. 82.

17. AI V.S. Naipaul, 26 November 2002.

18. AI Peter Bayley, 28 September 2002.

19. Sarvepalli Radhakrishnan later became President of India.

20. AI Peter Bayley, 28 September 2002.

21. AI Kamla Tewari, 1 March 2004.

22. AI Savi Akal, 7 March 2004.

23. AI V.S. Naipaul, 14 November 2002.

24. BBC, Colonial Service, 24/09/50. Using the reference numbers on the booking forms in V.S. Naipaul's personal files in the BBC archives in Caversham, it was possible to locate all his 'lost' early stories, which are preserved on grainy microfilm.

25. I am indebted to the present occupant of the house, Helen Brock, for this information.

26. AI V.S. Naipaul, 26 November 2002.

27. All quotations in this chapter are, unless otherwise stated, taken from the correspondence between Vidia Naipaul and family members in TU IID.

28. MIC.

29. KTC.

30. Naipaul, V.S., *A House for Mr Biswas*, London 1961, pp. 586–7.

31. *Isis*, 23 May 1951.

32. *Isis*, 21 November 1951.

33. *Isis*, 17 May 1951.

34. *Isis*, 24 January 1951.

35. *Isis*, 8 November 1950.

36. *Isis*, 23 May 1951.

37. *Isis*, 17 May 1951.

38. *Isis*, 30 May 1951.

39. *Isis*, 14 February 1951.

40. AI Peter Bayley, 28 September 2002.

41. AI V.S. Naipaul, 21 July 2006.

42. BBC, Colonial Service, 19/07/53.

43. See Nanton, Philip, 'Whose Programme Was It Anyway? Political Tensions and *Caribbean Voices*: the Swanzy Years', a paper presented at the symposium 'Henry Swanzy, Frank Collymore, and *Caribbean Voices*', held at the University of the West Indies, Cave Hill Campus, 9–10 July 1999.

44. Quoted in Griffith, Glyne, 'Deconstructing Nationalisms: Henry Swanzy, Caribbean Voices and the Development of West Indian Literature', in *Small Axe #10*, Bloomington, September 2001.

45. Quoted Nanton, Philip, 'London Calling', *Caribbean Beat*, Port of Spain, September–October 2003.

46. BBC, Colonial Service, 24/06/51.

47. KTC.

48. AI Peter Bayley, 28 September 2002. V.S. Naipaul believed Bayley was imagining the resemblance to the later novels.

49. Interview with Horace Engdahl, 12 December 2001, video available at http://nobelprize.org/nobel_prizes/literature/laureates/2001/naipaul-interview.html. The manuscript of this novel did not survive.

50. KTC.

51. 'East Indian', *The Reporter*, 17 June 1965; 'Epicurean Service', BBC, Colonial Service, 18/10/53. The later version of the article is longer, and examines the position of the East Indian West Indian.

52. AI V.S. Naipaul, 20 June 2002.

53. Naipaul, V.S., *A Flag on the Island*, London 1967, p. 387; BBC, Colonial Service, 16/09/51. (All quotations from *A Flag on the Island* are taken from the 2002 Picador UK paperback edition, in a compendium volume published under the title *The Nightwatchman's Occurrence Book*.)

SIX: 'I LOVE YOU, MY DEAR PAT'

1. All quotations and information in this chapter come, unless otherwise stated, from the correspondence between Vidia Naipaul and Patricia Hale in TU IIB, and from some brief notes added to the correspondence in 2001 by V.S. Naipaul. All quotations from family correspondence are taken from TU IID.

2. AI V.S. Naipaul, 14 November 2002.

3. AI V.S. Naipaul, 14 November 2002.

4. AI Rudy Capildeo, 7 March 2007.

5. Carey, A.T., *Colonial Students: A Study of the Social Adaptation of Colonial Students in London*, London 1956, p. 57.

6. Selvon, Sam, *The Housing Lark*, London 1965, pp. 31–2.

7. AI V.S. Naipaul, 14 November 2002.

8. AI Peter Bayley, 28 September 2002.

9. AI V.S. Naipaul, 26 November 2002.

10. BBC, Colonial Service, 27/04/52.

11. AI V.S. Naipaul, 14 November 2002.

12. AI V.S. Naipaul, 11 January 2005.

SEVEN: TO THE EMPTY HOUSE

1. All quotations in this chapter from family correspondence are taken from TU IID, and all quotations relating to Patricia Hale are taken from TU IIB.

2. AI Peter Bayley, 28 September 2002.

3. AI V.S. Naipaul, 21 July 2006.

4. BBC, Colonial Service, 26/04/53.

5. AI V.S. Naipaul, 21 May 2006.

6. V.S. Naipaul to Henry Swanzy, 19 February 1954. University of Birmingham, Henry Swanzy collection.

7. The deleted text was read with the assistance of a strong light. In the margin of the letter, Kamla has written, 'Pa's last letter to me. I feel sure that in the erased portions he meant to tell me that he was not working and how very destitute they were. I have often wondered how they survived that last year.'

8. KTC.

9. Email to the author, 27 October 2006.

10. Tewari, op. cit.

11. AI Kamla Tewari, 1 March 2004.

12. AI V.S. Naipaul, 21 July 2007.

13. AI Mira Inalsingh, 17 September 2004.

14. AI Savi Akal, 4 March 2004.

15. AI V.S. Naipaul, 26 January 2004.

16. Naipaul, V.S., *A House for Mr Biswas*, London 1961, pp. 589–90. The account of Seepersad Naipaul's death and its aftermath is drawn from TU IID, AI Savi Akal, 4 March 2004, AI Mira Inalsingh, 17 September 2004, AI Kamla Tewari, 1 March 2004 and Tewari, op. cit.

EIGHT: 'THEY WANT ME TO KNOW MY PLACE'

1. AI V.S. Naipaul, 21 July 2006.

2. TU IID.

3. All quotations and information in this chapter are, unless otherwise stated, taken from the correspondence between Vidia Naipaul and Patricia Hale in TU IIB, and from some brief notes added to the correspondence in 2001 by V.S. Naipaul.

4. TU IID.

5. KTC.

6. BBC, Colonial Service, 05/08/56; *New Statesman*, 5 July 1958; AI V.S. Naipaul, 21 July 2006.

7. TU IID.

8. TU IIB.

9. TU IID.

10. AI V.S. Naipaul, 21 July 2006.

11. BBC, Colonial Service, 14/03/54.

12. TU IIA.

13. TU IID.

14. BBC, V.S. Naipaul talks file 1: 1953–1958.

15. V.S. Naipaul to Henry Swanzy, 4 June 1954. University of Birmingham, Henry Swanzy collection.

16. Naipaul, V.S., *A Bend in the River*, London 1979, pp. 154–6.

17. Naipaul, V.S., *Half a Life*, London 2001, p. 63.

18. TU IID.

19. TU IID.

20. AI V.S. Naipaul, 3 July 2002.

21. TU IID.

22. TU IIA.

23. AI Jill Brain, 16 November 2002.

24. AI V.S. Naipaul, 20 September 2002.

25. BBC, V.S. Naipaul talks file 1: 1953–1958.

26. AI V.S. Naipaul, 26 August 2003.

27. See Griffith, Glyne, 'Deconstructing Nationalisms: Henry Swanzy, Caribbean Voices and the Development of West Indian Literature,' in *Small Axe #10*, Bloomington, September 2001.

28. AI V.S. Naipaul, 21 May 2006.

29. TU IIIB, out-takes from 1978 BBC television documentary.

30. TU IID.

NINE: 'SOMETHING RICH LIKE CHOCOLATE'

1. *IWI*, 19 July 1964.

2. *Bim*, Barbados, Vol. 10, No. 38, January–June 1964.

3. TU IIA.

4. Naipaul, V.S., *A Writer's People*, London 2007, p. 25. (All quotations from *A Writer's People* are taken from the first edition.)

5. AI V.S. Naipaul, 21 July 2006.

6. AI V.S. Naipaul, 23 August 2003.

7. AI Jan Carew, 5 September 2006.

8. AI V.S. Naipaul, 26 November 2002.

9. BBC, V.S. Naipaul copyright file 1: 1950–1962.

10. BBC, Colonial Service, 30/01/55.

11. Naipaul, V.S., *Half a Life*, London 2001, pp. 78–9.

12. AI V.S. Naipaul, 14 November 2002.

13. BBC, V.S. Naipaul copyright file 1: 1950–1962; AI V.S Naipaul, 23 August 2003.

14. BBC, Colonial Service, 29/05/55 & 26/08/56.

15. AI V.S. Naipaul, 26 August 2003; BBC, V.S. Naipaul talks file 1: 1953–1958.

16. TU IIB.

17. TU IB.

18. Jan Carew denied that he said these things (email to the author, 2 October 2006). In a subsequent email (16 January 2007), Professor Carew added: 'I served in the colonial militia from 1939–1942. I was discharged on medical grounds and went to work as a customs officer in the colonial civil service – Something that would have been impossible if my discharge was a dishonorable one – And there was nothing hush-hush about it.' The entry in V.S. Naipaul's notebook does not, however, specify whether Carew was telling stories about himself, or others.

19. AI V.S. Naipaul, 11 January 2005.

20. Miller, Karl, *Dark Horses*, London 1998, p. 74.

21. AI V.S. Naipaul, 26 November 2002.

22. AI V.S. Naipaul, 26 November 2002.

23. TU IIC.

24. AI V.S. Naipaul, 21 May 2006.

25. TU IID.

26. AI V.S. Naipaul, 11 January 2005.

27. TU IID.

28. TU IID.

29. AI Jill Brain, 16 November 2002.

30. AI V.S. Naipaul, 12 July 2002.

31. AI Jill Brain, 16 November 2002.

32. AI Jill Brain, 12 December 2003.

33. VSNC, red 'Bur-O-Class' aurora notebook, *c*.2001.

34. TU IID.

35. See http://www.thecaribbeanwriter. com/volume13/v13p190.html.

36. TU IIB.

37. AI V.S. Naipaul, 14 November 2002.

38. AI V.S. Naipaul, 3 July 2002.

39. See the beautifully written version of these events in 'Prologue to an Autobiography' in Naipaul, V.S., *Finding the Centre*, London 1984.

40. TU IB.

41. AI Kamla Tewari, 1 March 2004.

42. Naipaul, V.S., *Miguel Street*, London 1959, p. 44.

43. Naipaul, V.S., *Miguel Street*, London 1959, p. 93.

44. Naipaul, V.S., *Miguel Street*, London 1959, p. 34.

45. Naipaul, V.S., *Miguel Street*, London 1959, p. 61.

46. Naipaul, V.S., *Miguel Street*, London 1959, p. 106.

47. Naipaul, V.S., *Miguel Street*, London 1959, p. 58.

48. Naipaul, V.S., *Miguel Street*, London 1959, p. 167.

49. AI Diana Athill, 23 July 2003.

50. AI V.S. Naipaul, 28 October 2003.

51. AI V.S. Naipaul, 3 July 2002.

52. Naipaul, V.S., *The Mystic Masseur*, London 1957, p. 1. (All quotations from *The Mystic Masseur* are taken from the 2001 Picador UK paperback edition.)

53. Naipaul, V.S., *The Mystic Masseur*, London 1957, p. 8.

54. AI V.S. Naipaul, 14 November 2002.

55. TU IID.

56. AD.

57. TU IID.

58. TU IIA.

59. AI V.S. Naipaul, 26 November 2002. Today, a community day nursery has been built in the field opposite 593 Kingstanding Road; a signboard offers greetings in Hindi, among other languages.

60. AI Eleanor Hale, 13 June 2006.

61. EHC.

62. AI Eleanor Hale, 13 June 2006.

63. TU IIB.

64. *Gloucester Citizen*, August 1950.

65. TU IC.

66. TU IC.

TEN: BACK TO THE NEW WORLD

1. TU IID.

2. AI Kamla Tewari, 1 March 2004.

3. TU IID.

4. TU IID.

5. TU IIA.

6. All quotations in this chapter are taken from TU IIB unless otherwise stated.

7. TU IIIB 1.

8. See 'My Brother and I' in Naipaul, Shiva, *An Unfinished Journey*, London 1986.

9. AI Savi Akal, 4 March 2004.

10. See Figueira, op. cit., pp. 8–15. Bhadase Sagan Maraj was a thuggish early Indian politician in Trinidad. He began as a businessman and trade union leader on the sugar plantations in the 1950s; years later, it turned out that Tate & Lyle had been funding his political and union activities. He founded the PDP and the Sanatan Dharma Maha Sabha, which became the island's major Hindu organization.

11. AI V.S. Naipaul, 3 July 2002.

12. AI V.S. Naipaul, 26 January 2004.

13. AI V.S. Naipaul, 25 July 2002.

14. Quoted Meighoo, op. cit., p. 33.

15. Quoted Boodhoo, Ken, *The Elusive Eric Williams*, Port of Spain 2002, p. 130.

16. Quoted Meighoo, op. cit., p. 34.

17. See Boodhoo, op. cit., and Meighoo, op. cit., pp. 27–44.

18. Naipaul, V.S., *A Way in the World*, London 1994, p. 121.

19. AI V.S. Naipaul, 20 September 2002.

20. Naipaul, Seepersad, op. cit., p. 131.

21. AI Savi Akal, 4 March 2004.

22. AI Savi Akal, 4 March 2004.

23. AI V.S. Naipaul, 25 July 2002.

24. TU IIB.

25. AD.

26. AI V.S. Naipaul, 3 July 2002.

27. TU IID.

28. TU IID.

29. TU IID.

30. TU IID.

31. TU IID.

32. Athill, Diana, *Stet: An Editor's Life*, London 2000, p. 205. (All quotations from *Stet* are taken from the 2001 Granta UK paperback edition.)

33. AD cuttings. These extracts, and some subsequent press reviews of V.S. Naipaul's books, are taken from undated press cuttings in the André Deutsch archives (AD).

34. AI V.S. Naipaul, 3 July 2002.

35. Naipaul, V.S., *Half a Life*, London 2001, p. 123.

36. *Sunday Times*, 20 April 1958.

37. *Punch*, 30 April 1958.

38. Spectator, 2 May 1958.

39. BBC, Colonial Service, 25/05/58.

40. AI Lloyd Best, 2 March 2004. In 2007 the *Trinidad Guardian* ran extracts from *The Suffrage of Elvira*. The paper's front page lead on 2 March of that year concerned a 'jumbie chair' in the parliament building in Port of Spain that was apparently causing anyone who sat in it to fall ill or die; senators wanted the jumbie chair removed.

41. TU IIA.

42. *Times Literary Supplement*, 24 April 1959.

43. *Sunday Times*, 19 April 1959.

44. *News Chronicle*, AD cuttings.

45. *West Indian Gazette*, AD cuttings.

46. KTC.

ELEVEN: 'HE ASKED FOR 10 GNS!!'

1. AI V.S. Naipaul, 3 July 2002. References to Mary Treadgold by other people do not cast her in a racist light; she was, for instance, a close colleague of Una Marson.

2. TU IIA.

3. AI V.S. Naipaul, 20 September 2002.

4. BBC, V.S. Naipaul talks file 1: 1953–1958.

5. BBC, V.S. Naipaul talks file 1: 1953–1958.

6. BBC, Colonial Service, 31/08/58.

7. BBC, V.S. Naipaul talks file 1: 1953–1958.

8. AI V.S. Naipaul, 26 August 2003.

9. BBC, V.S. Naipaul talks file 2: 1959–1962.

10. BBC, V.S. Naipaul copyright file 1: 1950–1962.

11. Email to the author, 5 July 2002.

12. AI V.S. Naipaul, 3 July 2002.

13. AI V.S. Naipaul, 3 July 2002.

14. Letter to the author, 31 January 2006.

15. AI Ralph Ironman, 26 May 2006.

16. AI Jagdish Sondhi, 8 August 2006.

17. AI V.S. Naipaul, 3 July 2002.

18. AI Jill Brain, 12 December 2003.

19. AI V.S. Naipaul, 10 January 2005.

20. Athill, Diana, *Stet*, London 2000, p. 221.

21. AI Diana Athill, 23 July 2003.

22. AI V.S. Naipaul, 10 January 2005.

23. AI V.S. Naipaul, 11 January 2005.

24. AI V.S. Naipaul, 3 July 2002.

25. AI Kamla Tewari, 1 March 2004.

26. See Athill, Diana, *Stet*, London 2000.

27. AD.

28. AD.

29. Lewis, Jeremy, *Kindred Spirits: Adrift in Literary London*, London 1995, p. 58.

30. AD.

31. AI Diana Athill, 23 July 2003.

32. AD.

33. VSNC, cash book.

34. AI V.S. Naipaul, 21 February 2007.

35. AI Francis Wyndham, 27 August 2003.

36. *Hindu*, 17 March 2002.

37. http://www.anthonypowell.org.uk/ap/aptrivia.htm

38. AI V.S. Naipaul, 3 July 2002.

39. *IWI*, 28 June 1964.

40. *New Statesman*, 23 November 1957.

41. *New Statesman*, 21 December 1957.

42. *New Statesman*, 4 January 1958.

43. AI V.S. Naipaul, 29 August 2002.

44. TU IIA.

45. *New Statesman*, 16 July 1960.

46. *New Statesman*, 28 June 1958.

47. *New Statesman*, 25 January 1958.

48. *New Statesman*, 17 May 1958.

49. *New Statesman*, 12 July 1958.

50. *New Statesman*, 31 May 1958.

51. *New Statesman*, 4 October 1958.

52. *New Statesman*, 28 June 1958.

53. *New Statesman*, 6 December 1958.

54. AI V.S. Naipaul, 20 September 2002.

55. AI V.S. Naipaul, 29 August 2002

56. Lamming, George, *The Pleasures of Exile*, London 1960, p. 225.

57. *New Statesman*, 26 September 1959.

58. *New Statesman*, 16 July 1960.

59. *New Statesman*, 7 July 1961.

60. *New Statesman*, 28 March 1959.

61. *New Statesman*, 22 December 1961.

62. Naipaul, V.S., *An Area of Darkness*, London 1964, p. 42.

63. *New Statesman*, 7 July 1961.

64. *IWI*, 10 February 1963.

65. *Times*, 13 July 1961.

TWELVE: 'THERE WASN'T ANY KIND REMARK'

1. KTC.

2. AI V.S. Naipaul, 3 July 2002.

3. AI V.S. Naipaul, 23 August 2002.

4. AI V.S. Naipaul, 3 July 2002. In a Foreword to the 1983 edition of *A House for Mr Biswas*, V.S. Naipaul wrote a revealing account of the physical surroundings in which he wrote the book.

5. AI V.S. Naipaul, 22 January 2004.

6. Naipaul, V.S., *A House for Mr Biswas*, London 1961, p. 325.

7. Naipaul, V.S., *A House for Mr Biswas*, London 1961, p. 82.

8. Naipaul, V.S., *A House for Mr Biswas*, London 1961, p. 118.

9. Naipaul, V.S., *A House for Mr Biswas*, London 1961, p. 137.

10. Kumar, op. cit., p. 148.

11. Naipaul, V.S., *A House for Mr Biswas*, London 1961, p. 14.

12. AD.

13. TU IIA.

14. AI Francis Wyndham, 27 August 2003.

15. AI V.S. Naipaul, 26 September 2002.

16. AD.

17. Naipaul, V.S., *India: A Wounded Civilization*, London 1977, p. 18. (All quotations from *India: A Wounded Civilization* are taken from the first edition.)

18. TU IID.

19. AD.

20. TU IIA.

21. Capildeo, Vahni, 'Say If You Have Some Place in Mind', *The Caribbean Review of Books*, November 2005.

22. *Observer*, n.d.

23. *Observer*, 17 December 1961.

24. *New Statesman*, n.d.

25. *London Magazine*, October 1961.

26. *Trinidad Guardian*, n.d.

27. Brathwaite, Edward Kamau, *Roots*, Havana 1986, p. 39.

28. KTC.

29. TU IID.

30. TU IID.

31. TU IID.

32. AI Mira Inalsingh, 17 September 2004.

33. AI Savi Akal, 4 March 2004.

34. AI Savi Akal, 4 March 2004.

35. TU IIA.

36. Email to the author, 30 December 2006.

37. TU IID.

38. KTC.

39. TU IID.

40. AI Kamla Tewari, 2 March 2004.

41. TU IID.

42. TU IID.

43. TU IV.

44. RIC.

45. AI V.S. Naipaul, 3 July 2002. V.S. Naipaul kept a travel journal during this trip which no longer exists. It formed the basis of *The Middle Passage*.

46. Quoted Sandhu, Sukhdev, *London Calling: How Black and Asian Writers Imagined a City*, London 2003, p. 79; Naipaul, V.S., *The Middle Passage*, London 1962, p. 1; TU IID.

47. Naipaul, V.S., *The Middle Passage*, London 1962, p. 3.

48. Athill, Diana, *Stet*, London 2000, p. 217.

49. TU IIB.

50. AI V.S. Naipaul, 29 August 2002.

51. Naipaul, V.S., *The Middle Passage*, London 1962, p. 20.

52. Naipaul, V.S., *The Middle Passage*, London 1962, p. 40.

53. Naipaul, V.S., *The Middle Passage*, London 1962, pp. 62–3.

54. Naipaul, V.S., *The Middle Passage*, London 1962, p. 78.

55. Naipaul, V.S., *The Middle Passage*, London 1962, p. 69.

56. KTC.

57. AI Nella Chapman, 13 December 2007.

58. TU IIA.

59. AI Lloyd Best, 2 March 2004.

60. AI Margaret Walcott, 4 March 2004.

61. MAC.

62. TU IIA.

63. Naipaul, V.S., *The Middle Passage*, London 1962, p. 102.

64. Naipaul, V.S., *The Middle Passage*, London 1962, p. 160.

65. Naipaul, V.S., *The Middle Passage*, London 1962, p. 189.

66. Naipaul, V.S., *The Middle Passage*, London 1962, p. 205.

67. TU IIA.

68. AI Lloyd Best, 2 March 2004.

69. Naipaul, V.S., *The Middle Passage*, London 1962, p. 224.

70. Siewah, op. cit., pp. 613–14.

71. TU IID.

72. Read the document available at www.nalis.gov.tt/Independence/ T&TIndepConfRep.htm to see the roots of Dr Eric Williams's subsequent lock on the political system in Trinidad. No subsequent

prime ministers have changed this arrangement, including the first Indian occupant of the post, the dubious Basdeo Panday, who wanted to establish an executive presidency.

73. See Meighoo, op. cit., pp. 49–61, and Siewah, op. cit., pp. 97–114.

74. *New Commonwealth*, September 1962.

75. *Trinidad Guardian*, 3 February 1963.

76. *Month*, November 1962.

77. Mosley, Charlotte (ed.), *The Letters of Nancy Mitford and Evelyn Waugh*, London 1996, p. 474.

78. AI V.S. Naipaul, 20 September 2002.

79. TU IIIB, out-takes from 1978 BBC television documentary.

80. Natalie Galustian Rare Books catalogue.

81. RIC.

82. AI V.S. Naipaul, 11 January 2005.

83. AI Jan Carew, 5 September 2006.

84. RIC.

THIRTEEN: 'THE HOMECOMING'

1. AD.

2. TU IID.

3. TU IC2.

4. TU IID.

5. KTC.

6. Naipaul, V.S., *An Area of Darkness*, London 1964, p. 9.

7. I am indebted to the distinguished Lucknawi man of letters, Nasir Abid, for this observation.

8. Naipaul, V.S., *An Area of Darkness*, London 1964, p. 43.

9. AI V.S. Naipaul, 26 January 2004.

10. TU IC2.

11. AI Adil Jussawalla, 31 January 2003.

12. AI Ravi Dayal, 2 March 2003.

13. AI Ravi Dayal, 19 January 2004.

14. KTC.

15. TU IC2.

16. AI Khushwant Singh, 27 February 2003.

17. TU IC2.

18. TU IIA.

19. Naipaul, V.S., *An Area of Darkness*, London 1964, p. 70.

20. Naipaul, V.S., *An Area of Darkness*, London 1964, p. 201.

21. *Trinidad Guardian*, 7 March 1965.

22. TU IIA.

23. In *Alive and Well in Pakistan* (London 2004, p. 23), the self-declared Naipaul-obsessive Ethan Casey notes that Aziz was in fact Mr Butt's half-brother.

24. Naipaul, V.S., *An Area of Darkness*, London 1964, p. 107.

25. Naipaul, V.S., *An Area of Darkness*, London 1964, p. 111.

26. Naipaul, V.S., *An Area of Darkness*, London 1964, p. 156.

27. AI V.S. Naipaul, 20 October 2003.

28. RIC.

29. TU IIA.

30. *Sunday Telegraph*, 26 May 1963.

31. Naipaul, V.S., *Mr Stone and the Knights Companion*, London 1963, p. 307. (All quotations from *Mr Stone and the Knights Companion* are taken from the 2002 Picador UK paperback edition, in a compendium volume published under the title *The Nightwatchman's Occurrence Book*.)

32. *New Statesman*, 31 May 1963.

33. *Sunday Telegraph*, 26 May 1963.

34. TU IIA.

35. TU IC2.

36. AI Karan Singh, 29 March 2003.

37. TU IC2.

38. TU IIB.

39. TU IC2.

40. Naipaul, V.S., *An Area of Darkness*, London 1964, p. 162.

41. AI Zul Vellani, 30 January 2003.

42. AI V.S. Naipaul, 21 February 2007.

43. TU IID.

44. KTC.

45. TU IIB.

46. UWI, C.L.R. James Collection, Box 5, Folder 106. Thank you to Nicholas Laughlin for locating this letter.

47. RIC.

48. RIC.

49. AI Ravi Dayal, 2 March 2003.

50. AI Virendra Dayal, 28 March 2003.

51. Naipaul, V.S., *An Area of Darkness*, London 1964, p. 204.

52. TU IC2.

53. TU IIB.

54. TU IC2.

55. AI Khushwant Singh, 27 February 2003.

56. TU IID.

57. KTC.

58. AI Moni Malhoutra, 25 March 2003.

59. TU IC2.

60. TU IIB.

61. AD.

62. AD.

63. AI Vanraj Bhatia, 21 January 2003.

64. TU IIB.

65. TU IIA.

66. AI Moni Malhoutra, 25 March 2003.

67. TU IIB. Moni Malhoutra wrote an entertaining account of this adventure suggesting that V.S. Naipaul had narrowly avoided being eaten by a tiger. See 'Living Dangerously with V.S. Naipaul' in *First Proof: The Penguin Book of New Writing from India 1*, New Delhi 2005.

68. AI J.P. Singh, 19 January 2004.

69. TU IIB.

70. AI J.P. Singh, 19 January 2004.

71. TU IIB.

72. Naipaul, V.S., *An Area of Darkness*, London 1964, p. 260.

73. Naipaul, V.S., *An Area of Darkness*, London 1964, p. 263.

74. TU IIA.

75. TU IIB.

76. Letter in the private collection of Moni Malhoutra.

77. AI V.S. Naipaul, 26 January 2004.

FOURTEEN: 'LOVELY *VOGUE*, JUST BOUGHT'

1. Naipaul, V.S., *An Area of Darkness*, London 1964, p. 252.

2. TU IIA.

3. *Observer*, AD cuttings; *Times Literary Supplement*, 24 September 1964; *Daily Telegraph*, 17 September 1964; *New Statesman*, 11 September 1964.

4. Chandran, C. Sarat, 'Leveraging the Diaspora', newindpress.com, 9 February 2007.

5. AD.

6. Siewah, op. cit., pp. 189–90. Nissim Ezekiel's essay is available in Jussawalla, Adil, *New Writing in India*, London 1974.

7. Quoted Kumar, op. cit., p. 18.

8. *IWI*, 10 February 1963.

9. Naipaul's own copies of his 'Letters from London' were destroyed, and it was thought that no complete set of back issues of the *Illustrated Weekly of India* had survived. But I found a set on microfilm at the *Times of India* building in Mumbai.

10. *IWI*, 14 April 1963.

11. *IWI*, 12 May 1963.

12. *IWI*, 23 June 1963.

13. *IWI*, 28 July 1963.

14. *IWI*, 25 August 1963.

15. *IWI*, 29 September 1963.

16. *IWI*, 19 January 1964.

17. *IWI*, 27 December 1964.

18. AI V.S. Naipaul, 22 January 2007.

19. See Dhondy, Farrukh, *C.L.R. James: Cricket, the Caribbean, and World Revolution*, London 2001, & Dorn, Paul, *A Controversial Caribbean: C.L.R. James*, Spring 1995, http://www.runmuki.com/paul/CLR_James.html.

20. Naipaul, V.S., *A Writer's People*, London 2007, p. 12.

21. *IWI*, 28 July 1963.

22. *Encounter*, September 1963.

23. UWI, C.L.R. James Collection, Box 3, Folder 75.

24. UWI, C.L.R. James Collection, Box 5, Folder 106.

25. Quoted Dhondy, op. cit., p. 137.

26. KTC.

27. *New Statesman*, 28 October 1966.

28. *Spectator*, 16 October 1964.

29. *NYRB*, 4 March 1999.

30. KTC.

31. TU IIA.

32. KTC.

33. BBC, TVART 4. How prescient of Mr Burstall!

34. *Trinidadian*, February–March 1934.

35. NSA, NP346R.

36. See Hamner, Robert D. (ed.), *Critical Perspectives on V.S. Naipaul*, Washington, D.C. 1977, p. 147.

37. AI Pat Salkey, 11 April 2007.

38. Quoted Sandhu, op. cit., p. 97.

39. AI V.S. Naipaul, 21 February 2007.

40. Powell, Anthony, *Miscellaneous Verdicts: Writings on Writers 1946–1989*, London 1990, p. 391.

41. Quoted Stanford, Peter, *The Outcast's Outcast: A Biography of Lord Longford*, London 2003, p. 334.

42. Fraser, Antonia, and Pakenhams Elizabeth, Judith and Rachel, *The Pakenham Party Book*, London 1960, p. 40.

43. AI Antonia Fraser, 21 July 2003.

44. AFC.

45. AFC.

46. TU IIA.

47. AFC.

48. TU IIA.

49. Naipaul, V.S., *The Mystic Masseur*, London 1957, p. 195.

50. TU IIA.

51. AI V.S. Naipaul, 22 January 2004.

52. AI Francis Wyndham, 27 August 2003.

53. TU IV.

54. AI V.S. Naipaul, 22 January 2004.

55. *Trinidad Daily Mirror*, 7 March 1964.

56. Naipaul, Shiva, *Beyond the Dragon's Mouth*, London 1984, pp. 8–9.

57. Naipaul, Shiva, *An Unfinished Journey*, London 1986, p. 29. This page reference is from the 1988 edition.

58. AI Francis Wyndham, 27 August 2003.

59. KTC.

60. VSNC. Figures are missing for 1967.

61. AI V.S. Naipaul, 28 October 2003.

62. See Watson, Graham, *Book Society*, London 1980.

63. AI V.S. Naipaul, 26 September 2002 & 28 October 2003.

64. AI Richard Odgers, 13 December 2007.

65. AI V.S. Naipaul, 22 January 2004.

66. TU IIB.

67. SAC. V.S. Naipaul gave the early typescripts of *A Flag on the Island* to Savi and Mel Akal, having written it in their house.

68. Naipaul, V.S., *The Mimic Men*, London 1967, p. 216.

69. Naipaul, V.S., *The Mimic Men*, London 1967, p. 80.

70. *Observer*, 26 October 1969.

71. TU IIB.

72. *Trinidad Guardian*, 7 March 1965.

73. TU IIB.

74. AI V.S. Naipaul, 21 February 2007.

75. *Literary Review*, August 2001.

76. AI Mira Inalsingh, 17 September 2004.

77. AI Francis Wyndham, 27 August 2003.

78. AI Mira Inalsingh, 17 September 2004.

79. TU IID.

Fifteen: 'The Schintsky Method'

1. AI Paul Theroux, 21 September 2004.

2. AI V.S. Naipaul, 21 February 2007.

3. The early drafts of *The Mimic Men* survive in TU IB.

4. A note in TU IV by V.S. Naipaul dated 17 March 1995 reads: 'I borrowed the voice of the Trinidad minister (who wrote

the 1960 letter of invitation to me) for the colonial-politician narrator of *The Mimic Men* (1967). I knew his family as a child, and was to meet him in 1960 in Trinidad; but I borrowed the narrator's voice purely from this letter. I borrowed especially the word "interdigitating", which I had never heard before, but was trained by my Latin to understand.'

5. AD.

6. TU IIA.

7. AFC, 22 August 1966.

8. Email to the author, 28 September 2006.

9. Naipaul, V.S., *The Mimic Men*, London 1967, p. 11.

10. AI Jagdish Sondhi, 8 August 2006. The Sondhis were part of a small community of Indian and Pakistani professional families in Mombasa, mainly doctors, lawyers, bankers and architects, which included the Alvi family; Mr Alvi was the local president of the Muslim League. His daughter Nadira can be encountered in Chapter 25.

11. AFC, 9 June 1966.

12. AFC, 9 June 1966.

13. AD.

14. TU IIA.

15. TU IC.

16. TU IC2.

17. TU IIA. During the 1950s, Vidia had dealings with C. deGroot, the Commissioner for the West Indies, British Guiana and British Honduras in the United Kingdom.

18. AFC, 22 August 1966.

19. *Financial Times*, 4 May 1967.

20. AD, n.d.

21. *NYRB*, 11 April 1968.

22. *Kenyon Review*, November 1967.

23. Williams, Eric, *From Columbus to Castro: The History of the Caribbean 1492–1969*, London 1970, p. 502.

24. Michael Manley's letter was written in December 1977 while he was Jamaica's prime minister, and had been managing persistent violent unrest. John Hearne later described this period to Vidia as 'a six-year course of the very worst mimicry, fraudulent conversion of idealism and plain, degenerate buffoonery'. (TU IIA.)

25. TU IIA.

26. *Radio Times*, 24–30 March 1979.

27. TU IIA.

28. AD.

29. AI Francis Wyndham, 27 August 2003.

30. RIC.

31. AD.

32. AD. The final title was thought up by Piers Burnett of André Deutsch.

33. http://nobelprize.org/nobel_prizes/literature/laureates/2001/naipaul-lecture-e.html.

34. TU IIA.

35. *Guardian*, 20 November 1969.

36. Naipaul, V.S., *The Loss of El Dorado*, London 1969, p. 365. (All quotations from *The Loss of El Dorado* are taken from the 2001 Picador UK paperback edition.) In a letter to the Tulsa archivist Sid Huttner dated 10 July 1994, V.S. Naipaul wrote, 'The place was notorious; there were torture rooms. The young British governor who came out in 1810 changed all that. He made the Port of Spain jail part of the King's law. So there was an element of humanitarianism in the jail-gate legend, and it was an act of ignorance and vandalism on the part of independent Trinidad to take it down (apart, of course, from the great beauty of the Georgian cast-bronze lettering). I was told some years ago that the bronze letters have not been thrown away but are lying in some unknown cellar somewhere in Trinidad. The whole affair is full of ironies.'

37. *New Yorker*, 8 August 1970.

38. Quoted Hamner, op. cit., p. xxvii.

39. *Saturday Evening Post*, 3 June 1967.

40. TU IIA.

41. TU IIA.

42. AD.

43. TU IIB.

44. AI V.S. Naipaul, 1 November 2002.

45. TU IIA.

46. TU IIA.

47. TU IIA.

48. *Outlook India*, 4 October 1999.

49. TU IIB.

50. RIC.

51. PTC, 19 September 1967.

52. TU IIA.

53. TU IIA.

54. KTC.

55. KTC.

56. AI Peter Bayley, 28 September 2002.

57. KTC.

58. KTC.

59. AI Francis Wyndham, 27 August 2003.

60. AI David Pryce-Jones, 26 January 2005.

61. Email to the author, 28 September 2004.

62. TU IIA, 26 September 1966.

63. TU IIA, 6 November 1966.

64. TU IIA, 26 October 1966.

65. TU IIA, 30 October 1966.

66. TU IIA, 16 November 1968.

67. TU IIA, 26 October 1966.

68. TU IIA, 30 May 1967.

69. AI Paul Theroux, 21 September 2004.

70. PTC, 30 September 1966.

71. PTC, 18 October 1966.

72. PTC, 26 February 1967.

73. PTC, 21 February 1967.

74. AI V.S. Naipaul, 15 August 2002.

75. TU IIA, 22 July 1967.

76. TU IIA, 30 May 1967.

77. TU IIA, 25 October 1967.

78. TU IIA, 25 October 1967.

79. PTC, 16 November 1967.

80. PTC, 8 June 1968.

81. Email to the author, 31 May 2006; AI Anne Theroux, 3 June 2006.

82. TU IIA, 2 May 1970.

83. TU IIA, 18 December 1969.

84. TU IIA, 7 May 1969.

85. TU IIA, 18 December 1969.

86. PTC, 7 January 1970.

87. TU IIA, 2 May 1970.

88. TU IIA, 17 December 1970.

SIXTEEN: 'THE WORLD'

1. RIC.

2. AI Marisa Masters, 26 April 2004.

3. MARC.

4. PTC.

5. RIC.

6. AFC.

7. NSA, LP 34025, *The World at One*, 8 November 1968.

8. *Times*, 9 November 1968.

9. AI V.S. Naipaul, 26 January 2004.

10. AD.

11. AD. The phrase 'Black Power' would be taken up again in 2000 by followers of Robert Mugabe, when they invaded and occupied white-owned farms in Zimbabwe.

12. *NYRB*, 24 April 1969.

13. *Trinidad Guardian*, 28 November 1968.

14. TU IIIC.

15. Although V.S. Naipaul failed to listen to Dekker or Marley, they wrote on matching subjects. 'Emancipate yourself from mental slavery, None but ourselves can free our mind' sang Bob Marley in 'Redemption Song'.

16. TU IIA.

17. TU IIA.

18. AFC.

19. PTC.

20. AD.

21. AD.

22. *Telegraph Magazine*, April 1970.

23. AI Jill Brain, 12 December 2003.

24. AFC.

25. AI V.S. Naipaul, 26 January 2004.

26. TU IIA.

27. MARC.

28. TU IIA.

29. AI Marisa Masters, 26 April 2004.

30. Marisa Masters liked to collect the famous. When I interviewed her, she produced photographs of herself with, among others, Ivana Trump, Shere Hite and Mohamed al-Fayed.

31. AI Antonia Fraser, 21 July 2003.

32. AI Savi Akal, 4 March 2004.

33. AFC.

34. AFC.

35. TU IID.

36. PTC, 13 October 1970.

37. PTC, 26 May 1971.

38. TU IIA.

39. *Telegraph Magazine*, c.October 1972.

40. AI Eleanor Hale, 13 June 2006.

41. AI V.S. Naipaul, 26 January 2004.

42. KTC.

43. *Telegraph Magazine*, 10 December 1970.

44. Naipaul, V.S., *Magic Seeds*, London 2004, p. 267. (All quotations from *Magic Seeds* are taken from the first edition.)

45. Naipaul, V.S., *In a Free State*, London 1971, p. 26. (All quotations from *In a Free State* are taken from the 1973 Penguin UK paperback edition.)

46. Naipaul, V.S., *In a Free State*, London 1971, p. 29. No critic at the time of publication appears to have been aware that 'hubshi' was a term of abuse.

47. Naipaul, V.S., *In a Free State*, London 1971, p. 21. The narrative technique in this story leads to occasional absurdities. For instance: would an Indian (from India) think: 'A man came out from the kitchen with a tray. At first he looked like a fellow countryman, but in a second I could tell he was a stranger. "You are right," Priya said, when the stranger went back to the kitchen. "He is not of Bharat. He is a Mexican." '?

48. Naipaul, V.S., *In a Free State*, London 1971, p. 83.

49. AD.

50. AI V.S. Naipaul, 20 October 2003.

51. Naipaul, V.S., *In a Free State*, London 1971, pp. 104–7.

52. TU IIA.

53. TU IIA.

54. TU IIA.

55. AD.

56. TU IB.

57. *Times Educational Supplement*, 1 October 1971.

58. *NYRB*, 30 December 1971.

59. *New York Times Book Review*, 17 October 1971.

60. *Times*, October 1971.

61. MARC.

62. Theroux, Paul, *Sir Vidia's Shadow*, London 1998, p. 175. Stephen Tennant was in fact close to bankruptcy, and had to be bailed out from time to time by his brother.

63. RIC.

64. TU IID.

65. TU IID.

66. TU IB, *Black Power & National Reconstruction* by Lloyd Best.

67. *NYRB*, 3 September 1970.

68. TU IID.

69. *Sunday Times Magazine*, 12 May 1974 & 19 May 1974.

70. The ghost was Stephen John, author of *Roman Orgy*.

71. AI Farrukh Dhondy, 28 August 2004.

72. Lewis, op. cit., p. 72.

73. Athill, Diana, *Make Believe* (second edn.), London 2004, pp. 1–2.

74. Athill, Diana, *Make Believe* (second edn.), London 2004, pp. 5–6. I examine the story in more detail in an introduction to this edition of *Make Believe*.

75. TU IID.

76. KTC.

77. AD.

78. NSA, *The Arts This Week*, 29 October 1970.

79. BBC, RCONT 20, V.S. Naipaul Copyright File.

80. MIC.

81. TU IIA.

82. TU IIA.

83. TU IIA.

84. AI Margaret Drabble, 13 May 2005.

85. TU IIA.

86. BBC, RCONT 20, V.S. Naipaul Copyright File.

87. TU IIA.

88. The original *Bad Sign, Good Sign* song can be heard at www.montynorman.com.

89. NSA, T34250, *A Word in Edgeways*, 15 October 1971.

90. NSA, *The Arts and Africa*, 17 December 1971.

91. NSA, M3033R, Radio 3, 29 January 1973.

92. *Business Standard*, 16 October 2001.

93. TU IIB.

94. TU IID.

95. AD.

96. Tewari, op. cit.

97. Cliff Lashley was later beaten to death in Kingston, though not at V.S. Naipaul's instigation.

98. AI Kenneth Ramchand, 5 March 2004.

99. AI V.S. Naipaul, 21 July 2006.

100. *Sunday Times Magazine*, 16 July 1972.

101. AI V.S. Naipaul, 2 October 2003.

102. KTC.

103. TU IID.

104. AD.

105. AD. The judges for the Booker Prize that year were Saul Bellow, John Fowles, Antonia Fraser, John Gross and Malcolm Muggeridge.

106. *New Statesman*, 1 December 1972.

107. TU IIA.

108. TU IIA.

109. TU IIA.

110. TU IIA.

SEVENTEEN: 'WITH THE AID OF A CUTLASS BLADE'

1. All quotations in this chapter are taken from Patricia Naipaul's diary in TU IC2, unless otherwise stated.

2. PTC, 3 February 1972.

3. AI Mel Akal, 4 March 2004.

4. Athill, Diana, *Make Believe* (second edn.), London 2004, pp. 51–3.

5. Athill, Diana, *Instead of a Letter* (second edn.), London 2001, pp. 18–156.

6. Note by V.S. Naipaul in TU IB dated 13 February 1995.

7. AD.

8. AD.

9. AD.

10. TU IB.

11. AI V.S. Naipaul, 21 May 2006.

12. AI V.S. Naipaul, 28 October 2003.

13. AI Robert Silvers, 19 November 2003.

14. TU IIA.

15. Naipaul, V.S., *The Mimic Men*, London 1967, p. 82.

16. AI Savi Akal, 4 March 2004.

17. See Luna, Félix, *A Short History of the Argentinians*, Buenos Aires 2000.

18. AI Hermenegildo Sábat, 2 November 2004.

19. TU IB.

20. *NYRB*, 10 August 1972.

21. See di Giovanni, Norman Thomas, *The Lesson of the Master: On Borges and His Work*, London 2003.

22. AI Norman Thomas di Giovanni, 22 June 2004.

23. TU IB.

24. TU IB.

25. *NYRB*, 19 October 1972.

26. AI Norman Thomas di Giovanni, 22 June 2004.

27. AI V.S. Naipaul, 27 October 2003.

28. TU IB.

EIGHTEEN: MARGARITA

1. AI Norman Thomas di Giovanni, 22 June 2004.
2. MPS.
3. AI Norman Thomas di Giovanni, 22 June 2004.
4. AI V.S. Naipaul, 27 October 2003.
5. AI Norman Thomas di Giovanni, 29 June 2004.
6. TU IIB.
7. AI V.S. Naipaul, 27 October 2003.
8. AI Norman Thomas di Giovanni, 22 June 2004.
9. AI V.S. Naipaul, 10 January 2005.
10. TU IC2. All subsequent quotations and information in the chapter relating to Patricia Naipaul are taken from her diary in TU IC2, unless otherwise stated.
11. AI Savi Akal, 4 March 2004.
12. TU IIA.
13. PTC, 6 June 1972.
14. PTC, 2 July 1972.
15. TU IC.
16. *NYRB*, 10 August 1972.
17. TU IB.
18. TU IB.
19. AI Hermenegildo Sábat, 2 November 2004.
20. *NYRB*, 10 August 1972.
21. AI Andrew Graham-Yooll, 3 November 2004.
22. MPS.
23. AI Hermenegildo Sábat, 2 November 2004.
24. AI Michael Neill, 28 August 2005.
25. *Wellington Dominion*, 26 July 1972.
26. TU IIB.
27. AI V.S. Naipaul, 1 November 2002.
28. AI Pek Koon Heng, 31 May 2006.
29. AI Michael Neill, 28 August 2005.
30. MPS.
31. AI V.S. Naipaul, 25 July 2002.
32. TU IIA.
33. Private collection.
34. SAC.
35. TU IB.
36. PTC, 10 September 1972.
37. PTC, 18 September 1972.
38. TU IIA.
39. TU IV.
40. PTC, 22 October 1972.
41. AI Norman Thomas di Giovanni, 29 June 2004.
42. TU IIA.
43. AI Diana Athill, 23 July 2003.
44. AI Marisa Masters, 26 April 2004.
45. AI V.S. Naipaul, 10 January 2005.
46. AI V.S. Naipaul, 8 December 2006.
47. TU IIA.
48. KTC.
49. TU IID.

NINETEEN: ENGLAND AND ARGENTINA

1. RIC.
2. AI Michael Frayn, 21 September 2007.
3. AI V.S. Naipaul, 10 January 2005.
4. MPS.
5. AI Savi Akal, 4 March 2004.
6. TU IID.
7. TU IIB.
8. TU IIB.
9. VSNC, Task memo book.
10. *NYRB*, 12 June 1980.
11. TU IIA.
12. Michell, John (ed.), *Souvenir Programme for the Official Lynching of Michael Abdul Malik with Poems, Stories, Sayings by the Condemned*, Cambridge 1973.
13. *Sunday Times Magazine*, 12 May 1974 & 19 May 1974. The complete text of the article, together with an important postscript written in 1979 after Abbott's execution (from which part of this quotation is taken), can be found in Naipaul, V.S, *The Writer and the World*, London 2002. See also Humphry, Derek, and Tindall, David, *False Messiah: The Story of Michael X*, London 1977.
14. AD.
15. AI V.S. Naipaul, 10 January 2005.
16. *NYRB*, 4 April 1974.
17. TU IIA.

18. TU IIA.

19. AI Andrew Graham-Yooll, 3 November 2004.

20. AI V.S. Naipaul, 28 October 2003.

21. AI V.S. Naipaul, 10 January 2005.

22. AI Savi Akal, 4 March 2004.

23. AI Savi Akal, 7 March 2004.

24. VSNC, Task memo book.

25. TU IC2. All subsequent quotations and information in the chapter relating to Patricia Naipaul are taken from her diary in TU IC2, unless otherwise stated.

26. TU IIA.

27. MARC.

28. AFC.

29. McKay, Peter, *Inside Private Eye*, London 1986, p. 142.

30. TU IIA.

31. Naipaul, V.S., *Guerrillas*, London 1975, pp. 12–15. (All quotations from *Guerrillas* are taken from the 1976 Penguin UK paperback edition.)

32. TU IB.

33. Naipaul, V.S., *Guerrillas*, London 1975, p. 253.

34. Naipaul, V.S., *Guerrillas*, London 1975, pp. 242–3.

TWENTY: THE MARRIAGE OF MANDRAX AND VALIUM

1. TU IC2. All subsequent quotations and information in the chapter relating to Patricia Naipaul are taken from her diary in TU IC2, unless otherwise stated.

2. AI Hermenegildo Sábat, 2 November 2004.

3. MPS.

4. TU IB, draft letter in 'Kamikaze in Montevideo' notebook.

5. *NYRB*, 17 October 1974.

6. *NYRB*, 28 November 1974.

7. AD.

8. AI Diana Athill, 23 July 2003.

9. TU IIA.

10. TU IIA.

11. TU IV.

12. TU IIA.

13. *Mother Jones*, August 1980.

14. *Caribbean Contact*, November 1975.

15. *Spectator*, 13 September 1975 & *Observer*, 14 September 1975.

16. *Listener*, 25 September 1975.

17. TU IIA.

18. TU IIB.

19. *NYRB*, 19 September 1974.

20. TU IB.

21. AI Andrew Graham-Yooll, 3 November 2004.

22. AI V.S. Naipaul, 10 January 2005.

23. AI V.S. Naipaul, 27 October 2003.

24. AI V.S. Naipaul, 10 January 2005.

25. Theroux, Paul, *Sir Vidia's Shadow*, London 1998, pp. 214–28.

26. AI Michael Neill, 28 August 2005. See also C.K. Stead's 'Diary' in *London Review of Books*, 27 April 2000.

27. AI Pek Koon Heng, 31 May 2006.

28. AI Antonia Fraser, 21 July 2003.

29. Reproduced with permission from the unpublished diary of Antonia Fraser, © Antonia Fraser.

30. *Telegraph Magazine*, 12 October 2002, out-takes from interview with Mick Brown.

31. *Atlantic Unbound*, 31 March 2004, www.theatlantic.com/doc/200403u/int2004-03-31.

32. See Theroux, Paul, *My Secret History: A Novel*, London 1989, pp. 277–99.

33. See Theroux, Paul, *My Other Life: A Novel*, London 1996, pp. 175–6. In *My Other Life*, he describes a dinner at his house in London with the writer Anthony Burgess and a bibliophilic fan, Lettfish, which provoked (the real) Anne Theroux to write a letter to the *New Yorker* magazine disassociating herself from fictional comments she was meant to have made. See Stinson, John J., 'Burgess as Fictional Character in Theroux and Byatt', in *Anthony Burgess Newsletter: Issue 2*, http://

bu.univ-angers.fr/EXTRANET/
AnthonyBURGESS/NL2Theroux.htm.

34. Theroux, Paul, *Sir Vidia's Shadow*, London 1998, p. 24.

35. Theroux, Paul, *Sir Vidia's Shadow*, London 1998, p. 88.

36. Theroux, Paul, *Sir Vidia's Shadow*, London 1998, p. 51.

37. Theroux, Paul, *Sir Vidia's Shadow*, London 1998, p. 144.

38. The administrator of the Booker Prize, Martyn Goff, described Paul Theroux's account of the selection of the 1979 winner as 'pure invention . . . Theroux's account is a mile from the truth, nor could any vote of his have decided the outcome.' *Daily Telegraph*, 22 August 1998.

39. Theroux, Paul, *Sir Vidia's Shadow*, London 1998, p. 39.

40. Paul Theroux confirmed this to me during an interview, 21 September 2004.

41. See Theroux, Paul, *Sir Vidia's Shadow*, London 1998, p. 213, and the same text (from December 1971) in Jussawalla, Feroza (ed.), *Conversations with V.S. Naipaul*, Jackson 1997, p. 31. Theroux used this quotation in his 1972 profile of V.S. Naipaul in the *Telegraph Magazine*.

42. Theroux, Paul, *Sir Vidia's Shadow*, London 1998, p. 253.

43. Theroux, Paul, *Sir Vidia's Shadow*, London 1998, p. 358.

44. Theroux, Paul, *Sir Vidia's Shadow*, London 1998, p. 51.

45. AI Lloyd Best, 2 March 2004.

46. AI Paul Theroux, 21 September 2004.

47. AI V.S. Naipaul, 15 August 2002.

48. AI Sheila Rogers, 12 December 2007.

49. See Powell, Tristram and Georgia (eds.), *A Dedicated Fan: Julian Jebb 1934–1984*, London 1993.

50. AI Michael Holroyd, 13 May 2005.

51. AI Francis Wyndham, 27 August 2003.

52. AI Michael Neill, 28 August 2005.

53. *Time*, 11 August 1975.

54. *New Review*, November 1975.

55. AI David Pryce-Jones, 26 January 2005.

56. TU IIA.

57. AI Antonia Fraser, 21 July 2003.

58. TU IIA.

TWENTY-ONE: 'I WANT TO WIN AND WIN AND WIN'

1. AI Antonia Fraser, 21 July 2003.

2. AI Marisa Masters, 26 April 2004.

3. AI John Kasmin, 26 July 2004.

4. AI David Pryce-Jones, 26 January 2005.

5. AI V.S. Naipaul, 10 January 2005.

6. *NYRB*, 26 June 1975.

7. TU IIA.

8. TU IB.

9. TU IB.

10. *NYRB*, 26 June 1975.

11. TU IB.

12. AI Prem Shankar Jha, 15 January 2004.

13. AI V.S. Naipaul, 1 November 2002.

14. AI Vinod Mehta, 16 December 2002.

15. AI V.S. Naipaul, 1 November 2002.

16. AI Ravi Dayal, 2 March 2003.

17. TU IB.

18. AI V.S. Naipaul, 26 January 2004.

19. AI Sudhir Kakar, 2 March 2003.

20. AI Rahul Singh, 23 May 2004.

21. AI Shirish Patel, 31 January 2003.

22. AI V.S. Naipaul, 20 September 2003.

23. *New Statesman*, n.d. (October 1977).

24. *Times*, n.d., *Spectator*, 22 October 1977, *New Statesman*, n.d., *Sunday Telegraph*, 23 October 1977.

25. *New York Times*, 13 May 1979.

26. TU IIA.

27. Private collection, courtesy of Hugo Vickers.

28. TU IIA.

29. AI V.S. Naipaul, 11 January 2005.

30. *NYRB*, 11 October 1979. This article was written in 1977, but published in 1979.

31. *NYRB*, 30 January 1992.

32. *New Statesman*, 4 July 1980.

33. Amis, Martin, *Experience*, London 2000, p. 263.

34. Naipaul, V.S., *The Return of Eva Perón*, London 1980, p. 5.

35. *Observer*, 29 June 1980; *Daily Telegraph*, AD cuttings.

36. AI V.S. Naipaul, 20 September 2002.

37. *Harpers & Queen*, July 1980.

38. *NYRB*, 12 June 1980.

39. AI V.S. Naipaul, 10 January 2005.

40. AI Kamla Tewari, 1 March 2004.

41. AI Mira Inalsingh, 17 September 2004.

42. AI Savi Akal, 4 March 2004.

43. AI Suren Capildeo, 8 March 2004.

44. AI V.S. Naipaul, 8 December 2006.

45. Part of the seminar is transcribed at www.pancaribbean.com/banyan/naipaul.htm. Banyan Productions date it to 1974, but it appears to be from 1977.

46. TU IIA.

47. TU IC2. All subsequent quotations and information in the chapter relating to Patricia Naipaul are taken from her diary in TU IC2, unless otherwise stated.

48. TU IB.

49. Naipaul, V.S., *A Bend in the River*, London 1979, p. 135.

50. AI V.S. Naipaul, 21 May 2006.

51. AI V.S. Naipaul, 29 December 2006.

52. Naipaul, V.S., *A Bend in the River*, London 1979, p. 99.

53. AI Savi Akal, 4 March 2004.

54. Naipaul, V.S., *A Bend in the River*, London 1979, pp. 159–61.

55. Naipaul, V.S., *A Bend in the River*, London 1979, pp. 180–2.

56. MPS.

57. AI V.S. Naipaul, 12 July 2002.

58. TU IC.

59. Naipaul, V.S., *A Bend in the River*, London 1979, p. 287.

TWENTY-TWO: A HOUSE FOR MR NAIPAUL

1. TU IIA.

2. AI Phyllis Rose, 18 September 2004.

3. TU IIA.

4. *Sunday Telegraph Magazine*, 23 September 1979. This profile, by Linda Blandford, gives an unusually perceptive insight into V.S. Naipaul's behaviour and state of mind.

5. TU IIA.

6. TU IID.

7. TU IIA, 12 September 1978.

8. AI Phyllis Rose, 18 September 2004.

9. *Wesleyan: The Wesleyan University Alumnus*, Spring 1981.

10. TU IIA.

11. AI John Richardson, 16 September 2004.

12. *Vogue (USA)*, August 1981.

13. AD.

14. TU IIA.

15. TU IIA.

16. Shiva had won the Winifred Holtby Award for *Fireflies*, which may have been an additional consideration when it came to rejecting the prize.

17. *New York Times Book Review*, 13 May 1979; *Chicago Tribune Book World*, 13 May 1979; *Times*, 9 December 1979; *Evening Standard*, 25 September 1979; *Spectator*, 1 December 1979; *Guardian*, 14 February 2004.

18. Naipaul, V.S., *A Bend in the River*, London 1979, p. 9.

19. *Nation*, 3 May 1980.

20. *Wesleyan: The Wesleyan University Alumnus*, Spring 1981.

21. *New York Times*, 13 May 1979.

22. *Newsweek*, 18 August 1980.

23. BBC Radio 4, 11 May 1980, sound recording available in TU IIIB.

24. TU IID.

25. AD.

26. AD.

27. AD.

28. AD.

29. AD.

30. TU IIA.

31. TU IIA.

32. TU IIA.

33. AI Gillon Aitken, 13 August 2003.

34. AI V.S. Naipaul, 26 September 2002.

35. VSNC, cashbook.

36. VSNC, notebook. These deductions are approximate; precise comparable figures are not available for the different decades.

37. PTC, 5 April 1981.

38. *Vogue (UK)*, c.September 1979.

39. MPS.

40. AI V.S. Naipaul, 29 December 2006.

41. MPS.

42. TU IIA.

43. AFC.

44. TU IIA.

45. TU IIB.

46. *Private Eye*, 3 August 1979.

47. AI Francis Wyndham, 27 August 2003.

48. TU IC2. All subsequent quotations and information in the chapter relating to Patricia Naipaul are taken from her diary in TU IC2, unless otherwise stated.

49. TU IIA.

50. AI V.S. Naipaul, 29 December 2006.

51. AI V.S. Naipaul, 11 January 2005.

52. TU IIA.

53. RIC.

54. VSNC, Task memo book.

55. Recording from 1980 in TU IIIB.

56. *Sunday Times*, 4 October 1981.

57. TU IIA.

58. TU IIA, 8 April 1981.

59. *Washington Post*, 11 October 1981; *Times*, 4 December 1981; *Newsweek*, 16 November 1981.

60. *New Statesman*, 16 October 1981; *NYRB*, 24 June 1982; *Hudson Review*, Summer 1982. See also Bawer, Bruce, *Civilization and V.S. Naipaul* in *Hudson Review*, Autumn 2002.

61. Naipaul, V.S., *Among the Believers*, London 1981, p. 89. (All quotations from *Among the Believers* are taken from the 1982 Penguin UK paperback edition.)

62. TU IB.

63. TU IIA.

64. *Business Standard*, 16 October 2001.

65. TU IB.

66. AI Eleanor Hale, 13 June 2006.

67. TU IC. On 13 December 1981, Pat wrote in her diary: 'Started Boswell's Life of Johnson yesterday. I don't really like biography as an art form, but impressed.'

68. AI Selby Wooding, 5 March 2004.

69. *Salmagundi*, Fall 1981, quoted in Jussawalla, Feroza (ed.), *Conversations with V.S. Naipaul*, Jackson 1997, p. 77. The most convincing academic study of Naipaul's work is Hayward, Helen, *The Enigma of V.S. Naipaul*, Oxford 2002.

70. AI V.S. Naipaul, 20 September 2002.

71. AI V.S. Naipaul, 2 October 2003.

72. AI V.S. Naipaul, 8 September 2007.

73. *New Yorker*, 23 May 1994.

74. Hare, David, *A Map of the World*, London 1982, pp. 17–20.

75. Available at http://social.chass.ncsu.edu/wyrick/DEBCLASS/walsp.htm. My shortest interview while researching this book was with Derek Walcott: 'I feel jaded with him, I get increasingly irritated by him, I don't want to talk about him, I don't want to add to the legend of Naipaul.' (AI Derek Walcott, 16 September 2004.)

76. TU IIA.

77. TU IIA.

78. TU unclassified papers.

79. *Frankfurter Allgemeine Zeitung Magazin*, 23 December 1983. These answers are taken from V.S. Naipaul's original submission, written in English.

80. TU IB.

81. AI V.S. Naipaul, 11 January 2005.

82. VPRO-TV, 18 April 1982, video

recording available in TU IIIB. The ticket was economy class. After the trip, Cees Noteboom was quoted in *Het Parool* saying, 'As a writer you know that when you take a trip like this, you will be confronted with a bunch of idiots. If you haven't got the patience for it, you shouldn't go.'

83. TU IB.

84. TU IIA. The Cambridge University regulations specified that the bonnet needed to be taken off and put on from time to time during the ceremony: 'At this point the recipient again puts on his bonnet. The recipient does not speak at any point and is guided throughout the proceedings by the Esquire Bedells.'

85. TU IID.

86. TU IIA.

87. TU IA.

88. *Vanity Fair*, April 1983. The article was illustrated with family archive photographs and a new portrait of V.S. Naipaul by the 'jumped-up' photographer Lord Snowdon.

89. TU IA.

90. MPS.

91. *Daily Mail*, 7 May 1982.

92. Naipaul, V.S., *Finding the Centre*, London 1984, pp. 116–17.

93. TU IB.

94. MPS.

95. TU IIA.

96. MPS.

97. *Harper's*, March 1984.

98. Tewari, op. cit.

99. *NYRB*, 25 October 1984.

100. Naipaul, V.S., *Finding the Centre*, London 1984, p. 9.

101. *Daily Telegraph*, 11 May 1984.

102. *Dublin Sunday Tribune*, 6 May 1984.

103. *Observer*, 6 May 1984.

TWENTY-THREE: 'UNDOING MY SEMI-COLONS'

1. TU IV.

2. TU IID

3. KTC.

4. *Globe & Mail Magazine*, December 1988.

5. *New Statesman*, 18 December 1998.

6. TU unclassified papers.

7. AI Shalini Aleung, 2 March 2004.

8. KTC.

9. AI Nisha Inalsingh, 17 September 2004.

10. AI V.S. Naipaul, 8 December 2006.

11. TU IID.

12. AI Gillon Aitken, 13 August 2003.

13. AI Mira Inalsingh, 17 September 2004.

14. Hilary Mantel was the first young winner of the Shiva Naipaul Memorial Prize.

15. AD.

16. *Spectator*, 24 August 1985.

17. Naipaul, Shiva, *Black and White*, London 1980, pp. 3–4.

18. Naipaul, Shiva, *North of South*, London 1978, p. 44.

19. TU IID.

20. AI Vinod Mehta, 16 December 2002.

21. AI Nikhil Lakshman, 31 January 2003.

22. AI V.S. Naipaul, 20 September 2002.

23. AI V.S. Naipaul, 22 January 2004.

24. AFC.

25. KTC.

26. TU IID.

27. TU unclassified papers.

28. TU IC2.

29. VSNC, Task memo book; TU IB.

30. AI V.S. Naipaul, 10 January 2005.

31. *NYRB*, 9 April 1987.

32. Naipaul, V.S., *The Enigma of Arrival*, London 1987, p. 42.

33. Naipaul, V.S., *The Enigma of Arrival*, London 1987, pp. 152–3.

34. Naipaul, V.S., *The Enigma of Arrival*, London 1987, pp. 63–4.

35. Naipaul, V.S., *The Enigma of Arrival*, London 1987, pp. 56 & 27.

36. Naipaul, V.S., *The Enigma of Arrival*, London 1987, p. 203.

37. Naipaul, V.S., *The Enigma of Arrival*, London 1987, p. 60.

38. Naipaul, V.S., *The Enigma of Arrival*, London 1987, p. 186.

39. Naipaul, V.S., *The Enigma of Arrival*, London 1987, p. 209.

40. Naipaul, V.S., *The Enigma of Arrival*, London 1987, p. 278.

41. Naipaul, V.S., *The Enigma of Arrival*, London 1987, p. 252.

42. TU IIA.

43. *New Criterion*, October 1987.

44. *Boston Review*, June 1987.

45. TU unclassified papers.

46. TU IIA.

47. TU unclassified papers.

48. Powell, Anthony, *Journals: 1987–1989*, London 1996, p. 31.

49. *Times Literary Supplement*, 28 August 1987.

50. *Guardian*, 13 March 1987. Salman Rushdie was perceptive about the absence of the word 'love' in *The Enigma of Arrival*; remember that during the writing of *A Bend in the River*, Pat had noted in her diary: 'Vidia is so proud of never using the word love.'

51. *South Bank Show*, 1988, recording available in TU IIIB.

52. http://nobelprize.org/nobel_prizes/literature/laureates/2001/press.html.

53. *New Republic*, 13 April 1987.

54. 'The Schooner "Flight"' is available at http://www.cs.rice.edu/~ssiyer/minstrels/txt/1041.txt.

55. MARC.

56. *Chicago Tribune*, 30 November 1986.

57. TU IIA.

58. GAAA.

59. AI V.S. Naipaul, 11 January 2005.

60. AI Norman Thomas di Giovanni, 29 June 2004.

61. VSNC.

62. *Atlanta Constitution*, 28 May 1987.

63. TU IIA.

64. Naipaul, V.S., *A Turn in the South*, London 1989, p. 119. (All quotations from *A Turn in the South* are taken from the 2003 Picador UK paperback edition.)

65. Naipaul, V.S., *A Turn in the South*, London 1989, p. 125.

66. TU IV.

67. Naipaul, V.S., *A Turn in the South*, London 1989, p. 226.

68. *NYRB*, 30 March 1989.

69. GAAA.

70. GAAA.

71. GAAA.

72. AI Gillon Aitken, 26 July 2004.

73. AI Francis Wyndham, 27 August 2003.

74. GAAA.

75. AI Helen Fraser, 12 December 2007.

76. GAAA.

77. TU unclassified papers.

78. GAAA.

79. Powell, Anthony, *Journals: 1990–1992*, London 1997, p. 194 & Powell, Anthony, *Journals: 1982–1986*, London 1995, p. 291.

80. The recipe involved mutton and curry powder served with fried banana and dried coconut, and is available at http://www.anthonypowell.org.uk/ap/apcurry.htm, should you wish to eat it. 'If eggs are used they should be hard-boiled and set in halves on the curry. Odds and ends of potatoes and vegetables may also be called into play, though the last should be used in moderation.' One of Anthony Powell's relations told me his famous curry was 'absolutely disgusting, but we had to pretend we liked it'.

81. Naipaul, V.S., *A Writer's People*, London 2007, pp. 34–8.

82. AI Helen Fraser, 12 December 2007.

83. Powell, Anthony, *Journals: 1982–1986*, London 1995, p. 20.

84. TU IIA.

85. Powell, Anthony, *Journals: 1987–1989*, London 1996, p. 155.

86. Powell, Anthony, *Journals: 1987–1989*, London 1996, p. 126.

87. Powell, Anthony, *Journals: 1982–1986*, London 1995, p. 77.

88. Powell, Anthony, *Journals: 1987–1989*, London 1996, p. 127.

89. Powell, Anthony, *Journals: 1982–1986*, London 1995, p. 236.

90. AI David Pryce-Jones, 6 January 2005.

91. AD.

92. Kitty Giles; Bobby says the same thing to Linda in *In a Free State*.

93. TU IC.

94. TU IC2.

95. TU IC.

96. AI V.S. Naipaul, 22 January 2004.

97. TU IIA.

98. TU IV.

99. The material that follows is taken from TU unclassified papers.

100. *Independent*, 17 March 1989. These statements were first made to a *Sunday Observer* reporter in Bombay.

101. *Times*, 18 August 1993.

TWENTY-FOUR: ARISE, SIR VIDIA

1. AI Ralph Ironman, 26 May 2006.

2. AI Moni Malhoutra, 25 March 2003.

3. GAAA.

4. Luxury hotels in India were still comparatively cheap in 1988–9; V.S. Naipaul's hotel bills for the trip totalled around £13,000.

5. AI Vinod Mehta, 16 December 2002.

6. Naipaul, V.S., *India: A Million Mutinies Now*, London 1990, p. 1. (All quotations from *India: A Million Mutinies Now* are taken from the 1991 Minerva UK paperback edition.)

7. Naipaul, V.S., *India: A Million Mutinies Now*, London 1990, p. 6.

8. Naipaul, V.S., *India: A Million Mutinies Now*, London 1990, p. 37.

9. Naipaul, V.S., *India: A Million Mutinies Now*, London 1990, p. 15 & p. 60.

10. AI Nikhil Lakshman, 31 January 2003.

11. AI Charudatta Deshpande, 30 January 2003. Vithal Chavan was murdered in the chawl by a rival gang a year later. He is called Mr Ghate in *India: A Million Mutinies Now*.

12. AI Sadanand Menon, 11 January 2004.

13. AI H.V. Nathan, 31 January 2003. H.V. Nathan was for many years the right-hand man to Murli Deora, who ran the Congress Party's operation in Bombay.

14. AI Nasir Abid, 16 January 2004.

15. AI Sadanand Menon, 11 January 2004.

16. TU unclassified papers.

17. AI Nasir Abid, 16 January 2004.

18. AI V.S. Naipaul, 26 January 2004. Harinder Baweja denies being small.

19. AI Harinder Baweja, 27 March 2007.

20. AI Malavika Sanghvi, 29 March 2003.

21. AI Vir Sanghvi, 29 March 2003.

22. AI Malavika Sanghvi, 29 March 2003.

23. *Time*, 10 July 1989.

24. AI Nasir Abid, 16 January 2004.

25. GAAA. This letter was written at the end of 1991.

26. *Literary Review*, September 1990.

27. *Tatler*, October 1990.

28. *Financial Times*, 20 October 1990.

29. *New York Times*, 30 December 1990.

30. *Sunday Telegraph*, 30 September 1990.

31. *NYRB*, 14 February 1991.

32. TU unclassified papers.

33. AI V.S. Naipaul, 8 September 2007.

34. Tewari, op. cit.

35. AI Kenneth Ramchand, 5 March 2004. This trip may have taken place in 1984, but for narrative purposes I have left it here.

36. *Trinidad Guardian*, 7 March 1990.

37. AI Margaret Walcott, 4 March 2004.

38. AI Nella Chapman, 13 December 2007.

39. TU unclassified papers.

40. TU unclassified papers.

41. TU unclassified papers.

42. TU unclassified papers.

43. TU unclassified papers.

44. TU IC2.

45. *Evening Standard*, 15 October 1993.

46. NYRB, 31 January 1991.

47. TU unclassified papers.

48. TU unclassified papers.

49. Meyers, Jeffrey, *Privileged Moments: Encounters with Writers*, London 2000, p. 101.

50. TU unclassified papers.

51. GAAA.

52. AI V.S. Naipaul, 26 September 2002.

53. *Times of India*, 18 July 1993.

54. AI V.S. Naipaul, 2 October 2003 & 20 September 2003.

55. TU IIA.

56. TU IIA.

57. AI Eleanor Hale, 13 June 2006.

58. From a biographer's point of view, the most significant loss was the early novels, the Oxford diaries, the travel journals and the letters from friends and associates. V.S. Naipaul said later: 'What the documents that were lost in the warehouse would have reported, even the little journals that I kept – scrappy things – was the rage I felt. That came from my own unhappiness. I was capable of immense anger. I used to get angry very easily. Not only with Pat. I always got in rages, and often in public, entering the BBC, on a railway station – great rage, half mad. In Waterloo or some other station, if something happened to irritate me, probably someone might say something and I would be very angry . . . I was on the edge of anger all the time, and I never wrote about it. I wrote about it only once when I tried to define it in *An Area of Darkness* . . . I felt I was the defeated man, not seeing the way out. In a way, my father's rages had trained me for it, you understand. He was a great rager.' (AI V.S. Naipaul, 22 January 2004.)

59. AI V.S. Naipaul, 26 January 2004.

60. GAAA.

61. http://nobelprize.org/nobel_prizes/literature/laureates/1992/walcott-lecture.html.

62. TU IC2.

63. VSNC, purple Memorandum Book No 3. On the inside cover, V.S. Naipaul has written, 'An extraordinary, feeding little book. Always consulted by me during the writing of later books.'

64. VSNC, 'A Way in the World – notes 1990'.

65. TU unclassified papers.

66. Naipaul, V.S., *A Way in the World*, London 1994, p. 2.

67. Naipaul, V.S., *A Way in the World*, London 1994, p. 37.

68. Naipaul, V.S., *A Way in the World*, London 1994, p. 41.

69. Naipaul, V.S., *A Way in the World*, London 1994, p. 45.

70. Naipaul, V.S., *A Way in the World*, London 1994, p. 67.

71. Naipaul, V.S., *A Way in the World*, London 1994, p. 72.

72. Naipaul, V.S., *A Way in the World*, London 1994, p. 75.

73. Naipaul, V.S., *A Way in the World*, London 1994, pp. 77–94.

74. Calder Marshall, Arthur, *Glory Dead*, London 1939, p. 239.

75. Naipaul, V.S., *A Way in the World*, London 1994, p. 105.

76. Naipaul, V.S., *A Way in the World*, London 1994, p. 119.

77. Naipaul, V.S., *A Way in the World*, London 1994, p. 124.

78. Naipaul, V.S., *A Way in the World*, London 1994, p. 156.

79. Naipaul, V.S., *A Way in the World*, London 1994, p. 346.

80. Naipaul, V.S., *A Way in the World*, London 1994, pp. 367–8.

81. Naipaul, V.S., *A Way in the World*, London 1994, p. 369.

82. *Trinidad Guardian*, 26 June 1994.

83. *New York Times*, 17 May 1994.

84. *Sunday Times*, 8 May 1994.

85. *New York Times Book Review*, 22 May 1994.

86. *New Republic*, 13 June 1994.

87. TU IIIB.

88. GAAA.

89. *Independent on Sunday*, 28 March 1993.

90. *Publishers Weekly*, 6 June 1994.

91. *Der Spiegel*, 20 September 1993.

92. *New Yorker*, 23 May 1994.

93. AI V.S. Naipaul, 10 January 2005.

94. AI V.S. Naipaul, 11 January 2005.

95. *New Yorker*, 23 May 1994.

96. TU IIA.

97. AI V.S. Naipaul, 10 January 2005.

TWENTY-FIVE: THE SECOND LADY NAIPAUL

1. VSNC, small blue notebook.

2. GAAA.

3. VSNC.

4. VSNC.

5. MPS.

6. VSNC.

7. VSNC.

8. AI Gillon Aitken, 13 August 2003.

9. GAAA.

10. VSNC.

11. AI Ismail Merchant, 17 August 2004.

12. VSNC. V.S. Naipaul took eleven shirts with him, fifty-six fewer than Sir Francis Younghusband took to Tibet.

13. VSNC.

14. VSNC.

15. VSNC.

16. VSNC.

17. Naipaul, V.S., *Beyond Belief: Islamic Excursions Among the Converted Peoples*, London 1998, pp. 88, 222, 388–9. (All quotations from *Beyond Belief* are taken from the first edition.)

18. Naipaul, V.S., *Beyond Belief*, London 1998, p. 201.

19. Naipaul, V.S., *Beyond Belief*, London 1998, pp. 144 & 173–4.

20. *New York Times*, 7 June 1998.

21. *Financial Times*, 2 May 1998.

22. *Indian Review of Books*, 16 July 1998.

23. *Guardian*, n.d.

24. *Observer*, 3 May 1998.

25. *Sunday Telegraph*, 3 May 1998.

26. *Al-Ahram Weekly*, 6–12 August 1998.

27. *Sunday Times*, 3 May 1998.

28. GAAA.

29. VSNC.

30. TU IIB.

31. AI Angela Cox, 8 September 2007.

32. AI V.S. Naipaul, 27 October 2003 & 10 January 2005.

33. *Savvy*, January 2002.

34. VSNC.

35. AI Nadira Naipaul, 26 August 2007.

36. *Savvy*, January 2002.

37. This paragraph is based on AI Nadira Naipaul, 26 August 2007 and *Savvy*, January 2002.

38. *Frontier Post*, 13 February 1993.

39. *Savvy*, January 2002.

40. AI Nadira Naipaul, 26 August 2007.

41. Naipaul, V.S., *Beyond Belief*, London 1998, p. 355.

42. AI Minoo Bhandara, 2 September 2007.

43. AI Nadira Naipaul, 26 August 2007.

44. VSNC. His telephone bill for the quarter was £373.09, ten times its normal level.

45. AI Nadira Naipaul, 26 August 2007.

46. TU IV.

47. AI Mira Inalsingh, 17 September 2004.

48. AI Amar Inalsingh, 17 September 2004.

49. VSNC.

50. AI V.S. Naipaul, 8 September 2007.

51. AI Minoo Bhandara, 2 September 2007.

52. AI Nadira Naipaul, 26 August 2007.

53. AI Teresa Wells, 13 December 2007.

54. TU IV.

55. AI V.S. Naipaul, 26 January 2004.

56. AI V.S. Naipaul, 11 January 2005.

57. VSNC.

58. AI V.S. Naipaul, 8 September 2007.

59. VSNC.

60. PTC.

61. *Daily Telegraph*, 6 February 1996.

62. VSNC.

63. AI Eleanor Hale, 13 June 2006.

64. AI Eleanor Hale, 14 June 2006.

65. AI Nella Chapman, 13 December 2007.

66. AI Tristram Powell, 14 August 2003.

67. AI Angela Cox, 8 September 2007.

68. AI V.S. Naipaul, 11 January 2005.

69. VSNC.

70. AI Mira Inalsingh, 17 September 2004.

71. AI Nadira Naipaul, 7 January 2008.

72. VSNC.

73. TU IIB.

74. GAAA.

75. AI David Pryce-Jones, 26 January 2005.

76. *Daily Telegraph*, 20 April 1996.

77. *Times of India*, 23 June 1996.

78. AI V.S. Naipaul, 14 November 2002.

79. AI Nadira Naipaul, 26 August 2007.

80. Given his prominence as a writer on South Asia, it seems unlikely that Nadira Khannum Alvi had never heard of V.S. Naipaul, although it is possible that she had forgotten his name when Ahmed Rashid first mentioned his presence at the US consul general's house on 26 October 1995. A member of Nadira's family confirmed to me that she owned a well-thumbed copy of *India: An Area of Darkness*.

81. AI Eleanor Hale, 13 June 2006.

82. AI V.S. Naipaul, 11 January 2005.

83. VSNC.

84. AI Nadira Naipaul, 26 August 2007.

85. VSNC.

86. This translation of the *Fatiha* is not literal; it includes some extra words to make the sense clearer.

87. AI Nadira Naipaul, 26 August 2007.

88. For the moment.

Index

ADVERTISING
and Integrated Brand Pro

Fourth Edition

ADVERTISING
and Integrated Brand Promotion

Fourth Edition

Thomas C. O'Guinn
Professor, Department of Advertising
University of Illinois at Urbana-Champaign

Chris T. Allen
Arthur Beerman Professor of Marketing
University of Cincinnati

Richard J. Semenik
Professor of Marketing and Dean
Montana State University

THOMSON

SOUTH-WESTERN

Australia · Canada · Mexico · Singapore · Spain · United Ki

THOMSON

SOUTH-WESTERN

Advertising and Integrated Brand Promotion, Fourth Edition
Thomas C. O'Guinn, Chris T. Allen, Richard J. Semenik

VP/Editorial Director:
Jack W. Calhoun

VP/Editor-in-Chief:
Dave Shaut

Senior Publisher:
Melissa Acuña

Executive Editor:
Neil Marquardt

Senior Developmental Editor:
Mardell Toomey

Marketing Manager:
Nicole Moore

Production Editor:
Tamborah Moore

Manager of Technology, Editorial:
Vicky True

Technology Project Editor:
Pam Wallace

Web Coordinator:
Karen Schaffer

Senior Manufacturing Coordinator:
Diane Lohman

Production House:
Lachina Publishing Services

Printer:
CTPS

Art Director:
Stacy Jenkins Shirley

Internal Designer:
Craig LaGesse Ramsdell

Cover Designer:
Craig LaGesse Ramsdell

Cover Images:
© Lou Beach

Photography Manager:
John Hill

Photo Researcher:
Susan Van Etten

Library of Congress Control Number:
2004116550

For more information about our
products, contact us at:

Thomson Learning Academic
Resource Center

1-800-423-0563

Thomson Higher Education
5191 Natorp Boulevard
Mason, OH 45040
USA

Asia (including India)
Thomson Learning
5 Shenton Way
#01-01 UIC Building
Singapore 068808

Australia/New Zealand
Thomson Learning Australia
102 Dodds Street
Southbank, Victoria 3006
Australia

Canada
Thomson Nelson
1120 Birchmount Road
Toronto, Ontario
M1K 5G4
Canada

Latin America
Thomson Learning
Seneca, 53
Colonia Polanco
11560 Mexico
D.F.Mexico

UK/Europe/Middle East/Africa
Thomson Learning
High Holborn House
50/51 Bedford Row
London WC1R 4LR
United Kingdom

Spain (including Portugal)
Thomson Paraninfo
Calle Magallanes, 25
28015 Madrid, Spain

To

To my sister, Mary Jo Reed, and her husband of almost 60 years, Charles Hartford Reed. Mary Jo and Hartford have been rock solid in their love, support, and kindness. Mary Jo is the smart one of my family and has the soul of an angel. She raised four great kids and keeps everybody and everything together. Hartford fought in the Battle of the Bulge in the winter of 1944–1945, and to him and his fellow soldiers who truly saved the world, I am deeply grateful. Thank you.

My mom's sister, Flossie Pace, and her late husband, Larcus Pace, for their constant support and kindness.

Her daughter (my cousin) Caroline, and Caroline's husband, U.S. Marine, Korean War veteran, dusty-dry wit, life commentator, and great friend, Don Kelley, for their love and kindness.

And finally, to Jack Boland, farmer, father, and WWII veteran, for his service, for his family, and for his beautiful daughter Marilyn.
Thomas C. O'Guinn

To Linda, Gillian, and Maddy, my three reasons for being.
Chris Allen

To Molly and Andi. You support me through it all. I am a Lucky Man.
Rich Semenik

In Memoriam

Professor Kim B. Rotzoll.

Kim Rotzoll was my friend. He was also the best advertising educator and scholar I ever met. Many of you who teach this course knew him and loved him. He forgot more about advertising than most of us will ever know. Kim possessed a superb mind, but always deflected praise and attention. He was kind and gracious. He always tried to do the right thing, and he always acted with honor and dignity. Completely without hubris and guile, he was a truly great man. He is deeply missed.

—t.c.o.

PREFACE

In 2003, we launched the third edition of this book with a new title: *Advertising and Integrated Brand Promotion*. Some people questioned that title: "Isn't it supposed be Advertising and Integrated *Marketing Communication?*" We were convinced then that advertisers and agencies alike were focused on the brand and integrated *brand promotion* (IBP), and that integrated marketing communication (IMC) was really a thing of the past, and probably the wrong term in the first place. Our perspective proved to be correct. Advertising and promotion is *all* about the brand, and industry is pursing brand awareness and competitive advantage with an ever-expanding array of advertising and promotion brand building techiques—all of which we are proud and excited to present to you here in *Advertising and Integrated Brand Promotion, 4e*.

First, we have retained all the content and chapter features that students and instructors liked in our previous editions. Now more of a good thing: advertising as a brand–building process receives even greater emphasis in the fourth edition. The real ad world is about brands, and we cover the complete set of advertising and promotion tools. Once again, we lead the market in compelling, informative, and entertaining ads, and in illustrations, photos, and graphics (over 500!)—printed on the highest quality paper available—to highlight the features of each visual. Ads come first here.

We were very selective in choosing the content that received the heaviest revision and targeted those topics that reflect the important changes in the industry. Nearly every chapter has some new content and a lot of new visuals. But even in these cases, there is still a lot of familiar, foundation material. Some examples of the changes to the fourth edition will be helpful.

Chapter 1: The World of Advertising and Integrated Brand Promotion. The first chapter has a new name and was significantly revised to reflect the latest realities of industry practices and technological change. This change is evident in the annual reports of heavy users of advertising and promotion, like Procter & Gamble, who now proclaim that their core competitive capability is "branding."

Chapter 2: The Structure of the Advertising Industry: Advertisers, Advertising Agencies, and Support Organizations. Chapter 2 highlights some key changes in the industry affecting the way advertising and promotion are planned and executed. Examples of these changes include an increase in media consolidation, and the impact of consumers seizing control of their message environments with technology like **TiVo** and consumer-controlled information sources like **blogs.**

Chapter 3: The Evolution of Promoting and Advertising Brands. Here we offer extended coverage of the recent changes in advertising and IBP set in historical context. This allows students to see what is truly new, and what is recycled from the past.

Chapter 4: Social, Ethical and Regulatory Aspects of Advertising. Chapter 4 includes new restrictions on the advertising and promotion process such as the **"do not call"** list and **anti-spam** legislative movements, as well as an extensive discussion of privacy issues.

Chapter 5: Advertising, Integrated Brand Promotion, and Consumer Behavior. This revised chapter dedicates greater attention to the social and cultural perspectives of advertising and consumer behavior. These perspectives are shown in contrast to the psychological perspective offered in the first half of the chapter. No other book offers these dual and complementary perspectives. It tracks the changing views of advertising and promotion by both scholars and real world practitioners. It gives a clear explanation of how two very different ways of studying advertising, when taken together, yield a much better understanding of how advertising, IBP and branding work with real consumers. No other book offers this.

Chapter 7: Advertising and Promotion Research. This chapter has undergone significant revision. It has been updated to include current real-world changes in practice, as well as advances in the study of how advertising works. The move to better assess feelings generated by advertising and promotion is also covered. There is more interactive and web-based research treatment as well. While sophisticated in treatment, the text remains very accessible. It is material that can be used at several levels. This is the best chapter you'll find on this anywhere.

Chapter 9: Advertising Planning: An International Perspective. This material was revised to reflect the ever-changing cultural environment for advertising and promotion. This has never been more important than it is now.

Chapter 11: Message Strategy. The message strategy chapter has seen a moderate revision, allowing it to focus more on the order of clarifying, streamlining, tightening, and better differentiating nine key message strategies. The illustrations and accompanying support materials are also improved.

Chapter 14: Media Strategy and Planning for Advertising and IBP. Chapter 14 has been extensively revised—we mean *extensively*. We have updated it to better-fit industry practice, particularly all the recent changes in media, and provide a very real-world look at how media planning, selection, and placement really work. The chapter is also newly illustrated. It also presents the "real-deal" on industry practice: how things are really done, and why they are done that way.

Chapter 16: Media Planning: Advertising and IBP on the Internet. The information in this chapter basically had to be rewritten from scratch. In just three years since the release of the third edition, a full sixty percent of the web addresses cited in the book were dead links. The current treatment of the Internet highlights the reenergized growth of the medium, the emergence of **"paid search"** as a powerful new approach to using the Internet for advertising and promotion, and the new opportunities represented in technological advances like **WiFi, WiMax,** and **MobileFi.** The chapter also includes an extensive new discussion of security and privacy issues, and a very substantive discussion of measuring the effectiveness of using the Internet. No text offers such an extensive and contemporary view of the Internet in advertising and promotion issues.

Chapter 17: Support Media, Event Sponsorship, and Branded Entertainment. This chapter carries a new name to reflect the extensive changes in this area of promotion. In addition to understanding the role a wide range of media plays in supporting the main advertising effort, you'll learn about the emergence of strategies like **branded entertainment, advergaming,** and the ever expanding use of product (brand) placement in television and film production.

The above examples give you some idea of the new topical coverage and the discussions of contemporary topics which reflect the leading-edge coverage that *Advertising and Integrated Brand Promotion,* **4e** provides. In addition, we continue the practice, from prior editions, of the extensive use of examples to demostrate points throughout each chapter. Notice the large number of references throughout the book to literature from 2003 and 2004. Plus, over 50 percent of the ads, illustrations, and photos arc ncw in this edition. We work very hard to make the text current and relevant . . . and we think it shows.

But, even with these changes, the soul of the book remains the same. When we introduced the first edition of *Advertising,* we summed up our attitudes about our subject in this way:

Advertising is a lot of things. It's democratic pop culture, capitalist tool, oppressor, liberator, art, and theater, all rolled into one. It's free speech, it's creative flow, it's information, and it helps businesses get things sold. Above all, it's fun.

Advertising is fun, and this book reflects it. Advertising is also business, and this edition carries forward a perspective that clearly conveys that message as well. Like other aspects of business, advertising and integrated brand promotion are the result of hard work and careful planning. Creating good advertising is an enormous challenge . . . and we understand that. We understand advertising and promotion in its business and marketing context.

This book was written by three people with lots of experience in both academic and professional settings. We have collectively been consultants for many firms and their agencies. Thus, this book is grounded in real-world experience. It is not, however, a book that seeks to sell you a "show-and-tell coffee-table book" version of the advertising industry. Advertising and promotion, in the name of brands, is a worthy topic of academic attention. The story of the 20th century was in no small part the tale of the rise of consumer and advertising culture. Many academic disciplines want to understand how it works. We, as academic researchers, are in a unique and enviable position: We get to discuss advertising from the perspective of knowledge gathered in university settings as well as in daily practice. So, we wrote a book that is both practically engaging and academically solid.

Much has happened, since we released the first edition, that has strengthened our resolve to write and deliver the best advertising and promotions book on the market. First, we learned from our adopters (over 400 of you) and from our students that the book's (sometimes brutally) honest discussion of advertising practice was welcomed and applauded. We are not here to be cheerleaders for advertising, or to tell you we know what and where the magic bullets are. We truly love advertising, but we also know that it is not always wonderful. It can be frustrating to work with, particularly when you first learn there is *no* magic bullet. Advertising can also have a dark side. We understand that, and try to put it in a realistic context. We treat students like adults. When the best answer is "no one knows," we tell you that.

As much as we respected our academic and practitioner colleagues the first three times around, we respect them even more now. Research for the fourth edition turned up phenomenal industry talent, and we share our findings and surprises with you. This book is completely real-world, but the real world is also explained in terms of some really smart scholarship. This book copies no one, yet pays homage to many. More than anything, this book seeks to be honest, thoughtful, and imaginative. It acknowledges the complexity of human communication and consumer behavior while retaining a point of view.

We have tried our best to make life easier for the overworked instructor by offering a wide variety of ancillary materials that will assist in teaching from the book and in fully engaging students on this fascinating topic.

Students will like this book. You have liked the last three editions, and you'll like this one even more. We've spent considerable time reviewing student and instructor likes and dislikes of other advertising textbooks, in addition to examining their reactions to our own book. With this feedback, we've devoted pages and pictures, ideas and intelligence to creating a place for student and teacher to meet and discuss one of the most important and intrinsically interesting phenomena of contemporary times: advertising and promotion in the service of brands.

From Chapter 1 to Chapter 20.
As we said at the outset, *Advertising and Integrated Brand Promotion,* 4e is different in that it explicitly acknowledges that advertising and promotion are all about brands. Brands can be goods or services, things or people (for example, political candidates, performers), and advertising and promotion are about marketers projecting brands into the consciousness of consumers.

This fourth edition is also about taking a wider view of advertising and promotion. The truth these days is that any boundary between advertising and other forms of promotion is a pretty porous border. We acknowledge that point without making a big deal of it or moving away from traditional advertising. In fact, we have made it very easy for instructors to cover what they want. This is still, first and foremost, an advertising book. We think that advertising and promotion should be discussed between the covers of the same book, just as their coordinated integration should occur in practice.

Relevant, Intelligent Organization.
The fourth edition is divided into five parts. This feature of the book is unique and highly valued by adopters. Instructors and students alike find this organization relevant, intelligent, and easy to follow. The organization of the text is so popular because it lays out the advertising and promotion process the same way it unfolds in practice and application:

Part One: The Process: Advertising and Integrated Brand Promotion in Business and Society. Part One recognizes that students really need to understand just what advertising and IBP are all about, and have a good perspective on how the process works. This section contains the core fundamentals of the book (more about this in a minute). It describes the entire landscape of advertising and promotion, and provides a look at the structure of the industry and a historical perspective on the evolution of the process. Part One concludes with the key social, ethical, and regulatory issues facing practitioners and consumers.

Part Two: The Planning: Analyzing the Advertising and Integrated Brand Promotion Environment. Part Two provides all the essential perspectives to understand how to carry out effective advertising and IBP. Key strategic concepts of the process including consumer behavior analysis, market segmentation, brand differentiation, and brand positioning are considered. Then, this section proceeds to a discussion of the types of research advertising and promotion planners rely on to develop effective advertising and IBP. The final two chapters in this section provide the key components of developing both a domestic and international advertising and IBP plan.

Whether you are teaching/studying advertising and promotion in a business school curriculum or an advertising/journalism curriculum, the first two parts of the book provide the background and perspective that show how advertising and IBP have become the powerful business and society forces they are in the 21st century.

Part Three: Preparing the Message. Part Three is all about creativity: creativity in general, as a managerial issue, and as a part of art direction, copy writing, and message strategy. Most adopters in advertising and communication programs use this section, but some business-school adopters (particularly those on 6- and 10-week modules or classes) skip some of the creative chapters in Part Three. However, almost everyone uses Chapter 11, which focuses on message development and strategy.

Part Four: Placing the Message in Conventional and New Media. Part Four is all about using media—including the Internet—to reach target audiences. These chapters are key to understanding many of the execution aspects of good advertising and integrated brand promotion strategies. It is in this section that you will learn not just about the media per se, but also about the media environment and consumers' new found power in managing their information environments.

Part Five: Integrated Brand Promotion. Part Five covers the many tools of integrated brand promotion. Starting with the third edition, we bundled these four chapters together, since our business-school adopters often use them. We think they are good for everyone.

Our support package was designed and written for use in all advertising and/or promotion classes taught anywhere: in business and journalism schools, as well as in mass communication and advertising departments.

Compelling Fundamentals.
We fully expect our book to continue to set the standard for coverage of new topics and issues. It is loaded with features, insights, and common sense advertising perspectives about the ever-changing nature of the advertising and promotion industry. We were at the right place at the right time to build these issues into the first edition of *Advertising*. Now we have built on that competitive advantage and incorporated coverage of new issues in *every* chapter.

That said, a truly distinguishing strength of this book is its treatment of the fundamentals of advertising. You just *cannot* appreciate the role of the new media or new technologies today without a solid understanding of the fundamentals. If you doubt our commitment to the fundamentals, take a good look at Chapters 2 through 9. This is where we, once again, part company with other books on the market. *Advertising and Integrated Brand Promotion,* 4e, is the only book on the market that insures the deep economic roots of advertising and promotion are fully understood. And, we take the time to be sure that not just the business but also the social context of advertising are clear. Check out just how completely the foundational aspects are covered—you'll be impressed.

Also, notice that we don't wait until the end of the book to bring legal, ethical, social (Chapter 4), and international considerations (Chapter 9) into mainstream thinking about advertising and IBP. While most books put international issues as one of the last chapters—as if they are an afterthought—global topics are covered early and then integrated into every chapter throughout the text because today's decision makers must possess a global view.

Balanced New Media Coverage. Most chapters contain a boxed insert titled *IBP*. These furnish contemporary examples of how the new media and strategies are affecting various aspects of advertising practice. Every chapter also contains *e-Sightings*, which are application activities designed to bring chapter ads into real time, and the concepts of new media to life. Every chapter ends with *Using the Internet* exercises that can be pursued, via the Internet, to help students learn about advertising, generally, and the Internet, specifically. In-depth consideration of new media vehicles is provided in Part Four of the book, "Placing the Message in Conventional and New Media." Chapter 16 is all about advertising and marketing on the Internet and it reviews many technical considerations for working with this—now not-so-new, but still challenging and evolving—method for reaching and affecting consumers. Chapter 17 highlights all the new ways advertising and promotion can provide an "experiential" encounter with the brand.

IBP Coverage—The Integrated Cincinnati Bell Wireless Case. As we have said, advertising and IBP are all about the brand. The marketing and advertising worlds have always known this, but in the last few years have placed intense focus on branding. So we make things explicit: This book is about advertising and promotion in the service of brands. Further, it must be an integrated effort. Integrated efforts have come to be the norm.

But the IBP coverage doesn't stop with just our statement of philosophy—not by a long shot. Another unique feature of *Advertising and Integrated Brand Promotion,* 4e is the end-of-part case history, **"From Principles to Practice: A Comprehensive IBP Case,"** which we developed in conjunction with Cincinnati Bell and its former agency, Northlich. This five-part case takes you inside a real company and a real ad agency to learn how real IBP campaigns are planned and executed. The result illustrates the full array of considerations involved in implementing advertising and integrated brand promotion. As you will see, Cincinnati Bell provided us with all the planning, strategy, and implementation information from its campaign to introduce Cincinnati Bell Wireless services. We track the evolution of this campaign from its inception through its multimedia execution. This unique and comprehensive case history vividly illustrates what it means to speak to the customer with multiple tools, but *in a single voice,* to build and sustain a client's brand.

Student Engagement and Learning. You will find that this book provides a clear and sophisticated examination of advertising fundamentals in lively, concise language. We don't beat around the bush, and we're not shy about challenging conventions. In addition, the book features a stylish internal design (worthy of an advertising book!) and hundreds of illustrations. Reading this book will be an engaging experience for you.

The markers of our commitment to student learning are easily identified throughout the book. Every chapter begins with a statement of the *learning objectives* for that chapter. (For a quick appreciation of the coverage provided by this book, take a pass through it and read the learning objectives on the first page of each chapter.) Chapters are organized to deliver content that responds to each learning objective, and the *chapter summaries* are written to reflect what the chapter has offered with respect to each learning objective.

We also believe that students must be challenged to go beyond their reading to think about the issues raised in the book. Thus, you will note that the *Questions* at the end of each chapter demand thoughtful analysis rather than mere regurgitation, and the *Experiential Exercises* will help students put their learning to use in ways that will help them take more away from the course than just textbook learning. Complete use of this text and its ancillary materials will yield a dramatic and engaging learning experience for students of all ages who are studying advertising for the first time.

A Closer Look at Some Fourth Edition Features.

How the Text Is Organized. As we discussed earlier, *Advertising and Integrated Brand Promotion,* 4e is divided into five major parts:

- Part One: The Process: Advertising and Integrated Brand Promotion in Business and Society
- Part Two: The Planning: Analyzing the Advertising and Integrated Brand Promotion Environment
- Part Three: Preparing the Message
- Part Four: Placing the Message in Conventional and New Media
- Part Five: Integrated Brand Promotion

Now, let's call your attention to some important chapter highlights.

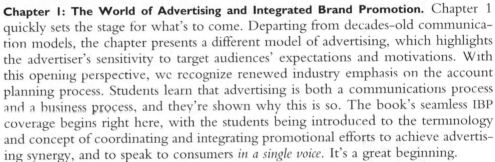

Part One: The Process: Advertising and Integrated Brand Promotion in Business and Society.

Chapter 1: The World of Advertising and Integrated Brand Promotion. Chapter 1 quickly sets the stage for what's to come. Departing from decades-old communication models, the chapter presents a different model of advertising, which highlights the advertiser's sensitivity to target audiences' expectations and motivations. With this opening perspective, we recognize renewed industry emphasis on the account planning process. Students learn that advertising is both a communications process and a business process, and they're shown why this is so. The book's seamless IBP coverage begins right here, with the students being introduced to the terminology and concept of coordinating and integrating promotional efforts to achieve advertising synergy, and to speak to consumers *in a single voice*. It's a great beginning.

This chapter has extensive discussions of the concepts of the brand, brand extensions, and brand equity. The concept of advertising and brand management is introduced here as the premise for the integrated brand promotion dimension of the text. IBP is the logical next step as a departure from integrated marketing communication (IMC).

Chapter 2: The Structure of the Advertising Industry: Advertisers, Advertising Agencies, and Support Organizations. In Chapter 2, you'll read about trends that are transforming the advertising industry today and the seismic changes the industry experienced at the end of the millennium. Students will see who are the participants in the ad industry today and the role each plays in the formulation and execution of ad campaigns.

The main point is that advertisers are rethinking the way they try to communicate with consumers. Fundamentally, there is a greater focus on integrating more tools with the overall advertising effort into brand promotion programs. More than ever, advertisers are looking to the full complement of promotional opportunities, including sales promotions, event sponsorships, new media options, and public relations, as means to support and enhance the primary advertising effort for brands. There is much more emphasis on the role of the trade in the communications effort. New to this treatment is the recognition that consumers are taking more control of their information environment with the use of new technologies like TiVo and PDAs.

Chapter 3: The Evolution of Promoting and Advertising Brands. Chapter 3 puts advertising in a historical context. But before the history lesson begins, students are given the straight scoop about advertising as a product of fundamental economic and social conditions—capitalism, the Industrial Revolution, manufacturers' pursuit of power, and modern mass communication—without which there would be no advertising process. Students then study the history of advertising through ten interesting and entertaining eras, seeing how advertising has changed and evolved, and how it is forged out of its social setting. This chapter is rich with some of the most interesting ads representing advertising as a faithful documentation of social life in America. Definitely an entertaining and provocative chapter, it also gives students a necessary and important perspective on advertising before launching into advertising planning concepts and issues. Most strategies were created decades ago, and if you can learn how advertisers took advantage of various social conditions and trends yesterday, you can learn a lot about how to do it today—and tomorrow.

Chapter 4: Social, Ethical, and Regulatory Aspects of Advertising. Advertising is dynamic and controversial. In Chapter 4, students will examine a variety of issues concerning advertising's effects on societal well being. Is advertising intrusive, manipulative, and deceptive? Does it waste resources, promote materialism, and perpetuate stereotypes? Or does it inform, give exposure to important issues, and raise the standard of living? After debating the social merits of advertising, students will explore the ethical considerations that underlie the development of campaigns and learn about the regulatory agencies that set guidelines for advertisers. Lastly, students are introduced to the concept of self-regulation and why advertisers must practice it.

There are a couple of important and extensive changes in the fourth edition. First, the issue of privacy is discussed extensively as both a social and ethical issue, given new technologies that can track and profile consumers through the communication process and the risks (such as easy access through WiFi) new technologies present. New material was also added on regulatory issues in direct marketing ("do not call" lists), in e-commerce (anti-spam legislation), in sales promotion, and in public relations.

Part Two: The Planning: Analyzing the Advertising and Integrated Brand Promotion Environment.

Chapter 5: Advertising, Integrated Brand Promotion, and Consumer Behavior. Chapter 5, which describes consumer behavior from two different perspectives, begins Part Two of the text. The first perspective portrays consumers as systematic decision makers who seek to maximize the benefits they derive from their purchases. The second portrays consumers as active interpreters of advertising, whose membership in various cultures, subcultures, societies, and communities significantly affects their interpretations of and responses to advertising. Students, shown the validity of both perspectives, learn that, like all human behavior, the behavior of consumers is complex, multifaceted, and often symbolic. Understanding buyer behavior is a tremendous challenge to advertisers, who should not settle for easy answers if they want good relationships with their customers. The chapter also includes information about brands, and the consumer behavior that makes or breaks them.

Chapter 6: Market Segmentation, Positioning, and the Value Proposition. Chapter 6 begins with the compelling story of how Gillette used segmentation, position, and targeting to grow into a global consumer products powerhouse. Students are introduced to the sequence of activities often referred to as STP marketing—segmenting, targeting, and positioning—and how advertising both affects and is affected by these basic marketing strategies. The remainder of the chapter is devoted to detailed analysis of how organizations develop market segmentation, positioning, and product differentiation strategies. The critical role of ad campaigns in successfully executing these strategies is emphasized over and over. Numerous examples of real-world campaigns that contrast different segmentation and positioning strategies keep the narrative fresh and fast moving. The chapter concludes by demonstrating that effective STP marketing strategies result in creating a perception of value in the marketplace.

Chapter 7: Advertising and Promotion Research. Chapter 7, which contains a lot of new content, covers the methods used in developmental research, the procedures used for pre-testing messages prior to the launch of a campaign, the methods used to track the effectiveness of ads during and after a launch, and the many sources of secondary data that can aid the ad-planning effort. This chapter also provides coverage of the agency's new emphasis on account planning as a distinct part of the planning process.

Chapter 8: Planning Advertising and Integrated Brand Promotion. Chapter 8 begins by recounting the sequence of events and strategies behind the launch of Apple's colorful iMac computers. Through this opening vignette, students see the importance of constructing a sound ad plan before launching any campaign. But in addition, this introductory campaign for the iMac is an extraordinary example of IBP at work. After reading this chapter, students will be familiar with the basic components of an ad plan. They will understand two fundamental approaches for setting advertising objectives—the budgeting process and the role of the ad agency in formulating an advertising plan. By the end of the chapter, students will understand the significance of the opening commentary in this chapter: ". . . you don't go out and spend $100 million promoting a new product that is vital to the success of a firm without giving the entire endeavor considerable forethought. Such an endeavor calls for a plan."

Chapter 9: Advertising Planning: An International Perspective. We begin Chapter 9 with a careful look at the challenges inherent in creating ad campaigns for cultures other than one's own. China, one of the world's growing economic powerhouses, is featured in a story that illustrates the challenge. The "stars" of this Chinese calamity are Toyota, and their ad agency Saatchi & Saatchi, showing that even the biggest and the best make mistakes on foreign soil. While many books bury their international chapter at the end, we chose to place this chapter in the heart of the book where it belongs, as part of the overall advertising planning effort. You'll find the chapter engaging in the way the fast-moving discussion unfolds: from a discussion of cultural barriers and overcoming them, to an examination of the creative, media, and regulatory challenges that international advertising presents. Of course, your students will also love the ad samples from Japan, Germany, Chile, the Czech Republic, and a host of other countries.

Part Three: Preparing the Message.

Chapter 10: Creativity, Advertising, and the Brand. Chapter 10 takes on the seemingly awkward task of "talking" about creativity. All you creatives out there know that this is a nearly impossible task. But what we have tried to do for students in this chapter is completely different from what is done in all other texts. Rather than just describing the creative *process* (we do that in Chapters 11 and 12), we have tried to discuss the essence of what creativity is. First, we portray the challenges of the creative effort by describing the conflicts that arise between the poets and the killers (we'll let you go to the chapter to see who these combatants are). Next, we highlight the commentary and achievements of creative geniuses—both within the advertising industry and completely removed from it. The result is a thought-provoking and enriching treatment like no other that students will find. We've also revised and refocused the material on the organizational and managerial realities of the creative/suit interface.

Chapter 11: Message Strategy. Building on Chapter 10, Chapter 11 explores the role of creativity in message strategy from a refreshingly honest perspective: No one knows exactly how advertising creativity works. Nine message strategy objectives are presented along with the creative methods used to accomplish the objectives, including humor, slice-of-life, anxiety, sexual-appeal, slogan, and repetition ads. This chapter makes excellent use of visuals to dramatize the concepts presented. Quite a bit of revision went into this signature chapter, and many ads are offered as concrete examples.

Chapter 12: Copywriting. Chapter 12 flows logically from the chapter on message development. In this chapter students learn about the copywriting process and the importance of good, hard-hitting copy in the development of print, radio, and television advertising. Guidelines for writing headlines, subheads, and body copy for print ads are given, as well as guidelines for writing radio and television ad copy. The chapter closes with a discussion of the most common mistakes copywriters make, and a discussion of the copy approval process. And, of course, this chapter also considers the issues surrounding the copywriting process in the highly constrained creative environment of the Internet.

Chapter 13: Art Direction and Production. The adopters of the first edition of *Advertising* told us that two chapters on art direction and production were overkill. We heeded your plea. Chapter 13 now combines discussion of both print and broadcast media. Here students learn about the strategic and creative impact of illustration, design, and layout, and the production steps required to get to the final ad. Numerous engaging full-color ads are included that illustrate important design, illustration, and layout concepts.

We also introduce students to what is often thought of as the most glamorous side of advertising: television advertising. Students learn about the role of the creative team and the many agency and production company participants involved in the direction and production processes. Students are given six creative guidelines for television ads, with examples of each. Radio is not treated as a second-class citizen in this chapter but is given full treatment, including six guidelines for the production of creative and effective radio ads. This chapter is comprehensive and informative without getting bogged down in production details.

Part Four: Placing the Message in Conventional and New Media.

Chapter 14: Media Strategy and Planning for Advertising and IBP. In Chapter 14, which begins Part Four, students see that a well-planned and creatively prepared campaign needs to be placed in media (and not just any media!) to reach a target audience and to stimulate demand. This chapter drives home the point that advertising placed in media that does not reach the target audience—whether new media or traditional media—will be much like the proverbial tree that falls in the forest with no one around: Does it make a sound? Students will read about the major media options available to advertisers today, the media-planning process, computer modeling in media planning, and the challenges that complicate the media-planning process. The chapter uses the "real-deal" headings to explain not how things should be done, but how they are done, and why.

Chapter 15: Media Planning: Print, Television, and Radio. The opening vignette for Chapter 15 highlights the ongoing battle for the favors of TV viewers. Cable television has slowly but surely made major inroads into the market share of broadcast television and both are battling for the most lucrative market segments, which are now migrating more and more to Web-based information sources. This chapter focuses on evaluating media as an important means for advertisers to reach audiences. The chapter details the advantages and disadvantages of newspapers, magazines, radio, and television as media classes and describes the buying and audience measurement techniques for each. New topics covered in this chapter highlight the impact of TiVo on television advertising and the potential impact of satellite radio on the radio medium.

Chapter 16: Media Planning: Advertising and IBP on the Internet. The first edition of *Advertising* was the first introductory advertising book to devote an entire chapter to advertising on the Internet, and this edition continues to set the standard for Internet coverage. Today's employers expect college advertising and promotion students to know about the Internet (inside and out) and the creative and selling opportunities it presents to advertisers as part of their IBP strategy. Chapter 16 presents a complete overview of advertising on the Internet and provides numerous Net activities to give students hands-on experience in visiting and analyzing advertisers' Web sites. The chapter describes who is using the Internet today and the ways they are using it, identifies the advertising and marketing opportunities presented by the Internet, discusses fundamental requirements for establishing sites on the World Wide Web, and lays out the challenges inherent in measuring the cost effectiveness of the Internet versus other advertising media. This chapter doesn't assume that all students are already Internet gurus, but it won't insult those who are.

What has been added to this chapter is a discussion of how the Internet has risen (the dot.com era), fallen (the dot.bomb era), and risen again. The Internet is here to stay. New applications by advertisers in paid search are propelling Internet advertising spending to new heights. In addition, the merging of Web site communication with sales promotion and sales transaction and fulfillment makes this a very powerful communications environment indeed. There is an extensive new discussion of security and privacy issues and a very substantive discussion of measuring the effectiveness of using the Internet. We believe this coverage is the most up-to-date and extensive you will find.

Part Five: Integrated Brand Promotion.

Chapter 17: Support Media, Event Sponsorship, and Branded Entertainment. Procter & Gamble, like many advertisers, will try just about anything to reach consumers with the right support for its brands. The wonder of P&G's Pottypalooza, a gleaming restroom on wheels dispensing Charmin toilet tissue, gets us off to a rousing start in this chapter. Chapter 17 then goes on to make students aware of the wide array of support media available to advertisers, including billboards, transit advertising, aerial advertising, and the good old Yellow Pages. If those aren't enough possibilities, this chapter also reviews the growing allure of event sponsorships and then takes a deep dive into the provocative subject of branded entertainment. We've come a long way from E.T. eating Reese's Pieces! If students didn't already appreciate the power of integrated brand promotion when they hit this chapter, they certainly will afterward. . .

Chapter 18: Sales Promotion and Point-of-Purchase Advertising. Sales promotion is a multibillion-dollar business in the United States and is emerging as a global force as well. Chapter 18 explains the rationale for different types of sales promotions. It differentiates between consumer and trade-sales promotions and highlights the risks and coordination issues associated with sales promotions—a consideration overlooked by other texts. All of the following are discussed: coupons, price off deals, premiums, contests, sweepstakes, sampling, trial offers, product (brand) placements, refunds, rebates, frequency programs, point-of-purchase displays, incentives, allowances, trade shows, and cooperative advertising.

This chapter has a new, extensive section on point of purchase. Point-of-purchase advertising is using new and powerful techniques at that precious moment when the consumer is making the final choice. A section, which was added during the last edition, "Sales Promotion, the Internet, and New Media," provides the most forward-thinking discussion of using new distribution and communication techniques for sales promotion.

PART FIVE

Chapter 19: Direct Marketing. Chapter 19 opens with a fable about direct marketing guru Les Wunderman and the magic of his little gold box, and then moves quickly on to L. L. Bean and the well-known L. L. Bean mail-order catalog. Students quickly learn about Bean's emphasis on building an extensive mailing list, which serves as a great segue to database marketing. Students will learn why direct marketing continues to grow in popularity, what media are used by direct marketers to deliver their messages, and how direct marketing creates special challenges for achieving integrated brand promotion.

Chapter 20: Public Relations and Corporate Advertising. This chapter provides a key discussion of the role of public relations in the overall integrated branding effort. Some firms have turned to PR as a new tool in their overall program. BUT, the argument that PR is rising to such prominence that the "death of advertising" is imminent (as some authors have suggested) literally made us laugh out loud. Advertising expenditures across all media are, once again, setting records. This chapter differentiates between proactive and reactive public relations and the strategies associated with each. You will learn that public relations are an important option in IBP, but they will never take the lead role.

This chapter concludes with a wide-ranging and complete discussion of corporate advertising. Various forms of corporate advertising are identified and the way each can be used as a means for building the reputation of an organization in the eyes of key constituents is discussed.

Inside Every Chapter.
Inside every chapter of *Advertising and Integrated Brand Promotion,* 4e you will find features that make this new book eminently teachable and academically solid, while at the same time fun to read. As we said earlier, this text was written and the examples were chosen to facilitate an effective meeting place for student and teacher. Who said learning has to be drudgery? It doesn't have to be and it shouldn't.

Dynamic Graphics and over 500 Ads and Exhibits. Ask any student and almost any instructor what an advertising book must include, and you will get as a top response—lots of ads. As you will see by quickly paging through *Advertising and Integrated Brand Promotion,* 4e, this book is full of ads and other instructional visuals. Over 500 ads, exhibits, illustrations and photos are used to highlight important points made in the chapters. Each exhibit is referenced in the text narrative, tying the visual to the concept being discussed.

As you can see, the book's clean, classic, graphic layout invites you to read it; it dares you to put it down without reading just one more caption or peeking at the next chapter.

Opening Vignettes. Every chapter includes a classic or current real-world advertising story to draw students into the chapter and to stimulate classroom discussions. Each vignette illustrates important concepts that will be discussed in the chapter. The chapters throughout the book continue with these types of lively introductions, ensuring that students get off to a good start with every chapter.

In-Chapter Features. Every chapter contains a minimum of three boxed features that highlight interesting, unusual, or just plain entertaining information as it relates to the chapter. The boxes are not diversions unrelated to the text; rather, they provide information that can be fully integrated into classroom lectures. The boxes are for teaching, learning, and reinforcing chapter content. Five types of boxes are included in the text: Ethics, Global Issues, Controversy, Creativity, and IBP. Let's take a look at each.

Ethics (New to this edition!): It is important that business decisions be guided by ethical practices, and advertising is a particularly interesting field to which ethics can be related. Because of the importance of ethics and its appeal to students' interests, we have added Ethics boxes to this edition. Students will gain insights into ethical business practices that will be useful not only in their advertising course, but in future business courses, as well as their careers.

Global Issues: The Global Issues boxes provide an insightful, real-world look at the numerous challenges advertisers face internationally. Many issues are discussed in these timely boxes, including the development of more standardized advertising across cultures with satellite-based television programming, how U.S.-based media companies such as MTV and Disney/ABC are pursuing the vast potential in global media, obstacles to advertising in emerging markets, and cross-cultural global research.

Controversy: Often related to ethics, these boxes call students' attention to some of the most interesting examples of chapter content as it applies in real life. These boxes strongly reinforce chapter content and increase student interest.

Creativity: Since creativity is often challenging both to teach and to learn, we have fortified the text with some compelling examples that will help students form a better understanding of this nebulous topic.

IBP: Much of the coverage in the IBP boxes focuses on issues related to advertising and its coordinated use with other promotional tools. These boxes highlight the strategic application and powerful impact IBP has had across a wide range of industries.

Also in each chapter:

e-Sightings. In keeping with the new media distinctiveness of this book, you will find all new "e-Sightings" in each chapter. You can spot these e-Sightings by looking for the e-Sighting logo found above selected exhibits in each chapter. Students are asked to go to the Web site addresses provided in the caption to explore the advertiser's home page, bringing the ad in the book online and into real time. Questions are provided to prompt students to explore, explain, describe, compare, contrast, summarize, rethink, or analyze the content or features of the advertiser's home page. You can think of these e-Sightings as in-chapter experiential exercises and real-time cases. Instructors can assign these e-Sightings as individual or group activities. They are also excellent discussion starters.

Concise Chapter Summaries. Each chapter ends with a summary that distills the main points of the chapter. Chapter summaries are organized around the learning objectives so that students can use them as a quick check on their achievement of learning goals.

Key Terms. Each chapter ends with a listing of the key terms found in the chapter. Key terms also appear in boldface in the text. Students can prepare for exams by scanning these lists to be sure they can define or explain each term.

Critical Thinking Questions. End-of-chapter questions, by B. J. Parker, contributing writer, are designed to challenge students' thinking and to go beyond the "read, memorize, and regurgitate" learning process. The *Questions for Review* and *Critical Thinking* sections require students to think analytically and to interpret data and information provided for them in the text. Detailed responses to these questions are provided in the Instructor's Manual.

Below is a sampling of the types of critical thinking questions found in *Advertising:*

- If a firm developed a new line of athletic shoes, priced them competitively, and distributed them in appropriate retail shops, would there be any need for advertising? Is advertising really needed for a good product that is priced right?

- The 1950s were marked by great suspicion about advertisers and their potential persuasive powers. Do you see any lingering effects of this era of paranoia in attitudes about advertising today?

- Some contend that self-regulation is the best way to ensure fair and truthful advertising practices. Why would it be in the best interest of the advertising community to aggressively pursue self-regulation?

- Identify several factors or forces that make consumers around the world similar to one another. Conversely, what factors or forces create diversity among consumers in different countries?

- Explain the two basic strategies for developing corporate home pages, exemplified in this chapter by Saturn and Absolut.

- Visit some of the corporate home pages described in this chapter, or think about corporate home pages you visited previously. Of those you have encountered, which would you single out as being most effective in giving the visitor a reason to come back? What conclusions would you draw regarding the best ways to motivate repeat visits to a Web site?

- Everyone has an opinion on what makes advertisements effective or ineffective. How does this fundamental aspect of human nature complicate a copywriter's life when it comes to winning approval for his or her ad copy?

Experiential Exercises. Prepared by B. J. Parker, contributing writer, these exercises found at the end of each chapter require students to apply the material they have just read by researching topics, writing short papers, preparing brief presentations, or interacting with professionals from the advertising industry. They require students to get out of the classroom to seek information not provided in the text. A number of these exercises are especially designed for teamwork, and many are classroom tested.

Experiencing the Internet. Prepared by B. J. Parker, contributing writer, this unique set of Internet exercises is designed to get students on to the Internet to examine the nature of the advertising that is there, to analyze the effectiveness of what they find, and to apply the Internet to fundamental advertising concepts presented in the text. Because the focus of these exercises is hands-on in nature, students will spend time accessing home pages using the Web site addresses provided, and then evaluating what they find. Application questions are provided for each exercise for students to answer after their Web site excursions. The application questions require students to apply the concepts taught in each chapter, making these surfing-the-Net exercises worthwhile and focused, not just browsing time. Suggested answers to all of the Internet exercises can be found in the Instructor's Manual.

 Learning Objectives and a Built-In Integrated Learning System. The text and test bank are organized around the learning objectives that appear at the beginning of each chapter, to provide you and your students with an easy-to-use, integrated learning system. A numbered icon like the one shown here identifies each chapter objective and appears next to its related material throughout the chapter. This integrated learning system can provide you with a structure for creating lesson plans as well as tests. A correlation table at the beginning of every chapter in the test bank enables you to create tests that fully cover every learning objective, or ones that emphasize just the objectives you feel are most important.

The integrated system also gives structure to students as they prepare for tests. The icons identify all the material in the text that fulfill each objective. Students can easily check their grasp of each objective by reading the text sections and reviewing the corresponding summary sections. They can also return to appropriate text sections for further review if they have difficulty with end-of-chapter questions.

End-of-Part Features:

Cincinnati Bell^{SM} **End-of-Part IBP Case History: Cincinnati Bell**^{SM} **Wireless.** No advertising text would be complete without giving special attention to integrated brand promotion. At the end of each of the five parts of this text is an ongoing case study of Cincinnati Bell and its Cincinnati Bell Wireless IBP campaigns. These sections will help students better understand IBP by examining the topic in two ways. First, each section begins by discussing the basics of IBP and methods for creating effective, integrated communications. Second, each section illustrates the basic principles of IBP in campaigns developed for Cincinnati Bell Wireless. As students will discover, Cincinnati Bell used a wide range of communication tools to support its goal of introducing and growing its brand. Of course, these IBP sections are fully and colorfully illustrated. And, as with a lot of the features that distinguish this book, we were in the right place at the right time. Cincinnati Bell Wireless's campaigns have been remarkably successful in an increasingly competitive marketplace.

Careers in Marketing Communications, IBP, and Advertising (New to this edition!). Prepared by B. J. Parker, contributing writer, this end-of-part feature personalizes each section's topics by featuring a real individual who students can relate to, explaining how the topics featured in that section affected their understanding of advertising and ultimately success in their career.

A Full Array of Teaching/Learning Supplementary Materials.

Supplements:

Instructor's Manual. The fourth edition's instructor's manual was prepared by one of the main text authors, Rich Semenik. The manual has been thoroughly revised to update all previous content including comprehensive lecture outlines that provide suggestions for using other ancillary products associated with the text, and suggested answers for all exercises found within the text. The quality is exceptional and includes many improvements to the last edition. These improvements include:

- Lecture notes inserted in chapter outlines
- Lecture notes to accompany all ads
- Many back stories or additional explanation *not* found in the text
- Answers to inductive discussion questions included in the PowerPoint® slide presentation
- A special new section on "How to use IBP," especially useful for business schools.
- Suggestions for using the experiential exercises, found at the end of each chapter.

PowerPoint®. This edition's PowerPoint® presentation is of the highest quality possible and was prepared by one of the main text authors, Rich Semenik. There are many improvements including additional ads with accompanying discussion questions (answers provided in instructor's manual). Many non-ad exhibits are now animated for increased interest and pedagogical value. Finally, streaming video from recent Super Bowl ads has been incorporated into the PowerPoint presentation. All ads are accompanied with commentary on how they illustrate theories and concepts presented in the text and include at least one inductive question to generate classroom discussion. This edition of PowerPoint includes a comprehensive version for instructor use only and a more basic student version that is available on our product website (see below).

Test Bank. Prepared by Ed Ackerly of the University of Arizona, this comprehensive test bank is organized around the main text's learning objectives. Each question is labeled according to the learning objective that is covered, the page number on which the answer can be found, and the type of question (definitional, conceptual, or application). Grouping the questions according to type allows for maximum flexibility in creating tests that are customized to individual classroom needs and preferences. The test bank includes true/false, multiple-choice, scenario application, and essay questions. There are a total of 2,000 questions. All questions have been carefully reviewed for clarity and accuracy. Improvements to this edition include a correlation grid for each chapter ranking questions according to difficulty and identifying types of questions (definitional, conceptual, application), more scenario application questions, and revised essay questions.

ExamView Testing Software. This electronic test bank allows instructors to easily manipulate the content found in our printed test bank supplement, and then creates customized tests to suit varying student levels and classroom needs.

Product Support Site (http://oguinn.swlearning.com). The product support site features "Instructor Resources" that include the instructor's manual, test bank, PowerPoint instructor's version, and, *new to this edition,* an integrative video guide to accompany "The 2004 Clios" video/DVD package and "The Advertising Process" video/DVD Collection. For students, we include for each chapter: learning objectives, crossword puzzles using key terms, Internet Applications exercises, interactive quizzes, and student PowerPoint. Many other additional resources are also available to instructors and students.

O'Guinn Xtra! This product provides additional support for students and special insights into the field of advertising that are not offered in the main text. Components include: Xtra! quizzing designed to prepare students for exams; and advertising documents such as an advertising plan, creative plan, media plan, research questionnaires, e-lectures, industry ads video clips, and additional 2003 Clio video clips.

Videos:

The 2004 Clios. Our award-winning video package is designed to show students how advertising works in the real world, showing the most current and creative examples of advertising worldwide. It's a dynamic, attention-getting, and engaging package you'll enjoy using in your classes. Also included with this edition is an extra DVD, the Clio's 40th Anniversary collection.

Other Products That Complement This Edition:

IMC: An Integrated Marketing Communications Exercise, 2nd Edition (0-324-01483-X). This comprehensive supplementary workbook puts students in the role of a client services manager at a major, full-service integrated marketing communications agency. The client, the Republic of Uruguay, wants the agency to create and manage a total marketing program for a new resort in Uruguay called Punta del Este. In approximately 80 pages, this semester-long project workbook includes step-by-step directions for students to follow. In addition to the traditional IMC mix, this exercise also takes students into the world of interactive media, because any successful presentation in the real world today will have to include a proposal integrating the Internet and other interactive media.

To begin the exercise, students are briefed on all aspects of the new resort: facts and details about Punta del Este, competition, research data, and the lore surrounding the resort. After the briefing, students are guided through the development of a four-part campaign recommendation for their client. They will create (1) a generalized communications statement complete with objectives and a strategy for segmentation, targeting, and product positioning; (2) a copy platform with their recommendations for TV and magazine ads; (3) a media plan, including interactive media; and (4) a promotion plan for travel industry intermediaries and travel consumers.

The correlating Instructor's Manual contains numerous suggestions and guidelines for the smooth implementation of this exercise into your course. It also offers suggestions for condensing the material, if you prefer a shorter exercise or one that focuses exclusively on advertising without the IMC topics.

This outstanding supplement was written by Bernard C. Jakacki of Ramapo College. In additional to writing this exercise, Professor Jakacki has tested it for years with many college students and advertising agency trainees. The response from users has been spectacular in terms of both its comprehensive content and the fun they have promoting Punta del Este. This tested and proven package is truly real-world in both orientation and design.

Campaign Planner for Promotion and IMC, 3rd Edition (0-324-32147-3). Developed by Shay Sayre, this text is designed to help students prepare and present a professional campaign in conjunction with *Advertising and Integrated Brand Promotion,* 4e. Using a 10-step guide, the Campaign Planner clearly explains the process of planning and executing a successful campaign. Acting as a simulated agency, students provide solutions for a chosen client's promotional problem. Problem solutions involve advertising, public relations, and promotional aspects to deliver a truly integrated marketing communications plan. Enhancements to the third edition include the following:

- Brand new "clients" and companies: the revised edition is up-to-date with companies that students are familiar with and can relate to, including Monster Energy Drink, Calloway Gold Equipment, Public Broadcast System, Napster Online, and more.
- Theory in Action: Simulating the real-life process agencies use to develop a campaign, the exercises allow you to see how objectives translate into strategies, and how strategies are then developed into usable tactics.
- Valuable Real-Life Experience: In order to complete their campaign, students are required to profile a target market, conduct primary and secondary research, analyze the competition, develop an industry overview, evaluate the product/service, and prepare media plans, creative strategies, and promotions.
- Guided Plans Book Development: Instructions on how to prepare and assemble a plans book provide you with important information needed to complete an end-of-term written proposal. A sample plans book appears at the back of the workbook.

http://oguinn.swlearning.com. Go online at http://oguinn.swlearning.com for additional resources, ideas, content, and lots and lots of links to great Web sites.

ACKNOWLEDGMENTS

The most pleasant task in writing a textbook is the expression of gratitude to people and institutions that have helped the authors. We appreciate the support and encouragement we received from many individuals, including the following:

- A VERY BIG thanks to a really great project manager: **Mandy Hetrick** at Lachina Publishing Services. Mandy is not only a great editor and manager, and a very smart one, but actually likes, listens to, and respects authors. She not only provided diligent editing work, but also showed a keen ability to actually understand all this stuff and provide quality substantive insights. And to her staff: copyeditor, **Christy Goldfinch;** compositor, **Carol Kurila;** art coordinator, **Pam Brossia;** and editorial assistant, **Kate Doman,** who are all excellent. We all thank you. You are the best.

- **Susan van Etten Lawson** in photo and ad research for her careful, creative, and conscientious effort. Susan is incredibly good at her job.

- **Neil Marquardt,** executive editor: Neil came on board right in the midst of revision and kept things rolling. Neil supports his authors. We thank you.

- Thank you also to production editor, **Tamborah Moore,** and developmental editor, **Mardell Toomey,** at Thomson South-Western for their efforts on this project.

- For great cover art: **Lou Beach** has created art for *The New York Times, Time,* David Bowie, Brian Eno, *The Big Lebowski,* and on and on. Lou is the hottest designer around. Thanks for the cover.

- For timely, patient, and expert computer support, and great graphics: **Barlow LeVold.**

- **Everyone at Cincinnati Bell and Northlich** who gave us tremendous help and support in creating and updating the IBP case. The updates to our IBP case in this 4th edition were made possible, first and foremost, by **Jack Cassidy,** Cincinnati Bell's President and CEO, and **Mark Serrianne,** President and CEO of Northlich. These two suberb brand builders have been generous in their support of this case and our textbook from the beginning. Two other individuls from Cincinnati Bell—**Don Daniels,** Vice President, Marketing, and **Libby Korosec,** Director of Corporate Communications—also made important contributions in updating our IBP case this time around. Thank you Don and Libby! And we must express our ongoing gratitude to all those persons who helped us create the IBP case in the first place. These include **Mike Vanderwoude,** then Director of Marketing at Cincinnati Bell, as well as the following people from Northlich: **Don Perkins,** Senior Vice President and Executive Creative Director; **Mandy Reverman,** Account Supervisor; **Mike Swainey,** Account Manager; **Scott Aaron,** Account Supervisor; **Susan Cheney,** Direct Marketing Account Supervisor; and **Jay Pioch,** Assistant Account Manager.

- **Marty Horn,** Senior Vice President, Group Director—Strategic Planning & Research, DDB-Chicago, for his thoughts and expert advice on our research chapter.
- **David Moore,** Vice President/Executive Producer at Leo Burnett, who gave us invaluable insights on the broadcast production process and helped us secure key materials for the text.
- **Kimberly Paul,** University of Texas at Austin and Intensity Designs, Austin, Texas, for her help with the creative chapters.
- **Xiaoyan Deng,** The Wharton School, University of Pennsylvania, for all her empirical efforts.
- **Ed Ackerly,** University of Arizona, for revising the test bank, assuring its accuracy and usefulness.
- **Matt Smith** of Arnold, Finnegan & Martin, for providing us with the Watermark ad and sketches in Chapter 13.
- **Peter Sheldon,** University of Illinois: Chief Exhibitionist (yes, he made us say this). Peter has contributed greatly to all four editions. He makes the book work creatively. He selected many of the ads for this book, and provided substantive editorial material and comments. Everybody says this, but in Peter's case it is really true: Without him, we couldn't have done it. He's a pro all the way. His vision, talent, and wonderful humor were our daily blessings. Thanks, Peter.
- **Professors Gray Swicegood** and **Gillian Stevens,** University of Illinois, for their help with consumer demography.
- **Cinda Robbins-Cornstubble, Janette Bradley Wright,** and **Robin Price,** University of Illinois at Urbana-Champaign, for their wonderful support and incredible competence.
- **Connie M. Johnson,** for years and years of great and loving observations about the human condition. Connie is connected to the Universe in some very special way.
- **Patrick Gavin Quinlan,** for years of great advice and best friendship.
- **Marilyn A. Boland,** for her love, creativity, smart suggestions, great questions, support, and wonderful images.
- **Martin, the 805 Group,** for his creativity and otherness.
- **David Bryan Teets,** University of Illinois, for help with the TV-commercial-director-becomes-movie-director lists and references. Dave knows film.
- **Mildred O'Guinn** (Tom's mom), who actually read every single word of the first edition and found the only misspelled word, one missed by countless computers, editors, authors, proofers, and so on: "Restritions," in Exhibit 9.16 on page 252. Very good job. Thanks.
- **Professor John Murphy II,** Joe C. Thompson Centennial Professor in Advertising at the University at Austin, who has given us great feedback and continued support. John went well beyond the call with efffort and creativity with the author interview film. John also keeps our feet on the ground. Thanks, John.
- **Steve Hall,** who supports, critiques, and gives his all to his students at The University of Illinois. Steve is a creative and gifted teacher, whose continued feedback helps us write better books for real students. Like John Murphy, Steve goes well beyond the call and is helping the team produce some really cool video projects for the fourth edition. Steve, thanks.
- **Nancy Roberts** for her office assistance, patience, and friendship.

We are also grateful to the following individuals from the business community:

Dianne Brown
Procter & Gamble

Julie Eddleman
Procter & Gamble

Roger Fishman
Creative Artists Agency

Melissa Hale
Procter & Gamble

Lauren Hellings
GJP Advertising

Jean Kendall
Lands' End

Beverly Larkin
Procter & Gamble

Greg Lechner
Luxottica Retail

Vicky Mayer
Procter & Gamble

Jackie Reau
Game Day Communications

Robyn Schroeder
Procter & Gamble

Jim Stengel
Procter & Gamble

We are particularly indebted to our reviewers—past and present—and the following individuals whose thoughtful comments, suggestions, and specific feedback shaped the content of *Advertising and Integrated Brand Promotion*. Our thanks go to:

Lynne Boles
Procter & Gamble

Anne Cunningham
University of Tennessee

Robert Dwyer
University of Cincinnati

Jon Freiden
Florida State University

Cynthia Frisby
University of Missouri–Columbia

Corliss L. Green
Georgia State University

Scott Hamula
Keuka College

Wayne Hilinski
Penn State University

E. Lincoln James
Washington State University

Karen James
Louisiana State University–Shreveport

Donald Jugenheimer
Southern Illinois University

James Kellaris
University of Cincinnati

Patricia Kennedy
University of Nebraska–Lincoln

Robert Kent
University of Delaware

Priscilla LaBarbera
New York University

William LaFief
Frostburg State University

Debbie Laverie
Texas Tech

Gail Love
California State University, Fullerton

Tina M. Lowrey
University of Texas at San Antonio

Nancy Mitchell
University of Nebraska–Lincoln

Cynthia R. Morton
University of Florida

Darrel Muehling
Washington State University

Andrew T. Norman
Iowa State

Marcella M. Norwood
University of Houston

James Pokrywczynski
Marquette University

John Purcell
Castleton State College

Joe Regruth
Procter & Gamble

Jim Rose
Bauder College

Debra Scammon
University of Utah

Kim Sheehan
University of Oregon

Alan Shields
Suffolk County Community College

Sloane Signal
University of Nebraska, Lincoln

Jan Slater
Syracuse University

Marla R. Stafford
University of Memphis

Patricia Stout
University of Texas–Austin

Lynn Walters
Texas A&M

Brian Wansink
University of Illinois

Jon P. Wardrip
University of South Carolina

Robert O. Watson
Quinnipiac University

Marc Weinberger
University of Massachusetts–Amherst

Professor Joan R. Weiss
Bucks County Community College

Gary B. Wilcox
University of Texas–Austin

Kurt Wildermuth
University of Missouri–Columbia

Christine Wright-Isak
Young & Rubicam

Molly Ziske
Michigan State University

Lara Zwarun
UT Arlington

Thomas C. O'Guinn
Chris T. Allen
Richard J. Semenik

BRIEF CONTENTS

CONTENTS

PART 2
The Planning: Analyzing the Advertising and Integrated Brand Promotion Environment   160

Chapter 6: Market Segmentation, Positioning, and the Value Proposition   210

PART 3
Preparing the Message   336

Collect all five.

Think different.

PART 4
Placing the Message in Conventional and "New" Media   480

Chapter 16: Media Planning: Advertising and IBP on the Internet   558

Delight in everyday perfection.

ELKAY. specialty collection sinks. Style that endures.

ADVERTISING
and Integrated Brand Promotion

Fourth Edition

The Process: Advertising and Integrated Brand Promotion in Business and Society

The first part of the book, "The Process: Advertising and Integrated Brand Promotion in Business and Society," sets the tone for our study of advertising. The chapters in this part of the book emphasize that advertising is much more than a wonderfully creative interpretation of important corporate marketing strategies. While it certainly serves that purpose, advertising is not just a corporate process; it is also a societal process that has evolved over time with culture, technology, and industry traditions.

To appreciate the true nature of advertising, we must first understand advertising as the complete dynamic business and social process it is. In this first part of the text, the roots of the advertising process are revealed. Advertising is defined as both a business *and* a communications process, and the structure of the industry through which modern-day advertising exists is described. The evolution of advertising is traced from modest beginnings through periods of growth and maturation. The complex and controversial social, ethical, and regulatory aspects of advertising conclude this opening part of the text.

The World of Advertising and Integrated Brand Promotion

Chapter 1, "The World of Advertising and Integrated Brand Promotion," introduces and defines advertising and the role it fulfills within a firm's overall marketing and brand promotion programs. This chapter also analyzes advertising as a marketing communications process. We introduce the concept of integrated brand promotion (IBP), which shows that firms communicate to consumers using a broad range of communications that often go far beyond advertising—sales promotion, event sponsorship, direct marketing, placing brands in movies and television programs, point-of-purchase displays, the Internet, and public relations—are used to help a firm compete effectively, to develop customer loyalty, and to generate profits.

1

The Structure of the Advertising Industry: Advertisers, Advertising Agencies, and Support Organizations

Chapter 2, "The Structure of the Advertising Industry: Advertisers, Advertising Agencies, and Support Organizations," shows that effective advertising requires the participation of a variety of organizations and specially skilled people, not just advertisers. Advertising agencies, research firms, production facilitators, designers, media companies, Web developers, public relations firms, and Internet portals are just some of the organizations that form the structure of the industry. Each plays a different role, and billions of dollars are spent every year for the services of these various participants. This chapter also highlights that the structure of the industry is in flux. New media options, like streaming video, and new types of organizations, like talent agencies, are forcing change. This chapter looks at the basic structure of the industry, the participants, and how both are evolving with the marketplace. Special attention is given to the rising prominence of promotion agencies as counterparts to advertising agencies.

2

The Evolution of Promoting and Advertising Brands

Chapter 3, "The Evolution of Promoting and Advertising Brands," sets the process of advertising and promotion into both a historical and contemporary context. Advertising has evolved and proliferated because of fundamental influences related to free enterprise, economic development, and tradition. Advertising as a business process and a reflection of social values has experienced many evolutionary periods of change as technology, business management practices, and social values have changed. Special attention is given to the evolution of technology and how new technologies are changing the development and delivery of advertising and promotion.

3

Social, Ethical, and Regulatory Aspects of Advertising

Chapter 4, "Social, Ethical, and Regulatory Aspects of Advertising," examines the broad societal aspects of advertising. From a social standpoint, we must understand that advertising has positive effects on the standard of living, addresses lifestyle needs, supports mass media, and is a contemporary art form. Critics argue that advertising wastes resources, promotes materialism, is offensive, and perpetuates stereotypes, or can make people do things they don't want to do. Ethical issues in advertising focus on truth in advertising, advertising to children, and the advertising of controversial products. Regulatory aspects highlight that while government organizations play a key role in regulating the process, nongovernment forces like consumer interest groups and societal values also put pressure on advertising to change and evolve with culture.

4

CHAPTER 1

After reading and thinking about this chapter, you will be able to do the following:

1

Know what advertising and integrated brand promotion (IBP) are and what they can do.

2

Discuss a basic model of advertising communication.

3

Describe the different ways of classifying audiences for advertising.

4

Explain the key roles of advertising as a business process.

5

Understand the concept of integrated brand promotion (IBP) and the role advertising plays in the process.

Introductory Scenario: When Does Something Free Cost $1.75 a Bottle?

The last time we checked, water still comes out freely from faucets and drinking fountains around the world. Yet the last time we checked, bottled-water brands like Aquafina and Dasani were priced at about $1.50 to $1.75 a bottle—often more than soft drinks in the same vending machine!

The bottled-water industry is truly a marvel of modern marketing, advertising, promotion, and branding. Not only has bottled water grown to be a $10 billion a year industry, but it is the fastest growing category in the beverage market—averaging double digit growth through 2005. How big is the industry other than the $10 billion in sales? It's huge on any dimension you can measure. Each year, about 1.5 billion cases of bottled water are consumed in the United States. That's about 36 billion eight-ounce bottles of water—120 bottles a year for each man, woman, and child in the United States! As the editor of *Beverage Digest* put it, "Bottled water growth over the last several years has been stunning, even shocking. . . ."[1]

What makes the dramatic growth of bottled water such a big deal? First, as we all know, water is free and yet a lot people choose to spend a lot of money for it anyway. Second, if people want their water in a bottle, you would think that they would simply buy the cheapest bottled water around, like Costco's Kirkland brand or the local grocery store brand of water. *Au contraire.* People don't just buy any bottled water. They buy *branded* bottle water that sells for a premium price, like Pepsi's Aquafina, Coca-Cola's Dasani, and Evian (see Exhibit 1.1). These premium brands aren't just a little more expensive. They usually sell for about twice as much as private-label brands like Kirkland. The top 10 branded bottled waters held 72.5 percent of the market share in the bottled water industry in 2002, a strengthening of market dominance from the 69.1 percent share they held in 2001.[2]

So why do we pay for water that we can get for free? And why do we buy more of the prominent, national brands than the less expensive private-label brands? Well, there are a lot of influences on why we are buying water instead of drinking the free stuff. First, every doctor in America is telling us to drink eight eight-ounce glasses of water a day. Second, most of us don't trust the water that comes from the tap from our local water treatment plant (how can something that smells that bad be doing anything good to the water?). Finally, when we have an urge to drink some nice cold water, we're probably closer to a vending machine or a convenience store than we are to our kitchen or a good drinking fountain.

So, in the end, drinking more bottled water might not be that hard to explain. But what's

L'original

EXHIBIT 1.1

Evian is one of the key competitors in the $10 billion bottled-water industry. http://www.evian.com

---

1.   Hillary Chura, "Water War Bubbling Among Top Brands," *Advertising Age,* July 7, 2003, 6.
2.   Hillary Chura, "Pricing Gets Slippery," *Advertising Age,* June 23, 2003, S20.

the explanation for buying high-priced bottled water as opposed to buying low-priced bottled water? Ah, herein lies the mystery and magic of the contents of this entire book—the world of advertising and integrated brand promotion. The reason you and I are inclined to buy well-known brands is that companies work hard to develop brands that have features that appeal to us and then advertise and promote those brands in such a way that we remember and like that brand better than others. Pepsi spends about $35 million per year advertising the Aquafina brand and Coke spends about $20 million advertising Dasani. That puts those brands as the number one and number two most heavily advertised brands of bottled water. Guess what? Aquafina is the leading brand in the market with about 15 percent market share, and Dasani is second with about 14 percent market share.[3]

Now it's not always true that the more you spend on advertising and promotion, the better the brand does in the market. But when a company works hard to develop a good brand *and* does a good job with the advertising and promotion, the probability increases that the brand will succeed and flourish. At this point, we will emphasize the nature of advertising and its effect on the way firms build their brands. Part Five of the text, "Integrated Brand Promotion," will go into great detail about the various other promotional tools firms use to build strong brands.

The World of Advertising.

The example of the bottled-water industry overall, and the success of Aquafina, Evian, and Dasani in particular, points to an important truth in the world of advertising—advertising is an important part of the brand-building process for a firm. And the role of advertising in communicating brand values is not reserved for big national or multinational companies like Pepsi and Coke. Marketers in organizations of all sizes and in all industries recognize the need for and invest in advertising and promotion as potent competitive tools. Company leaders appreciate that good advertising and solid brand promotion is key to driving sales and building brand value and market share.[4] For firms like Procter & Gamble (these are the folks who bring you Tide, Crest, Pringles, Folgers, and about 70 other brands) the concepts of advertising, promotion, and the brand are so central to the company that the opening of the firm's annual report starts with the company "promise": "Nearly 98,000 P&G people working in almost 80 countries worldwide make sure P&G brands live up to their promise to make everyday life just a little better."[5]

While companies believe in and rely heavily on advertising and promotion, they are not practices that the average person clearly understands or values. Most people have some significant misperceptions about the process of advertising and what it's supposed to do, what it can do, and what it can't do. But as average people, we do know what we like and want, and advertising helps expose us to brands that might meet our needs. And remember that a brand that does *not* meet our needs or is not advertised properly will not succeed. Consider the case of Cadillac. In the early 1950s, Cadillac held a stunning 75 percent share of the luxury car market. By 2001, that market share had fallen to about 9 percent—an unprecedented loss in the history of the automobile industry. What happened to the Cadillac brand? A series of product missteps (the 1986 Cimarron used a Chevy chassis and looked cheap, and the 1987 Allante sports car was slow and leaked like a sieve, as examples), confused the market's perception of the brand. And formidable competitors like Lexus and Infiniti entered the market with powerful and stylish alternatives that were effectively advertised. Now GM is reinvesting in Cadillac and has committed $4.3 billion

3.   Ibid.
4.   Clair Atkinson, "GM Ad Boss Takes Agencies to Task," *Advertising Age*, June 30, 2003, 1, 26.
5.   Procter & Gamble, "Sustaining Growth," *2003 Annual Report*, Cincinnati, Ohio, inside front cover.

WHERE PHYSICS AND METAPHYSICS CONVERGE

EXHIBIT 1.2

GM is reinvesting in the Cadillac brand with new designs and new advertising.
http://www.cadillac.com

to redesign and advertise the brand to change consumer's perceptions (see Exhibit 1.2). Advertising (featuring Led Zeppelin rock music) and effective product redesign (dramatic changes in styling and performance) are the key tools being used in revitalizing the brand.[6]

Another truth in the world of advertising is that there is no shortage of opinions about what it is and what it does. Many people think advertising deceives others, but rarely themselves. Most think it's a semi-glamorous profession, but one in which people are either morally bankrupt con artists or pathological liars. At worst, advertising is seen as hype, unfair capitalistic manipulation, banal commercial noise, mind control, postmodern voodoo, or outright deception. At best, the average person sees advertising as amusing, informative, helpful, and occasionally hip. Advertising often helps consumers see possibilities and meanings in the things they buy and in the services they use. It can connect goods and services to the culture and liberate meanings that lie below the surface. It can turn mere products into meaningful brand icons and important possessions. For example, the advertising of Doyle Dane Bernbach in the 1960s for Volkswagen (see Exhibit 1.3) helped turn an unlikely automobile into a mobile social statement.

Lemon.

EXHIBIT 1.3

Advertising can occasionally turn a mere brand into a social statement. Volkswagen used this ad in the 1960s to get consumers to replace the image of cars as "lemons" with the image of thrifty, dependable VWs.
http://www.vw.com

The truth about advertising lies somewhere between the extremes. Sometimes advertising is hard-hitting and powerful; at other times, it's boring and ineffective. Advertising can be enormously creative and entertaining, and it can be simply annoying. One thing is for sure: advertising is anything but unimportant. Advertising plays a pivotal role in world commerce and in the way we experience and live our lives. It is part of our language and our culture. It reflects the way we think about things and the way we see ourselves. It is both a complex communication process and a dynamic business process.

And, as a business process, it is relied on by companies big and small to build their brands—that is the central theme of this book. Advertising and integrated brand promotions are key to organizations' strategies designed to build awareness and preference for their brands (see Exhibit 1.4). Advertising is an important topic for you to study—so let's do that!

What Is Advertising? Advertising
means different things to different people. It's a business, an art, an institution, and a cultural phenomenon. To the CEO of a multinational corporation, like Pepsi, advertising is

---

6.   David Welch and Gerry Khermouch, "Can GM Save An Icon?" *BusinessWeek,* April 8, 2002, 60–67; David Welch, "The Second Coming of Cadillac," *BusinessWeek,* November 24, 2003, 79–80.

©2001 American Advertising Federation. The Intel logo is used with the express written permission of Intel and is a trademark of Intel Corporation. The AAF thanks Intel Corporation for their support and participation.

advert-tising

pentium® 4

It's what makes computers more powerful.

Advertising. The way great brands get to be great brands.

EXHIBIT 1.4

The American Advertising Federation (AAF) ran this ad touting the power of advertising's effect of brand building. The AAF used the Intel logo and brand "look" for this message because Intel is regarded as one of the most successful firms in using advertising to build brand name awareness and recognition. http://www.aaf.org

an essential marketing tool that helps create brand awareness and loyalty and stimulates demand. To the owner of a small retail shop, advertising is a way to bring people into the store. To the art director in an advertising agency, advertising is the creative expression of a concept. To a media planner, advertising is the way a firm uses the mass media to communicate to current and potential customers. To scholars and museum curators, advertising is an important cultural artifact, text, and historical record. Advertising means something different to all these people. In fact, sometimes determining just what is and what is not advertising is a difficult task. Keeping that in mind, we offer this straightforward definition:

Advertising *is a paid, mass-mediated attempt to persuade.*

As direct and simple as this definition seems, it is loaded with distinctions. First, advertising is *paid* communication by a company or organization that wants its information disseminated. In advertising language, the company or organization that pays for advertising is called the **client** or **sponsor.** If a communication is *not paid for,* it's not advertising. For example, a form of promotion called *publicity* is not advertising because it is not paid for. Let's say Will Smith appears on the *Late Show with David Letterman* to promote his newest movie. Is this advertising? No, because the producer or film studio did not pay the *Late Show with David Letterman* for airtime. In this example, the show gets an interesting and popular guest, the guest star gets exposure, and the film gets plugged. Everyone is happy, but no advertising took place—it might be public relations, but it is not advertising. But when the film studio produces and runs ads for the newest Will Smith movie on television and in newspapers across the country, this communication is paid for by the studio, it is placed in media to reach consumers, and therefore it most definitely is advertising.

For the same reason, public service announcements (PSAs) are not advertising either. True, they look like ads and sound like ads, but they are not ads. They are not commercial in the way an ad is because they are not paid for like an ad. They are offered as information in the public (noncommercial) interest. When you hear a message on the radio that implores you to "Just Say No" to drugs, this sounds very much like an ad, but it is a PSA. Simply put, PSAs are excluded from the definition of advertising because they are unpaid communication.

Consider the two messages in Exhibits 1.5 and 1.6. These two messages have similar copy and offer similar advice. Exhibit 1.5 has persuasive intent, is paid-for communication, and appears in the mass media. It is an advertisement. Exhibit 1.6 also has persuasive intent and appears in mass media outlets, but it is not advertising because it is not paid-for communication. PSAs are important and often strongly imitate their commercial cousins.

Second, advertising is *mass mediated.* This means it is delivered through a communication medium designed to reach more than one person, typically a large number—or mass—of people. Advertising is widely disseminated through familiar means—television, radio, newspapers, and magazines—and other media such as

The messages in Exhibits 1.5 and 1.6 communicate nearly identical information to the audience, but one is an advertisement and one is not. The message in Exhibit 1.5, sponsored by Trojan, is an advertisement because it is paid-for communication. The message in Exhibit 1.6, sponsored by the U.K.'s Health Education Authority, has a persuasive intent similar to the Trojan ad, but it is not advertising—Exhibit 1.6 is a PSA. Why isn't the Health Education Authority PSA message an ad?
http://www.trojancondoms.com

direct mail, billboards, the Internet, and CD-ROMs. The mass-mediated nature of advertising creates a communication environment where the message is not delivered in a face-to-face manner. This distinguishes advertising from personal selling as a form of communication.

Third, all advertising includes an *attempt to persuade*. To put it bluntly, ads are communications designed to get someone to do something. Even an advertisement with a stated objective of being purely informational still has persuasion at its core. The ad informs the consumer for some purpose, and that purpose is to get the consumer to like the brand and because of that liking to eventually buy the brand. Consider the Pur water filter ad in Exhibit 1.7. It doesn't carry a lot of product information. But it's interesting and most of us would say, "Yeah, I like that ad." With that reaction, this ad is persuasive. In the absence of a persuasive intent, a communication might be news, but it would not be advertising.

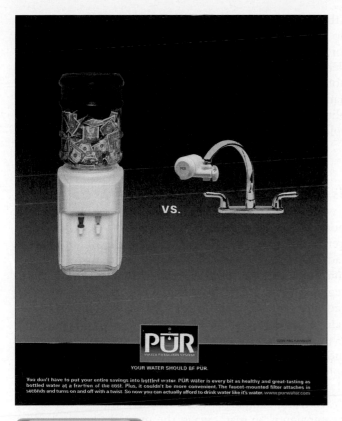

EXHIBIT 1.7

In order for a communication to be advertising it has to have a persuasive intent. Even though this PUR water filter ad is not overtly persuasive, the fact that it is interesting creates a positive reaction in the audience, which can persuade people to try the brand. http://www.purwater.com

At this point, we can say that for a communication to be classified as advertising, three essential criteria must be met:

1. The communication must be *paid for*.
2. The communication must be delivered to an audience via *mass media*.
3. The communication must be *attempting persuasion*.

It is important to note here that advertising can be persuasive communication not only about a product or service but also about an idea, a person, or an entire organization. When Colgate and Honda use advertising, this is product advertising and meets all three criteria. Likewise, when E-Trade, Delta Air Lines, Terminix, or your dentist runs advertisements, it is service advertising and meets all three criteria.

But what about political advertising? Political ads "sell" candidates rather than commercial goods or services. Political advertisements may seem special because they are the only completely unregulated form of advertising; they are viewed as "political speech" and thus enjoy complete First Amendment protection. Still, political advertising meets our definition because it is paid-for communication, is mass mediated, and has a persuasive intent. Not only does political advertising pass the definition test, but strategists also see advertising as a "brand" building process for political candidates.[7]

Consider political advertising represented by the Kerry and Edwards campaign effort (Exhibit 1.8).

EXHIBIT 1.8

The Kerry and Edwards presidential campaign uses advertising and promotion to promote ideas. This meets the definitional test for advertising in general—the ads are paid-for communications, are placed in mass media, and have a persuasive intent.

7. Erin Strout, "The Branding of a President," *Sales & Marketing Management*, October 2000, 54–62.

Although political ads, like those used in the Kerry and Edwards campaign in the 2004 presidential election, do not ask anyone to buy anything (in terms of spending money), they are (1) paid for, (2) placed in a mass medium, and (3) an attempt to persuade members of the electorate to view Kerry and Edwards and their agenda favorably. They represent another way advertising can persuade beyond the purchase of products and services. Many political candidates, environmental groups, human rights organizations, and political groups buy advertising and distribute it through mass media to persuade people to accept their way of thinking. They, too, are selling something.

Advertising, Advertisements, Advertising Campaigns, and Integrated Brand Promotion.

Now that we have a working definition of advertising, we turn our attention to other important distinctions in advertising. Let's start with the basics. An **advertisement** refers to a specific message that someone or some organization has placed to persuade an audience. An **advertising campaign** is a series of coordinated advertisements and other promotional efforts that communicate a reasonably cohesive and integrated theme. The theme may be made up of several claims or points but should advance an essentially singular theme. Successful advertising campaigns can be developed around a single advertisement placed in multiple media, or they can be made up of several different advertisements (more typically) with a similar look, feel, and message. You are probably familiar with the "Got Milk" campaign as an example. Another example is represented by the Lee Casuals ads in Exhibits 1.9 through 1.12. Notice the excellent use of similar look and feel in this advertising campaign. Advertising campaigns can run for a few weeks or for many years. The advertising campaign is, in many ways, the most challenging aspect of advertising execution. It requires a keen sense of the complex environments within which an advertiser must communicate to different audiences.

And think about this important aspect of advertising campaigns. Most individual ads would make little sense without the knowledge that audience members have accumulated from previous ads for a particular brand. Ads are interpreted by consumers through their experiences with a brand and previous ads for the brand. When you see a new Nike ad, you make sense of the ad through your history with Nike and its previous advertising. Even ads for a new brand or a new product are situated within audiences' broader knowledge of products, brands, and advertising. After years of viewing ads and buying brands, audiences bring a rich history and knowledge base to every communications encounter.

Related to advertising, but a bigger issue, is integrated brand promotion. **Integrated brand promotion** (IBP) is the use of many promotional tools, including advertising, in a coordinated manner to build and then maintain brand awareness, identity, and preference. When marketers combine contests, a Web site, event sponsorship, and point-of-purchase displays with advertising, this creates an integrated brand promotion. BMW did just that when the firm (re-) introduced the Mini Cooper auto to the U.S. market. The IBP campaign used billboards, print ads, an interactive Web site, and "guerrilla" marketing (a Mini was mounted on top of a Chevy Suburban and driven around New York City). Each part of the campaign was coordinated with all the others.[8] Note that the word *coordinated* is central to this definition. Without coordination among these various promotional efforts, there is not an integrated brand promotion. Rather, the consumer will merely encounter a series of unrelated (and often confusing) communications about a brand.

Integrated brand promotion will be a key concept throughout our discussion of advertising. The fact that this phrase is included in the title of the book signals its importance to the contemporary advertising effort. Make no mistake, all of marketing,

---

8.   John Gaffney, "Most Innovative Campaign," *Business 2.0*, May 2002, 98–99.

EXHIBITS 1.9 THROUGH 1.12

A well-conceived and well-executed advertising campaign offers consumers a series of messages with a similar look and feel. This series of ads for Lee Casuals is an excellent example of a campaign that communicates with similar images to create a unified look and feel. http://www.leejeans.com

including the advertising effort, is about brand building. As consumers encounter a daily blitz of commercial messages and appeals, brands and brand identity offer them a way to cope with the overload of information. Brands and the images they project allow consumers to quickly identify and evaluate the relevance of a brand to their lives and value systems. The marketer who does not use advertising and integrated brand promotion as a way to build brand meaning for consumers will, frankly, be ignored. We will develop this concept of integrated brand promotion throughout the text and demonstrate how advertising is central to the process. The encounters between consumers and advertisements, advertising campaigns, and integrated brand promotion underlie the discussion of our next topic.

2 Advertising as a Communication Process.

Communication is a fundamental aspect of human existence, and advertising is communication. To understand advertising at all, you must understand something about communication in general and about mass communication in particular. At the outset, it's important to understand the basics of how advertising works as a means of communication. To help with gaining this understanding, let's consider a contemporary model of mass communication. We'll apply this basic model of communication as a first step toward understanding advertising.

A Model of Mass-Mediated Communication.

As we said earlier, advertising is mass-mediated communication; it occurs, not face-to-face, but through a medium (such as radio, magazines, television, or a computer). While there are many valuable models of mass communication, a contemporary model of mass-mediated communication is presented in Exhibit 1.13. This model shows mass communication as a process where people, institutions, and messages interact. It has two major components, each representing quasi-independent processes: production and reception. Between production and reception are the mediating (interpretation) processes of accommodation and negotiation. It's not as complex as it sounds. Let's investigate each part of the model.

Moving from left to right in the model, we first see the process of communication production, where the content of any mass communication is produced. An advertisement, like other forms of mass communication, is the product of institutions (such as networks, corporations, advertising agencies, and governments) interacting to produce content (what physically appears on a page as a print ad, or on a videotape as a television ad, or on a computer screen at a company's Web site). The creation of the advertisement is a complex interaction of the advertiser's message; the advertiser's expectations about the target audience's desire for information; the advertiser's assumptions about how the audience will interpret the words and images

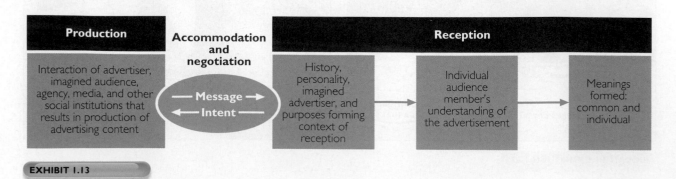

EXHIBIT 1.13

A model of mass-mediated communication

This ad is a good example of how the meaning of an ad can vary for different people. How would you interpret the meaning of this ad? Think of someone very different from you. What meaning might that person give this ad?
http://www.cocacola.com

in an ad; and the rules and regulations of the medium that transmits the message. Advertising is rarely (if ever) the product of any one individual. Rather, as this model shows, it is a collaborative (social) product between people receiving a message and the institutions (advertisers and media companies) that send them that message.

Continuing on to the right, we see that the mediating processes of accommodation and negotiation lie between the production and reception phases. Accommodation and negotiation are the ways in which consumers interpret ads. Audience members have some ideas about how the advertiser wants them to interpret the ad (we all know the rules of advertising—somebody is trying to persuade us to buy something). And consumers also have their own needs, agendas, and preferred interpretations. They also know about the way other consumers think about this product and this message, because brands have personalities and send social signals. Given all this, consumers who see an ad arrive at an interpretation of the ad that makes sense to them, serves their needs, and fits their personal history with a product category and a brand.

What's interesting about the whole progression of consumer receipt and interpretation of an ad is that it is usually wholly *incompatible* with the way the advertiser wanted consumers to see the ad! In other words, the receivers of the ad must *accommodate* these competing forces, meanings, and agendas and then *negotiate* a meaning, or an interpretation, of the ad. That's why we say that communication is inherently a *social* process: What a message means to any given consumer is a function, not of an isolated solitary thinker, but of an inherently social being responding to what he or she knows about the producers of the message (the advertisers), other receivers of it (peer groups, for example), and the social world in which the brand and the message about it resides. Now, admittedly, all this interpretation happens very fast and without much contemplation. Still, it happens. The level of conscious interpretation might be minimal (mere recognition) or it might be extensive (thoughtful, elaborate processing of an ad), but there is *always* interpretation.

It has to be emphasized that the processes of production and reception are partially independent. Although the producers of a message can control the placement of an ad in a medium, they cannot control or even closely monitor the circumstances that surround reception and interpretation of the ad. Audience members are exposed to advertising outside the direct observation of the advertiser and are capable of interpreting advertising any way they want. (Of course, most audience interpretations are not completely off the wall, either.) Likewise, audience members have little control over or input into the actual production of the message—the advertiser developed a message that audience members are *supposed* to like. Because of these aspects of communication, the model shows that both producers and receivers are thus "imagined," in the sense that the two don't have significant direct contact with each another but have a general sense of what the other is like.

The communication model in Exhibit 1.13 underscores a critical point: No ad contains a single meaning for all audience members. An ad for a pair of women's shoes means something different for women than it does for men. An ad that achieved widespread popularity (and controversy) is the ad for Diet Coke shown in Exhibit 1.14, which may be interpreted differently by men and women. For example, does the ad suggest that men drink Diet Coke so they can be the object of intense daily admiration by a group of female office workers? Or does the ad suggest that Diet Coke is a part of a modern woman's lifestyle, granting her "permission" to freely admire attractive men in the same way women have been eyed by male construction workers (or executives) for years? The audience decides. Keep in mind that although individual audience members' interpretations will differ to some extent, they may be close enough to the advertiser's intent to make the ad effective. When members of an audience are similar in their background, social standing, and goals, they generally yield similar enough meaning from an ad for it to accomplish its goals.

③ The Audiences for Advertising.

We've been referring to audiences, so now it's time to define them. In the language of advertising, an **audience** is a group of individuals who receive and interpret messages sent from advertisers through mass media. The audience could be made up of household consumers, college students, or business people. Any large group of people can be an audience. A **target audience** is a particular group of consumers singled out by an organization for an advertisement or advertising campaign. These target audiences are singled out for advertisements because the advertiser has discovered that audience members like or might like the product category being advertised. Target audiences are always *potential* audiences because advertisers can never be sure that the message will actually get through to them as intended. By the way, there is nothing sinister about the targeting process. Targeting audiences simply means that a company wants to reach you with a message. Do you feel like something bad happens to you when the Gap targets you with an ad and you see it on TV? Of course not! Somewhere along the line the word *targeting* and the phrase *target audience* have picked up some negative connotations—ignore them.

While advertisers can identify dozens of different target audiences, five broad audience categories are commonly described: household consumers, members of business organizations, members of a trade channel, professionals, and government officials and employees.

Audience Categories.

Household consumers are the most conspicuous audience in that most mass media advertising is directed at them. McDonald's, Nissan, Miller Brewing, the Gap, and AIG Insurance have products and services designed for the consumer market, and so their advertising targets household consumers. The most recent information indicates that there are about 109 million households in the United States and approximately 292 million household consumers.[9] Total yearly retail spending by these households is about $5.5 trillion in the United States.[10] This huge audience is typically where the action is in advertising. Under the very broad heading of "consumer advertising," very fine audience distinctions can be made by advertisers. A target audience definition such as men, 25 to 45, living in metropolitan areas, with incomes greater than $50,000 per year would be the kind of target audience description an advertiser might develop.

Members of business organizations are the focus of advertising for firms that produce business and industrial goods and services, such as office equipment, production machinery, supplies, and software. While products and services targeted to this audience often require personal selling, advertising is used to create an awareness and a favorable attitude among potential buyers. Not-for-profit businesses such

---

9.   "2004 Survey of Buying Power," *Sales and Marketing Management* (2004), 10, 15, 16.
10.   Ibid., 19.

THEY COME TO YOUR SITE LOOKING FOR SOMETHING DIFFERENT. GIVE IT TO THEM.

Everybody's different. When you know your customers—what they need, what they like and what may be of interest to them in the future—it's a lot easier to give them what they're looking for. Blue Martini has the power to make it all happen. Our applications analyze customer information, then deliver a highly personalized experience based on that analysis. The time spent interacting with your company is more relevant. It's quicker. And it's far more likely to produce a sale. To find out how Blue Martini's e-business solutions can improve your customer's experience, visit www.bluemartini.com/prism.

BLUE MARTINI
SOFTWARE

EXHIBIT 1.15

When members of business organizations use advertising to communicate, the ads often emphasize creating awareness of the company's brand name. Blue Martini, a software firm, is using high visual appeal to accomplish brand name recognition. http:// www.bluemartini.com

as universities, some research laboratories, philanthropic groups, and cultural organizations represent an important and separate business audience for advertising. Exhibit 1.15 is an example of an ad directed at members of business organizations. Blue Martini Software sells systems used by companies to cut sales costs and improve customer and channel loyalty.

Members of a trade channel include retailers, wholesalers, and distributors. They are a target audience for producers of both household and business goods and services. So, for example, if Microsoft cannot gain adequate retail and wholesale distribution through trade channels for the Xbox, the brand will not reach target customers. That being the case, it's important to direct advertising at the trade level of the market. Various forms of advertising and promotion can be used to develop demand among members of a trade channel. The promotional tool used most often to communicate with this group is personal selling. This is because this target audience represents a relatively small, easily identifiable group that can be reached with personal selling. When advertising is also directed at this target audience, it can serve an extremely useful purpose, as we will see later in the section on advertising as a business process.

Professionals form a special target audience and are defined as doctors, lawyers, accountants, teachers, or any other professional group that has special training or certification. This audience warrants a separate classification because its members have specialized needs and interests. Advertising directed to professionals typically highlights products and services uniquely designed to serve their more narrowly defined needs. The language and images used in advertising to this target audience often rely on esoteric terminology and unique circumstances that members of professions readily recognize. Advertising to professionals is predominantly carried out through trade publications. **Trade journals** are magazines published specifically for members of a trade and carry highly technical articles.

Government officials and employees constitute an audience in themselves due to the large dollar volume of buying that federal, state, and local governments do. Government organizations from universities to road maintenance operations buy huge amounts of various types of products. Producers of items such as office furniture, construction materials, vehicles, fertilizers, computers, and business services all target government organizations with advertising. Advertising to this target audience is dominated by direct mail, catalogs, and Web advertising.

Audience Geography. Audiences can also be broken down by geographic location. Because of cultural differences that often accompany geographic location, very few ads can be effective for all consumers worldwide. If an ad is used worldwide with only minor changes it is called **global advertising.** Very few ads can use global advertising. These are typically brands that are considered citizens of the world and whose manner of use does not vary tremendously by culture. Using a Sony television or a taking a trip on Singapore Airlines doesn't change much from culture to culture and

EXHIBITS 1.16 AND 1.17

Global advertising can be used for brands where there is little difference in use across cultures or geographic location. The only real difference in these two ads is language (German versus Italian), while other aspects—Rolex's appeal to an affluent elite who likely follow tennis and the Rolex brand imagery—remain the same. An interesting twist with Rolex is that it uses a Web site to describe, but not sell, its products (http://www.rolex.com). Instead, the Web site directs surfers to the retailers who carry the brand. Is the Web likely to be Rolex's best advertising channel, anyway?

geographic location to geographic location. Exhibits 1.16 and 1.17 show extremely similar appeals in two different ads for Rolex watches—another product category where product use across cultures is the same. Firms that market brands with global appeal, like Singapore Airlines, IBM, Sony, and Pirelli Tires, try to develop and place advertisements with a common theme and presentation in all markets around the world where the firm's brands are sold. Global placement is possible only when a brand and the messages about that brand have a common appeal across diverse cultures. Motorola had its agency, McCann-Erickson Worldwide, prepare global ads for its cell phones and pagers; their strategy is discussed in the Global Issues box. Note in this issues box that Motorola focused on the brand rather than product or technology issues as a way to appeal to the target market.

International advertising occurs when firms prepare and place different advertising in different national markets outside their home market. Each international market often requires unique or original advertising due to product adaptations or message appeals tailored specifically for that market. Unilever prepares different versions of ads for its laundry products for nearly every international market because consumers in different cultures approach the laundry task differently. Consumers in the United States use large and powerful washers and dryers and lots of hot water. Households in Brazil use very little hot water and hang clothes out to dry. Very few

GLOBAL ISSUES

Try This One on for Size

Here's a challenge of global proportions. Image that it is your job to develop the advertising for a retail store that sells women's lingerie. This shouldn't be too hard. After all, Victoria's Secret has done a great job with bold television advertising featuring Tyra Banks and Gisele Bundchen, not to mention those direct mail catalogs. It's a product category that's showing strong growth and is colorful and diverse visually, and the media are loosening up on restrictions for visuals.

Well, there is one other little detail that might make this a bit more difficult. The retail lingerie store's name is Al Mashat and it is located in Saudi Arabia. So, you ask? Lingerie is lingerie and women are women. That may be true, but Saudi Arabia is also Saudi Arabia and in Saudi Arabia the detail that is most problematic was well articulated by Margo Chase, founder and executive director of Chase Design Group design consulting firm: "The really huge problem is how to market lingerie in a country where you can't show photographs of women." Not being able to show women in lingerie is a somewhat important detail that would make this just a bit more difficult.

So, what *would* you do in a situation like this? One thing is for sure, there is no way that the religious culture of Saudi Arabia and the media restrictions it creates are going to change just because some retail store wants to more effectively advertise. But here are some details that might help you out: Saudi Arabia has an extremely young population, with 42.4 percent being under the age of 15. Additionally, shopping is one of the few recreations available to Saudi women. Finally, Saudi women are fascinated with all things French.

Have you figured out an advertising strategy yet? Well, let's take a look at what the U.S. consulting firm Chase Design Group came up with for advertising for Al Mashat. First, the design firm decided that if they could not use the images of women, then the advertising campaign would be carried by "language that was rich, textured, layered, and sensual." An example of the language was a poem featured both in advertising and store banners: "Wrap this beautiful robe of words around you and dream." Second, to carry through on the force of the language, a special font and characters were developed. Finally, advertising was launched using print ads, radio ads, and a direct mail piece featuring bags imprinted with the store logo and filled with potpourri and an invitation card printed on iridescent pearl-colored paper. As a follow-up, another direct mail campaign mailed out gift vouchers worth 50 riyals (about $13) to prospective customers.

How did it all work out? In the first year of the store's operations more than $3.2 million in revenue was generated. The owner expects revenue to grow to $5 million in the store's second full year.

The lesson here is that in global markets, any number of unique circumstances can restrict the way we might use advertising. But the other lesson is that even though there may be what seem to be huge barriers (like not showing women in ads for a product designed exclusively for women), the breadth and creativity of advertising can be used to overcome such barriers.

Source: Arundhati Parmar, "Out from Under," *Marketing News*, July 21, 2003.

firms enjoy the luxury of having a brand with truly cross-cultural appeal and global recognition as discussed in the previous section on global advertising.

National advertising reaches all geographic areas of one nation. National advertising is the term typically used to describe the kind of advertising we see most often in the mass media in the domestic U.S. market. Does international advertising use many different national advertising efforts? Yes, that is exactly the relationship between international advertising and national advertising.

Regional advertising is carried out by producers, wholesalers, distributors, and retailers that concentrate their efforts in a relatively large, but not national, geographic region. Albertson's, a regional grocery chain, has stores in 31 western, northwestern, midwestern, and southern states. Because of the nature of the firm's regional markets, it places advertising only in regions where it has stores.

Local advertising is much the same as regional advertising. **Local advertising** is directed at an audience in a single trading area, either a city or state. Exhibit 1.18 shows an example of this type of advertising. Daffy's is a discount clothing retailer with stores in the New York/New Jersey metropolitan area. Retailers with local markets like Daffy's use all types of local media to reach customers. Under special circumstances, national advertisers will share advertising expenses in a market with local dealers to achieve specific advertising objectives. This sharing of advertising expenses between national advertisers and local merchants is called **cooperative advertising** (or **co-op advertising**). Exhibit 1.19 illustrates a co-op advertisement run by TUMI luggage and one of its retailers, Shapiro. In a key strategy move several years ago, General Motors redesigned its co-op advertising program with dealers in an attempt to create a more fully coordinated integrated brand promotion.[11]

---

11.   Joe Miller, "Dealers Regain Ad Input as GM Revives Program," *Advertising Age*, October 16, 2000, 80.

EXHIBIT 1.18

Daffy's (http://www.daffys.com) is a clothing retailer with 12 shops in the New York/New Jersey metropolitan area. It services a local geographic market. Retailers that serve a small geographic area use local advertising to reach their customers and typically rely on newspaper and radio ads to reach their local target market.

EXHIBIT 1.19

National advertisers will often share advertising expenses with local retail merchants if the retailer features the advertiser's brand in local advertising. This sharing of expenses is called co-op advertising. Here a local retailer, Shapiro Luggage, is featuring TUMI brand luggage in this co-op ad. http://www.tumi.com

4 Advertising as a Business Process.
So far we have talked about advertising as a communication process and as a way companies reach diverse audiences with persuasive brand information. But we need to appreciate another aspect of advertising. Advertising is very much a business process as well as a communication process. For multinational organizations like Microsoft, as well as for small local retailers, advertising is a basic business tool that helps them communicate with current and potential customers. We need to understand advertising as a business process in three ways. First, we'll consider the role advertising plays in the overall marketing and brand promotion programs in firms. Second, we will look at the types of advertising used by firms. Finally, we will take a broader look at advertising by identifying the economic effects of the process.

The Role of Advertising in Marketing and Integrated Brand Promotion. To truly appreciate advertising as a business process, we have to understand the role advertising plays in a firm's marketing and integrated brand promotion effort. As the introductory scenario so clearly demonstrated, effective advertising as part of an overall integrated brand promotion is a key factor in the success of brands.

To begin with, realize that every organization *must* make marketing decisions. There simply is no escaping the need to develop brands, price them, distribute them, and advertise and promote them to a target audience. The role of advertising and brand promotion relates to four important aspects of the marketing process: (1) the marketing mix; (2) brand development and management; (3) achieving effective market segmentation, differentiation, and positioning; and (4) contributing to revenue and profit generation.

The Role of Advertising in the Marketing Mix. A formal definition of marketing reveals that advertising (as a part of overall promotion) is one of the primary marketing tools available to any organization:

Marketing *is the process of planning and executing the conception, pricing, promotion, and distribution of ideas, goods, and services to create exchanges that satisfy individual and organizational objectives.*[12]

Marketing people assume a wide range of responsibilities in an organization related to conceiving, pricing, promoting, and distributing goods, services, and even ideas. Many of you know that these four areas of responsibility and decision making in marketing are referred to as the **marketing mix.** The word *mix* is used to describe the blend of strategic emphasis on the product versus its price versus its promotion (including advertising) versus its distribution when a brand is marketed to consumers. This blend, or mix, results in the overall marketing program for a brand. Advertising is important, but it is only one of the major areas of marketing responsibility *and* it is only one of many different promotional tools relied on in the marketing mix.

Generally speaking, the role of advertising in the marketing mix is to focus on the ability of advertising to communicate to a target audience the value a brand has to offer. Value consists of more than simply the tangible aspects of the brand itself, though. Indeed, consumers look for value in the brand, but they also demand such things as convenient location, credit terms, warranties and guarantees, and delivery. In addition, a wide range of emotional values such as security, belonging, affiliation, excitement, and prestige can also be pursued in the brand choice process. If you have any doubts that emotion plays a role, think about the fact that a $10,000 Dodge Neon can get you from one place to another in pretty much the same way as an $80,000 BMW M5. Well, maybe without the same thrill and style—but that's the point. People look for more than function in a brand; they often buy the emotional kick that a brand and its features provide.

Because of consumers' search for such diverse values, marketers must determine which marketing-mix ingredients to emphasize and how to blend the mix elements in just the right way to attract and satisfy customers. These marketing mix decisions play a significant role in determining the message content and media placement of advertising.

Exhibit 1.20 lists factors typically considered in each area of the marketing mix. You can see that decisions under each of the marketing mix areas can directly affect the advertising message. The important point is that a firm's advertising effort must be consistent with and complement the overall marketing mix strategy being used by a firm.

The Role of Advertising in Brand Development and Management. One of the key issues to understand about the role of advertising is that it plays a critical role in brand development and management. We have been referring to the brand and integrated brand promotion throughout our discussion of the process of advertising so far. All of us have our own understanding of what a brand is. After all, we buy brands everyday. A formal definition of a **brand** is a name, term, sign, symbol, or any other feature that identifies one seller's good or service as distinct from those of other sellers. Advertising plays a significant role in brand development and management. A brand is in many ways the most precious business asset owned by a firm. It allows a firm to communicate consistently and efficiently with the market.[13]

---

12.   This definition of marketing was approved in 1995 by the American Marketing Association (http://www.marketingpower.com) and remains the official definition offered by the organization.

13.   Peter D. Bennett, *Dictionary of Marketing Terms,* 2nd ed. (Chicago: American Marketing Association, 1995), 4.

These are the factors that an organization needs to consider in creating a marketing mix. Advertising messages and media placement must be consistent with and complement strategies in all the other areas of the marketing mix.

Product	Promotion
Functional features	Amount and type of advertising
Aesthetic design	Number and qualifications of salespeople
Accompanying services	Extent and type of personal selling program
Instructions for use	Sales promotion—coupons, contests, sweepstakes
Warranty	Trade shows
Product differentiation	Public relations activities
Product positioning	Direct mail or telemarketing
	Event sponsorships
	Internet communications

Price	Distribution
Level:	Number of retail outlets
Top of the line	Location of retail outlets
Competitive, average prices	Types of retail outlets
Low-price policy	Catalog sales
Terms offered:	Other nonstore retail methods—Internet
Cash only	Number and type of wholesalers
Credit:	Inventories—extent and location
Extended	Services provided by distribution:
Restricted	Credit
Interest charges	Delivery
Lease/rental	Installation
	Training

BusinessWeek magazine in conjunction with Interbrand, a marketing analysis and consulting firm, has attached a dollar value to brand names based on a combination of sales, earnings, future sales potential and intangibles other than the brand that drive sales. The 20 most valuable brands in the world in 2004 are shown in Exhibit 1.21. Often, the brand name is worth much more than the annual sales of the brand. Coca-Cola, the most valuable brand in the world, is estimated to be worth about $67 billion even though sales of branded Coca-Cola products are only about $20 billion a year.

A brand can be put at a serious competitive disadvantage without effective communication provided by advertising. In fact, managers at ConAgra came to the startling realization that while they were doing a good job of using advertising to develop and manage the Marie Callender line of frozen entrées, they had "let the Healthy Choice brand wither on the vine."[14] To rectify that mistake, ConAgra invested $40 million in advertising for the more than 300 items in the Healthy Choice product line.

For every organization, advertising effects brand development and management in five important ways.

14. Stephanie Thompson, "ConAgra Cooks Up Stronger Identity," *Advertising Age,* November 6, 2000, 42.

EXHIBIT 1.21

The World's 20 Most
Valuable Brands in 2004

Rank	Brand	Brand Value 2004 (U.S. billions)	Brand Value 2003 (U.S. billions)	% Change
1	Coca-Cola	$67.39	$70.45	−4%
2	Microsoft	61.37	65.14	−6
3	IBM	53.79	51.76	4
4	GE	44.11	42.34	4
5	Intel	33.49	31.11	8
6	Disney	27.11	28.03	−3
7	McDonald's	25.00	24.69	1
8	Nokia	24.04	29.44	−18
9	Toyota	22.67	20.78	9
10	Marlboro	22.12	22.18	0
11	Mercedes	21.33	21.37	0
12	Hewlett-Packard	20.78	21.37	6
13	Citibank	19.97	18.57	8
14	American Express	17.68	16.83	5
15	Gillette	16.72	15.97	5
16	Cisco Systems	15.94	15.78	1
17	BMW	15.88	15.10	5
18	Honda	14.87	15.62	−5
19	Ford	14.47	17.06	−15
20	Sony	12.75	13.15	−3

Source: *Business Week,* August 2, 2004, 64–71.

Information and Persuasion. Target audiences learn about a brand's features and benefits through the message content of advertising and, to a lesser extent, other promotional tools (most other promotional tools, except the Web, are not heavy on content) that are used in the integrated brand promotion effort. But advertising has the best capability to inform or persuade target audiences about the values a brand has to offer. No other variable in the marketing mix is designed to accomplish this communication. As an example, persuasive brand communication is particularly competitive in the credit card market, where consumers often perceive no difference between services offered by one firm and another. Analysts agree that branding is crucially important in the multibillion dollar cell phone market as Verizon, Cellular One, AT&T, and Cingular compete for 150 million wireless subscribers.[15] In many ways, marketing and advertising a cellular service brand is much like marketing and advertising the bottled-water brands highlighted at the beginning of the chapter. One cell phone works just like another and there are plenty of alternatives.

Introduction of New Brand or Brand Extensions. Advertising is absolutely critical when organizations introduce a new brand or extensions of existing brands to the

15. Alice Z. Cuneo, "Cell Giants Plot $1.5B Ad Bonanza," *Advertising Age,* October 6, 2003, 1, 44.

Disney Color.

Magic by the gallon.

Visit the Disney Color display for a full selection of quality paints,

easy-to-use accessories and creative decorating ideas.

Call 888-304-DSNY for a Disney Color retailer near you.

EXHIBIT 1.22

Advertising helps companies with brand extension strategies. Here, the famous Disney brand name is being used as the company extends the brand name into paint products. How would you describe Yahoo! Shopping (http://www.shopping yahoo.com) in terms of brand extension strategy? What value does the widely recognized nature of these brand names lend to the extension process?

market. A **brand extension** is an adaptation of an existing brand to a new product area. For example, the Snickers Ice Cream Bar is a brand extension of the original Snickers candy bar, and Ivory Shampoo is a brand extension of Ivory Dishwashing Liquid. When brand extensions are brought to market, advertising and integrated brand promotion play a key role in attracting attention to the brand—so much so that researchers now suggest that "managers should favor the brand extension with a greater allocation of the ad budget.[16] This is often accomplished with advertising working in conjunction with other promotional activities such as sales promotions and point-of-purchase displays. Mars (famous for candy) invested heavily in advertising and promotion when it extended the Uncle Ben's Rice brand into ready-to-eat microwave Rice Bowls of all varieties, including Italian, Mexican, and Chinese.[17] Exhibit 1.22 shows another example of advertising being used to extend a famous brand name into a totally different product category.

Building and Maintaining Brand Loyalty among Consumers. Loyalty to a brand is one of the most important assets a firm can have. **Brand loyalty** occurs when a consumer repeatedly purchases the same brand to the exclusion of competitors' brands. This loyalty can result because of habit, because brand names are prominent in the consumer's memory, because of barely conscious associations with brand images, or because consumers have attached some fairly deep meanings to the brands they buy.

While brand features are the most important influence on building and maintaining brand loyalty, advertising plays a key role in the process as well. Advertising reminds consumers of the values—tangible and intangible—of the brand. Advertising and integrated brand promotions often provide an extra incentive to consumers to remain brand loyal. Direct marketing can tailor communications to existing customers. Other promotional tools can offer similarly valuable communications that will help build and strengthen lasting and positive associations with a brand—such as a frequent-flyer or frequent-buyer program. When a firm creates and maintains positive associations with the brand in the mind of consumers, the firm has developed **brand equity**.[18] While brand equity occurs over long periods of time, short-term advertising and promotional activities are key to long-term success.[19] This advertising fact of life became clear to strategists at food giant Kraft as it devised a strategy to defend its Kraft Miracle Whip brand against a new campaign by competitor Unilever for Imperial Whip. In order to protect Miracle Whip's $229 million in sales and brand equity with consumers, Kraft invested heavily in television advertising just before Unilever lowered prices on the Imperial Whip brand.[20]

16.   Douglas W. Vorhies, "Brand Extension Helps Parent Gain Influence," *Marketing News,* January 20, 2003, 25.
17.   Stephanie Thompson, "The Bowl Is Where It's At for New Frozen Meal Lines," *Advertising Age,* August 14, 2000, 4.
18.   Kevin L. Keller, *Strategic Brand Management: Building, Measuring, and Managing Brand Equity* (Upper Saddle River, N.J.: Prentice Hall, 1998), 2.
19.   Keller, "Conceptualizing, Measuring, and Managing Customer-Based Brand Equity," *Journal of Marketing,* vol. 57 (January 1993), 4.
20.   Stephanie Thompson, "Kraft Counters Unilever Launch," *Advertising Age,* August 25, 2003, 4.

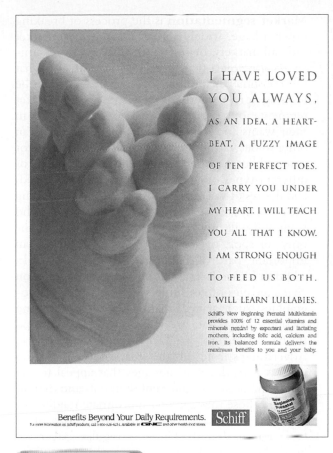

I HAVE LOVED
YOU ALWAYS,
AS AN IDEA, A HEART-
BEAT, A FUZZY IMAGE
OF TEN PERFECT TOES.
I CARRY YOU UNDER
MY HEART. I WILL TEACH
YOU ALL THAT I KNOW.
I AM STRONG ENOUGH
TO FEED US BOTH.
I WILL LEARN LULLABIES.

Schiff's New Beginning Prenatal Multivitamin
provides 100% of 12 essential vitamins and
minerals needed by expectant and lactating
mothers, including folic acid, calcium and
iron. Its balanced formula delivers the
maximum benefits to you and your baby.

Benefits Beyond Your Daily Requirements.   **Schiff**

For more information on Schiff products, call 1-800-526-6251. Available at **GNC** and other health food stores.

EXHIBIT 1.23

*The message in this Schiff ad
creates meaning for vitamins
that goes beyond the daily
nutrition role vitamins can
play. What are the many
meanings in this message
offered to consumers?*
http://www.schiffvitamins
.com

Creating an Image and Meaning for a Brand. As we
discussed in the marketing mix section, advertising
can communicate how a brand addresses certain
needs and desires and therefore plays an important
role in attracting customers to brands appear to be
useful and satisfying. But advertising can go further. It can help link a brand's image and meaning
to a consumer's social environment and to the
larger culture, and in this way actually delivers a
sense of personal connection for the consumer.

The Schiff ad for prenatal vitamins in Exhibit
1.23 is a clear example of how advertising can create an image and deeper meaning. The message in
this ad is not just about the health advantages of
using a nutritional supplement during pregnancy.
The message mines associations related to love and
caring for an unborn or recently born child. Even
the slogan for the brand, "Benefits Beyond Your
Daily Requirements," plays on the notion that a
vitamin is more than a vehicle for dosing up on
folic acid. Other promotional tools in the integrated brand promotion process, such as personal
selling, sales promotions, event sponsorship, or the
Internet, simply cannot achieve such creative
power or communicate all the potential meanings
a brand can have to a consumer.

**Building and Maintaining Brand Loyalty within the
Trade.** It might not seem as if wholesalers, retailers, distributors, and brokers would
be brand loyal, but they will favor one brand over others given the proper support
from a manufacturer. Advertising and particularly advertising integrated with other
brand promotions is an area where support can be given. Marketers can provide the
trade with sales training programs, collateral advertising materials, point-of-purchase
advertising displays, premiums (giveaways like key chains or caps), and traffic-building
special events. Exide, the battery company, spends several million dollars a year to
become the official battery of Nascar racing. Mike Dever, Exide's vice president of
marketing and product management, explains: "Both our distributors and our distributors' customers, for the most part, are race fans so it's the place we want to be."[21]

Also, remember that trade buyers (retailers, wholesalers, distributors, brokers) can
be key to the success of new brands or brand extensions, as we pointed out earlier
in the discussion of the trade market as a target audience. Marketers have little hope
of successfully introducing a brand if there is no cooperation in the trade channel
among wholesalers and retailers. This is where integrated brand promotion as a factor in advertising becomes prominent. This is because the trade is less responsive to
advertising messages than they are to other forms of promotion. Direct support to
the trade in terms of displays, contests, and other incentives combined with advertising in an IBP program helps ensure the success of a brand.

**The Role of Advertising Market Segmentation, Differentiation, and
Positioning.** For advertising to be effective, it must work to support an organization's basic marketing strategies. The most basic and important marketing strategies
for cultivating customers are market segmentation, differentiation, and positioning.
Advertising plays an important role in helping a firm execute these marketing strategies.

21. Beth Snyder Bulik, "The Company You Keep," *Sales & Marketing Management,* November 2003, 14.

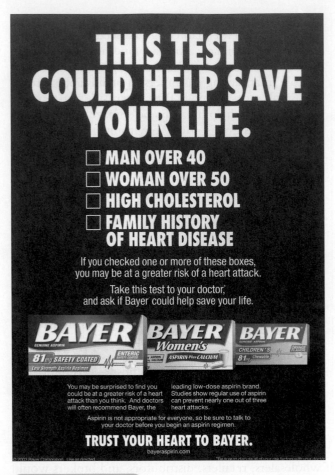

EXHIBIT 1.24

Advertising plays an important role in helping a firm segment the market based on needs and characteristics of consumers. Along with Bayer's regular aspirin for headache relief, Bayer offers these three additional versions of the brand that address both consumer needs (calcium-fortified aspirin for women) and consumer characteristics (a children's lower-dose aspirin). http://www.bayer aspirin.com

Market segmentation is the process of breaking down a large, widely varied *(heterogeneous)* market into submarkets, or segments, that are more similar *(homogeneous)* than dissimilar in terms of what the consumer is looking for or is presumed to be looking for. Underlying the strategy of market segmentation are the facts that consumers differ in their wants and that the wants of one person can differ under various circumstances. The market for automobiles can be divided into submarkets for different types of automobiles based on the needs and desires of various groups of buyers. Identifying those groups, or segments, of the population who want and will buy large or small, luxury or economy, or sport or sedan or minivan models is an important part of basic marketing strategy. In addition to needs, markets are often segmented on characteristics of consumers (referred to as demographics) such as age, marital status, gender, and income. These data are widely available and tend to be related to product preference and use. Advertising's role in the market segmentation process is to develop messages that appeal to the wants and desires of different segments and then to transmit those messages via appropriate media. For example, Bayer has four different versions of its basic aspirin brand. There is regular Bayer for headache relief; Bayer Enteric Safety Coated 81 mg aspirin for people with cholesterol and heart concerns; Women's Bayer, which includes a calcium supplement; and Children's Bayer, which is lower dose and chewable. Each of these versions of the Bayer brand of aspirin addresses both needs and characteristics of consumers in the market (see Exhibit 1.24). The Internet provides a new and highly efficient way to reach very well-defined market segments, as the Creativity box on page 28 demonstrates.

Differentiation is the process of creating a perceived difference, in the mind of the consumer, between an organization's brand and the competition's. Notice that this definition emphasizes that brand differentiation is based on *consumer perception*. The perceived differences can be tangible differences, or they may be based on image or style factors. Consider the Fendi watch ad in Exhibit 1.25. A $20 Timex and a $12,000 Fendi keep time in exactly the same way. But the two brands are differentiated on perceptions of style and the deeper meaning brands can have, as discussed earlier. The critical issue in differentiation is that consumers *perceive* a difference between brands. If consumers do not perceive a difference, then whether real differences exist or not does not matter. Differentiation is one of the most critical of all marketing strategies. If a firm's brand is not perceived as distinctive and attractive by consumers, then consumers will have no reason to choose that brand over one from the competition or to pay higher prices for the "better" or "more meaningful" brand.

When advertising is used to help create a difference in the mind of the consumer between an organization's brand and its competitors' brands, the ad may emphasize performance features, or it may create a distinctive image for the brand. The essential task for advertising is to develop a message that is different and unmistakably linked to the organization's brand. The ad in Exhibit 1.26 is distinctive and pursues product differentiation.

EXHIBIT 1.25

Advertising is key to the marketing strategy of differentiation—creating a perceived difference between the advertiser's brand and competitors' brands. This very expensive Fendi watch keeps time just like a $20 Timex. But you won't see an ad like this for a Timex. What is it about this ad that helps differentiate the Fendi brand from the Timex brand? http://www.fendi.it

EXHIBIT 1.26

An important role for advertising is to help a firm differentiate its brand from the competition with a distinctive message and presentation. The Hunter Fans ad in Exhibit 1.26 focuses on the function features of its air purifier line as the basis for differentiation.
http://www.hunterfan.com

Positioning is the process of designing a brand so that it can occupy a distinct and valued place in the target consumer's mind relative to other brands and then communicating this distinctiveness through advertising. Positioning, like differentiation, depends on a perceived image of tangible or intangible features. The importance of positioning can be understood by recognizing that consumers create a *perceptual space* in their minds for all the brands they might consider purchasing. A perceptual space is how one brand is seen on any number of dimensions—such as quality, taste, price, or social display value—in relation to those same dimensions in other brands.

There are really two positioning decisions. A firm must decide on the **external position** for a brand—that is, the niche the brand will pursue relative to all the competitive brands on the market. Additionally, an **internal position** must be achieved with regard to the other similar brands a firm markets. With the external-positioning decision, a firm tries to create a distinctive *competitive* position based on design features, pricing, distribution, or promotion or advertising strategy. Some brands are positioned at the very top of their competitive product category, such as BMW's 745i, priced around $85,000. Other brands seek a position at the low end of all market offerings, such as the Chevrolet Metro, whose base price is $10,000.

CREATIVITY

Wait! You Really Need Pickles!

When it comes to target marketing, the Internet can really deliver the goods. Think about this scenario. You go to the store and decide to pick up a few items. The store you shop at has given you a "loyalty card," which allows you to earn discount points, and you scan your card as you enter the store. No big deal, you say? Lots of stores have these loyalty cards, you say?

Well, a lot of stores may have loyalty cards, but few have integrated the loyalty card with the Internet like Stop & Shop Supermarket Company, which has created one of the most precise target marketing systems in the world. Imagine this as a shopping experience. You're making your way through the aisles of the Stop & Shop doing your normal grocery shopping. You stop in front of the deli counter and ask for a half pound of smoked turkey. Just then, the screen on your shopping cart computer beeps and a promotion pops up for Vlasic Dill Pickles! Talk about reaching the right target market at the right time!

The system is still in its early stages of trial, but works like this. A shopper starts by scanning a loyalty card through a reader on a specially computer-equipped shopping cart—"The Shopping Buddy." The computer then makes a wireless connection to the store's intranet, which downloads your product and brand preferences. The computer is also linking up to a GPS system that will track your progress through the store. That way, the computer knows just when to cue you to certain types of "compatible" products. Not only does the Shopping Buddy help companies target consumers right at the point of purchase, but the shopper gets a break, too. The Shopping Buddy scanner lets shoppers pay for their goods online and bypass check out lines completely. While there are still some bugs to be worked out, the system was being slowly introduced to all 334 Stop & Shops during 2004.

Source: Faith Arner, "Web Smart 50: Stop & Shop," *Business 2.0,* November 24, 2003, 96.

Effective internal positioning is accomplished by either developing vastly different products *within* the firm's own product line (Ben & Jerry's ice cream, for example, offers plenty of distinctive flavors, as shown in Exhibit 1.27) or creating advertising messages that appeal to different consumer needs and desires. Procter & Gamble successfully positions its many laundry detergent brands both internally and externally using a combination of product design and effective advertising. While some of these brands assume different positions within P&G's line due to substantive differences (a liquid soap versus a powder soap, for example), others with minor differences achieve distinctive positioning through advertising. One P&G brand is advertised as being effective on kids' dirty clothes, while another brand is portrayed as effective for preventing colors from running (see Exhibit 1.28). In this way, advertising helps create a distinctive position, both internally and externally.

The methods and strategic options available to an organization with respect to market segmentation, product differentiation, and positioning will be fully discussed in Chapter 6. For now, realize that advertising plays an important role in helping an organization put these most basic marketing strategies into operation.

The Role of Advertising in Revenue and Profit Generation. There are many who believe that the fundamental purpose of marketing (and the advertising that is used in marketing) can be stated quite simply: to generate revenue. No other part of an organization has this primary purpose. In the words of highly regarded management consultant and scholar Peter Drucker, "Marketing and innovation produce results: all the rest are 'costs.'"[22] The results Drucker is referring to are revenues. The marketing process is designed to generate sales and therefore revenues for the firm.

Creating sales as part of the revenue-generating process is where advertising plays a significant role. As we have seen, advertising communicates persuasive information to audiences based on the values created in the marketing mix related to the product, its price, or its distribution. This advertising communication, as you have seen throughout this chapter, then highlights these brand features, price, emotion, or availability through distribution and then attracts a target market. In this way, advertising makes a direct contribution to the marketing goal of revenue generation. Notice that advertising *contributes* to the process of creating sales and revenue. It can-

22.   Peter F. Drucker, *People and Performance: The Best of Peter Drucker* (New York: HarperCollins, 1997), 90.

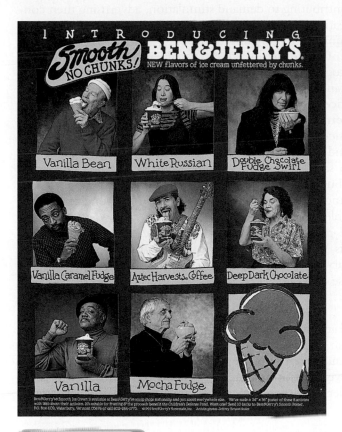

EXHIBIT 1.27

Firms with multiple brands in a single product category have to internally position these brands to differentiate them from each other in the minds of consumers. Ben & Jerry's achieves its product positioning by emphasizing the distinctly different flavors of each of its ice creams. http://www.benjerry.com

EXHIBIT 1.28

When a firm has multiple brands in a product category, it must be careful to position these brands distinctively so as to avoid cannibalization of one brand's sales by another. Procter & Gamble successfully achieves both a competitive external position and a distinctive internal product line position for Cheer laundry detergent by advertising the brand as the leader in preventing colors from running. http://www.pg.com

not be solely responsible for creating sales and revenue—it's not that powerful. Some organizations mistakenly see advertising as a panacea—the salvation for an ambiguous or ineffective overall marketing mix strategy. Advertising alone cannot be held responsible for sales. Sales occur when a brand has a well-conceived and complete marketing mix—including good advertising.

The effect of advertising on profits is a bit more involved and complicated. Its effect on profits comes about when advertising gives an organization greater flexibility in the price it charges for a product or service. Advertising can help create pricing flexibility by (1) contributing to economies of scale and (2) helping create inelasticity of demand. When an organization creates large-scale demand for its product, the quantity of product produced is increased, and **economies of scale** lead to lower unit production costs. Cost of production decreases because fixed costs (such as rent and equipment costs) are spread over a greater number of units produced.

How does advertising play a role in helping create economies of scale? When Colgate manufactures hundreds of thousands of tubes of its Colgate Total toothpaste and ships them in large quantities to warehouses, the fixed costs of production and shipping per unit are greatly reduced. With lower fixed costs per unit, Colgate can realize greater profits on each tube of toothpaste sold. Advertising contributes to demand stimulation by communicating to the market about the features and availability of a brand. By contributing to demand stimulation, advertising then contributes to the process of creating these economies of scale, which ultimately translates into higher profits per unit for the organization.

Remember the concept of brand loyalty we discussed earlier? Well, brand loyalty and advertising work together to create another important economic effect related to pricing flexibility and profits. When consumers are brand loyal, they are generally less sensitive to price increases for the brand. In economic terms, this is known as **inelasticity of demand.** When consumers are less price sensitive, firms have the flexibility to raise prices and increase profit margins. Advertising contributes directly to brand loyalty, and thus to inelasticity of demand, by persuading and reminding consumers of the satisfactions and values related to a brand. This argument related to the positive business effects of advertising was recently supported by a large research study. The study found that companies who build strong brands and raise prices are more profitable than companies who cut costs as a way to increase profits—by nearly twice the profit percentage. This research is supported by such real-world examples as Louis Vuitton. The maker of luxury handbags ($1,000 per bag or more) and other luxury items enjoys an operating margin of 45 percent and a 30 percent earnings increase in 2003.[23]

Types of Advertising.

So far, we've discussed advertising in a lot of different ways, from its most basic definition through how it can help an organization stimulate demand and generate profits. But to truly understand advertising, we need to go back to some very basic typologies that categorize advertising according to fundamental approaches to communication. Until you understand these aspects of advertising, you really don't understand advertising at all.

Primary versus Selective Demand Stimulation.

In **primary demand stimulation,** an advertiser is trying to create demand for an entire product *category.* Primary demand stimulation is challenging and costly, and research evidence suggests that it is likely to have an impact only for totally new products on the market—not brand extensions or product categories that have been around a long time (known as mature products). An example of effective primary demand stimulation was the introduction of the VCR to the consumer market in the 1970s. With a product that is totally new to the market, consumers need to be convinced that the product category itself is valuable and that it is, indeed, available for sale. When the VCR was first introduced in the United States, RCA, Panasonic, and Quasar (see Exhibit 1.29) ran primary demand stimulation advertising to explain to household consumers the value and convenience of taping television programs with this new product called a VHS video recorder—something no one had ever done before at home.

For organizations that have tried to stimulate primary demand in mature product categories, typically trade associations, the results have been dismal. Both the National Fluid Milk Processor Promotion Board and the Florida Department of Citrus have tried to use advertising to stimulate primary demand for the entire product categories of milk and orange juice. Examples of these campaigns are shown in Exhibits 1.30 and 1.31. While the "mustache" campaign is popular and wins awards, milk consumption has *declined* every year during the time of this campaign.[24] This is despite the fact that more than $1.5 billion in spending has been invested in the campaign (including a NASCAR race car!). Even if the attempts at primary demand have reduced the overall decline in milk consumption, this is still not a very impressive

23.   The research study is reported in Robert G. Docters, Michael R. Reopel, Jeanne-Mey Sun, and Stephen M. Tanney, *Winning the Profit Game: Smarter Pricing, Smarter Branding* (New York: McGraw-Hill, 2004); the information on Louis Vuitton was taken from Carol Matlack et al., "The Vuitton Machine," *BusinessWeek,* March 22, 2004, 98–102.

24.   U.S. Bureau of the Census, *Statistical Abstract of the United States: 1995,* 115th ed. (Washington, D.C.: U.S. Government Printing Office, 1995); "Got Results?" *Marketing News,* March 2, 1998, 1.

EXHIBIT 1.29

*When new, innovative products are first introduced to the market, a type of advertising called **primary demand stimulation** is often used. Primary demand stimulation attempts to stimulate demand for the entire product category by educating consumers about the values of the product itself, rather than the values of a brand within the product category. This ad from the early days of the VHS video cassette recorder is a classic example of primary demand stimulation in a new, innovative product category.*

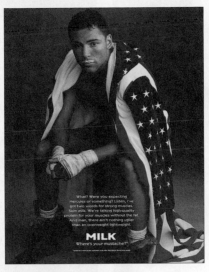

EXHIBIT 1.30

Advertising that attempts to stimulate primary demand is often tried by industry associations and advocacy groups, such as the National Fluid Milk Processor Promotion Board, rather than by specific manufacturers. Trouble is, it doesn't work. Primary demand stimulation has been shown to be ineffective in mature product categories, such as milk, but rather is appropriate for products totally new to the market. http://www.gotmilk.org *and* http://www.elsie.com

EXHIBIT 1.31

This ad promoting orange juice also attempts to stimulate primary demand, or demand for a product category rather than demand for a particular brand. Decades of literature demonstrate no relationship between aggregate levels of advertising in an industry and overall demand in an industry. It appears that advertising is indeed suited only to selective (brand) demand stimulation. http://www.floridajuice.com

result. This should come as no surprise, though. Research over decades has clearly indicated that attempts at primary demand stimulation in mature product categories (orange juice, beef, pork, and almonds have also been tried) have never been successful.[25]

While some corporations have tried primary demand stimulation, the true power of advertising is shown when it functions to stimulate demand for a particular company's brand. This is known as selective demand stimulation. The purpose of **selective demand stimulation** advertising is to point out a brand's unique benefits compared to the competition. For example, compare the Tropicana ad in Exhibit 1.32 touting the brand's superiority with the primary demand stimulation ad in Exhibit 1.31. Likewise, now that the VCR is past the stage of primary demand stimulation and is a mature product category, households accept the value of this product and each brand selectively appeals to different consumer needs. Selective demand stimulation advertising for VCRs emphasizes brand features such as hi-fi sound, remote control, and voice recognition programming, as Exhibit 1.33 illustrates. This is selective demand stimulation.

---

25.   For an excellent summary of decades of research on the topic, see Mark S. Abion and Paul W. Farris, *The Advertising Controversy: Evidence of the Economic Effects of Advertising* (Boston: Auburn House, 1981); and J. C. Luik and M. S. Waterson, *Advertising and Markets* (Oxfordshire, England: NTC Publications, 1996)

Amazing how lifting just 8 ounces a day can help keep your bones strong.

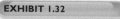

The best 9.3 seconds you could possibly spend on yourself. Everyday.

EXHIBIT 1.32

Selective demand stimulation advertising highlights a brand's superiority in providing satisfaction. In this ad, Tropicana touts its superiority as a brand of orange juice with very specific brand features. Compare this ad to the primary demand ad in Exhibit 1.31. http://www.tropicana.com

THIS IS THE HEART OF TOSHIBA'S REVOLUTIONARY VCR CHASSIS.

INTRODUCING V3. ONLY FROM TOSHIBA.

EXHIBIT 1.33

Once the VHS video cassette recorder became widely adopted, there was no longer a need for primary demand stimulation. Companies turned to the selective brand stimulation process represented by this Toshiba ad. How is this ad different in its message content from the ad in Exhibit 1.29? http://www.toshiba.com

Direct versus Delayed Response Advertising. Another important type of advertising involves how quickly we want consumers to respond. **Direct response advertising** asks consumers to act immediately. An ad that suggests that you "call this toll-free number" or "mail your $19.95 before midnight tonight" is an example of direct response advertising. In the ad in Exhibit 1.34, the company implores consumers to act quickly in order to obtain the Frank Sinatra collector's plate. That's direct response advertising.

While exceptions exist, direct response advertising is most often used for products that consumers are familiar with, that do not require inspection at the point of purchase, and that are relatively low-cost. The proliferation of toll-free numbers and the widespread use of credit cards have been a boon to direct response advertisers.

Delayed response advertising relies on imagery and message themes that emphasize the benefits and satisfying characteristics of a brand. Rather than trying to stimulate an immediate action from an audience, delayed response advertising attempts to develop awareness and preference for a brand over time. In general, delayed response advertising attempts to create brand awareness, reinforce the benefits of using a brand, develop a general liking for the brand, and create an image for a brand. When a consumer enters the purchase process, the information from delayed response advertising comes into play. Most advertisements we see on television and

Direct response advertising asks consumers to take some immediate action. Direct response advertising is most often used with low-price products with which consumers have extensive experience and don't need a lot of specific feature information.

Delayed response advertising attempts to reinforce the benefits of using a brand and create a general liking for the brand. This ad for "all" detergent is an example of delayed response advertising.

in magazines are of the delayed response type. Exhibit 1.35, an ad for hypoallergenic detergent, provides an example of this common form of advertising. In this ad, the message has as much to do with being a good parent (an image and delayed response–type message) as with the actual performance features of the brand.

Corporate versus Brand Advertising. Corporate advertising is not designed to promote a specific brand, but is meant to create a favorable attitude toward a company as a whole. Prominent users of corporate advertising are Microsoft, Phillips Petroleum, General Electric, and IBM. **Brand advertising,** as we have seen throughout this chapter, communicates the specific features, values, and benefits of a particular brand offered for sale by a particular organization. The firms that have long-established corporate campaigns are designed to generate favorable public opinion toward the corporation and its products. This type of advertising can also have an effect on the shareholders of a firm. When shareholders see good corporate advertising, it instills confidence and, ultimately, long-term commitment to the firm and its stock. We'll consider this type of advertising in great detail in Chapter 20.

Another form of corporate advertising is carried out by members of a trade channel, mostly retailers. When corporate advertising takes place in a trade channel it is referred to as *institutional advertising*. Retailers such as Nordstrom, The Home Depot,

A Little Plastic Packaging
Can Help Prevent Bruising.

PLASTIC MAKES IT POSSIBLE™

EXHIBIT 1.36

Advertising affects the competitive environment in an economy. This ad by a plastics manufacturers council is fostering competition with manufacturers of other packaging materials. http://www.americanplasticscouncil.org

and Wal-Mart advertise to persuade consumers to shop at their stores. While these retailers may occasionally feature a particular manufacturer's brand in the advertising (Nordstrom features Clinique cosmetics) the main purpose of the advertising is to get the audience to shop at their store. Federated Department Stores, for example, invested $387 million in 2003 to promote its national brand stores, Macy's and Bloomingdale's, as well as its many regional chains that include Rich's, Lazarus, and The Bon Marche. The thrust of Federated's brand strategy comes from marketing research findings that show their target audience "considers shopping an enjoyable activity."[26]

The Economic Effects of Advertising.
Our discussion of advertising as a business process so far has focused strictly on the use of advertising by individual business organizations. But you cannot *truly* understand advertising unless you know something about how advertising has effects across the entire economic system of a country. (This isn't the most fun you'll have reading this book, but it is one of the most important topics.)

Advertising's Effect on Gross Domestic Product. Gross domestic product (GDP) is
the measure of the total value of goods and services produced within an economic system. Earlier, we discussed advertising's role in the marketing mix. Recall that as advertising contributes to marketing mix strategy, it can contribute to sales along with the right product, the right price, and the right distribution. Because of this role, advertising is related to GDP in that it can contribute to levels of overall consumer demand when it plays a key role in introducing new products, such as VCRs, microcomputers, the Internet, or alternative energy sources. As demand for these new products grows, the resultant consumer spending fuels retail sales, housing starts, and corporate investment in finished goods and capital equipment. Consequently, GDP is affected by sales of products in new, innovative product categories.[27]

Advertising's Effect on Business Cycles. Advertising can have a stabilizing
effect on downturns in business activity. There is evidence that many firms increase advertising during times of recession in an effort to spend their way out of a business downturn.

Advertising's Effect on Competition. Advertising is alleged to stimulate com-
petition and therefore motivate firms to strive for better products, better production methods, and other competitive advantages that ultimately benefit the economy as a whole. Additionally, when advertising serves as a way to enter new markets, competition across the economic system is fostered. For example, Exhibit 1.36 shows an

26.   Mercedes M. Cardona, "Federated Focuses Campaign on Macy's," *Advertising Age,* December 8, 2003, 6.
27.   There are several historical treatments of how advertising is related to demand. See, for example, Neil H. Borden, *The Economic Effects of Advertising* (Chicago: Richard D. Irwin, 1942), 187–189; and John Kenneth Galbraith, *The New Industrial State* (Boston: Houghton Mifflin, 1967), 203–207.

ad in which plastics manufacturers present themselves as competitors to manufacturers of other packaging materials.

Advertising is not universally hailed as a stimulant to competition. Critics point out that the amount of advertising dollars needed to compete effectively in many industries is often prohibitive. As such, advertising can act as a barrier to entry into an industry; that is, a firm may have the capability to compete in an industry in every way except that the advertising dollars needed to compete are so great that the firm cannot afford to get into the business. In this way, advertising can actually serve to decrease the overall amount of competition in an economy.[28]

Advertising's Effect on Prices.   One of the widely debated effects of advertising has to do with its effect on the prices consumers pay for products and services. Since we have seen that firms spend millions or even billions of dollars on advertising, then products and services would cost much less if firms did no advertising. Right? Wrong!

First, across all industries, advertising costs incurred by firms range from about 1 percent of sales in the automobile and retail industries to about 15 percent of sales in the personal care and luxury products businesses. Exhibit 1.37 shows the ratio of advertising to sales for various firms in selected industries. Notice that there is no consistent and predictable relationship between advertising spending and sales. Honda spent $1.144 billion in advertising to generate about $40.3 billion in sales; L'Oréal spent about the same on advertising ($1.239 billion) but generated only $4.318 billion in sales; and Wal-Mart spent only $678 million on advertising to generate over $208 billion in sales! Different products and different market conditions demand that firms spend different amounts of money on advertising. These same conditions make it difficult to identify a predictable relationship between advertising and sales.

It is true that the cost of advertising is built into product costs, which are ultimately passed on to consumers. But this effect on price must be judged against a couple of cost savings that lower the price. First, there is the reduced time and effort a consumer has to spend in searching for a product or service. Second, economies of scale, discussed earlier, have a direct impact on cost and then on prices. Recall that economies of scale serve to lower the cost of production by spreading fixed costs over a large number of units produced. This lower cost can be passed on to consumers in terms of lower prices, as firms search for competitive advantage with lower prices. Nowhere is this effect more dramatic than the price of personal computers. In the early 1980s, an Apple IIe computer that ran at about 1 MHz and had 64K of total memory cost over $3,000. Today, you can get a computer that is several hundred times faster with vastly increased memory and storage for less than $800. And it is likely that companies like Gateway and Dell are spending more on advertising today than Apple did back in the 1980s.

Advertising's Effect on Value.   *Value* is the password for successful marketing. **Value,** in modern marketing and advertising, refers to a perception by consumers that a brand provides satisfaction beyond the cost incurred to obtain that brand. The value perspective of the modern consumer is based on wanting every purchase to be a "good deal." Value can be added to the consumption experience by advertising. Recall the discussion of bottled water at the beginning of the chapter. Advertising helps create enough value in the mind of consumers that they (we) will pay for water that comes free out of the tap.

Advertising also affects a consumer's perception of value by contributing to the symbolic value and the social meaning of a brand. **Symbolic value** refers to what a

---

28.   This fundamental argument about the effect of advertising on competition was identified and well articulated many years ago by Colston E. Warn, "Advertising: A Critic's View," *Journal of Marketing,* vol. 26, no. 4 (October 1962), 12.

Industry	Advertiser	2003 U.S. Ad Spending (millions)	2003 U.S. Sales (millions)	Advertising Spending as % of Sales
Automobiles				
	General Motors	$3,430	$133,897	2.55
	Ford	2,234	103,435	2.13
	Volkswagen	608	16,701	3.59
	Honda	1,144	40,306	2.72
Computers				
	IBM	862	33,762	2.37
	Dell	565	28,603	1.97
	Microsoft	1,147	22,100	4.98
	Intel	394	7,644	5.10
Drugs				
	Bristol-Myers Squibb	778	12,897	6.04
	Johnson & Johnson	1,996	25,274	7.89
	Bayer	434	7,567	5.71
Food				
	ConAgra	765	17,739	4.32
	Nestlé S.A.	1,113	20,527	5.40
	Altria Grp	1,311	40,298	3.23
	Sara Lee	583	10,662	5.44
Personal Care				
	Procter & Gamble	3,323	21,853	15.19
	Gillette	612	3,448	17.73
	Estée Lauder	906	2,953	30.71
	L'Oréal	1,239	4,318	28.53
Retail				
	JCPenney	1,025	17,786	5.73
	Home Depot	1,150	64,816	1.77
	Wal-Mart	678	208,757	.032

Source: Ad Age, Special Report: "U.S. Company Revenue Per 2003 Advertising Dollar," *Advertising Age*, June 28, 2004, 5–10.

EXHIBIT 1.37

Advertising spending as a proportion of sales in selected industries, 2003 (U.S. dollars in millions).

product or service means to consumers in a nonliteral way. For example, branded clothing such as Guess? jeans or Doc Martens shoes can symbolize self-concept for some consumers. Exhibit 1.38 shows an example of an ad seeking to create symbolic value for Ray-Ban sunglasses. In reality, all branded products rely to some extent on symbolic value; otherwise they would not be brands, but just unmarked commodities (like potatoes).

Social meaning refers to what a product or service means in a societal context. For example, social class is marked by any number of products used and displayed to

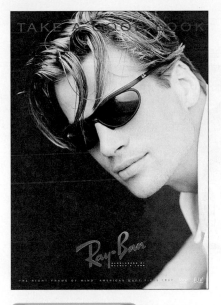

EXHIBIT 1.38

Advertising contributes to the symbolic value that brands have for consumers. What is it about the ad for Ray-Ban sunglasses in Exhibit 1.38 that contributes to the symbolic value of this brand? http://www.ray-ban .com

EXHIBIT 1.39

Ads communicate social meaning to consumers, as a product or service carries meaning in a societal context beyond its use or purpose. This ad for United Airlines puts the company's service into such a context. http://www.ual.com

signify class membership, such as cars, beverages, and clothes. Exhibit 1.39 shows an ad for a service with clear social-class connections. Often, the product's connection to a social class addresses a need within consumers to move up in class.

Researchers from various disciplines have long argued that objects (brands included) are never just objects. They take on meaning from culture, society, and consumers.[29] It is important to remember that these meanings often become just as much a part of the brand as the physical features. Since advertising is an essential way in which the image of a brand is developed, it contributes directly to consumers' perception of the value of the brand. The more value consumers see in a brand, the more they are willing to pay to acquire the brand. If the image of a Gucci watch, a Nissan coupe, or a Four Seasons hotel is valued by consumers, then consumers will pay a premium to acquire that value. Waterford crystal and Gucci watches, shown in Exhibits 1.40 and 1.41, are examples of brands that consumers pay a premium to own.

5 From Advertising to Integrated Marketing Communications to Integrated Brand Promotion.

As we discussed in the section on advertising's role in the marketing mix, it is important to recognize that advertising is only one of many promotional tools available to impress and persuade consumers. Now realize that it is not always even the *main* choice of some companies, because in many situations another tool, such as targeted e-mail, event

29.   For an historical perspective on culture, consumers, and the meaning of goods, see Ernest Ditcher, *Handbook of Consumer Motivations* (New York: McGraw-Hill, 1964), 6. For a contemporary view, see David Glenn Mic and Claus Buhl, "A Meaning-Based Model of Advertising Experiences," *Journal of Consumer Research,* vol. 19 (December 1992), 312–338.

EXHIBITS 1.40 AND 1.41

Waterford crystal and Gucci watches are two advertised products that consumers will pay premium prices to own. Both products have value in that they epitomize the highest levels of quality craftsmanship. Such craftsmanship, in itself, may not be enough to command premium prices in the marketplace. Advertising that creates an image of exclusivity may also be needed. In what way does the Gucci site (http://www.gucci.com) contribute directly to consumers' perceptions of a brand's value? Compare this site to Waterford's site (http://www.waterford.com) and determine which communicates its brand's social meaning more effectively.

sponsorship, or direct mail, is better suited to the task at hand (see the IBP box). For example, R. J. Reynolds Tobacco announced in September of 2003 that it would cease advertising two of its widely known brands, Winston and Doral, and focus instead on targeted e-mail to adult smokers and on pricing strategies.[30]

Another example is McDonald's. McDonald's spends over $1.3 billion a year in advertising.[31] But the firm also spends tens of millions of dollars a year on a wide range of promotions that include movie tie-in premiums featuring Disney Princesses and Power Rangers and event sponsorships like the 19-city Justin Timberlake European concert tour.

Beginning in about 1990, the concept of mixing various promotional tools has generally been referred to as integrated marketing communications.[32] **Integrated marketing communications** (IMC) is the process of using promotional tools in a unified way so that a synergistic communication effect is created. But as the discussion earlier in the chapter highlighted, the current thinking is that the emphasis on *communication* has given way to an emphasis on the *brand*. The result is a recent evolution from an integrated marketing communications perspective to an integrated brand promotion perspective.

30.   R.J. Reynolds Tobacco, "RJR Announces Restructuring Plan and Workforce Reduction; Revises Full-Year Earnings Guidance," press release available at http://www.rjrholdings.com/Investors/financials_otherview.asp?docID'425, accessed December 19, 2003.

31.   "100 Leading National Advertisers," *Advertising Age,* June 28, 2004, S2.

32.   Don E. Schultz, Stanley Tannenbaum, and Robert Lauterborn, *Integrated Marketing Communications* (Lincolnwood, Ill.: NTC Books, 1993).

IBP

Advertising and IBP: An ROI Perspective

All in all, you have to believe that advertising is a highly respected and trusted tool by marketers. After all, several organizations like General Motors, Procter & Gamble, and AOL spend over $2 billion a *year* on advertising. And what other way is there to reach hundreds of millions of people at the same time, not to mention all the beauty and drama you can create with advertising?

Well, while all that may be true, another perspective on advertising, return on investment (ROI), shows that a majority of marketers are not all that thrilled with advertising. A survey of marketing professionals showed that 26 percent thought that media advertising was the worst marketing tool for providing return on investment. Media advertising was followed by public relations (25 percent) and product placement (13 percent) as the next worst for providing return on investment. The best integrated brand promotion (IBP) tools for maximizing ROI turned out to be direct marketing, sales promotion, and coupons.

Before we jump to any conclusions that advertising is dead and will be totally replaced by other IBP tools, this survey is an excellent demonstration of the power of advertising versus the power of advertising tools—an issue that will be raised and discussed throughout the book. ROI is defined by the vast majority of survey respondents as sales or market share. The truth is that advertising and especially media advertising is not particularly easy to track relative to those definitions of ROI. Note that the most highly rated IBP tools—direct marketing, sales promotion, and coupons—*are* relatively easy to trace directly to sales.

So if marketing professionals do not like advertising from an ROI perspective, then why *do* they spend billions of dollars each year on advertising? There is a relatively straightforward answer: advertising does what no other IBP tool can do—it helps create an image and a position for a brand. You will learn throughout this text that advertising is powerful and useful but is very difficult to track. It can create a very special place in the mind of the consumer. Can you tell when or how this effect turns into a sale? Probably not. So despite the frustration with advertising from an ROI perspective, organizations will continue to invest heavily in this most ethereal of all communication tools.

Sources: Ad Age Special Report, "100 Leading National Advertisers," June 23, 2003, S2; Judann Pollack, "Marketers Slap Network TV in Survey on ROI," *Advertising Age*, October 13, 2003, 1, 66.

Recall from the definition earlier in the chapter that integrated brand promotion (IBP) is the use of various communication tools, including advertising, in a coordinated manner to build and maintain brand awareness, identity, and preference. The distinction between IBP and IMC is pretty obvious. IMC emphasizes the communication effort, per se, and the need for coordinated and synergistic messages. IBP retains the emphasis on coordination and synergy, but goes beyond the parameters of IMC. In integrated brand promotion, the emphasis is on the brand and not just the communication. With a focus on building brand awareness, identity, and ultimately preference, the IBP perspective recognizes that coordinated promotional messages need to have brand-building effects and not just communication effects.

Because of the growing importance of IBP to the advertising industry, IBP issues are raised throughout this book as it relates to various topics in advertising strategy and execution. In addition, each chapter has special IBP boxes that highlight the strategy and coordination challenges of every aspect of advertising. In addition, five distinct sections of this book are devoted to a rich case history that features a real-life application of IBP. These five sections conclude each of the major parts of the book, parallel the emphasis of the text, and feature the complete story of the application of IBP concepts by Cincinnati Bell in its marketing of a new, wireless phone service:

Part 1—Cincinnati Bell Wireless: From IMC to IBP

Part 2—Cincinnati Bell Wireless: Planning Advertising and Integrated Brand Promotion

Part 3—Cincinnati Bell Wireless: Preparing Advertising and Integrated Brand Promotion

Part 4—Cincinnati Bell Wireless: The Launch Campaign

Part 5—Cincinnati Bell Wireless: Sustaining and Growing the Brand after Launch

These special IBP sections are easy to find because each begins with the distinctive color scheme that designates our Cincinnati Bell Wireless case. These sections focus on the real-world challenges faced by Cincinnati Bell during the planning, development, and execution of nearly two years of brand-building activity for Cincinnati

ETHICS

Advertising Ethics

Corporate scandals are pretty common lately.

Steroids, corked bats, and bad lip sync on SNL.

Even the sacrosanct *News York Times* got caught printing the fabricated stories of one of its reporters.

Does everybody cheat now?

Does everyone look in the camera and lie?

In this environment the advertising industry is starting to look pretty good. Everyone knows ads try to put things in the best light, that they are trying to sell something.

Advertising has always been confronted with charges of poor ethical behavior. The criticisms range from fair to absurd, from justified and valid to shrill hyperbole and whiny victimhood.

So, when you think about the ethics of advertising, of doing the right thing, give it some thought.

The Ethics boxes you will see throughout the text are designed to get you think about this, and not just react. Hopefully, you will become more informed, knowledgeable, and sophisticated in your thinking about advertising, and you may change your mind a time or two over the course of reading our book.

Think about this:

"80% of American companies have a written Code of Ethics. And probably 100% of you do too, if you gave it some thought and wrote it down. Ethics happen, or don't, in our relationships with others. Advertisers are in the business of communicating with thousands, even millions, of 'others' all the time. That gives us thousands or millions of chances to practice what we believe every day. And try to get it right."

—Chris Moore, Ogilvy and Mather Advertising

Source: "Ethics in Advertising," Advertising Education Foundation, http://www.aef.com/05/speaker_pres/data/3001.

Bell Wireless. Cincinnati Bell, and its advertising agency, Northlich, have generously provided their advertising and other brand promotion materials for use in this text. We believe that IBP is an important enough consideration in contemporary communications and promotion that its role alongside the advertising effort deserves comprehensive assessment. The materials and expertise gained in working with our corporate partners allow us to provide a comprehensive case history that offers a truly unique learning opportunity on the forefront of advertising and integrated brand promotion.

SUMMARY

 Know what advertising and integrated brand promotion are and what they can do.

Since advertising has become so pervasive, it would be reasonable to expect that you might have your own working definition for this critical term. But an informed perspective on advertising goes beyond what is obvious and can be seen on a daily basis. Advertising is distinctive and recognizable as a form of communication by its three essential elements: its paid sponsorship, its use of mass media, and its intent to persuade. An advertisement is a specific message that an advertiser has placed to persuade an audience. An advertising campaign is a series of ads and other promotional efforts with a common theme also placed to persuade an audience over a specified period of time. Integrated brand promotion (IBP) is the use of many promotional tools, including advertising, in a coordinated manner to build and maintain brand awareness, identity, and preference.

 Discuss a basic model of advertising communication.

Advertising cannot be effective unless some form of communication takes place between the advertiser and the audience. But advertising is about mass communication. There are many models that might be used to help explain how advertising works or does not work as a communication platform. The model introduced in this chapter features basic considerations such as the message-production process versus the message-reception process, and this model says that consumers create their own meanings when they interpret advertisements.

 Describe the different ways of classifying audiences for advertising.

While it is possible to provide a simple and clear definition of what advertising is, it is also true that advertising takes many forms and serves different purposes from one application to another. One way to appreciate the complexity and diversity of advertising is to classify it by audience category or by geographic focus. For example, advertising might be directed at households or government officials. Using another perspective, it can be global or local in its focus.

 Explain the key roles of advertising as a business process.

Many different types of organizations use advertising to achieve their business purposes. For major multinational corporations, such as Procter & Gamble, and for smaller, more localized businesses, such as the San Diego Zoo, advertising is one part of a critical business process known as marketing. Advertising is one element of the marketing mix; the other key elements are the firm's products, their prices, and the distribution network. Advertising must work in conjunction with these other marketing mix elements if the organization's marketing objectives are to be achieved. It is important to recognize that of all the roles played by advertising in the marketing process, none is more important than contributing to building brand awareness and brand equity. Similarly, firms have turned to more diverse methods of communication beyond advertising that we have referred to as integrated brand promotion. That is, firms are using communication tools such as public relations, sponsorship, direct marketing, and sales promotion along with advertising to achieve communication goals.

 Understand the concept of integrated brand promotion (IBP) and the role advertising plays in the process.

Integrated brand promotion (IBP) is the use of various promotional tools like event sponsorship, the Internet, public relations, and personal selling, along with advertising, in a coordinated manner to build and maintain brand awareness, identity, and preference. When marketers use advertising in conjunction with other promotional tools, they create an integrated brand promotion that highlights brand features and value. Note that the word *coordinated* is central to this definition. Over the past 30 years, the advertising and promotion industry has evolved to recognize that integration and coordination of promotional elements is key to effective communication and lasting brand identity.

KEY TERMS

advertising
client, or sponsor
advertisement
advertising campaign
integrated brand promotion (IBP)
audience
target audience
household consumers
members of business organizations
members of a trade channel
professionals
trade journals
government officials and employees
global advertising
international advertising

national advertising
regional advertising
local advertising
cooperative advertising, or co-op
 advertising
marketing
marketing mix
brand
brand extension
brand loyalty
brand equity
market segmentation
differentiation
positioning
external position

internal position
economies of scale
inelasticity of demand
primary demand stimulation
selective demand stimulation
direct response advertising
delayed response advertising
corporate advertising
brand advertising
gross domestic product (GDP)
value
symbolic value
social meaning
integrated marketing communications (IMC)

QUESTIONS

1. Why do you think people will pay a premium price for bottled water when water from the tap is free? What is *symbolic value,* and how might it relate to the bottled-water phenomenon discussed at the opening of the chapter?

2. What does it mean when we say that advertising is intended to persuade? How do different ads persuade in different ways?

3. Explain the differences between regional advertising, local advertising, and cooperative advertising. What would you look for in an ad to identify it as a cooperative ad?

4. How do the goals of direct response and delayed response advertising differ? How would you explain marketers' growing interest in direct response advertising?

5. Differentiate between global advertising and international advertising. Do you think consumers in foreign markets would feel the same rock 'n' roll nostalgia for GM's Led Zeppelin–fueled Cadillac commercials as do American consumers? Why or why not?

6. Give an example of an advertising campaign that you know has been running for more than one year. Why do some advertising campaigns last for years, whereas others come and go in a matter of months?

7. If a firm developed a new line of athletic shoes, priced them competitively, and distributed them in appropriate retail shops, would there be any need for advertising? Is advertising really needed for a good product that is priced right?

8. Many companies now spend millions of dollars to sponsor and have their names associated with events such as stock-car races or rock concerts. Do these event sponsorships fit the definition for advertising given in this chapter?

9. How does the process of market segmentation lead an organization to spend its advertising dollars more efficiently and more effectively?

10. What is the concept of integrated brand promotion (IBP)? How are IBP and advertising related?

EXPERIENTIAL EXERCISES

1. In this chapter, audiences for advertising were divided into five broad audience categories. For each, find one ad that appears to be targeted to members of that audience. Analyze the message and style of each ad and determine whether the message seems effective, given the intended audience category. Why was the ad effective or ineffective? Did you have difficulty locating ads for any specific audience category? If so, explain why you think that might have occurred and what it reveals about the nature and methods of advertising to that audience category.

2. Very few advertisements or brands have the same appeal to all consumers worldwide. (Think about GM's decision to beef up Cadillac's image with rock 'n' roll from Led Zeppelin; how would that have gone over in foreign markets?) Advertisers must therefore strategically place ads based on geographic regions. List four favorite products or brands that you use in your everyday life. For each, decide whether it is appropriate to advertise the product at the global, international, national, regional, local, or cooperative level. Explain your answer.

EXPERIENCING THE INTERNET

1-1 What Is Advertising?

As a part of a settlement between the tobacco industry and attorneys general in 46 states, the Truth campaign is dedicated to distributing facts about the harmful effects of tobacco use, especially among young people. Run by the nonprofit American Legacy Foundation, the campaign gets its message out through TV, radio, magazines, and the Internet in the hopes of preventing the spread of tobacco use among its target audience while encouraging higher ethical standards for tobacco advertisers.

Truth: http://www.thetruth.com

1. Browse around the Truth Web site and describe its features. What audience category does the Truth campaign appear to be targeting?

2. What criteria need to be met for the Truth campaign to be considered advertising? Based on these criteria, should this campaign be classified as advertising?

3. Do you think the Truth campaign as it is presented on the Web site is effective? Explain your position.

1-2 Advertising as a Business Process

The wireless revolution is bringing about a whole new communications network based on computing devices that keep people connected to their work and lifestyle from almost any location. The race to supply consumers with instant e-mail and Internet access on handheld devices has increased the importance of advertising in the overall marketing and brand promotion programs of wireless-product manufacturers.

palmOne: http://www.palmone.com/us

1. What is a brand? Give reasons why the Palm brand name is so significant to the successful marketing of the company's computing products.

2. Using the text, list one of the ways advertising affects brand development and management, and give an example of how the palmOne site accomplishes this.

3. Explain how the term *value* relates to the popularity of wireless computing products among your peer groups. Use the concepts of *symbolic value* and *social meaning* in your answer.

CHAPTER 2

After reading and thinking about this chapter, you will be able to do the following:

1

Discuss important trends transforming the advertising and promotion industry.

2

Describe the advertising and promotion industry's size, structure, and participants.

3

Discuss the role played by advertising and promotion agencies, the services provided by these agencies, and how they are compensated.

4

Identify key external facilitators who assist in planning and executing advertising and integrated brand promotion campaigns.

5

Discuss the role played by media organizations in executing effective advertising and integrated brand promotion campaigns.

FJC and N

AIM HIGHER.

Introductory Scenario: Who's In Charge Here?

To say that there is a power struggle going on in the advertising industry might be the understatement of the new millennium. The power struggle really started back in 1999. It was about then that traditional advertising agencies were losing business to the new dot.com, interactive, totally hip (at the time) agencies. The big time advertising shops watched client after client be won over by the (over-)confident, techno-savvy, new era competitors. Well, the dot.com agencies got blown up in the dot.bomb explosion (implosion) of 2001–2002. So you would think that things must have returned to normal by now: dominance by the traditional big Madison Avenue (New York) and Wacker Drive (Chicago) agencies calling the shots. Not quite.

A whole new struggle has emerged in the advertising industry, and its roots go deep to the core of the structure of the industry. By the middle of 2002, the massive consolidation taking place among big agencies would provide an ideal opportunity for these big global agencies to dictate the way advertising and promotion would be done across the industry. After all, they controlled the majority of the nearly $500 billion a year that would be spent on media around the world.[1] But it hasn't worked out that way.

What has happened in the industry is that other players, beyond the agencies, have started to exert their own power and control. Not surprisingly, those other players are consumers and the advertisers themselves. After all, it is *their* money that ends up paying for advertising and, therefore, giving the big agencies their revenue.

But let's explore what's going on. First, from the consumer side. With the large number of media options available for news, information, and entertainment, media fragmentation is a boon to consumers and a huge headache for advertising agencies. The new generation of consumers are behaving very differently from the cable-TV generation that preceded them. This new generation of media users is insisting on the convenience and appeal (and control) of their PC, iPod, and TiVo.[2] The irony of the control that consumers are starting to exert is that it will make product branding even *more* important as consumers choose what and where they want to be exposed to persuasive messages. Again, the importance of the brand in advertising and promotion was a key theme in Chapter 1. And advertising agencies are struggling with just how to insert themselves and their clients' brands into this new environment controlled by the consumer. Some think better creative is the answer. Other advertisers, like Coca-Cola, feel that a much more radical solution is necessary. They believe that consumers will no longer tolerate passive television or magazine ads. Rather, the brand is going to have to become part of their daily lives in ways advertisers are only now trying to figure out. Part of Coke's approach: pay $20 million to have Coke cups on the desks of the judges during Fox Network's *American Idol* programming.[3] (See Exhibit 2.1.) More on this in Chapter 5 when we look at advertising and consumer behavior.

Now, let's consider the advertisers and their influence over the big advertising agencies. A wide range of changes are occurring and all of them end up hurting the bottom line of the agencies. First, advertisers are carefully scrutinizing their results and switching agencies with little hesitation. A case in point is the $110 million Tylenol account that Saatchi & Saatchi advertising held for nearly 30 years. As sales in the analgesic market flattened, Johnson & Johnson's McNeil division, makers of Tylenol, not only unceremoniously dumped Saatchi & Saatchi from the Tylenol account, but then proceeded to relieve the agency of another $85 million in annual billings.[4] Ouch! But the shake-up seemed to start to pay off almost immediately. The

---

1.   Stuart Elliot, "Advertising's Big Four: It's Their World Now," *New York Times,* March 21, 2002, Section 3, pp. 1, 10, 11.

2.   Martin Nisenholtz, "Control Shift Is Here," *Advertising Age,* December 15, 2003, 20.

3.   Dean Foust and Brian Grow, "Coke: Wooing the TiVo Generation," *BusinessWeek,* March 1, 2004, 77–78.

4.   Rich Thomaselli, "IPG Agencies Gun for Tylenol," *Advertising Age,* September 22, 2003, 1; *Advertising Age* Late News insert, "Incumbent Saatchi cut in $110 Million Tylenol review," *Advertising Age,* November 17, 2003, 1; Lisa Sanders and Rich Thomaselli, "J & J Yanks $85 million from Saatchi," *Advertising Age,* November 24, 2003, 1.

Big advertisers like Coca-Cola (which used to spend about $200 million a year on television advertising) realize that a large portion of the consumer market is gaining more and more control over their exposure to commercial messages like advertising. TiVo and other new technologies are allowing consumers to choose how and when they view such messages. In response, big advertisers are looking at more and varied ways to reach consumers and have their brands become more a part of consumers' lifestyles through promotional techniques like placing products within television shows and event sponsorships. http://www.cocacola.com

next year Tylenol sales reversed their downward trend.[5] Saatchi's problems and treatment by one of its biggest clients are not unique. Verizon, the wireless services giant, put $315 million of its $828 million advertising budget up for agency competition, saying flatly that "We are not completely satisfied with what we have received from IPG [Interpublic Group]."[6] In a slightly different demonstration of client control, General Motors Corporation (the largest advertiser in the world; see Exhibit 2.3) asked all of its agencies to define overhead costs using standardized components so the corporation could make judgments about the efficiency of its many supplier agencies. C. J. Fraleigh, GM's executive director of corporate advertising and marketing, called the big agencies "flabby organizations that have become more revenue models than consumer solutions models."[7] Double ouch! The exertion of this sort of control over agencies by clients is having an almost immediate and painful effect. In 2003, Interpublic Group (New York) posted a single-quarter loss of $327 million. Similarly, the Havas agency (Suresnes, France) posted a $64 million revenue decline and cut 850 jobs.[8]

This sort of change in the advertising industry is nothing new, as the section to follow highlights. But the pace of change and the complexity of the issues may be more challenging than any the industry has ever faced. We'll spend our time in this chapter considering the structure in the industry and all the "players" that are creating and being affected by change.

The Advertising Industry in Constant Transition.

The introductory scenario gives some examples of the deep and complex changes affecting the advertising industry. To say that the advertising industry is in *constant* transition might seem like an exaggeration, but it's not. If you consider changes in technology, economic conditions, culture, lifestyles, and business philosophies, one or more of these broad business and societal forces is always affecting the advertising and promotion effort. Aside from all these broad-based influences, we have to consider change in industry itself as the introductory scenario revealed.

This chapter highlights how the industry is changing now and has changed over time. But before we look at change and its effects, we first need to realize that the fundamental *process* of advertising and the role it plays in organizations remains steadfastly rooted in persuasive communications directed at target audiences—no matter what is happening with technology, economic conditions, society, or business philosophies. The underlying role and purpose of advertising and promotion has not changed and will not change.

To appreciate the way the advertising industry is in a state of constant transition and the level of complexity that transition can reach, it is necessary to appreciate that

5.   Rich Thomaselli, "Tylenol Remedy Sees Results," *Advertising Age*, February 9, 2004, 3, 51.
6.   Alice Z. Cuneo and Lisa Sanders, "Verizon Wireless Puts $315 Mil in Play," *Advertising Age*, January 12, 2004, 1.
7.   Lisa Sanders and Jean Halliday, "GM Hammers Agency Costs," *Advertising Age*, November 17, 2003.
8.   Laurel Wentz, "Havas to Cut 850 Jobs in Restucturing," *Advertising Age*, September 22, 2003, 3; Mercedes M. Cardona, "Interpublic's $327 Mil Loss Highlights Messy Situation," *Advertising Age*, November 17, 2003, 8.

advertising is an industry with great breadth and intricacy due to the fact that it is a communications process and therefore a communications industry. We will turn our attention to that issue now—understanding how advertising and other promotional tools are managed in a communications industry and how that effort is managed in a state of constant transition. First, we'll look at advertising as a fairly well-structured communications industry. Then, we'll consider all the different participants in the process, particularly the advertisers and their advertising agencies and the role they play in creating and executing advertising and integrated brand promotions.

Trends Affecting the Advertising and Promotion Industry.

Often advertisers struggle with whether to use traditional mass media, like television and radio, that have wide reach. Or whether they should use newer, highly targeted media like personalized e-mail, Web films, or other forms of promotion. But in the end what is important is not the Web or the new opportunities that technology has to offer, but rather the critical need to focus on the brand, its image, and a persuasive, integrated presentation of that brand to the target market. It might be the Web, it might not. It might be television, it might not. The point is that the right medium needs to be used to achieve the right persuasive impact.

To understand the change that is affecting the advertising and promotion industry and the use of promotional tools, let's consider four broad trends in the marketplace.

The "Undoing" of Agency Consolidation and Globalization?

As the introductory scenario alluded to, the advertising industry went through a period of extreme consolidation from 1999 through 2002. Full-service agencies acquired and merged with other full-service agencies and interactive shops. One such merger sequence began when Leo Burnett (the long-standing Chicago-based full-service agency) merged with the MacManus group to create a $1.7 billion-a-year agency known as Bcom3 Group, with 500 operating units in 90 countries and 16,000 employees.[9] Adding globalization to that merger, the Japanese agency Dentsu took a partnership position in the agreement as well. Then, two years later, the Paris-based global agency Publicis bought up the whole Bcom3 set. Another global agency, Interpublic Group, acquired more than 300 agencies from 1998 through 2002 at a cost of over $5 billion. It is fair to say that the advertising industry is now dominated by four giant, global agency groups: Publicis Groupe (Paris), Omnicom Group (New York), Interpublic Group (New York), and WPP Group (London).

But while this all consolidation and globalization provided an enormous array of services to clients, it has created problems as well. First, not all clients were impressed with the giant agencies. In a survey of nearly 300 major companies, only 43 percent said that it was "very important" to have a single agency offer fully integrated services. They felt they would be missing out on the creativity that small shops can offer through the specialization of services.[10] And, when agencies get very large, there are inevitably conflicts of interest when trying to go after new business because the potential new client is in the same business as an existing client. Too, bigger has not always meant better or more profitable. Interpublic's buying binge has not increased its net income, yet it has created crushing debt and made the agency unwieldy. Analysts are now saying that these big agencies need to consolidate, get rid of money-losing operations, and turn what's left "loose to pursue their own clients."[11]

9.   Laura Petrecca and Hillary Chura, "Merged Leo-MacManus Could Be Valued at $5 Billion," *Advertising Age,* November 8, 1999, 3.

10.   Hillary Chura, "Marketers: One-Stop Shops Could Compromise Creative," *Advertising Age,* June 16, 2003, 6.

11.   Gerry Khermouch, "Interpublic Group: Synergy—or Sinkhole," *BusinessWeek,* April 21, 2003, 76–77.

I want eMail that relates.

To connect with your customers, you'll need more than a catchy subject line. DoubleClick delivers the first truly integrated suite of eMail solutions, featuring all the tools you need to build relationships, deliver dynamic messages and manage multiple campaigns. Your eMail is waiting.

DoubleClick eMail Suite:
DARTmail Publisher. Leverage dynamic targeting and scalable delivery up to 500 million messages a day.
DARTmail Campaign Manager. Control your own campaigns with advanced reporting.
DoubleClick eMail List Services. Acquire targeted opt-in customers and monetize your lists.
DoubleClick eMail Network. Place your ad in the Web's premier collection of email publications.
PredictiveMail. Find your most responsive opt-in customers with statistical modeling.

Shape your own:
doubleclick.net/shape

| MEDIA | EMAIL | WIRELESS | TECHSOLUTIONS | **DoubleClick**

EXHIBIT 2.2

The proliferation of media alternatives has caused media fragmentation in the advertising and promotion industry. One effect of this change is that new specialized media organizations have emerged to sell and manage new media options. DoubleClick, one of these new media companies, manages targeted e-mail messages. http://www .doubleclick.net

It is unlikely that the giant agencies will dismantle all they have created. Some advertising clients are pleased to be able to consolidate all their integrated brand promotion (IBP) needs with one shop. But there is enough burden on the agencies from debt and conflict of interest that some unconsolidation will most certainly take place.

Media Proliferation and Consolidation.

The proliferation of cable television, direct marketing technology, Web options, and alternative new media has caused a proliferation of media options And while agency consolidation may be turning around, media consolidation may just be starting. Control of media has always been a driving force behind many media companies. But there has always been a legal barrier to just how much control any one media company could acquire. Well, in 2003, the Federal Communications Commission (FCC) relaxed a decades-old rule that had restricted media ownership. Now a single company can own television stations that reach up to 45 percent of U.S. households up from the 35 percent specified in the old rule. In addition, the FCC also voted to lift all "cross-ownership" restrictions, ending a ban on the joint ownership of a newspaper and broadcast station in a city.[12]

It is too soon to know what the effects of this new ruling will be. What we do know is that media companies tend to pursue more and more "properties" if they are allowed to. Consider the evolution of newspaper, satellite, and cable systems giant News Corp. The company's worldwide media holdings company generates $30 billion in revenue and reaches every corner of the earth.[13] And the Web has its own media conglomerate. InterActiveCorp (IAC) has amassed a media empire of Internet sites that is as diverse as it is successful. The holdings include Expedia, Hotels.com, Ticketmaster, Hotwire.com, and Lending Tree. Together, these sites generate about $6.2 billion in revenue, which makes IAC much bigger than better-known Internet merchants like eBay and Amazon.com.[14] In turn, the evolution of media options has spawned new specialized agencies to sell and manage these new media opportunities (see Exhibit 2.2). But fragmentation is only one aspect of the media evolution.

Media Clutter and Fragmentation.

While the media industry may be consolidating into fewer and fewer large firms with more control, that does not mean that there are fewer media options. Quite the contrary is true. There are more ways to *try* to reach consumers than ever before. In 1994 the consumer had access to about 27 television channels. Today, the average U.S. household has access to about 100 channels. In

12.   David Ho, "FCC Votes to Ease Media Ownership Rules," *Washington Post*, available at http://news.yahoo.com, accessed on June 2, 2003.
13.   Ronald Grover and Tom Lowry, "Rupert's World," *BusinessWeek*, January 19, 2004, 52–62.
14.   Timothy J. Mullaney and Ronald Grover, "The Web Mogul," *BusinessWeek*, October 13, 2003, 62–70.

1995, it took three well-placed TV spots to reach 80 percent of women television viewers. By 2003, it took 97 spots to reach them![15] From television ads to billboards to banner ads on the Internet, these new and increased media options have resulted in so much clutter that the probability of any one advertisement breaking through and making a real difference continues to diminish. Advertisers are developing a lack of faith in advertising alone, so promotion options such as online communication, brand placement in film and television, point-of-purchase displays, and sponsorships are more attractive to advertisers. For example, advertisers on the Super Bowl, notorious for its clutter and outrageous ad prices (about $2.5 million to $3 million for a 30-second spot), have turned instead to promotional tie-ins to enhance the effect of the advertising. To combat the clutter and expense at one Super Bowl, Miller Brewing distributed thousands of inflatable Miller Lite chairs by game day. The chairs were a tie-in with a national advertising campaign that began during the regular season before the Super Bowl.[16]

Given the backlash against advertising that clutter can cause, advertisers and their agencies are rethinking the way they try to communicate with consumers. Fundamentally, there is a greater focus on integrating more tools within the overall promotional effort in an attempt to reach more consumers in more different ways. As an example, just consider the kind of communication *plus* distribution channels that have emerged in the context of e-commerce. These new communication/distribution links include catalogs, TV shopping networks, and especially the online shopping and interactive television cited earlier. Consumers do not just want a communications experience; they are now expressing a desire for a *commerce* experience.[17] This topic is covered in detail in Chapter 17.

Advertisers are looking to the full complement of promotional opportunities in sales promotions (like the Miller chairs), event sponsorships, new media options, and public relations as means to support and enhance the primary advertising effort for brands. In fact, some advertisers are enlisting the help of Hollywood talent agencies in an effort to get their brands featured in television programs and films. The payoff for strategic placement in a film or television show can be huge. For example, getting Coca-Cola placed on *American Idol* is estimated to be worth up to $20 million in traditional media advertising.[18] This topic is covered in Chapter 17 when we consider branded entertainment in detail. The IBP box highlights how several firms in the luxury brand market are using public relations and brand placements in celebrity settings to grow brand visibility by using tools beyond mass media.

Consumer Control: From Blogs to TiVo. Historically, advertisers controlled information and the flow of information as a one-way communication through mass media. But, as the introductory scenario highlights, consumers are now in greater control of the information they receive about product categories and the brands within those categories. The simplest and most obvious example is when consumers log on to the Internet and visit sites they choose to visit for either information or shopping. But it gets a lot more complicated from there. The emergence of **blogs,** Web sites frequented by individuals with common interest where they can post facts, opinions, and personal experiences, are emerging as new and sophisticated sources of product and brand information. Once criticized as the "ephemeral scribble" of 13-year-old girls and the babble of techno-geeks, blogs are gaining greater sophistication and

15.   Matthew Boyle, "Brand Killers," *Fortune,* April 11, 2003, 89–100.
16.   Betsy Spethmann, "Pre-Game Warmups," *PROMO Magazine,* December 2000, 33–34; Bruce Horovitz, "Gee-Whiz Effects Make Super Bowl Ads Super Special," *USA Today,* January 30 ,2004, B1–B2.
17.   Lauren Barack, "Chiat's New Day," *Business 2.0,* December 1999, 130–132.
18.   Betsy Streisand, "Why Great American Brands Are Doing Lunch," *Business 2.0,* September 2003, 146–150.

organization. Web-based service firms like Blogline, Feedster, and Blogger are making blogs easier to use and accessible to the masses.[19]

IBP

See the Brand, Join the Club

Most advertisers have embraced the concept that a wide range of promotional tools is essential for reaching target markets and positively affecting brand awareness and image. But few advertisers have needed the full range of integrated brand promotion (IBP) strategies as much as luxury brand marketers, who need not only to maintain brand awareness but also to protect their brands from counterfeit brands. Knockoffs of luxury brands like Gucci, Hermes, and Rolex continue to be a problem. In the summer of 2000, Power Beads became a nationwide craze. The bead bracelet from New York design firm Stella Pace was the must-have accessory for the fashion conscious. But Zoe Metro, who conceived the bead designs and founded the company, lamented, "I've been a case study for these knockoffs." While the real thing, made from semi-precious stones, sold for $35 in upscale jewelry stores, knockoffs of the Power Beads were showing up in discount stores for as little as $5.

The answer to the knockoff problem? Experts say that the only solution is to continue to make the brand itself, not the object, the thing consumers covet. That, the experts continue, requires advertising plus a heavy investment in public relations, merchandising, and brand placements. The president of a brand consulting firm in New York argues, "There's a three dimensionality that builds these brands. It's not just advertising. Everything builds the brand from the advertising to the store experience to the Web site." The vice president of marketing for Louis Vuitton adds, "It's a top-to-bottom brand concept. PR is very important in helping these brands establish themselves. People are always trying to place their products in the right programs and with the right people because it adds validity to the brand." Metro credits the original success of Power Beads to celebrity plugs and coverage of the brand's popularity in the fashion media.

The formula of advertising plus IBP strategies must be working for these luxury brand marketers. Despite the aggressiveness of the counterfeiters, Interbrand research found that luxury brands like Louis Vuitton and Chanel have been enjoying 30 to 60 percent growth, while Gap and Nike have shown little or no growth in the past few years.

Source: Mercedes M. Cardona, "Trendsetting Brands Combat Knockoffs," *Advertising Age*, August 21, 2000, 20.

Another new and dramatic example of consumer control is the growth of personal video recorders (PVRs), like TiVo, which allow TV viewers to essentially skip broadcast advertising. Analysts expect that the use of PVRs will reduce ad viewership by as much as 30 percent by 2005. That translates into taking approximately $18 billion out of advertising industry revenue. And advertisers and their agencies can expect that by 2007, approximately one-quarter (27.4 million) of all U.S. television households will have "ad-skipping" capability.[20] Advertisers and their agencies will need to adapt to the concept that consumers are gaining greater control over the information they choose to receive. How will they adapt? Creativity is one answer. The more entertaining and informative an ad can be, the more likely consumers will be to want to actually watch the ads. Another technique, less creative but certainly effective, is to run advertising messages along the bottom of the programming. While effective, this method is sure to bring about the wrath of viewers and producers alike.[21]

Big advertisers are quickly recognizing that consumers are taking more and more control of their shopping and consumption experience. Big advertisers like Procter & Gamble have adopted the position that the "Consumer is Boss" and are developing new research methods to deal with this new, more independent, and harder to reach consumer.[22] You'll learn more about these research methods in Chapter 7 when we discuss advertising and promotion research.

For years to come, these trends and the changes they effect will force advertisers to think differently about advertising and IBP. Similarly, advertising agencies will need to think about the way they serve their clients and the way communications are delivered to audiences. As you have read already, big spenders such as Procter & Gamble, Miller Brewing, and General Motors are already demanding new and innovative programs to enhance the

19. John Battelle, "Why Blogs Mean Business," *Business 2.0*, January–February 2004, 62.
20. Stephen Baker, "My Son, the Ad-Zapper," *BusinessWeek*, November 10, 2003.
21. Ronald Grover, et. al., "Can Mad Ave Make Zap-Proof Ads?" *BusinessWeek*, February 2, 2004, 36–37.
22. Jim Stengel, keynote address to the AAAA Media Conference and Trade Show, February 12, 2004.

impact of their advertising and promotional dollars. The goal of creating persuasive communication remains intact—attract attention and develop preference for a brand—and so the dynamics of the communications environment and the changes in the structure of the advertising industry are the central topics of this chapter.

2 The Scope and Structure of the Advertising Industry. To

fully appreciate the structure of the advertising industry, let's first consider the size of the advertising industry. Remember from Chapter 1 that the advertising industry is huge: more than $250 billion spent in the United States alone on various categories of advertising, with nearly $550 billion spent worldwide. Spending on all forms of promotion exceeds a trillion dollars.[23]

Another indicator of the scope of advertising is the investment made by individual firms. Exhibit 2.3 shows spending for 2003 and 2002 among the top 20 U.S. advertisers. Hundreds of millions of dollars and, in the case of the largest spenders, even billions of dollars is truly a huge amount of money to spend annually on advertising. But we have to realize that the $3.7 billion spent by General Motors on advertising was just about 2 percent of GM's sales. Similarly, Unilever spent about

EXHIBIT 2.3

The 20 largest advertisers in the United States in 2003 (U.S. dollars in millions).

Company	2003 Ad Dollars (millions)	2002 Ad Dollars (millions)	% Change
General Motors	$3,429	$3,652	−6.1%
Procter & Gamble	3,322	2,673	24.3
Time Warner	3,097	2,922	6.0
Pfizer	2,838	2,566	10.6
DaimlerChrysler	2,317	2,031	14.1
Ford Motor Co.	2,233	2,251	−0.8
Walt Disney Co.	2,129	1,803	18.1
Johnson & Johnson	1,995	1,799	10.9
Sony Corp.	1,814	1,621	12.0
Toyota Motor	1,682	1,552	8.4
Verizon Communications	1,674	1,527	9.6
Sears Roebuck & Co.	1,633	1,661	−1.7
General Electric	1,575	1,181	25.4
Glaxo Smith Kline	1,553	1,554	0.0
SBC Communications	1,511	936	38.4
McDonald's	1,368	1,330	2.4
Unilever	1,332	1,640	−18.8
Altria	1,311	1,206	8.7
Nissan	1,300	845	34.6
Merck	1,264	1,158	9.1

Source: "100 Leading National Advertisers," *Advertising Age,* June 28, 2004, S-2.

23.   Hillary Chura, "Coen: 2005 Ad Spending Will Increase to $280 Billion," *Advertising Age,* June 28, 2004, 8.

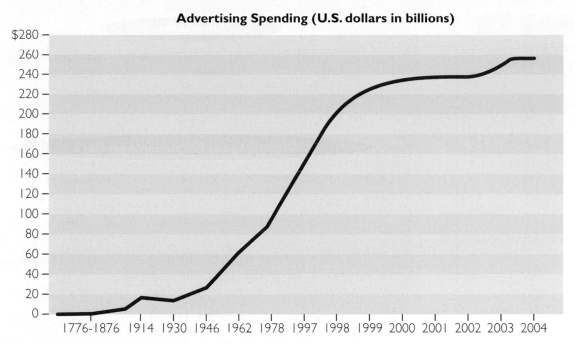

Advertising Spending (U.S. dollars in billions)

Source: "100 Leading National Advertisers," *Advertising Age*, annual estimates.

EXHIBIT 2.4

Advertising spending from the founding of the United States into the 21st century.

$1.6 billion, but this amount represented only about 3.2 percent of its sales. So while the absolute dollars are large, the relative spending is much more modest. Overall, the 100 leading advertisers in the United States spent just over $90 billion on advertising in 2003, which was a healthy 9 percent increase over 2002.[24] Still, there is no doubt that this rapidly increasing spending is related to increased clutter. Advertising may be quickly becoming its own worst enemy. Exhibit 2.4 shows the increase in advertising across the 20th century and into the 21st century.

Beyond the scope of spending, the structure of the industry is really the key issue. When we understand the structure of the advertising industry, we know *who* does *what, in what order,* during the advertising process. The advertising industry is actually a collection of a wide range of talented people, all of whom have special expertise and perform a wide variety of tasks in planning, preparing, and placing of advertising. Exhibit 2.5 shows the structure of the advertising industry by showing who the different participants are in the process.

Exhibit 2.5 demonstrates that *advertisers* (such as Kellogg) can employ the services of *advertising agencies* (such as Grey Global Group) that may (or may not) contract for specialized services with various *external facilitators* (such as Simmons Market Research Bureau), which results in advertising being transmitted with the help of various *media organizations* (such as the TNT cable network) to one or more *target audiences* (such as you!).

Note the dashed line on the left side of Exhibit 2.5. This line indicates that advertisers do not always employ the services of advertising agencies. Nor do advertisers or agencies always seek the services of external facilitators. Some advertisers deal directly with media organizations for placement of their advertisements or implementation of their promotions. This happens either when an advertiser has an internal advertising/promotions department that prepares all the materials for the process, or when media organizations (especially radio, television, and newspapers) provide technical assistance in the preparation of materials. The new interactive media formats also provide advertisers the opportunity to work directly with entertainment programming firms, such as Walt Disney, Sony, and SFX Entertainment,

24.   "100 Leading National Advertisers," , *Advertising Age,* June 28, 2004, S1.

*Structure of the advertising
industry and participants in
the process.*

Advertisers

| Manufacturers and service firms | *Trade resellers:* retailers, wholesalers, and distributors | Government and social organizations |

Advertising and Promotion Agencies

Advertising Agencies:
Full-service agencies
Creative boutiques
Interactive agencies
In-house agencies
Media specialists

Promotion Agencies:
Direct marketing and
    database agencies
E-commerce agencies
Sales promotion agencies
Event-planning agencies
Design firms
Public relations firms

Agency services:
Account services
Creative research
    and development
Creative and production
    services
Marketing services
Media planning, research,
    and buying services
Public relations
Direct-marketing and
    promotion services
Administrative services

Agency compensation:
Commission
Markup charges
Fee system
Pay-for-results

External Facilitators

| Marketing and advertising research firms | Production facilitators Consultants Information intermediators Software firms | Other communications organizations |

Media Organizations

| Broadcast media Print media Media specialists | Interactive media Support media | Media conglomerates Internet portals |

Target Audience(s)

to provide integrated programming that features brand placements in films and tele-vision programs or at entertainment events. And, as you will see, many of the new media agencies provide the creative and technical assistance advertisers need to implement campaigns through new media.

Each level in the structure of the industry is complex. So let's take a look at each level, with particular emphasis on the nature and activities of agencies. When you need to devise advertising or a fully integrated brand promotion, no source will be more valuable than the advertising or promotion agency you work with. Advertis-ing and promotion agencies provide the essential creative firepower to the process and represent a critical link in the structure.

Advertisers. First in the structure of advertising is the advertisers themselves. From your local pet store to multinational corporations, organizations of all types and sizes seek to benefit from the effects of advertising. **Advertisers** are business, not-for-profit, and government organizations that use advertising and other promotional techniques to communicate with target markets and to stimulate awareness and demand for their brands. Advertisers are also referred to as **clients** by their advertising and promotion agency partners. Different types of advertisers use advertising somewhat differently, depending on the type of product or service they market. The following categories describe the different types of advertisers and the role advertising plays for them.

Manufacturers and Service Firms. Large national manufacturers of consumer products and services are the most prominent users of promotion, often spending hundreds of millions of dollars annually. Procter & Gamble, General Foods, MCI, and Merrill Lynch all have national or global markets for their products and services. The use of advertising, particularly mass media advertising, by these firms is essential to creating awareness and preference for their brands. But advertising is useful not just to national or multinational firms; regional and local producers of household goods and services also rely heavily on advertising. For example, regional dairy companies sell milk, cheese, and other dairy products in regions usually comprising a few states. These firms often use ads placed in newspapers and regional editions of magazines. Further, couponing and sampling are ways to communicate with target markets with IBPs that are well suited to regional application. Several breweries and wineries also serve only regional markets. Local producers of products are relatively rare, but local service organizations are common. Medical facilities, hair salons, restaurants, auto dealers, and arts organizations are examples of local service providers that use advertising to create awareness and stimulate demand. What car dealer in America has not advertised a holiday event or used a remote local radio broadcast to attract attention!

Firms that produce business goods and services also use advertising on a global, national, regional, and local basis. IBM (computer and business services) and Deloitte (accounting and consulting services) are examples of global companies that produce business goods and services. At the national and regional level, firms that supply agricultural and mining equipment and repair services are common users of promotion, as are consulting and research firms. At the local level, firms that supply janitorial, linen, and bookkeeping services use advertising.

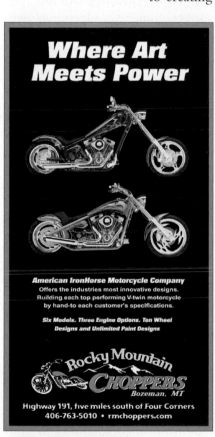

EXHIBIT 2.6

Advertising is not reserved for just big companies with national markets like Microsoft or Snapple. Organizations that serve regional and local markets, like Rocky Mountain Choppers, can make effective use of advertising as well. (http://www.rmchoppers .com)

Trade Resellers. The term **trade reseller** is simply a general description for all organizations in the marketing channel of distribution that buy products to resell to customers. As Exhibit 2.5 shows, resellers can be retailers, wholesalers, or distributors. These resellers deal with both household consumers and business buyers at all geographic market levels.

Retailers that sell in national or global markets are the most visible reseller advertisers. Sears, The Limited, and McDonald's are examples of national and global retail companies that use various forms of promotion to communicate with customers. Regional retail chains, typically grocery chains such as Albertson's or department stores such as Dillard's, serve multistate markets and use advertising suited for their regional customers. (See Exhibit 2.6.) At the local level, small retail shops of all sorts rely on newspaper, radio, television, and billboard advertising and special promotional events to reach a relatively small geographic area.

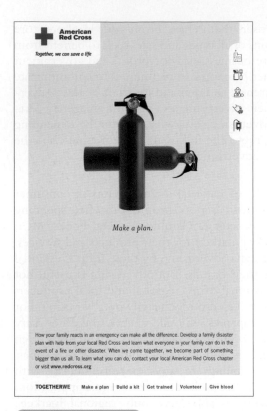

American Red Cross

Together, we can save a life

Make a plan.

How your family reacts in an emergency can make all the difference. Develop a family disaster plan with help from your local Red Cross and learn what everyone in your family can do in the event of a fire or other disaster. When we come together, we become part of something bigger than us all. To learn what you can do, contact your local American Red Cross chapter or visit www.redcross.org

TOGETHERWE   Make a plan | Build a kit | Get trained | Volunteer | Give blood

EXHIBIT 2.7

Government and social organizations can use advertising as effectively as corporations. Here the American Red Cross is using advertising to communicate to families the importance of having a "family disaster plan" in case of a fire or other catastrophe. Note how the American Red Cross is highlighting its logo in this ad as a way of developing "brand" recognition—just like corporations do!
(http://www.redcross.org)

Wholesalers and distributors, such as Ideal Supply, Inc. (a company that supplies contractors with blasting and surveying equipment), are a completely different breed of reseller. Technically, these types of companies deal only with business customers, since their position in the distribution channel dictates that they sell products either to producers (who buy goods to produce other goods) or to retailers (who resell goods to household consumers). Occasionally, an organization will call itself a wholesaler and sell to the public. Such an organization is actually operating as a retail outlet.

Wholesalers and distributors have little need for mass media advertising over media such as television and radio. Rather, they use trade publications, directory advertising such as the Yellow Pages and trade directories, direct mail, and their Internet Web sites as their main advertising media.

Federal, State, and Local Governments. At first, you might think it is odd to include governments as advertising users, but government bodies invest millions of dollars in advertising annually. The U.S. government often ranks as one of the 25 largest spenders on advertising in the United States, with expenditures typically exceeding $1.0 billion annually.[25] And that's just on advertising. If you add in other IBP expenses like brochures, recruiting fairs, and the personal selling expense of recruiting offices, the U.S. government easily spends well over $2 billion annually. The federal government's spending on advertising and promotion is concentrated in two areas: armed forces recruiting and social issues. As an example, the U.S. government regularly uses broad-based advertising campaigns for military recruiting.[26] The U.S. Army's "Army of One" campaign uses television, magazine, newspapers, and interactive games ("America's Army") hosted at the Army recruiting Web site (http://www.goarmy.com).

Social Organizations. Advertising by social organizations at the national, state, and local level is common. The Nature Conservancy, United Way, and American Red Cross use advertising to raise awareness of their organizations, seek donations, and attempt to shape behavior (deter drug use or encourage breast self-examination procedures, for example). National organizations such as these use both the mass media and direct mail to promote their causes and services (see Exhibit 2.7). Every state has its own unique statewide organizations, such as Citizens against Hunger, a state arts council, a tourism office, an economic development office, or a historical society. Social organizations in local communities represent a variety of special interests, from computer clubs to fraternal organizations to neighborhood child care organizations. The advertising used by social organizations has the same fundamental purpose as the advertising carried out by major multinational corporations: to stimulate demand and disseminate information. While big multinationals might use national or even global advertising, local organizations rely on advertising through local media to reach local audiences.

The Role of the Advertiser in IBP. Very few of the advertisers just discussed have the employees or financial resources to strategically plan and then prepare effective advertising and IBP programs. This is where advertising and promotion agencies play such an important role in the structure of the advertising industry. But there is an important role played by the advertiser *before* the services of an agency are enlisted. Advertisers

25.   Ibid.
26.   Elizabeth Boston, "Marketers Tweak Efforts on Fly," *Advertising Age,* June 23, 2003, 24.

of all sizes and types, as just discussed, have to be prepared for their interaction with an agency in order for the agency to do *its* job effectively. That is, it is the advertiser's role to

- Fully understand and describe the value that the firm's brand provides to users
- Fully understand and describe the brand's position in the market relative to competitive brands
- Describe the firm's objectives for the brand in the near term and long term (e.g., brand extensions, international market launches)
- Identify the target market(s) that are most likely to respond favorably to the brand
- Identify and manage the supply chain/distribution system that will most effectively reach the target markets
- Be committed to using advertising and other promotional tools as part of the organization's overall marketing strategy to grow the brand

Once an advertiser has done its job with respect to the six factors above, then and *only* then is it time to enlist the services of an agency to help effectively and creatively develop the market for the brand. This is not to say that an agency will not work with an advertiser to help better define and refine these factors. Rather, it is a mistake for an advertiser to enter a relationship with an agency (of any type) without first doing its homework and being prepared for a productive partnership.

3 **Advertising and Promotion Agencies.** Advertisers are fortunate to have a full complement of agencies that specialize in literally every detail of every advertising and promotion. Let's take a closer look at the types of agencies advertisers can rely on to help create their advertising and IBP campaigns.

Advertising Agencies. Most advertisers choose to enlist the services of an advertising agency. An **advertising agency** is an organization of professionals who provide creative and business services to clients in planning, preparing, and placing advertisements. The reason so many firms rely on advertising agencies is that agencies house a collection of professionals with very specialized talent, experience, and expertise that simply cannot be matched by in-house talent.

Most big cities and small towns in the United States have advertising agencies. Advertising agencies often are global businesses as well. As discussed in the section on trends affecting the advertising industry, megamergers between agencies have been occurring for several years. Exhibit 2.8 shows the world's 10 largest advertising organizations and their worldwide gross income. Worldwide revenue for ad agencies reached $20.54 billion in 2003.[27]

The types of agency professionals who help advertisers in the planning, preparation, and placement of advertising and other promotional activities include the following:

Account planners	Sales promotion and event planners
Marketing specialists	Copywriters
Account executives	Direct marketing specialists
Media buyers	Radio and television producers
Art directors	Web developers
Lead account planners	Researchers
Chief executive officers (CEOs)	Interactive media planners
Chief financial officers (CFOs)	Artists
Chief technology officers (CTOs)	Technical staff—printers, film editors,
Public relations specialists	and so forth
Creative directors	

27. "60th Annual Agency Report," *Advertising Age*, April 19, 2004, S1.

Rank		Company	Headquarters	Worldwide Gross Revenue, 2003 (millions)	% Change
2003	2002				
1	1	Omnicom Group	New York	$8,621	14.4
2	3	WPP Group	London	6,756	16.9
3	2	Interpublic Group	New York	5,863	–5.5
4	5	Publicis Groupe	Paris	4,408	7.3
5	4	Dentsu	Tokyo	2,545	11.0
6	6	Havas	Suresnes, France	1,877	–0.6
7	7	Grey Global Group	New York	1,307	9.0
8	8	Hakuhodo	Tokyo	1,208	0.0
9	9	Regis Group	London	1,067	21.9
10	10	Asatsu-DK	Tokyo	413	16.8

Source: "60th Annual Agency Report," *Advertising Age*, April 19, 2004, S-2.

EXHIBIT 2.8

The world's top 10 advertising organizations (ranked by worldwide gross revenue, U.S. dollars in millions).

As this list suggests, some advertising agencies can provide advertisers with a host of services, from campaign planning through creative concepts to e-strategies to measuring effectiveness. Also note from this list that an agency is indeed a business. Agencies have CEOs, CFOs, and CTOs just like any other business. Salaries in the positions listed above range from about $200,000 a year for a chief executive officer to about $50,000 for a media planner.[28] Of course, those salaries change depending on whether you're in a big urban market or a small regional market.

Several different types of agencies are available to the advertiser. Be aware that there are all sorts of agencies with varying degrees of expertise and services. It is up to the advertiser to dig deep into an agency's background and determine which agency or set of multiple agencies will fulfill the advertiser's needs. A short description of the major different types of agencies follows:

Full-Service Agencies. A **full–service agency** typically includes an array of advertising professionals to meet all the promotional needs of clients. Often, such an agency will also offer a client global contacts. Omnicom Group and Grey Global Group are examples. Full-service agencies are not necessarily large organizations employing hundreds or even thousands of people. Small local and regional shops can be full service with just a few dozen employees. At one point, when American Honda put its Acura account up for review, it wanted outstanding creative talent no matter what size agency did the work. The account went to a midsize agency in Santa Monica, California, well outside the mainstream of large agency cities.[29] Similarly, not every full-service agency is built on giant accounts worth hundreds of millions of dollars. Cramer-Krasselt, a midsize agency, has built a stable of international clients one small and medium account at a time. The agency rarely has accounts billing over $20 million. But by serving small accounts from clients such as AirTran, Allen-Edmonds shoes, Rexall, and Bombardier ATVs, the agency now has several million dollars in annual billings.[30]

28. R. Craig Endicott, "Agencies Mixed on '04 Pay Hikes," *Advertising Age,* December 8, 2003, S1.
29. *Advertising Age* Viewpoint editorial, "Why Mid-Size Shops Survive," *Advertising Age,* October 28, 1998, 26.
30. Hillary Chura and Kate MacArthur, "Cramer-Krasselt Thinks Small," *Advertising Age,* September 11, 2000, 32.

I am blue

How fast is online advertising changing? Whoops, you just lost ground to your biggest competitor. Yet the demands to provide rich, versatile, accountable, on-time solutions never seem to lessen. So you have a choice: Stay ahead, or you're toast. Whoops, they just did it to you again. That's why I am blue. JOHN BEHRMAN CEO BEYOND INTERACTIVE

bluestreak

Get Results, Get Serious. | www.bluestreak.com | 617-361-3300

EXHIBIT 2.9

The era of new media has spawned new interactive advertising agencies that specialize in developing banner ads and corporate Web sites. Bluestreak is an agency with the stated purpose of providing the infrastructure for marketers and agencies to create results-driven campaigns that generate dramatically higher click-through, conversion, and transaction rates. Check out their philosophy and purpose at http://www.bluestreak .com.

Creative Boutiques. A **creative boutique** typically emphasizes creative concept development, copywriting, and artistic services to clients. An advertiser can employ this alternative for the strict purpose of infusing greater creativity into the message theme or individual advertisement. As one advertising expert put it, "If all clients want is ideas, lots of them, from which they can pick and mix to their hearts' delight, they won't want conventional, full-service agencies. They all want fast, flashy fee-based idea factories."[31] Creative boutiques are these idea factories. Some large global agencies such as McCann-Erickson Worldwide and Leo Burnett have set up creative-only project shops that mimic the services provided by creative boutiques, with mixed results. The truth is that as the advertising industry continues to evolve, the creative boutiques may become a casualty of expansion-contraction-expansion by the big global multi-service agencies.[32] Be assured, there are still some great creative boutiques around, like E-volution Media (http:// www.e-volutionmedia.com) and Fusion Idea Lab (http://www.fusionidealab.com).

The creative boutique's greatest advantage, niche expertise, may be its greatest liability as well. As firms search for IBP programs and make a commitment to IBP campaigns, the creative boutique may be an extra expense and step that advertisers simply don't feel they can afford. But, as you will learn in Chapter 10 on creativity and advertising, the creative effort is so essential to effective brand building that creativity will rise to prominence in the process, and creative boutiques are well positioned to deliver that value.

Interactive Agencies. **Interactive agencies** help advertisers prepare communications for new media such as the Internet, interactive kiosks, CD-ROMs, and interactive television. Interactive agencies focus on ways to use Web-based solutions for direct marketing and target market communications (see Exhibit 2.9). Other cyberagencies, which we will talk about shortly, specialize in online promotions. One of the best interactive agencies in this regard is Ad4ever.com. This highly successful agency has created interactive campaigns for BMW, Oracle, Nintendo, and the U.S. Army. Check out their work at http://www.ad4ever.com and the story about their work in the Creativity box. But interactive agencies were not spared when the big shake out occurred among dot.coms in 1999. Many simply folded up shop; others were acquired by large agencies. Today, even a midsize full-service agency will offer interactive services to clients. This being the case, many firms have consolidated all their IBP needs, including interactive media, with their main full-service agency.

In-House Agencies. An **in-house agency** is often referred to as the advertising department in a firm and takes responsibility for the planning and preparation of advertising materials. This option has the advantage of greater coordination and control in all phases of the advertising and promotion process. Some prominent advertisers who do most of their work in-house are Gap, Calvin Klein, and Revlon. The

31.   Martin Sorell, "Agencies Face New Battle Grounds," *Advertising Age*, April 13, 1998, 22.
32.   Anthony Vagnoni, "Small Fries," *Advertising Age*, March 4, 2002, 20.

advertiser's own personnel have control over and knowledge of marketing activities, such as product development and distribution tactics. Another advantage is that the firm can essentially keep all the profits from commissions an external agency would have earned. While the advantages of doing advertising work in-house are attractive, there are two severe limitations. First, there may be a lack of objectivity, thereby constraining the execution of all phases of the advertising process. Second, it is highly unlikely that an in-house agency could ever match the breadth and depth of talent available in an external agency.

Media Specialists. While not technically agencies, **media specialists** are organizations that specialize in buying media time and space and offer media strategy consulting to advertising agencies and advertisers. The task of strategic coordination of media and promotional efforts has become more complex because of the proliferation of media options and extensive use of promotional tools beyond advertising.

An example of one of these specialists is Starcom MediaVest Group (SMG). SMG encompasses an integrated network of nearly 3,800 contact architects specializing in media management, Internet and digital communications, response media, entertainment marketing, sports sponsorships, event marketing, and multicultural media. A subsidiary of France-based Publicis Groupe, SMG's network of 110 offices in 76 countries focuses on brand building for many of the world's leading companies. In fact, its Web site prominently displays the slogan "Fueling Brand Power" (http://www.starcomworldwide.com).

CREATIVITY

The Four-Second Ad

When Eurocom Cellular Communications, sole agent for Nokia phones in Israel, wanted to launch the new Nokia 6210 mobile phone, the company turned to an interactive agency, Ad4ever Inc. (http://www.ad4ever.com). Eurocom was intrigued with Ad4ever's TopLayer Technology, which has been producing an unheard-of 25 percent click-through rate (CTR) in other campaigns. CTR measures the volume of traffic from exposure to the Web ad site.

Eurocom was not disappointed. Using the Internet's multimedia platform, Ad4ever created an interactive advertising campaign that emphasized the mobile phone's unique features. These included Internet access by WAP, high-speed data transmission, ability to synchronize with a computer, and an extended calendar.

The ads that were developed for the Nokia 6210 appear on a transparent layer above the conventional Web site on a user's screen. The ad is an interactive, animated, dynamic object complete with a greeting to the viewer. The ads are nonintrusive, lasting for only four seconds before disappearing from the middle of the monitor. The campaign then uses a friendly reminder that travels the screen as viewers scroll down the screen, staying with the user in a way that traditional banner ads do not. Users can choose to interact with the ad and request more information about the phone without leaving the Web site they originally came to visit.

Ophira Avisha, the MARCOM (Marketing Communications) manager at Eurocom, said, "We believe that by using Ad4ever's technology, we will be able to gain more effective use of the Internet as an integral part of our advertising."

Source: Ad4ever.com, "Interactive Online Advertising Campaign to Launch Nokia 6210," press release available at http://www.ad4ever.com/site/press/pr130602.html, accessed on January 8, 2004.

One additional advantage of using media specialists is that since they buy media in large quantities, they often acquire media time at a much lower cost than an agency or advertiser could. Also, media specialists often have time and space in inventory and can offer last-minute placement to advertisers. Media-buying services have been a part of the advertising industry structure for many years. In recent years, however, media planning has been added to the task of simply buying media space. At one point, Unilever decided to turn over its $575 million media-buying and planning tasks to a specialized agency, MindShare Worldwide. Firms are finding that the firm that buys space can provide keen insights into the media strategy as well.[33]

33. Richard Linnett, "Unilever Win Affirms MindShare Strategy," *Advertising Age*, December 4, 2000, 4.

Promotion Agencies. While advertisers often rely on an advertising agency as a steering organization for their promotional efforts, many specialized agencies often enter the process and are referred to as **promotion agencies.** This is because advertising agencies, even full-service agencies, will concentrate on the advertising process and often provide only a few key ancillary services for other promotional efforts. This is particularly true in the current era, in which new media are offering so many different ways to communicate to target markets. Promotion agencies can handle everything from sampling to event promotions to in-school promotional tie-ins. Descriptions of the types of agencies and their services follow.

Direct Marketing and Database Agencies. Direct marketing agencies and **database agencies** (sometimes also called **direct response agencies**) provide a variety of direct marketing services. These firms maintain and manage large databases of mailing lists as one of their services. These firms can design direct marketing campaigns either through the mail or via telemarketing, or direct response campaigns using all forms of media. These agencies help advertisers construct databases of target customers, merge databases, develop promotional materials, and then execute the campaign. In many cases, these agencies maintain **fulfillment centers,** which ensure that customers receive the product ordered through direct mail. Direct Media (http://www. directmedia.com) is the world's largest list management and list brokerage firm, providing clients with services in both the consumer and the business-to-business markets across the country and around the world.

Many of these agencies are set up to provide creative and production services to clients. These firms will design and help execute direct response advertising campaigns using traditional media such as radio, television, magazines, and newspapers. Also, there are some that can prepare **infomercials** for clients: a five- to 60-minute information program that promotes a brand and offers direct purchase to viewers. AdProducers.com is an online community that lists infomercial producers around the world. It is part of the Ad Producer.com/ Entertainment Producer.com network of advertising providers.

E-Commerce Agencies. There are so many new and different kinds of e-commerce agencies that it is hard to categorize all of them. **E-commerce agencies** handle a variety of planning and execution activities related to promotions using electronic commerce. Note that these agencies are different from the interactive agencies discussed earlier. They do not create Web sites or banner ads, but rather help firms conduct all forms of promotion through electronic media, particularly the Internet. They can run sweepstakes, issue coupons, help in sampling, and do direct response campaigns (see Exhibit 2.10). A firm like 24/7 Real Media (http://www.247media.com) offers advertisers the option of providing consumers with online coupons, contests, and loyalty programs.

EXHIBIT 2.10

E-commerce agencies provide highly specialized Internet-based services. XactMail (http://www.xactmail .com) provides opt-in e-mail communications programs for advertisers.

Old Navy, American Airlines, the World Wildlife Fund, Cisco, and 3M are a few of the firms that have signed on with e-commerce agencies to add another dimension to their IBP campaigns. Another of these new media e-commerce organizations is DoubleClick (featured in Exhibit 2.2 earlier in the chapter), which provides services related to Internet advertising, targeting technology, complete advertising management software solutions, direct response Internet advertising, and Internet advertising developed for regional and local businesses. The best way to view these new e-commerce agencies is to understand that they can provide all forms of promotion using new media technology and usually specializing in Internet solutions.

Sales Promotion Agencies. These specialists design and then operate contests, sweepstakes, special displays, or coupon campaigns for advertisers. It is important to recognize that these agencies can specialize in **consumer sales promotions** and will focus on price-off deals, coupons, sampling, rebates, and premiums. Other firms will specialize in **trade sales promotions** designed to help advertisers use promotions aimed at wholesalers, retailers, vendors, and trade resellers. These agencies are experts in designing incentive programs, trade shows, sales force contests, in-store merchandising, and point-of-purchase materials.

Event-Planning Agencies. Event sponsorship can also be targeted to household consumers or the trade market. **Event-planning agencies** and organizers are experts in finding locations, securing dates, and putting together a team of people to pull off a promotional event: audio/visual people, caterers, security experts, entertainers, celebrity participants, or whoever is necessary to make the event come about. The event-planning organization will also often take over the task of advertising the event and making sure the press provides coverage (publicity) of the event. When an advertiser sponsors an entire event, such as a PGA golf tournament, managers will work closely with the event-planning agencies. If an advertiser is just one of several sponsors of an event, such as a NASCAR race, then it has less control over planning.

Design Firms. Designers and graphics specialists do not get nearly enough credit in the advertising and promotion process. If you take a job in advertising or promotion, your designer will be one of your first and most important partners. While designers are rarely involved in strategy planning, they are intimately involved in the execution of the advertising or IBP effort. In the most basic sense, **designers** help a firm create a **logo**—the graphic mark that identifies a company—and other visual representations that promote an identity for a firm. This mark will appear on everything from advertising to packaging to the company stationery, business cards, and signage. But beyond the logo, graphic designers will also design most of the materials used in supportive communications such as the package design, coupons, in-store displays, brochures, outdoor banners for events, newsletters, and direct mail pieces. One of the largest consumer package goods firms in the world recently made a larger commitment to design across all aspects of its marketing and promotion, claiming that design was critical to "winning customers in the store with packaging and displays [being] major factors in the outcome."[34]

Public Relations Firms. Public relations firms manage an organization's relationships with the media, the local community, competitors, industry associations, and government organizations. The tools of public relations include press releases, feature stories, lobbying, spokespersons, and company newsletters. Most advertisers do not like to handle their own public relations tasks for two reasons. First, public relations takes highly specialized skills and talent not normally found in an advertising firm. Second, managers are too close to public relations problems and may not be

34.   Jack Neff, "P&G Boosts Design's Role in Marketing," *Advertising Age,* February 9, 2004, 1, 52.

capable of handling a situation, particularly a negative situation, with measured public responses. For these reasons, advertisers, and even advertising agencies, turn to outside public relations firms. In keeping with the movement to incorporate the Internet across all forms of promotion, there are even organizations that will handle putting all of a firm's news releases online. One such firm is PR Newswire (http://www.prnewswire.com).

In a search for more and distinctive visibility for their brands, advertisers have been turning to public relations firms to achieve a wide range of film and television placements.[35] William Morris, originally a talent agency and now a public relations firm, has 16 consultants working with top consumer brands like Anheuser-Busch. William Morris succeeded in getting Budweiser to be the first beer advertiser on the Academy Awards.

Agency Services. Advertising and promotion agencies offer a wide range of services. The advertiser may need a large, global, full-service advertising agency to plan, prepare, and execute its advertising and IBP campaigns. On the other hand, a creative boutique may offer the right combination of services. Similarly, a large promotion firm might be needed to manage events and promotions while a design firm is enlisted for design work, but nothing else. The most important issue, however, is for the advertiser and the agency to negotiate and reach agreement on the services being provided before any agency is hired. Exhibit 2.11 shows the typical organizational structure of a full-service advertising agency that also provides a significant number of IBP services. The types of services commonly offered by advertising and promotion agencies are discussed in the following sections.

Account Services. **Account services** includes managers who have titles such as account executive, account supervisor, or account manager, and who work with clients to determine how the brand can benefit most from promotion. Account services entail identifying the benefits a brand offers, its target audiences, and the best competitive positioning, and then developing a complete promotion plan. In some cases, account services in an agency can provide basic marketing and consumer behavior research, but the client should bring this information to the table. Knowing the target segment, the brand's values, and the positioning strategy are really the responsibility of the advertiser (more on this in Chapters 5 and 6).

Account services managers also work with the client in translating cultural and consumer values into advertising and promotional messages through the creative services in the agency. Finally, they work with media services to develop an effective media strategy for determining the best vehicles for reaching the targeted audiences. One of the primary tasks in account services is to keep the various agency teams' creative, production, and media on schedule and within budget (more about this in Chapter 8 when we look at the advertising plan).

Marketing Research Services. Research conducted by an agency for a client usually consists of the agency locating studies (conducted by commercial research organizations) that have bearing on a client's market or advertising and promotion objectives. The research group will help the client interpret the research and communicate these interpretations to the creative and media people. If existing studies are not sufficient, research may be conducted by the agency itself. As mentioned in the account services discussion, some agencies can assemble consumers from the target audience to evaluate different versions of proposed advertising and determine whether messages are being communicated effectively.

Many agencies have established the position of account planner to coordinate the research effort. An **account planner's** stature in the organization is on par with an

35.   Betsy Streisand, "Why Great American Brands Are Doing Lunch," *Business 2.0*, September 2003, 146–150.

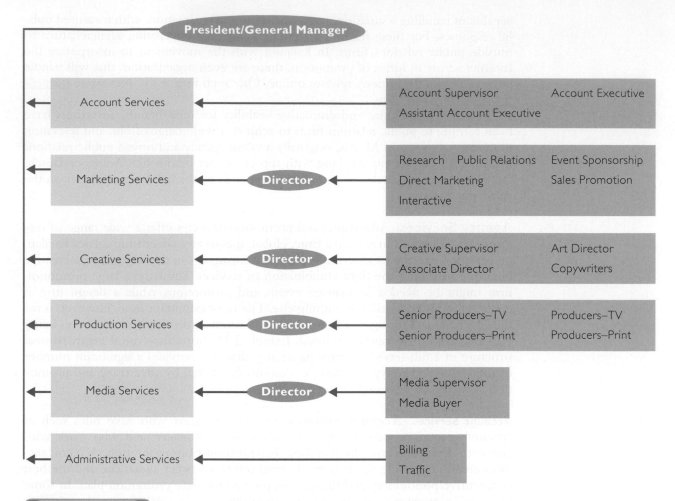

President/General Manager

Account Services	←	Account Supervisor	Account Executive
		Assistant Account Executive	

Marketing Services	← Director ←	Research Public Relations	Event Sponsorship
		Direct Marketing	Sales Promotion
		Interactive	

Creative Services	← Director ←	Creative Supervisor	Art Director
		Associate Director	Copywriters

Production Services	← Director ←	Senior Producers–TV	Producers–TV
		Senior Producers–Print	Producers–Print

Media Services	← Director ←	Media Supervisor
		Media Buyer

Administrative Services	←	Billing
		Traffic

EXHIBIT 2.11

The typical structure of a full-service advertising agency. Note that this structure includes significant integrated brand promotion (IBP) services as well as advertising services.

account executive. The account planner is assigned to clients to ensure that research input is included at each stage of development of campaign materials. Some agency leaders, like Jay Chiat of Chiat/Day, think that account planning has been the best new business tool ever invented.[36] Others are a bit more measured in their assessment. Jon Steel, director of account planning at Goody, Silverstein and Partners, described account planning this way: "[Account] planning, when used properly, is the best *old* business tool ever invented."[37] Either way, agencies are understanding that research, signaled by the appointment of an account planner, is key to successful promotional campaigns. The advertising research issue is considered in detail in Chapter 7.

Creative and Production Services. The **creative services** group in an agency comes up with the concepts that express the value of a company's brand in interesting and memorable ways. In simple terms, the creative services group develops the message that will be delivered though advertising, sales promotion, direct marketing, event sponsorship, or public relations. Howard Davis, retired CEO of the full-service advertising agency Tracy-Locke, refers to this process in the industry as the "art of commerce."[38]

Clients will push their agencies hard to come up with interesting and expressive ways to represent the brand. Geoffrey Frost, vice president of consumer communications for Motorola's Personal Communications Sector, expressed his company's

36.   John Steel, *Truth, Lies & Advertising: The Art of Account Planning* (New York: John Wiley & Sons, 1998), 42.
37.   Ibid, 43.
38.   Howard Davis expressed his views in this regard during a keynote speech at the Montana State University College of Business delivered on December 13, 2000.

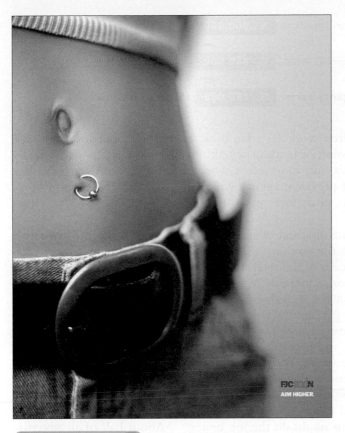

FJC*and*N
AIM HIGHER.

Advertising agencies, from large global agencies to smaller regional shops, provide a wide range of services for clients. Their greatest contribution to the process is, perhaps, their creative prowess. Here, FJCandN, a regional agency, once implored advertisers to "aim higher." A nice bit of creativity to tout the agency's creative talents.

approach to demanding creative excellence by saying, "What we've challenged the agencies to do was to help us to figure out how to position Motorola as the company that has really figured out the future. . . ."[39] That seems like a pretty tall creative order, indeed. The creative group in an agency will typically include a creative director, art director, illustrators or designers, and copywriters. In specialized promotion agencies, event planners, contest experts, and interactive media specialists will join the core group. Exhibit 2.12 shows how advertising agency FJCandN promotes its own creative services.

Production services include producers (and sometimes directors) who take creative ideas and turn them into advertisements, direct mail pieces, or events materials. Producers generally manage and oversee the endless details of production of the finished advertisement or other promotion material. Advertising agencies maintain the largest and most sophisticated creative and production staffs.

Media Planning and Buying Services. This service was discussed earlier as a specialized agency through which advertisers can contract for media buying and planning. Advertising agencies themselves provide **media planning and buying services** similar to those of the specialized agencies. The central challenge is to determine how a client's message can most effectively and efficiently reach the target audience. Media planners and buyers examine an enormous number of options to put together an effective media plan within the client's budget. But media planning and buying is much more than simply buying ad space, timing a coupon distribution, or scheduling an event. A wide range of media strategies can be implemented to enhance the impact of the message. Agencies are helping clients sort through the blizzard of new media options such as CD-ROMs, videocassettes, interactive media, and the Internet. Most large agencies, such as J. Walter Thompson, Chiat/Day, and Fallon McElligott, set up their own interactive media groups years ago in response to client demands that the Internet media option be included in nearly every IBP plan. The three positions typically found in the media area are media planner, media buyer, and media researcher. This is where most of the client's money is spent; it's very important.

Administrative Services. Like other businesses, agencies have to manage their business affairs. Agencies have personnel departments, accounting and billing departments, and sales staffs that go out and sell the agency to clients. Most important to clients is the traffic department, which has the responsibility of monitoring projects to be sure that deadlines are met. Traffic managers make sure the creative group and media services are coordinated so that deadlines for getting promotional materials to printers and media organizations are met. The job requires tremendous organizational skills and is critical to delivering the other services to clients.

Agency Compensation. The way agencies get paid is somewhat different from the way other professional organizations are compensated. While accountants, doctors,

---

39.   Tobi Elkin, "Motorola Tenders Brand Challenge," *Advertising Age*, August 14, 2000, 14.

Calculation of agency compensation using a traditional commission-based compensation system.

Agency bills client   **$1,000,000**   for television airtime

−

Agency pays television media   **$ 850,000**   for television airtime

=

Agency earns $ 150,000   15% commission

lawyers, and consultants often work on a fee basis, advertising agencies often base compensation on a commission or markup system. Promotion agencies occasionally work on a commission basis, but more often work on a fee or contract basis. We will examine the four most prevalent agency compensation methods: commissions, markup charges, fee systems, and newer pay-for-results plans.

Commissions. The traditional method of agency compensation is the **commission system,** which is based on the amount of money the advertiser spends on media. Under this method, 15 percent of the total amount billed by a media organization is retained by the advertising or promotion agency as compensation for all costs in creating advertising/promotion for the advertiser. The only variation is that the rate typically changes to 16 2/3 percent for outdoor media. Exhibit 2.13 shows a simple example of how the commission system works.

Over the past 15 years, and particularly in the past three years with the change in consumer media use, the wisdom of the commission system has been questioned by both advertisers and agencies themselves. As the chairman of a large full-service agency put it, "It's incenting us to do the wrong thing, to recommend network TV and national magazines and radio when other forms of communication like direct marketing or public relations might do the job better."[40] About half of all advertisers compensate their agencies using a commission system based on media cost. But only about 14 percent of advertisers responding to a recent survey still use the traditional 15 percent commission. More advertisers are using other percentage levels of commission, often negotiated levels, as the basis for agency compensation. But even the use of media-based commissions is under fire. Jim Stengel, global marketing officer for Procter & Gamble, told the American Association of Advertising Agencies members at a media conference that the media-based model dependent on the 30-second spot is "broken" and that the industry needs to understand the complexity of media use by contemporary consumers.[41] This message, indirectly, calls into question the whole issue of basing compensation on media billings at all.

Markup Charges. Another method of agency compensation is to add a percentage **markup charge** to a variety of services the agency purchases from outside suppliers. In many cases, an agency will turn to outside contractors for art, illustration, photography, printing, research, and production. The agency then, in agreement with the client, adds a markup charge to these services. The reason markup charges became prevalent in the industry is that many promotion agencies were providing services that did not use traditional media. Since the traditional commission method was based on media charges, there was no way for these agencies to receive payment for their work. This being the case, the markup system was developed. A typical markup on outside services is 17.65 to 20 percent.

Fee Systems. A **fee system** is much like that used by consultants or attorneys, whereby the advertiser and the agency agree on an hourly rate for different services provided. The hourly rate can be based on average salaries within departments or on some agreed-upon hourly rate across all services. This is the most common basis for

40.   Patricia Sellers, "Do You Need Your Ad Agency?" *Fortune,* November 15, 1993, 148.
41.   Jeff Neff and Lisa Sanders, "It's Broken," *Advertising Age,* February 16, 2004, 1, 30.

promotion agency compensation. GM, the largest U.S. advertiser, agreed to a fee system in which compensation will be based on an agency's work and thinking.[42] Many agencies went to a fee system when dot.coms were spending money like crazy to advertise themselves in some pretty expensive venues like the Super Bowl. That turned out to be a smart move in two ways: Many dot .com firms went bankrupt before the agencies would have received their commissions; and the vast majority of the new Internet firms that survived have dramatically curtailed their offline advertising expenditures from their peak spending in early 2000.[43]

Another version of the fee system is a fixed fee, or contract, set for a project between the client and the agency. It is imperative that the agency and the advertiser agree on precisely what services will be provided, by what departments in the agency, over what specified period of time. In addition, the parties must agree on which supplies, materials, travel costs, and other expenses will be compensated beyond the fixed fee. Fixed-fee systems have the potential for causing serious rifts in the client–agency relationship because out-of-scope work can easily spiral out of control when so many variables are at play.

Pay-for-Results. Recently, many advertisers and agencies alike have been working on compensation programs called **pay-for-results** that base the agency's fee on the achievement of agreed-upon results. Historically, agencies have not agreed to be evaluated on results because results have often been narrowly defined as sales. The key effects on sales are related to factors outside the agency's control such as product features, pricing strategy, and distribution programs (that is, the overall marketing mix, not just advertising or IBP). An agency may agree to be compensated based on achievement of sales levels, but more often (and more appropriately) communications objectives such as awareness, brand identification, or brand feature knowledge among target audiences will serve as the main results criteria.

One of the most difficult tasks in the compensation system is coordinating all the agencies and coordinating how they get paid. As you have seen, more advertisers are using more different forms of promotion and enlisting the help of multiple agencies. A key to IBP here is integrated agency communication. When all of an advertiser's

---

CONTROVERSY

Of Course I Trust You—Meet My Auditor

It used to be that advertisers and their agencies had long histories together and a handshake was the primary way deals got sealed. Well, times have changed. As you saw earlier in the chapter, agencies with 20- or even 30-year histories with a client are being dumped—usually with little ceremony. The days when the agency-advertiser relationship was build purely on trust seem to (sadly) be gone forever. When advertisers like General Motors refer to their agencies as "flabby organizations," you can be pretty sure that the atmosphere in the industry is changed for good. It doesn't help that recently a federal grand jury indicted two agency executives for defrauding the U.S. government with excess labor charges on a campaign developed for the Office of National Drug Control.

So what has replaced the handshake and the toast at dinner as the basis for the client/agency relationship? Guess who's coming to dinner—the auditor. Today, clients are using outside firms to scrutinize all aspects of agency work, from creative services to billing practices. One such scrutinizer is called Firm Decisions. It is an international ad-agency auditing firm that acts as an intermediary between advertisers and agencies. An example of the work done by Firm Decisions: On one agency project invoice, it found that an agency staffer had billed an average of 17 hours a day including weekends for an entire month. On one day, she even logged 26 hours. David Brocklehurst, founder of Firm Decisions, commented on this particular audit with the deadpan observation, "Even if it was true, how productive could she be?"

So the friendly partnership days are over and the auditor seems to be showing up more and more often. This is not to say that agencies are not productive and clients aren't happy with the agencies work. But it really isn't as much fun as it used to be.

Sources: Claire Atkinson, "GM Ad Boss Takes Agencies to Task," *Advertising Age*, June 30, 2003, 1, 26; Erin White, "Making Sure the Work Fits the Bill," *Wall Street Journal*, February 5, 2004, B8.

---

42.   Jean Halliday, "GM to Scrap Agency Commissions," *Advertising Age*, November 16, 1998, 1, 57.
43.   Jennifer Gilbert, "Dot-Com Shift," *Advertising Age*, September 25, 2000, 1, 24.

agencies are working together and coordinating their efforts, not only is integrated brand promotion achieved, but better relations between agencies are achieved.[44]

As if this long list of agencies and intricate compensation schemes weren't complicated enough, let's complicate things a bit more and consider a fairly long list of external facilitators and what their agencies rely on to create and execute promotional campaigns.

4 External Facilitators. While agencies offer clients many services and are adding more, advertisers often need to rely on specialized external facilitators in planning, preparing, and executing promotional campaigns. **External facilitators** are organizations or individuals that provide specialized services to advertisers and agencies. The most important of these external facilitators are discussed in the following sections.

Marketing and Advertising Research Firms. Many firms rely on outside assistance during the planning phase of advertising. Research firms such as Burke International and Simmons can perform original research for advertisers using focus groups, surveys, or experiments to assist in understanding the potential market or consumer perceptions of a product or services. Other research firms, such as SRI International, routinely collect data (from grocery store scanners, for example) and have these data available for a fee.

Advertisers and their agencies also seek measures of promotional program effectiveness after a campaign has run. After an advertisement or promotion has been running for some reasonable amount of time, firms such as Starch INRA Hooper will run recognition tests on print advertisements. Other firms such as Burke offer day-after recall tests of broadcast advertisements. Some firms specialize in message testing to determine whether consumers find advertising messages appealing and understandable.

Consultants. A variety of **consultants** specialize in areas related to the promotional process. Advertisers can seek out marketing consultants for assistance in the planning stage. Creative and communications consultants provide insight on issues related to message strategy and message themes. Consultants in event planning and sponsorships offer their expertise to both advertisers and agencies. Public relations consultants often work with top management. Media experts can help an advertiser determine the proper media mix and efficient media placement.

Three new types of consultants have emerged in recent years. One is a database consultant, who works with both advertisers and agencies. Organizations such as Shepard Associates help firms identify and then manage databases that allow for the development of integrated marketing communications programs. Diverse databases from research sources discussed earlier can be merged or cross-referenced in developing effective communications programs. Another new type of consultant specializes in Web site development and management. These consultants typically have the creative skills to develop Web sites and corporate home pages and the technical skills to advise advertisers on managing the technical aspects of the user interface. The final consultant helps firms integrate information across a wide variety of customer contacts and helps the firm organize all this information to achieve customer relationship management (CRM). Business Objects is one software firm that helps consultants create effective programs (http://www.businessobjects.com). (See Exhibit 2.14.)

Production Facilitators. External **production facilitators** offer essential services both during and after the production process. Production is the area where advertisers and their agencies rely most heavily on external facilitators. All forms of media advertising require special expertise that even the largest full-service agency, much less an advertiser, typically does not retain on staff. In broadcast production,

44.   Allen Winneker, "Avoiding Bonus Envy," *PROMO Magazine,* November 1999, 35–37.

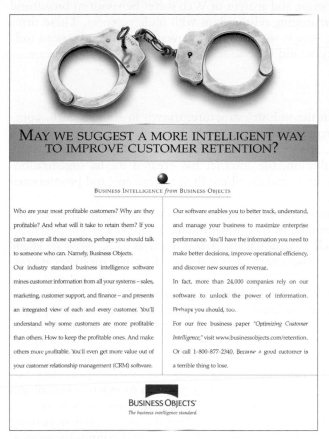

EXHIBIT 2.14

EXHIBIT 2.15

Business Objects is the world's leading business intelligence (BI) software company. Business intelligence enables organizations to track, understand, and manage enterprise performance. The company's solutions leverage the information that is stored in an array of corporate databases, enterprise resource planning (ERP), and customer relationship management (CRM) systems. http://www.businessobjects.com

Software firms like Hyperion are providing advertisers with key assistance in the areas of audience analysis or broadband communications. Hyperion specializes in gathering and analyzing online customer data from Web site visits. http://www.hyperion.com

directors, production managers, songwriters, camera operators, audio and lighting technicians, and performers are all essential to preparing a professional, high-quality radio or television ad. Production houses can provide the physical facilities, including sets, stages, equipment, and crews, needed for broadcast production. Similarly, in preparing print advertising, brochures, and direct mail pieces, graphic artists, photographers, models, directors, and producers may be hired from outside the advertising agency or firm to provide the specialized skills and facilities needed in preparing advertisements. In-store promotions is another area where designing and producing materials requires the skills of a specialty organization.

The specific activities performed by external facilitators and the techniques employed by the personnel in these firms will be covered in greater detail in Part 3 of the text. For now, it is sufficient to recognize the role these firms play in the advertising and promotions industry.

Software Firms. An interesting and complex new category of facilitator in advertising and promotion is composed of software firms. The technology in the industry, particularly new media technology, has expanded so rapidly that a variety of software firms facilitate the process. Some of these firms are well established and well known, such as Microsoft, Novell, and Oracle. But others, such as Hyperion (see Exhibit 2.15), L90, SAS, and Infinium, are new to the scene. These firms provide software ranging from the gathering and analysis of Web surfer behavior to broadband streaming audio and video to managing relationships with trade partners. These firms provide the kind of expertise that is so esoteric that even the most advanced full-service or e-commerce agency would have to seek their assistance.

④ Media Organizations. The next level in the industry structure, shown in Exhibit 2.16, comprises media available to advertisers. The media available for placing advertising, such as broadcast and print media, are well known to most of us simply because we're exposed to them daily. In addition, the Internet has created media organizations through which advertisers can direct and distribute their advertising and promotional messages.

Advertisers and their agencies turn to media organizations that own and manage the media access to consumers. In traditional media, major television networks such as NBC and Fox, as well as national magazines such as *U.S. News & World Report* and *People,* provide advertisers with time and space for their messages at considerable cost.

Other media options are more useful for reaching narrowly defined target audiences. Specialty programming on cable television, tightly focused direct mail pieces, and a well-designed Internet campaign may be better ways to reach a specific audience. One of the new media options, broadband, offers advertisers the chance to target very specific audiences. Broadband allows Internet users to basically customize their programming by calling on only specific broadcasts from various providers. For example, The FeedRoom (http://www.feedroom.com) is an interactive broadband television news network that allows Web users to customize their news broadcasts to their personal preference. Advertisers can target different types of audiences using broadband for interactive broadcasts. The next step in broadband communications is wireless broadband; firms are already developing technology and access for consumers (see Exhibit 2.17).

Note the inclusion of media conglomerates in the list shown in Exhibit 2.16. This category is included because organizations such as Viacom and Comcast own and operate companies in broadcast, print, and interactive media. Viacom brings you cable networks such as Nickelodeon, VH1, and TV Land. The recent merger of AOL and Time Warner (now referred to again as only Time Warner) has created the world's largest mega media conglomerate, one that provides broadcasting, cable, music, film, print publishing, and a dominant Internet presence. One analyst described the media environment as "AOL Time Warner Anywhere, Anytime, Anyhow."[45]

The support media organizations indicated in Exhibit 2.16 include all those places that advertisers want to put their messages other than mainstream traditional or interactive media. Often referred to as out-of-home media, these support media organizations include transit companies (bus and taxi boards), billboard organizations, specialized directory companies, and sports and performance arenas for sponsorships, display materials, and premium items.

Target Audiences. The structure of the promotion industry (check Exhibit 2.5 again) and the flow of communication would obviously be incomplete without an audience: no audience, no communication. One interesting thing about the audiences for promotional communications, with the exception of household consumers, is that they are also

45.   Frank Gibney Jr., "Score One for AOLTW," *Time,* December 25, 2000–January 1, 2001, 138.

EXHIBIT 2.16

Advertisers have an array of media organizations available to them. Notice that the choices range from traditional print and broadcast media to broadband and media conglomerates.

Broadcast

Television
Major network
Independent station
Cable
Broadband

Radio
Network
Local

Print

Magazines
By geographic coverage
By content

Direct Mail
Brochures
Catalogs
Videos

Newspapers
National
Statewide
Local

Specialty
Handbills
Programs

Interactive Media

Online Computer Services

Home-Shopping Broadcasts

**Interactive Broadcast
Entertainment Programming**

Kiosks

CD-ROMs

Internet

Support Media

Outdoor
Billboards
Transit
Posters

Directories
Yellow Pages
Electronic directories

Premiums
Keychains
Calendars
Logo clothing
Pens

Point-of-Purchase Displays

**Film and Program Brand
Placement**

Event Sponsorship

Media Conglomerates

Multiple Media Combinations
Time Warner
Viacom
Turner Broadcasting
Comcast
Disney
Clear Channel

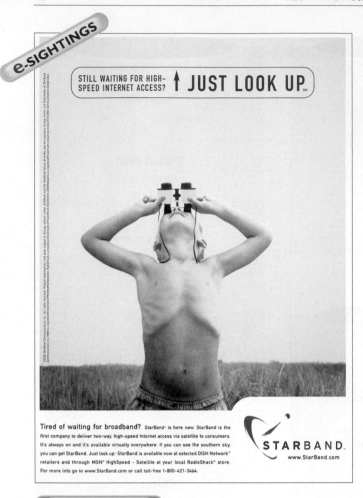

EXHIBIT 2.17

Broadband promises advertisers the opportunity to send audio and video through the Internet in a way that lets Web users customize their viewing and listening experiences. To learn more about various streaming services and media-rich content being developed for broadband, visit Akamai (http://www.akamai.com). http://www.starband.com

the advertisers who use advertising and IBP communications. We are all familiar with the type of advertising directed at us in our role as consumers: toothpaste, window cleaner, sport-utility vehicles, soft drinks, insurance, and on and on. The text is full of advertising by firms targeting household consumers.

But business and government audiences are key to the success of a large number of firms that sell only to business and government buyers. While many of these firms rely heavily on personal selling in their promotional mix, many also use a variety of advertising and IBP tools. KPMG Consulting uses high-profile television and magazine advertising and sponsors events. Many business and trade sellers regularly need public relations, and most use direct mail to communicate with potential customers as a prelude to a personal selling call.

SUMMARY

 Discuss important trends transforming the advertising and promotion industry.

Recent years have proven to be a period of dramatic change for the advertising and promotion industry. The late-1990s trend towards agency consolidation has seen a reversal as numerous industry acquisitions and mergers failed to impress clients or produce greater profitability. Next, the proliferation of media from cable television to the Internet has created new advertising options, and giant media conglomerates are expected to control a majority of these television, radio, and Internet properties. Media proliferation has in turn led to increasing media clutter and fragmentation, reducing the effectiveness of advertisements; as a result, advertisers are utilizing sales promotions, event sponsorships, and public relations to supplement and enhance the primary advertising effort. Finally, today's consumers have greater control over the information they receive about brands. New technology applications from blogs to TiVo empower consumers and diminish the role of advertising in the consumption process. These developments are forcing advertisers to think differently about advertising and IBP.

 Describe the advertising and promotion industry's size, structure, and participants.

Many different types of organizations make up the industry. To truly appreciate what advertising is all about, one must understand who does what and in what order in the creation and delivery of an advertising or IBP campaign. The process begins with an organization that has a message it wishes to communicate to a target audience. This is the advertiser. Next, advertising and promotion agencies are typically hired to launch and manage a campaign, but other external facilitators are often brought in to perform specialized functions, such as assisting in the production of promotional materials or managing databases for efficient direct marketing campaigns. These external facilitators also include consultants with whom advertisers and their agencies may confer regarding advertising and IBP strategy decisions. All advertising and promotional campaigns must use some type of media to reach target markets. Advertisers and their agencies must therefore also work with companies that have media time or space.

 Discuss the role played by advertising and promotion agencies, the services provided by these agencies, and how they are compensated.

Advertising and promotion agencies come in many varieties and offer diverse services to clients with respect to planning, preparing, and executing advertising and IBP campaigns. These services include market research and marketing planning, the actual creation and production of ad materials, the buying of media time or space for placement of the ads, and traffic management to keep production on schedule. Some advertising agencies appeal to clients by offering a full array of services under one roof; others such as creative boutiques develop a particular expertise and win clients with their specialized skills. Promotion agencies specialize in one or more of the other forms of promotion beyond advertising. New media agencies are proliferating to serve the Internet and other new media needs of advertisers. The four most prevalent ways to compensate an agency for services rendered are commissions, markups, fee systems, and the new pay-for-results programs.

 Identify key external facilitators who assist in planning and executing advertising and integrated brand promotion campaigns.

Marketing and advertising research firms assist advertisers and their agencies in understanding the market environment. Consultants of all sorts from marketing strategy through event planning and retail display are another form of external facilitator. Perhaps the most widely used facilitators are in the area of production of promotional materials. In advertising, a wide range of outside facilitators is used in the production of both broadcast and print advertising. In promotions, designers and planners are called on to assist in creation and execution of promotional mix tools. Software firms fill a new role in the structure of the industry. These firms provide expertise in tracking and analyzing consumer usage of new media technology.

 Discuss the role played by media organizations in executing effective advertising and integrated brand promotion campaigns programs.

Media organizations are the essential link in delivering advertising and IBP communications to target audiences. There are traditional media organizations such as television, radio, newspaper, and magazines. Interactive media options include not just the Internet but CD-ROMs, electronic kiosks, and less widely known communications companies. Media conglomerates such as AT&T, Time Warner, and Viacom control several different aspects of the communications system, from cable broadcast to Internet connections and emerging broadband communications technologies.

KEY TERMS

blog	database agency	account planner
advertiser	direct response agency	creative services
client	fulfillment center	production services
trade reseller	infomercial	media planning and buying services
advertising agency	e-commerce agency	commission system
full-service agency	consumer sales promotion	markup charge
creative boutique	trade sales promotion	fee system
interactive agency	event-planning agency	pay-for-results
in-house agency	designers	external facilitator
media specialists	logo	consultants
promotion agencies	public relations firm	production facilitator
direct marketing agency	account services	

QUESTIONS

1.   Briefly describe the power struggle now taking place in the advertising industry. Who, beyond the agencies, is exerting power in the industry, and in what ways?

2.   Do you think the increasing independence and control consumers gain through new technologies like TiVo, the Internet, digital music players, and cell phones will make advertising and product branding less important? Explain.

3.   As cable-TV channels continue to proliferate and the TV-viewing audience becomes ever more fragmented, how would you expect the advertising industry to be affected?

4.   The U.S. government spends millions of dollars each year trying to recruit young men and women into the armed services. What forms of advertising and IBP communication would be best suited to this recruiting effort?

5.   Huge advertisers such as Procter & Gamble spend billions of dollars on advertising every year, yet they still rely on advertising agencies to prepare most of their advertising. Why doesn't a big company like this just do all its own advertising in-house?

6.   What is the advertiser's role in IBP?

7.   As advertisers become more enamored with the idea of IBP, why would it make sense for an advertising agency to develop a reputation as a full-service provider?

8.   Explain the viewpoint that a commission-based compensation system may actually give ad agencies an incentive to do the wrong things for their clients.

9.   What makes production of promotional materials the area where advertisers and their agencies are most likely to call on external facilitators for expertise and assistance?

10. Give an example of how the skills of a public relations firm might be employed to reinforce the message that a sponsor is trying to communicate through other forms of promotion.

EXPERIENTIAL EXERCISES

1. Break up into groups and simulate a small business planning to advertise a new or innovative product. Once you have chosen a general industry and a product to advertise, perform the following tasks and present your answers to the class.

a. Pick the main trend in the advertising industry that you think would have the greatest effect for advertising your product.

b. Determine what advertiser category your business is classified under, and explain the role advertising plays for organizations in that category. How does this apply to your campaign?

c. Select one type of advertising or promotion agency that would be the most effective in providing appropriate services to achieve your advertising or promotion goals. Explain your choice.

d. Select one external facilitator that would provide specialization services to help ensure the success of your campaign and explain your reasoning.

e. Choose an available media organization that would be best suited for advertising and promoting your brand's identity. What makes it the best choice?

2. Choose a popular brand from a local or national advertiser and try to determine what media organizations the advertiser is using to target its audience. Does the brand have a special site on the Internet? Can you find television or billboard ads for your product? Are there media organizations you couldn't find that you believe would be suitable or innovative for advertising this brand? Explain.

EXPERIENCING THE INTERNET

2-1 The Advertising Industry in Transition

The advertising industry is in a state of constant transition, and numerous trends are forcing advertisers to rethink the way they communicate with consumers. In general, greater focus is being placed on the importance of integrating multiple tools with the overall advertising effort for effective brand promotion. As a communications services provider, XO Communications develops Internet applications and Web media tools that ultimately influence the methods and structure of the advertising industry.

xo Communications: http://www.xo.com

1. Of the four important trends that are altering the structure and processes of the advertising industry, which are most closely associated with the services of XO Communications? Explain your answer.

2. What is broadband, and how does it relate to XO Communications? What effect do you think broadband and DSL will have on advertising?

3. What adjustments might advertising agencies need to make to accommodate emerging trends in the industry?

2-2 Agencies

Advertisers have a broad pool of agencies from which to choose that help execute the details of advertising and promotion strategies. Each type of agency has its own specialized services that enable advertisers to effectively target audiences and build brand recognition.

24/7 Real Media: http://www.247realmedia.com

1. Is 24/7 Real Media a type of advertising agency, promotion agency, or both? What are the main differences between these two types of agencies?

2. Explain some of the services 24/7 Real Media provides to e-commerce companies, advertisers, and publishers. How do these services help attract and retain customers using the Internet?

3. Would 24/7 Real Media be considered an interactive agency? Why or why not?

CHAPTER 3

After reading and thinking about this chapter, you will be able to do the following:

1

Explain why advertising is an essential feature of capitalistic economic systems.

2

Describe manufacturers' dependence on advertising, promotion, and branding in achieving balanced relationships with retailers.

3

Discuss several significant eras in the evolution of advertising in the United States, and relate important changes in advertising practice to fundamental changes in society and culture.

4

Identify forces that will continue to affect the evolution of advertising.

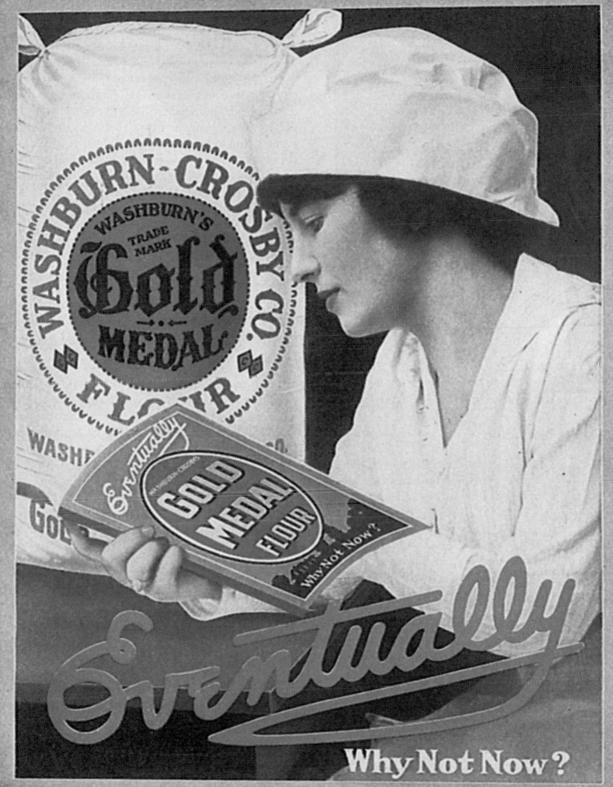

EXHIBIT 3.1

While this ad for Lux laundry powder may seem curious to us today, it reflected the anxiety of the 1930s, during the Great Depression. Just as today's advertising reflects the values of contemporary society, this ad emphasized some very real concerns of the time—the economic well-being and status of women.

The 1935 Lux advertisement shown in Exhibit 3.1 is undoubtedly curious to contemporary audiences. It is, however, typical of its time and probably made perfect sense to its original audience. In the 1930s, in the middle of the Great Depression, anxiety about losing one's husband—and thus one's economic well-being—to divorce was not unfounded. These ads were targeted to a new generation of stay-at-home housewives anxious about their exclusion from the modern world of their husbands, geographically separated from their usually agrarian parents, and living in a rapid and unsure urban environment. These ads went out to women at a time when losing one's source of income (husband) could mean abject poverty or worse. They were read by women in a society where daily bathing was still relatively rare but where self-doubt about personal hygiene was on the rise. Such an ad probably pushed just the right buttons. If Lux can "remove perspiration odor from underthings," it might save more than colors and fabrics. It might save affection; it might save marriages. If Bob's romantic indifference continues, Sally may soon be back home with Mom or even on the street. But with Lux on the scene, Bob goes home for dinner.

While some ads today use the very same general strategy to sell deodorants, soaps, and feminine-hygiene products, this ad is certainly not read the same way today as it was in 1935. Ads are part of their times. To really understand advertising and do well in the advertising business, you must understand that successful advertisements convey a particularly perceptive understanding of the contemporary social scene. If you are in the advertising business, you are in the culture and society business. The makers of this 1930s ad really understood and used the pressures bearing down on the young married women of that time. Today, Sally would likely have a job and be far less economically vulnerable and socially isolated—not to mention that Sally and Bob would both be bathing more. So we see the 1930s in this ad in the same way that students of the future will view ads of our time: as interesting, revealing, but still distorted reflections of daily life in the early 21st century. Even in the 1930s, consumers knew that ads were ads; they knew that ads were a little exaggerated; they knew that ads tried to sell things; and they knew that ads didn't exactly mirror everyday life. But ads look enough like life to work, sometimes. Good advertising is in touch with its time.

This chapter is about the evolution of advertising. Over the decades, advertisers have tried many different strategies and approaches, and you can learn a lot from their successes and failures. Just about every strategy used today came about decades ago—only the specifics have changed. Studying them will allow you to know when a given advertising technique is really something new or just reheated retro. (Not that re-heated retro can't sometimes sell). Besides being interesting, history is very practical.

Fundamental Influences on the Evolution of Advertising. In

many discussions of the evolution of advertising, the process is often portrayed as having its origins in ancient times, with even primitive peoples practicing some form of advertising. This is incorrect. Whatever those ancients were doing, they weren't advertising. Remember, advertising exists only as mass-mediated communication. As far as we know, there was no *Mesopotamia Messenger* or "Sparta: Live at Five." Although cavemen and cavewomen certainly were communicating with one another with persuasive intent, and maybe even in an exchange context, they were not using advertising. Advertising is a product of modern times and mass media.

Before we get into a brief social history of advertising in the United States, let's first consider some of the major factors in the evolution of this country that gave rise to advertising in the first place. Advertising came into being as a result of at least four major factors in the evolution of U.S. culture and economic development:

1. The rise of capitalism
2. The Industrial Revolution
3. Manufacturers' pursuit of power in the channel of distribution
4. The rise of modern mass media

The Rise of Capitalism.

The tenets of capitalism warrant that organizations compete for resources, called *capital,* in a free-market environment. Part of the competition for resources involves stimulating demand for the organization's goods or services. When an individual organization successfully stimulates demand, it attracts capital to the organization in the form of money (or other goods) as payment. One of the tools used to stimulate demand is advertising. So, as the United States turned to capitalism as the foundation of the country's economic system, the foundation was laid for advertising to become a prominent part of the business environment.

The Industrial Revolution.

The **Industrial Revolution** was an economic force that yielded the need for advertising. Beginning about 1750 in England, the revolution spread to the United States and progressed slowly until the early 1800s, when the War of 1812 boosted domestic production. The emergence of the principle of interchangeable parts and the perfection of the sewing machine, both in 1850, coupled with the Civil War a decade later, set the scene for widespread industrialization. The Industrial Revolution took American society away from household self-sufficiency as a method of fulfilling material needs to dependency on a marketplace as a way of life. The Industrial Revolution was a basic force behind the rapid increase in mass-production goods that required stimulation of demand, something that advertising can be very good at. By providing a need for advertising, the Industrial Revolution was a basic influence in its emergence and growth in the U.S. economy.

Other equally revolutionary developments were part of the broad Industrial Revolution. First, there was a revolution in transportation, most dramatically symbolized by the east-west connection of the United States in 1869 by the railroad. This connection represented the beginnings of the distribution network needed to move the mass quantities of goods for which advertising would help stimulate demand. In the 1840s, the **principle of limited liability,** which restricts an investor's risk in a business venture to only his or her shares in a corporation rather than all personal assets, gained acceptance and resulted in the accumulation of large amounts of capital to finance the Industrial Revolution. Finally, rapid population growth and urbanization began taking place in the 1800s. From 1830 to 1860, the population of the United States increased nearly threefold, from 12.8 million to 31.4 million. During the same period, the number of cities with more than 20,000 inhabitants grew to 43. Historically, there is a strong relationship between per capita outlays for advertising and an increase in the size of cities.[1] Overall, the growth and

---

1.   Julian Simon, *Issues in the Economics of Advertising* (Urbana: University of Illinois Press, 1970), 41–51.

concentration of population provided the marketplaces essential to the widespread use of advertising. As the potential grew for goods to be produced, delivered, and introduced to large numbers of people residing in concentrated areas, the stage was set for advertising to emerge and flourish.

② Manufacturers' Pursuit of Power in the Channel of Distribution. Another fundamental influence on the emergence and growth of advertising relates to manufacturers' pursuit of power in the channel of distribution. If a manufacturer can stimulate sizable demand for a brand, then that manufacturer can develop power in the distribution channel and essentially *force* wholesalers and retailers to sell that particular brand. Demand stimulation among consumers causes them to insist on the brand at the retail or wholesale level; retailers and wholesalers then have virtually no choice but to comply with consumers' desires and carry the desired item. Thus, the manufacturer has power in the channel of distribution and not only can force other participants in the channel to stock the brand, but also is in a position to command a higher price for the item. The marketing of Intel's Pentium chip is an excellent example of how one manufacturer, Intel, has developed considerable power in the computer distribution channel, establishing its product, the Pentium chip, as a premium brand.

A factor that turned out to be critical to manufacturers' pursuit of power was the strategy of **branding** products. Manufacturers had to develop brand names so that consumers could focus their attention on a clearly identified item. Manufacturers began branding previously unmarked commodities, such as work clothes and package goods. In the late 1800s, Ivory (1882), Coca-Cola (1886), Budweiser (1891), and Maxwell House (1892) were among the first branded goods to show up on shopkeepers' shelves. Once a product had a brand mark and name that consumers could identify, marketers gained power. Of course, an essential tool in stimulating demand for a brand was advertising. Even today, when Procter & Gamble and Altria spend many billions of dollars each year to stimulate demand for such popular brands as Crest, Charmin, and Velveeta, wholesalers and retailers carry these brands because advertising has stimulated demand and brought consumers into the retail store looking for and asking for those brands. It is just this sort of pursuit of power by manufacturers that is argued to have caused the widespread use of advertising in the United States.[2]

The Rise of Modern Mass Media. Advertising is also inextricably tied to the rise of mass communication. With the invention of the telegraph in 1844, a communication revolution was set in motion. The telegraph not only allowed the young nation to benefit from the inherent efficiencies of rapid communication, but also did a great deal to engender a sense of national identity and community. People began to know and care about people and things going on thousands of miles away. This changed not only commerce, but social consciousness as well.[3] Also, during this period, many new magazines designed for larger and less socially privileged audiences made magazines both a viable mass advertising medium and a democratizing influence on American society.[4] Through advertising in these mass-circulation magazines, national brands could be projected into national consciousness. National magazines made national advertising possible; national advertising made national brands possible. Without the rise of mass media, there would be no national brands, and no advertising.

2.   Vincent P. Norris, "Advertising History—According to the Textbooks," *Journal of Advertising,* vol. 9, no. 3 (1980), 3–12.

3.   James W. Carey, *Communication as Culture: Essays on Media and Society* (Winchester, Mass.: Unwin Hyman, 1989).

4.   Christopher P. Wilson, "The Rhetoric of Consumption: Mass-Market Magazines and the Demise of the Gentle Reader, 1880–1920," in *The Culture of Consumption: Critical Essays in American History, 1880–1980,* ed. Richard Weightman Fox and T. J. Jackson Lears (New York: Pantheon, 1983), 39–65.

It is critical to realize that for the most part, mass media in the United States are supported by advertising. Television networks, radio stations, newspapers, magazines, and Web sites produce shows, articles, films, programs, and Web content not for the ultimate goal of entertaining or informing, but to make a healthy profit from the sale of advertising. Media vehicles sell audiences to make money.

3 The Evolution of Advertising in the United States.

So far, our discussion of the evolution of advertising has identified the fundamental social and economic influences that fostered its rise. Now we'll turn our focus to the evolution of advertising in practice. Several periods in this evolution can be identified to give us various perspectives on the process of advertising.

The Preindustrialization Era (pre-1800).

In the 17th century, printed advertisements appeared in newsbooks (the precursor to the newspaper).[5] The messages were informational in nature and appeared on the last pages of the tabloid. In America, the first newspaper advertisement is said to have appeared in 1704 in the *Boston News Letter*. Two notices were printed under the heading "Advertising" and offered rewards for the return of merchandise stolen from an apparel shop and a wharf.[6]

Advertising grew in popularity during the 18th century in both Britain and the American colonies. The *Pennsylvania Gazette* printed advertisements and was the first newspaper to separate ads with blank lines, which made the ads both easier to read and more prominent.[7] As far as we know, it was also the first newspaper to use illustrations in advertisements. But advertising changed little over the next 70 years. While the early 1800s saw the advent of the penny newspaper, which resulted in widespread distribution of the news medium, advertisements in penny newspapers were dominated by simple announcements by skilled laborers. As one historian notes, "Advertising was closer to the classified notices in newspapers than to product promotions in our media today."[8] Advertising was about to change dramatically, however.

The Era of Industrialization (1800 to 1875).

In practice, users of advertising in the mid to late 1800s were trying to cultivate markets for growing production in the context of a dramatically increasing population. A middle class, spawned by the economic windfall of regular wages from factory jobs, was beginning to emerge. This newly developing populace with economic means was concentrated geographically in cities more than ever before.

By 1850, circulation of the **dailies,** as newspapers were then called, was estimated at 1 million copies per day. The first advertising agent—thought to be Volney Palmer, who opened shop in Philadelphia—basically worked for the newspapers by soliciting orders for advertising and collecting payment from advertisers.[9] This new opportunity to reach consumers was embraced readily by merchants, and at least one newspaper doubled its advertising volume from 1849 to 1850.[10]

With the expansion of newspaper circulation fostered by the railroads, a new era of opportunity emerged for the advertising process. Advertising was not universally hailed as an honorable practice, however. Without any formal regulation of advertising, the process was considered an embarrassment by many segments of society,

5.   Frank Presbrey, *The History and Development of Advertising* (Garden City, N.Y.: Doubleday, Doran & Company, 1929), 7.
6.   Ibid., 11.
7.   Ibid., 40.
8.   James P. Wood, *The Story of Advertising* (New York: Ronald Press, 1958), 45–46.
9.   Daniel Pope, *The Making of Modern Advertising and Its Creators* (New York: William Morrow, 1984), 14.
10.   Cited in Stephen Fox, *The Mirror Makers: A History of American Advertising and Its Creators* (New York: William Morrow, 1984), 14.

EXHIBIT 3.2

The expansion of newspaper circulation fostered more widespread use of advertising. Unfortunately, some of this new advertising did not contribute positively to the image of the practice. Ads like this one for a patent medicine carried bold claims, such as claiming to cure all liver ailments, including cancer.

including some parts of the business community. At one point, firms even risked their credit ratings if they used advertising—banks considered the practice a sign of financial weakness. This image wasn't helped much by advertising for patent medicines, which were the first products heavily advertised on a national scale. These advertisements promised a cure for everything from rheumatism and arthritis to cancer. Exhibit 3.2 shows a typical ad of this period.

The "P. T. Barnum Era" (1875 to 1918).

The only one who could ever reach me was the son of a preacher man.

—John Hurley and Ronnie Wilkins, "Son of a Preacher Man"; most notably performed by Dusty Springfield[11]

Shortly after the Civil War in the United States, modern advertising began. This is advertising that we would recognize as advertising. While advertising existed during the era of industrialization, it wasn't until America was well on its way to being an urban, industrialized nation that advertising became a vital and integral part of the social landscape. From about 1875 to 1918, advertising ushered in what has come to be known as **consumer culture,** or a way of life centered on consumption. True, consumer culture was advancing prior to this period, but during this age it really took hold, and the rise of modern advertising had a lot to do with it. Advertising became a full-fledged industry in this period. It was the time of advertising legends: Albert Lasker, head of Lord and Thomas in Chicago, possibly the most influential agency of its day; Francis W. Ayer, founder of N. W. Ayer; John E. Powers, the most important copywriter of the period; Earnest Elmo Calkins, champion of advertising design; Claude Hopkins, influential in promoting ads as "dramatic salesmanship"; and John E. Kennedy, creator of "reason why" advertising.[12] These were the founders, the visionaries, and the artists who played principal roles in the establishment of the advertising business. One interesting sidenote is that several of the founders of this industry had fathers who shared the very same occupation: minister. This very modern and controversial industry was founded in no small part by the sons of preachers.

By 1900, total sales of patent medicines had reached $75 million—providing an early demonstration of the power of advertising.[13] The stage was set for advertising's modern form. During this period, the first advertising agencies were founded and the practice of branding products became the norm. Advertising was motivated by the need to sell the vastly increased supply of goods brought on by mass production and by the demands of an increasingly urban population seeking social identity through (among other things) branded products. In earlier times, when shoppers went to the general store and bought soap sliced from a large locally produced cake, advertising had little or no place. But with advertising's ability to create enormous differences between near-identical soaps, advertising suddenly held a very prominent place in early consumer culture. Advertising made unmarked commodities into

---

11.   John Hurley and Ronnie Wilkins, "Son of a Preacher Man," Atlantic Recording Group, 1968.

12.   Fox, *The Mirror Makers,* op. cit.

13.   Presbrey, *The History and Development of Advertising,* 16.

DUCK PROFITS

Raise the best ducks. Our famous **big ducklings** (Pekin, white) are fattened on cheapest grain, weigh **FIVE** to **SIX LBS.** each marketed **10 weeks old**, taste delicious (not fishy, like sea-shore or lake)

DUCKS WITHOUT WATER WRITE FOR FREE BOOK

Ducks have **no lice** or any vermin, hawks will not touch them, they have no diseases. No swimming water needed, they do best without it. The **wonderful modern facts of ducks for business** have never been told fully, nor has plenty of good breeding stock before been obtainable. We tell the facts; we sell breeders and supplies. **Small cost to start.** We have an interesting book for **FREE** distribution, "**DUCK PROFITS.**" Send by mail for it, read the details, they **will astonish you.** Prices sent also. Write.

bred ducks and sell in all markets at big profit. No better way of turning grain, scraps, vegetables, green stuff into money than by feeding them to produce big ducklings from our stock. **Breed them anywhere for profits.** Write us for details.

American Pekin Duck Company
145 Pearl Street   Dept. 25   Boston, Mass.

EXHIBIT 3.3

Ads from the "P. T. Barnum era" were often densely packed with fantastic promises. This 1902 Saturday Evening Post advertisement featured many reasons why potential customers should get into the duck-raising business—even without water.

social symbols and identity markers, and it allowed marketers to charge far more money for them. Consumers are much more willing to pay more money for brands (for example, Ivory) than for unmarked commodities (generic soap wrapped in plain paper), even if they are otherwise identical. This is the power of brands.

The advertising of this period was, until 1906, completely unregulated. In that year, Congress passed the **Pure Food and Drug Act,** which required manufacturers to list the active ingredients of their products on their labels. Still, its effect on advertising was minimal; advertisers could continue to say just about anything—and usually did. Many advertisements took on the style of a sales pitch for snake oil. The tone and spirit of advertising owed more to P. T. Barnum—"There's a sucker born every minute"—than to any other influence. The ads were bold, carnivalesque, garish, and often full of dense copy that hurled fairly incredible claims at prototype "modern" consumers. A fairly typical ad from this era is shown in Exhibit 3.3.

Several things are notable about these ads: lots of copy (words); the prominence of the product itself and the relative lack of real-world context (pictures) in which the advertised product was to be consumed; ads were small; and they had little color, few photographs, and plenty of hyperbole. Over this period there was variation and steady evolution, but this is what ads were generally like up until World War I.

Consider the world in which these ads existed. It was a period of rapid urbanization, massive immigration, labor unrest, and significant concerns about the abuses of capitalism. Some of capitalism's excesses and abuses, in the form of deceptive and misleading advertising, were the targets of early reformers. It was also the age of suffrage, the progressive movement, motion pictures, and mass culture. The world changed rapidly in this period, and it was no doubt disruptive and unsettling to many—but advertising was there to offer solutions to the stresses of modern life, no matter how real, imagined, or suggested. Advertisers had something to fix just about any problem.

The 1920s (1918 to 1929). In many ways, the Roaring Twenties really began a couple of years early. After World War I, advertising found respectability, fame, and glamour. It was the most modern of all professions; it was, short of being a movie star, the most fashionable. According to popular perception, it was where the young, smart, and sophisticated worked and played. During the 1920s, it was also a place where institutional freedom rang. The prewar movement to reform and regulate advertising was pretty much dissipated by the distractions of the war and advertising's role in the war effort. During World War I, the advertising industry learned a valuable lesson: donating time and personnel to the common good is not only good civics but smart business.

The 1920s were prosperous times. Most Americans enjoyed a previously unequaled standard of living. It was an age of considerable hedonism; the pleasure principle was practiced and appreciated, openly and often. The Victorian Age was over, and a great social experiment in the joys of consumption was underway. Victorian repression and modesty gave way to a more open sexuality and a love affair with modernity. Advertising was made for this burgeoning sensuality; advertising gave people permission to enjoy. Ads of the era exhorted consumers to have a good time and instructed them how to do it. Consumption was not only respectable, but expected. Being a consumer became synonymous with being a citizen—and a good citizen.

During these good economic times, advertising instructed consumers how to be thoroughly modern and how to avoid the pitfalls of this new age. Consumers learned of halitosis from Listerine advertising and about body odor from Lifebuoy advertising (see Exhibit 3.4, a Lifebuoy ad from 1926). Not too surprisingly, there just happened to be a product with a cure for just about every social anxiety and personal failing one could imagine, many of which had supposedly been brought on as side effects of modernity. This was perfect for the growth and entrenchment of advertising as an institution: Modern times bring on many wonderful new things, but the new way of life has side effects that, in turn, have to be fixed by even more modern goods and services. For example, modern canned food replaced fresh fruit and vegetables, thus "weakening the gums," causing dental problems—which could be cured by a modern toothbrush. Thus, a seemingly endless consumption chain was created: Needs lead to products, new needs are created by new products, newer products solve newer needs, and on and on. This chain of needs is essential to a capitalist economy, which must continue to expand in order to survive. It also makes a necessity of advertising.

Other ads from the 1920s emphasized other modernity themes, such as the division between public workspace, the male domain of the office (see Exhibit 3.5), and the private, "feminine" space of the home (see Exhibit 3.6). Thus, two separate consumption domains were created, with women placed in charge of the latter, more economically important one. Advertisers soon figured out that women were responsible for as much as 80 percent of household purchases. While 1920s men were out

EXHIBIT 3.4

Many ads from the 1920s promised to relieve just about any social anxiety. Here, Lifebuoy offered a solution for people concerned that body odor could be standing in the way of career advancement.

EXHIBIT 3.5

This 1920s-era Gulf advertisement focuses on technological progress and the male prerogative in promoting its advancement. The work world is male space in this period's ads.

EXHIBIT 3.6

Ads from the 1920s often emphasized modernity themes, like the division between public and private workspace. This Fels-Naptha ad shows the private, "feminine" space of the home—where "her work" occurred.

in the "jungle" of the work world, women made most purchase decisions. So, from this time forward, women became advertising's primary target.

Another very important aspect of 1920s advertising, and beyond, was the role that science and technology began to play. Science and technology were in many ways the new religions of the modern era. The modern way was the scientific way. So one saw ads appealing to the popularity of science in virtually all product categories of advertising during this period. Ads even stressed the latest scientific offerings, whether in radio tubes or in "domestic science," as Exhibits 3.7 and 3.8 demonstrate.

The style of 1920s ads was much more visual than in the past. Twenties ads showed slices of life, or carefully constructed "snapshots" of social life with the product. In these ads, the relative position, background, and dress of the people using or needing the advertised product were carefully crafted. These visual lessons were generally about how to fit in with the "smart" crowd, how to be urbane and modern by using the newest conveniences, and how not to fall victim to the perils and pressure of the new fast-paced modern world. The social context of product use became critical, as one can see in Exhibits 3.9 through 3.12.

Advertising during the 1920s chronicled the state of technology and styles for clothing, furniture, and social functions. Advertising specified social relationships between people and products by depicting the social settings and circumstances into which people and products fit. Consider Exhibits 3.10 and 3.11. Note the attention to the social setting into which plumbing fixtures were to fit. Is the ad really about plumbing? Yes, in a very important way, because it demonstrates plumbing in a social context that works for both advertiser and consumer. Advertising was becoming

EXHIBITS 3.7 AND 3.8

The cultural theme of modernity in the 1920s emphasized science and technology. These ads for Sonatron Radio Tubes (Exhibit 3.7) and for Pet Milk (Exhibit 3.8) tout the science these brands brought to your home.

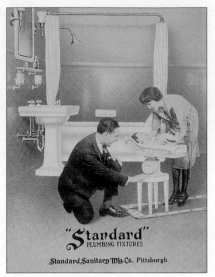

EXHIBITS 3.9 THROUGH 3.12

As the Kodak (Exhibit 3.9), Standard Sanitary (Exhibits 3.10 and 3.11) and Camay (Exhibit 3.12) ads illustrate, ads from the 1920s often showed carefully constructed "snapshots" of social life with the products. The social setting and the product blur together within one image. Setting becomes brand; brand becomes setting. Take a minute and study what's going on in these ads.

sophisticated and had discovered social context in a major way. In terms of pure art direction, the ads in Exhibits 3.13 through 3.15 are examples of the beauty of the period's look.

The J. Walter Thompson advertising agency was the dominant agency of the period. Stanley Resor, Helen Resor, and James Webb Young brought this agency to a leadership position through intelligent management, vision, and great advertising. Helen Resor was the first prominent female advertising executive and was instrumental in J. Walter Thompson's success. Still, the most famous ad person of the era was a very interesting man named Bruce Barton. He was not only the leader of BBDO but also a best-selling author, most notably of a 1924 book called *The Man Nobody Knows*.[14] The book was about Jesus and portrayed him as the archetypal ad man. This blending of Christian and capitalist principles was enormously attractive to a people struggling to reconcile traditional religious thought, which preached against excess, and the new religion of consumption, which preached just the opposite.

14.   Bruce Barton, *The Man Nobody Knows* (New York: Bobbs-Merrill, 1924).

EXHIBITS 3.13 THROUGH 3.15

These three ads are more examples of the beautiful and stylish art direction of the 1920s. (Actually, the Gold Medal ad was produced in the early 1930s, but it is of the 1920s style.) Many believe this was advertising's finest artistic moment. In an effort to make their advertising depict the technology and style of the era, advertisers in the 1920s enlisted the services of some of the best illustrators and artists of the time.

The Depression (1929 to 1941).

> *By 1932 a quarter of American workers were unemployed. But matters were worse than this suggests, for three quarters of those who had jobs were working part-time—either working short hours, or faced with chronic and repeated layoffs. . . . Perhaps half the working population at one time or another knew what it was like to lose a job. Millions actually went hungry, not once but again and again. Millions knew what it was like to eat bread and water for supper, sometimes for days at a stretch. A million people were drifting around the country begging, among them thousands of children, including numbers of girls disguised as boys. People lived in shanty towns on the fields at edges of cities, their foods sometimes weeds plucked from the roadside.[15]*

If you weren't there, you have no idea how bad it was. We don't, but our parents and grandparents did. The Depression was brutal, crushing, and mean. It killed people; it broke lives. Those who lived through it and kept their dignity are to be deeply admired. (See Exhibit 3.16.) It forever changed the way Americans thought about a great many things: their government, business, money, and, not coincidentally, advertising.

Just as sure as advertising was glamorous in the 1920s, it was villainous in the 1930s. It was part of big business, and big business, big greed, and big lust had gotten America into the great economic depression beginning in 1929—or so the story goes. The public now saw advertising as something bad, something that had tempted and seduced them into the excesses for which they were being punished.

Advertisers responded to this feeling by adopting a tough, no-nonsense advertising style. The stylish and highly aesthetic ads of the 1920s gave way to harsher and more cluttered ads. As one historian said, "The new hard-boiled advertising mystique brought a proliferation of 'ugly,' attention-grabbing, picture-dominated copy in the style of the tabloid newspaper."[16] Clients wanted their money's worth, and

15. James Lincoln Collier, *The Rise of Selfishness in America* (New York: Oxford University Press, 1991), 162.
16. Ibid., 303–304.

The very tough times of the Great Depression, depicted in this 1936 photo by Walker Evans, gave Americans reason to distrust big business and its tool, advertising.

agencies responded by cramming every bit of copy and image they could into their ads. This type of advertising persisted, quite likely making the relationship between the public and the institution of advertising even worse. The themes in advertisements traded on the anxieties of the day; losing one's job meant being a bad provider, spouse, or parent, unable to give the family what it needed (as seen in Exhibits 3.17 and 3.18).

Another notable event during these years was the emergence of radio as a significant advertising medium. During the 1930s, the number of radio stations rose

The themes in advertising during the 1930s traded on the anxieties of the day, as these ads for Paris Garters (Exhibit 3.17) and the Association of American Soap and Glycerine Producers, Inc. (Exhibit 3.18) illustrate.

from a handful to 814, and the number of radio sets in use more than quadrupled to 51 million. Radio was in its heyday as a news and entertainment medium, and it would remain so until the 1950s when television emerged. An important aspect of radio was its ability to create a new sense of community in which people thousands of miles apart listened to and became involved with their favorite radio soap opera, so named in reference to the soap sponsors of these shows.

Advertising, like the rest of the country, suffered dark days during this period. Agencies cut salaries and forced staff to work four-day weeks without being paid for the mandatory extra day off. Clients demanded frequent review of work, and agencies were compelled to provide more and more free services to keep accounts. Advertising would emerge from this depression, just as the economy itself did, during World War II. However, it would never again reach its pre-Depression status. It became the subject of a well-organized and angry consumerism movement. Congress passed real reform in this period. In 1938 the Wheeler-Lea Amendments to the Federal Trade Commission Act deemed "deceptive acts of commerce" to be against the law; this was interpreted to include advertising. Between 1938 and 1940, the FTC issued 18 injunctions against advertisers, including "forcing Fleischmann's Yeast to stop claiming that it cured crooked teeth, bad skin, constipation and halitosis."[17]

These government agencies soon used these new powers against a few large national advertisers, including Fleischmann's Yeast (consumers were being advised to eat yeast cakes for better health and vitality) and Lifebuoy and Lux soaps.

World War II and the '50s (1941 to 1960).

Almost one-half of all women married while they were still teenagers. Two out of three white women in college dropped out before they graduated. In 1955, 41 percent of women "thought the ideal number of children was four."[18]

Many people mark the end of the depression with the start of America's involvement in World War II in December 1941. During the war, advertising often made direct reference to the war effort, as the ad in Exhibit 3.19 shows, linking the product with patriotism and helping to rehabilitate the tarnished image of advertising. During the war, advertisers sold war bonds and encouraged conservation. In addition, they encouraged women to join the workforce, as seen in the so-called Rosie the Riveter ads. The ad in Exhibit 3.20 for the Penn Railroad is a good example. During the war years, many women joined the workforce; of course, many left it (both voluntarily and involuntarily) after the war ended in 1945.

Following World War II, the economy continued (with a few starts and stops) to improve, and the consumption spree was on again. This time, however, public sentiment toward advertising was fundamentally different from what it had been in the 1920s, following WWI. After WWII, there was widespread belief that America's

EXHIBIT 3.19

Advertisers often used America's involvement in World War II as a way to link their products with patriotism. This link provides advertising with a much-needed image boost after the dark period of the late 1930s. http://www .cocacola.com

17. Fox, *The Mirror Makers*, 168.
18. Wini Breines, *Young, White and Miserable: Growing Up Female in the Fifties* (Boston: Beacon, 1992).

EXHIBIT 3.20

EXHIBIT 3.21

During the war, advertisers encouraged women to join the workforce, as this ad for Penn Railroad illustrates.

During the 1950s, with fears of communist mind control and a very real nuclear arms race, frightened people built bomb shelters in their backyards and became convinced of advertising's hidden powers.

successful propaganda experts at the War Department simply moved over to Madison Avenue and started manipulating consumer minds. At the same time, there was great concern about the rise of communism and its use of "mind control." Perhaps it was only natural to believe that advertising was involved in the same type of pursuit, but to get you to buy things rather than become a communist. The United States was filled with suspicion related to McCarthyism, the bomb, repressed sexual thoughts (a resurgence of Freudian thought), and even aliens from outer space. Otherwise normal people were building bomb shelters in their backyards (see Exhibit 3.21), wondering whether their neighbors were communists and whether listening to "jungle music" (a.k.a. rock 'n' roll) would make their daughters less virtuous.

In this environment of mass fear, stories began circulating in the 1950s that advertising agencies were doing motivation research and using the "psychological sell," which served only to fuel an underlying suspicion of advertising. It was also during this period that Americans began to fear they were being seduced by **subliminal advertising** (subconscious advertising) to buy all sorts of things they didn't really want or need. There had to be a reason that homes and garages were filling up with so much stuff; it must be all that powerful advertising—and so a great excuse for lack of self-control was born. In fact, a best-selling 1957 book, *The Hidden Persuaders,* offered the answer: Slick advertising worked on the subconscious.[19] Suspicions about

19.   Vance Packard, *The Hidden Persuaders* (New York: D. McKay, 1957). With respect to the effects of "subliminal advertising," researchers have shown that while subliminal *communication* is possible, subliminal *persuasion,* in the typical real-world environment, remains all but impossible. As it was discussed, as mind control, in the 1950s, it remains a joke. See Timothy E. Moore, "Subliminal Advertising: What You See Is What You Get," *Journal of Marketing,* vol. 46 (Spring 1982), 38–47.

slick advertising still persist, and is still a big business for the "aren't consumers dumb/aren't advertisers evil" propagandists. Selling fears about advertising has always been good business. (See the IBP box.)

IBP

Not Snake Oil—But Still Pretty Slick

Marketers and advertisers long ago gave up the snake-oil—"it cures all"—claims of eras past like the old ad in Exhibit 3.2. But modern technology enables advertisers to use multiple media to integrate their marketing communications in a way that is, well, pretty slick.

Let's say your grandmother suffers from arthritis and really needs to take medication to relieve her pain, but all the prescription arthritis pain medications upset her stomach. Magically, a coupon for $1.00 off Zantac antacid shows up in her mailbox. The reason? Glaxo-SmithKline, the maker of Zantac, knows that various forms of prescription arthritis medication lead to nausea in a high percentage of cases. It just so happens that Granny is in a GlaxoSmithKline database of arthritis medication users and—voilà—the coupon gets sent out for Zantac.

Until recently, pharmaceutical marketers did not know, and could not know, who their prescription customers were. Doctors and pharmacists were sworn to keep the names of patients confidential. But recent changes in advertising regulations have relaxed restrictions. Now, about 300 new database marketing programs are available that track drug use. With this information, direct mail campaigns, magazine placement of ads, and even certain television media placements can be made with greater efficiency in reaching target customers.

Acquiring names and other vital information about target customers is not a matter of doctors and pharmacists violating confidentiality, though. In many cases, drug companies get the names of people who suffer from such sensitive conditions as depression and impotence from an unlikely source—the patients themselves. Many people give out their names and addresses when they call toll-free numbers, subscribe to magazines, or fill out pharmacy questionnaires. For example, *Reader's Digest* sent a survey to 15 million of its subscribers asking them about their health problems. More than 3 million subscribers responded, and now *Reader's Digest* can target mailings to people with high cholesterol, to smokers, and to arthritis sufferers. Many patients are outraged at the invasion of privacy, even though they gave out their names freely.

For the time being, firms such as GlaxoSmithKline are trying to understand the best way to use database information to the benefit of both the firm and the patient without violating the patient's sense of privacy and confidentiality.

Sources: William M. Bulkeley, "Prescriptions, Toll-Free Numbers Yield a Gold Mine for Marketers," *Wall Street Journal*, April 17, 1998, B1; Sally Beatty, "*Reader's Digest* Targets Patients by Their Ailments," *Wall Street Journal*, April 17, 1998, B1.

The most incredible story of the period involved a man named James Vicary. According to historian Stuart Rogers, in 1957 Vicary convinced the advertising world, and most of the U.S. population, that he had successfully demonstrated a technique to get consumers to do exactly what advertisers wanted. He claimed to have placed subliminal messages in motion picture film, brought in audiences, and recorded the results. He claimed that the embedded messages of "Eat Popcorn" and "Drink Coca-Cola" had increased sales of popcorn by 57.5 percent and Coca-Cola by 18.1 percent. He held press conferences and took retainer fees from advertising agencies. Later, he skipped town, just ahead of reporters who had figured out that none of his claims had ever happened. He completely disappeared, leaving no bank accounts and no forwarding address. He left town with about $4.5 million ($22.5 million in today's dollars) in advertising agency and client money.[20]

Wherever you are, Jim, it appears that you pulled off the greatest scam in advertising history. The big problem is that a lot of people, including regulators and members of Congress, still believe in the hype you were selling and that advertisers can actually do such things. That's the real crime.

The 1950s were also about sex, youth culture, rock 'n' roll, and television. In terms of sex, volumes could be written about the very odd and paradoxical '50s. On one hand, this was the time of neo-Freudian pop psychology and *Beach Blanket Bingo,* with sexual innuendo everywhere; at the same time, very conservative pronouncements about sexual mores were giving young Americans very contradictory messages. What's more, they would be

advertised to with a singular focus and force never seen before, becoming, as a result, the first "kid" and then "teen" markets. Because of their sheer numbers, they would

---

20. Stuart Rogers, "How a Publicity Blitz Created the Myth of Subliminal Advertising," *Public Relations Quarterly* (Winter 1992–1993), 12–17.

EXHIBIT 3.22

At first, advertisers didn't know what to do with television, the pre–World War II science experiment that reached 90 percent of U.S. households by 1960.

EXHIBIT 3.23

This is an ad from the famous Rosser Reeves at the Ted Bates agency. His style dominated the 1950s: harsh, abrasive, repetitive, diagrammatic, etc. He believed that selling the brand had virtually nothing to do with art or winning creative awards. His style of advertising is what the creative revolution revolted against.

ultimately constitute an unstoppable youth culture, one that everyone else had to deal with and try to please—the baby boomers. They would, over their parents' objections, buy rock 'n' roll records in numbers large enough to revolutionize the music industry. Now they buy golf clubs, SUV's, and mutual funds.

And then there was TV (Exhibit 3.22). Nothing like it had happened before. Its rise from pre–World War II science experiment to 90 percent penetration in U.S. households occurred during this period. At first, advertisers didn't know what to do with it and did two- and three-minute commercials, typically demonstrations. Of course, they soon began to learn TV's look and language.

This era also saw growth in the U.S. economy and in household incomes. The suburbs emerged, and along with them there was an explosion of consumption. Technological change was relentless and was a national obsession. The television, the telephone, and the automatic washer and dryer became common to the American lifestyle. Advertisements of this era were characterized by scenes of modern life, social promises, and reliance on science and technology.

Into all of this, 1950s advertising projected a confused, often harsh, at other times sappy presence. It is rarely remembered as advertising's golden age. Two of the most significant advertising personalities of the period were Rosser Reeves of the Ted Bates agency, who is best remembered for his ultra-hard-sell style (see Exhibit 3.23), and consultant Ernest Dichter, best remembered for his motivational research, which focused on the subconscious and symbolic elements of consumer desire. Exhibits 3.24 through 3.28 are representative of the advertising from this contradictory and jumbled period in American advertising

These ads show mythic nuclear families, well-behaved children, our "buddy" the atom, the last days of unquestioned faith in science, and rigid gender roles, while the rumblings of the sexual revolution of the 1960s were just barely audible. In a few short years, the atom would no longer be our friend; we would question science; youth would rebel; women and African-Americans would demand inclusion and fairness; bullet bras would be replaced with no bras.

Peace, Love, and the Creative Revolution (1960 to 1972).

You say you want a revolution, well, you know, we all want to change the world.

—John Lennon and Paul McCartney, "Revolution"[21]

As you well know, there was a cultural revolution in the 1960s. It affected just about everything—including advertising. Ads started to take on the themes, the language, and the look of the 1960s. But as an institution, advertising in the United States during the 1960s was actually slow to respond to the massive social revolution going on all around it. While the nation was struggling with civil rights, the Vietnam War, and the sexual revolution, advertising was often still portraying women and other

21. John Lennon and Paul McCartney, "Revolution," Northern Songs, 1968.

EXHIBITS 3.24 THROUGH 3.28

These five ads show the 1950's as they were: contradictory, family-dominated, but titillating, and science obsessed. Exhibit 3.28 shows evidence of the 1950s' paradoxical view on sex: titillating, but still "just an underwear ad."

minorities in subservient roles. Advertising agencies remained one of the whitest industries in America, despite what the ads looked like. And in ads, much of the sexual revolution just made women into boy toys. Gays and lesbians, as far as advertising was concerned, didn't exist.

The only thing truly revolutionary about 1960s advertising was the **creative revolution.** This revolution was characterized by the "creatives" (art directors and copywriters) having a bigger say in the management of their agencies. The emphasis in advertising turned "from ancillary services to the creative product; from science and research to art, inspiration, and intuition."[22] The look of this revolutionary advertising was clean and minimalist, with simple copy and a sense of self-effacing humor. More than anything, the creative revolution was about self-awareness, that is, saying, "OK, here's an ad, you know it's an ad—and so do we." It often went even further, even making fun of itself. The 1960s was also a time when advertising began to understand that it was all about hip, cool, and youth. Whatever

22. Fox, *The Mirror Makers*, 218.

EXHIBITS 3.29 AND 3.30

The new era of advertising in the 1960s was characterized by the creative revolution, during which the creative side of the advertising process rose to new prominence. Note the clean look and minimal copy in the Kellogg's ad in Exhibit 3.29, prepared by Leo Burnett in Chicago. The Rolls-Royce ad in Exhibit 3.30, from David Ogilvy of Ogilvy and Mather, was considered "revolutionary" for its copy, (not its look) which took the consumer more seriously than the ads of the 1950s did. http://www.kelloggs.com *and* http://www.rollsroyce.com

became cool, ads had to incorporate into their message. The '60s cultural revolution soon became ad copy. Everything became rebellion; even an un-hip brand like Dodge traded successfully on the "Dodge Rebellion."[23] Once advertising learned that it could successfully attach itself to youth, hipness, and revolution, it never went back.

The creative revolution, and the look it produced, is most often associated with four famous advertising agencies: Leo Burnett in Chicago; Ogilvy & Mather in New York (a little less so); Doyle Dane Bernbach in New York (the most); and Wells Rich and Green in New York. They were led in this revolution by agency heads Leo Burnett, David Ogilvy, Bill Bernbach, and Mary Wells. The Kellogg's Special K cereal, Rolls-Royce, Volkswagen, and Braniff ads pictured in Exhibits 3.29 through 3.32 are 1960s ads prepared by these four famous agencies, respectively.

Of course, it would be wrong to characterize the entire period as a creative revolution. Many ads in the 1960s still reflected traditional values and relied on relatively uncreative executions. Typical of many of the more traditional ads during the era is the Goodyear ad in Exhibit 3.33. Pepsi (Exhibit 3.34), traded on youth and the idea of youth.

23.   Thomas Frank, *The Conquest of Cool: Business Culture, Counterculture, and the Rise of Hip Consumerism* (Chicago: University of Chicago Press, 1997).

This is one of Mary Wells's famously futuristic (and fashionable) ads.

Through innovative advertising, Volkswagen has, over the years, been able to continually refuel its original message that its cars aren't expensive luxuries but as much a household staple as broccoli and ground round (and, at $1.02 a pound, cheaper than either!). These ads from DDB also acknowledged a sophisticated consumer. http://www.vw.com

Not all the advertising in the 1960s was characterized by the spirit of the creative revolution. The ad in Exhibit 3.33 relies more on traditional styles and values. http://www.goodyear.com

Pepsi "created" a generation and traded on the discovery of the vast youth market. Pepsi claimed youth as its own. http://www.pepsiworld.com

A final point that needs to be made about the era from 1960 to 1972 is that this was a period when advertising became generally aware of its own role in consumer culture—that is, advertising was an icon of a culture fascinated with consumption. While advertising played a role in encouraging consumption, it had become a symbol of consumption itself. While the creative revolution did not last long, advertising was forever changed. After the 1960s it would never again be quite as naïve about its own place in society; it has since become much more self-conscious. It also learned that, at least in America and probably most of the world, people (particularly youth) play out their revolutionary period *through* consumption—even when it's an anti-consumption revolution, you've got to have the right look, the right clothes, the right revolutionary garb. In a very significant way, advertising learned how to forever dodge the criticism of capitalism: Hide in plain sight.

Every few years, it seems, the cycles of the sixties repeat themselves on a smaller scale, with new rebel youth cultures bubbling their way to a happy replenishing of the various culture industries' depleted arsenal of cool. New generations obsolete the old, new celebrities render old ones ridiculous, and on and on in an ever-ascending spiral of hip upon hip. As adman Merle Steir wrote back in 1967, "Youth has won. Youth must always win. The new naturally replaces the old." And we will have new generations of youth rebellion as certainly as we will have generations of mufflers or toothpaste or footwear.[24]

My son's
the reason we
switched to Crest.

I'm going to be involved with my son as much as I can. Whether it's taking the time to teach him to tie his tie the right way, or making sure he brushes with a toothpaste we trust. That's why we switched to Crest. We learned there's no better cavity fighter than the fluoristat in Crest. And that's important to us. And, there are 3 great-tasting flavors to choose from...regular, mint and gel...and that's important to him.

Aren't your kids worth *Crest*?

EXHIBIT 3.35

While a bad economy and a national malaise caused a retreat to the tried-and-true styles of decades before, a bright spot of 1970s advertising was the portrayal of people of color. Thomas Burrell created ads that portrayed African-Americans with "positive realism."

The 1970s (1973 to 1980).

Mr. Blutarski, fat, drunk, and stupid is no way to go through life.

—Dean Vernon Wormer (John Vernon) in National Lampoon's *Animal House*, 1978

Dean Wormer's admonition to John Belushi's character in *Animal House* captured essential aspects of the 1970s, a time of excess and self-induced numbness. This was the age of polyester, disco, and driving 55. The re-election of Richard Nixon in 1972 marked the real start of the 1970s. America had just suffered through its first lost war, four student protesters had been shot and killed by the National Guard at Kent State University in the spring of 1970, Mideast nations appeared to be dictating the energy policy of the United States, and we were, as President Jimmy Carter suggested late in this period, in a national malaise. In this environment, advertising again retreated into the tried-and-true but hackneyed styles of decades before. The creative revolution of the 1960s gave way to a slowing economy and a return to the hard sell. This period also marked the beginning of the second wave of the American feminist movement. In the 1970s, advertisers actually started to present women in "new" roles and to include people of color, as the ad in Exhibit 3.35 shows.

The '70s was the end of "the '60s" and the end of whatever revolution one wished to speak of. This period became known as the era of self-help and selfishness. "Me" became the biggest word in the 1970s. What a great environment for advertising. All of society was telling

24. Frank, *The Conquest of Cool*, 235.

people that it was not only OK to be selfish, but it was the right thing to do. Selfishness was said to be natural and good. A refrain similar to "Hey babe, I can't be good to you if I'm not good to me," became a '70s mantra. Of course, being good to oneself often meant buying stuff—always good for advertising. Funny how that worked out.

Somewhat surprisingly, the '70s also resulted in added regulation and the protection of special audiences. Advertising encountered a new round of challenges on several fronts. First, there was growing concern over what effect $200 million a year in advertising had on children. A group of women in Boston formed **Action for Children's Television (ACT),** which lobbied the government to limit the amount and content of advertising directed at children. Established regulatory bodies, in particular the **Federal Trade Commission (FTC)** and the industry's **National Advertising Review Board,** demanded higher standards of honesty and disclosure from the advertising industry. Several firms were subject to legislative mandates and fines because their advertising was judged to be misleading. Most notable among these firms were Warner-Lambert (for advertising that Listerine mouthwash could cure and prevent colds), Campbell's (for putting marbles in the bottom of a soup bowl to bolster its look), and Anacin (for advertising that its aspirin could help relieve tension).

While advertising during this period featured more African-Americans and women, the effort to adequately represent and serve these consumers was minimal; advertising agency hiring and promotion practices with respect to minorities were formally challenged in the courts and informally known to be very, very white. Two important agencies owned and managed by African-Americans emerged and thrived: Thomas J. Burrell founded Burrell Advertising, and Byron Lewis founded Uniworld. Burrell is perhaps best known for ads that rely on two principles: "positive realism" and "psychological distance." Positive realism is "people working productively; people engaging in family life . . . people being well-rounded . . . and thoughtful; people caring about other people; good neighbors, good parents . . . people with dreams and aspirations; people with ambition." Psychological distance is "a feeling of separation between the black consumer and a mainstream product." One of Burrell's well-known ads is shown in Exhibit 3.35. (Go to http://www.little africa.com/resources/advertising.htm for a current list of major African-American advertising agencies and resources.)

The 1970s also signaled a period of growth in communications technology. Consumers began to surround themselves with devices related to communication. The development of the VCR, cable television, and the laserdisc player all occurred during the 1970s. Cable TV claimed 20 million subscribers by the end of the decade. Similarly, cable programming grew in quality, with viewing options such as ESPN, CNN, TBS, and Nickelodeon. As cable subscribers and their viewing options increased, advertisers learned how to reach more specific audiences through the diversity of programming on cable systems.

The process of advertising was being restricted by both consumer and governmental regulatory challenges, yet technological advances posed unprecedented opportunities. It was the beginning of the merger mania that swept the industry throughout the end of the decade and into the next, a movement that saw most of the major agencies merge with one another and with non-U.S. agencies as well. It was also the birth of what were essentially program-length commercials, particularly in children's television. Product/show blends for toys like Strawberry Shortcake made regulation more difficult: If it's a show about a product, then it's not really an ad (and can't be regulated as an ad)—or is it? This drove regulators crazy, but program-length commercials were incredibly smart marketing.[25] They were generally treated by regulators as shows and opened the door for countless numbers of imitators.

---

25.   Tom Engelhardt, "The Shortcake Strategy," in Todd Gitlin, ed., *Watching Television* (New York: Pantheon, 1986), 68–110.

One of the significant differences between advertising prepared in the 1960s and in the 1970s is that ads began focusing on the product itself rather than on creative techniques. The Jensen ad in Exhibit 3.36 and the Listerine ad in Exhibit 3.37 represent this product-focused feature of 1970s advertising, which reflects the fact that advertising agency management took control back from creatives during this era. What do current advertising trends tell us about the role of management in today's agencies?

This period in the evolution of advertising presented enormous challenges. In all of this, the look of advertising was about as interesting as it was in the 1950s. Often, advertisements focused on the product itself, rather than on creative technique, as illustrated in the product-focused ads in Exhibits 3.36 and 3.37. During this period, management took control and dominated agency activities. In agencies used to creative control, the idea of "bottom-liners" struck deep at the soul. Of course, all that money they made in the 1980s made them feel much better about the whole thing.

The Designer Era (1980 to 1992).

Greed, for a lack of a better word, is good.

—Gordon Gekko (Michael Douglas) in *Wall Street,* 1987

"In 1980, the average American had twice as much real income as his parents had had at the end of WWII."[26] Consumers had a lot of real income to spend. The political, social, business, and advertising landscape changed in 1980 with the election of Ronald Reagan. The country made a right, and conservative politics were the order of the day. There was, of course, some backlash and many countercurrents, but the

---

26.   Collier, *The Rise of Selfishness in America,* 230.

EXHIBIT 3.38

An ad that embodied the tone and style of 1980s advertising was Ronald Reagan's 1984 re-election campaign ad "Morning in America." The ad is soft in texture but firm in its affirmation of the conservative values of family and country.

EXHIBIT 3.39

This MasterCard ad demonstrates the social-class and design consciousness of the 1980s.

EXHIBIT 3.40

I want my MTV.

conservatives were in the mainstream. Greed was good, stuff was good, advertising was good.

Many ads from the Republican era are particularly social-class and values conscious. They openly promote consumption, but in a conservative way, all wrapped up in "traditional American values." The quintessential 1980s ad may be the 1984 television ad for President Ronald Reagan's reelection campaign called "Morning in America." The storyboard for this ad is shown in Exhibit 3.38. This ad is soft in texture, but it is a firm reaffirmation of family and country—and capitalism. Other advertisers quickly followed with ads that looked similar to "Morning in America." The 1980s were also about designer labels, social-class consciousness, and having stuff, as the ad in Exhibit 3.39 demonstrates.

At the same time, several new communication technology trends were emerging, which led to more-creative, bold, and provocative advertising. Television advertising of this period was influenced by the rapid-cut editing style of MTV. George Lois, himself of the 1960s creative revolution, was hired by MTV to save the fledgling network after a dismal first year. After calling a lot of people who were unwilling to take the chance, he got Mick Jagger to proclaim, "I want my MTV" (see Exhibit 3.40). The network turned around and music television surged into popular consciousness. Most importantly for us, television ads in the 1980s started looking like MTV videos: rapid cuts with a very self-conscious character.

This was also the age of the **infomercial,** a long advertisement that looks like a talk show or a half-hour product demonstration. If you watch late-night cable television, you've probably seen some guy lighting his car on fire as part of a demonstration for car wax. These very long ads initially aired in late-night television time slots, when audiences were small in number and airtime was relatively inexpensive. Infomercials have since spread to other off-peak time slots, including those with somewhat larger audiences, and they have gained respect along the way. The Psychic Friends Network, Bowflex, and a wide assortment of automotive, weight loss, and hair care products are all examples of products and services recently promoted on infomercials. You might check out http://www.as-on-tv-ads.com for more examples.

The Second '90s (1993 to 2000).

Modern advertising had entered its second century, and it was more self-conscious than ever before. In the '90s, self-parody was the inside joke of the day, except everyone was "inside." Winks and nods to the media-savvy audience were becoming pretty common. Advertising was fast, and it was everywhere. Some said it was "dead," killed by the World Wide Web and other new media, but that turned out to be a pretty large exaggeration. By the end of the decade, ads were still ads, and they were very much alive.

Still, there were scary moments. In May 1994, Edwin L. Artzt, then chairman and CEO of Procter & Gamble, the $40-billion-a-year marketer of consumer packaged goods, dropped a bomb on the advertising industry. During an address to participants at the American Association of Advertising Agencies (4As) annual conference, he warned that agencies must confront a "new media" future that won't be driven by traditional advertising. While at that time P&G was spending about $1 billion a year on television advertising, Artzt told the 4As audience, "From where we stand today, we can't be sure that ad-supported TV programming will have a future in the world being created—a world of video-on-demand, pay-per-view, and subscription TV. These are designed to carry no advertising at all."[27] An icy chill filled the room. Then, just when the industry had almost recovered from Artzt's dire proclamation, William T. Esrey, chairman and CEO of Sprint, gave it another jolt a year later at the same annual conference. Esrey's point was somewhat different but equally challenging to the industry. He said that clients are "going to hold ad agencies more closely accountable for results than ever before. That's not just because we're going to be more demanding in getting value for our advertising dollars. It's also because we know the technology is there to measure advertising impact more precisely than you have done in the past."[28] Esrey's point: **Interactive media** will allow direct measurement of ad exposure and impact, quickly revealing those that perform well and those that do not. Secondly, the agency will be held accountable for results. Well, the former (precise measurement) didn't really work out, but the latter (accountability) became the order of the day. That did change. Ad agencies are now said to be operating with fewer staff and a smaller margin than ever before. Clients are more tight-fisted than at any time since the Great Depression.

The saga continues. Still unsure of what could be delivered and what could be counted, in August 1998 Procter & Gamble hosted an Internet "summit," due to "what is widely perceived as the poky pace of efforts to eliminate the difficulties confronted by marketers using on-line media to pitch products."[29] Some of these

---

27.   This quote and information from this section can be found in Steve Yahn, "Advertising's Grave New World," *Advertising Age,* May 16, 1994, 53.

28.   Kevin Goodman, "Sprint Chief Lectures Agencies on Future," *Wall Street Journal,* April 28, 1995, B6.

29.   Stuart Elliot, "The Media Business: Advertising; Procter and Gamble Calls Internet Marketing Executives to Cincinnati for a Summit Meeting," *New York Times,* August 19, 1998, D3; available at http://www.nytimes.com, accessed February 20, 1999.

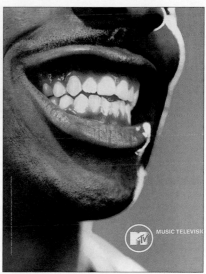

EXHIBITS 3.41 AND 3.42

1990s ads were generally more visual and self-aware. They didn't try to be realistic; they said "this is an ad."

problems were technological: incompatible technical standards; limited bandwidth; and disappointing measurement of audience, exposure, and subsequent behavior. Others were the result of naïveté. Advertisers such as P&G want to know what they are getting and what it costs when they place an Internet ad. Does anyone notice these ads, or do people click right past them? What would "exposure" in this environment mean? How do you use this medium to build brand relationships? At the end of this summit, P&G reaffirmed its commitment to the Internet.

But history again showed that measurement of bang for buck (return on investment, ROI) in advertising (Internet or not) is still elusive. While better than TV, the Internet is fundamentally unable to accommodate precise measurements of return on investment in advertisement. Too many variables, too much noise in the system, too many lagged (delayed) effects, and too many uncertainties about who is really there (online) abound.

Not a big surprise for those who pay attention to history: Advertising's impact is always tough to measure. Even with all this technology, it still is. What bump in sales comes from where is still elusive (more about this in Chapter 15).

Another change has come in the form of a significant challenge on New York's claim as the center of the advertising universe. In the United States, the center has moved west, with the ascendancy of agencies in California, Minnesota, Oregon, and Washington, not to mention international hot spots such as London and Singapore. In the 1990s these agencies tended to be more creatively oriented and less interested in numbers-oriented research than those in New York. Other hot or nearly hot ad-shop markets include Minneapolis, Austin, Atlanta, Houston, and Dallas. Outside the United States, London emerged as the key player (Exhibit 3.41), with Singapore a close second. Nineties ads were generally more visually oriented and much more self-aware. They said "this is an ad" in their look and feel. They had a young and ironic flavor. Some call them "postmodern." Exhibits 3.41 and 3.42 are good examples of this '90s style.

4 The '00s: More Hip Ads and More Technology (2001–present). As for the creative trends in ads, ads of the '00s have become even more self-aware and self-referential. They are ads that are very aware of being ads. Everyone is in on it (see

EXHIBITS 3.43 THROUGH 3.46

Exhibits 3.43 through 3.46 are good examples of recent advertising. They are visual, usually self-aware, young, and stylish. They are ads that are comfortable being ads.

Exhibits 3.43 through 3.46). They are comfortable being ads. They are also visual, young, and stylish. But people should not kid themselves: Straightforward traditional ads are still a big part of the mix (see Exhibits 3.47 and 3.48).

Technology and Advertising. The technological changes that occurred during the early years of the 21st century have been and will continue to be intoxicating and somewhat frightening. But despite all the creative opportunities that technology offers, the volatility in ad markets demonstrates some harsh realities of the complex-

EXHIBITS 3.47 AND 3.48   **EXHIBIT 3.49**

Despite the surge in creativity, there are still lots of traditional ads like these.   *Nice ads, but company is gone.*

ity of global commerce. No place has that harsh reality been felt more severely than in the dot.coms. In a phenomenon often referred to as the "dot.bomb," many Internet firms that once had billion-dollar valuations and many believers—such as Pets.com (see Exhibit 3.49)—declared bankruptcy in 2000 and 2001. For one example, see the Creativity box.

The demise of Web sites that were totally dependent on online advertising for revenue does not mean that online advertising is dead. It's just not going to be as all-encompassing (and nowhere near as easy) as early predictions made by P&G and Sprint (and others) might have suggested. From 1998 to 2000, online advertising revenues exploded from about $2.0 billion annually to over $8.0 billion. When the slump in online advertising hit bottom in 2002, revenues stood at about $5.8 billion—not exactly peanuts. And the turnaround appears real—at least for now. Online advertising revenues are expected to climb back to nearly $9.0 billion in 2005.[30] And don't forget about business-to-business promotion on the Web, known as e-business. **E-business** is another form of e-advertising and/or promotion in which companies selling to business customers (rather than to household consumers) rely on the Internet to send messages and close sales (we'll cover this in detail in Chapter 16). E-business revenues transactions reached $2.4 trillion by 2003 and are expected to experience strong growth through the first decade of the 21st century, at least.[31]

The main impetus for such spending on Web advertising is focused on three aspects of technology that will continue to foster growth—interactive, wireless, and broadband technologies. Because of advances in technology, firms like Procter & Gamble continue to invest heavily in this means of sending messages and reaching target customers. P&G has developed and maintains dozens different Web sites for the company's approximately 300 brands to serve and interact with customers.[32] P&G also has gone beyond just product-oriented sites and has launched "relationship building" sites like beinggirl.com, a teen community site (Exhibit 3.50). With such a site, the firm can gather data, test new product ideas, and experiment with interactivity.

30.   Heather Green and Pallavi Gogoi, "Online Ads Take Off—Again," *BusinessWeek,* May 5, 2003, 75.
31.   Timothy Mullaney et al., "The E-Biz Surprise," *BusinessWeek,* May 12, 2003, 60–68.
32.   Beth Snyder Bulik, "Procter & Gamble's Great Web Experiment," Business 2.0, November 28, 2000, 48-54.

CREATIVITY

Start the E-volution without Me

During the latter part of the 1990s and the early days of the 2000s, nearly every advertiser made a commitment to the Internet. The (fairly sound) logic was that this new medium was gaining more and more favor, with more consumers and households getting "wired" every day. Surely this would be an ideal opportunity to reach a large number of consumers, through a new medium and in a much more personalized way.

Whirlpool was just the sort of company to use that logic. As one of the oldest U.S. companies and one that held a leading market share, not to mention a great brand image, Whirlpool wanted to be sure the opportunities to use the Internet effectively were not overlooked. Managers' thinking went something like this. Millions of people were scouring the Web in search for the best deals on books, air travel, and even cars. Surely some of these millions of people would want to search the Web for a deal on a refrigerator or washing machine.

With that strategic orientation, Whirlpool launched Brandwise.com, the first comparative-shopping Web site for appliances. Brandwise.com would be consumers' trusted source for up-to-the-minute product information and reviews of all kinds of appliances made by all kinds of manufacturers. And Brandwise could make arrangements, right there on the Web site, for consumers to buy their dream appliance by connecting them to a nearby retailer. Whirlpool was so certain that Brandwise.com would be a runaway hit with consumers that the firm hired Kathy Misunas, former CEO of American Airlines' Sabre Reservations Group. At Brandwise.com's launch, Misunas crowed, "Brandwise.com represents the next step in the evolution of e-commerce."

Wrong. Within eight months, Brandwise.com was shut down. The site attracted so few visitors—less than 200,000 per month—that Media Metrix wouldn't even follow it on its Web traffic–counting system. What went wrong and how could it go wrong so fast? The answer is actually painfully simple. Brandwise was conceived and executed with the attitude that the Web is so hot and hip that anything on the Web will not just survive but flourish. But what happened was that Whirlpool botched the marketing effort, failed to establish good relations with retailers, and underestimated the difficulty of setting up and maintaining a good Web site. In addition, the consumer behavior analysis was botched as well. Eighty percent of appliance purchasers are replacing something that broke. They don't want to go to a Web site, they want to go to a store and get a new appliance—now. In the end, what wrecked this new economy idea was an old economy challenge—execution.

Source: Amy Kover, "Brandwise Was Brand Foolish," *Fortune*, November 13, 2000, 201–208.

For example, if a visitor wants to know what nail polish will match the lipstick she just saw in a commercial, she can go to the Web site and get an immediate answer. Thus, target audiences do not have to be broadly defined by age or geographic groups—individual households can be targeted through direct interaction with the audience member. Also note that P&G can reach a global audience through beinggirl.com without the cost and time-consuming effort of placing traditional media ads in dozens of markets.

Chapter 2 raised the issues of wireless and broadband technologies as trends that will be affecting the future of advertising. To follow up on that discussion, wireless penetration into U.S. households has experienced tremendous growth. High-speed Internet access (primarily broadband) now reaches about 40 million households (about 40 percent of all households). In addition, "**wi-fi**" provides speedy wireless technology that beams a radio signal connection out 300 feet and allows Web surfers to roam around their homes, offices, or local coffee shops without being tethered to a phone line.[33]

Branded Entertainment. There is no aspect of the evolution of advertising more significant than the emergence of "branded entertainment." **Branded Entertainment** is the blending of advertising and integrated brand promotion with entertainment, primarily film and television programming. A subset of branded entertainment is *product placement,* the significant placement of brands within films or television programs. When Tom Cruise wore Ray-Bans in the film *Top Gun*, when James Bond switched to the BMW Z-8 from his beloved Aston-Martin (by the way, he has switched back), and when the cast of *Friends* drank Pepsi, audiences took notice. Well, branded entertainment takes the process of getting attention for brands by placing them in film and television scenes a quantum leap forward. With branded entertainment, a brand is not just a bit player; it is the "star" of the program. An early

---

33.   Mullaney et al., "The E-Biz Surprise"; Heather Green et al., "WiFi Means Business," *BusinessWeek,* April 28, 2003, 86–92; Cliff Edwards, et al., "Digital Homes," *BusinessWeek,* July 21, 2003, 58–64.

participant in branded entertainment and still a leader in using the technique is BMW. BMW launched the BMW Web film series in 2001 and has featured the work of well-known directors, including Wong Kar-Wai, Ang Lee, John Frankenheimer, Guy Ritchie, and Alejandro González Iñárritu (Exhibit 3.51). Other sites featuring entertainment by featuring the brand include Lipton Tea (http://www.lipton.com), Oldsmobile with Tiger Woods in "Tiger Trap" (http://www.oldsmobile.com), and the U.S. Army at its Web-based computer game (http://www.goarmy.com). There are many advantages to branded entertainment—not running into the consumer's well-trained resistance mechanisms to ads, and not having to go through all the ad regulations. In an ad BMW has to use a disclaimer ("closed track, professional driver") when it shows its cars tearing around, but in *The Italian Job,* no such disclaimer is required. Also, movies have been seen by the courts as artistic speech, not as the less protected "commercial speech." Branded entertainment, therefore, gets more First Amendment protection than ordinary advertising does. This is an important distinction, since regulation and legal fights surrounding ads represent a large cost of doing business.

But the Web is only one part of the branded entertainment process. Recently, firms are seeing the beauty of partnering with film studios. For example, the highly successful 2003 film *Pirates of the Caribbean* can easily be argued as a 90-minute advertisement for Disneyland. Going the other way, Universal Studios now has an Indiana Jones ride at its Universal Studios park in Orlando. In this case, the film came first and the amusement ride was developed based on the success of the film.

EXHIBIT 3.50

P&G's communal Web site beinggirl.com is a good example of online brand community building with global reach. http://www.beinggirl.com

EXHIBIT 3.51

The ultimate in branded entertainment, the BMW Web films entertain viewers by featuring BMW cars in short Web-accessed films. The films have attracted millions of viewers who stay at the BMW site for an average of 16 to 20 minutes— far longer viewership than any traditional advertising could ever hope for. http://www.bmwfilms.com

As you can imagine, advertisers love the exposure that branded entertainment can provide. And entertainment venues are fully protected (as artistic expression) by the First Amendment provisions of free speech and therefore skirt much of the regulation imposed on traditional advertising. But not all consumers are wildly enthusiastic about the blurring line between advertising and entertainment. One survey showed that 52 percent of respondents were worried about advertisers influencing entertainment content. The same survey showed that 62 percent of respondents found product placement distracting rather than entertaining.[34]

Advertisers should take note of this generally negative attitude among consumers. What happens if branded entertainment gets to be too prominent, too intrusive? Consumers will turn to solutions like TiVo. **TiVo** is a service that automatically records a consumer's favorite television shows every time they air. With technology like TiVo, consumers can skip commercials, and 63 percent of TiVo users report that they do just that.[35]

The Value of an Evolutionary Perspective.

As intriguing as new technology like wi-fi is and as exciting as new communications options like Web films may be, we shouldn't jump to the conclusion that the very nature of advertising as a process will change. So far, it hasn't. Advertising will still be a paid, mass-mediated attempt to persuade. As a business process, advertising will still be one of the primary marketing mix tools that contribute to revenues and profits by stimulating demand and nurturing brand loyalty. Even though the executives at P&G believe there is a whole new world of communication and have developed dozens of Web sites to take advantage of this new world, the firm still spends over $3 billion a year on traditional advertising through traditional media.[36] It is also safe to argue that consumers will still be highly involved in some product decisions and not so involved in others, so that some messages will be particularly relevant and others will be completely irrelevant to forming and maintaining beliefs and feelings about brands. To this date, technology (particularly e-commerce) has changed the way people shop, gather information, and purchase. And while the advance in online advertising continues, so far the big winners in the resurgence of advertising spending have been traditional media. Recall that online advertising is estimated to be about $9 billion in 2005. Well, spending in traditional media like television, radio, newspapers, and magazines will be about $260 billion in 2005.[37] Maybe things will change, maybe not.

In this chapter, we have tried to offer an evolutionary perspective on advertising. We strongly believe that to understand advertising in an evolutionary perspective is to appreciate the reasons for advertising's use in a modern industrialized society. Advertising was spawned by a market-driven system and grew through free market economies. Efficient methods of production made advertising necessary; commodities had to become brands. Urbanization, transportation expansion, and communications advancements all facilitated the use and growth of advertising. The result is that advertising has become firmly entrenched as a business function, with deeply rooted economic and cultural foundations. This evolutionary perspective allows us to understand the more basic aspects of the role and impact of advertising. An important chapter in any discussion of the evolution of advertising is, of course, the evolution of integrated brand promotion. While the advances in technology have taken center stage in our discussion of the latest era in advertising, integrated brand promotion (IBP) strategies and tactics have evolved as well. Remember from Chapter 2 that more and more money is being allocated to IBP tools other than advertising. And the evolution of advertising and IBP is truly a global evolution, as the Global Issues box highlights. Stay tuned.

34.   Claire Atkinson, "Ad Distraction Up, Say Consumers," *Advertising Age,* January 6, 2003, 1, 19.
35.   Ibid., 19.
36.   "100 Leading National Advertisers," *Advertising Age,* June 28, 2004, S4.
37.   Projections provided by Bob Coen each year in *Advertising Age* and at Adage.com.

SUMMARY

Explain why advertising is an essential feature of capitalistic economic systems.

Although some might contend that the practice of advertising began thousands of years ago, it is more meaningful to connect advertising as we know it today with the emergence of capitalistic economic systems. In such systems, business organizations must compete for survival in a free market setting. In this setting, it is natural that a firm would embrace a tool that assists it in persuading potential customers to choose its products over those offered by others. Of course, advertising is such a tool. The explosion in production capacity that marked the Industrial Revolution gave demand-stimulation tools added importance.

Describe manufacturers' dependence on advertising, promotion, and branding in achieving balanced relationships with retailers.

Advertising and branding play a key role in the ongoing power struggle between manufacturers and their retailers. U.S. manufacturers began branding their products in the late 1800s. Advertising could thus be used to build awareness of and desire for the various offerings of a particular manufacturer. Retailers have power in the marketplace deriving from the fact that they are closer to the customer. When manufacturers can use advertising to build customer loyalty to their brands, they take part of that power back. Of course, in a capitalistic system, power and profitability are usually related.

Discuss several significant eras in the evolution of advertising in the United States, and relate important changes in advertising practice to more fundamental changes in society and culture.

Social and economic trends, along with technological developments, are major determinants of the way advertising is practiced in any society. Before the Industrial Revolution, advertising's presence in the United States was barely noticeable. With an explosion in economic growth around the turn of the century, modern advertising was born: The "P. T. Barnum era" and the 1920s established advertising as a major force in the U.S. economic system. With the Great Depression and World War II, cynicism and paranoia regarding advertising began to grow. This concern led to refinements in practice and more careful regulation of advertising in the 1960s and 1970s. Consumption was once again in vogue during the designer era of the 1980s. The new communication technologies that emerged in the 1990s era seem certain to effect significant changes in future practice. Finally, the interactive, wireless, and broadband technologies that are leading advertising into the 21st century hold great promise but a hard-to-predict future.

Identify forces that will continue to affect the evolution of advertising.

Integrated, interactive, and *wireless* have become the advertising buzzwords of the early 21st century. These words represent notable developments that are reshaping advertising practice. This is so because the technologies present advertisers with new options like Web films or feature films that highlight brands—a process known as advertainment. In addition, consumers can use wi-fi systems, limited-area wireless access systems, to provide more mobility in their use of computers. Integrated brand promotion may continue to grow in importance as advertisers work with more-varied media options to reach markets that are becoming even more fragmented. A variety of advertisers are using interactive media to reach consumers in the digital realm, while services like TiVo demonstrate a consumer backlash against the ubiquity of advertising. As for creative, the ads of the '00s have become more self-aware and self-referential—they are ads that are very aware of being ads. Advertising in the next decade will continue to be a vibrant and challenging profession.

KEY TERMS

Industrial Revolution	subliminal advertising	infomercial
principle of limited liability	creative revolution	interactive media
branding	Action for Children's Television	e-business
dailies	(ACT)	wi-fi
consumer culture	Federal Trade Commission (FTC)	branded entertainment
Pure Food and Drug Act	National Advertising Review Board	TiVo

QUESTIONS

1. As formerly communist countries make the conversion to free market economies, advertising typically becomes more visible and important. Why would this be the case?

2. Explain why there is a strong relationship between increasing urbanization and per capita spending.

3. How do manufacturers gain or lose power in the channel of distribution? What other parties are involved in this power struggle?

4. Describe the various factors that produced an explosion of advertising activity in the "P. T. Barnum era."

5. The 1950s were marked by great suspicion about advertisers and their potential persuasive powers. Do you see any lingering effects of this era in attitudes about advertising today?

6. There were many important developments in the 1970s that set the stage for advertising in the Reagan era. Which of these developments are likely to have the most enduring effects on advertising practice in the future?

7. Ed Artzt, then chairman and CEO of Procter & Gamble, made a speech in May 1994 that rattled the cages of many advertising professionals. What did Artzt have to say that got people in the ad business so excited?

8. Review the technological developments that have had the greatest impact on the advertising business. What new technologies are emerging that promise more profound changes for advertisers in the next decade?

9. What creative trends in ads have emerged in the period from 2001 to the present?

EXPERIENTIAL EXERCISES

1. Advertising has changed throughout the past century, reflecting the social, economic, and cultural forces of the times. The ads of the '00s are becoming more hip and self-referential. Many of today's most prominent ads are full of irony and quirky attempts at comedy with a wink. Select three prominent ads from television, radio, or new media, and analyze the content and themes used in the ads to communicate the brands. For each, answer the following questions: Does the theme rely on high fashion, comedy, patriotism, or pop-culture trends? How well does the ad communicate the value of the brand? In what way is the ad a product of the times in which we live?

2. In this chapter, manufacturers' pursuit of power in the channel of distribution is listed as an important influence on the emergence and growth of advertising. Man-ufacturers depend on other members of the distribution channel (such as retailers and wholesalers) for the success of their brands. Hoping to pressure channel members to purchase manufacturers' brands, advertisers use ads to stimulate demand for their products at the consumer level, which in turn spurs retailers to purchase from manufacturers to meet that demand.

Contact a local retail store and set up a brief phone interview with the manager or retail buyer. Ask the manager what role customer requests and fashion trends play in determining the store's product offerings. Find out how they keep track of those requests and trends and how they respond to them. Finally, ask the manager to describe the role of advertisers in stimulating consumer demand and how that places leverage on them to carry certain brands. Ask for real-world examples.

3. During the period from 1980 to 1992, half-hour television product demonstrations known as infomercials emerged and became popular. Infomercials sell a variety of popular products—from diets and cosmetics to housewares and body training—and are designed to prompt a direct response from viewers. While many viewers question the integrity of these advertising programs, they have earned respect for their success in eliciting spontaneous purchases from broad target audiences.

The Carlton Sheets infomercial for his *No Down Payment* real estate investment program is seen all over the country on late-night television. Go to a search engine and search for the Carlton Sheets Internet site. Compare and contrast the message of the infomercial with the message of the site. Do you think these two media reach the same target audience? Which medium do you think is more persuasive for this particular kind of product advertisement? Why? What social and economic conditions of the 1980s produced the advertising method known as the infomercial? If you are not familiar with Carlton Sheets, pick any infomercial and answer these same questions.

EXPERIENCING THE INTERNET

3-1 The Value of an Evolutionary Perspective

While many aspects of advertising have remained constant over the course of its evolution, other aspects have changed dramatically. Emerging forces in technology and globalization have challenged advertisers to develop and promote brands in widely fragmented markets. As the evolutionary perspective of the history of advertising demonstrates, social, cultural, and economic shifts of the past have radically influenced the overall progression of the industry. As we would expect, many of today's important trends will guide the future evolution of advertising.

InfoWorld: http://www.infoworld.com

1. The final sections of the chapter examine some of the forces that will shape the next decade of advertising. What changes can be expected for the advertising industry, and why? What aspects of advertising are likely to remain constant?

2. Since new technologies will continue to play an important role in shaping the evolution of advertising, choose a relevant news story from InfoWorld and explain how you think the news might relate to the future evolution of the industry.

3-2 Important Eras in the Evolution of Advertising

The practice of advertising has emerged in modern times, owing its development largely to the social and economic changes of recent centuries and the rise of modern mass media. During the history of the United States, many important advertising eras evolved, each reflecting fundamental changes in society and culture. One of the world's largest searchable databases of classic print ads, adflip.com, features ads from the 1940s to the present. Fans of advertising history visit adflip.com to enjoy these retro ads and the evolution of pop culture they represent.

adflip: http://www.adflip.com

1. Browse adflip and select two ads from various decades of advertising history. Briefly describe the ads and explain how they fit the general characteristics of advertisements for their era as defined in the chapter.

2. Select an ad from the site that does not seem to reflect the general characteristics of its era. How does it differ from ads typical to this period? Would it fit better in a different general era of advertising history? Explain.

CHAPTER 4

After reading and thinking about this chapter, you will be able to do the following:

Identify the benefits and problems of advertising and promotion in a capitalistic society and debate a variety of issues concerning their effects on society's well-being.

Explain how ethical considerations affect the development of advertising and IBP campaigns.

Discuss the role of government agencies in the regulation of advertising and promotion.

Explain the meaning and importance of self-regulation for a firms that develop and use advertising and promotion.

Discuss the regulation of the full range of techniques used in the IBP process.

Miller

MILLER BREWING CO.
SINCE *1855*
MILWAUKEE, WIS. USA

NOT EVEN THE IRISH RELY ON LUCK.

DON'T DRIVE DRUNK.
DESIGNATE A DRIVER THIS ST. PATRICK'S DAY.

Miller Brewing Company and its distributors share a commitment to live responsibly.

 Live Responsibly **Miller**

Introductory Scenario: I Didn't Sign Up for This!

Has this ever happened to you? You see an ad in a magazine or the newspaper that announces a "Big Sweepstakes" where you can win a fabulous vacation to Hawaii, a killer speedboat, or $1 million in a drawing. You fill in the entry form, mail it, and wait. After a few months, it dawns on you that you haven't won the sweepstakes, but what you have won is a mailbox (or e-mail box) full of stuff from advertisers who got your name from the outfit that ran the sweepstakes!

This is exactly what happened to Anne Marie when she saw the Eddie Bauer edition of a Ford Explorer as a sweepstakes giveaway. It was her dream car and she entered the sweepstakes. But in the end, she decided that entering the sweepstakes created a nightmare. "Every Jeep dealer in the Galaxy was calling me after that," she said. "There was a span of about two weeks that a different car dealer called or mailed something [every day] about me coming in to test drive a car. I was furious."[1]

What happened to Anne Marie happens to millions of Americans every day. Advertisers call it "database marketing." Contests, sweepstakes, supermarket discount cards, and product warranty cards are common methods used by marketers to gather information about customers and create a database to be used for advertising and integrated brand promotion (IBP) strategies.[2] Big data "warehouse" companies such as Metromail, Acxiom, and R. L. Polk specialize in collecting massive amounts of consumer information. They then sell the data—including names, addresses, phone numbers, and e-mail addresses—to companies that use direct marketing, such as catalog publishers, Internet companies, charities, credit card issuers, book clubs, and music clubs—you know, the ones who send you all the stuff in the (e-)mail. (See Exhibit 4.1.) Some companies, however, do not infringe on customer privacy because they do not collect individual data. One such company is Watchfire. At Watchfire (http://www.watchfire.com), the firm provides aggregate data only on visitors to a company's Web site with respect to where the visitors came from and what behavior they exhibited while at the site.

While marketers call this process database marketing, some consumer advocates are calling it an invasion of privacy. The leader of Junkbusters, a consumer advocacy group that opposes invasions of consumer privacy, calls the practice of database development "Orwellian" because "George Orwell's *1984* described a world where each home had a television-like device that actually watched what individuals were doing."[3] And there is ample and growing evidence that consumers are getting more and more aggravated with these database marketing efforts. A recent survey by Planetfeedback.com showed that 80 percent of respondents were "very annoyed" by pop-up ads and spam e-mail; in comparison, only about 10–15 percent of these respondents reported being "very annoyed" by print or TV ads.[4]

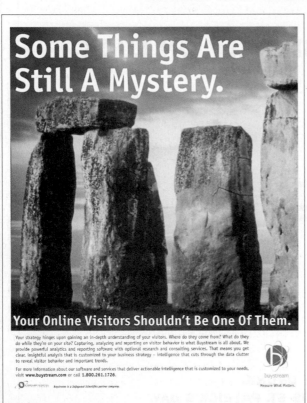

EXHIBIT 4.1

Many firms are in the business of providing information for advertisers to effectively and efficiently deliver advertising and integrated brand promotion messages to target audiences. Firms like Buystream (now owned by Watchfire) sell consumers names and addresses they have gathered and organized into easy-to-use databases.

---

1. Teena Massingill, "Buyer Beware: Retailers Sharing Data," *Knight Ridder News Service,* September 17, 1999.
2. Alissa Quart, "Ol' College Pry," *Business 2.0,* April 3, 2001, 68.
3. Bradley Johnson, "Gov't Agencies Eye Online Profiling," *Advertising Age,* November 8, 1999, 102.
4. Jack Neff, "Spam Research Reveals Disgust with Pop-Up Ads," *Advertising Age,* August 23, 2003, 1, 21.

But advertisers defend themselves by saying that good marketing research (including database development) leads to greater efficiency and more value for customers. As one direct marketer put it, "The more effective direct marketers get, the more they know about you, the better they can serve you."[5] For example, grocers argue that with the databases they can target coupons and other specially advertised offers to the people most likely to use them, instead of wasting money on coupons and mailings that are never used.

Consumer advocates argue that any good that might come from the "data mining" process is far outweighed by the annoyance created by the avalanche of offers plaguing consumers. These advocates are arguing for "permission marketing," in which marketers can direct advertising and promotions *only* to people who give them express permission to do so by indicating clearly that they "opt-in" to receiving offers through the mail or e-mail.[6]

The repercussions of database marketing and not heeding consumers' frustration are already being felt in the form of new regulations. The year 2004 saw the implementation of two restrictive pieces of legislation. The "do-not-call list" devised by the Federal Trade Commission is expected to include 60 million American phone numbers registered in an attempt to restrict telemarketing calls.[7]

We have to realize that nothing about database development or sending advertising messages and promotional offers to consumers is unethical or illegal—yet. We will need to wait and see whether any restrictions are placed on the database process by either government mandate or consumer pressure. Or we could all do what some people do. They don't enter sweepstakes, they never shop on the Internet, they throw junk mail and surveys directly into the trash, and they have unlisted phone numbers.

The story of Anne Marie (and perhaps even your own experience) highlights that the social, ethical, and regulatory aspects of advertising are as dynamic and controversial as any of the strategic or creative elements of the process. What is socially responsible or irresponsible, ethically debatable, politically correct, or legal? The answers are constantly changing. As a society changes, so, too, do its perspectives. Like anything else with social roots and implications, advertising will be affected by these changes.

Advertising history includes all sorts of social, ethical, and legal lapses on the part of advertisers. However, advertising has also had its triumphs, moral as well as financial. Whether justified or not, many criticisms of advertising can be naïve and simplistic, often failing to consider the complex social and legal environment in which contemporary advertising operates. Don't get us wrong; sometimes criticisms of advertising are right on. Other times, the criticism comes from intuition and emotion not supported by facts or reality. In this chapter, we will consider a wide range of social, ethical, and legal issues related to advertising and the many tools of integrated brand promotion in an analytical and straightforward fashion.

The Social Aspects of Advertising.
The social aspects of advertising are often volatile. For those who feel that advertising and promotion are intrusive and manipulative, the social aspects usually provide the most fuel for heated debate.

We can consider the social aspects of advertising in several broad areas. On the positive side, we'll consider advertising's effect on consumers' knowledge, standard of living, and feelings of happiness and well-being, and its potential positive effects on the mass media. On the negative side, we'll examine a variety of social criticisms of advertising, ranging from the charge that advertising wastes resources and promotes materialism to the argument that advertising perpetuates stereotypes.

5.   Erika Rasmusson, "What Price Knowledge?" *Sales and Marketing Management,* December 1998, 56.
6.   Stephen Baker, "Where Danger Lurks," *BusinessWeek,* August 25, 2003, 114–118.
7.   Ira Teinowitz, "FCC Extends Do-Not-Call-List," *Advertising Age,* June 30, 2003, 1, 29.

Our approach is to offer the pros and cons on several issues that critics and advertisers commonly argue about. Be forewarned—these are matters of opinion, with no clear right and wrong answers. You will have to draw your own conclusions. But above all, be analytical and thoughtful. These are important issues and without understanding and contemplating these issues, you really haven't studied advertising and promotion at all.

Advertising Educates Consumers.
Does advertising provide valuable information to consumers, or does it seek only to confuse or entice them? Here's what the experts on both sides have to say.

Pro: Advertising Informs.
Supporters of advertising argue that advertising educates consumers, equipping them with the information they need to make informed purchase decisions. By regularly assessing information and advertising claims, consumers become more educated regarding the features, benefits, functions, and value of products. Further, consumers can become more aware of their own tendencies toward being persuaded and relying on certain types of product information. The argument has been offered that advertising is "clearly an immensely powerful instrument for the elimination of ignorance."[8] Now, that might be a *little* bit overstated, but according to this argument, better-educated consumers enhance their lifestyles and economic power through astute marketplace decision making.

A related argument is that advertising *reduces product search time*—that is, the amount of time an individual must spend to search for desired products and services is reduced because of advertising. The large amount of information readily available through advertising allows consumers to easily assess the potential value of brands without spending time and effort traveling from retail store to retail store trying to evaluate each one. The information contained in an advertisement "reduces drastically the cost of search."[9]

Another aspect of informing the public has to do with the role advertising can play in communicating about important social issues. Miller Brewing devotes millions of dollars a year promoting responsible drinking with both print and television advertisements like the one shown in Exhibit 4.2. As described in the IBP box, there is also a unique Web site at http://www.beeresponsible.com as part of an IBP campaign designed to combat drunk driving, underage drinking, and binge drinking.

Con: Advertising Is Superficial and Intrusive.
Critics argue that advertising does not provide good product information at all and that it is so pervasive and intrusive to daily life that it is impossible to escape. The basic criticism of advertising with respect to it being superficial focuses on the claim that many ads carries little, if any, actual product infor-

EXHIBIT 4.2

Advertising can be used to inform the public about important social issues. Miller Brewing spends millions of dollars a year promoting responsible drinking behavior (http://www .millerbrewing.com).

---

8.   George J. Stigler, "The Economics of Information," *Journal of Political Economy* (June 1961), 213–220.
9.   Ibid., 220.

mation (Exhibit 4.3). What it does carry is said to be hollow ad-speak. Ads are rhetorical; there is no pure "information." All information in an ad is biased, limited, and inherently deceptive.

Critics of advertising believe that ads should contain information on brands that relates to functional features and performance results. Advertisers argue in response that, in many instances, consumers are interested in more than a physical, tangible material good with performance features and purely functional value. The functional features of a brand may be secondary in importance to consumers in both the information search and the choice process and emotional factors play an important role in consumer's choices (Exhibit 4.4). The advertisers' point is that critics often dismiss or ignore the totality of brand benefits, including emotional, hedonic (pleasure-seeking), or aesthetic aspects. The relevant information being used by a buyer relates to criteria being used to judge the satisfaction potential of the product, and that satisfaction is quite often nonutilitarian or nonfunctional in nature. On the other hand, defenders of advertising often don't really understand how limited this sort of "information" really is. As evidence, analysts note how often the truth about brands comes about only after regulatory or legal action. In truth, advertisers don't have the best record.

With respect to the intrusive aspect of advertising, the argument is that advertising has become so widespread (in some critics' view, ubiquitous) that consumers are starting to revolt. In the same Planetfeedback.com survey where respondents

EXHIBITS 4.3 AND 4.4

Critics of advertising complain that ads often carry little, if any, product information and would prefer that all advertising be rich in "information" like the Toyota ad in Exhibit 4.3. Is the Honda ad in Exhibit 4.4 devoid of "information"?

expressed their annoyance with pop-ups, the study found that over 95 percent of consumers considered themselves "angry" or "furious" over spam and pop-up ads.[10] Similarly, consumers are getting increasingly concerned and frustrated with brands working their way into entertainment programming. The so-called commerce-content crossover—product placement and the like—was rated as allowing advertising to become too pervasive by 72 percent of consumers surveyed.[11] Despite widespread consumer aggravation, it would seem that advertisers really aren't paying much attention. On the one hand, consumers seem to be saying loud and clear that advertising is getting just too widespread and intruding on their lives and lifestyles. On the other hand, big advertisers like American Express are pushing to become more "relevant" to consumers than a mere 30-second advertising spot and to make their brands part of consumer lifestyles. So much so that the chief marketing officer at American Express said in a keynote speech to a large advertising audience, "We need to adapt to the new landscape by thinking not in dayparts [referring to television advertising schedules] but to mindparts."[12] We'll let you decide what you think of that one.

IBP

Tackling Alcohol Abuse through Integrated Brand Promotion

Since 1982, when Anheuser-Busch launched its "Know When to Say When" ad campaign, the firm has spent over $500 million on advertising and other programs to promote responsible drinking among adults who choose to drink. In November 1997, Anheuser-Busch celebrated the 15-year anniversary of this campaign by launching the Web site http://www.beeresponsible.com to continue the fight against alcohol abuse "one person at a time."

Anheuser-Busch's approach to fighting alcohol abuse is no different from its philosophy about selling beer: They want to be the best and they want to get results. The firm has been at the forefront of alcohol awareness and education initiatives since the early 1900s, when it ran a series of print ads reminding Americans to drink responsibly, with the slogan "Budweiser Means Moderation." In 1982, with the launch of the now famous "Know When to Say When" campaign, Anheuser-Busch began a new era in its efforts to fight alcohol abuse and underage drinking by promoting personal responsibility.

Successful promotions to prevent drunk driving through the use of designated drivers and cab rides home began in 1984. The following year, Anheuser-Busch was the first in the alcohol beverage industry to bring responsible drinking messages to television. Their efforts have helped to make *designated driver* a household term and changed public attitudes about drinking and driving.

Anheuser-Busch's strong opposition to underage drinking then led to the development in 1990 of the "Let's Stop Underage Drinking Before It Starts" campaign. Ads in this campaign were focused on helping parents (who children say are the leading influence in their decision whether to drink) address this important issue with their children and are also designed to be used with students in schools.

In the fall of 1999, a new chapter in its awareness and education efforts began with the launch of its "We All Make a Difference" advertising campaign. "We All Make a Difference" reinforces the good practices of drinkers who exercise personal responsibility, designate a driver, or call a cab; salutes those parents who talk to their children about illegal underage drinking; and builds on the momentum of the positive downward trend in drunk driving fatalities and the decline in teen drinking.

Anheuser-Busch is a good example of a firm that has made a commitment to social responsibility and has used advertising and promotion in a consistent manner over many years to achieve a positive effect. This is IBP applied to a social issue rather than to promote the company's brands.

Source: http://www.beeresponsible.com, accessed March 22. 2004.

Advertising Improves the Standard of Living.
Whether advertising raises or lowers the general standard of living is hotly debated. Opinions vary widely on this issue and go right to the heart of whether advertising is a good use or a waste of energy and resources.

Pro: Advertising Lowers the Cost of Products.
First, supporters argue that due to the economies of scale (it costs less to produce products in large quantities) produced by advertising, products cost less than if there were no advertising at all. As broad-

10. Jack Neff, "Spam Research Reveals Disgust with Pop-Up Ads," *Advertising Age,* August 23, 2003, 1, 21.

11. Clair Atkinson, "Ad Intrusion Up, Say Consumers," *Advertising Age,* January 6, 2003, 1, 19.

12. Hank Kim, "Just Risk It," *Advertising Age,* February 9, 2004, 1, 51.

based demand stimulation results in lower production and administrative costs per unit produced, lower prices are passed on to consumers. Second, it is also argued that consumers have a greater variety of choice in products and services because advertising increases the probability of success that new products will succeed. Third, the pressures of competition and the desire to have fresh, marketable brands stimulates firms to produce improved products and brands. Fourth, the speed and reach of the advertising process aids in the diffusion of innovations. This means that new discoveries can be communicated to a large percentage of the marketplace very quickly. Innovations succeed when advertising communicates their benefits to the customer.

All four of these factors can contribute positively to the standard of living and quality of life in a society. Advertising may be instrumental in bringing about these effects because it serves an important role in demand stimulation and keeping customers informed.

Con: Advertising Wastes Resources and Raises the Standard of Living Only for Some.

One of the traditional criticisms of advertising is that it represents an inefficient, wasteful process that channels monetary and human resources in a society to the "shuffling of existing total demand," rather than to the expansion of total demand.[13] Advertising thus brings about economic stagnation and a *lower* standard of living, not a higher standard of living. Critics say that a society is no better off with advertising because it does not stimulate demand—it only shifts demand from one brand to another. Similarly, critics argue that brand differences are trivial and the proliferation of brands does not offer a greater variety of choice, but rather a meaningless waste of resources, with confusion and frustration for the consumer. Further, they argue that advertising is a tool of capitalism that just helps widen the gap between rich and poor, creating strife between social classes.

Advertising Affects Happiness and General Well-Being.

Critics and supporters of advertising differ significantly in their views about how advertising affects consumers' happiness and general well-being. As you will see, this is a complex issue with multiple pros and cons.

Con: Advertising Creates Needs.

A common cry among critics is that advertising creates needs and makes people buy things they don't really need or even want. The argument is that consumers are relatively easy to seduce into wanting the next shiny bauble offered by marketers. Critics would say, for example, that a quick examination of any issue of *Seventeen* magazine reveals a magazine intent on teaching the young women of the world to covet slim bodies and a glamorous complexion. Cosmetics giants like Estée Lauder and Revlon typically spend from 15 to 30 cents from every dollar of sales to promote their brands as the ultimate solution for those in search of the ideal complexion.

Pro: Advertising Addresses a Wide Variety of Basic Human Needs.

A good place to start in discussing whether advertising can create needs or not is to consider the basic nature of human needs. Abraham Maslow, a pioneer in the study of human motivation (and someone you probably read about in your psych class), conceived that human behavior progresses through the following hierarchy of need states:[14]

- *Physiological needs:* Biological needs that require the satisfaction of hunger, thirst, and basic bodily functions.

13. Richard Caves, *American Industry: Structure, Conduct, Performance* (Englewood Cliffs, N.J.: Prentice-Hall, 1964), 102.
14. A. H. Maslow, *Motivation and Personality* (New York: Harper & Row, 1970).

- *Safety needs:* The need to provide shelter and protection for the body and to maintain a comfortable existence.
- *Love and belonging needs:* The need for affiliation and affection. A person will strive for both the giving and receiving of love.
- *Esteem needs:* The need for recognition, status, and prestige. In addition to the respect of others, there is a need and desire for self-respect.
- *Self-actualization needs:* This is the highest of all the need states and is achieved by only a small percentage of people, according to Maslow. The individual strives for maximum fulfillment of individual capabilities.

It must be clearly understood that Maslow was describing *basic* human needs and motivations, not consumer needs and motivations. But in the context of an affluent society, individuals will turn to goods and services to satisfy needs. Many products are said to directly address the requirements of one or more of these need states. Food and health care products, for example, relate to physiological needs (see Exhibit 4.5). Home security systems and smoke detectors help address safety needs. Many personal care products, such as the skin care system shown in Exhibit 4.6, promote feelings of self-esteem, confidence, glamour, and romance.

In the pursuit of esteem, many consumers buy products they perceive to have status and prestige: expensive jewelry, clothing, automobiles, and homes are exam-

EXHIBIT 4.5

An ad like this appeals to our physiological needs (protecting our health) in Maslow's Hierarchy of Human Needs.

EXHIBIT 4.6

"All you need is Guinot." In what sense might a person need Guinot? Does the Guinot site (http://www.guinotusa.com) tie in to consumers' happiness and general well-being? Click around the site and identify message and design elements that target consumers' various need states.

ples. Though it may be difficult to buy self-actualization, educational pursuits and high-intensity leisure activities (e.g., extreme sports) can certainly foster the feelings of pride and accomplishment that contribute to self-actualization. Supporters maintain that advertising may be directed at many different forms of need fulfillment, but it is in no way powerful enough to create basic human needs.

Con: Advertising Promotes Materialism. It is also claimed that individuals' wants and aspirations may be distorted by advertising. The long-standing argument is that in societies characterized by heavy advertising, there is a tendency for conformity and status-seeking behavior, both of which are considered materialistic and superficial.[15] Material goods are placed ahead of spiritual and intellectual pursuits. Advertising, which portrays products as symbols of status, success, and happiness, contributes to the materialism and superficiality in a society. It creates wants and aspirations that are artificial and self-centered. This results in an overemphasis on the production of private goods, to the detriment of public goods (such as highways, parks, schools, and infrastructure).[16] It is also thought by some that long-term exposure to advertising will destroy your soul and blind you to what really matters in life.

Pro: Advertising Only Reflects Society's Priorities. Although advertising is undeniably in the business of promoting the good life, defenders of advertising argue that it did not create the American emphasis on materialism. For example, in the United States, major holidays such as Christmas (gifts), Thanksgiving (food), and Easter (candy and clothing) have become festivals of consumption. This is the American way. Historian and social observer Stephen Fox concludes his treatise on the history of American advertising as follows:

One may build a compelling case that American culture is—beyond redemption—money-mad, hedonistic, superficial, rushing heedlessly down a railroad track called Progress. Tocqueville and other observers of the young republic described America in these terms in the early 1800s, decades before the development of national advertising. To blame advertising now for these most basic tendencies in American history is to miss the point. . . . The people who have created modern advertising are not hidden persuaders pushing our buttons in the service of some malevolent purpose. They are just producing an especially visible manifestation, good and bad, of the American way of life.[17]

While we clearly live in the age of consumption, goods and possessions have been used by all cultures to mark special events, to play significant roles in rituals, and to serve as vessels of special meaning long before there was modern advertising. Still, have we taken it too far? Is excess what we do best in consumer cultures?

Advertising: Demeaning and Deceitful, or Liberating and Artful?

Without a doubt, advertisers are always on the lookout for creative and novel ways to grab and hold the attention of their audience. Additionally, many times an advertiser has a particular profile of the target customer in mind when an ad is being created. Both of these fundamental propositions about how ads get developed can spark controversy.

Con: Advertising Perpetuates Stereotypes. Advertisers often portray people in advertisements that look like members of their target audience with the hope that people who see the ad will be more prone to relate to the ad and attend to its message. Critics charge that this practice yields a very negative effect—it perpetuates stereotypes. The portrayal of women, the elderly, and ethnic minorities is of particular

15.   Vance Packard, *The Status Seekers* (New York: David McKay, 1959).
16.   See, for example, George Katona, *The Mass Consumption Society* (New York: McGraw-Hill, 1964), 54–61; and John Kenneth Galbraith, *The Affluent Society* (Boston: Houghton Mifflin, 1958).
17.   Stephen Fox, *The Mirror Makers: A History of American Advertising and Its Creators* (New York: William Morrow, 1984), 330.

concern. It is argued that women are still predominantly cast as homemakers or objects of desire (see Exhibit 4.7), despite the fact that women now hold top management positions and deftly head households. The elderly are often shown as helpless or ill, even though many active seniors enjoy a rich lifestyle. Critics contend that advertisers' propensity to feature African-American or Latin athletes in ads is simply a more contemporary form of stereotyping.

Pro: Advertisers Are Showing Much More Sensitivity. Much of this sort of stereotyping is becoming part of the past. Advertisements from prior generations do show a vivid stereotyping problem. But in today's setting, the ad in Exhibit 4.8 shows that women can be featured as strong and feminine in contemporary advertising. Advertisers are realizing that a diverse world requires diversity in the social reality that ads represent and help construct. However, many remain dissatisfied with the pace of change; the Body Shop ad in Exhibit 4.9, promoting something other than the body of a supermodel as a valid point of reference for women, is still the exception, not the rule.

Con: Advertising Is Often Offensive. A pervasive and long-standing criticism of advertising is that it is often offensive and the appeals are in poor taste. Moreover, some would say that the trend in American advertising is to be rude, crude, and sometimes lewd, as advertisers struggle to grab the attention of consumers who have learned to tune out the avalanche of advertising messages they are confronted with

EXHIBIT 4.7

What is the advertiser claiming in this ad? How about—a Versace gown is the ultimate in chic. http://www.versace.com

EXHIBIT 4.8

Advertisers today realize the diverse reality of consumers' lives. This Dove ad is a beautiful example of advertisers' efforts to represent diversity. http://www.dovespa.com

EXHIBIT 4.9

*The Body Shop (*http://www.bodyshop.com*) is bucking trends by protesting the "supermodel" imagery often used in product advertising. While men's magazine sites, such as Playboy (*http://www.playboy.com*), triumphantly display airbrushed perfection and countless companies adorn everything from automobiles to breakfast cereal with the svelte and athletic, the Web is (currently) a rather low-fidelity medium for transmitting glossy photographs. Sex may sell, but simple, bold, and clever graphics may be as useful for "eye candy" as anything ever exhibited by Versace Couture.*

Oddly, frank talk about real-life issues is not all that common in advertising. Do you know anyone who would be put off by such frankness?
http://www.tampax.com

each day.[18] Of course, taste is just that, a personal and inherently subjective evaluation. What is offensive to one person is merely satiric to another. What should we call an ad prepared for the Australian market that shows the owner of an older Honda Accord admiring a newer model? The owner's admiration of the new car spurs the old version to lock its doors, rev its motor, and drive off a cliff—with the owner still inside. Critics decry the ad as trivializing suicide—an acute problem among young people, who are also the target market for this ad.[19]

But not all advertising deemed offensive has to be as extreme as these examples. Many times, advertisers get caught in a firestorm of controversy because certain, and sometimes relatively small, segments of the population are offended. The history of advertising is loaded with examples. The AIDS prevention campaign run by the Centers for Disease Control and Prevention (CDC), a highly respected government agency, has been criticized for being too explicit. A spokesperson for the Family Research Council said about the ads, "They're very offensive—I thought I was watching *NYPD Blue*." A highly popular ad seen as controversial by some was the "People Taking Diet Coke Break" ad (this ad was featured in Exhibit 1.14 in Chapter 1). In this television spot, a group of female office workers is shown eyeing a construction worker as he takes off his T-shirt and enjoys a Diet Coke. Coca-Cola was criticized for using reverse sexism in this ad. While Coca-Cola and the CDC may have ventured into delicate areas, consider these advertisers, who were caught completely by surprise in finding that their ads were deemed offensive:[20]

- In a public service spot developed by Aetna Life & Casualty insurance for a measles vaccine, a wicked witch with green skin and a wart was cause for a challenge to the firm's ad from a witches' rights group.
- A Nynex spot was criticized by animal-rights activists because it showed a rabbit colored with blue dye.
- A commercial for Black Flag bug spray had to be altered after a war veterans' group objected to the playing of "taps" over dead bugs.

It should be emphasized that most consumers probably did not find these ads particularly offensive. Perhaps the spirit of political correctness causes such scrutiny, or maybe consumers are so overwhelmed with ads that they have simply lost their tolerance. Or maybe some people just have too much time on their hands. And sometimes they correctly point to insensitivity on the part of advertisers. Whatever the explanation, marketers today are well advised to take care in broadly considering the tastefulness of their ads. Expect the unexpected. An unpretentious ad like that in Exhibit 4.10, featuring frank copy about mundane aspects of menstruation, could be expected to breach some consumers' sensibilities. However, the marketer in this case is willing to take the risk in the hopes that the frank approach will get attention and ring true with the target customer.

In the end, we have to consider whether advertising is offensive or whether society is merely pushing the limits of what is appropriate for freedom of speech and expression. The now infamous "costume malfunction" that plagued Janet Jackson

18.   Stuart Elliott, "A New Pitch for US Ads: Lewd, Crude and Rude," *Herald International Tribune,* June 20, 1998, 1, 4.

19.   Normandy Madden, "Honda Pulls Suicide Car Ad from Australian TV Market," *Advertising Age,* September 22, 2003, 3.

20.   Kevin Goldman, "From Witches to Anorexics, Critical Eyes Scrutinize Ads for Political Correctness," *Wall Street Journal,* May 19, 1994, B1, B10.

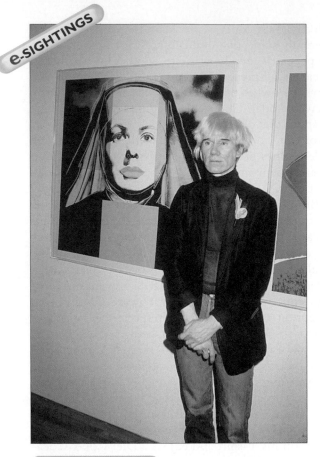

e-SIGHTINGS

EXHIBIT 4.11

Artist Andy Warhol demonstrated that the most accessible art was advertising. Intel (Blue Man Group) and Microsoft (butterflies) have both used art in their advertising. What message would Intel seek to convey about its Pentium brand by associating its processor with this innovative, critically acclaimed theater troupe (http://www.blueman.com)?

during a Super Bowl halftime show and incidents like shock radio DJs' profanity are drawing attention not just from fed-up consumers, but from the U.S. Congress as well.[21] And while Congress may move to provide a legal remedy to deter offensive broadcasts—advertising messages or programming—the fact is that what is acceptable and what is offensive changes over time in a culture.

Pro: Advertising Is a Source of Fulfillment and Liberation. On the other end of the spectrum, some argue that the consumption that advertising glorifies is actually quite good for society. Most people sincerely appreciate modern conveniences that liberate us from the more foul facets of everyday life, such as body odor, close contact with dirty diapers, and washing clothes by hand. Furthermore, this view holds that consumption is more likely to set one free than the slavish worship of an unpleasant, uncomfortable, and likely odoriferous—but natural—condition. Some observers remind us that when the Berlin Wall came down, those in East Germany did not immediately run to libraries and churches—they ran to department stores and shops. Before the modern consumer age, the consumption of many goods was restricted by social class. Modern advertising has helped bring us a "democracy" of goods. Observers argue that there is a liberating quality to advertising and consumption that should be appreciated and encouraged.

Con: Advertisers Deceive via Subliminal Stimulation. There is much controversy, and almost a complete lack of understanding, regarding the issue of subliminal (below the threshold of consciousness) communication and advertising. Since there is much confusion surrounding the issue of subliminal advertising, perhaps this is the most appropriate point to provide some clarification: No one ever sold anything by putting images of breasts in ice cubes or the word *sex* in the background of an ad. Furthermore, no one at an advertising agency, except the very bored or the very eager to retire, has time to sit around dreaming up such things (see the Controversy box). We realize it makes for a great story, but hiding pictures in other pictures doesn't work to get anyone to buy anything. Although there is some evidence for some types of unconscious ad processing, these effects are very short-lived and found only in laboratories, not the Svengali-type hocus-pocus that has become advertising mythology.[22] If the rumors are true that advertisers are actually using subliminal messages in their ads, the conclusion should be that they're wasting their money.[23] As of yet, there is no practical application of subliminal advertising.

Pro: Advertising Is Democratic Art. Some argue that one of the best aspects of advertising is its artistic nature. The pop art movement of the late 1950s and 1960s, particularly in London and New York, was characterized by a fascination with commercial culture. Some of this art critiqued consumer culture and simultaneously celebrated it. Above all, Andy Warhol (see Exhibit 4.11), himself a com-

21.   Ann Oldenburg, "TV Indecency Draws Congress' Icy Stare," *USA Today,* February 12, 2004, D1.

22.   Murphy, Monahan, and Zajonc, "Additivity of Nonconscious Affect: Combined Effects of Priming and Exposure," *Journal of Personality and Social Psychology,* vol. 69 (1995), 589–602.

23.   Timothy E. Moore, "Subliminal Advertising: What You See Is What You Get," *Journal of Marketing,* vol. 46 (Spring 1982), 38–47; Timothy E. Moore, "The Case Against Subliminal Manipulation," *Psychology and Marketing,* vol. 5, no. 4 (Winter 1988), 297–317.

mercial illustrator, demonstrated that art was for the people and that the most accessible art was advertising. Art was not restricted to museum walls; it was on Campbell's soup cans, LifeSavers candy rolls, and Brillo pads. Advertising is anti-elitist, democratic art. As Warhol said about America, democracy, and Coke,

What's great about this country is that America started the tradition where the richest consumers buy essentially the same things as the poorest. You can be watching TV and see Coca-Cola, and you can know that the President drinks Coke, Liz Taylor drinks Coke, and just think, you can drink Coke, too. A Coke is a Coke and no amount of money can get you a better Coke than the one the bum on the corner is drinking. All the Cokes are the same and all the Cokes are good. Liz Taylor knows it, the President knows it, the bum knows it, and you know it.[24]

CONTROVERSY

Subliminal Advertising: A Really Bad Idea

Every few years, a story will surface claiming that an advertiser tried to sell a brand by putting subliminal (below the conscious threshold of awareness) messages or images in an ad. To set the record straight, subliminal advertising doesn't work—and you'll get in a lot of trouble if you try it.

This is how subliminal *communication* does work. Research has shown that people can, indeed, process information that is transmitted to them below the level of conscious awareness, that is, subliminally. What is not proven is that you can send a *persuasive* message subliminally. Ever since a crack-pot inserted the phrases "eat popcorn" and "drink Coca-Cola" in a movie back in the 1950s, the world has been terrified that unscrupulous marketers will use the technique to sell products. Well, you can rest easy. Subliminal advertising doesn't work, but it does make for some really interesting stories:

- French TV network M6 and its production house Expand got in hot water in 2001 with French regulators over the alleged insertion of 33 subliminal images of a Kodak disposable camera during the airing of an episode of a hit reality TV show called "Popstars."
- Russian TV network ATN was pulled off the air in 2000 when Russian officials discovered that the broadcaster had been inserting the message "sit and watch only ATN" into every 25th frame of its broadcasting during the summer of 2000. The station was off the air for nearly two years.
- During the 2000 presidential election campaigns in the United States, Democrats accused Republicans of using subliminal advertising in the so-called Rats ad, which attacked Democratic candidate Al Gore's prescription drug plan. The allegation charged that during the ads the word "bureaucrats" was reduced to the word "rats," visible for a split second.

Whether subliminal advertising works or not, it does provide some great entertainment. And as long as people are suspicious of advertising, claims will surface that subliminal advertising is being used on unsuspecting consumers.

Sources: Lawrence J. Speer, "Off in a Flash," *Ad Age Global*, February 2002, 6; Bob Garfield, "Subliminal Seduction and Other Urban Myths," *Advertising Age*, September 18, 2000, 41.

Advertising Has a Powerful Effect on the Mass Media.

One final issue that advertisers and their critics debate is the matter of advertising's influence on the mass media. Here again, we find a very wide range of viewpoints.

Pro: Advertising Fosters a Diverse and Affordable Mass Media. Advertising fans argue that advertising is the best thing that can happened to an informed democracy. Magazines, newspapers, and television and radio stations are supported by advertising expenditures. In 2003, advertising expenditures in the United States reached nearly $270 billion.[25] Much of this spending went to support television, radio, magazines, and newspapers. If you include online advertising, the number approaches $300 billion. With this sort of monetary support of the media, citizens have access to a variety of information and entertainment sources at low cost. Network television and radio broadcasts would not be free commodities, and newspapers and magazines would likely cost two to four times more in the absence of advertising support.

Others argue that advertising provides invaluable exposure to issues. When non-commercial users of advertising rely on the advertising process, members of society

24. Andy Warhol, *The Philosophy of Andy Warhol: From A to B and Back Again* (New York: Harcourt Brace Jovanovich, 1975), 101.

25. "100 Leading National Advertisers," *Advertising Age*, June 28, 2004, S1.

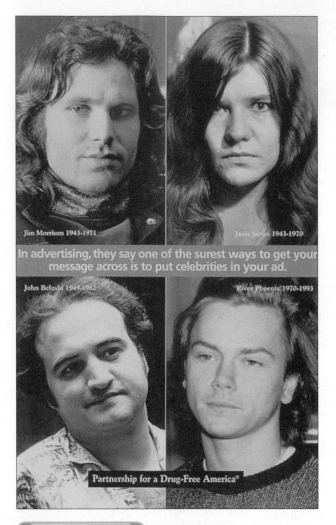

Jim Morrison 1943-1971   Janis Joplin 1943-1970

In advertising, they say one of the surest ways to get your
message across is to put celebrities in your ad.

John Belushi 1949-1982   River Phoenix 1970-1993

Partnership for a Drug-Free America®

EXHIBIT 4.12

*This ad both appeals to our
fascination with celebrity and
shocks the viewer with the
realization that drug use can
be fatal. At* http://www
.drugfreeamerica.org, *the
Partnership for a Drug-Free
America hones its message
that drug use is anything but
glamorous.*

receive information on important social and political issues. A dramatic example of the noncommercial use of advertising was the multimedia campaign launched in 1998 by the U.S. government, working in conjunction with the Partnership for a Drug-Free America.[26] At the campaign's launch in July 1998, President Clinton pledged to outspend major advertisers such as Nike and Sprint to remind the American public of the ruinous power of drugs such as heroin. Estimates at that time indicated that spending on the campaign over five years could approach $1 billion. A stockpile of nearly 400 ads was available for use in this comprehensive campaign. Some, like the one shown in Exhibit 4.12, involved powerful messages about the ultimate consequence of drug abuse.

Con: Advertising Affects Programming.
Critics argue that advertisers who place ads in media have an unhealthy effect on shaping the content of information contained in the media. For example, if a magazine that reviews and evaluates stereo equipment tests the equipment of one of its large advertisers, the contention is that the publication will hesitate to criticize the advertiser's equipment. This allegation would seem to be supported when you consider the decision by ESPN network to cancel a highly rated series about a fictional football team. The series was criticized by the commissioner of the NFL and owners of NFL teams because it occasionally featured story lines about drug and spousal abuse. While the show drew an audience for ESPN of nearly 1.65 million households, ESPN had to consider its $600 million annual rights fee to broadcast NFL games.[27]

Another charge leveled at advertisers is that they purchase air time only on programs that draw large audiences. Critics argue that these mass market programs lower the quality of television because cultural and educational programs, which draw smaller and more selective markets, are dropped in favor of mass market programs. Additionally, television programmers have a difficult time attracting advertisers to shows that may be valuable, yet controversial. Programs that deal with abortion, sexual abuse, or AIDS may have trouble drawing advertisers who fear the consequences of any association with controversial issues.

2 The Ethical Aspects of Advertising. Many of the ethical aspects of advertising border on and interact with both the social and legal considerations of the advertising process. **Ethics** are moral standards and principles against which behavior is judged. Honesty, integrity, fairness, and sensitivity are all included in a broad definition of ethical behavior. Much of what is judged as ethical or unethical comes down to personal judgment. We will discuss the ethical aspects of advertising in three areas: truth in advertising, advertising to children, and advertising controversial products.

26.   B. G. Gregg, "Tax Funds Bankroll New Anti-Drug Ads," *Cincinnati Enquirer,* July 10, 1998, A1, A17.
27.   Rudy Martzke, "NFL's Ire with 'Playmakers' Causes ESPN to Pull the Plug," *USA Today,* February 4, 2004, C1.

Truth in Advertising. While truth in advertising is a key legal issue, it has ethical dimensions as well. The most fundamental ethical issue has to do with **deception**—making false or misleading statements in an advertisement. The difficulty regarding this issue, of course, is in determining just what is deceptive. A manufacturer who claims a laundry product can remove grass stains is exposed to legal sanctions if the product cannot perform the task. Another manufacturer who claims to have "The Best Laundry Detergent in the World," however, is perfectly within its rights to employ superlatives. Just what constitutes "The Best" is a purely subjective determination; it cannot be proved or disproved. The use of absolute superlatives such as "Number One" or "Best in the World" is sometimes called **puffery** and is considered completely legal. The courts have long held that superlatives are understood by consumers as simply the standard language of advertising and are interpreted by consumers as such.

We also need to be aware that various promotional tools are often challenged as being deceptive. The "small print" that accompanies many contests or sweepstakes are often challenged by consumers. Similarly, the appeal of a "free" gift for listening to a pitch on a resort condo or time share often draws a harsh reaction from consumers. Now, a consumer watchdog group is challenging brand placements in television shows as deceptive. The group Commercial Alert argues that television networks are deceiving consumers by not disclosing that they are taking money for highlighting brands within shows like NBC's "The Restaurant," which features Coors beer and American Express credit cards.[28] This could cause a bit of conflict for government agencies that regulate television programming since another branch of the government, the U.S. Treasury, used product placement in TV quiz shows and late night talks shows to help introduce the new colorized $20 bills in late 2003.

Another area of debate regarding truth in advertising relates to emotional appeals. It is likely impossible to legislate against emotional appeals such as those made about the beauty- or prestige-enhancing qualities of a brand, because these claims are unquantifiable (take another look at Exhibit 4.6). Since these types of appeals are legal, the ethics of such appeals fall into a gray area. Beauty and prestige, it is argued, are in the eye of the beholder, and such appeals are neither illegal nor unethical. Although there are some narrowly defined legal parameters for truth in advertising (as we will discuss shortly), the ethical issues are not as clear-cut.

Advertising to Children. The desire to restrict advertising aimed at children is based on a wide range of concerns, particularly since it is estimated that children between two and 11 years old may see over 20,000 advertisements in a year. One concern is that advertising promotes superficiality and values founded in material goods and consumption, as we discussed earlier in the broader context of society as a whole. Another is that children are inexperienced consumers and easy prey for the sophisticated persuasions of advertisers, and as such, advertising influences children's demands for everything from toys to snack foods. These demands, in turn, create an environment of child-parent conflict. Parents find themselves having to say no over and over again to children whose desires are piqued by effective advertising. Most recently, child psychologists are contending that advertising advocates violence, is responsible for child obesity, creates a breakdown in early learning skills, and results in a destruction of parental authority.[29]

There is also concern that many programs aimed at children constitute program-length commercials. Many critics argue that programs featuring commercial products, especially products aimed at children, are simply long advertisements. This movement began in 1990 when critics argued that 70 programs airing at the time were based on commercial products such as He-Man, the Smurfs, and the

28.   Claire Atkinson, "Watchdog Group Hits TV Product Placement," *Advertising Age,* October 6, 2003, 12.
29.   Richard Linnett, "Psychologists Protest Kids' Ads," *Advertising Age,* September 11, 2000, 4.

Muppets.[30] A similar charge was leveled at elaborate, hour-long television productions such as *Treasure Island: The Adventure Begins,* which features a young boy's vacation at the Las Vegas resort Treasure Island. Critics claim that programs such as this blur the boundary between programming and advertising: The *Treasure Island* program was produced by the owners of the Treasure Island resort, and the one-hour time slot was purchased from a major network, as advertising time, for an estimated $1.7 million.[31] While the program looks like an adventure show, critics argue that it merely promotes the theme park and casino to kids, without ever revealing its sponsor. There have been several attempts by special-interest groups to strictly regulate this type of programming aimed at children, but, to date, the Federal Communications Commission permits such programming to continue.

One restriction on advertising to children that was successfully implemented came about due to the efforts of the special-interest group Action for Children's Television. The group disbanded in 1992, but before it did, it helped get the Children's Television Act passed in 1990. This regulation restricts advertising on children's programming to 10.5 minutes per hour on weekends and 12 minutes per hour on weekdays.[32]

Finally, the issue of advertising and promotion in schools has come about as public schools face declining government support and are cash strapped for needed resources like books and computer technology. One of the most active organizations involved in placing advertising in schools is Channel One. Channel One provides direct broadcasting of news shows and commercials to 12,000 middle, junior, and high schools reaching about 8 million students.[33]

A broad coalition of companies, organizations, and activists, ranging from Focus on the Family to Ralph Nader, have kicked off a campaign to stop Channel One from what they call exploiting school children for commercial gain. The coalition is asking all Channel One's advertisers to stop advertising on Channel One and asking the top 50 U.S. advertising agencies not to place ads on Channel One. Other promotions are also used in and around schools like advertising on the sides of school buses and on textbook covers.

Advertising Controversial Products. Some people question the wisdom of allowing the advertising of controversial goods and services, such as tobacco, alcoholic beverages, gambling and lotteries, and firearms.

Critics charge that tobacco and alcoholic beverage firms are targeting adolescents with advertising and with making dangerous and addictive products appealing.[34] This is, indeed, a complex issue. Many medical journals have published survey research that claims that advertising "caused" cigarette and alcohol consumption—particularly among teenagers.[35]

It is interesting to note, however, that these recent studies contradict research conducted since the 1950s carried out by marketing, communications, psychology, and economics researchers—including assessments of all the available research by the Federal Trade Commission.[36] These early studies (as well as several Gallup polls dur-

30.   Patrick J. Sheridan, "FCC Sets Children's Ad Limits," *1990 Information Access Company,* vol. 119, no. 20 (1990), 33.

31.   Laura Bird, "NBC Special Is One Long Prime-Time Ad," *Wall Street Journal,* January 21, 1994, B1, B4.

32.   For more information on this act and other acts related to advertising and children go to the Federal Trade Commission Web site, http://www.ftc.gov.

33.   Information obtained from Channel One at the company Web site, http://www.channelone.com, accessed March 14, 2004.

34.   Kathleen Deveny, "Joe Camel Ads Reach Children, Research Finds," *Wall Street Journal,* December 11, 1991, B1, B6.

35.   See, for example, Joseph R. DiFranza et al., "RJR Nabisco's Cartoon Camel Promotes Camel Cigarettes to Children," *Journal of the American Medical Association,* vol. 266, no. 22 (1991), 3168–3153.

36.   For a summary of more than 60 articles that address the issue of alcohol and cigarette advertising and the lack of a relationship between advertising and cigarette and alcohol industry demand, see Mark Frankena et al., "Alcohol, Consumption, and Abuse," Bureau of Economics, Federal Trade Commission, March 5, 1985. For a similar listing of research articles where the same conclusions were drawn during Congressional hearings on the topic, see "Advertising of Tobacco Products," Hearings before the Subcommittee on Health and the Environment, Committee on Energy and Commerce, House of Representatives, Ninety-Ninth Congress, July 18 and August 1, 1986, Serial No. 99–167.

ing the 1990s) found that family, friends, and peers—not advertising—are the primary influence on the use of tobacco and alcohol products. Studies published in the late 1990s and early in this decade have reaffirmed the findings of this earlier research.[37] While children at a very early age can, indeed, recognize tobacco advertising characters like "Joe Camel," they also recognize as easily the Energizer Bunny (batteries), the Jolly Green Giant (canned vegetables), and Snoopy (life insurance)—all characters associated with adult products. Kids are also aware that cigarettes cause disease and know that they are intended as an adult product. Research in Europe offers the same conclusion: "Every study on the subject [of advertising effects on the use of tobacco and alcohol] finds that children are more influenced by parents and playmates than by the mass media."[38]

Why doesn't advertising cause people to smoke and drink? The simple answer is that advertising just isn't that powerful. Eight out of 10 new products fail and if advertising were so powerful, no new products would fail. The more detailed answer is that advertising cannot create primary demand in mature product categories. **Primary demand** is demand for an entire product category (recall the discussion from Chapter 1). With mature products—like milk, automobiles, toothpaste, cigarettes, and alcohol—advertising isn't powerful enough to have that effect. Research across several decades has demonstrated repeatedly that advertising does not create primary demand for tobacco or alcohol.[39]

No one has ever said that smoking or drinking is good for you. (Except for maybe that glass of wine with dinner.) That's not what we're saying here, either. The point is that these behaviors emerge in a complex social context, and the vast weight of research evidence over 40 years suggests that advertising is not a significant causal influence on initiation behavior (e.g., smoking, drinking). Rather, advertising plays its most important role in consumers' choice of brands (e.g., Camel, Coors) after they have decided to use a product category (e.g., cigarettes, beer).

Gambling and state-run lotteries represent another controversial product area with respect to advertising. What is the purpose of this advertising? Is it meant to inform gamblers and lottery players of the choices available? This would be selective demand stimulation. Or is such advertising designed to stimulate demand for engaging in wagering behavior? This would be primary demand stimulation. What about compulsive gamblers? What is the state's obligation to protect "vulnerable" citizens by restricting the placement or content of lottery advertising? When these vulnerable audiences are discussed, questions as to the basis for this vulnerability can become complex and emotionally charged. Those on one side of the issue argue that special audiences are among the "information poor," while those on the other side find such claims demeaning, patronizing, and paternalistic. And a new era of gaming is upon us with its own set of problems and controversies. Online gambling is widespread and providing a fast and easy way for people to lose their life savings. The most recent estimates put total online gaming revenues at $4.2 billion with some sites boasting more than 300,000 active members.[40] Stories of out-of-control online gambling are

---

37.   For examples of the more recent studies that reaffirm peers and family rather than advertising as the basis for smoking initiation see Charles R. Taylor and P. Greg Bonner, "Comment on 'American Media and the Smoking-Related Behaviors of Asian Adolescents,'" *Journal of Advertising Research* (December 2003), 419–430; Bruce Simons Morton, "Peer and Parent Influences on Smoking and Drinking Among Early Adolescents," *Journal of Health Education and Behavior* (February 2000); and Karen H. Smith and Mary Ann Stutz, "Factors that Influence Adolescents to Smoke," *Journal of Consumer Affairs*, vol. 33, no. 2 (Winter 1999), 321–357.

38.   With regard to cartoon characters see, for example, Lucy L. Henke, "Young Children's Perceptions of Cigarette Brand Advertising: Awareness, Affect and Target Market Identification," *Journal of Advertising*, vol. 24, no. 4 (Winter 1995), 13–27; and Richard Mizerski, "The Relationship between Cartoon Trade Character Recognition and Attitude toward the Product Category," *Journal of Marketing*, vol. 59 (October 1995), 58–70. The evidence in Europe is provided by Jeffrey Goldstein, "Children and Advertising—the Research," *Commercial Communications*, July 1998, 4–8.

39.   For research on this topic across several decades, see Richard Schmalensee, *The Economics of Advertising* (Amsterdam-London: North-Holland, 1972); Mark S. Albion and Paul W. Farris, *The Advertising Controversy* (Boston: Auburn House, 1981); and Michael J. Waterson, "Advertising and Tobacco Consumption: An Analysis of the Two Major Aspects of the Debate," *International Journal of Advertising*, 9 (1990), 59–72.

40.   Ralph King, "On-line Gambling's 'Mr. Big,'" *Business 2.0*, April 2003, 87–91.

widespread.[41] And whose responsibility is it to control people's gambling behavior—the Internet portal or the individual who chooses to log on and give his or her credit card information?

The issue of advertising controversial products is complex. This is something we wrote for the previous edition of this text published in 2003:

But consider this as you contemplate the role advertising plays in people's decisions regarding these types of products. Currently, one in three children in the United States is diagnosed as clinically obese.[42] Will parents of these kids begin to sue McDonald's, Coca-Cola, Kellogg's, and General Mills because they advertise food products to children? Think this is unbelievable? Think again.

Now that's a little spooky! As you are now well aware, this is *exactly* what has happened. McDonald's and other food companies have had to prepare themselves for lawsuits where people are claiming food providers "made them fat." The food industry has countered with the proposition that kids are fat because of unconcerned parents, underfunded school systems that have dropped physical activity programs, and sedentary entertainment like home video games.[43] This issue is troublesome enough that the U.S. government has had to pass legislation barring people from suing food companies for their obesity. In March 2004, the U.S. House of Representatives overwhelmingly approved legislation nicknamed the "cheeseburger bill" that would block lawsuits blaming the food industry for making people fat. During the debate on the bill, one of the bill's sponsors said it was about "common sense and personal responsibility." [44] That certainly seems to make sense.

While we can group these ethical issues of advertising into some reasonable categories, it is not as easy to make definitive statements about the status of ethics in advertising. Ethics will always be a matter of personal values and personal interpretation. And as long as there are unethical people in the world, there will be ethics problems in advertising just like in every other phase of business and life.

3 The Regulatory Aspects of Advertising.

The term *regulation* immediately brings to mind government scrutiny and control of the advertising process. Indeed, various government bodies do regulate advertising. But consumers themselves and several different industry organizations exert as much regulatory power over advertising as government agencies. Three primary groups—consumers, industry organizations, and government bodies—regulate advertising in the truest sense: Together they shape and restrict the process. The government relies on legal restrictions, while consumers and industry groups use less-formal controls. Like the other topics in this chapter, regulation of advertising can be controversial, and opinions about what does and doesn't need to be regulated can be highly variable. Moreover, the topic of regulation could easily be an entire course of study in its own right, so here we present just an overview of major issues and major players.

First we'll consider the areas of regulation pursued most ardently, whether it be by the government, consumers, or industry groups. Then we'll examine the nature of the regulation and influence exerted by these groups.

Areas of Advertising Regulation.

There are three basic areas of advertising regulation: deception and unfairness in advertising, competitive issues, and advertising to children. Each area is a focal point for regulation.

41. Ira Singer, et al., "The Underground Web," *BusinessWeek*, September 2, 2002, 67–74.
42. Pat Wingert et al., "Generation XXL," *Newsweek*, July 3, 2000, 40–47.
43. Mercedes M. Cardona, "Marketers Bite Back as Fat Fight Flares Up," *Advertising Age*, March 1, 2004, 3, 35.
44. Rep. Ric Keller (R–Florida), quoted in Joanne Kenen, "U.S. House Backs Ban on Obesity Lawsuits," Reuters, published on the Internet at http://biz.yahoo.com/rc/040310/congress_obesity_3.html on March 10, 2004; accessed March 14, 2004.

Deception and Unfairness. Agreement is widespread that deception in advertising is unacceptable. The problem, of course, is that it is as difficult to determine what is deceptive from a regulatory standpoint as it is from an ethical standpoint. The Federal Trade Commission's (FTC's) policy statement on deception is the authoritative source when it comes to defining deceptive advertising. It specifies the following three elements as essential in declaring an ad deceptive:[45]

1. There must be a representation, omission, or practice that is likely to mislead the consumer.
2. This representation, omission, or practice must be judged from the perspective of a consumer acting reasonably in the circumstance.
3. The representation, omission, or practice must be a "material" one. The basic question is whether the act or the practice is likely to affect the consumer's conduct or decision with regard to the product or service. If so, the practice is material, and consumer injury is likely because consumers are likely to have chosen differently if not for the deception.

If this definition of deception sounds like carefully worded legal jargon, that's because it is. It is also a definition that can lead to diverse interpretations when it is actually applied to advertisements in real life. Fortunately, the FTC now provides highly practical advice for anticipating what can make an ad deceptive (go to http://www.ftc.gov/bcp/guides/guides.htm under the section "Frequently Asked Advertising Questions"). One critical point about the FTC's approach to deception is that both implied claims and information that is *missing* from an ad can be bases for deeming an ad deceptive. Obviously, the FTC expects any explicit claim made in an ad to be truthful, but it also is on the lookout for ads that deceive through allusion and innuendo or ads that deceive by not telling the whole story.

Many instances of deceptive advertising and packaging have resulted in formal government programs designed to regulate such practices. But as we discussed earlier, there can be complications in regulating puffery. Conventional wisdom has argued that consumers don't actually believe extreme claims and realize that advertisers are just trying to attract attention. There are those, however, who disagree with this view of puffery and feel that it actually represents "soft-core" deception, because some consumers may believe these exaggerated claims.[46]

While the FTC and the courts have been reasonably specific about what constitutes deception, the definition of unfairness in advertising has been left relatively vague until recently. In 1994, Congress ended a long-running dispute in the courts and in the advertising industry by approving legislation that defines **unfair advertising** as "acts or practices that cause or are likely to cause substantial injury to consumers, which is not reasonably avoidable by consumers themselves, and not outweighed by the countervailing benefits to consumers or competition."[47] This definition obligates the FTC to assess both the benefits and costs of advertising, and rules out reckless acts on the part of consumers, before a judgment can be rendered that an advertiser has been unfair.

Competitive Issues. Because the large dollar amounts spent on advertising may foster inequities that literally can destroy competition, several advertising practices relating to maintaining fair competition are regulated. Among these practices are cooperative advertising, comparison advertising, and the use of monopoly power.

---

45. For additional discussion of the FTC's definition of deception, see Gary T. Ford and John E. Calfee, "Recent Developments in FTC Policy on Deception," *Journal of Marketing*, vol. 50 (July 1986), 82–103.

46. Ivan Preston, *The Great American Blow Up* (Madison: University of Wisconsin Press, 1975), 4.

47. Christy Fisher, "How Congress Broke Unfair Ad Impasse," *Advertising Age*, August 22, 1994, 34. For additional discussion of the FTC's definition of unfairness, see Ivan Preston, "Unfairness Developments in FTC Advertising Cases," *Journal of Public Policy and Marketing*, vol. 14, no. 2 (1995), 318–321.

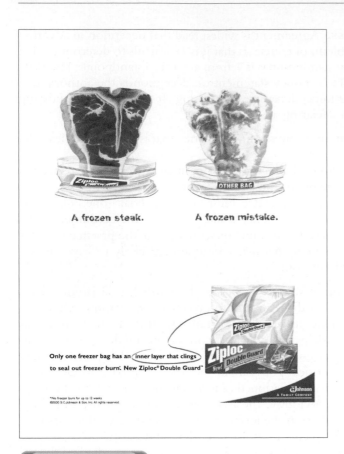

A frozen steak.   A frozen mistake.

Only one freezer bag has an inner layer that clings to seal out freezer burn. New Ziploc® Double Guard

*No freezer burn for up to 12 weeks
©2000 S.C.Johnson & Son, Inc. All rights reserved.

EXHIBIT 4.13

The advertising industry provides guidelines to advertisers to ensure that comparison ads, like this one, offer fair comparisons between brands. http://www .ziploc.com

Vertical cooperative advertising is an advertising technique whereby a manufacturer and dealer (either a wholesaler or retailer) share the expense of advertising. This technique is commonly used in regional or local markets where a manufacturer wants a brand to benefit from a special promotion run by local dealers. There is nothing illegal, per se, about the technique, and it is used regularly. The competitive threat inherent in the process, however, is that dealers (especially since the advent of first department store chains and now mega retailers like Wal-Mart, Target, and Home Depot) can be given bogus cooperative advertising allowances. These allowances require no effort or expenditure on the part of the dealer/retailer and thus represent hidden price concessions. As such, they are a form of unfair competition and are deemed illegal. If an advertising allowance is granted to a dealer, that dealer must demonstrate that the funds are applied specifically to advertising.

The potential exists for firms to engage in unfair competition if they use comparison ads inappropriately. **Comparison advertisements** are those in which an advertiser makes a comparison between the firm's brand and competitors' brands. The comparison may or may not explicitly identify the competition. Again, comparison ads are completely legal and are used frequently by all sorts of organizations. The ad in Exhibit 4.13 is a example of straightforward and completely legal comparison advertising.

But in recent years, the frequency of use of comparison ads has resulted in a similarly large increase in complaints to the National Advertising Division of the Better Business Bureau from marketers who dispute the competitive comparative claims.[48] If an advertisement is carried out in such a way that the comparison is not a fair one, then there is an unfair competitive effect. The American Association of Advertising Agencies (4As) has issued a set of guidelines, shown in Exhibit 4.14, regarding the use of comparison ads. Further, the FTC may require a firm using comparison to substantiate claims made in an advertisement and prove that the claims do not tend to deceive.[49] A slightly different remedy is the use of a disclaimer to help consumers understand comparative product claims. That's what Duracell had to do when it claimed its "Coppertop" battery lasted longer than Energizer's heavy duty battery. While the claim was technically true, the Coppertop is an alkaline battery and was not being compared to Energizer's alkaline battery. Gillette, makers of Duracell, agreed to include a disclaimer in subsequent ads and then finally pulled the campaign altogether.[50]

Finally, some firms are so powerful in their use of advertising that **monopoly power** by virtue of their advertising spending can become a problem. This issue normally arises in the context of mergers and acquisitions. As an example, the U.S. Supreme Court blocked the acquisition of Clorox by Procter & Gamble because the advertising power of the two firms combined would (in the opinion of the Court) make it nearly impossible for another firm to compete.

48.   Jack Neff, "Household Brands Counter Punch," *Advertising Age,* November 1, 1999, 26.

49.   Maxine Lans Retsky, "Lanham Have It: Law and Comparative Ads," *Marketing News,* November 8, 1999, 16.

50.   Daniel Golden and Suzanne Vranica, "Duracell's Duck Will Carry Disclaimer," *Wall Street Journal,* February 7, 2002, B2.

EXHIBIT 4.14

American Association of Advertising Agencies guidelines for comparison advertising. http://www .aaaa.org

The Board of Directors of the American Association of Advertising Agencies recognizes that when used truthfully and fairly, comparative advertising provides the consumer with needed and useful information. However, extreme caution should be exercised. The use of comparative advertising, by its very nature, can distort facts and, by implication, convey to the consumer information that misrepresents the truth. Therefore, the Board believes that comparative advertising should follow certain guidelines:

1. The intent and connotation of the ad should be to inform and never to discredit or unfairly attack competitors.
2. When a competitive product is named, it should be one that exists in the marketplace as significant competition.
3. The competition should be fairly and properly identified, but never in a manner or tone of voice that degrades the competitive product or service.
4. The advertising should compare related or similar properties or ingredients of the product, dimension to dimension, feature to feature.
5. The identification should be for honest comparison purposes and not simply to upgrade by association.
6. If a competitive test is conducted, it should be done by an objective testing source, preferably an independent one, so that there will be no doubt as to the veracity of the test.
7. In all cases, the test should be supportive of all claims made in the advertising based on the test.
8. The advertising should never use partial results or stress insignificant differences to cause the consumer to draw an improper conclusion.
9. The property being compared should be significant in terms of value or usefulness of the product to the consumer.
10. Comparatives delivered through the use of testimonials should not imply that the testimonial is more than one individual's thought unless that individual represents a sample of the majority viewpoint.

Source: American Association of Advertising Agencies.

Advertising to Children. As we discussed in the area of ethics, critics argue that continually bombarding children with persuasive stimuli can alter their motivation and behavior. While government organizations such as the FTC have been active in trying to regulate advertising directed at children, industry and consumer groups have been more successful in securing restrictions. Recall that the consumer group known as Action for Children's Television (disbanded in 1992) was actively involved in getting Congress to approve the Children's Television Act (1990). This act limits the amount of commercial airtime during children's programs to 10.5 minutes on weekends and 12 minutes on weekdays. The Council of Better Business Bureaus established a Children's Advertising Review Unit and has issued a set of guidelines for advertising directed at children. These guidelines emphasize that advertisers should be sensitive to the level of knowledge and sophistication of children as decision makers. The guidelines also urge advertisers to make a constructive contribution to the social development of children by emphasizing positive social standards in advertising, such as friendship, kindness, honesty, and generosity. Similarly, the major television networks have set their own guidelines for advertising aimed at children. The guidelines restrict the use of celebrities, prohibit exhortative language (such as "Go ask Dad"), and restrict the use of animation to one-third of the total time of the commercial.

Regulatory Agents. Earlier in this section, it was noted that consumer and industry groups as well as government agencies all participate in the regulation of advertising. We will now

Primary government agencies regulating advertising.

Government Agency	Areas of Advertising Regulation
Federal Trade Commission (FTC)	Most widely empowered agency in government. Controls unfair methods of competition, regulates deceptive advertising, and has various programs for controlling the advertising process.
Federal Communications Commission (FCC)	Prohibits obscenity, fraud, and lotteries on radio and television. Ultimate power lies in the ability to deny or revoke broadcast licenses.
Food and Drug Administration (FDA)	Regulates the advertising of food, drug, cosmetic, and medical products. Can require special labeling for hazardous products such as household cleaners. Prohibits false labeling and packaging.
Securities and Exchange Commission (SEC)	Regulates the advertising of securities and the disclosure of information in annual reports.
U.S. Postal Service (USPS)	Responsible for regulating direct mail advertising and prohibiting lotteries, fraud, and misrepresentation. It can also regulate and impose fines for materials deemed to be obscene.
Bureau of Alcohol, Tobacco, Firearms, and Explosives (ATF)	Most direct influence has been on regulation of advertising for alcoholic beverages. This agency was responsible for putting warning labels on alcoholic beverage advertising and banning active athletes as celebrities in beer ads. It has the power to determine what constitutes misleading advertising in these product areas.

discuss examples of each of these agents along with the kinds of influence they exert. Given the multiple participants, this turns out to be a highly complex activity that we can only overview in this discussion. Additionally, our discussion focuses on regulatory activities in the United States, but advertising regulation can vary dramatically from country to country. Chapter 9, Advertising Planning: An International Perspective, provides additional insights on advertising regulation around the world, but we must caution that becoming an expert on the complex and dynamic topic of global ad regulation would literally require a lifetime of study.

Government Regulation. Governments have a powerful tool available for regulating advertising: the threat of legal action. In the United States, several different government agencies have been given the power and responsibility to regulate the advertising process. Exhibit 4.15 identifies the six agencies that have legal mandates concerning advertising and their areas of regulatory responsibility.

Several other agencies have minor powers in the regulation of advertising, such as the Civil Aeronautics Board (advertising by air carriers), the Patent Office (trademark infringement), and the Library of Congress (copyright protection). The agencies listed in Exhibit 4.15 are the most directly involved in advertising regulation. Most active among these agencies is the Federal Trade Commission, which has the most power and is most directly involved in controlling the advertising process. The FTC has been granted legal power through legislative mandates and also has developed programs for regulating advertising.

The FTC's Legislative Mandates. The Federal Trade Commission was created by the FTC Act in 1914. The original purpose of the agency was to prohibit unfair methods of competition. In 1916, the FTC concluded that false advertising was one way in which a firm could take unfair advantage of another, and advertising was established as a primary concern of the agency.

It was not until 1938 that the effects of deceptive advertising on consumers became a key issue for the FTC. Until the passage of the Wheeler–Lea Amendment (1938), the commission was primarily concerned with the direct effect of advertising on competition. The amendment broadened the FTC's powers to include regulation of advertising that was misleading to the public (regardless of the effect on competition). Through this amendment, the agency could apply a cease-and-desist order, which required a firm to stop its deceptive practices. It also granted the agency specific jurisdiction over drug, medical device, cosmetic, and food advertising.

Several other acts provide the FTC with legal powers over advertising. The Robinson–Patman Act (1936) prohibits firms from providing phantom cooperative-advertising allowances as a way to court important dealers. The Wool Products Labeling Act (1939), the Fur Products Labeling Act (1951), and the Textile Fiber Products Identification Act (1958) provided the commission with regulatory power over labeling and advertising for specific products. Consumer protection legislation, which seeks to increase the ability of consumers to make more-informed product comparisons, includes the Fair Packaging and Labeling Act (1966), the Truth in Lending Act (1969), and the Fair Credit Reporting Act (1970). The FTC Improvement Act (1975) expanded the authority of the commission by giving it the power to issue trade regulation rules.

Recent legislation has expanded the FTC's role in monitoring and regulating product labeling and advertising. For example, the 1990 Nutrition Labeling and Education Act (NLEA) requires uniformity in the nutrition labeling of food products and establishes strict rules for claims about the nutritional attributes of food products. The standard "Nutrition Facts" label required by the NLEA now appears on everything from breakfast cereals to barbecue sauce. The NLEA is a notable piece of legislation from the standpoint that two government agencies—the FTC and the FDA—play key roles in its enforcement.

Of course, the Internet has spawned all sorts of scrutiny by the FTC. One area of particular scrutiny regarding children is privacy, which led to the Children's Online Privacy Act of 1998 in which the FTC states explicitly that

It is unlawful for an operator of a website or online service directed to children, or any operator that has actual knowledge that it is collecting personal information from a child, to collect personal information from a child in a manner that violates the regulations prescribed under subsection (b).[51]

Subsection (b) mandates that full disclosure of the Web site's information gathering (if any) must plainly appear on the Web site.

Regulations also provide the FTC and other agencies with various means of recourse when advertising practices are judged to be deceptive or misleading. The spirit of all these acts relates to the maintenance of an equitable competitive environment and the protection of consumers from misleading information. It is interesting to note, however, that direct involvement of the FTC in advertising practices more often comes about from its regulatory programs and remedies than from the application of legal mandates.

---

51.   The full text and specifications of the Children's Online Privacy Act can be found at http://www.ftc.gov/ogc/coppa1.htm.

The FTC's Regulatory Programs and Remedies. The application of legislation has evolved as the FTC exercises its powers and expands its role as a regulatory agency. This evolution of the FTC has spawned several regulatory programs and remedies to help enforce legislative mandates in specific situations.

The **advertising substantiation program** of the FTC was initiated in 1971 with the intention of ensuring that advertisers make supporting evidence for their claims available to consumers. The program was strengthened in 1972 when the commission forwarded the notion of "reasonable basis" for the substantiation of advertising. This extension suggests not only that advertisers should substantiate their claims, but also that the substantiation should provide a reasonable basis for believing the claims are true. [52] Simply put, before a company runs an ad, it must have documented evidence that supports the claim it wants to make in that ad. The kind of evidence required depends on the kind of claim being made. For example, health and safety claims will require competent and reliable scientific evidence that has been examined and validated by experts in the field (go to http://www.ftc.gov for additional guidance).

The consent order and the cease-and-desist order are the most basic remedies used by the FTC in dealing with deceptive or unfair advertising. In a **consent order,** an advertiser accused of running deceptive or unfair advertising agrees to stop running the advertisements in question, without admitting guilt. For advertisers who do not comply voluntarily, the FTC can issue a **cease-and-desist order,** which generally requires that the advertising in question be stopped within 30 days so that a hearing can be held to determine whether the advertising is deceptive or unfair. For products that have a direct effect on consumers' health or safety (for example, foods), the FTC can issue an immediate cease-and-desist order.

Affirmative disclosure is another remedy available to the FTC. An advertisement that fails to disclose important material facts about a product can be deemed deceptive, and the FTC may require **affirmative disclosure,** whereby the important material absent from prior ads must be included in subsequent advertisements. The absence of important material information may cause consumers to make false assumptions about products in comparison to the competition.

The most extensive remedy for advertising determined to be misleading is **corrective advertising.**[53] In cases where evidence suggests that consumers have developed incorrect beliefs about a brand based on deceptive or unfair advertising, the firm may be required to run corrective ads in an attempt to dispel those faulty beliefs. The commission has specified not only the message content for corrective ads, but also the budgetary allocation, the duration of transmission, and the placement of the advertising. The goal of corrective advertising is to rectify erroneous beliefs created by deceptive advertising, but it hasn't always worked as intended. Corrective advertising has a long history ranging from Warner Lambert's Listerine mouthwash claims that it could "cure and prevent colds" (which it couldn't) to more recent ad campaigns that tout new flavors and other brand features.

Another area of FTC regulation and remedy involves **celebrity endorsements.** The FTC has specific rules for advertisements that use an expert or celebrity as a spokesperson for a product. In the case of experts (those whose experience or training allows a superior judgment of products), the endorser's actual qualifications must justify his or her status as an expert. In the case of celebrities (such as Tiger Woods as a spokesperson for Buick or Nike), FTC guidelines state that the celebrity must be an actual user of the product, or the ad is considered deceptive.

52.   For a discussion of the FTC advertising substantiation program and its extension to require reasonable basis, see Debra L. Scammon and Richard J. Semenik, "The FTC's 'Reasonable Basis' for Substantiation of Advertising: Expanded Standards and Implications," *Journal of Advertising,* vol. 12, no. 1 (1983), 4–11.

53.   A history of the corrective-advertising concept and several of its applications are provided by Debra L. Scammon and Richard J. Semenik, "Corrective Advertising: Evolution of the Legal Theory and Application of the Remedy," *Journal of Advertising,* vol. 11, no. 1 (1982), 10–20.

These regulatory programs and remedies provide the FTC a great deal of control over the advertising process. Numerous ads have been interpreted as questionable under the guidelines of these programs, and advertisements have been altered. It is likely also that advertisers and their agencies, who are keenly aware of the ramifications of violating FTC precepts, have developed ads with these constraints in mind.

Yet it is certainly fair to conclude that advertising regulation is a dynamic endeavor that will challenge regulators far into the future. Of course, the most notable new challenge that regulators around the world must learn to cope with is advertising on the Internet. For instance, while U.S. government agencies such as the FTC and FDA intend to extend their jurisdiction to the Internet, they clearly have a tiger by the tail.

State Regulation.   State governments do not have extensive policing powers over the promotional activities of firms. Since the vast majority of companies are involved in interstate marketing of goods and services, any violation of fair practice or existing regulation is a federal government issue.

There is typically one state government organization, the attorney general's office, that is responsible for investigating questionable promotional practices. It was the attorneys general offices in Texas and New York that launched an investigation of claims made by Kraft that its Cheez Whiz spread used real cheese.[54] Similarly, it was the state attorney general's office in Texas that claimed a demonstration used by Volvo was misleading. In the ad, a monster truck with oversized tires was shown rolling over the roofs of a row of cars, crushing all of them except a Volvo. The problem was, the Volvo in the test had its roof reinforced while the other cars' roof supports had been weakened.[55]

Since the 1980s, the National Association of Attorneys General, whose members include the attorneys general from all 50 states, has been active as a group in monitoring advertising and sharing its findings. In 1988, attorneys general from 22 states challenged the safety of Honda's three-wheeled ATV, claiming that the vehicle posed an unreasonable risk of injury. Part of the challenge was that Honda advertising encouraged dangerous riding behavior.[56] Overall, states will rely on the vigilance of the federal agencies discussed earlier to monitor promotional practices and then act against firms with questionable activities.

Finally, in 1995, thirteen states passed prize notification laws regarding sweepstakes and contests. The new laws require marketers to make full disclosure of rules, odds, and retail value of prizes. The states were responding to what they felt was widespread fraud and deception. Some states aggressively prosecuted the sweepstakes companies in court.

 Industry Self-Regulation.   The promotion industry has come far in terms of self-control and restraint. Some of this improvement is due to tougher government regulation, and some to industry self-regulation. **Self-regulation** is the promotion industry's attempt to police itself. Supporters say it is a shining example of how unnecessary government intervention is, while critics point to it as a joke, an elaborate shell game. According to the critics, meaningful self-regulation occurs only when the threat of government action is imminent. How you see this controversy is largely dependent on your own personal experience and level of cynicism.

Several industry and trade associations and public service organizations have voluntarily established guidelines for promotion within their industries. The reasoning is that self-regulation is good for the promotion community as a whole and creates credibility for, and therefore enhances the effectiveness of, promotion itself. Exhibit

54.   "Deceptive Ads: The FTC's Laissez-Faire Approach Is Backfiring," *BusinessWeek,* December 2, 1985, 130.

55.   Steven W. Colford and Raymond Serafin, "Scali Pays for Volvo Ad: FTC," *Advertising Age,* August 26, 1991, 4.

56.   Paul Harris, "Will the FTC Finally Wake Up?" *Sales and Marketing Management,"* January 1988, 57.

EXHIBIT 4.16

Selected business organizations and industry associations with advertising self-regulation programs

Organization	Code Established
Advertising Associations	
American Advertising Federation	1965
American Association of Advertising Agencies	1924
Association of National Advertisers	1972
Business/Professional Advertising Association	1975
Special Industry Groups	
Council of Better Business Bureaus	1912
Household furniture	1978
Automobiles and trucks	1978
Carpet and rugs	1978
Home improvement	1975
Charitable solicitations	1974
Children's Advertising Review Unit	1974
National Advertising Division/National Advertising Review Board	1971
Media Associations	
American Business Press	1910
Direct Mail Marketing Association	1960
Direct Selling Association	1970
National Association of Broadcasters	
Radio	1937
Television	1952
Outdoor Advertising Association of America	1950
Selected Trade Associations	
American Wine Association	1949
Wine Institute	1949
Distilled Spirits Association	1934
United States Brewers Association	1955
Pharmaceutical Manufacturers Association	1958
Proprietary Association	1934
Bank Marketing Association	1976
Motion Picture Association of America	1930
National Swimming Pool Institute	1970
Toy Manufacturers Association	1962

4.16 lists some organizations that have taken on the task of regulating and monitoring promotional activities, and the year when each established a code of standards.

The purpose of self-regulation by these organizations is to evaluate the content and quality of promotion specific to their industries. The effectiveness of such organizations depends on the cooperation of members and the policing mechanisms used.

Each organization exerts an influence on the nature of promotion in its industry. Some are particularly noteworthy in their activities and warrant further discussion.

The National Advertising Review Board. One important self-regulation organization is the National Advertising Review Board (NARB). The NARB is the operations arm of the National Advertising Division (NAD) of the Council of Better Business Bureaus. Complaints received from consumers, competitors, or local branches of the Better Business Bureau (BBB) are forwarded to the NAD. Most such complaints come from competitors. After a full review of the complaint, the issue may be forwarded to the NARB and evaluated by a panel. The complete procedure for dealing with complaints is detailed in Exhibit 4.17.

The NAD maintains a permanent professional staff that works to resolve complaints with the advertiser and its agency before the issue gets to the NARB. If no resolution is achieved, the complaint is appealed to the NARB, which appoints a panel made up of three advertiser representatives, one agency representative, and one public representative. This panel then holds hearings regarding the advertising in question. The advertiser is allowed to present the firm's case. If no agreement can be reached by the panel either to dismiss the case or to persuade the advertiser to change

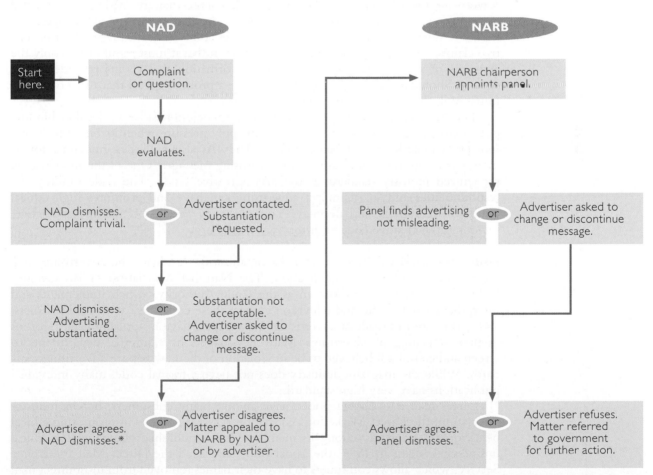

*If the complaint originated outside the system, the outside complainant can appeal at this point to the NARB chairperson for a panel adjudication. Granting of such an appeal is at the chairperson's discretion.

EXHIBIT 4.17

The NAD and NARB regulatory process.

the advertising, then the NARB initiates two actions. First, the NARB publicly identifies the advertiser, the complaint against the advertiser, and the panel's findings. Second, the case is forwarded to an appropriate government regulatory agency (usually the FTC).

The NAD and the NARB are not empowered to impose penalties on advertisers, but the threat of going before the board acts as a deterrent to deceptive and questionable advertising practices. Further, the regulatory process of the NAD and the NARB is probably less costly and time-consuming for all parties involved than if every complaint were handled by a government agency.

State and Local Better Business Bureaus. Aside from the national BBB, there are more than 140 separate local bureaus. Each local organization is supported by membership dues paid by area businesses. The three divisions of a local BBB—merchandise, financial, and solicitations—investigate the advertising and selling practices of firms in their areas. A local BBB has the power to forward a complaint to the NAD for evaluation.

Beyond its regulatory activities, the BBB tries to avert problems associated with advertising by counseling new businesses and providing information to advertisers and agencies regarding legislation, potential problem areas, and industry standards.

Advertising Agencies and Associations. It makes sense that advertising agencies and their industry associations would engage in self-regulation. An individual agency is legally responsible for the advertising it produces and is subject to reprisal for deceptive claims. The agency is in a difficult position in that it must monitor not only the activities of its own people, but also the information that clients provide to the agency. Should a client direct an agency to use a product appeal that turns out to be untruthful, the agency is still responsible.

The American Association of Advertising Agencies (4As) has no legal or binding power over its agency members, but it can apply pressure when its board feels that industry standards are not being upheld. The 4As also publishes guidelines for its members regarding various aspects of advertising messages. One of the most widely recognized industry standards is the 4As' Creative Code. The code outlines the responsibilities and social impact advertising can have and promotes high ethical standards of honesty and decency. You can view the 4As standards of practice, including the creative code, at http://www.aaaa.org.

Media Organizations. Individual media organizations evaluate the advertising they receive for broadcast and publication. The National Association of Broadcasters (NAB) has a policing arm known as the Code Authority, which implements and interprets separate radio and television codes. These codes deal with truth, fairness, and good taste in broadcast advertising. Newspapers have historically been rigorous in their screening of advertising. Many newspapers have internal departments to screen and censor ads believed to be in violation of the newspaper's advertising standards. While the magazine industry does not have a formal code, many individual publications have very high standards.

Direct mail may have a poor image among many consumers, but its industry association, the Direct Marketing Association (DMA), is active in promoting ethical behavior and standards among its members. It has published guidelines for ethical business practices. In 1971, the association established the Direct Mail Preference Service, which allows consumers to have their names removed from most direct mail lists.

A review of all aspects of industry self-regulation suggests not only that a variety of programs and organizations are designed to monitor advertising, but also that many of these programs are effective. Those whose livelihoods depend on advertising are just as interested as consumers and legislators in maintaining high standards. If advertising deteriorates into an unethical and untrustworthy business activity, the economic vitality of many organizations will be compromised. Self-regulation can help prevent such a circumstance and is in the best interest of all the organizations discussed here.

Internet Self-Regulation. Because there are few federal guidelines established for advertising and promotion on the Internet (with the exception of anti-spam legislation), the industry itself has been the governing body. So far, no industry-wide trade association has emerged to offer guidelines or standards. You will see later in this chapter that several special interest groups are questioning the ethics of some Internet promotional practices. And there are those who are skeptical that the industry can regulate itself.

A new group, the Global Business Dialog on Electronic Commerce (GBDe), is trying to establish itself as a trade association for the online industry. But while it counts some big companies among its 200 members—Time Warner, Daimler-Chrysler, Toshiba—not one of the Internet heavyweights, like Amazon.com or Yahoo!, have joined the ranks. The GBDe has drawn up a proposal for dealing with harmful content (pornography), protecting personal information, enforcing copyrights, and handling disputes in e-commerce. But the organization's efforts have not created great enthusiasm. Lester Thurow, the prominent public policy professor from MIT, said, "Self-regulation can play a role if you have real regulation that will come piling in if you don't do it."[57]

Consumers as Regulatory Agents. Consumers themselves are motivated to act as regulatory agents based on a variety of interests, including product safety, reasonable choice, and the right to information. Advertising tends to be a focus of consumer regulatory activities because of its conspicuousness. Consumerism and consumer organizations have provided the primary vehicles for consumer regulatory efforts.

Consumerism, the actions of individual consumers or groups of consumers designed to exert power in the marketplace, is by no means a recent phenomenon. The earliest consumerism efforts can be traced to 17th-century England. In the United States, there have been recurring consumer movements throughout the 20th century. *Adbusters* magazine and Web site is a recent example.

In general, these movements have focused on the same issue: Consumers want a greater voice in the whole process of product development, distribution, and information dissemination. Consumers commonly try to create pressures on firms by withholding patronage through boycotts. Some boycotts have been effective. Firms as powerful as Procter & Gamble, Kimberly-Clark, and General Mills all have historically responded to threats of boycotts by pulling advertising from programs consumers found offensive. Sparked by the Janet Jackson Super Bowl incident, advertisers themselves are threatening to withhold their advertising dollars unless they can be assured of decency in programming by producers and networks.[58]

Consumer Organizations. The other major consumer effort to bring about regulation is through established consumer organizations. The following are the most prominent consumer organizations and their prime activities:

- *Consumer Federation of America (CFA).* This organization, founded in 1968, now includes more than 200 national, state, and local consumer groups and labor

57.   Neal Boudette, "Internet Self-Regulation Seen Lacking Punch," Reuters News Services, September 14, 1999, accessed via the Internet at biz.yahoo.com/ on September 14, 1999.
58.   An Advertising Age Roundup, "Upstaged Advertisers Riled by Bowl Stunt," *Advertising Age,* February 9, 2004, 1.

unions as affiliate members. The goals of the CFA are to encourage the creation of consumer organizations, provide services to consumer groups, and act as a clearinghouse for information exchange between consumer groups (http://www.consumerfed.org).

- **Consumers Union.** This nonprofit consumer organization is best known for its publication of *Consumer Reports*. Established in 1936, Consumers Union has as its stated purpose "to provide consumers with information and advice on goods, services, health, and personal finance; and to initiate and cooperate with individual and group efforts to maintain and enhance the quality of life for consumers."[59] This organization supports itself through the sale of publications and accepts no funding, including advertising revenues, from any commercial organization (http://www.consumersunion.org).

- **Consumer Alert.** Founded in 1977, Consumer Alert champions consumer causes through testimony and comments to legislative and regulatory bodies, legal action, issues management, and media outreach. In addition, the organization promotes the need for sound science and sound economic data in public policy decisions (http://www.consumeralert.org).

- **Commercial Alert.** Commercial Alert is headed by Ralph Nader, a historic figure in consumer rights and protection. The organization's stated mission is to keep the commercial culture within its proper sphere and to prevent it from exploiting children and subverting the higher values of family, community, environmental integrity, and democracy (http://www.commercialalert.org).

These four consumer organizations are the most active and potent of the consumer groups, but there are hundreds of such groups organized by geographic location or product category. Consumers have proven that when faced with an organized effort, corporations can and will change their practices. In one of the most publicized events in recent times, consumers applied pressure to Coca-Cola and, in part, were responsible for forcing the firm to re-market the original formula of Coca-Cola (as Coca-Cola Classic). If consumers are able to exert such a powerful and nearly immediate influence on a firm such as Coca-Cola, one wonders what other changes they could effect in the market.

5 The Regulation of Other Promotional Tools. As firms broaden the scope of the promotional effort beyond advertising, the regulatory constraints placed on other IBP tools become relevant. We will consider the current and emerging regulatory environment for direct marketing, e-commerce, sales promotion, and public relations.

Regulatory Issues in Direct Marketing and E-Commerce.
The most pressing regulatory issue facing direct marketing and e-commerce was actually discussed at the outset of the chapter—database development and the privacy debate that accompanies the practice. But that discussion just scratched the surface. The real privacy issue has to do with the developing ability of firms to merge offline databases with the online Web search and shopping behavior of consumers.

Privacy. E-commerce privacy issues focus on a wide range, from database development (talked about earlier in this chapter) to **cookies,** those online tracking markers that advertisers place on a Web surfer's hard drive to track that person's online behavior. The current environment is annoying and feels like a huge invasion of privacy. But it is nothing compared to the emerging possibilities. Currently, cookies do not reveal a person's name or address. But what is looming as a real possibility is the widespread use of offline databases that *do* include a consumer's name, address,

---

59.   This statement of purpose can be found inside the cover of any issue of *Consumer Reports*.

EXHIBIT 4.18

Web sites like eBay are very conscientious about protecting the privacy of their customers and have detailed privacy statements that explain their efforts. http://pages .ebay .com/help/privacycentral2 .html

phone number, credit card numbers, medical records, credit records, and Social Security number that are merged with online tracking data from Web browsing behavior.[60] With this combination of data, the following could easily happen: You are browsing a Web page on mutual funds and seconds later, you get a phone call from a telemarketer trying to sell you financial services!

This scenario may not be too far in the future, and the data/ browsing merge has already occurred. The merger of Double-Click with Abacus Direct created a database that contains transactional data from 1,700 cataloguers, retailers, and publishers—data that chronicles more than 3.6 *billion* transactions by 90 million U.S. households. (By the way, there are only about 102 million households in the United States.) DoubleClick has signed up more than 275 online retailers who contribute detailed transaction, geographic, and demographic information to the database.[61] Sure feels like an invasion of privacy. Firms are searching for ways to guarantee to consumers that their privacy will be preserved (see Exhibit 4.18). In the meantime, the concern is great enough that Congress and the FTC are carefully scrutinizing mergers of firms that would create such comprehensive online and offline databases and privacy advocates are trying to alert people to the invasion.[62] We have to realize, though, that while this tracking of behavior seems pretty scary, many people don't really seem to care. A recent survey of Web surfers asked if they read a site's privacy policy before making a purchase—only 6 percent responded that they always do, and 77 percent said they rarely or never do. The story in the IBP box certainly supports those results.

Spam. Few of us would argue with the allegation that **spam,** unsolicited commercial messages sent through the e-mail system, is the scourge of the Internet. To put spam into perspective, it is estimated that 10.4 million spam e-mails are sent every *minute* worldwide—that comes out to about 15 billion messages a day.[63] Spam can be so bad it has actually shut down a company's entire operations. To cope with the onslaught, individuals and companies are turning to spam filtering software to stem flow and take back control of their e-mail systems. The rise in spam has prompted Internet services providers to form a coalition against spammers. In the spring of 2003, Yahoo!, AOL, and MSN announced a joint anti-spam offensive relying on technological and legal remedies. About that same time, the FTC convened a brainstorming session to determine what, if anything, could be done legally.[64] Then in October of 2003, the U.S. Senate voted unanimously 97–0 to implement the CAN SPAM Act. The Senate followed in November of 2003 with its support, voting

60. Marcia Stepanek, "Protecting E-Privacy: Washington Must Step In," *Business Week E.Biz,* July 26, 1999, EB30; Michael Krauss, "Get a Handle on the Privacy Wild Card," *Marketing News,* February 28, 2000, 12.

61. G. Beato, "Big Data's Big Business," *Business 2.0,* February 2001, 62.

62. Jennifer Gilbert and Ira Teinowitz, "Privacy Debate Continues to Rage," *Advertising Age,* February 7, 2000, 44; Ann Harrison, "Privacy? Who Cares," *Business 2.0,* June 12, 2001, 48–49.

63. Stephen Baker, "The Taming of the Internet," *BusinessWeek,* December 15, 2003, 78–82

64. Lorraine Woellert et al., "Slamming Spam," *BusinessWeek,* May 12, 2003, 40.

392–5 in favor of the legislation. The act does not outlaw all unsolicited e-mail, but rather targets fraudulent, deceptive, and pornographic messages, which is estimated to make up about two-thirds of all commercial unsolicited e-mail.[65] Violators face jail time and fines up to $1 million.

Spammers are not taking the legislation lying down, as you might expect. They are challenging the legislation on legal grounds, claiming that it violates First Amendment free speech rights. And they are doing what they do best—slamming their opponents with a barrage of e-mails.[66] The concern of course is that legitimate marketers and advertisers who could use e-mail in a reasonable way will caught in this legislation.

Contests and Sweepstakes. While privacy and spam are huge direct marketing and e-commerce issues, they are not the only ones. The next biggest legal issue has to do with sweepstakes and contests. Because of the success and widespread use of sweepstakes in direct marketing (such as the Publishers Clearing House sweepstakes), Congress has imposed limits on such promotions. The limits on direct mail sweepstakes include the requirement that the phrases "No purchase is necessary to win" and "A purchase will not improve an individual's chance of winning" must be repeated three times in letters to consumers and again on the entry form. In addition, penalties can be imposed on marketers who do not promptly remove consumers' names from mailing lists at the consumer's request.[67]

The online version of sweepstakes and contests also has the attention of the U.S. Congress. Sweepstakes, like the ones promoted at LuckySurf.com (shown in Exhibit 4.19), play a lot like traditional sweepstakes, lotteries, games, or contests. At the LuckySurf site, you merely need to register (providing name, home address, e-mail address, and password), pick seven numbers, then click on one of four banner ads to activate your entry in a $1 million a day drawing. So far, these online games have avoided both lawsuits and regulation, but they have attracted the attention of policymakers.[68]

IBP

Privacy? What Privacy?

What does it take to get 200 college students to surrender their e-mail addresses and other personal information to a company in a single day? Would you guess $50 each? $100 each? Maybe even $200 each? How about some mouse pads and T-shirts? That's all it took for Kangaroo.net (now Entopia) to get a couple of college kids to sign up 200 other college kids for a Web-based research effort for its client The Magma Group, a youth marketing firm in Brighton, Massachusetts.

Despite all the hoopla and hand-wringing over the threat of privacy invasions that new technology may be bringing, over 46 percent of online shoppers *never* read a site's privacy statement and another 31 percent rarely read it. Only 6 percent of online shoppers say they always read the privacy policy of the merchants with whom they do business. If privacy were such a big deal, you would expect a lot more people to act a lot more carefully to protect their privacy.

With this little protest, you can be sure that firms will proceed posthaste with creating large and comprehensive databases—especially databases containing information on young adults in the United States. In 2004, U.S. teens spent over $200 billion on everything from clothes to cell phones to movie tickets. In addition, college students spent another nearly $100 billion on products from books to food and clothing to cell phones. But that's not the really good news. The really good news is that this "peer to peer" marketing, as it is called, costs peanuts. Peer programs, where kids sign up other kids, cost from $25,000 at the low end to $300,000 at the very top end—not a lot of money in today's world of marketing and advertising.

What may be driving this willing invasion of privacy, though, is the fact that there is usually something in it for the "invadee." In the simplest terms, one of Kangaroo.com's willing participants put it this way: "I don't have to give them any money, I get a free T-shirt, and if I am interested in the product, I'll get an e-mail about it and find out more." Well, there you have it—direct and personal, and not that big a deal for some people.

Sources: Alissa Quart, "Ol' College Pry," *Business 2.0*, April 3, 2001, 68; Business 2.0.com Snapshot, *Business 2.0*, January 23, 2001, 17.

---

65.   "Senate Approves Antispam Bill," Reuters News, reported on the Internet on October 22, 2003 at http://news.reuters.com.
66.   Stephen Baker, "The Taming of the Internet," op. cit., 82.
67.   Ira Teinowitz, "Congress Nears Accord on Sweepstakes Limits," *Advertising Age*, August 9, 1999, 33.
68.   James Heckman, "Online, but Not on Trial, though Privacy Looms Large," *Marketing News*, December 6, 1999, 8.

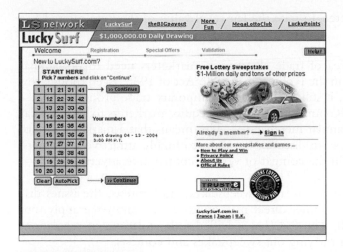

Online contests and sweepstakes are being monitored by government regulatory agents.
http://www.luckysurf.com

Telemarketing.   Another legal issue in direct marketing that has hit the headlines in recent years has to do with telemarketing practices. The first restriction on telemarketing was the Telephone Consumer Fraud and Abuse Prevention Act of 1994 (later strengthened by the FTC in 1995) which requires telemarketers to state their name, the purpose of the call, and the company they work for. The guidelines in the act prohibit telemarketers from calling before 8 AM and after 9 PM, and they cannot call the same customer more than once every three months. In addition, they cannot use automatic dialing machines that contain recorded messages, and they must keep a list of consumers who do not want to be called.

That original telemarketing law was benign compared to recent legislation aimed at telemarketers. At the center of new regulation restricting telemarketing is the "Do Not Call Law," which allows consumers to sign up for a Do Not Call Registry (see Exhibit 4.20) (http://www.donotcall.gov). The Federal Trade Commission, the Federal Communications Commission, and states started to enforce the registry on October 1, 2003. The program exempts political and charitable fund-raisers as well as pollsters. When the program was launched, about 60 million phone numbers were registered by consumers as "do not call" numbers.[69]

There is much at stake in this regulation, and firms dependent on telemarketing for their main promotional communication are not taking this legislation lightly. Estimates put telemarketing revenues at $700 billion annually, and this sort of legislation will be a huge compromise in telemarketers' processes.[70] Telemarketers are challenging the legislation as a compromise of their First Amendment rights to free speech. And the legislation does not stop all calls. Those with rights to keep calling include[71]

- Charities, politicians, pollsters, and market researchers
- Companies you do business with
- Companies that have sold you something or delivered something to you within the previous 18 months
- Businesses *you've* contacted in the past three months
- Companies that obtain your permission to call you

The Federal Trade Commission, the Federal Communications Commission, and states started to enforce the Do Not Call Registry on October 1, 2003. Registering your phone number(s) with the registry blocks a wide variety of telemarketers from calling you with a sales pitch. http://www.donotcall.gov

Regulatory Issues in Sales Promotion.   Regulatory issues in sales promotion focus on three areas: premium offers, trade allowances, and contests and sweepstakes.

Premium Offers.   With respect to **premiums** (an item offered for "free" or at a greatly reduced price with the purchase of another item), the main area of regulation

69.   Ira Teinowitz, "FCC Extends Do-Not-Call List," *Advertising Age,* June 30, 2003, 3.

70.   Ibid.

71.   Lorraine Woellert, "The Do-Not-Call Law Won't Stop the Calls," *BusinessWeek,* September 29, 2003, 89.

has do with requiring marketers to state the fair retail value of the item offered as a premium.

Trade Allowances. In the area of trade allowances, marketers need to be familiar with the guidelines set forth in the Robinson-Patman Act of 1936. Even though this is an old piece of legislation, it still applies to contemporary trade promotion practices. The guidelines of the Robinson-Patman Act require marketers to offer similar customers similar prices on similar merchandise. This means that a marketer cannot use special allowances as a way to discount the price to highly attractive customers. This issue was raised earlier in the context of vertical cooperative advertising.

Contests and Sweepstakes. In the area of sweepstakes and contests, the issues discussed in the previous section under direct marketing and e-commerce apply, but there are other issues as well. The FTC has specified four violations of regulations that marketers must avoid in carrying out sweepstakes and contests:

• Misrepresentations about the value (for example, stating an inflated retail price) of the prizes being offered
• Failure to provide complete disclosure about the conditions necessary to win (are there behaviors required on the part of the contestant?)
• Failure to disclose the conditions necessary to obtain a prize (are there behaviors required of the contestant after the contestant is designated a "winner"?)
• Failure to ensure that a contest or sweepstakes is not classified as a lottery, which is considered gambling—a contest or sweepstakes is a lottery if a prize is offered based on chance and the contestant has to give up something of value in order to play

Product/Brand Placement. The area of sales promotion to receive attention most recently in the regulatory arena is brand/product placement in television programs and films. As discussed earlier, consumer groups feel that unless television networks and film producers reveal that brands are placed into a program or film for a fee, consumers could be deceived into believing that the product use is natural and real. The industry counterclaim is, "There is a paranoia about our business that shouldn't be there. We don't control the storyline, or the brands that are included. The writers and producers do."[72]

Regulatory Issues in Public Relations. Public relations is not bound by the same sorts of laws as other elements of the promotional mix. Because public relations activities deal with public press and public figures, much of the regulation relates to these issues. The public relations activities of a firm may place it on either side of legal issues with respect to privacy, copyright infringement, or defamation through slander and libel.

Privacy. The privacy problems facing a public relations firm center on the issue of appropriation. **Appropriation** is the use of pictures or images owned by someone else without permission. If a firm uses a model's photo or a photographer's work in an advertisement or company brochure without permission, then the work has been appropriated without the owner's permission. The same is true of public relations materials prepared for release to the press or as part of a company's public relations kit.

Copyright Infringement. Copyright infringement can occur when a public relations effort uses written, recorded, or photographic material in public relations materials. Much as with appropriation, written permission must be obtained to use such works.

---

72.   Claire Atkinson, "Watchdog Group Hits TV Product Placement," *Advertising Age*, October 6, 2003, 12.

Defamation. When a communication occurs that damages the reputation of an individual because the information in the communication was untrue, this is called **defamation** (you many have heard it referred to as "defamation of character"). Defamation can occur either through slander or libel. **Slander** is oral defamation and in the context of promotion would occur during television or radio broadcast of an event involving a company and its employees. **Libel** is defamation that occurs in print and would relate to magazine, newspaper, direct mail, or Internet reports.

The public relations practitioner's job is to protect clients from slanderous or libelous reports about a company's activities. Inflammatory TV "investigative" news programs are often sued for slander and libel and are challenged to prove the allegations they make about a company and personnel working for a company. The issues revolve around whether negative comments can be fully substantiated.[73] Erroneous reports in major magazines and newspapers about a firm can result in a defamation lawsuit as well. Less frequently, public relations experts need to defend a client accused of making defamatory remarks.

---

73.   One of the most widely publicized lawsuits of this time involved Philip Morris's $10 billion libel suit against ABC's news program *DayOne*. For a summary of this suit, see Steve Weinberg, "ABC, Philip Morris and the Infamous Apology," *Columbia Journalism Review*, November/December 1995, available at http://www.cjr.org, accessed December 7, 1999.

SUMMARY

 Identify the benefits and problems of advertising and promotion in a capitalistic society and debate a variety of issues concerning their effects on society's well-being.

Advertisers have always been followed by proponents and critics. Proponents of advertising argue that it offers benefits for individual consumers and society at large. At the societal level, proponents claim, advertising helps promote a higher standard of living by allowing marketers to reap the rewards of product improvements and innovation. Advertising also "pays for" mass media in many countries and provides consumers with a constant flow of information not only about products and services, but also about political and social issues.

Over the years critics have leveled many charges at advertising and advertising practitioners. Advertising expenditures in the multibillions are condemned as wasteful, offensive, and a source of frustration for many in society who see the lavish lifestyle portrayed in advertising, knowing they will never be able to afford such a lifestyle. Critics also contend that advertisements rarely furnish useful information but instead perpetuate superficial stereotypes of many cultural subgroups. For many years, some critics have been concerned that advertisers are controlling us against our will with subliminal advertising messages.

 Explain how ethical considerations affect the development of advertising and IBP campaigns.

Ethical considerations are a concern when creating advertising, especially when that advertising will be targeted to children or will involve controversial products such as firearms, gambling, alcohol, or cigarettes. While ethical standards are a matter for personal reflection, it certainly is the case that unethical people can create unethical advertising. But there are also many safeguards against such behavior, including the corporate and personal integrity of advertisers.

 Discuss the role of government agencies in the regulation of advertising and promotion.

Governments typically are involved in the regulation of advertising. It is important to recognize that advertising regulations can vary dramatically from one country to the next. In the United States, the Federal Trade Commis-

sion (FTC) has been especially active in trying to deter deception and unfairness in advertising. The FTC was established in 1914, and since then a variety of legislation has been passed to clarify its powers. The FTC has also developed regulatory remedies that have expanded its involvement in advertising regulation, such as the advertising substantiation program.

 Explain the meaning and importance of self-regulation for firms that develop and use advertising and promotion.

Some of the most important controls on advertising are voluntary; that is, they are a matter of self-regulation by advertising and marketing professionals. For example, the American Association of Advertising Agencies has issued guidelines for promoting fairness and accuracy when using comparative advertisements. Many other organizations, such as the Better Business Bureau, the National Association of Broadcasters, and the Direct Marketing Association, participate in the process to help ensure fairness and assess consumer complaints about advertising and promotion.

 Discuss the regulation of the full range of techniques used in the IBP process.

The regulation of other tools in the IBP process focuses on direct marketing, e-commerce, sales promotions, and public relations. In direct marketing and e-commerce, the primary concern has to do with consumer privacy. New legislation, like the Do Not Call Registry and the CAN SPAM Act, is restricting ways in which companies can contact consumers with a sales offer. The legislation is a reaction to new technologies that have enabled firms to match consumers' online behavior with offline personal information. Another aspect of e-commerce has to do with contests and sweepstakes and the potential for such games to actually be gambling opportunities. In sales promotions, premium offers, trade allowances, and offline contests and sweepstakes are subject to regulation. Firms are required to state the fair value of "free" premiums, trade allowances must follow the guidelines of fair competition, and contests and sweepstakes must follow strict rules specified by the FTC. The regulation of public relations efforts has to do with privacy, copyright infringement, and defamation. Firms must be aware of the strict legal parameters of these factors.

KEY TERMS

ethics	advertising substantiation program	cookies
deception	consent order	spam
puffery	cease-and-desist order	premiums
primary demand	affirmative disclosure	appropriation
unfair advertising	corrective advertising	defamation
vertical cooperative advertising	celebrity endorsements	slander
comparison advertisements	self-regulation	libel
monopoly power	consumerism	

QUESTIONS

1.   How does consumer involvement with sweepstakes, contests, discount cards, warranty registrations, and other marketing initiatives lead to an increase in spam and junk mail?

2.   What are the pros and cons of database marketing, and what can consumers do to protect themselves and their privacy from unwanted or intrusive advertising and promotion campaigns?

3.   Advertising has been a focal point of criticism for many decades. In your opinion, what are some of the key factors that make advertising controversial?

4.   You have probably been exposed to hundreds of thousands of advertisements in your lifetime. In what ways does exposure to advertising make you a better or worse consumer?

5.   Use Maslow's Hierarchy of Needs to address critics' concerns that too much advertising is directed at creating demand for products that are irrelevant to people's true needs.

6.   One type of advertising that attracts the attention of regulators, critics, and consumer advocates is advertising

directed at children. Why is it the focus of so much attention?

7.   What is comparison advertising, and why does this form of advertising need a special set of guidelines to prevent unfair competition?

8.   Explain why a marketer might be tempted to misuse cooperative-advertising allowances to favor some kinds of retailers over others. What piece of legislation empowered the FTC to stop these bogus allowances?

9.   The Nutrition Labeling and Education Act of 1990 is unique for a number of reasons. How has this act affected the day-to-day eating habits of many U.S. consumers? What makes this a special piece of legislation from an enforcement standpoint?

10. Some contend that self-regulation is the best way to ensure fair and truthful advertising practices. Why would it be in the best interests of the advertising community to aggressively pursue self-regulation?

EXPERIENTIAL EXERCISES

1.   The Federal Trade Commission's National Do Not Call Registry is one of the most popular and successful consumer initiatives undertaken by the federal government, attracting millions of registrants and permitting consumers to block most telemarketers from calling their personal telephone numbers. Violators face steep fines. While the registry's popularity is without question, its constitutionality is not. Commerce groups have taken the FTC to court, claiming that the registry violates free speech rights—in this case, commercial speech. The case could eventually make it all the way to the Supreme Court. Write a report on the current progress of the National Do Not Call Registry (http://www.donotcall.gov), and be sure to discuss the latest court judgments concerning its constitutionality. Provide your opinion on whether the registry violates the constitutional right to free speech, and defend your position. Finally, discuss the effect it is having on the direct marketing industry.

2.   Cut out an ad from a magazine. Choose three pros or cons in the social aspects of advertising. Explain how the ad you chose educates consumers, affects the standard of living, affects happiness, influences mass media, and is demeaning or artful.

3.   List two product categories (other than cigarettes) that you think require some kind of advertising regulation and explain why. Do you think they require government regulation, industry self-regulation, or consumer regulation? Explain. Based on your answer, list regulatory agents that might get involved in controlling the advertising process for these products. Finally, go to the Internet and do a search for one or more agency or watchdog sites that would be relevant to the regulatory process. How does the site encourage consumers to get involved, and what resources does the site offer to empower their participation in the process?

EXPERIENCING THE INTERNET

4-1 Social and Ethical Considerations of Advertising

Although all advertising has pros and cons, one particularly divisive issue in the past 50 years has been the promotion of cigarettes. Critics claim that cigarette manufacturers create ads that target children and make potentially dangerous or addictive products seem appealing. The ongoing clash between the industry and the federal government resulted in the 1998 Master Settlement Agreement. This legislation requires manufacturers to take down advertising from billboards and sports arenas and to stop using cartoon characters to sell cigarettes. The tobacco companies also agreed to not market or promote their products to young people. This strict regulatory environment is a far cry from the heyday of the tobacco advertising of past decades. Truth in Advertising, a site that contains historic ads for well-known cigarette products, is a virtual shrine to the *laissez-faire* days of tobacco advertising.

Truth in Advertising: http://www.chickenhead.com/truth

1.   Go to this site and choose an ad from the 1940s or 1950s and describe how it reflects the priorities of society in that era. Is the advertisement guilty of promoting materialism? Explain.

2.   In what way does the ad inform the consumer? In what way is the ad superficial?

3.   What needs does the product claim to satisfy? How does the advertisement create artificial needs?

4.   What do you think is the advertiser's ethical and social responsibility concerning the promotion of cigarettes? Apply relevant chapter concepts in your answer.

4-2 Advertising to Children

Protecting children's privacy online is a hot topic in advertising regulation. Advertisers routinely acquire important market information from Internet users, gathering data from consumer registration forms as well as from hidden browser cookie files. The Children's Online Privacy Protection Act of 1998 sets guidelines for Internet businesses, requiring full disclosure of their sites' data-gathering procedures. Sites like popsicle.com are a good example of how online brands seek to comply with regulatory standards and conduct socially responsible marketing and advertising practices.

Popsicle: http://www.popsicle.com

1.   Using the text, list some of the main concerns regarding advertising targeted to children.

2.   Describe the purpose and features of popsicle.com. How might the site's marketers help protect children from the potentially harmful effects of advertising and marketing?

3.   Click on Popsicle's "privacy policy" link and describe the types of information disclosed about the site's data-gathering practices.

PART I

Cincinnati Bell℠

Cincinnati Bell Wireless: From IMC to IBP
Client: Cincinnati Bell
Agency: Northlich

Background and Participants. In Chapter 1, we introduced the concept of integrated brand promotion (IBP) as an extension of conventional thinking about integrated marketing communication (IMC). The rise in prominence of IBP makes it essential that this evolving perspective on marketing communication be understood in conjunction with traditional mass media advertising. On the client side, sophisticated marketers such as Procter & Gamble, McDonald's, American Express, and General Motors are integrating communication tools such as direct marketing, event sponsorship, sales promotions, the Internet, and public relations, with or without mass media advertising, to build their brands.[1] On the agency side, new organizational designs continue to evolve in search of just the right mix that will deliver clients the integrated expertise they need for building their brands.[2] Coordination and synergy in communication have become the key themes in a world where the advertiser with the strongest brand is the winner in the marketplace.

The five sections at the end of each part of this text will help you better understand advertising and integrated brand promotion by examining topics in two ways. First, each section will discuss IBP relative to each part of the text to provide more concepts and principles for understanding this important approach. Second, we will bring these concepts to life through an in-depth and ongoing case history. This in-depth case history features the working relationship between a client and an ad agency in pursuit of the initial launch and subsequent growth of a wireless phone-service brand (Cincinnati Bell Wireless). The featured client and agency are Cincinnati Bell and Northlich. You will learn a great deal about these two organizations over the course of our five-part, five-year case history. More important, by closely examining the work of Northlich in launching and growing Cincinnati Bell Wireless, we can gain a concrete appreciation for the challenges and benefits of sophisticated advertising and IBP campaigns.

1. For discussions of how these and other marketers are using multiple communications options in an integrated way, see Betsy Spethmann, "Is Advertising Dead?" *PROMO Magazine,* September 1998, 32–36, 159–162; Suzanne Vranica, "For Big Marketers Like AmEx, TV Ads Lose Starring Role," *Wall Street Journal,* May 17, 2004, B1, B3; Anthony Bianco, "The Vanishing Mass Market," *BusinessWeek,* July 12, 2004, 61–68.
2. For example, see Kate Fitzgerald, "Beyond Advertising," *Advertising Age,* August 3, 1998, 1, 14; Kathryn Kranhold, "FCB Makes Itself a New Economy Shop," *Wall Street Journal,* June 14, 2000, B8; Suzanne Vranica, "Y&R's Partilla Reshapes Ad Approach," *Wall Street Journal,* November 29, 2000, B6; Peter Breen, "Six Degrees of Integration," *PROMO* Magazine, October 2001, 75–80; Lisa Sanders, "Brand Buzz Gains 'Independence,'" *Advertising Age,* March 22, 2004, 8.

INTEGRATED BRAND PROMOTION

INTEGRATED BRAND PROMOTION

From IMC to IBP. There is always some risk in advancing new terminology to replace existing terminology, as we are doing here. As champions of advertising and integrated brand promotion, we are not arguing that integrated marketing communication is no longer a valid perspective. The emphasis on synergy and coordination that are at the heart of IMC are also at the heart of IBP. Moreover, we draw explicitly on the analysis of IMC provided by Esther Thorson and Jeri Moore in their 1996 book *Integrated Communication: Synergy of Persuasive Voices.* In their words,

IMC is the strategic coordination of multiple communication voices. Its aim is to optimize the impact of persuasive communication on both consumer and nonconsumer (e.g., retailers, sales personnel, opinion leaders) audiences by coordinating such elements of the marketing mix as advertising, public relations, promotions, direct marketing, and package design.[3]

However, Thorson and Moore also make it clear that achieving synergy and coordination must be based on an understanding of the brand. They note that the first task in planning an integrated communications campaign is to "define and understand in detail the brand itself and the 'equity' it possesses . . . [one] must explore extensively the brand's essence—both current and intended."[4] We concur with this view that a clear focus on a brand's current and desired brand equity is essential for creating effective, integrated campaigns. Branding gurus like Donald Schultz and Kevin Keller also endorse this position with their recommendations to "align all [marketing] actions with the brand's value proposition"[5] and evaluate marketing communication options strategically to determine how they can contribute to brand equity.[6] Without an explicit focus on brand building, there can be no integrated communication. Hence, the task at hand is not simply integrated marketing communication, but rather advertising and integrated brand promotion.

Factors Contributing to the Need for an Integrated Approach. Why have synergy and coordination of communication tools for brand-building purposes become a necessity? Several significant and pervasive changes in the communications environment have contributed to the need for an integrated approach:[7]

- *Fragmentation of media.* Media options available to marketers have proliferated at an astounding rate. Broadcast media now offer "narrowcasting" so specific that advertisers can reach consumers at precise locations, such as airports and supermarket checkout counters. The print media have proliferated dramatically as well. At one point, there were 197 different sports magazines on the market in the United States! The proliferation and fragmentation of media have resulted in less reliance on mass media and more emphasis on other promotional options, such as point-of-purchase promotions and event sponsorship.
- *Better audience assessment.* More-sophisticated research methods have made it possible to more accurately identify and target specific market segments such as Asian-Americans, teenagers, Hispanics, and dual-income households with no kids (DINKs). This leads the marketer away from mass media to promotional tools that reach only the segment that has been targeted.
- *Consumer empowerment.* Consumers today are more powerful and sophisticated than their predecessors. Fostering this greater power are more single-person households, smaller families, higher education levels, and more experienced con-

3.   Esther Thorson and Jeri Moore, *Integrated Communication: Synergy of Persuasive Voices* (Mahwah, N.J.: Lawrence Erlbaum, 1996), l.
4.   Thorson and Moore, *Integrated Communication: Synergy of Persuasive Voices,* 3.
5.   Don E. Schultz, "A Boatload of Branders," *Marketing Management,* Fall 2000, 9.
6.   Kevin Keller, *Strategic Brand Management* (Upper Saddle River, N.J.: Prentice Hall, 2003), ch. 6.
7.   In the opening chapter of his influential book *Permission Marketing* (New York: Simon & Schuster, 1999), Seth Godin argues that increasing fragmentation of the mass media and rampant ad clutter are due to cause a cataclysmic decline in the effectiveness of conventional mass media advertising. Perhaps that day has arrived. In an influential speech delivered at the meetings of the American Association of Advertising Agencies, Jim Stengel, P&G's chief marketing officer, declared any marketing approach based on mass media advertising as "broken." See "Stengel's Call to Arms," *Advertising Age,* February 16, 2004, 16, 17.

sumers. Empowered consumers are more skeptical of commercial messages and demand information tailored to their needs. Technology plays a huge role here as well. PVR/DVR/TiVo systems, which make ad zapping quick and easy, put the consumer in total control.

- ***Increased advertising clutter.*** Not only are consumers becoming more sophisticated, they are becoming more jaded as well. The proliferation of advertising stimuli has diluted the effectiveness of any single message. There is no end in sight to this "message" proliferation.
- ***Database technology.*** The ability of firms to generate, collate, and manage databases has created diverse communications opportunities beyond mass media. These databases can be used to create customer and noncustomer profiles. With this information, highly targeted direct response and telemarketing programs can be implemented. Growth of the Internet will foster more of this type of marketing activity.
- ***Channel power.*** In many product and market categories, there has been a shift in power away from big manufacturers toward big retailers. The new "power retailers," such as Wal-Mart and Home Depot, are able to demand promotional fees and allowances from manufacturers, which diverts funds away from advertising and into special events or other retail promotions.
- ***Accountability.*** In an attempt to achieve greater accountability, firms have reallocated marketing resources from advertising to more short-term and more easily measurable methods, such as direct mail and sales promotion.

All these factors have contributed to an increase in the diversity and complexity of the communication tools used by firms in building their brands. Mass media advertising still plays an important role for many companies, but the opportunity to use other communication and promotional tools makes coordination and integration ever more challenging. Learning to cope with this challenge is what our book and this case history is all about.

Sounds Great . . . **So What's So Hard about Advertising and Integrated Brand Promotion?** Exhibit IBP 1.1 presents a hierarchy of participants that helps to illustrate the challenges that marketers will encounter when attempting to surround current or prospective customers with a "wall" of advertising and integrated brand promotion. Notice that the marketer typically brings to the process a marketing plan, goals and objectives, and perhaps a database that will identify current and prospective customers. The advertising agency will help research the market, suggest creative strategies, and produce persuasive messages. In addition, agencies can assist in placing these messages in outlets that range from conventional mass media to event sponsorship to Internet advertising. The exhibit also shows a number of specialized marketing communication organizations that may need to be hired in conjunction with or in place of the firm's ad agency to execute a comprehensive campaign. Back in Chapter 2 we referred to such specialists as promotion agencies and external facilitators. This is where the process starts to get messy.

Most ad agencies simply do not have all the internal expertise necessary to develop and manage every marketing communication tool. First and foremost, the ad agency is the expert in the development and placement of mass media advertising. This is especially the case for large advertising agencies. Mega-agencies such as those listed in Exhibit 2.8 became mega-agencies because of their prowess in mass media advertising. Because they have a lot invested in their mass media expertise, large ad agencies are often criticized for the tendency to push mass media as the best communication solution for any and all clients.[8]

8. For example, see Fitzgerald, "Beyond Advertising"; Spethmann, "Is Advertising Dead?"; Daniel Klein, "Disintegrated Marketing," *Harvard Business Review,* March 2003, 18, 19; Joe Cappo, *The Future of Advertising* (Chicago, IL: Crain Communications, 2003), ch. 8.

Hence, when marketers want other communication options, they often must turn to specific types of promotion agencies to get the expertise they are looking for. For example, companies including Avon and Ford's Lincoln Mercury division have retained Wunderman Cato Johnson–Chicago just to help them with event management, and Pepsi and Philip Morris have hired Cyrk-Simon Worldwide to design and run their Pepsi Stuff and Marlboro Miles branded-merchandise reward programs.[9] As reflected by the dashed line in Exhibit IBP 1.1, in many instances marketing organizations must bypass their traditional advertising agency to get the expertise they require for building their brands.

Coordination and integration of a marketing communications program becomes much more complex as various promotion agencies are brought into the picture. These diverse specialists often will view one another as competitors for clients' marketing dollars, and will most likely champion their particular specialty, be it event

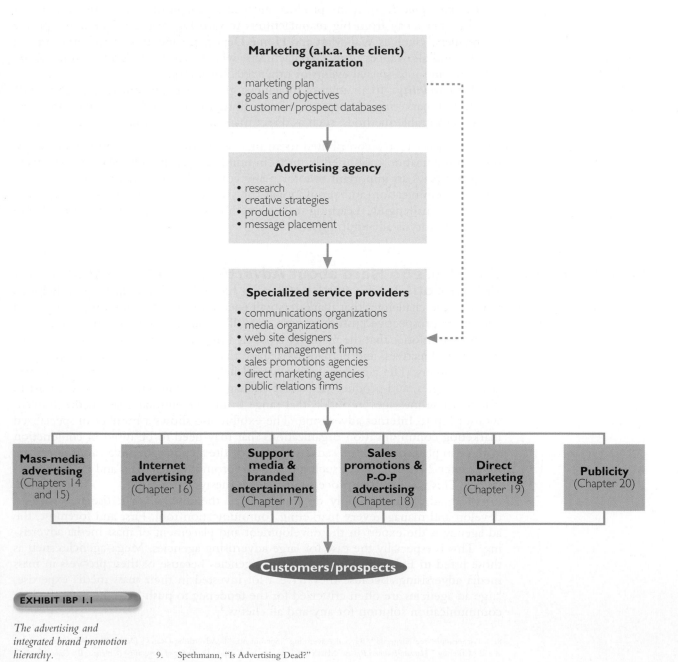

EXHIBIT IBP 1.1

The advertising and integrated brand promotion hierarchy.

9.   Spethmann, "Is Advertising Dead?"

sponsorship, sales promotions, Web site development, direct marketing, or whatever. This is just human nature in a free enterprise system. But instead of ending up with coordination and integration, we often find the situation characterized by conflict and disintegration.[10] Of course, conflict and disintegration are *not* what the marketer wants for his or her brand.

Advertising agencies of all sizes are well aware of these challenges, and as we noted in Chapter 2, many are attempting to redesign themselves to add more expertise that can foster the goals of IBP. Sometimes this redesign comes in the form of a new unit launched within the traditional agency under a nifty name, such as Young & Rubicam's Brand Buzz—a unit now totally devoted to guerrilla marketing.[11] Other times, expertise is added when big companies buy out smaller specialist firms to supplement their range of services.[12] As you can see, this whole business of advertising and IBP is about bringing together the right combination of expertise to serve a client's brand-building needs. This is always a complex undertaking with no easy answers.

The process depicted in Exhibit IBP 1.1 shows a complex array of participants and tools. Our Cincinnati Bell Wireless case history will bring this process to life for you. Additionally, each of the chapters in Parts Four and Five of the book will examine different tools to help you master the complexity of advertising and integrated brand promotion. Specifically, Chapters 14 and 15 will emphasize traditional mass media tools; Chapter 16 looks at advertising and IBP on the Internet; Chapter 17 will consider support media and branded entertainment; Chapter 18 reviews the array of possibilities in sales promotion and point-of-purchase advertising; Chapter 19 provides a comprehensive look at direct marketing; and Chapter 20 completes the set by discussing the public relations function. So if Exhibit IBP 1.1 is not completely clear to you at this point, fear not. There's more to come on all this! But enough about what's to come. Now let's meet the participants in our comprehensive case history.

An Agency in Pursuit of Integrated Brand Promotion . . .

Northlich, http://www.northlich.com. Northlich (pronounced "North-lick"), based in Cincinnati, Ohio, was founded in 1949. Still one of a small group of blue-chip, independent agencies, Northlich defines its essence as "Innovating for business growth and brand value." This essence is implemented via a unique business model that brings together two distinct entities—Northlich, a full-service IBP agency, and BrandStorm, a new-product and brand revitalization consultancy. The expressed purpose of the total organization is to generate inspiring ideas that then deliver a measurable return on investment for clients.

As of 2003, Northlich ranked No. 89 in *Adweek* magazine's ranking of the top 100 U.S. agencies. In 2003 Northlich enjoyed a 12 percent increase in billings over the previous year to nearly $127 million, which generated revenues for the company of about $19 million. Northlich and BrandStorm's client base is diverse and includes familiar names like Ashland, Valvoline, KeyCorp, Humana, Jacuzzi, Procter & Gamble, Chiquita, and Sara Lee Corp., to name a few. Northlich is also the agency behind the highly recognized Ohio anti-smoking campaign appealing to the state's youth. A few samples of Northlich's recent work are shown in Exhibit IBP 1.2.

10. Klein, "Disintegrated Marketing."

11. Vranica, "Y&R's Partilla Reshapes Ad Approach"; Sanders, "Brand Buzz Gains 'Independence.'"

12. Spethmann, "Is Advertising Dead?"; Gerry Khermouch, "Interpublic Group: Synergy—Or Sinkhole?" *BusinessWeek,* April 21, 2003, 76, 77.

Recent Northlich advertising samples.

Used with permission from Northlich. All rights reserved.

Northlich executives attribute their success as a full-service advertising and IBP agency to their people and their underlying shared purpose. The following six values are displayed proudly throughout the Northlich office complex:

1. A visceral connection to our clients' consumers and constituents.
2. A reverence for breakthrough ideas as the nourishment of growth.
3. Agility in our thinking and action.
4. A captivating work environment.
5. An independent spirit.
6. Great style, fine taste, and a big heart.

Other elements of the Northlich model include the following:

- Relentless pursuit of audience insights that leads to distinctive and preemptive value propositions for clients' brands.
- Building equity by soaking up the consumer's mind-space, leaving little room for the competition.
- Methods for helping companies "find their voice" and understand the drama of their business strategies.
- Superior visualization of benefits.
- Delivery of holistic programs designed to reach internal and external stakeholders.

While the folks at Northlich usually refer to their company as an advertising agency, it is probably more accurate to think of them as an IBP agency and consultancy. Integration at Northlich means using whatever marketing tools are appropriate for the brand-building problem at hand. That could mean that direct marketing must be used in conjunction with image-oriented advertising, or that PR alone is the best way to proceed. To truly leverage the power of a brand name and motivate consumers, it takes an intimate understanding of how to orchestrate different media and messages. The overriding goal is always to build the strength of the client's brand.

Northlich employs about 125 full-time people. The agency's leadership team, featured in Exhibit IBP 1.3, gives an indication of the range of expertise that Northlich can marshal to serve clients' brand-building needs. This starts with an extensive client-service capability that includes strategic marketing planning, product positioning, and market research expertise. Northlich also provides a full line of creative and production services for development of media advertising, collateral, packaging, point-of-purchase, direct marketing, and other IBP materials. The client services team will assist with program design, strategy development, program oversight, measurement, and effectiveness evaluation. Northlich offers complete media planning, buying, and post-buy evaluation, and has additional expertise in interactive marketing with specific capabilities in Web site design and construction. The public relations group also has full-service capabilities including media and community relations, employee relations, and crisis management. The combination of Northlich's unique business model, its value system, its manageable size, its collocation of diverse capabilities, a team-oriented work environment, and its excellent range and depth of expertise puts it in an excellent position to fulfill its promise of integrated brand builder.

In 1998, after 23 years with the agency, Mark Serrianne was named Northlich's president and CEO. He is clearly an advocate for IBP. As executive vice president in 1987, Serrianne began the redesign of Northlich from a conventional, mass media–oriented ad agency to a full-service IBP firm. One conclusion should be obvious: The transformation from conventional to integrated does not happen overnight. In Serrianne's view, Northlich has created an internal culture that embraces and rewards integration. Simple aspects of the daily work environment feed into the drive for integration. For example, no one, including the CEO, has a private office. In Serrianne's view, the open-office policy "has created more energy . . . culturally sends a good message to everyone . . . and breaks down barriers between departments."

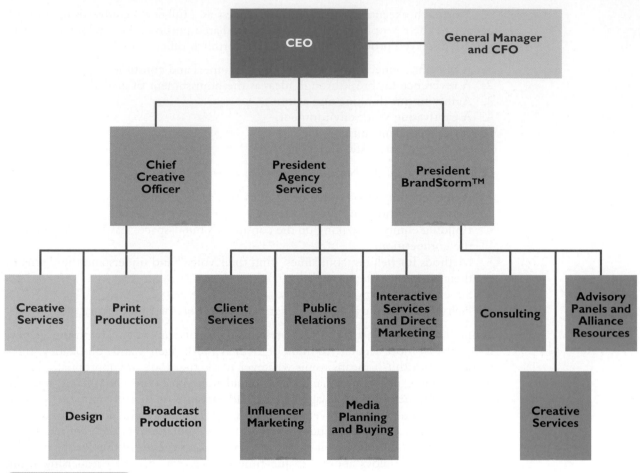

EXHIBIT IBP 1.3

Northlich's organizational structure.

At the same time, Northlich's office complex is filled with numerous breakout rooms of various sizes that allow teams of employees to retreat and focus on clients' problems from a cross-departmental perspective. "Clients are convinced to buy integrated services," says Serrianne, "once you have some pretty good case histories and they have experience with our multidisciplinary teams."[13] We will see those multidisciplinary teams at work in the case history of the launch of Cincinnati Bell Wireless.

A Client in Pursuit of Integrated Brand Promotion . . .

Cincinnati Bell, http://www.cincinnatibell.com. The other key player in our ongoing IBP case history is Cincinnati Bell, a diversified and innovative telecommunications company that began in 1873 as the City & Suburban Telegraph Association. Today, Cincinnati Bell supplies the Greater Cincinnati region with an array of services and business solutions that cannot be found anywhere else in the United States, such as local, long distance, wireless, Internet, and broadband services from a single source,

13.   Sue Fulton, "Local to National: One Agency's Strategy," *Ad Business Report,* June 1998, 1.

billed together with one point of contact. Cincinnati Bell's residential customers routinely score the company among the highest in the country for customer service, as measured in the annual J. D. Power & Associates customer satisfaction survey. In fact, Cincinnati Bell is the only company in Greater Cincinnati to ever win a J. D. Power award, and is the only telecommunications provider to ever win three awards in one year. Additionally, Cincinnati Bell's high-speed, asymmetrical digital subscriber line service, called ZoomTown, helps make Cincinnati one of the most wired communities in America, with service available to more than 85 percent of households, versus a 70 percent national average. Here we'd expect you to conclude that Cincinnati Bell is a lot more than just a sleepy little telephone service provider nestled on the banks of the Ohio River.

Cincinnati Bell has launched numerous brand-building campaigns for innovative products like ZoomTown, Fuse Internet Access, Cincinnati Bell Any Distance, Complete Connections and Custom Connections. Sample ads for some of these branded services are displayed in Exhibit IBP 1.4. However, the star of our case history is Cincinnati Bell's wireless category. Although now combined and led by CEO John F. (Jack) Cassidy, Cincinnati Bell originally launched wireless as a separate subsidiary. Our case history officially begins in late fall 1997, when Cincinnati Bell Wireless (CBW) was conceived.

In the fourth quarter of 1997, having already hired Jack Cassidy from Cantel Cellular Services in Canada to become the subsidiary's president, Cincinnati Bell signed a landmark agreement with AT&T Wireless Services that marked the birth of CBW (http://www.cbwireless.com). The stage was set for a tumultuous six-month period in which Northlich and CBW would prepare to launch advanced personal communication services: voice, paging, and e-mail messaging, with other features and associated products. The strategy formulation that occurred in the period from November 1997 through the spring of 1998 will be described in the next installment of this IBP case history, at the end of Part Two.

IBP EXERCISES

1. What is it about integrated brand promotion that extends and better focuses the perspective previously referred to as integrated marketing communication? What do these two perspectives have in common?

2. A major challenge in executing advertising and integrated brand promotion is to speak to the customer via multiple communications tools in a single voice. What does *single voice* mean, and what's so hard about achieving a single voice in an IBP campaign?

3. Examine the Northlich organizational structure, shown in Exhibit IBP 1.3. How do you think this structure would compare to the structure of a more traditional advertising agency? How does the structure of Northlich lend itself to the execution of the Cincinnati Bell Wireless launch campaign?

4. Why would a regional company like Cincinnati Bell seek out an advertising agency with IBP capabilities to launch its new wireless service? Why might Cincinnati Bell not want to rely on mass media advertising alone to promote its new service? (*Hint:* Refer to the discussion of the factors contributing to the need for integration: fragmentation of media, better audience assessment, consumer empowerment, increased advertising clutter, database technology, channel power, and accountability.)

EXHIBIT IBP 1.4

Recent Cincinnati Bell advertising samples.

**Darcy Ervick
Account Supervisor,
Freedman, Gibson & White**

Does life imitate art? For Darcy Ervick, account supervisor at Freedman, Gibson & White, the question has a certain professional relevance. Ms. Ervick's decision to pursue a career in advertising was influenced in part by *Melrose Place,* the *Beverly Hills 90210* spin-off that became one of the most popular nighttime soaps of the 1990s and of television history. "Advertising always sounded like an interesting profession to me," recalls Ervick, "and this was compounded by my obsession in college with *Melrose Place* and Amanda's career at D&D Advertising." Whatever other factors might have shaped Ms. Ervick's career ambitions, the star power provided by *Melrose* cast member Amanda Woodward (played by Heather Locklear) was enough to pique the young Ohio University student's interest and set her off in pursuit of life in the advertising world.

As with many other successful advertising professionals, Ms. Ervick followed a well-trodden path to Madison Avenue. Her journey to account supervisor passed through a series of stops along the way that included receptionist, traffic manager, print-production manger, and account executive. But it was her work for former client Subway Restaurants that was perhaps most important in earning the promotion to her current position. At a time when Subway was emerging as the market leader in health-conscious, low-carb fast food, Ms. Ervick began writing and executing annual plans for the international deli chain, functioning essentially as a marketing manager for her region. This extensive QSR (Quick Service Restaurant) experience was a key factor in being recruited to her current position with Freedman, Gibson & White, a full-service marketing communications agency that oversees advertising accounts for corporations like U.S. Bank, Supervalu Pharmacies, and Fazoli's.

As a supervisor in the account services department, Ms. Ervick provides end-to-end service for her clients. From the early strategic-planning stages to the execution and evaluation of integrated brand campaigns, Ervick maintains regular contact with clients and manages their advertising budgets in the development of copy-tested, on-target creative that produces results. "The greatest thing about advertising, and my job in particular, is seeing the results of a well-executed plan," says the account supervisor. "Clients are looking at the bottom line to measure their successes. When the goal is to increase weekly sales by x% and your plan helped sales increase $x+1$%, it's a great feeling." Of course, limited budgets and increasing demands for measurable results put pressure on today's advertising professionals to accomplish the impossible. "Clients expect miracles for minimal budgets and somehow you have to figure out a way to get it done," says Ervick.

Account-services work can be demanding, but the many job-related perks keep things fun and interesting. "There are lots of opportunities for free tickets to a variety of events such as concerts, plays, and sporting events," Ervick remarks. Her responsibility for overseeing the creative process also provides the occasional brush with fame, such as when Ervick's PR efforts centered on Jared Fogle, the Subway spokesperson and weight-loss icon who lost 245 pounds in a single year eating sub sandwiches. "Because of my association with Subway Restaurants, I got to hang out with Jared," says Ervick. On occasion, she even gets the spotlight to herself, such as when clients use her as "talent" in television spots or outdoor advertising.

Darcy Ervick enjoys her career, especially working with clients and being part of an ever-changing, well-respected industry. Asked what advice she could offer to students considering advertising as a profession, the Freedman, Gibson & White account supervisor replies, "Do anything it takes to get in: intern, answer phones, start in the mailroom—whatever it takes." She adds, "It's a difficult industry to get into without experience, but once you're in, soak up all the knowledge you can."

The Planning: Analyzing the Advertising and Integrated Brand Promotion Environment

Successful advertising and integrated brand promotion rely on a clear understanding of how and why consumers make their purchase decisions. Successful campaigns are also rooted in sound marketing strategies and careful research about a brand's market environment. This understanding of the market, sound marketing strategy, and research are brought together in a formal advertising plan. Part Two, "The Planning: Analyzing the Advertising and Integrated Brand Promotion Environment," discusses several important bases for the development of an advertising plan and concludes with a look at planning challenges in international markets.

PART TWO

Advertising, Integrated Brand Promotion, and Consumer Behavior
Chapter 5, "Advertising, Integrated Brand Promotion, and Consumer Behavior," begins with an assessment of the way consumers make product and brand choices. These decisions depend on consumers' involvement and prior experiences with the product in question. This chapter also addresses consumer behavior and advertising from both psychological and sociological points of view. It concludes with a discussion of how culture affects consumer behavior and advertising. This includes a discussion of ads as social texts.

5

Market Segmentation, Positioning, and the Value Proposition
Chapter 6, "Market Segmentation, Positioning, and the Value Proposition," details how these three fundamental planning efforts are developed by an organization. With a combination of audience and competitive information, products and services are developed to provide benefits that are both valued by target customers and different from those of the competition. Finally, the way advertising contributes to communicating value to consumers is explained and modeled.

6

Advertising and Promotion Research
Chapter 7, "Advertising and Promotion Research," discusses the types of research conducted by advertisers and the role information plays in planning an advertising effort. Advertisers do research before messages are prepared, during the preparation process, and after messages are running in the market. The new "account planning process" is also covered in this chapter.

7

Planning Advertising and Integrated Brand Promotion
Chapter 8, "Planning Advertising and Integrated Brand Promotion," explains how formal advertising plans are developed. The inputs to the advertising plan are laid out in detail, and the process of setting advertising objectives—both communications and sales objectives—is described. The methods for setting an advertising budget are presented, including the widely adopted and preferred objective-and-task approach.

8

Advertising Planning: An International Perspective
Chapter 9, "Advertising Planning: An International Perspective," introduces issues related to planning advertising targeted to international audiences. Global forces are creating more accessible markets. In the midst of this trend toward international trade, marketers are redefining the nature and scope of the markets for their goods and services while adjusting to the creative, media, and regulatory challenges of competing across national boundaries.

9

CHAPTER 5

After reading and thinking about this chapter, you will be able to do the following:

Describe the four basic stages of consumer decision making.

Explain how consumers adapt their decision-making processes as a function of involvement and experience.

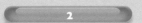

Discuss how advertising may influence consumer behavior through its effects on various psychological states.

Discuss the interaction of culture and advertising.

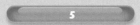

Discuss the role of sociological factors in consumer behavior and advertising response.

Discuss how advertising transmits sociocultural meaning.

Introductory Scenario: Bringing Joy to Japan

The Japanese marketplace is one of the toughest competitive arenas in the world. Japanese consumers are among the most affluent and educated in the world. Giant U.S. corporations such as Procter & Gamble often struggle in this challenging environment. Up until 1995, P&G—maker of dishwashing products such as Dawn, Joy, Ivory, and Cascade—did not sell any dish soap in Japan.[1] Soaps are P&G's core business; P&G aspires to market all its brands around the world; and P&G is one of the most sophisticated companies in the world when it comes to executing multimillion-dollar advertising campaigns. But how to get started in Japan?

P&G used a tried-and-true formula. They sent their managers into the field to talk to consumers and study Japanese dishwashing rituals. They watched the Japanese wash their dishes, videotaped them washing dishes, and talked to them before, during, and after dishwashing. As a result of this careful observation, P&G researchers discovered one critical habit: Japanese homemakers, one after another, squirted out more liquid than was called for, more than was needed, and more than was effective. P&G managers interpreted this as a clear sign of consumers' frustrations with existing products. Implicitly, these consumers wanted a more powerful cleaning liquid, and were trying to get it by simply using more of their current brand. But it wasn't working.

P&G's chemical engineers in Kobe, Japan, went to work on a new, highly concentrated soap formula just for the frustrated Japanese consumer. The marketing pitch would be simple and to the point: A little bit of Joy cleans better, yet is easier on the hands. Encouraged by positive results in test marketing, P&G prepared for a nationwide launch in Japan.

For its advertising campaign P&G settled on a documentary-style TV ad in which a famous Japanese comedian named Junji Takada dropped in on unsuspecting homemakers (see Exhibit 5.1), with his camera crew in tow, to test Joy on the household's dirty dishes. Television ads featured a shot of a grease slick in a sink full of dirty dishes. One squirt of Joy and the grease disappeared. With this simple visual demonstration the ad communicated to consumers that the new Joy was more potent than their old brand. It wasn't long before Joy began racking up impressive market share gains throughout Japan.

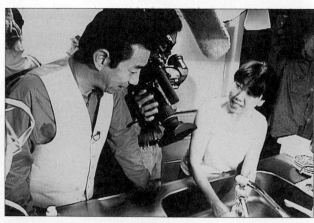

EXHIBIT 5.1

P&G used a documentary-style advertising campaign for its launch of Joy in Japan: on the road in search of greasy dishes. The interviewer is comedian Junji Takada. His celebrity status and sense of humor were important elements in creating likable and persuasive TV commercials.
http://www.pg.com

---

1.   Norihiko Shirouzu, "P&G's Joy Makes an Unlikely Splash in Japan," *Wall Street Journal,* December 10, 1997, B1.

Of course, P&G's Japanese competitors were quick to notice the success of Joy. The Kao Corporation (think of Kao as the P&G of Japan) conducted research to better understand Joy's success. Kao's research showed that more than 70 percent of Joy's users began using it because the TV ads persuaded them that this new brand offered superior performance. Now that's effective advertising! Kao's management admitted: "We had mistakenly assumed Japanese didn't care much about grease-fighting power in dish soaps. The reality was that people were eating more meat and fried food and were frustrated about grease stains on their plastic dishes and storage containers."[2] Kao's lack of understanding of what was important to the customer led to a predictable outcome: Joy became Japan's best-selling dishwashing soap.

Many things must go right for a new brand to enter a crowded marketplace and achieve market leadership, as Joy did in Japan. The product's performance, its packaging, its pricing, and the advertising campaign must work synergistically to achieve this level of success. But success can commonly be traced back to understanding consumers, creating products that address their needs, and executing ad campaigns that persuade consumers that only one brand has just what they're looking for. As with Joy in Japan, insights about the behavior of consumers are crucial to advertising professionals. Before advertisers initiate campaigns for any product or service, they need a thorough understanding of what's important to the customer. This understanding greatly increases the advertiser's chance of affecting purchase behavior.

Chapters 1 through 4 provided important background and perspectives about the business of advertising. With this background in place, we are now ready to begin consideration of how one actually goes about planning for an advertising campaign. Where to begin? How does one get started? As you saw in the preceding success story about marketing dishwashing liquids in Japan, a great place to start is with unique insights about your consumers.

Consumer behavior is defined as the entire broad spectrum of things that affect, derive from, or form the context of human consumption. Like all human behavior, the behavior of consumers is complicated, rich, and varied. However, advertisers must make it their job to understand consumers if they want to experience sustained success in creating effective advertising. Sometimes this understanding comes in the form of comprehensive research efforts; other times in the form of years of experience and implicit theories; other times in the form of blind, dumb luck (rarely attributed as such). However this understanding comes about, it is a key factor for advertising success.

This chapter summarizes the concepts and frameworks we believe are most helpful in trying to understand consumer behavior. We will describe consumer behavior and attempt to explain it, in its incredible diversity, from two different perspectives. The first portrays consumers as reasonably systematic decision makers who seek to maximize the benefits they derive from their purchases. The second views consumers as active interpreters (meaning-makers) of advertising, whose membership in various cultures, societies, and communities significantly affects their interpretation and response to advertising. These two perspectives are different ways of looking at the exact same people and the exact same behaviors. Though different in essential assumptions, both of these perspectives offer something valuable to the task of actually getting the work of advertising done.

The point is that no one perspective can adequately explain consumer behavior. Consumers are psychological, social, cultural, historical, and economical at the same time. For example, suppose a sociologist and a psychologist both saw someone buying a car. The psychologist might explain this behavior in terms of attitudes, decision criteria, and the like, while the sociologist would probably explain it in terms of the buyer's social environment and circumstances (that is, income, housing conditions, social class, the social value or "cultural capital" the brand afforded, and so

2.   Ibid.

on). Both explanations may be valid, but each is incomplete. The bottom line is that all consumer behavior is complex and multifaceted. Why you or any other consumer buys a movie ticket rather than a lottery ticket, or Pepsi rather than Coke, or KFC rather than Wendy's, is a function of psychological, economic, sociological, anthropological, historical, textual, and other forces. No single explanation is sufficient. With this in mind, we offer two basic perspectives on consumer behavior.

Perspective One: The Consumer as Decision Maker.

One way to view consumer behavior is as a logical, sequential process culminating with the individual's reaping a set of benefits from a product or service that satisfies that person's perceived needs. In this basic view, we can think of individuals as purposeful decision makers who take matters a step at a time. All consumption episodes might then be conceived as a sequence of four basic stages:

1. Need recognition
2. Information search and alternative evaluation
3. Purchase
4. Postpurchase use and evaluation

The Consumer Decision-Making Process. A brief discussion of what typically happens at each stage will give us a foundation for understanding consumers, and it can also illuminate opportunities for developing powerful advertising.

EXHIBIT 5.2

Every season has its holidays, and with those holidays come a particular array of consumption needs. How many jellybean flavors can you name? Hint: ham is definitely not one of them.

Need Recognition. The consumption process begins when people perceive a need. A **need state** arises when one's desired state of affairs differs from one's actual state of affairs. Need states are accompanied by a mental discomfort or anxiety that motivates action; the severity of this discomfort can be widely variable depending on the genesis of the need. For example, the need state that arises when one runs out of toothpaste would involve very mild discomfort for most people, whereas the need state that accompanies the breakdown of one's automobile on a dark and deserted highway in Minnesota in mid-February can approach true desperation.

One way advertising works is to point to and thereby activate needs that will motivate consumers to buy a product or service. For instance, in the fall, advertisers from product categories as diverse as autos, snowblowers, and footwear roll out predictions for another severe winter and encourage consumers to prepare themselves before it's too late. Every change of season brings new needs, large and small, and advertisers are always at the ready. The coming of spring is typically a cause for celebration, which for some will include Starburst jellybeans (per Exhibit 5.2), along with a delicious Honeybaked Ham for Easter dinner. Isn't life juicy?

Many factors can influence the need states of consumers. For instance, Maslow's hierarchy of needs suggests that a consumer's level of affluence can have a dramatic impact on the types of needs he or she might perceive as relevant. The less fortunate are concerned with fundamental needs, such as food and shelter; more-affluent consumers may fret over which new piece of Williams-Sonoma kitchen gadgetry or other accoutrement to place in their uptown condo. The former's needs are predominantly for physiological survival and basic comfort, while the latter's may have more to do with seeking to validate personal accomplishments and derive status and recognition through consumption. While income clearly matters in this regard, it would be a mistake to believe that the poor have no aesthetic concerns, or that the rich are always oblivious to the need for basic essentials. The central point is that a variety of needs can be fulfilled through consumption, and it is reasonable to suggest that consumers are looking to satisfy needs when they buy products or services.

Products and services should provide benefits that fulfill consumers' needs; hence, one of the advertiser's primary jobs is to make the connection between the two for the consumer. Benefits come in many forms. Some are more functional—that is, they derive from the more objective performance characteristics of a product or service. Convenience, reliability, nutritiousness, durability, and energy efficiency are descriptors that refer to **functional benefits.**

Some day soon, he'll have a superhero ... a seat on the bus, and a new best friend.

Now, while you can, Johnson's Baby him.

Johnson's Baby Bath: still the mildest baby bath you can buy. And now the number one choice of hospitals. Today, teach him the meaning of gentle, with Johnson's Baby Bath. The mildest you can buy, it's clinically proven as gentle to his eyes as pure water—yet cleans far better than water ever could. It's hypoallergenic and carefully pH-balanced, too. No wonder it's the number one choice of hospitals. He'll grow up soon enough. For now, just Johnson's Baby him.

Protect them.
Shelter them.
Johnson's Baby them.

EXHIBIT 5.3

All parents want to be good to their child. This ad promises both functional benefits and emotional rewards for diligent parents.
http://www.jnj.com

Consumers may also choose products that provide **emotional benefits;** these are not typically found in some tangible feature or objective characteristic of a product. Emotional benefits are more subjective and may be perceived differently from one consumer to the next. Products and services help consumers feel pride, avoid guilt, relieve fear, and experience intense pleasure. These are powerful consumption motives that advertisers often try to activate. Can you find the emotional benefits promised in Exhibit 5.3?

Advertisers must develop a keen appreciation for the kinds of benefits that consumers derive from their brands. Even within the same product category, the benefits promised may vary widely. For instance, as shown in Exhibit 5.4, the makers of Colgate Total portray their toothpaste as the epitome of good hygiene. Twelve-hour protection from nasty bacteria is the functional benefit promised by Colgate. Conversely, for Crest Whitening Expressions, shown in Exhibit 5.5, the pictures speak for themselves. Here the benefit promise is an invigorating usage experience and a beautiful smile. Toothpaste is all about looking and feeling good. These dramatically disparate ads simply illustrate that consumers will look for different kinds a benefits, even in a simple product category like toothpaste. To create advertising that resonates with your consumers, you better have a good handle on the benefits they are, or could be, looking for.

Information Search and Alternative Evaluation. Given that a consumer has recognized a need, it is often not obvious what would be the best way to satisfy that need. For example, if you have a fear of being trapped in a blizzard in upstate New York, a condo on Miami Beach may be a much better solution than a Jeep or new snow tires. Need recognition simply sets in motion a process that may involve an extensive information search and careful evaluation of alternatives

Strange. It's only breakfast and your toothpaste has already called it a day.

Unless you use Colgate Total. Most toothpastes can't fight plaque after you eat or drink,* when teeth become more vulnerable to bacteria. But Colgate Total is different. Its unique formula has an antibacterial ingredient that attaches to teeth to protect for 12 hours. Even after eating and drinking.

Colgate Total

12-Hour Protection

*Most toothpastes can't affect plaque after brushing.

EXHIBIT 5.4

Functional benefits rule in this ad. Colgate Total keeps on working, even after a big plate of pancakes!

EXHIBIT 5.5

Has brushing your teeth ever been this exciting? If not, perhaps you could use a little Cinnamon Rush!

prior to purchase. Of course, during this search and evaluation, there are numerous opportunities for the advertiser to influence the final decision.

Once a need has been recognized, information for the decision is acquired through an internal or external search. The consumer's first option for information is to draw on personal experience and prior knowledge. This **internal search** for information may be all that is required. When a consumer has considerable prior experience with the products in question, attitudes about the alternatives may be well established and determine choice, as is suggested in the ad for Campbell's soup shown in Exhibit 5.6.

An internal search can also tap into information that has accumulated in one's memory as a result of repeated advertising exposures. Affecting people's beliefs about a brand before their actual use of it, or merely establishing the existence of the brand in the consumer's consciousness, is a critical function of advertising. As noted in Chapter 1, the purpose of delayed response advertising is to generate recognition of and a favorable predisposition toward a brand so that when consumers enter into search mode, that brand will be one they immediately consider as a possible solution to their needs. If the consumer has not used a brand previously and has no recollection that it even exists, then that brand probably will not be the brand of choice.

It is certainly plausible that an internal search will not turn up enough information to yield a decision. The consumer then proceeds with an **external search.** An external search involves visiting retail stores to examine the alternatives, seeking input from friends and relatives about their experiences with the products in ques-

EXHIBIT 5.6

For a cultural icon such as Campbell's soup, an advertiser can assume that consumers have some prior knowledge. Here the advertiser seeks to enhance that knowledge to lead people to use more canned soup. http://www.campbellsoups.com

tion, or perusing professional product evaluations furnished in various publications such as *Consumer Reports* or *Car and Driver*. In addition, when consumers are in an active information-gathering mode, they may be receptive to detailed, informative advertisements delivered through any of the print media, or they may deploy a shopping agent or a search engine to scour the Internet for the best deal.

During an internal or external search, consumers are not merely gathering information for its own sake. They have some need that is propelling the process, and their goal is to make a decision that yields benefits. The consumer searches and is simultaneously forming attitudes about possible alternatives. This is the alternative-evaluation component of the decision process, and it is another key phase for the advertiser to target.

Alternative evaluation will be structured by the consumer's **consideration set** and evaluative criteria. The consideration set is the subset of brands from a particular product category that becomes the focal point of the consumer's evaluation. Most product categories contain too many brands for all to be considered, so the consumer finds some way to focus the search and evaluation. For example, for autos, consumers may consider only cars priced less than $20,000, or only cars that have antilock brakes, or only foreign-made cars, or only cars sold at dealerships within a five-mile radius of their work or home. A critical function of advertising is to make consumers aware of the brand and keep them aware so that the brand has a chance to be part of the consideration set. Virtually all ads try to do this.

As the search-and-evaluation process proceeds, consumers form evaluations based on the characteristics or attributes that brands in their consideration set have in common. These product attributes or performance characteristics are referred to

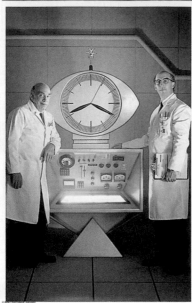

RECENTLY, SCIENTISTS IN BRAUNSCHWEIG, GERMANY, SET THE ATOMIC CLOCK BACK ONE FULL SECOND.

OUR FLIGHT SCHEDULES HAVE BEEN ADJUSTED ACCORDINGLY.

Every 365 days, more or less, the earth completes another revolution around the sun. It is a ritual as predictable as it is beautiful.

And for the last three of those revolutions, almost as predictably, Northwest has been the #1 on-time airline among the four largest U.S. carriers.

(Based on U.S. Department of Transportation consumer reports for the years 1990, 1991 and 1992.)

This sort of record should be expected from an airline that has made punctuality a sort of corporate mission.

For information or reservations, call your travel agent or Northwest at 1-800-225-2525.

And you'll soon understand why, in Switzerland, they say that a good watch "should run like a Northwest flight."

NORTHWEST AIRLINES
Some People Just Know How to Fly

EXHIBIT 5.7

Advertisers must know the relevant evaluative criteria for their products. For an airline, on-time arrival is certainly an important matter.
http://www.nwa.com

---

as **evaluative criteria.** Evaluative criteria differ from one product category to the next and can include many factors, such as price, texture, warranty terms, service support, color, scent, or carb content. As Exhibit 5.7 suggests, one traditional evaluative criterion for judging airlines has been on-time arrivals.

It is critical for advertisers to have as complete an understanding as possible of the evaluative criteria that consumers use to make their buying decisions. They must also know how consumers rate their brand in comparison with others from the consideration set. Understanding consumers' evaluative criteria furnishes a powerful starting point for any advertising campaign and will be examined in more depth later in the chapter.

Purchase. At this third stage, purchase occurs. The consumer has made a decision, and a sale is made. Great, right? Well, to a point. As nice as it is to make a sale, things are far from over at the point of sale. In fact, it would be a big mistake to view purchase as the culmination of the decision-making process. No matter what the product or service category, the consumer is likely to buy from it again in the future. So, what happens after the sale is very important to advertisers.

Postpurchase Use and Evaluation. The goal for marketers and advertisers must not be simply to generate a sale; it must be to create satisfied and, ultimately, loyal customers. The data to support this position are quite astounding. Research shows that about 65 percent of the average company's business comes from its present, satisfied customers, and that 91 percent of dissatisfied customers will never buy again from the company that disappointed them.[3] Thus, consumers' evaluations of products in use become a major determinant of which brands will be in the consideration set the next time around.

Customer satisfaction derives from a favorable postpurchase experience. It may develop after a single use, but more likely it will require sustained use. Advertising can play an important role in inducing customer satisfaction by creating appropriate expectations for a brand's performance, or by helping the consumer who has already bought the advertised brand to feel good about doing so.

Advertising plays an important role in alleviating the **cognitive dissonance** that can occur after a purchase. Cognitive dissonance is the anxiety or regret that lingers after a difficult decision. Often, rejected alternatives have attractive features that lead people to second-guess their own decisions. If the goal is to generate satisfied customers, this dissonance must be resolved in a way that leads consumers to conclude that they did make the right decision after all. Purchasing high-cost items or choosing from categories that include many desirable and comparable brands can yield high levels of cognitive dissonance.

When dissonance is expected, it makes good sense for the advertiser to reassure buyers with detailed information about its brands. Postpurchase reinforcement programs might involve direct mail, e-mail, or other types of personalized contacts with

---

3.   Terry G. Vavra, *Aftermarketing: How to Keep Customers for Life through Relationship Marketing* (Homewood, IL.: Business One Irwin, 1992), 13.

the customer. This postpurchase period represents a great opportunity for the advertiser to have the undivided attention of the consumer and to provide information and advice about product use that will increase customer satisfaction. That's the name of the game: customer satisfaction. Without satisfied customers, we can't have a successful business.

② Four Modes of Consumer Decision Making. As you may be thinking about now, consumers aren't always deliberate and systematic; sometimes they are hasty, impulsive, or even irrational. The search time that people put into their purchases can vary dramatically for different types of products. Would you give the purchase of a toothbrush the same amount of effort as the purchase of a new MP3 player? Probably not, unless you've been chastised by your dentist recently. Why is that T-shirt you bought at a Dave Matthews concert more important to you than the brand of orange juice you had for breakfast this morning? Does buying a Valentine's gift from Victoria's Secret create different feelings than buying a newspaper for your father?

EXHIBIT 5.8

The emotional appeal in this Casio ad is just one of the many involvement devices. The play on water resistance also increases involvement as the reader perceives the double meaning. Describe how these devices work. How does Casio use involvement devices at its Web site, http://www.casio -usa.com, to encourage visitors to further explore its products on the site? Describe the involvement devices used by competitor Timex at its home page, http://www .timex.com.

When you view a TV ad for car batteries, do you carefully memorize the information being presented so that it will be there to draw on the next time you're evaluating the brands in your consideration set?

Let's face it; some purchase decisions are just more engaging than others. In the following sections we will elaborate on the view of consumer as decision maker by explaining four decision-making modes that help advertisers appreciate the richness and complexity of consumer behavior. These four modes are determined by a consumer's involvement and prior experiences with the product or service in question.

Sources of Involvement. To accommodate the complexity of consumption decisions, those who study consumer behavior typically talk about the involvement level of any particular decision. **Involvement** is the degree of perceived relevance and personal importance accompanying the choice of a certain product or service within a particular context. Many factors have been identified as potential contributors to an individual's level of involvement with a consumption decision.[4] People can develop interests and avocations in many different areas, such as cooking, photography, pet ownership, or exercise and fitness. Such ongoing personal interests can enhance involvement levels in a variety of product categories. Also, any time a great deal of risk is associated with a purchase—perhaps as a result of the high price of the item, or because the consumer will have to live with the decision for a long period of time—one should also expect elevated involvement.

Consumers can also derive important symbolic meaning from products and brands. Ownership or use of some products can help people reinforce some aspect of their self-image or make a statement to other people who are important to them. If a purchase carries great symbolic and real consequences—such as choosing the right gift for a special someone on Valentine's Day—it will be highly involving.

Some purchases can also tap into deep emotional concerns or motives. For example, many marketers, from Wal-Mart to Marathon Oil, have solicited consumers with an appeal to their patriotism. The ad for Casio watches (a Japanese product) in Exhibit 5.8 demonstrates that a product doesn't have to be American to wrap itself in the Stars and Stripes. And from the Global Issues box it should be

4. Michael R. Solomon, *Consumer Behavior* (Upper Saddle River, N.J.: Pearson/Prentice Hall, 2004), ch. 4.

clear that patriotic appeals resonate with consumers around the world, not just the United States. The passions of patriotism can have significant impact on many things, including a person's level of involvement with a consumption decision.

GLOBAL ISSUES

Validating Global Brands in China

In a world that has become increasingly sensitive to national pride and prejudice, it is always a salient issue to consider how your import will be received in another country, and whether or not your "foreign brand" will be considered friend or foe. Savvy global brand builders typically take steps to validate their presence by supporting high-profile events that tap into the passions of patriotism. Recent examples from China demonstrate the effectiveness of this strategy.

For example, when China received the highly coveted honor of hosting the 2008 Olympic games, McDonald's was there front and center to celebrate this proud moment with the Chinese. McDonald's, aspiring to be a hip hangout for Chinese teens, invited customers to watch the Olympic announcement ceremony on TVs in its restaurants, and the following day offered free hamburgers as part of the celebration of China's victory. Similarly, Adidas helped the Chinese commemorate their qualification into the World Cup soccer tournament by launching an ad campaign featuring China's football hero, Fan Zhiyi. The ad also highlighted people from all over China wearing the Chinese team's official Adidas-sponsored shirt, but each with their own unique number ranging from 100 to 1.2 billion. The idea here was to promote a message of inclusion and pride, suggesting that each and every person shared in China's great accomplishment. Of course, that sharing is more self-evident for any person wearing some item of clothing sporting the Adidas logo.

Global brands like Nike, Coke, Disney, Wrigley, Adidas, and McDonald's have fared well in China. One reason is because of their skillful use of patriotic themes. But times will change. As China's economy matures, and local brand builders in China become more sophisticated and establish their own reputations for quality, competition will become fierce. And who knows . . . one day soon you may find Jianlibao cola or Li Ning athletic gear marketed in a store near you, using an appeal to your national pride. After all, turnabout is fair play when it comes to global brand building.

Sources: "Just Do It, Chinese-Style," *The Economist*, August 2, 2003, 59; and "Chinese Youth Aren't Patriotic Purchasers," *Advertising Age*, January 5, 2004, 6.

Involvement levels vary not only among product categories for any given individual, but also among individuals for any given product category. For example, some pet owners will feed their pets only the expensive canned products that look and smell like people food. IAMS, whose ad is featured in Exhibit 5.9, understands this and made a special premium dog food for consumers who think of their pets as humans. Many other pet owners, however, are perfectly happy with the 50-pound, economy-size bag of dry dog food.

Now we will use the ideas of involvement and prior experience to help conceive four different types of consumer decision making. These four modes are shown in Exhibit 5.10. Any specific consumption decision is based on a high or low level of prior experience with the product or service in question, and a high or low level of involvement. This yields the four modes of decision making: (1) extended problem solving; (2) limited problem solving; (3) habit or variety seeking; and (4) brand loyalty. Each is described in the following sections.

Extended Problem Solving. When consumers are inexperienced in a particular consumption setting yet find the setting highly involving, they are likely to engage in **extended problem solving.** In this mode, consumers go through a deliberate decision-making process that begins with explicit need recognition, proceeds with careful internal and external search, continues through alternative evaluation and purchase, and ends with a lengthy postpurchase evaluation.

Examples of extended problem solving come with decisions such as choosing a home or a diamond ring, as suggested by Exhibit 5.11. These products are expensive, are publicly evaluated, and can carry a considerable amount of risk in terms of making an uneducated decision. Buying one's first new automobile and choosing a college are two other consumption settings that may require extended problem solving. Extended problem solving is the exception, not the rule.

Limited Problem Solving. In this decision-making mode, experience and involvement are both low. **Limited problem solving** is a more common mode of

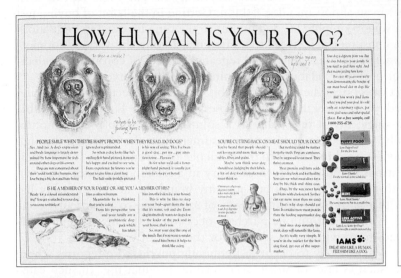

EXHIBIT 5.9

When people think of their pets as human beings, they take their selection of pet food very seriously. IAMS offers serious pet food for the serious dog owner. http://www.iams.com

EXHIBIT 5.11

High involvement and low experience typically yield extended problem solving. Buying an engagement ring is a perfect example of this scenario. This ad offers lots of advice for the extended problem solver. http://www.adiamondisforever.com

EXHIBIT 5.10

Four modes of consumer decision making.

	High Involvement	**Low Involvement**
Low Experience	Extended problem solving	Limited problem solving
High Experience	Brand loyalty	Habit or variety seeking

decision making. In this mode, a consumer is less systematic in his or her decision making. The consumer has a new problem to solve, but it is not a problem that is interesting or engaging, so the information search is limited to simply trying the first brand encountered. For example, let's say a young couple have just brought home a new baby, and suddenly they perceive a very real need for disposable diapers. At the hospital they received complimentary trial packs of several products, including Pampers disposables. They try the Pampers, find them an acceptable solution to their messy new problem, and take the discount coupon that came with the sample to their local grocery, where they buy several packages. In the limited problem-solving mode, we often see consumers simply seeking adequate solutions to mundane problems. It is also a mode in which just trying a brand or two may be the most efficient way of collecting information about one's options. Of course, smart marketers realize that trial offers can be a preferred means of collecting information, and they facilitate trial of their brands through free samples, inexpensive "trial sizes," or discount coupons.

Habit or Variety Seeking. Habit and variety seeking occur in settings where a decision isn't involving and a consumer repurchases from the category over and over again. In terms of sheer numbers, habitual purchases are probably the most common decision-making mode. Consumers find a brand of laundry detergent that suits their needs, they run out of the product, and they buy it again. The cycle repeats itself many times per year in an almost mindless fashion. Getting in the habit of buying just one brand can be a way to simplify life and minimize the time invested in "nuisance" purchases. When a consumer perceives little difference among the various competitive brands, it is easier to buy the same brand repeatedly. A lot of consumption decisions are boring but necessary. Habits help us minimize the inconvenience.

In some product categories where a buying habit would be expected, an interesting phenomenon called variety seeking may be observed instead. Remember, **habit** refers to buying a single brand repeatedly as a solution to a simple consumption problem. This can be very tedious, and some consumers fight the boredom through variety seeking. **Variety seeking** refers to the tendency of consumers to switch their selection among various brands in a given category in a seemingly random pattern. This is not to say that a consumer will buy just any brand; he or she probably has two to five brands that all provide similar levels of satisfaction to a particular consumption problem. However, from one purchase occasion to the next, the individual will switch brands from within this set, just for the sake of variety.

Variety seeking is most likely to occur in frequently purchased categories where sensory experience, such as taste or smell, accompanies product use. In such categories, no amount of ad spending can overcome the consumer's basic desire for fresh sensory experience.[5] Satiation occurs after repeated use and leaves the consumer looking for a change of pace. Product categories such as soft drinks and alcoholic beverages, snack foods, breakfast cereals, and fast food are prone to variety seeking, so marketers in these categories must constantly be introducing new possibilities to consumers to feed their craving for variety. The new line of salads from McDonald's featured in Exhibit 5.12 looks like a good match for the carb-conscious variety seeker.

Brand Loyalty. The final decision-making mode is typified by high involvement and rich prior experience. In this mode, **brand loyalty** becomes a major consideration in the purchase decision. Consumers demonstrate brand loyalty when they repeatedly purchase a single brand as their choice to fulfill a specific need. In one sense, brand-loyal purchasers may look as if they have developed a simple buying habit; however, it is important to distinguish brand loyalty from simple habit. Brand loyalty is based on highly favorable attitudes toward the brand and a conscious commitment to find this brand each time the consumer purchases from this category. Conversely, habits are merely consumption simplifiers that are not based on deeply held convictions. Habits can be disrupted through a skillful combination of advertising and sales promotions. Spending advertising dollars to persuade truly brand-loyal consumers to try an alternative can be a great waste of resources.

Brands such as Sony, Starbucks, eBay, Apple, Gerber, Oakley, Coke, Heineken, IKEA, Calvin Klein, Tide, Harley-Davidson, Puma, FedEx, JBL, and Bath & Body

Calories: 250
Taste: 800

"Okay, so I'm crazed at work, I squeeze in a workout and then attempt a social life. That doesn't leave much time to eat. Let alone research quick, wholesome meal options. What's a girl to do? I mean, time I don't have, but I've still got an appetite."

Sounds like someone's a perfect fit for McDonald's® new Grilled Chicken Caesar Premium Salad. Mixed baby greens, warm grilled chicken, and total calories are just 250 when you add Newman's Own® all-natural low fat Balsamic Vinaigrette dressing. Problem solved.

At participating McDonald's. ©2003 McDonald's Corporation.
Sodium for Grilled Chicken Caesar is 680 mg. Sodium for low fat Balsamic Vinaigrette is 730 mg.

i'm lovin' it.™

EXHIBIT 5.12

New menu items are a must for most fast-food businesses and become a focal point in their advertising. Out with the old and in with the new is a fact of life for menu planners at McDonald's.

5.   Shirley Leung, "Fast-Food Firms Big Budgets Don't Buy Consumer Loyalty," *Wall Street Journal,* July 24, 2003, B4.

Works have inspired loyal consumers. Brand loyalty is something that any marketer aspires to have, but in a world filled with more-savvy consumers and endless product proliferation, it is becoming harder and harder to attain. Brand loyalty may emerge because the consumer perceives that one brand simply outperforms all others in providing some critical functional benefit. For example, the harried business executive may have grown loyal to FedEx's overnight delivery service as a result of repeated satisfactory experiences with FedEx—and as a result of FedEx's advertising that has repeatedly posed the question, "Why fool around with anyone else?"

Perhaps even more important, brand loyalty can be due to the emotional benefits that accompany certain brands. One of the strongest indicators for brand loyalty has to be the tendency on the part of some loyal consumers to tattoo their bodies with the insignia of their favorite brand. While statistics are not kept on this sort of thing, it would be reasonable to speculate that the worldwide leader in brand-name tattoos is Harley-Davidson. What accounts for Harley's fervent following? Is Harley's brand loyalty simply a function of performing better than its many competitors? Or does a Harley rider derive some deep emotional benefit from taking that big bike out on the open road and leaving civilization far behind? To understand loyalty for a brand such as Harley, one must turn to the emotional benefits, such as feelings of pride, kinship, and nostalgia that attend "the ride." Owning a Harley—perhaps complete with tattoo—makes a person feel different and special. Harley ads are designed to reaffirm the deep emotional appeal of this product.

Strong emotional benefits might be expected from consumption decisions that we classify as highly involving, and they are major determinants of brand loyalty. Indeed, with so many brands in the marketplace, it is becoming harder and harder to create loyalty for one's brand through functional benefits alone. To break free of this brand-parity problem and provide consumers with enduring reasons to become or stay loyal, advertisers are investing more and more effort in communicating the emotional benefits that might be derived from brands in categories as diverse as greeting cards (Hallmark—"When you care enough to send the very best") and vacation hot spots (Las Vegas—"What happens here, stays here.")

In addition, as suggested by the Creativity box, many companies are exploring ways to use the Internet to create dialogue and community with customers. To do this, one must look for means to connect with customers at an emotional level.

3 Key Psychological Processes. To complete our consideration of the consumer as a thoughtful decision maker, one key issue remains. We need to examine the explicit psychological consequences of advertising. What does advertising leave in the minds of consumers that ultimately may influence their behavior? For those of you who have taken psychology courses, many of the topics in this section will sound familiar.

As we noted earlier in the chapter, a good deal of advertising is designed to ensure recognition and create favorable predispositions toward a brand so that as consumers search for solutions to their problems, they will think of the brand immediately. The goal of any delayed-response ad is to affect some psychological state that will subsequently influence a purchase.

Two ideas borrowed from social psychology are usually the center of attention when discussing the psychological aspects of advertising. First is attitude. **Attitude** is defined as an overall evaluation of any object, person, or issue that varies along a continuum, such as favorable to unfavorable or positive to negative. Attitudes are learned, and if they are based on substantial experience with the object or issue in question, they can be held with great conviction. Attitudes make our lives easier because they simplify decision making; that is, when faced with a choice among several alternatives, we do not need to process new information or analyze the merits of the alternatives. We merely select the alternative we think is the most favorable.

We all possess attitudes on thousands of topics, ranging from political candidates to underage drinking. Marketers and advertisers, however, are most interested in one particular class of attitudes—brand attitudes.

Brand attitudes are summary evaluations that reflect preferences for various products and services. The next time you are waiting in a checkout line at the grocery, take a good look at the items in your cart. Those items are a direct reflection of your brand attitudes.

CREATIVITY

Creative Brand Building: Digital Storytelling Unleashes the Power of Emotion

The premise of interactive media seems ideally suited for brand development. After all, *interactive* by definition is a two-way communication between buyer and seller; communication builds relationships, and relationships translate into brand loyalty. Right? Well, the rules of online marketing are far from established, but the Internet may prove to be the most powerful tool ever in creating long-term relationships with brand-conscious consumers. And maybe, just maybe, it can be as simple as asking consumers to tell their own stories. Traditional brand builders such as Coca-Cola, McDonald's, and Ford Motor Company are determined to find out.

Digital StoryTelling (DST)—which combines the glamour and reach of the Internet with the emotional appeal of personal stories—is surely among the most innovative applications of the Web for brand-building purposes. While advertisers have always used stories in an effort to sell their products, this is not business as usual. Unlike conventional mass media, wherein company-created stories are told in an effort to persuade customers, DST seeks to build community around a brand by inviting consumers to share their experiences with the brand. This sharing leads to stories that are much more authentic and interactive than just another TV testimonial.

How does one foster this unique form of storytelling? Any number of ways. Coca-Cola hires the Web equivalent of a TV ad producer to seek out, record, and produce customer stories that are Web-ready. Coke also features the best of these stories at its DST exhibit inside its Atlanta headquarters. According to Coke's chief DST archivist, "You simply can't buy advertising as emotionally potent as a good customer story. DST helped us pop the lid on a lot of emotional ties that we just hadn't been able to capture in our marketing before the Internet." With no real prospects of differentiating its brand on the basis of functional benefits, it's easy to understand the enthusiasm of Coke execs for unleashing emotional ties.

But what is the basis for these summary evaluations? Where do brand attitudes come from? Here we need a second idea from social psychology. To understand why people hold certain attitudes, we need to assess their specific beliefs. **Beliefs** represent the knowledge and feelings a person has accumulated about an object or issue. They can be logical and factual in nature, or biased and self-serving. A person might believe that the Mini Cooper is cute, that garlic consumption promotes weight loss, and that pet owners are lonely people. For that person, all these beliefs are valid and can serve as a basis for attitudes toward Minis, garlic, and pets.

If we know a person's beliefs, it is usually possible to infer attitude. Consider the two consumers' beliefs about Cadillac summarized in Exhibit 5.13. From their beliefs, we might suspect that one of these consumers is a prospective Cadillac owner, while the other will need a dramatic change in beliefs to ever make Cadillac part of his or her consideration set. It follows that the brand attitudes of the two individuals are at opposite ends of the favorableness continuum.

Sources: "Tell Me a (Digital) Story," *BusinessWeek E.Biz*, May 15, 2000, EB92–EB94 and http://www2.coca-cola.com/heritage/stories/.

EXHIBIT 5.13

An example of two consumers' beliefs about Caddies.

Consumer 1	Consumer 2
Cadillacs are clumsy to drive.	Cadillacs are luxurious.
Cadillacs are expensive.	Cadillacs have great resale value.
Cadillacs are gas guzzlers.	Cadillacs have OnStar.
Cadillacs are large.	Cadillacs TV ads rock!
Cadillacs are for senior citizens.	Cadillacs aren't what they used to be.

Changing consumers' beliefs is never an easy task. And the challenge is always made more complex by the fact that your best competition will only keep getting better. So for Cadillac the question becomes, even with a series of dramatic improvements, can they ever catch the Ultimate Driving Machine? It's the job of everyone who works for BMW to make sure that they don't. . . .

You may be aware that in recent years General Motors has spent billions of dollars on its Cadillac brand in a determined effort to take on Japanese and German models like the exquisite BMW 5 Series, which is exalted on the Toronto billboard in Exhibit 5.14. Simply put, the folks at General Motors will need to change a lot of consumers' beliefs about Cadillac if they are to have success in regaining market share from the likes of Lexus and BMW. Among other things, our beliefs determine the cars we drive (subject of course to the limitations of our pocketbooks).

People have many beliefs about various features and attributes of products and brands. Some beliefs are more important than others in determining a person's final evaluation of a brand. Typically, a small number of beliefs—on the order of five to nine—underlie brand attitudes.[6] These beliefs are the critical determinants of an attitude and are referred to as **salient beliefs.**

Clearly, we would expect the number of salient beliefs to vary between product categories. The loyal Harley owner who proudly displays a tattoo will have many more salient beliefs about his bike than he has about his brand of shaving cream. Also, salient beliefs can be modified, replaced, or extinguished. Exhibit 5.15 is a two-page ad from a Sears campaign designed to modify the salient beliefs of its target audience.

Belief change is a common goal in advertising. With its "Softer Side" campaign, Sears attempted to change beliefs about its stores as a source for women's fashions. http://www.sears.com

Since belief shaping and reinforcement can be one of the principal goals of advertising, it should come as no surprise that advertisers make belief assessment a focal point in their attempts to understand consumer behavior.

6.   Icek Ajzen and Martin Fishbein, *Understanding Attitudes and Predicting Social Behavior* (Englewood Cliffs, N.J.: Prentice Hall, 1980), 63.

Multi-Attribute Attitude Models (MAAMS). **Multi-attribute attitude models (MAAMS)** provide a framework and a set of research procedures for collecting information from consumers to assess their salient beliefs and attitudes about competitive brands. Here we will highlight the basic components of a MAAMs analysis and illustrate how such an analysis can benefit the advertiser.

Any MAAMs analysis will feature four fundamental components:

- *Evaluative criteria* are the attributes or performance characteristics that consumers use in comparing competitive brands. In pursuing a MAAMs analysis, an advertiser must identify all evaluative criteria relevant to its product category.
- *Importance weights* reflect the priority that a particular evaluative criterion receives in the consumer's decision-making process. Importance weights can vary dramatically from one consumer to the next; for instance, some people will merely want good taste from their bowl of cereal, while others will be more concerned about fat and fiber content.
- The *consideration set* is that group of brands that represents the real focal point for the consumer's decision. For example, the potential buyer of a luxury sedan might be focusing on Acura, BMW, and Lexus. These and comparable brands would be featured in a MAAMs analysis. Cadillac could have a model, such as its new STS sedan, that aspired to be part of this consideration set, leading General Motors to conduct a MAAMs analysis featuring the STS and its foreign rivals. Conversely, it would be silly for GM to include the Chevy Malibu in a MAAMs analysis with this set of luxury/performance imports.
- *Beliefs* represent the knowledge and feelings that a consumer has about various brands. In a MAAMs analysis, beliefs about each brand's performance on all relevant evaluative criteria are assessed. Beliefs can be matters of fact—a 12-ounce Pepsi has 150 calories; a 12-ounce Coke Classic has 140—or highly subjective—the Cadillac XLR roadster is the sleekest, sexiest car on the street. It is common for beliefs to vary widely among consumers.

In conducting a MAAMs analysis, we must specify the relevant evaluative criteria for our category, as well as our direct competitors. We then go to consumers and let them tell us what's important and how our brand fares against the competition on the various evaluative criteria. The information generated from this survey research will give us a better appreciation for the salient beliefs that underlie brand attitudes, and it may suggest important opportunities for changing our marketing or advertising to yield more favorable brand attitudes.

Three basic attitude-change strategies can be developed from the MAAMs framework. First, a MAAMs analysis may reveal that consumers do not have an accurate perception of the relative performance of our brand on an important evaluative criterion. For example, consumers may perceive that Crest is far and away the best brand of toothpaste for fighting cavities, when in fact all brands with a fluoride additive perform equally well on cavity prevention. Correcting this misperception could become our focal point if we compete with Crest.

Second, a MAAMs analysis could uncover that our brand is perceived as the best performer on an evaluative criterion that most consumers do not view as very important. The task for advertising in this instance would be to persuade consumers that what our brand offers (say, lower carb content than any other light beer) is more important than they had thought previously.

Third, the MAAMs framework may lead to the conclusion that the only way to improve attitudes toward our brand would be through the introduction of a new attribute to be featured in our advertising. In some instances we could just add that attribute or feature (e.g., 10X, through the lens, optical zoom) to an existing product (e.g., our Olympus digital camera), and make that the centerpiece in our next ad campaign. Alternatively, if the attribute in question has emerged to be highly valued by 30 million Americans, we may want to reinvent an entire product line to feature this critical attribute. That's exactly what Unilever Bestfoods (makers of Ragu, Lip-

INTRODUCING
DELICIOUS NEW OPTIONS
YOU CAN COUNT ON.

CARB OPTIONS™ STEAK SAUCE
1 G CARBS 5 CAL PER SERVING
SEE ALL PRODUCTS >

EXHIBIT 5.16

When fads emerge as major marketplace trends, marketers must respond or risk dramatic erosion in their customer base. Such has been the case in the food business, where carb-consciousness has affected the marketing of everything from peanut butter to steak sauce. Learn more at http://www .carboptions.com.

ton, Skippy and Wish-Bone) decided to do for carb-crazed consumers when it introduced a line of products like the one in Exhibit 5.16.

When marketers use the MAAMs approach, good things can result in terms of more-favorable brand attitudes and improved market share. When marketers carefully isolate key evaluative criteria, bring products to the marketplace that perform well on the focal criteria, and develop ads that effectively shape salient beliefs about the brand, the results can be dramatic—as we saw in the case of Joy in Japan.

Information Processing and Perceptual Defense. At this point you may have the impression that creating effective advertising is really a straightforward exercise. We carefully analyze consumers' beliefs and attitudes, construct ads to address any problems that might be identified, and choose various media to get the word out to our target customers. Yes, it would be very easy if consumers would just pay close attention and believe everything we tell them, and if our competition would kindly stop all of its advertising so that ours would be the only message that consumers had to worry about. Of course, these things aren't going to happen.

Why would we expect to encounter resistance from consumers as we attempt to influence their beliefs and attitudes about our brand? One way to think about this problem is to portray the consumer as an information processor who must advance through a series of stages before our message can have its intended effect. If we are skillful in selecting appropriate media to reach our target, then the consumer must (1) pay attention to the message, (2) comprehend it correctly, (3) accept the message exactly as we intended, and (4) retain the message until it is needed for a purchase decision. Unfortunately, problems can and do occur at any or all of these four stages, completely negating the effect of our advertising campaign.

There are two major obstacles that we must overcome if our message is to have its intended effect. The first—the **cognitive consistency** impetus—stems from the individual consumer. Remember, a person develops and holds beliefs and attitudes for a reason: They help him or her make efficient decisions that yield pleasing outcomes. When a consumer is satisfied with these outcomes, there is really no reason to alter the belief system that generated them (e.g., why bother with a Cadillac if you love your BMW!). New information that challenges existing beliefs can be ignored or disparaged to prevent modification of the present cognitive system. The consumer's desire to maintain cognitive consistency can be a major roadblock for an advertiser that wants to change beliefs and attitudes.

The second obstacle—**advertising clutter**—derives from the context in which ads are processed. Even if a person wanted to, it would be impossible to process and integrate every advertising message that he or she is exposed to each day. Pick up today's newspaper and start reviewing every ad you come across. Will you have time today to read them all? The clutter problem is further magnified by competitive brands making very similar performance claims.[7] Was it Advil, Anacin, Aveda,

---

7.   Clutter creates a variety of problems that compromise the effectiveness of advertising. For instance, research has shown that clutter interferes with basic memory functions, inhibiting a person's ability to keep straight which brands are making what claims. For more details see Anand Kumar and Shanker Krishnan, "Memory Interference in Advertising: A Replication and Extension," *Journal of Consumer Research*, vol. 30 (March 2004), 602–612.

Aleve, Avia, Aflexa, Aveya, Actonel, Motrin, Nuprin, or Tylenol Gelcaps that promised you 12 hours of relief from your headache? (Can you select the brands from this list that aren't a headache remedy?) The simple fact is that each of us is exposed to hundreds of ads each day, and no one has the time or inclination to sort through them all.

Consumers thus employ perceptual defenses to simplify and control their own ad processing. It is important here to see that the consumer is in control, and the advertiser must find some way to engage the consumer if an ad is to have any impact. Of course, the best way to engage consumers is to offer them information about a product or service that will address an active need state. Simply stated, it is difficult to get people to process a message about your headache remedy when they don't have a headache. **Selective attention** is certainly the advertiser's greatest challenge and produces tremendous waste of advertising dollars. Most ads are simply ignored by consumers. They turn the page, change the station, mute the sound, head for the refrigerator, or just daydream or doze off—rather than process the ad.

Advertisers employ a variety of tactics to break through the clutter. Popular music, celebrity spokespersons, sexy models, rapid scene changes, and anything that is novel are devices for combating selective attention. Remember, as we discussed in Chapter 4, advertisers constantly walk that fine line between novel and obnoxious in their never-ending battle for the attention of the consumer. They really don't want to insult you or anyone else; they just want to be noticed. Of course, they often step over the annoyance line.

The battle for consumers' attention poses another dilemma for advertisers. Without attention, there is no chance that an advertiser's message will have its desired impact; however, the provocative, attention-attracting devices used to engage consumers often become the focal point of consumers' ad processing. They remember seeing an ad featuring 27 Elvis Presley impersonators, but they can't recall what brand was being advertised or what claims were being made about the brand. If advertisers must entertain consumers to win their attention, they must also be careful that the brand and message don't get lost in the shuffle.

Let's assume that an ad gets attention and the consumer comprehends its claims correctly. Will acceptance follow and create the enduring change in brand attitude that is desired, or will there be further resistance? If the message is asking the consumer to alter beliefs about the brand, expect more resistance. When the consumer is involved and attentive and comprehends a claim that challenges current beliefs, the cognitive consistency impetus kicks in, and cognitive responses can be expected. **Cognitive responses** are the thoughts that occur to individuals at that exact moment in time when their beliefs and attitudes are being challenged by some form of persuasive communication. Remember, most ads will not provoke enough mental engagement to yield any form of cognitive response, but when they occur, the valence of these responses is critical to the acceptance of one's message. As we shall see in the next section, cognitive responses are one of the main components of an influential framework for understanding the impact of advertising labeled the **elaboration likelihood model (ELM).**

The Elaboration Likelihood Model (ELM). The ELM is another of those ideas that has been borrowed from social psychology and applied to advertising settings.[8] It is a model that pertains to any situation where a persuasive communication is being sent and received, and it has particular relevance in this chapter because it incorporates ideas such as involvement, information processing, cognitive responses, and attitude formation in a single, integrated framework. The basic premise of the

---

8.   For an expanded discussion of these issues, see Richard E. Petty, John T. Cacioppo, Alan J. Strathman, and Joseph R. Priester, "To Think or Not to Think: Exploring Two Routes to Persuasion," in *Persuasion: Psychological Insights and Perspectives,* ed. Sharon Shavitt and Timothy C. Brock (Boston: Allyn & Bacon, 1994), 113–147.

EXHIBIT 5.17

Two routes to attitude change.

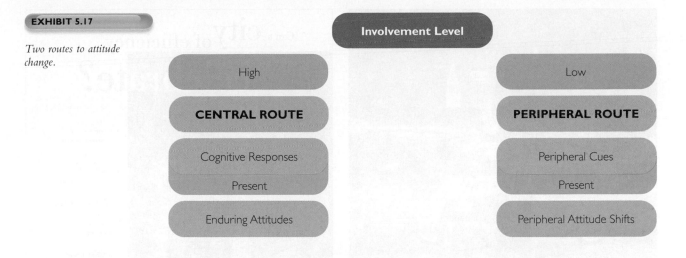

ELM is that to understand how a persuasive communication may affect a person's attitudes, we must consider his or her motivation and ability to elaborate on the message during processing. For most advertising contexts, motivation and ability will be a function of how involved the person is with the consumption decision in question. Involving decisions will result in active, mental elaboration during ad processing, whereas uninvolving decisions will implicate passive ad processing.

As indicated in Exhibit 5.17, the ELM uses the involvement dichotomy in spelling out two unique routes to attitude change. These are typically referred to as the central and peripheral routes to persuasion.

When involvement is high, we should expect the consumer to draw on prior knowledge and experience and scrutinize or elaborate on the message arguments that are central to the advertiser's case. The nature of the individual's effortful thinking about the issues at hand could be judged from the cognitive responses that the ad provokes. These cognitive responses may be positive or negative in tone, and can be reactions to specific claims or any executional element of the ad.

Messages designed to reinforce existing beliefs, or shape beliefs for a new brand that the consumer was unaware of previously, are more likely to win uncritical acceptance. Compare the ads in Exhibits 5.18 and 5.19. In this example, think of the cities Cleveland and Singapore as two brands competing for a tourist's attention (and ultimately, dollars). Each of these ads tries to affect beliefs and attitudes about its focal city. The cognitive consistency impetus that manifests in cognitive responses will work against the city that is more well known, especially when the ad challenges existing beliefs. Which ad do you find more challenging to your beliefs?

If the cognitive responses provoked by one's ad are primarily negative in tone, the ad has backfired: The consumer is maintaining cognitive consistency by disparaging your ad, and that person's negative thoughts are likely to foster negative evaluation of your brand. However, when positive attitudes can be affected through the central route, they have very appealing properties. Because they are based on careful thought, central-route attitudes will (1) come to mind quickly for use in product selection, (2) resist the change efforts of other advertisers, (3) persist in memory without repeated ad exposures, and (4) be excellent predictors of behavior. These properties cannot be expected of attitudes that are formed in the peripheral route.

For low-involvement products, such as batteries or tortilla chips, cognitive responses to advertising claims are not expected. In such situations, attitude formation will often follow a more peripheral route, and peripheral cues become the focal point for judging the ad's impact. **Peripheral cues** refer to features of the ad other than the actual arguments about the brand's performance. They include an attractive

Cities can also engage in persuasive communications. Does this ad present an image of Cleveland that is compatible with your prior beliefs? http://www.travelcleveland.com/ohio

*Singapore's Tourism Board uses this ad to educate readers about its broad cultural diversity, and to tickle their curiosity (*http://www. newasia-singapore.com*). Is Singapore an Asian city? Yes, but with influences from many cultures. The ad invites the reader to break out of a conceptual box, just as the Florida orange growers did with their "Orange juice: It's not just for breakfast anymore" campaign.*

or comical spokesperson, novel imagery, humorous incidents, or a catchy jingle. Any feature of the ad that prompts a pleasant emotional response could be thought of as a peripheral cue.

In the peripheral route the consumer can still learn from an advertisement, but the learning is passive and typically must be achieved by frequent association of the peripheral cue (for example, the Eveready Energizer Bunny) with the brand in question. It has even been suggested that classical conditioning principles might be employed by advertisers to facilitate and accelerate this associative learning process.[9] As consumers learn to associate pleasant feelings and attractive images with a brand, their attitude toward the brand should become more positive.

What do LeAnn Rimes, James Carville, Queen Latifah, Jerry Seinfeld, Mr. Peanut, Jay-Z, Shakira, Junji Takada, Michelin Man, LeBron (a.k.a. King) James, Paige Davis, the Geico Gecko, Missy Elliott, and the song "Instant Karma" by John Lennon have in common? They and hundreds of others like them have been used as peripheral cues in advertising campaigns. When all brands in a category offer similar benefits, the most fruitful avenue for advertising strategy is likely to be the peripheral route, where the advertiser merely tries to maintain positive or pleasant associations with the brand by constantly presenting it with appealing peripheral cues. Of course, peripheral cues can be more than merely cute, with the right ones

9.   For additional discussion of this issue, see Frances K. McSweeney and Calvin Bierley, "Recent Developments in Classical Conditioning," *Journal of Consumer Research*, vol. 11 (September 1984), 619–631.

adding an undeniable level of "hipness" to aging brands.[10] Selecting peripheral cues can be especially important for mature brands in low-involvement categories where the challenge is to keep the customer from getting bored;[11] however, this is an expensive tactic because any gains made along the peripheral route are short-lived. TV air time, lots of repetition, sponsorship fees, and a never-ending search for the freshest, most popular peripheral cues demand huge budgets. When you think of the peripheral route, think of the advertising campaigns for high-profile, mature brands such as Coke, Pepsi, Budweiser, Gap, McDonald's, Nike, and Doritos. They entertain in an effort to keep you interested.

Perspective Two: The Consumer as Social Being.

The creditable human being must have not only the things needed for decent life, but something extra, something superfluous or sentimental or luxurious. The human being, to be human, must show that he or she is not just an animal or brute, not just biological, and must in some manner make the non-animal nature visible.[12]

—Michael Schudson, famous advertising scholar and sociologist

The view of the consumer as decision maker and information processor has been a popular one. It is not, however, without its limitations or its critics. In fact, its critics are getting louder. So we want to give you the other side of the story, a second perspective.

First, don't throw the baby out with the bathwater. While we are going to point out limitations and shortcomings, we are *not* telling you that what you just learned is wrong or useless. Far from it, there is undeniable value in the perspective presented above—no doubt about it. What goes on in consumers' minds is obviously important. But just as certainly it tells only part of the story of consumer behavior and advertising. Advertising and consumer behavior is so many things, and operates on so many levels, that a single-perspective approach is completely inadequate. So we offer more, a second perspective.

What the first perspective is best at is advancing understanding about how consumers make decisions. It is reasonably good at that. For example, it tells us that in general, consumers tend to use less as opposed to more information. That might seem odd, but it's true. Consumers *say* that more information is best, but tend to *actually use* less rather than more. If you think about it, this makes perfect sense. Consumers store and retrieve previously made judgments (e.g., *Honda is the best value*) in order to not have to decide all over again every time they make a purchase. If this were not true, a quick trip to the convenience store would take hours: "Let's see, Trident versus Bubble Yum . . . hmmm . . . let me think." In order to make their lives easier, consumers employ all sorts of mental short-cuts and effort-saving strategies. So, with this situation, and many others the perspective described above has helped advertisers understand consumer decision making.

But what of understanding advertising and how it works with consumers? In their effort to isolate psychological mechanisms, information-processing researchers typically take consumer behavior (and consumers) out of its (their) natural environment in favor of a laboratory. As you may have already guessed, few consumers actually

10.   Associations like Jay-Z with Heineken, Missy Elliott with the Gap, and Queen Latifah with Cover Girl illustrate the influence of Russell Simmons in bringing hip-hop into the advertising mainstream. (See "The CEO of Hip Hop," *BusinessWeek,* October 27, 2003, 91–98.) It is fair to say that Simmons found great success by lining up hip-hop icons as peripheral cues for all sorts of big-name advertisers.

11.   The rationale for cultivating brand interest for mature brands is discussed more fully in Karen A. Machleit, Chris T. Allen, and Thomas J. Madden, "The Mature Brand and Brand Interest: An Alternative Consequence of Ad-Evoked Affect," *Journal of Marketing,* vol. 57 (October 1993), 72–82.

12.   (1984), "An Anthropology of Goods," in *Advertising, The Uneasy Persuasion: Its Dubious Impact on American Society,* New York: Basic Books, 133.

watch ads and buy things in laboratories. In fact, under such obviously unrealistic conditions, some argue that these researchers are no longer studying ads at all, but only "stimulus material." Those who criticize this approach believe that ads really exist *only* in the real social world and natural environment. When removed from that environment they are no longer ads in any meaningful sense. Think about it for yourself; when you watch advertising on television, you usually see eight to ten ads in a commercial break. You may or may not be listening, or watching. You might be talking to friends or family, reading, or just about anything else. Chances are you are not watching an ad on a computer monitor for class credit. To seriously believe these are the same thing is to believe in some pretty odd notions of reality. More importantly, what the ad means is often completely lost in the quest for "information" being "processed." But the allure of science and its symbols (e.g., labs) is one of the modern period's most well-known seductions. The trappings of science give people feelings of certainty and truth, whether it is deserved or appropriate. And to be fair, the aims of academic experimental research (to advance basic knowledge and theory) are often quite different from the aims of the advertising industry (to make ads that sell things).

Industry critics and more and more academic researchers alike believe that much of the psychological research (most popular in the industry in the 1950s) has significantly less to do with the advertising and consumption of real goods and services in the real world than with advancing psychological theory—a completely worthy goal for some college professors, but not necessarily important to the actual practice of advertising. In the real world of advertising, real consumers matter, as does how they respond to real ads in real environments.

The move away from purely psychological approaches has been going on in the advertising industry for quite some time, at least 30 years. It gathered enormous momentum in the 1980s. At that time U.S. West Coast agencies began adopting what they called "British Research," which was really just qualitative research as has been practiced by anthropologists, sociologists, and others for well over a century. The only thing really "British" about it at all is that some very hot London agencies had been doing research this way all along. (Actually, many had been, but these agencies used it as a point of differentiation.) Judie Lannon's emphasis on meaning is a good example.

And if Advertising contributes to the meaning of inanimate goods, then the study of these values and meanings are of prime importance . . . the perspective of research must be what people use advertising for.[13]

—Judie Lannon, then creative research director,
J. Walter Thompson, London

This industry trend also resonated with a similar move in academic research toward more qualitative field work, interpretive, and textual approaches to the study of human behavior, including consumer behavior. People began to see consumers as more than "information processors" and ads as more than socially isolated attempts at attitude manipulation. **Meaning** became more important than attitudes. Perhaps, consumers do "process" information, but they also do a whole lot more (see Exhibit 5.20). Furthermore, "information" itself is a rich and complex textual product, bound by history, society, and culture, and interpreted in very sophisticated ways by very human beings. Advertising practice is not engineering or chemistry. It is about knowing how to connect with human beings around their consumption practices with advertising. That's why advertising agencies like and hire people who know about material culture (anthropology), demography and social process (sociology), the history of brands and consumption practices (history), memory (psychology), communication, text (literature), and art (what a lot of ads are). Understanding people and ads will not be the same as counting kilos of sulfur, concentrations of acids, or stars

13.   Davidson, Martin (1992), "Objects of Desire: How Advertising Works," in Martin Davidson, *The Consumerist Manifesto: Advertising in Postmodern Times,* London: Routledge, 23–60.

in a galaxy. Humans and their creations (like ads and branded goods) are not just processors of information. They are much more.

In this section we present a second perspective on consumer behavior, a perspective concerned with social and cultural processes. It should be considered another part of the larger story of how advertising works. Remember, this is just another perspective. We are still talking about the same consumers discussed in the preceding section; we are just viewing their behavior from a different vantage point. When it comes to the complexities of consumer behavior and advertising, we really can't have too many perspectives.

Consuming in the Real World.
Let's consider some major components of real consumer's lives:

Culture. If you are in the ad business, you are in the culture business.

Culture infuses, works on, is part of, and generally lands on all consumption. You need to understand what culture is, and what culture does.

Culture is what a people do, or "the total life ways of a people, the social legacy the individual acquires from his (her) group."[14] It is the way we eat, groom ourselves, celebrate, and mark our space and position. It is the way things are done. Cultures are often thought of as large and national, but in reality cultures are usually smaller, and not necessarily geographic, such as *urban hipster culture, teen tech-nerd culture, goth culture, Junior League culture,* and so on. It's usually easier to see and note

culture when it's more distant and unfamiliar. For most people, this is when they travel to another place. For example, if you've traveled beyond your own country, you have no doubt noticed that people in other cultures do things differently. If you were to point this out to one of the locals—for example, to a Parisian—and say something like, "Dude, you guys sure do things funny over here in France," you would no doubt be struck (perhaps literally) with the locals' belief that it is not they, but you, who behave oddly. This is a manifestation of culture and points out that members of a culture find the ways they do things to be perfectly natural. Culture

EXHIBIT 5.20

Real consumers do not consume in a vacuum. Consumers are inherently social beings, connected to other consumers through social identities, families, rituals, cultures, symbols, and shared histories. To have any hope of understanding how real consumers will respond to real ads, you must first consider them and their consumption practices, and not in isolation.

is thus said to be invisible to those who are immersed in it. Everyone around us behaves in a similar fashion, so we do not easily think about the existence of some large and powerful force acting on us all. But it's there; this constant background force is the force of culture. To really see the culture that is all around you, to really see what you take as ordinary, to see it like you were a visitor to a strangle land, is what the socio-cultural perspective offers.

Make no mistake, culture is real, and it affects every aspect of human behavior, including consumer behavior and advertising. Culture surrounds the creation, transmission, reception, and interpretation of ads and brands, just as it touches every aspect of consumption. It is about as "real world" as it gets. For example, if you are

14.   Gordon Marshall, ed., *The Concise Oxford Dictionary of Sociology* (New York: Oxford University Press, 1994), 104–105.

Ocean Spray, you want to understand how the U.S. Thanksgiving holiday works so that you can sell more cranberries, and make more profit. Why cranberries? Why cranberries on Thanksgiving, but not on St. Patrick's Day? What is the deal with cranberries? Why do we have the particular rituals we perform on that day? Are there market opportunities in those rituals? Or who makes up the rules of gift giving? If you are Tiffany, Barnes & Noble, or Hallmark, you have a very good reason to understand why people do things a certain way (for example, buy things for one holiday, but not for another).

When advertisers consider just why consumers consume certain goods or services, or why they consume them in a certain way, they are considering culture. Culture informs consumers' views about food, the body, gifts, possessions, a sense of self versus others, mating, courtship, death, religion, family, jobs, art, holidays, leisure, satisfaction, work—just about everything.

Values are the defining expressions of culture. They express in words and deeds what is important to a culture. For example, some cultures value individual freedom, while others value duty to the society at large. Some value propriety and restrained behavior, while others value open expression. Values are cultural bedrock. Values are enduring. They cannot be changed quickly or easily. They are thus different from attitudes, which can be changed through a single advertising campaign or even a single ad. Think of cultural values as the very strong and rigid foundation on which much more mutable attitudes rest. Exhibit 5.21 illustrates this relationship. Values are the foundation of this structure. Attitudes are, in turn, influenced by values, as well as by many other sources. Advertising has to be consistent with, but cannot easily or quickly change, values. It is thus senseless for an advertiser to speak of using advertising to change values in any substantive way. Advertising influences values in the same way a persistent drip of water wears down a granite slab—very slowly and through cumulative impact, over years and years. It is also the case that cultural values change advertising.

Typically, advertisers try to either associate their product with a cultural value or criticize a competitor for being out of step with one. For example, in America, to say that a product "merely hides or masks odors" would be damning criticism, because it suggests that anyone who would use such a product doesn't really value cleanliness and thus isn't like the rest of us.

Advertisements must be consistent with the values of a people. If they are not, they will likely be rejected. Many argue that the best (most effective) ads are those that best express and affirm core cultural values. For example, one core American value is said to be individualism, or the predisposition to value the individual over the group. This value has been part of American culture for a very long time. Thus, advertisements that celebrate or affirm this value are more likely to succeed than ones that denigrate or ignore it. Exhibit 5.22 shows an ad that leans heavily on this value. But you should also be aware that current thinking on globalization makes a fly for this ointment. Those seeing globalization everywhere hold that the world is becom-

EXHIBIT 5.21

Cultural values, attitudes, and consumer behavior. Some believe that advertising can directly affect consumer behavior and, over time, cultural values as well.

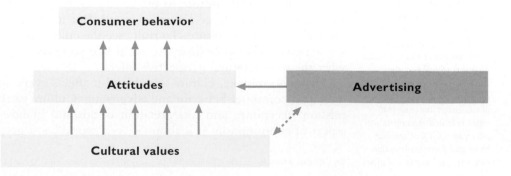

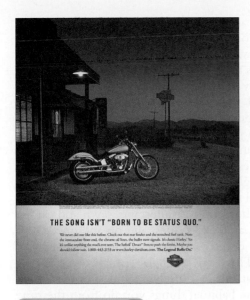

THE SONG ISN'T "BORN TO BE STATUS QUO."

What could be more thoroughly individual?

Global brandscape. From Tucson to Tucumcari, Madrid to Cork (photo above), the global brandscape is there.

ing more alike . . . the local is being gobbled up by the global brands and a global culture of marketing, branding, advertising and consuming. In fact, this is referred to as the "globalization and homogenization" of everyday life. Travel just about anywhere on this planet and you will be met by the *global brandscape* (see Exhibit 5.23). It may turn out that cultural values become global values, at least in the consumption context. We are not there yet; we will have to wait and see.

Rituals are "often-repeated formalized behaviors involving symbols."[15] Cultures participate in rituals; consumers participate in rituals. Rituals are core elements of culture. Cultures affirm, express, and maintain their values through rituals. They are a way in which individuals are made part of the culture, and a method by which the culture constantly renews and perpetuates itself. For example, ritual-laden holidays such as Thanksgiving, Christmas, Hanukah, and the Fourth of July help perpetuate aspects of American culture through their repeated reenactment (tradition). In Europe, there are a myriad of very important cultural rituals, all involving consumption (e.g., feasts and gift giving). In fact, this is true all over the world, and rituals help intertwine culture and consumption practices in a very real way. For example, Jell-O may have attained the prominence of an "official" American holiday food because of its regular usage as part of the Thanksgiving dinner ritual.[16] In the American South, it is common to eat black-eyed peas on New Year's Day to ensure good luck. In one sense it is "just done," but in another it is just done because it is a ritual embedded in a culture. If you are a canned-goods manufacturer, understanding this particular ritual is not a trivial concern at all. (See Exhibits 5.24 and 5.25.)

we make it *Simple* so you can make it a *Holiday*

The Holiday Flavors of Kraft.

This ad promotes Kraft products as an integral part of family rituals and traditions. http://www.kraftfoods .com

15. Ibid., 452.
16. Melanie Wallendorf and Eric J. Arnould, "We Gather Together: Consumption Rituals of Thanksgiving Day," *Journal of Consumer Research*, vol. 18, no. 1 (June 1991), 13–31.

The dance of the
SPLENDA· PLUM FAIRY

Now SPLENDA· No Calorie Sweetener comes in a large Baker's Bag. Almost anywhere you can use sugar, you can use SPLENDA. Made from sugar, so it tastes like sugar. *Think* SUGAR, *say* SPLENDA.

EXHIBIT 5.25

In this ad, Splenda is made part of holiday ritual.

Rituals also occur every day in millions of other contexts. For example, when someone buys a new car or a new home, they do all sorts of "unnecessary" things to make it theirs. They clean the carpets even if they were just cleaned, they trim trees that don't need trimming, they hang things from the mirror of the used car they just bought, they change oil that was just changed—all to make the new possession theirs and remove any trace of the former owner. These behaviors are not only important to anthropologists, they are also important to those making and trying to sell products such as paint, rug shampoos, household disinfectants, lawn and garden equipment, auto accessories, and on and on.

Rituals don't have to be the biggest events of the year. There are everyday rituals, such as the way we eat, clean ourselves, and groom. Think about all the habitual things you do from the time you get up in the morning until you crawl into bed at night. These things are done in a certain way; they are not random. Members of a common culture tend to do them one way, and members of other cultures do them other ways. Again, if you've ever visited another country, you have no doubt noticed significant differences. An American dining in Paris might be surprised to have sorbet to begin the meal and a salad to end it.

Daily rituals seem inconsequential because they are habitual and routine, and thus "invisible." If, however, someone tried to get you to significantly alter the way you do these things, he or she would quickly learn just how important and resistant to change these rituals are. If a product or service cannot be incorporated into an already-existing ritual, it is very difficult and expensive for advertisers to effect a change. If, on the other hand, an advertiser can successfully incorporate the consumption of its good or service into an existing ritual, then success is much more likely. Imagine how important rituals are to the global beauty industry (Exhibit 5.26). Cleaning and beauty practices are highly ritualized.

Clearly, there are incredible opportunities for marketers who can successfully link their products to consumption rituals. In Exhibits 5.27 and 5.28 we see two advertisers incorporating their brands into Easter rituals.

5   **Stratification (social class)** refers to a person's relative standing in a social system as produced by systematic inequalities in things such as wealth, income, education, power, and status. For example, some members of society exist within a richer group (stratum), others within a less affluent stratum. Race and gender are also unequally distributed across these strata: for example, men generally have higher incomes than women. Thus a cross-section, or slice, of American society would reveal many different levels (or strata) of the population along these different dimensions. Sociologists used to prefer the term "social class," but many have gotten away from it lately. It seems that contemporary societies have less stable or easy to define classes than was once thought. Also, it is argued that the emergence of the *New Class,* a class of technologically skilled and highly educated individuals with great access to information and information technology, has changed the way we define social class: "Knowledge of, and access to, information may begin to challenge property as a determinant of social class."[17]

17.   Alvin W. Gouldner, "The Future of Intellectuals and the Rise of the New Class," in *Social Stratification in Sociological Perspective: Class, Race and Gender,* ed. David B. Grusky (San Francisco: Westview Press, 1994), 711–729.

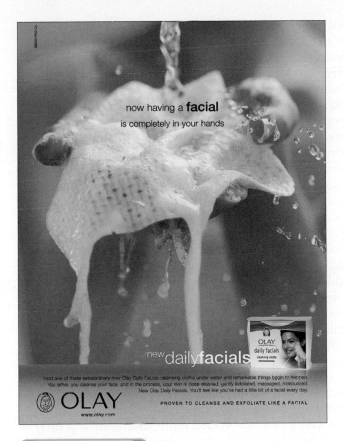

This ad helps Olay become part of an already existing ritual.

"Social class" was typically thought most strongly determined by income: higher-income Americans tended to be of a higher "social class," and lower-income Americans were considered in a lower class. But that was a clearly imperfect relationship. For example, successful plumbers often had much higher incomes than college professors, but their occupation was (perhaps) less prestigious, and thus their "social class" designation was lower. So, the prestige of one's occupation also entered into what we called "social class." Education also has something to do with "social class," but a person with a little college experience and a lot of inherited wealth will probably rank higher than an insurance agent with an MBA. Thus income, education, and occupation are three important variables for indicating "social class," but are still individually, or even collectively, inadequate at capturing its full meaning. Then there are rock stars, professional athletes, and successful actors, all with high incomes, but generally thought to be completely outside the "social class" system. This is another reason the term has been falling to the more preferred "stratification" term.

Important to marketers is the belief that members of social strata tend to live in similar ways, have similar views and philosophies, and, most critically, tend to consume in similar ways. You can supposedly tell "social class" from what people consume and how they consume; at least, that's what lots of marketers and advertisers believe. Markers of social class include what one wears, where one lives, and how one speaks. In a consumer society, consumption marks or indicates stratification in a myriad of ways. Stratification related consumption preferences reflect value differences and different ways of seeing the world and the role of things in it; they reflect taste. What do you think? Put it to the test, go to a mall, walk around and check people out: Do you think you could guess their income, education, occupation, whether they live downtown or in the 'burbs from the way they look, what they are wearing, and the stores they shop in? Most advertisers think you can, and that's why stratification matters.

This brings us to taste. **Taste** refers to a generalized set or orientation to consumer preferences. Social class affects consumption through tastes, including media habits, and thus exposure to various advertising media vehicles—for example, *RV Life* versus *Wine Spectator*. We think of tennis more than bowling as belonging to the upper classes, chess more than checkers, and brie more than Velveeta. Ordering

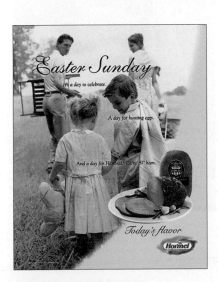

Two advertisers incorporate Easter rituals.

wine instead of beer has social significance, as does wearing Tommy Hilfiger rather than Lee jeans, or driving a Volvo rather than a Chevy. Social stratification and taste are intertwined. In fact, cultural theorist Pierre Bourdieu argues that social class is such a powerful socializing factor that it "structures the whole experience of subjects," particularly when it comes to consumption.[18] Again, this is because of the relationship between social stratification (or social class) and taste. Yet, remember, the argument is made that contemporary consumer societies have a much more fluid sense of class, and strata themselves are more in flux and have more permeable boundaries than we once believed. We come down on this in the following way: Yes, in contemporary society there is a more fluid character to social stratification (class) and its consumption markers, but it is still there and still matters. Fashion and taste cycle faster than they once did, and consumers may be more playful in their use of class markers than they once were, but we think the shopping mall test still generally works, and the stratification of taste still matters to advertisers.

A related concept is *cultural capital,* the value that cultures place on certain consumption practices. For example, a certain consumption practice, say snowboarding, has a certain capital or value (like money) for some segment of the population. If you own a snowboard (a certain amount of cultural capital) and can actually use it (more cultural capital), and look good while using it (even more capital), then this activity is like cultural currency or cultural money in the bank. You can "spend" it. It gets you things you want. A Porsche has a certain cultural capital among some groups, as does wearing khakis, drinking Bud, ordering the right pinot noir, knowing how to hail a cab, flying first class, or knowing the latest band. This capital may exist within a hipster culture, or a 40-something wine-snob culture, or a redneck culture. These are all cultures, and certain consumer practices are favored or valued more in each. Advertisers need to figure out which ones are valued more, and why, and how to make their product sought after because it has higher cultural capital. This is what "taste" is all about; having good taste gives you cultural capital. These ads try to emphasize the cultural capital, style, and taste to be found in the product (see Exhibits 5.29 and 5.30), and then on to the consumer.

EXHIBITS 5.29 AND 5.30

These two ads point to the high cultural capital of the products.

18.   Pierre Bourdieu, "Distinction: A Social Critique of the Judgment of Taste," in *Social Stratification in Sociological Perspective: Class, Race and Gender,* ed. David B. Grusky (San Francisco: Westview Press, 1994), 404–429.

Consider some examples. Think about the purchases of equivalently priced cars, say a Saab and a Cadillac. The Saab is owned by a young architect, the Cadillac by the owner of a small construction company. These two consumers don't frequent the same restaurants, drink in the same bars, or eat the same kinds of foods. They don't belong to the same "social strata," and it is evident in their consumption. Think about the contents of the living rooms of those in various social classes. The differences are not due to money only, or the lack of it. Clearly, there is another dynamic at work here.

"Social class" also becomes apparent when a person moves from one class into another. Consider the following example: Bob and Jill move into a more expensive neighborhood. Both grew up in lower-middle-class surroundings and moved into high-paying jobs after graduate school. They have now moved into a fairly upscale neighborhood, composed mostly of "older money." On one of the first warm Sundays, Bob goes out to his driveway and begins to do something he has done all his life: change the oil in his car. One of Bob's neighbors comes over and chats, and ever so subtly suggests to Bob that people in this neighborhood have "someone else" do "that sort of thing." Bob gets the message: It's not cool to change your oil in your own driveway. This is not how the new neighbors behave. It doesn't matter whether you like to do it or not; it is simply not done. To Bob, paying someone else to do this simple job seems wasteful and uppity. He's a bit offended, and a little embarrassed. But, over time, he decides that it's better to go along with the other people in the neighborhood. Over time, Bob begins to see the error of his ways and changes his attitudes and his behavior.

This is an example of the effect of social class on consumer behavior. Bob will no longer be a good target for Fram, Purolator, AutoZone, or any other product or service used to change oil at home. On the other hand, Bob is now a perfect candidate for quick-oil-change businesses such as Jiffy Lube. Consider the ads in Exhibits 5.31 and 5.32 in terms of social-class considerations. Which social strata (income, education, etc.) do you believe are being targeted by these ads?

EXHIBITS 5.31 AND 5.32

These ads speak to two different social classes. Compare the sites of Chivas (http://www.chivas.com) and Miller Lite (http://www.millerlite.com). What activities and interests are featured at each? How does leisure-oriented content at each site create a context of social class that reinforces each brand's meaning? Which brand appeals to you most?

RÉSUMÉS: $40

SUIT: $210

MORE RÉSUMÉS: $40

HANGING UP YOUR WAITER'S APRON FOR THE LAST TIME:

PRICELESS

THERE ARE SOME THINGS MONEY CAN'T BUY.
FOR EVERYTHING ELSE THERE'S MASTERCARD.

TO LEARN MORE, OR APPLY FOR A CARD,
VISIT OUR WEB SITE AT WWW.MASTERCARD.COM/COLLEGE

MasterCard.

EXHIBIT 5.33

Aspirations play a large part in the message of this MasterCard ad. http://www.mastercard.com

Reference groups are also important. Obviously, other people and their priorities can have a dramatic impact on our consumption priorities, as suggested by the MasterCard ad in Exhibit 5.33. A **reference group** is any configuration of other people that a particular individual uses as a point of reference in making his or her own consumption decisions.

Reference groups can be small and intimate (you and the people sharing your neighborhood) or large and distant (people wanting to become rich and powerful advertising executives). Reference groups can also vary in their degree of formal structure. They can exist as part of some larger organization—such as any business or employer—with formal rules for who must be part of the group and what is expected of the group in terms of each day's performance. Or they may be informal in their composition and agenda, such as a group of casual friends who all live in the same apartment complex.

Another way of categorizing reference groups involves the distinction between membership groups and aspirational groups.[19] **Membership groups** are those that we interact with in person on some regular basis; we have personal contact with the group and its other members. **Aspirational groups** are made up of people we admire or use as role models, but it is likely we will never interact with the members of this group in any meaningful way. However, because we aspire to be like the members of this group, they can set standards for our own behavior. Professional athletes, movie stars, rock stars, and successful business executives become role models whether they like it or not. Of course, advertisers are keenly aware of the potential influence of aspirational groups, and they commonly employ celebrities as endorsers for their products. After all, who wouldn't want to be, to paraphrase another ad, like Michael Jordan? But aspirational reference groups may also show up in ads as "ideal types," or "regular people" who seem to have the lives (and stuff) we want.

Family. The consumer behavior of families is also of great interest to advertisers. Advertisers want not only to discern the needs of different kinds of families, but also to discover how decisions are made within families. The first is possible; the latter is much more difficult. For a while, consumer researchers tried to determine who in the traditional nuclear family (that is, Mom, Dad, and the kids) made various purchasing decisions. This was largely an exercise in futility. Due to errors in reporting and conflicting perceptions between husbands and wives, it became clear that the family purchasing process is anything but clear. While some types of purchases are handled by one family member, many decisions are actually diffuse nondecisions, arrived at through what consumer researcher C. W. Park aptly calls a "muddling-through" process.[20] These "decisions" just get made, and no one is really sure who

19.   For additional explanation of this distinction, see Michael R. Solomon, *Consumer Behavior* (Upper Saddle River, N.J.: Prentice Hall, 1996), 342–344.
20.   C. Whan Park, "Joint Decisions in Home Purchasing: A Muddling-Through Process," *Journal of Consumer Research,* vol. 9 (September 1982), 151–162.

EXHIBIT 5.34

Who are the Cleavers?

made them, or even when. For an advertiser to influence such a diffuse and vague process is indeed a challenge. The consumer behavior of the family is a complex and often subtle type of social negotiation. One person handles this, one takes care of that. Sometimes specific purchases fall along gender lines, but sometimes they don't.[21] While they may not be the buyer in many instances, children can play important roles as initiators, influencers, and users in many categories, such as cereals, clothing, vacation destinations, fast-food restaurants, and technology (like computers). Still, some advertisers capitalize on the flexibility of this social system by suggesting in their ads who *should* take charge of a given consumption task, and then arming that person with the appearance of expertise so that whoever wants the job can take it and defend his or her purchases.

We also know that families have a lasting influence on the consumer preferences of family members. One of the best predictors of the brands adults use is the ones their parents used. This is true for cars, toothpaste, household cleansers, and many more products. Say you go off to college. You eventually have to do laundry, so you go to the store, and you buy Tide. Why Tide? Well, you're not sure, but you saw it around your house when you lived with your parents, and things seemed to have worked out okay for them, so you buy it for yourself. The habit sticks, and you keep buying it. This is called an **intergenerational effect.**

Advertisers often focus on the major or gross differences in types of families, because different families have different needs, buy different things, and are reached by different media. Family roles often change when both parents (or a single parent) are employed outside the home. For instance, a teenage son or daughter may be given the role of initiator and buyer, while the parent or parents serve merely as influences. Furthermore, we should remember that Ward, June, Wally, and the Beaver (Exhibit 5.34) are not the norm (see Exhibit 5.35). There are a lot of single parents and second and third marriages. *Family* is a very open concept. In addition to the "traditional" nuclear family and the single-parent household, there is the extended family (nuclear family plus grandparents, cousins, and others) and the so-called alternative family (single parents and gay and lesbian households with and without children, for example).

Beyond the basic configuration, advertisers are often interested in knowing things such as the age of the youngest child, the size of the family, and the family income. The age of the youngest child living at home tells an advertiser where the family is in terms of its needs and obligations (that is, toys, investment instruments for college savings, clothing, and vacations). When the youngest child leaves home, the consumption patterns of a family radically change. Advertisers love to track the age of the youngest child living at home and use it as a planning criterion. This is called a **life-stage** variable, and is used frequently in advertising planning.

Celebrity is a unique sociological category, and it matters a great deal to advertisers. Twenty-first-century society is all about celebrity. While there are all sorts of

---

21.   For an excellent article on this topic, see Craig J. Thompson, William B. Locander, and Howard R. Pollio, "The Lived Meaning of Free Choice: An Existential-Phenomenological Description of Everyday Consumer Experiences of Contemporary Married Women," *Journal of Consumer Research,* vol. 17 (December 1990), 346–361.

Characteristics	All house-holds	Family households					Nonfamily households		
		Total	Married couple	Other families			Total	Female house-holder	Male house-holder
				Female house-holder	Male house-holder				
All households	104,705	72,025	55,311	12,687	4,028		32,680	18,039	14,641
Race and Hispanic origin									
White	87,671	60,251	48,790	8,380	3,081		27,420	15,215	12,204
White not Hispanic	78,819	53,066	43,865	6,732	2,468		25,753	14,475	11,278
Black	12,849	8,664	4,144	3,814	706		4,185	2,309	1,876
Hispanic	9,319	7,561	5,133	1,769	658		1,758	783	974
Size of household									
1 person	26,724	N/A	N/A	N/A	N/A		26,724	15,543	11,181
2 people	34,666	29,834	22,899	5,206	1,730		4,832	2,225	2,607
3 people	17,152	16,405	11,213	4,086	1,106		746	177	570
4 people	15,309	15,064	12,455	1,927	682		245	66	179
5 people	6,981	6,894	5,723	864	307		87	17	70
6 people	2,445	2,413	1,916	366	130		32	6	26
7 or more people	1,428	1,415	1,105	237	73		13	5	8
Average size	2.62	3.24	3.26	3.17	3.16		1.25	1.17	1.34
Presence of own									
children under 18	34,605	34,605	25,248	7,571	1,786		N/A	N/A	N/A

Note: Data are not shown separately for the American Indian and Alaska Native population because of the small size in the Current Population Survey in March 2000.

Source: U.S. Census Bureau, Current Population Survey, March 2000.

EXHIBIT 5.35

American households by type and selected characteristics, 2000. Numbers are in thousands, except for averages. Note: there are a lot of "non-traditional" families.

celebrities, they can be both self-expressive and aspirational for consumers. Current thinking is that in a celebrity-based culture, celebrities help contemporary consumers with identity. Identity in a consumer culture becomes a "fashion accessory" prop for a day—lesbian chic, head banger, corporate slave at work, and so forth. The idea is that contemporary consumers are very good at putting on and taking off, trying on, switching, and trading various identities, in the same way that they have clicked through the channels since they could reach the remote. E-generation (www generation) children have become who they are, in no small part, through celebrity-inspired identities—the way they do their hair, the way they think about their bodies, their relationships, their aspirations, and certainly their styles. Of course, style is often purchased and accessorized. This means that celebrities and images of them are used moment to moment to help in a personal parade of identity. For this reason, the understanding of the celebrity is much more complex and vital than merely thinking in terms of similar attitudes and behaviors. It's who we are, minute to minute, ad to ad, mall to mall, purchase to purchase (Exhibits 5.36 through 5.39).

Cool. A lot of what advertising is all about is figuring out what is cool, and then injecting that meaning into the brand. What is cool is determined through a social process. Consumers have a great deal of power in this way, because they along with advertisers determine the meaning of cool. Sometimes the last person to know what is cool (or not) is the advertiser. These days some marketers actually go out into various areas known for the hot spot on the cool map (like certain urban settings),

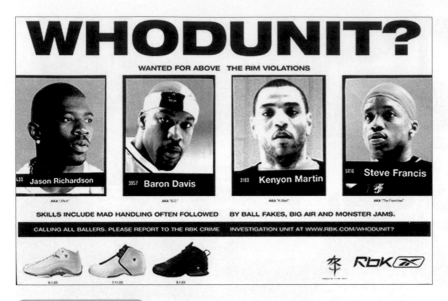

EXHIBIT 5.40

Does this ad successfully capture and project cool onto the brand?

and see what the "kids" are wearing, and doing, and saying. These "coolhunts" are then translated into brands and ads (see Exhibit 5.40).

Race and Ethnicity. Race and ethnicity provide other ways to think about important social groups. Answering the question of how race figures into consumer behavior is very difficult. Our discomfort stems from having, on the one hand, the desire to say, "Race doesn't matter, we're all the same," and on the other hand not wanting (or not being able) to deny the significance of race in terms of reaching ethnic cultures and influencing a wide variety of behaviors, including consumer behavior. The truth is we are less and less sure what *race* is, what it means. Obviously, a person's pigmentation, in and of itself, has almost nothing to do with preferences for one type of product over another. But because race has mattered in culture, it does still matter in consumer behavior. To the extent that race is part of culture, it matters. But it is true that the United States is becoming an increasingly diverse culture (Exhibit 5.41), and the empirical reality does not always conform to stereotypes. But how do we (and should we) deal with this reality?

There probably isn't an area in consumer behavior where research is more inadequate. This is probably because everyone is terrified to discuss it, and because most of the findings we do have are suspect. What is attributed to race is often due to another factor that is itself associated with race. For example, consumer behavior textbooks commonly say something to the effect that African-Americans and Hispanics are more brand loyal than their Anglo counterparts. Data on the frequency of brand switching is offered, and lo and behold, it does appear that white people switch brands more often. But why? Some ethnic minorities live in areas where there are fewer retail choices. When we statistically remove the effect of income dis-

Year	White	Black	Hispanic	Asian	American Indian
1996	194.4 (73.3%)	32.0 (12.1%)	27.8 (10.5%)	9.1 (3.4%)	2.0 (0.7%)
2000	197.1 (71.8%)	33.6 (12.2%)	31.4 (11.4%)	10.6 (3.9%)	2.1 (0.7%)
2010	202.4 (68.0%)	37.5 (12.6%)	41.1 (13.8%)	14.4 (4.8%)	2.3 (0.8%)
2020	207.4 (64.3%)	41.5 (12.9%)	52.7 (16.3%)	18.6 (5.7%)	2.6 (0.8%)
2030	210.0 (60.5%)	45.4 (13.1%)	65.6 (18.9%)	23.0 (6.6%)	2.9 (0.8%)
2040	209.6 (56.7%)	49.4 (13.3%)	80.2 (21.7%)	27.6 (7.5%)	3.2 (0.9%)
2050	207.9 (52.8%)	53.6 (13.6%)	96.5 (24.5%)	32.4 (8.2%)	3.5 (0.9%)

Source: U.S. Census Bureau.

EXHIBIT 5.41

Ethnic diversity in America: projected U.S. population by race in millions (and percentage of total population by race).

parities between white people and people of color, we see that the brand-switching effect often disappears. This suggests that brand loyalty is not a function of race, but of disposable income and shopping options.

But race does inform one's social identity to varying degrees. One is not blind to one's own ethnicity. African-Americans, Hispanics, and other ethnic groups have culturally related consumption preferences. Certain brands become associated with racial or ethnic groups. It is not enough, however, for advertisers to say one group is different from another group, or that they prefer one brand over another simply because they are members of a racial or ethnic category. If advertisers really want a good, long-term relationship with their customers, they must acquire, through good consumer research, a deeper understanding of who their customers are and how this identity is affected by culture, felt ethnicity, and race. In short, advertisers must ask why groups of consumers are different, or prefer different brands, and not settle for an easy answer. It wasn't until the mid to late 1980s that most American corporations made a concerted effort to court African-American consumers, or even to recognize their existence.[22] Efforts to serve the Hispanic consumer have been intermittent and inconsistent. Sample ads directed at diverse audiences are shown in Exhibits 5.42, 5.43, and 5.44.

Gender.   Gender is the social expression of sexual biology, sexual choice, or both. Obviously, gender matters in consumption. But are men and women really that different in any meaningful way in their consumption behavior, beyond the obvious?

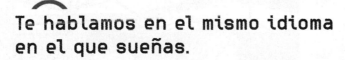

EXHIBITS 5.42, 5.43, AND 5.44

These ads are directed at Hispanics, Asian, and African American consumers.

22.   Jannette L. Dates, "Advertising," in *Split Image: African Americans in the Mass Media,* ed. Jannette L. Dates and William Barlow (Washington, D.C.: Howard University Press, 1990), 421–454.

Again, to the extent that gender informs a "culture of gender," the answer is yes. As long as men and women are the products of differential socialization, then they will continue to be different in some significant ways. There is, however, no definitive list of gender differences in consumption, because the expression of gender, just like anything else social, depends on the situation and the social circumstances. In the 1920s, advertisers openly referred to women as less logical, more emotional, the cultural stewards of beauty.[23] (Some say that the same soft, irrational, emotional feminine persona is still invoked in advertising.) Advertising helps construct a social reality, with gender a predominant feature. Not only is it a matter of conscience and social responsibility to be aware of this construction, but it is good business as well. Advertisers must keep in mind, though, that it's hard to keep the business of people you patronize, insult, or ignore.

Obviously, gender's impact on consumer behavior is not limited to heterosexual men and women. Gay men and lesbians are large and significant markets. Of late, these markets have been targeted by corporate titans such as IBM, United Airlines, and Citibank.[24] Again, these are markets that desire to be acknowledged and served, but not stereotyped and patronized. Exhibits 5.45 and 5.46 are ads directed at lesbian and gay audiences.

EXHIBIT 5.45

Some advertisers are beginning to recognize the advantages of marketing to gay and lesbian consumers. Here, American Express recognizes the special financial challenges faced by lesbian couples. http://www.american express.com.

EXHIBIT 5.46

Here, Alizé attempts to represent and appeal to gay consumers.

23.   Roland Marchand, *Advertising: The American Dream* (Berkeley: University of California Press, 1984), 25.
24.   Laura Koss-Feder, "Out and About: Firms Introduce Gay-Specific Ads for Mainstream Products, Services," *Marketing News,* May 25, 1998, 1, 20.

In the late 1970s, advertisers discovered working women. In the 1980s, marketers discovered African-American consumers, about the same time they discovered Hispanic consumers. Later they discovered Asian-Americans, and just lately they discovered gays and lesbians. Of course, these people weren't missing. They were there all along. These "discoveries" of forgotten and marginalized social groups create some interesting problems for advertisers. Members of these groups, quite reasonably, want to be served just like any other consumers. To serve these markets, consider what Wally Snyder of the American Advertising Federation said:

Advertising that addresses the realities of America's multicultural population must be created by qualified professionals who understand the nuances of the disparate cultures. Otherwise, agencies and marketers run the risk of losing or, worse, alienating millions of consumers eager to buy their products or services. Building a business that "looks like" the nation's increasingly multicultural population is no longer simply a moral choice, it is a business imperative.[25]

Attention and representation without stereotyping from a medium and a genre that is known for stereotyping might be a lot to expect, but it's not that much. Web sites such as Commercial Closet (Exhibit 5.47) offer reviews and opinions on LGBT representation in ads.

Community. **Community** is a powerful and traditional sociological concept. Its meaning extends well beyond the idea of a specific geographic place. Communities can be imagined or even virtual. Community members believe that they belong to a group of people who are similar to them in some important way, and different from those not in the community. Members of communities often share rituals and traditions, and feel some sort of responsibility to one another and the community.

Advertisers are becoming increasingly aware of the power of community. It is important in at least two major ways. First, it is where consumption is grounded, where consumption literally lives. Products have social meanings, and community is the quintessential social domain, so consumption is inseparable from the notion of where we live (actually or virtually). Communities may be the fundamental reference group, and they exhibit a great deal of power. A community may be your neighborhood, or it may be people like you with whom you feel a kinship, such as members of social clubs, other consumers who collect the same things you do, or people who have, use, or admire the same brands you do.

Brand communities are groups of consumers who feel a commonality and a shared purpose grounded or attached to a consumer good or service.[26]

When owners of Doc Martens, Saabs, Mountain Dews, or Saturns experience a sense of connectedness by virtue of their common ownership or usage, a brand community exists. When two perfect strangers stand in a parking lot and act like old friends simply because they both own Saturns, a type of community is revealed. Many of these communities exist online, and some reveal a certain level of brand fanaticism:

Coke is the best drink ever created. . . . And with popularity, the imitators came. These imitators make money, are not as good as the Real Thing, they gained popularity and must be stopped. This is why we must rally around our beverage in its time of need. We cannot see the horrible things pepsico does anymore. It is times these crimes stop.

Join the Coke Army.

—from the Web site of a 16-year-old male in Belgium

Other times, these communities reveal an important and more "mainstream" connection between owners, users or admirers of brands, that with the rise of the Internet, has made these communities and this type of community conversation anything but trivial:

Truth be told, I just "found" this group and I'm a happy little person now that I've found there are other people out there like me that love their Miatas!

—from a WWW Miata user group post

25.   Wally Snyder, "Advertising's Ethical and Economic Imperative," *American Advertising* (Fall 1992), 28.
26.   Albert Muniz, Jr., and Thomas O'Guinn, "Brand Community," *Journal of Consumer Research,* vol. 27 (2001), 412–432.

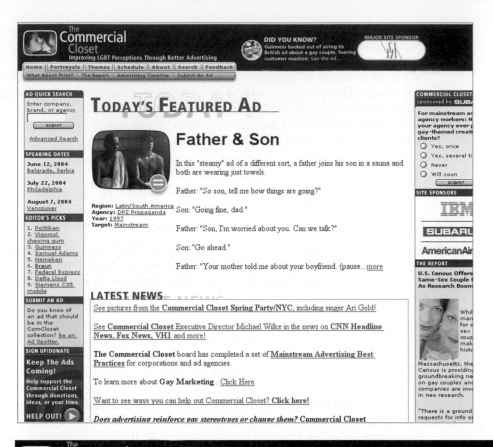

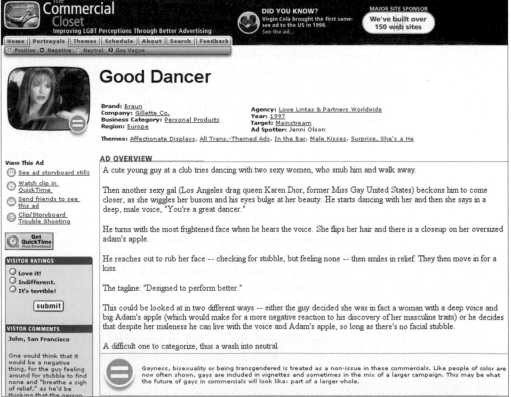

EXHIBIT 5.47

Commercial Closet reviews two ads here. What do you think?

This quote reveals the writer's joy at realizing that there are others out there who get it—who see what this "happy little person" sees in this material object, this car, this brand: Miata. The promise of community—not to be alone, to share appreciation and admiration of something or someone, no matter how odd or inappropriate others feel it to be—is fulfilled in online communities. The language looks much like that of people pleased that they discovered others with the same sexual orientation, the same health problems, or the same religion, in this case a brand and model of car. It is a rewarding and embracing social collective centered on a brand. This should not surprise us too much given how central consumption and branding have become in contemporary society. Brands matter.

Indeed, Saturn's Spring Hill Homecoming, described in the IBP box, is considered a great marketing success story in the area of cultivating brand community. Exhibit 5.48 shows how Saturn reinforces its communal appeal.

Object Meaning and the Social Life of Brands.

Things always stand for other values; and the advertiser is merely making sure the translation is vivid and to the product's advantage.

—Michael Schudson

The entire human record consists of no place where materiality and meaning are strangers. Such a place, such a time, are fictions. So things always have social meaning. But, brands go even further, are particularly marked, and have a special relationship to modern market economies, those economies marked by marketing, advertising and consumption.

—O'Guinn and Muñiz,
Inside Consumption, 2005[27]

The one thing a brand can never be is just a box on the shelf.[28]

—Martin Davidson

GM's Saturn division has been a leader in promoting a sense of community among its owners. In this ad, that sense of community is cultivated through photographs from the Spring Hill Homecoming. Savvy Saturn marketers used the homecoming as a feature in advertising campaigns to show that the bond between Saturn owners and their cars is something special. http://www.saturncars.com

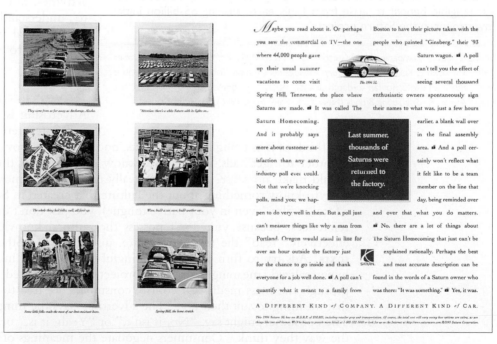

27. Thomas C. O'Guinn and Albert M. Muñiz, Jr., "Consumption Communities" in *Inside Consumption: Frontiers of Research on Consumer Motives, Goals, and Desires*, David Glen Mick and S. Ratneshwar (eds.), New York: Routledge, 2005.
28. Davidson, Martin (1992), "Objects of Desire: How Advertising Works," in Martin Davidson, *The Consumerist Manifesto: Advertising in Postmodern Times*, London: Routledge, 23–60.

The things we buy, the things we consume, have meaning. All consumed objects (in fact, all material things) have sociocultural meaning. They are not just things. Look around you: The things in your home, the things in your room, the things in your car, your car itself, all things material, derive their meaning from society and culture. A Fender is not just a piece of wood with some wires and strings. It is also not just a fine musical instrument. It is an electric guitar. It is a Fender. It is the kind of guitar that Stevie Ray Vaughan, Eric Clapton, Kurt Cobain, Jimi Hendrix, and other famous guitarists have played (Exhibit 5.49). It has a social history. People give it meaning, and history gives it meaning. A tuxedo is not just a coat and pants combo. It is worn on certain social occasions. Paper plates (not even Chinette) are not just plates made of paper. If you serve your guests a fine meal on them, they will notice. A Tag Heuer watch is not just a timepiece; neither is a Timex or a $30 Casio. They all mean something, and this meaning is derived socially. Advertisers try to influence this process. Sometimes they succeed; other times they don't. Just remember, all material things have meaning, as do activities. Smart advertisers must hope to understand relevant and widely shared social meaning in order to get consumers to appreciate their brand.

IBP

Coming Together . . . Over Saturn

It sounded like a goofy idea: Invite every Saturn owner (about 600,000) to a "homecoming" at the Spring Hill, Tennessee, plant where their cars were "born." After all, who in their right mind would plan their vacation around a remote manufacturing facility? About 44,000 Saturn owners, that's who. Owners came from as far away as Alaska and Taipei; one couple ended up getting married by a United Auto Workers chaplain, with the Saturn president there to give away the bride. Another 100,000 Saturn owners participated in related dealer-sponsored programs all over the United States. Add in the national publicity provided from the news media and ensuing Saturn ads depicting the event, and the idea isn't so goofy anymore. It's a masterful integrated brand promotion campaign that has helped build an allegiance to the Saturn brand that is the envy of the automotive industry.

The genius of the Spring Hill Homecoming (and subsequent ads, such as the one shown in Exhibit 5.49) is that Saturn's primary marketing strategy revolves around strong customer relations and service. The four-day event at the Tennessee plant rewarded customers for their purchase behavior and provided reassurance for new-car shoppers seeking the trust and relationships that allay service-related fears and the general mystery of new-car buying. Saturn's innovative approach is also integral to the overall strategy of its parent company, General Motors: The overwhelming majority of Saturn sales come from previous import owners, and not at the expense of other GM divisions. Actually, Saturn's retention programs just may be the greatest tangible benefit to arise from GM's earth-shaking $5 billion initial investment in the Saturn project.

Sources: "Savvy Companies Hold Customer," *Sales & Marketing Management*, December 1994, 15; Kevin L. Keller, *Strategic Brand Management* (Upper Saddle River, N.J.: Prentice Hall: 1998), 244–245; for an in-depth analysis of Saturn's brand-building programs, see David Aaker, *Building Strong Brands* (New York: Free Press, 1996), ch. 2.

Advertising as Social Text.

Advertising is also a text. It is "read" and interpreted by consumers. You can think of it as being like other texts, books, movies, posters, paintings, and so on. In order to "get" ads, you have to know something of the cultural code, or they would make no sense. In order to really understand a movie, to really get it, you have to know something about the culture that created it. Sometimes when you see a foreign film (even in your native tongue), you just don't quite get all the jokes and references, because you don't possess the cultural knowledge necessary to really effectively "read" the text. So ads are, just like these other forms, **sociocultural texts.** Ads try to turn already meaningful things into things with very special and hyperrealized meaning: carefully projected and crafted meaning concentrated through the mass media. Of course, consumers are free to accept, reject, or adjust that meaning to suit their taste. The advertisers says the thing they are selling is cool. The consumer might say, "No, it isn't," or "Yeah, it is," or "Well, yeah, but not in the way they think." Consumers negotiate the meanings of ads and brands with the advertisers. Ultimately, consumers determine what is or is not cool.

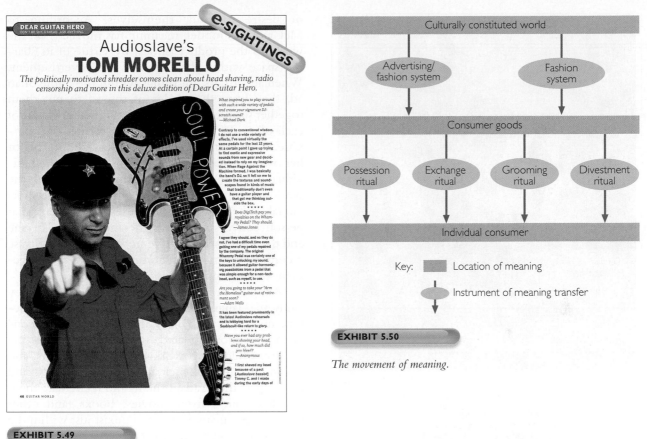

EXHIBIT 5.49

A Fender is not just a guitar.

The movement of meaning.

  How Ads Transmit Sociocultural Meaning.

Start work in an ad agency and the first thing they teach you is the difference between a product and a brand. That is because it is advertising's job to turn one into another.

—Martin Davidson

That's right: Ads turn products into brands. They do this, in large part, by trying to wrap material objects with a certain meaning—a meaning that comes from culture. The link between culture and advertising is key. Anthropologist Grant McCracken has offered the model in Exhibit 5.50 to explain how advertising (along with other cultural agents) functions in the transmission of meaning. To understand advertising as a mechanism of cultural meaning transfer is to understand a great deal about advertising. In fact, one could legitimately say that advertisers are really in the meaning-transfer business.

Think about McCracken's model as you examine the ad for Johnston and Murphy in Exhibit 5.51. The product—in this case, shoes—exists "out there" in the culturally constituted world, but it needs advertising to link it to certain social representations, certain slices of life. The advertiser places the advertised product and the slice of social life in an ad to get the two to rub off on each other, to intermingle, to become part of the same social scene. In other words, the product is given social meaning by being placed within an ad that represents an idealized context. This slice of life, of course, is the type of social setting in which potential customers might find,

You've got a life.   We've got a style.

JOHNSTON & MURPHY

For locations, call 1.800.515.3668, ext. 3000

EXHIBIT 5.51

A Johnston & Murphy shoe is not just any shoe. One goal of this advertisement is to create a special meaning for this brand of men's shoes. http://www.johnstonmurphy.com

or desire to find, themselves. According to McCracken's model, meaning has moved from the world to the product (shoes) by virtue of its sharing space within the frame of the advertisement. When advertisers put things within the frame of an ad, they want the reader of the ad to put them together seamlessly, to take them together as part of each other. When a consumer purchases or otherwise incorporates that good or service into his or her own life, the meaning is transferred to the individual consumer. Meaning is thus moved from the world to the product (via advertising) to the individual. When the individual uses the product, that person conveys to others the meaning he or she and the advertisement have now given it. Their use incorporates various rituals that facilitate the movement of meaning from good to consumer.

Ads also become part of consumers' everyday landscape, language, and everyday reality. Characters, lines, and references all become part of conversations, thoughts, and—coming full circle—the culture. Children, coworkers, family members, and talk-show hosts all pick up things from ads, and then replay them, adapt them, and recirculate them just like things from movies, books, and other texts. Ads, in many ways, don't exist just within the sociocultural context; they *are* the sociocultural context of our time (Exhibit 5.52 is a particularly poignant example). If you want to do well in the real ad world, it's a very good idea to understand that.

EXHIBIT 5.52

The Berlin Wall is now a place for ads.

ETHICS

Abercrombie & Fitch's Controversial Advertising and Promotion

Abercrombie & Fitch uses advertising and brand promotion aimed at a younger market. We're sure you are familiar with them. Their advertising and IBP efforts have raised the ire of consumer activist groups and regulators. The controversial approach may work for Abercrombie & Fitch; it certainly generates free publicity.

Abercrombie & Fitch actually sells its catalogs—the 2003 Christmas catalog, titled "280 pages of Moose, Ice Hockey, Chivalry, Group Sex & More," sold for $7. The catalog features ripped and stained jeans for $69.50, men's boxer shorts for $14.50, and women's boxer shorts for $19.50.

It seems that those upset with Abercrombie & Fitch don't like the party attitude and the skin.

Maybe they're not in the target market.

- Does this advertising and IBP hurt anyone?
- Does it diminish morality in any significant way?
- How do you think it plays in "blue" vs. "red" states?
- Should it be banned or heavily regulated?
- Should this be protected free as free speech?
- Do you care?

SUMMARY

 Describe the four basic stages of consumer decision making.

Advertisers need a keen understanding of their consumers as a basis for developing effective advertising. This understanding begins with a view of consumers as systematic decision makers who follow a predictable process in making their choices among products and brands. The process begins when consumers perceive a need, and it proceeds with a search for information that will help in making an informed choice. The search-and-evaluation stage is followed by purchase. Postpurchase use and evaluation then become critical as the stage in which customer satisfaction is ultimately determined.

 Explain how consumers adapt their decision-making processes as a function of involvement and experience.

Some purchases are more important to people than others, and this fact adds complexity to any analysis of consumer behavior. To accommodate this complexity, advertisers often think about the level of involvement that attends any given purchase. Involvement and prior experience with a product or service category can lead to four diverse modes of consumer decision making. These modes are extended problem solving, limited problem solving, habit or variety seeking, and brand loyalty.

 Discuss how advertising may influence consumer behavior through its effects on various psychological states.

Advertisements are developed to influence the way people think about products and brands. More specifically, advertising is designed to affect consumers' beliefs and brand attitudes. Advertisers use multi-attribute attitude models to help them ascertain the beliefs and attitudes of target consumers. However, consumers have perceptual defenses that allow them to ignore or distort most of the commercial messages to which they are exposed. When consumers are not motivated to thoughtfully process an advertiser's message, it may be in that advertiser's best interest to feature one or more peripheral cues as part of the message.

 Discuss the interaction of culture and advertising.

Advertisements are cultural products, and culture provides the context in which an ad will be interpreted. Advertisers who overlook the influence of culture are bound to struggle in their attempt to communicate with the target audience. Two key concepts in managing the impact of culture are values and rituals. Values are enduring beliefs that provide a foundation for more-transitory psychological states, such as brand attitudes. Rituals are patterns of behavior shared by individuals from a common culture. Violating cultural values and rituals is a sure way to squander advertising dollars.

 Discuss the role of sociological factors in consumer behavior and advertising response.

Consumer behavior is an activity that each of us undertakes before a broad audience of other consumers. Advertising helps the transfer of meaning. Reference groups of various types have a dramatic influence on the consumption behavior of their individual members. Gender, ethnicity, and race are important influences on consumption. Who consumers are—their identity—is changeable; consumers can change aspects of who they are rapidly and frequently through what they buy and use. Celebrities are particularly important in this regard.

 Discuss how advertising transmits sociocultural meaning.

Advertising transfers a desired meaning to the brand by placing them within a carefully constructed social world respresented in an ad, or "slice of life." The advertiser paints a picture of the ideal social world, with all the meanings they want to impart to their brand. Then, the brand is carefully placed in that picture, and the two (the constructed social world and the brand) rub off on each other, becoming a part of each other. Meaning is thus transferred from the carefully constructed social world within the ad to the brand.

KEY TERMS

consumer behavior
need state
functional benefits
emotional benefits
internal search
external search
consideration set
evaluative criteria
customer satisfaction
cognitive dissonance
involvement
extended problem solving
limited problem solving
habit
variety seeking

brand loyalty
attitude
brand attitudes
beliefs
salient beliefs
multi-attribute attitude models
    (MAAMs)
cognitive consistency
advertising clutter
selective attention
cognitive responses
elaboration likelihood model (ELM)
peripheral cues
movement of meaning
culture

values
rituals
stratification (social class)
taste
reference group
membership groups
aspirational groups
intergenerational effect
life-stage
celebrity
gender
community
brand communities
global consumer culture
sociocultural text

QUESTIONS

1. When consumers have a well-defined consideration set and a list of evaluative criteria for assessing the brands in that set, they in effect possess a matrix of information about that category. Drawing on your experiences as a consumer, set up and fill in such a matrix for the category of fast-food restaurants.

2. Is cognitive dissonance a good thing or a bad thing from an advertiser's point of view? Explain how and why advertisers should try to take advantage of the cognitive dissonance their consumers may experience.

3. Most people quickly relate to the notion that some purchasing decisions are more involving than others. What kinds of products or services do you consider highly involving? What makes these products more involving from your point of view?

4. Explain the difference between brand-loyal and habitual purchasing. When a brand-loyal customer arrives at a store and finds her favorite brand out of stock, what would you expect to happen next?

5. Describe three attitude-change strategies that could be suggested by the results of a study of consumer behavior using multi-attribute attitude models. Provide examples of different advertising campaigns that have employed each of these strategies.

6. Watch an hour of prime-time television and for each commercial you see, make a note of the tactic the advertiser employed to capture and hold the audience's attention. How can the use of attention-attracting tactics backfire on an advertiser?

7. What does it mean to say that culture is invisible? Explain how this invisible force serves to restrict and control the activities of advertisers.

8. Give three examples of highly visible cultural rituals practiced annually in the United States. For each ritual you identify, assess the importance of buying and consuming for effective practice of the ritual.

9. Are you a believer in the intergenerational effect? Make a list of the brands in your cupboards, refrigerator, and medicine cabinet. Which of these brands would you also expect to find in your parents' cupboards, refrigerator, and medicine cabinet?

10. "In today's modern, highly educated society, there is simply no reason to separate men and women into different target segments. Gender just should not be an issue in the development of marketing and advertising strategies." Comment.

EXPERIENTIAL EXERCISES

1.   Create a list of three products or services to which you are brand-loyal. For each, explain why you have highly favorable attitudes toward the brand and consciously seek to buy it whenever you make a purchase from that product category. Describe what factors could cause you to change your loyalty and switch to a competing brand.

2.   Visit a friend or family member and identify the types of products they use. Examine apparel, bath and personal care products, foods and beverages, or any other product category of your choosing. Based on what you've learned about consumption contexts, describe what their preferred products reveal about their values and rituals. Be sure to identify how their consumer

choices are related to concepts such as stratification, cultural capital, reference groups, cool, race and ethnicity, and gender. Based on your analysis, suggest two or three new brands that your friend might be inclined to try out or use on a regular basis, and support your reasoning.

3.   Find ads that address the following four modes of decision making: extended problem solving, limited problem solving, habit or variety seeking, and brand loyalty. Explain why each ad fits with that particular decision-making mode and state whether you think the ad is effective in persuading consumers. Be sure to include the concepts of involvement and prior experience in your answer.

EXPERIENCING THE INTERNET

5-1 Comparison Shopping: Evaluating Prices and Products

Once a consumer has recognized a need, a process is set in motion involving an extensive product-information search and a careful evaluation of alternatives prior to purchase. Consumers usually conduct searches by comparison shopping, choosing between brands in a certain product category as they focus in on individual product attributes. In the real world, this information search and evaluation takes place in an interactive environment where consumers can consult the opinions of others as well as test products. But how does this process take place on the Web? Hundreds of sites have emerged on the Internet to aid consumers, re-creating the real-world decision-making process on the Web.

Epinions: http://www.epinions.com

mySimon: http://www.mysimon.com

1.   Briefly describe the purpose of these sites. How are they similar? How are they different?

2.   Do these sites help consumers with an internal search or an external search? What's the difference between the two? Can an internal search be conducted online? Explain.

3.   Compare online product evaluation with the traditional brick-and-mortar evaluation process. What advantage does each have in terms of convenience and usefulness?

5-2 Two Perspectives on Consumer Behavior

This chapter attempts to explain consumer behavior from two basic perspectives. The consumer can be understood as a decision maker walking through a logical process of analyzing needs and evaluating products to meet those needs at the cost-to-rewards level of consciousness. Another valuable perspective views the consumer as a product of social surroundings and forces that invariably lead to the purchase of products consistent with that consumer's culture, values, and beliefs. While no single perspective can fully explain the complicated and multifaceted phenomenon of consumer behaviors, these broad perspectives help advertisers create ads that are more likely to be effective in promoting brands and persuading audiences.

URB1: http://www.urb1.com

CCS: http://www.ccs.com

1.   Describe the characteristics of these two shopping sites. Which of the two perspectives on consumer behavior do they appear to represent?

2.   Describe the role of values and rituals as they relate to the consumer culture of URB1 and CCS. How do advertisers accommodate—and even create—sociocultural consumption contexts to benefit the promotion of brands?

3.   What is cultural capital and why is it important to advertisers? Explain the role of membership groups and aspirational groups in creating cultural capital. Give a real-world example of this from one of these sites.

CHAPTER 6

After reading and thinking about this chapter, you will be able to do the following:

1

Explain the process known as STP marketing.

2

Describe different bases that marketers use to identify target segments.

3

Discuss the criteria used for choosing a target segment.

4

Identify the essential elements of an effective positioning strategy.

5

Review the necessary ingredients for creating a brand's value proposition.

  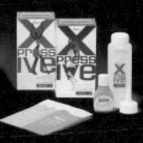

Introductory Scenario: Finding More Wet Shavers.

It would be fair to say that executives at The Gillette Company in Boston, Massachusetts, have become prisoners of their own success. King C. Gillette invented the safety razor in 1903, and since that time male grooming habits and the "wet shave" have been the company's obsession. Few companies can demonstrate the growth rates and global success that Gillette achieved in the 20th century. By the end of the century Gillette was able to claim that roughly two-thirds of all wet shaves around the world involved one of its razors, and that the company's profit growth was averaging nearly 15 percent annually.[1] Its advertising slogan—"Gillette: The Best a Man Can Get"— and products such as its SensorExcel and Mach3 shaving systems were ubiquitous. Thus, the challenge for Gillette executives was how to maintain their company's success at growing sales and profits around the world. They could keep introducing more expensive (and more profitable) shaving systems like the Mach3, and try to reach every last wet-shaving male on the face of the planet, but at some point they literally would run out of new faces.

Many companies large and small share Gillette's problem: How do you keep growing when there are always natural limits to growth? Or, how do you keep growing in the face of effective competitors who also want to grow just as much as you do? Companies anticipate and address this problem through a process we will refer to as STP marketing. It is a critical process from an advertising standpoint because it leads to decisions about *who* we need to advertise to, and *what* value proposition we will want to present to them.

To find sources for new growth, Gillette would need to identify new markets— someone other than wet-shaving males—to target with its new products and advertising campaigns. To make a long story short, Gillette decided to target wet-shaving females. The quintessential male-focused company would finally devote some of its considerable resources to address the unique shaving needs of women. And not just men's razors with pink handles (like the Daisy disposable razor, a failed Gillette product in the mid-1970s), but a complete line of products developed by women for women.

In effect, Gillette had discovered women as a focal point for its considerable marketing and advertising efforts. But not all women; more specifically, Gillette would emphasize women in the 15-to-24-year-old range—a new target segment for Gillette. The thinking was that winning over youthful, wet-shaving females would create customers for life. Additionally, Gillette had the global marketplace in mind when it launched its "Gillette for Women: Are You Ready?" campaign. While women around the world are less likely to remove body hair than their counterparts in the United States, younger women worldwide are most receptive to the idea. Gillette set out to tap the growth potential represented by the target segment of 15-to-24-year-old females around the world.

The program Gillette launched for these young women was multifaceted. It started with the Sensor shaving system for women, created by a female industrial designer, which featured a flat, wafer-shaped handle to give women better control while shaving. Other products followed, such as a high-end disposable razor named Agility and a line of shaving creams and after-shave products marketed under the brand name Satin Care. More money was allocated for global ad campaigns featuring ads such as those shown in Exhibits 6.1 and 6.2. This advertising, with the theme "Gillette for Women: Are You Ready?" was based on market research showing that most women perceive shaving as a nuisance or chore. Hence, they treat razors as a

---

1.   Mark Maremont, "Gillette Finally Reveals Its Vision of the Future, and It Has 3 Blades," *Wall Street Journal,* April 14, 1998, A1, 10.

EXHIBIT 6.1

This was one of the first ads featured in Gillette's aggressive marketing program to young women. As suggested by the ad, most of each year's ad budget was concentrated on the peak season—summertime.
http://www.gillette.com

EXHIBIT 6.2

Gillette marketing executives were intent on elevating the role of shaving from the practical realm to the emotional realm. Would you agree that emotional benefits are promised by this ad? http://www.gillette.com

EXHIBIT 6.3

Here we see Schick zig to counteract Gillette's zag. Recall that Gillette wanted to take wet shaving for women to a new, emotional realm. Schick's point of emphasis in more about function and simplicity. With this all-in-one razor, shaving's never been so simple. So, trust your intuition! http://www.schickintuition.com

commodity item and are satisfied with inexpensive disposables. Gillette's advertising was designed to make this routine grooming chore more important and more glamorous, and, in the words of Gillette's VP of female shaving, "elevate the role of shaving beyond the practical to a more emotional realm."[2]

By targeting wet-shaving young women, Gillette executives found a way to keep the company's sales and profits growing. This success convinced Gillette management that distinctive brands just for females were critical to the future of the company, and product development efforts were intensified to perfect the wet shave for women. More new product launches followed, including Venus, Venus Passion, and Venus Divine.[3] In addition, in perhaps the clearest indicator of Gillette's success, archrival Schick launched its own version of a wet-shaving system for women. The Schick Intuition is an all-in-one product with three blades embedded in a skin conditioner. As suggested by Exhibit 6.3, Intuition was designed to take the soap opera out of shaving. The simple fact that Schick was willing to devote $120 million on advertising to launch Intuition tells us that Gillette got it right when they decided to target wet-shaving women around the world.[4]

STP Marketing and the Evolution of Marketing Strategies.
The Gillette example illustrates the process that marketers use to decide whom to advertise to and what to say in that advertising. Gillette executives started with the diverse market of all women, and they broke the market down by age segments. They then selected 15-to-24-year-old females as their target segment. The

2.   Mark Maremont, "Gillette's New Strategy Is to Sharpen Pitch to Women," *Wall Street Journal,* May 11, 1998, B1, B16.
3.   Charles Forelle, "Schick Seeks Edge with Four-Blade Razor," *Wall Street Journal,* August 12, 2003, B1, B9.
4.   Suzanne Vranica, "Schick Challenges Gillette with $120 Million Campaign," *Wall Street Journal,* April 7, 2003, A18.

target segment is the subgroup (of the larger market) chosen as the focal point for the marketing program and advertising campaign.

While markets are segmented, products are positioned. To pursue the target segment, a firm organizes its marketing and advertising efforts around a coherent positioning strategy. **Positioning** is the process of designing and representing one's product or service so that it will occupy a distinct and valued place in the target consumer's mind. **Positioning strategy** involves the selection of key themes or concepts that the organization will feature when communicating this distinctiveness to the target segment. In Gillette's case, its executives first designed a line of products for the youthful female wet-shaver. They then came up with the positioning theme "Gillette for Women: Are You Ready?" to clearly distinguish this new line from their traditional male-oriented shaving systems. Finally, through skillful advertising, they communicated distinctive functional and emotional benefits to the target segment.

Notice the specific sequence, illustrated in Exhibit 6.4, that was played out in the Gillette example: The marketing strategy evolved as a result of *segmenting, targeting,* and *positioning.* This sequence of activities is often referred to as **STP marketing,** and it represents a sound basis for generating effective advertising.[5] While no formulas or models guarantee success, the STP approach is strongly recommended for markets characterized by diversity in consumers' needs and preferences. In markets with any significant degree of diversity, it is impossible to design one product that would appeal to everyone, or one advertising campaign that would communicate with everyone. Organizations that lose sight of this simple premise often run into trouble.

Indeed, in most product categories one finds that different consumers are looking for different things, and the only way for a company to take advantage of the sales potential represented by different customer segments is to develop and market a different brand for each segment. No company has done this better than cosmetics juggernaut Estée Lauder. Lauder has more than a dozen cosmetic brands, each developed for a different target segment.[6] For example, there is the original Estée

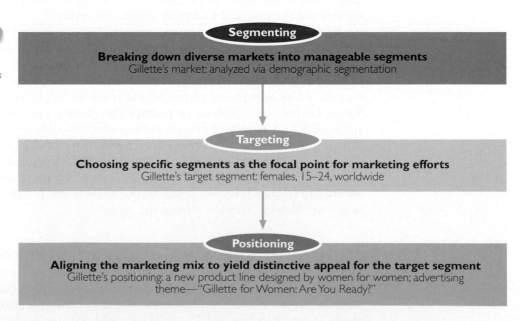

EXHIBIT 6.4

Laying the foundation for effective advertising campaigns through STP marketing.

Segmenting

Breaking down diverse markets into manageable segments
Gillette's market: analyzed via demographic segmentation

Targeting

Choosing specific segments as the focal point for marketing efforts
Gillette's target segment: females, 15–24, worldwide

Positioning

Aligning the marketing mix to yield distinctive appeal for the target segment
Gillette's positioning: a new product line designed by women for women; advertising theme—"Gillette for Women: Are You Ready?"

---

5.   For a more extensive discussion of STP marketing, see Philip Kotler, *Marketing Management* (Upper Saddle River, N.J.: Prentice Hall, 2003), ch. 10, 11.

6.   Nina Munk, "Why Women Find Lauder Mesmerizing," *Fortune,* May 25, 1998, 96–106.

Lauder brand, for women with conservative values and upscale tastes. Then there is Clinique, a no-nonsense brand that represents functional grooming for Middle America. Bobbi Brown is for the working mom who skillfully manages a career and her family and manages to look good in the process. M.A.C. is a brand for those who want to make a bolder statement: its spokespersons have been RuPaul, a 6-foot-7-inch drag queen, and k. d. lang, the talented lesbian vocalist. Prescriptives is marketed to a hip, urban, multiethnic target segment, and Origins, with its earthy packaging and natural ingredients, is for consumers who are concerned about the environment. These are just some of the cosmetics brands that Estée Lauder has marketed to appeal to diverse target segments. You can check out their entire lineup at http://www.elcompanies.com.

We offer the Estée Lauder example to make two key points before we move on. First, the Gillette story about wet-shavers may have made things seem too simple: STP marketing is a lot more complicated than just deciding to target women or men. Gender alone is rarely specific enough to serve as a complete identifier of a target segment. Second, the cosmetics example shows that many factors beyond just age and gender can come into play when trying to identify valid target segments. For these diverse cosmetics brands we see that considerations such as attitudes, lifestyles, and basic values all may play a role in identifying and describing customer segments.

To illustrate these points, examine the two ads in Exhibits 6.5 and 6.6. Both of these ads ran in *Seventeen* magazine, so it is safe to say that in each case the advertiser

EXHIBIT 6.5

The U.S. Armed Forces, including the Marines, are very aggressive and sophisticated advertisers. Here the Marines direct a message to basically the same target segment (from an age and gender standpoint) that was the focal point in Gillette's "Are You Ready?" campaign. http://www.usmc.mil

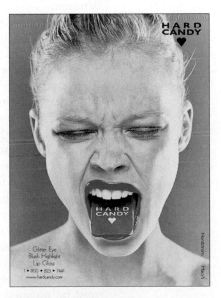

EXHIBIT 6.6

*Hard Candy comes by its hip style perhaps in large part because of its uninhibitedly energetic founding by Gen-Xer Dineh Mohajer, who was unhappy with the choices traditional cosmetics firms offered her and her market demographic (*http://www.hardcandy.com*). There must be something in that California air. Internet technology company Cisco co-founder Sandy Lerner created Urban Decay (*http://www.urbandecay.com*)—another alternative for the fashion-mad—out of a similar dissatisfaction with the offerings of companies like Lancôme (*http://www.lancome.com*).*

was trying to reach adolescent females. But as you compare these exhibits, it should be pretty obvious that the advertisers were really trying to reach out to very different segments of adolescent females. To put it bluntly, it is hard to imagine a marine captain wearing Hard Candy lip gloss. These ads were designed to appeal to different target segments, even though the people in these segments would seem the same if we considered only their age and gender.

Beyond STP Marketing. If an organization uses STP marketing as its framework for strategy development, at some point it will find the right strategy, develop the right advertising, make a lot of money, and live happily ever after. Right? As you might expect, it's not quite that simple. Even when STP marketing yields profitable outcomes, one must presume that success will not last indefinitely. Indeed, an important feature of marketing and advertising—a feature that can make these professions both terribly interesting and terribly frustrating—is their dynamic nature. To paraphrase a popular saying, shifts happen—consumer preferences shift. Competitors improve their marketing strategies, or technology changes and makes a popular product obsolete. Successful marketing strategies need to be modified or may even need to be reinvented as shifts occur in the organization's competitive environment.

To maintain the vitality and profitability of its products or services, an organization has two options. The first entails reassessment of the segmentation strategy. This may come through a more detailed examination of the current target segment to develop new and better ways of meeting its needs, or it may be necessary to adopt new targets and position new products to them, as was the case with Gillette for Women.

The second option is to pursue a product differentiation strategy. As defined in Chapter 1, product differentiation focuses the firm's efforts on emphasizing or even creating differences for its brands to distinguish them from the offerings of established competitors. Advertising plays a critical role as part of the product differentiation strategy because often the consumer will have to be convinced that the intended difference is meaningful. For example, Schick's response to Gillette's Mach3 Turbo was the Schick Quattro, with, you guessed it, four blades instead of three. But does that fourth blade really deliver a better shave? How could it be better than The Best a Man Can Get? Following a product differentiation strategy, the role for Schick's advertising is to convince the wet-shaving male that that fourth blade is essential for a close shave. And if they succeed, can the Gillette Mach5 Super Turbo be far behind?

The basic message is that marketing strategies and the advertising that supports them are never really final. Successes realized through proper application of STP marketing can be short-lived in highly competitive markets where any successful innovation is almost sure to be copied or "one-upped" by competitors. Thus, the value creation process for marketers and advertisers is continuous; STP marketing must be pursued over and over again and may be supplemented with product differentiation strategies.

Virtually every organization must compete for the attention and business of some customer groups while de-emphasizing or ignoring others. In this chapter we will examine in detail the way organizations decide whom to target and whom to ignore in laying the foundation for their marketing programs and advertising campaigns. The critical role of advertising campaigns in executing these strategies is also highlighted.

2 Identifying Target Segments.

The first step in STP marketing involves breaking down large, heterogeneous markets into more manageable submarkets or customer segments. This activity is known as **market segmentation.** It can be accomplished in many ways, but keep in mind that advertisers need to identify a segment with common characteristics that will lead the members of that segment to respond distinctively to a marketing program. For a segment to be really useful, advertisers also must be able to reach that segment with information about the product. Typically this means that advertisers must be able to identify the media the segment uses that will allow them to get an advertising message to the segment. For example, teenage males can be reached through media such as MTV; selected rap, contemporary rock, or alternative radio stations; and the Internet. The favorite syndicated TV show among highly affluent households (i.e., annual household income over $100,000) is *Seinfeld,* making it a popular choice for a host of advertisers.

In this section we will review several ways that consumer markets are commonly segmented. Markets can be segmented on the basis of usage patterns and commitment levels, demographic and geographic information, psychographics and lifestyles, or benefits sought. Many times, segmentation schemes evolve in such a way that multiple variables are used to identify and describe the target segment. Such an outcome is desirable because more knowledge about the target will usually translate into better marketing and advertising programs.

Usage Patterns and Commitment Levels.
One of the most common ways to segment markets is by consumers' usage patterns or commitment levels. With respect to usage patterns, it is important to recognize that for most products and services, some users will purchase much more frequently than others. It is common to find that **heavy users** in a category account for the majority of a product's sales and thus become the preferred or primary target segment. For example, Campbell Soup Company discovered what it refers to as its extra-enthusiastic core users: folks who buy nearly 320 cans of soup per year.[7] That's enough soup to serve Campbell's at least six days a week every week. To maintain this level of devotion to the product, standard marketing thought holds that it is in Campbell's best interest to know these heavy users in great detail and make them a focal point of the company's marketing strategy.

While being the standard wisdom, the heavy-user focus has some potential downsides. For one, devoted users may need no encouragement at all to keep consuming. In addition, a heavy-user focus takes attention and resources away from those who do need encouragement to purchase the marketer's brand. Perhaps most important, heavy users may be significantly different in terms of their motivations to consume, their approach to the product, or their image of the product.

Another segmentation option combines prior usage patterns with commitment levels to identify four fundamental segment types—brand-loyal customers, switchers (or variety seekers), nonusers, and emergent consumers.[8] Each segment represents a unique opportunity for the advertiser. **Nonusers** offer the lowest level of opportunity relative to the other three groups. **Brand-loyal users** are a tremendous asset if they are the advertiser's customers, but they are difficult to convert if they are loyal to a competitor.

Switchers, or **variety seekers,** often buy what is on sale or choose brands that offer discount-coupons or other price incentives. Whether they are pursued through price incentives, high-profile advertising campaigns, or both, switchers turn out to be a costly target segment. Much can be spent in getting their business merely to have it disappear just as quickly as it was won.

Emergent consumers, however, offer the organization an important business opportunity. In most product categories, there is a gradual but constant influx of

7.   Rebecca Piirto, *Beyond Mind Games: The Marketing Power of Psychographics* (Ithaca, N.Y.: American Demographics Books, 1991), 230.

8.   Further discussion of this four-way scheme is provided by David W. Stewart, "Advertising in Slow-Growth Economies," *American Demographics* (September 1994), 40–46.

EXHIBIT 6.7

Emergent consumers represent an important source of long-term opportunity for many organizations. Have you ever thought of yourself as an emergent consumer? http://www.wellsfargo.com

first-time buyers. The reasons for this influx vary by product category and include purchase triggers such as puberty, college graduation, marriage, a new baby, divorce, job promotions, and retirement. Immigration can also be a source of numerous new customers for many product categories, and, as indicated by the Global box, companies could learn a lot from Western Union with respect to courting immigrants around the world. Generation X also attracted the attention of marketers and advertisers because it was a large group of emergent adult consumers. But inevitably, Generation X lost its emergent status and was replaced by a new age cohort—you guessed it, Generation Y—who took their turn as advertisers' darlings.[9]

Emergent consumers are motivated by many different factors, but they share one important characteristic: Their brand preferences are still under development. Targeting emergents with messages that fit their age or social circumstances may produce modest effects in the short run, but it eventually may yield a brand loyalty that pays handsome rewards for the discerning organization. Of course, this was part of Gillette's rationale in targeting youthful females. As another example, banks actively recruit college students who have limited financial resources in the short term, but excellent potential as long-term customers. Exhibit 6.7 shows an ad from Wells Fargo Bank with an appeal to emergent consumers at the University of Arizona.

Demographic Segmentation. Demographic segmentation is widely used in selecting target segments and includes basic descriptors such as age, gender, race, marital status, income, education, and occupation (see the array of possibilities at http://www.factfinder.census.gov). Demographic information has special value in market segmentation because if an advertiser knows the demographic characteristics of the target segment, choosing media to efficiently reach that segment is much easier.

Demographic information has two specific applications. First, demographics are commonly used to describe or profile segments that have been identified with some other variable. If an organization had first segmented its market in terms of product usage rates, the next step would be to describe or profile its heavy users in terms of demographic characteristics such as age or income. In fact, one of the most common approaches for identifying target segments is to combine information about usage patterns with demographics.

Mobil Oil Corporation used such an approach in segmenting the market for gasoline buyers and identified five basic segments: Road Warriors, True Blues, Generation F3, Homebodies, and Price Shoppers.[10] Extensive research on more than 2,000 motorists revealed considerable insight about these five segments. At one extreme, Road Warriors spend at least $1,200 per year at gas stations; they buy premium gasoline and snacks and beverages and sometimes opt for a car wash. Road Warriors are generally more affluent, middle-aged males who drive 25,000 to 50,000

9.   Bonnie Tsui, "Generation Next," *Advertising Age,* January 15, 2001, 14, 16.
10. Allanna Sullivan, "Mobil Bets Drivers Pick Cappuccino over Low Prices," *Wall Street Journal,* January 30, 1995, B1.

miles per year. (Note how Mobil combined information about usage patterns with demographics to provide a detailed picture of the segment.) In contrast, Price Shoppers spend no more than $700 annually at gas stations, are generally less affluent, rarely buy premium, and show no loyalty to particular brands or stations. In terms of relative segment sizes, there are about 25 percent more Price Shoppers on the highways than Road Warriors. If you were the marketing vice president at Mobil, which of these two segments would you target? Think about it for a few pages—we'll get back to you.

Second, demographic categories are used frequently as the starting point in market segmentation. This was the case in the Gillette example, where teenage females turned out to be the segment of interest. Demographics will also be a major consideration in the tourism industry, where families with young children are often the marketer's primary focus. For instance, the Bahamian government launched a program to attract families to their island paradise. But instead of reaching out to mom and dad, Bahamian officials made their appeal to kids by targeting the 2-to-11-year-old viewing audience of Nickelodeon's cable television channel.[11] Marketing to and through children is always complex, and as we saw in Chapter 4, is often controversial as well. The IBP box offers some guidelines for approaching young consumers in a professional manner.

Another demographic group that is receiving renewed attention from advertisers is the "woopies," or well-off older people. In the United States, consumers over 50 years old control two-thirds of the country's wealth, around $28 trillion. The median net worth of households headed by persons 55 to 64 is 15 times larger than the net worth for households headed by a person under age 35. Put in simple terms, for most people age 20, $100 is a lot of money. For woopies, $100 is change back from the purchase of a $10,000 home theatre system. Marketers such as Ford, Sony, Target, Anheuser-Busch, Walt Disney, and Virgin Entertainment Group are all reconsidering their product offerings with woopies in mind.[12] And, by 2025, the number of people over 50 will grow by 80 percent to become a third of the U.S. population. Growth in the woopie segment will also be dramatic in other countries, such as Japan and the nations of Western Europe. Still, like any other age segment, older consumers are a diverse group, and the temptation to stereotype must

GLOBAL ISSUES

Nothin' Says Lovin' Like a Money-Gram!

Western Union Financial Services is best known for helping people move money quickly when they find themselves in a tight squeeze. But recently they discovered that their electronic money transfers are often associated with significant emotional episodes for families with loved ones in another country. In a strategy reminiscent of Gillette's outreach to wet-shaving females, Western Union decided to take the money transfer business from a purely functional to a more emotional realm. As part of its new global campaign, Western Union revised its positioning strategy from "The Fastest Way to Send Money" to "Uniting People with Possibilities." Note the change from functional to emotional.

Two new TV spots created for the $300 million dollar campaign relied on visual metaphors to symbolize the act of reaching out to a loved one. One showed a Latino café owner sending a flock of lemon-yellow birds to a daughter moving into a new apartment. Another used a beam of light leaping from the laptop of an African-American man across a continent to the college graduation ceremony of his brother. In each of these cases Western Union and its agency J. Walter Thompson hopes the symbolism in the ads will be "translated" the same way by people all over the world.

$300 million sounds like a lot, but goes fast when pursuing markets the size of North America, China, India, and the Ukraine. Fortunately, Western Union has another key asset that will assist in making the new positioning strategy resonate at the local level in diverse cultures. It will rely on its 50,000 agents in the U.S. and Canada along with 100,000 agents in other key markets to bring the new strategy to life. "Uniting People with Possibilities" is a strong promise, and with 150,000 agents around the world, it is a promise that Western Union is uniquely equipped to fulfill.

Source: Brian Steinberg, "Western Union to Court Immigrants," *Wall Street Journal*, May 2, 2003, B2.

11.   Sally Beatty, "Nickelodeon Sets $30 Million Ad Deal with the Bahamas," *Wall Street Journal*, March 14, 2001, B6.
12.   Kelly Greene, "Marketing Surprise: Older Consumers Buy Stuff, Too," *Wall Street Journal*, April 6, 2004, A1, A12.

be resisted. Some marketers advocate partitioning older consumers into groups aged 50–64, 65–74, 75–84, and 85 or older, as a means of reflecting important differences in needs. Still, more thorough knowledge of this population is clearly needed.

IBP

Take Special Care with Promotions to Kids

Kids' discretionary income grows as societies become more affluent. Kids also exert significant influence in purchasing decisions made by moms, dads, grandmas, grandpas, aunts, uncles, and so forth and so on. When you add it all up, kids either control or influence the expenditure of hundreds of billions of dollars every year. So it is logical that in many instances, tykes, tweens, and/or teens are identified as primary target markets for planning special promotions. When targeting kids for special promotions, here are three good principles to live by.

- *Play by their tools.* When targeting a generation that takes computers, high-tech video games, and the Internet for granted, marketers must learn how to play by their tools. This will usually mean incorporating the Internet as part of the promotion. For example, even a low-tech baseball card giveaway can be moved to the Internet. Skippy peanut butter developed such a promotion featuring its baseball star spokesperson—Derek Jeter of the New York Yankees. Skippy jar tops directed kids to peanutbutter.com, where they entered "the secret code" to receive downloadable cards known as Digibles. These digital baseball cards provided both sound and video featuring baseball's MVP.
- *Treat them like family.* When moving your promotions to the Internet, privacy should always be a concern, and this goes double for promotions to kids. We encourage you to respect young consumers' privacy because it is the right thing to do, and because there are numerous laws that require it. The Children's Online Privacy Protection Act (COPPA), which is enforced by the FTC, restricts kid-focused Web sites in the areas of data collection, spamming, sweepstakes, and contests. According to Susan Bennett, director of promotions for foxkids.com, "If you're in the kids marketplace, you better know what COPPA is."
- *Look for the high road.* Something really cool is happening among young people. Kids are less likely to be ridiculed by their peers for being interested in learning about math, science, reading, and especially the environment and all living things. In other words, it's hip to be smart. Thus, educationally themed promotions are increasingly common among kids' brands, and there are abundant opportunities to build on the premise of engaging kids through participative learning. For instance, in the case of the Bahamas' campaign directed at kids and their families, a featured element was learning about a coral reef in the Bahamas and identifying actions that children can take to help protect endangered waterways. Giveaways are nice, but don't forget to look for the high road.

Sources: John Palmer, "Connecting to Kids," *PROMO Magazine*, March 2001, 21–33; and Nancy Keates, "Catering to Kids," *Wall Street Journal*, May 3, 2002, W1, W6.

Geographic Segmentation.

Geographic segmentation needs little explanation other than to emphasize how useful geography is in segmenting markets. Geographic segmentation may be conducted within a country by region (for example, the Pacific Northwest versus New England in the United States), by state or province, by city, or even by neighborhood. Climate and topographical features yield dramatic differences in consumption by region for products such as snow tires and surfboards, but geography can also correlate with other differences that are not so obvious. Eating and food preparation habits, entertainment preferences, recreational activities, and other aspects of lifestyle have been shown to vary along geographic lines. Exhibits 6.8 and 6.9 show U.S. consumption patterns for Twinkies and for Obsession versus Old Spice. As you can see, where one lives does seem to affect preferences.

In recent years, skillful marketers have merged information on where people live with the U.S. Census Bureau's demographic data to produce a form of market segmentation known as geodemographic segmentation. **Geodemographic segmentation** identifies neighborhoods (by ZIP codes) around the country that share common demographic characteristics. One such system, known as PRIZM (potential rating index by ZIP marketing), identifies 62 market segments that encompass all the ZIP codes in the United States.[13] Each of these segments has similar lifestyle characteristics and can be found throughout the country.

For example, the American Dreams segment is found in many metropolitan neighborhoods and comprises upwardly mobile ethnic minorities, many of

---

13. Christina Del Valle, "They Know Where You Live—and How You Buy," *BusinessWeek*, February 7, 1994, 89; Amy Merrick, "Counting on the Census," *Wall Street Journal*, February 14, 2001, B1.

EXHIBIT 6.8

People who eat Hostess Twinkies (red marks the highest consumption).

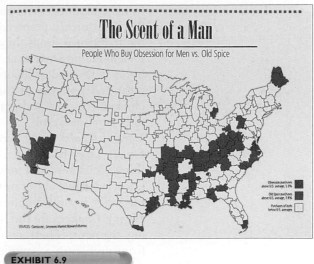

EXHIBIT 6.9

People who buy Obsession for Men (red) versus Old Spice (blue).

whom were foreign-born. This segment's product preferences are different from those of people belonging to the Rural Industria segment, who are young families with one or both parents working at low-wage jobs in small-town America. Systems such as PRIZM are very popular because of the depth of segment description they provide, along with their ability to precisely identify where the segment can be found (for more details, search for PRIZM at http://www.clusterbigip1.claritas.com).

Psychographics and Lifestyle Segmentation. **Psychographics** is a term that advertisers created in the mid-1960s to refer to a form of research that emphasizes the understanding of consumers' activities, interests, and opinions (AIOs).[14] Many advertising agencies were using demographic variables for segmentation purposes, but they wanted insights into consumers' motivations, which demographic variables did not provide. Psychographics were created as a tool to supplement the use of demographic data. Because a focus on consumers' activities, interests, and opinions often produces insights into differences in the lifestyles of various segments, this approach usually results in a **lifestyle segmentation.** Knowing details about the lifestyle of a target segment can be valuable for creating advertising messages that ring true to the consumer.

Lifestyle, or psychographic, segmentation can be customized with a focus on the issues germane to a single product category, or it may be pursued so that the resulting segments have general applicability to many different product or service categories. An example of the former is research conducted for Pillsbury to segment the eating habits of American households.[15] This "What's Cookin'" study involved consumer interviews with more than 3,000 people and identified five segments of the population, based on their shared eating styles:

- *Chase & Grabbits,* at 26 percent of the population, are heavy users of all forms of fast food. These are people who can make a meal out of microwave popcorn; as long as the popcorn keeps hunger at bay and is convenient, this segment is happy with its meal.
- *Functional Feeders,* at 18 percent of the population, are a bit older than the Chase & Grabbits but no less convenience-oriented. Since they are more likely

14.   Michael R. Solomon, *Consumer Behavior* (Upper Saddle River, N. J.: Pearson Prentice Hall, 2004), 204–207.
15.   Piirto, *Beyond Mind Games,* 222–23.

to have families, their preferences for convenient foods involve frozen products that are quickly prepared at home. They constantly seek faster ways to prepare the traditional foods they grew up with.

- **Down-Home Stokers,** at 21 percent of the population, involve blue-collar households with modest incomes. They are very loyal to their regional diets, such as meat and potatoes in the Midwest and clam chowder in New England. Fried chicken, biscuits and gravy, and bacon and eggs make this segment the champion of cholesterol.

- **Careful Cooks,** at 20 percent of the population, are more prevalent on the West Coast. They have replaced most of the red meat in their diet with pastas, fish, skinless chicken, and mounds of fresh fruit and vegetables. They believe they are knowledgeable about nutritional issues and are willing to experiment with foods that offer healthful options.

- **Happy Cookers** are the remaining 15 percent of the population but are a shrinking segment. These cooks are family-oriented and take substantial satisfaction from preparing a complete homemade meal for the family. Young mothers in this segment are aware of nutritional issues but will bend the rules with homemade meat dishes, casseroles, pies, cakes, and cookies.

Even these abbreviated descriptions of Pillsbury's five psychographic segments should make it clear that very different marketing and advertising programs are called for to appeal to each group. Exhibits 6.10 and 6.11 show ads from Pillsbury. Which segments are these ads targeting?

EXHIBIT 6.10

EXHIBIT 6.11

Which lifestyle segment is Pillsbury targeting with this ad? It looks like a toss-up between Chase & Grabbits and Functional Feeders. Does Pillsbury's site (http://www.pillsbury.com) target the same lifestyle segment as the ads? What features at the site are designed to build customer loyalty? Based on the site's message and design, what lifestyle choices does Pillsbury seem to assume that its target segment has made?

The convenience-oriented Functional Feeders seem the natural target for this novel ad. That Pillsbury Doughboy sure gets around!
http://www.pillsbury.com

EXHIBIT 6.12

The eight VALS™ segments. http://www .sric-bi.com

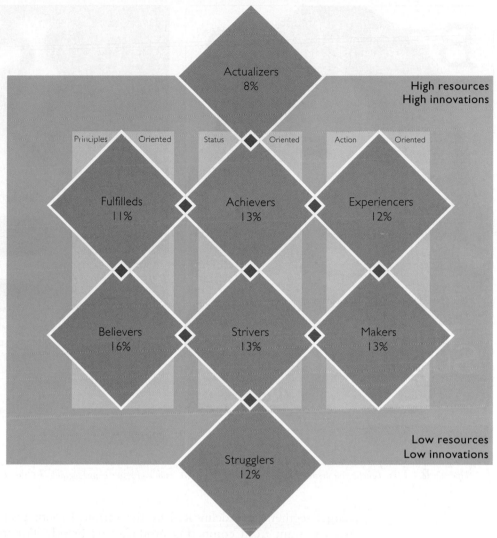

As noted, lifestyle segmentation studies can also be pursued with no particular product category as a focus, and the resulting segments could prove useful for many different marketers. A notable example of this approach is the VALS™ (for values and lifestyles) system developed by SRI International and marketed by SRI Consulting Business Intelligence of Menlo Park, California.[16] The VALS™ framework was first introduced in 1978 with nine potential segments, but in recent years it has been revised to feature eight segments.

As shown in Exhibit 6.12, the segments are organized in terms of resources (which include age, income, and education) and primary motivation. For instance, the Experiencer is relatively affluent and action-oriented. This enthusiastic and risk-taking group has yet to establish predictable behavioral patterns. Its members look to sports, recreation, exercise, and social activities as outlets for their abundant energy. SRI Consulting Business Intelligence sells detailed information and marketing recommendations about the eight segments to a variety of marketing organizations.

Benefit Segmentation.   Another segmentation approach developed by advertising researchers and used extensively over the past 30 years is **benefit segmentation.** In benefit segmentation,

16.   Ibid.; see ch. 3, 5, and 8 for an extensive discussion of the VALS system.

EXHIBIT 6.13

Benefit segmentation really comes to life in this ad for Bed Head. If that Superstar look is the benefit you desire, Think Thick!

EXHIBIT 6.14

Catwalk promises 3-D benefits: Defrizz—Define—Detangle. And the end result is unDeniable—Curls Rock!

target segments are delineated by the various benefit packages that different consumers want from competing products and brands. For instance, different people want different benefits from their automobiles. Some consumers want efficient and reliable transportation; others want speed, excitement, and glamour; and still others want luxury, comfort, and prestige. One product could not possibly serve such diverse benefit segments. Exhibits 6.13 and 6.14 feature two hair care products that promise different kinds of benefits to potential consumers.

This notion of attempting to understand consumers' priorities and assess how different brands might perform based on criteria deemed important by various segments should have a familiar ring. If not, turn back to Chapter 5 and revisit our discussion of multi-attribute attitude models (MAAMs). The importance weights collected from individual consumers in MAAMs research often provide the raw material needed for identifying benefit segments.

Segmenting Business-to-Business Markets. Thus far, our discussion of segmentation options has focused on ways to segment **consumer markets.** Consumer markets are the markets for products and services purchased by individuals or households to satisfy their specific needs. Consumer marketing is often compared and contrasted with business-to-business marketing. **Business markets** are the institutional buyers who purchase items to be used in other products and services or to be resold to other businesses or households. Although advertising is more prevalent in consumer markets, products and services such as wireless phones, Web hosting, consulting services,

EXHIBIT 6.15

Xerox: The Document Company has taken its brand name and products like the printer/copier/fax machine around the world with great success. "Multifuncionales" is a feature that business people appreciate in North and South America. http://www.xerox.cl

EXHIBIT 6.16

If you have a package that needs to be there on time, FedEx has always been a good choice. FedEx Ground promises date-definite, door-to-door delivery to any and all business addresses in the United States, Canada, and Puerto Rico. Relax, it's FedEx. http://www.fedex.com

and a wide array of business machines and package-delivery services (see Exhibits 6.15 and 6.16) are commonly promoted to business customers around the world. Hence, segmentation strategies are also valuable for business-to-business marketers.

Business markets can be segmented using several of the options already discussed.[17] For example, business customers differ in their usage rates and geographic locations, so these variables may be productive bases for segmenting business markets. Additionally, one of the most common approaches uses the Standard Industrial Classification (SIC) codes prepared by the U.S. Census Bureau. SIC information is helpful for identifying categories of businesses and then pinpointing the precise locations of these organizations.

Some of the more sophisticated segmentation methods used by firms that market to individual consumers do not translate well to business markets.[18] For instance, rarely would there be a place for psychographic or lifestyle segmentation in the business-to-business setting. In business markets, advertisers fall back on simpler strategies that are easier to work with from the perspective of the sales force. Segmentation by a potential customer's stage in the purchase process is one such strategy. It turns out that first-time prospects, novices, and sophisticates want very different

---

17.   Kotler, *Marketing Management,* 296–298.
18.   Thomas S. Robertson and Howard Barich, "A Successful Approach to Segmenting Industrial Markets," *Planning Forum* (November–December 1992), 5–11.

packages of benefits from their vendors, and thus they should be targeted separately in advertising and sales programs.

3 Prioritizing Target Segments.

Whether it is done through usage patterns, demographic characteristics, geographic location, benefit packages, or any combination of options, segmenting markets typically yields a mix of segments that vary in their attractiveness to the advertiser. In pursuing STP marketing, the advertiser must get beyond this potentially confusing mixture of segments to a selected subset that will become the target for its marketing and advertising programs. Recall the example of Mobil Oil Corporation and the segments of gasoline buyers it identified via usage patterns and demographic descriptors. What criteria should Mobil use to help decide between Road Warriors and Price Shoppers as possible targets?

Perhaps the most fundamental criterion in segment selection revolves around what the members of the segment want versus the organization's ability to provide it. Every organization has distinctive strengths and weaknesses that must be acknowledged when choosing its target segment. The organization may be particularly strong in some aspect of manufacturing, like Gillette, which has particular expertise in mass production of intricate plastic and metal products. Or perhaps its strength lies in well-trained and loyal service personnel, like those at FedEx, who can effectively implement new service programs initiated for customers, such as next-day delivery "absolutely, positively by 10:30 AM." To serve a target segment, an organization may have to commit substantial resources to acquire or develop the capabilities to provide what that segment wants. If the price tag for these new capabilities is too high, the organization must find another segment.

Another major consideration in segment selection entails the size and growth potential of the segment. Segment size is a function of the number of people, households, or institutions in the segment, plus their willingness to spend in the product category. When assessing size, advertisers must keep in mind that the number of people in a segment of heavy users may be relatively small, but the extraordinary usage rates of these consumers can more than make up for their small numbers. In addition, it is not enough to simply assess a segment's size as of today. Segments are dynamic, and it is common to find marketers most interested in devoting resources to segments projected for dramatic growth. As we have already seen, the purchasing power and growth projections for people age 50 and older have made this a segment that many companies are targeting.

So does bigger always mean better when choosing target segments? The answer is a function of the third major criterion for segment selection. In choosing a target segment, an advertiser must also look at the **competitive field**—companies that compete for the segment's business—and then decide whether it has a particular expertise, or perhaps just a bigger budget, that would allow it to serve the segment more effectively.

When an advertiser factors in the competitive field, it often turns out that smaller is better when selecting target segments. Almost by definition, large segments are usually established segments that many companies have identified and targeted previously. Trying to enter the competitive field in a mature segment isn't easy because established competitors can be expected to respond aggressively with advertising campaigns or price promotions in an effort to repel any newcomer.

Alternatively, large segments may simply be poorly defined segments; that is, a large segment may need to be broken down into smaller categories before a company can understand consumers' needs well enough to serve them effectively. Again, the segment of older consumers—age 50 and older—is huge, but in most instances it would simply be too big to be valuable as a target. Too much diversity exists in the needs and preferences of this age group, so further segmentation based on other

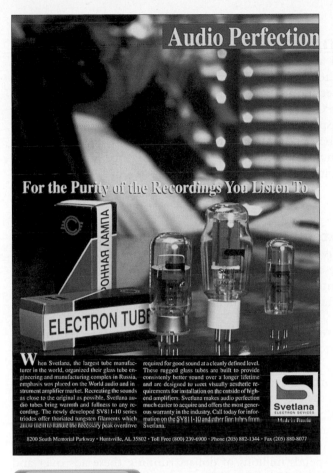

Audio Perfection

For the Purity of the Recordings You Listen To

When Svetlana, the largest tube manufacturer in the world, organized their glass tube engineering and manufacturing complex in Russia, emphasis was placed on the World audio and instrument amplifier market. Recreating the sounds as close to the original as possible, Svetlana audio tubes bring warmth and fullness to any recording. The newly developed SV811-10 series triodes offer thoriated tungsten filaments which allow them to handle the necessary peak overdrive required for good sound at a cleanly defined level. These rugged glass tubes are built to provide consistently better sound over a longer lifetime and are designed to meet visually aesthetic requirements for installation on the outside of high-end amplifiers. Svetlana makes audio perfection much easier to acquire and offers the most generous warranty in the industry. Call today for information on the SV811-10 and other fine tubes from Svetlana.

Svetlana
ELECTRON DEVICES
Made in Russia

8200 South Memorial Parkway • Huntsville, AL 35802 • Toll Free (800) 239-6900 • Phone (205) 882-1344 • Fax (205) 880-8077

EXHIBIT 6.17

Niche marketers are usually able to charge a premium price for their distinctive products. If you decide to go with Svetlana the next time you are buying amplifier tubes, expect to pay a little extra.

demographic variables, or perhaps via psychographics, is called for before an appropriate target can be located.

The smaller-is-better principle has become so popular in choosing target segments that it is now referred to as niche marketing. A market niche is a relatively small group of consumers who have a unique set of needs and who typically are willing to pay a premium price to the firm that specializes in meeting those needs.[19] The small size of a **market niche** often means it would not be profitable for more than one organization to serve it. Thus, when a firm identifies and develops products for market niches, the threat of competitors developing imitative products to attack the niche is reduced. Exhibit 6.17 is an example of an ad directed toward a very small niche, those who prefer imported Russian tubes for their high-end tube stereo amplifiers.

Niche marketing will continue to grow in popularity as the mass media splinter into a more and more complex and narrowly defined array of specialized vehicles. Specialized cable programming—such as the Health & Fitness Channel, the History Channel, or the 24-hour Golf Channel—attracts small and very distinctive groups of consumers, providing advertisers with an efficient way to communicate with market niches.[20] Additionally, perhaps the ideal application of the Internet as a marketing tool is in identifying and accessing market niches.[21]

But now let's return to the question faced by Mobil Oil Corporation. Whom should it target—Road Warriors or Price Shoppers? Hopefully you will see this as a straightforward decision. Road Warriors are a more attractive segment in terms of both segment size and growth potential. Although there are more Price Shoppers in terms of sheer numbers, Road Warriors spend more at the gas station, making them the larger segment from the standpoint of revenue generation. Road Warriors are much more prone to buy those little extras, such as a sandwich and a car wash, that could be extremely profitable sources of new business. Mobil also came to the conclusion that too many of its competitors were already targeting Price Shoppers. Mobil thus selected Road Warriors as its target segment and developed a positioning strategy it referred to as "Friendly Serve." Gas prices went up at Mobil stations, but Mobil also committed new resources to improving all aspects of the gas-purchasing experience.[22] Cleaner restrooms and better lighting alone yielded sales gains between 2 percent and 5 percent. Next, more attendants were hired to run between the pump and the snack bar to get Road Warriors in and out quickly—complete with their sandwich and beverage. Early results indicated that helpful attendants boosted station sales by another 15 to 20 percent. The Mobil case is a good example of how the application of STP marketing can rejuvenate sales, even in a mundane product category such as gasoline.

19. Kotler, *Marketing Management,* 280–281.
20. Timothy Aeppel, "For Parker Hannifin, Cable Is Best," *Wall Street Journal,* August 7, 2003, B3.
21. Heather Green, "How to Reach John Q. Public," *BusinessWeek,* March 26, 2001, 132, 133.
22. Chad Rubel, "Quality Makes a Comeback," *Marketing News,* September 23, 1996, 10.

4 **Formulating the Positioning Strategy.** Now that we have discussed the ways markets are segmented and the criteria used for selecting specific target segments, we turn our attention to positioning strategy. If a firm has been careful in segmenting the market and selecting its targets, then a positioning strategy—such as Mobil's "Friendly Serve" or Gillette's "The Best a Man Can Get"—should occur naturally. In addition, as an aspect of positioning strategy, we will begin to entertain ideas about how a firm can best communicate to the target segment what it has to offer. This is where advertising plays its vital role. A positioning strategy will include particular ideas or themes that must be communicated effectively if the marketing program is to be successful.

Essentials for Effective Positioning Strategies.

Any sound positioning strategy includes several essential elements. Effective positioning strategies are based on meaningful commitments of organizational resources to produce substantive value for the target segment. They also are consistent internally and over time, and they feature simple and distinctive themes. Each of these essential elements is described and illustrated in this section.

Let's begin with the issue of substance. For a positioning strategy to be effective and remain effective over time, the organization must be committed to creating substantive value for the customer. Take the example of Mobil Oil Corporation and its target segment, the Road Warriors. Road Warriors are willing to pay a little more for gas if it comes with extras such as prompt service or fresh coffee. So Mobil must create an ad campaign that depicts its employees as the brightest, friendliest, most helpful people you'd ever want to meet. The company asks its ad agency to come up with a catchy jingle that will remind people about the great services they can expect at a Mobil station. It spends millions of dollars running these ads over and over and wins the enduring loyalty of the Road Warriors. Right? Well, maybe, and maybe not. Certainly, a new ad campaign will have to be created to make Road Warriors aware of what the company has to offer, but it all falls apart if they drive in with great expectations and the company's people do not live up to them.

Effective positioning begins with substance. In the case of Mobil's "Friendly Serve" strategy, this means keeping restrooms attractive and clean, adding better lighting to all areas of the station, and upgrading the quality of the snacks and beverages available in each station's convenience store. It also means hiring more attendants, outfitting them in blue pants, blue shirts, ties, and black Reeboks, and then training and motivating them to anticipate and fulfill the needs of the harried Road Warrior.[23] Effecting meaningful change in service levels at thousands of stations nationwide is an expensive and time-consuming process for Mobil, but without some substantive change, there can be no hope of retaining the Road Warrior's lucrative business.

A positioning strategy also must be consistent internally and consistent over time. Regarding internal consistency, everything must work in combination to reinforce a distinct perception in the consumer's eyes about what a brand stands for. If we have chosen to position our airline as the one that will be known for on-time reliability, then we certainly would invest in things like extensive preventive maintenance and state-of-the-art baggage-handling facilities. There would be no need for exclusive airport lounges as part of this strategy, nor would any special emphasis need to be placed on in-flight food and beverage services. If our target segment wants reliable transportation, then this and only this should be the obsession in running our airline. This particular obsession has made Southwest Airlines a very formidable competitor,

23.   Ibid.

HARD WORK, ATTENTION TO DETAIL,
PERSONAL SERVICE. SOUND FAMILIAR?
WE LIVE WHERE YOU LIVE.™

State Farm® agents are business owners too. That's why they know how to take care of you
and your business insurance needs with comprehensive coverage, reasonable rates and monthly
payments. Call your State Farm agent to find out if you qualify for up to
30% off your premium.

LIKE A GOOD NEIGHBOR   STATE FARM IS THERE.℠

Call your neighborhood State Farm Agent, or visit statefarm.com®

Providing Insurance and Financial Services

EXHIBIT 6.18

Consistency is a definite virtue in choosing and executing a positioning strategy. State Farm's "Good Neighbor" theme has been a hallmark of its advertising for many years. Does State Farm's site (http://www.statefarm .com) produce substantive value for its target segment? How? What simple and distinctive themes can you find? Why are these elements essential to State Farm's positioning strategy?

even against much larger airlines, as it has expanded its routes to different regions of the United States.[24]

A strategy also needs consistency over time. As we saw in Chapter 5, consumers have perceptual defenses that allow them to screen or ignore most of the ad messages they are exposed to. Breaking through the clutter and establishing what a brand stands for is a tremendous challenge for any advertiser, but it is a challenge made easier by consistent positioning. If year in and year out an advertiser communicates the same basic themes to the target segment, then the message may get through and shape the way consumers perceive the brand. An example of a consistent approach is the long-running "Good Neighbor" ads of State Farm Insurance. While the specific copy changes, the thematic core of the campaign does not change. Exhibit 6.18 shows a contemporary ad from this long-running campaign, including the "We Live Where You Live" extension to their "Good Neighbor" premise.

Finally, there is the matter of simplicity and distinctiveness. Simplicity and distinctiveness are essential to the advertising task. No matter how much substance has been built into a product, it will fail in the marketplace if the consumer doesn't perceive what the product can do. Keep in mind, in a world of harried consumers who can be expected to ignore, distort, or completely forget most of the ads they are exposed to, complicated, imitative messages simply have no chance of getting through. The basic premise of a positioning strategy must be simple and distinctive if it is to be communicated effectively to the target segment.

The value of simplicity and distinctiveness in positioning strategy is nicely illustrated by the approach of GM's Pontiac division, starting in the mid-1980s. This was a period when Japanese automakers were taking market share from their U.S. counterparts, and no American car company was being hit harder than General Motors. Pontiac, however, grew its market share in this period with a positioning strategy that involved a return to Pontiac's heritage from the 1960s as a performance car. Pontiac's positioning strategy involved a number of different variations of an "excitement" promise, including, "We Build Excitement," "We Are Driving Excitement," and "Grand Am—Excitement Well Built."

It was that last phrase ("Well Built") that ultimately led to erosion in the effectiveness of Pontiac's strategy. While simple, distinctive, and consistent, their strategy began to suffer when their product didn't live up to the promise. Plastic fenders, under-powered engines borrowed from GM's Chevy and Buick divisions, and premium pricing turned off the customer segment looking for excitement.[25] But to the credit of the Pontiac division, they didn't back down on the basic premise. Models like the legendary GTO (Gran Turismo Omologato, Italian for a race car that has been made street legal) were rebuilt and re-launched to deliver substance again. Distinctive affiliations like the Official Performance Machines of the NCAA supported Pontiac's updated positioning message: "Fuel for the Soul." Embedding the Pontiac brand as a regular fixture and supporter of "March Madness" (see Exhibit 6.19) was a real coup for Pontiac marketers. Pontiac continues to impress with the simplicity,

24.   Scott McCartney, "Profit for Southwest Air Is Industry Rarity," *Wall Street Journal,* October 18, 2002, B4.
25.   David Welch, "An 'American BMW'? Don't Hold Your Breath," *BusinessWeek,* March 17, 2003, 98.

PONTIAC Official Performance Machines of the *NCAA*

EXHIBIT 6.19

"We Build Excitement" is a good example of a single-benefit positioning theme. More recently Pontiac has updated that theme as "Fuel for the Soul," and a great relationship with NCAA basketball creates a unique identity for Pontiac. But to compete in today's automotive marketplace, models like the GTO must deliver legendary performance. http://www .gto.com

consistency, and distinctiveness of their positioning strategy. It can work for them again, but they must deliver on "Well Built."

Fundamental Positioning Themes.

Positioning themes that are simple and distinctive help an organization make internal decisions that yield substantive value for customers, and they assist in the development of focused ad campaigns to break through the clutter of competitors' advertising. Thus, choosing a viable positioning theme is one of the most important decisions faced by marketers and advertisers. In many ways, the raison d'être for STP marketing is to generate viable positioning themes.

Positioning themes take many forms, and like any other aspect of marketing and advertising, they can benefit from creative breakthroughs. Yet while novelty and creativity are valued in developing positioning themes, some basic principles should be considered when selecting a theme. Whenever possible, it is helpful if the organization can settle on a single premise—such as "Good Neighbor" or "We Build Excitement" or "Friendly Serve" or "Relax, It's FedEx"—to reflect its positioning strategy.[26] In addition, three fundamental options should always be considered in selecting a positioning theme: benefit positioning, user positioning, and competitive positioning.[27]

"We Build Excitement" and "Friendly Serve" are examples of **benefit positioning.** Notice in these premises that a distinctive customer benefit is featured. This single-benefit focus is the first option that should be considered when formulating a positioning strategy. As we saw in Chapter 5, consumers purchase products to derive functional, emotional, or self-expressive benefits, so an emphasis on the primary benefit they can expect to receive from a brand is fundamental. While it might seem that more compelling positioning themes would result from promising consumers a wide array of benefits, keep in mind that multiple-benefit strategies are hard to implement. Not only will they send mixed signals within an organization about what a brand stands for, but they will also place a great burden on advertising to deliver and validate multiple messages.

Functional benefits are the place to start in selecting a positioning theme, but in many mature product categories, the functional benefits provided by the various brands in the competitive field are essentially the same. In these instances the organization may turn to emotion in an effort to distinguish its brand. Emotional benefit positioning may involve a promise of exhilaration, like "Exciting Armpits" (see Exhibit 6.20), or may feature a way to avoid negative feelings—such as the embarrassment felt in social settings due to bad breath, dandruff, or coffee-stained teeth.

Another way to add an emotional benefit in one's positioning is by linking a brand with important causes that provoke intense feelings. Avon Products' former CEO, James E. Preston, insisted that tie-ins with high-profile social issues can cut

26.   A more elaborate case for the importance of a single, consistent positioning premise is provided in Ries and Trout's classic, *Positioning: The Battle for Your Mind* (New York: Warner Books, 1982).

27.   Other positioning options are discussed in Philip Kotler, *Kotler on Marketing: How to Create, Win, and Dominate Markets* (New York: Free Press, 1999), ch. 4.

When the functional benefits of 24-hour protection and no white residue become old hat, then the advertiser may have no choice but to try to engage consumers through a promise of emotional benefits, as we see in this ad for Lady Speed Stick. http://www.mennen.com

Bonus points for children is the motto of Germany's first charitable credit card. Card users earn PAYBACK points on every transaction, which are then automaticaly credited to UNICEF. UNICEF, the United Nations Children's Fund, supports programs for children in 158 countries around the world, in an effort to bring more smiles. Learn more at http://www.unicef.de *and* http://www.payback.de.

through the clutter of rivals' marketing messages.[28] Not surprising then that Avon has been a regular sponsor of important causes, such as the Avon Walk for Breast Cancer. Likewise, Sears helped raise money for the homeless, Star-Kist has promoted dolphin-safe fishing practices, Coors Brewing has funded public literacy programs, and Visa in Germany supported the Friendship Card, featured in Exhibit 6.21. There's a meaningful trend here: In a survey of executives from 211 companies, 69 percent said that their companies planned to increase participation in cause-related marketing, as a way to build emotional bonds with their consumers.[29]

Self-expressive benefits can also be the bases for effective positioning strategies. With this approach, the purpose of an advertising campaign is to create distinctive images or personalities for brands, and then invite consumers into brand communities.[30] These brand images or personalities can be of value to individuals as they use the brands to make statements about themselves to other people. For example, feelings of status, pride, and prestige might be derived from the imagery associated with brands such as BMW, Rolex, and Gucci. Brand imagery can also be valued in gift-giving contexts. A woman who gives Lauder Intuition for Men Pure Magnetism is

28.   Geoffrey Smith and Ron Stodghill, "Are Good Causes Good Marketing?" *BusinessWeek,* March 21, 1994, 64–65.

29.   Stephanie Thompson, "Good Humor's Good Deeds," *Advertising Age,* January 8, 2001, 6.

30.   Albert M. Muniz, Jr., and Thomas C. O'Guinn, "Brand Community," *Journal of Consumer Research,* vol. 27 (2001), 412–432.

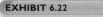

EXHIBIT 6.22

While this ad is busy with competing images and diverse product claims, it still communicates an unmistakable message about who should use this new line of coloring products from Bigen Xpressive.

EXHIBIT 6.23

Obviously, Myoplex is for the guy who has reached new heights but wants to keep going.

expressing something very different than the woman who gives Old Spice. Advertisers help brands acquire meaning and self-expressive benefits to distinguish them beyond their functional forms.

Besides benefit positioning, another fundamental option is **user positioning.** Instead of featuring a benefit or attribute of the brand, this option takes a specific profile of the target user as the focal point of the positioning strategy. Ads like those shown in Exhibits 6.22 and 6.23 make unequivocal statements about who should consider the possibilities offered by Bigen Xpressive and Myoplex Original. Notice how these ads attempt to speak to clearly identifiable user segments.

The third option for a positioning theme is **competitive positioning.** This option is sometimes useful in well-established product categories with a crowded competitive field. Here, the goal is to use an explicit reference to an existing competitor to help define precisely what your brand can do. Many times this approach is used by smaller brands to carve out a position relative to the market share leader in their category. For instance, in the analgesics category, many competitors have used market leader Tylenol as an explicit point of reference in their positioning strategies. Excedrin, for one, has attempted to position itself as the best option to treat a simple headache, granting that Tylenol might be the better choice to treat the various symptoms of a cold or the flu. As shown in Exhibit 6.24, Excedrin's strategy must have been effective, because Tylenol came back with a very pointed reply.

Now that you've seen the three fundamental options for creating a positioning strategy, we need to make matters a bit messier. There is nothing that would prevent an advertiser from combining these various options to create a hybrid involv-

In mature saturated markets where the performance features of brands don't change much over time, it is common to see competitors making claims back and forth in an effort to steal market share from one another. Powerhouse brands such as Tylenol usually don't initiate these exchanges, because they have the most to lose. This ad is a reply from the makers of Tylenol, responding to a campaign of a smaller competitor. http://www.tylenol.com

The beauty of this ad for Xootr is its simple, unequivocal message. Ours versus Theirs equates to Joy versus Toy. http://www.xootr.com

ing two or more of them working together. The combination of benefit and user is common in creating positioning strategies. For example, the two Gillette ads you examined at the beginning of the chapter are hybrids involving the benefit/user combination. And the Xootr ad in Exhibit 6.25 is a superb example of user and competitive positioning combined. Do keep in mind that we're looking for a strategy that reflects substance, consistency, simplicity, and distinctiveness. But the last thing we'd want to do is give you guidelines that would shackle your creativity. So don't be shy about looking for creative combinations.

Repositioning. STP marketing is far from a precise science, so marketers do not always get it right the first time. Furthermore, markets are dynamic. Things change. Even when marketers do get it right, competitors can react, or consumers' preferences may shift for any number of reasons, and what once was a viable positioning strategy must be altered if the brand is to survive. One of the best ways to revive an ailing brand or to fix the lackluster performance of a new market entry is to redeploy the STP process to arrive at a revised positioning strategy. This type of effort is commonly referred to as **repositioning.**

   While repositioning efforts are a fact of life for marketers and advertisers, they present a tremendous challenge. When brands that have been around for some time are forced to reposition, perceptions of the brand that have evolved over the years must be changed through advertising. This problem is common for brands that become popular with one generation but fade from the scene as that generation ages and emergent consumers come to view the brand as passé. So, for several years, the makers of Oldsmobile tried to breathe new life into their brand with catchy ad slogans such as "This is not your father's Oldsmobile," "Demand better," and "Defy convention." Ultimately, none of these efforts were able to save a brand that had become passé in a crowded marketplace.[31]

On the other hand there are numerous examples of brands that have been able to get consumers to take a fresh look at them. Mazda found itself in a funk in the '90s when it tried to go head-to-head with Toyota and Honda around dependability and good value. So Mazda's new CEO decided to return the brand to its roots as a stylish and fun-to-drive vehicle, targeting the 25 percent of the car-buying market that consider themselves auto enthusiasts. The "Zoom Zoom" theme was the outcome of this application of STP marketing, and with it the Mazda brand got its groove back. [32]

5 Capturing Your Strategy in a Value Proposition. In this chapter we have presented several important concepts for understanding how marketers develop strategies for their brands that then have major implications for the advertising and integrated promotion campaigns that are executed to build those brands. One needs to think about and research customer segments and target markets along with the competitive field to make decisions about various kinds of positioning themes that might be appropriate in guiding the creation of a campaign. Yes, as noted up front, it can get complicated. Furthermore, as time passes, and as new people from both the client and agency side are brought in to work on the brand team, it can be easy to lose sight of what the brand used to stand for in the eyes of the target segment. Of course, if the people who create the advertising and promotion programs for a brand get confused about the brand's desired identity, then the consumer is bound to get confused as well. This is a recipe for disaster. Thus, we need a way to capture and keep a record of what our brand is supposed to stand for in the eyes of the target segment. While there are many ways to capture one's strategy on paper, we recommend doing just that by articulating the brand's value proposition. If we are crystal clear in our own minds on what value we believe our brand offers to consumers, and everyone on the brand team shares that clarity, the foundation is in place for creating effective advertising and integrated brand promotion.

At this point you should find the following definition of a **value proposition** a natural extension of concepts that are already familiar; it simply consolidates the emphasis on customer benefits that has been featured in this and the previous chapter:

A brand's value proposition is a statement of the functional, emotional, and self-expressive benefits delivered by the brand that provide value to customers in the target segment. A balanced value proposition is the basis for brand choice and customer loyalty, and is critical to the ongoing success of a firm.[33]

Exhibit 6.26 emphasizes the point in our definition that we must have a balanced value proposition to be successful in the marketplace. On the one hand, if the set of benefits provided by the brand does not justify its price relative to competitive brands, then we've obviously got a problem. On the other hand, if our price is too low relative to the benefits the brand offers, then we are essentially giving away profits. Balance is optimal.

---

31. Vanessa O'Connell and Joe White, "After Decades of Brand Bodywork, GM Parks Oldsmobile—For Good," *Wall Street Journal,* December 13, 2000, B1, B4.

32. Jean Halliday, "Mazda Repositioning Begins to Show Results," *Advertising Age,* January 6, 2003, 4.

33. This definition is adapted from David Aaker, *Building Strong Brands* (New York: Free Press, 1996), ch. 3.

EXHIBIT 6.26

Don't let your value proposition get out of balance!

Benefits?
- functional
- emotional
- self-expressive

- relative price

Here are the extensive value propositions for two global brands that are likely familiar to you.[34]

McDonald's Value Proposition
- **Functional benefits:** Good-tasting hamburgers, fries, and drinks served fast; extras such as playgrounds, prizes, premiums, and games.
- **Emotional benefits:** Kids—fun via excitement at birthday parties; relationship with Ronald McDonald and other characters; a feeling of special family times. Adults—warmth via time spent enjoying a meal with the kids; admiration of McDonald's social involvement such as McDonald's Charities and Ronald McDonald Houses.

Nike's Value Proposition
- **Functional benefits:** High-technology shoe that will improve performance and provide comfort.
- **Emotional benefits:** The exhilaration of athletic performance excellence, feeling engaged, active, and healthy; exhilaration from admiring professional and college athletes as they perform wearing "your brand"—when they win, you win a little bit, too.
- **Self-expressive benefits:** Using the brand endorsed by high-profile athletes lets your peers know your desire to compete and excel.

Notice from these two statements that over time many different aspects can be built into the value proposition for a brand. Brands like Nike may offer benefits in all three benefit categories, McDonald's from two of the three. Benefit complexity of this type is extremely valuable when the various benefits reinforce one another. In these examples, this cross-benefit reinforcement is especially strong for Nike, with all levels working together to deliver the desired state of performance excellence. The job of advertising is to carry the message to the target segment

---

ETHICS

Prepaid Cards and Young Consumers

In 2004 MasterCard announced the introduction of two new prepaid cards, one picturing pop icon Usher and the other featuring the cartoon character Hello Kitty. Credit card companies are interested in tapping into the estimated 25 million 13-to-19-year-olds in the United States who have a collective spending power of $175 billion. The cards can deliver big profits and/or bad press.

Visa, MasterCard, Discover, and American Express generated $2.6 billion in prepaid card sales in 2003, a 73 percent increase over the previous year. Companies also charge fees for replenishment and monthly maintenance. In addition, 17 percent of balances on prepaid cards go unused, so the card companies keep those dollars as well.

Ethical considerations:

- Do the cards promote spending and keep users from building a credit history? Or do they cultivate responsible spending habits among teens who cannot get credit cards and checking accounts?
- Does this train young consumers that they don't ever have to wait for something they want?
- Should this practice and/or its advertising be banned, or heavily regulated?
- Does this practice bother you?

---

34.   These examples are adapted from Aaker, *Building Strong Brands*, ch. 3.

about the value that is offered by the brand. However, for brands with complex value propositions such as McDonald's and Nike, no single ad could be expected to reflect all aspects of the brand's value. However, if any given ad is not communicating some selected aspects of the brand's purported value, then we have to ask, why run that ad?

So from now on, every time you see an ad, ask yourself, what kind of value or benefits is that ad promising the target customer? What is the value proposition underlying this ad? We very definitely expect you to carry forward an ability to select target segments and isolate value propositions.

One gains tremendous leverage from the process of STP marketing because it is all about anticipating and servicing customers' wants and needs. But targeting groups for focused advertising and promotion efforts has a controversial side, as do many things in today's complex marketplace. So we end here with another appeal to your ethical sensibilities, which hopefully will be heightened by the Controversy box on this page.

CONTROVERSY

Avoid Targeting's Dark Side

Targeting is all about finding your best prospects and appealing to them very directly to attract their business. As we've noted before, it is often true that a small group of heavy users will drive the success of your business, if you come to know them and are able to reach them efficiently. But sometimes the heavy user can be attracted to your product or service for the wrong reason. That reason may entail a physical or psychological addiction, or may be based in a lack of education that yields misunderstanding about the real benefits of your product. In such instances, you face an ethical dilemma that can't be ignored.

Let's take a concrete example. If you are in the casino and gaming business (and this is very big business, and not just in Las Vegas), you will need to make an explicit decision on whether you will deploy marketing tactics to attract pathological gamblers. These are folks who in a very real sense are addicted to the rush that comes when they put their money on the line in hopes of scoring that next big win. They are the ultimate heavy user who lacks the ability to say no, even if it means blowing an entire paycheck. A common tactic for attracting these people is the payday bonanza. Offering special jackpots, free food, and show tickets for gamblers who bring their paychecks or welfare or Social Security checks right to the casino to be cashed appeals to the pathological gambler. And once in the casino with that cash in their pocket, there is little chance that they will take any of it home.

The good news is that major players such as Harrah's Entertainment are coming forth with codes of conduct that ban advertising that could appeal to pathological gamblers and other vulnerable market segments such as young consumers. Harrah's has banned all promotions in college newspapers and in any media that could reach children, and it explicitly bans paycheck promotions that appeal to the addicted gambler. Instead, Harrah's targets people between ages 45 and 70 who spend $1,000 to $2,000 a year on gambling. While these may be thought of as heavy users, Harrah's executives believe that this spending level is far less than what could be expected from a pathological gambler. The thoughtfulness and thoroughness reflected in Harrah's code of conduct nicely illustrates what we mean by the phrase *avoid targeting's dark side.*

Source: Christina Binkley, "Harrah's New Code to Restrict Marketing," *Wall Street Journal,* October 19, 2000, B16.

SUMMARY

 Explain the process known as STP marketing.

The term STP marketing refers to the process of segmenting, targeting, and positioning. Marketers pursue this set of activities in formulating marketing strategies for their brands. STP marketing also provides a strong foundation for the development of advertising campaigns. While no single approach can guarantee success in marketing and advertising, STP marketing should always be considered when consumers in a category have heterogeneous wants and needs.

 Describe different bases that marketers use to identify target segments.

In market segmentation, the goal is to break down a heterogeneous market into more manageable subgroups or segments. Many different bases can be used for this purpose. Markets can be segmented on the basis of usage patterns and commitment levels, demographics, geography, psychographics, lifestyles, benefits sought, SIC codes, or stages in the purchase process. Different bases are typically applied for segmenting consumer versus business-to-business markets.

 Discuss the criteria used for choosing a target segment.

In pursuing STP marketing, an organization must get beyond the stage of segment identification and settle on one or more segments as a target for its marketing and advertising efforts. Several criteria are useful in establishing the organization's target segment. First, the organization must decide whether it has the proper skills to serve the segment in question. The size of the segment and its growth potential must also be taken into consideration.

Another key criterion involves the intensity of the competition the firm is likely to face in the segment. Often, small segments known as market niches can be quite attractive because they will not be hotly contested by numerous competitors.

 Identify the essential elements of an effective positioning strategy.

The P in STP marketing refers to the positioning strategy that must be developed as a guide for all marketing and advertising activities that will be undertaken in pursuit of the target segment. As exemplified by Pontiac's "We Build Excitement" and "Fuel for the Soul" campaigns, effective positioning strategies should be linked to the substantive benefits offered by the brand. They are also consistent internally and over time, and they feature simple and distinctive themes. Benefit positioning, user positioning, and competitive positioning are options that should be considered when formulating a positioning strategy.

 Review the necessary ingredients for creating a brand's value proposition.

Many complex considerations underlie marketing and advertising strategies, so some device is called for to summarize the essence of one's strategy. We advance the idea of the value proposition as a useful device for this purpose. A value proposition is a statement of the various benefits (functional, emotional, and self-expressive) offered by a brand that create value for the customer. These benefits as a set justify the price of the product or service. Clarity in expression of the value proposition is critical for development of advertising that sells.

KEY TERMS

target segment
positioning
positioning strategy
STP marketing
market segmentation
heavy users
nonusers
brand-loyal users

switchers, or variety seekers
emergent consumers
demographic segmentation
geodemographic segmentation
psychographics
lifestyle segmentation
benefit segmentation
consumer markets

business markets
competitive field
market niche
benefit positioning
user positioning
competitive positioning
repositioning
value proposition

QUESTIONS

1.   While STP marketing often produces successful out-comes, there is no guarantee that these successes will last. What factors can erode the successes produced by STP marketing, forcing a firm to reformulate its marketing strategy?

2.   Why does the persuasion required with a product differentiation strategy present more of a challenge than the persuasion required with a market segmentation strategy?

3.   Explain the appeal of emergent consumers as a target segment. Identify a current ad campaign targeting an emergent-consumer segment.

4.   It is often said that psychographics were invented to overcome the weaknesses of demographic information for describing target segments. What unique information can psychographics provide that would be of special value to advertisers?

5.   What criteria did Mobil Oil Corporation weigh most heavily in its selection of Road Warriors as a target segment? What do you think will be the biggest source of frustration for Mobil in trying to make this strategy work?

6.   Explain why smaller can be better when selecting segments to target in marketing strategies.

7.   What essential elements of a positioning strategy can help overcome the consumer's natural tendency to ignore, distort, or forget most of the advertisements he or she is exposed to?

8.   On which aspect of its positioning strategy did Pontiac fail to deliver, thus eroding its effectiveness and turning off consumers? How did Pontiac recover?

9.   Identify examples of current advertising campaigns featuring benefit positioning, user positioning, and competitive positioning.

10. Carefully examine the Gillette ads displayed in Exhibits 6.1 and 6.2. What positioning theme (benefit, user, or competitive) is the basis for these ads? If you say benefit positioning, what form of benefit promise (functional, emotional, or self-expressive) is being made in these ads? Write a statement of the value proposition that you believe is reflected by these two ads.

EXPERIENTIAL EXERCISES

1.   Move over, Barbie—here come the Bratz. The race to win the hearts of little girls everywhere has heated up recently as MGA Entertainment's ultra-fashionable Bratz dolls aim to reduce Mattel's Barbie to little more than "the doll mom used to play with." Complete with bare midriffs, bee-stung lips, trendy duds, and funky names, the Bratz are the epitome of the 21st century girl—sassy and self-aware. Using concepts from the STP marketing approach, analyze the Bratz phenomenon in light of the threat it poses to Barbie's position in the toy-doll market. To find research for your analysis, visit the dolls' respective Web sites, look up news articles on the Internet, and contact a toy-store manager to find out which doll brand is most popular.

2.   Discount pioneer Kmart is repositioning to stay competitive in a challenging retail sector where stores like Wal-Mart and Target are ahead of the pack. Kmart suffered in the past from poor customer service and a lack of consumer enthusiasm toward its brands, but the company is currently making a turnaround. Since emerging out of bankruptcy in 2003, the creator of the blue-light special has been on a tear, cutting costs and boosting profits. Analysts claim that Kmart, having been outmatched by everyday-low-price giant Wal-Mart, has abandoned the superstore concept, and is instead concentrating on its core competency of merchandising. Kmart's new marketing strategy continues to emphasize popular

exclusive brands like Martha Stewart Everyday and Joe Boxer, while promoting products related to the WB television network and fashions from Latina pop idol Thalia. Visit Kmart's e-tail site (http://www.kmart.com) and describe how the company seeks to reconnect with customers through the promotion of its exclusive brands and services. How does the site compare to others by Target (http://www.target.com) and Wal-Mart (http://www.walmart.com)? Finally, interview someone who is older and ask that person to describe his or her perception of Kmart over the past couple of decades. How do those perceptions compare to the ones you are gathering through your analysis? Do you think Kmart will be successful with its repositioning strategy given its previous track record with consumers?

3.   Break up into teams and imagine you are creating an e-business. Choose your business and identify and break down relevant heterogeneous markets into manageable subgroups. Identify your target segment. Which criteria did you use to identify your target and why? Choosing from among the benefit, user, and competitive positioning options, select your positioning theme. Why will this theme be most effective for your advertising and marketing efforts? Formulate your brand's value proposition. Present your answers and reasoning to the class.

EXPERIENCING THE INTERNET

6-1 Segmentation

Community sites are popular Internet hangouts for Web users who share common interests, hobbies, and lifestyles. The enhanced technology features of these sites allow for live interaction with others via message boards, chat rooms, personal home pages, clubs, Web-based e-mail, and instant messaging services. In addition, interactive games, polls, and streaming broadcasts engage users and promote user loyalty, making community sites powerful entities that deliver ready-made audiences for savvy marketers.

Bolt: http://www.bolt.com

TalkCity: http://www.talkcity.com

gURL: http://www.gurl.com

1.   What broad consumer market do these sites share in common?

2.   Describe the target segment for each of these sites. On what basis are these markets segmented (usage pattern, psychographics, etc.)?

3.   How does the positioning reflected in each Web site match with the target segment?

4.   For each site, list one advertiser or corporate sponsor. Why might it be more beneficial for advertisers to place ads at these sites instead of at high-traffic portal sites like Yahoo?

6-2 Positioning

Once a firm has carefully segmented its market and selected target segments, a positioning strategy should evolve naturally. The positioning strategy includes particular ideas and themes that must be communicated effectively if the marketing program is going to be successful.

Match: http://www.match.com

eHarmony: http://www.eharmony.com

AfroConnections: http://www.afroconnections.com

1.   What are the essential elements of an effective positioning strategy? Which do you think is most important for these sites? Explain.

2.   Which of the three positioning options do these sites seem to favor (benefit, user, competitive)? In what sense can they be viewed as having a hybrid of these three positioning options?

3.   Pick one of these sites and define, in your own words, its value proposition. What is the importance of a brand's value proposition in creating effective advertising and integrated brand promotion?

CHAPTER 7

After reading and thinking about this chapter, you will be able to do the following:

Explain the purposes served by and methods used in developmental advertising research.

Identify sources of secondary data that can aid the IBP planning effort.

Discuss the purposes served by and methods used in copy research.

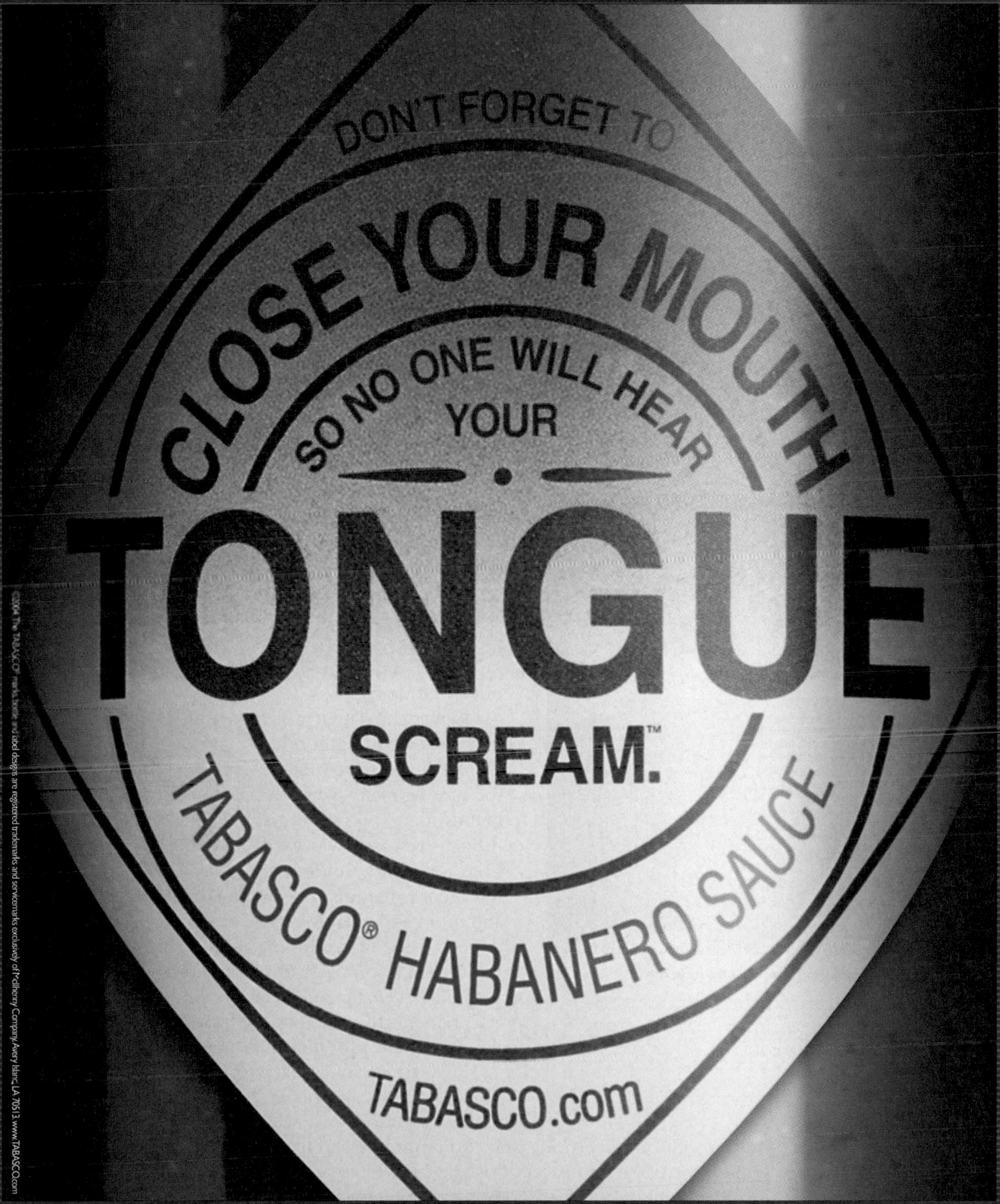

DON'T FORGET TO
CLOSE YOUR MOUTH
SO NO ONE WILL HEAR
YOUR
TONGUE
SCREAM.™
TABASCO® HABANERO SAUCE
TABASCO.com
©2004 The TABASCO® marks, bottle and label designs are registered trademarks and servicemarks exclusively of McIlhenny Company, Avery Island, LA 70513. www.TABASCO.com

Coca-Cola discovered that consumers generally preferred Pepsi—in blind taste tests. Coke had apparently conducted thousands of taste tests, and knew it was true: When consumers didn't know which cola they were drinking, most preferred Pepsi. To make the point more painful, Coke had been losing market share to Pepsi. What to do?

The answer was a new formula. After conducting 190,000 more blind taste tests, Coca-Cola discovered that consumers preferred New Coke over both Pepsi and Coke. So they announced the switch: New Coke replaced Coke. As you know, it was a disaster. Consumers were outraged and demanded their friend Coca-Cola back. They stayed away from New Coke in droves.

I do not drink alcoholic beverages, I don't smoke, and I don't chase other women, my only vice has been Coke. Now you have taken that pleasure from me.

Would it be right to rewrite the Constitution? The Bible? To me, changing the Coke formula is of such a serious nature.

—From letters sent to The Coca-Cola Company in 1985 following the introduction of New Coke, which announced the end of "old" Coke.[1]

Why? Didn't the "scientific" research lead to the right decision? No, it did not. Didn't the psychologists provide all the rights answers? No, they didn't.

Why? Because the right question was never asked. No one bothered to find out if consumers would mind Coke being taken away. And Coca-Cola and its advertising experts broke a cardinal rule of advertising and marketing. They confused the objective taste tests with cultural reality. They confused sociocultural meaning with physical reality. Coke possessed cultural meaning way beyond simple taste.

As others have noted, never, ever, ever confuse a brand and a product. The blind taste tests were about products; the market reaction of real consumers was about a brand—a brand that had enormous cultural meaning.

Never forget the difference: meaning makes brands out of products.

Never think that just throwing research at a problem does anything good.[2]

Ad luminaries such as Bill Bernbach (responsible for, among many other things, the amazing creative for brands like Volkswagen in the 1960s; see Exhibit 7.1) thought research was worse than a waste, while others have found it absolutely essential. Lately, with shrinking agency margins, research has been regarded as more and more expendable by the bean counters. At any rate, there is a lot of confusion about what advertising and promotion research is, if it does any good, and whether it should even be practiced at all. We won't end the research controversy, but we hope to make things a little clearer and provide some perspective.

First, to clarify our terms: Advertising and promotion research is any research that helps in the development, execution, or evaluation of advertising and promotion. Good advertising and promotion research moves one closer to producing good advertising and promotion, that is, effective (i.e., *on strategy*) advertising. That includes judging what is good or bad, effective or ineffective.

"It was the only thing to do after the mule died."

Three years back, the Hinsleys of Dora, Missouri, had a tough decision to make.

To buy a new mule. Or invest in a used bug. They weighed the two possibilities. First there was the problem of the bitter Ozark winters. Tough on a warm-blooded mule. Not so tough on an air-cooled VW.

Then, what about the eating habits of the two contenders? Hay vs. gasoline. As Mr. Hinsley puts it: "I get over eighty miles out of a dollar's worth of gas and I get where I want to go a lot quicker."

Then there's the road leading to their cabin. Many a mule pulling a wagon and many a conventional automobile has spent many an hour stuck in the mud. As for shelter, a mule needs a barn. A

bug doesn't. "It just sets out there all day and the paint job looks near as good as the day we got it."

Finally, there was maintenance to think about. When a mule breaks down, there's only one thing to do: Shoot it.

But if and when their bug breaks down, the Hinsleys have a Volkswagen dealer only two gallons away.

EXHIBIT 7.1

Bill Bernbach created some of the best advertising of all time, and he did it without research. In fact, he thought research got in the way of good advertising.

1.   See Mark Pendergrast, "The Marketing Blunder of the Century," in *For God, Country and Coca-Cola: The Definitive History of the Great American Soft-Drink and the Company That Makes It* (New York: Basic Books, 2000), 356.
2.   Ibid., p. 347–363.

Advertising research came to us from the 1950s, a period where science was popularized to ridiculous heights and was commonly misapplied. Unfortunately, that legacy influenced the advertising industry for decades to come.

Advertising research had its biggest growth in the "mind control" fears and pop psychology of the 1950s. Unfortunately, this legacy lasted a long time.

Although some advertising agencies have had research departments for 90 years or more, their growth occurred in the mid-20th century, with the 1950s being their real heyday. During this period, agencies adopted research departments for three basic reasons: (1) The popularity of science in the culture during this time legitimized anything called "science" or "research," (2) other agencies had research departments, and (3) there was a real information vacuum concerning ads, consumers, and consuming.

During the 1950s, advertising research established and legitimized itself in the industry. The popular adoration of science was at its height; the books, the plays, the movies, and the ads (see Exhibit 7.2) of this period are full of popular science. It was a period of great faith in the power of science and technology, and great concern about its misuse for evil and destructive ends.

Due in large part to popular belief in the success of propaganda and psychological warfare in World War II, there was a ready made acceptance of the "science of persuasion." This was a widely held belief that sophisticated mind-control techniques used in the war effort were now being turned into Madison Avenue mind control through sophisticated advertising. A belief in hidden mass persuasion was a cornerstone of cold-war ideology. Into this already strange social context, add a popular renaissance in everything Freud, particularly his obsession with the repressed subconscious (typically sexual in flavor). It was a period of fear about mind control, seduction, moral and mental subversion, and repressed desires (see Exhibit 7.3).

So into this social environment were born the great advertising research departments. In the 1950s, advertising agencies and their clients clamored for more research, more science, more hidden messages. Agency research departments were justified by the sacred name of "science" and the reality of scared consumers. We tell you all this because this history still absolutely influences what we call advertising and promotion research. This legacy is still with us. There are those who still insist on using 1950s-era methods, appropriate or not.

But, there is change. In the early 1980s advertising agencies began to openly voice their distrust for the sacred research methods established in the 1950s. These voices of dissent began in London, moved to the U.S. West Coast, and lately are heard just about everywhere. In fact, in the past several years some advertising agencies have come to believe that stand-alone research departments are a luxury that they can no longer afford. At least two things are being seen as replacements: the account planning system in which research is a more integral part of planning advertising and promotion strategy and execution, and secondly, much greater research outsourcing, that is, going outside the agency for specific advertising research when and only when the need arises. Now, don't get us wrong: Science is valuable in general, and can be in advertising, but not in the immodest and all encompassing way previously thought (or at least practiced).

There are a lot of ways to judge research. Exhibit 7.4 gives you some terms and concepts that are very useful when talking about research.

Advertising and Promotion Research.
A lot of things are called "advertising and promotion research." Not all of it is done on the actual ads or promotions themselves. Quite a bit of this research is really done in preparation for making the ads and promotions. So, we divide the research world into two parts: (1) developmental advertising and promotion research and (2) copy research.

Developmental Advertising and Promotion Research.
Developmental advertising and promotion research is used to generate opportunities and messages. It helps the creatives and the account team figure out things such as the target audience's identity, "street language," usage expectations, history, and context. It provides critical information used by creatives in actually producing ads and promotions. It is conducted early in the process so there is still an opportunity to influence the way the ads or promotions come out. Because of this, many consider it the most valuable kind of research.

EXHIBIT 7.4

Words to judge research by.

- **Reliability** means that the method generates generally consistent findings over time.

- **Validity** means that the information generated is relevant to the research questions being investigated. In other words, the research investigates what it seeks to investigate.

- **Trustworthiness** is a term usually applied to qualitative data, and it means exactly what it implies: Can one, knowing how the data were collected, trust them, and to what extent?

- **Meaningfulness** is the most difficult of all these terms. Just what does a piece of research really mean (if anything)? Meaningfulness is determined by asking what the methods and measures really have to do with determining a good ad. This simple question is not asked enough.

Good advertising and promotions research can actually help make better advertising and promotions.

Now it smells best on glass, too.

New Windex Mountain Berry
smells as good as it cleans.
For a streak-free shine every time,
Windex is best on glass.

EXHIBIT 7.5

Ideas sometimes turn into products. Research can reveal the good ideas consumers have. http://www.scjohnson.com

Purposes of Developmental Advertising Research.

The purposes served by developmental research include the following:

Idea Generation. Sometimes an ad agency is called on to invent new ways of presenting an advertised good or service to a target audience. Sometimes the brand is being **repositioned,** or having its meaning changed relative to its competitors. The outcome might take the form of a new product launch or a repositioning strategy for an advertiser. For example, after many years of representing its parks as the ultimate family destination, Disney and its ad agencies have now positioned its theme parks as adult vacation alternatives for couples whose children have grown and gone off on their own. In Exhibit 7.5 Windex and its advertising agency found a new way to differentiate its old familiar product from other window cleaners.

Where does an advertiser get ideas for new and meaningful ways to portray a brand? Direct contact with the customer can be an excellent place to start. Qualitative research involving observation of customers, and extended interviewing of customers can be great devices for fostering fresh thinking about a brand. (Disney probably got its idea for repositioning by simply observing how many older couples were visiting its parks without children in tow!) Direct contact with and aggressive listening to the customer can fuel the creative process at the heart of any great advertising campaign. It can also be a great way to anticipate and shape marketplace trends, as seen in the Global Issues box.

Concept Testing. Many times advertisers also need feedback about new ideas before they spend a lot of money to turn the idea into a new marketing or advertising initiative. A **concept test** seeks feedback designed to screen the quality of a new idea, using consumers as the final judge and jury. Concept testing may be used to screen new ideas for specific advertisements or to assess new product concepts. How the product fits current needs and how much consumers are willing to pay for the new product are questions a concept test attempts to answer. For example, are consumers willing to cover their teeth with white flexible strips in order to brighten up their smiles? Crest certainly hoped so (see Exhibit 7.6), and they were right. Concept tests of many kinds are commonly included as part of the agenda of focus groups to get quick feedback on new product or advertising ideas. Concept testing is also executed via survey research when more generalizable feedback is desired.

Audience Definition. Market segmentation and targeting are among the first and most important marketing decisions a firm must make. As discussed in the previous chapter, the goal of market segmentation is to identify target audiences that represent the best match between the firm's market offering and consumers' needs and desires, and then target them with effective advertising. Basic data about audience sizes along with their demographic profiles are absolutely critical in this process. Furthermore, new market opportunities are commonly discovered when you get to know your audience.

Audience Profiling. Perhaps the most important service provided by developmental advertising research is the profiling of target audiences for the creatives. Creatives

need to know as much as they can about the people to whom their ads will speak. This research is done in many ways. One of the most popular is through lifestyle research. Lifestyle research, also known as AIO (activities, interests, and opinions) research, uses survey data from consumers who have answered questions about themselves. From the answers to a wide variety of such questions, advertisers can get a pretty good profile of the consumers they are most interested in talking to. Since the data also contain other product usage questions, advertisers can account for a consumption lifestyle as well. For example, it may turn out that the target for a brand of roach killer consists of male consumers, age 35 to 45, living in larger cities, who are more afraid of "unseen dirt" than most people and who think of themselves as extremely organized and bothered by messes. Maybe they also tend to enjoy hunting more than average, and tend to be gun owners. They read *Guns and Ammo* and watch *America's Most Wanted*. Profiles like this present the creative staff with a finer-grained picture of the target audience and their needs, wants, and motivations. Of course, the answers to these questions are only as valuable as the questions are valid. In-depth interviews with individual consumers provide an excellent source of information to supplement the findings from AIO research, and vice versa.

Developmental Advertising Research Methods.

Several methods are used in developmental advertising research; they will be discussed next. They are generally used to help form, shape, and tune the creative effort.

Focus Groups.

A **focus group** is a discussion session with (typically) six to 12 target customers who have been brought together to come up with new insights about the good or service. With a professional moderator guiding the discussion, the consumers are first asked some general questions; then, as the session progresses, the questioning becomes more focused and moves to detailed issues about the brand in question. Advertisers tend to like focus groups because they can understand them and observe the data being collected. While focus groups provide an opportunity for in-depth discussion with consumers, they are not without limitations. Even multiple focus groups represent a very small sample of the target audience and are prone to all sorts of "errors" caused by group dynamics. But remember that generalization is not the goal. The real goal is to get or test a new idea and gain depth of information. Greater depth of information allows for a greater understanding of the context of actual usage and its subtleties. More than once in a while, what ends up being actual ad copy comes from the mouths of focus group members.

It takes great skill to lead a focus group effectively. If the group does not have a well-trained and experienced moderator, some individuals will completely dominate the others. Focus group members also feel empowered and privileged; they have been made experts by their selection, and they will sometimes give the moderator all sorts of strange answers that may be more a function of trying to impress other group members than anything having to do with the product in question.

Projective techniques are designed to allow consumers to project thoughts and feelings (conscious or unconscious) in an indirect and unobtrusive way onto a theoretically neutral stimulus. (Seeing zoo animals in clouds, or faces in ice cubes, is an example of projection.) Projective techniques share a history with Freudian psychology and depend on notions of unconscious or even repressed thoughts. Projective techniques often consist of offering consumers fragments of pictures or words and asking them to complete the fragment. The most common projective techniques are association tests, dialogue balloons, story construction, and sentence or picture completion.

Dialogue balloons offer consumers the chance to fill in the dialogue of cartoonlike stories, much like those in the comics in the Sunday paper. The story usually has to do with a product use situation. The idea is that the consumers will "project" appropriate thoughts into the balloons.

Story construction is another projective technique. It asks consumers to tell a story about people depicted in a scene or picture. Respondents might be asked to tell a story about the personalities of the people in the scene, what they are doing, what they were doing just before this scene, what type of car they drive, and what type of house they live in. Again, the idea is to use a less direct method to less obtrusively bring to the surface some often unconscious mapping of the brand and its associations.

Another method of projection is **sentence and picture completion.** Here a researcher presents consumers with part of a picture or a sentence with words deleted and then asks that the stimulus be completed. The picture or sentence relates to one or several brands of products in the category of interest. For example, a sentence completion task might be *Most American-made cars are* _____. The basic idea is to elicit honest thoughts and feelings. Of course, consumers usually have some idea of what the researcher is looking for. Still, researchers can get some pretty good information from this method.

Another method that has enjoyed growing popularity in advertising and promotional developmental is the **Zaltman Metaphor Elicitation Technique (ZMET).**[3] It is also projective in nature. This technique claims to draw out people's buried

---

GLOBAL ISSUES

Japan's Marketing Bellwether: The Teenage Girl

For many marketers in Japan, aggressive listening to the customer begins and ends with adolescent females. It seems that high school girls in Japan have an unusual ability to predict consumer product successes, and, when targeted with special promotions, are also able to create favorable hype for products that can turn those products into family favorites. For example, Coca-Cola used focus groups of teenage girls to help fine-tune the marketing program for its fermented-milk drink Lactia. The girls suggested a light and smooth consistency for the product, and a short, stubby bottle with a pink label. Coke followed this advice and then handed out 30,000 of the stubby bottles to high school girls to help generate favorable word-of-mouth during the brand's launch. Lactia is now one of Japan's most popular beverages.

What could account for this special status of young women as a focal point in market research? Japanese marketing executives say that the girls are simply much more open and honest than their modest and tradition-bound elders. Additionally, these young women are very value-conscious consumers, and thus have good insights when inexpensive products are the focal point of the research. And they often have a substantial say in their mothers' selections of food items for the entire family. When Meiji Milk Products of Japan introduced its breath-cleansing Chinese tea under the brand name Oolong Socha, it did so with the advice of teenage girls. It soon became a family favorite. Yasuo Olo, a Meiji Milk brand manager, commented: "We were flabbergasted. We didn't think high school girls were that close with their parents these days."

And what about teenage boys? One market research consultant in Tokyo put it this way: "Most Japanese high school boys have trouble articulating. They're no help for our purposes."

Source: Norihiko Shirouzu, "Japan's High-School Girls Excel in Art of Setting Trends," *Wall Street Journal*, April 24, 1998, B1.

---

3. For three different viewpoints on ZMET, compare Kevin Lane Keller, *Strategic Brand Management* (Upper Saddle River, N. J.: Prentice-Hall, 1988), 317–320; Ronald B. Liever, "Storytelling: A New Way to Get Close to Your Customer," *Fortune,* February 3, 1997, 102–108; and Gerald Zaltman,"Rethinking Market Research: Putting People Back In," *Journal of Marketing Research,* vol. 34 (Novermber 1997), 424–437.

Cookies aren't the only things
that can be dipped with milk.

Nothing keeps me going during a night out,
like the refreshing sensation of milk.
It tastes great and keeps my body limber
and my bones strong – necessities for
the twists and twirls of the tango!

got milk?

EXHIBIT 7.7

*This campaign was largely
inspired by qualitative
research: researchers actually
went out into the "field" and
found that there was nothing
worse than having a cookie/
brownie/etc., but no milk.*

thoughts and feelings about products and brands by encouraging participants to think in terms of metaphors. A metaphor simply involves defining one thing in terms of another. ZMET draws metaphors from consumers by asking them to spend time thinking about how they would visually represent their experiences with a particular product or service. Participants are asked to make a collection of photographs and pictures from magazines that reflect their experience. For example, in research conducted for DuPont, which supplies raw material for many pantyhose marketers, one person's picture of spilled ice cream reflected her deep disappointment when she spots a run in her hose. In-depth interviews with several dozen of these metaphor-collecting consumers can often reveal new insights about consumers' consumption motives, which then may be useful in the creation of products and ad campaigns to appeal to those motives.

Field work is conducted outside the agency (i.e., in the "field"), usually in the home or site of consumption. Its purpose is to learn from the experiences of the consumer and from direct observation. Consumers live real lives, and their behavior as consumers is intertwined throughout these real lives. Their consumption practices are **embedded;** that is, they are tightly connected to (embedded within) their social context. To study them outside of that context makes little sense. More and more, researchers are attempting to capture more of the real embedded experiences of consumers.[4] This research philosophy and related methods are very popular today. Campaigns such as the award-winning and successful Got Milk? campaign (see Exhibit 7.7) used field work to get at the real consumption opportunity for milk—a mouth full of cookies and an empty milk carton. This helped form, and then drive, the strategy and creative execution. Often times the essential creative strategy is referred to as a **creative brief,** a document that outlines and channels the essential creative idea and objective.[5]

Consumers began to remember to be sure to have milk at home, to ask themselves when at the grocery store, "Got milk?" Other advertisers and their agencies shoot, or have consumers themselves, shoot home movies on digital video to get at the real usage opportunities and consumption practices or real consumers in real settings. Dell and their agency used this to create the Dell Dude, Steven. Advertising researchers can make better messages if they understand the lives of their target audience, and understand it in some rich context.

Field research uses prolonged observation and in-depth study of individuals or small groups of consumers in their own social environment. The advertising industry has long appreciated the value of qualitative data and is currently moving to even more strongly embrace extended types of fieldwork.

Coolhunts do this by getting researchers to actually go to the site where they believe cool resides, stalk it, and bring it back to be used in the product and its advertising. Exhibit 7.8 gives an example of coolhunting.

---

4.   Craig J. Thompson, William B. Locander, and Howard Pollio, "Putting Consumer Experience Back into Consumer Research: The Philosophy and Method of Existential Phenomenology," *Journal of Consumer Research,* vol. 16 (June 1989), 133–147.
5.   Karen Whitehill King, John D. Pehrson, and Leonard N. Reid, "Pretesting TV Commercials: Methods, Measures, and Changing Agency Roles," *Journal of Advertising,* vol. 22 (September 1993), 85–97.

Internal Company Sources. Some of the most valuable data are available within a firm itself and are, therefore, referred to as "internal company sources." Commonly available information within a company includes strategic marketing plans, research reports, customer service records, warranty registration cards, letters from customers, customer complaints, and various sales data (broken down by region, by customer type, by product line). All of these provide a wealth of information relating to the proficiency of the company's advertising programs and, more generally, changing consumer tastes and preferences. Sometimes really great data are right there under the client's or agency's nose.

Government Sources. Various government organizations generate data on factors of interest to advertising planners; information on population and housing trends, transportation, consumer spending, and recreational activities in the United States is available through government documents.[6] Go to http://www.lib.umich.edu/govdocs/federal.html for a couple hundred or so pages of great links to data from federal, state, and international government sources. The Census of Population and Housing is conducted every 10 years in years ending in 0. The data (actually tables, not the data itself, unfortunately) are released at various times over the following handful of years after the census. The Census Bureau has a great Web site with access to numerous tables and papers (http://www.census.gov/).

A great new source of data is the American Community Survey, which the Census Bureau actually hopes will replace many aspects of the census in 2010. It came online in 2003. The ACS is a new approach for collecting accurate, timely information. It is designed as an ongoing survey that will replace the so-called long form in the 2010 census. The ACS provides estimates of demographic, housing, social, and economic characteristics every year for states, cities, counties, metropolitan areas, and population groups of 65,000 people or more (http://www.factfinder.census.gov/home/en/acsdata.html). (See Exhibit 7.9, from the ACS.)

There is also the commonly used Current Population Survey, which is a national survey that has been conducted monthly since 1940 by the Bureau of the Census for the Department of Labor Statistics. It provides information on unemployment, occupation, income, and sources of income, as well as a rotating set of topics such as health, work schedules, school enrollment, fertility, households, immigration, and language (http://www.bls.census.gov/cps/cpsmain.htm).

You might also check out the International Social Survey Programme at http://www.issp.org. Here you could get valuable data on the feelings of consumers from 30 or so nations on, for example, environmental issues, quite a find for companies trying to market "green products." Another very cool site is the National Archives and Records Administration, http://www.nara.gov. This site has an incredible array of information about Americans and American culture—all available, for no charge, from any computer. The array of consumer data available from government sources is a wonderful resource in advertising and planning for businesses of all sizes. These publications/sites are reasonably current. Print versions are available at public libraries. This means that even a small business owner can access large amounts of information for advertising planning purposes at little or no cost. Again, the Internet has changed the world and the practice of advertising and promotion.

Commercial Sources. Since information has become such a critical resource in marketing and advertising decision making, commercial data services have emerged to provide data of various types, and to package existing data. Firms specializing in this sort of information tend to concentrate their data-gathering efforts on household level consumption. PRIZM NE (New Evolution), a geo-demographic, lifestyle segmentation system, is a good example. Its founder, Claritas Inc., a leading market research firm and the pioneer of geo-demography, collects data at the household

---

6. We would like to thank Professor Gillian Stevens of the University of Illinois for her assistance with government data sources.

COOLHUNT

Baysie Wightman met DeeDee Gordon, appropriately enough, on a coolhunt. It was 1992. Baysie was a big shot for Converse, and DeeDee, who was barely twenty-one, was running a very cool boutique called Placid Planet, on Newbury Street in Boston. Baysie came in with a camera crew—one she often used when she was coolhunting—and said, "I've been watching your store, I've seen you, I've heard you know what's up," because it was Baysie's job at Converse to find people who knew what was up and she thought DeeDee was one of those people. DeeDee says that she responded with reserve—that "I was like, 'Whatever' "—but Baysie said that if DeeDee ever wanted to come and work at Converse she should just call, and nine months later DeeDee called. This was about the time the cool kids had decided they didn't want the hundred-and-twenty-five-dollar basketball sneaker with seventeen different kinds of high-technology materials and colors and air-cushioned heels anymore. They wanted simplicity and authenticity, and Baysie picked up on that. She brought back the Converse One Star, which was a vulcanized, suede, low-top classic old-school sneaker from the nineteen-seventies, and, sure enough, the One Star quickly became the signature shoe of the retro era. Remember what Kurt Cobain was wearing in the famous picture of him lying dead on the ground after committing suicide? Black Converse One Stars. DeeDee's big score was calling the sandal craze. She had been out in Los Angeles and had kept seeing the white teenage girls dressing up like cholos, Mexican gangsters, in tight white tank tops known as "wife beaters," with a bra strap hanging out, and long shorts and tube socks and shower sandals. DeeDee recalls, "I'm like, 'I'm telling you, Baysie, this is going to hit. There are just too many people wearing it. We have to make a shower sandal.' " So Baysie, DeeDee, and a designer came up with the idea of making a retro sneaker-sandal, cutting the back off the One Star and putting a thick outsole on it. It was huge, and amazingly, it's still huge.

Today, Baysie works for Reebok as general-merchandise manager—part of the team trying to return Reebok to the position it enjoyed in the mid-nineteen-eighties as the country's hottest sneaker company. DeeDee works for an advertising agency in Del Mar called Lambesis, where she puts out a quarterly tip sheet called the L Report on what the cool kids in major American cities are thinking and doing and buying. Baysie and DeeDee are best friends. They talk on the phone all the time. They get together whenever Baysie is in L.A. (DeeDee: "It's, like, how many times can you drive past O.J. Simpson's house?"), and between them they can talk for hours about the art of the coolhunt. They're the Lewis and Clark of cool.

What they have is what everybody seems to want these days, which is a window on the world of the street. Once, when fashion trends were set by the big couture houses—when cool was trickle-down—that wasn't important. But sometime in the past few decades things got turned over, and fashion became trickle-up. It's now about chase and flight—designers and retailers and the mass consumer giving chase to the elusive prey of street cool—and the rise of coolhunting as a profession shows how serious the chase has become. The sneakers of Nike and Reebok used to come out yearly. Now a new style comes out every season. Apparel designers used to have an eighteen-month lead time between concept and sale. Now they're reducing that to a year, or even six months, in order to react faster to new ideas from the street. The paradox, or course, is that the better coolhunters become at bringing the mainstream close to the cutting edge, the more elusive the cutting edge becomes. This is the first rule of the cool: The quicker the chase, the quicker the flight. The act of discovering what's cool is what causes cool to move on, which explains the triumphant circularity of coolhunting: because we have coolhunters like DeeDee and Baysie, cool changes more quickly, and because cool changes more quickly, we need coolhunters like DeeDee and Baysie.

One day last month, Baysie took me on a coolhunt to the Bronx and Harlem, lugging a big black canvas bag with twenty-four different shoes that Reebok is about to bring out, and as we drove down Fordham Road, she had her head out the window like a little kid, checking out what everyone on the street was wearing. We went to Dr. Jay's, which is the cool place to buy sneakers in the Bronx, and Baysie crouched down on the floor and started pulling the shoes out of her bag one by one, soliciting opinions from customers who gathered around and asking one question after another, in rapid sequence. One guy she listened closely to was maybe eighteen or nineteen, with a diamond stud in his ear and a thin beard. He was wearing a Polo baseball cap, a brown leather jacket, and the big, oversized leather boots that are everywhere uptown right now. Baysie would hand him a shoe and he would hold it, look at the top, and move it up and down and flip it over. The first one he didn't like: "Oh-kay." The second one he hated: he made a growling sound in his throat even before Baysie could give it to him, as if to say, "Put it back in the bag—now!" But when she handed him a new DMX RXT—a low-cut run/walk shoe in white and blue and mesh with a translucent "ice" sole, which retails for a hundred and ten dollars—he looked at it long and hard and shook his head in pure admiration and just said two words, dragging each of them out: "No doubt."

Baysie was interested in what he was saying, because the DMX RXT she had was a girls' shoe that actually hadn't been doing all that well. Later, she explained to me that the fact that the boys loved the shoe was critical news, because it suggested that Reebok had a potential hit if it just switched the shoe to the men's section. How she managed to distill this piece of information from the crowd of teenagers around her, how she made any sense of the two dozen shoes in her bag, most of which (to my eyes, anyway) looked pretty much the same, and how she knew which of the teens to really focus on was a mystery. Baysie is a Wasp from New England, and she crouched on the floor in Dr. Jay's for almost an hour, talking and joking with the homeboys without a trace of condescension or self-consciousness.

Near the end of her visit, a young boy walked up and sat down on the bench next to her. He was wearing a black woolen cap with white stripes pulled low, a blue North Face pleated down jacket, a pair of baggy Guess jeans, and on his feet, Nike Air Jordans. He couldn't have been more than thirteen. But when he started talking you could see Baysie's eyes light up, because somehow she knew the kid was the real thing.

"How many pairs of shoes do you buy a month?" Baysie asked.

"Two," the kid answered. "And if at the end I find one more I like I get to buy that, too."

Baysie was on to him. "Does your mother spoil you?"

The kid blushed, but a friend next to him was laughing. "Whatever he wants, he gets."

Baysie laughed, too. She had the DMX RXT in his size. He tried them on. He rocked back and forth, testing them. He looked back at Baysie. He was dead serious now: "Make sure these come out."

Baysie handed him the new "Rush" Emmitt Smith shoe due out in the fall. One of the boys had already pronounced it "phat," and another had looked through the marbleized-foam cradle in the heel and cried out in delight, "This is bug!" But this kid was the acid test, because this kid knew cool. He paused. He looked at it hard. "Reebok," he said, soberly and carefully, "is trying to get butter."

When Baysie comes back from a coolhunt, she sits down with marketing experts and sales representatives and designers, and reconnects them to the street, making sure they have the right shoes going to the right places at the right price. When she got back from the Bronx, for example, the first thing she did was tell all these people they had to get a new DMX RXT out, fast, because the kids on the street loved the women's version. "It's hotter than we realized," she told them. The coolhunter's job in this instance is very specific. What DeeDee does, on the other hand, is a little more ambitious. With the L Report, she tries to construct a kind of grand matrix of cool, comprising not just shoes but everything kids like, and not just kids of certain East Coast urban markets but kids all over. DeeDee and her staff put it out four times a year, in six different versions—for New York, Los Angeles, San Francisco, Austin-Dallas, Seattle, and Chicago—and then sell it to manufacturers, retailers, and ad agencies (among others) for twenty thousand dollars a year. They go to each city and find the coolest bars and clubs, and ask the coolest kids to fill out questionnaires. The information is then divided into six categories—You Saw It Here First, Entertainment and Leisure, Clothing and Accessories, Personal and Individual, Aspirations, and Food and Beverages—which are, in turn, broken up into dozens of subcategories, so that Personal and Individual, for example, include Cool Date, Cool Evening, Free Time, Favorite Possession, and on and on. The information in those subcategories is subdivided again by sex and by age bracket (14–18, 19–24, 25–30), and then, as a control, the L Report gives you the corresponding set of preferences for "mainstream kids."

What DeeDee argues, though, is that cool is too subtle and too variegated to be captured with these kind of broad strokes. Cool is a set of dialects, not a language. The L Report can tell you, for example, that nineteen-to-twenty-four-year-old male trendsetters in Seattle would most like to meet, among others, King Solomon and Dr. Seuss, and that nineteen-to-twenty-four-year-old female trendsetters in San Francisco have turned their backs on Calvin Klein, Nintendo Game Boy, and sex. What's cool right now? Among male New York trendsetters: North Face jackets, rubber and latex, khakis, and the rock band Kiss. Among female trendsetters: ska music, old-lady clothing, and cyber tech. In Chicago, snowboarding is huge among trendsetters of both sexes and all ages. Women over nineteen are into short hair, while those in their teens have embraced mod culture, rock climbing, tag watches, and bootleg pants. In Austin-Dallas, meanwhile, twenty-five-to-thirty-year-old women trendsetters are into hats, heroin, computers, cigars, Adidas, and velvet, while men in their twenties are into video games and hemp. In all, the typical L Report runs over one hundred pages. But with the flood of data comes an obsolescence disclaimer: "The fluctuating nature of the trendsetting market makes keeping up with trends a difficult task." By the spring, in other words, everything may have changed.

The key to coolhunting, then, is to look for cool people first and cool things later, and not the other way around. Since cool things are always changing, you can't look for them, because the very fact they are cool means you have no idea what to look for. What you would be doing is thinking back on what was cool before and extrapolating, which is about as useful as presuming that because the Dow rose ten points yesterday it will rise another ten points today. Cool people, on the other hand, are a constant.

Source: From Malcolm Gladwell, "The Coolhunt," in *The Consumer Society Reader,* Juliet B. Schor and Douglas B. Holt, eds. (New York: New Press, 2000), 360–374.

EXHIBIT 7.8

This is a description of coolhunting.

EXHIBIT 7.9

The American Community Survey is a great resource for defining target audiences.

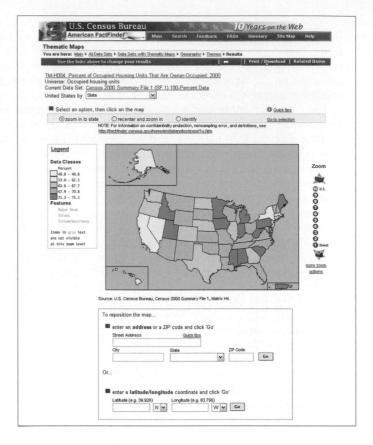

level on consumption. This way, a marketer can see a pretty interesting profile of who is most likely to consume a given good or service, and also *where* (see Exhibit 7.10). This is based on the premise that most consumers within a given ZIP Code are more alike than different in their consumption habits. However, this assumption is not accepted universally. Sometimes there are significant variations in consumer practices within a given geographic area. But that is the exception. More often than not, people living in close proximity to one another are more like each other (in consumption practices) than people living in different geographic areas. That simple reality is what makes geographic clustering research methods work at all.

Information from commercial data vendors is reasonably comprehensive and is normally gathered using reasonably sound methods. Information from these sources costs more than information from government sources, but is specifically designed to be of benefit to advertisers and marketers. Exhibit 7.11 details several of the major companies and their offerings.

Professional Publications. Another secondary data source is professional publications. Professional publications are periodicals in which marketing and advertising professionals report significant information related to industry trends or new research findings.

The Internet. It probably goes without saying for today's Web-savvy college student that the Internet can be an advertiser's best friend when looking for secondary data of almost any kind. The Internet has revolutionized developmental research, particularly for smaller agencies and advertisers. Common search engines allow the search of enormous amounts of data previously available only to the wealthiest agencies. Human search costs have been slashed. Beyond commonly available engines, some companies buy customized engines to search the Web for their own particular needs. Of particular value are Web-based interest groups, or online communities. Google Groups are a great resource (see Exhibit 7.12).

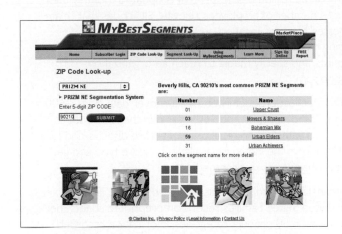

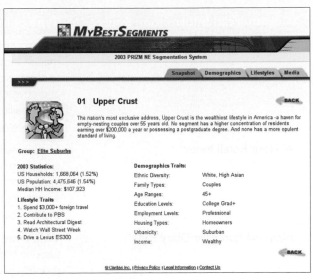

EXHIBIT 7.10

Here is the ZIP Code consumer data from PRIZM NE. Nice ZIP Code: 90210. Here is the listing of five of "My Best Segments" and three of the "best" segments for Beverly Hills, California.

3 Copy Research. The second major type of advertising and promotion research is known as copy research, or *evaluative research*. It is the kind that people usually think of when one says "advertising research." It is research on the actual ads or promotional texts themselves, finished or unfinished. It is used to judge or *evaluate* ads and promotions. Even though most contemporary ads are more pictures than words, the name "copy" still reflects the time when it was the effect of advertising copy (words) that was supposed to be most important.

In the best case, reliable, valid, trustworthy, and meaningful tests are appropriately applied. In the worst case, tests in which few still believe continue to survive because they represent "the way we have always done things." The pressure of history and the felt need for normative data (which allows comparisons with the past) significantly obscure questions of appropriateness and meaningfulness. This makes

Commercial Information Source	Type of Information
Dun & Bradstreet Market Identifiers	DMI is a listing of 4.3 million businesses that is updated monthly. Information includes number of employees, relevant SIC codes that relate to the businesses' activities, location, and chief executive. Marketing and advertising managers can use the information to identify markets, build mailing lists, and specify media to reach an organization. http://www.dnb.com
Nielsen Retail Index	Nielsen auditors collect product inventory turnover data from 1,600 grocery stores, 750 drugstores, and 150 mass merchandise outlets. Information is also gathered on retail prices, in-store displays, and local advertising. Data from the index are available by store type and geographic location. http://www.nielsenmedia.com
National Purchase Diary Panel	With more than 13,000 families participating, NPD is the largest diary panel in the United States. Families record on preprinted sheets their monthly purchases in 50 product categories. Information recorded includes brand, amount purchased, price paid, use of coupons, store, specific version of the product (flavor, scent, etc.), and intended use.
Consumer Mail Panel	This panel is operated by a firm called Market Facts. There are 45,000 active participants at any point in time. Samples are drawn in lots of 1,000. The overall panel is said to be representative of different geographic regions in the United States and Canada, then broken down by household income, urbanization, and age of the respondent. Data are provided on demographic and socioeconomic characteristics as well as type of dwelling and durable goods ownership. http://www.marketfacts.com

EXHIBIT 7.11

Examples of the commercial data sources available to advertisers.

for an environment in which the best test is not always done, the wrong test is done, and the right questions are not always asked.

This brings us to motives and expectations of the agency and the client: Why are certain tests done? Just what is it that advertising professionals want out of their copy research? The answer, of course, depends on who you ask. Generally speaking, the account team wants some assurance that the ad does essentially what it's supposed to do, or at least is defensible in terms of copy test scores. Many times, the team simply wants whatever the client wants. The client typically wants to see some numbers, generally meaning **normative test scores**—scores relative to the average for a category of ads. In other words, the client wants to see how well a particular ad scored against average commercials of its type that were tested previously. From a purely practical standpoint, having a good normative copy test scores (above the average for the category) lowers the probability of getting fired later. You can point to the score, and say it "tested well," and then assert that you (and/or your agency) should not be fired. There is a lot of cover in these scores, perhaps in reality their greatest value. If things go bad, one can always point to the high test scores, and say, "Well, it tested well. It's not my fault."

How about the people who actually make the ads, the creatives? What do they want in all of this? Well, generally they hate copy testing and wish it would go away. They are uninterested in normative tests. The creatives who actually produced the

EXHIBIT 7.12

At Google Groups you will find thousands and thousands of discussion groups, many of them consumer- and brand-based. Here, advertisers can gain incredibly rich, unobtrusive, and sophisticated data from real consumers at virtually no cost. Sophisticated newsreader programs can quickly search and organize these data.

ad typically believe there is no such thing as the average commercial, and they are quite sure that if there are average commercials, theirs are not among them. Besides benefiting the sales of the advertised product or service, the creatives wouldn't mind another striking ad on their reel or in their book, another Addy or Clio on their wall. But copy research scores are unlikely to predict awards, which are the unofficial currency of creatives. So creatives don't tend to be fans of copy tests. Creatives want awards. Copy tests often stand in the way and seem meaningless.

Copy tests generate a type of report card, and some people, particularly on the creative side of advertising, resent getting report cards from people in suits. (Who wouldn't?) Creatives also argue that these numbers are often misleading and misapplied. More often than not, they're right. Further, they argue that ads are artistic endeavors, not kitchen appliances to be rated by *Consumer Reports*. Again, they have a point. Because of these problems, and the often conflicting agenda of creatives (awards, career as a filmmaker) and account managers (keep your job, sell more stuff, maybe get to move to the brand side), copy research is often the center of agency tensions. Other than corner offices, copy tests have probably been at the center of more agency fights than just about anything.

Whenever people begin looking at the numbers, there is a danger that trivial differences can be made monumental. Other times, the mandatory measure is simply inappropriate. Still other times, creatives wishing to keep their jobs simply give the client what he or she wants, as suggested in Exhibit 7.13. If simple recall is what the client wants, then increasing the frequency of brand mentions might be the answer. It may not make for a better commercial, but it may make for a better score and, presumably, a happy client in the short run. A lot of games are played with copy tests.

EXHIBIT 7.13

Creative pumps up DAR numbers.

Bob, a creative at a large agency, has learned from experience how to deal with lower-than-average day-after recall (DAR) scores. As he explains it, there are two basic strategies: (1) Do things that you know will pump up the DAR. For example, if you want high DARs, never simply super (superimpose) the brand name or tag at the end of the ad. Always voice it over as well, whether it fits or not. You can also work in a couple of additional mentions in dialogue; they may stand out like a sore thumb and make consumers think, "Man, is that a stupid commercial," because people don't talk that way. But it will raise your DARs. (2) Tell them (the account executive or brand manager and other suits) that this is not the kind of product situation that demands high DARs. In fact, high DARs would actually hurt them in the long run due to quick wearout and annoyance. Tell them, "You're too sophisticated for that ham-handed kind of treatment. It would never work with our customers." You can use the second strategy only occasionally, but it usually works. It's amazing.

Despite the politics involved, message testing research is *probably* a good idea, at least some of the time. Properly conceived (almost never), correctly conducted (about half the time), and appropriately applied (rare), such research can yield important data that management can then use to determine the suitability of an ad. Knowing when it is appropriate, when it is not, and sticking to your guns is, quite simply, very hard in the advertising and promotion world—too many careers and too much money are on the line. *Doesn't the Emperor look grand in his new clothes?*

Evaluative Criteria: What Is Being Assessed.

There are a few common ways ads are judged. They are, more than anything else, traditional. Some make a great deal of sense and are very useful for integrated brand advertising and promotion, others are horribly overused and misapplied. Below we go through and discuss the major evaluative criteria. Later will we describe the major methods of assessing ads and promotions on these criteria.

Getting It.

Sometimes advertisers just want to know if audience members "get" the ad. Do they generally understand it, get the joke, see the connection, or get the main point? The reasoning behind this assessment is so obvious it hurts. It makes sense, it can be easily defended—even to copy-research-hating creatives. Brand managers understand this criterion; so do account executives. Do you get the ads in Exhibits 7.14 and 7.15?

Cognitive Residue.

It assumed that if the consumer was exposed to the ad, something of that ad remains in the consumer's mind: cognitive residue. It might be a memory of the headline, the brand name, the joke in the TV spot, a piece of copy, a vague memory trace of an executional element in the ad, or just about anything. So advertisers have for decades scored the cognitive residue, or the things left in consumer's minds. If "remembering stuff" from the ad matters, this makes sense at some basic level, yet we have known for at least 30 to 40 years that most memory measures don't tend to predict actual sales very well at all. Why is this? Well, for one thing, consumers may remember all sorts of things in ads, and not care for the advertised brand at all. Or they remember things that are completely irrelevant to the advertiser's intended message, or some of their thoughts actually interfere with associating the advertiser's brand name with the ad itself. Humorous ads are great example of this. The consumer remembers what is funny, but not the brand name—or worse yet, remembers the competitor's brand name.

It is also the case that these tests are premised on an increasingly out-of-fashion view of human memory. Not so long ago, psychologists thought that whatever a human experienced made its way into memory pretty much like streaming video or an unedited movie of one's life. So the focus of lots of advertising research was on the accurate and faithful retrieval of an ad, as if it existed unaltered in memory . . . or at least pieces of it. Lately though, a new way of thinking about human memory has emerged. Inspired from research into false memories in child abuse cases, psychologists now know that human memory is much messier than previously assumed. Psychologists now believe memory to be more fluid, and highly subject to motivation: remembering things as we care to remember them, even things that never happened. Memory appears to be much more of an interpretive act than previously thought. Advertising researcher Kathryn Braun-LaTour has shown that one can actually be fairly easily made to remember brands that don't exist and consumption experiences that never happened.[7] This work tells us that to rely so strongly on memory as a

---

7.   Kathryn A. Braun, "Postexperience Advertising Effects on Consumer Memory," *Journal of Consumer Research*, vol. 25 (March 1999), 319–334.

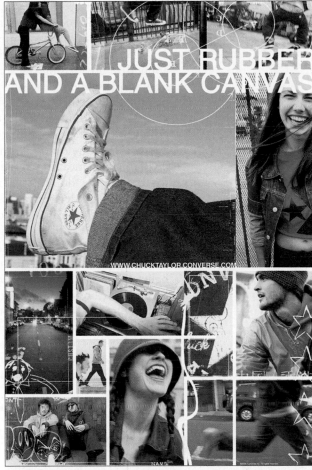

EXHIBITS 7.14 AND 7.15

Do you get it? Does the main message come across? Is the right image projected? http://www.cocacola.com *and* http://www.converse .com

measure of advertising effectiveness is a very bad idea. There are certainly times when such measures are appropriate, but nowhere near as much as they are used at present.

Knowledge. Knowledge is one big step up from fairly random cognitive residue. To have knowledge about a brand that could have come only from an ad is a much more meaningful measure of advertising effectiveness. This knowledge may take several forms. It could be a brand claim, or a belief about the brand. For example, the advertisers may believe that Brand X cleans twice as well as Brand Y. If Brand X's advertising and promotion has been stressing this very fact, then we may generally assume that the consumer has learned something from the promotion and advertising, and that brand knowledge has been created.

Attitude Change. Attitudes suggest where a brand stands in the consumer's mind. Attitudes can be influenced both by what people know and by what people feel about a brand. In this sense, attitude or preference is a summary evaluation that ties together the influences of many different factors. Advertisers thus may view attitude change as an important dimension for assessing advertising.

The biggest problem with attitude assessment is that it is overused and poorly applied in advertising research. Common sense tells us that sometimes attitudes are very worthwhile in assessing ads. Yet it also tells us that there are plenty upon plenty of times when they are not. Decades ago, when ads were mostly claimed-based and verbal, attitudes made more sense than in a real contemporary ad world, where most communication is done through picturing, and explicit claims are less and less the norm. Also, one cannot assume that a favorable attitude toward the ad will lead to a favorable and meaningful attitude toward the brand. We can all think of ads we love for brands we don't. Still, in the right circumstance, when the correct attitude dimensions are defined, assessing summary evaluations makes sense. There will more on this when we discuss specific methods and message strategies in Chapter 11.

Feelings and Emotions. Advertisers have always had a special interest in feelings and emotions. Ever since the "atmospheric" ads of the 1920s, there has been the belief that feelings may be more important than thoughts as a reaction to certain ads. Recent research by business professor Michel Pham and others[8] have shown that feelings have three distinct properties that makes them very powerful in reactions to advertisements and the advertised goods and services: (1) Consumers monitor and access feelings very quickly—consumers often know how they feel before they know what they think; (2) there is much more agreement in how consumers feel about ads and brands than in what they think about them; and (3) feelings are very good predictors of thoughts. This research adds a great deal of support to the argument that, in many ways, feelings are more important than thoughts when it comes to advertising. It also appears that ads that use feelings produce stronger and more lasting effects than those that try to persuade by thought alone. For example, the way a consumer feels about the imagery in the ads in Exhibits 7.16 and 7.17 may be far more important than any attitudinal component of the communication.

There is a lot of current interest in developing better measures of the feelings and emotions generated by advertising.[9] This has included better paper-and-pencil measures as well as dial-turning devices with which those watching an ad turn a dial in either a positive or negative direction to indicate their emotional response to the ad. Assessment of feelings evoked by ads is becoming much more important goal of the advertising industry.

Physiological Changes. Every few years there will be renewed interest in the technology of physiological assessment of advertising. Then, just as surely, the excitement falls way. The reasons for the recurring infatuation have to do with our general cultural fascination with technology, and the fairly reasonable belief that ads that really impact consumers must impact them at the physiological level

EXHIBIT 7.16

This ad is supposed to work with images and feelings.

8.   Michel Tuan Pham, Joel B. Cohen, John W. Pracejus, and G. David Hughes, "Affect Monitoring and the Primacy of Feelings in Judgment," *Journal of Consumer Research,* vol. 28 (September 2001), 167–188.

9.   Stuart J. Agres, Julie A. Edell, and Tony M. Dubitsky, eds., *Emotion in Advertising* (Westport, Conn.: Quorum Books, 1990). See especially Chapters 7 and 8.

EXHIBIT 7.17

*Words and arguments are not
what makes this ad work.*

YOUR LEFT HAND IS THE SENSIBLE ONE. YOUR RIGHT HAND IS THE CRAZY ONE. YOUR LEFT HAND DOES WHAT IT SHOULD. YOUR RIGHT HAND DOES WHAT IT PLEASES. YOUR LEFT HAND WILL SUPPORT YOU. YOUR RIGHT HAND WILL SURPRISE YOU. **WOMEN OF THE WORLD, RAISE YOUR RIGHT HAND.**

THE NEW DIAMOND RIGHT HAND RING. ROMANTIC, MODERN VINTAGE, FLORAL AND CONTEMPORARY STYLES AT ADIAMONDISFOREVER.COM

as well. So, technologies come and go that seek to capture changes in the bodies of people exposed to ads. Typically this is in terms of eye movement or dimensions measured by lie-detector-like devices such as skin conductivity, respiration, and pulse. Even PT scans (a procedure where subjects breathe radioactive isotopes) of the brain have been used experimentally, not in routine practice. Bottom line: They have not proven to be of much practical value.

Behavioral Intent. This is essentially what consumers say they intend to do. If, after exposure to Brand X's advertising, stated intent to purchase Brand X goes up, there is some evidence to believe that the tested advertising had something to do with it. Of course, we all know the problem with intended behavior: It's a poor substitute for actual behavior. Think about it: You really intended to call your mom, put the check in the mail, and all those other things. But it just didn't work out that way. The same thing is true when these are the criteria for testing consumer response to advertising. On a relative basis (say, percentage who intend to buy Pepsi vs. percentage who intend to buy Coke), these measures can be meaningful and helpful, particularly if the changes are really large. Beyond that, don't take them to the bank.

Actual Behavior. Other advertisers really want to see evidence that the new ads will actually get people to do something: generally, to buy their product. It is, to some, the gold standard. But for reasons explained earlier, there are so many things that can affect sales that the use of actual sales as a measure of advertising effectiveness is considered inherently flawed, but not flawed enough not to be used. Here is a place where advertising and promotion are really different. In the case of the more easily and precisely tracked effects of promotions, sales are the gold standard. In the case of media advertising, statistical models are employed to try to isolate the effect of advertising on sales. A host of other variables that might also affect sales, from the weather to competing advertising, are factored into these mathematical models. Even with all this sophistication, industry experts acknowledge that they are very far from perfect, and far less reliable and meaningful than those constructed for sales promotions. But they do generally help more than hurt. Another of their downsides is that they typically are done long after the fact, long after the ad campaign to be assessed has been in place, and sales data have come in. To get around this, behavioral data are sometimes derived from test markets, situations where the advertising is tested in a few select geographic areas before its wider application. While expensive, these tests can be very telling. Ideally, measures of actual behavior would come from tightly controlled field experiments. It's just that meaningfully controlled field experiments are incredibly difficult and expensive, and thus very rare. The area of greatest hope for those who believe real behavior is the best test of advertising effectiveness is the use of the Internet for experiments, although that is still in its infancy.

Copy Research Methods.
Now that we have discussed what criteria or measures advertising promotion professionals typically care about, let's take a look at how those criteria are actually assessed, that is, the methods actually used in copy research.

Communication Tests.
These test the "getting it" dimension. A **communication test** simply seeks to discover whether a message is communicating something close to what the advertiser desired. They are most often used with television. Communication tests are usually done in a group setting, with data coming from a combination of pencil-and-paper questionnaires and group discussion. Members of the target audience are shown the ad, or some preliminary or rough version of it. They typically see it several times. Then a discussion is held. One reason communication tests are performed is to prevent a major disaster, to prevent communicating something completely wrong, something the creators of the ad are too close to see but that is entirely obvious to consumers. This could be an unintended double entendre, an inadvertent sexual allusion, or anything else "off-the-wall." With more transnational or global advertising, it could be an unexpected interpretation of the imagery that emerges as that ad is moved from country to country around the world. Remember, if the consumer sees things, it doesn't matter whether they're intended or not—to the consumer, they're there. However, advertisers should balance this against the fact that communication test members feel privileged and special, and thus they may try too hard to see things. This is another instance where well-trained and experienced researchers must be counted on to draw a proper conclusion from the testing. These tests are most often conducted in-house (at advertising agency itself) as opposed to being outsourced to a commercial testing service.

Resonance Tests.
In a **resonance test** the goal is to determine to what extent the message resonates or rings true with target-audience members.[10] The question becomes: Does this ad match consumers' own experiences? Does it produce an affinity reaction? Do consumers who view it say, "Yeah, that's right; I feel just like that" (Exhibit 7.18)? Do

Wisk tablets remove dirt like it never happened.

If only they could do the same for your daughter's new tattoo.

Introducing Wisk® Dual Action Tablets with blue stain-fighting enzymes. So powerful, it's as if dirt never happened at all.

© 2001 Lever Brothers Company

EXHIBIT 7.18

Some ads are judged by their resonance, or how true they ring. http://www.wisk.com

10.   David Glenn Mick and Claus Buhl, "A Meaning-Based Model of Advertising Experiences," *Journal of Consumer Research*, vol. 19 (December 1992), 317–338.

consumers read the ad and make it their own?[11] The method is pretty much the same as a communication test. Consumers see an ad in a group several times, and then discuss it. It is usually done in-house by agency planners and researchers. In addition to resonance, the criteria typically being assessed are knowledge, feelings, and emotions.

Thought Listings. It is commonly assumed that advertising and promotions generate thoughts during and following exposure. Copy research that tries to identify specific thoughts that were generated by an ad is referred to as **thought listing,** or **cognitive response analysis.** These are tests of knowledge, cognitive residue, and to a lesser degree feelings and emotions. Thought-listing tests are either conducted in-house or obtained from a commercial testing service. They are most often used with television ads, although they can be applied to all ads. Here the researcher is interested in the thoughts that an ad or promotion generates in the mind of the audience. Typically, cognitive responses are collected by having individuals watch the commercial in groups and, as soon as it is over, asking them to write down all the thoughts that were in their minds while watching the commercial. They are then asked about these thoughts and asked to explain or amplify them. The hope is that this will capture what the potential audience members made of the ad and how they responded, or "talked back to it in their head."

These verbatim responses can then be analyzed in a number of ways. Usually, simple percentages or box scores of word counts are used. The ratio of favorable to unfavorable thoughts may be the primary interest of the researcher. Alternatively, the number of times the person made a self-relevant connection—that is, "That would be good for me" or "That looks like something I'd like"—could be tallied and compared for different ad executions. This method gets at several things: "getting it," knowledge acquired, attitude shifts, and emotions and feelings. The idea itself is very appealing: getting at people's stream of thoughts about an ad at time of exposure. But in its actual execution problems arise. These thoughts are in reality more retrospective than online; in other words, people are usually asked to write these down seconds to minutes after their thoughts actually occurred. They are also highly self-edited—some of your thoughts are not very likely to be shared. These thoughts are obtained in artificial environments and mental states typically unlike those in which real people actually are exposed to ads in real environments, such as sitting in their living room, talking, half-listening to the TV, and so on. But the researchers asked; you have to tell them something. Still, even with all these problems, there is something of value in these thoughts. They do tend to reveal something. The trick is, of course, knowing what is valuable and what is just "noise." A lot has to do with how well matched the ad and the procedure are. Some ads, for example, are designed in such a way that the last thing the advertiser really wants is a lot of deep thought (more on this in Chapter 11). For other ads (those where certain conclusions and judgments are the desired goal), it's a good test.

Recall Tests. These are the most commonly employed test in advertising, and the most controversial. They are used to get at the cognitive residue of ads. The basic idea is that if the ad is to work, it has to be remembered. Following on this premise is the further assumption that the ads best remembered are the ones most likely to work. Thus the objective of these tests is to see just how much, if anything, the viewer of an ad remembers of the message. Recall is used most in testing television advertising. In television **recall tests** the big companies are Ipsos-ASI and Burke. In print, the major recall testing services are Gallup & Robinson and Mapes and Ross. In print, however, **recognition** is generally the industry standard. Recognition simply means that the audience members indicate that they have seen an ad before

11.   Linda Scott, "The Bridge from Text to Mind: Adapting Reader Response Theory for Consumer Research," *Journal of Consumer Research,* vol. 21 (December 1994), 461–486.

(i.e., recognize it), whereas recall requires more actual memory (recalling from memory) of an ad. Recall is more common for television, recognition for print. But, as we note, there are exceptions.

In television, the basic recall procedure is to recruit a group of individuals from the target market who will be watching a certain channel during a certain time on a test date. They are asked to participate ahead of time, and simply told to watch the show. A day after exposure, the testing company calls the individuals on the phone and determines, of those who actually saw the ad, how much they can recall. The day-after-recall (DAR) procedure generally starts with questions such as, "Do you remember seeing a commercial for any laundry detergents? If not, do you remember seeing a commercial for Tide?" If the respondent remembers, he or she is asked what the commercial said about the product: What did the commercial show? What did the commercial look like? The interview is recorded and transcribed. The verbatim interview is coded into various categories representing levels of recall, typically reported as a percentage. *Unaided recall* is when the respondent demonstrates that he or she saw the commercial and remembered the brand name without having the brand name mentioned. If the person had to be asked about a Tide commercial, it would be scored as *aided recall*. Industry leader Burke Company reports two specific measures: *claim-recall* (percent who claim seeing the ad), and *related-recall* (percent who accurately recall specific elements of the ad).[12] Ipsos-ASI uses a similar procedure, but with one major difference. Like Burke, Ipsos-ASI recruits a sample, but tells the participants that they are really evaluating potential new television shows. What they are really evaluating are the ads. The shows are mailed to the sample audience members' home and they are given instructions. One day after viewing, the company contacts the viewers and asks them questions about the shows and the ads. From their responses, various measures are gathered, including recall. The advantage is the deception. If audience members think they are evaluating the shows, the researchers may get a more realistic assessment of the ads. It is not the same as a truly natural exposure environment, but it's probably an improvement.

Recall is done a bit differently in print. Remember, recognition is considered the standard test in print, not recall. But when recall is assessed for print, it is done in the following way. In a typical print recall test, a consumer is recruited from the target market, generally at a shopping mall. He or she is given a magazine to take home. Many times the magazine is an advance issue of a real publication; other times it is a fictitious magazine created only for testing purposes. The ads are "tipped in," or inserted, into the vehicle. Some companies alter the mix of remaining ads; others do not. Some rotate the ads (put them in different spots in the magazine) so as not to get effects due to either editorial context or order. The participants are told that they should look at the magazine and that they will be telephoned the following day and asked some questions. During the telephone interview, aided recall is assessed. This involves a product category cue, such as, "Do you remember seeing any ads for personal computers?" The percentage who respond affirmatively and provide some evidence of actually remembering the ad are scored as exhibiting aided recall. Other tests go into more detail by actually bringing the ad back to the respondent and asking about various components of the ad, such as the headline and body copy. Sometimes a deck of cards with brand names is given to consumers, and they are asked to stop if they can remember any ads from the brands on the cards. If they can, then they are asked to describe everything they can remember about the ad. These are scored in a manner similar to television day-after recall (DAR) tests.

Recognition Tests. Recognition tests are the standard cognitive residue test for print ads and promotions. Rather than asking you if you recall something, they ask

---

12.   Shimp, Terence A., *Advertising, Promotion and Supplemental Aspects of Integrated Marketing Communications* (Cincinnati: South-Western, 2002).

Recognition testing uses the ad itself to test whether consumers remember it and can associate it with its brand and message. This unusual, comically fanciful image would likely make this ad easy to recognize. But imagine this ad with the Altoids brand name blacked out. If consumers remember the ad, will they also remember the Altoids brand name? Novel imagery sometimes actually distracts readers, enticing them to overlook brand names. Visit the Altoids site (http://www.altoids.com) and evaluate how it reinforces or dilutes recognition in the minds of consumers. Are the interactive features useful or distracting? Does the site achieve "cool," or is it too over-the-top to reinforce brand recognition?

if you *recognize* an ad, or something in an ad. This type of testing attempts to get at little more than evidence of exposure residue. Recognition tests ask magazine readers and (sometimes television viewers) whether they remember having seen particular advertisements and whether they can name the company sponsoring the ad. For print advertising, the actual advertisement is shown to respondents, and for television advertising, a script with accompanying photos is shown. For instance, a recognition test might ask, "Do you remember seeing [the ad in Exhibit 7.19]?" This is a much easier task than recall in that respondents are cued by the very stimulus they are supposed to remember, and they aren't asked to do anything more than say yes or no. Do you think any complications might arise in establishing recognition of the ad displayed in Exhibit 7.20?

Companies such as **Starch Readership Services** that do this kind of research follow some general procedures. Subscribers to a relevant magazine are contacted and asked if an interview can be set up in their home. The readers must have at least glanced at the issue to qualify. Then each target ad is shown, and the readers are asked if they remember seeing the ad (if they *noted* it), if they read or saw enough of the ad to notice the brand name (if they *associated* it), if they *read any* part of the ad copy, or if they claim to have read at least 50 percent of the copy *(read most)*. This testing is usually conducted just a few days after the current issue becomes available. The *noted, associated,* and *read most* scores are calculated (see Exhibit 7.21). With print ads, Starch is the major supplier of recognition (they also term them "readership") tests.

Bruzzone Research Company provides recognition scores for TV ads. Essentially a sample of television viewers is selected. A photoboard (a board with still frames from the actual ad) of the TV commercial is sent out to a sample of viewers, but the brand name is obscured (both in picture and copy). Then recognition questions such as "Do you remember seeing this commercial on TV?" are asked. The respondent is asked to identify the brand and answer some attitude items. A recognition score is then presented to the client, along with attitude data. This method has advantages in that it is fairly inexpensive (and may be becoming less so through use of the Internet), and, due to its manner of blocking brand names, may provide a more valid measure of recognition (see Exhibit 7.22).

Recognition scores have been collected for a long time, which allows advertisers to compare their current ads with similar ones done last week, last month, or 50 years ago. This is a big attraction of recognition scores. The biggest problem with this test is that of a yea-saying bias. In other words, many people say they recognize an ad that in fact they haven't seen. After a few days, do you really think you could correctly remember which of the three ads in Exhibits 7.23, 7.24, and 7.25 you really saw, if you saw the ads under natural viewing conditions? Still, on a relative basis, these tests may tell which ads are way better or way worse than others.

Now comes the rub: Considerable research indicates there is little relation between recall and recognition scores and sales effectiveness.[13] But doesn't it make sense that the best ads are the ads best remembered? Well, the evidence for that is simply not there. This seeming contradiction has perplexed academics and practitioners

13. Rajeev Batra, John G. Meyers, and David A. Aaker, *Advertising Management,* 5th ed. (Upper Saddle River, N.J.: Prentice Hall, 1996), 469.

EXHIBIT 7.20

Though the correlation between seduction and candy is not new, consumers might mistake this imagery for a valentine, not an advertisement. What is the advantage to the product placement in this ad?

STARCH™ AD-AS-A-WHOLE		
Noted %	Associated %	Read Most %
W 55	50	23–

EXHIBIT 7.21

55% of Starch respondents said they noticed an ad, 50% said they associated it with the advertised brand, and 23% said they read more than half the body copy.

for a long time. And as ads become more and more visual, recall of words and claims is more and more irrelevant. The fact is that, as measured, the level of recall for an ad seems to have relatively little (if anything) to do with sales. This may be due to highly inflated and artificial recall scores. It may also be that ads that were never designed to elicit recall are being tested as if they were. By doing this, by applying this test so widely and so indiscriminately, it makes the test itself look bad. We believe that when, but only when, recall or recognition is the desired result, are these tests appropriate and worthwhile.

A recall does make sense when simple memory goals are the aim of the commercial. For example, saying "Kibbles and Bits" 80 times or so in 30 seconds indicates an ad aimed at one simple goal: Remember "Kibbles and Bits." That's all. For an ad like that, recall is the perfect measure. But as advertising moves to fewer words and more pictures, recognition tests, good recognition tests, may become much more valuable than recall. And for most ads, ads that operate at a far more sophisticated and advanced level than either recall or recognition, these measures are insufficient and often inappropriate.

EXHIBIT 7.22

Try the test: http://www .brcsurvey.com/brc_demo survey4.htm

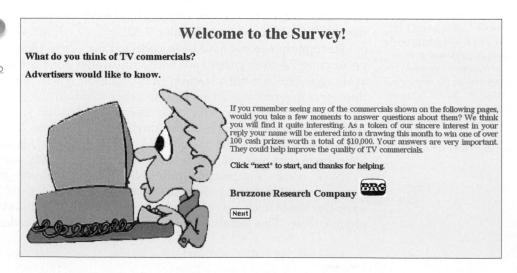

Welcome to the Survey!

What do you think of TV commercials?

Advertisers would like to know.

If you remember seeing any of the commercials shown on the following pages, would you take a few moments to answer questions about them? We think you will find it quite interesting. As a token of our sincere interest in your reply your name will be entered into a drawing this month to win one of over 100 cash prizes worth a total of $10,000. Your answers are very important. They could help improve the quality of TV commercials.

Click "next" to start, and thanks for helping.

Bruzzone Research Company BRC

Next

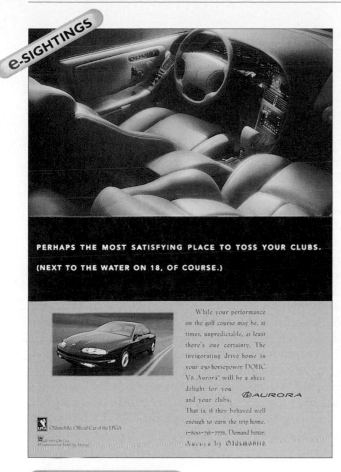

EXHIBITS 7.23, 7.24, AND 7.25

All of these ads, so strikingly similar, do little to (1) differentiate the product, (2) make it memorable for the consumer, or (3) promote the brand, though presumably GM and Ford had intended to do all three with these ads. Compare and contrast the new Cadillac models (http://www .cadillac.com) with the Ford luxury models (http://www.lincolnvehicles.com). Has either company broken any new ground in its approach to advertising these vehicles? Do you think in a few days you could distinguish between these models or remember the message of these Web sites?

Attitude Studies. The typical industry **attitude study** measures consumer attitudes after exposure to an ad. Television ads are typically seen in a group setting; print ads are often shown one-on-one. The studies may also be administered by survey, including Internet surveys. Essentially, people from the target market are recruited, and their attitudes toward the advertised brand as well as toward competitors' brands are noted. Ideally, there would be pre- and postexposure attitude measurement, so that one could see the change related to seeing the ad in question. Unfortunately, industry practice and thinner agency profit margins have created a situation in which only postexposure measures are now typically taken. True prepost tests are rare.

To the extent that attitudes measure something meaningful, and the most important things, these tests may be very useful. Their validity is typically premised on a single ad exposure (sometimes two) in an unnatural viewing environment (such as a theater). Many advertisers believe that commercials don't register their impact until after three, four, or more exposures. Still, a significant swing in attitude scores with a single exposure suggests that something is going on, and that some of this effect might be expected when the ad reaches real consumers in the comfort of their homes. But this method is expensive and may be waning in popularity. John Philip

Jones of Syracuse University has conducted analyses on these data and his conclusions are actually very supportive of attitude studies.[14] He contends that even if this form of message pretesting yields some incorrect predictions about ads' potential effectiveness (as it surely will), an advertiser's success rate is bound to improve with this tool. On the other hand, it is difficult to really know whether the respondent is expressing feelings toward the ad itself or the product advertised, and these can be very different things.

To test attitude change in print ads, test ads can be dropped off at the participants' homes in the form of magazines. The test ads have been tipped in. Subjects are told that the researcher will return the next day for an interview. They are also told that as part of their compensation for participating, they are being entered in a drawing. At that point, they are asked to indicate their preferences on a wide range of potential prizes. The next day when the interviewer returns, he or she asks for these preferences a second time. This is the postexposure attitude measure.

As you may remember from above, Bruzzone's recognition tests also collect attitude measures. This is a postexposure measure, but because it is linked to recognition scores, it may prove quite useful. Similarly, ASI Next★TV collects postexposure attitude scores. To our knowledge the only prominent testing service to offer true pre-post attitude testing is **ARS Persuasion Method.** This is a theater-type test in which commercials are embedded in television shows. Audience members indicate brand attitude as preference for brands should they win a basket of free items. Because they are asked this same question before and after exposure, attitude change scores can be determined. While this is a significant improvement over post-only attitude measurement, there is still the pesky problem of the very artificial setting and manner in which these TV ads are viewed. First, they are not on TV, and most of us rarely watch TV with a few hundred other people, knowing that we are supposed to pay attention.

Tracking Studies. **Tracking studies** are one of the most commonly used advertising and promotion research methods. Basically, they "track" the apparent effect of advertising over time. They typically assess attitude change, knowledge, behavioral intent, and self-reported behavior. They assess the performance of advertisements before, during, or after the launch of an advertising campaign. This type of advertising research is almost always conducted as a survey. Members of the target market are surveyed on a fairly regular basis to detect any changes. Any change in awareness, belief, or attitude is usually attributed (rightly or wrongly) to the advertising effort. Even though the participants are susceptible to other influences (e.g., news stories about the brand or category), these are fairly valuable tests because they do occur over time and provide ongoing assessment, rather than the one-time, one-shot approach of so many other methods. Their weakness resides largely in the meaningfulness of the specific measures. Sometimes attitudes shift a bit, but translate into no noticeable increase in sales and no return on investment (ROI).

Frame-by-Frame Tests. **Frame-by-frame tests** are usually employed for ads where the affective or emotional component is seen as key, although they may also be used to obtain thought listing as well. These tests typically work by getting consumers to turn dials (like/dislike) while viewing television commercials in a theater setting. The data from these dials are then collected, averaged, and later superimposed over the commercial for the researchers in the form of a line graph. The height of the line reflects the level of interest in the ad. The high points in the line represent periods of higher interest in the ad, and the dips show where the audience had less interest in that particular point of the ad. While some research companies

14.   John Philip Jones, "Advertising Pre-Testing: Will Europe Follow America's Lead?" *Commercial Communications,* June 1997, 21–26.

Here consumers' interest levels are measured while they watch an ad in real time.

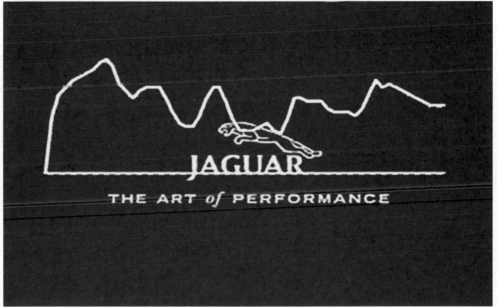

do ask consumers what they were thinking or feeling at certain points along the trace, and sometimes these responses are diagnostic, others do not. In those cases (such as the one shown in Exhibit 7.26), what the trace line really does then is measure the levels of interest at each specific moment in the execution—it does not explain whether or why consumers' reactions were positive or negative. The downside of frame-by-frame tests is that they involve somewhat higher costs than other methods, and there are some validity concerns in that you are asking consumers to do something they do not normally do while watching television. On the other hand, the method has quite a few fans. We believe it will grow in importance due to the heightened interest in assessing emotions and feelings in ads. Most researchers and advertising professionals believe that useful data can be gathered in this way.

Physiological Tests. Physiological measures detect how consumers react to messages, based on physical responses. **Eye-tracking systems** have been developed to monitor eye movements across print ads. With one such system, respondents wear a gogglelike device that records (on a computer system) pupil dilations, eye movements, and length of view by sectors within a print advertisement. Voice response analysis is another medium-tech research procedure. The idea here is that inflections in the voice when discussing an ad indicate excitement and other physiological states. In a typical application, a subject is asked to respond to a series of ads. These responses are tape-recorded and then computer-analyzed. Deviations from a flat response are claimed to be meaningful. Other, less frequently used physiological measures record brain wave activity, heart rate, blood pressure, and muscle contraction.

All physiological measures suffer from the same drawbacks. While we may be able to detect a physiological response to an advertisement, there is no way to determine whether the response is to the ad or the product, or which part of the advertisement was responsible for the response. In some sense, even the positive-negative dimension is obscured. Without being able to correlate specific effects with other dimensions of an ad, physiological measures are of minimal benefit.

Since the earliest days of advertising, there has been a fascination with physiological measurement. Advertising's fascination with science is obvious, with early attempts at physiological measurement being far more successful as a sales tool than as a way to actually gauge ad effectiveness. There is something provocative about scientists (sometimes even in white lab coats) wiring people up; it seems so precise and legitimate. Unfortunately—or fortunately, depending on your perspective—these measures tell us little beyond the simple degree of arousal attributable to an ad. For most advertisers, this minimal benefit doesn't justify the expense and intrusion involved with physiological measurement.

Pilot Testing. Before committing to the expense of a major campaign, advertisers sometimes test their messages in the marketplace via **pilot testing.** There are three major types of pilot testing. **Split-transmission** (often on cable television systems) is where different signals (or ads) can be sent to different neighborhoods or households. This allows testing of two different versions of an advertisement through direct transmission to two separate samples of similar households. This method provides exposure in a natural setting for heightened realism. Factors such as frequency of transmission and timing of transmission can be carefully controlled. The advertisements are then compared on measures of cognitive residue, recall, attitude change, and behavioral intent.

Split-run distribution uses the same technique as split-cable transmission, except the print medium is used. An ad is placed in half the copies of, say, the January issue of a magazine and a different version of the ad runs in the other half. This method of pilot testing has the advantage of using direct response as a test measure. Ads can be designed with a reply card that can serve as a basis of evaluation. Coupons and toll-free numbers can also be used. The realism of this method is a great advantage in the testing process. Expense is, of course, a major drawback.

Finally, a **split-list experiment** tests the effectiveness of various aspects of direct mail advertising pieces. Multiple versions of a direct mail piece are prepared and sent to various segments of a mailing list. The version that *pulls* (produces sales) the best is deemed superior. The advantage of all the pilot testing methods is the natural and real setting within which the test takes place. A major disadvantage is that competitive or other environmental influences in the market cannot be controlled and may affect the performance of one advertisement without ever being detected by the researcher.

Direct Response. **Direct response** measures actual behavior. Advertisements in print, the Internet, and broadcast media that offer the audience the opportunity to place an inquiry or respond directly through a Web site, reply card, or toll-free phone number produce **inquiry/direct response measures.** An example is displayed in Exhibit 7.27. These measures are quite straightforward in the sense that

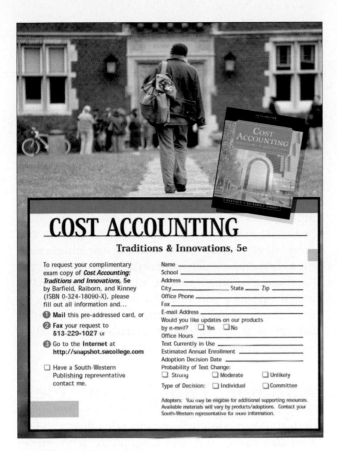

EXHIBIT 7.27

An ad like this allows for a very simple kind of advertising response management. The advertiser knows if they call, click, or write.

advertisements that generate a high number of inquiries or direct responses, compared to historical benchmarks, are deemed effective. Additional analyses may compare the number of inquiries or responses to the number of sales generated. For example, some print ads will use different 800 numbers for different versions of the ad so that the agency can compute which ad is generating more inquiries. These measures are not relevant for all types of advertising, however. Ads designed to have long-term image building or brand identity effects should not be judged using such short-term response measures.

Single-Source Data. With the advent of universal product codes (UPCs) on product packages and the proliferation of cable television, research firms are now able to engage in *single-source research* to document the behavior of individuals— or, more typically, households—in a respondent pool by tracking their behavior from the television set to the checkout counter. **Single-source data** provide information from individual households about brand purchases, coupon use, and television advertising exposure by combining grocery store scanner data with TV-viewing data from monitoring devices attached to the households' televisions. With these different types of data combined, a better case can be made for assessing the real impact of advertising and promotion on consumers' actual purchases. This is not an inexpensive method of assessment, and it still remains difficult (if not impossible) to know exactly what specific aspects of advertising had what effects on consumers. The best-known supplier if this type of testing is **iri BehaviorScan.**

Account Planning versus Advertising Research. Jon Steel, director of account planning and vice chairman of Goodby, Silverstein and Partners—its clients include Anheuser-Busch, the California Milk Processors Board ("Got Milk?"), Nike, Porsche, and Hewlett-Packard—has called account planning "the biggest thing to hit American advertising since Doyle Dane Bernbach's Volkswagen campaign."[15] That is stretching it a bit, but account planning is a big story in the industry. What is it? Well, good question. (See Exhibit 7.28.)

    Account planning is defined in contrast to traditional advertising research. It differs mostly in three ways. First, in terms of organization, agencies that use this system typically assign an "account planner" to work cooperatively with the account executive on a given client's business. Rather than depending on a separate research department's occasional involvement, the agency assigns the planner to a single client (just like an advertising executive) to stay with the projects on a continuous basis—even though, in this organizational scheme, there is typically an account planning department. In the more traditional system, the research department would get involved from time to time as needed, and members of the research department would work on several different clients' advertising. (There are several variations on this theme.)

    Another difference is that this organizational structure puts research in a different, more prominent role. In this system, researchers (or "planners") seem to be more actively involved throughout the entire advertising process and seem to have

15. Jon Steel, *Truth, Lies & Advertising: The Art of Account Planning* (New York: John Wiley & Sons, 1998), jacket.

EXHIBIT 7.28

Much ado is made about the account planner versus traditional advertising research.

a bigger impact on it as well. (Of course, some of the difference is more agency self-promotion than reality.) Agencies that practice "account planning" tend to do more developmental and less evaluative research. Third, "planning agencies" tend to do more qualitative and naturalistic research than their more traditional counterparts. But these differences, too, seem fairly exaggerated—even though Jay Chiat called planning "the best new business tool ever invented."[16] There is another, more cynical side to this story: Many advertising agencies have decided that they simply cannot afford the cost of a full-time research staff. It's cheaper and maybe even better to outsource the work. But a quieter and more devious way of downsizing (or eliminating these expensive departments) is to go to the "account planning" system, in which a researcher will always be a part of the team. Then, there's no need for a centralized research department, and it appears as if the agency is actually demonstrating more commitment to research.

Another Thought on Message Testing.
None of these methods is perfect. There are challenges to reliability, validity, trustworthiness, and meaningfulness with all of them. Advertisers sometimes think that consumers watch new television commercials the way they watch new, eagerly awaited feature films, or that they listen to radio spots like they listen to a symphony, or read magazine ads like a Steinbeck novel. We watch TV while we work, talk, eat, and study; we use it as a night light, background noise, and babysitter. Likewise, we typically thumb through magazines very, very quickly. While these traditional methods of message testing have their strengths, more naturalistic methods are clearly recommended. Still, it would be a mistake to throw the baby out with the bath water; good and appropriate social science can produce better advertising.

What We Need.
Advertising research could do with some change. The way we think about ads is certainly changing. Qualitative research is now the norm. Agencies known best for their creativity have been attractive to hot creatives because of the lack of old-style quantitative attitude copy research. In fact, across the industry, the view that ads are complex social texts has caught on. The move to an almost complete visual advertising style has also put into question the appropriateness of a set of tests that focus on the acceptance of message claims, as well as remembrance.

The account planning way of thinking merges the research and brand management business. Good research can play an important role in this; it can be very helpful or an enormous hindrance, as advertisers are realizing more and more. Top-down delivered marketing is not considered realistic by many in the industry. With this new realization comes new terms. One is the idea of account planning as a substitute for the traditional research efforts of an agency. There has been a very recent but very significant turn in thinking about research and its role in advertising, promotion, and brand management.

16.   Ibid., p. 42.

ETHICS

Research and Healthy Fast Food

Awareness of the health concerns associated with obesity has grown lately in the United States, but advertising healthy fast food has been a losing battle for the industry. Approximately 127 million adults in the United States are overweight and 60 million of them are obese, according to the American Obesity Association (evaluate their objectivity and disinterest yourself).

So advertisers did research, followed their findings, and did what seemed best for people—yet it was not successful. In fact, advertising fast food as "healthy" is often detrimental to chain restaurants.

Research, focus groups, and interviews led Taco Bell to offer products with less fat and calories. Taco Bell took their research one step further and conducted blind taste tests. Repeatedly, individuals preferred the low-fat items—but they bombed in the market. Likewise, the use of health and nutrition information in milk advertising was a failure. The switch from "It does a body good" to "Got milk?" has been a success because customers do not like to be lectured about nutrition and drinking their white medicine.

- So, what are the ethics here?
- What should fast food advertisers do?
- Do you give customers what they want, what they need, or just not tell them when it's actually good for them?

As you can see, advertising and promotion research is used to judge advertising, but who judges advertising research, and how? First of all, not enough people, in our opinion, question and judge advertising research. Research is not magic or truth, and it should never be confused with such. Issues of reliability, validity, trustworthiness, and meaningfulness should be seriously considered when research is used to make important decisions. Otherwise, you're just using research as some sort of mystical ritual that you know really has limited meaning, mouthing the words, and faithfully uttering the chant too. Research can be a wonderful tool when applied correctly, but is routinely poorly matched to the real world situation. Things are getting better on this front.

SUMMARY

1 Explain the purposes served by and methods used in developmental advertising research.

Advertising and promotion research can serve many purposes in the development of a campaign. There is no better way to generate fresh ideas for a campaign than to listen carefully to the customer. Qualitative research involving customers is essential for fostering fresh thinking about a brand. Audience definition and profiling are fundamental to effective campaign planning and rely on advertising research. In the developmental phase, advertisers use diverse methods for gathering information. Focus groups, projective techniques, the ZMET, and field work are trusted research methods that directly involve consumers and aid in idea generation and concept testing.

2 Identify sources of secondary data that can aid the IBP planning effort.

Because information is such a critical resource in the decision-making process, several sources of data are widely used. Internal company sources such as strategic marketing plans, research reports, customer service records, and sales data provide a wealth of information on consumer

tastes and preferences. Government sources generate a wide range of census and labor statistics, providing key data on trends in population, consumer spending, employment, and immigration. Commercial data sources provide advertisers with a wealth of information on household consumers. Professional publications share insider information on industry trends and new research. Finally, the Internet is a revolutionary research tool that delivers rich data at virtually no cost. In particular, advertisers can obtain sophisticated research data at thousands of consumer- and brand-based online community sites.

3 Discuss the purposes served by and methods used in copy research.

Copy research (evaluative research) aims to judge the effectiveness of actual ads. Advertisers and clients try to determine if audiences "get" the joke of an ad or retain key knowledge concerning the brand. Tracking changes in audience attitudes, feelings and emotions, behavior, and physiological response is important in gauging the overall success of an ad, and various methods are employed before and after the launch of a campaign to assess the impact on audiences. Communication tests, recall testing, pilot testing, and the thought-listing technique are a few of the methods that try to measure the persuasiveness of a message. Some agencies, attempting to bypass the high cost and inconclusive results of research, substitute account planning for traditional advertising and promotion research. Advocates of this trend believe an account planning system merges the best in research and brand management.

KEY TERMS

repositioned
concept test
focus group
projective techniques
dialogue balloons
story construction
sentence and picture completion
Zaltman Metaphor Elicitation Technique (ZMET)
field work
embedded
creative brief
coolhunts

normative test scores
communication test
resonance test
thought listing, or cognitive response analysis
recall tests
recognition
recognition tests
Starch Readership Services
attitude study
ARS Persuasion Method
tracking studies
frame-by-frame test

physiological measures
eye-tracking systems
pilot testing
split-transmission
split-run distribution
split-list experiment
direct response
inquiry/direct response measures
single-source data
single-source tracking measures
IRI BehaviorScan
account planning

QUESTIONS

1.   Read the chapter opening and list two important lessons that can be learned from Coca-Cola's advertising and promotion research blunder with New Coke.

2.   What historic factors led to the development and prominence of advertising and promotion research departments during the mid-1900s?

3.   Focus groups are one of the advertising researcher's most versatile tools. Describe the basic features of focus group research that could lead to inappropriate generalizations about the preferences of the target audience.

4.   ZMET is a technique that advertisers may use in place of focus groups. What aspects of ZMET and focus groups are similar? What particular features of ZMET could foster richer understanding of consumers' motives than is typically achieved with focus groups?

5.   List the sources and uses of secondary data. What are the benefits of secondary data? What are the limitations?

6.   Identify issues that could become sources of conflict between account managers and advertising creatives in the message-testing process. What could go wrong if people in an ad agency take the position that what the client wants, the client gets?

7.   Criteria for judging ad effectiveness include "getting it," cognitive residue, knowledge, attitude change, feelings and emotions, physiological changes, and behavior. Identify specific evaluative advertising research methods that could be used to test an ad's impact on any of these dimensions.

8.   How would you explain the finding that ads that achieve high recall scores don't always turn out to be ads that do a good job in generating sales? Are there some features of ads that make them memorable but could also turn off consumers and dissuade them from buying the brand? Give an example from your experience.

9.   What is single-source research, and what is its connection to the universal product codes (UPCs) one finds on nearly every product in the grocery store?

10. Explain the industry trend of substituting account planning for traditional advertising and promotion research. Why do some agency directors claim that this trend is the biggest thing in advertising since the famous Bernbach Volkswagen campaign? Do you tend to believe the hype surrounding this trend, or are you cynical that forces of downsizing are driving it? Explain your reasoning.

EXPERIENTIAL EXERCISES

1. Conduct an informal advertising research test on a popular television commercial of your choice. First, determine the evaluative criteria you think would be most relevant for determining the ad's effectiveness. Next, design a test to evaluate the commercial's effectiveness by selecting one of the least-involved research methods and typing up a short pencil-and-paper questionnaire (you can draw upon ideas from the chapter). Ask a classmate or partner to watch the commercial and complete the questionnaire. Once the questionnaire is completed, write a short evaluation of the commercial based on the results of your survey.

2. Search the Internet or local phone directory and identify a company that conducts advertising and promotion research. Investigate the background of the company and type a one-page paper describing the information and services the organization provides. Who would be likely to benefit from the firm's services? List one of the firm's clients, and explain how advertising research helped guide that client's advertising and promotion initiatives.

EXPERIENCING THE INTERNET

7-1 Developmental Advertising and Promotion Research

Developmental advertising research provides key information used by creatives in producing ads. A brand's optimal advertising and promotion effort depends on accurate information about trends, target audience, product usage expectations, and other data that are useful during the production of the advertising message.

Clairol delivers integrated brand promotion for many of its product lines and develops effective campaigns based on important research. Clairol's research has led to the development of its Herbal Essences products, which target a very specific consumer niche within the broad category of personal care products.

Herbal Essences: http://www.herbalessences.com

1. Explain the role of *audience profiling* and how it guides the uses and message of the Herbal Essences Web site.

2. What is the main concept behind the Herbal Essences product line? Do you believe that concept testing played an important role for Clairol in the development of Herbal Essences? Explain.

3. What trends do you believe had to be measured quantitatively by trustworthy research in order for Clairol to develop and advertise Herbal Essences? Identify the developmental advertising research method that you think would be the most important to guide Clairol's efforts to advertise and promote Herbal Essences. Explain why you picked this method.

7-2 Conducting Research in the Real World

The Got Milk? advertising campaign, which recently celebrated its 10th anniversary, has become an American icon, boasting a 90 percent consumer awareness rate for the milk industry while taking home many prestigious advertising awards. First conceived in 1993 by the California Milk Processor Board (CMPB) in conjunction with Goodby, Silverstein & Partners, Got Milk? changed the course of the U.S. dairy industry after a decade of sagging milk sales. With its growing international presence, promotional tie-ins to food-industry giants like McDonald's, and celebrity backing from pop-culture icons such as Paris Hilton and Dr. Phil, the Got Milk? campaign is well-positioned for another great decade of delicious success.

Got Milk?: http://www.gotmilk.com/

1. According to your text, which developmental advertising research method played a key role in the formulation of the Got Milk? advertising theme?

2. What does it mean that consumption practices are *embedded,* and how did this principle lead to the success of the Got Milk? campaign?

3. Visit the Got Milk? Web site and list some of the newest developments in the campaign. What celebrities are currently endorsing milk? What IBP efforts are lending support to the Got Milk? ads?

CHAPTER 8

After reading and thinking about this chapter, you will be able to do the following:

1

Describe the basic components of an advertising plan.

2

Compare and contrast two fundamental approaches for setting advertising objectives.

3

Explain various methods for setting advertising budgets.

4

Discuss the role of the advertising agency in formulating an advertising plan.

Introductory Scenario: Polishing the Apple.

In his book *The End of Advertising As We Know It,* Sergio Zyman, one-time chief marketing officer at Coca-Cola, has a lot to say about many high-profile ad campaigns, including Apple's "Think Different." Launched in the fall of 1997, the Apple campaign featured billboards of innovators like Albert Einstein, Amelia Earhart, Muhammad Ali, and Pablo Picasso. TV ads were black and white mini-documentaries explaining how each of these persons took a different path and changed the world. The ads ended with the Apple logo and the printed phrase "Think Different," suggesting that you, too, can chart a different path, as long as you take a bite from the Apple. Critics loved the campaign. Apple's ad agency picked up an Emmy, a Clio, and a Silver Lion at the Cannes International Advertising Festival. Unfortunately, the company's revenues dropped for the next three quarters and by June of 1998, Apple's U.S. retail market share had fallen to a mere 2 percent.[1] The company that had once rocked the computer business with its innovative Macintosh was doing award-winning advertising, and facing extinction.

Apple found itself in a real mess. And we want to emphasize that the severity of its problems went well beyond what one might be able to fix with a fresh advertising campaign and a catchy slogan like "Think Different." To rebound, Apple would need inspired leadership and, most important, a series of innovative new products to capture the imagination of consumers around the world. The leadership would have to come from its celebrated founder and on-again/off-again CEO—Steve Jobs. The new product designed to salvage the company was the iMac personal computer.

Put yourself in the shoes of Steve Jobs. The company that you helped create is adrift and you desperately need a major new product success to turn things around. You have decided to stake the future of your company on a new product called iMac. Launching a great new product via a comprehensive advertising and IBP campaign is your best hope for reviving the company. Jobs held nothing back in his determined effort to save Apple.

The iMac was the first in a new generation of Internet appliances. It was a system designed first and foremost to get households hooked to the Net. As described by Steve Jobs, "iMac does for Internet computing what the original Macintosh did for personal computing. Macintosh let anyone use a computer and iMac lets anyone get on to the Internet quickly and easily." Regarding his advertising and IBP campaign, Jobs went on to say, "We're launching this campaign because we want the world to know that iMac is the computer for the tens of millions of consumers who want to get to the Internet easily, quickly, and affordably."[2] Jobs, of course, was not just grasping at straws: His market research at the time was telling him that one of consumers' primary motives for buying a personal computer was to hook up to the Internet.

While the iMac actually went on sale August 14, 1998, its launch campaign was initiated three months earlier at a surprise unveiling of the machine before an audience of media types in the same auditorium where the Macintosh was introduced. In other parallels with the 1984 launch of the Macintosh, Jobs departed from his usual dress code by wearing a suit and kept the iMac prototype behind a veil on stage until he was ready to spring it on his unsuspecting audience. Jobs stated at the time: "We figured we'd have a surprise and then let people feed on it before they could get it."[3] In the weeks leading up to August 14, Jobs's sneak preview had the desired effect of creating an iMac buzz across Web sites frequently visited by loyal Mac users.

Steve Jobs and his public relations machine continued to strut their stuff in the hours leading up to the first public sale of the iMac at 12:01 AM on August 14.

1.   Sergio Zyman, *The End of Advertising As We Know It* (Hoboken, N.J.: John Wiley & Sons, 2002), 18–19; Bradley Johnson, "Jobs Orchestrates Ad Blitz for Apple's New iMac PC," *Advertising Age,* August 10, 1998, 6.
2.   Apple Computer, "Apple Launches Its Largest Marketing Campaign Ever for iMac," press release, August 13, 1998.
3.   Jim Carlton, "From Apple, a New Marketing Blitz," *Wall Street Journal,* August 14, 1998, B1.

Working with loyal retailers, Apple's PR people created 20-foot-high inflatable iMac balloons to fly above retail stores at the Midnight Madness event on August 14, 1998. A Cupertino, California, retailer added giant searchlights and scheduled part of its midnight iMac delivery using four new Volkswagen Beetles on loan from a local dealer. Of course, TV crews from every station in the Bay Area were there to cover the action and report it all to the world the next day. Summarizing the state of affairs on launch day, one salesperson at a CompUSA Superstore in San Francisco said: "I don't think even Apple expected it to be this crazy. We're having trouble keeping iMacs on the shelves."[4]

And that was just for starters. As the new iMac was going on sale, Apple executives also announced the start of the largest advertising campaign in their history, where paid media advertising costs were expected to run more than $100 million between August 15 and December 31, 1998. (Yes, Steve Jobs was betting the future of his company on the success of the iMac.) These are just some of the key elements of the campaign:[5]

- **Television advertising.** National TV ads began August 16 on *The Wonderful World of Disney* and continued on programs such as *NewsRadio* and *The Drew Carey Show,* and on cable shows such as *South Park* and *Larry King Live.* TV ads were also placed in the top 10 metro markets—Boston; Chicago; Los Angeles; New York; San Francisco; Philadelphia; Washington, D.C.; Seattle; Minneapolis; and Denver. TV ads began airing in Europe and Asia in September 1998.
- **Outdoor advertising.** Billboards also went up in the top 10 metro markets. As shown in Exhibit 8.1, they featured a photo of the iMac and one of the following copy lines: "Chic. Not Geek"; "Sorry, no beige"; "Mental floss"; and "I think, therefore iMac." This last copy line was attributed to Mr. Magic—Steve Jobs.
- **Magazine advertising.** An informative 12-page iMac insert was distributed through leading magazines such as *Time, People, Sports Illustrated,* and *Rolling Stone.* More than 15 million copies were put in consumers' hands in the first few weeks after launch. This more than doubled the amount of inserts ever distributed by Apple in any prior campaign. Four pages from this insert are displayed in Exhibit 8.2.

EXHIBIT 8.1

Apple's iMac launch used outdoor billboards like this one in the 10 top metro markets across the United States. What value proposition do you see being addressed by this billboard? Does this value proposition relate to a larger trend in the computer and technology industry?
http://www.apple.com

4.   "iMac Makes a Midnight Debut," http://www.macweek.com, accessed August 15, 1998.
5.   Apple Computer, "Apple Launches Its Largest Marketing Campaign Ever for iMac," press release, August 13, 1998.

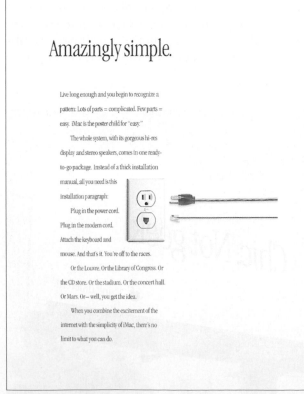

EXHIBIT 8.2

Apple has consistently broken new ground in its product advertising. Former Chairman John Sculley, who came to Apple from PepsiCo, contrasted the company with his former margin-focused employer, as an agent of incessant innovation and radical change. Apple ads certainly seem to find endless ways to herald the new, the innovative, the unordinary—better, perhaps, than any others.

EXHIBIT 8.3

Of course, Apple's home page featured the iMac in November 1998. The interactivity of the Web makes it the perfect medium for anticipating and answering questions about the technical features of a product such as a new personal computer.

EXHIBIT 8.4

The original candy-colored iMac resonated with consumers from a design standpoint. New generations of the iMac have continued to feature elegant design as a primary point of differentiation.

- *Radio advertising.* A five-day countdown to the iMac launch was executed through a network of 20 nationwide radio companies. This promotion featured iMac giveaways each day of the week preceding Midnight Madness. Apple's was the most comprehensive radio campaign in the United States the week of August 10, 1998.
- *Cooperative advertising.* Apple also joined forces with its local retailers in cooperative advertising efforts around the United States. For example, Apple worked with the New York dealer DataVisions Inc. to help sponsor iMac ads on movie screens in all 600 of Long Island's theaters. Other dealers participated in software and T-shirt giveaways, and CompUSA launched newspaper ads that for the first time promoted Apple products exclusively.
- *Web site features and promotions.* Of course, everything you could ever want to know about the iMac and the iMac product launch was available for the world to peruse at http://www .apple.com. Exhibit 8.3 shows the Apple home page as of November 1998.

The iMac launch campaign yielded the kind of results that Steve Jobs needed for reviving his company. In November 1998 the iMac was the best-selling personal computer in the consumer market, with about a third of iMac buyers being first-time owners of any type of personal computer. And it wasn't just a faddish success: The iMac would propel Apple Computer Inc. to 11 consecutive quarters of profitable growth. But just to illustrate the point that nothing in marketing and advertising is ever permanent, by the summer of 2000 media pundits of all kinds began asking questions like, "Yes, Steve, you fixed it. Congrats! Now what's Act Two?"[6] Jobs came up with several answers to that question, including stylish remakes of the original iMac (see Exhibit 8.4), and, more recently, a whole new product strategy built around iTunes and iPod, designed to revolutionize the world of online music.[7]

As the high-profile CEO of Apple, Jobs received a good deal of the praise for iMac's original launch campaign. However, he quickly demurred and assigned the credit to his advertising agency—TBWA Chiat/Day of Venice, California. Said Jobs: "Creating great advertising, like creating great products, is a team effort. I am lucky to work with the best talent in the industry."[8] Indeed, it would be impossible to launch a campaign of this scale without great teamwork between agency and client.

While we have merely scratched the surface in describing all that was involved in the campaign that launched the iMac, we hope this example gives you a taste for the complexity that can be involved in executing a comprehensive advertising and IBP effort. You don't go out and spend $100 million promoting a new product that is vital to the success of a firm without

6.   For a thorough debriefing on Apple's situation post-iMac, see Peter Burrows, "Apple," *BusinessWeek,* July 31, 2000, 102–113; Pui-Wing Tam, "Apple's Growth beyond Traditional Base Is Called into Question," *Wall Street Journal,* October 2, 2000, B26.
7.   Ronald Glover and Tom Lowry, "Show Time!" *BusinessWeek,* February 2, 2004, 56–64.
8.   Johnson, "Jobs Orchestrates Ad Blitz for Apple's New iMac PC."

giving the entire endeavor considerable forethought. Such an endeavor will call for a plan. As you will see in this chapter, Jobs, Apple, and Chiat/Day followed the process of building an advertising effort based on several key features of the advertising plan. An advertising plan is the culmination of the planning effort needed to deliver effective advertising.

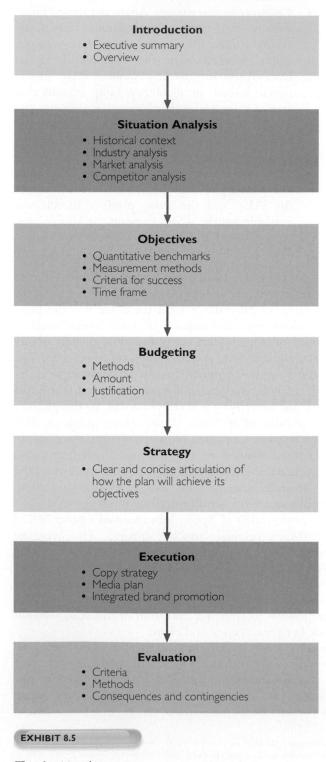

Introduction
- Executive summary
- Overview

Situation Analysis
- Historical context
- Industry analysis
- Market analysis
- Competitor analysis

Objectives
- Quantitative benchmarks
- Measurement methods
- Criteria for success
- Time frame

Budgeting
- Methods
- Amount
- Justification

Strategy
- Clear and concise articulation of how the plan will achieve its objectives

Execution
- Copy strategy
- Media plan
- Integrated brand promotion

Evaluation
- Criteria
- Methods
- Consequences and contingencies

EXHIBIT 8.5

The advertising plan.

The Advertising Plan and Its Marketing Context.

An ad plan should be a direct extension of a firm's marketing plan. As suggested in the closing section of Chapter 6, one device that can be used to explicitly connect the marketing plan with the advertising plan is the statement of a brand's value proposition. A statement of what the brand is supposed to stand for in the eyes of the target segment derives from the firm's marketing strategy, and will guide all ad-planning activities. The advertising plan, including all integrated brand promotion, is a subset of the larger marketing plan. The IBP component must be built into the plan in a seamless and synergistic way. Everything has to work together, whether the plan is for Apple or for a business with far fewer resources. And as Steve Jobs noted about his iMac campaign, there is no substitute for good teamwork between agency and client in the development of compelling marketing and advertising plans.

An **advertising plan** specifies the thinking, tasks, and timetable needed to conceive and implement an effective advertising effort. We particularly like the iMac example because it illustrates the wide array of options that can be deployed in creating interest and communicating the value proposition for a brand. Jobs and his agency choreographed public relations activities, promotions and give-aways, cooperative advertising, broadcast advertising, billboard advertising, Web site development, and more, as part of the iMac launch. Advertising planners should review all the options before selecting an integrated set to communicate with the target audience. It is critical to think beyond traditional broadcast media when considering the best way to break through the clutter of the modern marketplace and get a message across to the focal customer. Miami's Crispin Porter & Bogusky is an agency that built its reputation on finding novel ways to register clients' messages with consumers. CPB's rules for breaking all the rules are summarized in the Creativity box.

Exhibit 8.5 shows the components of an advertising plan. It should be noted that there is a great deal of variation in advertising plans from advertiser to advertiser. Our discussion of the advertising plan will focus on the seven major sections shown in Exhibit 8.5: the introduction, situation analysis,

CREATIVITY

Hot Agencies "Think Different"

Hot agencies come and go, but Crispin Porter & Bogusky may be a prototype for the agency of the future. That is, although many have bemoaned the increasing inadequacy of traditional broadcast media for reaching today's time-starved consumers, Madison Avenue is commonly criticized for not changing with the times. Through its innovative IBP campaigns for clients like Mini, IKEA, Virgin Atlantic Airways, and Molson beer, CPB has proven time and again that they know how to deliver results for clients without relying on costly TV ads. At CPB they try to follow a few soft and loose rules to help them "Think Different."

Rule #1: Zero in on the product. CPB's Alex Bogusky believes the product is the thing, and recommends close inspection of the product. Find out every good thing about the product and then invent more. Come up with ideas to spruce up the product through packaging, displays, little giveaways, and so on.

Rule #2: Use loads of design. Hire lots of graphic designers and let them do their thing creating leaflets, posters, packaging, and new gear.

Rule #3: Find the sweet spot. Draw two circles. One contains all the characteristics of a given product; the other holds the list of needs and aspirations of your target market. The overlap of the circles is where the best ideas for a new campaign will be found.

Rule #4: Surprise equals buzz equals exposure. Create a stunt (e.g., put a Mini on the roof of an SUV and drive it around town). If it's surprising enough, people will start talking about it and the news media will want to cover it. That sounds like free exposure!

Rule #5: Don't be timid (but don't be an ass either). Sex, violence, and bathroom humor have a short shelf life. Be smart. Be sly. CPB's anti-tobacco ad, "Shards O' Glass Freeze Pop" spoofed the tobacco industry's attempts to justify their products. It got people talking without fart jokes or wardrobe malfunctions. (Remember that Super Bowl fiasco?)

Rule #6: Conspire with the customer. Convince people you're on their side. CPB helped male Molson drinkers break the ice with women by printing pickup lines on the labels of its beer bottles. That's definitely thinking different!

Rule #7: Make yourself useful. Nobody needs an ad, but everybody likes free stuff. Keep your designers busy inventing inexpensive giveaways, like the IKEA poster that doubled as holiday gift-wrap.

Rule #8: Think of advertising as a product, not a service. Stop wasting time schmoozing the client. Instead of being a paid pal, be a factory focused on turning out the best product. But remember, advertising is never an assembly-line product; it's always custom made.

Rule #9: Good ideas can come from anyone, anywhere. Throw lots of people at the problem. Listen. Sometimes even the client (gasp) can have a good idea.

Rule #10: Rules are lame. Break the rules.

Sources: Jack Neff and Lisa Sanders, "It's Broken," *Advertising Age*, February 16, 2004, 1,30; Hillary Chura, "Madison Ave. Out of Touch?" *Advertising Age*, April 12, 2004, 18; and Warren Berger, "Dare-Devils," *Business 2.0*, April 2004, 111–116.

objectives, budgeting, strategy, execution, and evaluation. Each component is discussed in the following sections.

Introduction. The introduction of an advertising plan consists of an executive summary and an overview. An executive summary, typically two paragraphs to two pages in length, is offered to state the most important aspects of the plan. This is the takeaway; that is, it is what the reader should remember from the plan. It is the essence of the plan.

As with many documents, an overview is also customary. An overview ranges in length from a paragraph to a few pages. It sets out what is to be covered, and it structures the context. All plans are different, and some require more setup than others. Don't underestimate the benefit of a good introduction. It's where you can make or lose a lot of points with your boss or client.

Situation Analysis. When someone asks you to explain a decision you've made, you may say something like, "Well, here's the situation. . . ." In what follows, you try to distill the situation down to the most important points and how they are connected in order to explain why you made the decision. An ad plan **situation analysis** is no different. It is where the client and agency lay out the most important factors that define the situation, and then explain the importance of each factor.

A lengthy list of potential factors (e.g., demographic, social and cultural, economic, and political/regulatory) can define a situation analysis. Some books offer long but incomplete lists. We prefer to play it straight with you: There is no complete or perfect list of situational factors. The idea is not to be exhaustive or encyclopedic when writing a plan, but to be smart in choosing the few important factors that really describe the situation, and then explain how the factors relate to the advertising task at hand. Market segmentation and consumer behavior research provide the organization with insights that can be used for a situation analysis, but ultimately you have to decide which of the many factors are really the most critical to address in your advertising. This is the essence of smart management.

Let's say you represent American Express. How would you define the firm's current advertising situation? What are the most critical factors? What image has prior advertising, like that in Exhibit 8.6, established for the card? Would you consider the changing view of prestige cards to be critical? What about the problem of hanging onto an exclusive image while trying to increase your customer base by having your cards accepted at discount stores? Does the proliferation of gold and platinum cards by other banks rate as critical? Do the diverse interest rates offered by bank cards seem critical to the situation? What about changing social attitudes regarding the responsible use of credit cards? What about the current high level of consumer debt?

Think about how credit card marketing is influenced by the economic conditions of the day and the cultural beliefs about the proper way to display status. In the 1980s, it was acceptable for advertisers to tout the self-indulgent side of plastic (for example, MasterCard's slogan "MasterCard, I'm bored"). Today, charge and credit card ads often point out just how prudent it is to use your card for the right reasons. Now, instead of just suggesting you use your plastic to hop off to the islands when you feel the first stirrings of a bout with boredom, credit card companies often detail functional benefits for their cards with a specific market segment in mind, as reflected by the American Express ad in Exhibit 8.7.

EXHIBIT 8.6

What is the image this ad establishes for the American Express card? How is this image a response to the company's situation analysis? Link your answer to a discussion of market segmentation and product positioning. Who is reached by this ad and how does reaching this segment fit into the overall strategy for American Express? http://www.americanexpress.com

EXHIBIT 8.7

Here we see American Express offering a specific package of benefits to a well-defined target segment. Obviously, the folks at American Express understand STP marketing (per Chapter 6).

Basic demographic trends may be the single most important situational factor in advertising plans. Whether it's baby boomers or Generation X, Y, or Z, where the people are is usually where the sales are. As the population distribution varies with time, new markets are created and destroyed. The baby boom generation of post–World War II disproportionately dictates consumer offerings and demand simply because of its size. As the boomers age, companies that offer the things needed by tens of millions of aging boomers will have to devise new appeals. Think of the consumers of this generation needing long-term health care, geriatric products, and things to amuse themselves in retirement. Will they have the disposable income necessary to have the bountiful lifestyle many of them have had during their working years? After all, they aren't the greatest savers. And what of today's twenty-somethings? When do you tend to model your parents? When do you look to put space between yourself and your parents? Knowing which generation(s) you are targeting is critical in your situation analysis.

Historical Context. No situation is entirely new, but all situations are unique. Just how a firm arrived at the current situation is very important. Before trying to design Apple's iMac campaign, an agency should certainly know a lot about the history of all the principal players, the industry, the brand, the corporate culture, critical moments in the company's past, its big mistakes and big successes. All new decisions are situated in a firm's history, and an agency should be diligent in studying that history. For example, would an agency pitch new business to Green Giant without knowing something of the brand's history and the rationale behind the Green Giant character? The history of the Green Giant dates back decades, as suggested in Exhibit 8.8. The fact is that no matter what advertising decisions are made in the present, the past has a significant impact.

Apart from history's intrinsic value, sometimes the real business goal is to convince the client that the agency knows the client's business, its major concerns, and its corporate culture. A brief history of the company and brand are included to demonstrate the thoroughness of the agency's research, the depth of its knowledge, and the scope of its concern.

e-SIGHTINGS

EXHIBIT 8.8

Knowing a brand's history can guide the development of future campaigns. Visit the Green Giant corporate site (http://www.greengiant .com) and read all about the history of the Green Giant character. He first appeared in advertising in 1928. How might this history determine future Green Giant ads? Is it time to ditch the Green Giant? Can you think of brands that made drastic changes in their popular icons? What might motivate a company to modernize or change its animated character icon?

Industry Analysis. An **industry analysis** is just that; it focuses on developments and trends within an entire industry and on any other factors that may make a difference in how an advertiser proceeds with an advertising plan. An industry analysis should enumerate and discuss the most important aspects of a given industry, including the supply side of the supply-demand equation. When great advertising overstimulates demand that can't be matched by supply, one can end up with lots of unhappy customers.

No industry faces more dramatic trends and swings in consumers' tastes than the food business. In recent years the low-carb craze has challenged industry giants from Nestlé to Hershey Foods to H.J. Heinz Co. to McDonald's to come up with new products and reposition old ones to satisfy consumers' growing concerns about sugar and white flour. When your industry research tells you that 30 million Americans describe themselves as being on a low-carb diet, and another 100 million are

EXHIBIT 8.9

Pizzeria Uno built its business around the classic, Chicago-style, deep dish pizza. But in a world gone mad with carb counting, the deep dish pizza was bound to lose some appeal. Enter Uno Chicago Grill and Lemon Basil Salmon with just 7 net carbs. Can carb counters and deep dish pizza lovers find a way to peacefully co-exist? For Uno's sake, let's hope so.

expected to join them in a matter of months, it's time to reposition and reformulate.[9] It is hard to imagine the marketing and advertising plans of any food maker not giving some consideration to the carb issue as part of an analysis of their industry. As suggested by Exhibit 8.9, no one is immune.

Market Analysis. A **market analysis** complements the industry analysis, emphasizing the demand side of the equation. In a market analysis, an advertiser examines the factors that drive and determine the market for the firm's product or service. First, the advertiser needs to decide just exactly what the market is for the product. Most often, the market for a given good or service is simply defined as current users. The idea here is that consumers figure out for themselves whether they want the product or not and thus define the market for themselves, and for the advertiser. This approach has some wisdom to it. It's simple, easy to defend, and very conservative. Few executives get fired for choosing this market definition. However, it completely ignores those consumers who might otherwise be persuaded to use the product.

A market analysis commonly begins by stating just who the current users are, and (hopefully) why they are current users. Consumers' motivations for using one product or service but not another may very well provide the advertiser with the means toward a significant expansion of the entire market. If the entire pie grows, the firm's slice usually does as well. The advertiser's job in a market analysis is to find out the most important market factors and why they are so important. It is at this stage in the situation analysis that account planning can play an important role.

Competitor Analysis. Once the industry and market are studied and analyzed, attention turns to **competitor analysis.** Here an advertiser determines just exactly who the competitors are, discussing their strengths, weaknesses, tendencies, and any threats they pose.

Suppose you are creating advertising for Fuji 35-mm film. Who are your competitors? Is Kodak, with its dominant market share, your only real competitor? Are Agfa and Konica worth worrying about? Would stealing share from these fairly minor players be productive? What has Kodak done in the past when Fuji has made a move? What are Kodak's advantages? For one, it may have successfully equated memories with photographs and with trusting the archiving of these memories to Kodak film. Does Kodak have any weaknesses? Could Kodak be characterized as stodgy and old-fashioned? What of recent product innovations? What level of commitment is Kodak making to digital photography? What about financial resources? Can Kodak swat Fuji like a fly? Or does Fuji have deep pockets, too? What would happen if Fuji tripled its advertising and directly compared its product to Kodak's? These are the kinds of questions that would be addressed in a thorough analysis of the competitive field.

Objectives. Advertising objectives lay the framework for the subsequent tasks in an advertising plan and take many different forms. Objectives identify the goals of the advertiser in concrete terms. The advertiser, more often than not, has more than one objective for an ad

9.   Stephanie Thompson, "Low-Carb Craze Blitzes Food Biz," *Advertising Age,* January 5, 2004, 1, 22.

EXHIBIT 8.10

The makers of Bose audio equipment have the philosophy that sound reproduction is a matter of science, so it follows that the best way to impress a consumer is to simply lay out the facts. Learn more about Dr. Amar Bose and the philosophy behind his company at http://www.bose.com.

EXHIBIT 8.11

In the world of the beauty, art rules over science. Hence, this simple ad for Dove's daily exfoliating bar is composed like a still-life painting, but look inside and the message is clear.

campaign. An advertiser's objective may be (1) to increase consumer awareness of and curiosity about its brand, (2) to change consumers' beliefs or attitudes about its product, (3) to influence the purchase intent of its customers, (4) to stimulate trial use of its product or service, (5) to convert one-time product users into repeat purchasers, (6) to switch consumers from a competing brand to its brand, or (7) to increase sales. (Each of these objectives is discussed briefly in the following paragraphs.) The advertiser may have more than one objective at the same time. For example, a swimwear company may state its advertising objectives as follows: to maintain the company's brand image as the market leader in adult female swimwear and to increase revenue in this product line by 15 percent.

Creating or maintaining brand awareness and interest is a fundamental advertising objective. Brand awareness is an indicator of consumer knowledge about the existence of the brand and how easily that knowledge can be retrieved from memory. For example, a market researcher might ask a consumer to name five insurance companies. **Top-of-the-mind awareness** is represented by the brand listed first. Ease of retrieval from memory is important because for many goods or services, ease of retrieval is predictive of market share. This proved to be the case for AFLAC, an insurance company (American Family Life Assurance Co.) who used a determined duck quacking *aaa-flack* in its ad campaign as a means to building brand awareness. If you've seen these ads, we suspect that you'll never forget that duck. If you haven't seen them, you might be thinking, a duck as your primary spokesperson sounds pretty dopey. Maybe yes, maybe no, but that duck helped AFLAC become a major player in the U.S. insurance market.[10]

Creating, changing, or reinforcing attitudes is another important function of advertising, and thus makes for a common advertising objective. As we saw in Chapter 5, one way to go about changing people's attitudes is to give them information designed to alter their beliefs. There are many ways to approach this task. One way is exemplified by the Bose ad in Exhibit 8.10. Here we see an information-dense approach where a number of logical arguments are developed to shape beliefs regarding the QuietComfort 2 Noise-Cancelling Headphones. For the consumer willing to digest this complex, text-based ad, the arguments are likely to prove quite compelling. Conversely, a very different approach is taken in the elegant ad for the Dove beauty bar in Exhibit 8.11. Here the approach depends on the visual imagery and the consumer's willingness to solve the riddle of what a bar of soap has in common with a walnut. If you solve the puzzle, you learn something about Dove, shaping or reinforcing a belief about the performance of this soap. Whether through direct, logical arguments, or thought-provoking

10. Zyman, *The End of Advertising As We Know It*, 20.

visual imagery, advertisements are frequently designed to deliver their objective of belief and attitude change.

Purchase intent is another popular criterion in setting objectives. Purchase intent is determined by asking consumers whether they intend to buy a product or service in the near future. The appeal of influencing purchase intent is that intent is closer to actual behavior, and thus closer to the desired sale, than are attitudes. While this makes sense, it does presuppose that consumers can express their intentions with a reasonably high degree of reliability. Sometimes they can, sometimes they cannot. Purchase intent, however, is fairly reliable as an indicator of relative intention to buy, and it is, therefore, a worthwhile advertising objective.

Trial usage reflects actual behavior and is commonly used as an advertising objective. Many times, the best that we can ask of advertising is to encourage the consumer to try our brand. At that point, the product or service must live up to the expectations created by our advertising. In the case of new products, stimulating trial usage is critically important. In the marketing realm, the angels sing when the initial purchase rate of a new product or service is high.

The **repeat purchase,** or conversion, objective is aimed at the percentage of consumers who try a new product and then purchase it a second time. A second purchase is reason for great rejoicing. The odds of long-term product success go way up when this percentage is high.

Brand switching is the last of the advertising objectives mentioned here. In some brand categories, switching is commonplace, even the norm. In others it is rare. When setting a brand-switching objective, the advertiser must neither expect too much, nor rejoice too much, over a temporary gain. Persuading consumers to switch brands can be a long and arduous task.

2   Communications versus Sales Objectives.
Some analysts argue that as a single variable in a firm's overall marketing mix, it is not reasonable to set sales expectations for advertising when other variables in the mix might undermine the advertising effort or be responsible for sales in the first place. In fact, some advertising analysts argue that communications objectives are the *only* legitimate objectives for advertising. This perspective has its underpinnings in the proposition that advertising is but one variable in the marketing mix and cannot be held solely responsible for sales. Rather, advertising should be held responsible for creating awareness of a brand, communicating information about product features or availability, or developing a favorable attitude that can lead to consumer preference for a brand. All of these outcomes are long term and based on communications impact.

There are some major benefits to maintaining a strict communications perspective in setting advertising objectives. First, by viewing advertising as primarily a communications effort, marketers can consider a broader range of advertising strategies. Second, they can gain a greater appreciation for the complexity of the overall communications process. Designing an integrated communications program with sales as the sole objective neglects aspects of message design, media choice, public relations, or sales force deployment that should be effectively integrated across all phases of a firm's communication efforts. Using advertising messages to support the efforts of the sales force and/or drive people to your Web site is an example of integrating diverse communication tools to build synergy that then may ultimately produce a sale.

Yet there is always a voice reminding us that there is only one rule: *Advertising must sell.*[11] Nowhere is the tension between communication and sales objectives better exemplified than in the annual debate about what advertisers really get for the tremendous sums of money they spend on Super Bowl ads. Each year great hoopla

11. Zyman, *The End of Advertising As We Know It.*

accompanies the ads that appear during the Super Bowl, and numerous polls are taken after the game to assess the year's most memorable ads. One such study showed that among the five most memorable ads (for Budweiser, Pepsi, VW, E★Trade, and Doritos) that ran during a Super Bowl, only the Doritos ad moved people to say that they were much more likely to purchase the product as a result of seeing the ad.[12] If a super-cool Pepsi ad featuring Britney Spears doesn't affect consumers' purchase intentions, can it really be worth the millions of dollars it takes to produce and air it?

While there is a natural tension between those who advocate sales objectives and those who push communications objectives, nothing precludes a marketer from using both types when developing an advertising plan. Indeed, combining sales objectives such as market share and household penetration with communication objectives such as awareness and attitude change can be an excellent means of motivating and evaluating an advertising campaign.[13]

Objectives that enable a firm to make intelligent decisions about resource allocation must be stated in an advertising plan in terms specific to the organization. Articulating such well-stated objectives is easier when advertising planners do the following:

1. *Establish a quantitative benchmark.* Objectives for advertising are measurable only in the context of quantifiable variables. Advertising planners should begin with quantified measures of the current status of market share, awareness, attitude, or other factors that advertising is expected to influence. The measurement of effectiveness in quantitative terms requires a knowledge of the level of variables of interest before an advertising effort, and then afterward. For example, a statement of objectives in quantified terms might be, "Increase the market share of heavy users of the product category using our brand from 22 to 25 percent." In this case, a quantifiable and measurable market share objective is specified.

2. *Specify measurement methods and criteria for success.* It is important that the factors being measured be directly related to the objectives being pursued. It is of little use to try to increase the awareness of a brand with advertising and then judge the effects based on changes in sales. If changes in sales are expected, then measure sales. If increased awareness is the goal, then change in consumer awareness is the legitimate measure of success. This may seem obvious, but in a classic study of advertising objectives, it was found that claims of success for advertising were unrelated to the original statements of objective in 69 percent of the cases.[14] In this research, firms cited increases in sales as proof of success of advertising when the original objectives were related to factors such as awareness, conviction to a brand, or product-use information. But maybe that just says when sales do go up, we forget about everything else.

3. *Specify a time frame.* Objectives for advertising should include a statement of the period of time allowed for the desired results to occur. In some cases, as with direct response advertising, the time frame may be related to a seasonal selling opportunity like the Christmas holiday period. For communications-based objectives, the measurement of results may not be undertaken until the end of an entire multiweek campaign. The point is that the time period for accomplishment of an objective and the related measurement period must be stated in advance in the ad plan.

These criteria for setting objectives help ensure that the planning process is organized and well directed. By relying on quantitative benchmarks, an advertiser has guidelines

12.   Bonnie Tsui, "Bowl Poll: Ads Don't Mean Sales," *Advertising Age,* February 5, 2001, 33.
13.   John Philip Jones, "Advertising's Crisis of Confidence," *Marketing Management,* vol. 2, no. 1 (1993), 15–24.
14.   Stewart Henderson Britt, "Are So-Called Successful Advertising Campaigns Really Successful?" *Journal of Advertising Research,* vol. 9 (1969), 5.

for making future decisions. Linking measurement criteria to objectives provides a basis for the equitable evaluation of the success or failure of advertising. Finally, the specification of a time frame for judging results keeps the planning process moving forward. As in all things, however, moderation is a good thing. A single-minded obsession with watching the numbers can be dangerous in that it minimizes or entirely misses the importance of qualitative and intuitive factors.

③ Budgeting. One of the most agonizing tasks is budgeting the funds for an advertising effort. Normally, the responsibility for the advertising budget lies with the firm itself. Within a firm, budget recommendations come up through the ranks; e.g., from a brand manager to a category manager and ultimately to the executive in charge of marketing. The sequence then reverses itself for the allocation and spending of funds. In a small firm, such as an independent retailer, the sequence just described may include only one individual who plays all the roles.

In many cases, a firm will rely on its advertising agency to make recommendations regarding the size of the advertising budget. When this is done, it is typically the account executive in charge of the brand who will analyze the firm's objectives and its creative and media needs and then make a recommendation to the company. The account supervisor's budget planning will likely include working closely with brand and product-group managers to determine an appropriate spending level.

To be as judicious and accountable as possible in spending money on advertising and IBP, marketers rely on various methods for setting an advertising budget. To appreciate the benefits (and failings) of these methods, we will consider each of them in turn.

Percentage of Sales. A **percentage-of-sales approach** to advertising budgeting calculates the advertising budget based on a percentage of the prior year's sales or the projected year's sales. This technique is easy to understand and implement. The budget decision makers merely specify that a particular percentage of either last year's sales or the current year's estimated sales will be allocated to the advertising process. It is common to spend between 2 and 12 percent of sales on advertising.

While simplicity is certainly an advantage in decision-making, the percentage-of-sales approach is fraught with problems. First, when a firm's sales are decreasing, the advertising budget will automatically decline. Periods of decreasing sales may be precisely the time when a firm needs to increase spending on advertising; if a percentage-of-sales budgeting method is being used, this won't happen. Second, this budgeting method can easily result in overspending on advertising. Once funds have been earmarked, the tendency is to find ways to spend the budgeted amount. Third, the most serious drawback from a strategic standpoint is that the percentage-of-sales approach does not relate advertising dollars to advertising objectives. Basing spending on past or future sales is devoid of analytical evaluation and implicitly presumes a direct cause-and-effect relationship between advertising and sales. But here, we have sales "causing" advertising. That's backward!

A variation on the percentage-of-sales approach that firms may use is the **unit-of-sales approach** to budgeting, which simply allocates a specified dollar amount of advertising for each unit of a brand sold (or expected to be sold). This is merely a translation of the percentage-of-sales method into dollars per units sold. The unit-of-sales approach has the same advantages and disadvantages as the percentage-of-sales approach.

Share of Market/Share of Voice. With this method, a firm monitors the amount spent by various significant competitors on advertising and allocates an amount equal to the amount of money spent by competitors or an amount proportional to (or slightly greater than) the firm's market share relative to the competi-

EXHIBIT 8.12

Share of market versus share of voice, major car manufacturers in 2002 (U.S. dollars in millions).

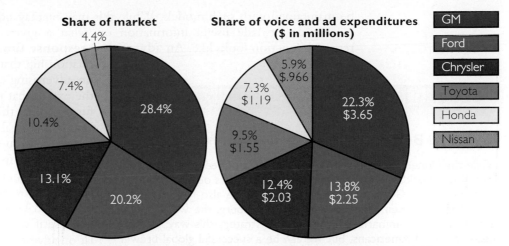

Source: Market share information taken from *Market Share Report, 2004* (Los Angeles Times, January 4, 2003, p. C1). Share of voice/ad expenditures calculated from *100 Leading National Advertisers*, AdAge, Special Report, 6.23.03 and *Domestic Advertising Spending by Category*, AdAge, 2002.

tion.[15] Exhibit 8.12 shows the relationship between share of market and share of voice for automakers in the U.S.

With this method, an advertiser will achieve a **share of voice,** or an advertising presence in the market, equal to or greater than the competitors' share of advertising voice. This method is often used for advertising budget allocations in new-product introductions. Conventional wisdom suggests that some multiple, often 2.5 to 4 times the desired first year market share, should be spent in terms of share-of-voice advertising expenditures. For example, if an advertiser wants a 2 percent first-year share, it would need to spend up to 8 percent of the total dollar amount spent in the industry (for an 8 percent share of voice). The logic is that a new product will need a significant share of voice to gain notice among a group of existing, well-established brands.[16] So if you brew beer in Denmark and wanted to promote your Carlsberg brand in North America, how much money will you have to spend to steal market share from the likes of Anheuser–Busch and Miller? As explained in the Global Issues box, executives at Carlsberg decided the right answer for them was $0.

Although the share-of-voice approach is sound in its emphasis on competitors' activities, there are important challenges to consider with this approach. First, it may be difficult to gain access to precise information on competitors' spending. Second, there is no reason to believe that competitors are spending their money wisely or in a way even remotely related to what the decision-making firm wants to accomplish. Third, the flaw in logic in this method is the presumption that every advertising effort is of the same quality and will have the same effect from a creative-execution standpoint. Nothing could be further from the truth. Google spends something like $2.5 million on advertising per year; AT&T spends at a rate of over $900 million.[17] Are both getting the same rate of return on their investment in advertising? Not likely.

Response Models.   Using response models to aid the budgeting process is a fairly widespread practice among larger firms.[18] The belief is that greater objectivity can

15.   The classic treatment of this method was first offered by James O. Peckham, "Can We Relate Advertising Dollars to Market-Share Objectives?" in Malcolm A. McGiven, ed., *How Much to Spend for Advertising* (New York: Association of National Advertisers, 1969), 24.

16.   James C. Shroer, "Ad Spending: Growing Market Share," *Harvard Business Review* (January–February 1990), 44.

17.   Hillary Chura, "Madison Ave. Out of Touch?" *Advertising Age,* April 12, 2004, 18.

18.   James E. Lynch and Graham J. Hooley, "Increasing Sophistication in Advertising Budget Setting," *Journal of Advertising Research* (February–March 1990), 72.

be maintained with such models. While this may or may not be the case, response models do provide useful information on what a given company's advertising response function looks like. An **advertising response function** is a mathematical relationship that associates dollars spent on advertising and sales generated. To the extent that past advertising predicts future sales, this method is valuable. Using marginal analysis, an advertiser would continue spending on advertising as long as its marginal spending was exceeded by marginal sales. Margin analysis answers the advertiser's question, "How much more will sales increase if we spend an additional dollar on advertising?" As the rate of return on advertising expenditures declines, the wisdom of additional spending is challenged.

Theoretically, this method leads to a point where an optimal advertising expenditure results in an optimal sales level and, in turn, an optimal profit. The relationship between sales, profit, and advertising spending is shown in the marginal analysis graph in Exhibit 8.13. Data on sales, prior advertising expenditures, and consumer awareness are typical of the numerical input to such quantitative models.

Unfortunately, the advertising-to-sales relationship assumes simple causality, and we know that that assumption isn't true. Many other factors, in addition to advertising, affect sales directly. Still, some feel that the use of response models is a better budgeting method than guessing or applying the percentage-of-sales or other budgeting methods discussed thus far.

GLOBAL ISSUES

Trying to Be King Is Not the Danish Way. . .

While the United States is at the top of the list of beer drinking countries in the world, there are plenty of beer drinkers outside of North America. China, Germany, Brazil, and Russia are also huge markets. Thus, Nils Andersen, chief executive of Carlsberg, the world's fifth-largest brewer, summarizes his company's strategy this way: "I don't mean to offend Americans, but we can be a successful global brewer without the U.S."

Some industry analysts criticize Carlsberg for this strategy; however, it is also salient to consider that the four largest beer marketers in the world spend heavily to support their brands (e.g., Budweiser, Miller Lite, Heineken, Labatt Blue) in the United States, on the order of a billion dollars in beer advertising among them. (Those are some deep pockets.) One of the essential decisions that global marketers are always faced with is how much of the globe can we really cover with the advertising funds that our company has available. Andersen's priorities for supporting his brand are clear. For example, he recently commissioned a new analysis of the fast-growing beer market in Serbia. He has no plans for spending any money on further investigation of the United States any time soon.

But in marketing and advertising, the analysis of one's situation is an ongoing process, so executives at Carlsberg won't rule out the possibility of someday making a big advertising push in North America. If they do, it is likely to be a unique campaign, because the Danes seem to think different when it comes to positioning their brands. As expressed by one Carlsberg executive, "We don't like to brag about ourselves. We would never be so bold and say that our beer is king." Probably a good idea to stay away from that line anyway, because last time we checked, "King of Beers" was already taken.

Source: Dan Bilefsky, "Not on Tap: Carlsberg Skips U.S. Beer Market for . . . Serbia?" *Wall Street Journal*, October 7, 2003, B1.

Objective and Task. The methods for establishing an advertising budget just discussed all suffer from the same fundamental deficiency: a lack of specification of how expenditures are related to advertising goals. The only method of budget setting that focuses on the relationship between spending and advertising objectives is the **objective-and-task approach.** This method begins with the stated objectives for an advertising effort. Goals related to production costs, target audience reach, message effects, behavioral effects, media placement, duration of the effort, and the like are specified. The budget is formulated by identifying the specific tasks necessary to achieve different aspects of the objectives.

There is a lot to recommend this procedure for budgeting. A firm identifies any and all tasks it believes are related to achieving its objectives. Should the total dollar figure for the necessary tasks be beyond the firm's financial capability, reconciliation must be found. But even if reconciliation and a subsequent reduction of the budget results, the firm has at least identified what *should* have been budgeted to pursue its advertising objectives.

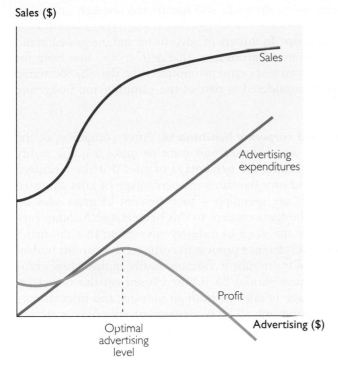

Sales ($)

Sales

Advertising expenditures

Profit

Optimal advertising level

Advertising ($)

Source: David A. Aaker, Rajeev Batra, and John G. Meyers, *Advertising Management*, 4th ed. (Englewood Cliffs, N.J.: Prentice-Hall, 1992), 469. Reprinted by permission of Prentice-Hall, Inc., Upper Saddle River, N.J.

EXHIBIT 8.13

Sales, profit, and advertising curves used in marginal analysis.

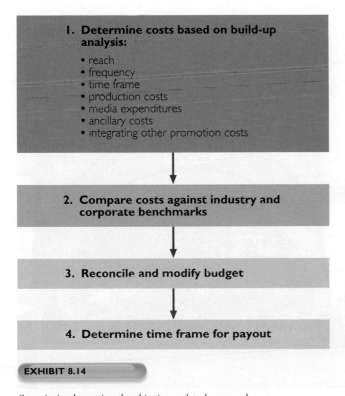

1. **Determine costs based on build-up analysis:**

   • reach
   • frequency
   • time frame
   • production costs
   • media expenditures
   • ancillary costs
   • integrating other promotion costs

2. **Compare costs against industry and corporate benchmarks**

3. **Reconcile and modify budget**

4. **Determine time frame for payout**

EXHIBIT 8.14

Steps in implementing the objective-and-task approach.

The objective-and-task approach is the most logical and defensible method for calculating and then allocating an advertising budget. It is the only budgeting method that specifically relates advertising spending to the advertising objectives being pursued. It is widely used among major advertisers. For these reasons, we will consider the specific procedures for implementing the objective-and-task budgeting method.

Implementing the Objective-and-Task Budgeting Method. Proper implementation of the objective-and-task approach requires a data-based, systematic procedure. Since the approach ties spending levels to specific advertising goals, the process depends on proper execution of the objective-setting process described earlier. Once a firm and its agency are satisfied with the specificity and direction of stated objectives, a series of well-defined steps can be taken to implement the objective-and-task method. These steps are shown in Exhibit 8.14 and summarized in the following sections.

Determine costs based on build-up analysis. Having identified specific objectives, an advertiser can now begin determining what tasks are necessary for the accomplishment of those objectives. In using a **build-up analysis**—building up the expenditure levels for tasks—the following factors must be considered in terms of costs:

• *Reach.* The advertiser must identify the geographic and demographic exposure the advertising is to achieve.
• *Frequency.* The advertiser must determine the number of exposures required to accomplish desired objectives.
• *Time frame.* The advertiser must estimate when communications will occur and over what period of time.
• *Production costs.* The decision maker can rely on creative personnel and producers to estimate the costs associated with the planned execution of advertisements.
• *Media expenditures.* Given the preceding factors, the advertiser can now define the appropriate media, media mix, and frequency of insertions that will directly address objectives. Further, differences in geographic allocation, with special attention to regional or local media strategies, are considered at this point.
• *Ancillary costs.* There will be a variety of related costs not directly accounted for in the preceding factors. Prominent among these are

costs associated with advertising to the trade and specialized research unique to the campaign.

- ***Integrating other promotional costs.*** In this era of advertising and integrated brand promotion, sometimes it is the novel promotion that delivers the best bang for the buck. New and improved forms of brand promotion, like the one illustrated in Exhibit 8.15, must also be considered as part of the planning and budgeting process.

Compare costs against industry and corporate benchmarks. After compiling all the costs through a build-up analysis, an advertiser will want to make a quick reality check. This is accomplished by checking the percentage of sales that the estimated set of costs represents relative to industry standards for percentage of sales allocated to advertising. If most competitors are spending 4 to 6 percent of gross sales on advertising, how does the current budget compare to this percentage? Another recommended technique is to identify the share of industry advertising that the firm's budget represents. Another relevant reference point is to compare the current budget with prior budgets. If the total dollar amount is extraordinarily high or low compared to previous years, this variance should be justified based on the objectives being pursued. The use of percentage of sales on both an industry and internal corporate basis provides a reference point only. The percentage-of-sales figures are not used for decision making per se, but rather as a benchmark to judge whether the budgeted amount is so unusual as to need reevaluation.

Reconcile and modify the budget. It is always a fear that the proposed budget will not meet with approval. It may not be viewed as consistent with corporate policy related to advertising expense, or it may be considered beyond the financial capabilities of the organization. Modifications to a proposed budget are common, but having to make radical cuts in proposed spending is disruptive and potentially devastating. The objective-and-task approach is designed to identify what a firm will need to spend

EXHIBIT 8.15

What could be better on a warm summer day than a stroll down Chicago's Navy Pier? Smart marketers like Best Buy want to be part of your day, and thus they bring their Best Buy High Tech Playground right to where the action is. The idea here is to build deeper relationships with potential customers by contributing to their good times in a special venue. Concerts, sporting events, fairs, and carnivals are all great places to show off your brand.

in order to achieve a desired advertising impact. To have the budget level compromised after such planning can result in an impotent advertising effort because necessary tasks cannot be funded.

Every precaution should be taken against having to radically modify a budget. Planners should be totally aware of corporate policy and financial circumstance *during* the objective-setting and subsequent task-planning phases. This will help reduce the extent of budget modification, should any be required.

Determine a time frame for payout. It is important that budget decision makers recognize when the budget will be available for funding the tasks associated with the proposed effort. Travel expenses, production expenses, and media time and space are tied to specific calendar dates. For example, media time and space are often acquired and paid for far in advance of the completion of finished advertisements. Knowing when and how much money is needed improves the odds of the plan being carried out smoothly.

If these procedures are followed for the objective-and-task approach, an advertiser will have a defendable budget with which to pursue key objectives. One point to be made, however, is that the budget should not be viewed as the final word in funding an advertising effort. The dynamic nature of the market and rapid developments in media require flexibility in budget execution. This can mean changes in expenditure levels, but it can also mean changes in payout allocation.

Like any other business activity, a marketer must take on an advertising effort with clearly specified intentions for what is to be accomplished. Intentions and expectations for advertising are embodied in the process of setting objectives. Armed with information from market planning and an assessment of the type of advertising needed to support marketing plans, advertising objectives can be set. These objectives should be in place before steps are taken to determine a budget for the advertising effort, and before the creative work begins. Again, this is not always the order of things, even though it should be. These objectives will also affect the plans for media placement.

Strategy. Returning now to the other major components of the advertising plan (revisiting Exhibit 8.5 is a good idea at this point), next up is strategy. Strategy represents the mechanism by which something is to be done. It is an expression of the means to an end. All of the other factors are supposed to result in a strategy. Strategy is what you do, given the situation and objectives. There are numerous possibilities for advertising strategies. For example, if you are trying to get more top-of-the-mind awareness for your brand of chewing gum, a simple strategy would be to employ a high-frequency, name-repetition campaign (Double your pleasure with Doublemint, Doublemint, Doublemint gum). Exhibit 8.16 presents an ad from Danskin's campaign designed to address a more ambitious objective; that is, broadening the appeal of the brand beyond dance accessories to the much larger fitness-wear market. Danskin's advertising strategy thus features unique "fitness" celebrities as implicit endorsers of the brand.

More sophisticated goals call for more sophisticated strategies. You are limited only by your resources: financial, organizational, and creative. Ultimately, strategy formulation is a creative endeavor. It is best learned through the study of what others have done in similar situations and through a thorough analysis of the focal consumer. To assist in strategy formulation, a growing number of ad agencies have created a position called the account planner. This person's job is to synthesize all relevant consumer research and draw inferences from it that will help define a coherent advertising strategy. You will learn a great deal more about the connection between ad objectives and strategy options when you get to Chapter 11.

This ad provides an excellent example of repositioning. The slogan says it all: "Danskin—Not Just for Dancing." http://www.danskin.com

Execution. The actual "doing" is the execution of the plan. It is the making and placing of ads across all media. To quote a famous bit of advertising copy from a tire manufacturer, this is where "the rubber meets the road." There are two elements to the execution of an advertising plan: determining the copy strategy and devising a media plan.

Copy Strategy. A copy strategy consists of copy objectives and methods, or tactics. The objectives state what the advertiser intends to accomplish, while the methods describe how the objectives will be achieved. Part Three of this text will deal extensively with these executional issues.

Media Plan. The media plan specifies exactly where ads will be placed and what strategy is behind their placement. In an integrated communications environment, this is much more complicated than it might first appear. Back when there were just three broadcast television networks, there were already more than a million different combinations of placements that could be made. With the explosion of media and promotion options today, the permutations are almost infinite.

It is at this point—devising a media plan—where all the money is spent, and so much could be saved. This is where the profitability of many agencies is really determined. Media placement strategy can make a huge difference in profits or losses and is considered in great depth in Part Four of this text.

Integrated Brand Promotion. Many different forms of brand promotion may accompany the advertising effort in launching or maintaining a brand; these should be spelled out as part of the overall plan. There should be a complete integration of all communication tools in working up the plan. For example, in the launch of its Venus shaving system for women, Gillette had the usual multimillion-dollar budget allocation for traditional mass media. But along with its aggressive advertising effort, several other promotional tools were deployed.[19] At http://www.GilletteVenus .com, shown in Exhibit 8.17, women could sign up for an online sweepstakes to win vacations in Hawaii, New York City, and Tuscany, and provide friends' e-mail addresses (a tactic known as viral e-mail) to increase their own chances of winning. Gillette also put a pair of 18-wheelers on the road (see Exhibit 8.18) to spread the word about Venus at beaches, concerts, colleges campuses, and store openings. So the launch of Venus integrated tools that ran the gamut from TV ads to the World Wide Web to Interstate 95. You'll learn much more about a variety of IBP tools in Part Five.

Evaluation. Last but not least in an ad plan is the evaluation component. This is where an advertiser determines how the agency will be graded: what criteria will be applied and how long the agency will have to achieve the agreed-upon objectives. It's critically important for the advertiser and agency to align around evaluation criteria up front.

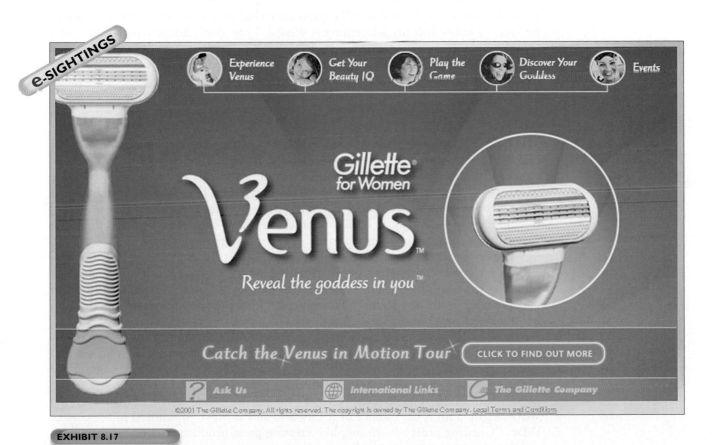

EXHIBIT 8.17

The Venus Web site has offered many possibilities, including the prospect of winning a great vacation, a beauty IQ test, and a way to "Reveal the goddess in you." Compare these examples of integrated brand promotion with attempts by competitors Norelco (http://www.norelco.com) and Schick (http://www.schick.com). Are these promotions integrated in a way that supports the image of the brand?

19.   Betsy Spethmann, "Venus Rising," *PROMO Magazine,* April 2001, 52–61.

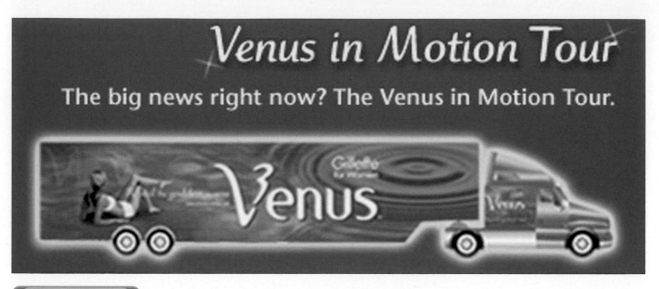

EXHIBIT 8.18

Hard to imagine goddesses going on the road in an 18-wheeler, but in today's world of integrated brand promotion, just about anything goes.

John Wanamaker's classic line still captures the challenge associated with evaluation; he said, "I know half my advertising is wasted, I just don't know which half." In a world where the pressures on companies to deliver short-term profitability continue to intensify, advertising agencies find themselves under increasing pressure to show quantifiable outcomes from all advertising and IBP activities.[20]

4 The Role of the Advertising Agency in Advertising Planning.

Now that we have covered key aspects of the advertising planning process, one other issue should be considered. Because many marketers rely heavily on the expertise of an advertising agency, understanding the role an agency plays in the advertising planning process is important. As implied by the IBP box, various agencies will approach their craft with different points of emphasis. But while not everyone does it the same way, it is still important to ask: What contribution to the planning effort can and should an advertiser expect from its agency?

The discussion of advertising planning to this point has emphasized that the marketer is responsible for the marketing-planning inputs as a type of self-assessment that identifies the firm's basis for offering value to customers. This assessment should also clearly identify, in the external environment, the opportunities and threats that can be addressed with advertising. A firm should bring to the planning effort a well-articulated statement of a brand's value proposition and the marketing mix elements designed to gain and sustain competitive advantage. However, when client and agency are working in harmony, the agency may take an active role in helping the client formulate the more general marketing plan. Indeed, when things are going right, it can be hard to say exactly where the client's work ended and the agency's work began. This is the essence of teamwork, and as Steve Jobs noted in the case of iMac: "Creating great advertising, like creating great products, is a team effort."

But the advertising agency's crucial role is to translate the current market and marketing status of a firm and its advertising objectives into advertising strategy and,

---

20.   Laura Q. Hughes, "Measuring Up," *Advertising Age,* February 5, 2001, 1, 34; Kate Fitzgerald, "Event Marketing Seeks Measurement," *Advertising Age,* September 2, 2002, 6, 7.

ultimately, finished advertisements and IBP materials. An agency can serve its clients best by taking charge of the preparation and placement stages. Here, message strategies and tactics for the advertising effort and for the efficient and effective placement of ads in media need to be hammered out. At this point, the firm (as a good client) should turn to its agency for the expertise and talent needed for planning and executing at the stage where design and creative execution brings marketing strategies to life. There are two basic models for the relationship between agencies and their clients: adversarial or partnering. The former is too common; the latter is certainly preferred.

IBP

The Fundamentals Never Go Out of Style

The dot.com debacle that marked the dawning of the new millennium sent shock waves through the ad agency business. Many high-profile agencies suffered from the demise of the dot.coms because they had built up large interactive units with catchy names like Darwin Digital and Zentropy Partners, in search of Internet advertising riches. These units then had to be downsized or discontinued after the dot.com crash. One agency that didn't follow the pack in search of Internet riches was Goodby, Silverstein & Partners, San Francisco (http://www.goodbysilverstein.com). You've seen their work: "Got Milk?," the Budweiser lizards, E*Trade's singing chimp, and many more.

But here's the irony. As the dust settled after all the interactive downsizing, Goodby, Silverstein's stable of clients included companies such as TiVo, eBay, eLuxury.com, and Loudcloud, some of the best performers in the Internet sector. Turns out that slow-moving, old-fashioned Goodby, Silverstein had timeless skills that marketers of all types need for building their brands, whether they are based in the physical or the digital world. Industry analysts claim that Goodby's lack of Internet hype and its enduring focus on brand building via breakthrough advertising campaigns are the things that won it loyal digital clients. Here are a few fundamental rules for creating great ad campaigns, inspired by Goodby, Silverstein & Partners:

- *Simplicity is key.* Complexity fuels confusion. Trying to say too much is the number one pitfall, even among advertising veterans.
- *Don't talk down.* Assume your audience is paying attention, is as smart as you are, and has a sense of humor. This is how you win their respect.
- *Don't be invisible.* Make your communication different. Take risks. Better to take risks and be noticed than to spend money on something that is technically correct, but practically invisible.
- *Refresh Yourself.* Nitpicking old ideas is a sure sign that you are creating tired advertising. When you find yourself in nitpicking mode, refresh yourself by starting over.

Source: Beth Snyder Bulik, "As Goodby as It Gets," *Business 2.0*, May 1, 2001, 58–60.

SUMMARY

 Describe the basic components of an advertising plan.

An advertising plan is motivated by the marketing planning process and provides the direction that ensures proper implementation of an advertising campaign. An advertising plan incorporates decisions about the segments to be targeted, communications and/or sales objectives with respect to these segments, and salient message appeals. The plan should also specify the dollars budgeted for the campaign, the various communication tools that will be employed to deliver the messages, and the measures that will be relied on to assess the campaign's effectiveness.

 Compare and contrast two fundamental approaches for setting advertising objectives.

Setting appropriate objectives is a crucial step in developing any advertising plan. These objectives are typically stated in terms of communications or sales goals. Both types of goals have their proponents, and the appropriate types of objectives to emphasize will vary with the situation. Communications objectives feature goals such as building brand awareness or reinforcing consumers' beliefs about a brand's key benefits. Sales objectives are just that: They hold advertising directly responsible for increasing sales of a brand.

 Explain various methods for setting advertising budgets.

Perhaps the most challenging aspect of any advertising campaign is arriving at a proper budget allocation. Companies and their advertising agencies work with several different methods to arrive at an advertising budget. A percentage-of-sales approach is a simple but naive way to deal with this issue. In the share-of-voice approach, the activities of key competitors are factored into the budget-setting process. A variety of quantitative models may also be used for budget determination. The objective-and-task approach is difficult to implement, but with practice it is likely to yield the best value for a firm's advertising dollars.

 Discuss the role of the advertising agency in formulating an advertising plan.

An advertising plan will be a powerful tool when firms partner with their advertising agencies in its development. The firm can lead this process by doing its homework with respect to marketing strategy development and objective setting. The agency can then play a key role in managing the preparation and placement phases of campaign execution.

KEY TERMS

advertising plan
situation analysis
industry analysis
market analysis
competitor analysis
top-of-the-mind awareness

purchase intent
trial usage
repeat purchase
brand switching
percentage-of-sales approach
unit-of-sales approach

share of voice
advertising response function
objective-and-task approach
build-up analysis

QUESTIONS

1. Review the materials presented in this chapter (and anything else you may be able to find) about Apple's launch of the iMac. Based on the advertising utilized, what do you surmise must have been the value proposition for iMac at the time of its launch?

2. Find an example of cooperative advertising in your local newspaper. Why would computer manufacturers

such as Apple, IBM, or Compaq want to participate in cooperative advertising programs with their retailers?

3. Explain the connection between marketing strategies and advertising plans. What is the role of target segments in making this connection?

4. Describe five key elements in a situation analysis and provide an example of how each of these elements may ultimately influence the final form of an advertising campaign.

5. How would it ever be possible to justify anything other than sales growth as a proper objective for an advertising campaign? Is it possible that advertising could be effective yet not yield growth in sales?

6. What types of objectives would you expect to find in an ad plan that featured direct response advertising?

7. Write an example of a workable advertising objective that would be appropriate for a product like Crest White Strips.

8. In what situations would share of voice be an important consideration in setting an advertising budget? What are the drawbacks of trying to incorporate share of voice in budgeting decisions?

9. What is it about the objective-and-task method that makes it the preferred approach for the sophisticated advertiser? Describe how build-up analysis is used in implementing the objective-and-task method.

10. Briefly discuss the appropriate role to be played by advertising agencies and their clients in the formulation of marketing and advertising plans.

EXPERIENTIAL EXERCISES

1. Five of the most common objectives for advertising are described in this chapter: top-of-the-mind awareness, purchase intent, trial usage, repeat purchase, and brand switching. For each, find an ad in a magazine or newspaper that you think aims to accomplish this objective and analyze whether or not the ad is successful.

2. The advertising plan consists of seven basic components: the introduction, situation analysis, objectives,

budgeting, strategy, execution, and evaluation. Break up into teams and choose a popular television advertising campaign familiar to everyone in the group. Analyze the commercial and explain how you think the goals of the advertisement relate to each basic component of the advertising plan. Based on your analysis of the commercial, speculate on how each of the seven components might have been developed in the advertiser's original planning process.

EXPERIENCING THE INTERNET

8-1 Situation Analysis

No industry faces more dramatic swings in consumers' tastes than the food business. The low-carb craze is challenging industry giants like McDonald's and Anheuser-Busch to come up with new products or reposition old ones to satisfy consumers. In particular, low-carb beer is the biggest thing to hit the brew sector since light beer, and all the big brewing companies are in on the action.

Michelob Ultra: http://www.michelobultra.com

1. Name at least two low-carb beers that compete against Anheuser-Busch's low-carb Michelob Ultra.

2. In what ways does Anheuser-Busch seek to distinguish its low-carb Michelob Ultra from the competition? How does the Michelob Ultra Web site communicate its distinctive features?

3. What effect might the proliferation of low-carb beer products have on the overall alcoholic beverages industry?

8-2 Communications versus Sales Objectives

Advertising objectives provide a framework for the advertising plan, defining the goals of the advertiser in concrete terms. Advertisers usually have multiple objectives at one time, and often set goals for effective communication as well as for sales.

Xootr: http://www.xootr.com

1. What objectives do you think are most common for the advertising in the scooter industry?

2. Briefly explain the difference between communications and sales objectives. Does the Xootr site reflect sales objectives?

3. Describe how an advertisement for scooters might achieve both sales and communications objectives. Why do some analysts believe that communications objectives are the only legitimate objectives for advertising?

CHAPTER 9

After reading and thinking about this chapter, you will be able to do the following:

1

Explain the types of audience research that are useful for understanding cultural barriers that can interfere with effective communication.

2

Identify three distinctive challenges that complicate the execution of advertising in international settings.

3

Describe the three basic types of advertising agencies that can assist in the placement of advertising around the world.

4

Discuss the advantages and disadvantages of globalized versus localized advertising campaigns.

NOKIA
3650

Pořiď si obrázky, video- nebo zvukové klipy.
Pošli je jako e-mail nebo na jiný telefon, který
umožňuje jejich zobrazení, a uvidíš, co se stane.

Club
NOKIA

Přidej se k nám a užij si výhod!
Na webových stránkách www.club.nokia.cz nebo
prostřednictvím WAP na adrese mobile.club.nokia.cz.

NOKIA
CONNECTING PEOPLE

www.nokia.cz

Introductory Scenario: The China Challenge.

By now it should be apparent to you that marketers are ready, willing, and able to go where the consumers are, anywhere in the world. And no country has more potential consumers than China. With a population of well over a billion people, a robustly growing economy, new global status associated with hosting the 2008 Olympic games, and greater acceptance of capitalistic ways and means, it follows that many companies large and small have turned to China as a new source of business opportunity. It also follows that advertising spending in China is growing at unprecedented rates. Many experts are already predicting that in this decade China will overtake Japan as the second largest advertising market in the world.[1] Anyone with an interest in advertising should also be interested in China.

But China presents many incredible challenges for advertisers from around the world. Some of these derive from the gargantuan nature of this country.[2] China has 31 provinces, 656 cities, and 48,000 districts. There is no one Chinese language; rather, there are seven major tongues with 80 spoken dialects. The north of China is a frozen plateau and the south of China is tropical. There are huge income and lifestyle differences between city-dwellers and farmers, and between the prosperous east and the impoverished west. When you come right down to it, there really is no such thing as a single "China." And that's just the obvious stuff.

Matters get even more complex when one factors in the unique aspects of the Chinese culture, where the norms of a Confucian society often are in conflict with the drive toward economic reform and Western lifestyles. The Chinese are also keenly aware and proud of their rich history, which spans thousands of years. (Recall that Marco Polo set out to explore the mysteries of China in the 13th century.) For any outsider China presents many mysteries, which will need to be solved in the development of appropriate and effective advertising.

Toyota's launch of the Prado Land Cruiser in China provides a nice example of the challenges one must overcome in developing advertising to reach across national (and cultural) boundaries.[3] Now keep in mind, this is Toyota, from just across the East China Sea in Toyota City, Japan, not some newcomer to the Asian continent. To launch its big SUV in China, Toyota's ad agency Saatchi & Saatchi created a print campaign showing a Prado driving past two large stone lions, which were saluting and bowing to the Prado. This seems to make sense because the stone lion is a traditional sign of power in the Chinese culture. As one Saatchi executive put it, "These ads were intended to reflect Prado's imposing presence when driving in the city: You cannot but respect the Prado."[4]

Chinese consumers saw it differently. For starters, Chinese words often have multiple meanings, and Prado can be translated into Chinese as *badao,* which means "rule by force" or "overbearing." In addition, the use of the stone lions prompted scathing commentary on the Internet about a contentious time in China's relationship with Japan. Some thought the stone lions in the Prado ad resembled those that flank the Marco Polo Bridge in China, a site near Beijing that marked the opening battle of Japan's invasion of China in 1937. These of course are not the kind of reactions that an advertiser is looking for when launching a new product; the automaker quickly pulled 30 magazine and newspaper ads and issued a formal apology. And Saatchi & Saatchi went back to work trying to resolve the China Challenge.

The Toyota mishap in China illustrates the difficulties that even the savviest companies must overcome as they take their products and brands to new markets. This is but one modest example of the perils in international advertising. **International advertising** is advertising that reaches across national and cultural bound-

1. Geoffrey Fowler, "China's Edgy Advertising," *Wall Street Journal,* October 27, 2003, B1, B4.
2. Sameena Ahmad, "A Billion Three, But Not for Me," *The Economist,* March 20, 2004, 5,6.
3. Geoffrey Fowler, "China's Cultural Fabric Is a Challenge to Marketers," *Wall Street Journal,* January 21, 2004, B7.
4. Ibid.

aries. In the past, a great deal of international advertising was nothing more than translations of domestic advertising. Often these simple translations were ineffective, and sometimes they were even offensive. The day has passed—if there ever was such a day— when advertisers based in industrialized nations could simply "do a foreign translation" of their ads. Today, international advertisers have learned they must pay greater attention to local cultures. Communicating with consumers around the world involves immersing yourself in the subtleties and mysteries of culture.

As we said in Chapter 5, culture is a set of values, rituals, and behaviors that define a way of life. Culture is typically invisible to those who are immersed within it. Communicating *across* cultures is not easy. It is, in fact, one of the most difficult of all communication tasks, largely because there is no such thing as culture-free communication. Advertising is a cultural product; it means nothing outside of culture. Culture surrounds advertising, informs it, gives it meaning. To transport an ad across cultural borders, one must respect, and hopefully understand, the power of culture.

Ads depend on effective communication, and effective communication depends on shared meaning. The degree of shared meaning is significantly affected by cultural membership. When an advertiser in culture A wants to communicate with consumers in culture B, it is culture B that will surround the created message, form its cultural context, and significantly affect how it will be interpreted, as in the Toyota Prado example.

Some products and brands may belong to a global consumer culture more than to any one national culture. Such brands travel well, as do their ads, because there is already common cultural ground on which to build effective advertising. The LG and Jack Daniel's ads in Exhibits 9.1 and 9.2 provide examples of products and

EXHIBIT 9.1

Electronics is a product category that lends itself to global brands (e.g., LG, Sony, Panasonic, Nintendo, Phillips, Nokia, Apple) because, for consumers who have the disposable income to afford them, performance is performance, whether you watch, play, or listen in Montreal, Moscow, or Mexico City. To get a good appreciation of the scale and reach of a company like LG Electronics, check out their global network at http://www.lge.com/general/globalsite.jsp *Oh, yeah—Life's Good.*

EXHIBIT 9.2

You don't need to be able to read Japanese to get the point here, in part because this ad follows the same style as other Jack Daniel's ads around the world. If you want a smooth sippin' whiskey, it can't be rushed. And in the back hills of Tennessee, no one is rushing anything. . . .

brands with wide, if not "global," appeal. Jack Daniels began distilling whiskey in 1866. With ads like the one in Exhibit 9.2, the legend of Jack Daniel's spread around the world, and Tennessee became associated with smooth, sippin' whiskey. One common bond among Jack Daniel's drinkers worldwide is the nostalgic premise that their whiskey is distilled the old-fashioned way. Tennessee pride guarantees it!

LG Electronics, headquartered in Seoul, Korea, markets its products in dozens of countries around the world. If you're in the market for a new plasma TV with a 7-foot screen and high definition DVR, they've got the perfect product for you, just as they do for consumers in Asia, Europe, Latin America, and the rest of the world. But brands like Jack Daniel's and LG are more the exceptions rather than the rule, and as "global" as they may be, they are still affected by local culture as to their use and, ultimately, their meaning.

This chapter augments and extends the advertising planning framework offered in Chapter 8. We add some necessary international planning tools along with additional insights about the special challenges found in advertising around the world. There is likely to be a China in your future, so now's the time to begin thinking about these things.

GLOBAL ISSUES

From Salsa to Cinco de Mayo

When it comes to fast food in Mexico, the taco remains supreme. Steak, pork, chicken, and fish tacos are always available, broiled or steamed, with corn or flour tortillas, piled high with chilies and salsa. Vendors set up for the breakfast crowd and usually stay in place till about midnight. But sales of the taco in Mexico have been slumping of late. Why? Because Mexican fast-food consumers can now also choose from pizza at Domino's and Pizza Hut, hamburgers at McDonald's and Jack in the Box, and cold sandwiches at their local Subway. Hungry yet?

In the United States, "Americanized" Mexican food continues to grow in popularity. "Tex-Mex" has become a food genre that is popular around the world. U.S. consumers chow down on chili dogs, nachos, Doritos, Tostitos, and salsa brands such as Victoria and Ortega, to get their taste of Old Mexico. The irony, of course, is that products such as these are largely invented in the United States to appeal to the U.S. consumer's idealized sense of what Mexican food must be like.

The ultimate staple of the native Mexican diet is salsa and fresh chilies. They are at the table for breakfast, lunch, and dinner. Here we clearly observe the homogenization effect on consumer preferences that evolves between close trading partners. Salsa brands made in the United States now fill the shelves of grocery stores in Mexico, side by side with Mexican brands. Now Mexican consumers can choose the salsa with a taste of Old USA to spice up their fish tacos at breakfast.

Holiday exports/imports are another excellent example of this relentless cultural fusion. Cinco de Mayo, which commemorates a Mexican victory over French invaders on May 5, 1862, is not one of Mexico's major fiestas. However, it appears destined to take its place with other "ethnic" celebrations like Oktoberfest and St. Patrick's Day as cause for "shared" rejoicing. Turns out that Cinco de Mayo is timed perfectly for the U.S. celebrant: May 5 is ideally positioned about halfway between Easter and Memorial Day. And while few people from Mexico would recognize their fiesta as it is practiced in the United States, it has become a major point of emphasis in the marketing plan for Corona beer, Mexico's top-selling brand. Like it or not, commercialization of culture is a fact of life in today's global economy.

Sources: Ignacio Vazquez, "Mexicans Are Buying 'Made in USA' Food," *Marketing News*, August 31, 1998, 14; Joel Millman, "U.S. Marketers Adopt Cinco de Mayo as National Fiesta," *Wall Street Journal*, May 1, 2001, B1.

① Overcoming Cultural Barriers.

Global trade initiatives such as the General Agreement on Tariffs and Trade (GATT) and the North American Free Trade Agreement (NAFTA) are designed to facilitate trade and economic development across national borders. These initiatives signal the emergence of international markets that are larger, more accessible, and perhaps more homogeneous. A couple of nice examples of this emerging homogenization between two NAFTA trading partners are discussed in the Global Issues box. In the midst of this trend toward more and more international trade, marketers are redefining the nature and scope of the markets for their goods and services, which in turn redefines the nature and scope of advertising and the advertising planning effort. This means that firms must be more sensitive to the social and economic differences of various international markets.

Exhibit 9.3 offers perspective on the kinds of companies that are most committed and successful in marketing and advertising around the world. Brazil, China,

Brazil Advertiser	2002	2001	% chg
Telefonica	$91.70	$86.68	5.8
Casas Bahia	72.85	60.08	21.2
Unilever	67.64	58.81	15.0
Volkswagen	66.57	86.23	−22.8
Fiat	66.45	68.06	−2.4
Ford Motor Co.	62.63	53.04	18.1
General Motors Corp.	59.33	63.32	−6.3
Co. de Bebidas das Americas	49.38	57.77	−14.5
Lojas Marabraz	47.61	23.84	99.7
Banco do Brasil	46.11	44.41	3.8

China Advertiser	2002	2001	% chg
Procter & Gamble Co.	$404.33	$204.91	97.3
Gai Zhong Gai	243.33	66.72	264.7
Jiante Biology Invest. Hldg. Co.	192.52	105.32	82.8
ShenZhen Taitai Pharm. Ind. Co.	157.63	113.08	39.4
Medical treatment information	148.48	101.09	46.9
Hutong Pharmaceutical	141.78	85.35	66.1
Xiuzheng Pharmaceutical Co.	137.90	68.83	100.4
Arche Cosmetics Co.	131.74	45.70	188.3
Hangzhou Wahaha Group Co.	113.01	70.33	60.7
Diaopai	106.58	110.82	−3.8

Germany Advertiser	2002	2001	% chg
Procter & Gamble Co.	$250.45	$182.86	37.0
Unilever	209.93	163.27	28.6
Volkswagen	194.50	189.99	2.4
Ferrero	185.02	186.16	−0.6
Henkel	177.86	170.37	4.4
Media Markt	167.18	156.04	7.1
Deutsche Telekom	159.79	158.75	0.7
L'Oreal	151.88	127.37	19.2
Springer Verlag	151.83	104.32	45.5
PSA Peugeot Citroen	149.29	139.29	7.2

United Kingdom Advertiser	2002	2001	% chg
Procter & Gamble Co.	$250.45	$196.04	27.8
Unilever	246.35	218.88	12.5
Ford Motor Co.	224.87	190.31	18.2
Government of the U.K.	178.96	215.54	−17.0
BT Group	144.51	147.52	−2.0
Volkswagen	132.89	132.99	−0.1
General Motors Corp.	124.14	102.74	20.8
PSA Peugeot Citroen	122.54	127.41	−3.8
Dixons Group	113.83	133.32	−14.6
L'Oreal	106.06	75.11	41.2

Source: *Advertising Age*, November 10, 2003, 26.

EXHIBIT 9.3

Advertising leaders in four major global markets (U.S. dollars in millions).

Germany, and the U.K. are huge but diverse markets. In Exhibit 9.3 you will see many familiar names that span the globe in their quest for consumers. These are corporate titans such as Procter & Gamble, Unilever, Volkswagen, and General Motors. It is also interesting to note that in China, the predominant advertisers are mainly Chinese, suggesting that many global marketers (e.g., Toyota) are still trying to solve the mysteries of China. But the key point is that most companies today consider their markets to extend beyond national boundaries and across cultures. Hence, advertisers must come to terms with how they are going to effectively overcome cultural barriers in trying to communicate with consumers around the world.

Barriers to Successful International Advertising.

Adopting an international perspective is often difficult for marketers. The reason is that experiences gained over a career and a lifetime create a cultural "comfort zone"—that is, one's own cultural values, experiences, and knowledge serve as a subconscious guide for decision making and behavior. International advertisers are particularly beset with this problem.

Managers must overcome two related biases to be successful in international markets. **Ethnocentrism** is the tendency to view and value things from the perspective of one's own culture. A **self-reference criterion (SRC)** is the unconscious reference to one's own cultural values, experiences, and knowledge as a basis for decisions. These two closely related biases are primary obstacles to success when conducting marketing and advertising planning that demand a cross-cultural perspective.

A decision maker's SRC and ethnocentrism can inhibit his or her ability to sense important cultural distinctions between markets. This in turn can blind advertisers to their own culture's "fingerprints" on the ads they've created. Sometimes these are offensive or, at a minimum, markers of "outsider" influence. Outsiders aren't always welcome; other times, they just appear ignorant.

For example, AT&T's "Reach Out and Touch Someone" advertising campaign was viewed as much too sentimental for most European audiences. Similarly, AT&T's "Call USA" campaign, aimed at Americans doing business in Europe, was negatively perceived by many Europeans. The ad featured a harried American businessman whose language skills were so poor that he could barely ask for assistance to find a telephone in a busy French hotel. European businesspeople are typically fluent in two or three languages and have enough language competence to ask for a telephone. This ad, with its portrayal of Americans as culturally inept and helpless, created a negative association for AT&T among European businesspeople. Granted, the target market was Americans in foreign assignments, but the perspective of the ad was still decidedly ethnocentric and offensive to Europeans.

The only way you can have any hope at all of counteracting the negative influences that ethnocentrism and SRC have on international advertising decision making is to be constantly sensitive to their existence and to the virtual certainty of important differences between cultures that will somehow affect your best effort. Even with the best cross-cultural research, it is still likely that problems will present themselves. However, without it, problems are a virtual certainty.

Cross-Cultural Audience Research.

Analyzing audiences in international markets can be a humbling task. If firms have worldwide product distribution networks—like Nestlé, Unilever, and Procter & Gamble—then international audience research will require dozens of separate analyses. There really is no way to avoid the task of specific audience analysis. This typically involves research in each different country, generally from a local research supplier. There are, however, good secondary resources that provide broad-based information to advertisers about international markets. The U.S. Department of Commerce has an International Trade Administration (ITA) division, which helps companies based in the United States develop foreign market opportunities for their products and services. The ITA publishes specialized reports that cover most of the major markets in the world and provide economic and regulatory information (see http://www.ita.doc.gov/). The United Nations' *Statistical Yearbook* is another source of general economic and population data (http://unstats .un.org/unsd/). The yearbook, updated annually, provides information for more than 200 countries. These sources provide helpful information for the international advertiser. Unfortunately, it's rarely enough.

An international audience analysis will also involve evaluation of economic conditions, demographic characteristics, values, custom and ritual, and product use and preferences.

Economic Conditions.

One way to think about the economic conditions of a potential international audience is to break the world's markets into three broad classes of economic development: less-developed countries, newly industrialized countries, and highly industrialized countries. These categories provide a basic understanding of the economic capability of the average consumer in a market and thus help place consumption in the context of economic realities. Exhibit 9.4 lists gross domestic product (GDP) per capita for 22 countries to give you additional appreciation for the vast differences in resources available to consumers around the world.

EXHIBIT 9.4

Gross domestic product (GDP) per capita of selected countries, 2001 (U.S. dollars).

United States	$34,788	Argentina	5,267
Switzerland	34,274	World Average	5,052
Japan	32,809	Malaysia	3,748
Denmark	29,833	South Africa	2,550
Ireland	26,503	Turkey	2,136
Germany	22,507	Thailand	1,865
Canada	22,385	Egypt	1,390
France	22,168	China	918
Israel	18,930	Ukraine	771
New Zealand	13,470	India	467
Portugal	10,968	Nigeria	435
Mexico	6,144		

Source: United Nations Statistical Division, http://www.unstats.un.org/unsd, accessed May 18, 2004.

Less-developed countries represent nearly 75 percent of the world's population. Some of these countries are plagued by drought and civil war, and their economies lack almost all the resources necessary for development: capital, infrastructure, political stability, and trained workers. Many of the products sold in these less-developed economies are typically not consumer products, but rather business products used for building infrastructure (such as heavy construction equipment) or agricultural equipment.

Newly industrialized countries have economies defined by change; they are places where traditional ways of life that have endured for centuries are changing and modern consumer cultures have emerged in a few short years. This creates a very particular set of problems for the outside advertiser trying to hit a moving target, or a culture in rapid flux.

Rapid economic growth in countries such as Singapore, China, Taiwan, and South Korea has created a new middle class of consumers with radically different expectations than their counterparts of a mere decade ago. Asian consumers are relatively heavy users of media-based information. The latest global trends in fashion, music, and travel have shorter and shorter lag times in reaching this part of the world. Many U.S. firms already have a strong presence in these markets with both their products and their advertising, like the Tropicana brand featured in Exhibit 9.5.

The **highly industrialized countries** of the world are those with mature economies and high levels of affluence as indicated by data such as GDP per capita (several are apparent in Exhibit 9.4). These countries have also invested heavily over many years in infrastructure—roads, hospitals, airports, power-generating plants, educational institutions, and the Internet. Within this broad grouping, an audience assessment will focus on more-detailed analyses of the market, including the nature and extent of competition, marketing trade channels, lifestyle trends, and market potential. Firms pursuing opportunities in highly industrialized countries proceed with market analysis in much the same way that they would in the United States. While the advertising in these countries will often vary based on unique cultural and lifestyle factors, consumers in these markets are accustomed to seeing a full range of creative appeals for goods and services. Heineken and McDonald's ads in Exhibits 9.6 and 9.7 provide familiar examples.

Demographic Characteristics. Information on the demographic characteristics of nations is generally available. Both the U.S. Department of Commerce and the

EXHIBIT 9.5

This ad for Tropicana exemplifies the rapid changes occurring in many Asian countries. Traditional values are giving way to focus on consumption and consumer culture. http://www.tropicana.com

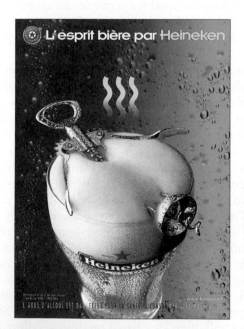

EXHIBIT 9.6

Heineken's distinctive red star is a logo known around the world. Here Heineken challenges partygoers in France to choose the bottle opener over the corkscrew for their next celebration. http://www.heineken.com

EXHIBIT 9.7

Big Mac Tuesdays play well in many places. In this instance it's Toronto, so that's $1.69, Canadian.

United Nations publish annual studies of population for hundreds of countries. Advertisers must be sensitive to the demographic similarities and differences in international markets, along with key trends. Demographics, including size of population, age distribution, income distribution, education levels, occupations, literacy rates, and household size, can dramatically affect the type of advertising prepared for a market. And it is always true that advertising dollars flow to where the purchasing power resides. Those planning advertising for international markets should keep in mind that roughly 20 percent of the world's population, generally residing in the highly industrialized countries, controls 75 percent of the world's wealth and accounts for 75 percent of all consumption.[5]

However, the world's wealthy nations are, for the most part, getting older, and this creates the potential for wealth redistribution around the world.[6] It could work this way: While the United States, Japan, and Western Europe will struggle in the future with pension plan shortfalls and rising health care costs, countries like China, Brazil, and Mexico have an opportunity to surge ahead economically because of something referred to as the **demographic dividend.** In these developing nations, falling labor costs, a younger and healthier population, and the entry of millions of women into the work force produce a favorable climate for economic expansion. The experts say that these developing nations have about a 30-year window to capitalize on their demographic dividend. Better education for more of their populations will be an essential element in realizing this dividend.

Here again the point is simply that understanding fundamental demographic trends around the world is essential for marketing and advertising planning. Increases and decreases in the proportion of the population in specific age groups are closely related to the demand for particular products and services. As populations continue to increase in developing countries, new market opportunities emerge for products and services for young families and teens. Similarly, as advanced-age groups continue to increase in countries with stable population rates, the demand for consumer services such as health care, travel, and retirement planning will increase. It is fair to conclude that knowing the age segment you want to target is especially critical for developing effective international advertising.

Values. Cultural values are enduring beliefs about what is important to the members of a culture. They are the defining bedrock of a culture. They are an outgrowth of the culture's history and its collective experience. (Even though there are many cultures within any given nation, many believe that there are still enough shared values to constitute a meaningful "national culture," such as "American culture.") For example, the value of individualism enjoys a long and prominent place in American history and is considered by many to be a core American value. Other cultures seem to value the group or collective more. Even though a "collectivist" country like Japan may be becoming more individualistic, there is still a Japanese tradition that favors the needs of the group over those of the individual. In Japan, organizational loyalty and social interdependence are values that promote a group mentality. Japanese consumers are thus thought to be more sensitive to appeals that feature stability, longevity, and reliability, and they find appeals using competitive comparisons to be confrontational and inappropriate.[7] Some researchers believe this continuum from individualism to collectivism to be a stable and dependably observed difference among the people of the world, or at least stable enough for crafting different ads for different cultures.[8]

5.   Clive Cook, "Catching Up," *The Economist,* Winter 1993, 15–16.
6.   Gautam Naik, "Leveraging the Age Gap," *Wall Street Journal,* February 27, 2003, B1, B4.
7.   Johny Johansson, "The Sense of Nonsense: Japanese TV Advertising," *Journal of Advertising* (March 1994), 17–26.
8.   S. Han and S. Shavitt, "Persuasion and Culture: Advertising Appeals in Individualistic and Collectivistic Societies," *Journal of Experimental Social Psychology,* vol. 30 (1994), 326–350.

EXHIBIT 9.8

In many European countries it is common to create a "homemade" batch of breakfast cereal each morning with natural grains and fresh fruit. In this ad from Switzerland's Movenpick, we see the advertiser attempting to align the convenient packaging of its new product with the homemade tradition. The headline reads, "At the end, you'll even think that you made it yourself." Or, more simply, tastes like homemade! When was the last time you looked for a breakfast cereal that "tastes like homemade"?

Custom and Ritual. Among other things, rituals perpetuate a culture's connections to its core values. They seem perfectly natural to members of a culture, and they can often be performed without much thought (in some cases, none at all) regarding their deeper meaning. Many consumer behaviors involve rituals, such as grooming, gift giving, or food preparation. As reflected in Exhibit 9.8, something as simple as preparing breakfast cereal can entail different rituals from one culture to another (and, of course, in many cultures breakfast cereal is a totally foreign concept). To do a good job in cross-cultural advertising, the rituals of other cultures must be not only appreciated, but also understood. This requires in-depth and extended research efforts. Quick marketing surveys rarely do anything in this context except invite disaster.

One of the most devastating mistakes an advertiser can make is to presume that consumers in one culture have the same rituals as those in another. Religion is an obvious expression of values in a culture. In countries adhering to the precepts of the Islamic religion, which includes most Arab nations, traditional religious beliefs restrict several products from being advertised at all, such as alcohol and pork. Other restrictions related to religious and cultural values include not allowing women to appear in advertising and restricting the manner in which children can be portrayed in advertisements. Each market must be evaluated for the extent to which prevalent customs or values translate into product choice and other consumer behaviors.

Understanding values and rituals can represent a special challenge (or opportunity) when economic development in a country or region creates tensions between the old and the new. The classic example is the dilemma advertisers face as more wives leave the home for outside employment, creating tensions in the home about who should do the housework. This tension over traditional gender assignments in household chores has been particularly acute in Asia, and advertisers there have tried to respond by featuring husbands as homemakers. For example, an ad for vacuum cleaners made by Korea's LG Electronics showed a woman lying on the floor exercising and giving herself a facial with slices of cucumbers, while her husband cleaned around her. The ad received mixed reviews from women in Hong Kong and South Korea, with younger women approving, but their mothers disapproving.[9] (Sound familiar?) The advertiser's dilemma in situations like these is how to make ads that reflect real changes in a culture without alienating important segments of consumers by appearing to push the changes. Not an easy task!

Product Use and Preferences. Information about product use and preferences is available for many markets. The major markets of North America, Europe, and the Pacific Rim typically are relatively heavily researched. In recent years, A. C. Nielsen has developed an international database on consumer product use in 26 countries. Also, Roper Starch Worldwide has conducted "global" studies on product preferences, brand loyalty, and price sensitivity in 40 countries. The Roper study revealed, for example, that consumers in India were the most brand loyal, and that German and Japanese consumers showed the greatest tendency for price sensitivity.[10]

Studies by firms such as Nielsen and Roper document that consumers around the world display different product use characteristics and preferences. One area of great variation is personal-care products. There is no market in the world like the United States, where consumers are preoccupied with the use of personal-care products such as toothpaste, shampoo, deodorant, and mouthwash. Procter & Gamble, maker of

9.   Louise Lee, "Depicting Men Doing Housework Can Be Risky for Marketers in Asia," *Wall Street Journal,* August 14, 1998, B6.
10.   Leah Rickard, "Ex-Soviet States Lead World in Ad Cynicism," *Advertising Age,* May 5, 1995, 3.

brands such as Crest, Pert, Secret, and Scope, among others, learned the hard way in Russia with its Wash & Go shampoo. Wash & Go (comparable to Pert in the United States) was a shampoo and conditioner designed for the consumer who prefers the ease, convenience, and speed of one-step washing and conditioning. Russian consumers, accustomed to washing their hair with bar soap, didn't understand the concept of a hair conditioner, and didn't perceive a need to make shampooing any more convenient.

Other examples of unique and culture-specific product uses and preferences come from Brazil and France. In Brazil, many women still wash clothes by hand in metal tubs, using cold water. Because of this behavior, Unilever must specially formulate its Umo laundry powder and tout its effectiveness under these washing conditions.

In France, men commonly use cosmetics like those used by women in the United States. Advertising must, therefore, be specifically prepared for men and placed in media to reach them with specific male-oriented appeals. As another example, Exhibit 9.9 shows an ad directed toward French women—some of whom are relatively less accustomed (compared to women in the United States) to shaving their legs and underarms—for a razor designed for just such a purpose. The ad uses both pictures and text to promote the behavior. Perfume is another product category that inspires distinctive approaches around the world. As exemplified by Exhibit 9.10, the French have a passion for perfume that transforms their advertisements in this category to near works of art.

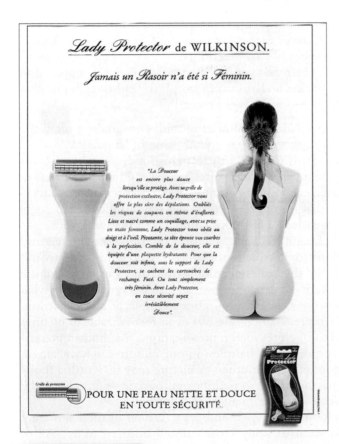

EXHIBIT 9.9

It's been said that "all politics are local," but so too is personal hygiene. The United Kingdom's Wilkinson might encounter difficulties in selling its Lady Protector, specifically designed for shaving women's legs and underarms, in France. The company's Web site (http://www .wilkinson-sword.com) is admirably multilingual, though, appealing to Spanish, British, French, Portuguese, and German speakers.

EXHIBIT 9.10

Thumb through a French fashion magazine and you'll appreciate both the passion for art and the passion for perfume that are hallmarks of French culture.

2 The Challenges in Executing Advertising Worldwide.

Cross-cultural audience research on basic economic, social, and cultural conditions is an essential starting point for planning international advertising. But even with excellent audience analysis, three formidable and unique challenges face the advertiser: the creative challenge, the media challenge, and the regulatory challenge.

The Creative Challenge. Written or spoken language is a basic barrier to cross-cultural communication. Ads written in German are typically difficult for those who speak only Spanish—this much is obvious. But language issues will always be a formidable challenge. We've all heard stories of how some literal translation of an ad said something very different than what was intended. International blunders are a rich part of advertising lore, and the anecdotes are plentiful:[11]

- The name *Coca-Cola* in China was first rendered as "Ke-kou-ke-la." Unfortunately, Coke did not discover until after thousands of signs had been printed that the phrase means "bite the wax tadpole" or "female horse stuffed with wax," depending on the dialect. Coke then researched 40,000 Chinese characters and found a close phonetic equivalent, "ko-kou-ko-le," which can be loosely translated as "happiness in the mouth."
- In Taiwan, the translation of the Pepsi slogan "Come alive with the Pepsi generation" came out as "Pepsi will bring your ancestors back from the dead."
- Scandinavian vacuum manufacturer Electrolux used the following in an American ad campaign: "Nothing sucks like an Electrolux."
- When Parker Pen marketed a ballpoint pen in Mexico, its ads were supposed to say, "It won't leak in your pocket and embarrass you." Instead the ads said that "It won't leak in your pocket and make you pregnant."

True or not, such tales remind us that communicating with consumers around the world is a special challenge, just in terms of the obvious issue of language.

What is less obvious, however, is the role of **picturing** in cross-cultural communication. There is a widely held belief that pictures are less culturally bound than are words, and that pictures can speak to many cultures at once. International advertisers are increasingly using ads that feature few words and rely on pictures to communicate. This is, as you might expect, a bit more complicated than it sounds.

First, picturing is culturally bound. Different cultures use different conventions or rules to create representations (or pictures) of things. Pictures, just like words, must be "read" or interpreted, and the "rules of reading" pictures vary from culture to culture. People living in Western cultures often assume that everyone knows what a certain picture means. This is not true and is another example of ethnocentrism. Photographic two-dimensional representations are not even recognizable as pictures to those who have not learned to interpret such representations. Symbolic representations that seem so absolute, common, and harmless in one culture can have varied, unusual, and even threatening meaning in another. A picture may be worth a thousand words, but those words may not mean something appropriate—or they may be entirely unintelligible or tasteless—to those in another culture.

Think about the ads in Exhibits 9.11, 9.12, and 9.13. Which of these ads seem culture-bound? Which would seem to easily cross cultural borders? Why? All of these ads depend on knowing the way to correctly interpret the ad, but some require more cultural knowledge than others. For U.S. consumers, the message of the Visa ad in Exhibit 9.11 is perfectly clear: Visa will help you acquire more stuff. But in less materialistic cultures, the premise of collecting material possessions as an expression

---

11.   Robert Kirby, "Kirby: Advertising Translates Into Laughs," *Salt Lake Tribune,* http://www.sltrib.com, accessed February 24, 1998.

EXHIBITS 9.11 THROUGH 9.13

Which of these ads seem most bound to specific cultures, based on the pictures in the ads? Are any of them not culturally bound?

of self may be completely incomprehensible. Exhibit 9.12 is a stylized ad created to present a romantic vision of a vacation in Thailand, with German consumers as the target segment. Do you suppose that this ad has any meaning to the average person in Thailand? And the ad in Exhibit 9.13 promises that Sears has everything you need to be the shining star at your high school prom. But while this ad ran in Spanish speaking countries throughout South America, the high school prom is a more common ritual in North America. Can a teen in Santiago spark to the offer of a formal prom dress when she has no cultural context for interpreting the meaning of "prom"? Not likely.

A few human expressions, such as a smile, are widely accepted to mean a positive feeling. Such expressions and their representations, even though culturally connected, have widespread commonality. But cultureless picture meanings do not exist. A much larger contributor to cross-cultural commonalities are those representations that are a part of a far-flung culture of commerce and have thus taken on similar meanings in many different nations. With sports playing an ever-larger role in international commerce, the sports hero is often used to symbolize common meaning across the world. What do you think? Is Tiger Woods Tiger Woods, no matter what he is selling or where he is selling it? Can the Williams sisters revive the Avon cosmetics brand around the world? Avon signed the tennis champs to an endorsement deal to do just that.[12]

The Media Challenge.   Of all the challenges faced by advertisers in international markets, the media challenge may be the greatest. Exhibit 9.14 shows a sampling of traditional media options for reaching consumers around the world.

Media Availability and Coverage.   Some international markets simply have too few media options. In addition, even if diverse media are available in a particular international market, there may be severe restrictions on the type of advertising that can be done or the way in which advertising is organized in a certain medium.

Many countries have dozens of subcultures and language dialects within their borders, each with its own newspapers and radio stations. This complicates the problem

12.   Mercedes Cardona, "Venus and Serena Become Avon's New Leading Ladies," *Advertising Age,* January 22, 2001, 8.

EXHIBIT 9.14

Advertising Age*'s global media lineup.*

Media	Ownership	Circulation or Number of Households
PRINT		
BusinessWeek	The McGraw-Hill Cos.	1.08 million
Computerworld/InfoWorld	IDG	1.9 million
The Economist	The Economist Group	684,416
Elle	Hachette Filipacchi	5.1 million
Elle Deco	Hachette Filipacchi	1.5 million
Financial Times	Pearson PLC	363,525
Forbes Global Business & Finance	Forbes	860,000**
Fortune	Time Warner	915,000
Harvard Business Review	Harvard Business School Publishing	220,000
International Herald Tribune	The New York Times/ The Washington Post Co.	222,930
National Geographic	National Geographic Society	8.8 million
Newsweek Worldwide	The Washington Post Co.	4.2 million
PC World	IDG	3.6 million
Reader's Digest	Reader's Digest Association	26 million
Scientific American	Yerlagsgruppe Hoitzbrinck	562,150
Time	Time Warner	5.6 million
USA Today International	Gannett Co.	2.2 million† (Mon.–Thurs.) 2.6 million (Friday edition)
The Wall Street Journal	Dow Jones & Co.	4.3 million
TV		
Animal Planet	Discovery Communications/BBC	4.9 million*
BBC World	BBC Worldwide	60 million
Cartoon Network	Time Warner	125.5 million
CNBC	NBC/Dow Jones & Co. (only 100% NBC-owned in U.S.)	136 million**
CNN International	Time Warner	221 million
Discovery Networks International	Discovery Communications	144 million
ESPN	Walt Disney Co./Hearst Corp.	242 million
MTV Networks	Viacom	285 million
TNT	Time Warner	104.2 million

* Includes 45 million homes in the United States
** Excludes Latin America
† For international edition only

Source: *Advertising Age International,* February 8, 1999, 23. Reprinted with permission from the February 8, 1999, issue of *Advertising Age International.* Copyright © Crain Communications Inc., 1999.

of deciding which combination of newspapers or radio stations will achieve the desired coverage of the market. The presence of a particular medium in a country does not necessarily make it useful for advertisers if there are restrictions on accepting advertising. A prominent example is the BBC networks in the United Kingdom, where advertising is still not accepted. While the U.K. does have commercial networks in both radio and television, the BBC stations are still widely popular. Or consider the situation with regard to television advertising in Germany and the Netherlands. On the German government-owned stations, television advertising is banned on Sundays and holidays and restricted to four five-minute blocks on other days. In the Netherlands, television advertising cannot constitute more than 5 percent of total programming time, and most time slots must be purchased nearly a year in advance. Similar circumstances exist in many markets around the world.

Newspapers are actually the most localized medium worldwide, and they require the greatest amount of local market knowledge to be used correctly as an advertising option. In Mexico, for example, advertising space is sold in the form of news columns, without any notice or indication that the "story" is a paid advertisement. This situation influences both the placement and layout of ads. Turkey has hundreds of daily newspapers; the Netherlands has only a handful. Further, many newspapers (particularly regional papers) are positioned in the market based on a particular political philosophy. Advertisers must be aware of this, making certain that their brand's position with the target audience does not conflict with the politics of the medium.

The best news for advertisers from the standpoint of media availability and coverage is the emergence of several global television networks made possible by cable and satellite technology. Viacom bills its combined MTV Networks (MTVN) as the largest TV network in the world, with a capability to reach over 300 million households worldwide.[13] MTVN also offers expertise in developing special promotions to Generations X, Y, and Z around the world. MTVN has facilitated international campaigns for global brands such as Pepsi, Swatch, Sega, and BMX Bikes. Additionally, MTV has proven expertise in producing programs for specific country markets, like "Mochilao," a backpack travel show hosted by a popular Brazilian model, as well as programming designed to appeal to its key demographic across cultures.[14] If there is such a thing as a "global consumer," MTVN offers an efficient means for reaching them.

Another development affecting Europe and Asia is direct broadcast by satellite (DBS), via systems like SkyPort (see Exhibit 9.15). DBS transmissions are received through the small, low-cost receiving dishes that have become a familiar sight on rooftops around the world. STAR, which stands for Satellite Televisions Asian Region, sends BBC, U.S., Bollywood, and local programming to 300 million households in 53 countries across Asia.[15] With literally billions more people in its viewing area, STAR has the potential to become one of the world's most influential broadcasting systems.

EXHIBIT 9.15

Direct broadcast by satellite allows households to receive television transmission via a small, low-cost receiving dish. This is an ad for Skyport TV promoting its satellite service in the Asian market.

13.   "On-Air Opportunities," *Television Business International*, vol. 49 (January 1998), 1.
14.   Charles Goldsmith, "MTV Seeks Global Appeal," *Wall Street Journal*, July 21, 2003, B1, B3.
15.   From the STAR Web site, http://www.startv.com, accessed May 20, 2004.

Media Costs and Pricing. Confounding the media challenge is the issue of media costs and pricing. As discussed earlier, some markets have literally hundreds of media options (recall the Turkish newspapers). Whenever a different medium is chosen, separate payment and placement must be made. Additionally, in many markets, media prices are subject to negotiation—no matter what the official rate cards say. The time needed to negotiate these rates is a tremendous cost in and of itself.

Global coverage is an expensive proposition. For example, a four-color ad in *Reader's Digest* costs on the order of half a million dollars. Should the advertiser desire to achieve full impact in *Reader's Digest,* then the ad should be adapted in all 20 of the different languages for the international editions—again, generating substantial expense. Both ad rates and the demand for ad space are on the increase. In some markets, advertising time and space are in such short supply that, regardless of the published rate, a bidding system is used to escalate the prices. As you will see in Chapter 14, media costs represent the majority of costs in an advertising budget. With the seemingly chaotic buying practices in some international markets, media costs are indeed a great challenge in executing cost-effective advertising campaigns.

The Regulatory Challenge. The regulatory restrictions on international advertising are many and varied, reflecting diverse cultural values, market by market. The range and specificity of regulation can be aggravatingly complex. Tobacco and liquor advertising are restricted (typically banned from television) in many countries, although several lift their ban on liquor after 9 or 10 PM. With respect to advertising to children, Austria, Canada, Germany, and the United States have specific regulations. Other products and topics monitored or restricted throughout the world are drugs (Austria, Switzerland, Germany, Greece, and the Netherlands), gambling (United Kingdom, Italy, and Portugal), and religion (Germany, United Kingdom, and the Netherlands).

This regulatory complexity, if anything, continues to grow. For instance, the European Union, the world's largest trading bloc, has strict regulations protecting citizens' privacy, thus limiting marketers' access to data that are readily available in North America. To cope with these regulations many global companies have dozens of employees in Europe whose job is to keep their companies in compliance with various regulations.[16] Generally, advertisers must be sensitive to the fact that advertising regulations can, depending on the international market, impose limitations on the following:

- The types of products that can be advertised
- The kinds of data that can be collected from consumers
- The types of message appeals that can be used
- The times during which ads for certain products can appear on television
- Advertising to children
- The use of foreign languages (and talent) in advertisements
- The use of national symbols, such as flags and government seals, in advertisements
- The taxes levied against advertising expenditures

In short, just about every aspect of advertising can be regulated, and every country has some peculiarities with respect to ad regulation. As explained in the IBP box, these restrictions and regulations may also apply to a host of common promotional tactics, such as couponing and loyalty rewards programs.

3 Advertising Agencies around the World. An experienced and astute agency can help an advertiser deal with the creative, media, and regulatory challenges just discussed. In Brazil, using a local agency is essential to getting the creative

---

16.   David Scheer, "Europe's New High-Tech Role: Playing Privacy Cop to the World," *Wall Street Journal,* October 10, 2003, A1, A16.

style and tone just right. In Australia, Australian nationals must be involved in certain parts of the production process. And in China, trying to work through the government and media bureaucracy is nearly impossible without the assistance of a local agency. There are nearly 80,000 to choose from in China.[17]

Advertisers have three basic alternatives in selecting an agency to help them prepare and place advertising in other countries: They can use a global agency, an international affiliate, or a local agency.

IBP

Releasing That Pent-Up Urge to Clip Coupons

A few years ago, a court in Düsseldorf blocked a drugstore there from giving away 75-cent shopping bags in celebration of the anniversary of its opening. The bags featured a lovable penguin holding a birthday cake ... pretty dangerous stuff! The German court ruled this was a violation of the Free Gift Act. The court reasoned that since most German retailers sell shopping bags, giving them away was *verboten*. Half-price happy-hour drinks didn't fare any better with the courts in Germany. Since the Discount Law there forbids price breaks of more than 3 percent off list, a half-price offer on drinks is strictly *verboten*. These are just two examples of a myriad of laws and regulations in Germany controlling many kinds of price promotions that American consumers take for granted.

Oftentimes laws like these are remnants of another era. Many such German regulations date back to the Nazi regime when the intent was to eliminate deals and discounting because these tactics were associated with the soft economic policies of the Marxist movement. The wild part of it is, 75 years later, these laws are still enforced aggressively. As hard as it may be to get laws passed in any culture, it is probably always harder to make them go away, even when it is not clear what purpose they are serving in modern times.

But fear not, there is hope for the German coupon clipper. Coupons and other familiar promotional tactics are on the way, thanks to the Internet. Although the majority of German consumers do not shop via the Internet, there is a growing concern that the Internet will introduce discounting practices that will be hard for traditional retailers to match if they are shackled by regulations like the Free Gift Act and the Discount Law. So how will German consumers react to the prospect of free shopping bags, happy-hour specials, coupons, or buy-one-get-one-free offers? They'll probably be pretty excited at first, given that these things will be something new and different. But it shouldn't take long for things to settle down, with coupon clipping becoming the tedious chore that many consumers around the world already know it to be.

Source: David Wessel, "German Shoppers Get Coupons," *Wall Street Journal*, April 5, 2001, 1.

The Global Agency.
The consolidation and mergers taking place in the advertising industry are creating more and more **global agencies,** or worldwide advertising groups. The "big four" are Omnicom Group, Interpublic Group, WPP Group, and Publicis Groupe. The lineup of companies affiliated with Omnicom and Interpublic is detailed in Exhibit 9.16. Note how these multi-billion dollar businesses have assembled a network of diverse service providers to deliver advertising and integrated brand promotion for clients who demand global reach.

The great advantage of a global organization is that it will know the advertiser's products and current advertising programs (presuming it handles the domestic advertising duties). With this knowledge, the agency can either adapt domestic campaigns for international markets or launch entirely new campaigns. Another advantage is the geographic proximity of the advertiser to the agency headquarters, which can often facilitate planning and preparation of ads. The size of a global agency can be a benefit in terms of economies of scale and political leverage.

Their greatest disadvantage stems from their distance from the local culture. Exporting meaning is never easy. This is no small disadvantage to agencies that actually believe they can do this. Most, however, are not that naive, and they have procedures for acquiring local knowledge.

The International Affiliate.
Many agencies do not own and operate worldwide offices, but rather have established foreign-market **international affiliates** to handle clients' international advertising needs. Many times these agencies join a network of foreign agencies

---

17. Normandy Madden, "Culture Clash Thwarts Shops from Enjoying China's Boom," *Advertising Age*, May 3, 2004, 20.

*Advertising agencies affiliated
with the top two global
agencies, 2004.*

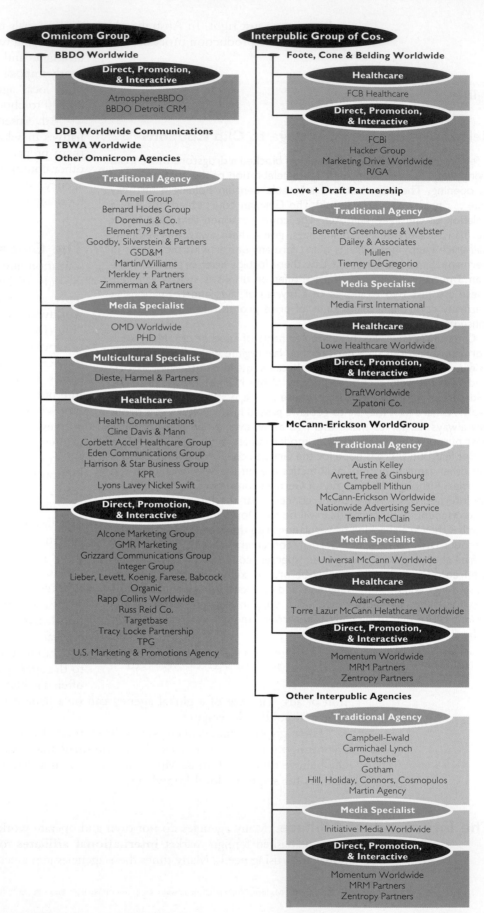

or take minority ownership positions in several foreign agencies. The benefit of this arrangement is that the advertiser typically has access to a large number of international agencies that can provide local market expertise. These international agencies are usually well established and managed by foreign nationals, which gives the advertiser a local presence in the international market, while avoiding any resistance to foreign ownership. This was the reasoning behind Coca-Cola's decision to give local creative responsibility for advertising its Coke Classic brand in Europe to the French agency Publicis.[18] Although Coke Classic is a global brand, Coke felt that the French agency was better suited to adapt U.S. ad campaigns for Europe.

The risk of these arrangements is that while an international affiliate will know the local market, it may be less knowledgeable about the advertiser's brands and competitive strategy. The threat is that the real value and relevance of the brand will not be incorporated into the foreign campaign.

The Local Agency. The final option is for an advertiser to choose a **local agency** in every foreign market where advertising will be carried out. Local agencies have the same advantages as the affiliate agencies just discussed: They will be knowledgeable about the culture and local market conditions. Such agencies tend to have well-established contacts for market information, production, and media buys. But the advertiser that chooses this option is open to administrative problems. There is less opportunity for standardization of the creative effort; each agency in each market will feel compelled to provide a unique creative execution. This lack of standardization can be expensive, and potentially disastrous for brand imagery when the local agency seeks to make its own creative statement without a good working knowledge of a brand's heritage.[19] Finally, working with local agencies can create internal communication problems, which increases the risk of delays and errors in execution.

4 Globalized versus Localized Campaigns.

One additional issue needs to be considered in advertising planning for international markets. This key issue involves the extent to which a campaign will be standardized across markets versus localized by market. In discussions of this issue, the question is often posed as: How much can the advertiser globalize the approach? **Globalized campaigns** use the same message and creative execution across all (or most) international markets. Exhibit 9.17 shows an ad from a globalized campaign that you'll find familiar, even though this version appeared in a magazine targeting the Spanish-speaking countries of South America. By contrast, **localized campaigns** involve preparing specific messages and/or creative executions for a particular market. Compare Exhibits 9.17 and 9.18. It should be evident that the dairy producers of Deutschland wanted an ad campaign focused on their local market, not something for a global stage.

The issue is more complex than simply a question of globalized versus localized advertising. Both the brand and its overall marketing strategy must be examined. The marketer must first consider the extent to which the brand can be standardized across markets, and then the extent to which the advertising can be globalized across markets. The degree to which advertising in international markets can use a common appeal, versus whether the ads prepared for each market must be customized, has been a widely debated issue.

Those who favor the globalized campaign assume that similarities as well as differences between markets can be taken into account. They argue that standardization of messages should occur whenever possible, adapting the message only when absolutely necessary. For example, Mars's U.S. advertisements for Pedigree dog food

---

18.   Daniel Tilles, "Publicis Gets a Sip of Coke Account," *International Herald Tribune*, July 7, 1995, 13.
19.   Leon E. Wynter, "Global Marketers Learn to Say No to Bad Ads," *Wall Street Journal*, April 1, 1998, B1.

Globalized advertising campaigns maintain a similar look and feel across international markets. This "got milk" ad could easily work in San Antonio or San Diego, even though it ran in Santiago, Chile.

Here the key message is that German dairy products are best for Germans. And perhaps, "got butter"?

have used golden retrievers, while poodles were deemed more effective for the brand's positioning and image in Asia. Otherwise, the advertising campaigns were identical in terms of basic message appeal.

Those who argue for the localized approach see each country or region as a unique communication context, and claim that the only way to achieve advertising success is to develop separate campaigns for each market.

The two most fundamental arguments for globalized campaigns are based on potential cost savings and creative advantages. Just as organizations seek to gain economies of scale in production, they also look for opportunities to streamline the communication process. Having one standard theme to communicate allows an advertiser to focus on a uniform brand or corporate image worldwide, develop plans more quickly, and make maximum use of good ideas. Thus, while Gillette sells hundreds of different products in more than 200 countries around the world, its corporate philosophy of globalization is expressed in its "Gillette—The Best a Man Can Get" theme. This theme is attached to all ads for men's toiletry products, wherever they appear.[20]

Several trends in the global marketplace are working in combination to create conditions that are supportive of globalized campaigns, in that they facilitate the creation of a global consumer. Some of the conditions which support the use of globalized ad campaigns are as follows.[21]

20. Mark Maremont, "Gillette Finally Reveals Its Vision of the Future, and It Has 3 Blades," *Wall Street Journal,* April 14, 1998, A1, A10; Charles Forelle, "Schick Puts a Nick in Gillette's Razor Cycle," *Wall Street Journal,* October 3, 2003, B7.

21. This list is updated from Henry Assael, *Consumer Behavior and Marketing Action,* 5th ed. (Cincinnati: South-Western/International Thomson Publishing, 1995), 491–494.

- **Global communications.** Worldwide cable and satellite networks have resulted in television becoming a truly global communications medium. MTVN's 200 European advertisers almost all run English-language-only campaigns in the station's 28-nation broadcast area. These standardized messages will themselves serve to homogenize the viewers within these market areas. Similarly, common experience and exposure on the Internet serves to create shared values around the world, especially among young people.

- **Global youth.** As suggested by the Nokia ad from the Czech Republic in Exhibit 9.19, young people around the world have a lot in common. Global communications, global travel, and the demise of communism are argued to have created common norms and values among teenagers around the world.[22] One advertising agency videotaped the rooms of teenagers from 25 countries, and it was hard to tell whether any given room belonged to an American, German, or Japanese teen. And it's not just teenagers. Toy makers like Mattel, Hasbro, and Lego once worked under the assumption that children around the world would value different toys that carried some local flavor. No more. The large toymakers now create and launch standardized products for children worldwide.[23]

- **Universal demographic and lifestyle trends.** Demographic and related lifestyle trends that emerged in the 1980s in the United States are now manifesting themselves in markets around the world. More working women, more single-person households, increasing divorce rates, and fewer children per household are now widespread demographic phenomena that are effecting common lifestyles worldwide, with advertisers sure to follow. For instance, the rising number of working women in Japan caused Ford Motor Company to prepare ads specifically targeted to this audience.

- **The Americanization of consumption values.** Perhaps of greatest advantage to U.S. advertisers has been the Americanization of consumption values around the world. American icons have gained popularity worldwide, especially due to the exportation of pop culture fueled by the U.S. entertainment industry. American brands often benefit. However, dramatic events in recent years like 9/11 and the Afghan and Iraqi wars are altering America's image around the world. As discussed in the Controversy box, these dramatic events could serve to undermine the appeal of global brands, especially those associated with Brand America.

Many factors have created an environment where a common message across national boundaries becomes more plausible. To the extent that consumers in various countries hold the same interests and values, "standardized" images and themes can be effective in advertising.

EXHIBIT 9.19

You don't need to speak Czech to appreciate the intent of this ad. As with any Nokia product, it's all about "connecting people" (especially young people).

Arguments against globalization tend to center on issues relating to local market requirements and cultural constraints within markets. The target audiences in different countries must understand and place the same level of importance on brand features or attributes for a globalized campaign to be effective. In many cases, different features are valued at different levels of intensity, making a common message

22.   Arundhati Parmar, "Global Youth United," *Marketing News*, October 28, 2002, 1, 49.

23.   Lisa Bannon, "One-Toy-Fits-All: How Industry Learned to Love the Global Kid," *Wall Street Journal*, April 29, 2003, A1, A12.

inappropriate. Also, if a globalized campaign defies local customs, values, and regulations, or if it ignores the efforts of local competition, then it has little chance of being successful.

CONTROVERSY

Brand America in Decline?

American companies and brands are well known globally. Inevitably, they get connected with other dramatic events occurring around the world. Of late, there can be little doubt that the image of Brand America has suffered worldwide, raising deep concerns among leaders in the advertising profession. Keith Reinhard, chairman of DDB Worldwide, has conducted research to probe the question, "Why do they hate us?" Here are some of the issues his group identified.

- *Exploitation by American companies.* There is a widespread feeling that American companies take more than they give back in foreign markets.
- *Hyperconsumerism.* There is also a sentiment that Americans want to make money, and nothing more. This leads to aggressive marketing of products that are not wanted or needed in other cultures.
- *Corrupting influence.* American brands are often associated with an attempt to subvert the local culture and promote behaviors that conflict with local customs and religious norms.
- *Arrogance and insensitivity.* There is a perception around the world that Americans believe that everyone else wants everything that America has and would gladly give up their local language and culture for a chance to live in America.

It is sobering to point out that all the concerns above were identified in research conducted *before* the start of the Iraqi war.

To try to help address the growing negativity, in January 2004 Reinhard founded a group called Business for Diplomatic Action (BDA). He launched the group with 150 other executives from the advertising profession around a simple premise: "There is a role for business and for us as citizens to try to become more proactive in countering the negative imagery" that exists worldwide regarding America. BDA's early priorities involved an Internet clearinghouse of best practices for being a good ambassador for the United States (versus being a clumsy tourist), along with educational programs aimed at high school and college students designed to foster cultural sensitivity. The group is also working with media companies to plan television shows that better represent how people in America really live, versus "Baywatch"-like programs, which have been disseminated worldwide.

Reputation is reality. There are obviously no simple solutions to the decline in America's reputation worldwide. For business, and for a wide variety of other reasons, we wish Reinhard and his group much success.

Sources: Dennis Dunlap, "Hate the Policy, Love the Product," *Marketing News,* May 15, 2004, 9; Hillary Chura, "Marketing Execs Try to Polish Brand USA," *Advertising Age,* May 17, 2004, 12.

It is also the case that local managers do not always appreciate the value of globalized campaigns. Since they did not help create the campaign, they may drag their feet in implementing it. Without the support of local managers, no globalized campaign can ever achieve its potential.

Developing global brands through standardized campaigns can be successful only when advertisers can find similar needs, feelings, or emotions as a basis for communication across cultures. Understanding consumers around the world is the critical success factor. As expressed by Bob Wehling, Procter & Gamble's former chief of global marketing: "When you bring consumers in every part of the world what they want and you present it in an arresting and persuasive manner, success will follow. And when you don't, the consumer will be the first to tell you to fix it."[24]

Finally, global marketers need to distinguish between strategy and execution when using a global approach to advertising. The basic need identified may well be universal, but communication about the product or service that offers satisfaction of the need may be strongly influenced by cultural values in different markets, and thus may work against globalization. Recall the example of AT&T's "Reach Out and Touch Someone" campaign. The campaign was highly successful in the United States in communicating the need to keep in touch with loved ones, but was viewed by European audiences as too sentimental in style and execution. For another executional example, take a look at Exhibit 9.20. What do you think of this Italian ad for Yokohama tires? Would it play in Peoria? Everyone wants a tire that performs well, but for Peoria, there are better ways to execute a performance claim for your tire.

24. Jack Neff, "Rethinking Globalism," *Advertising Age,* October 9, 2000, 100.

Using standardized campaigns for global brands is difficult. This Italian Yokohama ad (http://www.yokohamatire.com) may suit Italian sensibilities, but how will it play in Peoria? Many American tire ads stress safety (for example, the ad showing a baby securely nestled in a solid, sensible tire) and performance in adverse weather, not a torrid romance with the road. Might this be a consequence of differences in who buys tires? When both mom and dad drive (and take for service) their own cars, the whole of the family's considerations come into play.

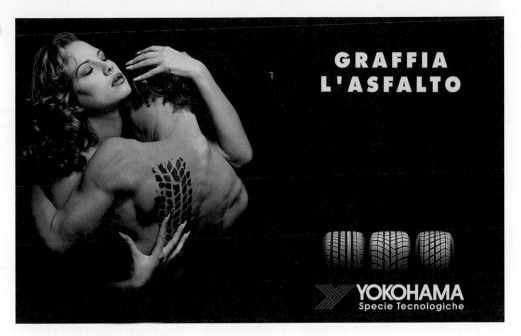

SUMMARY

 Explain the types of audience research that are useful for understanding cultural barriers that can interfere with effective communication.

All of us wear cultural blinders, and as a result we must overcome substantial barriers in trying to communicate with people from other countries. This is a major problem for international advertisers as they seek to promote their brands around the world. To overcome this problem and avoid errors in advertising planning, cross-cultural audience analysis is needed. Such analyses involve evaluation of economic conditions, demographic characteristics, customs, values, rituals, and product use and preferences in the target countries.

 Identify three distinctive challenges that complicate the execution of advertising in international settings.

Worldwide advertisers face three distinctive challenges in executing their campaigns. The first of these is a creative challenge that derives from differences in experience and meaning among cultures. Even the pictures featured in an ad may be translated differently from one country to the next. Media availability, media coverage, and media costs vary dramatically around the world, adding a second complication to international advertising. Finally, the amount and nature of advertising regulation vary dramatically from country to country and may force a complete reformulation of an ad campaign.

 Describe the three basic types of advertising agencies that can assist in the placement of advertising around the world.

Advertising agencies provide marketers with the expertise needed to develop and execute advertising campaigns in international markets. Marketers can choose to work with global agencies, local agencies in the targeted market, or an international affiliate of the agency they use in their home country. Each of these agency types brings different advantages and disadvantages on evaluative dimensions such as geographic proximity, economies of scale, political leverage, awareness of the client's strategy, and knowledge of the local culture.

 Discuss the advantages and disadvantages of globalized versus localized advertising campaigns.

A final concern for international advertising entails the degree of customization an advertiser should attempt in campaigns designed to cross national boundaries. Globalized campaigns involve little customization among countries, whereas localized campaigns feature heavy customization for each market. Standardized messages bring cost savings and create a common brand image worldwide, but they may miss the mark with consumers in different nations. As consumers around the world become more similar, globalized campaigns may become more prevalent. Teenagers in many countries share similar values and lifestyles and thus make a natural target for globalized campaigns.

KEY TERMS

international advertising	highly industrialized countries	local agency
ethnocentrism	demographic dividend	globalized campaigns
self-reference criterion (SRC)	picturing	localized campaigns
less-developed countries	global agencies	
newly industrialized countries	international affiliates	

QUESTIONS

1. Why are so many companies looking to China as a new source of business opportunity, and what challenges do they face there?

2. What perils did Japanese automaker Toyota face during its campaign to launch the Prado Land Cruiser in China? How did Toyota ad agency Saatchi & Saatchi respond to the controversy?

3. From the various facts and figures presented throughout this chapter, which did you find most compelling in making the case for the global nature of the advertising business?

4. In this chapter we discuss the challenges advertisers face in Asia when it comes to representing husbands and wives in ads for products such as laundry detergents and vacuum cleaners. Why is this a challenging issue in Asia today? Would you expect that advertisers face this same challenge in other parts of the world? Where?

5. If you were creating a media strategy for a global advertising campaign, what emphasis would you put on newspapers in executing your strategy? What factors complicate their value for achieving broad market coverage?

6. Explain the appeal of new media options such as direct broadcast by satellite and the Internet for marketers who have created globalized advertising campaigns.

7. Compare and contrast the advantages of global versus local ad agencies for implementing international advertising.

8. Identify several factors or forces that make consumers around the world more similar to one another. Conversely, what factors or forces create diversity among consumers in different countries?

9. Teens and retired people are two market segments found worldwide. If these two segments of European consumers were each being targeted for new advertising campaigns, which one would be most responsive to a globalized ad campaign? Why?

EXPERIENTIAL EXERCISES

1.   Select a particular brand or product category that you think would succeed internationally given the right advertising and brand promotion effort, and imagine you are a marketer planning to launch that brand globally. You are looking for the right spokesperson to endorse your product and communicate the value of your brand to international audiences. Based on the information you learned from this chapter as well as your general knowledge of global marketing opportunities, select someone to represent your brand internationally—perhaps a Hollywood star, sports icon, or other high-profile celebrity—and explain why he or she would be an ideal spokesperson.

2.   Conduct a study on the concept of *picturing* in cross-cultural communication. Go to the library and find any magazine from another country that has numerous ads with photographic representations. Based on what you learned about picturing in this chapter, analyze the photographic messages of the ads and compare them to the messages you would commonly find in ads targeted to your own culture. What contrasts or similarities did you find? What can you infer about the values of a culture based on the types of photographic images that are used?

EXPERIENCING THE INTERNET

9-1 Agencies for International Advertising

Boasting clients such as Mitsubishi Motors, Toshiba, Konica, and Sega Corporation, Tokyo-based Dentsu is the number one ad firm in Japan and one of the largest advertising agencies in the world. While many ad agencies leave a number of communications activities to specialized companies, Dentsu offers clients comprehensive, integrated solutions designed to serve all their brand needs. Dentsu is a market leader in interactive media communications, and its trademark "Total Communications Services" approach is key to the agency's success.

Dentsu: http://www.dentsu.com

1.   Visit the Dentsu Web site and list specific services the firm offers to its clients.

2.   List some advantages and disadvantages of globalized versus localized advertising campaigns. In an era of globalization, do you think the "local" will lose its identity, or will the dynamism of globalization help create new "local" ideas?

3.   Based on the information given in the text, determine whether Dentsu is best characterized as a global agency, an international affiliate, or a local agency.

9-2 Challenges in Executing Worldwide Advertising

Advertisers seeking to reach a global audience face distinctive challenges in executing their campaigns. Differences in meaning between cultures, availability of media,

and advertising regulations across borders can cause a lot of headaches for advertisers. Nowhere is this more evident than on the Web, where quick access to international audiences is too tempting for advertisers to pass up. Maybelline, one of the leaders in the cosmetics industry, has produced numerous international sites to develop integrated brand promotion for its products. Visit the link and compare Maybelline's international sites by clicking on the links from the home page.

Maybelline: http://www.maybelline.com

1.   What creative challenges do you think Maybelline is likely to encounter as it tries to promote its makeup products internationally? What is *picturing*, and how essential is it to the success of Maybelline's global sites?

2.   What are typical media challenges that companies have to overcome when advertising globally? Which of Maybelline's current international sites do you think has the most media challenges? Why?

3.   List some of the promotional tactics employed by Maybelline at its sites. Does the company use the same promotions in every country? What regulatory challenges does Maybelline face with its sites and with its promotion strategies?

INTEGRATED BRAND PROMOTION

Cincinnati Bell℠

PART 2
Cincinnati Bell Wireless: Planning Advertising and IBP

It has become common for marketers to deploy a variety of communication tools to build their brands. Depending on a firm's objectives and resources, many different combinations of tools may be used. For example, TV advertising is relied on heavily for establishing brand awareness; print advertising may carry specific information about terms or features of an offering; sales promotions are used to cause short-term spikes in demand; direct marketing is used to motivate action from a well-defined target audience; and public relations can help a firm manage media reports about its activities. We will see all these tools and more put in play in the launch of Cincinnati Bell Wireless.

This range of promotional devices and their application under different conditions is common. But achieving desired outcomes (for example, sales and brand loyalty) through sophisticated advertising and IBP campaigns will always require careful planning. Here we will thoroughly review the planning process that served as the platform for launching Cincinnati Bell Wireless.

A Model for Planning Advertising and Integrated Brand Promotion.
There are many different models that one might use for direction in the process of planning a launch campaign. To put the Cincinnati Bell Wireless campaign in a proper context, and to be consistent with our discussion of planning issues in the last five chapters, we will frame this discussion using the strategic planning triangle proposed by advertising researchers Esther Thorson and Jeri Moore.[1] As reflected in Exhibit IBP 2.1, the apexes of the planning triangle entail the segment(s) selected as targets for the campaign, the brand's value proposition, and the array of persuasion tools that might be deployed to achieve campaign objectives.

In planning an IBP campaign, a firm starts with the customer or prospect and works backward, identifying what the customer deems important information. Hence, we place identification and specification of the target segment as the paramount apex in the triangle. Building a consensus between the client and the agency about which customer segments will be targeted is essential to the campaign's effectiveness. Complex IBP campaigns may end up targeting multiple segments; when this is so, it is critical to analyze if and how different target segments will interact to support or disparage the campaign. As suggested in Chapter 6, compelling advertising begins with descriptions and insights about one's target segment(s) that are both personal and precise.

---

1. Esther Thorson and Jeri Moore, *Integrated Communication: Synergy of Persuasive Voices* (Mahwah, NJ: Erlbaum, 1996).

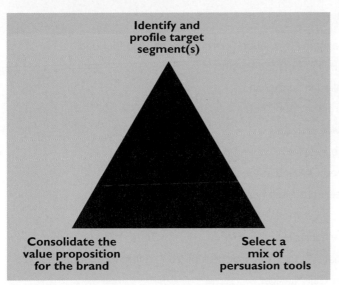

Identify and
profile target
segment(s)

Consolidate the
value proposition
for the brand

Select a
mix of
persuasion tools

Adapted from Esther Thorson and Jeri Moore, *Integrated Communication: Synergy of Persuasive Voices*
(Mahwah, N.J.: Erlbaum, 1996).

EXHIBIT IBP 2.1

*Thorson and Moore's
strategic planning triangle.*

The second important apex in the planning triangle entails specification of the brand's value proposition. Per Chapter 6, a brand's value proposition is a statement of the functional, emotional, and self-expressive benefits delivered by the brand that provide value to customers in the target segment. In formulating the value proposition, one should consider both what a brand has stood for or communicated to consumers in the past, and what new types of value or additional benefits one wants to claim for the brand going forward. For mature and successful brands, reaffirming the existing value proposition may be the primary objective for any campaign. When launching a new brand, there is an opportunity to start from scratch in establishing the value proposition. For Cincinnati Bell Wireless (CBW), which was a combination of something old (Cincinnati Bell) and something new (wireless), the challenge was to draw on the strengths of the old as a foundation for claims about the new.

The final apex of the planning triangle considers the various persuasion tools that may be deployed in executing the campaign. A complete description of the tools is yet to come. Chapters 14 and 15 will emphasize traditional mass media tools; Chapter 16 looks at the Internet advertising option; Chapter 17 will consider support media, event sponsorship, and branded entertainment; Chapter 18 reviews the array of possibilities in sales promotion and point-of-purchase advertising; Chapter 19 provides a comprehensive look at direct marketing; and Chapter 20 completes the set by discussing the public relations function. The mix of tools used will depend on the objectives that are set for the campaign in question. For example, building awareness of and excitement about a new brand such as CBW will be accomplished most effectively via mass media and event sponsorship, whereas bringing consumers into retail stores with an intent to purchase may require a sales promotion, delivered to the targeted customer via a direct mail offer, with a telemarketing follow-up. As you will see, one of the most admirable aspects of the IBP campaign designed by Northlich for the CBW launch was its skillful use of multiple persuasion tools working in harmony to sell the product. That's right, we want to emphasize: *to sell the product.* Marketers such as Cincinnati Bell fund IBP campaigns to get results that affect their companies' revenues and profitability. The campaign that launched CBW did just that.

Assessing CBW'S Situation Prior to Launch.
As described in Chapter 8, an effective campaign begins with a keen appreciation for the critical elements of one's situation. There is an infinite list of potential factors (for example, demographic, social and cultural, economic, political/regulatory) that may be considered in analyzing the situation. However, the idea is to be smart in choosing the few important factors that really describe the situation, and then explain how the factors relate to the task at hand. To appreciate the task that Northlich faced in planning the campaign to launch CBW requires an appreciation for several key elements of the situation.

Historical Context.
Cincinnati Bell officially launched its wireless phone service on May 11, 1998. However, this particular launch was just one in a continuing series of new products

INTEGRATED BRAND PROMOTION

EXHIBIT IBP 2.2

Cincinnati Bell: Celebrating 125 years of innovation.

A Corporate Timeline . . .

1873—City & Suburban Telegraph Association (now Cincinnati Bell) founded

1876—Alexander Graham Bell invents the telephone

1877—First telephone installed in Cincinnati

1907—First Yellow Pages directory published

1975—911 emergency service activated

1984—First fiber optic cable installed

1990—Cincinnati Reds sweep Oakland in the World Series

1992—Cincinnati Bell pioneered the self-healing fiber optic network

1996—First telecommunication company to offer Internet access: Fuse

1997—1,000,000th access line installed

1997—Ranked one of the nation's top two providers of trouble-free local phone service

1998—First to offer Internet Call Manager

1998—Ranked highest independent telecommunications company for Web technology

1998—Cincinnati Bell: Celebrating 125 years of innovation

and services involving the Cincinnati Bell brand name. Moreover, in 1998 Cincinnati Bell celebrated its 125-year anniversary in the Greater Cincinnati metropolitan market under the banner "Celebrating 125 Years of Innovation." Some important milestones in the history of the company are listed in Exhibit IBP 2.2. In addition, as illustrated by the sample ads in Exhibit IBP 2.3, a common theme across ads for its various products and services was the slogan "People you know you can rely on." Obviously, the launch of CBW should not be viewed as an isolated event, and the Cincinnati Bell brand name carried with it equities that provided a sound foundation for the launch of a wireless service. Certainly, it was a name widely known in the local market, and one that connoted superior service, quality, innovation, and

EXHIBIT IBP 2.3

Cincinnati Bell: Celebrating 125 years of innovation.

value. These types of connections to the Cincinnati Bell brand would of course be tremendous assets in the launch of CBW.

Industry Analysis. Telecommunications is a dynamic, technical, and complex business. Building a product and service network that would deliver good value to the wireless phone customer was the responsibility of Cincinnati Bell and its partners. Although it is beyond the scope of this discussion to explain the interworkings of the telecommunications business, some familiarity with key industry issues is essential for appreciating the business opportunity that CBW sought to capitalize on in May of 1998.

In the winter of 1998, the wireless phone marketplace in Cincinnati and, for that matter, nationwide, was on the brink of bedlam. As one writer put it at the time:

Well, the future of [wireless] is now. And while some of its promises are already being fulfilled, all of the new (and sometimes incompatible) gear and advanced services have had an unintended impact: It's wireless chaos out there.[2]

Executives at Cincinnati Bell realized that in a marketplace typified by chaos, the rewards would go to companies that offered consumers simple solutions and good value. Out of chaos often comes wonderful business opportunity.

Critical to understanding this opportunity is the distinction between analog cellular and digital PCS (personal communication services) wireless phones. CBW would launch a new digital PCS offering to the Greater Cincinnati marketplace. Its primary competition at launch would be analog cellular providers. Analog cellular was the established technology that introduced most of us to the concept of a wireless phone. Across the United States, analog service providers all rely on the same transmission methods and thus can handle calls for each others' customers, for a heavy "roaming fee." Hence, you can make an analog cellular call almost anywhere in the United States. The common transmission standard for analog also meant that consumers could select from a wide variety of phone models, ranging from the low-cost Nokia 232 to the pricey ($800 to $1,200) but chic Motorola StarTAC 8600.[3]

Digital PCS was the new kid on the block, and offered some important advantages over analog. Digital PCS can be marketed at lower prices vis-à-vis analog because digital technology allows providers to expand capacity to handle calls much more easily than is the case for analog service. Also, because digital service always relies on a computer-mediated stream of ones and zeros, digital messages can be more easily encrypted, thus eliminating many forms of "cellular fraud" that plague analog systems. Digital technology also opens the door for add-on services such as e-mail and Internet access, and the sound quality for digital is superior to that of analog. Finally, the agreement that Cincinnati Bell Inc. signed with AT&T Wireless Services in the fourth quarter of 1997 made Cincinnati Bell Wireless part of a nationwide system that would allow CBW customers to use their phones in 400 cities across the United States. Opportunity was knocking, but only if CBW could get its value proposition in front of consumers before the competition.

Local Competition. In the winter of 1998 Cincinnati Bell worked closely with its ad agency in an effort to capitalize on the competitive advantages in digital PCS. At the time, only one other PCS provider existed in the Cincinnati market, under the brand name GTE Wireless. However, GTE Wireless had not been aggressive in convincing Cincinnatians of the benefits of digital PCS, and was further hampered by a very limited calling area. More established competition came from analog cellular providers, and two of these—Ameritech Cellular and AirTouch Cellular—had strong brand

2.   Chris O'Malley, "Sorting Out Cellphones," *Popular Science*, February 1998, 55.
3.   Ibid.

INTEGRATED BRAND PROMOTION

identity in the local market. As part of the planning process, CBW and Northlich would have to resolve a fundamental dilemma created by the local competition. That is, should they concentrate the launch campaign on signing up first-time wireless phone users, or should they seek to steal customers away from entrenched analog competition? The resolution of this dilemma would come through a thorough segmentation analysis.

Market Analysis. CBW was preparing to launch its service in the face of surging demand for both digital PCS and analog cellular. Nationwide, the market for these services had more than doubled from 1995 to 1998, to over 60 million subscribers.[4] Market growth rates approaching 30 percent annually had several companies scrambling to take advantage of this opportunity (for example, Sprint would introduce its PCS service to the Cincinnati market in November 1998), so CBW executives pressed for their launch as soon as was humanly possible. The Federal Communications Commission estimates the Cincinnati marketplace to be about 1.9 million people. Given a national penetration rate of 25 percent,[5] this translates into a potential market of 475,000 wireless phone subscribers in Greater Cincinnati. Who among these should be targeted in the CBW launch? How many of these could CBW hope to sign on to its service in the first 90 days after launch? These would be pivotal questions hotly debated by Northlich and CBW personnel leading up to their May 11 blastoff.

Pinpointing the Target Segment for Launch.
Northlich and CBW would draw on various forms of market research in preparing for the spring launch. Both quantitative and qualitative research tools uncovered important consumer insights that benefited the planning process. For example, survey research established that the number one motivation for sign-up among new users was concern for safety of a family member. Hence, if the decision was to target nonusers, alleviating concerns about safety when a family member is traveling or away from home would have to be the primary appeal. Additionally, focus group research established that many consumers felt confused and overwhelmed by the growing number of wireless phone deals and options. Consumers don't like marketplace chaos, so the supplier that can make things simple would have almost instant appeal. Moreover, in a finding that had to warm the hearts of executives at Cincinnati Bell, consumers also rated corporate identity and credibility as becoming increasingly important in the decision about which wireless service to choose.

Synthesizing the various market research studies and developing a consensus between client and agency about who should be the primary launch target for the campaign was achieved, as described in Chapter 6, via an in-depth segmentation analysis. The general framework that was developed to structure this analysis is summarized by the diagram in Exhibit IBP 2.4. As reflected there, usage considerations and demographic factors were combined to isolate a number of different market segments. Guided by this framework, an analysis was pursued that ultimately produced consensus about the primary launch target. In the discussion that follows, two specific segments will be profiled to provide an appreciation for the details that must be considered in planning for a major new product launch. As we noted earlier, compelling advertising begins with descriptions and insights about one's target segment(s) that are both personal and precise.

- *Midlevel executives—profile and motivations.* One market segment carefully assessed as the launch target was midlevel executives who were current users of another wireless service. This segment was primarily college-educated males who

---

4.   Mike Boyer, "Wireless Wars," *Cincinnati Enquirer,* November 15, 1998, E1, E4.
5.   Ibid.

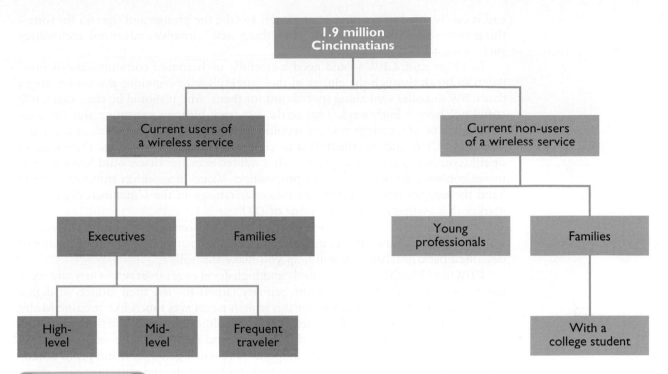

EXHIBIT IBP 2.4

The CBW/Northlich segmentation framework: Spring 1998.

embraced technology and were early adopters of many advanced technologies, including the Internet. These individuals looked at their wireless phone as a productivity-enhancing device for their work, and were receptive to any features in a wireless phone, such as e-mail, voice mail, or text messaging, that could make them more productive. Most of these executives indicated that price was a key factor that would make them switch carriers, and many also acknowledged that they probably could find a better deal if they spent the time to comparison shop. Poor customer service, erratic sound quality, and restrictive calling zones were also concerns among those in this market segment.

- *Families with a child in college—profile and motivations.* Families with one or more children in college represented an important segment of nonusers. Here, the purchaser of the service would most likely be the parent, whereas the primary user was projected to be the student. Both parents and students looked to a wireless phone as offering safety and security. Parents also wanted to be able to reach their student at a moment's notice and expressed a lack of confidence in roommates or other means of passing on important messages to their college student. However, parents expressed concerns about the phone being misused once it was out of their control; they wanted to realize the security and convenience of a wireless phone while controlling costs. Parents as primary purchasers did not represent early adopters of new technologies and thus were especially intimidated by various options regarding contracts, pricing, coverage zones, and add-on features. They just wanted an easy and safe way to get direct access to their son or daughter at college. Hence, for this market segment, a familiar brand name that parents already trusted would be a great asset in winning their new business.

The two market segments profiled here reflect the dilemma faced by CBW and Northlich as they approached the launch date in May 1998. Should they attempt to steal savvy customers from established competitors such as Ameritech Cellular and AirTouch Cellular, or appeal to the novice customer who had previously never used wireless? This is a tough choice because it can be hard to get savvy customers to switch when they already have a product or service that is filling their requirements, and it can be hard to get novice customers to take the plunge and sign on for something new, especially when that "something new" involves advanced technology such as digital PCS.

In either case, CBW would need a carefully orchestrated communications campaign to break through the clutter of the marketplace to convince the launch target that CBW did offer something special, just for them. And it should be clear that CBW could not have it both ways. That is, the fast-track business executive and the concerned parent of a college student would require very different appeals and persuasion tools. CBW and Northlich had to choose one target segment for their launch, or risk coming to the marketplace with a diluted message that would leave all segments confused about CBW's value proposition. Value-proposition ambiguity would hand the opportunity of taking first-mover advantage in the Cincinnati digital PCS market to a competitor such as Sprint or GTE.

So which would you choose—current users or nonusers? Before you read on, stop and give this some thought. Reflecting on the example of Mobil Oil that was described back in Chapter 6 will help you make this call.

CBW and Northlich selected mid- and high-level executives who currently were using another wireless service as the primary targets for the their launch of digital PCS in Cincinnati. The rationale for this launch target was much like the one Mobil Oil used in targeting Road Warriors. Recall that although Road Warriors were outnumbered by Price Shoppers, Road Warriors spend more at the gas station, making them the larger segment from the standpoint of revenue generation and profit potential. Likewise for MOPEs (managers, owners, professionals, and entrepreneurs) when it comes to use of a wireless phone: They make much heavier use of the wireless service in terms of minutes called per month, versus household users. And the way Cincinnati Bell makes money on a service like this is when customers are actually using the phone. Having a phone at home in the kitchen drawer that no one ever uses unless there is an emergency was not the usage scenario that excited CBW management. Hence, MOPEs became the launch target.

Launch Strategy and the CBW Value Proposition.
The launch strategy was set: MOPEs using another wireless service would be targeted for conversion to digital PCS from Cincinnati Bell. The value proposition to be advanced through a diversified advertising and IBP campaign would feature the functional benefits of this new service. Various media and methods would be deployed to communicate a compelling value proposition around these benefit claims:

- **Simple pricing, better value.** No contracts to sign; subscribers choose a simple pricing plan, such as 500 minutes for $49 per month or 1,600 minutes for $99 per month.
- **Member of the AT&T Wireless Network.** As a member of AT&T's nationwide network, CBW offered customers complete wireless access in over 400 cities at one "hometown rate."
- **Worry-free security.** Business transactions that may be compromised over analog cellular are secure over digital PCS.
- **The coolest phone on the planet.** CBW launched its service with the feature-laden Nokia 6160 wireless phone. It was the kind of phone that you wanted to be seen with in 1998. (Of course, by your standards today, the 6160 looks like an antique.)

Cincinnati Bell had several important benefit claims to make for its service in comparison to the analog cellular competition. In addition, it had a tremendous advantage from the standpoint of the combined brand equities of its strategic partners, which surely contributed to the credibility of all its claims. Specifically, its claim of a nationwide network was instantly validated by its association with AT&T, and the

EXHIBIT IBP 2.5

Another asset in the CBW launch: The Nokia 6100 series digital phone.

Another Nokia discovery:

Dead batteries are inconvenient.

That's why we make the Nokia 6100 Series digital phones with long battery life. Up to eight hours of talk time and 14 days of standby time. So whether you're talking with a client or playing one of the phone's built-in games, you'll have plenty of time. Once again, we got a jump on the competition.

NOKIA
CONNECTING PEOPLE

quality of its phone gear per se was supported by brand-building ads (see Exhibit IBP 2.5) and high-visibility event sponsorship (for example, the Nokia Sugar Bowl) that made Nokia one of the best-known portable phone brands at the time of launch. In combination, the Cincinnati Bell, AT&T, and Nokia brand names were an imposing triad that would establish instant credibility for Cincinnati Bell Wireless.

Objectives and Budget. With all this opportunity staring them in the face, the Northlich team was clearly challenged to produce dramatic results with the launch of CBW. Jack Cassidy, CBW's president at the time, stated the initial objective for launch simply and forcefully: "Get me activations!" Although activating a customer does not necessarily create a satisfied or profitable customer, everything starts with an activation. And while the distinction between communication and sales objectives discussed in Chapter 8 was not lost on Cassidy, he clearly was just interested in the sale. Since it is the client that pays the bills, it is the client's prerogative to determine a campaign's objectives. Northlich's work would be judged initially on the basis of the number of new customers who signed on for CBW's service. Cassidy and his associates at Cincinnati Bell specified as their goal 16,868 new CBW customers for the calendar year 1998. Given the estimate of 475,000 potential wireless customers in the Greater Cincinnati market, Cassidy was looking for an immediate market penetration in excess of 3.5 percent.

The initial thinking was that the first eight months of advertising for CBW would be supported by a $3 million budget. Starting in May 1998, all marketing communications would be directed at the Greater Cincinnati market, but about 90 days after launch the market space would be expanded to include the Dayton, Ohio, market, which would increase the scope of the overall market from 1.9 to 3.2 million people. This $3 million budget for May through December may not seem all that impressive on first glance, but if we project it to a year-long nationwide campaign we can immediately grasp the level of importance Cincinnati Bell was placing on this launch. If such a campaign were to be executed for 12 months in the top 50 metro markets across the United States, the $3 million budget would translate into a $225 million program. Per Chapter 8, this would be a commitment on par with that made by Steve Jobs in launching his new iMac in the second half of 1998. Clearly, the folks at Cincinnati Bell were committed to making a "big-time" investment in their launch of CBW, and they were expecting "big-time" results. These expectations would create many sleepless nights for the Northlich personnel working on CBW.

The Mix of Persuasion Tools. While the folks at Northlich knew that their work would be evaluated initially on the basis of Cassidy's "Get me activations!," they first conceived their challenge in terms of more fundamental communication objectives. To get new customers, the campaign would first have to create brand awareness, then generate interest in the brand, and finally bring people into retail outlets where they could buy their Nokia 6160 phone (at a special introductory price of $99) and activate their service. In Part 4 of this case history, substantial details will be provided about the various elements of the campaign that were deployed to launch CBW. For example, television, radio, and outdoor ads were created to build brand awareness for CBW; print ads were used to provide information about specific features; event sponsorships were placed to create excitement and visibility for the new service; and a sophisticated direct marketing effort was launched in conjunction with sales promotion to motivate MOPEs to visit retail stores and close the deal. Indeed, nearly all the persuasion tools discussed in Chapters 14 through 20 were considered as part of this comprehensive campaign. But would they really produce the kind of results that the client was looking for? Stay tuned. . . .

IBP EXERCISES

1. Refer to Exhibit IBP 2.1, Thorson and Moore's planning triangle. Whom did Cincinnati Bell Wireless (CBW) identify as the primary market segments for its new wireless phone service? How did it profile each market segment? What was the value proposition CBW planned to communicate to its targeted market?

2. One of the ways Northlich and CBW gather data is through focus group research. Develop a list of 10 questions you would use in a focus group of potential wireless phone users to identify their preferences and values related to wireless phone use. If you are a wireless phone user, think back to the reasons why you decided to subscribe. Recalling your own reasons for subscribing will assist you in drafting your questions.

3. In Chapter 5, we learned that products and services should provide benefits that fulfill consumers' needs. List three functional and three emotional benefits a consumer might derive from subscribing to a wireless phone service.

4. What kinds of associations come to your mind when you think of the brand names Nokia and AT&T? In what ways did Cincinnati Bell hope to capitalize on the brand equity of its partners as part of the launch of CBW?

Kimberly Kohus
Retail Coordinator,
Jones Apparel Group

Jones Apparel Group, Inc. provides attractive fashions that suit a variety of lifestyle needs for women. As a leading designer of clothing, footwear, and accessories, the New York-based manufacturer dresses style-conscious customers in its esteemed apparel lines such as Jones New York, Nine West, Anne Klein, and Evan-Picone. The company also markets famous licensed brands like Polo Jeans, Givenchy, and ESPRIT. Jones draws upon the cache of iconic models like Brooke Shields and Claudia Schiffer to promote its distinguished apparel and accessories, and the firm's advertising campaigns integrate brand images and messages throughout various media, including careful coordination with the retail environment.

Since retail operations are vital to the business of Jones Apparel Group, advertising strategies must be coordinated all the way to the retail level for campaigns to be effective. Kimberly Kohus, a retail coordinator at Jones, is responsible for making sure that the company's national brand campaigns are fully integrated within the retail environment. "The main responsibility of my job is to ensure that our brands are appropriately represented in department stores," says Ms. Kohus. The Jones coordinator makes certain that in-store graphics and visuals are up to date, and that prime real estate is secured within department stores to prominently display brands. Coordinating local retail environments with the schematic created by national campaign planners means seeing to it that print ads, in-store fashion shows, gift-with-purchase programs, and other promotions work together to make a personal impact upon consumers in the local setting.

Ms. Kohus has long admired clothing designers and been intrigued by the creative ways brands could be represented in the department stores. "I've always been fascinated with fashion, advertising, and marketing," says Kohus. After three years of working in merchandising and apparel for Polo Ralph Lauren at the store level, she interviewed for a position with the Polo Jeans division of Ralph Lauren and was hired as a regional retail coordinator. Jones Apparel Group later purchased the license for that brand, and she has worked for Jones ever since.

Being a retail coordinator has its perks, and the position keeps Ms. Kohus right on the pulse of the latest trends and activities in the fashion-design industry. "I am doing something that I love," remarks Kohus. "I get to see all of the newest trends and products before they hit the stores." As coordinator, Kohus gets to meet many high-profile models that are the face of Jones brands. "Through special events and trips to New York . . . I have met several models and celebrities," says Kohus. "It is very exciting to see them in person." Spying out the latest trends and meeting famous designers are among Kohus's favorite perks, but she points out that wearing the newest fashions is a nice bonus as well. "The annual clothing allowance allows us to wear the most current product from our company to help promote brands," states Kohus.

When asked what advice she might offer to students looking for a career in her field, Ms. Kohus reflects on how her in-store experience was crucial toward her success: "Learning every aspect of the business is important. My past experience with in-store selling helps me understand what customers are looking for and what attracts them to certain brands." Ms. Kohus adds, "Relationships and networking are also very important—others can help you be a success in your job."

Preparing the Message

Part Three, "Preparing the Message," marks an important passage in our study of advertising. The topics to this point have raised the essential process and planning issues that make advertising what it is as a business communication tool. Now we need to take the plunge into the actual *preparation* of advertising.

Creativity is the soul of advertising. Without the creative function, there is no advertising. It's the one thing advertising could not get by without. Yet most advertising books treat it as either a bunch of creative "rules" or dry lectures about the value of various fonts. We take a different approach. We first consider the idea of creativity itself: what is it, what distinguishes it, what is its beauty, when is it a beast? What makes creative people creative? We then quickly present the organizational and managerial/creative interface. We discuss honestly what many textbooks don't mention at all: the problem of the competing reward systems of brand managers, account executives, and creatives. We then offer a chapter like no other: message strategy, where we detail nine time-honored message strategies and their strategic pluses and minuses. We then offer the best basic chapters on copywriting and art direction available. These chapters have been developed and refined with constant input from industry professionals. If you read them carefully, you will know a lot about art direction and copywriting.

Creativity, Advertising, and the Brand A famous dancer once said, "If I could describe dancing, I wouldn't have to do it." Well, we feel the same way about creativity in advertising—it really is impossible to describe fully. But in Chapter 10, "Creativity, Advertising, and the Brand," we do our best to give you insights into the creative process by giving examples of how the creative process is worked out in an advertising context—how the "creatives" work with the "strategists." But we also try to provide insight into this wonderfully slippery thing called creativity. We do it by drawing on many sources and the examples of some of the most creative minds of the past century, from physics to painting. While creativity is creativity, we move from the general to discussing the particular context of advertising creativity and its unique opportunities and problems. Creativity is the soul of advertising, and this chapter tries to reveal the magic of advertising.

10

Message Strategy Chapter 11, "Message Strategy," is a chapter like no other anywhere. We take nine key and primary message objectives and their matching strategies and explore them. We give you lots of specific real-world examples and walk you through each one. We discuss their advantages and disadvantages and tell you when they should be used and when they should not.

11

Copywriting Chapter 12, "Copywriting," explores the development of copy from the creative plan through dealing with the constraints and opportunities of the medium that will carry the message. This chapter also highlights guidelines for writing effective copy and common mistakes in copywriting. A full discussion of radio and television advertising formats, which provide the context for copy development, is provided. Writing for the web is covered. At the end of this chapter is a discussion of a typical copy approval process used by advertisers and agencies. This chapter received enormous input from real live advertising professionals with years of copywriting experience in real advertising agencies. It's a very experience-driven chapter.

12

Art Direction and Production In Chapter 13, "Art Direction and Production," you will first learn about creating effective print advertisements destined for magazines, newspapers, and direct-marketing promotions. The nature of the illustration, design, and layout components of print advertising are considered. Then the exciting and complex process of creating broadcast advertising is discussed. This part of the chapter describes the people and techniques involved in creating television and radio ads. The emphasis in this chapter is on the creative team and how creative concepts are brought to life. The chapter follows a preproduction, production, and postproduction sequence. Also highlighted in this chapter are the large numbers of people outside the agency who facilitate the production effort. Again, this chapter was overseen by advertising professionals who have worked in art direction for years. This is experience talking.

13

CHAPTER 10

After reading and thinking about this chapter, you will be able to do the following:

1

Describe the core characteristics of great creative minds.

2

Contrast the role of an advertising agency's creative department with that of its business managers/account executives and explain the tensions between them.

Maybe traffic jams happen because cars like to be with other cars.

EXHIBIT 10.1

Nissan's "Mr. K" campaign pitted the poets against the killers (http://www.nissan driven.com). Compare Nissan's Web site to those of Mitsubishi (http://www .mitsubishi.com) and Honda (http://www.honda.com). Do these sites give off any signs of the behind-the-scenes creative battles that rage between the poets and the killers? Are these advertisers integrating their Internet initiatives with their most current ad campaigns?

This is the kind of conference room that can be very scary. When you enter the room, the lights come on like magic. But they don't burst on in a blaze. They come up very, very slowly. A spooky kind of slowly. When the lights are full, the room is perfectly lit—no shadows, no glare. Then there are the floor-to-ceiling windows—tall enough so that Shaq would need a ladder to clean them. What's more, this corner conference room on the 50th floor gives you a 120-degree view of Manhattan (or L.A., or Dallas, or Chicago, or Seattle). All very intimidating.

But not as intimidating as the meetings that go on here. You see, this is sort of a modern-day Colosseum. It's not supposed to be that way in this era of "relationships" and "partnering." But like the lions and the Christians, this is where the poets meet the killers.[1] There is no real bloodshed, but there are battered egos and bloodied relationships.

The poets are the creatives from the ad agency—the art directors, copywriters, graphic artists, and account planners who are dedicated to making advertising exciting, aesthetic, compelling, and edgy. The poets are dedicated to conceiving advertising that makes clients nervous enough to rise out of their seats, pace the floor, and jingle the change in their pockets.[2]

The killers are the clients—or, more specifically, the marketing and strategy-trained managers from the client who wield the anything-but-aesthetic bottom-line sword against the poets' creative prowess. It's not that the killers don't like the poets. It's not that they don't like advertising. It is that they like sales and want the poets to talk about sales. But the poets have a higher calling. Neither side means to wage a bloody battle, and the meetings never start with either side intending it to be that way. But these are tense times: new media, more old media, monster databases, astute audiences, shareholders clamoring for higher earnings per share.

No ad campaign in recent history has locked the poets against the killers in mortal battle like Nissan's "Mr. K" campaign (see Exhibit 10.1). Mr. K was the kindly guy who used to show up at the end of Nissan ads. The creative community loved the campaign, but the Nissan dealers were sitting on unmoved inventory. The result was the resignation of Nissan USA president Bob Thomas. The battle lines drawn around this campaign were so severe that ad agency types didn't even want to talk about it. One creative director said that talking about the Mr. K campaign with his clients "was kind of like the McCarthy hearings. You know, 'Are you now, or have you ever been, an admirer of Nissan's advertising.'"[3] The latest casualties of unmoved inventory were "Ads by Dick." These were the offbeat Miller Lite ads, like the one featured in Exhibit 10.2, that featured rampaging beavers and furry animals living in armpits. The light-beer category grew 2.7 percent in 1998, while Miller Lite's volume grew only 2.4 percent—oops.[4]

1.   Anthony Vagnoni, "Creative Differences," *Advertising Age,* November 17, 1997, 1, 28, 30.
2.   This description of clients' nervous reactions is credited to Mike Dunn, founder and principal of Dunn Communications, Salt Lake City, Utah.
3.   Vagnoni, "Creative Differences," 28–30.
4.   Sally Beatty, "Remember Dick? He Was Miller's Attempt to Woo Cool Drinkers," *Wall Street Journal,* May 4, 1999, 1.

("Naked/Texas" :60 Radio)

(SFX: MILLER TIME MUSIC)
ANNCR.: Not long ago we asked Dick, the Creative Superstar behind Miller Lite advertising, to come up with a Miller Time radio concept just for beer-loving Texans. Dick said, "OK." Dick said he liked radio ads because you could get away with more naughty stuff than in TV. We weren't sure what Dick meant by this, so we asked him to explain. Dick said, for example, that you can't show naked people in TV commercials. But by merely saying the words "naked people" in a radio commercial, you force listeners to picture naked people in their minds. Here is what Dick wants you to picture in your mind while listening to his commercial. Naked people. Naked people in Texas. Naked Texans going to the refrigerator and getting a Miller Lite. Wearing nothing . . . except cowboy boots . . . with spurs, drinking Miller Lite. Naked. This has been a very naughty Miller Time presentation for Texas by Dick. Thank you for your time.
SINGERS: Miller Time.
ANNCR.: Miller Brewing Company, Fort Worth, Texas.

Fallon McElligott (Minneapolis, MN), ad agency
Miller Lite, client

Still not convinced that battles such as these are being fought every day through the halls of agencies and businesses? How about the great Chihuahua war? Surely you remember the campaign (see Exhibit 10.3). Client Taco Bell and agency TBWA/Chiat/Day were trying to position Taco Bell as a cool place for teenagers and twentysomethings to eat. The themeline of the campaign, "Yo quiero Taco Bell" ("I want Taco Bell"), was on its way to becoming a national catchphrase.

We'll let the press coverage of the campaign tell the rest of the story. The head-line on March 29, 1999 "Taco Bell Chihuahua is an advertising triumph."[5] A quote

5.   Greg Johnson, "Taco Bell Chihuahua Is an Advertising Triumph," *Lexington* [Kentucky] *Herald-Leader,* March 22, 1999, http://www.Kentuckyconnect.com, accessed June 16, 2001.

from the client? "If we keep it exciting, (the Chihuahua) can last forever."[6] And from the agency? "We never set out to create an icon for the company, but that's what it became."[7] Sales rose 3 percent over the year, and during the time period when Chihuahua plush toys were sold at franchises, sales were up 9 percent. Over time, 20 million of the fuzzy things were sold. Clearly, just about everyone was "yo quiero-ing" the little dog.

But then sales slowed. After rising 4 percent in the first quarter of 1999, they shrank to 1 percent growth in the second.[8] The killers began nipping at the Chihuahua's heels. A new headline announced a bit of a change in the role of the advertising icon. It read, "Top Dog No More."[9] Taco Bell indicated that the focus in its ads was shifting from the dog to the food. A spokesperson stated, "We'll use the dog in a different sense to draw attention to the food."[10] There was no reaction from the agency to the change in the article. Nine months later, the killers finished off the dog. Headline? "Taco Bell replaces top executive and Chihuahua, too."[11] It seems that the Chihuahua that "can last forever" couldn't. The president of Taco Bell was replaced. The agency was canned. According to the head of the agency, Taco Bell had clearly made an error. "People liked the dog," he said. "It's that simple."[12]

But the debate doesn't center on offbeat, unusual ads. The debate is much more central to the entire advertising process. It centers on the creative role of advertising. One side says you must sell with advertising, and selling means giving consumers facts they can use to make decisions. The other side says you have to build an emotional bond[13] between consumers and brands, and that process requires communicating much more than product attributes. Bob Kuperman, former president and CEO of TBWA/Chiat/Day North America, puts it quite simply: "Before you can be believed, you have to be liked."[14] The killers who favor selling—and believe that there are plenty of killer/rationalists on the agency side as well as the client side—point to the historic failures of emotional advertising: any Alka-Seltzer campaign, Joe Isuzu, Mr. K, and Ads by Dick. They say that such campaigns are creatively self-indulgent and grossly inefficient. Fortunately, the poets and killers are not always working at cross purposes.

While the killers call creative advertising inefficient, the poets are starting to lose their patience. In a speech to the European Association of Advertising Agencies, CEO of Saatchi & Saatchi Worldwide Kevin Roberts said, "[I]t seems like it's open season on attacking agencies nowadays, everyone's jumping on the bandwagon. Clients, management consultants, Silicon Valley hot shot technic nerds and even Rance Crain of *Ad Age*. Enough's enough! In the words of my New Zealand compatriot, Xena, Warrior Princess: 'Stop staring at me before I take your eyes out.'"[15]

These scenarios are not unusual. There has been a tension between poets and killers for as long as there have been poets and killers. In the world of advertising and promotion, it happens all the time, even filtering into Web advertising, as evidenced in the Creativity box. The reasons are at once simple (often conflicting

6.   Ibid.
7.   Ibid.
8.   Associated Press, "Top Dog No More: Taco Bell Pushes Chihuahua to Side in New Campaign," ABC News Internet Ventures, October 11, 1999, http://www.abcnews.com, accessed June 16, 2001.
9.   Ibid.
10. Ibid.
11. Associated Press, "Taco Bell Replaces Top Executive and Chihuahua, Too," July 19, 2000, http://www.cnn.com, accessed June 16, 2001.
12. Ibid.
13. Marc Gobe, Emotional Branding: The New Paradigm for Connecting Brands to People (New York: Allworth, 2001).
14. Vagnoni, "Creating Differences," 1.
15. Kevin Roberts, "Making Magic" (keynote address to the European Advertising Agencies Association Conference, Budapest, Hungary, October 16, 1998), available at http://www.saatchikevin.com/talkingit/magic.html.

target.com

reward systems), and complex (the nature of creative professionals and those not so designated).

Creating Brands. Brands are all about creativity (see Exhibit 10.4). They always have been. Marketers use advertising and promotion to invent and reinvent brands all the time. Remember, advertising and promotion professionals are in the brand-meaning creation and management business. The people who actually create the ads and shape the brand image can have a huge input into what the brand comes to mean. Making ads and promotions is one of the most important functions in the creation, growth, and survival of brands.

Advertisers try to get consumers to see the brand their way. But of course there are always those pesky consumers. They want to have a say in it too. A brand is not just some object; it is an incredibly complicated social creation. Advertisers and consumers themselves struggle with each other to make a brand mean what it means. Think about Mountain Dew: Was it just the advertising that made it the official Gen-X soft drink, or Birkenstock the official counter-culture brand, or Tommy Hilfiger the official hip-hop brand? No, it was consumers, maybe more than advertisers. A lot of what Apple Macintosh, Coke, Skechers, Nike, Prada, Palm, Pepsi, Guinness, and on and on, are, is derived through a process of social meaning creation. Advertisers get a say, consumers get a say, then advertisers get another say, then consumers respond, on and on. So a brand has to have a creative force behind it, or it is dead or lost at sea, the sea of thousands of ads a day, every day, trying to create meaning in a brand that will resonate with the consumer long enough to be purchased and repurchased. And all the while, the competition doesn't sleep. So, of course, creativity matters.

Creativity in General. To understand how the creative function plays out in the advertising and promotion world, it might be best to take a brief look at creativity in general.

Any book on advertising, promotion, and branding really needs some attention paid to creativity, the thing that most people think about when they think about advertising. And, in reality, it is the thing that makes the promotion and advertising world go round. Without it, there is really no promotion or advertising. There is no branding. Creativity is advertising's soul . . . it is branding's soul. Yet most textbooks say relatively little about it. They give you some technical information on typefaces, T-squares, and film production, but they tell you little about creativity itself. We will tell you more.

We will first discuss creativity in general, then creativity in the advertising and promotion world, and then the creative-management interface/friction zone. It's an entertaining story, but it doesn't always support the myth of orderly business. It's way too messy, way too human; avert your eyes if the sight of disorder makes you squeamish. But it is the way it is in that messy REAL WORLD out there.

CREATIVITY

Online Advertising: Creativity Takes a Back Seat

While the promise of interactive advertising may still spark hopes for tech-minded creatives, the current reality of Web advertising is downright gloomy. Most people accept that advertising is necessary to support the content that they want, but the onslaught of online casino ads, X10 pop-ups, and other downscale advertising is quickly wearing out Net-advertising's welcome. Advertisers realize that they must do more than merely support valuable content—they have to provide value itself. Since Web ads are integrated into the Net's user experience, online ads need to do more than just get in the way.

Yet at this stage of the Web's development, creativity has suffered at the hands of account managers and impatient clients. While "poet" creatives may desire to make online advertising better, there are signs that "killer" brand managers are winning the day. The emphasis on the Internet's enhanced measurement capabilities has forced advertisers into a cutthroat competition over click-through and direct-response results. One prominent interactive service finds itself mired in the thick of the issue. E-commerce firm Gator.com is suing the Interactive Internet Advertising Bureau for asserting that its practices violate contract interests of Web publishers and advertisers. Gator is a plug-in application that makes browsing and online shopping more customizable for the end user. However, the technology also allows advertisers to advertise directly over a competing company's advertisement with banners, pop-ups, and other creative formats, effectively blocking the publisher's intended ad from being seen. Such advertising tricks and gizmos have devalued Web media and offended the sensibilities of users.

How are consumers responding to the Vegas-styled clutter of Web advertising? Boycott. Services that enable Web users to filter all unwanted advertising are gaining popularity. One service, Guidescope, uses patent-pending technology to filter advertisements and other unwanted graphics from Web pages; it even limits the ability of Web companies to track one's surfing. Another service, AdSubtract, lets you "subtract ads" by blocking pop-ups, cookies, daughter windows, and animation. Siemens AG's WebWasher service is designed to fight excessive advertising and claims more than a thousand corporate customers.

Whatever the future holds for online advertising, one thing is clear: As long as clients are mesmerized by the measurement and tracking capabilities of the Web, creativity will continue to take a back seat to crass marketing strategies inspired by the bottom line.

Sources: Kevin Featherly, "Gator Chomps First, Sues Interactive Advertising Bureau," *Newsbytes*, http://www.newsbytes.com, accessed August 28, 2001; Jeffrey Graham, "Why Online Advertising Has to Get Better," *ClickZ*, http://www.clickz.com, accessed October 17, 2001.

Creativity across Domains.

The creative mind plays with the objects it loves.

—C. G. Jung[16]

Creativity, in its essence, is the same no matter what the domain. People who create, create, whether they write novels, take photographs, ponder the particle physics that drives the universe, craft poetry, write songs, play a musical instrument, dance, make films, design buildings, paint, or make ads. Great ads can be truly great creative accomplishments.

Creativity is generally seen as a gift, a special way of seeing the world. It is. Throughout the ages, creative people have been seen as special, revered and reviled, loved and hated. They have served as powerful political instruments (for good and evil), and they have been ostracized, imprisoned, and killed for their art. For example, creativity has been associated with various forms of madness:

Madness, provided it comes as the gift of heaven, is the channel by which we receive the greatest blessings. . . . [T]he men of old who gave their names saw no disgrace or reproach in madness; otherwise they would not have connected it with the name of the noblest of all arts, the art of discerning the future, and called by our ancestors, madness is a nobler thing than sober sense. . . . [M]adness comes from God, whereas sober sense is merely human.

—Socrates[17]

Creativity reflects early childhood experiences, social circumstances, and mental styles. In one of the best books ever written on creativity, *Creating Minds,* Howard Gardner examines the lives and works of seven of the greatest creative minds of the 20th century: Sigmund Freud, Albert Einstein, Pablo Picasso (see Exhibit 10.5), Igor Stravinsky, T. S. Eliot, Martha Graham, and Mahatma

16.   Carl G. Jung, cited in Astrid Fitzgerald, An Artist's Book of Inspiration: A Collection of Thoughts on Art, Artists, and Creativity (New York: Lindisfarne, 1996), 58.
17.   Socrates, cited in Plato, *Phaedrus and the Seventh and Eighth Letters,* Walter Hamilton, trans. (Middlesex, England: Penguin, 1970), 46–47, cited in Kay Redfield Jamison, *Touched with Fire: Manic-Depressive Illness and the Artistic Temperament* (New York: Free Press, 1993), 51.

e-SIGHTINGS

EXHIBIT 10.5

*Pablo Picasso, seen here in a self-portrait, was one of the greatest creative minds of the 20th century. Read about the life of Pablo Picasso at Artcyclopedia (*http://www.artcyclopedia.com*), or visit the official Pablo Picasso Web site (*http://www.picasso.fr*).*

Gandhi.[18] His work reveals fascinating similarities among great creators. All seven of these individuals, from physicist to modern dancer, were

self confident, alert, unconventional, hardworking, and committed obsessively to their work. Social life or hobbies are almost immaterial, representing at most a fringe on the creators' work time.[19]

Apparently, total commitment to one's craft is the rule. While this commitment sounds positive, there is also a darker reflection:

[T]he self confidence merges with egotism, egocentrism, and narcissism: highly absorbed, not only wholly involved in his or her own projects, but likely to pursue them at costs of other individuals.[20]

Let's be clear: One should not stand between a great creator and his or her work. It's not safe; you'll have tracks down your back. Or maybe the creator will just ignore you to death. Not coincidentally, these great creative minds had troubled personal lives and simply did not have time for the more ordinary people (such as their families). According to Gardner, they were generally not very good to those around them. This was true even of Gandhi.[21]

All seven of these great creatives were also great self-promoters.[22] Widely recognized creative people are not typically shy about getting exposure for their work. Apparently, fame in the creative realm rarely comes to the self-effacing and timid.

All seven of these great creators were, very significantly, childlike in a critical way. All of them had the ability to see things as a child does. Einstein spent much of his career revolutionizing physics by pursuing in no small way an idea he produced as a child: What would it be like to move along with a strand of pure light? Picasso commented that it ultimately was his ability to paint like a child (along with amazingly superior technical skills) that explained much of his greatness.[23] Freud's obsession with and interpretation of his childhood dreams had a significant role in what is one of his most significant works, *The Interpretation of Dreams.*[24] T. S. Eliot's poetry demonstrated imaginative abilities that typically disappear past childhood. The same is true of Martha Graham's modern dance. Even Gandhi's particular form of social action was formulated with a very simple and childlike logic at its base. These artists and creative thinkers never lost the ability to see the ordinary as extraordinary, to not have their particular form of imagination beaten out of them by the process of "growing up."

Of course, the problem with this childlike thinking is that these individuals also behaved as children throughout most of their lives. Their social behavior was egocentric and selfish. They expected those around them to be willing sacrifices at the

---

18.   Howard Gardner, *Creating Minds: An Anatomy of Creativity Seen through the Lives of Freud, Einstein, Picasso, Stravinsky, Eliot, Graham, and Gandhi* (New York: Basic Books, 1993).

19.   Gardner, *Creating Minds,* 364.

20.   Ibid.

21.   Ibid.

22.   Ibid.

23.   Ibid.

24.   Gardner, *Creating Minds,* 145; Sigmund Freud, *The Interpretation of Dreams,* in A. A. Brill, ed., *The Basic Writings of Sigmund Freud* (New York: Modern Library, 1900/1938).

altar of their gift. Gardner put it this way: "[T]he carnage around a great creator is not a pretty sight, and this destructiveness occurs whether the individual is engaged in solitary pursuit or ostensibly working for the betterment of humankind."[25] They can, however, be extraordinarily charming when it suits their ambitions. They could be monsters at home, and darlings when performing.

Apparently they actually desire marginality;[26] they love being outsiders. They revel in it. This marginality seems to have been absolutely necessary to these people, and provided them with some requisite energy.

Emotional stability did not mark these creative lives either. All but Gandhi had a major mental breakdown at some point in their lives, and Gandhi suffered from at least two periods of severe depression. Extreme creativity, just as the popular myth suggests, seems to come at some psychological price.

Can One Become Creative?

This is a very big question. The popular answer in a democratic society would be to say, "Yes, sure; you too can be Picasso." Well, it's not quite that way. It really depends on what one means by *creativity*. For starters, determining creativity is about as simple as nailing Jell-O to a wall. Is a person creative because he or she can produce a creative result? Or is a person creative because of the way he or she thinks? Further, who gets to determine what is creative and what is not? When an elephant paints holding a brush with its trunk, and the paintings sell for thousands of dollars, does it mean that the elephant is creative? Or is the next teen-throb band creative because they sell a gazillion albums? Clearly, public acceptance may not be the best measuring stick. Yet is it inconsequential? No.

Creativity in the Business World.

The difficulty of determining who is creative and who is not, or what is creative and what is not, in the artistic world is paralleled in the business world. Certainly, no matter how this trait is defined, creativity is viewed in the business world as a positive quality for employees.[27] It's been said that "creative individuals assume almost mythical status in the corporate world."[28] Everybody needs them, but no one is sure who or what they are. Furthermore, business types often expect that working with creative people will not be easy. Often, they are right.

Against Stereotype.

While we are discussing the general traits of seven extraordinary creative people, a couple of notes of caution are in order. First, it should be understood that just because you are in a "creative" job, it doesn't always follow that you are creative. Conversely, just because you are on the account side (a.k.a. "a suit") does not mean you are not creative (see Exhibit 10.6). In fact, great strategy is all about creativity.

Some people who study creativity in business believe that everybody is creative, albeit in different ways. For example, *adaptation/innovation theory* maintains that the way people think when facing creative tasks places them on a continuum between being an adaptor and being an innovator.[29] **Adaptors** tend to work within the existing paradigm, whereas innovators treat the paradigm as part of the problem. In other words, adaptors try to do things better. **Innovators** try to do things differently.[30] It can be argued that adaptors and innovators are equally creative.[31] However, between

25. Gardner, *Creating Minds*, 369.

26. Ibid.

27. Bernd H. Schmitt, *Experiential Marketing: How to Get Customers to Sense, Feel, Think, Act, and Relate to Your Company and Brands* (New York: Free Press, 1999).

28. T. A. Matherly and R. E. Goldsmith, "The Two Faces of Creativity," *Business Horizons*, 1985, 8–11.

29. M. Kirton, "Adaptors and Innovators: A Description and Measure," *Journals of Applied Psychology*, vol. 61, no. 5 (1976), 622–629.

30. M. Kirton, "Adaptors and Innovators in Organizations," *Human Relations*, vol. 33, no. 4 (1980), 213–224.

31. Ibid.; Matherly and Goldsmith, "The Two Faces of Creativity."

Artist David Ross's Swimming Suits, a view of corporate individuality and creativity that is often shared by art directors and copywriters.

and within organizations, one mode of creative problem solving may be more conducive to success than the other.[32] An example of this is presented in the Global Issues box.

This approach has a certain commonsense appeal. The CEO of an airline might reward and promote an employee who created a way to get customers through the ticket line faster using technology the airline was using in a different part of its oper ations. However, the same CEO might not respond as favorably to an employee who created a rising set of service expectations on the part of customers. The commonsense appeal has its limitations—especially if you were an employee at a bank in 1970 who figured out a way to keep customers out of the bank. You might have gotten laughed out of a job. Luckily, ten years later you could deposit your unemployment checks at the ATM around the corner.

Creativity is the ability to consider and hold together seemingly inconsistent elements and forces. This ability to step outside of everyday logic, to free oneself of thinking in terms of "the way things are" or "the way things have to be," apparently allows creative people to put things together in a way that, once we see it, makes sense, is interesting, is creative. To see love and hate as the same entity, to see "round squares," or to imagine time bending like molten steel is to have this ability. Ideas born of creativity reveal their own logic, and then we all say, "Oh, I see."

Advertising Agencies, the Creative Process, and the Product.

As an employee in an agency creative department, you will spend most of your time with your feet up on a desk working on an ad. Across the desk, also with his feet up, will be your partner—in my case, an art director. And he will want to talk about movies.

In fact, if the truth be known, you will spend fully one-fourth of your career with your feet up talking about movies.

32. Kirton, "Adaptors and Innovators in Organizations."

The ad is due in two days. The media space has been bought and paid for. The pressure's building. And your muse is sleeping off a drunk behind a dumpster somewhere. Your pen lies useless. So you talk movies.

That's when the traffic person comes by. Traffic people stay on top of a job as it moves through the agency. Which means they also stay on top of you. They'll come by to remind you of the horrid things that happen to snail-assed creative people who don't come through with the goods on time. . . .

So you try to get your pen moving. And you begin to work. And working, in this business, means staring at your partner's shoes.

That's what I've been doing from 9 to 5 for almost 20 years. Staring at the bottom of the disgusting tennis shoes on the feet of my partner, parked on the desk across from my disgusting tennis shoes. This is the sum and substance of life at an agency.

—Luke Sullivan,
copywriter and author[33]

GLOBAL ISSUES

Europe: The Birthplace of the 30-Minute Ad?

Creatives have their work cut out for them in the next five years. The emergence of interactive digital television (iDTV) as Europe's "next big thing" is sending major reverberations to the heads of global advertising agencies. A recent research study says that within the next few years, most Europeans will use televisions instead of PCs as their main points of Internet access. Researchers predict that by 2005, 50 percent of European households will use iDTV. Current iDTV services are offered on private networks operated by broadcasters such as BSkyB's SkyDigital TV, and technology giants such as Time Warner and Microsoft are set to lead the expansion of this new medium around the globe.

iDTV's interactive capabilities are changing the way advertisers think of creativity, and agency conglomerates such as Bcom3 are getting positioned to pioneer the interactive ads of the future. The group announced its strategic investment in Spring Communications, a London-headquartered agency dedicated to offering brand owners best-of-breed iDTV marketing services. Marcus Vinton, chief creative officer of Spring, said, "Interactivity at the brand level will only extend the advertising experience beyond mainstream media opportunities. The next five years are about the birth of the 30-minute ad, not the demise of the 30-second spot."

Exactly how will iDTV influence the creative capabilities of advertisers? Advertising is likely to become more varied as it becomes more targeted. Pundits generally agree that it will carry more content. There will be less focus on 30- and 60-second spots and more of everything and anything else: sponsorships, branded games, quizzes, and unusual spots—you name it. It will be less intrusive, more focused, and integrated, and will offer the viewer a lot more because it will need to attract and hold attention.

iDTV is the mainstream entertainment medium of the future; its interactive capabilities hold great promise for advertisers. Mark Iremonger of the digital advertising production firm Sleeper said, "What I can't understand is why iDTV is often sold as a direct response advertising tool. Sure, it'll be used for DR, but why focus on this when iDTV will fulfill all the advertising and marketing communication that linear TV does today?"

Sources: David Barry, "Interactive TV to Dominate European E-Commerce," *E-Commerce Times*, http://www.ecommercetimes.com, accessed March 27, 2000; Mark Iremonger, "iDTV Advertising: A Future to Look Forward To?," *Digitrends*, http://www.digitrends.com, accessed October 18, 2001; "Bcom3 Backs Future of Television through New Global Interactive Digital Venture," http://www.bcom3.com, accessed October 18, 2001.

Exhibit 10.7 is illustrative of many creative pursuits: lots of time trying to get an idea, or the right idea. You turn things over and over in your head, trying to see the light. You try to find that one way of seeing it that makes it all fall into place. Or it just comes to you, real easy, just like that. Magic. Every creative pursuit involves this sort of thing. However, advertising and promotion, like all creative pursuits, are unique in some respects. Ad people come into an office and try to solve a problem, always under time pressure, given to them by some businessperson. Often this problem is poorly defined, and there are competing agendas. They work for people who seem not to be creative at all, and doing their best not to let them be creative. They are housed in the "creative department," which makes it seem as if it's some sort of warehouse where the executives keep all the creativity so they can find it when they need it, and so it won't get away. This implies that one can pick some up, like getting extra batteries at Wal-Mart.

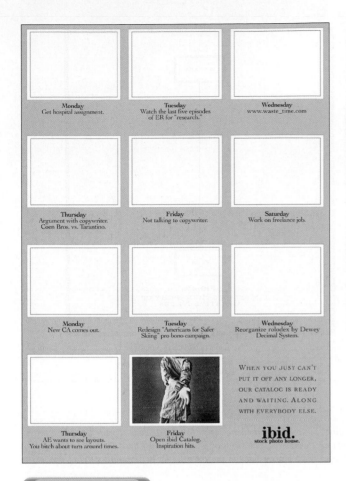

Companies like ibid (http://www.ibidphoto.com) cater to the creative: The ibid catalog offers images to jumpstart the imagination.

Oil and Water: The Essential Organizational Behavior of the Creative/Management Interface.

Here are some thoughts on management and creativity by two advertising greats:

The majority of businessmen are incapable of original thinking, because they are unable to escape from the tyranny of reason. Their imaginations are blocked.

—William Bernbach[34]

If you're not a bad boy, if you're not a big pain in the ass, then you are in some mush in this business.

—George Lois[35]

As you can see, this topic rarely yields tepid, diplomatic comments. Advertising is produced through a social process. As a social process, however, it's marked by struggles for control and power that occur within departments, between departments, and between the agency and its clients on a daily basis.

Most research concerning the contentious environment in advertising agencies places the creative department in a central position within these conflicts. We know of no research that has explored conflict within or between departments in an advertising agency that doesn't place the creative department as a focus of the conflict. One explanation hinges on reactions to the uncertain nature of the product of the creative department. What is it they do? From the outside it sometimes appears that they are having a lot of fun and just screwing around while everyone else has to wear a suit to the office and try to sell more stuff for their client. But you really can't replace them . . . you need them. This creates a great deal of tension between the creative department and the account service department. In addition, individuals in the account service department and in the creative department of an advertising agency do not always share the same ultimate goals for advertisements. Individuals in the creative department see an advertisement as a vehicle to communicate a personal creative ideology that will further their careers. (See Exhibit 10.8.) The account manager, serving as liaison between client and agency, sees the goal of the communication as achieving some predetermined objective in the marketplace.[36] Another source of conflict is attributed to differing perspectives due to differing background knowledge of the members of creative groups and the account service team. Account managers must be generalists with broad knowledge, whereas creatives (copywriters and art directors) are specialists who must possess great expertise in a single area.[37]

Regardless of its role as a participant in conflict, the creative department is recognized as an essential part of an advertising agency's success. It is the primary

34.   William Bernbach, cited in Thomas Frank, *The Conquest of Cool: Business Culture, Consumer Culture, and the Rise of Hip Consumerism* (Chicago: University of Chicago Press, 1997).

35.   George Lois, cited in Randall Rothenberg, *Where the Suckers Moon* (New York: Knopf, 1994), 135–172.

36.   Elizabeth Hirschman, "The Effect of Verbal and Pictorial Advertising Stimuli on Aesthetic, Utilitarian and Familiarity Perceptions," *Journal of Advertising,* 1985, 27–34.

37.   B. G. Vanden Berg, S. J. Smith, and J. W. Wickes, "Internal Agency Relationships: Account Service and Creative Personnel," *Journal of Advertising,* vol. 15, no. 2 (1986), 55–60.

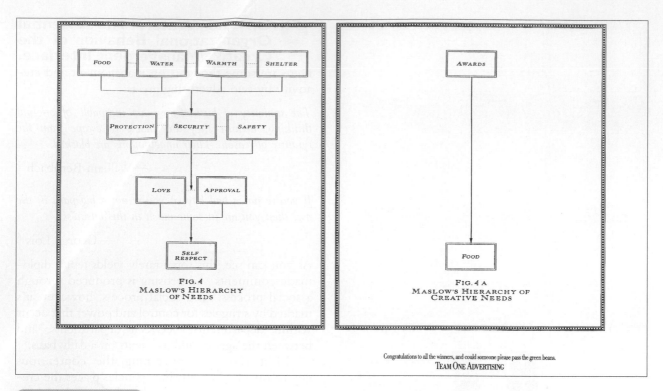

Congratulations to all the winners, and could someone please pass the green beans.
TEAM ONE ADVERTISING

EXHIBIT 10.8

Team One Advertising (http://www.teamoneadv.com) has an interesting spin on what motivates agency creatives; here, it parodies Maslow's hierarchy to make its point. Compare this print advertisement with the imagery, words, and ideas on display at Team One's Web site. Both are, in part, self-promotional and self-congratulatory. When an agency is both client and creator, how do the struggles for power and control of the creative product change?

consideration of potential clients when they select advertising agencies.[38] Creativity has been found to be crucial to a positive client/advertiser relationship. Interestingly, clients see creativity as an overall agency trait, whereas agency people place the responsibility for it firmly on the shoulders of the creative department.[39] However, there is evidence that, although clients may hold the entire agency responsible for the creative output, they may still unknowingly place the creative department in a position of primary responsibility. An interview with 20 of the largest advertising clients in the United States found that failing to produce effective advertisements was the single unforgivable shortcoming an agency could have.[40]

However, many clients don't recognize their role in killing the very same effective ideas that they claim to be looking for (see Exhibit 10.9). Anyone who has worked in the creative department of an advertising agency for any length of time has a full quiver of client stories—like the one about the client who wanted to produce a single 30-second spot for his ice cream novelty company. The creative team went to work and brought in a single spot that everyone agreed delivered the strategy perfectly, set up further possible spots in the same campaign, and, in the words of the copywriter, was just damn funny. It was the kind of commercial that you actually look forward to seeing on television. During the storyboard presentation, the client laughed in all the right places, and admitted the spot was on strategy. Then the client rejected the spot.

38.   D. West, "Restricted Creativity: Advertising Agency Work Practices in the U.S., Canada and the U.K.," *Journal of Creative Behavior,* vol. 27, no. 3 (1993), 200–213.

39.   P. C. Michell, "Accord and Discord in Agency-Client Perceptions of Creativity," *Journal of Advertising Research,* vol. 24, no. 5 (1984), 9–24.

40.   M. Kingman, "A Profile of a Bad Advertising Agency," *Advertising Age,* November 23, 1981, 53–54.

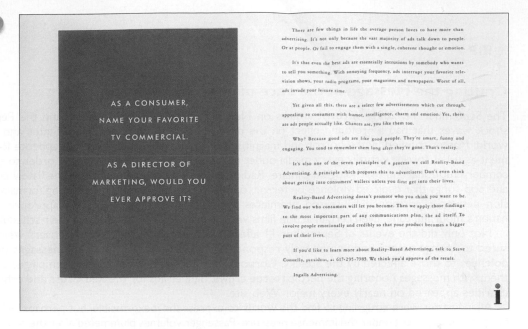

AS A CONSUMER,
NAME YOUR FAVORITE
TV COMMERCIAL.

AS A DIRECTOR OF
MARKETING, WOULD YOU
EVER APPROVE IT?

There are few things in life the average person loves to hate more than advertising. It's not only because the vast majority of ads talk down to people. Or at people. Or fail to engage them with a single, coherent thought or emotion.

It's that even the best ads are essentially intrusions by somebody who wants to sell you something. With annoying frequency, ads interrupt your favorite television shows, your radio programs, your magazines and newspapers. Worst of all, ads invade your leisure time.

Yet given all this, there are a select few advertisements which cut through, appealing to consumers with humor, intelligence, charm and emotion. Yes, there are ads people actually like. Chances are, you like them too.

Why? Because good ads are like good people. They're smart, funny and engaging. You tend to remember them long after they're gone. That's reality.

It's also one of the seven principles of a process we call Reality-Based Advertising. A principle which proposes this to advertisers: Don't even think about getting into consumers' wallets unless you first get into their lives.

Reality-Based Advertising doesn't promote who you think you want to be. We find out who consumers will let you become. Then we apply those findings to the most important part of any communications plan, the ad itself. To involve people emotionally and credibly so that your product becomes a bigger part of their lives.

If you'd like to learn more about Reality-Based Advertising, talk to Steve Connelly, president, at 617-295-7985. We think you'd approve of the result.

Ingalls Advertising.

The client said the agency was trying to force him into a corner where he had to approve the spot, since they didn't show him any alternatives. The agency went back to work. Thirty-seven alternatives were presented over the next six months. Thirty-seven alternatives were killed. Finally, the client approved a spot, the first spot from half a year earlier. There was much rejoicing. One week later, he canceled the production, saying he wanted to put the money behind a national couponing effort instead. Then he took the account executive out to lunch and asked why none of the creatives liked him.

Or the potato chip client that told an agency that the next campaign they came up with needed to be the best work they had ever done. The new product the client was introducing was crucial to the overall success of the company. The agency put every team in the house to work on it for 16 hours a day, two weeks straight. The result? The client loved the work, saying it was indeed the best work he had ever seen. In fact, instead of the single product-introduction ad he had asked for, the client approved four ads. There was a client/agency group hug. One week later, the client fired the agency, asking why they hadn't ever presented this kind of work before.

Or the newspaper client that wanted to encourage people who didn't read the newspaper to read the newspaper. Only one mandate, though. The ads had to appear in the client's newspaper since the space was free.

It's easy and sometimes fun to blame clients for all of the anxieties and frustrations of the creatives. Especially if you work in a creative department. You can criticize the clients all you want and, since they aren't in the office next to you, they can't hear you. But, despite the obvious stake that creative departments have in generating superior advertising, it should be mentioned that no creative ever put $200 million of his own money behind a campaign. Clients not only foot the bills, they also approach agencies with creative problems in the first place. Take, for instance, the challenge faced by many advertisers following the terrorist attacks of September 11, 2001, as discussed in the IBP box.

Indeed, you can't always blame the clients. Sometimes the conflicts and problems that preclude wonderful creative work occur within the walls of the advertising agency itself. To say there can be a bit of conflict between the creative department and the other departments of an advertising agency is a bit like saying there can be a bit of conflict when Jerry Springer walks into a studio. In advertising, the conflict often centers on the creative department and the account management department. It's no wonder that creatives feel as if their creative output is put under a microscope.

IBP

Crafting the Message in the Face of Tragedy

The September 11, 2001, terrorist attacks on New York's World Trade Center and the Pentagon sent shock waves that had a profound effect on the mood of audiences in the United States and around the world. Masses stunned by the horror and magnitude of the tragedy quickly lost the appetite for entertainment-as-usual, forcing virtually every media outlet to radically change programming in order to adjust to the somber emotional and psychological climate. Radio stations around the country immediately censored rap and pop songs that depicted violence or terror, opting for more patriotic and uplifting formats, and television networks postponed fall-season premieres to revise scripts that seemed inappropriate given the nation's mournful tone. Even certain action films were postponed indefinitely from their scheduled releases.

Not only did the events of September 11 affect media programming, but advertisers were also pressured to change course and immediately respond. Agency creatives crafted new messages offering condolences to those affected by the attacks. Corporations pulled ads from current campaigns and replaced them with messages honoring the heroic rescue crews. Banner ads for the Red Cross and other nonprofit charities appeared on nearly every major Web site.

All industries were struggling to find the words to express the inexpressible, but perhaps airline advertising was buckling most under the immense pressure. Passenger volumes plummeted after the terrorist attacks, with flights booked as much as 40 percent empty as jittery travelers opted to stay home or travel by car and train. United Airlines' first TV ads after the events spoke openly with viewers about the attacks, but received mixed reviews from marketing experts. United's agency, Fallon Worldwide, ran spots for the airlines titled "Family" and "Passion," hoping to instill themes of renewal, camaraderie, a passion for flying, and confidence in the company. In the ads, airline workers talked about the thrill of flying and the "freedom" to travel anywhere, anytime in the United States. "We're not gonna let anyone take that away from us," a pilot stated. "We're Americans, and this is not going to beat us down," added an airline executive. While United's employees expressed heartfelt boldness in the face of airline tragedy, many critics rebuffed the campaign as a brilliant execution of the wrong strategy. One critic from the New England Consulting Group claimed United was "reminding people of what [United] wanted them to forget." Some reviewers, however, applauded the airline for being out there at all, recognizing the futility in hiding when the impact of the attack was so massive.

Adopting an integrated brand promotion strategy was crucial for United. With the industry facing billions in losses, marketers had to attempt to strike a balance between expressions of confidence in the airlines and subtle encouragement to fly. Jerry Dow, United's director of worldwide marketing, said, "Our customers want us out there talking to them, but they don't want the hard sell just yet." In order to stimulate business, United relied heavily on print and electronic media to offer discounts for business and leisure travelers.

For creatives, wielding advertising's powers of persuasion with such delicate precision was daunting—many advertisers just stayed home. In fact, United's two largest competitors, American Airlines and Delta, sat on the sidelines, opting to let time heal wounds before encouraging consumers to fly the friendly skies once again.

Sources: Jack Feuer, "TV Watchers More Sensitive," *AdWeek,* http://www.adweek.com, accessed September 25, 2001; "United Speaks on Attacks in TV Ad," Associated Press, http://www.adweek.com, accessed October 18, 2001.

The creative department is recognized as an essential part of an advertising agency's success. What does a potential client consider to be of primary importance when choosing an advertising agency? Creativity. What is one of the crucial factors in a positive client/ agency relationship? Again, creativity.[41] So why doesn't everybody pull together and love each other within an agency?

When a client is unhappy, it fires the agency. Billings and revenue drop. Budgets are cut. And pink slips fly. It's no wonder that conflict occurs. When someone is looking out for his or her job, it's tough not to get involved in struggles over control of the creative product. Account managers function as the conduit from agency to client and back. Every day when they walk in the door, their prime responsibility is to see that the client is purring and happy. Since clients hold the final power

41. D. C. West, "Cross-National Creative Personalities, Processes, and Agency Philosophies," *Journal of Advertising Research,* vol. 33, no. 5 (1993), 53–62.

of approval over creative output, the members of the account team see an advertisement as a product they must control before the client sees it.[42] Members of the creative department resent the control. They feel as if their work is being judged by a group whose most creative input should be over what tie or scarf goes best with a pinstriped suit. Members of the account management team perceive the creatives as experts in the written word or in visual expression. However, they believe that creatives don't understand advertising strategy or business dealings.

As with most things, the truth probably lies somewhere in the murky middle. Unfortunately, except at a few fortunate agencies (see Exhibit 10.10), the chances for total recognition of each department's talents are slim. As stated earlier, the backgrounds of the people in each department are just too different, the organizational structures too much of a problem.

So how does an agency successfully address this tension? The ad in Exhibit 10.11 suggests that it can be done with the right computer software. In most instances, though, the truth may be that it can't, not even with the world's largest supercomputer. Beyond the philosophy may be a simple fact: Individuals in the account service departments and creative departments of advertising agencies do not always (even usually) share the same ultimate goals for advertisements. Sorry, but that's often the way it is.

For an account manager to rise in his or her career, he or she must excel in the care and feeding of clients. It's a job of negotiation, gentle prodding, and ambassadorship. For a creative to rise, the work must challenge. It must arrest attention. It must provoke. At times, it must shock. It must do all the things a wonderful piece

---

EXHIBIT 10.10

How to identify a good advertising executive.

For some 25 years I was an advertising agency "AE," eventually rising through the crabgrass to become a founder, president, chairman and now chairman emeritus of Borders, Perrin and Norrander, Inc.

During all those years, I pondered the eternal question: Why do some advertising agencies consistently turn out a superior creative product while others merely perpetuate mediocrity? Is the answer simply to hire great writers and art directors? Well, certainly that has a lot to do with it, but I would suggest that there is another vital component in the equation for creative success.

Outstanding creative work in an ad agency requires a ferocious commitment from all staffers, but especially from the account service person. The job title is irrelevant—account executive, account manager, account supervisor—but the job function is critical, particularly when it comes to client approvals. Yes, I am speaking of the oft-maligned AE, the "suit" who so frequently is the bane of the Creative Department.

So how in the wide world does one identify this rare species, this unusual human being who is sensitive to the creative process and defends the agency recommendations with conviction and vigor? As you might expect, it is not easy. But there are some signals, some semihypothetical tests that can be used as diagnostic tools:

To begin with, look for unflappability, a splendid trait to possess in the heat of battle. In Australia last year I heard a chap tell about arriving home to "find a bit of a problem" under his bed. An eight-foot python had slithered in and coiled around the man's small dog. Hearing its cries, he yanked the snake out from under the mattress, pried it loose from the mutt, tossed it out the door and "dispatched it with a garden hoe." Was he particularly frightened or distressed? Not at all. "I've seen bigger snakes," he said, helping himself to another Foster's Lager. Now, that's the kind of disposition which wears well in account service land.

Source: Wes Perrin, "How to Identify a Good AE," *Communication Arts Advertising Annual* 1988 (Palo Alto, Calif: Coyne and Blanchard, Inc., 1988), 210.

---

42. A. J. Kover and S. M. Goldberg, "The Games Copywriters Play: Conflict, Quasi-Control, a New Proposal," *Journal of Advertising Research,* vol. 25, no. 4 (1995), 52–62.

e-SIGHTINGS

"Our shop grows because our creative side and our business side work together. That's why we use Clients & Profits."

Successful **ad agencies** and **design studios** get that way when everyone **works together**. Over 800 of today's smartest shops do it with Clients & Profits,® the best-selling **job tracking, costing, billing** and **accounting** software for the **Macintosh**. It's designed only for creative businesses, so it works just like you do. Call **800 272-4488** today for a **free guided tour** and complete information. *Or fax (619) 945-2365.*

WORKING COMPUTER
The Triangle Building
4755 Oceanside Blvd., Suite 200
Oceanside, CA 92056
(619) 945-4334

EXHIBIT 10.11

Companies like Working Computer (http://www.clientsandprofits .com) provide tools to help manage some of the most complex machinery imaginable: the human being. Why do you think the Clients & Profits ad highlights that the software runs on the Macintosh, given that so many of the computers in the world aren't Macs?

of art must do. Yet, as we indicated earlier, this is all the stuff that makes for nervous clients. And that is an account executive's nightmare.

This nightmare situation for the account executives produces the kind of ads that win awards for the creatives. People who win awards are recognized by the award shows in the industry. Their work gets published in *The One Show* and *Communication Arts* and appears on the Clios. These people become in demand and they are wined and dined by rival agencies (see Exhibit 10.12). And they become famous and, yes, rich by advertising standards. Are they happier, better people? Some are. Some aren't. Ask one sometime. In the most honest moments, do they think about sales as much as *One Shows* and Addys? (See Exhibit 10.13.) So the trick is, how do you get creatives to want to pursue cool ads that also sell? Let them win awards even though it may have nothing to do with boosting sales, or, more simply, let them keep their job?

The difficulty of assessing the effectiveness of an advertisement has also created antagonism between the creative department and the research department.[43] Vaughn states that the tumultuous social environment between creative departments and research departments represents the "historical conflict between art and science . . . these polarities have been argued philosophically as the conflict between Idealism and Materialism or Rationalism

EXHIBIT 10.12

Foote, Cone & Belding (http://www.fcb.com) is in the hunt for creatives, using a bit of sassy, pun-in-cheekiness to signal that résumés are wanted. What challenges do you think the Foote, Cone & Belding HR department faces in hiring and retaining the best and brightest (beyond borrowing some of the company's creative time to produce clever recruitment ads)?

WE'D LIKE TO TELL ALL OF TONIGHT'S AWARD HUNGRY, SMART ASS, HOLIER-THAN-THOU ADDY WINNERS EXACTLY WHERE THEY CAN GO.

FCB   (312) 440-5101

CATHY J. WALEJESKI
CREATIVE RECRUITER

FOOTE, CONE & BELDING
FCB CENTER, 101 EAST ERIE
CHICAGO, IL 60611-2897, FAX (312) 751-3501

43.   Ibid.

Fox Trot

Research on an ad's effectiveness is an important, difficult, and unpopular task.

and Empiricism."[44] In the world of advertising, people in research departments are put in the unenviable position of judging the creatives (see Exhibits 10.14 and 10.15). So, again, "science" judges art. Creatives don't like this, particularly when it's usually pretty bad science, or not science at all. Of course, researchers are sometimes creative themselves, and they don't typically enjoy being an additional constraint on those in the creative department.

44.   R. L. Vaughn, "Point of View. Creatives versus Researchers—Must They Be Adversaries?" *Journal of Advertising Research,* vol. 22, no. 6 (1983), 45–48.

One of the advantages of being a practitioner-turned-educator is the opportunity to interact with a large number of agencies. Much like Switzerland, an academic is viewed as a neutral in current affairs and not subject to the suspicions of a potential competitor.

The result of my neutral status has been the opportunity to watch different agencies produce both great and poor work. And, as a former associate creative director, I'd like to share the trends I've seen in the development of bad creative. The revelation: Bad work is more a matter of structure than talent. Here are 12 pieces of advice if you want to institutionalize bad creative work in your agency:

1. Treat your target audience like a statistic.

Substituting numbers for getting a feel for living, breathing people is a great way to make bad work inevitable. It allows you to use your gut instinct about "women 55 to 64" rather than the instinct that evolves from really understanding a group of folks. The beauty with staying on the statistical level is that you get to claim you did your homework when the creative turns out dreadful. After all, there were 47 pages of stats on the target.

2. Make your strategy a hodgepodge.

Good ads have one dominant message, just one. Most strategies that result in lousy work have lots more than one. They are political junkyards that defy a creative wunderkind to produce anything but mediocrity. So make everybody happy with the strategy and then tell your creatives to find a way to make it all work. You'll get bad work, for sure.

3. Have no philosophy.

William Bernbach believed in a certain kind of work. His people emulated his philosophy and produced a consistent kind of advertising that built a great agency. Now, to be controversial, I'll say the exact same thing about Rosser Reeves. Both men knew what they wanted, got it, and prospered.

The agency leaders who do hard sell one day, then new wave the next, create only confusion. More important, the work does not flow from a consistent vision of advertising and a code of behavior to achieve that advertising. Instead, there is the wild embrace of the latest fashion or the currently faddish bromide making the rounds at conventions. So beware of those who have a philosophy and really are true to it. They are historically at odds with lousy work.

4. Analyze your creative as you do a research report.

The cold, analytical mind does a wonderful job destroying uncomfortable, unexpected work. Demand that every detail be present in every piece of creative and say it is a matter of thoroughness. The creative work that survives your ice storm will be timid and compromised and will make no one proud.

5. Make the creative process professional.

"Creative types collect a paycheck every two weeks. They'd better produce and do it now. This is, after all, a business." The corporate performance approach is a highly recommended way of developing drab print and TV. Treating the unashamedly artistic process of making ads as if it were an offshoot of the local oil filter assembly plant promises to destroy risk-taking and morale. Your work will become every bit as distinctive as a gray suit. More important, it will be on schedule. And both are fine qualities in business and we are a business, aren't we?

6. Say one thing and do another.

Every bad agency says all the right things about risk-taking, loving great creative, and admiring strong creative people. It is mandatory to talk a good game and then do all the things that destroy great work. This will help keep spirits low and turnover high in the creatives who are actually talented. And then you'll feel better when they leave after a few months because you really do like strong creative people—if they just weren't so damn defensive.

7. Give your client a candy store.

To prove how hard you work, insist on showing numerous half-thought-out ideas to your client. The approved campaign will have lots of problems nobody thought about and that will make the final work a mess.

Campaigns with strong ideas are rare birds, and they need a great deal of thinking to make sure they're right. So insist on numerous campaigns and guarantee yourself a series of sparrows rather than a pair of eagles.

8. Mix and match your campaigns.

Bring three campaigns to your client, and then mix them up. Take a little bit of one and stick it on another. Even better, do it internally. It's like mixing blue, red, and green. All are fine colors, but red lacks the coolness of blue. Can't we add a little? The result of the mix will be a thick muddy clump. Just like so many commercials currently on the air.

Continued

9. Fix it in production.

Now that your procedure has created a half-baked campaign that is being mixed up with another, tell the creative to make it work by excellent production values. Then you can fire the incompetent hack when the jingle with 11 sales points is dull.

10. Blame the creative for bad creative.

After all, you told them what they should do. ("Make it totally unexpected, but use the company president and the old jingle.") The fault lies in the fact that you just can't find good talent anymore. Never mind that some creative departments have low turnover and pay smaller salaries than you do.

11. Let your people imitate.

"Chiat/Day won awards and sales for the Apple *1984* commercial, so let's do something like that for our stereo store account." This approach works wonders because your imitation appears lacking the original surprise that came from a totally expected piece of work. You can even avoid the controversy that surrounded Chiat/Day when half the industry said the ad was rotten. Your imitation can blend right in with all the other imitations and, even better, will have no strategic rationale for your bizarre execution.

12. Believe posttesting when you get a good score.

That way you can be slaughtered by your client when your sensitive, different commercial gets a score 20 points below norm. The nice things you said about posttesting when you got an excellent score with your "singing mop" commercial cannot be taken back. If you want to do good work, clients must somehow be made to use research as a tool. If you want to do bad creative, go ahead, and believe that posttesting rewards excellent work.

Naturally, a lot of bad creative results from egomania, laziness, incompetence, and client intractability—but a lot less than most believe. I have found that bad work usually comes from structures that make talented people ineffective and that demand hard work, human dedication, and tremendous financial investment to produce work that can be topped by your average high school senior.

John Sweeney, a former associate creative director at Foote, Cone & Belding, Chicago, teaches advertising at the University of North Carolina–Chapel Hill.

EXHIBIT 10.16

Assuring poor creative.

Why Does Advertising Need Creativity?

Who needs creativity? Clients do. Humans do. Creativity allows the consumer to see the brand in new and desired ways. It can accomplish the increasingly elusive breakthrough. Most marketing is about establishing brand relationships—creating and maintaining brand image and position. It is the creative execution that really allows this to happen. Advertising makes brands and relationships, and creative makes advertising. It puts the brand in a social context. It makes things into brands. And, as suggested by Exhibit 10.16, "bad" creatives will surely destroy a client's brand.

With all this talk of competition, envy, madness, constraint, and frustration, we could have written a do-it-yourself marriage counseling book. But we had to tell you the truth. Too many books make it seem that if you just follow their good management flow chart, everything will be fine: peace, love, and profits. Sorry, it's not that way. Still, maybe by understanding the reasons for and the nature of the tensions, you will be able to do better. More importantly, even with all its problems, the world of advertising is, as Jerry Della Femina said, "The most fun you can have with your pants on."[45] It's one of the few places left where really creative people can go to express themselves and make a living.

And remember:

What lies behind us and what lies before us are tiny matters compared to what lies within us.

—Ralph Waldo Emerson[46]

45.   Jerry Della Femina, *From Those Wonderful Folks Who Gave You Pearl Harbor, Front-Line Dispatches from the Advertising War* (New York: Simon and Schuster, 1970), 244.

46.   Ralph Waldo Emerson, cited in The Quotations Archive, http://www.aphids.com/quotes.

SUMMARY

 1 Describe the core characteristics of great creative minds.

A look at the shared sensibilities of great creative minds provides a constructive starting point for assessing the role of creativity in the production of great advertising. What Picasso had in common with Gandhi, Freud, Eliot, Stravinsky, Graham, and Einstein—including a strikingly exuberant self-confidence, (childlike) alertness, unconventionality, and an obsessive commitment to the work—both charms and alarms us. Self-confidence, at some point, becomes crass self-promotion; an unconstrained childlike ability to see the world as forever new devolves, somewhere along the line, into childish self-indulgence. Without creativity, there can be no advertising. How we recognize and define creativity in advertising rests on our understanding of the achievements of acknowledged creative geniuses from the worlds of art, literature, music, science, and politics.

 2 Contrast the role of an advertising agency's creative department with that of its business managers/account executives and explain the tensions between them.

What it takes to get the right idea (a lot of hard work), and the ease with which a client or agency manager may dismiss that idea, underlies the contentiousness between an agency's creative staff and its managers and clients—between the poets and the killers. Creatives provoke. Managers control. Ads that win awards for creative excellence don't necessarily fulfill a client's business imperatives. All organizations deal with the competing agendas of one department versus another, but in advertising agencies, this competition plays out at an amplified level. The difficulty of assessing the effectiveness of an advertisement only adds to the antagonism between departments. Advertising researchers are put in the unenviable position of judging the creatives, pitting "science" against art. None of these tensions changes the fact that creativity is essential to the vitality of brands. Creativity makes a brand, and it is creativity that reinvents established brands in new and desired ways.

KEY TERMS

adaptors
innovators

QUESTIONS

1. Over the years, creativity has been associated with various forms of madness and mental instability. In your opinion, what is it about creative people that prompts this kind of characterization?

2. Think about a favorite artist, musician, or writer. What is unique about the way he or she represents the world? What fascinates you about the vision he or she creates?

3. A lot of credence is given in this chapter to the idea that tension (of various sorts) fuels creative pursuits. Explain the connection between creativity and tension.

4. What role should critics play in determining what is creative and what is not?

5. Which side of this debate do you have more affinity for: Are people creative because they can produce creative results, or are they creative because of the way they think? Explain.

6. Do you think everybody is creative, yet in different ways? According to the adaptation/innovation theory, what is the difference between the creativity of adaptors and that of innovators? Are both modes of creativity of equal benefit in every situation? Explain.

7. What forces inside an advertising agency can potentially compromise its creative work? Is compromise always to be avoided? Imagine that you are an agency creative. Define compromise. Now imagine that you are an account executive. How does your definition of compromise change?

8. Describe the conflict between the creative department and the research department. Do you think creatives are justified in their hesitancy to subject their work to advertising researchers? Why? Is science capable of judging art any more than art is capable of judging science? Explain.

9. Choose an ad from the book that represents exemplary creativity to you. Explain your choice.

10. Examine Exhibit 10.16. Using this exhibit as your guide, generate a list of ten principles to facilitate creativity in an advertising agency.

EXPERIENTIAL EXERCISES

1. Creativity with brands is often directly related to the names marketers choose for their products and services. Identify and research two brands that have especially creative names. For each, describe tangible ways that the brand's name influences the creativity expressed in its advertising and promotion themes and campaigns.

2. Write a one-page analysis of a creative song, video, or piece of art created by an artist or musician. In your own words, describe what makes the work uniquely creative (be sure to use chapter concepts concerning creativity and creative personalities). Finally, given the contentious conflicts between creativity and management in the advertising industry, do you think this artist or musician could have succeeded in a career in advertising? Explain.

3. This chapter discussed the natural friction that occurs within the organizational structure of the advertising industry, highlighting conflicts that arise between creatives and management. Typically, creatives are experts in the written word and visual expression, but they often don't understand business strategy. Account managers, on the other hand, are trained in business strategy and client relations, but they lack an understanding of the creative process. Reread the section of this chapter concerning the tensions and challenges that occur in the industry between the creative and account management departments. Contact an employee at an advertising agency, the advertising department at your school, or any advertising professional that you know and schedule a brief phone interview concerning this issue. Ask this person for his or her professional opinion regarding organizational challenges that exist in balancing the creative and business goals of advertising, and ask for specific examples that affect the overall effectiveness of the agency.

EXPERIENCING THE INTERNET

10-1   Eureka!

The Eureka Institute is a think tank of strategic inventors whose mission includes inspiring breakthrough ideas in the workplace and enabling people to develop them into successful products and campaigns. Eureka! Ranch is the magical place where executives from organizations such as Nike, Walt Disney, Procter & Gamble, and other megacorporations convene for creativity training seminars focused on "capitalist creativity," the art and science of inspiring and articulating ideas that make money. Founded by famously barefooted master inventor Doug Hall, Eureka! Inventing continues to revolutionize the creative development and marketing of brands, including quantitative metrics to calculate their chances of success.

Eureka! Inventing: http://www.eurekaranch.com

1. Visit Eureka! Inventing online and briefly describe the mission, activities, and aims of this think tank.

2. What assumptions about the nature of creativity make a resort like the Eureka! successful or even possible?

3. Describe one of the Eureka! Inventing patented services such as Merwyn, and explain how it relates to enhancing creativity.

10-2   Creativity across Domains

Thousands of sites on the Web are devoted to developing creativity in business, arts, education, and entertainment. The Innovation Network, a creative online thinkspace based firmly upon the motivational philosophies of Maslow and other humanistic psychologists, is dedicated to rethinking conditions around the workplace to produce more innovative creative environments for business success. Browse the following creativity site and answer the questions.

Innovation Network: http://www.thinksmart.com

1. What is the purpose of this site? Comment on the creativity displayed on this site in terms of design and artistic appeal.

2. Do you think creativity is a personality trait that resides naturally in some people but not in others, or can anyone develop creativity? Explain your answer.

3. Name and describe two or three of the site's interactive tools and functions that are designed to give your creativity a workout online. What uses might these resources have for developing creativity in advertising and promotion?

CHAPTER 11

After reading and thinking about this chapter, you will be able to do the following:

1

Identify nine objectives of message strategy.

2

Identify methods for executing each message strategy objective.

3

Discuss the strategic implications of various methods used to execute each message strategy objective.

Most say it was brilliant and inspired. Others argue it was an arrogant and expensive exercise in grandstanding. In January 1984, during the third quarter of the Super Bowl, Apple Computer introduced the Macintosh with a 60-second spot. The ad, known as "1984," climaxed with a young athletic woman hurling a mallet through a huge projection screen in a monochromatic vision of a hypercorporate and ugly future.[1] On the big screen was an Orwellian Big Brother instructing the masses. As the ad closed, with the near-soulless masses obediently chanting the corporate-state mantra in the background, the following simple statement appeared on the television screens of millions of viewers: "On January 24th, Apple Computer will introduce Macintosh. And you'll see why 1984 won't be like 1984."

What made this advertisement particularly newsworthy is that it cost $400,000 to produce (very expensive for its day) and another $500,000 to broadcast, yet it was broadcast only *once*. It was a creative superevent. The three major networks covered the event on the evening news, and the ad went on to become *Advertising Age*'s Commercial of the Decade for the 1980s. But why? It wasn't just its high cost and single play. It wasn't just its very stylish but disturbing look (directed by Ridley Scott [*Blade Runner, Alien, Gladiator, G.I. Jane, Black Hawk Down*]). It wasn't just another ad that told us who or what we could be. The ad captured and expressed something important lying just below the surface of early 1980s American culture. It was about us versus them, threatened individuals versus faceless corporations. It was about the defiant rejection of sterile corporate life and the celebration of individuality through, of all things, a computer. Archrival IBM was implicitly cast as the oppressive Big Blue (that is, Big Brother) and Apple as the good and liberating anticorporate corporation. The ad captured the moment and, most critically, served up a consumer product as popular ideology. Apple became the hip, the young, the cool, the democratic, the antiestablishment computer. It was the computer of the nonsellout, or at least of those who wished to think of themselves that way.

The really great ads of all time have captured the cultural moment, have wrapped their brands in the words and pictures of that cultural moment, and then served that package up for sale to that very same culture. If you can also serve a large and underserved market segment (for example, cyber-insecure consumers unwilling to deal with DOS, ready to use a mouse, and generally anti-button-down corporate), even better. Steve Hayden, the "1984" copywriter, described the ad this way: "We thought of it as an ideology, a value set. It was a way of letting the whole world access the power of computing and letting them talk to one another. The democratization of technology—the computer for the rest of us."[2]

With "1984," Apple and advertising agency Chiat/Day wanted to focus attention on a new product and completely distinguish Apple and the Macintosh from Big Blue, IBM. Macintosh was going to offer computing power to the people. This declaration of computing independence was made on the most-watched broadcast of the year. Forty-six percent of all U.S. households tuned into the 1984 Super Bowl. With the Macintosh, Apple offered an alternative and very hip cyber-ethos for those who felt alienated or intimidated by the IBM world. The "1984" ad offered a clear choice, a clear instruction: *Buy a Mac, keep your soul.* And it worked. Macintosh and Apple grew and prospered. For quite a while, "the rest of us" was a pretty big group.

Of course, there is another lesson here: Nothing lasts forever, not even a great creative idea. Things change. Advertising has to evolve along with the situation, or the brand may suffer. As great as this ad was (and it was) and as much success as the Mac and Apple had (they did), things didn't stay so good. Some believe that the seeds of Apple's own near demise were sown with the "rest of us" idea. Apple effectively cultivated an us-versus-them ethic, which worked well to help establish a

---

1.   The term *ugly future* was first used in this context (and beautifully so) by Connie Johnson, University of Illinois, in the late 1970s. We thank her.
2.   This quote appears in Bradley Johnson, "10 Years after 1984: The Commercial and the Product That Changed Advertising," *Advertising Age,* January 10, 1994, 12.

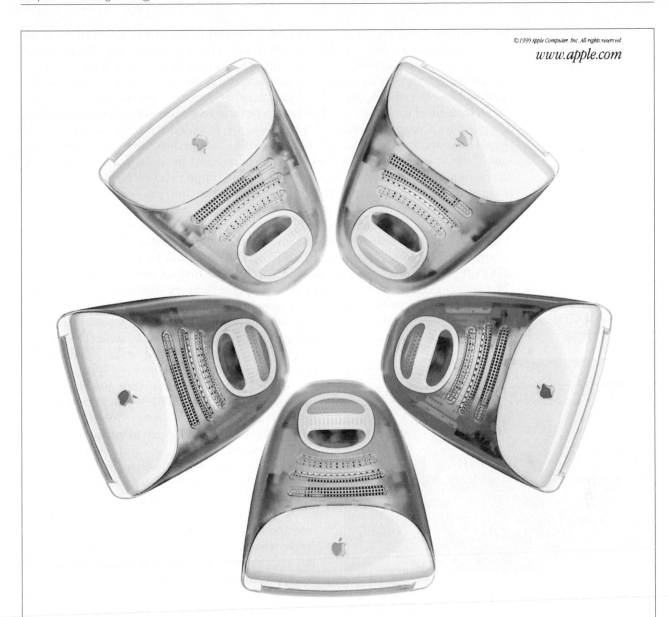

www.apple.com

Collect all five.

Think different.™

The launch of the iMac. http://www.apple.com

brand position and even a sense of brand community, but Apple failed to keep the Apple tent inclusive and big. The rest-of-us ethos became something of a problem.

By 2000, Apple's market share had dropped to mid single digits. Many believed that Apple was forever damaged by a failure to recognize and adapt to changes in the marketplace. Because Apple refused to license its operating system until 1995 (and then changed its mind again), Macs became a relatively expensive alternative to PCs. Coupled to a premium price, they came to be regarded by some as evidence of Apple's snooty and elitist nature. The "rest of us" seemed to think they were better (more hip, cooler, more arty, and so on) than us—not necessarily a desirable product attribute if a company hopes to sell a lot of computers. Once the skid hit software availability, Apple came perilously close to extinction.

Then came the iMac. With the return of co-founder Steve Jobs to the company, Apple once again teamed up with TBWA/Chiat/Day to launch the iMac (see Exhibit 11.1), and things turned around (a bit). The company made a profit of around $309 million after a loss of $1 billion in the previous Jobs-less year. And over 278,000 people took iMacs home with them in the first six weeks on the market.[3] The stylish iMac started a trend in the computer industry similar to what General Motors did in the 1920s, when all cars were black and were in some danger of eventually becoming undifferentiated commodities—GM began to produce them in color and introduced elements of style. This created brand distinctiveness, added value, and period obsolescence (style change).

In the 1990s, computers were quickly becoming low-margin commodities—so, taking a page from GM 70 years previously, Apple introduced style and color. This was very smart marketing and required smart advertising. But within a few months, everyone else was offering style and design as product benefits as well. Still, Apple was there first, and still "owns" the computer "style segment."

What about the present? Is Apple back tapping into the soul of American culture? Well, sort of; Apple and its advertising is highly regarded, but still only three to five percent of the market buys an Apple computer. So, while doing pretty well, Apple computers have not conquered the American consciousness the way they did in 1984. Back then, Apple's advertising was unquestionably amazing. No one can ever take that away. It was truly creative, and it advanced Apple's strategy. Apple and Chiat/Day deserve a great deal of credit. But now the world is different, and the computer market is different. In 1984 it was still an open question as to who would win the operating system platform race; that race has been over for a long time now. Expecting people to switch platforms at this point is an entirely different marketing and advertising problem. Now Apple is more than computers. Perhaps more importantly, small share, or "micro-brands" have turned out to be both popular and profitable. Apple is still reinventing itself. Apple is many things, including the wildly successful iPod and iTunes, and still trading on its brand equity of cyber-cool (see Exhibit 11.2). Don't weep for Apple.

EXHIBIT 11.2

Twenty-some years after 1984, Apple has become much more than a company that just makes computers.

Message Strategy. So, now we come to talking about message, how to create a message with advertising and integrated brand promotion that advances the marketers' strategy, that helps sell more stuff. One major component of the larger advertising and promotion advertising strategy is the **message strategy.** The message strategy consists of objec-

3.   David Kirkpatrick, "The Second Coming of Apple," *Fortune,* November 9, 1998, 86–92.

EXHIBIT 11.3

Message strategy objectives and methods.

Objective: What the Advertiser Hopes to Achieve	Method: How the Advertiser Plans to Achieve the Objective
Promote brand recall: To get consumers to recall its brand name(s) first; that is, before any of the competitors' brand names	Repetition Slogans and jingles
Link a key attribute to the brand name: To get consumers to associate a key attribute with a brand name and vice versa	Unique selling proposition (USP)
Persuade the consumer: To convince consumers to buy a product or service through high-engagement arguments	Reason-why ads Hard-sell ads Comparison ads Testimonials Demonstration Advertorials Infomercials
Instill brand preference: To get consumers to like or prefer its brand above all others	Feel-good ads Humor ads Sexual-appeal ads
Scare the consumer into action: To get consumers to buy a product or service by instilling fear	Fear-appeal ads
Change behavior by inducing anxiety: To get consumers to make a purchase decision by playing to their anxieties; often, the anxieties are social in nature	Anxiety ads Social anxiety ads
Transform consumption experiences: To create a feeling, image, or mood about a brand that is activated when the consumer uses the product or service	Transformational ads
Situate the brand socially: To give the brand meaning by placing it in a desirable social context	Slice-of-life ads Product placement/ short Internet films Light-fantasy ads
Define the brand image: To create an image for a brand by relying predominantly on visuals rather than words and argument	Image ads

tives and methods. The message strategy defines the goals of the advertiser (objectives) and how those goals will be achieved. This chapter offers nine message strategies, and then discusses and illustrates the methods most often used to satisfy them. This is not an exhaustive list, but it covers many of the most common and important message strategies. Exhibit 11.3 summarizes the nine message strategies presented here.

We will take these in an order from simple to complex. Also, you must understand that you will certainly see ads that are not pure cases, and ads that are combinations of strategies. We offer these nine pure types as examples. When you see an ad you should ask: What is this ad trying to do, and how is trying to accomplish that? What is its *main* method?

Essential Message Objectives and Strategies.
Again, these are presented from simplest to most complex. For each one we will tell you about the logic behind the strategy, the mechanisms involved or how it works, how success or failure is typically determined, and a strategic summary of those methods.

① Objective #1: Promote Brand Recall. This is the simplest type of advertising there is. Since modern advertising's very beginning, getting consumers to remember the advertised brand's name has been a goal. The obvious idea behind this objective is that if consumers remember the brand name, and can easily recall it, they are more likely to buy it. It's a pretty simple and straightforward idea.

Although human memory is a very complex topic, the relationship between repetition and recall has been pretty well understood for a long time. We know that repetition generally increases the odds of recall. So, by repeating a brand name over and over, the odds of recalling that brand name go up—pretty simple.

But advertisers typically don't just want consumers to remember their name, they want their name to be the *first* brand consumers remember, or what advertisers call *top of mind*. At a minimum, they want them to be in the *evoked set,* a small list of brand names (typically less than five) that come to mind when a product or service category (for example, airlines [United, American, Delta], soft drinks [Coke, Pepsi], or toothpaste [Crest, Colgate]) is mentioned. So, if someone says "soft drink," the folks in Atlanta (Coke headquarters) want you to say "Coke."

Again, the odds of being either top of mind or in the evoked set increase with recall. In the case of parity products (those with few major objective differences between brands—for example, laundry soaps) and other "low-involvement" goods and services, the first brand remembered is often the most likely to be purchased. First-remembered brands are often the most popular brands. In fact, consumers may actually infer popularity, desirability, and even superiority from the ease with which they recall brands. The most easily recalled brand may be seen as the leading brand (most popular, highest market share), even when it isn't. Of course, in time if people think a brand is the leading brand, it generally becomes the leading brand. For things purchased routinely, you can't expect consumers to deliberate and engage in extensive consideration of product attributes. Instead, in the real world of advertising and brand promotion, you rely on recall of the brand name, recall of a previously made judgment (e.g., *I like Tide*), or even habit to get the advertised brand in the shopping cart. Sometimes, the simplest strategy is the best strategy.

So, how do advertisers promote easy recall? There are two popular methods: repetition and the use of memory encoding (storing in memory) and retrieval (remembering) aids: slogans and jingles.

CoverGirl Wal-Mart Spring Endcap '02
Alliance, A Rock-Tenn Company
Procter & Gamble Cosmetics
Temporary ▪ Bronze

EXHIBIT 11.4

Point-of-purchase (POP) displays are great for promoting recall.

② Method A: Repetition. Repetition is a tried-and-true way of gaining easier retrieval of brand names from consumer's memory. Advertisers do this by buying lots of ads and/or by repeating the brand name within the ad itself. This is typically a strategy for television and radio, but can be accomplished visually in print, with promotional placement, and on the Web. The idea is that things said (or shown) more often will be remembered more easily than things said (or shown) less frequently. So the advertiser repeats the brand name over and over and over again. Then, when the consumer stands in front of, say, the cosmetic aisle, the advertised brand name is recalled from memory. In the contemporary IBP world, marketers often use point-of-purchase displays (see Exhibit 11.4) that help trigger, or cue, the brand name from memory.

In other cases, the aisle itself (its look, smells, etc.) or the packaging may cue the category (say, detergent), and the advertised brand (say, *Tide*). The more accessible (easier to remember) brand names are retrieved first and fastest from memory, making them (all else being equal) more likely to end up in the shopping cart. Getting into the consumer's evoked set gets you close to actual purchase, and achieving top of mind gets you even closer. So memory is key, and thus the message strategy becomes one of achieving simple brand name recall. This type of advertising tries to keep existing users as much as it tries to get new ones. Repetition strategies are being used use on the Internet as well: Familiar names are placed so that consumers will see them over and over. IPB promotional efforts do this too. Seeing a name over and over (and having it in a TV shot) is certainly one of the ideas behind named arenas: Qualcom Park, SBC Park, Enron (sorry, Minute-Maid) Park, and so on. In fact, having brand names become the wallpaper of contemporary society is everyday evidence of the popularity of this strategy.

Does this method always work? No, of course it doesn't. There are plenty of times when consumers remember one brand, and then buy another. Still, this type of advertising plays a probability game—being easily recalled tilts the odds of being purchased in favor of the advertisers willing to pay for the recall that repetition buys.

By the way: We think the all-time record for most brand mentions in a single ad might be a tie: either "Kibbles and Bits, Kibbles and Bits, I gotta get me some Kibbles and Bits" over and over and over (see Exhibit 11.5), or the endless "Meow, Meow, Meow, Meow" for Meow-Mix.

Method B: Slogans and Jingles. Slogans are one small step up from raw repetition in degree of complexity. Here, slogans and jingles are used as ways of enhancing the odds of recalling the brand name The basic mechanism at work here is still memory, and the goal is still brand name recall. Slogans are linguistic devices that link a brand name to something memorable due to the slogan's simplicity, meter, rhyme, or some other factor. Jingles do the same thing, just set to music. Examples are numerous: "You Deserve a Break Today"; "You're in Good Hands with Allstate"; "Like a Good Neighbor, State Farm Is There"; "We Love to Fly and It Shows"; "Two, Two, Two Mints in One"; "Get Met, It Pays"; and "It Keeps on Going and Going and Going." No doubt you've heard a few of these before. Slogans and jingles provide rehearsal because they are catchy, or prone to repeating, and the inherent properties of the slogan or jingle provide a retrieval cue for the brand name. As testament that sometimes less is more, some clever advertisers make the brand name itself, and just the brand name, into a slogan of sorts: two

EXHIBIT 11.5

This ad may hold the all-time record for most brand mentions in a single :30 ad. Kibbles and Bits, Kibbles and Bits . . .

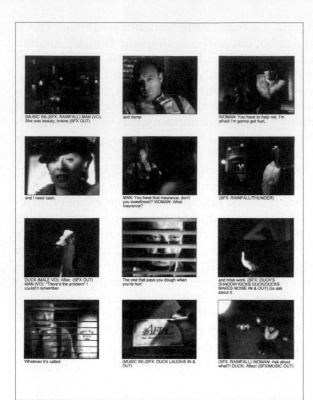

EXHIBIT 11.6

AF-LAC: these ads provided very effective brand name rehearsal.

famous examples come to mind: Bud–Weis–er, and AF–LAC. Remember, rehearsal leads to remembering (see Exhibit 11.6).

Or consider a practical application of the human need to complete or "close" a verse: For example, when you say, "Like a good neighbor," you pretty much are compelled to say "State Farm is there." As you know, slogans and jingles are hard to get out of your head. That's the idea.

Evaluation of repetition, slogans, and jingles is typically done through day-after-recall (DAR) tests and tracking studies emphasizing recall (e.g., "name three detergents"). In other words, these ads are evaluated with the most traditional ad copy research there is: simple recall measures. This is one time when the method of evaluation actually makes perfect sense: You are trying to get recall, you test for recall.

Strategic Implications of Repetition, Slogans, and Jingles.

Extremely resistant. Once a high level of memory is achieved, it becomes virtually impossible to forget the brand.

Efficient for consumer. For routinely purchased items, where the harm in a bad choice is minimal, consumers rely on simple and easy decision "rules": Buy what you remember. So, this kind of advertising works well in repeat purchase and low involvement items.

Big carryover. Once established, the residual amount of impact from the campaign is huge. If some advertisers stopped advertising today, you would remember their slogans, jingles, and names for a long, long time.

Long-term commitment/initial expense. To achieve this carryover, advertisers have to sign on for a lot of advertising, at least initially. It's not easy in a cluttered media environment to build this type of resistant recall. It takes lots and lots of repetition, particularly early on, or a very memorable slogan or jingle. Once advertisers have achieved a high recall level, they can fine tune their spending so that they are spending just enough to stay where they want. But they have to get there first, and it can be a very expensive trip.

Competitive interference. This is less a problem with repetition, but sometimes consumers learn a slogan or jingle only to associate it with the wrong brand. This has happened more times that you might imagine. For example, "It keeps on going, and going, and going. . . ." It's Duracell, right? Wait, maybe it's Eveready? Not absolutely sure? Not good.

Creative resistance. Creatives generally hate this type of advertising. Can you imagine why? These ads are rarely called creative and don't usually win a lot of creative awards. So creatives are less likely to enjoy working on them.

Objective #2: Link Key Attribute(s) to the Brand Name. Sometimes advertisers want consumers to remember the brand and associate it with one or two attributes. This type of advertising is most closely identified with the **unique selling proposition (USP)** style, a type of ad that strongly emphasizes a supposedly unique quality (or qualities) of the advertised brand. It is more complicated than simple brand recall, and a bit more challenging. It requires more of the consumer, a little more thought, a little more learning. The ads provide a reason to buy, but don't require the consumer to think too much about that reason, just associate it with the brand name. In fact, many experts believe these ads work best if consumers don't think too much

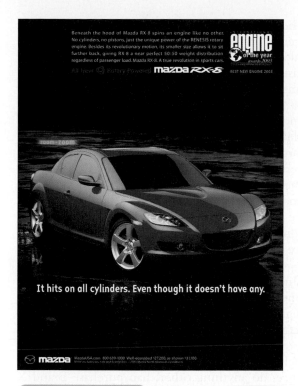

EXHIBIT 11.7

Here we have a very clear USP.

about the claim. The primary mechanisms are memory and learning. The appeal may be through words (copy), or pictures (art direction). Contemporary advertising relies more and more on visuals to communicate key brand attributes. This type of ad is typically evaluated through tracking studies that measure attitudes, beliefs, and preferences, as well as through qualitative field work and communications tests.

Method: USP. The idea of emphasizing one and only one brand attribute is a very good idea—sometimes two are used if they are complementary, such as "strong but gentle." Ads that try to link several attributes to a brand while working to establish recall generally fail—they are too confusing and give too much information. Too much is attempted. Consider the Mazda ad in Exhibit 11.7. Clearly, the USP is the rotary engine. The headline delivers the single-minded message. The body copy explains it further. Why buy an RX-8? It has a rotary engine. That's all you have to know. This type of advertising relies on a soft-logic: The ad makes sense, but don't think too much about it. Other examples of unique selling propositions: Volvo is safe, Listerine is strong, Ivory is pure. Success or failure with this method is demonstrated by successful recall of an attribute linked to a brand. Evaluation of the USP method is typically done through recall tests and tracking studies.

Strategic Implications of the USP Method.

- *Very resistant.* If you can strongly link one attribute with one brand, it is incredibly resistant to competitive challenge. Generations of consumers have been born, lived, and died remembering that Ivory is pure. Being the first to claim an attribute can be a huge advantage. Professionals will often say "Brand X owns that space" (meaning that attribute). For example, "Ivory owns the purity space."
- *Big carryover.* For the reason just mentioned, the efficiency of this advertising is great, once this link has been established. An investment in this kind of advertising can carry you through some lean times.
- *Long-term commitment.* If advertisers are going to do this, they have to be in it for the long haul. You can't keeps switching strategies and expect this to work.
- *Expense.* It will be very expensive, at least initially.
- *Competitive interference.* A lot of advertisers may be trying to link the same single attribute to their brand. If others stay out of your attribute "space," great. But if they crowd in, it can get very confusing for consumers, and inefficient for the advertiser. Again, think of batteries.
- *Some creative resistance.* Creatives tend not to hate this quite as much as simple repetition, but it does seem to get old with them pretty fast. Don't expect a thank-you note.

Objective #3: Persuade the Consumer.

This style of advertising is about arguments. In this type of advertising we move up from linking one (possibly two) attributes to a brand name with soft-logic and simple learning to actually posing several logical arguments to an engaged consumer. This is high-engagement advertising. That is, it assumes an actively engaged consumer, a consumer who is actually paying attention and considering the presented arguments. Its goal is to convince the consumer through arguments that the advertised brand is superior, the right choice. The advertiser says, in effect, you should buy my brand because of x, y, and z reasons. These arguments have typically been thought of as verbal (copy), but have in the past few decades come to use visual arguments (visual rhetoric) as well. As detailed below, there are several forms of this genre of advertising.

For this general type of advertising to work as planned the receiver has to think about what the advertiser is saying, a least to some degree. The receiver must "get" the ad, understand the argument, and agree with it. In a persuasion ad there is an assumed dialogue between the ad and the receiver and some of the dialogue is the consumer disagreeing and counter-arguing with the message. This and its inherent wordiness are the reasons such advertising is becoming less popular. Consider the very short attention span of consumers, sophisticated media surfers, and incredible media clutter. These ads are still found in the earliest phases of a technological inno-vation, where a new good or service has to be explained to consumers, or in cate-gories where the very nature of the product or service is complex. But generally, ads that resemble high school debates are going the way of the eight-track tape.

Method A: Reason-Why Ads. In a reason-why ad, the advertiser reasons with the potential consumer. The ad points out to the receiver that there are good rea-sons why this brand will be satisfying and beneficial. Advertisers are usually relent-less in their attempt to reason with consumers when using this method. They begin with some claim, like "Seven great reasons to buy Brand X," and then proceed to list all seven, finishing with the conclusion (implicit or explicit) that only a moron would, after such compelling evidence, do anything other than purchase Brand X (see Exhibit 11.8). Other times, the reason or reasons why to use a product can be presented deftly. The biggest trick to this method is making sure that the reason makes sense and that consumers care. The reason-why approach is used in direct mail and other forms of IBP (see Exhibit 11.9).

Strategic Implications of Reason-Why Ads.

👍 Gives consumer "permission to buy."

👍 Gives the consumer a socially acceptable defense for making the purchase.

👎 Assumes a high level of involvement; consumers have to be paying attention for these ads to work.

👎 Generates considerable counterarguments. May convince consumers why *not* to buy.

👎 Legal/regulatory challenges/exposure; the makers of these ads tend to get dragged into court quite a bit. You'd better make sure that all your reasons why can stand up in court. Many haven't.

Method B: Hard-Sell Ads. Hard-sell ads are a subcategory of reason-why ads. They are characteristically high pressure and urgent. Phrases such as "act now," "limited time offer," "your last chance to save," and "one-time-only sale" are rep-resentative of this method. The idea is to create a sense of urgency so consumers will act quickly (see Exhibit 11.10). Sometimes these are done as IBP, and include "call or click *now*." Of course, many consumers have learned to ignore or otherwise dis-count these messages.

Strategic Implications of Hard-Sell Approaches.

👍 Gives consumer "permission to buy NOW."

👍 Gives the consumer a socially acceptable defense for making a potentially poor choice: "I had to act"; "It was on sale that day"; "It was such a good deal."

👎 Legal/regulatory challenges/exposure; the makers of these ads tend to get dragged into court quite a bit.

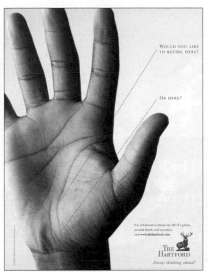

EXHIBIT 11.8

Kia uses reason-why.

EXHIBIT 11.9

The insurance category tends to use reason-why. Makes sense, right?

EXHIBIT 11.10

Hurry! You better act fast to get the benefits of JCPenney. http://www.jcpenney.com

Method C: Comparison Ads. Comparison advertisements are another form of advertising designed to persuade the consumer. Comparison ads try to demonstrate a brand's ability to satisfy consumers by comparing its features to those of competitive brands. Comparisons can be an effective and efficient means of communicating a large amount of information in a clear and interesting way, or they can be extremely confusing. Comparison as a technique has traditionally been used by marketers of convenience goods, such as pain relievers, laundry detergents, and household cleaners. Advertisers in a wide range of product categories have tried comparison advertising from time to time. For several years, AT&T and MCI had a long-running feud over whose rates were lower for household consumers. The ads seemed to have thoroughly confused everyone. Luxury car makers BMW and Lexus have targeted each other with comparative claims.[4] In one ad, BMW attacks the sluggish performance of Lexus with the message, "According to recent test results, Lexus' greatest achievement in acceleration is its price." Not to be left out, the Acura dealers of Southern California entered the luxury car advertising skirmish by stating, "We could use a lesser leather in our automobiles, but then we'd be no better than Rolls-Royce." Evaluation of comparison ads is typically done through tracking studies that measure attitudes, beliefs, and preferences; focus groups are also used.

Using comparison in an advertisement can be direct and name competitors' brands, or it can be indirect and refer only to the "leading brand" or "Brand X."

- Direct comparison by a low-share brand to a high-share brand increases the attention on the part of receivers and increases the purchase intention of the low-share brand.
- Direct comparison by a high-share brand to a low-share brand does not attract additional attention and increases awareness of the low-share brand.

---

4.   Jim Henry, "Comparative Ads Speed Ahead for Luxury Imports," *Advertising Age,* September 12, 1994, 10.

EXHIBIT 11.11

A straight comparison ad.
http://www.castrolusa.com

EXHIBIT 11.12

Considering buying a Rolls Royce or a Bentley? Perhaps you might re-think your decision after you compare them directly to the Lexus LS 430. http://www.finestsedan.com

- Direct comparison is more effective if members of the target audience have not demonstrated clear brand preference in their product choices.[5]

For these reasons, established market leaders almost never use comparison ads. What do you think of the ads in Exhibits 11.11 and 11.12?

Strategic Implications of Comparison Ads.

👍 Can help a low-share brand, largely through awareness.

👍 Provides social justification for purchase.

👎 Significant legal/regulatory exposure.

👎 Not done much outside the United States; in much of the world, they are either outlawed, not done by mutual agreement, or simply considered in such poor taste as to never be done.

👎 Not for established market leaders.

👎 These ads are sometimes evaluated as more offensive and less interesting than noncomparative ads.

5.   Conclusions in this list are drawn from William R. Swinyard, "The Interaction between Comparative Advertising and Copy Claim Variation," *Journal of Marketing Research* 18 (May 1981), 175–186; Cornelia Pechmann and David Stewart, "The Effects of Comparative Advertising on Attention, Memory, and Purchase Intentions," *Journal of Consumer Research* (September 1990), 180–191; and Sanjay Petruvu and Kenneth R. Lord, "Comparative and Noncomparative Advertising: Attitudinal Effects under Cognitive and Affective Involvement Conditions," *Journal of Advertising* (June 1994), 77–90.

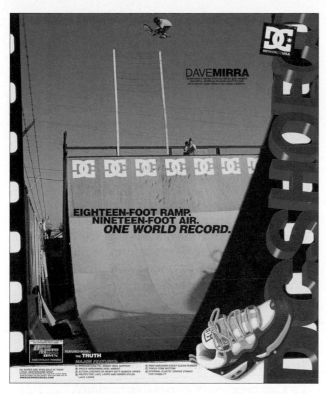

EXHIBIT 11.13

Dave Mirra is known as the Miracle Boy of freestyle BMX riding. What type of audience might find his testimonials persuasive?

Method D: Testimonials. Testimonials are another type of persuade-the-consumer type of ad. A frequently used message tactic is to have a spokesperson who champions the brand in an advertisement, rather than simply providing information. When an advocacy position is taken by a spokesperson in an advertisement, this is known as a **testimonial.** The value of the testimonial lies in the authoritative presentation of a brand's attributes and benefits by the spokesperson. There are three basic versions of the testimonial message tactic.

The most conspicuous version is the *celebrity testimonial.* Sports stars such as Michael Jordan (McDonald's) and Arnold Palmer (Pennzoil, Cadillac) are favorites of advertisers. Supermodels such as Cindy Crawford (Pepsi) are also widely used. The belief is that a celebrity testimonial will increase an ad's ability to attract attention and produce a desire in receivers to emulate or imitate the celebrities they admire (see Exhibit 11.13).

Whether this is really true or not, the fact remains that a list of top commercials is dominated by ads that feature celebrities.[6] Of course, there is the ever-present risk that a celebrity will fall from grace, as several have in recent years, and potentially damage the reputation of the brand for which he or she was once the champion.

Expert spokespeople for a brand are viewed by the target audience as having expert product knowledge. The GM Parts Service Division created an expert in Mr. Goodwrench, who was presented as a knowledgeable source of information. A spokesperson portrayed as a doctor, lawyer, scientist, gardener, or any other expert relevant to a brand is intended to increase the credibility of the message being transmitted. There are also real experts. Advertising for the Club, a steering-wheel locking device that deters auto theft, uses police officers from several cities to demonstrate the effectiveness of the product. Some experts can also be celebrities. This is the case when Michael Jordan gives a testimonial for Nike basketball shoes.

There is also the *average-user testimonial.* Here, the spokesperson is not a celebrity or portrayed as an expert but rather as an average user speaking for the brand. The philosophy is that the target market can relate to this person. Solid theoretical support for this testimonial approach comes from reference group theory. An interpretation of reference group theory in this context suggests that consumers may rely on opinions or testimonials from people they consider similar to themselves, rather than on objective product information. Simply put, the consumer's logic in this situation is, "That person is similar to me and likes that brand; therefore, I will also like that brand." In theory, this sort of logic frees the receiver from having to scrutinize detailed product information by simply substituting the reference group information (see Exhibit 11.14). Of course, in practice, the execution of this strategy is rarely that easy. Consumers are very sophisticated at detecting this attempt at persuasion. Evaluation is usually through tracking studies; focus groups and communications tests are also used.

Strategic Implications of Testimonial Advertising.

👍 Very popular people can generate popularity for the brand.

👍 Can make more attribute-related reasons important (e.g., "If it's good enough for Michael Jordan, it's good enough for me").

6.   Kevin Goldman, "Year's Top Commercials Propelled by Star Power," *Wall Street Journal,* March 16, 1994, B1.

EXHIBIT 11.14

This testimonial is done with facial expression, body attitude and "look." These days even testimonials don't have to have words. There is no doubt they are testifying.
http://www.skechers.com

👎 Generally, poor memorability for who is promoting what. Consumers often forget who likes what.

👎 Can generate more popularity for the star than for the brand.

👎 Celebrities, being human, are not as easy to manage as packages or cartoon characters: think Tony the Tiger versus Martha Stewart.[7]

Method E: Demonstration. How close an electric razor shaves, how green a fertilizer makes a lawn, or how easy an exercise machine is to use are all product features that can be demonstrated by using a method known simply as demonstration. "Seeing is believing" is the motto of this school of advertising. When it's done well, the results are striking (see Exhibit 11.15). Evaluation of demonstration ads is typically done through tracking studies that measure attitudes, beliefs, and preferences; focus groups and communication tests are also used.

Strategic Implications of Demonstration Ads.

👍 Can create very retrievable memory.

👍 Inherent credibility of "seeing is believing," however slight.

👍 Can be used as social justification; helps the consumer defend his or her decision to buy.

👎 Heavy regulatory/legal exposure.

👎 Faces a cynical audience, suspicious of special effects "tricks."

Method F: Infomercials. With the **infomercial,** an advertiser buys from five to 60 minutes of television time and runs a documentary/information/entertainment program that is really an extended advertisement. Real estate investment programs, weight-loss and fitness products, motivational programs, and cookware have dominated the infomercial format. A 30-minute infomercial can cost from $50,000 to a few million to put on the air. The program usually has a host who provides information about a product and typically brings on guests to give testimonials about how successful they have been using the featured product. Most infomercials run on cable stations, although networks have sold early-morning and late-night time as well. Recently, even big and very traditional firms have used infomercials..

Not all advertisers have had such good success with infomercials. After spending nearly half a million dollars to produce and air a 30-minute infomercial promoting a Broadway show, the producers pulled the ad after three weeks. The toll-free number to order tickets drew an average of only 14 calls each time the ad ran.[8] However, infomercials can have tremendous sales impact. Many leading infomercials rely on celebrity spokespeople as part of the program. Infomercials are often used in an integrated communications effort with promotional efforts. The infomercial sucks you in; mail and telephone promotions follow up; and then some type of sales promotion effort, such as a "free" trip to hear more about this amazing offer, concludes the approach.

7.   See Susan Fournier, Harvard Business School Case: Martha Stewart.
8.   Kevin Goldman, "Broadway Hopeful Flops with Debut of Infomercial," *Wall Street Journal,* April 1992, 1.

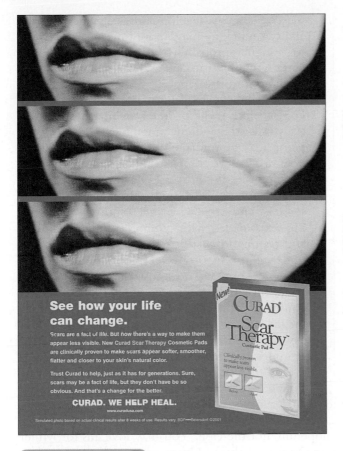

EXHIBIT 11.15

Straight demonstration of a product benefit by Curad.
www.curadusa.com

Strategic Implications of Infomercials.

👍 Long format gives advertisers plenty of time to make their case.

👍 As network ratings fall, day-parts (e.g., Sunday mornings 9–11) previously unaffordable have now opened up, making infomercials better deals for advertisers.

👎 The genre of ads has a somewhat negative public image, which doesn't help build credibility or trust in the advertised brand.

Others. There are other persuade-the-consumer formats, including ads posing as newspaper articles (advertorials), but all have the same basic mechanism at their core.

Objective #4: Affective Association: Get the Consumer to Feel Good about the Brand. Advertisers want consumers to like their brand. They believe that liking leads to preference. But rather than provide the consumer with hard reasons to like the brand, these ads work more through feelings—although let's be clear about this, completely separating thoughts and feelings in real-world human responses to advertising is next to impossible. Instead, what we are talking about here are ads that are *more* geared toward eliciting feelings relative to those *more* designed to elicit thought.

There are several well-known approaches to getting the consumer to like one's brand. Let's look at some of the general approaches; most specific executions are finer distinctions within these more general ones.

Method A: Feel-Good Ads. These ads are supposed to work through affective (feeling) association. They are supposed to link the good feeling elicited by the ad with the brand: You like the ad, you like the brand. While the actual theory and mechanics of this seemingly simple association are far more complex than you can imagine, the basic idea is that by creating ads with positive feelings, advertisers will lead consumers to associate those positive feelings with the advertised brand, leading to a higher probability of purchase. As Steve Sweitzer of the Hal Riney and Partners advertising agency said:

[C]onsumers want to do business with companies they LIKE. If they LIKE us, they just may give us a try at the store. What a concept. Sometimes just being liked is a strategy.[9]

Of course, getting from liking the ad to liking the brand is one big jump. Still many try, typically by making a "feel good" ad and assuming that the feeling for the ad will find its way to the consumer's attitude toward the brand. The evidence on how well this method works is mixed. It may be that positive feelings are transferred to the brand, or it could be that they actually interfere with remembering the message or the brand name. Liking the ad doesn't necessarily mean liking the brand. But

---

9.   The One Club e-mail discussion, July 27, 1997, as published in *One: A Magazine for Members of the One Club for Art and Copy*, vol. 1, no. 2 (Fall 1997), 18.

(MUSIC IN) MAN SINGS: Like a rock...

standing arrow-straight.

Like a rock...

charging from the gate.

Like a rock.

MALE ANNCR: Last year, more than 6 million people

got into a Chevy truck.

This year.

it'll be even

easier.

Chevy, the most dependable, longest-lasting trucks on the road.

MAN SINGS: Oh, like a rock. (MUSIC OUT)

EXHIBIT 11.16

Chevy's feel-good "Like a Rock" truck ads create positive association for working-class Americans.
http://www.chevrolet.com

message strategy development is a game of probability, and liking may, more times than not, lead to a higher probability of purchase. There are certainly practitioners who believe in the method's intuitive appeal.

We believe that ultimately what creates a good feeling is the product of interpretation on the part of the audience member. This interpretation may be informed by fairly simple associations or by more complex and elaborated thoughts. The interpretive processes of humans are, however, very sophisticated. Humans can make sense of and otherwise "get" complex advertising texts loaded with symbols, innuendo, jokes, and so on, in a split second. While we don't understand why some feel-good ads work and others do not, we do know that paying greater attention to the social context of likely target consumers, and the manner in which consumers "read" ads, is critical. Some positive attitudes toward the ad don't seem to result in positive attitudes toward the brand because they are not "read" for that purpose, or, it could be that consumers easily separate their feelings for the ad and their feelings for the brand. If the theory was as simple (and consumers as simple minded) as some believe, seeing *The Producers* would make you like Nazis more. Clearly not the intent, hopefully not the case. You may love ads for Miller Lite but be a Budweiser drinker. You may think, "Nice ads—wish they made a good beer." Or you might love the new iMac ads, but don't ever want to be an Apple owner.

Still, other feel-good advertising campaigns do work. For example, the long-running and apparently successful Chevrolet truck television campaign "Like a Rock," shown in Exhibit 11.16, features the music of Bob Seger and scenes of hard-working, patriotic Americans and their families. It seems to work for a lot of consumers. The good feeling it produces may be the result of widely shared patriotic associations and the celebration of working-class Americans evoked by the advertising. It may map easily onto the brand because sophisticated consumers know that the brand and the advertising are symbolically consistent in theory and practice—and consumer experience.

Delta Air Lines could show how often its planes depart and arrive on schedule. Instead, it shows the happy reunion of family members and successful business meetings, which create a much richer message, a wider field of shared meanings. The emotions become the product attribute linked to the brand, as long as the ad resonates (as true) with common lived experience—in other words, is that kind of what flying on Delta is like? Hopefully, the consumer makes the desired linkage. Consider Kodak's highly successful print and television campaign that highlighted the "Memories of Our Lives" with powerful scenes: a son coming home from the military just in time for Christmas dinner, a father's reception dance with his newly married daughter. Here, Kodak makes it clear that it is in the memory business, and Kodak memories are good memories. In Exhibit 11.17, Martex attempts to evoke warm feelings associated with the relationship between a father and son.

Evaluation of feel-good ads is typically done by measuring attitude change via pre-/postexposure tests, tracking studies, theater dial-turning tests, focus groups, communication tests, and qualitative field studies.

OUR KIDS
ARE FULL OF SURPRISES.
FROM **TOWELS** TO TOYBOXES,
THEY **TREAT** EVERYTHING
LIKE AN ADVENTURE.
SAME WITH **YOU** AND
YOUR KIDS, **RIGHT**?

M A R T E X
BATH & BEDDING | IN TOUCH WITH YOU.

EXHIBIT 11.17

A touching ad for Martex Bath and Bedding. http:// www.martex.com

Recently, there has been progress in understanding the mechanisms involved in feel-good advertising.[10] It is becoming clearer that thought and feelings are, at some basic level, separate systems. Feelings are believed to be a more "primitive" system. That is, they emanate from a part of the brain that responds quickly to stimuli in the environment. The classic example is that a loud noise frightens (feeling) us, before we know what we are frightened of (thought). So emotions are faster than thought, and sometimes even stronger. There is also evidence that as the media environment gets more cluttered, the affective (or feeling ads) may actually do better than thought-based ads that require a great deal of processing. The feelings may even outlast the thought. Feeling ads may have a leg up in the contemporary media environment, but there are still many "feel-good" ads that fail, and fail miserably.

Strategic Implications of Feel-Good Advertising.
👍 Eager creatives.
👍 May perform better in cluttered media environment.
👍 May render thought about the brand and its claimed superiority unnecessary.
👎 Can have wearout problems if the emotional appeal is very strong.
👎 Audience reaction difficult to reliably predict for the long term.
👎 Only moderate success in copy-testing.

Method B: Humor Ads. The goal of a humor ad is pretty much the same as that of other feel-good ads, but humor is a bit of a different animal. Generally, the goal of humor in advertising is to create in the receiver a pleasant and memorable association with the product. Recent advertising campaigns as diverse as those for ESPN ("This Is SportsCenter"), California Milk Processor Board ("Got Milk?") and Las Vegas ("What Happens Here, Stays Here") have all successfully used humor as the primary message theme. But research suggests that the positive impact of humor is not as strong as the intuitive appeal of the approach. Quite simply, humorous versions of advertisements often do not prove to be more persuasive than nonhumorous

10. See Michel Tuan Pham, Joel B. Cohen, John W. Pracejus and G. David Hughes, "Affect Monitoring and the Primacy of Feelings in Judgment," *Journal of Consumer Research,* vol. 28 (September 2001), 167–188.

versions of the same ad—or research is simply inadequate to detect the difference. We think it's the former more than the latter.

How many times have you been talking to friends about your favorite ads, and you say something like, "Remember the one where the guy knocks over the drink, and then says. . . ." Everybody laughs, and then maybe someone says something like, "I can't remember who it's for, but what a great ad." Wrong; this is not a great ad. You remember the gag, but not the brand. Not good. How come with some other funny ads you can recall the brand? The difference may be that ads in which the payoff for the humor is an integral part of the message strategy better ensure the memory link between humor and brand. If the ad is merely funny and doesn't link the joke (or the punch line) to the brand name, then the advertiser may have bought some very expensive laughs. Hint: Clients rarely consider this funny.

An example of an explicitly linked payoff is the Bud Light "Give Me a Light" campaign of the early 1980s. "Miller Lite" was quickly becoming the generic term for light beer. To do something about this, Bud Light came up with the series of "Give Me a Light" ads to remind light beer drinkers that they had to be a little more specific in what they were ordering. The ads showed customers ordering "a light" and getting spotlights, landing lights, searchlights, and other types of lights. The customer would then say, "No, a Bud Light." The ads not only were funny, but also made the point perfectly: Say "Bud Light," not just "a light," when ordering a beer. In addition, the message allowed thousands of customers and would-be comedians in bars and restaurants to repeat the line in person, which amounted to a lot of free advertising. The campaign by Needham, Harper and Steers–Chicago (now DDB Chicago) was a huge success.

Miller Brewing is an advertiser that has both reaped the benefits of humor in its recent ad campaigns and suffered from its risks. The original "Less Filling—Tastes Great" campaigns that pitted famous retired athletes against one another rose to great prominence in the late 1970s and through nearly the entire decade of the 1980s. Sports fans could hardly wait for the next installment of the campaign. But the campaign, while highly successful overall, ultimately ran into the problem of wearout. The brand began to lose market share and is still struggling to regain past glories.

Parody and self-parody are also forms of humor advertising. The 7-UP taste-test ad, the classic VW ads of the 1960s, and the unforgettable Joe Isuzu are great examples of having some fun with advertising in general. (See Exhibit 11.18.) Evaluation of humor ads is typically done through pre-/postexposure tests; dial-turning attitude tests; tracking studies that measure attitudes, beliefs, and preferences; communication tests; and focus groups.

Strategic Implications of Humor Advertising.

👍 If the joke is integral to the copy platform, can be very effective.

👍 Very eager creatives.

👎 Humorous messages may adversely affect comprehension.

👎 Humorous messages can wear out as quickly as after three exposures, leaving no one laughing, especially the advertiser.[11]

👎 Humorous messages may attract attention but may not increase the effectiveness or persuasive impact of the advertisement.

👎 Can be very expensive entertainment.

Method C: Sexual Appeal Ads. Sex ads are a type of feelings-based advertising. Because they are directed toward humans, ads tend to focus on sex from time to time. Not a big surprise. They are thought not to require much thought, just arousal

---

11.   This claim is made by Video Storyboards Tests, based on its extensive research of humor ads, and cited in Kevin Goldman, "Ever Hear the One about the Funny Ad?" *Wall Street Journal,* November 2, 1993, B11.

Pretty funny, eh? Is it good advertising?

BOY:	Dan Patrick? At TGI Friday's? Can I have your autograph, please?
DAN:	Sure, buddy.
BOY:	Thanks, Mr. Patrick.
DAN:	Uh-huh. Don't mention it.
SUPER:	In here, it's always Friday.

MERIT AWARD: Consumer Television :20 and Under: Single
ART DIRECTOR: Manuel Moreno
WRITER: Mike Fiddleman
AGENCY PRODUCER: Harvey Lewis
PRODUCTION COMPANY: Five Union Square Productions
DIRECTOR: Tom Schiller
CLIENT: TGI Friday's
AGENCY: Publicis/Dallas
ID 00 0672A

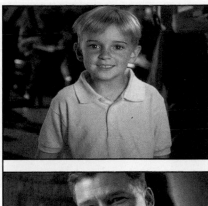

and affect. But does sex sell? In a literal sense, the answer is no, because nothing, not even sex, *makes* someone buy something. However, sexual appeals are attention getting and occasionally arousing, which may affect how consumers feel about a product. The advertiser is trying to get attention and link some degree of sexual arousal to the brand. Some believe in a type of classical conditioning involving sex in ads. Evidence for the effect is mixed. Like all other interpretation of ads by humans, context is extremely important in sexual-appeal messages. Knowing just what constitutes sex appeal is not easy. Is it showing skin? How much skin? What's the difference between the celebration of a beautiful body and its objectification? Motive? Politics? Who says? What of the Nipple-Gate scandal of the 2004 Super Bowl?

Can you use sex to help create a brand image? Sure you can. Calvin Klein and many other advertisers have used sexual imagery successfully to mold brand image. But these are for products such as clothes and perfumes, which emphasize how one looks, feels, and smells. Does the same appeal work as well for cars, telephones, computer peripherals, or file cabinets? How about breakfast cereals? In general, no. But because humans are complex and messy creatures, we cannot say that sex-appeal ads never work in such categories. Sometimes they do. In 1993, the print ads rated most successful in *Starch Tested Copy,* a publication of the market-research firm Starch INRA Hooper, were ads using muted sexual appeal (see Exhibit 11.19).[12] As recently noted by Professor Tom Reichert at the University of Georgia,[13] traditional wisdom

12.   Leah Richard, "Basic Approach in Ads Looks Simply Superior," *Advertising Age,* October 10, 1994, 30.
13.   Reichert, Tom (2004), *The Erotic History of Advertising,* Amherst, NY: Prometheus.

EXHIBIT 11.19

Historically, muted sex ads have scored well in recall tests. http://www.motorola.com/ phonefeel/

in the ad business was that the use of sex is "amateurish and sophomoric, and a desperate–not to mention ineffective–attempt to rescue plummeting sales." But, in the very next breath, advertising professionals will recount several examples where it has worked wonderfully. So, which is it? This may be one of those classic examples of what is said (by ad industry spokespeople) being very different from what is actually done, or at least somewhat different. This should not be too surprising in that humans in general, and Americans in particular, are chronically vexed by the topic, and their own ambivalence on the topic shows.

The most important aspect for effectiveness seems to be the match (or appropriateness) of the category and the appeal. The ads shown in Exhibit 11.20 use a sexual-appeal message to one degree or another. How effective do you think these ads are in fulfilling the objective of instilling brand preference? Are they gratuitous? Are they on target strategically? In which of these is the sex appeal relevant, appropriate, distracting, sexist, demeaning, fun, innocent, playful, or good advertising? What do you think? Sex appeals are certainly used in all sorts of promotional efforts: remember wet T-shirt contests? But what is sexy or constitutes a sex appeal seems to vary widely according to audience members' gender, appropriateness for the product or service category, and so on. There is

EXHIBIT 11.20

Sex appeals are among the most common and the most controversial in advertising. But often the issues of "what is appropriate" and "why" get completely mixed up and confused. Here, we provide 9 current ads for your inspection and discussion. As future advertising professionals, which do you think are good, sound on-strategy advertising? Which do you think use sex inappropriately? Which are in poor taste? Which may do the brand more harm than good? What might women think and feel about these ads and the companies that sponsor them? How about men? Should there be more regulations, or not? What do you think? http://www.cutty-sark.co.uk, http://www.michaelkors.com, http://www .azzuredenim.com, *and* http://www.rockport.com

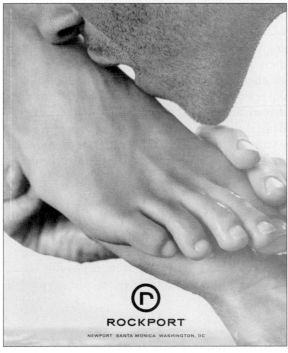

What do you think? Puritainism, good taste, bad taste, desperate for ratings?

more discussion of sex in advertising than just about any other topic. So look at these and think about what is good, bad, effective, ineffective, OK, not OK, and why. Talk about which of these ads are good advertising, gratuitous advertising, demeaning, appropriate, and so on. You will be engaging in the same debate that advertising professionals do all the time. It's good training.

One of the biggest problems that all agencies have is the headache of censorship. There is simply no reason to it. Censorship, any kind of censorship, is pure whim and fancy. It's one guy's idea of what is right for him. It's based on everything arbitrary. . . . There's a classic Lenny Bruce bit. He's doing a father talking to his son while they're both watching a pornographic film. Bruce says, "Son, I can't let you watch this. This is terrible and disgusting. Son, I'm going to have to cover your eyes now. That man is going to kiss that woman and they're going to make love and there's going to be pleasure and everything else and this is terrible, it's not for you until you are at least twenty-one. Instead son, I am going to take you to a nice war movie."

—Famous adman Jerry Della Femina[14]

No kidding. If you use sex in an ad, you will probably have "issues" with clients, or regulators, or advocacy groups, or lawmakers, or municipalities, on and on. You will hear of all the harms that can occur if you use sex. Some on the political right will tell you to avoid promoting promiscuity (and lost sales), and some on the political left will tell you to protect women from degrading images (and lost sales). Whatever your politics, the fear of losing sales is an entirely reasonable concern, but rarely a very realistic problem in practice. Just as consumers do not typically buy something (like a lawn mower) because of a poor-fitting sex appeal, they will rarely refrain from buying it either. After Nipple-Gate the advertising industry wondered publicly whether we were entering a new age of puritanical thought (see Exhibit 11.21).

Evaluation of sex-appeal ads is typically done through communication tests, focus groups, pre-/postexposure tests, and tracking studies that measure attitudes, beliefs, and preferences.

Strategic Implications of Sexual-Appeal Advertising.

👍 Higher attention levels.
👍 Higher arousal affective feeling levels.
👎 Poor memorability due to interference at the time of exposure is possible.
👎 Product–theme continuity excludes many goods and services.
👎 Legal, political, and regulatory exposure.

Objective #5: Scare the Consumer into Action. Sometimes the advertising strategy is to scare the consumer into acting. Fear appeals are typically designed to illicit a specific feeling (fear) as well as thought. Fear is an extraordinarily powerful emotion and may be used to get consumers to take some very important action. But this fear must be

14.   Jerry Della Femina, "Censorship," in *From Those Wonderful Folks Who Gave You Pearl Harbor: Front-Line Dispatches from the Advertising War,* with Charles Sopkin, ed. (New York: Simon and Schuster, 1970), 179, 190.

coupled with some degree of thought in order for it to work. That's why we place this strategy a bit higher up the ladder in terms of its degree of complexity. It is generally considered hard to use effectively, and is fairly limited in application. The place you are most likely to encounter a fear appeal is in a public service announcement, rather than ads per se. Still, you should know how they work.

Method: Fear-Appeal Ads. A fear appeal highlights the risk of harm or other negative consequences of not using the advertised brand or not taking some recommended action. The appeal is usually a combination of reason-why and affect attachment. It's a little bit of thought coupled with a little bit of fear. Getting the balance right can be very tricky. The intuitive belief about fear as a message tactic is that fear will motivate the receiver to buy a product that will reduce or eliminate the portrayed threat. For example, Radio Shack spent $6 million to run a series of ads showing a dimly lit unprotected house, including a peacefully sleeping child, as a way to raise concerns about the safety of the receiver's valuables as well as his or her family. The campaign used the theme "If security is the question, we've got the answer." The ad closed with the Radio Shack logo and the National Crime Prevention Council slogan, "United against Crime."[15] Similarly, the ad in Exhibit 11.22 for Body Alarm cuts right to the chase: It capitalizes on fears of not being able to cry for help during a bodily attack.

The contemporary social environment has provided advertisers with an ideal context for using fear appeals. In an era of drive-by shootings, carjackings, gang violence, and terrorism, Americans fear for their personal safety. Manufacturers of security products such as alarm and lighting security systems play on this fearful environment.[16] Other advertisers have recently tried fear as an appeal. One such advertiser, the Asthma Zero Mortality Coalition, urges people who have asthma to seek professional help and uses a fear appeal in its ad copy: "When those painful, strained breaths start coming, keep in mind that any one of them could easily be your last."[17] The creator of the ad states, "Sometimes you have to scare people to save their lives." In Exhibit 11.23, Electrolux shows us what lives in all our carpets, and how to get rid of them.

EXHIBIT 11.22

How does this ad for the Body Alarm embody the scare-the-consumer-into-action objective? Does this ad have ethical implications? How so?

EXHIBIT 11.23

Just to look at a dust mite close up is a little scary.

15.   Jeffrey D. Zbar, "Fear!," *Advertising Age,* November 14, 1994, 18.

16.   Ibid.

17.   Emily DeNitto, "Healthcare Ads Employ Scare Tactics," *Advertising Age,* November 7, 1994, 12.

Research indicates that until one gets to very high fear levels, more is better. So, moderate levels of fear appear to work better than low levels. However, the effect of truly intense levels of fear is either unknown or thought to be counterproductive. Because they are so rarely used, either in a research setting or in the real world, no one is entirely sure. Traditional wisdom held that intense fear appeals actually short-circuit persuasion and result in a negative attitude toward the advertised brand.[18] Other researchers argue that the tactic is beneficial to the advertiser.[19] So no one really knows. What is fairly clear, though, is that two other factors seem to produce better results when moderate fear appeals are used: that the message is plausible, and that the ad presents a very clear action to be taken to avoid harm. The ideal fear-appeal ad would thus be a moderate (but not severe) level of fear that is entirely believable[20] (one that people can't easily say doesn't apply to them or seems unlikely to be a real threat), and has a very clear (completely obvious) and very easy way to avoid the bad thing threatened by the ad. Evaluation of fear-appeal ads is typically done through tracking studies that measure attitudes, beliefs, and preferences; pre-/postexposure tests; communication tests; and focus groups.

Strategic Implications of Fear-Appeal Advertising.

👍 Moderate level of fear works well.

👍 A plausible threat motivates consumers.

👍 Reliable solution is to buy the advertised brand.

👎 Legal, regulatory, and ethical exposure and problems.

👎 Some fear ads are just ridiculous and have low impact.

Objective #6: Change Behavior by Inducing Anxiety.

Anxiety is fear's cousin. Anxiety is not quite outright fear, but it is uncomfortable and can last longer. While it's hard to keep people in a state of outright fear, people can feel anxious for a good long time. People try to avoid feeling anxious. They try to minimize, moderate, and alleviate anxiety. Often people will buy or consume things to help them in their continuing struggle with anxiety. They might watch television, smoke, exercise, eat, or take medication. They might also buy mouthwash, deodorant, condoms, a safer car, or even a retirement account, and advertisers know this. Advertisers pursue a change-behavior-by-inducing-anxiety objective by playing on consumer anxieties. The ads work through both thought and feelings.

Method A: Anxiety Ads.

There are many things to be anxious about. Advertisers realize this and use many settings to demonstrate why you should be anxious and what you can do to alleviate the anxiety. Social, medical, and personal-care products frequently use anxiety ads. The message conveyed in anxiety ads is that (1) there is a clear and present problem, and (2) the way to avoid this problem is to buy the advertised brand. When Head & Shoulders dandruff shampoo is advertised with the theme "You never get a second chance to make a first impression," the audience realizes the power of Head & Shoulders in saving them the embarrassment of having dandruff.

Other anxiety ads tout the likelihood of being stricken by gingivitis, athlete's foot, calcium deficiency, body odor, and on and on. The idea is that these anxiety-

18.   Irving L. Janis and Seymour Feshbach, "Effects of Fear Arousing Communication," *Journal of Abnormal Social Psychology* 48 (1953), 78–92.

19.   Michael Ray and William Wilkie, "Fear: The Potential of an Appeal Neglected by Marketing," *Journal of Marketing*, vol. 34, no. 1 (January 1970), 54–62.

20.   E. H. H. J. Das, J. B. F. de Wit, and W. Strobe, "Fear Appeals Motivate Acceptance of Action Recommendations: Evidence for a Positive Bias in the Processing of Persuasive Messages," *Personality and Social Psychology Bulletin*, vol. 29 (2003), 650–664.

This ad is designed to produce anxiety. What is the target market supposed to worry about? http://www.lvidocs.com

*Here is another example of a social anxiety ad. Also, antiperspirant brands are a natural fit for advertising messages that play upon social anxiety. Do product sites for Old Spice (*http://www.oldspice.com*) or Secret (*http://www.secretstrength.com*) capitalize on faux pas anxieties?*

producing conditions are out there, and they may affect you unless you take the appropriate action. What anxieties might the ad in Exhibit 11.24 arouse?

Method B: Social Anxiety Ads. This is a subcategory of anxiety ads where the danger is negative social judgment. Procter & Gamble has long relied on such presentations for its household and personal-care brands. In fact, Procter & Gamble has used this approach so consistently over the years that in some circles the anxiety tactic is referred to as the P&G approach. One of the more memorable P&G social anxiety ads is the scene where husband and wife are busily cleaning the spots off the water glasses before dinner guests arrive because they didn't use P&G's Cascade dishwashing product, which, of course, would have prevented the glasses from spotting. Most personal-care products have used this type of appeal. In Exhibit 11.25, Eclipse suggests that you might be sharing unwanted leftovers from lunch. Feel a touch of anxiety? How's your breath? Evaluation of anxiety ads is typically done by measuring attitudes and beliefs arousal and anxiety through tracking studies, focus groups, communication tests, and other qualitative methods.

Strategic Implications of Anxiety Advertising.

👍 Can generate perception of widespread threat and thus motivate action (buying and using the advertised product).

⚐ The brand can become the solution to the ever-present problem, and this results in long-term commitment to the brand.

⚐ Efficient: A little anxiety goes a long way.

⚐ Too much anxiety, like fear, may overwhelm the consumer, and the ad and the brand may be avoided because it's just too much discomfort.

⚐⚐ If the anxiety-producing threat is not linked tightly enough to the brand, you may increase category demand and provide business for your competitors. The strategy typically works best for the brand leaders. If total category share goes up, you get most of it. If you are a small-share brand, much of your advertising and IBP may end up helping category growth, most of which will end up in the market leader's numbers.

⚐ Ethical issues: Some believe there is enough to feel anxious about without advertisers adding more.

⚐ Typically targeted at women. Critics note that advertising has historically targeted women with ads designed to induce feelings of inadequacy.

Objective #7: Transform Consumption Experiences.

You know how sometimes it's hard to explain to someone else just exactly why a certain experience was so special, why it felt so good? It wasn't just this thing, or that thing; the entire experience was somehow better than the sum of the individual facets. Sometimes, that feeling is at least partly due to your expectations of what something will be like, your positive memories of previous experiences, or both. Sometimes advertisers try to provide that anticipation and/or familiarity, bundled up in a positive memory of an advertisement, to be activated during the consumption experience itself. It is thus said to have transformed the consumption experience.

Method: Transformational Ads.

The idea behind transformational advertising is that it can actually make the consumption experience better. For example, after years of advertising by McDonald's, the experience of eating at McDonald's is actually transformed or made better by virtue of what you know and feel about McDonald's each time you walk in. Transformational advertising messages attempt to create a brand feeling, image, and mood that are activated when the consumer uses the product or service. Transformational ads that are acutely effective are said to connect the experience of the advertisement so closely with the brand that consumers cannot help but think of the advertisement (or in a more general sense, be informed by the memory of many ads) when they think of the brand. Exhibit 11.26 is as much about the fun feelings connected with having a Miller Lite with friends as it is about the taste of beer. Also check out Exhibit 11.27. Evaluation of transformational ads is typically done through field studies, tracking studies, ethnographic methods, focus groups, and communication tests.

Strategic Implications of Transformational Advertising.

⚐ Can be extremely powerful due to a merging of ad and brand experience.

⚐ Requires long term commitment.

⚐ Can ring absolutely false.

Objective #8: Situate the Brand Socially.

Maybe you haven't given it much thought, but if you're ever going to understand advertising, you have to get this: Objects have social meanings. While it applies to all cultures, this simple truth is at the very center of

Does this ad actually transform the consumption experience? That's the idea.

If the strategy is right, your first trip to the Magic Kingdom should be different (and better) by virtue of what you have learned (from ads like these) before getting there. http://www.disneyworld.com

consumer cultures. In consumer cultures such as ours, billions of dollars are spent in efforts to achieve specific social meanings for advertised brands. Advertisers have long known that when they place their product in the right social setting, their brand takes on some of the characteristics of its surroundings. These social settings are created within ads. In advertising, a product is placed into a custom-created social setting perfect for the brand, a setting in which the brand excels. Hopefully, this becomes the way in which the consumer remembers the brand, as fitting into this manufactured and desirable social reality. Let us say it again: Objects have social meaning; they are not just things. Advertising lets us shape that meaning. As amazing as it seems, many forget this.

Method A: Slice-of-Life Ads. By placing a brand in a social context, it gains social meaning by association. Slice-of-life advertisements depict an ideal usage situation for the brand. The social context surrounding the brand rubs off and gives the brand social meaning (see Exhibit 11.28). Consumers may, of course, reject or significantly alter that meaning, but often they accept it. Think about it. You put the brand into a social setting and transfer meaning from that social setting to the brand. Look at Exhibits 11.29 and 11.30. Think about them, how they work. Evaluation of slice-of-life ads is typically done through tracking studies that measure attitudes, beliefs, and preferences; pre-/postexposure tests; communication tests; and focus groups.

EXHIBIT 11.28

By carefully constructing a social world within the frame of the ad into which the product is carefully placed, meaning is transferred to the product. "Background" and product meanings merge. This is the sophistication behind "slice-of-life" advertising. http://www.louisboston.com

EXHIBIT 11.30

This is an excellent slice-of-life ad. It shows the phone in an idealized social context. Great ad. http://www.verizon.com

EXHIBIT 11.29

Think of the message the carefully constructed choice of newspaper and background scene transfers to the line of hair care products.

Strategic Implications of Slice-of-Life Ads.

👍 Generally, less counterargument.

👍 Enduring memory trace. In other words, pieces of this ad will hang around in consumer's memory for a long time.

👍 Legal/regulatory deniability. Advertisers' attorneys like pictures more than words because determining the truth or falsity of a picture is much tougher than words.

👍 Iconic potential. To make your brands another Coca-Cola is many advertisers' dream. Socially set pictures of a brand give you this chance.

👍 Creation of ad-social-realities. You can create the desired social worlds for your brand on the page.

👎 Fairly common, can get lost in clutter.

👎 If not done very well, rejected as clearly false.

👎 Don't tend to copy-test well.

Method B: Product Placement/Short Internet Films. One way to integrate the product into a desired setting is to place the product in either a television show or film. An actor picks up a can of Coke, rather than just any soda, and hopefully the correct image association is made. Even more explicit are short films (usually less than 10 minutes) made for the Internet. Recently BMW released six such films showing its cars in dramatic contexts (http://www.bmwfilms.com). The most famous was a film starring Madonna and directed by her husband, British film director Guy Ritchie (*Lock, Stock, and Two Smoking Barrels; Snatch*). There are no standard ways of assessing the success of these methods.

Strategic Implications of Product Placement and Internet Films.

👍 Low counterargument, if not too obvious.

👍 Outside normal ad context; may reduce all sorts of defensive measures by consumers, such as source discounting.

👍 Virtually no regulation.

👎 Can be horribly ineffective when obvious.

👎 Nonstandardized rate structure; hard to price these.

Objective #9: Define the Brand Image.
Madonna has an image; Michael Jordan has an image; so do Prada and Pepsi. Even fictional characters such as the wildly popular Harry Potter have images. Just like people, brands have images. Images are the most apparent and most prominently associated characteristics of a brand. They are the thing consumers most remember or associate with a brand. Advertisers are in the business of creating, adjusting, and maintaining images—in other words, they often engage in the define-the-brand-image objective.

Method: Image Ads. Image advertising means different things to different people. To some, it means the absence of hard product information (see Exhibit 11.31). To others, it refers to advertising that is almost exclusively visual (see Exhibit 11.32).

EXHIBIT 11.32

Stylish visual ads for stylish Prada.

EXHIBIT 11.31

Image.

This is an oversimplification, but it is true that most image advertising tends toward the visual. In both cases, it means an attempt to link certain attributes to the brand rather than to engage the consumer in any kind of extended thought. Sometimes these linkages are quite explicit, such as using a tiger to indicate the strength of a brand. Other times, the linkages are implicit and subtle, such as the colors and tones associated with a brand. Check out the ads in Exhibit 11.33. Evaluation of image ads can be difficult. Usually qualitative methods are employed; sometimes associative tests are used, along with attribute-related tracking studies. Much advertising since the 1960s has been about figuring out what is cool, representing that cool social context in an ad, and then putting them together with the brand, transferring cool to the brand. Of course, what is cool is all about society, politics, and culture. It is the skillful use of this social knowledge that turn brands into very successful brands, or even brand icons, the distilled image of cool itself.[21]

What is often really needed is a very cultural connected creative, and management wise enough to either help them, or leave them alone.

Strategic Implications of Image Advertising.

👍 Enduring memory.
👍 Generally, less counterargument.
👍 Low legal/regulatory exposure.
👍 Iconic potential.
👎 Very common, can get lost in clutter.
👎 Can be rejected as clearly false.
👎 Don't tend to copy-test well.

In the End. In the end, message development is where the advertising and IBP battle is usually won or lost. It's where real creativity exists. It's where the agency has to be smart and figure out just how to turn the wishes of the client into effective advertising. It is where the creatives have to get into the minds of consumers, realizing that the advertisement will be received by different people in different ways. It is where advertisers merge culture, mind, and brand. Great messages are developed by people who can put themselves into the minds of their audience members and anticipate their response, leading to the desired outcomes.

---

21.   Douglas B. Holt, "What Becomes an Icon Most?" *Harvard Business Review* (March 2003).

EXHIBIT 11.33

These are all image ads. Even though some people think of these ads as light and fluffy, they are anything but that. They are carefully constructed to yield the right set of connections and the right images. To "get them," the reader/viewer has to give them a little thought. Think about these. Do you get it?

SUMMARY

 Identify nine objectives of message strategy.

Advertisers can choose from a wide array of message strategy objectives as well as methods for implementing these objectives. Three fundamental message objectives are promoting brand recall, linking key attributes to the brand name, and persuading the customer. The advertiser may also wish to create an affective association in consumers' minds by linking good feelings, humor, and sex appeal with the brand itself. Such positive feelings associated with the advertised brand can lead consumers to a higher probability of purchase. The advertiser may try to scare the consumer into action or change behavior by inducing anxiety, using negative emotional states as the means to motivate purchases. Transformational advertising aims to transform the nature of the consumption experience so that a consumer's experience of a brand becomes connected to the glorified experiences portrayed in ads. A message may also situate the brand in an important social context to heighten the brand's appeal. Finally, advertisers seek to define a brand's image by linking certain attributes to the brand, mostly using visual cues.

 Identify methods for executing each message strategy objective.

Advertisers employ any number of methods to achieve their objectives. To get consumers to recall a brand name, repetition, slogans, and jingles are used. When the advertiser's objective is to link a key attribute to a brand, USP ads emphasizing unique brand qualities are employed. If the goal is to persuade a consumer to make a purchase, reason-why ads, hard-sell ads, comparison ads, testimonials, demonstrations, and infomercials all do the trick. Feel-good ads, humorous ads, and sexual-appeal ads can raise a consumer's preferences for one brand over another through affective association. Fear-appeal ads, judiciously used, can motivate purchases, as can ads that play on other anxieties. Transformational ads attempt to enrich the consumption experience. With slice-of-life ads, product placement, and short Internet films, the goal is to situate a brand in a desirable social context. Finally, ads that primarily use visuals work to define brand image.

 Discuss the strategic implications of various methods used to execute each message strategy objective.

Each method used to execute a message strategy objective has pros and cons. Methods that promote brand recall or link key attributes to a brand name can be extremely successful in training consumers to remember a brand name or its specific, beneficial attributes. However, these methods require long-term commitment and repetition to work properly, and advertisers can pay high expense while generating disdain from creatives. Methods used to persuade consumers generally aim to provide rhetorical arguments and demonstrations for why consumers should prefer a brand, resulting in strong, cognitive loyalty to products. However, these methods assume a high level of involvement and are vulnerable to counterarguments that neutralize their effectiveness—more-sophisticated audiences tune them out altogether, rejecting them as misleading, insipid, or dishonest. Methods used in creating affective association have short-term results and please creatives; however, the effect on audiences wears out quickly and high expense dissuades some advertisers from taking the risk. Methods designed to play on fear or anxiety are compelling, but legal and ethical issues arise, and most advertisers wish to avoid instigating consumer panic. Finally, methods that transform consumption experiences, situate the brand socially, or define brand image have powerful enduring qualities, but often get lost in the clutter and can ring false to audiences.

KEY TERMS

message strategy
unique selling proposition (USP)

comparison advertisements
testimonial

infomercial

QUESTIONS

1. Review the chapter opener about the success of Apple's "1984" commercial. What was the idea at the heart of this ad that helped make the Macintosh a success? A decade later, Apple's big idea had failed to pan out. What went wrong?

2. Once again, reflect on the "1984" commercial. As this chapter suggested, consumers are active interpreters of ads, and one of the virtues of the "1984" ad was that it invited the audience to become involved and make an interpretation. What sorts of interpretations could a viewer of the "1984" ad make that would benefit the brand? Conversely, what sorts of interpretations might a person make, after a single exposure to this ad, that would be detrimental to Macintosh?

3. How has Apple reinvented itself and tapped back into the soul of American culture since the near-demise of the Macintosh back in the mid-'90s?

4. Explain the difference between brand recall and affective association as message objectives. Which of these objectives do you think would be harder to achieve, and why?

5. Discuss the merits of unique selling proposition (USP) ads. Is it possible to have a USP that is not the "big idea" for an ad campaign?

6. Review the do's and don'ts of comparison advertising and then think about each of the brand pairs listed here. Comment on whether you think comparison ads would be a good choice for the product category in question, and if so, which brand in the pair would be in the most appropriate position to use comparisons: Ford versus Chevy trucks; Coors Light versus Bud Light beer; Nuprin versus Tylenol pain reliever; Brut versus Obsession cologne; Wendy's versus McDonald's hamburgers.

7. Procter & Gamble has had considerable success with the message strategy involving anxiety arousal. How does P&G's success with this strategy refute the general premise that the best way to appeal to American consumers is to appeal to their pursuit of personal freedom and individuality?

8. What are some of the ways advertisers can use the Internet to execute message strategy objectives?

9. Do you think product placement and short Internet films are effective in executing the message strategy of situating the brand socially? Have you ever consciously made a correlation between the products actors used during a film and your own brand preferences?

10. Think of a major purchase you have made recently. Which of the nine message strategy objectives do you think were the most effective in influencing your purchase decision? Explain.

EXPERIENTIAL EXERCISES

1. Choose a popular radio or television slogan or jingle and evaluate its effectiveness based on what you learned in the chapter. Does the slogan or jingle immediately make you think of the brand? Does the slogan or jingle evoke a positive response? If not, does this matter? Do you think you will remember this slogan or jingle years from now? Why might creatives in the industry be averse to repetition, slogans, and jingles?

2. Beer advertisers often use ad strategy methods that are designed to achieve the objective of "affective association." Keen advertisers recognize that consumers purchase products based on their general liking of the prod-uct; such a "liking" can be prompted through good feelings evoked by advertisements. Describe a current television beer advertisement that aims to achieve affective association. Which specific method is applied in the commercial to achieve the objective? What response did you personally have to the commercial? Do you think you'd be more inclined to try this product based on the ad? What are some of the positive and negative implications of this message strategy?

EXPERIENCING THE INTERNET

11-1   Short Internet Films: The Adventures of Seinfeld & Superman

American Express made business and entertainment news in the spring of 2004 when it released the second install-ment of its Web-only video ad series titled *The Adventures of Seinfeld & Superman*. The animated "Webisode" paired up comedian Jerry Seinfeld and DC Comics hero Superman to entertain audiences with quirky adventures while touting the advantages of the American Express Card. In sponsoring short Internet films featuring Sein-feld and the Man of Steel, American Express joins a growing list of marketers creating ads that can be seen only by computer users. The idea for portraying the odd-couple friendship between Seinfeld and the famous superhero was first hatched during an American Express Super Bowl commercial in 1998, and the ongoing series now continues to attract large audiences online. Watch one or both of the five-minute Webisodes of *The Adventures of Seinfeld & Superman* and answer the following questions.

The Adventures of Seinfeld & Superman:
http://www.jerry.digisle.tv/room.html

1. What does American Express seek to accomplish through its online episodes of *Seinfeld & Superman*?

2. Why do you think American Express selected Web-only ad films to communicate the benefits of its credit card services?

3. How might American Express use integrated brand promotion to draw attention to upcoming Webisodes of *The Adventures of Seinfeld & Superman*?

11-2   The Necessity of Healthy Hair

Pantene Pro-V is a collection of vitamin-enriched hair care products designed to produce beautiful and healthy hair. The distinct feature of Pantene Pro-V is its focus on an individual's styling needs instead of hair type. The Pantene Pro-V collection includes a shampoo, condi-tioner, treatment, and styler to provide the best care for individual styling preferences. Advertisers have recog-nized that the brand's emphasis on individuality and style fits well with the ethic of style and self-expression cham-pioned by popular female artists and musicians. Pantene capitalizes on this similarity by cosponsoring its Pro-Voice music competition—an annual talent showcase that celebrates talented female performers.

Pantene Pro-Voice: http://www.pro-voice.com

Pantene Pro-V: http://www.pantene.com

1. What message-strategy objective do you think is being applied for Pantene Pro-V, and what specific methods are being used to achieve this?

2. What social meanings does Pantene hope the consumer will associate with its product? Explain. Do you think this approach will produce brand recall?

3. What are some of the pros and cons of Pantene's message strategy?

CHAPTER 12

After reading and thinking about this chapter, you will be able to do the following:

1

Explain the need for a creative plan in the copywriting process.

2

Detail the components of print copy, along with important guidelines for writing effective print copy.

3

Describe various formatting alternatives for radio ads and articulate guidelines for writing effective radio copy.

4

Describe various formatting alternatives for television ads and articulate guidelines for writing effective television copy.

WHY
SPACE
ALIENS
STEAL OUR COWS.

WARNING: The Difference Between Copywriters And Art Directors May Not Be As Great As You Think.

We live in an age when just about everything carries a warning label of some sort. Objects in rearview mirrors may be closer than they appear. Hair dryers should not be used in the shower. Using a lawn mower to trim the hedge may result in injury.

In this spirit, the authors of this book urge you to read the warning label in Exhibit 12.1. Yet, unlike the examples given earlier, the truth expressed here may not be quite so obvious, the danger not so clear. You know how some people just have to divide up the world into neat little parcels and categories. These are the same people who neatly place copywriters in one box on the organizational chart, and art directors in another. But in practice, it's not that simple. It's far too simplistic to state that copywriters are responsible for the verbal elements in an ad and art directors are responsible for the visual elements. In fact, copywriters and art directors function as partners and are referred to as the **creative team** in agencies. The creative team is responsible for coming up with the **creative concept** and for guiding its execution. The creative concept, which can be thought of as the unique creative thought behind a campaign, is then turned into individual advertisements. During this process, copywriters often suggest the idea for magnificent, arresting visuals. Likewise, art directors often come up with killer headlines.

As you can see in Exhibits 12.2 and 12.3, some ads have no headlines at all; some have no pictures. Still, in most cases, both a copywriter and an art director are equally involved in creating an ad. This doesn't mean that copywriting and art directing are one and the same. This chapter and the next will show that the talent and knowledge needed to excel in one area differ in many ways from those needed to excel in the other. Still, one must recognize that not all copywriting is done by copywriters and not all art directing is done by art directors.

Understanding copywriting is as much about the people who write copy as it is about the product studies, audience research, and other information that copywriters draw upon to create effective copy. Copywriting is, in fact, mostly about the fairly magical relationship between creator and creation, between writer and text, writer and brand. It is more about art than science. Copywriting is writing, and writing is a form of crafted magic. Magic cannot be taught. If (and it's a big if) you have a gift to begin with, then you can learn technique. But technique alone is not enough. Gifts are gifts—they come from somewhere else. Writing long paragraphs won't make you William Faulkner any more than writing self-effacing copy will make you Bill Bernbach. Likewise, trying to treat a discussion of copywriting like a step-by-step discussion of how to change the oil in your car is sadly silly and thoroughly useless. Still, there are things—some of them

Where are the ugly rockstars?

They were once a shining beacon of hope to oddballs everywhere who figured, "man if I'm ever going to get laid I'd better grab a guitar." All you see on music television these days are models, socialites, and "the beautiful people." If this trend continues millions of uglies everywhere will be left in the dark, never aware that they too can "get some" with dizzying regularity. If you're remotely ugly, please get back in the game.

RollingStone

Some ads have no copy.

principles, some of them hints and tips—that can be learned from the creators of some of the greatest advertising of all time. Furthermore, even if you don't plan to be a copywriter, knowing something about the craft is essential to any working understanding of advertising. Knowing something about the craft is also essential to selling good ideas in global markets, as shown in the Global Issues box.

Let's begin with some fairly general thoughts on copywriting from some of the most influential people in the history of advertising:

If you think you have a better mousetrap, or shirt, or whatever, you've got to tell people, and I don't think that has to be done with trickery, or insults, or by talking down to people. . . . The smartest advertising is the advertising that communicates the best and respects consumers' intelligence. It's advertising that lets them bring something to the communication process, as opposed to some of the more validly criticized work in our profession which tries to grind the benefits of a soap or a cake mix into a poor housewife's head by repeating it 37 times in 30 seconds.

—Lee Clow, creator of the Apple Macintosh "1984" advertisement[1]

As I have observed it, great advertising writing either in print or television is disarmingly simple. It has the common touch without being or sounding patronizing. If you are writing about baloney, don't try to make it sound like Cornish hen, because that is the worst kind of baloney. Just make it darned good baloney.

—Leo Burnett, founder of the Leo Burnett agency, Chicago[2]

Why should anyone look at your ad? The reader doesn't buy his magazine or tune his radio and TV to see and hear what you have to say. . . . What is the use of saying all the right things in the world if nobody is going to read them? And, believe me, nobody is going to read them if they are not said with freshness, originality and imagination.

—William Bernbach, cofounder of one of the most influential
agencies during the 1960s, Doyle Dane Bernbach[3]

---

1.   Jennifer Pendleton, "Bringing New Clow-T to Ads, Chiat's Unlikely Creative," *Advertising Age,* February 7, 1985, 1.
2.   Leo Burnett, "Keep Listening to That Wee, Small Voice," in *Communications of an Advertising Man* (Chicago: Leo Burnett, 1961), 160.
3.   Cited in Martin Mayer, *Madison Avenue, U.S.A.* (New York: Pocket Books, 1954), 66.

GLOBAL ISSUES

You Know That Kissing Thing—It Works for Global Ads, Too

Years ago, some management guru said, "Keep It Simple, Stupid," giving birth to the KISS rule in American management philosophy. Well, it turns out that KISS has a place in global advertising as well.

Over the past decade, advertisers have been getting better and better at creating advertising campaigns that succeed on a global level. The International Advertising Festival at Cannes demonstrates that fact annually. More and more of the winning campaigns are global campaigns, not just domestic market campaigns. They work as well in Boston as they do in Brussels. What is also a demonstrated fact annually is that these winning campaigns are actually quite simple in terms of message theme and visual structure. Certainly, particular product categories lend themselves more readily to a global stage than do others. Lifestyle products such as soft drinks, jeans, sneakers, and candy translate well across cultures. Nike, Pepsi, and Levi's speak to the world and each has been the subject of memorable, award-winning campaigns. But what makes these brands so well suited to a global audience—even beyond the natural fit of lifestyle product categories?

The campaigns that work best on a global scale are those where the brand and its imagery are inextricably one and the same. Innovative product demonstrations or images where the pictures tell the story are the foundation of effective global advertising. Advertising that succeeds in the global arena draws on four constants: Simplicity, Clarity, Humor, and Clever demonstration. SCHC doesn't exactly spell KISS, but the reason that global ads that highlight these qualities can bridge the complexities and distinctiveness of one culture to another is simple. Granted, what is funny to a Brit may be lost on a Brazilian, but the key is to find not the culturally bound humor in a demonstration, but the culturally shared humor. When it comes to copy, simplicity and clarity rule. Aside from their inherent value, their ability to communicate across cultures is, well, clear. In short, actually *trying* to bridge cultures may be just the thing that complicates the situation. Reducing a brand and its message to the simplest and most common human values has a great chance of succeeding.

Source: Jay Schulberg, "Successful Global Ads Need Simplicity, Clarity," Advertising Age, June 30, 1997, 17.

Never write an advertisement which you wouldn't want your family to read. Good products can be sold by honest advertising. If you don't think the product is good, you have no business to be advertising it. If you tell lies, or weasel, you do your client a disservice, you increase your load of guilt, and you fan the flames of public resentment against the whole business of advertising.

—David Ogilvy's ninth of eleven commandments of advertising[4]

Finally, the following observation on the power of a good advertisement, brilliant in its simplicity, is offered by one of the modern-day geniuses of advertising:

Imagination is one of the last remaining legal means to gain an unfair advantage over your competition.

—Tom McElligott, cofounder of a highly creative and successful Minneapolis advertising agency[5]

Good copywriters must always bring spirit and imagination to advertising. Lee Clow, Leo Burnett, William Bernbach, and David Ogilvy have created some of the most memorable advertising in history: the "We're Number 2, We Try Harder" Avis campaign (William Bernbach); the Hathaway Shirt Man ads (David Ogilvy); the Jolly Green Giant ads (Leo Burnett); and the "1984" Apple Macintosh ad (Lee Clow). See Exhibits 12.4 and 12.5 for samples of their work. When these advertising legends speak of creating good ads that respect the consumer's intelligence and rely on imagination, they assume good copywriting.

① Copywriting and the Creative Plan.

Writing well, rule #1: Write well.

—Luke Sullivan, copywriter and author

Copywriting is the process of expressing the value and benefits a brand has to offer, via written or verbal descriptions. Copywriting requires far more than the ability to string product descriptions together in coherent sentences. One apt description of copywriting is that it is a never-ending search for ideas combined with a never-ending search for new and different ways to express those ideas.

4.   David Ogilvy, *Confessions of an Advertising Man* (New York: Atheneum, 1964), 102.
5.   Tom McElligott is credited with making this statement in several public speeches during the 1980s.

When you're only No.2, you try harder. Or else.

Avis can't afford to relax.

Little fish have to keep moving all of the time. The big ones never stop picking on them.

Avis knows all about the problems of little fish.

We're only No.2 in rent a cars. We'd be swallowed up if we didn't try harder.

There's no rest for us.

We're always emptying ashtrays. Making sure gas tanks are full before we rent our cars. Seeing that the batteries are full of life. Checking our windshield wipers.

And the cars we rent out can't be anything less than spanking new Plymouths.

And since we're not the big fish, you won't feel like a sardine when you come to our counter.

We're not jammed with customers.

© AVIS RENT A CAR SYSTEM, INC.

EXHIBIT 12.4

One of the great names in advertising is William Bernbach, and the memorable and highly effective "We try harder" campaign for Avis Rent a Car was produced by his agency, Doyle Dane Bernbach.
http://www.avis.com

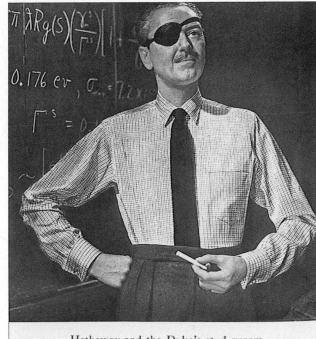

Hathaway and the Duke's stud groom

IT ALL STARTED with Richard Tattersall, the Duke of Kingston's stud groom. He dressed his horses in magnificent check blankets. Then English tailors started using Mr. Tattersall's checks for gentlemen's waistcoats.

Now Hathaway takes the Tattersall one step further. With the help of an old Connecticut mill, we have scaled down this classic pattern to miniature proportions, so that you can wear it in New York. Yet its implication of landed gentry still remains.

You can get this Hathaway miniature Tattersall in red and grey (as illustrated), navy and blue, or mahogany and beige. Between board meetings you can amuse yourself counting the various hallmarks of a Hathaway shirt: 22 single-needle stitches to the inch, big buttons, square-cut cuffs. And so forth.

The price is $8.95. For the name of your nearest store, write C. F. Hathaway, Waterville, Maine. In New York, call OXford 7-5566.

EXHIBIT 12.5

David Ogilvy, to many a guru in advertising, created the Hathaway Shirt Man (complete with an eye patch) as a way to attract attention and create an image for the Hathaway brand many years ago.

Imagine you're a copywriter on the MasterCard account. You've sat through meeting after meeting in which your client, account executives, and researchers have presented a myriad of benefits one gets from using a MasterCard for online purchases. You've talked to customers about their experiences. You've even gone online to try the card out for yourself. All along, your boss has been reminding you that the work you come up with must be as good as the work that focuses on the general use of the card (see Exhibit 12.6). Now your job is simple. Take all the charts, numbers, and strategies and turn them into a simple, emotionally involving, intellectually challenging campaign such as the one in Exhibits 12.7 and 12.8.

Effective copywriters are well-informed, astute advertising decision makers with creative talent. Copywriters are able to comprehend and then incorporate the complexities of marketing strategies, consumer behavior, and advertising strategies into a brief yet powerful communication. They must do so in such a way that the copy does not interfere with but rather enhances the visual aspects of the message.

An astute advertiser will go to great lengths to provide copywriters with as much information as possible about the objectives for a particular advertising effort. The responsibility for keeping copywriters informed lies with the client's marketing managers in conjunction with account executives and creative directors in the ad agency. They must communicate the foundations and intricacies of the firm's marketing strategies to the copywriters. Without this information, copywriters are left without guidance and direction, and they must rely on intuition about what sorts of information

EXHIBIT 12.6

Your boss has been reminding you that the work you come up with must be as good as the work that focuses on the general use of the card. http://www.mastercard.com

EXHIBITS 12.7 AND 12.8

Take all the charts, numbers, and strategies and turn them into a simple, emotionally involving, intellectually challenging campaign. http://www.mastercard.com

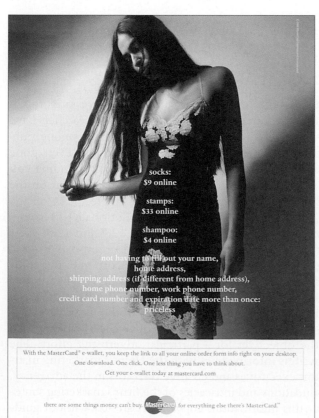

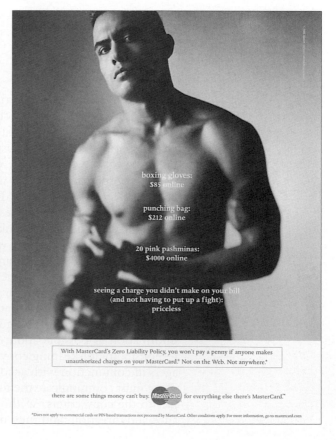

Expected product feature, unexpected creative delivery.

are relevant and meaningful to a target audience. Sometimes that works; most of the time, it does not.

A **creative plan** is a guideline used during the copywriting process to specify the message elements that must be coordinated during the preparation of copy. These elements include main product claims, creative devices, media that will be used, and special creative needs a product or service might have. One of the main challenges faced by a copywriter is to make creative sense out of the maze of information that comes from the message development process. Part of the challenge is creating excitement around what can otherwise be dull product features. For example, just about any razor can claim to shave your face smooth. But the creative team responsible for the ad in Exhibit 12.9 made the claim in an unexpected way. In the ad in Exhibit 12.10, the expected feature of insect-killing ability in an insecticide was presented in an unexpected fashion.

Another aspect of the challenge is bringing together various creative tools (such as illustration, color, sound, and action) and the copy. Copy must also be coordinated with the media that will be used. All of these factors are coordinated through the use of a creative plan. Some of the elements considered in devising a creative plan are the following:

- The single most important thought you want a member of the target market to take away from the advertisement
- The product features to be emphasized
- The benefits a user receives from these features
- The media chosen for transmitting the information and the length of time the advertisement will run
- The suggested mood or tone for the ad
- The ways in which mood and atmosphere will be achieved in the ad
- The production budget for the ad[6]

These considerations can be modified or disregarded entirely during the process of creating an ad. For example, sometimes a brilliant creative execution demands that television, rather than print, be the media vehicle of choice. Occasionally, a particular creative thought may suggest a completely different mood or tone than the one listed in the creative plan. A creative plan is best thought of as a starting point, not an endpoint, for the creative team. Like anything else in advertising, the plan should evolve and grow as new insights are gained. Once the creative plan is devised, the creative team can get on with the task of creating the actual advertisement.

2 Copywriting for Print Advertising.

In preparing copy for a print ad, the first step in the copy development process is deciding how to use (or not use) the three separate components of print copy: the headline, the subhead, and the body copy. Be aware that the full range of components applies most directly to print ads that appear in magazines, newspapers, or direct mail pieces. These guidelines also apply to other "print" media such as billboards, transit advertising, and specialty advertising, but all media are in effect different animals. More detail on these "support" media is presented in Chapter 17. The Creativity box describes how the advertising industry itself is using print advertising to convince corporate executives of the merits of using advertising to build brands.

The Headline.

The **headline** in an advertisement is the leading sentence or sentences, usually at the top or bottom of the ad, that attracts attention, communicates a key selling point, or achieves brand identification. Many headlines fail to attract attention, and the ad itself then becomes another bit of clutter in consumers' lives. Lifeless headlines do not compel the reader to examine other parts of the ad. Simply stated, a headline can either motivate a reader to move on to the rest of an ad or lose the reader for good.

Purposes of a Headline. In preparing a headline, a copywriter begins by considering the variety of purposes a headline can have in terms of gaining attention or actually convincing the consumer. In general, a headline can be written to pursue the following purposes:

- ***Give news about the brand.*** A headline can proclaim a newsworthy event focused on the brand. "Champion Wins Mt. Everest Run" and "25 of 40 Major Titles Won with Titleist" are examples of headlines that communicate news-

---

6.   The last two points in this list were adapted from A. Jerome Jewler, *Creative Strategy in Advertising*, 3rd ed. (Belmont, Calif.: Wadsworth, 1989), 196.

CREATIVITY

Advertising Sells Itself

Ad icons like the Sunkist orange and the Energizer bunny are taking center stage in a campaign aimed to sell corporate executives on using advertising to build brands. The multiyear print advertising campaign by the American Advertising Federation (AAF) highlights the success of top brands, hoping to reinforce advertising's strategic importance in the changing business environment. A survey of top-level executives conducted by the AAF validates the need for the campaign: The survey found that while CEOs appreciated that advertising drove sales, they didn't have a complete understanding of its importance in building brands.

The new AAF campaign alters familiar ads of well-respected brands, using a persuasive mix of copy and visual to get the point across that advertising is vital to brand success. For the visual, Energizer, Sunkist, Coca-Cola, Anheuser-Busch, and Intel signed off on an unprecedented modification of their logos. The logos in the AAF ads are modified to read "Advertising" and then a specific question or statement is put forth. The copy ends with the same tagline, prompting audiences to reflect on the value of advertising.

Energizer's copy asks, "What makes one battery more powerful than another?" Sunkist's copy states, "The average grocery store carries 16,875 brands. Why do you recognize this one?" Coca-Cola's copy states, "The secret formula, revealed." Intel's copy states, "It's what makes computers more powerful." For each, the AAF tag is the same: "Advertising. The way great brands get to be great brands." The idea behind the creative was born out of the notion that advertising helped build the world's most recognized brands. "If you put your hand over the logo, you would still recognize who it was," said Randy Hughes, the creative director of the campaign.

Now seems to be an important time for advertising to sell itself, and the fact that top brands have allowed cherished logos to be altered shows the solidarity of advertisers in making their case to CEOs. Advertising currently ranks low in strategic importance among top executives, and less than half of those surveyed by the AAF believe that the importance of advertising will increase in the future. That mindset isn't likely to change soon. In fact, 27 percent of the marketers surveyed said advertising would be among the first budget items cut in a sales downturn. The AAF hopes that a little shameless self-promotion can force executives to change their minds—and, more important, their budgets.

Sources: AAF, "AAF's Next 'Great Brands' Campaign Features Intel," press release available at http://www.aaf.org, accessed October 31, 2001; Wendy Milillo, "AAF Debuts Print Campaign," *Advertising Week*, available at http://www.aaf.org, accessed October 31, 2001.

worthy events about Champion spark plugs and Titleist golf balls. The Tanqueray No. Ten ad in Exhibit 12.11 uses this approach in a powerful, straightforward manner.

- *Emphasize a brand claim.* A primary and perhaps differentiating feature of the brand is a likely candidate for the headline theme. "30% More Mileage on Firestone Tires" highlights durability. Exhibit 12.12 reminds people of how durable a HUMMER is.

- *Give advice to the reader.* A headline can give the reader a recommendation that (usually) is supported by results provided in the body copy. "Increase Your Reading Skills" and "Save up to 90% on Commissions" both implore the reader to take the advice of the ad. The headline in Exhibit 12.13 advises readers to make sure that bad radio stations don't ever ruin a road trip.

- *Select prospects.* Headlines can attract the attention of the intended audience. "Good News for Arthritis Sufferers" and "Attention June Graduates" are examples of headlines designed to achieve prospect selection. The headline in the women.com ad shown in Exhibit 12.14 suggests in no uncertain terms who the intended audience is for the site.

- *Stimulate the reader's curiosity.* Posing a riddle with a headline can serve to attract attention and stimulate readership. Curiosity can be stimulated with a clever play on words or a contradiction. Take, for example, the headline "With MCI, Gerber's Baby Talk Never Sounded Better." The body copy goes on to explain that Gerber Products (a maker of baby products) uses the high technology of MCI for its communication needs. Does the headline in the ad shown in Exhibit 12.15 get your attention? It was written for that purpose.

- *Set a tone or establish an emotion.* Language can be used to establish a mood that the advertiser wants associated with its product. Teva sports sandals has an ad with the headline "When you die, they put you in a nice suit and shiny shoes. As if death didn't suck enough already." Even though there is no direct reference to

EXHIBIT 12.11

This ad gives important news about the brand.

EXHIBIT 12.13

This headline offers advice. http://www.roxio.com

EXHIBIT 12.12

This headline emphasizes a straight-ahead brand feature. http://www.hummer.com

for every hundred women

42 have their mother's eyes.

17 own a "#1 MOM" coffee mug.

61 swore they'd never turn into their mother.

60 have turned into their mother.

55 say their mom is their best friend.

There's one place for all of us.   **w men com** Where women are going.

www.women.com   AOL keyword: women.com

EXHIBIT 12.14

The headline in this ad suggests in no uncertain terms who the intended audience is for the site. http://www .women.com

the product being advertised, the reader has learned quite a bit about the company doing the advertising and the types of people expected to buy the product. The headline in the ad shown in Exhibit 12.16 accomplishes the same objective.

- *Identify the brand.* This is the most straightforward of all headline purposes. The brand name or label is used as the headline, either alone or in conjunction with a word or two. The goal is to simply identify the brand and reinforce brand-name recognition. Advertising for Brut men's fragrance products often uses merely the brand name as the headline.

Guidelines for Writing Headlines. Once a copywriter has firmly established the purpose a headline will serve in an advertisement, several guidelines can be followed in preparing the headline. The following are basic guidelines for writing a good headline for print advertisements:

- Make the headline a major persuasive component of the ad. Five times as many people read the headline as the body copy of an ad. If this is your only opportunity to communicate, what should you say? The headline "New Power. New Comfort. New Technology. New Yorker" in a Chrysler ad communicates major improvements in the product quickly and clearly.
- Appeal to the reader's self-interest with a basic promise of benefits coming from the brand. For example, "The Temperature Never Drops

EXHIBIT 12.15

A headline that creates curiosity motivates readers to continue reading, perhaps after a slight disconcerting pause. http://www.milk .co.uk

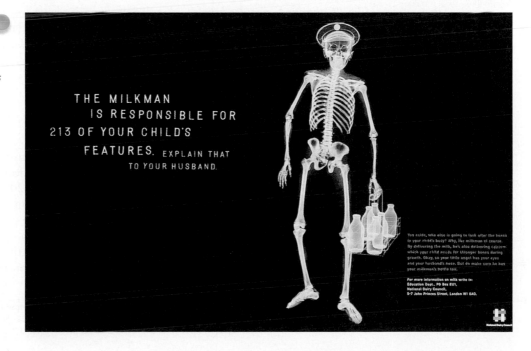

IF YOU BUILD IT, THEY WILL CLICK.

The latest scores, in-depth analysis, global coverage. SportsLine.com offers depth of content no fan can resist. And to help them deliver it all, they turn to AT&T. Every day SportsLine.com averages over 25 million page views from fans looking to download streaming video, get real-time scores and more. AT&T's broadband technology helps to deliver it, 24x7. Today, thousands of businesses are playing smarter and faster with the help of AT&T. It's a whole new game. Enjoy.

AT&T | BOUNDLESS

att.com/boundless

EXHIBIT 12.16

Even though there is no direct reference to the product being advertised, the reader has learned quite a bit about the company doing the advertising and the types of people expected to buy the product. http://www.att.com/boundless

Below Zerex" promises engine protection in freezing weather from Zerex antifreeze.

- Inject the maximum information in the headline without making it cumbersome or wordy.
- Limit headlines to about five to eight words.[7] Research indicates that recall drops off significantly for sentences longer than eight words.
- Include the brand name in the headline.
- Entice the reader to read the body copy.
- Entice the reader to examine the visual in the ad. An intriguing headline can lead the reader to carefully examine the visual components of the ad.
- Never change typefaces within a headline. Changing the form and style of the print can increase the complexity of visual impression and negatively affect the readership.
- Never use a headline whose persuasive impact depends on reading the body copy.
- Use simple, common, familiar words. Recognition and comprehension are aided by words that are easy to understand and recognize.

This set of guidelines is meant only as a starting point. A headline may violate one or even all of these basic premises and still be effective. And it is unrealistic to try to fulfill the requirements of each guideline in every headline. This list simply offers general safeguards to be considered. Test the list for yourself using the ads in Exhibits 12.17 through 12.19. Which, if any, of these ten guidelines do these ads comply with? And which ones do they torch? Which of these guidelines would you say are most important for creating effective headlines?

A truly great piece of advice:

Certain headlines are currently checked out. You may use them when they are returned. Lines like "Contrary to popular belief . . ." or "Something is wrong when . . ." These are dead. Elvis is dead. John Lennon is dead. Deal with it. Remember, anything that you even think you've seen, forget about it. The stuff you've never seen? You'll know when you see it, too. It raises the hair on the back of your neck.

—Luke Sullivan[8]

Originality is good.

The Subhead. A **subhead** consists of a few words or a short sentence and usually appears above or below the headline. It includes important brand information not included in the headline. The subhead in the ad for Clorox in Exhibit 12.20 is an excellent example of how a subhead is used to convey important brand information not communicated in the headline. A subhead serves basically the same purpose as a headline—to communicate key selling points or brand information quickly. A subhead is normally in print smaller than the headline, but larger than the body copy. In many cases, the subhead is more lengthy than the headline and can be used to communi-

7.   Based in part on Jewler, *Creative Strategy in Advertising*, 232–233; Albert C. Book, Norman D. Cary, and Stanley I. Tannenbaum, *The Radio and Television Commercial* (Lincolnwood, Ill.: NTC Business Books, 1984), 22–26.
8.   Luke Sullivan, *Hey Whipple, Squeeze This: A Guide to Creating Great Ads* (New York: Wiley, 1998), 78.

There are ten general guidelines for writing headlines. How do you rate the headlines in these ads relative to the guidelines? http://www .landrover.com, http://www.waterfrontbluesfest.com, *and* http://www.beefitswhatsfordinner.com

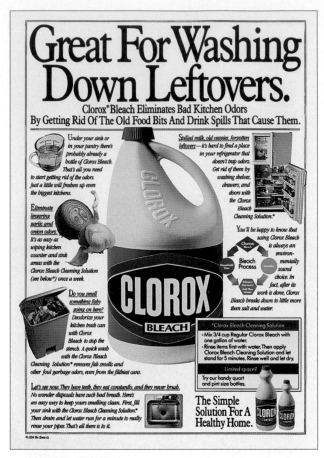

EXHIBIT 12.20

Subheads include important brand information not included in the headline. Where is the subhead in this Clorox ad? What does the subhead accomplish that the headline does not?
http://www.clorox.com

cate more complex selling points. The subhead should reinforce the headline and, again, entice the reader to proceed to the body copy.

Subheads can serve another important purpose: stimulating a more complete reading of the entire ad. If the headline attracts attention, the subhead can stimulate movement through the physical space of the ad, including the visual. A good rule of thumb is the longer the body copy, the more appropriate the use of subheads. Most creative directors try to keep the use of subheads to the barest minimum, however. They feel that if an ad's visual and headline can't communicate the benefit of a product quickly and clearly, the ad isn't very good.

The Body Copy. More good advice:

I don't think people read body copy. I think we've entered a frenzied era of coffee-guzzling, fax-sending channel surfers who honk the microsecond the light turns green and have the attention span of a flashcube. If the first five words of body copy aren't "May we send you $700.00?," word 6 isn't read. Just my opinion, mind you.

—Luke Sullivan[9]

It's our opinion too.

Body copy is the textual component of an advertisement and tells a more complete story of a brand. Effective body copy is written in a fashion that takes advantage of and reinforces the headline and subhead, is compatible with and gains strength from the visual, and is interesting to the reader. Whether body copy is interesting is a function of how accurately the copywriter and other decision makers have assessed various components of message development, and how good the copywriter is. The most elaborate body copy will probably be ineffective if it is "off strategy." It will not matter if it's very clever, but has little to do in advancing the strategy.

There are several standard techniques for preparing body copy. The **straight-line copy** approach explains in straightforward terms why a reader will benefit from use of a brand. This technique is used many times in conjunction with a benefits message strategy. Body copy that uses **dialogue** delivers the selling points of a message to the audience through a character or characters in the ad. The Nicorette ad shown in Exhibit 12.21 is an example of the testimonial technique. A **testimonial** uses dialogue as if the spokesperson is having a one-sided conversation with the reader through the body copy. Dialogue can also depict two people in the ad having a conversation, a technique often used in slice-of-life messages.

Narrative as a method for preparing body copy simply displays a series of statements about a brand. A person may or may not be portrayed as delivering the copy. It is difficult to make this technique lively for the reader, so the threat of writing a dull ad using this technique is ever present. **Direct response copy** is, in many ways, the least complex of copy techniques. In writing direct response copy, the copywriter is trying to highlight the urgency of acting immediately. Hence, the range of

9.   Ibid, 85.

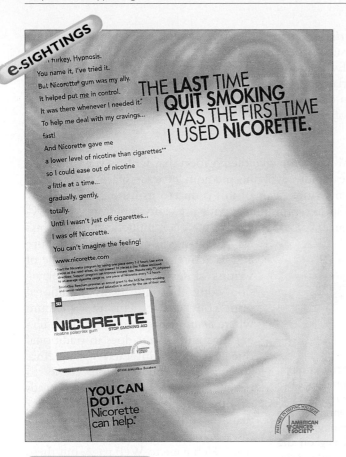

...turkey, Hypnosis.
You name it, I've tried it.
But Nicorette® gum was my ally.
It helped put _me_ in control.
It was there whenever I needed it.
To help me deal with my cravings...

fast!

And Nicorette gave me
a lower level of nicotine than cigarettes**
so I could ease out of nicotine
a little at a time...
gradually, gently,
totally.
Until I wasn't just off cigarettes...
I was off Nicorette.
You can't imagine the feeling!

www.nicorette.com

THE LAST TIME I QUIT SMOKING WAS THE FIRST TIME I USED NICORETTE.

NICORETTE®
nicotine polacrilex gum
STOP SMOKING AID

YOU CAN DO IT.
Nicorette can help.®

AMERICAN CANCER SOCIETY

EXHIBIT 12.21

In this testimonial ad from Nicorette (http://www.nicorette.com), a spokesperson tells his story directly to the reader. Is this same copy technique used at the Nicorette site? What does Nicorette offer to its customers at the Committed Quitters resource site (http://www.committedquitters.com), and is the copy at this site more geared toward eliciting a direct response from consumers?

possibilities for direct response copy is more limited. In addition, many direct response advertisements rely on sales promotion devices, such as coupons, contests, and rebates, as a means of stimulating action. Giving deadlines to the reader is also a common approach in direct response advertising.

These techniques for copywriting establish a general set of styles that can be used as the format for body copy. Again, be aware that any message objective can be employed within any particular copy technique. There are a vast number of compatible combinations.

Guidelines for Writing Body Copy. Regardless of the specific technique used to develop body copy, the probability of writing effective body copy can be increased if certain guidelines are followed. However, guidelines are meant to be just that—guidelines. Copywriters have created excellent ads that violate one or more of these recommendations. Generally, however, body copy for print ads has a better chance of being effective if these guidelines are followed:

- _**Use the present tense whenever possible.**_ Casting brand claims in the past or future reduces their credibility and timeliness. Speaking to the target audience about things that have happened or will happen sounds like hollow promises.
- _**Use singular nouns and verbs.**_ An ad is normally read by only one person at a time, and that person is evaluating only one brand. Using plural nouns and verbs simply reduces the focus on the item or brand attribute being touted and makes the ad less personal.
- _**Use active verbs.**_ The passive form of a verb does little to stimulate excitement or interest. The use of the active verb in Pontiac's "We Build Excitement" slogan suggests that something is happening, and it's happening _now_.
- _**Use familiar words and phrases.**_ Relying on familiar words and phrases to communicate in an interesting and unique way poses a formidable challenge for a copywriter. Familiar words can seem common and ordinary. The challenge is to creatively stylize what is familiar and comfortable to the reader so that interest and excitement result.
- _**Vary the length of sentences and paragraphs.**_ Using sentences and paragraphs of varying lengths not only serves to increase interest but also has a visual impact that can make an ad more inviting and readable.
- _**Involve the reader.**_ Talking at the receiver or creating a condescending mood with copy results in a short-circuited communication. Copy that impresses the reader as having been written specifically for him or her reduces the chances of the ad being perceived as a generalized, mass communication.
- _**Provide support for the unbelievable.**_ A brand may have features or functions that the reader finds hard to believe. Where such claims are critical to the brand's positioning in the market and value to the consumer, it is necessary to document (through test results or testimonials) that the brand actually lives up to the claims made. Without proper support of claims, the brand will lose its credibility and therefore its relevance to the consumer.

- *Avoid clichés and superlatives.* Clichés are rarely effective or attention-getting. The average consumer assumes that a brand touted through the use of clichés is old-fashioned and stale. Even though the foundation for puffery as a message method is the use of superlatives (*best, superior, unbeatable*), it is wise to avoid their use. These terms are worn out and can signal to the consumer that the brand has little new or different to offer.[10]

Copywriting for Cyberspace.

While some take the position that writing is writing, we see enough evidence that the rapidly evolving medium of cyberspace has its own style, its own feel, and its own writing. Part of this is due to its history. Cybercopy evolved from a very techno-speak community, with a twentysomething, Gen-X-meets-techno-nerd kind of voice. Cybercopy's style has been influenced by this history. The medium itself, its structure and its active nature, suggests a type of writing closer to print than to television copy, but not really traditional print copy either. This is a medium where *audience* has a significantly different meaning than it does in traditional one-way (noninteractive) media. Audience members often come to cyberads, that is they seek out the ads or other online IBP material, rather than the other way around. In other cases, cyberads pop up as one moves from Web page to Web page, but these pop-ups are fortunately going the way of the eight-track. The medium itself (online computer) is a fundamentally more user-directed medium than print, television, or radio. This means that consumers approach (and read) cyberads somewhat differently than other ads. Most believe there is still more incentive to read cybercopy than traditional print advertising. Further, much cybercopy is direct response, thus dictating copy style. At this point we believe that the basic principles of good print advertising discussed earlier in the chapter (and reconsidered in the Creativity box) generally apply, but a type of copy that assumes an active and engaged audience is preferred. Still, remember that odds are that they are not there for your ads, and they have a mouse in their hands. Consider the cyberads in Exhibits 12.22 through 12.25. What do these different forms suggest to you about cyberwriting?

CREATIVITY

Writing Cybercopy: Don't Abandon All the Old Rules

Writing effective copy for print and broadcast media is difficult enough, but what kind of copy does the average Net surfer find appealing? No one really knows, but we do know a few things about early users of the Internet and World Wide Web. First, users of the Internet are there first and foremost because it is an information environment. It is hard to imagine someone getting up in the morning, turning on the computer, and seeking out ads. Quite to the contrary, the beauty of the Internet in the minds of many has been its freedom from advertising.

Second, when Internet users visit a site, that visit may last only a few seconds. *HotWired* magazine says that on a good day, it can have 600,000 "hits," or visits, some lasting only a few seconds—just long enough for the visitor to quickly scan what is available and then, if not intrigued, move on to another site. The chance to communicate online thus may be even more fleeting than the opportunity offered by radio or television. Third, advertisers have to accept that cyberspace may become just as cluttered with competing ads as the traditional media.

In the end, the rules for writing effective copy in cyberspace may not be all that different from the general rules for copywriting. Once a browser is attracted to a site for the information it offers, he or she will, oh by the way, bump into ads. The new opportunity is to make these ads and their copy interactive according to an individual consumer's interest. If an IBM advertisement can lead a consumer through a series of alternative click-and-proceed paths, then customization of ads is the new copywriting opportunity offered by the interactive environment.

Sources: "Cerfin' the Net," *Sales and Marketing Management,* March 1995, 18–23; Julie Chao, "Tallies of Web-Site Browsers Often Deceive," *Wall Street Journal,* June 12, 1995, B1; Bruce Judson, "Luring Advertisers' Prospects to Web," *Advertising Age,* August 7, 1995, 16; Steven Oberbeck, "Continued Growth in Internet Ads, Users Forecast," *Salt Lake Tribune,* March 21, 1999, http://www.sltrib.com, accessed March 22, 1999.

---

10.   The last three points in this list were adapted from Kenneth Roman and Jan Maas, *The New How to Advertise* (New York: St. Martin's Press, 1992), 18–19.

EXHIBITS 12.22 THROUGH 12.25

Cybercopy represents a new type of ad writing—closer to print than to television copy, but not really traditional print copy either. What do these four cyberads suggest to you about cyberwriting? http://www.garageband.com, http://www.johnsonville.com, http://www.columbia.com, *and* http://www.woodentoy.com.

Copywriting for Broadcast Advertising.

Relative to the print media, radio and television present totally different challenges for a copywriter. It is obvious that the audio and audiovisual capabilities of radio and television provide different opportunities for a copywriter. The use of sound effects and voices on radio and the ability to combine copy with color and motion on television provide vast and exciting creative possibilities.

Compared to print media, however, broadcast media have inherent limitations for a copywriter. In print media, a copywriter can write longer and more involved copy to better communicate complex brand features. For consumer shopping goods such as automobiles or home satellite systems, a brand's basis for competitive differentiation and positioning may lie with complex, unique functional features. In this case, print media provide a copywriter the time and space to communicate these details, complete with illustrations. In addition, the printed page allows a reader to dwell on the copy and process the information at a personalized, comfortable rate.

These advantages do not exist in the broadcast media. Radio and television offer a fleeting exposure. In addition, introducing sound effects and visual stimuli can distract the listener or viewer from the copy of the advertisement. Despite the additional creative opportunities that radio and television offer, the essential challenge of copywriting remains.

3　Writing Copy for Radio.

Your spot just interrupted your listener's music. It's like interrupting people having sex. If you're going to lean in the bedroom door to say something, make it good: "Hey your car's on fire."

—Luke Sullivan[11]

Some writers consider radio the ultimate forum for copywriting creativity. Because the radio is restricted to an audio-only presentation, a copywriter is free from some of the harsher realities of visual presentations. Yet it has been said that radio *is* visual. The copywriter must (it is almost inevitable) create images in the minds of listeners. The creative potential of radio rests in its ability to stimulate a theater of the mind, which allows a copywriter to create images and moods for an audience that transcend those created in any other medium.

Despite these creative opportunities, the drawbacks of this medium should never be underestimated. Few radio listeners ever actively listen to radio programming, much less the commercial interruptions. (Talk radio is an obvious exception.) Radio may be viewed by some as the theater of the mind, but others have labeled it audio wallpaper—wallpaper in the sense that radio is used as filler or unobtrusive accompaniment to reading, driving, household chores, or homework. If it were absent, the average person would miss it, but the average person would be hard-pressed to recall the radio ads aired during dinner last evening.

The most reasonable view of copywriting for radio is to temper both the enthusiasm of the theater-of-the-mind perspective and the pessimism of the audio-wallpaper view. (Of course, "reasonable" creative solutions often are destined to be mind-numbingly dull.) A radio copywriter should recognize the unique character of radio and exploit the opportunities it offers. First, radio adds the dimension of sound to the copywriting task, and sound (other than voices) can become a primary tool in creating copy. Second, radio can conjure images in the mind of the receiver that extend beyond the starkness of the brand "information" actually being provided. Radio copywriting should, therefore, strive to stimulate each receiver's imagination.

Writing copy for radio should begin the same way that writing copy for print begins. The copywriter must review components of the creative plan so as to take advantage of and follow through on the marketing and advertising strategies specified and integral to the brand's market potential. Beyond that fundamental task, there are particular formats for radio ads and guidelines for copy preparation the writer can rely on for direction.

Radio Advertising Formats. There are four basic formats for radio advertisements, and these formats provide the structure within which copy is prepared: the music format, the dialogue format, the announcement format, and the celebrity announcer format. Each of these formats is discussed here.

Music. Since radio provides audio opportunities, music is often used in radio ads. One use of music is to write a song or jingle in an attempt to communicate in an attention-getting and memorable fashion. Songs and jingles are generally written specifically to accommodate unique brand copy. On occasion, an existing tune can be used, and the copy is fit to its meter and rhythm. This is especially true if the

11.　Sullivan, *Hey Whipple, Squeeze This: A Guide to Creating Great Ads,* 131.

music is being used to capture the attention of a particular target segment. Tunes popular with certain target segments can be licensed for use by advertisers. Advertisements using popular tunes by Garbage and Barry Manilow would presumably attract two very different audiences. Singing and music can do much to attract the listener's attention and enhance recall. Singing can also create a mood and image with which the product is associated. Modern scores can create a contemporary mood, while sultry music and lyrics create a totally different mood.

But what of jingles? While some love them—and let's face it, they have survived for over a hundred years in advertising—there are some hazards in the use of singing or jingles. Few copywriters are trained lyricists or composers. The threat is ever present that a musical score or a jingle will strike receivers as amateurish and silly. To avoid this, expert songwriters are often used. Further, ensuring that the copy information dominates the musical accompaniment takes great skill. The musical impact can easily overwhelm the persuasion and selling purposes of an ad. Still, just try to get a really good jingle out of your head. You may go to your grave with it on your mind.

Another use of music in radio commercials is to open the ad with a musical score and/or have music playing in the background while the copy is being read. The role of music here is generally to attract attention. This application of music, as well as music used in a song or jingle, is subject to an ongoing debate. If a radio ad is scheduled for airing on music-format stations, should the music in the ad be the same type of music the station is noted for playing, or should it be different? One argument says that if the station format is rock, for example, then the ad should use rock music to appeal to the listener's taste. The opposite argument states that using the same type of music simply buries the ad in the regular programming and reduces its impact. There is no good evidence to suggest that music similar to or different from station programming is superior.

Dialogue. The dialogue technique, described in the section on print copywriting, is commonly used in radio. There are difficulties in making narrative copy work in the short periods of time afforded by the radio medium (typically 15 to 60 seconds). The threat is that dialogue will result in a dull drone of two or more people having a conversation. (You hear enough of that, right?) To reduce the threat of boredom, many dialogues are written with humor, like the one in Exhibit 12.26. Of course, some believe that humor is overused in radio.

Announcement. Radio copy delivered by an announcer is similar to narrative copy in print advertising. The announcer reads important product information as it has been prepared by the copywriter. Announcement is the prevalent technique for live radio spots delivered by disc jockeys or news commentators. The live setting leaves little opportunity for much else. If the ad is prerecorded, sound effects or music may be added to enhance the transmission.

CLIENT 01145.4 SWAIR dh **TITLE** "Nope"
MEDIUM Radio SWM10383 **LENGTH/SIZE** :30
DATE 2/6/01; Rev. 3/19 A **WRITER/PRODUCER** MR/Su Cl

GSD&M

AS RECORDED

MAN:	October second?
WOMAN:	Nope.
MAN:	October 20th?
WOMAN:	Nope.
MAN:	November 18th.
WOMAN:	(THROUGH PHONE RECEIVER) Nope.
MAN:	November 19th?
WOMAN:	Nope.
MAN:	December second?
WOMAN:	Nope.
MAN:	December 25th?
WOMAN:	Are you kidding?
MAN:	January 17th?
WOMAN:	Nope.

ANNCR: What good are frequent flyer miles if you can't use them? With Rapid Rewards from Southwest Airlines, you can fly where you want, when you want. No seat restrictions. Very few blackout dates.

MAN:	June 22nd?
WOMAN:	Nope.
MAN:	This doesn't bother you at all, does it?
WOMAN:	Nope.

ANNCR: So don't miss out. Visit southwest.com to learn how to become a Rapid Rewards Member. Southwest Airlines.

SFX: **DING**

PILOT: You are now free to move about the country.

EXHIBIT 12.26

To reduce the threat of boredom, many dialogues are written with humor.

Celebrity Announcer. Having a famous person deliver the copy is alleged to increase the attention paid to a radio ad. Most radio ads that use celebrities do not fall into the testimonial category. The celebrity is not expressing his or her satisfaction with the product, but merely acting as an announcer. Some celebrities (such as James Earl Jones) have distinctive voice qualities or are expert at the emphatic delivery of copy. It is argued that these qualities, as well as listener recognition of the celebrity, increase attention to the ad.

Guidelines for Writing Radio Copy. The unique opportunities and challenges of the radio medium warrant a set of guidelines for the copywriter to increase the probability of effective communication. The following are a few suggestions for writing effective radio copy:

- *Use common, familiar language.* The use of words and language easily understood and recognized by the receiver is even more important in radio than in print copy preparation.
- *Use short words and sentences.* The probability of communicating verbally increases if short, easily processed words and sentences are used. Long, involved, elaborate verbal descriptions make it difficult for the listener to follow the copy.
- *Stimulate the imagination.* Copy that can conjure up concrete and stimulating images in the receiver's mind can have a powerful impact on recall.
- *Repeat the name of the product.* Since the impression made by a radio ad is fleeting, it may be necessary to repeat the brand name several times before it will register. The same is true for location if the ad is being used to promote a retail organization.
- *Stress the main selling point or points.* The premise of the advertising should revolve around the information that needs to be presented. If selling points are mentioned only in passing, there is little reason to believe they'll be remembered.
- *Use sound and music with care.* By all means, a copywriter should take advantage of all the audio capabilities afforded by the radio medium, including the use of sound effects and music. While these devices can contribute greatly to attracting and holding the listener's attention, care must be taken to ensure that the devices do not overwhelm the copy and therefore the persuasive impact of the commercial.
- *Tailor the copy to the time, place, and specific audience.* Take advantage of any unique aspect of the advertising context. If the ad is specified for a particular geographic region, use colloquialisms unique to that region as a way to tailor the message. The same is true with time-of-day factors or unique aspects of the audience.[12]

The Radio Production Process. Radio commercial production highlights the role of the copywriter. There is no art director involved in the process. Further, the writer is relatively free to plan nearly any radio production he or she chooses because of the significantly reduced costs of radio execution compared to television. In radio, there are far fewer expert participants than in television. This more streamlined form of production does not mean, however, that the process is more casual. Successful fulfillment of the objectives of an advertisement still requires the careful planning and execution of the production process.

Exhibit 12.27 lists the stages and timetable of a fairly complex radio production: a fully produced commercial. Again, this is a realistic and reasonable timetable once script and budget approval have been secured. The production process for radio is quite similar to the production process for television. Once the copy strategy and methods for the commercial are approved, the process begins with soliciting bids from production houses. The producer reviews bids and submits the best bid for advertiser approval. When the best bid (not always the lowest-priced bid) is identified, the agency submits an estimate to the advertiser for approval. The bid estimate includes both the production house bid and the agency's estimates of its own costs associated with production. When the agency and the advertiser agree, then the producer can award the job to a production house.

12.   Book, Cary, and Tannenbaum, *The Radio and Television Commercial*.

The timetable of a fully produced radio commercial, once script and budget approval have been secured.

Activity	Time
Solicit bids from production houses/other suppliers	1 week
Review bids, award job, submit production estimate to advertiser	1 week
Select a cast (announcer, singers, musicians)	1 week
Plan special elements (e.g., sound effects); make final preparations; produce tape	1 week
Edit tape	Less than 1 week
Review production (advertiser)	1 week
Mix sound	Less than 1 week
Duplicate tape; ship to stations	1 week
Total	6 to 7 weeks

After awarding the job to a production house, the next step is to cast the ad. A radio ad may have only an announcer, in which case the casting job is relatively simple. If the dialogue technique is used, two or more actors and actresses may be needed. Additionally, musical scores often accompany radio ads, and either the music has to be recorded, which includes a search for musicians and possibly singers, or prerecorded music has to be obtained for use by permission. Securing permission for existing music, especially if it is currently popular, can be costly. Much music is in the public domain—that is, it is no longer rigidly protected by copyright laws and is available for far less cost. Closely following the casting is the planning of special elements for the ad, which can include sound effects or special effects, such as time compression or stretching, to create distinct sounds.

Final preparation and production entails scheduling a sound studio and arranging for the actors and actresses to record their pieces in the ad. If an announcer is used in addition to acting talent, the announcer may or may not record with the full cast; her or his lines can be incorporated into the tape at some later time. Music is generally recorded separately and simply added to the commercial during the sound-mixing stage.

It is during the actual production of the ad that the copywriter's efforts become a reality. As in television production, the copywriter will have drawn on the copy platform plans approved in the message development stage to write copy for the radio spot. The script used in the production of a radio advertisement serves the same purpose that the storyboard does in television production. Exhibit 12.28 shows a typical radio script.

Note that the copywriter must indicate the use of sound effects (SFX) on a separate line to specify the timing of these devices. Further, each player in the advertisement is listed by role, including the announcer if one is used.

One important element of writing radio copy not yet discussed is the number of words of copy to use given the length of the radio ad. As a general rule, word count relative to airtime is as follows:

10 seconds	20 to 25 words
20 seconds	40 to 45 words
30 seconds	60 to 65 words
60 seconds	120 to 125 words
90 seconds	185 to 190 words[13]

13.   Sandra E. Moriarty, *Creative Advertising: Theory and Practice,* 2nd ed. (Englewood Cliffs, N. J.: Prentice Hall, 1991), 293.

MERIT AWARD: Consumer Radio: Single
WRITER: Adam Chasnow
AGENCY PRODUCER: Andy Lerner
CLIENT: Hollywood Video
AGENCY: Cliff Freeman & Partners/New York
ID 00 0542A

ANNOUNCER:	Hollywood Video presents "Sixty Second Theater," where we try, unsuccessfully, to pack all the action and suspense of a two-hour Hollywood production into 60 seconds. Today's presentation, "The Matrix."
SFX:	TECHNO/ACTION MUSIC; KNOCK KNOCK.
TRINITY:	(CARRIE-ANN MOSS SOUNDALIKE; FROM BEHIND DOOR) Hello, Neo?
NEO:	(KEANU REEVES SOUNDALIKE) Yeah.
TRINITY:	You gotta come with me to meet Morpheus and learn about the Matrix.
NEO:	But I don't know you.
TRINITY:	I'm wearing a skin-tight leather catsuit.
SFX:	DOOR OPENS.
NEO:	Oh, I'll get my coat.
SFX:	TECHNO/ACTION MUSIC TRANSITION.
TRINITY:	Morpheus, this is Neo. He's going to save the world from the machines that control the virtual reality the entire human race believes they live in.
MORPHEUS:	(LAURENCE FISHBURNE SOUNDALIKE) Hi, Neo.
NEO:	(VERY KEANU) Hey, dude.
MORPHEUS:	(TO TRINITY UNDER HIS BREATH) This guy's going to save the world?
TRINITY:	Yeah. Isn't he hot?
MORPHEUS:	We better get started. Plug the computer into his head.
SFX:	PLUG INTO HEAD.
NEO:	Ouch!
SFX:	COMPUTER SOUNDS.
MORPHEUS:	Download everything he needs to know. First, kung fu.
SFX:	COMPUTER SOUNDS.
NEO:	Hi-yah!
MORPHEUS:	Now, judo.
SFX:	KARATE SOUNDS; BODY SLAM.
NEO:	Whoa!
MORPHEUS:	And wine tasting.
SFX:	COMPUTER SOUNDS; WINE POURING FROM BOTTLE.
NEO:	Mmm. Is this a merlot or a cabernet?
MORPHEUS:	Cabernet.
SFX:	WINE GLASSES CLINKING. TECHNO/ACTION MUSIC TRANSITION.
MORPHEUS:	Now you're ready to save the world, which doesn't exist.
NEO:	Wait. This isn't actually happening?
MORPHEUS:	It is, but it isn't.
NEO:	You mean, I don't know kung fu?
MORPHEUS:	No.
NEO:	And that wasn't a cabernet?
MORPHEUS:	Sorry.
NEO:	What about her leather catsuit?
MORPHEUS:	I'm afraid not.
NEO:	Dude!
SFX:	HOLLYWOOD VIDEO THEME MUSIC.
ANNOUNCER:	If this doesn't satisfy your urge to see "The Matrix," and we can't say we blame you, then rent it today at Hollywood Video. The only place to get five-day rentals on new releases like "Prince of Egypt" and "The Mummy," available September 28th. Welcome to Hollywood. Hollywood Video. Celebrity voices impersonated.

EXHIBIT 12.28

A typical radio script. http://www.hollywoodvideo.com

The inclusion of musical introductions, special effects, or local tag lines (specific information for local markets) reduces the amount of copy in the advertisement. Special sound effects interspersed with copy also shorten copy length. The general rules for number of words relative to ad time change depending on the form and structure of the commercial.

After production, the tape goes through editing to create the best version of the production. Then, after advertiser approval, a sound mix is completed in which all music, special sound effects, and announcer copy are mixed together. The mixing process achieves proper timing between all audio elements in the ad and ensures that all sounds are at the desired levels. After mixing, the tape is duplicated and sent to radio stations for airing.

Expenses for a radio ad should be in the $30,000 to $50,000 range, although big-name talent can push that cost way up.

The most loosely structured production option essentially requires no production at all. It is called a fact sheet. A **fact sheet radio ad** is merely a listing of important selling points that a radio announcer can use to ad-lib a radio spot. This method works best with radio personalities who draw an audience because of their lively, entertaining monologues. The fact sheet provides a loose structure so the announcer can work in the ad during these informal monologues. The risk, of course, is that the ad will get lost in the chatter and the selling points will not be convincingly delivered. On the positive side, radio personalities many times go beyond the scheduled 30 or 60 seconds allotted for the ad.

Another loosely structured technique is the live script. The **live script radio ad** involves having an on-air radio personality, such as a DJ or talk-show host, read the detailed script of an advertisement. Normally there are no sound effects, since such effects would require special production. The live script ensures that all the selling points are included when the commercial is delivered by the announcer. These scripts are not rehearsed, however, and the emphasis, tone, and tempo in the delivery may not be ideal. The advantage of a live script is that it allows an advertiser to submit a relatively structured commercial for airing in a very short period of time. Most stations can work in a live script commercial in a matter of hours after it is received. Exhibit 12.29 shows that a live script is, indeed, read right over the air.

EXHIBIT 12.29

A live script radio ad has an on-air personality read a detailed script over the air. Normally, there are no sound effects or music to accompany the ad—just the announcer's voice.

4   Writing Copy for Television.

Great print can make you famous. Great TV can make you rich.

—Anonymous[14]

Rule #1 in producing a great TV commercial. First, you must write one.

—Luke Sullivan[15]

The ability to create a mood or demonstrate a brand in use gives television wonderful capabilities; it also affords you the ability to really screw up in magnificent fashion for a very large and expensive audience (no pressure here!). Obviously, copy for television must be highly sensitive to the ad's visual aspects. It is a visual medium; you should try to not let the words get in the way.

The opportunities inherent to television as an advertising medium represent challenges for the copywriter as well. Certainly, the inherent capabilities of television can do much to bring a copywriter's words to life. But the action qualities of television can create problems. First, the copywriter must remember that words do not stand alone. Visuals, special effects, and sound techniques may ultimately convey a message far better than the cleverest turn of phrase. Second, television commercials represent a difficult timing challenge for the copywriter. It is necessary for the copy to be precisely coordinated with the video. If the video portion were one continuous illustration, the task would be difficult enough. Contemporary television ads, however, tend to be heavily edited (that is, lots of cuts), and the copywriting task can be a nightmare. The copywriter not only has to fulfill all the responsibilities of proper information inclusion (based on creative platform and strategy decisions), but also has to carefully fit all the information within, between, and around the visual display taking place. To make sure this coordination is precise, the copywriter, producer, and director assigned to a television advertisement work together closely to make sure the copy supports and enhances the video element. The road map for this coordination effort is known as a **storyboard.** A storyboard is a important shot-by-important-shot sketch depicting in sequence the visual scenes and copy that will be used in a television advertisement. The procedures for coordinating audio and visual elements through the use of storyboards will be presented in Chapter 13, when television production is discussed.

Television Advertising Formats.   Because of the broad creative capability of the television medium, there are several alternative formats for a television ad: demonstration, problem and solution, music and song, spokesperson, dialogue, vignette, and narrative. Each is discussed here. Again, this is not an exhaustive list, but rather a sampling of popular forms.

Demonstration.   Due to television's abilities to demonstrate a brand in action, demonstration is an obvious format for a television ad. Do it if you can. Brands whose benefits result from some tangible function can effectively use this format. Copy that accompanies this sort of ad embellishes the visual demonstration. The copy in a demonstration is usually straight-line copy, but drama can easily be introduced into this format, such as with the Radio Shack home security system that scares off a burglar or the Fiat braking system that saves a motorist from an accident. Demonstration with sight and sound lets viewers appreciate the full range of features a brand has to offer. The commercial in Exhibit 12.30 was created at an agency in São Paulo, Brazil, but the clarity of the demonstration is convincing in just about any culture.

14.   Cited in Sullivan, *Hey Whipple, Squeeze This: A Guide to Creating Great Ads,* 103.
15.   Sullivan, *Hey Whipple, Squeeze This: A Guide to Creating Great Ads,* 104.

Demonstration with sight and sound lets viewers appreciate the full range of features a brand has to offer. This commercial created by an ad agency in Brazil is a good example. http://www .honda.com

(SFX: MOTORCYCLE SOUNDS)	
SUPER:	Honda C-100 Dream. Up to 700 Km per liter or 30 seconds with a single drop.
SUPER:	C-100 Dream, Start It, Ride It, And Love It.
SUPER:	Honda. The World's Best Emotion.

Honda C-100 Dream. Up to 70Km per liter or 30 seconds with a single drop.

Problem and Solution. In this format, a brand is introduced as the savior in a difficult situation. This format often takes shape as a slice-of-life message, in which a consumer solves a problem with the advertised brand. Dishwashing liquids, drain openers, and numerous other household products are commonly promoted with this technique. A variation on the basic format is to promote a brand on the basis of problem prevention. A variety of auto maintenance items and even insurance products have used this approach.

Music and Song. Many television commercials use music and singing as a creative technique. The various beverage industries (soft drinks, beer, and wine) frequently use this format to create the desired mood for their brands. Additionally, the growth of image advertising has resulted in many ads that show a product in action accompanied by music and only visual overlays of the copy. This format for television advertising tends to restrict the amount of copy and presents the same difficulties for copywriting as the use of music and song in radio copywriting. Did you wonder if Burger King would ever run out of pop songs to use to peddle fast food? A logo, a few captions, a product shot, and songs ranging from "Tempted" to "So Hot" to the theme from *Welcome Back, Kotter* have been used to great success for the franchise.

Spokesperson. The delivery of a message by a spokesperson can place a heavy emphasis on the copy. The copy is given precedence over the visual and is supported by the visual, rather than vice versa. Expert, average-person, and celebrity testimonials fall into this formatting alternative. An example of the effective use of an expert spokesperson is Tiger Woods for Titleist.

Dialogue. As in a radio commercial, a television ad may feature a dialogue between two or more people. Dialogue-format ads pressure a copywriter to compose dialogue that is believable and keeps the ad moving forward. Most slice-of-life ads in which a husband and wife or friends are depicted using a brand employ a dialogue format.

Vignette. A vignette format uses a sequence of related advertisements as a device to maintain viewer interest. Vignettes also give the advertising a recognizable look, which can help achieve awareness and recognition. The Taster's Choice couple featured in a series of advertisements in the United States and Great Britain is an example of the vignette format.

Narrative. A narrative is similar to a vignette but is not part of a series of related ads. Narrative is a distinct format in that it tells a story, like a vignette, but the mood of the ad is highly personal, emotional, and involving. A narrative ad often focuses on storytelling and only indirectly touches on the benefits of the brand. Many of the "heart-sell" ads by McDonald's, Kodak, and Hallmark use the narrative technique to great effect. (See Exhibit 12.31.)

Guidelines for Writing Television Copy. Writing copy for television advertising has its own set of unique opportunities and challenges. The following are some general guidelines:

- *Use the video.* Allow the video portion of the commercial to enhance and embellish the audio portion. Given the strength and power of the visual presentation in television advertising, take advantage of its impact with copy.

EXHIBIT 12.31

A narrative ad often focuses on storytelling and indirectly touches on the benefits of the brand. http://www .jhancock.com

SUPER:	Your parents, your children, yourself.
SIGOURNEY	
WEAVER:	You owe it to your parents, for they brought you into this world.
SUPER:	Who do you love the least?
WEAVER:	You owe it to your children, for you did the same for them. But the day may arrive when both debts come due. When you may have no choice but to borrow from your own retirement to educate a child or care for a parent. Into whose eyes can you look and say you just can't help?
SUPER:	Insurance for the unexpected.
WEAVER:	For in both, you will surely see your own.
SUPER:	Investments for the opportunities.
SUPER:	John Hancock (Olympic rings) worldwide sponsor.

- ***Support the video.*** Make sure that the copy doesn't simply hitchhike on the video. If all the copy does is verbally describe what the audience is watching, an opportunity to either communicate additional information or strengthen the video communication has been lost.
- ***Coordinate the audio with the video.*** In addition to strategically using the video, it is essential that the audio and video do not tell entirely different stories.
- ***Sell the product as well as entertain the audience.*** Television ads can sometimes be more entertaining than television programming. A temptation for the copywriter and art director is to get caught up in the excitement of a good video presentation and forget that the main purpose is to deliver persuasive communication.
- ***Be flexible.*** Due to media-scheduling strategies, commercials are produced to run as 15-, 20-, 30-, or 60-second spots. The copywriter may need to ensure that the audio portion of an ad is complete and comprehensive within varying time lengths.
- ***Use copy judiciously.*** If an ad is too wordy, it can create information overload and interfere with the visual impact. Ensure that every word is a working word and contributes to the impact of the message.
- ***Reflect the brand personality and image.*** All aspects of an ad, copy and visuals, should be consistent with the personality and image the advertiser wants to build or maintain for the brand.
- ***Build campaigns.*** When copy for a particular advertisement is being written, evaluate its potential as a sustainable idea. Can the basic appeal in the advertisement be developed into multiple versions that form a campaign?[16]

Slogans.

Copywriters are often asked to come up with a good slogan or tagline for a product or service. A **slogan** is a short phrase in part used to help establish an image, identity, or position for a brand or an organization, but mostly used to increase memorability. A slogan is established by repeating the phrase in a firm's advertising and other public communication as well as through salespeople and event promotions. Slogans are often used as a headline or subhead in print advertisements, or as the tagline at the conclusion of radio and television advertisements. Slogans typically appear directly below the brand or company name, as "The Brand That Fits" does in all Lee jeans advertising. Some memorable and enduring ad slogans are listed in Exhibit 12.32.

A good slogan can serve several positive purposes for a brand or a firm. First, a slogan can be an integral part of a brand's image and personality. BMW's slogan, "The Ultimate Driving Machine," does much to establish and maintain the personality and image of the brand. Second, if a slogan is carefully and consistently developed over time, it can act as a shorthand identification for the brand and provide information on important brand benefits. The long-standing slogan for Allstate Insurance, "You're in Good Hands with Allstate," communicates the benefits of dealing with a well-established insurance firm. A good slogan also provides continuity across different media and between advertising campaigns. Nike's "Just Do It" slogan has given the firm an underlying theme for a wide range of campaigns and other promotions throughout the 1990s. In this sense, a slogan is a useful tool in helping to bring about thematic integrated marketing communications for a firm. Microsoft's slogan—"Where do you want to go today?"—is all about freedom, but the company approach to integrated communications is more sophisticated than just brandishing its slogan with a vengeance.

---

16.   The last three points in this list were adapted from Roman and Maas, *The New How to Advertise.*

EXHIBIT 12.32

Slogans used for brands and organizations.

Brand/Company	Slogan
Allstate Insurance	You're in Good Hands with Allstate.
American Express	Don't Leave Home without It.
AT&T (consumer)	Reach Out and Touch Someone.
AT&T (business)	AT&T. Your True Choice.
Beef Industry Council	Real Food for Real People.
Best Buy	Turn on the Fun.
BMW	The Ultimate Driving Machine.
Budweiser	This Bud's for You.
Chevrolet trucks	Like a Rock.
Cotton Industry	The Fabric of Our Lives.
DeBeers	Diamonds Are Forever.
Ford	Have You Driven a Ford Lately?
Goodyear	The Best Tires in the World Have Goodyear Written All Over Them.
Harley-Davidson	The Legend Rolls On.
Lincoln	What a Luxury Car Should Be.
Maybelline	Maybe She's Born with It. Maybe It's Maybelline.
Microsoft (online)	Where Do You Want to Go Today?
Panasonic	Just Slightly Ahead of Our Time.
Prudential Insurance	Get a Piece of the Rock.
Rogaine	Stronger Than Heredity.
Saturn	A Different Kind of Company. A Different Kind of Car.
Sharp	From Sharp Minds Come Sharp Products.
Toshiba	In Touch with Tomorrow.
VH1	Music First.
Visa	It's Everywhere You Want to Be.
VW	Drivers Wanted.

Common Mistakes in Copywriting.

The preceding discussions have shown that print, radio, and television advertising present the copywriter with unique challenges and opportunities. Copy in each arena must be compatible with the various types of ads run in each medium and the particular capabilities and liabilities of each medium and format. Beyond the guidelines for effective copy in each area, some common mistakes made in copywriting can and should be avoided:

- *Vagueness.* Avoid generalizations and words that are imprecise in meaning. To say that a car is stylish is not nearly as meaningful as saying it has sleek, aerodynamic lines.
- *Wordiness.* Being economical with descriptions is paramount. Copy has to fit in a limited time frame (or space), and receivers bore easily. When boredom sets in, effective communication often ceases.

ETHICS

Copywriting and Ethical Issues

Advertisers must be careful when they write copy. Advertisers can claim attributes and superiority only if they can substantiate the claims. When Procter & Gamble advertised that its Tampax Pearl tampons offered better protection, absorbency, and comfort than rival Playtex's Gentle Glide brand, Playtex filed a lawsuit to stop P&G from saying its product was superior to Playtex's. The Lanham Act, passed in 1946, bans advertisers from misrepresenting qualities of its product and prohibits false and misleading advertisements. It does not ban advertising that is mere puffery and has vague assertions of superiority. In this case, however, P&G was stating it had a product that was better than its competitor's.

At trial, a federal jury awarded Playtex $2.96 million in damages for the misleading advertising, and the court issued a permanent injunction against Procter & Gamble that bars the company "from communicating that its Tampax Pearl tampons are superior in any way to those" of Playtex. The order requires Procter & Gamble to immediately recall all offending promotional products and displays from retailers and distributors and to immediately halt all television and print advertising, packaging, direct mail, sales presentations, and coupons that make such claims. P&G said it would appeal both the order and the damage award.

Would you suggest that P&G appeal? What is the best way for a company to act when faced with an ethical problem? How would you suggest that P&G proceed after being told its copywriting was a violation of the Lanham Act?

- *Triteness.* Using clichés and worn-out superlatives was mentioned as a threat to print copywriting. The same threat (to a lesser degree, due to audio and audiovisual capabilities) exists in radio and television advertising. Trite copy creates a boring, outdated image for a brand or firm.

- *Creativity for creativity's sake.* Some copywriters get carried away with a clever idea. It's essential that the copy in an ad remain true to its primary responsibility: communicating the selling message. However, copy that is extraordinarily funny or poses an intriguing riddle yet fails to register the main selling theme will simply produce another amusing advertising failure.

The Copy Approval Process.

"The client has some issues and concerns about your ads." This is how account executives announce the death of your labors: "issues and concerns." To understand the portent of this phrase, picture the men lying on the floor of that Chicago garage on St. Valentine's Day. Al Capone had issues and concerns with these men.

I've had account executives beat around the bush for 15 minutes before they could tell me the bad news. "Well, we had a good meeting."

"Yes," you say, "but are the ads dead?"

"We learned a lot?"

"But are they dead?"

"Wellll, . . . They're really not dead. They are just in a new and better place."

—Luke Sullivan[17]

The final step in copywriting is getting the copy approved. For many copywriters, this is the most dreaded part of their existence. During the approval process, the proposed copy is likely to pass through the hands of a wide range of client and agency people, many of whom are ill-prepared to judge the quality of the copy. The challenge at this stage is to keep the creative potency of the copy intact. As David Ogilvy suggests in his commandments for advertising, "Committees can criticize advertisements, but they can't write them."[18]

The copy approval process usually begins within the creative department of an advertising agency. A copywriter submits draft copy to either the senior writer or the creative director, or both. From there, the redrafted copy is forwarded to the

17. Sullivan, *Hey Whipple, Squeeze This: A Guide to Creating Great Ads,* 182.
18. Ogilvy, *Confessions of an Advertising Man,* 101.

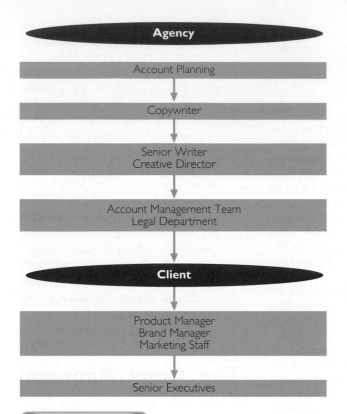

EXHIBIT 12.33

The copy approval process.

account management team within the agency. The main concern at this level is to evaluate the copy on legal grounds. After the account management team has made recommendations, a meeting is likely held to present the copy, along with proposed visuals, to the client's product manager, brand manager, and marketing staff. Inevitably, the client representatives feel compelled to make recommendations for altering the copy. In some cases, these recommendations realign the copy in accordance with important marketing strategy objectives. In other cases, the recommendations are amateurish and problematic. From the copywriter's point of view, they are rarely welcome, although the copywriter usually has to act as if they are.

Depending on the assignment, the client, and the traditions of the agency, the creative team may also rely on various forms of copy research. Typically, copy research is either developmental or evaluative. **Developmental copy research** can actually help copywriters at the early stages of copy development by providing audience interpretations and reactions to the proposed copy. **Evaluative copy research** is used to judge copy after it's been produced. Here, the audience expresses its approval or disapproval of the copy used in an ad. Copywriters are not fond of these evaluative report cards. In our view, they are completely justified in their suspicion; for many reasons, state-of-the-art evaluative copy research just isn't very good. Most of the time, it's awful, maybe even a crime. Just because someone calls it science doesn't mean a thing.

Finally, copy should always be submitted for final approval to the advertiser's senior executives. Many times, these executives have little interest in evaluating advertising plans, and they leave this responsibility to middle managers. In some firms, however, top executives get very involved in the approval process. The various levels of approval for copy are summarized in Exhibit 12.33 and parodied in Exhibit 12.34. For the advertiser, it is best to recognize that copywriters, like other creative talent in an agency, should be allowed to exercise their creative expertise with guidance but not overbearing interference. Copywriters seek to provide energy and originality to an often dry marketing strategy. To override their creative effort violates their reason for being.

EXHIBIT 12.34

Advertisers should allow copywriters to exercise their creative expertise with guidance but not overbearing interference, as this Dilbert cartoon illustrates. http://www.dilbert.com

SUMMARY

 Explain the need for a creative plan in the copywriting process.

Effective ad copy must be based on a variety of individual inputs and information sources. Making sense out of these diverse inputs and building from them creatively is a copywriter's primary challenge. A creative plan is used as a device to assist the copywriter in dealing with this challenge. Key elements in the creative plan include product features and benefits that must be communicated to the audience, the mood or tone appropriate for the audience, and the intended media for the ad.

 Detail the components of print copy, along with important guidelines for writing effective print copy.

The three unique components of print copy are the headline, subhead, and body copy. Headlines need to motivate additional processing of the ad. Good headlines communicate information about the brand or make a promise about the benefits the consumer can expect from the brand. If the brand name is not featured in the headline, then that headline must entice the reader to examine the body copy or visual material. Subheads can also be valuable in helping lead the reader to and through the body copy. In the body copy, the brand's complete story can be told. Effective body copy must be crafted carefully to engage the reader, furnish supportive evidence for claims made about the brand, and avoid clichés and exaggeration that the consumer will dismiss as hype.

 Describe various formatting alternatives for radio ads and articulate guidelines for writing effective radio copy.

Four basic formats can be used to create radio copy. These are the music format, the dialogue format, the announcement format, and the celebrity announcer format. Guidelines for writing effective radio copy start with using simple sentence construction and language familiar to the intended audience. When the copy stimulates the listener's imagination, the advertiser can expect improved results as long as the brand name and the primary selling points don't get lost. When using music or humor to attract and hold the listener's attention, the copywriter must take care not to shortchange key selling points for the sake of simple entertainment.

 Describe various formatting alternatives for television ads and articulate guidelines for writing effective television copy.

Several formats can be considered in preparing television ad copy. These are demonstration, problem and solution, music and song, spokesperson, dialogue, vignette, and narrative. To achieve effective copy in the television medium, it is essential to coordinate the copy with the visual presentation, seeking a synergistic effect between audio and video. Entertaining to attract attention should again not be emphasized to the point that the brand name or selling points of the ad get lost. Developing copy consistent with the heritage and image of the brand is also essential. Finally, copy that can be adapted to various time lengths and modified to sustain audience interest over the life of a campaign is most desirable.

KEY TERMS

creative team
creative concept
copywriting
creative plan
headline
subhead

straight-line copy
dialogue
testimonial
narrative
direct response copy
fact sheet radio ad

live script radio ad
storyboard
slogan
developmental copy research
evaluative copy research

QUESTIONS

1. Explain the applications for copy research in the copywriting process. What other forms of consumer or market research might be particularly helpful in developing effective ad copy?

2. Pull 10 print ads from your favorite magazine. Using the classifications offered in this chapter, what would you surmise was the copywriter's intended purpose for each of the headlines in your 10 print ads?

3. How does audience influence the style of writing exhibited in cyberads? How do you characterize the writing at http://www.garageband.com shown in Exhibit 12.22?

4. Discuss the advantages and disadvantages of music as a tool for constructing effective radio ads.

5. Listen with care to the radio ads in 30 minutes of programming on your favorite radio station. Then do the same for 30 minutes of programming on a parent's or grandparent's favorite station. Identify ads that did the best job of using terms and jargon familiar to the target audience of each station. What differences in mood or tone did you detect among ads on the two stations?

6. Compare and contrast the dialogue and narrative formats for television ads. What common requirement must be met to construct convincing TV ads using these two formats?

7. Entertainment is both the blessing and the curse of a copywriter. Is it conceivable that ads that merely entertain could actually prove valuable in stimulating sales? If so, how so?

8. Describe the four common categories of mistakes that copywriters must avoid. From your personal experience with all types of ads, are there other common mistakes that you believe copywriters are prone to make on a regular basis?

9. Everyone has his or her own opinion on what makes advertisements effective or ineffective. How does this fundamental aspect of human nature complicate a copywriter's life when it comes to winning approval for his or her ad copy?

EXPERIENTIAL EXERCISES

1. Divide into groups. Your team assignment is to study and improve upon local car-dealer television advertising. Watch two or three television commercials by local car dealers. Discuss what you found good or bad about the ads. Seize upon the worst commercial and develop a list of suggestions to improve it. Apply your thoughts to the generation of a storyboard for a much-improved commercial.

2. Find two print ads that do not use a subhead. Craft three subheads for each ad and defend the role each plays in improving the ads.

12-1   Basic Components of Copy

Several major elements are used when producing advertising copy. Visit the following sites and click around individual pages in the site to read and analyze copy.

L'eggs: http://www.leggs.com

Sirius: http://www.sirius.com

MINI: http://www.miniusa.com

Puffs: http://www.puffs.com

1.   Do these sites have headlines on the home page? What do you think makes a headline for a Web page effective?

2.   Do you think that the body copy for each site supports the headline? What aspects of the body copy do you think are most effective? Least effective?

3.   Does the copy support the overall creative plan of the site by integrating with various design elements such as color, illustration, sound, and interactive?

12-2   Careers for Copywriters

Ad agencies too busy with clients to get bogged down in the hunt for creative talent need only make a trip to the zoo. Atlanta-based Talent Zoo is a popular online recruitment firm specializing in the job placement of skilled professionals for the advertising industry. Finding good talent takes time and resources, and Talent Zoo is the quickest and easiest way for agencies to find experienced, qualified job candidates. Talent Zoo saves advertising firms the cost of having to recruit new people every few months, and eliminates the long, painful process of pouring over reams of resumes.

Talent Zoo: http://www.talentzoo.com

1.   Visit Talent Zoo and briefly describe the site and some of its career resources. Who is likely to use these resources?

2.   Search Talent Zoo's site and identify a career opportunity for a copywriter. Who is the agency looking for copy talent, and what are the requirements for the open position?

3.   Using Talent Zoo's "salary monitor" tool, list the job description and salary range for a junior copywriter in your area. Do you think you would enjoy working for an advertising agency as a copywriter or in some other position? Explain.

CHAPTER 13

After reading and thinking about this chapter, you will be able to do the following:

1

Identify the basic purposes, components, and formats of print ad illustrations.

2

Describe the principles and components that help ensure the effective design of print ads.

3

Detail the stages that art directors follow in developing the layout of a print ad.

4

Discuss the activities and decisions involved in the final production of print ads.

5

Identify the various players who must function as a team to produce television ads.

6

Discuss the specific stages and costs involved in producing television ads.

7

Describe the major formatting options for television ad production.

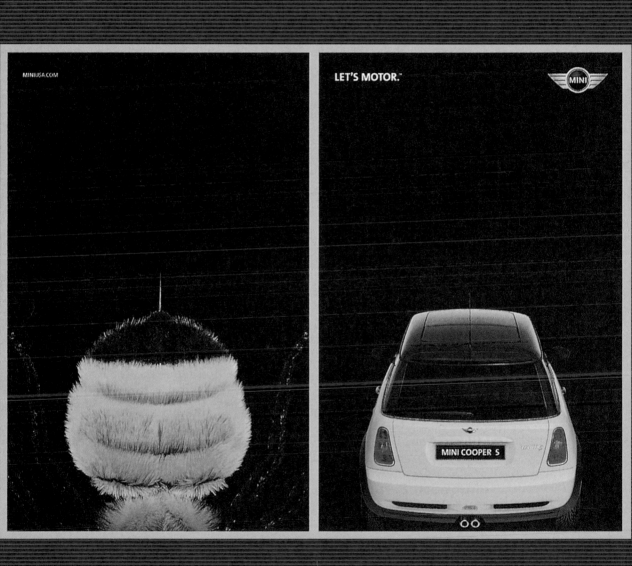

A hundred years ago advertisers largely relied on words to persuade consumers. They argued with consumers, attempted to reason with them, pleaded with them, and cajoled them. Then sometime in the early 20th century, particularly noticeable after about 1910, advertisers began to move away from words and toward pictures. This trend would extend throughout the 20th century and into the 21st. Advertising has become more and more visual. There are several reasons for this. Among them are (1) improved technologies, which facilitate better and more affordable illustration; (2) the inherent advantage of pictures to quickly demonstrate goods and services; (3) the ability to build brand "images" through visuals; (4) the legalistic advantage of pictures over words in that the truth or falsity of a picture is almost impossible to determine; (5) the widely held belief that pictures, although just as cultural as words, permit a certain type of portability that words do not; and (6) the fact that pictures allow advertisers to place brands in desired social contexts, thus transferring important social meaning to them.

Not coincidentally, the role of the art director has grown more and more important relative to the copywriter. This is a visual age, and like it or not, the primacy of the word has been challenged by pictures in contemporary advertising. Make no mistake, copywriting is still vital. This is a place where we can learn from the experience of real advertising practice. So, let's show and tell.

Illustration, Design, and Layout.
We begin with a discussion of three primary visual elements of a print ad: illustration, design, and layout. We then identify aspects of each that should be specified, or at least considered, as a print ad is being prepared. An advertiser must appreciate the technical aspects of coordinating the visual elements in an ad with the mechanics of the layout and ultimately with the procedures for print production. A discussion of illustration, design, and layout brings to the fore the role of art direction in print advertising.

Initially, the art director and copywriter decide on the content of an illustration. Then the art director, often in conjunction with a graphic designer, takes this raw idea for the visual and develops it further. Art directors, with their specialized skills and training, coordinate the design and illustration components of a print ad. The creative director oversees the entire process. Most often, the copywriter is still very much in the loop.

Illustration.
Illustration, in the context of print advertising, is the actual drawing, painting, photography, or computer-generated art that forms the picture in an advertisement.

Illustration Purposes. There are several specific, strategic purposes for illustration, which can greatly increase the chances of effective communication. The basic purposes of an illustration are the following:

- To attract the attention of the target audience
- To make the brand heroic
- To communicate product features or benefits
- To create a mood, feeling, or image
- To stimulate reading of the body copy
- To create the desired social context for the brand

Attract the Attention of the Target Audience. One of the primary roles of an illustration is to attract and hold attention. With all the advertising clutter out there today, this is no easy task. In some advertising situations (for example, the very early stages of a new product launch or very "low-involvement" repeat purchase items), just being noticed by consumers may almost be enough. In most cases, however,

EXHIBITS 13.1 AND 13.2

What do you think of the impact of these ads? http://www.homestore.com *and* http://www.oddbins.com

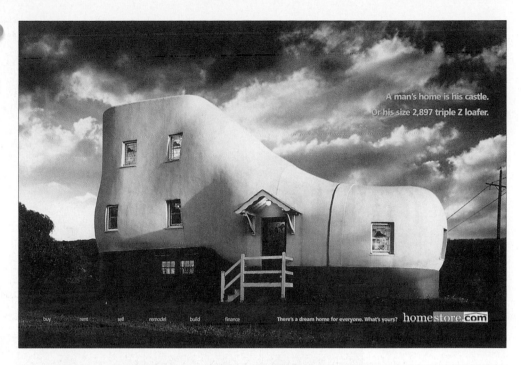

being noticed is a necessary, but not sufficient, goal. An illustration is made to communicate with a particular target audience and, generally, must support other components of the ad to achieve the intended communication impact. So, what do you think of the impact of the ads in Exhibits 13.1 and 13.2? Will they get noticed?

Make the Brand Heroic. One traditional role of art direction is to make the brand heroic. Very often this is done by the manner in which the brand is presented via illustration. Visual techniques such as backlighting, low-angle shots, and dramatic use of color can communicate heroic proportions and qualities. (See Exhibit 13.3.) David Ogilvy suggests that if you don't have a particular story to tell in the ad, then

What makes this ad have impact? Lighting? Color? What?

Butter made with seasalt

Sometimes a photograph of a product in use can present brand features or benefits in a simple, powerful manner.

make the package the subject of the illustration.[1] The Creativity box tells how OshKosh B'Gosh incorporated the tragic events of the September 11, 2001, terrorist attacks into its advertising to make its brand heroic.

Communicate Product Features or Benefits. Perhaps the most straightforward illustration is one that simply displays brand features, benefits, or both (see Exhibit 13.4). Even though a print ad is static, the product can be shown in use through an "action" scene or even through a series of illustrations. The benefits of product use can be demonstrated with before-and-after shots or by demonstrating the result of having used the product.

1.   David Ogilvy, *Ogilvy on Advertising* (New York: Vintage Books, 1985), 77.

Create a Mood, Feeling, or Image. Brand image is projected through illustration. The myriad of ways this is done is beyond enumeration, but the illustration interacts with the packaging, associated brand imagery (for example, the brand logo), and evoked feelings, which all contribute. The "mood" of an ad can help this along. Whether these goals are achieved with a print ad depends on the technical execution of the illustration. The lighting, color, tone, and texture of the illustration can have a huge impact. In Exhibit 13.5, the photograph used as the illustration in the print ad for a video rental store that specializes in horror movies captures an eerie, disconcerting feeling with its contrast and lighting.

CREATIVITY

We Could Be Heroes

In October 2001, children's clothier OshKosh B'Gosh launched a national ad campaign—"What the future wears"—that produced two New York City–specific ads reflecting on the terrorist events that crippled the city on September 11, 2001. Laughlin/Constable in Milwaukee produced the ads for OshKosh B'Gosh and placed them on outdoor boards in New York City and in two magazines.

For the huge Times Square board, the agency produced a simple message in a childlike scrawl: "Every kid needs heroes. Thanks N.Y.C." The second ad depicted a young boy standing before an American flag and wearing a pair of OshKosh B'Gosh overalls, holding a crayon in his hand. Beneath him, also written in a child's hand, the tag says, "Land that I love." That ad ran in New York bus shelters, in *The New York Times Magazine,* and in *People* magazine.

In the wake of the terrorist attacks, advertisers were faced with difficult creative choices: run ads similar to what was running before the events, or address the tragic events head-on? For OshKosh, choosing to tip its hat to New York City created many strategic opportunities for the brand. First, the visual component tapped into an event that already had immediate worldwide attention. Second, the international community viewed the response efforts of the firefighting and rescue teams as a display of unparalleled heroism (a heroism every manufacturer could only dream of having transferred to its products). Finally, the ads showed patriotic fervor and boldly discussed the future in the face of an event that creates anxiety about what lies ahead. The message? OshKosh B'Gosh creates rugged products worn by the next generation of heroes and patriots.

While some critics are cynical about various post-tragedy marketing efforts, OshKosh B'Gosh believed audiences would be receptive. Chief executive officer Douglas Hyde said he didn't think his company's message would be misinterpreted: "We have a reputation as this company that comes from the Midwest. We care about families and children."

Sources: Doris Hajewski, "Attacks Spur OshKosh to Change Holiday Ad Campaign in New York," *Milwaukee Journal Sentinel,* http://www.jsonline.com, accessed October 24, 2001; Barry Janoff, "OshKosh Tips Hat to New York," *Media Week,* accessed October 25, 2001.

Stimulate Reading of the Body Copy. Just as a headline can stimulate examination of the illustration, the illustration can stimulate reading of the body copy. Since body copy generally carries the essential selling message, any tactic that encourages reading is useful. (See Exhibit 13.6.) Illustrations can create curiosity and interest in readers. To satisfy that curiosity, readers may proceed to the body copy for clarification. (This is not easy; body copy often looks boring and tedious.) Normally, an illustration and headline need to be fully coordinated and play off each other for this level of interest to occur. One caution is to avoid making the illustration too clever a stimulus for motivating copy reading. Putting cleverness ahead of clarity in choosing an illustration can confuse the receiver and cause the body copy to be ignored. As one expert puts it, such ads win awards but can camouflage the benefit offered by the product.[2]

Create the Desired Social Context for the Brand. As described earlier, advertisers need to associate or situate their brand within a type of social setting, thereby linking it with certain "types" of people and certain lifestyles. Establishing desired social contexts is probably the most important function of modern art direction. Look at the ad in Exhibit 13.7 and then think about what it would mean if the product were divorced from the social context. (See Exhibit 13.8.) See what we mean? Context can be (and usually is) everything.

2.   Tony Antin, *Great Print Advertising* (New York: Wiley, 1993), 38.

Contrast and eerie lighting work here.

Illustration Components. Various factors contribute to the overall visual presentation and impact of an illustration. Size, color, and medium affect viewers. Individual decisions regarding size, color, and medium are a matter of artistic discretion and creative execution. There is some evidence of the differing effects of various decisions made in each of these areas. But remember, the interpretation and meaning of any visual representation cannot be explained completely by a series of rules or prescriptive how-tos. Thankfully, it's not that simple.

Size. Does doubling the size of an illustration double the probability that the illustration will achieve its intended purpose? The answer is probably no. There is no question that greater size in an illustration may allow an ad to compete more successfully for the reader's attention, especially in a cluttered media environment. Generally speaking, illustrations with a focal point immediately recognizable by the reader are more likely to be noticed and comprehended. Conversely, illustrations that arouse curiosity or incorporate action score high in attracting attention but have been found to score low in inducing the reading of the total ad.[3]

Color. While not every execution of print advertising allows for the use of color (because of either expense or the medium being employed), color is a creative tool with important potential. Some products (such as furniture, floor coverings, or expensive clothing) may depend on color to accurately communicate a principal value. Color can also be used to emphasize a product feature or attract the reader's attention to a particular part of an ad. But remember, color has no fixed meaning, so no hard rules can be offered. Color is cultural, situational, and contex-

This ad tries to get you to read the body copy. Does it work? http://www.becks -beer.com

3.   Daniel Starch, *Measuring Advertising Readership and Results* (New York: McGraw-Hill, 1966), 83.

Context is (almost) everything. When you remove the advertised brand from the advertiser created context, it isn't the same, is it?

tual. To say that red always means this or blue always means that is to rely on a popular but unfounded myth. It's simply not true.

Medium. The choice of **medium** for an illustration is the decision regarding the use of drawing, photography, or computer graphics.[4] Drawing represents a wide range of creative presentations, from cartoons to pen-and-ink drawings to elaborate watercolor or oil paintings. Photos have an element of believability as representations of reality (even though they can be just as manipulated as any other form of representation). Further, photos can often be prepared more quickly and at much less expense than other forms of art. Photographers all over the world specialize in different types of photography: landscape, seascape, portrait, food, or architecture, for example. The American Society of Media Photographers (originally the Society of Magazine Photographers and later the American Society of Magazine Photographers) is a trade association for more than 5,000 photographers whose work is primarily used for publication.[5] This society can help buyers find professional photographers. Buyers can also purchase photographs from various stock agencies, such as Corbis, Getty Images, or PhotoEdit. These photographs can usually be cropped to

4.   This section is adapted from Sandra E. Moriarty, *Creative Advertising: Theory and Practice,* 2nd ed. (Englewood Cliffs, N.J.: Prentice-Hall, 1991), 139–141.
5.   G. Robert Cox and Edward J. McGee, *The Ad Game: Playing to Win* (Englewood Cliffs, N.J.: Prentice Hall, 1990), 44.

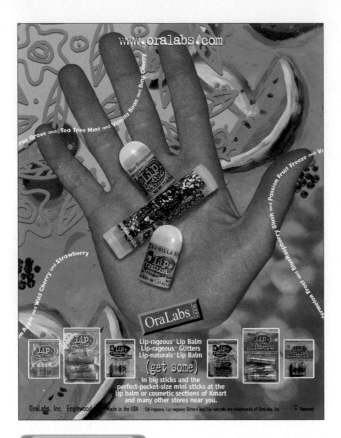

Computer graphics make this ad. http://www.oralabs .com

any size or shape, retouched, color-corrected, and doctored in a number of ways to create the user's desired effect.

With advancing technology, artists have discovered the application of computer graphics to advertising illustrations. Computer graphics specialists can create and manipulate images. With respect to illustrations for print advertising, the key development has been the ability to digitize images. Digitizing is a computer process of breaking an image (illustration) into a grid of small squares. Each square is assigned a computer code for identification. With a digitized image, computer graphics specialists can break down an illustration and reassemble it or import other components into the original image. Age can be added to or taken away from a model's face, or the Eiffel Tower can magically appear on Madison Avenue. The creative possibilities are endless with computer graphics. Exhibit 13.9 is an example of an ad with multiple images imported through computer graphics. Some art directors are very fond of these software solutions.

The size, color, and media decisions regarding an illustration are difficult ones. It is likely that strategic and budgetary considerations will heavily influence choices in these areas. Once again, advertisers should not constrain the creative process more than is absolutely necessary, and even then they should probably back off a bit.

Illustration Formats. The just-discussed components represent a series of decisions that must be made in conceiving an illustration. Another important decision is how the product or brand will appear as part of the illustration. **Illustration format** refers to the choices the advertiser has for displaying its product. There are product shots of all sorts: Some emphasize the social context and meaning of the product or service; others are more abstract (see Exhibit 13.10). Obviously, the illustration format must be consistent with the copy strategy set for the ad. The creative department and the marketing planners must communicate with one another so that the illustration format selected helps pursue the specific objectives set for the total ad campaign.

The Strategic and Creative Impact of Illustration. Defining effectiveness is a matter of first considering the basic illustration purposes, components, and formats we've just discussed. Next, these factors need to be evaluated in the context of marketing strategy, consumer behavior, and campaign planning. At this point there is a lot of negotiation, discussion, and explaining. If everything works out, the ad goes forward.

2   **Design.** **Design** is "the structure itself and the plan behind that structure" for the aesthetic and stylistic aspects of a print advertisement.[6] Design represents the effort on the part of creatives to physically arrange all the components of a printed advertisement in such a way that order and beauty are achieved—order in the sense that the illustration, headline, body copy, and special features of the ad are easy to read; beauty in the sense that the ad is visually pleasing to a reader.

6.   This discussion is based on Roy Paul Nelson, *The Design of Advertising,* 5th ed. (Dubuque, Iowa: Wm. C. Brown, 1985), 126.

Some ads are more abstract.
http://www.boeriusa.com

Certainly, not every advertiser has an appreciation for the elements that constitute effective design, nor will every advertiser be fortunate enough to have highly
skilled designers as part of the team creating a print ad. As you will see in the following discussions, however, there are aspects of design that directly relate to the
potential for a print ad to communicate effectively based on its artistic form. As such,
design factors are highly relevant to creating effective print advertising.

Principles of Design. Principles of design govern how a print advertisement
should be prepared. The word *should* is carefully chosen in this context. It is used
because, just as language has rules of grammar and syntax, visual presentation has
rules of design. The **principles of design** relate to each element within an advertisement and to the arrangement of and relationship between elements as a whole.[7]
Principles of design suggest the following:

- A design should be in balance.
- The proportion within an advertisement should be pleasing to the viewer.
- The components within an advertisement should have an ordered and direc-
  tional pattern.
- There should be a unifying force within the ad.
- One element of the ad should be emphasized above all others.

We will consider each of these principles of design and how they relate to the development of an effective print advertisement. Of course, as surely as there are rules,
there are occasions when the rules need to be broken. An experienced designer
knows the rules and follows them, but is also prepared to break the rules to achieve
a desired outcome. But first, you learn the rules.

Balance. **Balance** in an ad is an orderliness and compatibility of presentation. Balance can be either formal or informal. **Formal balance** emphasizes symmetrical
presentation—components on one side of an imaginary vertical line through the ad
are repeated in approximate size and shape on the other side of the imaginary line.

7. Ibid., 129–136.

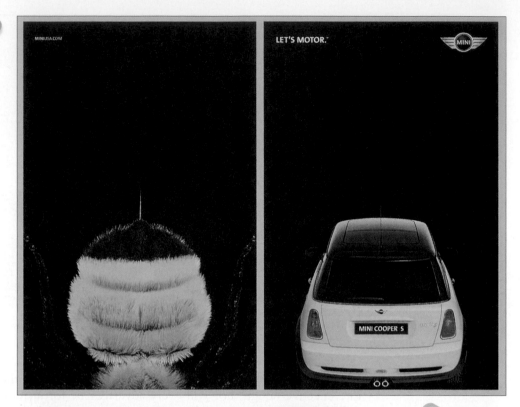

Formal balance creates a mood of seriousness and directness and offers the viewer an orderly, easy-to-follow visual presentation (see Exhibit 13.11).

Informal balance emphasizes asymmetry—the optical weighing of nonsimilar sizes and shapes. Exhibit 13.12 shows an advertisement using a range of type sizes, visuals, and colors to create a powerful visual effect that achieves informal balance. Informal balance in an ad should not be interpreted as imbalance. Rather, components of different sizes, shapes, and colors are arranged in a more complex relationship

EXHIBIT 13.13

Proportion, when expertly controlled, can result in an inspired display of the oversized versus the undersized. http://www .parmalat.com

providing asymmetrical balance to an ad. Informal balance is more difficult to manage in that the placement of unusual shapes and sizes must be precisely coordinated.

Proportion. Proportion has to do with the size and tonal relationships between different elements in an advertisement. Whenever two elements are placed in proximity, proportion results. In a printed advertisement, proportional considerations include the relationship of the width of an ad to its depth; the width of each element to the depth of each element; the size of one element relative to the size of every other element; the space between two elements and the relationship of that space to a third element; and the amount of light area as opposed to the amount of dark area. Ideally, factors of proportion vary so as to avoid monotony in an ad. Further, the designer should pursue pleasing proportions, which means the viewer will not detect mathematical relationships between elements. In general, unequal dimensions and distances make for the most lively designs in advertising (see Exhibit 13.13).

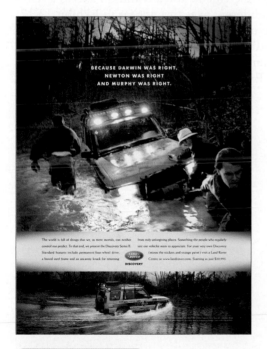

EXHIBIT 13.14

The order of elements in this ad for the Land Rover controls the reader's eye, moving it from the top of the ad through the body copy and logo, then down to the product shot at the bottom. http://www.landrover .com

Order. Order in an advertisement is also referred to as sequence or, in terms of its effects on the reader, "gaze motion." The designer's goal is to establish a relationship among elements that leads the reader through the ad in some controlled fashion. A designer can create a logical path of visual components to control eye movement. The eye has a "natural" tendency to move from left to right, from up to down, from large elements to small elements, from light to dark, and from color to noncolor. Exhibit 13.14 is an example of an ad that takes advantage of these tendencies. The bright lights on top of the Land Rover and the white headline against a dark background initially attract the gaze. The eye then moves down the shape of the car and the headlights bring the gaze down to the body copy and logo. The natural tendency for the eye to move from up to bottom leads the eye to a final shot of the Land Rover. Order also includes inducing the reader to jump from one space in the ad to another, creating a sense of action. The essential contribution of this design component is to establish a visual format that results in a focus or several focuses.

Unity. Ensuring that the elements of an advertisement are tied together and appear to be related is the purpose of unity. Considered the most important of the design principles, unity results in harmony among the diverse components of print advertising: headline, subhead, body copy, and illustration. Several design techniques contribute to unity. The **border** surrounding an ad keeps the ad elements from spilling over into other ads or into the printed matter next to the ad. **White space** at the outside edges creates an informal border effect. The indiscriminate use of white space within an ad can separate elements and give an impression of disorder. The proper use of white space can be dramatic and powerful and draw the receiver's attention to the most critical elements of an ad. Exhibit 13.15 shows a classic example of the effective use of white space. Exhibit 13.16 shows that it wasn't just the look of the Beetle that made a comeback decades later: The effective use of white space came along for the ride, too.

The final construct of unity is the axis. In every advertisement, an axis will naturally emerge. The **axis** is a line, real or imagined, that runs through an ad and from which the elements in the advertisement flare out. A single ad may have one, two, or even three axes running vertically and horizontally. An axis can be created by blocks of copy, by the placement of illustrations, or by the items within an illustration, such the position and direction of a model's arm or leg. Elements in an ad may violate the axes, but when two or more elements use a common axis as a starting point, unity is enhanced. Note all the different axes that appear in Exhibit 13.17. A design can be more forceful in creating unity by using either a three-point layout or a parallel layout. A **three-point layout structure** establishes three elements in the ad as dominant forces. The uneven number of prominent elements is critical to creating a gaze motion in the viewer (see Exhibit 13.18.) **Parallel layout structure**

EXHIBIT 13.15 AND 13.16

The effective use of white space—past and present—to highlight the critical aspect of the ad: the product. http://www.vw.com

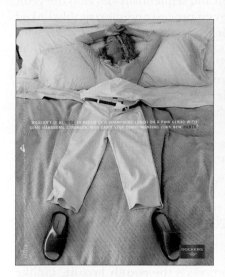

EXHIBIT 13.17

EXHIBIT 13.18

Look at all the different axes that appear in this ad. http://www.dockers.com

There are three prominent visual elements here.

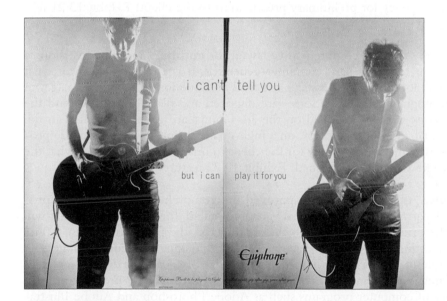

EXHIBIT 13.19

Here, the visual layout on the left is repeated on the right. http://www .epiphone.com

employs art on the right-hand side of the page and repeats the art on the left-hand side. This is an obvious and highly structured technique to achieve unity (see Exhibit 13.19).

Emphasis. At some point in the decision-making process, someone needs to decide which major component—the headline, subhead, body copy, or illustration—will be emphasized. The key to good design relative to emphasis is that one item is the primary but not the only focus in an ad. If one element is emphasized to the total exclusion of the others, then a poor design has been achieved, and ultimately a poor communication will result.

Balance, proportion, order, unity, and emphasis are the basic principles of design. As you can see, the designer's objectives go beyond the strategic and message-development elements associated with an advertisement. Design principles relate to the aesthetic impression an ad produces. Once a designer has been informed of the components that will make up the headline, subhead, body copy, and illustration to be included in the ad, then advertising and marketing decision makers *must* allow the designer to arrange those components according to the principles of creative design.

③ Layout. In contrast to design, which emphasizes the structural concept behind a print ad, layout is the mechanical aspect of design—the physical manifestation of design concepts. A **layout** is a drawing or digital rendering of a proposed print advertisement, showing where all the elements in the ad are positioned. An art director uses a layout to work through various alternatives for visual presentation and sequentially develop the print ad to its final stages. It is part and parcel of the design process and inextricably linked to the development of an effective design. While some art directors still work with traditional tools—layout tissue, T-square, triangle, and markers—many work in computerized layout programs, such as QuarkXPress.

An art director typically proceeds through various stages in the construction of a final design for an ad. The following are the different stages of layout development, in order of detail and completeness, that an art director typically uses.

Thumbnails. **Thumbnails** are the first drafts of an advertising layout. The art director will produce several thumbnail sketches to work out the general presentation of the ad. While the creative team refines the creative concept, thumbnails represent placement of elements—headline, images, body copy, and tagline. Headlines are often represented with zigzag lines and body copy with straight, parallel lines. An example of a thumbnail is shown in Exhibit 13.20. Typically, thumbnails are drawn at one-quarter the size of the finished ad.

Rough Layouts. The next step in the layout process is the **rough layout.** Unlike a thumbnail sketch, a rough layout is done in the actual size of the proposed ad and is usually created with a computer layout program, such as QuarkXPress. This allows the art director to experiment with different headline fonts and easily manipulate the placement and size of images to be used in the ad. A rough layout is often used by the advertising agency for preliminary presentation to the client. Exhibit 13.21 features a rough layout.

Comprehensives. The comprehensive layout, or **comp,** is a polished version of an ad. Now, for the most part, computer-generated, it is a representation of what the final ad will look like. At this stage, the final headline font is used, the images to be used—photographs or illustrations—are digitized and placed in the ad, and the actual body copy is often included on the ad. Comps are generally printed in full color, if the final ad is to be in color, on a high-quality printer. Comps that are produced in this way make it very easy for the client to imagine (and approve) what the ad will look like when it is published. Exhibit 13.22 features a comp layout.

Mechanicals. After the client has approved the comprehensive layouts, the production art department creates the final version of an ad, the **mechanical,** that will be sent to the printer. Working with the art director, the production artist refines the ad by adjusting the headline spacing (kerning), making any copy changes the client has requested, and placing high-quality digitized (scanned or digitally created) versions of images (illustrations or photographs) to be used. The production artist uses a variety of computer programs such as Adobe Photoshop and Adobe Illustrator to create the ad. A layout program is used to assemble all of the elements of the ad—images and type. Although there are many programs available to perform these tasks, QuarkXPress is the standard for the advertising industry, along with the Macintosh computer platform.

The client will make one last approval of the mechanical before it is sent to the printer. Changes that a client requests, prior to the ad being sent to the printer, are still easily and quickly made. A digital file is then sent either electronically or by mail to the printer. (Prior to the use of computers to generate mechanicals, a small copy change could result in hours of work on the part of the production artists and a large bill to the client.)

The stages of layout development discussed here provide the artistic blueprint for a print advertisement (see Exhibit 13.23). At this point, the practical matters of choosing the look and style of a print ad can be considered. We now turn our attention to the matter of print production.

A thumbnail showing the transition from idea to advertisement.

A rough layout.

A comp layout.

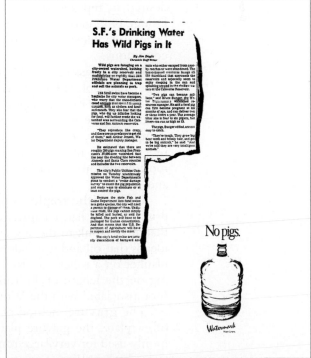

The finished ad.

4   Production in Print Advertising.

The production process in print advertising represents the technical and mechanical activities that transform a creative concept and rough layout into a finished print advertisement. While the process is fundamentally technical, some aspects of print production directly relate to the strategic and design goals of the print ad. Different type styles can contribute to the design quality, readability, and mood in an advertisement. Our purpose in this section, however, is to provide a basic familiarity with production details. Here we will outline the sequence of activities and proper time frame related to print production and the various options available for print preparation.

The Print Production Schedule.

The advertiser is only partly in control of the timing of the print advertisement. While plans can be made to coordinate the appearance of the ad with overall marketing strategies, it must be recognized that the print media have specifications regarding how far in advance and in what form an ad must be received to appear in print. The deadline for receipt of an ad is referred to as the **closing date.** Closing dates for newspapers can be one or two days before publication. For magazines, the closing date may be months ahead of publication.

Advertisers must be aware that advance planning is necessary to accommodate the basic nature of print production. Computers have certainly speeded things up, but there are still pressures (often more financial than anything else) to close earlier than is truly necessary from a production standpoint.

Print Production Processes.

Seven major processes can be used in print production.[8] Depending on the medium (newspaper, magazine, direct mail, or specialty advertising), the length of the print run (quantity), the type of paper being used, and the quality desired in reproduction, one of the following processes is used: letterpress, offset lithography, gravure, flexography, electronic, laser, and inkjet printing. Advances in technology have made computer print production an ideal alternative under certain conditions.

Letterpress draws its name from the way it "presses" type onto a page. Typesetters hand-placed, or *set,* each letter for a printed page in a tray, separating lines of text with bars of lead. These trays would then be inked and "pressed" onto the paper to transfer the ink type or image, similar to how we might currently use a rubber stamp. Today, handset type is a thing of the past, and individual metal type has been replaced with metal or rubber plates that are typeset from a computer program. The most common use for the letterpress today is finishing activities, such as embossing and scoring.

Offset lithography is by far the most common printing method. This process prints from a flat, chemically treated surface—a plate—wrapped around a cylinder that attracts ink to the areas to be printed and repels ink from other areas; the basic idea is that oil and water don't mix. The inked image is then transferred to a rubber blanket on a roller and from this roller the impression is carried to paper. Depending on the length of the run (quantity of pieces needed), either a sheetfed or web (not associated with the World Wide Web) press would be used.

The **gravure** method of printing also prints from a plate. However, unlike the offset plate, the gravure plate is engraved. This method of printing is most commonly used for very large runs, such as the Sunday newspaper supplements, to maintain a high quality of printing clarity.

---

8.   This discussion is based in part on Michael H. Bruno, ed., *Pocket Pal: A Graphic Arts Production Handbook,* 19th ed. (New York: Graphic Arts Technical Foundation, 2004).

Flexography is similar to offset lithography because it also uses a rubber blanket to transfer images. It differs from offset in that this process uses water-based ink instead of oil-based ink, and printing can be done on any surface. Because of this versatility of printing surface, flexography is most commonly used in packaging.

Electronic, laser, and inkjet printing are also known as plateless printing. The widespread use of computer technology has made printing very small runs, as few as one piece, in full color or black and white, with very sharp image quality on a variety of different papers, very easy. The advertising industry often uses software connected to a color photocopier to generate color comps for clients. The colors may not be exactly as they would be if a printer had produced the piece, but for comping purposes this method is both timely and inexpensive. Laser and inkjet printing are also plateless printing processes that are directly connected to a computer to transfer information. However, unlike the large color comping machines, laser and inkjet printers are affordable for home use. On a larger scale, both *Time* and *Fortune* use inkjet printers to address magazines to their subscribers.

Computer Print Production. Integrating the printing production process with the computer has changed the printing business considerably. First, by having digital files, printers no longer need to photograph pasted-up versions of ads. Film can be generated directly from digital files and, in turn, printing plates are made from the film. Second, the proofing process—double-checking that the colors to be printed are correct—can be performed well before the print job is on the press. Iris prints, polar proofs, and watermark prints are all extremely high-quality proofing methods. Though these proofing methods are expensive, their cost is only a small fraction of the cost to reprint a piece. Last, with the increasing use of electronic file transfer, files can be sent quickly to printers.

As stated earlier, choice of the proper printing process depends on the requirements of the advertisement with regard to the medium being used, the quantity being printed, the type of paper being printed on, and the level of quality needed. With respect to magazines, the production process is mandated by the publisher of a particular vehicle within the medium. Print production processes are independent publishing decisions.

Typography in Print Production. The issues associated with typography have to do with the typeface chosen for headlines, subheads, and body copy, as well as the various size components of the type (height, width, and running length). Designers agonize over the type to use in a print ad because decisions about type affect both the readability and the mood of the overall visual impression. For our purposes, some knowledge of the basic considerations of typography is useful for an appreciation of the choices that must be made.

Categories of Type. Typefaces have distinct personalities, and each can communicate a different mood and image. A **type font** is a basic set of typeface letters. For those of us who do word processing on computers, the choice of type font is a common decision. In choosing type for an advertisement, however, the art director has thousands of choices based on typeface alone.

There are six basic typeface groups: blackletter, roman, script, serif, sans serif, and miscellaneous. The families are divided by characteristics that reflect the personality and tone of the font. **Blackletter,** also called *gothic,* is characterized by the ornate design of the letters. This style is patterned after hand-drawn letters in monasteries where illuminated manuscripts were created. You can see blackletter fonts used today in very formal documents, such as college diplomas. **Roman** is the most common group of fonts used for body copy because of its legibility. This family is characterized by the use of thick and thin strokes in the creation of the letter forms.

Script is easy to distinguish by the linkage of the letters in the way that cursive handwriting is connected. Script is often found on wedding invitations and documents that are intended to look elegant or of high quality. **Serif** refers to the strokes or "feet" at the ends of the letter forms. Notice the serifs that are present in these letters as you read. Their presence helps move your eye across the page, allowing you to read for a long time without losing your place or tiring your eyes. **Sans serif** fonts, as the name suggests, do not have serifs, hence the use of the French word *sans,* meaning "without." Sans serif fonts are typically used for headlines and not for body copy. **Miscellaneous** includes typefaces that do not fit easily into the other categories. Novelty display, garage, and deconstructed fonts all fall into this group. These fonts were designed specifically to draw attention to themselves and not necessarily for their legibility. The following example displays serif and sans serif type:

This line is set in serif type.
This line is set in sans serif type.

Type Measurement.   There are two elements of type size. **Point** refers to the size of type in height. In the printing industry, type sizes run from 6 to 120 points. Now, with computer layout programs such as QuarkXPress, the range is much larger, between 2 and 720 points. Exhibit 13.24 shows a range of type sizes for comparison purposes. **Picas** measure the width of lines. A pica is 12 points wide, and each pica measures about one-sixth of an inch. Layout programs make it very easy for the art director to fit copy into a designated space on an ad by reducing or enlarging a font with a few strokes on the keyboard.

Readability.   It is critical in choosing type to consider readability. Type should facilitate the communication process. The following are some traditional recommendations when deciding what type to use (however, remember that these are only guidelines and should not necessarily be followed in every instance):

- Use capitals and lowercase, NOT ALL CAPITALS.
- Arrange letters from left to right, not up and down.
- Run lines of type horizontally, not vertically.
- Use even spacing between letters and words.

This is 8 point type

This is 12 point type

This is 18 point type

This is 36 point type

This is 60 point type

EXHIBIT 13.24

A range of type point sizes.

Different typefaces and styles also affect the mood conveyed by an ad. Depending on the choices made, typefaces can connote grace, power, beauty, modernness, simplicity, or any number of other qualities.

Art Direction and Production in Cyberspace. Cyberspace is its own

space. It is its own medium, too. It's not television or radio, but, at this point, it's closer to print than to anything else. It's an active medium rather than a passive one (people generally come to it rather than the other way around). While the basic principles of art direction (design and concept) apply, the medium is fundamentally different in the way its audience comes to it, navigates it, and responds to it. This is one of the real challenges of electronic advertising.

In most respects, cyberproduction does not differ significantly from print, radio, or television production, but it does differ from these traditional media in how aspects of production are combined with programming language, such as HTML, and with each other. Advances in streaming audio and digital video keep art direction and production in cyberspace a moving target. Still, at this point, most Internet advertising is, essentially, print advertising. Most is either produced in traditional ways and then digitized and combined with text or created entirely with computer design packages. Exhibits 13.25 through 13.28 are pretty representative of what's out there.

All media have to find their own way, their own voice. This is not just an aesthetic matter. It's figuring out what works, which has something to do with design. How the information is laid out matters. If you go back and look at the first few years of television advertising, you have to say that they really didn't fully understand the medium or the ways audiences would use this new technology. The ads went on forever and seemed to be written for radio. In fact, many of the early TV writers were radio writers. They tried to make television radio.

This same phenomenon seems to be happening with Web sites. They look more like print ads than something truly Web-ish. Yet, unlike print ads, Web sites have the ability to change almost immediately. If a client wants to change a copy point, for example, it can happen many times in one afternoon. And Web consumers demand change. Though frequent changes may seem time consuming and expensive, they ensure return visits from audiences. Many clients, however, are slow to integrate the Web into their overall communication strategy. Thus, many sites appear to be neglected, distant relatives to their high-profile cousins, TV and print.

There is also a rapidly growing clutter problem. Web pages are often very busy, with lots of information crammed into small spaces. Advertisers, while not yet knowing what this medium can do, are convinced that they must be in it. In short, the Web is not print *or* television: It is electronic and fluid, and must be thought of in this way. In terms of design, this means trying to understand why people come to various sites, what they are looking for, what they expect to encounter, what they expect in return for their very valuable click. The design has to be an expression of this.

Art Direction and Production in Television Advertising. There

have been few (if any) things that have more changed the face of advertising (or contemporary culture) than television. Like other media, television first struggled to find its best form, but soon did. In many ways, television was simply made for advertising. It is everywhere, serving as background to much of daily life. If you are in a room and a television is on, you will find yourself watching it. Want to kill a good party? Turn on a television. Did you ever try to talk to someone sitting across from you when your back is to the television? You just about have to offer money to get their attention. In the Oscar-winning film *Network,* a television anchorman believes

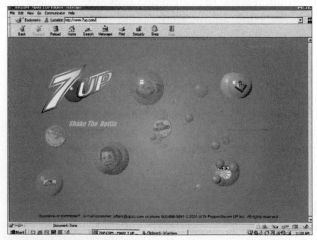

EXHIBITS 13.25 THROUGH 13.28

These ads are pretty typical of contemporary cyberads. Visit the promotion site for pop group They Might Be Giants (http://www.tmbg.com) and its companion site (http://www.dialasong.com). Do these sites suggest that the future of art direction and production in cyberspace will be more like television than print, or do the interactive features make the medium unique? Do you think highly interactive Web sites add clutter, or do they make browsing a more efficient experience? Does the average Internet user have the patience to wait for interactive graphics to load and display?

that God has chosen him as a modern-day prophet. When he asks God, "Why me?" God replies, "Because you're on television, dummy." Everybody watches TV, no matter what they tell you.

Television is about moving visuals. Sometimes, it's just about leaving impressions, or setting moods, or getting you to notice; sometimes it tells stories. Many believe that the very best television ads work just as well with the sound turned off, that the best television tells its story visually. Of course, this is what film critics have said about master film directors, such as John Ford (Exhibit 13.29) and Alfred Hitchcock (Exhibit 13.30), both of whom learned their craft in silent films.

Still, it must be said that an awful lot of TV spots are very reliant on copy. In fact, entire genres of television ads rely heavily on repetitive brand mentions, or dialogue-dependent narratives. Of late, rapid cuts and sparse dialogue seem to be the way of the TV creatives, but this phase will probably change before the next full moon. Advertising is, in so many respects, fashion.

Art Direction in Television Advertising. The primary creative directive for TV is the same as for other media: effective communication. Television presents some unique challenges, however. Due to its complexity, television production involves a lot of people. These people have different but often overlapping expertise, responsibility, and authority. This makes for a myriad of complications and calls for tremendous organizational skills. At some point, individuals who actually shoot the film or the tape are brought in to execute the copywriter's and art director's concepts. At this point, the creative process becomes intensely collaborative: The film director applies his or her craft and is responsible for the actual production. The creative team (that is, the art director and copywriter) rarely relinquishes control of the project, even though

EXHIBITS 13.29 AND 13.30

Two of the very best filmmakers—and storytellers—ever: John Ford and Alfred Hitchcock.

GLOBAL ISSUES

Ad Queen to Boost U.S.'s Global Image

She has been called the queen of Madison Avenue and the most powerful woman in advertising. She's the only woman to have served as chairman of two top-10 worldwide advertising agencies, J. Walter Thompson and Ogilvy & Mather. She helped shape brands such as Uncle Ben's Rice and Head & Shoulders, and has graced the cover of leading magazines such as *Fortune*. Now Charlotte Beers is faced with the branding challenge of a lifetime—enhancing the global image of the United States.

The Bush administration's appointment of longtime ad executive Charlotte Beers as undersecretary of state for public affairs came with the unique objective of fighting the international war on terrorism. Using an unlikely arsenal of weapons, Beers and the State Department hope to accomplish the repositioning of the quintessential global brand—the United States.

For a country with the biggest marketing industry on earth, the United States has done a surprisingly poor job of managing its own image abroad, a problem that has shifted sharply into focus in the propaganda war surrounding the September 11, 2001, terrorist attacks. "Loyal brand users" see the United States as a beacon of freedom, democracy, and tolerance. Users of the competing "brands" see the United States as a monster of self-absorption, crass commercialism, and blatant hypocrisy. The solution to this brand-identity crisis? Advertising.

The State Department has announced plans to buy television advertising on Qatar-based news channel Al Jazeera, a favored broadcast venue of well-known terrorists such as Osama bin Laden. The Arab-language station is said to have some 40 million viewers around the world. Ideas being tested for effectiveness include spotlighting famous athletes and entertainers, interviewing American Muslims about the virtues of the American system, and explaining that the United States is not a pagan paradise but a country that respects all religions. "The immediate problem is getting the message articulated and understood," said Beers.

Certainly, the stakes for directing effective television ads have never been higher. The State Department has developed an advisory council of Arab and Muslim leaders to help craft what the United States should communicate in foreign countries. In addition, Beers is working with international media-reaction teams and public affairs officers in embassies around the world to ensure that the message remains front and center.

Deeply entrenched perceptions of the United States will be hard to budge, and politicians accustomed to quick fixes could blanch under long-range branding approaches to international affairs. For Beers, this is a battle for the mind: "We are having people who are not our friends define America in negative terms. It is time for us to reignite the understanding of America."

Sources: Ira Teinowitz, "U.S. Considers Advertising on Al Jazeera TV," *Ad Age*, http://www.adage.com, accessed October 15, 2001; Rick Stengel, "It Is Coke vs. Pepsi," *Time*, http://www.time.com, accessed November 8, 2001.

the film director may prefer exactly that. But who really has creative authorship is typically unclear. Getting the various players to perform their particular specialty at just the right time, while avoiding conflict with other team members, is an ongoing challenge in TV ad production.

5 **The Creative Team in Television Advertising.** The vast and ever-increasing capability of the broadcast media introduces new challenges and complexities to the production process. One aspect of these complexities is that aside from the creative directors, copywriters, and art directors who assume the burden of responsibility in the production of print advertising, we now encounter a host of new and irreplaceable creative and technical participants. The proper and effective production of broadcast advertising depends on a team of highly capable creative people: agency personnel, production experts, editorial specialists, and music companies. An advertiser and its agency must consider and evaluate the role of each of these participants. Descriptions of the roles played by the participants in television advertising are provided in Exhibit 13.31. The Global Issues box on this page describes how Charlotte Beers, probably the most powerful woman in advertising, faces the challenge of assembling a creative team to enhance the global image of the United States.

Creative Guidelines for Television Advertising.

Just as for print advertising, there are general creative principles for television advertising.[9] These principles are not foolproof or definitive, but they certainly represent good advice. Again, truly great creative work has no doubt violated some or all of these conventions.

---

9.   These guidelines were adapted from A. Jerome Jewler, *Creative Strategy in Advertising*, 3rd ed. (Belmont, Calif.: Wadsworth, 1989), 210–211; Nelson, *The Design of Advertising*, 296.

Agency Participants

Creative director (CD): The creative director manages the creative process in an agency for several different clients. Creative directors typically come from the art or copywriting side of the business. The main role of the CD is to oversee the creative product of an agency across all clients.

Art director (AD): The art director and the copywriter work together to develop the concept for a commercial. The AD either oversees the production of the television storyboard or actually constructs the storyboards. In addition, the AD works with the director of the commercial to develop the overall look of the spot.

Copywriter: The copywriter is responsible for the words and phrases used in an ad. In television and radio advertising, these words and phrases appear as a script from which the director, creative director, and art director work during the production process. Together with the AD, the copywriter also makes recommendations on choice of director, casting, and editing facility.

Account executive (AE): The account executive acts as a liaison between the creative team and the client. The AE has the responsibility for coordinating scheduling, budgeting, and the various approvals needed during the production process. The AE can be quite valuable in helping the advertiser understand the various aspects of the production process. Account executives rarely have direct input into either the creative or technical execution of an ad.

Executive producer: The executive producer in an agency is in charge of many line producers, who manage the production at the production site. Executive producers help manage the production bid process. They also assign the appropriate producers to particular production jobs.

Producer: The producer supervises and coordinates all the activities related to a broadcast production. Producers screen director reels, send out production bid forms, review bids, and recommend the production house to be used. The producer also participates in choosing locations, sets, and talent. Normally, the producer will be on the set throughout the production and in the editing room during postproduction, representing agency and client interests.

Production Company Participants

Director: The director is in charge of the filming or taping of a broadcast advertising production. From a creative standpoint, the director is the visionary who brings the copy strategy to life on film or tape. The director also manages the actors, actresses, musicians, and announcers used in an ad to ensure that their performances contribute to the creative strategy being pursued. Finally, the director manages and coordinates the activities of technical staff. Camera operators, sound and lighting technicians, and special effects experts get their assignments from the director.

Producer: The production company also has a producer present, who manages the production at the site. This producer is in charge of the production crew and sets up each shoot. The position of cameras and readiness of production personnel are the responsibility of this producer.

Production manager: The production manager is on the set of a shoot, providing all the ancillary services needed to ensure a successful production. These range from making sure that food service is available on the set to providing dressing rooms and fax, phone, and photocopy services. The production manager typically has a production assistant (PA) to help take care of details.

Camera department: Another critical part of the production team is the camera department. This group includes the director of photography, camera operator, and assistant camera operator. This group ensures that the lighting, angles, and movement are carried out according to the plan and the director's specification.

Art department: The art department that accompanies the production company includes the art director and other personnel responsible for creating the set. This group designs the set, builds background or stunt structures, and provides props.

Editors: Editors enter the production process at the postproduction stage. It is their job, with direction from the art director, creative director, producer, or director, to create the finished advertisement. Editors typically work for independent postproduction houses and use highly specialized equipment to cut and join frames of film or audiotape together to create the finished version of a television or radio advertisement. Editors also synchronize the audio track with visual images in television advertisements and perform the transfer and duplication processes to prepare a commercial for shipping to the media.

EXHIBIT 13.31

The creative team for television advertising production.

- *Use an attention-getting and relevant opening.* The first few seconds of a television commercial are crucial. A receiver can make a split-second assessment of the relevance and interest a message holds. An ad can either turn a receiver off or grab his or her attention for the balance of the commercial with the opening. Remember, remote controls are rarely too far away. This truism should not be ignored. Channel surfing is a very real phenomenon. It is getting so incredibly easy to avoid commercials that you, as an advertiser, must have a good hook to suck viewers in. Ads just don't get much time to develop. Of course, there is the belief that "slower" ads (ads that take time to develop) don't wear out as quickly as the quick hit-and-run ads. So, if you have a huge (almost inexhaustible) supply of money, an ad that "builds" might be best. If you don't, go for the quick hook. In Exhibit 13.32, the PBS spot opens with a goldfish watching a PBS TV show about salmon returning upriver. It's hard to not wonder what's going to come next.

- **Emphasize the visual.** The video capability of television should be highlighted in every production effort. To some degree, this emphasis is dependent on the creative concept, but the visual should carry the selling message even if the audio portion is ignored by the receiver. In Exhibit 13.33, Bahlsen Cookies tells its story with a minimum of words. Exhibit 13.34 shows one of the most famous political ads of all time, an ad that helped cement Lyndon Johnson's win over Barry Goldwater in 1964 by painting Goldwater as a near madman who might get us into a nuclear war.

- **Coordinate the audio with the visual.** The images and copy of a television commercial must reinforce each other rather than pursue separate objectives. Such divergence between the audio and visual portions of an ad only serves to confuse and distract the viewer. In Exhibit 13.35, Miller High Life uses both words and visuals to create the world of a High Life man.

- **Persuade as well as entertain.** It is tempting to produce a beautifully creative television advertisement rather than a beautifully effective television advertisement. The vast potential of film lures the creative urge in all the production participants. Creating an entertaining commercial is an inherently praiseworthy goal *except* when the entertainment value of the commercial completely overwhelms its persuasive impact. In Exhibit 13.36, Hewlett-Packard sells its photo-quality

EXHIBIT 13.32

Would a scene of goldfish watching TV be enough to keep you from reaching for the remote?

EXHIBIT 13.33

A TV ad that succeeds without words.

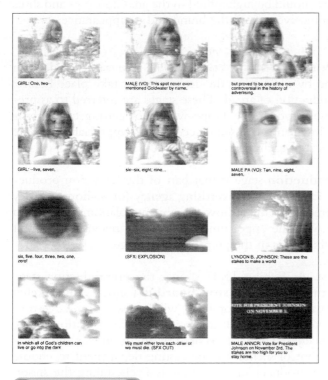

GIRL: One, two--

MALE (VO): This spot never even mentioned Goldwater by name,

but proved to be one of the most controversial in the history of advertising.

GIRL: --live, seven,

six--six, eight, nine...

MALE PA (VO): Ten, nine, eight, seven.

six, five, four, three, two, one, zero!

(SFX: EXPLOSION)

LYNDON B. JOHNSON: These are the stakes to make a world

in which all of God's children can live or go into the dark

We must either love each other or we must die. (SFX OUT)

MALE ANNCR: Vote for President Johnson on November 3rd. The stakes are too high for you to stay home.

EXHIBIT 13.34

The most famous political ad of all time (Doyle Dane Bernbach).

(single and part of series)

"Donut" :30

(OPEN ON A CLOSE-UP OF BEER, DONUTS AND A MAN'S DIRTY HANDS ON TABLE. HE PICKS UP A DONUT)

ANNCR. (VO):   Sometimes a man gets too hungry to clean his hands properly.

(CUT TO CLOSE-UP OF DONUTS)

ANNCR. (VO):   The powdered sugar on this donut puts a semi-protective barrier between your fingerprint and your nutrition.

(CUT TO A MAN HOLDING BEER, EATING DONUTS)

ANNCR. (VO):   But even if some grease does get on that donut, that's just flavor to a High Life man.

TITLE CARD: (FADE UP) Miller Time logo.

ART DIRECTOR: Jeff Williams
WRITER: Jeff Kling
CREATIVE DIRECTOR: Susan Hoffman
PRODUCER: Jeff Selis
DIRECTOR: Errol Morris
PRODUCTION COMPANY: @radical.media
AD AGENCY: Wieden & Kennedy (Portland, OR)
CLIENT: Miller Brewing Company

EXHIBIT 13.35

An ad that creates the world of the High Life man. http://www.millerbrewing.com

---

EXHIBIT 13.36

Humor meets demonstration. http://www.hp.com

(SFX: QUIET TICKING OF CLOCK)
(SFX: WRESTLING ON TV)
GRANDPA: Ohhhhhh!
(SFX: THUD)
BABY: Wahhhhhhhhhhh!
GRANDPA: Don't worry, honey. Mom and Dad will be right back.
GRANDPA: Pretty baby!
BABY: Wahhhhhhhhhhh!
(SFX: SUDDEN QUIET)
(SFX: CLOCK TICKING)
ANNCR: HP photo-quality printers. Good enough to fool almost anyone.
SUPER: BUILT BY ENGINEERS. USED BY NORMAL PEOPLE.

printers with a humorous yet persuasive demonstration of their reproductive powers.

- **Show the product.** Unless a commercial is using intrigue and mystery surrounding the product, the product should be highlighted in the ad. Close-ups and shots of the brand in action help receivers recall the brand and its appearance.

 The Production Process in Television Advertising. The television production process can best be understood by identifying the activities that take place before, during, and after the actual production of an ad. These stages are referred to as preproduction, production, and postproduction. (Hope we're not getting too technical.) By breaking the process down into this sequence, we can appreciate both the technical and the strategic aspects of each stage.

Preproduction. The **preproduction** stage is that part of the television production process in which the advertiser and the advertising agency (or in-house agency staff) carefully work out the precise details of how the creative planning behind an ad can best be brought to life with the opportunities offered by television. Exhibit 13.37 shows the sequence of six events in the preproduction stage.

Storyboard and Script Approval. As Exhibit 13.37 shows, the preproduction stage begins with storyboard and script approval. A **storyboard** is a shot-by-shot sketch depicting, in sequence, the visual scenes and copy that will be used in an advertisement. A **script** is the written version of an ad; it specifies the coordination of the copy elements with the video scenes. The script is used by the producer and director to set the location and content of scenes, by the casting department to choose actors and actresses, and by the producer in budgeting and scheduling the shoot. Exhibit 13.38 is part of a storyboard from the Miller Lite "Can Your Beer Do This?" campaign, and Exhibit 13.39 shows the related script. This particular spot was entitled "Ski Jump" and involved rigging a dummy to a recliner and launching the chair and the dummy from a 60-meter ski jump.

The art director and copywriter are significantly involved at this stage of production. It is important that the producer has discussed the storyboard and script with the creative team and fully understands the creative concept and objectives for the advertisement before production begins. Since it is the producer's responsibility to solicit bids for the project from production houses, the producer must be able to fully explain to bidders the requirements of the job so that cost estimates are as accurate as possible.

Budget Approval. Once there is agreement on the scope and intent of the production as depicted in the storyboard and script, the advertiser must give budget approval. The producer needs to work carefully with the creative team and the advertiser to estimate the approximate cost of the shoot, including production staging, location costs, actors, technical requirements, staffing, and a multitude of other

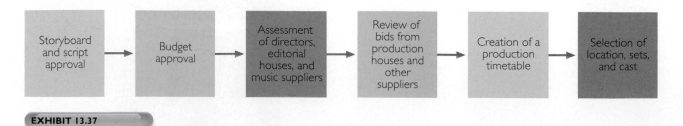

EXHIBIT 13.37

Sequence of events in the preproduction stage of television advertising.

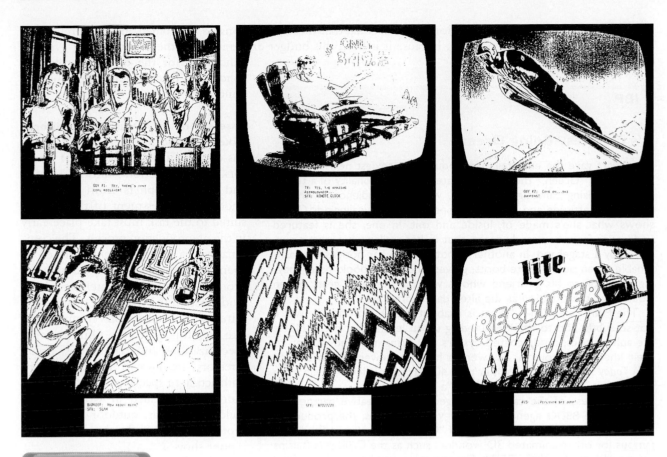

EXHIBIT 13.38

How does this storyboard for a Miller Lite Beer ad save the advertiser time and money during the television production process?
http://www.millerlite.com

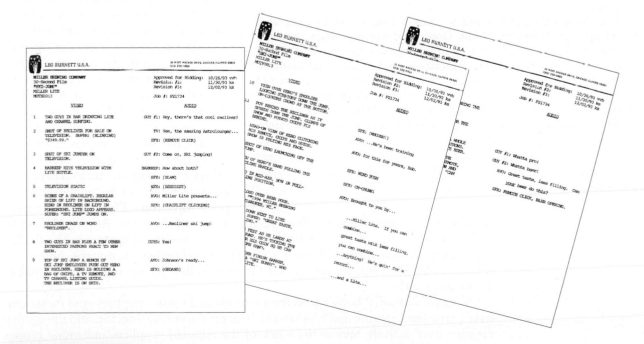

EXHIBIT 13.39

This is the script for the Miller Lite "Can Your Beer Do This?" ad shown in Exhibit 13.38. The producer and director use the script to set locations and the content of scenes and for budgeting and scheduling. The script is also used to choose actors and actresses.

considerations. It is essential that these discussions be as detailed and comprehensive as possible, because it is from this budget discussion that the producer will evaluate candidates for the directing role and solicit bids from production houses to handle the job.

IBP

It's Not Easy Being Green

M&M/Mars gave the entertainment industry its sexiest new star—the green M&M. "Green," the sassy animated M&M personality of a television advertising campaign by BBDO, won over audiences with her hard-nosed attitude and smart sex appeal. In the revealing ads Green shows what she's made of, inside and out. In one, she is featured undressing from her candy-green coat in her trailer when she is surprised by a stagehand. In another, a hot guy at a bar notices her fashionable green outfit, white boots, gloves, and pocketbook, barely paying attention to his girlfriend who is wearing the same gear. Green gloats over the situation as the jilted date storms out.

The M&M campaign—"What is it about the Green ones?"—was a not-so-subtle nod to the longstanding urban legend that green M&Ms are aphrodisiacs, candy-coated oysters that bring men and women to their knees. The colorful ads were a hit with viewers. According to *USA Today*'s Ad Track consumer poll, 40 percent of viewers—up from the average 22 percent—liked them "a lot."

The success of the campaign hinged on the creative partnership between the BBDO agency and Will Vinton Studios, the production house responsible for the creation of "Green." Will Vinton Studios is famous for other animated 3D wonders such as the California Raisins (of the "I Heard It through the Grapevine" campaign) and "The PJs," Fox television's funny Claymation family. The firm's award-winning work in the world of dimensional animation offers advertisers memorable ways of building brand equity through characterization and storytelling.

The ripple effect of Green's success is seen in M&M's integrated brand promotion efforts. While Green and her sexy ways remain a popular myth in the ads and in urban legends, her popularity also reaches into licensed goods, interactive media, and entertainment. M&M says she is one of the biggest movers of merchandise at its site (http://www.m-ms.com). Nevertheless, it's the whole assortment of colors that's popular at candy counters. The M&Ms brand in its many varieties is the number one–selling confection across the United States.

Sources: Theresa Howard, "Green Signals Go for Ad Watchers," *USA Today*, http://www.usatoday.com, accessed October 29, 2001; Press information on Will Vinton Studios, http://www.vinton.com, accessed November 2, 2001.

Assessment of Directors, Editorial Houses, Music Suppliers. A producer has dozens (if not hundreds) of directors, postproduction editorial houses, and music suppliers from which to choose. An assessment of those well-suited to the task must take place early in the preproduction process. The combination of the creative talents of ad agencies and production houses can produce creative, eye-catching ads, as evidenced in the IBP box on this page. Directors of television commercials, like directors of feature films, develop specializations and reputations. Some directors are known for their work with action or special effects. Others are more highly skilled in working with children, animals, outdoor settings, or shots of beverages flowing into a glass ("pour shots").

The director of an advertisement is responsible for interpreting the storyboard and script and managing the talent to bring the creative concept to life. A director specifies the precise nature of a scene, how it is lit, and how it is filmed. In this way, the director acts as the eye of the camera. Choosing the proper director is crucial to the execution of a commercial. Aside from the fact that a good director commands a fee anywhere from $8,000 to $25,000 per day, the director can have a tremendous effect on the quality and impact of the presentation. An excellent creative concept can be undermined by poor direction. The agency creative team should be intimately involved in the choice of directors. Among the now-famous feature film directors who have made television commercials are Ridley Scott (Apple), John Frankenheimer (AT&T), Woody Allen (Campari), Spike Lee (Levi's, Nike, the Gap, Barney's), and Federico Fellini (Coop Italia). (See Exhibits 13.40 and 13.41.)

Similarly, editorial houses (and their editors) and music suppliers (and musicians) have particular expertise and reputations. The producer, the director, and the agency creative team actively review the work of the editorial suppliers and music houses that are particularly well suited to the production. In most cases, geographic proximity to the agency facilities is important; as members of the agency team try to maintain a tight schedule, editorial and music services that are nearby facilitate the

EXHIBITS 13.40 AND 13.41

Examples of famous feature film directors who have made television commercials are Ridley Scott, director of Apple's "1984" campaign and the 1982 movie Blade Runner, *and Spike Lee, who directed 1989's* Do the Right Thing *as well as the "Morris Blackman" Nike ads.* http://www.apple.com *and* http://www.nike.com

timely completion of an ad. Because of this need, editorial and music suppliers have tended to cluster near agencies in Chicago, New York City, and Los Angeles.

Review of Bids from Production Houses and Other Suppliers. Production houses and other suppliers, such as lighting specialists, represent a collection of specialized talent and also provide needed equipment for ad preparation. The expertise in production houses relates to the technical aspects of filming a commercial. Producers, production managers, sound and art specialists, camera operators, and others are part of a production house team. The agency sends a bid package to several production houses. The package contains all the details of the commercial to be produced and includes a description of the production requirements and a timetable for the production. An accurate timetable is essential because many production personnel work on an hourly or daily compensation rate.

To give you some idea of the cost of the technical personnel and equipment available from production houses, Exhibit 13.42 lists some key production house personnel who would participate in shooting a commercial, and the typical daily

EXHIBIT 13.42

Sample costs for production personnel and equipment.

Personnel	Cost
Director	$8,000–25,000/day
Director of photography	3,000/day
Producer	800/day
Production assistant	200/day
Camera operator	600/day
Unit manager	450/day
Equipment	
Production van (including camera, lighting kit, microphones, monitoring equipment)	$2,500–4,000/day
Camera	750–1,000/day
Grip truck with lighting equipment and driver	400–500/day
Telescript with operator	600–700/day
Online editing with editor and assistant editor	250–400/hour

rates (for a 10-hour day) for such personnel and related equipment. Also listed are the rental costs of various pieces of equipment. These costs vary from market to market, but it is obvious why production expenses can run into the hundreds of thousands of dollars. The costs listed in the exhibit represent only the daily rates for production time or postproduction work. In addition to these costs are overtime costs, travel, and lodging (if an overnight stay is necessary).

Most agencies send out a bid package on a form developed by the agency. An example of such a bid form is provided in Exhibit 13.43. By using a standardized form, an agency can make direct comparisons between production house bids. A similar form can be used to solicit bids from other suppliers providing editorial or music services. The producer reviews each of the bids and revises them if necessary. From the production house bids *and* the agency's estimate of its own costs associated with production (travel, expenses, editorial services, music, on-camera talent, and agency markups), a production cost estimate is prepared for advertiser review and approval. Once the advertiser has approved the estimate, one of the production houses is awarded the job. The lowest production bid is not always the one chosen. Aside from cost, there are creative and technical considerations. A hot director costs more than last year's model. The agency's evaluation of the reliability of a production house also enters into the decision.

EXHIBIT 13.43

Advertising agencies use a bid form to make comparisons between production house bids and provide the client with an estimate of production costs.

CLIENT:		DATE:			
PRODUCT:		A. E.:			
		ACCT. SUP.:			
		WRITER:			
		A. D.:			
		C. D.:			

NAME / LENGTH	TYPE	TALENT COUNT			
		OC	EXT	VO	
1					
2					
3					
4					
		ESTIMATE	ACTUAL		
PRODUCTION CO.					
EDITING					
MUSIC					
TALENT					
ARTWORK/CC PACKAGES					
RECORDING STUDIO					
VIDEOTAPE TRANSFERS					
ANIMATION					
CASTING					
SUB TOTAL NET					
% A. C.					
TRAVEL					
SHIPPING					
TOTAL GROSS COST					
NOTES:					

Creation of a Production Timetable. In conjunction with the stages of preproduction just discussed, the producer will be working on a **production timetable.** This timetable projects a realistic schedule for all the preproduction, production, and postproduction activities. To stay on budget and complete the production in time to

Example of a reasonable timetable for shooting a 30-second television advertisement.

Activity	Time
Assess directors/editorial houses/music suppliers	1 week
Solicit bids from production houses/other suppliers	1 week
Review bids, award jobs to suppliers, submit production estimate to advertiser	1 week
Begin preproduction (location, sets, casting)	1 to 2 weeks
Final preparation and shooting	1 to 2 weeks
Edit film	1 week
Agency/advertiser review of rough-cut film	1 week
Postproduction (final editing, voice mix, record music, special effects, etc.) and transfer of film to video; ship to media	2 weeks
Transfer film to videotape; ship to stations	1 week
Total	10 to 12 weeks

ship the final advertisement to television stations for airing, an accurate and realistic timetable is essential. A timetable must allow a reasonable amount of time to complete all production tasks in a quality manner. Exhibit 13.44 is a timetable for a national 30-second spot, using location shooting.

Realize that a reasonable timetable is rarely achieved. Advertisers often request (or demand) that an agency provide a finished spot (or even several spots) in times as short as four or five weeks. Because of competitive pressures or corporate urgency for change, production timetables are compromised. Advertisers have to accept the reality that violating a reasonable timetable can dramatically increase costs and puts undue pressure on the creative process—no matter what the reason for the urgency. In fact, a creative director at one agency often told clients that they could pick any two selections from the following list for their television commercials: good, fast, and reasonably priced.[10]

Selection of Location, Sets, and Cast. Once a bid has been approved and accepted, both the production house and the agency production team begin to search for appropriate, affordable locations if the commercial is to be shot outside a studio setting. Studio production warrants the design and construction of the sets to be used.

A delicate stage in preproduction is casting. While not every ad uses actors and actresses, when an ad calls for individuals to perform roles, casting is crucial. Every individual appearing in an ad is, in a very real sense, a representative of the advertiser. This is another reason why the agency creative team stays involved. Actors and actresses help set the mood and tone for an ad and affect the image of the brand. The successful execution of various message strategies depends on proper casting. For instance, a slice-of-life message requires actors and actresses with whom the target audience can readily identify. Testimonial message tactics require a search for particular types of people, either celebrities or common folks, who will attract attention and be credible to the audience. The point to remember is that successfully casting a television commercial depends on much more than simply picking people with good acting abilities. Individuals must be matched to the personality of the brand, the nature of the audience, and the scene depicted in the ad. A young male actor who makes a perfect husband in a laundry detergent ad may be totally inappropriate as a rugged outdoorsman in a chainsaw commercial.

10. Peter Sheldon, former creative director and head of creative sequences, University of Illinois Advertising Department.

Script Specification	Meaning
CU	Close-up.
ECU	Extreme close-up.
MS	Medium shot.
LS	Long shot.
Zoom	Movement in or out on subject with camera fixed.
Dolly	Movement in or out on subject moving the camera (generally slower than a zoom).
Pan	Camera scanning right or left from stationary position.
Truck	Camera *moving* right or left, creating a different visual angle.
Tilt	Camera panning vertically.
Cut	Abrupt movement from one scene to another.
Dissolve	Smoother transition from one scene to another, compared to a cut.
Wipe	Horizontal or vertical removal of one image to replace it with a new image (inserted vertically or horizontally).
Split screen	Two or more independent video sources occupying the screen.
Skip frame	Replacement of one image with another through pulsating (frame insertion of) the second image into the first. Used for dramatic transitions.
Key insert, matte, chromakey	Insertion of one image onto another background. Often used to impose product over the scene taking place in the commercial.
Super title	Lettering superimposed over visual. Often used to emphasize a major selling point or to display disclaimers/product warnings.
SFX	Sound effects.
VO	Introducing a voice over the visual.
ANN	Announcer entering the commercial.
Music under	Music playing in the background.
Music down and out	Music fading out of commercial.
Music up and out	Music volume ascending and abruptly ending.

EXHIBIT 13.45

Instructions commonly appearing in television commercial scripts.

Production. The **production stage** of the process, or the **shoot,** is where the storyboard and script come to life and are filmed. The actual production of the spot may also include some final preparations before the shoot begins. The most common final preparation activities are lighting checks and rehearsals. An entire day may be devoted to *prelight,* which involves setting up lighting or identifying times for the best natural lighting to ensure that the shooting day runs smoothly. Similarly, the director may want to work with the on–camera talent along with the camera operators to practice the positioning and movement planned for the ad. This work, known as *blocking,* can save a lot of time on a shoot day, when many more costly personnel are on the set.

Lighting, blocking, and other special factors are typically specified by the director in the script. Exhibit 13.45 is a list of common directorial specifications that show up in a script and are used by a director to manage the audio and visual components of a commercial shoot.

Shoot days are the culmination of an enormous amount of effort beginning all the way back at the development of the copy platform. They are the execution of all the well–laid plans by the advertiser and agency personnel. The set on a shoot day is a world all its own. For the uninformed, it can appear to be little more than high-energy chaos, or a lot of nothing going on between camera setups. For the professionals involved, however, a shoot has its own tempo and direction, including a whole lot of nothing going on.

Production activities during a shoot require the highest level of professionalism and expertise. A successful shoot depends on the effective management of a large number of diverse individuals—creative performers, highly trained technicians, and skilled laborers. Logistical and technical problems always arise, not to mention the ever-present threat of a random event (a thunderstorm or intrusive noise) that disrupts filming and tries everyone's patience. There is a degree of tension and spontaneity on the set that is a necessary part of the creative process but must be kept at a manageable level. Much of the tension stems from trying to execute the various tasks of production correctly and at the proper time.

Another dimension to this tension, however, has to do with expense. As pointed out earlier, most directors, technicians, and talent are paid on a daily rate plus overtime after 10 hours. Daily shooting expenses, including director's fees, can run $80,000 to $120,000 for just an average production, so the agency and advertiser, understandably, want the shoot to run as smoothly and quickly as possible.

There is the real problem of not rushing creativity, however, and advertisers often have to learn to accept the pace of production. For example, a well-known director made a Honda commercial in South Florida, where he shot film for only one hour per day—a half-hour in the morning and a half-hour at twilight. His explanation? "From experience you learn that cars look flat and unattractive in direct light, so you have to catch the shot when the angle [of the sun] is just right."[11] Despite the fact that the cameras were rolling only an hour a day, the $9,000-per-hour cost for the production crew was charged all day for each day of shooting. Advertisers have to accept, on occasion, that the television advertising production process is not like an assembly line production process. Sweating the details to achieve just the right look can provoke controversy—and often does.

The Cost of Television Production. Coordinating and taking advantage of the skills offered by creative talent is a big challenge for advertisers. The average 30-second television commercial prepared by a national advertiser can run up production charges from $100,000 to $500,000 and even more if special effects or celebrities are used in the spot.[12] The cost of making a television commercial increased nearly 400 percent between 1979 and 1993.[13] Now it's even more. Part of that increase is attributed to the escalating cost of creative talent, such as directors and editors. Other aspects of the cost have to do with more and better equipment being used at all stages of the production process, and longer shooting schedules to ensure advertiser satisfaction.

The average expense for a 30-second spot tends to be higher for commercials in highly competitive consumer markets, such as beer, soft drinks, autos, and banking, where image campaigns (which require high-quality production) are commonly used. Conversely, average production costs tend to be lower for advertisements in which functional features or shots of the product often dominate the spot, as with household cleansers and office equipment.

The high and rising cost of television production has created some tensions between advertisers and their ad agencies. Most agencies and production companies respond by saying that advertisers are demanding to stand out from the clutter, and to do so requires complex concepts and high-priced talent.[14] Conversely, when an advertiser is not so image conscious, ways can be found to stand out without spending huge dollar amounts.

11.   Jeffrey A. Trachtenberg, "Where the Money Goes," *Forbes,* September 21, 1987, 180.
12.   Joe Mandese, "Study Shows Cost of TV Spots," *Advertising Age,* August 1, 1994, 32.
13.   Information for the average cost of a 30-second ad in 1979 was taken from Ronald Alsop, "Advertisers Bristle as Charges Balloon for Splashy TV Spots," *Wall Street Journal,* June 20, 1985, 29. Information for the average cost of a 30-second ad in 1993 was taken from Peter Caranicas, "4A's Survey Shows Double-Digit Hike in Spot Production Costs," *Shoot,* July 15, 1994, 1, 40–42.
14.   Caranicas, "4A's Survey Shows Double-Digit Hike in Spot Product Costs," 42.

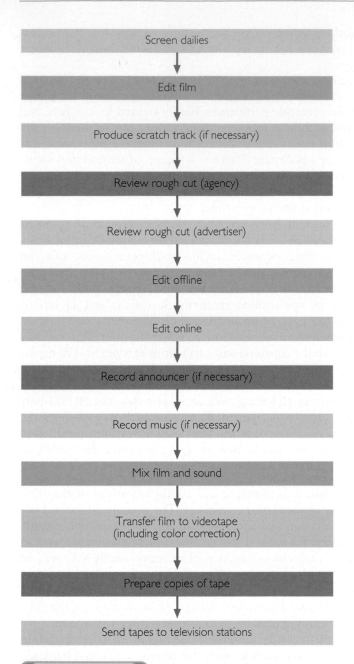

Screen dailies

Edit film

Produce scratch track (if necessary)

Review rough cut (agency)

Review rough cut (advertiser)

Edit offline

Edit online

Record announcer (if necessary)

Record music (if necessary)

Mix film and sound

Transfer film to videotape
(including color correction)

Prepare copies of tape

Send tapes to television stations

EXHIBIT 13.46

Sequence of events in television commercial postproduction.

The important issue in the preparation of all television advertising, regardless of cost, is that the production process has direct and significant effects on the communication impact of a finished advertisement. A well-conceived copy strategy can fall flat if the execution at the point of production is poor. As one advertiser put it, "We don't want to be penny wise and pound foolish. If we're spending $10 million to buy TV time, we shouldn't threaten creative integrity just to cut production cost to $140,000 from $150,000."[15] One rule of thumb is to ask for 10 percent of the planned media buy for production. They may not give it to you, but it's nice if you can get it, unless they are planning a very small media buy.

Postproduction. Once filming is completed, several postproduction activities are required before the commercial is ready for airing. At this point, a host of additional professional talent enters the process. Film editors, audio technicians, voice-over specialists, and musicians may be contracted. Exhibit 13.46 shows the sequence of events in the postproduction phase.

The first step in postproduction is review of the **dailies**—scenes shot during the previous day's production. Such screening may result in reshooting certain segments of the ad. Once dailies are acceptable to the agency, the editing process begins. **Editing** involves piecing together various scenes or shots of scenes, called *takes,* to bring about the desired visual effect. Most editing involves making decisions about takes shot at different angles, or subtle differences in the performance of the talent. If music is to be included, it will be prepared at this point using a **scratch track,** which is a rough approximation of the musical score using only a piano and vocalists.

A rough cut of the commercial is then prepared by loading the video dailies into an *Avid computer* to digitize and timecode the tape. The **rough cut** is an assembly of the best scenes from the shoot edited together using the quick and precise access afforded by digital technology. Using the offline Avid computer on the digitized rough cut, various technical aspects of the look of a commercial can be refined—color alterations and background images, for example. The final editing of the advertisement—which includes repositioning of elements, correcting final color, and adding fades, titles, blowups, dissolves, final audio, and special effects—is done with online equipment in online rooms equipped for final editing. **Online editing** involves transferring the finalized rough cut onto one-inch videotape, which is of on-air quality suitable for media transmission.

The personnel and equipment required for postproduction tasks are costly. Film editors charge about $150 to $200 per hour, and an editing assistant is about $50 per hour. An offline computer costs about $100 per hour. When online editing begins, the cost goes up, with online rooms running about $700 per hour. The reason for the dra-

15.   Alsop, "Advertisers Bristle as Charges Balloon for Splashy TV Spots."

matic difference in cost between offline editing and online editing is that offline edits are done on a single machine to produce a rough, working version of an ad. The online room typically includes many specialized machines for all the final effects desired in the ad. Additionally, a mixing room for voice and music costs about $400 per day.

In all, it is easy to see why filmed television commercials are so costly. Scores of people with specialized skills and a large number of separate tasks are included in the process. The procedures also reflect the complexity of the process. Aside from the mechanics of production, a constant vigil must be kept over the creative concept of the advertisement. Despite the complexities, the advertising industry continues to turn out high-quality television commercials on a timely basis.

7   Production Options in Television Advertising. Several production options are available to an advertiser in preparing a television commercial. Eighty percent of all television commercials prepared by national advertisers use film as the medium for production. The previous discussion of production procedures, in fact, described the production process for a filmed advertisement. **Film** (typically 35-mm) is the most versatile medium and produces the highest-quality visual impression. It is, however, the most expensive medium for production and is also the most time consuming.

A less expensive option is **videotape.** Videotape is not as popular among directors or advertisers for a variety of reasons. Tape has far fewer lines of resolution, and some say videotape results in a flatter image than film. Its visual impressions are more stark and have less depth and less color intensity. While this can sometimes add to the realism of a commercial, it can also detract from the appearance of the product and the people in the ad. New **digital video (DV)** formats are replacing traditional videotape, and even challenging film in some productions due to DV's much lower cost and high-quality look. It doesn't look like film exactly, but it sure looks better than videotape.

There is always the choice of live television commercial production. **Live production** can result in realism and the capturing of spontaneous reactions and events that couldn't possibly be recreated in a rehearsed scene. It is clear, however, that the loss of control in live settings threatens the carefully worked-out objectives for a commercial. On occasion, local retailers (such as auto dealers) use live commercials to execute direct response message strategies. Such a technique can capture the urgency of an appeal.

Two techniques that do not neatly fit the production process described earlier are animation and stills. **Animation** (and the variation known as Claymation) is the use of drawn figures and scenes (such as cartoons) to produce a commercial. Keebler cookie and California Raisin commercials use characters created by animators and Claymation artists. Animated characters, such as Tony the Tiger, are frequently incorporated into filmed commercials for added emphasis. A newer form of animation uses computer-generated images. Several firms, such as TRW, have developed commercials totally through the use of computers. The graphics capabilities of giant-capacity computers make futuristic, eye-catching animation ads an attractive alternative. And the actors show up on time.

Still production is a technique whereby a series of photographs or slides is filmed and edited so that the resulting ad appears to have movement and action. Through the use of pans, zooms, and dissolves with the camera, still photographs can be used to produce an interesting yet low-cost finished advertisement.

The production option chosen should always be justified on both a creative and a cost basis. The dominance of filmed commercials is explainable by the level of quality of the finished ad and the versatility afforded by the technique. A local retailer or social service organization may not need or may not be able to afford the quality of film. In cases where quality is less significant or costs are primary, other production techniques are available.

SUMMARY

 Identify the basic purposes, components, and formats of print ad illustrations.

With few exceptions, illustrations are critical to the effectiveness of print ads. Specifically, illustrations can serve to attract attention, make the brand heroic, communicate product features or benefits, create a mood and enhance brand image, stimulate reading of the body copy, or create the desired social context for the brand. The overall impact of an illustration is determined in part by its most basic components: size, use of color, and the medium used to create the illustration. Another critical aspect of the illustration's effectiveness has to do with the format chosen for the product in the illustration. Obviously, a print ad cannot work if the consumer doesn't easily identify the product or service being advertised.

 Describe the principles and components that help ensure the effective design of print ads.

In print ad design, all the verbal and visual components of an ad are arranged for maximum impact and appeal. Several principles can be followed as a basis for a compelling design. These principles feature issues such as balance, proportion, order, unity, and emphasis. The first component of an effective design is focus—drawing the reader's attention to specific areas of the ad. The second component is movement and direction—directing the reader's eye movement through the ad. The third component is clarity and simplicity—avoiding a complex and chaotic look that will deter most consumers.

 Detail the stages that art directors follow in developing the layout of a print ad.

The layout is the physical manifestation of all this design planning. An art director uses various forms of layouts to bring a print ad to life. There are several predictable stages in the evolution of a layout. The art director starts with a hand-drawn thumbnail, proceeds to the digitized rough layout, and continues with a tight comp that represents the look of the final ad. With each stage, the layout becomes more concrete and more like the final form of the advertisement. The last stage, the mechanical, is the form the ad takes as it goes to final production.

 Discuss the activities and decisions involved in the final production of print ads.

Timing is critical to advertising effectiveness: Advertisers must have a keen understanding of production cycles to have an ad in the consumer's hands at just the right time. In addition, there are many possible means for actually printing an ad. These range from letterpress to screen printing to computer print production. As with many aspects of modern life, the computer has had a dramatic impact on print ad preparation and production. Before a print ad can reach its audience, a host of small but important decisions need to be made about the type styles and sizes that will best serve the campaign's purposes.

 Identify the various players who must function as a team to produce television ads.

The complexity of ad production for television is unrivaled and thus demands the inputs of a variety of functional specialists. From the ad agency come familiar players such as the art director, copywriter, and account executive. Then there are a host of individuals who have special skills in various aspects of production for this medium. These include directors, producers, production managers, and camera crews. Editors will also be needed to bring all the raw material together into a finished commercial. Organizational and team-management skills are essential to make all these people and pieces work together.

 Discuss the specific stages and costs involved in producing television ads.

The intricate process of TV ad production can be broken into three major stages: preproduction, production, and postproduction. In the preproduction stage, scripts and storyboards are prepared, budgets are set, production houses are engaged, and a timetable is formulated. Production includes all those activities involved in the actual filming of the ad. The shoot is a high-stress activity that usually carries a high price tag. The raw materials from the shoot are mixed and refined in the postproduction stage. Today's editors work almost exclusively with computers to create the final product—a finished television ad. If all this sounds expensive, it is!

 Describe the major formatting options for television ad production.

Film is the preferred option for most TV ads because of the high-quality visual impression it provides. Videotape suffers on the quality issue, and live television is not practical in most cases. Animation is probably the second most popular formatting option. With continuing improvements in computer graphics, computer-generated images may one day become a preferred source of material for TV ad production. Still production can be an economical means to bring a message to television.

KEY TERMS

illustration
medium
illustration format
design
principles of design
balance
formal balance
informal balance
border
white space
axis
three-point layout structure
parallel layout structure
layout
thumbnails
rough layout
comp

mechanical
closing date
letterpress
offset lithography
gravure
flexography
electronic, laser, and inkjet printing
type font
blackletter
roman
script
serif
sans serif
miscellaneous
point
picas
preproduction

storyboard
script
production timetable
production stage, or shoot
dailies
editing
scratch track
rough cut
online editing
film
videotape
digital video (DV)
live production
animation
still production

QUESTIONS

1. Is there anyone out there who would rather watch black-and-white television than color? If not, why would any advertiser choose to run a black-and-white print ad in a medium that supports color? Can you think of a situation where a black-and-white ad might be more effective than a color ad?

2. "Effective" turns out to be a very elusive concept in any discussion of advertising's effects. In what ways might an illustration in a print ad prove to be effective from the point of view of a marketer?

3. This chapter reviewed five basic principles for print ad design: balance, proportion, order, unity, and emphasis. Give an example of how each of these principles might be employed to enhance the selling message of a print ad.

4. Creativity in advertising is often a matter of breaking with conventions. Peruse an issue of your favorite magazine or newspaper to find examples of ads that violate the five basic principles mentioned in the previous question.

5. Why is it appropriate to think of print as a static medium? Given print's static nature, explain how movement and direction can be relevant concepts to the layout of a print ad.

6. For an art director who has reached the mechanicals stage of the ad layout process, explain the appeal of computer-aided design versus the old-fashioned paste-up approach.

7. Explain the role of the production company in the evolution of a television commercial. As part of this explanation, be certain you have identified each of the unique skills and specialties that people in the production company bring to the ad development process.

8. Compare and contrast the creative guidelines for TV offered in this chapter with those offered for print ads in the previous chapter. Based on this analysis, what conclusions would you offer about the keys to effective communication in these two media?

9. Identify the six steps involved in the preproduction of a television ad and describe the issues that an art director must attend to at each step if his or her goals for the ad are to be achieved.

10. Without a doubt, a television ad shoot is one of the most exciting and pressure-packed activities that any advertising professional can take part in. List the various factors or issues that contribute to the tension and excitement that surrounds an ad shoot.

11. Review the formatting options that an art director can choose from when conceiving a television ad. Discuss the advantages of each option and describe the situation for which each is best suited.

EXPERIENTIAL EXERCISES

1.   The production process in television advertising is highly involved and requires advertisers to work with a range of production partners to be successful. Television ads develop through preproduction, production, and postproduction stages, and each stage requires careful project management on the part of advertisers. In particular, advertisers must carefully select production houses and other suppliers to create the actual ads. AMVF Productions is a full-service television-advertising production firm that many advertisers trust to help them communicate messages across a range of visual media options. Visit AMVF's Web site (http://www.amvfproductions.com) to learn more about how television production companies can help advertisers. Who are AMVF's clients? Which production options for television advertising listed at the end of this chapter does AMVF offer to clients? What can you learn about AMVF from the portfolio section of its site, and how does that information help advertisers during the preproduction stage?

2.   Advertisers that have a strong Internet component to their businesses often list a Web address at the end of television commercials, prompting viewers to visit the site. For this exercise, evaluate a television advertisement that lists a Web address during the commercial. First, discuss whether you think the ad follows the general creative principles for television advertising listed in this chapter and cite examples. Next, visit the Web site and evaluate it based on the principles of illustration also listed in this chapter. Does the particular Web site design resemble print, or does it seem to have interactive features unique to the Internet medium? Finally, comment on how well the advertiser integrates the television ad with the Web site to communicate a single, clear message to consumers.

EXPERIENCING THE INTERNET

13-1   Elements of Illustration

Hillmancurtis is one of the premier design companies in the world, specializing in brand development and advertising for some of the most famous brands. The firm's regard for the power of visual design has earned it a list of clients such as Adobe, Fox SearchLight, MTV, RollingStone.com, and AOL. Hillmancurtis has won prestigious honors for its work in print, broadcast, and Web media. Visit the Hillmancurtis site and browse the firm's online portfolio samples to answer the following questions.

Hillmancurtis: http://www.hillmancurtis.com

Adobe: http://www.adobe.com

1.   Good illustration can make a brand more heroic. Choose a portfolio sample from the hillmancurtis.com portfolio section and explain how the firm accomplished this for its client's brand.

2.   Visit Adobe's Web site and explain how Hillmancurtis designed the illustration at the site to create a mood, feeling, and image that appeal to graphic designers. How does the illustration at the site support Adobe's reputation as a leading manufacturer of publishing software and graphic design tools?

3.   Browse and identify portfolio examples of Web animation at hillmancurtis.com, and describe how advancing computer technology is enabling design firms to produce endless creative possibilities for illustration.

13-2   Art Direction in Cyberspace

At this stage in the development of the Internet, cyberspace is often compared to print and television, yet it possesses unique qualities as well. The medium is interactive, and new technology is making it possible for a variety of rich media to be used for advertising purposes. Blitz Digital Studios is on the pioneering edge of the Web's progression toward full-motion interactive capabilities.

Blitz Digital Studios: http://www.blitzds.com

1.   What industries are most likely to rely heavily on the enhanced interactive design capabilities provided by Blitz Digital Studios?

2.   Describe how the Blitz Digital Studios site combines elements of television and print into one new media experience for the user. What challenges still exist in making cyberspace a fully interactive experience for many Web users?

3.   Do you think traditional advertising agencies are capable of providing such advanced Internet production services to clients? Is interactive Web design influencing design elements in print or television advertising? Cite one example of a print or television ad that was influenced by the booming popularity of the Internet.

INTEGRATED BRAND PROMOTION

PART 3

Cincinnati Bell℠

Cincinnati Bell Wireless: Preparing Advertising and IBP

In Parts 1 and 2 of our comprehensive IBP case, we introduced you to a client and an ad agency who together, in the spring of 1998, were preparing for the launch of a new digital phone service in the Greater Cincinnati market.

Now it is time to take an inside look at the process of actually preparing the elements of an integrated communications campaign. This stressful, stop-and-go process must be managed in such a way that the tension and stress do not stifle the creativity that is always required for breakthrough advertising. Many different types of expertise must be folded into the process to take advantage of multiple communication tools, and countless details must be attended to if the various tools are to work together to produce the synergy that is the reason for pursuing an IBP campaign in the first place. Collaboration between agency and client is key to ensure that the approval process proceeds in a timely fashion, but with all the planning and forethought there still needs to be an element of spontaneity that allows both client and agency to capitalize on the last-minute big ideas that always infiltrate the process just when it seems everything is decided.

Tension, stress, creativity, deadlines, collaboration, synergy, conflict, misunderstandings, expertise, complexity, details, details, details . . . these are all things that characterize the process of preparing to launch an IBP campaign. How is it possible for people to survive and work through the array of challenges that characterize campaign preparation? How is it possible, in the people-intensive business of advertising design and production, for order ever to emerge from the chaos?

Making Beautiful Music Together: Coordination, Collaboration, and Creativity.
Metaphors help us understand, so let's use a metaphor to appreciate the challenge of executing sophisticated IBP campaigns. Executing an IBP campaign is very much like the performance of a symphony orchestra. To produce glorious music, many individuals must make their unique contributions to the performance, but it sounds right only if the maestro brings it all together at the critical moment. The next time you attend the performance of a symphony orchestra, get there early so that you can hear each individual musician warming up his or her instrument. Reflect on the many years of dedicated practice that this individual put in to master that instrument. Reflect on the many hours of practice that this individual put in to learn his or her specific part for tonight's performance. As you sit there listening to the warm-up, notice how the random collection of sounds becomes increasingly painful to the ears. With each musician doing his or her own thing, the sound is a collection of hoots and clangs that grows louder as the performance approaches. Mercifully, the maestro finally steps to the podium to quell the cacophony. All is quiet for a moment. The musicians focus on their sheet music for reassurance, even though by now they could play their individual parts in their sleep.

Finally, the maestro calls the orchestra into action. As a group, as a collective, as a team, with each person executing a specific assignment as defined by the composer, under the direction of the maestro, they make beautiful music together.

So it goes in the world of advertising. Preparing and executing breakthrough IBP campaigns is a people-intensive business. Many different kinds of expertise will be needed to pull it off, and this means many different people must be enlisted to play a variety of roles. But some order must be imposed on the collection of players. Frequently, a maestro will need to step in to give the various players a common theme or direction for their work. Beyond this need for leadership, the effort must also be guided by a strategy if this collective is to produce beautiful music together. Of course, the goal for this kind of music is a persuasive harmony that makes the cash register sing!

Without a doubt, the coordination and collaboration required for IBP execution require sophisticated teamwork. Moreover, the creative essence of the campaign can be aided and elevated by a thoughtful team approach. Teams possess a potential for synergy that allows them to rise above the talents of their individual members on many kinds of tasks.[1] (Yes, the whole can be greater than the sum of the individual parts.)

Our Cincinnati Bell Wireless example is replete with stories of successful teamwork. We will share some of those stories subsequently; however, we'd first like to make the point that successful teamwork can't be left to chance. It must be planned for and facilitated if it is to occur with regularity. In the remainder of this section we will introduce several concepts and insights about teams that are offered to encourage you to take teamwork more seriously. We will review research concerning what makes teams effective, along with basic principles for effective teamwork. Then we will turn to our Cincinnati Bell Wireless example to bring the concepts to life.

What We Know about Teams. We fully expect that all college students, by the time they read this textbook, will have taken a class where part of their grade was determined by teamwork. Get used to it. More and more instructors in all sorts of classes are incorporating teamwork as part of their courses because they know that interpersonal skills are highly valued in the real world of work. In fact, an impressive body of evidence from research on management practices indicates that teams have become essential to the effectiveness of modern organizations. In their book *The Wisdom of Teams,* management consultants Jon Katzenbach and Douglas Smith review many valuable insights about the importance of teams in today's world of work. Here we summarize several of their key conclusions.[2]

Teams Rule! There can be little doubt that teams have become the primary means for getting things done in a growing number and variety of organizations. The growing number of performance challenges faced by most businesses—as a result of factors such as more demanding customers, technological changes, government regulation, and intensifying competition—demand speed and quality in work products that are simply beyond the scope of what an individual can hope to offer. In many instances, teams are the only valid option for getting things done. This is certainly the case for executing IBP campaigns.

It's All about Performance. Research shows that teams are effective in organizations where senior management makes it perfectly clear that teams will be held accountable for performance. Teams are expected to produce results that satisfy the

1. Arthur B. VanGundy, *Managing Group Creativity* (New York: American Management Association, 1984).
2. Jon R. Katzenbach and Douglas K. Smith, *The Wisdom of Teams: Creating the High-Performance Organization* (Boston: Harvard Business School Press, 1993).

client and yield financial gains for the organization. As we will see in subsequent examples, this performance motive as the basis for teams is a perfect fit in an advertising and IBP agency such as Northlich.

Synergy through Teams. Modern organizations require many kinds of expertise to get the work done. The only reliable way to mix people with different expertise to generate solutions where the whole is greater than the sum of the parts is through team discipline. Research shows that blending expertise from diverse disciplines often produces the most innovative solutions to many different types of business problems.[3] The "blending" must be done through teams.

The Demise of Individualism? Rugged individualism is the American Way. Always look out for number one! But are we suggesting that a growing reliance on teams in the workplace must mean a devaluation of the individual and a greater emphasis on conforming to what the group thinks? Not at all. Left unchecked, of course, an "always look out for number one" mentality can destroy teams. But teams are not incompatible with individual excellence. To the contrary, effective teams find ways to let each individual bring his or her unique contributions to the forefront as the basis for their effectiveness. When an individual does not have his or her own contribution to make, then one can question that person's value to the team. Or, as Northlich CEO Mark Serrianne is fond of saying, "If you and I both think alike, then one of us is unnecessary."

Teams Promote Personal Growth. Finally, an added benefit of teamwork is that it promotes learning for each individual team member. In a team, people learn about their own work styles and observe the work styles of others. This learning makes them more effective team players in their next assignment.

Leadership in Teams.

A critical element in the equation for successful teams is leadership. Leadership in teams is a special form of leadership; it is not a matter of the most senior person in the team giving orders and expecting others to follow. Leadership in teams is not derived from the power and authority granted by one's standing in an organization. It is not a function of some mysterious accident at birth that grants some of us the ability to lead, while others must be content to follow. All of us can learn to be effective team leaders. It is a skill worth learning.

Leaders do many things for their teams to help them succeed.[4] Teams ultimately must reach a goal to justify their standing, and here is where the leader's job starts. The leader's first job is to help the team build consensus about the goals they hope to achieve and the approach they will take to reach those goals. Without a clear sense of purpose, the team is doomed. Once goals and purpose are agreed upon, then the leader plays a role in ensuring that the work of the team is consistent with the strategy or plan. This is a particularly important role in the context of creating IBP campaigns because there must always be a screen or filter applied to ensure that each element is supporting the overriding communication goal.

Leaders may also specify roles for various individuals and set and reaffirm ground rules that facilitate open communication in the team. Additionally, team leaders may serve as the point of contact for the team with others in the organization or a client outside the organization.

Finally, team leaders must help do the real work of the team. Here the team leader must be careful to contribute ideas without dominating the team. There are

3.   Dorothy Leonard and Susaan Straus, "Putting Your Company's Whole Brain to Work," *Harvard Business Review*, July–August 1997, 111–121.
4.   Katzenbach and Smith, *The Wisdom of Teams*, ch. 7.

also two key things that team leaders should never do: *They should not blame or allow specific individuals to fail, and they should never excuse away shortfalls in team performance.*[5] Mutual accountability must always be emphasized over individual performance.

Teams as the Engine for Coordination, Collaboration, and Creativity in the Launch of Cincinnati Bell Wireless.

A multimillion-dollar product launch requires the coordination and collaboration of hundreds of individuals. The Cincinnati Bell Wireless launch will include employees from Cincinnati Bell and Northlich plus a variety of outside vendors, each contributing their own particular expertise to make the launch a success. Without skillful teamwork involving dozens of discrete teams working at various levels and on various tasks, there could be no hope of executing an integrated campaign.

That team effort has many manifestations, but it must begin with a partnership between agency and client. When Mark Serrianne of Northlich was asked what one needs to be successful in executing an IBP campaign, the first thing he said was, "You have to have a great client—a client that wants a partnership role." In the launch of Cincinnati Bell Wireless, we see client and agency working as partners to execute a successful launch. Cincinnati Bell brought to the table exactly those things that any good client must provide: technical expertise in their product category, financial resources, keen insights about competitive strategy, and a deep appreciation for the critical role of retailer support. From the agency side, Northlich brought a tireless commitment to understanding the consumer as a basis for effective communication, and a depth of expertise and experience in the design, preparation, and placement of a broad array of communication tools. Each looked to the other to do its job; in particular, we see in this example a client that trusted its agency to do the job of preparing and placing a full-scale IBP campaign. That trust is critical because it frees the agency to do its most crucial task: creating breakthrough communications that will disrupt the category and drive business results.

The Account Team.

As expressed by Mark Serrianne, the Northlich philosophy on teamwork is embodied by the account team. This team of experts from the various disciplines within the agency is charged with bringing a campaign into being for its focal client. Every account team must have a leader, or account supervisor, who becomes the critical communication liaison to the client and who seeks to facilitate and coordinate a dialogue among the disciplines represented on the team. But, consistent with our earlier discussion about team leadership, the Northlich account supervisor is definitely not identified as the highest-ranking person on the team, whose job it is to give orders, sit back, and let other people do all the work. The account supervisor is a working member of the team who also is responsible for encouraging and coordinating the efforts of other team members.

Half the battle in making teams work is getting the right people on the team in the first place. This begins with the account supervisor. The Northlich account team for the CBW launch was led by Mandy Reverman. Reverman was hired by Northlich from Campbell-Ewald, Advertising–Detroit, to direct the CBW launch. Over a seven-year period with Campbell-Ewald, Reverman had gained considerable experience in account management and team leadership through her work for Chevrolet and Toyota auto dealerships. Automotive retailer groups are a demanding clientele who expect to see a direct effect on sales from the advertising they sponsor in specific metro markets. As it turns out, these were the same kinds of expectations that CBW had for its advertising in the Greater Cincinnati metro market in the

---

5. Katzenbach and Smith, *The Wisdom of Teams*, 144.

spring of 1998. Reverman thus had the right background to oversee the CBW account team.

Reverman views the role of team leader as the hub of a wheel, with various spokes that reach out to diverse disciplinary expertise. The hub connects the spokes and ensures that all of them work in tandem to make the wheel roll smoothly. Using Reverman's wheel metaphor, her spokes are represented by team members from direct marketing, public relations, broadcast media, graphic design, creative, and accounting. To illustrate the multilayered nature of the team approach to IBP, each team member can also be thought of as a hub in his or her very own wheel. For example, the direct marketing member on the account team was team leader for her own set of specialists charged with preparing direct marketing materials for the CBW launch. Through this type of multilevel "hub-and-spokes" design, the coordination and collaboration essential for effective IBP campaigns can be achieved.

Teams Moderate Tension in the Copy Approval Process. In the deadline-driven and pressure-packed activity of campaign preparation, one predictable source of tension between agency and client is the copy approval process. This was certainly evident in the CBW launch, not only because of the time pressures that accompanied this launch, but also because of the unique partnership between Cincinnati Bell and AT&T that was forged in the creation of CBW. While the AT&T network was critical to the credibility of the CBW service, the partnership with AT&T also gave executives from that organization a say in the copy approval process. This turned out to be one of the most frustrating aspects of the launch for the Northlich creative team, because AT&T's executives were far removed from the actual process of ad development. According to one Northlich insider, this is the painstaking part of the process: "It is hard to keep people motivated to work the details when what appear to be insignificant changes are requested by a distant third party."

So how do you keep people motivated when these last-minute requests to shift scenes and sentences are made on work that you thought was finished? First of all, the communication that is facilitated through teamwork is essential to working through the copy approval process. Delays caused by miscommunication are certain to heighten tensions and create dysfunctional outcomes. Moreover, the mutual accountability that goes with effective teams must also come into play. The copywriters or art directors that have to respond with last-minute changes must accept their roles as team players, and move forward on the changes for the sake of the team.

Teams Liberate Decision Making. When the right combination of expertise is assembled on a team, what appears to be casual or spur-of-the-moment decision making can turn out to be more creative decision making. The value of divergent, spontaneous input as a basis for decisions is beautifully illustrated by the team-oriented approach that Northlich and CBW employed during the shoot of their television commercials. Key members of the "shoot team" included the account supervisor from Northlich, Mandy Reverman, and her steadfast partner from the client side, Mike Vanderwoude, marketing director at CBW. They joined the production manager, art director, and copywriter to create a working team that didn't just bring their storyboards to life in the shoot. Through a lively give-and-take on the site, they created engaging video that was on strategy and delivered a message that wireless customers in Cincinnati were ready and waiting to hear.

Exhibit IBP 3.1 is an example of one of the storyboards that this working team started with at a shoot. This ad, titled "Classroom," is seeded with the core strategy that drove much of the advertising for the launch. The message of the ad was that Cincinnati Bell Wireless is a superior solution because it is both simpler and more

Classroom:30 (pricing/affordability)

(We open on our spokesman in classroom. He's in front of a chalkboard with a bunch of complicated formulas on it.)

Have you ever tried to figure out how much cellular service actually costs?

Hmm. Maybe you should have taken Advanced Calculus after all.

Here's a better answer:

Cincinnati Bell Wireless.

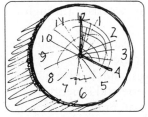

No peak calling hours. No extra charges.

(Hands of school clock spin rapidly.)

Just one low rate that's way more affordable than cellular.

(Holds up flash cards of the less than symbol., fractions)

Stop by the Store at Cincinnati Bell and see if wireless is right for you.

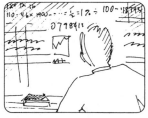

Unless, of course, you like homework.

EXHIBIT IBP 3.1

Cincinnati Bell Wireless storyboard: "Classroom."

economical than cellular. You don't need to know advanced calculus to figure out the benefits of Cincinnati Bell Wireless. But the final ad that evolved from this board shows many departures from its rather languid script. This is because, during the shoot, the working team fed off one another's ideas to continue to develop and refine the ad's expression of "simple terms" and "it's just a better deal [than cellular]." Individual scenes were shot over and over again, testing various deliveries of new executions that the working team was creating on the spur of the moment. This liberated the team, the talent, and the director to produce a final product that delivers on the simplification message in a most compelling way.

More about Teams and Creativity. As the preceding example reflects, creativity in the preparation of an IBP campaign can be fostered by the trust and open communication that are hallmarks of effective teams. But it is also true that the creativity required for breakthrough campaigns will evolve as personal work products generated by individuals laboring on their own. Both personal and team creativity are critical in the preparation of IBP campaigns. The daunting task of facilitating both usually falls in the lap of an agency's creative director.

The position of creative director in any ad agency is very special because, much like the maestro of the symphony orchestra, the creative director must encourage personal excellence but at the same time demand team accountability. Don Perkins, senior VP and executive creative director at Northlich, sees his job as channeling the creative energies of the dozens of individuals in his group. Perkins acknowledges that

INTEGRATED BRAND PROMOTION

creativity has an intensely personal element; in his view, original creation is motivated by the desire to satisfy one's own ego or sense of self. But despite the intimate character he ascribes to creativity, Perkins clearly appreciates the need for team unity. Many of the principles he relies on for channeling the creativity of his group could in fact be portrayed as key tenets for team leadership. In orchestrating Northlich's creative teams, Perkins relies on the following principles:

- Take great care in assigning individuals to a team in the first place. Be sensitive to their existing workloads and the proper mix of expertise required to do the job for the client.
- Get to know the work style of each individual. Listen carefully. Since creativity can be an intensely personal matter, one has to know when it is best to leave people alone, versus when one needs to support them in working through the inevitable rejection.
- Make teams responsible to the client. Individuals and teams are empowered when they have sole responsibility for performance outcomes.
- Beware of adversarial relationships between individuals and between teams. They can quickly lead to mistrust that destroys camaraderie and synergy.
- In situations where the same set of individuals will work on multiple teams over time, rotate team assignments to foster fresh thinking.

To Ensure the Uniform Look, Turn to Teams. While we're probably starting to sound like a broken record on this team thing, let's take just one more example. Exhibits IBP 3.2, 3.3, and 3.4 show point-of-purchase brochures, a direct mail piece, and a billboard facing that were created by three different Northlich designers for the CBW

EXHIBIT IBP 3.2

CBW launch: P-O-P brochures.

launch. These and dozens of other elements of the launch campaign were created to have a uniform look that supported the integrated premise of the campaign. But how does one get this uniform look when in fact these dozens of different items will inevitably be the work products of dozens of different individuals? Sure. You guessed it. If you want a uniform look, you must rely on teamwork.

The materials in the three exhibits feature several common design elements, including colors, line art, fonts, background, and of course, the CBW logo. These elements were selected through an internal competition that Don Perkins and his design director orchestrated in the Northlich design department. From this competition, a design standard was chosen, and the graphic artist who created that design became the leader of an ad hoc design team. That artist thereafter coordinated the efforts of different designers as they prepared various materials for the campaign, and served the critical role that leaders often fulfill as filters to ensure collaboration, which in this specific case emerged as the "uniform look." Here we see once again that the fundamentals of effective teams—communication, trust, complementary expertise, and leadership—produce the desired performance outcome. There's simply no alternative. Teams rule!

EXHIBIT IBP 3.3

CBW launch: Direct mail piece.

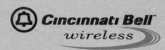

EXHIBIT IBP 3.4

CBW launch: Billboard facing.

IBP EXERCISES

1. Advertising always has been a team sport, but the advent of advertising and IBP has made effective teamwork more important than ever. It also has made it more difficult to achieve. Explain how the growing emphasis on IBP makes effective teamwork more difficult to achieve.

2. What insight(s) about teams does Mark Serrianne, CEO of Northlich, provide when he states, "If you and I both think alike, then one of us is unnecessary"?

3. In the launch of Cincinnati Bell Wireless, we see client and agency working together as a partnership to execute a product launch. What did each "bring to the table" to create the partnership? In your opinion, who plays the greater role in creating a successful partnership: the client or the agency?

4. The creative director in an advertising agency has the daunting task of channeling the creative energies of dozens of individuals, while demanding team accountability. If the expression of creativity is personal and highly individualized, how can teamwork possibly foster creativity? What might a creative director do to "allow creativity to happen" in a team environment? Explain how the saying "The whole is greater than the sum of its parts" fits into a discussion of creativity and teamwork.

Calvin Soh
President and Creative Director,
Fallon Singapore and Hong Kong

When the Toyota Motor Corporation wanted to promote its latest Corolla series to consumers throughout the Asia-Pacific region, the Japanese automaker selected Fallon Worldwide to develop a print-ad campaign that accentuated the enhanced safety features of its sporty, best-selling model. Each full-page ad features an Asian preschool child gazing directly into the camera with a look of perplexity: A girl sits on a tricycle modified with four extra training wheels; a toddler wearing a bubble-wrap jumpsuit sits at play with his bubble-wrap covered blocks; a child stands in an inflatable baby pool sporting six arm floaties and multiple inner tubes around the waist. The tagline: "Corolla. For overprotective parents."

Such genius is indispensable in the world of advertising, and Calvin Soh, president and creative director of Fallon Singapore/Hong Kong, is a fount of never-ending creativity. Over the years, Soh has racked up creative awards, including Gold and Silver Pencils in New York's prestigious One Show, Lions in Cannes, Clios, and top honors at Asian regional shows. In 2000, Soh was ranked No. 1 creative in Asia by advertising magazine *Campaign Brief*. Soh's talented career traces back through top agencies like Ogilvy and Mather, Dentsu Young and Rubicam, and Saatchi & Saatchi, and the young advertising whiz has been the creative go-to guy for international campaigns featuring brands like Volkswagen, United Airlines, Georgio Armani, and Lexus.

As a seasoned professional experienced in developing effective international ad campaigns, Calvin Soh understands the challenge of communicating brands across national and cultural boundaries. He points out that his creative work tends to rely heavily on the visual component of advertising. "The work is quite visual—that's because in Asia, you have multiple languages," remarks Soh. "You can have an idea in an English headline and then translate it into Thai, Malay, and Cantonese, but more likely than not, the essence and subtle nuances would be lost." The solution, according to Soh, is to communicate visual ideas based on "a universal truth which crosses cultural and geographic borders." Soh's results speak for themselves. In the case of the Toyota Corolla campaign, the sheer comedic value of the visuals is matched only by the universal insight the ads so effectively communicate: all parents are protective of their children. Therefore, the ads persuade, since Corollas are now extra safe, buy a Corolla.

Soh's success and boundless creativity are attributable to a combination of his background, work ethic, raw determination, and sense of humor. Soh says that his two-and-a-half years of compulsory military service as a marksman and sergeant in the 35th Battalion Singapore Combat Engineers gave him the determination and confidence to make something out of his talent. Soh worked as a fast-food chef, electronics salesman, and telemarketer before finally getting a foothold in the advertising world. "I started in Traffic, which in the grand scheme of things was above amoeba but below plankton and paid peanuts," Soh offers with characteristic humor. "But I put in the hours and stayed late." Soh's big break came when he leveraged his love of English Literature in his handwritten application for the copywriter position at Ogilvy Direct. He captured their attention by quoting both George Bernard Shaw's "unreasonable man" theory of human progress and agency pioneer David Ogilvy's "We sell, or else" philosophy of advertising. The rest, as they say, is history. After being hired by Ogilvy, Soh worked his way up the ranks in various agencies and now shoulders both creative and executive duties for Fallon's operations in Singapore and Hong Kong.

Yet perhaps Soh's greatest creative asset is his natural curiosity and lust for life. He has a unique way of looking at the world around him and blurs the line between work and living. "The greatest thing about my job is that it isn't a job," says the Fallon chief. "I love studying people. You're almost an evolutionary anthropologist, or more accurately, a cultural peeping Tom." In his travels, Soh has brushed up against celebrities like Ron Howard and J. Lo, and he tells the story about sitting in a restaurant next to Lou Reed, the solo artist and former guitar player for the Velvet Underground: Soh and guest followed Reed in lighting up a smoke inside the restaurant, only to be promptly escorted outside. When Soh protested that Reed was not equally interrupted and shown the door, the waiter glibly replied, "He's Lou Reed."

Soh likes to cut up and doesn't take himself too seriously, but the energy that drives his creativity has deep reserves. Soh believes that good advertising is ultimately about understanding people and hatching big ideas: "The more you study people, the more you realize how different we are on the outside; but stripped of the veneer of skin, we're all remarkably similar." Soh continues, "Advertising is beyond a print or TV ad. It's not about mediums, it's about the idea."

When asked what advice he would give to students interested in pursuing a career in advertising, Soh offers, "Don't get misled by technobabble and naysayers. The death of advertising was predicted because TV would kill radio, the Web will kill TV, TiVo will kill everyone." From Soh's perspective, the future viability of advertising rests on something far more permanent: human creativity, ingenuity, and hard work.

Placing the Message in Conventional and "New" Media

Once again we pass into a new and totally different area of advertising, "Placing the Message in Conventional and 'New' Media." We are now at the point where reaching the target audience is the key issue.

Beyond the basic and formidable challenge of effectively choosing the right media to reach a target audience, contemporary advertisers are demanding even more from the media placement decision: synergy and integration. Throughout the first three parts of the text, the issue of integrated brand communications has been raised whenever the opportunity existed to create coordinated communications. Indeed, the Cincinnati Bell sections at the end of each part are included to highlight the IBP issue. But nowhere is IBP more critical than at the media placement. Here, audiences may be exposed to an advertiser's messages through a wide range of different media each with a unique quality and tone to the communication. The advertiser is challenged to ensure that if diverse communications media options are chosen for placing the message, there is still a "one-voice" quality to the overall communication program.

Media Strategy and Planning for Advertising and IBP. Maintaining integration is indeed a challenge in the contemporary media environment. Chapter 14, "Media Strategy and Planning for Advertising and IBP," begins with a discussion of the major changes that have altered and now define the contemporary media landscape. Next the fundamentals of media planning are explained, followed by the details. We then tell it like it really is in the real world by discussing the "real deals" of media planning. Next, we discuss how the real world environment impacts the entire process, followed by particular attention to IBP's impact. We finish with a reminder of the value of traditional advertising.

14

Media Planning: Print, Television, and Radio. Chapter 15, "Media Planning: Print, Television, and Radio," offers an analysis of the major media options available to advertisers. The vast majority of the creative effort—and money—is expended on print and broadcast advertising campaigns. Despite the many intriguing opportunities that new media options offer, print and broadcast media will likely form the foundation of most advertising campaigns for years to come. The chapter follows a sequence in which the advantages and disadvantages of each medium are discussed, followed by considerations of costs, buying procedures, and audience measurement techniques.

15

Media Planning: Advertising and IBP on the Internet. The newest and perhaps greatest challenge for advertisers has recently presented itself—the Internet. Chapter 16, "Media Planning: Advertising and IBP on the Internet," describes this relatively new and formidable technology available to advertisers. This chapter is key to understanding the contemporary advertising environment. Basic terminology and procedures are described. Most of the discussion in this chapter focuses on two fundamental issues: the structure of the Internet and the potential of the Internet as an advertising medium. Through these discussions, we will come to a better understanding of how to use the Internet as part of an effective advertising and integrated brand promotion effort. We will consider a short history of the Internet, an overview of cyberspace, the different types of advertising that can be used, and some of the technical aspects of the process. We also discuss where the (r)evolution stands, including triumphs, disappointments and strategic re-thinking and redeployment. A multitude of Web sites are offered for exploration.

16

CHAPTER 14

After reading and thinking about this chapter, you will be able to do the following:

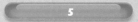

Describe the important changes that have altered the advertising and IBP media landscape: such as agency compensation, ROI demands, ethnic media, and globalization.

Describe the fundamentals of media planning.

Discuss the "real deals" in media planning.

Discuss the essentials of the contemporary media planning environment.

Know the bottom line of IBP's impact on media planning.

Discuss the value of traditional advertising.

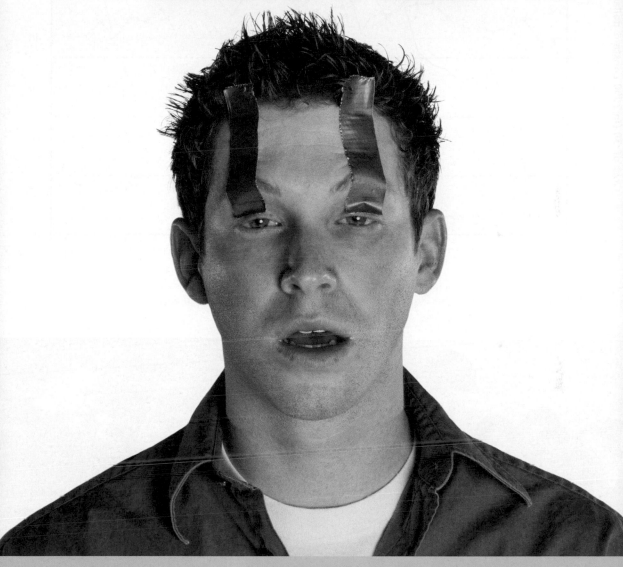

whatever it takes

CRAM you snooze, you lose.

hosted by
Graham Elwood & Icey

the new season
premieres june 15
every night @ 10:30pm

to get cable, call
(1800 OK CABLE)

GAME
SHOW
network

www.gsn.com

Super Bowl, 1967–2001
Media Cost/Delivery Trends

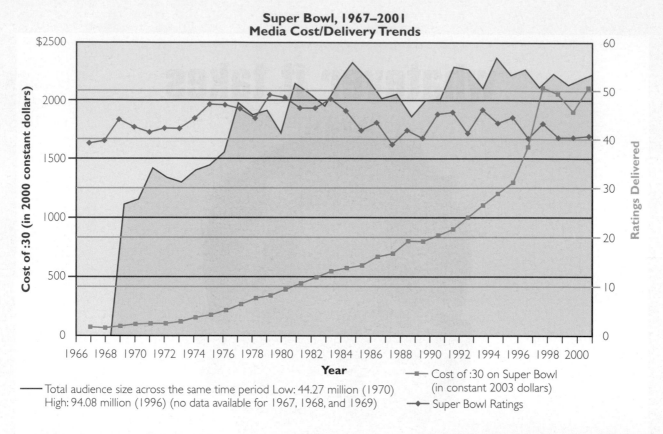

—— Total audience size across the same time period Low: 44.27 million (1970)
High: 94.08 million (1996) (no data available for 1967, 1968, and 1969)

■— Cost of :30 on Super Bowl
(in constant 2003 dollars)

◆— Super Bowl Ratings

(1967 Super Bowl)

(2003 Super Bowl)

EXHIBIT 14.1

In 1967 the Super Bowl reached 41 percent of U.S. households. It still reaches about 41 percent of U.S. households. Now it just costs ten times as much for a :30 ad. TV advertising has become very expensive.

In 1967, Super Bowl I was simultaneously telecast on CBS and NBC. It reached about 41 percent of U.S. households (a 41 rating), or about 43 million people. A 30-second ad on Super Bowl I cost $42,000, or about $208,000 in current (2003 inflation-corrected) dollars. In 2003, Super Bowl XXXVII still reached about 41 percent of U.S. households, now about 88 million people, but 30 seconds of advertising now costs $2.1 million dollars—that's right, $2.1 million dollars for a 30-second ad that in 1967 cost (in real dollars) one-tenth that amount. (See Exhibit 14.1.) That means

EXHIBIT 14.2

As you can see, TV ad rights for the really mass audiences are not in decline.

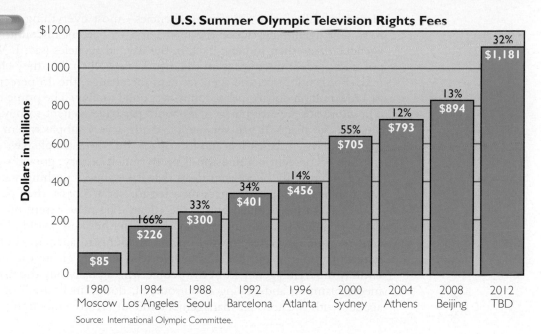

U.S. Summer Olympic Television Rights Fees

Dollars in millions

Year	City	Amount	%
1980	Moscow	$85	
1984	Los Angeles	$226	166%
1988	Seoul	$300	33%
1992	Barcelona	$401	34%
1996	Atlanta	$456	14%
2000	Sydney	$705	55%
2004	Athens	$793	12%
2008	Beijing	$894	13%
2012	TBD	$1,181	32%

Source: International Olympic Committee.

that network television advertising over the past 37 years has gotten about 10 times more expensive, even though its total audience has gone up only twofold and its rating (41 percent of U.S. households) has not changed at all. Television advertising has become very expensive. More than a few people have noticed. This trend is not confined to the Super Bowl. It is true of TV advertising generally, particularly for truly mega-audience events like the Olympics. (See Exhibit 14.2.)

A few years ago a few people were saying, "Advertising is dead; long live new media." While some traditional forms have been challenged, and other new forms emerged, advertising is still very much alive. There are now more ways to promote brands than ever before. It's still a little unclear where this is all heading. On the one hand, there is certainly a big effort to broaden what we think of as advertising. On the other hand, there are countervailing forces trying to enforce traditional boundaries. As an example of the latter, Anheuser-Busch told its long time agency, DDB Chicago, that it should stick to what it does best (advertising), and let other specialists handle promotions.[1] This issue is still in play.

The Very Wide World of Promotional Media. Now let's talk about

placing ads and IBP. It turns out that the decisions involved in placing messages are just as big as the ones involved in producing them, maybe bigger.

Enter the world of promotional media, a world in which professionals match message and media. Media selection is where the money is spent, invested wisely, or wasted. It is also a land where much has changed, and changed recently. We begin by noting the changes and discussing their real-world implications.

Important Changes.

Agency Compensation. Twenty-five years ago it was a pretty simple system: Around 80 percent of

all advertising and promotional dollars went to media advertising (television, radio, newspapers, magazines, and outdoor). The advertising was created, produced, and

1. *Advertising Age,* August 21, 2004.

placed by full-service advertising agencies—most everything was done under one roof. The agency purchased the media at a 15 percent discount, and that's how ad agencies made their money. Back in the day, ad agencies (say, J. Walter Thompson) got a 15 percent discount from the media (e.g., NBC), but they charged their clients (e.g., Ford) full price; the agencies kept the change, the 15 percent. Fifteen percent of a few million dollars (per account) was good money. The prime directive was clear: The more ads advertising agencies could persuade a client to buy, the more money the agencies made. It was very simple math, a very simple system. And, not surprisingly, this system begat lots and lots of ads. But those simple days are long gone.

The 15 percent commission is pretty much history, gone away. In its place is a sea of individually negotiated deals that have almost nothing standard about them. Most clients now pay agencies on a fee-for-service basis; they pay for specific jobs. Lots of staff time is billed out to the client. The new system more resembles a law firm's billing system than anything else in the business world. There is still significant revenue generated through media discounts to agencies, but it is neither constant nor uniform. Further, the people who actually create the ads may work at an entirely different agency from the people who actually buy the media. Quite a bit of media planning and buying is outsourced, done "in-house," or split off from the agency with the account management and/or creative function.

More Media. Even more fundamentally challenging to the old system is that "media" now include all sorts of new species: the Internet, cross-promotions, product placements, buzz marketing, movies that are really feature-length commercials, and so on. The line between public relations and advertising has become almost no line at all, just a blur. In fact, Sergio Zyman, former chief marketing officer at The Coca-Cola Company, recently defined "advertising" under the new rules as "everything."[2] Well, while we stop short of that all-inclusive definition, it's closer to the new reality than we could have ever imagined just a few years ago. If you defined advertising only in terms of media placement, or where promotional messages appear, then advertising is pretty much everything. Of course, there's more to the definition than that (as explained in Chapter 1).

Still, many traditional lines are blurred or have been erased altogether. For example, companies supply and push "news" stories about their brands or categories to media outlets as part of their overall integrated brand promotion effort. These "news" stories cost the companies nothing other than the salaries of the staff writers and placement specialists, so in a pure sense, no ads are actually purchased. But IBP is clearly being done; it is "advertising" of a sort. The most obvious examples occur around holidays when food stories (let's say about cooking turkeys) show up on the local early news as a feature story. These "stories" are often written and produced by a poultry or seasoning marketer and sent out to the news media as news, not advertising. Lazy journalists are usually more than willing to let marketers write and produce their stories for them. Journalistic ethics don't seem to get in the way very often. We know of at least one major U.S. package goods advertiser that has very quietly moved a significant percentage of its overall promotional budget into this type of news/media/advertising. A senior executive says that the growth of ads as "news" is fast, strong, and significant, and suggests the model of the future. Of course, the same is true in entertainment, where movies can work as promotional vehicles for products while still entertaining. (See Exhibit 14.3.)

Consolidation and Shifting Channel Power. It is also true that media and agency consolidation (mergers) has changed the **channel power,** or who has the most power in terms

---

2.   Harvard Business School Professor John Deighton has also made this point.

Advertising? IBP? Did it sell shoes?

■ **MADISON+VINE**

GOLDEN GIRL: Sales of Uma's Asics have taken off in Asia, Europe and the U.S.

Asics sneaks are 'Kill Bill' sleeper hit

of setting prices in favor of the media. Several media companies and ad agencies are now considerably larger than their average advertiser or client, and that means power. It's not the old days when one advertiser went to one agency for help with its advertising. Now, the typical situation is for a brand that is part of a family of brands to go to an agency that is itself part of some enormous holding company of other ad agencies, public relations firms, direct mail companies, and assorted other media–promotion entities that buy media at a significant discount by virtue of their size and efficiencies. The agency can thus be tougher with its clients because there are simply fewer and fewer places for disgruntled clients to go. Also, due to their large size and affiliated agencies, the contemporary ad agency can better absorb the loss of clients. Through all of this, advertising agencies have gained some serious clout relative to their clients, although they will almost never admit this.

Thinner Margins/Thinner Shops. But clout does not always translate one-to-one to profit. In fact, agency revenue margins are generally a little smaller than they were thirty years ago. There are lots of reasons for this, but the loss of the 15 percent standard commission is probably the biggest. Media buying is still profitable for agencies, but what was once a 15 percent guaranteed return is now something much smaller and less certain in terms of contributing to the agency's bottom line. Not too surprisingly, and absolutely related to this change in agency compensation, mass media has become less popular for all involved. If you are not going to get the fat 15 percent commission, regardless of its effect on sales, why do it, why buy them? These days the majority of promotion and advertising dollars are found not in traditional media advertising (TV, radio, magazines) but rather in other forms of integrated brand promotion. One reason for this switch is that agencies often make more profit on these "alternative" promotional buys than from traditional (e.g., television, radio, magazines) buys. That's another reason why IBP is so vital to any understanding of contemporary advertising and promotion. It's where most of the money is, and where even more of it is going.

Ad agencies also employ fewer people to do more work that they used to. This, again, has to do with several factors. The truth is, due in part to the change in how agencies make money, more people work longer hours than they used to for no more money. Agencies have become much leaner operations, and part of the reason is the demise of the 15 percent commission. Another reason is that when agencies moved from being privately held corporations to publicly traded companies, there was simply more stockholder pressure on short-term profitability. In the ad world, the two quickest routes to greater short-term profit are (a) to fire staff, and (b) to make more money on media buys. It's all connected to media. To understand media is to understand a great deal about real-world advertising and marketing practice.

Greater Accountability: Return on Investment (ROI). Another big change directly related to media is agency accountability. In the past, the standard reply from advertising agencies to client questions concerning results was, "Well, there is really no way to precisely isolate the effects of advertising from all the other things going on in the consumer's environment—maybe sales went up/down because of weather, a change in packaging, or a competitor's actions. But clearly our advertising is doing great things for your brand. Trust us."

Well, trust is in short supply these days. One big reason for the shift out of traditional media advertising and into other forms of IBP is the at least perceived greater accountability of other promotional forms. For example, proponents of direct mail advertising say that they can pretty much determine the effect of each promotional mailing in real dollar terms. This answer makes brand managers much happier than the traditional "don't know, don't care, got to trust us" answer from traditional media. Also, advances in mathematical modeling and access to better data have increased the ability of sophisticated marketers to determine the return on investment (ROI) of most forms of IBP. In fact, these days the pressure to produce a documented ROI for all forms of advertising and IBP is huge. ROI is the demand *du jour* and is driving many of the changes in media today.

Globalization. Then there is globalization. More and more, advertising and IBP media are truly worldwide. These days media are not controlled by national borders, or even bothered by them. Transnational corporations, particularly media, don't really care much about the borders of nation-states. From CNN to Al Jazeera, media exist in transnational space, and must be thought of that way. This is the new media reality. Even vehicles strongly associated with one certain country are more and more trying to soften that association. From the 2.9 million daily readers of the *Wall Street Journal* around the world (see Exhibit 14.4) to the estimated 250 million viewers of MTV, global reach with highly accessible media is a reality. Many of these global media organizations have large audiences outside of North America. BBC Worldwide TV, based in London, has more than 7.2 million viewers throughout Asia, and NBC has 65 million viewers in Europe. Likewise, *Time* magazine is actively expanding all over the globe. The British magazine *The Economist* can be found on magazine racks all over the world. As the European Union solidifies (if it does), the big media muscle of united Europe will be felt all over the globe.

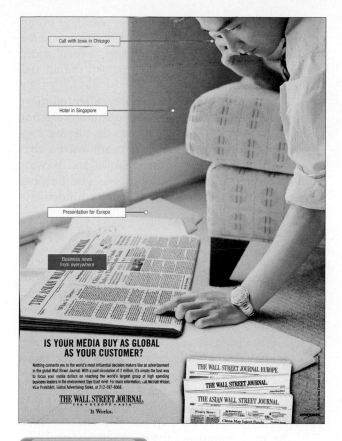

Call with boss in Chicago

Hotel in Singapore

Presentation for Europe

Business news from everywhere

IS YOUR MEDIA BUY AS GLOBAL AS YOUR CUSTOMER?

Nothing connects you to the world's most influential decision makers like an advertisement in the global Wall Street Journal. With a paid circulation of 2 million, it's simply the best way to focus your media dollars on reaching the world's largest group of high spending business leaders in the environment they trust most. For more information, call Michael Wilson, Vice President, Global Advertising Sales, at 212-597-6068.

THE WALL STREET JOURNAL
U S A • E U R O P E • A S I A
It Works.

THE WALL STREET JOURNAL EUROPE.

THE WALL STREET JOURNAL.

THE ASIAN WALL STREET JOURNAL.

EXHIBIT 14.4

The Wall Street Journal *is read all around the globe. Media are going global.*

But there is a very big fly in the transnational ointment: The lack of international standardized audience measurement and pricing makes for a very complicated and anything-but-optimal situation. We are, however, optimistic about this getting better: There is a large economic incentive to come up with a common media currency. But for now, it is a big mess. While the ad world is clearly going transnational, advertising media data have simply not kept up. On the global media planning front there is a lot of guessing, a lot of sloppiness, and a ton of waste. We think things will get better sooner rather than later.

Free Content. Maybe the single biggest change in the media world is the flood of "free" media content. Largely due to the Internet and other telecommunications changes, consumers are getting used to getting cool stuff for free, or next to free. So, why should they buy a magazine at a bookstore for $4.50 that's full of ads? They can go online and get much of the same, maybe better, content without paying a dime, and can avoid the ads—if there are any ads at all. This is making traditional ad-supported paid media vehicles an increasingly endangered species. So advertisers are putting more of their total promotional budget into nontraditional media, media environments contemporary consumers clearly enjoy and use more. Exhibit 14.5 shows how much media usage has shifted in just a seven-year period.

E-Commerce/E-Media. While Internet advertising is still trying to find its exact form (discussed in Chapter 16), e-commerce has been wildly successful. It has truly revolutionized the way consumers consume. Its impact has been far more than technological; it has been cultural and economic. It has given consumers considerably more power in the marketing channel: access to more and better information, access to millions of other consumers and their opinions of goods and services, and much higher expectations of finding good deals (see Exhibit 14.6). In fact, two of the biggest changes the Internet has wrought are the rise of **deal-proneness** in consumers and **price/cost transparency**. It is now so incredibly easy to get a deal, to know what a good deal is, to operate with knowledge of what a good price would be, and even to know what the seller's cost is. A new car buyer can very easily find out online what the local car dealer's invoice price was (how much it paid for the car), and what the breakeven point is for the dealer. Consumers can do the same for countless goods and services through the Worldwide Web. It's now cool to talk about how little you paid for

Measured Media	1997	2004
Radio	18	21
Broadcast TV	18	15
Cable & Satellite TV	12	19
Internet	1	4
Newspapers	4	3
Consumer Magazines	3	2
Total	56	63

Source: Veronis Suhler Stevenson Communications Industry Forcast – July 2003

EXHIBIT 14.5

Consumer Use of Media, 1997–2004. Chart shows hours per week with these media.

EXHIBIT 14.6

It's become much easier to find the best deal. http://www.shopping.com

something. Consumers have now become prone to seek deals more than ever before. E-commerce (shopping and consuming online), much more than e-advertising per se, has changed the ad and promotion world.

This gives the consumer unprecedented marketplace power. This is power consumers are not going to give up. So this means that going forward consumers are going to want media that gives them this kind of information and power, often for free and without obtrusive ads. This has changed the media environment in a fundamental way.

Hyper-Clutter. While it has always been the case that consumers felt there were lots of ads in their environment, it has now become the stuff of serious industry concern. It is probably most threatening to network television and magazines. Before, consumers pretty much had no choice. Now they do. They can watch no-ad premium channels such as HBO for shows like *Six Feet Under* and *The Sopranos,* or they can "TiVo" out the ads from network television shows such as *ER.* On the Internet, pop-up ad filters are some of the most popular software offerings available. People will pay to avoid ads, and this is quickly becoming a little too close to the rule, at least as far as the advertising industry is concerned. Too many ads have made advertising in general less powerful.

Ethnic Media. If you haven't noticed, there is a lot more ethnic media these days. There are many reason for this, but in the United States, one of the most obvious is the growing population of several prominent ethnic groups. In the United States, the most attention is on the Hispanic/Latino(a) market, due mostly to its size and growth rate. Most major advertisers are paying lots of attention to this. Exhibit 14.7 shows an ad for Telemundo, a major Spanish-language channel.

② The Fundamentals of Media Planning. OK, so a lot has changed in media

land. But not everything. There are still some ideas, names, concepts, and principles that are just as they always were. Traditional concepts still matter. Some basic tools remain the same. So now we are going to talk about what has stayed the same and still matters. There are those things that endure, particularly principles. One of them is the principle of good planning.

PRIME ATTRACTION.

■ **Weekday Prime audience** up **99%**

■ **Primetime is** up **11 share points**

75% of Telemundo's primetime shows are original. No wonder people can't take their eyes off us.

Call Steve Mandala, EVP Sales. 212-664-3500.

Gabriela Spanic, Prisionera

FRESH ORIGINAL TELEMUNDO

EXHIBIT 14.7

Telemundo is one example of the growing ethnic diversity in media.

Good planning remains good planning regardless of the media employed. We'll give you an example. While I was writing an earlier version of this chapter, I went downstairs to get the mail. One envelope was from "Unique Customized Dog Food." Enclosed was a bright blue bag labeled "Stool Sample Collection Instructions." That's right; these guys wanted me to send them some dog feces for customized analysis, so they could make some dog food that would be "optimized for your dog's DNA (Digestive Nutrient Absorption)." I'm not making this up. This is a form of promotion. The marketer selected me to receive this offer, betting that I would be more likely than others to scoop up some of Fido's fertilizer and send it in. Of course, there is a problem—I don't have a dog. I used to, but I haven't for a while. Clearly, this company relied on some bad data.

No matter how new the media are, how great a marketing plan is, and how insightful or visionary advertising strategists are, poor message placement will undermine even the best-laid plans. Advertising placed in media that do not reach the target audience—whether via new media or traditional media—will be much like the proverbial tree that falls in the forest with no one around: Does it make a sound? From an advertising standpoint, no. Advertising placed in media that do not reach target audiences will not achieve the communications or sales impact an advertiser desires.

Media Planning. First, let's talk about these different media, and try to make some useful distinctions.

The Big Pie. Think of all the money used to promote a brand as a big pie. The big pie (see Exhibit 14.8) includes advertising, direct mail, point of purchase promotion, coupons, promotional e-mails, buzz marketing—everything spent to promote a good or service. This is a very big pie. Let's call that pie the Total Promotions Pie. Within that pie is traditional media advertising (at 42.5 percent), traditional promotions (42.5 percent), and what we call extended promotions (15 percent). These are estimates, but we think they pretty accurately mirror reality. The completely unvarnished truth is that no one really knows exactly how much is spent on all things promotional, but we have a pretty good idea about the size of the slices. We're dead serious when we say no one knows these numbers for sure because there are so many different ways different companies (and their creative accountants) list these items. But we think we are pretty close to reality.

You're probably saying: Wait, I don't see the IBP slice. Where does IBP fit in? Where is the IBP slice? Good question. Answer: Integrated brand promotions are not a slice of the pie, but the effort to keep the pie together, to make it a whole, to make

The Big Pie

Media Advertising include: "measured" or "above the line" expenditures for: all magazines (including Sunday magazines), all television (except local cable spots and DBS), radio, outdoor, and Internet.

Traditional Promotion includes: direct mail, sales promotion, co-op, couponing, catalogs, business-to-business publications, farm publications, and special events. It also includes some unspecified expenditures as determined by *Advertising Age* as a simple difference between reported total company advertising/promotion spending and measured media advertising (Media Advertising category above).

Extended Promotions is our estimate of the total amount of everything else, including product placement, targeted public relations, brand/category promoting news stories, appearances, and event venue signage.

According to *AdAge*: in 2003, if one only counts the first categories the ratio is 52.3% advertising, 47.7% promotion.

Source: 100 Leading National Advertisers, *Advertising Age*, June 28, 2004, 1–4.

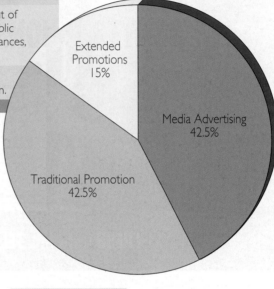

EXHIBIT 14.8

The Total Promotions Pie.

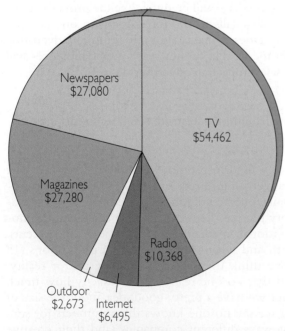

Source: 100 Leading National Advertisers, *Advertising Age*, June 28, 2004, 1–4.

EXHIBIT 14.9

This is how media advertising in the U.S. breaks down by medium.

the whole pie taste good. IBP, if you will, is the shell that holds the promotional pie together.

If you break things down a bit more, you can see the relative standing of the different media (see Exhibit 14.9). Television is King, by a long, long way in terms of dollars received by advertisers, about the size of newspapers and magazines combined. The Internet, which is growing, still amounts to only 5.1 percent of media advertising spending. That 5.1 percent is very significant, but it's still just 5.1 percent.

It is also interesting to see who spends where (see Exhibit 14.10). Marketers in some product categories spend more on media and rely more on certain types of media than others. For example, compare how the two industries shown in Exhibit 14.11 spread around their media money.

Domestic Advertising Spending by Category
By media bought in 2003 and 2002

RANK			U.S. MEASURED MEDIA BREAKOUT FOR 2003						
'03	CATEGORY	MEASURED MEDIA 2003	MAGAZINE	NEWSPAPER	OUTDOOR	TV	CABLE NETS	RADIO	INTERNET
1.	Automotive	$18,393.3	$2,196.7	$6.271.0	$339.4	$7,878.2	$1,058.4	$434.1	$215.5
2.	Retail	16,204.9	1,364	6,685	291	5,127	873	750	1,115
3.	Movies, media, advertising	8,319.4	1,539	2,301	231	2,252	589	353	1,055
4.	Medicines & proprietary remedies	6,863.2	1,882	200	13	3,382	953	215	218
5.	Food, beverages, confectionery	6,403.0	1,551	40	50	3,366	1,158	172	67
6.	Financial services	6,236.0	918	1,482	193	1,725	802	200	916
7.	Home furnishings, supplies, appliances	5,927.4	2,178	181	14	2,300	1,065	126	63
8.	Telecommunications	5,592.3	358	1,924	107	2,005	530	372	296
9.	Personal care	5,045.6	1,773	47	8	2,417	713	46	41
10.	Airlines, hotels, car rental	4,690.5	1,083	1,607	264	820	463	119	334
11.	Direct response cos.	4,489.0	1,715	380	2	1,005	1,256	41	89
12.	Restaurants and fast food	4,130.8	106	149	206	3,034	471	150	15
13.	Computers, software, Internet	3,985.7	1,664	378	26	797	391	86	644
14.	Insurance and real estate	3,278.5	359	1,200	195	931	315	119	158
15.	Apparel	2,300.4	1,648	26	20	332	195	16	64

Notes: Dollars in millions. Table includes measured media from the TNS Media Intelligence/CMR. Yellow Pages is excluded from these totals as are local radio, spot cable and FSIs. Some categories are aggregated from the CMR classifications as follows: Apparel; Ready to-wear/Underclothing & hosiery/Apparel NEC/Jewelry & watches/Apparel accessories/Footwear; Toiletries, cosmetics & personal care: Cosmetics & beauty aids-wmn, m&w, Unisex/Personal hygiene & health-wmn, m&w, unisex/Hair products & access-wmn, m&w, unisex/Toiletries, hygienic goods & skin care-men; Food, beverages & confectionery: Beverages/Confectionery & snacks/Dairy, produce, meat & bakery goods/Prepared foods/Ingredients, mixes & seasonings; Home furnishings, appliances, supplies: household soaps, cleansers & polishes/Household furnishings and accessories/Building materials, equipment & fixtures/Home & building/Household appliances, equipment & utensils/Household supplies; Medicines & proprietary remedies: Pharmaceutical houses/Medicines & proprietary remedies/Drugs, toiletries & fitness/Eye glasses, medical equip & supplies; Retail: Discount departments & variety stores/Department stories/Retail/Shopping centers & catalog showrooms. Consumer magazine includes Sunday magazine, local magazine and business publication; TV includes network, spot, syndicated and Spanish-language TV; radio is network and national spot; newspaper includes national newspaper.

Source: 100 Leading National Advertisers, *Advertising Age*, June 28, 2004, 1–4.

EXHIBITS 14.10 AND 14.11

Different categories spend advertising in different media. Whereas fast food spends the vast majority of its budget on TV, financial services spread theirs around, and are particularly big users of print media. Why do you think that is? Could it be just about everyone eats fast food, but the financial services market can more narrowly target with print? Yes. Look at the other categories and think about why these advertisers place their ads where they do.

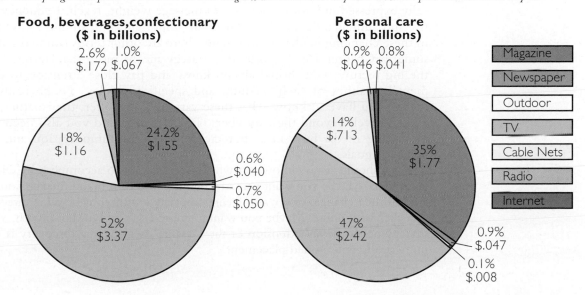

Food, beverages, confectionary ($ in billions)

- 2.6% $.172
- 1.0% $.067
- 18% $1.16
- 24.2% $1.55
- 0.6% $.040
- 0.7% $.050
- 52% $3.37

Personal care ($ in billions)

- 0.9% $.046
- 0.8% $.041
- 14% $.713
- 35% $1.77
- 47% $2.42
- 0.9% $.047
- 0.1% $.008

Legend: Magazine, Newspaper, Outdoor, TV, Cable Nets, Radio, Internet

③ The Media-Planning Process.

The ad world can be a pretty peculiar place. Media planning is particularly peculiar these days. While everyone knows this is the place where vast fortunes can be saved by better media buying, media jobs are neither glamorous (like being a creative), nor high paying (like account executives). A lot of people enter the ad industry through the media department, but relatively few stay. It has traditionally been a job of numbers, schedules, and deadlines, and relatively low salaries. But as the world of media has opened up, it has become considerably more interesting, more desirable, and even a little better paying.

True, the big matrix of media options demands attention to detail in the media-planning process. But, at that same time, you should never lose sight of what it is you are really trying to do. Media planning requires creativity and strategic thinking. Sure, you should need to know how to do the basic math, and know the key terms, but you should never let the raw numbers and techno-buzzwords obscure the strategy. What you need to understand is what you are trying to do with media, why, and the key aspects of the various tools at your disposal. You should also realize with all the "new" media and the way things have opened up, you can do some pretty amazing and pretty cool things (see Exhibit 14.12).

A **media plan** specifies the media in which advertising messages will be placed to reach the desired target audience. A **media class** is a broad category of media, such as television, radio, or newspapers. A **media vehicle** is a particular option for placement within a media class. For example, *Newsweek* is a media vehicle within the magazine media class. The **media mix** is the blend of different media that will be used to effectively reach the target audience.

A media plan includes strategy, objectives, media choices, and a media schedule for placing a message. And remember: Everything must fit together. The advertising plan (Chapter 8) is developed during the planning stage of the advertising effort, and is the driving force behind a media plan. Market and advertising research determines that certain media options hold the highest potential for shaping the consumer behavior (Chapter 5) of the target audience. The message strategy (Chapter 11) has enormous implications for where to place the messages, that is, in which media. Thus, in reality, the media-planning process takes place soon after the overall development of the advertising plan.

Media Strategies.

The true power of a media plan is in the media strategy. This strategy is typically expressed in traditional terms of message weight, reach, frequency, continuity, and audience duplication. These are important; you should know them. But in these changing media environment, there are other terms (some discussed here, some in Chapter 16). Importantly, strategy means more than terms. Don't miss the big picture; you should always know and pay close attention to the fundamental qualities of each medium and specific vehicles. To be really good in media, you have to know what these various forms offer, their nature, and their qualities well beyond their numbers. To be really good you also need to be able to see the media buys in a strategic context of communication and consumer behavior goals.

You should always know just what is it you want to accomplish by selecting certain media. Maybe you want name recognition for your brand, maybe you want specific attitude change, or a warm feeling associated with your brand, a direct response, or a click of a mouse. Maybe you want to create *buzz*, or word of mouth. Your media strategy has to be an extension of the message itself. Media discovery is more than numerically determined placement.

WHEREVER THEY ARE,
WE ARE TOO.

EXHIBIT 14.12

The WWF gets pretty creative with all sorts of offerings for advertisers.

Perhaps the most obvious media objective is that the vehicle chosen *reaches the target audience*. Recall that a target audience can be defined by demographics, geography, or lifestyle or attitude dimensions. But this is actually where a lot of problems happen in the real advertising and IBP world.

Here's what happens too often. The people making the ads, the creatives, along with (maybe) account planners and/or folks from the research department, account executives, and brand mangers, have "determined" a target market of something similar to this example: "housewives 18–49, who hate cooking, long for the day when their children are out of the house, typically vote Republican, and need a better nonstick cooking spray for baking." Now, unfortunately, most media are bought and sold with a much, much shorter list of variables: age, income, family size—in other words, very basic demographics associated with the total audience of that particular vehicle, say *Newsweek*. All that other stuff helps the creatives, but doesn't do much for the media buyer. You really can't call a salesperson at *Newsweek* and say, "Give me just those women who meet this very specific profile." Sorry, can't do it. So media planners are often (very often) put in the awkward and unenviable position of trying to deliver very specific audience characteristics based on inadequate data from media organizations. This is a common industry-wide problem. Most of the time, there is simply no way to identify which television shows are watched by "women who really like strawberries" and who "regularly shop at Bed Bath & Beyond." Those data are not routinely collected, are not available. And no matter how many times you tell account executives and creatives this, they seem to still think these data exist. No, generally speaking, they are not available. Media buyers have to use their creativity to figure out what the next best thing would be. A lot of the creativity involved in media planning is trying to find that next best thing.

Having said that, having described the typical media-buying situation, let's be sure to say that sometimes you can find very good and very relevant data are linked to media exposure data. The trick is getting them in the same data set, that is, knowing which women really like strawberries, *and* regularly shop at Bed Bath & Beyond, *and* watch, read, browse, or in some way are exposed to specific advertising vehicles. It's usually easy to get one or the other, but not all. Sometimes, however, if advertisers are willing to spend the money, and you are reasonably lucky in terms of what you asked for, the data will be available from a media research organization. These organizations don't cover everything, but they sometimes cover what you are looking for. This information can greatly increase the precision and usefulness of media buys. The two most prominent providers of demographic information correlated

Aftershave Lotion & Cologne for Men																			
		Eternity for Men				Jovan Musk				Lagerfeld				Obsession for Men					
	TOTAL U.S. '000	A '000	B % DOWN	C % ACROSS	D INDEX	A '000	B % DOWN	C % ACROSS	D INDEX	A '000	B % DOWN	C % ACROSS	D INDEX	A '000	B % DOWN	C % ACROSS	D INDEX		
BASE: MEN																			
All Men	92674	2466	100.0	2.7	100	3194	100.0	3.4	100	1269	100.0	1.4	100	3925	100.0	4.2	100		
Men	92674	2466	100.0	2.7	100	3194	100.0	3.4	100	1269	100.0	1.4	100	3925	100.0	4.2	100		
Women	—	—	—	—	—	—	—	—	—	—	—	—	—	—	—	—	—		
Household Heads	77421	1936	78.5	2.5	94	2567	80.4	3.3	96	1172	92.4	1.5	111	2856	72.7	3.7	87		
Homemakers	31541	967	39.2	3.1	115	1158	36.3	3.7	107	451	35.5	1.4	104	1443	36.8	4.6	108		
Graduated College	21727	583	23.7	2.7	101	503	15.8	2.3	67	348	27.4	1.6	117	901	23.0	4.1	98		
Attended College	23842	814	33.0	3.4	128	933	29.2	3.9	113	*270	21.3	1.1	83	1283	32.7	5.4	127		
Graduated High School	29730	688	27.9	2.3	87	1043	32.7	3.5	102	*460	36.3	1.5	113	1266	32.2	4.3	101		
Did not Graduate H.S.	17374	*380	15.4	2.2	82	*715	22.4	4.1	119	*191	15.0	1.1	80	*475	12.1	2.7	65		
18–24	12276	754	30.6	6.1	231	*391	12.2	3.2	92	*7	0.5	0.1	4	747	19.0	6.1	144		
25–34	20924	775	31.4	3.7	139	705	22.1	3.4	98	*234	18.5	1.1	82	1440	36.7	6.9	162		
35–44	21237	586	23.8	2.8	104	1031	32.3	4.9	141	*311	24.5	1.5	107	838	21.3	3.9	93		
45–54	14964	*202	8.2	1.4	51	*510	16.0	3.4	99	*305	24.0	2.0	149	481	12.3	3.2	76		
55–64	10104	*112	4.6	1.1	42	*215	6.7	2.1	62	*214	16.9	2.1	155	*245	6.2	2.4	57		
65 or over	13168	*37	1.5	0.3	10	*342	10.7	2.6	75	*198	15.6	1.5	110	*175	4.4	1.3	31		
18–34	33200	1529	62.0	4.6	173	1096	34.3	3.3	96	*241	19.0	0.7	53	2187	55.7	6.6	156		
18–49	62950	2228	90.4	3.5	133	2460	77.0	3.9	113	683	53.9	1.1	79	3315	84.5	5.3	124		
25–54	57125	1563	63.4	2.7	103	2246	70.3	3.9	114	850	67.0	1.5	109	2758	70.3	4.8	114		
Employed Full Time	62271	1955	79.3	3.1	118	2141	67.0	3.4	100	977	77.0	1.6	115	2981	76.0	4.8	113		
Part-time	5250	*227	9.2	4.3	163	*141	4.4	2.7	78	*10	0.8	0.2	14	*300	7.7	5.7	135		
Sole Wage Earner	21027	554	22.5	2.6	99	794	24.9	3.8	110	332	26.2	1.6	115	894	22.8	4.3	100		
Not Employed	25153	*284	11.5	1.1	42	912	28.6	3.6	105	*281	22.2	1.1	82	643	16.4	2.6	60		
Professional	9010	*232	9.4	2.6	97	*168	5.3	1.9	54	*143	11.3	1.6	116	504	12.8	5.6	132		
Executive/Admin./Mgr.	10114	*259	10.5	2.6	96	*305	9.6	3.0	88	*185	14.6	1.8	134	353	9.0	3.5	82		
Clerical/Sales/Technical	13212	436	17.7	3.3	124	*420	13.2	3.2	92	*231	18.2	1.7	128	741	18.9	5.6	132		
Precision/Crafts/Repair	12162	624	25.3	5.1	193	*317	9.9	2.6	76	*168	13.2	1.4	101	511	13.0	4.2	99		
Other Employed	23022	631	25.6	2.7	103	1071	33.5	4.7	135	*261	20.6	1.1	83	1173	29.9	5.1	120		
H/D Income																			
$75,000 or More	17969	481	19.5	2.7	101	*320	10.0	1.8	52	413	32.5	2.3	168	912	23.2	5.1	120		
$60,000–74,999	10346	*368	14.9	3.6	134	*309	9.7	3.0	87	*142	11.2	1.4	100	495	12.6	4.8	113		
$50,000–59,999	9175	*250	10.2	2.7	103	*424	13.3	4.6	134	*153	12.1	1.7	122	*371	9.4	4.0	95		
$40,000–49,999	11384	*308	12.5	2.7	102	*387	12.1	3.4	99	*134	10.6	1.2	86	580	14.8	5.1	120		
$30,000–39,999	12981	*360	14.6	2.8	104	542	17.0	4.2	121	*126	10.0	1.0	71	*416	10.6	3.2	76		
$20,000–29,999	13422	*266	10.8	2.0	75	*528	16.5	3.9	114	*164	12.9	1.2	89	*475	12.1	3.5	84		
$10,000–19,999	11867	*401	16.3	3.4	127	*394	12.3	3.3	96	*67	5.3	0.6	41	*481	12.3	4.1	96		
Less than $10,000	5528	*31	1.3	0.6	21	*291	9.1	5.3	153	*69	5.4	1.2	91	*194	4.9	3.5	83		

Source: Mediamark Research Inc., Mediamark Research Men's, Women's Personal Care Products Report (Mediamark Research Inc., Spring 1997), 16.

EXHIBIT 14.13

Commercial research firms can provide advertisers with an evaluation of a brand's relative strength within demographic segments. This typical data table from Mediamark Research shows how various men's aftershave and cologne brands perform in different demographic segments. http://www.mediamark.com

with product usage data are Mediamark Research (MRI) and Simmons Market Research Bureau (SMRB). An example of the type of information supplied is shown in Exhibit 14.13, where market statistics for four brands of men's aftershave and cologne are compared: Eternity for Men, Jovan Musk, Lagerfeld, and Obsession for Men. The most-revealing data are contained in columns C and D. Column C shows each brand's strength relative to a demographic variable, such as age or income. Column D provides an index indicating that particular segments of the population are heavier users of a particular brand. Specifically, the number expresses each brand's share of volume as a percentage of its share of users. An index number above 100 shows particular strength for a brand. The strength of Eternity for Men as well as Obsession for Men is apparent in both the 18–24 and the 25–34 age cohorts.

Even more sophisticated data have become available. Research services such as A. C. Nielsen's Home*Scan and Information Resources' BehaviorScan are referred to as **single-source tracking services,** which offer information not just on demographics but also on brands, purchase size, purchase frequency, prices paid, and media exposure. BehaviorScan is the most comprehensive, in that exposure to particular television programs, magazines, and newspapers can be measured by the service. With demographic, behavioral, and media-exposure correlates provided by research services like these, advertising and media planners can address issues such as the following:

- How many members of the target audience have tried the advertiser's brand, and how many are brand-loyal?
- What appears to affect brand sales more—increased amounts of advertising, or changes in advertising copy?
- What other products do buyers of the advertiser's brand purchase regularly?
- What television programs, magazines, and newspapers reach the largest number of the advertiser's audience?

Another critical element in setting advertising objectives is determining the **geographic scope** of media placement. In some ways, this is a relatively easy objective to set. Media planners merely need to identify media that cover the same geographic area as the advertiser's distribution system. Obviously, spending money on the placement of ads in media that cover geographic areas where the advertiser's brand is not distributed is wasteful.

Some analysts suggest that when certain geographic markets demonstrate unusually high purchasing tendencies by product category or by brand, then geo-targeting should be the basis for the media placement decision. **Geo-targeting** is the placement of ads in geographic regions where higher purchase tendencies for a brand are evident. For example, in one geographic area the average consumer purchases of Prego spaghetti sauce were 36 percent greater than the average consumer purchases nationwide. With this kind of information, media buys can be geo-targeted to reinforce high-volume users.[3]

Another media objective is **message weight,** the total mass of advertising delivered. Message weight is the gross number of advertising messages or exposure opportunities delivered by the vehicles in a schedule. Media planners are interested in the message weight of a media plan because it provides a simple indication of the size of the advertising effort being placed against a specific market.

Message weight is typically expressed in terms of gross impressions. **Gross impressions** represent the sum of exposures to the entire media placement in a media plan. Planners often distinguish between two types of exposure. *Potential ad impressions* or *opportunities* to be exposed to ads are the most common meanings and refer to exposures by the media vehicle carrying advertisements (for example, a program or publication). *Message impressions,* on the other hand, refers to exposures to the ads themselves. Information on ad exposure probabilities can be obtained from a number of companies, including Nielsen, Simmons, Roper-Starch, Gallup & Robinson, Harvey Research, and Readex. This information can pertain to particular advertisements, campaigns, media vehicles, product categories, ad characteristics, and target groups.

For example, consider a media plan that, in a one-week period, places ads on three television programs and in two national newspapers. The sum of the exposures to the media placement might be as follows:

---

3.   This section and the example are drawn from Erwin Ephron, "The Organizing Principle of Media," *Inside Media,* November 2, 1992.

| | Gross Impressions | |
	Media Vehicle	Advertisement
Television		
Program A audience	16,250,000	5,037,500
Program B audience	4,500,000	1,395,000
Program C audience	7,350,000	2,278,500
Sum of TV exposures	28,100,000	8,711,000
Newspapers		
Newspaper 1	1,900,000	376,200
Newspaper 2	450,000	89,100
Sum of newspaper exposures	2,350,000	465,300
Total gross impressions	**30,450,000**	**9,176,300**

The total gross impressions is the media weight.

Of course, this does not mean that 30,450,000 separate people were exposed to the programs and newspapers or that 9,176,300 separate people were exposed to the advertisements. Some people who watched TV program A also saw program B and read newspaper 1, as well as all other possible combinations. This is called **between-vehicle duplication** (remember, "vehicles" are shows, newspapers, magazines—things that carry ads). It is also possible that someone who saw the ad in newspaper 1 on Monday saw it again in newspaper 1 on Tuesday. This is **within-vehicle duplication.** That's why we say that the total *gross* impressions number contains audience duplication. Data available from services such as SMRB report both types of duplication so that they may be removed from the gross impressions to produce the *unduplicated* estimate of audience, called *reach*. (You should know, however, that the math involved in such calculations is fairly complex.) The concept of reach is discussed in the next section.

The message weight objective provides only a broad perspective for a media planner. What does it mean when we say that a media plan for a week produced more than 30 million gross impressions? It means only that a fairly large number of people were potentially exposed to the advertiser's message. It provides a general point of reference. When Toyota Motors introduced the Avalon in the U.S. market, the $40 million introductory ad campaign featured 30-second television spots, newspaper and magazine print ads (see Exhibit 14.14 for an example), and direct mail pieces. The highlight of the campaign was a nine-spot placement on a heavily watched Thursday evening TV show, costing more than $2 million. The message weight of this campaign in a single week was enormous—just the type of objective Toyota's media planners wanted for the brand introduction.[4]

Reach and Frequency. Reach refers to the number of people or households in a target audience that will be exposed to a media vehicle or schedule at least one time during a given period of time. It is often expressed as a percentage. If an advertisement placed on the hit network television program *ER* is watched at least once by 10 percent of the advertiser's target audience, then the reach is said to be 10 percent. Media vehicles with broad reach are ideal for consumer convenience goods, such as toothpaste and cold remedies. These are products with fairly simple features, and they are frequently purchased by a broad cross-section of the market. Broadcast

---

4.   Bradley Johnson, "Toyota's New Avalon Thinks Big, American," *Advertising Age,* November 14, 1994, 46.

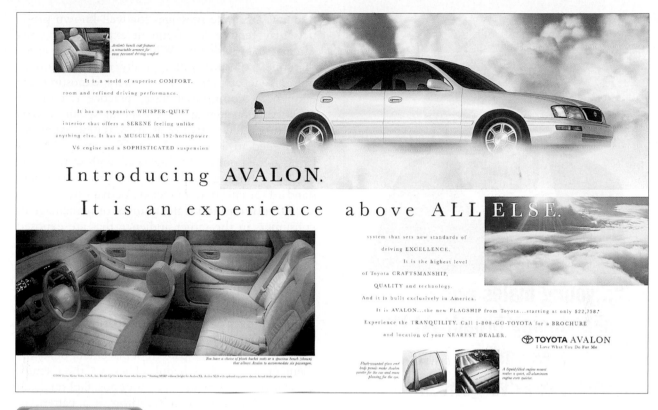

Introducing AVALON.
It is an experience above ALL ELSE.

EXHIBIT 14.14

What is the importance of message weight for the introduction of a new product such as the Avalon? Is it important that the advertiser be able to distinguish between gross impressions and audience reach in this type of campaign?
http://www.toyota.com

television, cable television, and national magazines have the largest and broadest reach of any of the media, due to their national and even global coverage. But their audiences have been shrinking. Now, vehicles like MTV (Exhibit 14.15) are claiming respectable reach among selected but prized "demos" (demographics).

Frequency is the average number of times an individual or household within a target audience is exposed to a media vehicle in a given period of time (typically a week or a month). For example, say an advertiser places an ad on a weekly television show with a 20 rating (20 percent of households) four weeks in a row. The show has an (unduplicated) reach of 43 (percent) over the four-week period. So, frequency is then equal to $(20 \times 4)/43$, or 1.9. This means that an audience member had the opportunity to see the ad an average of 1.9 times.

An important measure for media planners related to both reach and frequency is **gross rating points (GRP).** GRP is the product of reach times frequency (GRP = $r \times f$). When media planners calculate the GRP for a media plan, they multiply the rating (reach) of each vehicle in a plan times the number of times an ad will be inserted in the media vehicle and sum these figures across all vehicles in the plan. Exhibit 14.16 shows the GRP for a combined magazine and television schedule.

The GRP number is used as a relative measure of the intensity of one media plan versus another. Whether a media plan is appropriate is ultimately based on the judgment of the media planner.

Advertisers often struggle with the dilemma of increasing reach at the expense of frequency, or vice versa. At the core in this struggle are the concepts of effective frequency and effective reach. **Effective frequency** is the number of times a target audience needs to be exposed to a message before the objectives of the advertiser are met—either communications objectives or sales impact. Many factors affect the level of effective frequency. New brands and brands laden with features may demand high

Ashton Kutcher returns for another season of "Punk'd" on MTV.

"...young males are abandoning broadcast TV in droves, and we know where they've gone..."

Reach is an important measure of a media vehicle's effectiveness. Who you reach is very important.

frequency. Simple messages for well-known products may require less frequent exposure for consumers to be affected. While most analysts agree that one exposure will typically not be enough, there is debate about how many exposures are enough. A common industry practice is to place effective frequency at three exposures, but analysts argue that as few as two or as many as nine exposures are needed to achieve effective frequency. This is being argued quite a bit just now, with some pushing for a number larger than three to be the new standard for effective frequency, perhaps five.

Effective reach is the number or percentage of consumers in the target audience that are exposed to an ad some minimum number of times. The minimum-number estimate for effective reach is based on a determination of effective frequency. If effective reach is set at four exposures, then a media schedule must be devised that achieves at least four exposures over a specified time period within the target audience.

Continuity is the pattern of placement of advertisements in a media schedule. There are three strategic scheduling alternatives: continuous, flighting, and pulsing. **Continuous scheduling** is a pattern of placing ads at a steady rate over a period of time. Running one ad each day for four weeks during the soap opera *General Hospital* would be a continuous pattern. Similarly, an ad that appeared in every issue of *Redbook* magazine for a year would also be continuous. **Flighting** is another media-scheduling strategy. Flighting is achieved by scheduling heavy advertising for a period of time, usually two weeks, then stopping advertising altogether for a period, only to come back with another heavy schedule.

Gross rating points (GRP) for a media plan.

Media Class/Vehicle	Rating (reach)	Number of Ad Insertions (frequency)	GRP
Television			
ER	25	4	100
Law & Order	20	4	80
Good Morning America	12	4	48
Days of Our Lives	7	2	14
Magazines			
People	22	2	44
Travel & Leisure	11	2	22
U.S. News & World Report	9	6	54
Total			**362**

EXHIBIT 14.17

An example of a print ad that was flighted during December—a month in which whipped-cream dessert toppings figure prominently.
http://www.reddi-wip .com

Flighting is often used to support special seasonal merchandising efforts or new product introductions, or as a response to competitors' activities. The financial advantages of flighting are that discounts might be gained by concentrating media buys in larger blocks. Communication effectiveness may be enhanced because a heavy schedule can achieve the repeat exposures necessary to achieve consumer awareness. For example, the ad in Exhibit 14.17 was run heavily in December issues of magazines, to take advantage of seasonal dessert-consumption patterns.

Finally, **pulsing** is a media-scheduling strategy that combines elements from continuous and flighting techniques. Advertisements are scheduled continuously in media over a period of time, but with periods of much heavier scheduling (the flight). Pulsing is most appropriate for products that are sold fairly regularly all year long but have certain seasonal requirements, such as clothing.

Continuity and the Forgetting Function.

While many may not know it, industry media continuity practices were actually strongly influenced by academic research in the area of human memory. When people first started trying to understand how and when to place ads, the idea of forgetting soon came into play. It makes sense. Very early in advertising's history, this very useful piece of psychological research was recognized. It turns out that people's forgetting is fairly predictable; that is, all else being equal, we know at about what interval things fade from people's memory. It seems to obey a mathematical function pretty well; thus it is often called the **"forgetting function."** The original work for this was done over a century ago by psychologist Hermann Ebbinghaus in the late 19th century, and most notably in the advertising world by Hubert Zielske in 1958. In his very famous study, Zielske sent food ads to two randomly selected groups of women. One received the ad every four weeks for 52 weeks (13 total exposures), the other received the ad once every week for 13 straight weeks (13 total exposures). Exhibit 14.18 shows what happened. The group that received all 13 ads in the first 13 weeks (called a flighting schedule) scored much higher in terms of peak unaided recall, but the level of recall fell off very fast, and by halfway through the year was very low. The group that got the ads at an evenly spaced schedule (called a continuous schedule) never attained as a high a level of recall as the other group, but finished much higher at the end of the year, and had an overall higher average recall.

This research has been very influential in terms of guiding industry media planners for several decades. The real-world implications are pretty clear. If you need rapid and very high levels of recall—say for the introduction of a new product, a strategic move to block the message of a competitor, or a political ad campaign, where there is only one day of actual shopping (election day)—use a flighting (sometimes called "heavy-up") schedule. A continuous schedule would be more broadly effective, and would be used for established brands with an established message.

We do, however, offer a note of caution here. This work has not been completely validated outside the realm of simple recall. And, as you know, the idea of recall and its measurement have received considerable criticism from both industry

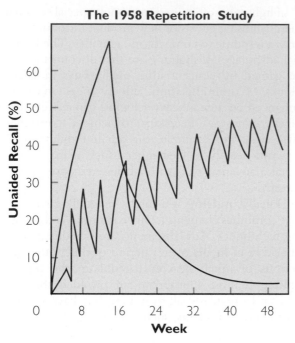

The 1958 Repetition Study

Source: Adapted from Hubert A. Zielske, "The Remembering and Forgetting of Advertising," *Journal of Marketing*, American Marketing Association, January 23, 1959, 239–243. Reprinted in R. Batra, J. Myers, and D. Aaker, *Advertising Management*, 4th ed. (Englewood Cliffs, N.J.: Prentice Hall, 1992).

EXHIBIT 14.18

Work your way through this graph of a very important and influential piece of media research. It links what we know about the manner in which humans forget things with the optimal frequency of advertising.

managers and academic researchers. We also don't know as much about how more emotional or affective ads work over time, particularly with respect to repetition and "affective memory." Still, we have to think that forgetting has to play a significant role in most types of advertising response.

Length or Size of Advertisements. Beyond whom to reach, how often to reach them, and in what pattern, media planners must make strategic decisions regarding the length of an ad in electronic media or the size of an ad in print media. Certainly, the advertiser, creative director, art director, and copywriter have made determinations in this regard as well. Television advertisements (excluding infomercials) can range from 10 seconds to 60 seconds, and sometimes even two minutes, in length. Is a 60-second television commercial always six times more effective than a 10-second spot? Of course, the answer is no. Is a full-page newspaper ad always more effective than a two-inch, one-column ad? Again, this is not necessarily so. Some research shows an increase in recognition scores of print advertising with increasing image size. Some call this the **square root law;** that is, "the recognition of print ads increases with the square of the illustration."[5] So a full-page ad should be twice as memorable as a quarter-page ad. Such "laws" should not be considered laws, but rather general guidelines; they show a general relationship, but should not be taken with such precision. Too much depends on other variables. Still, advertisers use full-page newspaper ads when a product claim, brand image, or market situation warrants it.

The decision about the length or size of an advertisement depends on the creative requirements for the ad, the media budget, and the competitive environment within which the ad is running. From a creative standpoint, ads attempting to develop an image for a brand may need to be longer in broadcast media or larger in print media to offer more creative opportunities. On the other hand, a simple, straightforward message announcing a sale may be quite short or small, but it may need heavy repetition. From the standpoint of the media budget, shorter and smaller ads are, with few exceptions, much less expensive. If a media plan includes some level of repetition to accomplish its objectives, the lower-cost option may be mandatory. From a competitive perspective, matching a competitor's presence with messages of similar size or length may be essential to maintain the share of mind in a target audience. Once again, the size and length decisions are a matter of judgment between the creative team and the media planner, tempered by the availability of funds for media placement.

Media Context. This used to be referred to as "editorial climate." It refers to the feel, spirit, look, or image of the media vehicle. There is the belief that you are known by the company you keep, and that an ad is colored, to some extent, by where it appears. These are sometimes called **context effects**. It means that some of the meaning of your ad's surroundings rubs off on it. So advertisers and media professionals have to be very aware of the social meaning of context. Some advertisers will not do direct mail because they feel it is beneath them, that to do so would tarnish their brand's upper-crust image. Others will not use certain magazines, or

---

5.   John R. Rossiter, "Visual Imagery: Applications to Advertising," *Advances in Consumer Research* (Provo, Utah: Association for Consumer Research, 1982), 101–106.

Characteristics	Medium								
	Broadcast TV	Cable TV	Radio	News-paper	Maga-zines	Direct Mail	Outdoor	Transit	Directory
Reach									
Local	M	M	H	H	L	H	H	H	M
National	H	H	L	L	H	M	L	L	M
Frequency	H	H	H	M	L	L	M	M	L
Selectivity									
Audience	M	H	H	L	H	H	L	L	L
Geographic	L	M	H	H	M	H	H	H	H
Audience reactions									
Involvement	L	M	L	M	H	M	L	L	H
Acceptance	M	M	M	H	M	L	M	M	H
Audience data	M	L	L	M	H	H	L	L	M
Clutter	H	H	H	M	M	M	M	L	H
Creative flexibility	H	H	H	L	M	M	L	L	L
Cost factors									
Per contact	L	L	L	M	M	H	L	L	M
Absolute cost	H	H	M	M	H	H	M	M	M

H = High, M = Moderate, L = Low

EXHIBIT 14.19

Basic evaluation of media options.

sponsor a NASCAR driver, or cross-promote certain kinds of movies. Conversely, some purposefully choose exclusive magazines or other media, including sponsorships, precisely because they want to be elevated by their surroundings. While there have been attempts to grade, quantify, and automate editorial climate in media selection models, it has proven to be a task best suited for knowledgeable human interpretation. You should always make media context a consideration in media strategy. Quantifiable or not, it counts.

Media Choices. The advertiser and the agency team determine which media class is appropriate for the current effort, based on criteria similar to those listed in Exhibit 14.19. These criteria give a general orientation to major media and the inherent capabilities of each media class.

Media Efficiency. Each medium under consideration in a media plan must be scrutinized for the efficiency with which it performs. In other words, which media deliver the largest target audiences at the lowest cost? A common measure of media efficiency is **cost per thousand (CPM),** which is the dollar cost of reaching 1,000 (the M in CPM comes from the roman numeral for 1,000) members of an audience using a particular medium. The CPM calculation can be used to compare the relative efficiency of two media choices within a media class (magazine versus magazine) or between media classes (magazine versus radio). The basic measure of CPM is fairly straightforward; the dollar cost for placement of an ad in a medium is divided by the total audience and multiplied by 1,000. Let's calculate the CPM for a full-page black-and-white ad in the Friday edition of *USA Today:*

$$\text{CPM} = \frac{\text{cost of media buy}}{\text{total audience}} \times 1{,}000$$

$$\text{CPM for } USA\ Today = \frac{\$72{,}000}{5{,}206{,}000} \times 1{,}000 = \$13.83$$

These calculations show that *USA Today* has a CPM of $13.83 for a full-page black-and-white ad. But this calculation shows the cost of reaching the entire readership of *USA Today.* If the target audience is college graduates in professional occupations, then the **cost per thousand–target market (CPM–TM)** calculation might be much higher for a general publication such as *USA Today* than for a more specialized publication such as *Fortune* magazine:

$$\text{CPM–TM for } USA\ Today = \frac{\$72{,}000}{840{,}000} \times 1{,}000 = \$85.71$$

$$\text{CPM–TM for } Fortune = \frac{\$54{,}800}{940{,}000} \times 1{,}000 = \$58.30$$

You can see that the relative efficiency of *Fortune* is much greater than that of *USA Today* when the target audience is specified more carefully and a CPM–TM calculation is made. An advertisement for business services appearing in *Fortune* will have a better CPM–TM than the same ad appearing in *USA Today.*

Information about ad cost, gross impressions, and target audience size is usually available from the medium itself. Detailed audience information to make a cost per thousand–target market analysis also is available from media research organizations, such as Simmons Market Research Bureau (for magazines) and A. C. Nielsen (for television). Cost information also can be obtained from Standard Rate and Data Service (SRDS) and Bacon's Media Directories, for example.

Like CPM, a **cost per rating point (CPRP)** calculation provides a relative efficiency comparison between media options. In this calculation, the cost of a media vehicle, such as a spot television program, is divided by the program's rating. (A rating point is equivalent to 1 percent of the target audience—for example, television households in the designated rating area tuned to a specific program.) Like the CPM calculation, the CPRP calculation gives a dollar figure, which can be used for comparing TV program efficiency. The calculation for CPRP is as follows, using television as an example.

$$\text{CPRP} = \frac{\text{dollar cost of ad placement on a program}}{\text{program rating}}$$

For example, an advertiser on WLTV (Univision 23) in the Miami–Ft. Lauderdale market may wish to compare household CPRP figures for 30-second announcements in various dayparts on the station. The calculations for early news and prime-time programs are as follows.

$$\text{CPRP for WLTV early news} = \frac{\$2{,}205}{9} = \$245$$

$$\text{CPRP for WLTV prime time} = \frac{\$5{,}100}{10} = \$510$$

Clearly an early news daypart program delivers households more efficiently at $245 CPRP, less than half that of prime time, with 90 percent of the typical prime-time rating.

It is important to remember that these efficiency assessments are based solely on costs and coverage. They say nothing about the quality of the advertising and thus should not be viewed as indicators of advertising effectiveness. When media efficiency measures such as CPM and CPM–TM are combined with an assessment of media objectives and media strategies, they can be quite useful. Taken alone and out of the broader campaign-planning context, such efficiency measures may lead to ineffective media buying.

3 The Real Deal.

The Real Deal: Data Quality. A problem that gets way too little attention, at least in textbooks, is this: GIGO. This is an old, but still very appropriate, rule in computer data management: garbage in, garbage out. In other words, no matter how much you process data, if it was garbage coming in to the system, it is still garbage going out. In media planning, there is enormous reliance on very sophisticated mathematical models and computer programs to optimize media schedules. But throwing the calculus book at the problem isn't sufficient. We have a big cultural hang-up about numbers. In fact, let us say that again: We have a big cultural hang-up about numbers. When we put a number to something it makes it appear more precise, more scientific, and more certain. But that is often pure illusion. Yes, these optimization programs are good, they are valuable, they save clients billions of dollars—but they also distract attention from a more basic problem: Media exposure data are often just not very good. We are not saying that media data are complete trash, but we are saying that what it means to be exposed to an advertisement is not adequately addressed by most exposure data. This is a sad reality, and one that is well known but rarely acknowledged until fairly recently. With the radically changing media landscape, clients are less willing to pay for, or rely on, an even highly "optimized" media schedule when the data going into those calculations are highly suspect. There are now too many other games in town with better and more meaningful exposure estimates and ROIs to have to pay for poor data. This is now a common industry complaint. It is almost at crisis stage.

Think about it: Is being in the room when a TV is on sufficient to say you were exposed to the ad? Did you see it in any meaningful way? Shouldn't "exposure" be more, mean more than that? Well, sure it should. But the media measurement companies argue that (1) it's the best we have, (2) everyone is playing by the same rules, and if you use the measures simply to judge *relative* strengths, then they are OK, and (3) they are always working on better methods. They are right about the second point: If used only for relative measurement (one schedule against another), exposure data are probably reasonably good. Unfortunately, most exposure data in all mass media are a long way from capturing and delivering what it means to see or hear an ad. You need to keep this in mind when you see all those precise-looking numbers.

Nielsen, which holds a virtual monopoly on national television ratings in the United States, has been under pressure to improve the accuracy of its ratings. Indeed, several firms, including General Electric (the parent of NBC), Disney/ABC, and CBS, have paid for a statistical analysis to examine ways of improving the ratings process.[6] Some television stations have even dropped out of the Nielsen rating program, claiming that the measurement periods, known as sweep periods, create an artificial

6.   See Joe Mandese, "Rivals' Ratings Don't Match Up," *Advertising Age,* February 24, 1992, 50.

measurement context. Some question Nielsen for the accuracy of its methods and their appropriateness in markets outside the United States.

Finally, media organizations often provide information to advertisers in ways that are only marginally useful. While it is possible to get detailed information on the age, gender, and geographic location of target audiences, these characteristics may not be relevant to audience identification. Not all brands show clear tendencies among consumer groups based on Simmons or MRI data. Rather, consumer behavior is much more often influenced by peer groups, lifestyles, attitudes, and beliefs—which don't show up on commercial media reports. If we base our target marketing on these behavioral and experiential factors, then we would logically want to choose our media in the same way. But such information is often not generally available from media organizations, nor is it likely to be forthcoming (due to the cost of gathering these data). In fairness, some media kits from magazines targeted to upper-income consumers (such as *Smithsonian Magazine*) provide fairly detailed information on past purchase behaviors and some leisure activities. This information is the exception rather than the rule, however, and even then a lot is being assumed.

The Real Deal: Ads For Advertisers. Another thing that is generally poorly covered in other books is the institutional sales function. How do media vehicles sell themselves to advertisers and advertising agencies? What is the role of this business-to-business (B2B) advertising? Well, it's a big effort, and a big role. Media companies spend lots of money selling their time and space to advertisers thorough their ad agencies. Pick up any issue of *Ad Age* and count the ads. Who is spending the money? Exhibits 14.20 through 14.23 are some pretty creative ads for media vehicles placed in *Ad Age* to attract advertisers. This is an important part of the real-world of advertising and IBP media.

The Real Deal: The Media Lunch. It's the real world. It's Friday afternoon, and *Big National Magazine* is throwing a party at your agency. Wow, what nice folks: free drinks, great food, nice socializing. One of the sales reps took some of us to a bar afterward. Wow, those reps over at *Big National Magazine* are sure some great guys.

But wait, why the party? Well, let's look at the guest list: The party is being held on the floor of the building where the media buyers work. Look around the room. There are some account people, the occasional hungry creative, but almost everyone there is a media planner or buyer. Hmm. Well, yes, that's because a lot of media buying does not depend on sophisticated math from a computer program, but on good old-fashioned schmoozing and sales pitches. The media planner has options beyond what the canned software recommends—he/she can make deals, can and does play favorites. This is why, despite the relatively low pay, entry-level ad people tend to like the job. It has good perks. It's also why certain ads get in certain vehicles.

④ Contemporary Essentials.

Internet Media. We cover the topic of Internet media in considerable detail in Chapter 16. We devote an entire chapter to it because Internet media has its own terms, its own unique calculation issues. Exhibit 14.24 gives a good glossary of Internet media terms. An excellent free resource for exploring Internet media planning and buying is Ad Resource (http://adres.internet.com). Check it out. Many Internet portals post their advertising rates. Other good resources include the Interactive Advertising Bureau (http://www.iab.net) and Iconocast (http://www.iconocast.com). The bottom line on Internet advertising, at this point, is that it has grown tremendously as a new medium, but rates have not. This is largely due to the difficulty in assessing the size of the Internet advertising audience and in determining what it means

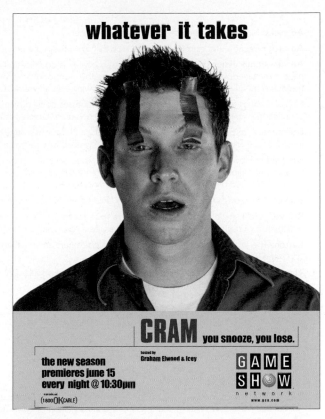

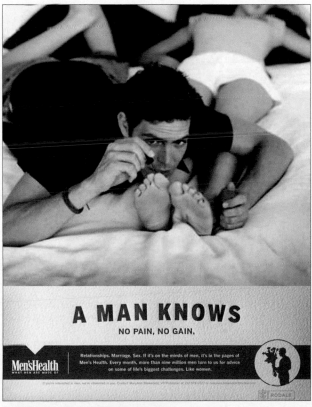

EXHIBITS 14.20 THROUGH 14.23

These are ads for advertising professionals, particularly media buyers. They tell why their particular vehicle is the best at reaching some desired audience.

Ad clicks: Number of times users click on an ad banner.

Ad click rate: Sometimes referred to as "click-through," this is the percentage of ad views that resulted in an ad click.

Ad views (impressions): Number of times an ad banner is downloaded and presumably seen by visitors. If the same ad appears on multiple pages simultaneously, this statistic may understate the number of ad impressions, due to browser caching. Corresponds to net impressions in traditional media. There is currently no way of knowing if an ad was actually loaded. Most servers record an ad as served even if it was not.

B2B: B2B stands for "business-to-business," as in businesses doing business with other businesses. The term is most commonly used in connection with e-commerce and advertising, when you are targeting businesses as opposed to consumers.

Backbone: A high-speed line or series of connections that forms a large pathway within a network. The term is relative to the size of network it is serving. A backbone in a small network would probably be much smaller than many nonbackbone lines in a large network.

Bandwidth: How much information (text, images, video, sound) can be sent through a connection. Usually measured in bits per second. A full page of text is about 16,000 bits. A fast modem can move approximately 15,000 bits in one second. Full-motion full-screen video requires about 10,000,000 bits per second, depending on compression. (See also: 56K, bit, modem, T1)

Banner: An ad on a Web page that is usually "hot-linked" to the advertiser's site.

Browser caching: To speed surfing, browsers store recently used pages on a user's disk. If a site is revisited, browsers display pages from the disk instead of requesting them from the server. As a result, servers undercount the number of times a page is viewed.

Button: The term used to reflect an Internet advertisement smaller than the traditional banner. Buttons are square in shape and usually located down the left or right side of the site.

The IAB and CASIE have recognized these sizes as the most popular and most accepted on the Internet:

Standard internet ad sizes (in pixels):

468 × 60	Full banner
392 × 72	Full banner/vertical navigation bar
234 × 60	Half banner
125 × 125	Square button
120 × 90	Button #1
120 × 60	Button #2
88 × 31	Micro button
120 × 240	Vertical banner

CASIE: CASIE stands for the Coalition for Advertising Supported Information and Entertainment. It was founded in May 1994 by the Association of National Advertisers (ANA) and the American Association of Advertising Agencies (AAAA) to guide the development of interactive advertising and marketing.

CGI: Common Gateway Interface. An interface-creation scripting program that allows Web pages to be made on the fly based on information from buttons, checkboxes, text input, etc.

Click-through: The percentage of ad views that resulted in an ad click.

CPC: Cost-per-click is an Internet marketing formula used to price ad banners. Advertisers will pay Internet publishers based on the number of clicks a specific ad banner gets. Cost usually runs in the range of $0.10–$0.20 per click.

CPM: CPM is the cost per thousand for a particular site. A Web site that charges $15,000 per banner and guarantees 600,000 impressions has a CPM of $25 ($15,000 divided by 600). For more information on the average CPM rates of sites around the Web.

Cyberspace: Coined by author William Gibson in his 1984 novel *Neuromancer*, *cyberspace* is now used to describe all of the information available through computer networks.

Domain name: The unique name of an Internet site; for example, www.cyberatlas.com. There are six top-level domains widely used in the United States: .com (commercial) .edu (educational), .net (network operations), .gov (U.S. government), .mil (U.S. military) and .org (organization). Other two-letter domains represent countries: .uk for the United Kingdom and so on.

DTC: DTC stands for "direct-to-consumer." The term is commonly used to denote advertising that is targeted to consumers, as opposed to businesses. Television ads, print ads in consumer publications, and radio ads are all forms of DTC advertising.

Hit: Each time a Web server sends a file to a browser, it is recorded in the server log file as a "hit." Hits are generated for every element of a requested page (including graphics, text and interactive items). If a page containing two graphics is viewed by a user, three hits will be recorded—one for the page itself and one for each graphic. Webmasters use hits to measure their server's workload. Because page designs vary greatly, hits are a poor guide for traffic measurement.

Host: An Internet host used to be a single machine connected to the Internet (which meant it had a unique IP address). As a host it made available to other machines on the network certain services. However, virtual hosting now means that one physical host can now be actually many virtual hosts.

HTML: Hypertext Markup Language is a coding language used to make hypertext documents for use on the Web. HTML resembles old-fashioned typesetting code, where a block of text is surrounded by codes that indicate how it should appear. HTML allows text to be "linked" to another file on the Internet.

Hypertext: Any text that can be chosen by a reader and that causes another document to be retrieved and displayed.

IAB: IAB stands for the Interactive Advertising Bureau. The IAB is a global nonprofit association devoted exclusively to maximizing the use and effectiveness of advertising on the Internet. The IAB sponsors research and events related to the Internet advertising industry.

Continued

EXHIBIT 14.24

A handy glossary of media terms. http://www.internet.com/glossary

Internet: A collection of approximately 60,000 independent, interconnected networks that use the TCP/IP protocols and that evolved from ARPANet of the late '60s and early '70s.

Interstitial: Meaning "in between," refers to an advertisement that appears in a separate browser window while you wait for a Web page to load. Interstitials are more likely to contain large graphics, streaming presentations, and applets than conventional banner ads, and some studies have found that more users click on interstitials than on banner ads. Some users, however, have complained that interstitials slow access to destination pages.

IP address: Internet Protocol address. Every system connected to the Internet has a unique IP address, which consists of a number in the format A.B.C.D where each of the four sections is a number from 0 to 255. Most people use domain names instead, and the resolution between domain names and IP addresses is handled by the network and domain name servers. With virtual hosting, a single machine can act like multiple machines (with multiple domain names and IP addresses).

IRC: Internet Relay Chat is a worldwide network of people talking to each other in real time.

ISDN: Integrated Services Digital Network is a digital network that moves up to 128,000 bits per second over a regular phone line at nearly the same cost as a normal phone call.

Java: Java is a general-purpose programming language with a number of features that make the language well suited for use on the World Wide Web. Small Java applications are called Java applets and can be downloaded from a Web server and run on your computer by a Java-compatible Web browser, such as Netscape Navigator or Microsoft Internet Explorer.

Javascript: Javascript is a scripting language developed by Netscape that can interact with HTML source code, enabling Web authors to spice up their sites with dynamic content.

Jump page: A jump page, also known as a "splash page," is a special page set up for visitors who clicked on a link in an advertisement. For example, by clicking on an ad for Site X, visitors go to a page in Site X that continues the message used in the advertising creative. The jump page can be used to promote special offers or to measure the response to an advertisement.

Link: An electronic connection between two Web sites (also called "hot link").

Listserv:* The most widespread of maillists. Listervs started on BITNET and are now common on the Internet.

Log file: A file that lists actions that have occurred. For example, Web servers maintain log files listing every request made to the server. With log file analysis tools, it's possible to get a good idea of where visitors are coming from, how often they return, and how they navigate through a site. Using cookies enables Webmasters to log even more detailed information about how individual users are accessing a site.

Newsgroup: A discussion group on Usenet devoted to talking about a specific topic. Currently, there are over 15,000 newsgroups.

Opt-in e-mail: Opt-in e-mail lists are lists where Internet users have voluntarily signed up to receive commercial e-mail about topics of interest.

Page: All Web sites are a collection of electronic "pages." Each Web page is a document formatted in HTML (Hypertext Markup Language) that contains text, images or media objects such as RealAudio player files, QuickTime videos, or Java applets. The "home page" is typically a visitor's first point of entry and features a site index. Pages can be static or dynamically generated. All frames and frame parent documents are counted as pages.

Page views: Number of times a user requests a page that may contain a particular ad. Indicative of the number of times an ad was potentially seen, or "gross impressions." Page views may overstate ad impressions if users choose to turn off graphics (done to speed browsing).

RealAudio: A commercial software program that plays audio on demand, without waiting for long file transfers. For instance, you can listen to National Public Radio's entire broadcast of *All Things Considered* and *Morning Edition* on the Internet.

Rich media: *Rich media* is a term for advanced technology used in Internet ads, such as streaming video, applets that allow user interaction, and special effects.

ROI: ROI stands for "return on investment," one of the great mysteries of online advertising, and indeed, advertising in general. ROI is trying to find out what the end of result of the expenditure (in this case, an ad campaign) is. A lot depends on the goal of the campaign, building brand awareness, increasing sales, etc. Early attempts at determining ROI in Internet advertising relied heavily on the click-through of an ad.

Server: A machine that makes services available on a network to client programs. A file server makes files available. A WAIS server makes full-text information available through the WAIS protocol (although WAIS uses the term *source* interchangeably with *server*).

Splash page: See *jump page.*

Sponsorship: Sponsorships are increasing in popularity on the Internet. A sponsorship is when an advertiser pays to sponsor content, usually a section of a Web site or an e-mail newsletter. In the case of a site, the sponsorship may include banners or buttons on the site, and possibly a tagline.

Sticky: "Sticky" sites are those where the visitors stay for an extended period of time. For instance, a banking site that offers a financial calculator is stickier than one that doesn't because visitors do not have to leave to find a resource they need.

T1: A high-speed (1.54 megabits/second) network connection.

T3: An even higher-speed (45 megabits/second) Internet connection.

TCP: Transmission Control Protocol works with IP to ensure that packets travel safely on the Internet.

Unique users: The number of different individuals who visit a site within a specific time period. To identify unique users, Web sites rely on some form of user registration or identification system

Unix: A computer operating system (the basic software running on a computer, underneath things like databases and word processors). Unix is designed to be used by many people at once ("multi-user") and has TCP/IP built-in. Unix is the most prevalent operating system for Internet servers.

Valid hits: A further refinement of hits, valid hits are hits that deliver all information to a user. Excludes hits such as redirects, error messages and computer-generated hits.

Visits: A sequence of requests made by one user at one site. If a visitor does not request any new information for a period of time, known as the "time-out" period, then the next request by the visitor is considered a new visit. To enable comparisons among sites, I/PRO, a provider of services and software for the independent measurement and analysis Web site usage, uses a 30-minute time-out.

Source: ADResources, 2001.

*Listserv is a trademark of L-Soft International, used to describe its electronic mailing list software, using it as a generic term infringes on L-Soft's trademark rights. It is however, commonly used in a generic fashion.

to say that someone was "exposed" to an ad on the Internet. It is also true that this medium is struggling to find its way in terms of what kind of ads really work. In the early days of radio and television, those media struggled to find the forms that would be best for advertising. The Internet is no different. Pop-ups came, pop-ups pretty much went away.

Competitive Media Assessment. While media planners normally do not base an overall media plan on how much competitors are spending or where competitors are placing their ads, a competitive media assessment can provide a useful perspective. A competitive media assessment is particularly important for product categories in which all the competitors are focused on a narrowly defined target audience. This condition exists in several product categories in which heavy-user segments dominate consumption— for example, snack foods, soft drinks, beer and wine, and chewing gum. Brands of luxury cars and financial services also compete for common-buyer segments.

When a target audience is narrow and attracts the attention of several major competitors, an advertiser must assess its competitors' spending and the relative share of voice its brand is getting. **Share of voice** is a calculation of any one advertiser's brand expenditures relative to the overall spending in a category:

$$\text{Share of voice} = \frac{\text{one brand's advertising expenditures in a medium}}{\text{total product category advertising expenditures in a medium}}$$

This calculation can be done for all advertising by a brand in relation to all advertising in a product category, or it can be done to determine a brand's share of product category spending on a particular advertising medium, such as network television or magazines. For example, athletic-footwear marketers spend approximately $310 million per year in measured advertising media. Nike and Reebok are the two top brands, with approximately $160 million and $55 million respectively in annual expenditures in measured advertising media. The share-of-voice calculations for both brands follow.

$$\text{Share of voice, Nike} = \frac{\$160 \text{ million}}{\$310 \text{ million}} \times 100 = 51.6\%$$

$$\text{Share of voice, Reebok} = \frac{\$55 \text{ million}}{\$310 \text{ million}} \times 100 = 17.7\%$$

Together, both brands dominate the product category advertising with a nearly 70 percent combined share of voice. Yet Nike's share of voice is nearly three times that of Reebok.

Research data, such as that provided by Competitive Media Reporting, can provide an assessment of share of voice in up to 10 media categories. A detailed report shows how much a brand was advertised in a particular media category versus the combined media category total for all other brands in the same product category. Knowing what competitors are spending in a medium and how dominant they might be allows an advertiser to strategically schedule within a medium. Some strategists believe that scheduling in and around a competitor's schedule can create a bigger presence for a small advertiser.[7]

7.   Andrea Rothman, "Timing Techniques Can Make Small Ad Budgets Seem Bigger," *Wall Street Journal,* February 3, 1989, B4; see also Robert J. Kent and Chris T. Allen, "Competitive Interference Effects in Consumer Memory for Advertising: The Role of Brand Familiarity," *Journal of Marketing* (July 1994), 97–105.

Computer Media-Planning Models. The explosion of available data on markets and consumers has motivated media planners to rely heavily on electronic databases, computers, and software to assist with the various parts of the media-planning effort.

Nearly all of the major syndicated research services offer electronic data to their subscribers, including advertisers, agencies, and media organizations. These databases contain information helpful in identifying target markets and audiences, estimating or projecting media vehicle audiences and costs, and analyzing competitive advertising activity, among many others. Companies that offer data electronically, such as Nielsen, Arbitron, MRI, SMRB, Scarborough, and the Audit Bureau of Circulations, also typically provide software designed to analyze their own data. Such software often produces summary reports, tabulations, ranking, reach-frequency analysis, optimization, simulation, scheduling, buying, flowcharts, and a variety of graphical presentations.

Advertisers that use a mix of media in their advertising campaigns often subscribe to a variety of electronic data services representing the media they use or consider using. However, the various syndicated services do not provide standardized data, reports, and analyses that are necessarily comparable across media categories. Also, individual syndicated service reports and analyses may not offer the content and depth that some users prefer. Nor do they typically analyze media categories that they do not measure. Consequently, media software houses such as Interactive Market Systems (IMS) and Telmar Information Services Corp. (Telmar) offer hundreds of specialized and standardized software products that help advertisers, agencies, and media organizations worldwide develop and evaluate markets, audiences, and multimedia plans. Exhibit 14.25 shows typical screens from one such computer program. The first screen is reach and cost data for spot TV ads, and the second screen is the combined reach and cost data for spot TV and newspaper ads.

Computerization and modeling can never substitute for planning and judgment by media strategists. Computer modeling does, however, allow for the assessment of a wide range of possibilities before making costly media buys. It can, and does, save advertisers a lot of money.

One of the most important aspects of the media-scheduling phase involves creating a visual representation of the media schedule. Exhibit 14.26 shows a media schedule flowchart that includes both print and electronic media placement. With this visual representation of the schedule, the advertiser has tangible documentation of the overall media plan.

Making the Buy. Once an overall media plan and schedule are in place, the focus must turn to **media buying.** Media buying entails securing the electronic media time and print media space specified in the schedule. An important part of the media-buying process is the agency of record. The **agency of record** is the advertising agency chosen by the advertiser to purchase time and space. The agency of record coordinates media discounts and negotiates all contracts for time and space. Any other agencies involved in the advertising effort submit insertion orders for time and space within those contracts.

Rather than using an agency of record, some advertisers use a **media-buying service,** which is an independent organization that specializes in buying large blocks of media time and space and reselling it to advertisers (see Exhibit 14.27). Some agencies have developed their own media-buying units to control both the planning and the buying process. Regardless of the structure used to make the buys, media buyers evaluate the audience reach, CPM, and timing of each buy. The organization responsible for the buy also monitors the ads and estimates the actual audience reach delivered. If the expected audience is not delivered, then media organizations have to *make good* by repeating ad placements or offering a refund or price reduction on future

```
ADplus(TM) RESULTS: SPOT TV (30S)
Walt Disney World                     Frequency (f) Distributions
Off-Season Promotion
Monthly                                    VEHICLE        MESSAGE
Target: 973,900              f        % f+      % f+       % f     % f+
Jacksonville DMA Adults

                             0        5.1        -        9.1       -
Message/vehicle = 32.0%      1        2.0       94.9      7.5      90.9
                             2        2.2       92.9      8.1      83.4
                             3        2.3       90.7      8.1      75.2
                             4        2.4       88.3      7.8      67.1
                             5        2.4       85.9      7.2      59.3
                             6        2.5       83.5      6.6      52.1
                             7        2.5       81.0      6.0      45.5
                             8        2.5       78.5      5.3      39.5
                             9        2.5       76.0      4.7      34.2
                            10+      73.5       73.5     29.5      29.5
                            20+      49.8       49.8      6.1       6.1

Summary Evaluation
Reach 1+ (%)                         94.9%               90.9%
Reach 1+ (000s)                      923.9               885.3

Reach 3+ (%)                         90.7%               75.2%
Reach 3+ (000s)                      882.9               732.8

Gross rating points (GRPs)          2,340.0              748.8
Average frequency (f)                 24.7                8.2
Gross impressions (000s)           22,789.3            7,292.6
Cost-per-thousand (CPM)               6.10               19.06
Cost-per-rating point (CPP)            59                 186

Vehicle List      RATING  AD COST  CPM-MSG  ADS  TOTAL COST  MIX %
WJKS-ABC-AM        6.00     234     12.51    30    7,020      5.1
WJXT-CBS-AM        6.00     234     12.51    30    7,020      5.1
WTLV-NBC-AM        6.00     234     12.51    30    7,020      5.1
WJKS-ABC-DAY       5.00     230     14.76    60   13,800      9.9
WJXT-CBS-DAY       5.00     230     14.76    60   13,800      9.9
WTLV-NBC-DAY       5.00     230     14.76    60   13,800      9.9
WJKS-ABC-PRIM     10.00     850     27.27    30   25,500     18.4
WJXT-CBS-PRIM     10.00     850     27.27    30   25,500     18.4
WTLV-NBC-PRIM     10.00     850     27.27    30   25,500     18.4
                        Totals:    19.06    360  138,960    100.0
```

EXHIBIT 14.25

The explosion of data about markets and consumers has caused advertisers to rely more on computerized media-planning tools.

```
ADplus(TM) RESULTS: DAILY NEWSPAPERS (1/2 PAGE), SPOT TV (30S)
Walt Disney World                     Frequency (f) Distributions
Off-Season Promotion
Monthly                                    VEHICLE        MESSAGE
Target: 973,900              f        % f+      % f+       % f     % f+
Jacksonville DMA Adults

                             0        1.2        -        4.0       -
Message/vehicle = 28.1%      1        0.8       98.8      4.9      96.0
                             2        0.9       98.0      5.9      91.1
                             3        0.9       97.2      6.5      85.2
                             4        1.0       96.2      6.7      78.7
                             5        1.1       95.2      6.8      72.0
                             6        1.1       94.2      6.6      65.2
                             7        1.2       93.0      6.3      58.6
                             8        1.3       91.8      5.9      52.4
                             9        1.3       90.6      5.5      46.5
                            10+      89.3       89.3     41.0      41.0
                            20+      73.3       73.3      9.6       9.6

Summary Evaluation
Reach 1+ (%)                         98.8%               96.0%
Reach 1+ (000s)                      962.6               934.6

Reach 3+ (%)                         97.2%               85.2%
Reach 3+ (000s)                      946.5               829.7

Gross rating points (GRPs)          3,372.0              948.0
Average frequency (f)                 34.1                9.9
Gross impressions (000s)           32,839.9            9,232.3
Cost-per-thousand (CPM)              10.96               38.99
Cost-per-rating point (CPP)           107                 380

Vehicle List        RATING  AD COST  CPM-MSG  ADS  TOTAL COST  MIX %
1 Daily Newspapers          Totals:  114.00    80   221,040    61.4

Times-Union          42.00   8,284   104.93    20   165,680    46.0
Record                4.00     866   115.18    20    17,320     4.8
News                  3.20     926   153.95    20    18,520     5.1
Reporter              2.40     976   216.35    20    19,520     5.4

2 Spot TV (30s)             Totals:   19.00   360   138,960    38.6

WJKS-ABC-AM           6.00     234    12.51    30     7,020     2.0
WJXT-CBS-AM           6.00     234    12.51    30     7,020     2.0
WTLV-NBC-AM           6.00     234    12.51    30     7,020     2.0
WJKS-ABC-DAY          5.00     230    14.76    60    13,800     3.8
WJXT-CBS-DAY          5.00     230    14.76    60    13,800     3.8
WTLV-NBC-DAY          5.00     230    14.76    60    13,800     3.8
WJKS-ABC-PRIM        10.00     850    27.27    30    25,500     7.1
WJXT-CBS-PRIM        10.00     850    27.27    30    25,500     7.1
WTLV-NBC-PRIM        10.00     850    27.27    30    25,500     7.1
                           Totals:   38.99   440   360,000   100.0
```

ads. For example, making good to advertisers because of shortfalls in delivering 1998 Winter Olympics prime-time cost CBS an estimated 400 additional 30-second spots.[8]

Interactive Media. The media environment has gotten considerably more challenging as interactive media have been refined. **Interactive media** reach beyond television and include kiosks. Exhibit 14.28 shows an award-winning interactive kiosk in shopping malls or student unions. Also included are interactive telephones, interactive CDs, online services, the Internet, and online versions of magazines. Absolut Vodka has developed a successful interactive Internet campaign. Even such traditional, upscale outlets as Christie's auction house have started using home pages on the World Wide Web to publicize upcoming events (see Exhibit 14.29). The confounding factor for media placement decisions is that if consumers truly do begin to spend time with interactive media, they will have less time to spend with traditional media such as

8.   "CBS Faces Olympics Make-Goods," http://www.adage.com, February 19, 1998.

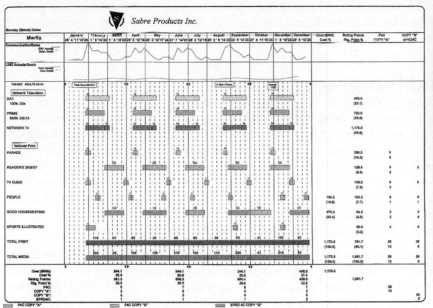

Source: Telmar Information Services Corp., FlowMaster for Windows™, New York, 1999. Reprinted with permission.

EXHIBIT 14.26

A media flowchart gives an advertiser a visual representation of the overall media plan.

EXHIBIT 14.27

An example of a media-buying service. Internet based media-buying services enable media professionals to purchase advertising more efficiently for print, online, and broadcast media. Explore the services and capabilities of Marketron International (http://www .marketron.com) and Advertise123 (http:// www.advertise123.com). How do these Web-based advertising-exchange services increase the efficiency of media scheduling and buying?

EXHIBIT 14.28

This example of point-of-purchase advertising won an award from the Point-of-Purchase Advertising Institute.

EXHIBIT 14.29

Online and interactive media have become popular even among upscale, traditional organizations. http://www.christies.com

television and newspapers. This will force advertisers to choose whether to participate in (or develop their own) interactive media. (Chapter 16 deals exclusively with the Internet, media buying on the Internet, and audience measurement problems.)

5 Media Choice and Integrated Brand Promotions.

A final complicating factor in the media environment is that more firms are adopting an integrated brand promotion perspective, which relies on a broader mix of communication tools. As you know, IBP is the use of various promotional tools, including advertising, in a coordinated manner to build and maintain brand awareness, identity, and preference. Promotional options such as event sponsorship, direct marketing, sales promotion (see Exhibit 14.30), and public relations are drawing many firms away from traditional mass media advertising. But even these new approaches will still require coordination with the advertising that remains. Some of the more significant implications for media planning to achieve IBP are as follows:

- The reliance on mass media will be reduced as more highly targeted media are integrated into media plans. Database marketing programs and more sophisticated single-source data research will produce more tightly focused efforts through direct marketing and interactive media options.
- More precise media impact data, not just media exposure data, will be needed to compare media alternatives. Advertisers will be looking for proof that consumers exposed to a particular medium are buyers, not just prospects.

EXHIBIT 14.30

Sunglass Hut and American Pie 2 *cross-promote.*

- Media planners will need to know much more about a broader range of communication tools: event sponsorship, interactive media, direct marketing, and public relations. They will need to know more about the impact and capabilities of these other forms of promotion to fully integrate communications.
- Central control will be necessary for synergistic, seamless communication. At this point, it is unclear who will provide this central control—the advertiser, the advertising agency, the copywriter, or the media planner. There is some reason to believe that, because of the need for integration and coordination, media planners will emerge as more critically important to the communications process than they have ever been in the past.[9]

6 In Defense of Traditional Advertising. While it is absolutely undeniable that the world of media advertising and promotion has changed a great deal, we would like to throw a bit of cold water (maybe more like a mist) on the media revolution. Traditional advertising, even the "30 Net-TV" (30-second network television) ad and the magazine ad, are not dead. They still perform a very valuable function. There are just some things you can't accomplish without them. Sometimes their unique qualities get lost in the optimized promotional numbers. Brand building still needs traditional ads. Yet the traditional ad world has learned that it can never rest on its laurels, nor can the traditional media. But throwing around planning buzzwords doesn't work either. As Kevin Roberts, CEO of Saatchi and Saatchi, recently said in obvious rebuke of the integrated communication frenzy: "If I hear the words 'touchpoints' or 'holistic' one more time, I'm going to throw up."

The world of media selection is where that revolution will continue to be fought. Stay tuned.

---

9.   Adapted from Sissors and Bumba, *Advertising Media Planning,* 6–7, 51–60.

SUMMARY

 Describe the important changes that have altered the advertising and IBP media landscape.

The demise of the 15% commission means that there is less economic incentive for agencies to buy media advertising. With more media of all sorts of advertising and IBP out there, dollars get spread around a lot more than they used to. Also, due to industry consolidation there are simply fewer places for disgruntled clients to go, thus making agencies more powerful. The consolidated media buying allows agencies to get better deals and exert more power on the media. Still, agencies now operate with fewer staff to do even bigger jobs, thus making the newer and more lucrative types of media more attractive than traditional media. Further, the globalization of media is exerting considerable pressure on the industry to standardize media measurement across the globe, and it is nowhere close to doing so. Also, consumers who are spoiled by free content are less and less interested in obtrusive advertising, thus favoring alternative forms going forward. Further, the increasing deal-proneness and cost transparency provided by the WWW has made consumers considerably more powerful in their ability to get consumer information without having to rely on traditional media advertising. Add to this the incredibly adcluttered state of traditional media, and you can see why nothing in advertising media is sacred, nothing. Further, don't forget the growing influence of ethnic media available across the globe. It's a new world of media out there.

 Describe the fundamentals of media planning.

Although many important changes are taking place in the advertising industry, the components of the media-planning process remain essentially the same. A media plan specifies the media vehicles that will be used to deliver the advertiser's message. Developing a media plan entails setting objectives such as effective reach and frequency and determining strategies to achieve those objectives. Media planners use several quantitative indicators, such as CPM and CPRP, to help them judge the efficiency of prospective media choices. The media-planning process culminates in the scheduling and purchase of a mix of media vehicles expected to deliver the advertiser's message to specific target audiences at precisely the right time to affect their consumption decisions. While media planning is a methodical process, it cannot be reduced to computer decision-making models and statistical measurements; data quality and human and personal factors prohibit media planning from being an exact science.

 Discuss the "real deals" in media planning.

In the real ad and IBP world there is an illusion of precision because of all the numbers used. In reality there is a lot of slop in the media measurement system. Data quality is just not all that great. They are good enough for some purposes, but don't be fooled into thinking numbers equal truth. Not so. Bad measurement is still bad measurement no matter how many computers crunch the data. Also, a lot of real world media planning comes from ads for advertisers. Media planners are the target market of lots of ads for lots of media outlets. And never forget the power of the media lunch: the "free lunch" or cocktail party hosted by your friendly media rep. That's how a lot of media get planned. Truth.

 Discuss the essentials of the contemporary media planning environment.

You should know the particular measurement demands and essential terms of Internet media. You should also know the importance of share-of-voice calculations; they allow you to see, across all kinds of contemporary media, what percent your brand's spending is of the total category, and they provide quick and easy competitive comparisons. You should also understand that standard practice these days involves the uses of computer-media models that optimize media schedules for the most mathematically cost efficient media buy. This should be used as a tool, but not a substitute for media strategy. You should also understand that the growing category of interactive media demands special attention from media planners and will probably make traditional media less important over time. You should also know that more and more media buys are made by a stand-alone media buying company.

Know the bottom line of IBP's impact on media planning.

You should know that there is the very real possibility of a continued decline in advertising's reliance on traditional media. IBP efforts that rely on database efforts are very attractive due to their highly selective targeting and measured response. It's also true that better and better measures of advertising effectiveness will be required with more reliance on IBP. To work in the contemporary ad and IBP environment you will have to know a lot about a much wider array of "media." Further, central control of these far-flung promotional efforts is a must. Things can really get away from you in this new environment.

 Discuss the value of traditional advertising.

You should know that a lot of very smart, creative, and powerful people believe in traditional advertising, and don't see it going away . . . at all, ever.

KEY TERMS

channel power
deal-proneness
price/cost transparency
media plan
media class
media vehicle
media mix
single-source tracking services
geographic scope
geo-targeting
message weight
gross impressions

between-vehicle duplication
within-vehicle duplication
reach
frequency
gross rating points (GRP)
effective frequency
effective reach
continuity
continuous scheduling
flighting
pulsing
"forgetting function"

square-root law
context effects
cost per thousand (CPM)
cost per thousand–target market
 (CPM–TM)
cost per rating point (CPRP)
share of voice
media buying
agency of record
media-buying service
interactive media

QUESTIONS

1.   The opening section of this chapter describes radical changes that have taken place in the world of media planning. Compare and contrast the way things used to be and the way they are now. What factors contributed to this shift? Do you think the job of media planning has become more or less complicated? Explain.

2.   Of all the changes taking place in the in the world of media planning, which do you think will continue to have the greatest impact on the future of the advertising industry?

3.   The proliferation of media options has created increasing complexities for media planners, but useful distinctions can still be made concerning the relative standing of the different choices available to advertisers. What advertising and brand promotion options dominate the "big pie" of total promotion options? Who is doing the most ad spending?

4.   Media plans should of course take a proactive stance with respect to customers. Explain how geo-targeting can be used in making a media plan more proactive with respect to customers.

5.   Media strategy models allow planners to compare the impact of different media plans, using criteria such as reach, frequency, and gross impressions. What other kinds of criteria should a planner take into account before deciding on a final plan?

6.   Review the mathematics of the CPM and CPRP calculations, and explain how these two indicators can be used to assess the efficiency and effectiveness of a media schedule.

7.   Why is data quality becoming an increasingly important issue in real-world media planning?

8.   In the real world, do media planners always make strategic decisions based on sophisticated data, or are there other influences that sway their media-buying decisions? Explain.

9.   Assume that you are advising a regional snack-food manufacturer whose brands have a low share of voice. Which pattern of continuity would you recommend for such an advertiser? Would you place your ads in television programming that is also sponsored by Pringles and Doritos? Why or why not?

10. Discuss the issues raised in this chapter that represent challenges for those who champion integrated brand promotions. Why would central control be required for achieving IBP? If media planners wish to play the role of central controller, what must they do to qualify for the role?

EXPERIENTIAL EXERCISES

1.   Carefully watch one hour of television and record the time length of each advertisement. Using your perceptions about the most and least persuasive ads during this hour of television, develop a hypothesis about the value of long versus short advertising messages. When should an advertiser use long instead of short ads?

2.   Choose two of your favorite magazines or newspapers and visit their Web sites to find information pertaining to ad rates. To do this, search for links on the home pages that say "advertising" or "media kit" (you may have to browse various magazine and newspaper sites until you find this information). Once you locate the advertising information at the site, describe the type of data that is available to potential advertisers and media buyers. List two or three specific examples of data and explain how this information helps media buyers make effective decisions during the media-planning process.

EXPERIENCING THE INTERNET

14-1   Strategies for Promoting Hip Brands

Hi Frequency is a national youth-marketing company that implements custom-built campaigns through a nationwide organization of teams that operate at street level to make a connection to today's media-savvy youth market. The firm's army of hip young reps appear at music stores, skateboarding parks, and shopping malls with a mission to create a buzz over a pop star's latest CD or a designer's new clothing line. By sparking interest in new concepts through guerrilla marketing methods, Hi Frequency has been instrumental in the success of alternative bands such as Radiohead and Limp Bizkit, and continues to be a favorite promotion firm for the entertainment industry.

Hi Frequency Marketing:
http://www.hifrequency.com

1. Describe Hi Frequency's clients, and explain why the firm's campaigns provide some of the most targeted message placement available for these clients.

2. Read about the firm's services at the site. Name three unique methods the company employs to reach influential trendsetters and consumers of youth culture.

3. Briefly define the concept of media efficiency, and explain why there are difficulties in determining the efficiency of the advertising and promotion techniques that are employed by Hi Frequency.

CHAPTER 15

After reading and thinking about this chapter, you will be able to do the following:

1

Detail the pros and cons of newspapers as a media class, identify newspaper categories, and describe buying and audience measurement for newspapers.

2

Detail the pros and cons of magazines as a media class, identify magazine categories, and describe buying and audience measurement for magazines.

3

Detail the pros and cons of television as a media class, identify television categories, and describe buying and audience measurement for television.

4

Detail the pros and cons of radio as a media class, identify radio categories, and describe buying and audience measurement for radio.

Where Are the 18-to-34-Year-Olds?   Thanks, ladies. You've done a great job.

Since the mid-1970s, you've pretty much dominated cable TV viewership and helped cable grow into the powerful media force it is today. Cable companies have catered to you since the very beginning with programming appearing on networks like the History Channel, QVC, and A&E Network. In recent years, new networks like Lifetime, Oxygen, and WE have provided even more female-oriented shows. Sure, the guys have always had MTV and ESPN, but that was about it—until now. Cable executives are in a mad dash to try to capture the lucrative—and illusive—18-to-34-year-old male market. It turns out that males 18–34 are the smallest audience watching prime time TV of any kind (cable or network) behind teenagers. What's worse for advertisers is that when you ask young men where they first hear about brands they are likely to buy, only 51 percent cite television versus 70 percent of young women.[1]

But this aversion to television is about to change if cable programmers have their way. A new wave of cable channels directly targeted at the 18-to-34-year-olds is being launched. Most prominent among these is Spike TV, dubbed "The First Network for Men." Spike TV features spy movies, extreme sports shows, and adult-themed cartoons, as well as reruns of "guy" shows like *Star Trek* and *CSI*. The focus on this group of men is key for advertisers because 18–34 are considered the "free spending" years for men. Albie Hecht, president of Spike TV, is planning a programming line-up that will help advertisers attract and keep this key market segment. In Hecht's words, "We want to be a real home base for young men from fashion to finance."[2] It would seem he has every opportunity to succeed. Spike TV is taking over the old TNN channel distribution and that reaches about 90 million households. By late 2004, the initial response to the new network was very strong, with 38 new advertisers putting up over $40 million in additional advertising media buys versus the old TNN line-up (see Exhibit 15.1).

But Spike TV is by no means the only nonsports male-oriented channel in the works for the younger male market. *Maxim* and *Men's Health* magazines are experimenting with programming with an eye toward launching networks of their own. Bravo cable network, long recognized as the home for opera, ballet, and other programming most young males wouldn't be caught dead watching, is reaching out to the 18-to-34-year-old segment as well. While Bravo is already considered a solid success with 70 million subscribers, the president of Bravo is determined to "stretch" the network's genre and significantly expand viewership. The first step in that direction, "Queer Eye for the Straight Guy," in which gay men help fashion-challenged straight guys remodel their apartments (and their lives), has been a huge success. Bravo increased its 25–45 audience 13 percent during prime time in just one year.[3] Of course increases in viewership always attract more advertisers, and for Bravo that has meant new advertisers like eBay, Citibank, Moen, and TD Waterhouse.

The beauty of cable TV is reflected in this pursuit of young men by cable networks. Cable is a medium through which programmers and advertisers can reach very well-defined segments of consumers. From the serious news programming that appears on CNN and CNBC through children's programming on Nickelodeon to the extreme sports programming on pay-per-view, cable can home in on very well-defined segments of consumers.

But cable and, indeed, television do not nearly tell the whole story of media and its role in advertising and promotion. Simply stated, without media there is no advertising and there would be very little promotion. Media carry the messages and the appeals that let consumers know the excitement and value of brands. And the

---

1.   Tom Lowry, "Young Man, Your Couch is Calling," *BusinessWeek,* July 28, 2003, 68.
2.   Ibid.
3.   Daisy Whitney, "Bravo Stretches, Adds Viewers & Advertisers," *Advertising Age,* June 9, 2003, S14.

EXHIBIT 15.1

A wide range of advertisers are interested in reaching the 18-to-34-year-old male segment of consumers. Young men in this age category are said to be in their "free spending" years. Cable television is an ideal medium to reach this age group with programming on cable networks like Spike TV. http://www.spiketv .com

features and capabilities of various media enhance and expand the power of these messages and appeals. This chapter offers a survey and evaluation of the wide range of media options available to advertisers from the far-reaching broadcast media to the highly targeted print and radio options.

Which Media? Strategic Planning Considerations. Media

decisions made by advertisers are critically important for two reasons. First, advertisers need media advertisers to reach the audiences that are likely to buy the advertiser's brand. Not much of a mystery there. Second, when advertisers choose their media, then these choices ultimately determine which media companies earn the billions of dollars spent on newspaper magazine, television/cable, and radio advertising slots. This chapter focuses on the challenge advertisers face in evaluating these major print and broadcast media options as key ways to reach their audiences. As the discussion of media planning in the previous chapter emphasized, even great advertising can't achieve communications and sales objectives if the media placement misses the target audience.

Our discussion of print, television, and radio media will concentrate on several key aspects of using these major media. With respect to the print media—newspapers and magazines—we'll first consider the advantages and disadvantages of the media themselves. Both newspapers and magazines have inherent capabilities and limitations that advertisers must take into consideration in building a media plan. Next, we'll look at the types of newspapers and magazines from which advertisers can choose. Finally, we will identify buying procedures and audience measurement techniques.

After we look at the print media, we will consider television and radio. First, the types of television and radio options are described. Next, the advantages and disadvantages of television and radio are examined. The buying procedures and audience measurement techniques are identified. Finally, the future of television and radio in the context of new Internet, satellite, and broadband technology is considered.

Print, television, and radio media represent major alternatives available to advertisers for reaching audiences. While much has been said—and more will be said in the following chapters—about increased spending on new media, about 50 percent of all advertising dollars in the United States still go to traditional print, radio, and television media.[4] In addition, the vast majority of the creative effort—and money— is expended on print and broadcast advertising campaigns. Despite the many intriguing opportunities that new media offer, print and broadcast media will likely form the foundation of most advertising campaigns for years to come. The discussions in this chapter will demonstrate why these media represent such rich communication alternatives for advertisers.

Print Media. You might think that the print media—newspapers and magazines—are lifeless lumps and lack impact compared to dynamic broadcast media options like Spike TV. Think

again. Consider the problems that faced Absolut vodka. In 1980, Absolut was on the verge of extinction. The Swedish brand was selling only 12,000 cases a year in the United States—not enough to even register a single percentage point of market share. The name Absolut was seen as gimmicky; bartenders thought the bottle was ugly and hard to pour from; and to top things off, consumers gave no credibility at all to a vodka produced in Sweden, which they knew as the land of boxy-looking cars and hot tubs.

ETHICS

Audience-Size Inflation

Recently, numerous newspapers have admitted they artificially pumped up circulation figures. The *Dallas Morning News* and *Chicago-Sun Times* both admitted they had inflated circulation. Advertising rates for print media are closely tied to circulation figures. In order to justify their advertising rates, newspaper publishers need to document their readership. The scandals come at a time when U.S. newspapers are emerging from a long advertising slump. As noted in the text, in order to survive, newspapers will have to evolve with the demands of consumers and advertisers. In addition, to attract advertisers, publishers of newspapers will have to demonstrate they can measure the size of their audience more accurately. Like newspapers, most magazines rely on advertising revenues to support their operations. But publishers recognize that newspaper and magazine circulation does not equal readership, since a single copy of a paper or magazine in circulation may be read by many different people. Therefore, publishers use consumer surveys to document the quantity of their readers.

There have been many studies on the appropriate method for measuring magazine and newspaper readership. One common approach is a two-step process. In the first step, consumers are asked if they have ever read the publication. Those who answer "yes" are asked when they last read the publication. A reader is then defined as someone who has read the publication within the publication period (e.g., within the past seven days for a weekly; within the past month for a monthly). The two-step process is needed because research demonstrates that with only the second question, readership numbers become significantly inflated.

- Should circulation numbers for magazine and newspapers be audited? Why or why not?
- Whose responsibility is it to make sure of the numbers? Should the buyer beware?
- Should we just assume that these numbers are a little inflated and live with it?
- Why does it matter?
- Who gets hurt?

The TBWA advertising agency in New York set about the task of overcoming these liabilities of the brand and decided to rely on print advertising *alone*—primarily because spirits ads were banned from broadcast at the time. The agency took on the challenge of developing magazine and newspaper ads that would build awareness, communicate quality, achieve credibility, and avoid Swedish clichés etched in the minds of American consumers. The firm came up with one of the most famous and successful print campaigns of all time. The concept was to feature the strange-shaped Absolut bottle as the hero of each ad, in which the only copy was a two-word tag line always beginning with *Absolut* and ending with a "quality" word such as *perfection* or *clarity*. The two-word description evolved from the original quality concept to a variety of clever combinations. "Absolut Centerfold" appeared in *Playboy* and featured an Absolut bottle with all the printing removed, and "Absolut Wonderland" was a Christmas-season ad with the bottle in a snow globe like the ones that feature snowy Christmas scenes.

In the end, the Absolut campaign was not only a creative masterpiece but also a resounding market success. Absolut has become one of the leading imported vodkas in the United States. The vodka with no credibility and the ugly bottle has become sophisticated and fashionable with a well-conceived and well-placed print campaign.[5] To this day, the Absolut brand still relies heavily on magazine advertising in the IBP mix with continued success.

 **Newspapers.** The newspaper is the still the medium that is most accessible to the widest range of advertisers. Advertisers big and small—even you and I when we want to sell that old bike or snowboard—can use newspaper advertising. In fact, investment in news-

5.   Historical information about the *Absolut* vodka campaign was adapted from information in Nicholas Ind, "Absolut Vodka in the U.S.," in *Great Advertising Campaigns* (Lincolnwood, Ill.: NTC Business Books, 1993), 15–32.

Top 10 newspaper advertisers (U.S. dollars in millions).

Rank	Advertiser	National Newspaper Ad Spending		
		2003	**2002**	**% Change**
1	Verizon	$513.9	$376.9	36.3
2	ATT Wireless	510.4	419.4	21.7
3	Federated Dept. Stores	493.7	521.3	−5.3
4	Sprint	477.0	271.6	75.6
5	SBC Comm.	441.7	309.9	42.5
6	May Dept. Stores	440.3	459.1	−4.1
7	Time Warner	381.0	316.7	20.3
8	Walt Disney	313.0	250.7	24.8
9	General Motors	274.3	228.3	20.1
10	Daimler/Chrysler	264.9	141.1	87.7

Source: *Advertising Age*, June 18, 2004, S-20.

paper advertising reached $48.2 billion in 2004—second only to direct mail in attracting advertising dollars.[6] Exhibit 15.2 shows the top 10 advertisers in newspapers. Several national newspapers reach primarily business audiences. Newspapers are, of course, ideally suited to reaching a narrow geographic area—precisely the type of audience retailers want to reach.

There are some sad truths, however, about the current status of newspapers as a medium. Since the 1980s, newspapers across the United States have been suffering circulation declines, and the trend has continued into the 21st century. What may be worse is that the percentage of adults reading daily newspapers is also declining. About 58 percent of adults in the United States read a daily newspaper, compared with about 78 percent in 1970.[7] Much of the decline in both circulation and readership comes from the fact that both morning and evening newspapers have been losing patronage to television news programs. While shows such as *Good Morning America* and *Fox Nightly News* cannot provide the breadth of coverage that newspapers can, they still offer news, and they offer it in a lively multisensory format.

Advantages of Newspapers. Newspapers may have lost some of their luster over the past two decades, but they do reach more than 50 percent of U.S. households, representing about 150 million adults. And, as mentioned earlier, the newspaper is still an excellent medium for retailers targeting local geographic markets. But broad reach isn't the only attractive feature of newspapers as a medium. Newspapers offer other advantages to advertisers:

- *Geographic selectivity.* Daily newspapers in cities and towns across the United States offer advertisers the opportunity to reach a well-defined geographic target audience. Some newspapers are beginning to run zoned editions, which target even more narrow geographic areas within a metropolitan market. Zoned editions are typically used by merchants doing business in the local area; national marketers such as Kellogg and Colgate can use the paper carrier to deliver free samples to these zoned areas.
- *Timeliness.* The newspaper is one of the most timely of the major media. Because of the short time needed for producing a typical newspaper ad and the regularity

---

6.   "Marketing Fact Book 2004 Edition," *Marketing News,* June 15, 2004, 14.
7.   Data on newspaper readership is available at the Newspaper Association of America Web site, http://www.naa.org. Data cited here were drawn from that site accessed on April 25, 2004.

The newspaper medium offers a large format for advertisers. This is important when an advertiser needs space to provide the target audience with extensive information, as Tire America has done with this ad featuring tire sizes and prices.

of daily publication, the newspaper allows advertisers to reach audiences in a timely way. This doesn't mean on just a daily basis. Newspaper ads can take advantage of special events or a unique occurrence in a community.

- *Creative opportunities.* While the newspaper page does not offer the breadth of creative options available in the broadcast media, there are things advertisers can do in a newspaper that represent important creative opportunities. Since the newspaper page offers a large and relatively inexpensive format, advertisers can provide a lot of information to the target audience at relatively low cost. This is important for products or services with extensive or complex features that may need lengthy and detailed copy. The Tire America ad in Exhibit 15.3 needs just such a large format to provide detail about tire sizes and prices.

- *Credibility.* Newspapers still benefit from the perception that "if it's in the paper it must be the truth." This credibility element played a key role in the decision by Glaxo Wellcome and SmithKline Beecham to announce their megamerger (creating the $73 billion GlaxoSmithKline corporation) using newspapers.[8]

- *Audience interest.* Newspaper readers are truly interested in the information they are reading. While overall readership may be down in the United States, those readers that remain are loyal and interested. Many readers buy the newspaper specifically to see what's on sale at stores in the local area, making this an ideal environment for local merchants. And newspapers are the primary medium for local classified advertising despite an early concern that the Internet would cut deeply into classified revenue, as the IBP box on page 528 suggests.

- *Cost.* In terms of both production and space, newspapers offer a low-cost alternative to advertisers. The cost per contact may be higher than with television and radio options, but the absolute cost for placing a black-and-white ad is still within reach of even a small advertising budget.

Disadvantages of Newspapers. Newspapers offer advertisers many good opportunities. Like every other media option, however, newspapers have some significant disadvantages.

- *Limited segmentation.* While newspapers can achieve good geographic selectivity, the ability to target a specific audience ends there. Newspaper circulation simply cuts across too broad an economic, social, and demographic audience to allow the isolation of specific targets. The placement of ads within certain sections can achieve minimal targeting by gender, but even this effort is somewhat fruitless. Some newspapers are developing special sections to enhance their segmentation capabilities (see Exhibit 15.4). Many papers are developing sections on e-business and film reviews to target specific audiences.[9] In addition, more and more newspapers are being published to serve specific ethnic groups, which is another form of segmentation. The industry feels it has made great progress in this regard and is approaching advertisers with the argument that newspaper advertising, if purchased strategically, can rival the targeting capability of magazines.[10]

- *Creative constraints.* The opportunities for creative executions in newspapers are certainly outweighed by the creative constraints. First, newspapers have poor reproduction quality. Led by *USA Today,* most newspapers now print some of their pages in color. But even the color reproduction does not enhance the look of most products in advertisements. For advertisers whose brand images depend on accurate, high-quality reproduction (color or not), newspapers simply have severe limitations compared to other media options. Second, newspapers are a unidimensional medium—no sound, no action. For brands that demand a broad creative execution, this medium is often not the best choice.
- *Cluttered environment.* The average newspaper is filled with headlines, subheads, photos, and announcements—not to mention the news stories. This presents a terribly cluttered environment for an advertisement. To make things worse, most advertisers in a product category try to use the same sections to target audiences. For example, all the home equity loan and financial services ads are in the business section, and all the women's clothing ads are in the metro, or local, section.
- *Short life.* In most U.S. households, newspapers are read quickly and then discarded (or, hopefully, stacked in the recycling pile). The only way advertisers can overcome this limitation is to buy several insertions in each daily issue, buy space several times during the week, or both. In this way, even if a reader doesn't spend much time with the newspaper, at least multiple exposures are a possibility.

The newspaper has creative limitations, but what the average newspaper does, it does well. If an advertiser wants to reach a local audience with a simple black-and-white ad in a timely manner, then the newspaper is the superior choice.

Many newspapers are trying to increase their target selectivity by developing special sections for advertisers, such as a NASCAR section for race fans.

9.   Jon Fine, "Tribune Seeks National Ads with 3 New Special Sections," *Advertising Age,* October 9, 2000, 42.
10.   Jon Fine, "Papers' Ad Group Goes on Offensive," *Advertising Age,* February 9, 2004, 6.

Categories of Newspapers. All newspapers enjoy the same advantages and suffer from the same limitations to one degree or another. But there are different types of newspapers from which advertisers can choose. Newspapers are categorized by target audience, geographic coverage, and frequency of publication.

- *Target audience.* Newspapers can be classified by the target audience they reach. The five primary types of newspapers serving different target audiences are general-population newspapers, business newspapers, ethnic newspapers, gay and lesbian newspapers, and the alternative press. **General-population newspapers** serve local communities and report news of interest to the local population. Newspapers such as the *Kansas City Star,* the *Dayton Daily News,* and the *Columbus Dispatch* are examples. **Business newspapers** such as the *Wall Street Journal, Investor's Business Daily* (United States), and the *Financial Times* (United Kingdom) serve a specialized business audience. **Ethnic newspapers** that target specific ethnic groups are growing in popularity. Most of these newspapers are published weekly. The *New York Amsterdam News* and the *Michigan Chronicle* are two of the more than 200 newspapers in the United States that serve African-American communities. The Hispanic community in the United States has more than 300 newspapers. One of the most prominent is *El Diario de las Americas* in Miami. **Gay and lesbian newspapers** exist in most major (and many smaller) markets. Readership typically extends considerably beyond gay and lesbian readers. So-called **alternative press newspapers,** such as *L.A. Weekly* (http://www.laweekly.com), the *Austin Chronicle* (http://www.austinchronicle.com), and *Gambit Weekly* (http://www.bestofneworleans.com), are very viable vehicles for reaching typically young and entertainment-oriented audiences.

- *Geographic coverage.* As noted earlier, the vast majority of newspapers are distributed in a relatively small geographic area—either a large metropolitan area or a state. Newspapers such as the *Tulsa World* and the *Atlanta Journal-Constitution,* with circulations of 170,000 and 400,000, respectively, serve a local geographic area. The other type of newspaper in the United States is a national newspaper. *USA Today* and the *Wall Street Journal* were,

---

IBP

Myth: The Web Will Dominate Classified Advertising. Reality: Newspapers Don't Have to Worry—They're Going Digital, Too.

Classified advertising is the lifeblood of local newspapers. It often represents 30 to 40 percent of a newspaper's total revenues. Currently, classifieds bring in about $16.0 billion a year, according to the Newspaper Association of America.

It is no wonder that when big portals like Yahoo!, Microsoft, and America Online began creating local sites to compete with newspapers, there was serious concern that Web-based classifieds would seriously cut into newspaper revenues. After all, wasn't the Web a better and more accessible venue for classified ads? A consumer-seller could submit a photo of the house or the bike or the dog that was for sale. This is a much enhanced presentation over the itty-bitty box with the three terse lines of description. Similarly, the consumer-buyer could come to the classified advertising environment anytime—no need to trek out onto the lawn to grab the paper that never quite seems to make it to the front porch. It seemed like such a much better idea than newspaper-based classifieds that dot.com companies such as Monster.com (help wanted/employees available) and autobytel.com (automobile classifieds) were attracting outside investors and establishing a foothold online by offering classified ads free of charge supported by banner ads. How could newspapers ever compete with a better presentation format *and* free advertising space?

Well, there are a few reality checks in order. First, while classified advertising is down a bit over the past couple of years (and that probably has to more with circulation than with Web competition), the prospect of the Web swallowing up all the classified advertising dollars never turned into a reality. Second, local newspapers have combated the Web attack by providing their own localized version of ads on the Internet. Third, the really big newspaper chains like Knight Ridder and newspapers like the *Washington Post* are investing in online social networks like Friendster, MeetUp, and Tribe. These online venues reach local audiences but in a networking context rather than with merely a classified ad.

Sources: Dan Mitchell, "Hello Webmaster—Get Me a Rewrite," *Business 2.0,* March 6, 2001, 42; Tobi Elkin, "Newspaper Giants Buy into Tribe," *Advertising Age,* December 8, 2003, 36.

Sunday supplements such as Parade (http://www.parade .com) and USA Weekend (http://www.usaweekend .com) offer advertisers another alternative for placing newspaper ads. How do these differ from alternative press weeklies such as the Village Voice (http://www.village voice.com)? Does USA Weekend's Web site offer any features that attract repeat visits from readers, thus increasing the life of the weekly publication?

from their inception, designed to be distributed nationally, and have a circulation of about 2.2 million and 1.8 million respectively. The *New York Times* and the *Los Angeles Times,* each with a circulation of about 1.0 million, have evolved into national newspapers.[11]

- *Frequency of publication.* The majority of newspapers in the United States are called *dailies* because they are published each day of the week, including Sunday. There are a smaller number of *weeklies,* and these tend to serve smaller towns or rural communities. Finally, another alternative for advertisers is the Sunday supplement, which is published only on Sunday and is usually delivered along with the Sunday edition of a local newspaper. The most widely distributed Sunday supplements—*Parade* magazine and *USA Weekend*—are illustrated in Exhibit 15.5.

Categories of Newspaper Advertising. Just as there are categories of newspapers, there are categories of newspaper advertising: display advertising, inserts, and classified advertising.

Retailers who feature a particular brand can receive co-op advertising money for media placement. http:// www.ebel.com

- *Display advertising.* Advertisers of goods and services rely most on display advertising. **Display advertising** in newspapers includes the standard components of a print ad—headline, body copy, and often an illustration—to set it off from the news content of the paper. An important form of display advertising is co-op advertising sponsored by manufacturers. In **co-op advertising,** a manufacturer pays part of the media bill when a local merchant features the manufacturer's brand in advertising. Co-op advertising can be done on a national scale as well. (See Exhibit 15.6.) Intel invests heavily in co-op advertising with computer manufacturers who feature the "Intel Inside" logo in their print ads.

- *Inserts.* There are two types of insert advertisements. Inserts do not appear on the printed newspaper page but rather are folded into the newspaper before distribution. An advertiser can use a **preprinted insert,** which is an advertisement delivered to the newspaper fully printed and ready for insertion into the newspaper

11.   Lisa Singhania, "Newspaper Circulation Holds Steady," *Editor & Publisher,* available at http://www.editorandpublisher.com, accessed on April 26, 2004.

EXHIBIT 15.7

This example of a free-standing insert (FSI) from Pizza Hut shows how an ad can be delivered via a newspaper distribution system without having to become part of the paper itself. What are the production and attention-getting advantages that this insert provides?
http://www.pizzahut.com

The second type of insert ad is a **free-standing insert (FSI),** which contains cents-off coupons for a variety of products and is typically delivered with Sunday newspapers. The Pizza Hut ad in Exhibit 15.7 is part of a free-standing insert.

• *Classified advertising.* **Classified advertising** is newspaper advertising that appears as all-copy messages under categories such as sporting goods, employment, and automobiles. Many classified ads are taken out by individuals, but real estate firms, automobile dealers, and construction firms also buy classified advertising.

Costs and Buying Procedures for Newspaper Advertising. When an advertiser wishes to place advertising in a newspaper, the first step is to obtain a rate card from the newspaper. A **rate card** contains information on costs, closing times (when ads have to be submitted), specifications for submitting an ad, and special pages or features available in the newspaper. The rate card also summarizes the circulation for the designated market area and any circulation outside the designated area.

The cost of a newspaper ad depends on how large the advertisement is, whether it is black-and-white or color, how large the total audience is, and whether the newspaper has local or national coverage. Advertising space is sold in newspapers by the **column inch,** which is a unit of space one inch deep by one column wide. Each column is $2^1/_{16}$ inches wide. Most newspapers have adopted the **standard advertising unit (SAU)** system for selling ad space, which defines unit sizes for advertisements. There are 57 defined SAU sizes for advertisements in the system, so that advertisers can prepare ads to fit one of the sizes. Many newspapers offer a volume discount to advertisers who buy more than one ad in an issue or buy multiple ads over some time period.

When an advertiser buys space on a **run-of-paper (ROP)** basis, which is also referred to as a *run-of-press basis,* the ad may appear anywhere, on any page in the paper. A higher rate is charged for **preferred position,** in which the ad is placed in a specific section of the paper. **Full position** places an ad near the top of a page or in the middle of editorial material.

Measuring Newspaper Audiences. There are several different dimensions to measuring newspaper audiences. The reach of a newspaper is reported as the newspaper's circulation. **Circulation** is the number of newspapers distributed each day (for daily newspapers) or each week (for weekly publications). **Paid circulation** reports the number of copies sold through subscriptions and newsstand distribution. **Controlled circulation** refers to the number of copies of the newspaper that are given away free. The Audit Bureau of Circulations (ABC) is an independent organization that verifies the actual circulation of newspapers.

Rates for newspaper advertising are not based solely on circulation numbers, however. The Newspaper Association of America estimates that about 2.2 people read each copy of a daily newspaper distributed in the United States. **Readership** of a newspaper is a measure of the circulation multiplied by the number of readers of a copy. This number, of course, is much higher than the circulation number and provides a total audience figure on which advertisers base advertising rates. To give

Nothing attracts online shoppers to your website like newspapers.

Newspapers can help your website achieve the critical mass it needs to drive your business. According to a recent study, daily newspapers reached over 59% of those who had made a purchase on the Internet within the previous 30 days.* No other medium delivers this amount of traffic with greater velocity. So if you're looking for shoppers you'll find them browsing through newspapers. For more information call the number below. **Nobody delivers the paper like we do.**

newspaper national network*

Call Jack Grandcolas, VP of High Tech advertising, at 415-454-9168 or e-mail granj@nnn-naa.com

The future of newspapers will be greatly enhanced if the medium adapts to the demands of a new media environment and particularly if newspapers can become part of the integrated brand promotion process that includes new media. This ad touts just such a role for newspapers in IBP. http://www.nnn-naa.com

you some idea of costs, a full-page four-color ad in *USA Today* costs about $100,000, and a full-page black-and-white ad in the *Wall Street Journal* costs about $175,000. A full-page ad in your local newspaper is, of course, considerably less—probably around $10,000 to $15,000 for a good-sized city and much less for small-town newspapers. Remember, though, that few advertisers, national or local, purchase an entire page.

The Future of Newspapers. At the outset of this chapter, we talked about the fact that newspaper circulation has been in a long, sustained downward trend, and that readership is following the same pattern. To survive as a viable advertising medium, newspapers will have to evolve with the demands of both audiences and advertisers, who provide them with the majority of their revenue. Primarily, newspapers will have to exploit their role as a source for local news—something new media like the Web cannot do effectively. To compete in the future as a viable advertising medium, newspapers will have to do the following:

- Continue to provide in-depth coverage of issues that focus on the local community.
- Increase coverage of national and international news.
- Provide follow-up reports of news stories.
- Maintain and expand their role as the best local source for consumers to find specific information on advertised product features, availability, and prices.
- Provide the option of shopping through an online newspaper computer service.
- Offer new options to readers using new media such as online "classified" auctions similar to e-Bay.
- Become more mainstream in integrated brand promotions particularly relating to new media (see Exhibit 15.8).

② Magazines. The marketing director for Schwinn Cycling & Fitness wanted to resurrect the company's bicycle division. Schwinn had been pummeled by worthy competitors such as Trek and Specialized, and he felt certain that one of the underlying problems was that the image of the Schwinn brand was outdated. To begin solving this image problem, the marketing director first instructed the firm's advertising agency to develop a $10 million magazine campaign. One of Schwinn's ads from this campaign is shown in Exhibit 15.9. The ads were placed in specialty biking magazines and were aimed at mountain-biking and race-biking enthusiasts. Schwinn created an integrated brand promotion supporting the magazine campaign with event sponsorships and interactive mall kiosks. While Schwinn is still behind the leaders in the U.S. bike market, sales climbed 18.4 percent during the restructured IBP period that featured magazine ads.

Schwinn's emphasis on magazine advertising was part of an effort to upgrade the brand image and turned out to be an excellent strategic decision. Magazines, more than any other media option, provide advertisers with a choice of highly selective alternatives that offer a wide variety of formats and contexts. Magazines are a highly valued media choice with advertisers spending over $32.4 billion for advertising

EXHIBIT 15.10

Top 10 magazines by circulation for 2003.

Rank	Publication	Circulation	% Change
1	AARP The Magazine	20,018,227	14.1
2	Reader's Digest	11,090,349	−9.2
3	TV Guide	9,026,852	−0.5
4	Better Homes & Gardens	7,611,005	0.1
5	National Geographic	6,685,685	−3.0
6	Good Housekeeping	4,603,989	−2.2
7	Family Circle	4,578,589	−2.0
8	My Generation	4,269,163	11.0
9	Ladies' Home Journal	4,100,068	0.0
10	Time	4,095,935	−0.4

Source: FactPack 2004, Advertising Age, 36.

space in the top 300 magazines annually.[12] The top 10 magazines in the United States, based on circulation, are listed in Exhibit 15.10. This list suggests the diversity of magazines as a media class. Exhibit 15.11 shows the top 10 advertisers in magazines.

Like newspapers, magazines have advantages and disadvantages, come in different types, offer various ad costs and buying procedures, and measure their audiences in specific ways. We will consider these issues now.

Advantages of Magazines. Magazines have many advantages relative to newspapers. These advantages make them more than just an ideal print medium—many analysts conclude that magazines are, in many ways, superior to even broadcast media alternatives.

12.   R. Craig Endicott, "Top 300 Revenue a Record $32.5 Billion," *Advertising Age,* September 24, 2004, S2.

Top 10 magazine advertisers for 2003 (U.S. dollars in millions).

Rank	Advertiser	Magazine Ad Spending		
		2003	2002	% Change
1	Procter & Gamble	$582.3	$499.0	16.7
2	General Motors	453.8	394.4	15.0
3	Altria	367.8	383.6	–4.1
4	Johnson & Johnson	306.9	257.2	19.3
5	Daimler/Chrysler	299.0	268.3	11.4
6	Ford Motor Co.	278.4	258.1	7.9
7	Time Warner	273.1	268.8	1.6
8	L'Oreal	271.7	250.2	8.6
9	Toyota	253.9	223.0	13.9
10	Pfizer	212.8	153.7	38.5

Source: Advertising Age, June 28, 2004, S-20

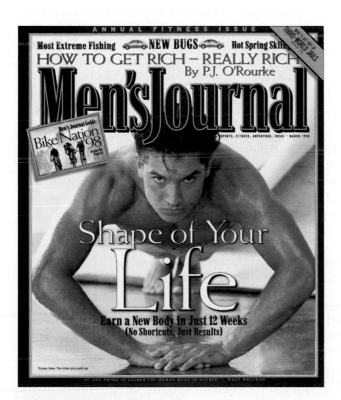

One distinct advantage of magazines over most other media options is the ability to attract and target a highly selective audience. Magazines such as Men's Journal attract an audience based on special interests and activities—in this case, readers interested in health issues and exercise.

- *Audience selectivity.* The overwhelming advantage of magazines relative to other media—print or broadcast—is the ability of magazines to attract, and therefore target, a highly selective audience. This selectivity can be based on demographics *(Woman's Day),* lifestyle *(Muscle & Fitness),* or special interests *(Men's Journal),* as shown in Exhibit 15.12. The audience segment can be narrowly defined, as is the one that reads *Modern Bride,* or it may cut across a variety of interests, as does the one for *Newsweek.* Magazines also offer geographic selectivity on a regional basis, as does *Southern Living,* or city magazines, such as *Atlanta,* which highlight happenings in major metropolitan areas. Also, large national publications have multiple editions for advertisers to choose from. *Better Homes & Gardens* has 85 different specific market editions, and *Time* offers advertisers a different edition for each of the 50 states.

- *Audience interest.* Perhaps more than any other medium, magazines attract an audience because of content. While television programming can attract audiences through interest as well, magazines have the additional advantage of voluntary exposure to the advertising. Golfers are interested in golf equipment like that shown in Exhibit 15.13 and advertised in *Golf Digest,* while auto enthusiasts find the auto accessory equipment advertised in *Car and Driver* appealing.

- *Creative opportunities.* Magazines offer a wide range of creative opportunities. Because of the ability to vary the size of an ad, use color, use white space, and play off the special interests of

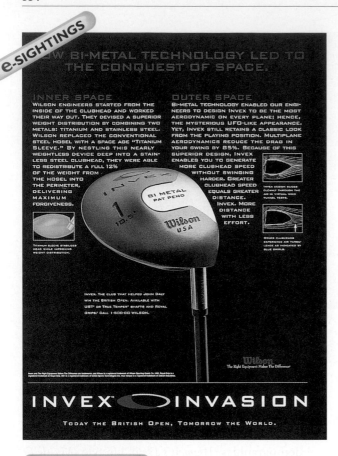

EXHIBIT 15.13

Magazines can attract readers with specialized content, and in so doing, they attract advertisers. This ad by Wilson (http://www.wilson sports.com) appeared in Golf Digest. *Does* Golf Digest*'s site (http://www. golfdigest.com) follow the same monthly publication cycle as the magazine? Do advertisers benefit from the digital versions of popular magazines? What useful interactive features does* Golf Digest *offer to golf enthusiasts? What does the magazine hope to accomplish with such interactive site features?*

the audience, magazines represent a favorable creative environment. Also, because the paper quality of most magazines is quite high, color reproduction can be outstanding—another creative opportunity.

These factors are precisely why Infiniti invests nearly $60 million annually in magazines. A case in point was when the firm introduced its full size QX56 SUV. Magazines offered the perfect combination of audience selectivity and high-quality visual presentation to effectively advertise the brand.[13] In an attempt to expand the creative environment even further, some advertisers have tried various other creative techniques: pop-up ads, scratch-and-sniff ads, ads with perfume scent strips, and even ads with small computer chips that have flashing lights and play music. The Clarins ad in Exhibit 15.14 shows how an advertiser can take advantage of the creative opportunities offered by magazines.

- *Long life.* Many magazines are saved issue-to-issue by their subscribers. This means that, unlike newspapers, a magazine can be reexamined over a week or a month. Some magazines are saved for long periods for future reference, such as *Architectural Digest, National Geographic,* and *Travel & Leisure.* In addition to multiple subscriber exposure, this long life increases the chance of pass-along readership as people visit the subscriber's home (or professional offices) and look at magazines.

Many magazines are experiencing some difficulty in growing both circulation and revenue. Business magazines in general have suffered from poor business conditions and a sporadic investment environment. Conversely, specialty magazines with narrow target audiences, such as *Maxim* and *Car and Driver,* have recently shown solid gains in circulation of up to 20 percent.[14] It would appear that the main advantage of magazines—their appeal to a selective audience—is translating into market success.

Disadvantages of Magazines. The disadvantages of magazines as a media choice have to do with their being too selective in their reach and with the recent proliferation of magazines.

- *Limited reach and frequency.* The tremendous advantage of selectivity discussed in the previous section actually creates a limitation for magazines. The more narrowly defined the interest group, the less overall reach a magazine will have.

Since most magazines are published monthly or perhaps every two weeks, there is little chance for an advertiser to achieve frequent exposure using a single magazine. To overcome this limitation, advertisers often use several magazines targeted at the same audience. For example, many readers of *Better Homes & Gardens* may also be readers of *Architectural Digest.* By placing ads in both publications, an advertiser can increase both reach and frequency within a targeted audience.

13. Jean Halliday, "Auto Industry Pushes Print's Creative Limits," *Advertising Age,* March 8, 2004, 4.
14. Ibid.

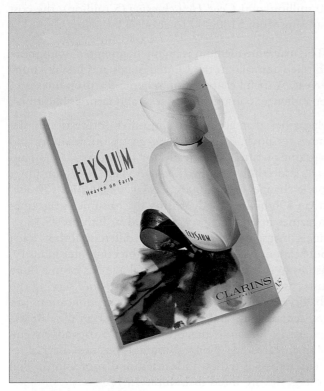

Magazines offer unique creative opportunities to advertisers. Perfume marketers such as Clarins include scent strips in the magazine ads for consumers to sample.

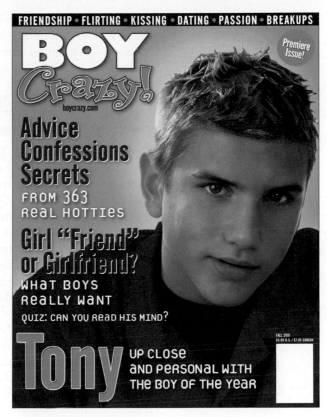

In the consumer magazine category, publishers try to appeal to target audiences' special interests. Boy Crazy! is one of many titles targeted to teenagers.

- **Clutter.** Magazines are not quite as cluttered as newspapers, but they still represent a fairly difficult context for message delivery. The average magazine is about half editorial and entertainment content and half advertising material, but some highly specialized magazines, like *Bride*, can have as much as 80 percent of their pages devoted to advertising. And given the narrowly defined audiences, this advertising tends to be for brands in direct competition with each other. In addition to this clutter, there is another sort of clutter that has recently begun to plague magazines. As soon as a new market segment is recognized, there is a flood of "me too" magazines. The teen magazine market suffered precisely this problem from 2000 to 2005. Traditional titles like *Seventeen* and *YM* suddenly found themselves amid a glut of teen girl magazines including *Teen, Teen People, Teen Vogue, Cosmo Girl, Elle Girl,* and *Boy Crazy!*. (See Exhibit 15.15.) This may be good in terms of coverage, but it may devalue individual ads, and the magazines in which they appear may reach fewer consumers than the advertiser expected.[15]

- **Long lead times.** Advertisers are required to submit their ads as much as 90 days in advance of the date of publication. If the submission date is missed, there can be as much as a full month's delay in placing the next ad. And once an ad is submitted, it cannot be changed during that 90-day period, even if some significant event alters the communications environment.

- **Cost.** While the cost per contact in magazines is not nearly as high as in some media (direct mail in particular), it is more expensive than most newspaper space, and many times the cost per contact in the broadcast media. The absolute cost

15. Jon Fine, "Teen Title Crush Leads to Circ Cuts," *Advertising Age,* July 7, 2003, 21.

for a single insertion can be prohibitive. For magazines with large circulations, such as *Modern Maturity* (20 million) and *Good Housekeeping* (5 million), the cost for a one-time four-color ad runs from $100,000 to about $250,000.

Categories of Magazines. The magazine medium is highly fragmented, with more than 12,000 magazine titles published annually in the United States and literally hundreds of titles introduced every year. A useful classification scheme for magazines is to categorize them by major target audience: consumer, business, and farm publications.

- *Consumer publications.* Magazines that appeal to consumer interests run the gamut from international news to sports, education, age-group information, and hobbies. These include magazines written specifically for men (like *Men's Journal*), women (*Woman's Day*), and ethnic groups (*Ebony*). Many new consumer magazines appeal to the lifestyle changes of the 2000s: *Cooking Light, Men's Health.* Advertisers invested more than $26 billion in advertising in consumer magazines in 2002.[16] The top five magazines in this category are listed in Exhibit 15.16.
- *Business publications.* Business magazines come in many different forms. Each major industry has a trade publication, such as *PC World* in the computer industry, that highlights events and issues in that industry. The digital age has been a huge boon to the magazine industry with dozens of new titles, like *Wired* serving the needs of Internet and Web service professionals.[17] Professional publications are written for doctors, lawyers, accountants, and other professional groups. *American Family Physician* publishes articles for family practitioners and carries advertising from many pharmaceutical manufacturers. General-interest business magazines such as *Fortune* and *Forbes* cut across all trades, industries, and professions. The leading business magazine categories are listed in Exhibit 15.17.
- *Farm publications.* The three major farm publications in the United States and their approximate paid circulations are *Farm Journal* (175,000), *Successful Farming* (450,000), and *Progressive Farmer* (250,000). These magazines provide technical information about farming techniques as well as business management articles to improve farmers' profitability. In addition to national publications, regional farm magazines and publications focus on specific aspects of the industry.

Costs and Buying Procedures for Magazine Advertising. The cost for magazine space varies dramatically. As with newspapers, the size of an ad, its position in a publication, its creative execution (black-and-white or color or any special techniques), and its placement in a regular or special edition of the magazine all affect costs. The main cost, of course, is based on the magazine's circulation. A full-page four-color ad in *Reader's Digest* costs about $226,000 (based on 11 million readers); a full-page four-color ad in *People* costs about $200,000; a full-page ad in *Skiing* costs about $35,000; and a full-page ad in *UpHere,* the magazine about Canada's northern frontier with a circulation of about 20,000, is only $3,000.

Each magazine has a rate card that shows the cost for full-page, half-page, two-column, one-column, and half-column ads. A rate card also shows the cost for black-and-white, two-color, and four-color ads. Rate cards for magazines, as with newspapers, have been the standard pricing method for many years. In recent years, however, more and more publishers have been willing to negotiate rates and give deep discounts for volume purchases—discounts as large as 30 to 40 percent off the published card rate.

In addition to standard rates, there is an extra charge for a **bleed page.** On a bleed page, the background color of an ad runs to the edge of the page, replacing the standard white border. **Gatefold ads**, or ads that fold out of a magazine to display an extra-wide advertisement, also carry an extra charge. Gatefolds are often used by advertisers on the inside cover of upscale magazines. An example is the ad for dishes and flatware in Exhibit 15.18.

16.   Ibid.
17.   Gary Wolf, "The Magazine That Launched a Decade," *Business 2.0,* July 2003, 87–91.

Magazine Category	Total Revenue	Ad Revenue	Ad Revenue 2002–2003 % Change	Top Magazine in Classification
Women's	$5,874.0	$4,233.0	7.5	*InStyle*
Newsweeklies	5,460.0	3,388.0	0.1	*People*
General editorial	3,808.0	2,437.0	2.6	*N.Y. Times Magazine*
Home service and home	2,974.0	2,143.0	0.9	*Better Homes & Gardens*
Business and finance	1,739.0	1,351.0	−6.3	*Forbes*

Source: *Advertising Age*, September 20, 2004, S2. Reprinted with permission from the September 20, 2004, issue of *Advertising Age*. Copyright © Crain Communications Inc. 2004.

EXHIBIT 15.16

Top five consumer magazine categories, ranked by revenue, 2003 (U.S. dollars in millions).

Magazine Category	Total Revenue	Ad Revenue	Ad Revenue 2002–2003 % Change	Top Magazine in Classification
Computers/Internet	$1,164.0	$1,041.0	0.0	*CRN*
Business	336.0	211.0	−4.6	*The Economist*
Electronic gaming	150.0	62.0	−0.8	*PC Gamer*
Travel	149.0	149.0	−21.5	*Travel Agent*
Electronic engineering	141.0	141.0	0.0	*EE Times*

Source: *Advertising Age*, September 20, 2004, S2. Reprinted with permission from the September 20, 2004, issue of *Advertising Age*. Copyright © Crain Communications Inc. 2004.

EXHIBIT 15.17

Top five business magazine categories, ranked by revenue, 2003 (U.S. dollars in millions).

EXHIBIT 15.18

Gatefold ads display extra-wide advertisements, like this one for Lenox dishes. http://www.lenox.com

When buying space in a magazine, advertisers must decide among several placement options. A run-of-paper advertisement, as mentioned earlier, can appear anywhere in the magazine, at the discretion of the publisher. The advertiser may pay for several preferred positions, however. **First cover page** is the front cover of a magazine; **second cover page** is the inside front cover; **third cover page** is the inside back cover; and **fourth cover page** is the back cover. When advertisers prepare **double-page spreads**—advertisements that bridge two facing pages—it is important that no headlines or body copy run through the *gutter,* which is the fold between the magazine pages.

Buying procedures for magazine advertising demand that an advertiser follow several guidelines and honor several key dates. A **space contract** establishes a rate for all advertising placed in a publication by an advertiser over a specified period. A **space order,** also referred to as an *insertion order,* is a commitment by an advertiser to advertising space in a particular issue. It is accompanied by production specifications for the ad or ads that will appear in the issue. The dates that an advertiser must be aware of are as follows:

- **Closing date:** The date when production-ready advertising materials must be delivered to a publisher for an ad to appear in an issue.
- **On-sale date:** The date on which a magazine is issued to subscribers and for newsstand distribution. Most magazines put issues on sale far in advance of the cover date.
- **Cover date:** The date of publication appearing on a magazine.

Measuring Magazine Audiences. Most magazines base their published advertising rates on **guaranteed circulation,** which is a stated minimum number of copies of a particular issue that will be delivered to readers. This number guarantees for advertisers that they are achieving a certain minimum reach with an ad placement. In addition, publishers estimate **pass-along readership,** which is an additional number of people, other than the original readers, who may see a publication. Advertisers can verify circulation through the Audit Bureau of Circulations, which reports total and state-by-state circulation for magazines, as well as subscriber versus newsstand circulation. When an advertiser wants to go beyond basic circulation numbers, the syndicated magazine research services such as Simmons Market Research Bureau and Mediamark Research can provide additional information. Through personal interviews and respondent-kept diaries, these services provide advertisers with information on reader demographics, media use, and product usage.

The Future of Magazines. Magazines have had a roller-coaster history over the past 10 to 15 years. The most recent data show that circulation is, once again, in a downward trend but that ad revenues are either up slightly or down slightly depending on the year. The revenue figure is testimony to the fact that advertisers still find the advantages of magazines well suited to their current needs.

Three factors need to be considered as influences on magazines as an advertising medium in the future. First, magazines will, like other media options, have to determine how to adapt to new media options. In the late 1990s, there was a rush to online posting of magazines with more than 250 magazines offered in online versions. As discussed earlier, these electronic versions were touted as having several advantages to both the publisher and the subscriber, but it appears that neither readers nor advertisers are particularly happy with the "digizine." Consider the fact that the paid circulation for the print version of *Reader's Digest* is 11 million copies, while there are only 86,000 subscribers online.[18] And, in 2003, Ziff Davis, one of the largest newspaper publishers, dropped *Yahoo! Internet Life* from its publication lineup.

---

18. Jon Fine, "Magazines Recorded Declines in Late 2003," *Advertising Age,* February 23, 2004, 39.

EXHIBIT 15.19

While the rush to "digizines" (online versions of magazines) was pretty much a bust, magazine publishers are encouraged by the introduction of the Tablet PC as a vehicle for digital delivery of magazine content.

To date, these digizines have attracted minimal ad spending and fewer are being offered. But the recent introduction by Microsoft of the Tablet PC—a sleek and portable part laptop, part digital notepad—is encouraging some publishers to reconsider digital formats for their magazines. (See Exhibit 15.19.) *The New Yorker,* the *Financial Times,* and *Forbes* are all preparing digital versions for Tablet PC application.[19]

The second factor affecting the future of magazines is a robust environment for mergers and acquisitions. Recent years have seen dozens of merger and acquisition deals each year in the magazine industry. Buyers are looking for two benefits in acquiring publications: economies of scale in traditional print publication and new media outlets. In the past few years, the pursuit of these advantages has resulted in over $2 billion a year in mergers and acquisitions. The U.S. unit of German publisher Bertelsmann alone invested $600 million in acquiring new titles during the early part of this century.[20]

Third, magazines, perhaps more than any other medium, seem to be caught in the move by advertisers to expand their IBP spending beyond major media and into more varied promotional efforts such event sponsorship and interactive marketing. An analysis of the auto industry shows that across all advertisers, pages of magazine advertising declined about 15 percent in 2004.[21]

Magazines are not alone in the move by advertisers to use more diverse tools in their IBP efforts, and we will investigate this trend in great detail in Part Five, Integrated Brand Promotion.

Television and Radio: Strategic Planning Considerations.

When you say the word *advertising,* the average person thinks of television and radio advertising. It's easy to understand why. Television advertising can be advertising at its very best. With the benefit of sight and sound, color and music, action and special effects, television advertising can be the most powerful advertising of all. It has some other advantages as well. In many parts of the world, particularly in the United

19.   Tobi Elkin, "Publishers Bet on Tablet PC Content," *Advertising Age,* January 6, 2003, 17.
20.   Tom Lowry, "How Many Magazines Did We Buy Today?" *BusinessWeek,* January 22, 2001, 98–99.
21.   Jean Halliday, "Auto Industry Slashes Q1 Ad Spending," *Advertising Age,* April 5, 2004, 1, 37.

States, television is the medium most widely used by consumers for entertainment and information. Radio advertising also has key advantages. The ability to reach consumers in multiple locations and the creative power of radio rank as important communications opportunities. Advertisers readily appreciate the power of television and radio advertising and invest billions of dollars a year in these media.

③ Television. To many, television is the medium that defines what advertising is. With its multisensory stimulation, television offers the chance for advertising to be all that it can be. Television presents two extraordinary opportunities to advertisers. First, the diversity of communication possibilities allows for outstanding creative expression of a brand's value. Dramatic color, sweeping action, and spectacular sound effects can cast a brand in an exciting and unique light. Second, once this expressive presentation of a brand is prepared, it can be disseminated to millions of consumers, often at a fraction of a penny per contact.

These opportunities have not been lost on advertisers. In the United States in 2004, advertisers invested about $68 billion in television advertising for media time alone—this does not include the many billions of dollars spent on production costs.[22] To fully appreciate all that television means to advertisers, we need to understand much more about this complex medium.

Television Categories. Without careful evaluation, the natural tendency is to classify television as a single type of broadcast medium. When we turn on the television, we simply decide what program we find interesting and then settle in for some entertainment. The reality is that over the past 15 to 20 years, several distinct versions of television have evolved, from which consumers can choose for entertainment and advertisers can choose for reaching those consumers. There are four different alternatives: network, cable, syndicated, and local television. Exhibit 15.20 shows the spending in these television categories for 2002 and 2003. Notice that while all the options with the exception of syndication showed solid growth in advertising receipts, the fastest growth by far was in spot television placement. This can be explained by the ability of spot placement to efficiently and effectively reach well-defined geographic segments.

Let's examine the nature of each of the four options for television advertising and the growing satellite/closed-circuit option as well.

Network Television. **Network television** broadcasts programming over airwaves to affiliate stations across the United States under a contract agreement. Advertisers can buy time within these programs to reach audiences in hundreds of markets. There

---

EXHIBIT 15.20

Spending by advertisers in the four major television categories (U.S. dollars in billions).

	Total Measured Advertising Spending		
	2003	**2002**	**% Change**
Spot TV	$6.1	$6.4	−4.7
Network TV	15.2	14.5	4.7
Cable TV	6.7	5.7	17.6
Syndicated TV	2.3	2.0	15.9

Source: *Advertising Age,* June 28, 2004, S-21.

---

22. "Marketing Fact Book 2004 Edition," *Marketing News,* June 15, 2004, 14.

arc currently six major broadcast television networks in the United States. The original big three networks were American Broadcasting Company (ABC, now owned by Disney), the Columbia Broadcasting System (CBS), and the National Broadcasting Company (NBC). The next broadcast company to be added was the Fox network. Two additional competitors in network television began to broadcast in 1995: The WB, financed by Time Warner (now part of AOL), and United Paramount Network (UPN). Each network estimates that it now reaches more than 90 percent of U.S. households. Exhibit 15.21 shows the top 10 advertisers on network television.

Despite speculation over the last decade that alternative television options (discussed next) would ultimately undermine broadcast television, the broadcast networks still continue to flourish—mostly due to innovative programming. For example, the final episode of *Survivor 2001* on CBS drew an audience of 35.8 million viewers (more recent versions of *Survivor* have drawn audiences in the range of 20 million viewers) and the Super Bowl annually draws over 50 million viewers.[23] No other television option gives advertisers that sort of breadth of reach.

Cable Television. From its modest beginnings as community antenna television (CATV) in the 1940s, cable television has grown into a worldwide communications force. **Cable television** transmits a wide range of programming to subscribers through wires rather than over airwaves. In the United States, more than 73 million basic cable subscribers (nearly 68 percent of all U.S. households) are wired for cable reception and receive on average more than 30 channels of sports, entertainment, news, music video, and home-shopping programming.[24] Cable's power as an advertising option has grown enormously over the past decade as cable's share of the prime-time viewing audience has grown.

Aside from more programming on cable, which distinguishes this category of television from the networks, another aspect is the willingness of cable networks to invest in original programming. With the success of programs such as USA network's *JAG*, cable networks are investing record dollar amounts in new programs to continue to attract well-defined audiences (see Exhibit 15.22).

Syndicated Television. Television syndication is either original programming or programming that first appeared on network television. It is then rebroadcast on either

Top 10 network TV advertisers (U.S. dollars in millions).

Rank	Advertiser	Network TV Ad Spending		
		2003	2002	% Change
1	Procter & Gamble	$873.6	$723.7	15.2
2	General Motors	641.4	727.2	−11.8
3	Johnson & Johnson	527.5	508.5	3.7
4	Ford Motor Co.	449.6	437.9	2.7
5	Pfizer	442.4	429.1	3.1
6	Time Warner	428.8	351.7	21.9
7	Pepsi Co.	423.2	369.3	14.6
8	Walt Disney	409.7	345.8	18.5
9	Sony	338.0	303.8	11.2
10	Yum Brands	322.4	293.1	10.0

Source: *Advertising Age*, June 28, 2004, S-20

23. Associated Press News Release, available at http://www.wsj.com, accessed May 5, 2001.

24. Data drawn from the National Cable & Telecommunications Association, Industry Overview, http://www.ncta.com, accessed on April 18, 2004.

Like car shows?
We've got 'em Monday thru Thursday. 8PM/ET 11PM/PT

Go to speedtv.com for programs and times. To get SPEED Channel call 1-888-22-SPEED today.

SPEED CHANNEL
FUEL YOUR PASSION

EXHIBIT 15.22

The power and success of cable comes from offering very specific programming through a wide range of cable networks. An example is the Speed Channel, which offers all forms of motor sports programming and commentary.

network or cable stations. Syndicated programs provide advertisers with proven programming that typically attracts a well-defined, if not enormous, audience. There are several types of television syndication. **Off-network syndication** refers to programs that were previously run in network prime time. Some of the most popular off-network syndicated shows are *Home Improvement* and *Seinfeld*. The most popular of the off-network syndication shows command significant ad dollars—$175,000 to $225,000 for a 30-second ad. Less popular shows are more affordable with prices set between about $25,000 and $60,000.[25] **First-run syndication** refers to programs developed specifically for sale to individual stations. The most famous first-run syndication show is *Star Trek: The Next Generation.* **Barter syndication** takes both off-network and first-run syndication shows and offers them free or at a reduced rate to local television stations, with some national advertising presold within the programs. Local stations can then sell the remainder of the time to generate revenues. This option allows national advertisers to participate in the national syndication market conveniently. Some of the most widely recognized barter syndication shows are *Jeopardy* and *Wheel of Fortune.*

Local Television. Local television is the programming other than the network broadcast that independent stations and network affiliates offer local audiences. Completely independent stations broadcast old movies, sitcoms, or children's programming. Network affiliates get about 90 hours of programming a week from the major networks, but they are free to broadcast other programming beyond that provided by the network. News, movies, syndicated programs, and community-interest programs typically round out the local television fare.

Satellite/Closed-Circuit. New technology offers another version of television available to advertisers. Programming can now be transmitted to highly segmented audiences via **satellite and closed-circuit** transmission. The best known of these systems is the CNN Airport Network, which transmits news and weather programming directly to airport terminals around the world. A growing segment in this area is programming being delivered via satellite to college campuses. CTN (College Television Network) reaches 5 million college students each week through closed-circuit programming delivered by satellite to thousands of TV monitors on 720 college and university campuses.[26]

As you can see, while all television may look the same to the average consumer, advertisers actually have five distinct options to consider. Regardless of which type of television transmission advertisers choose, television offers distinct advantages to advertisers as a way to communicate with target audiences.

Advantages of Television. Throughout the book, we have referred to the unique capability of television as an advertising medium. There must be some very

25.   Richard Linnett, "Host of TV Superstars Boost Bullish Syndication Market," *Advertising Age,* March 8, 2004, S4.
26.   "SES Americom Distributes MTV Networks' CTN: College Television Network via AMC-3," Business PR Newswire, September 11, 2003, available at http://www.collegiatepresswire.com, accessed on May 1, 2004.

good reasons why advertisers such as AT&T, General Motors, and Procter & Gamble invest hundreds of millions of dollars annually in television advertising. The specific advantages of this medium are as follows:

- *Creative opportunities.* The overriding advantage of television compared to other media is, of course, the ability to send a message using both sight and sound. With recent advances in transmission and reception equipment, households now have brilliantly clear visuals and stereo-enhanced audio to further increase the impact of television advertising. In addition, special effects perfected for films such as *The Matrix* are now making their way into advertising prepared for television.

- *Coverage, reach, and repetition.* Television, in one form or another, reaches more than 98 percent of all households in the United States—an estimated 290 million people. These households represent every demographic, economic, and ethnic segment in the United States, which allows advertisers to achieve broad coverage. We have also seen that the cable television option provides reach to hundreds of millions of households throughout the world. Further, no other medium allows an advertiser to repeat a message as frequently as television.

- *Cost per contact.* For advertisers that sell to broadly defined mass markets, television offers a cost-effective way to reach millions of members of a target audience. The average prime-time television program reaches 11 million households, and top-rated shows can reach more than 20 million households. This brings an advertiser's cost-per-contact figure down to an amount unmatched by any other media option—literally fractions of a penny per contact.

- *Audience selectivity.* Television programmers are doing a better job of developing shows that attract well-defined target audiences. **Narrowcasting** is the development and delivery of specialized programming to well-defined audiences. Cable television is far and away the most selective television option. Cable provides not only well-defined programming, but also entire networks—such as MTV and ESPN—built around the concept of attracting selective audiences. The ability to narrowcast is enhanced ever further when cable is combined with other media, as the Creativity box highlights.

Disadvantages of Television. Television has great capabilities as an advertising medium, but it is not without limitations. Some of these limitations are serious enough to significantly detract from the power of television advertising.

- *Fleeting message.* One problem with the sight and sound of a television advertisement is that it is gone in an instant. The fleeting nature of a television message, as opposed to a print ad (which a receiver can contemplate), makes message impact difficult. Some advertisers invest huge amounts of money in the production of television ads to overcome this disadvantage.

- *High absolute cost.* While the cost per contact of television advertising is the best of all media, the absolute cost may be the worst. The average cost of air time for a single 30-second television spot during prime time in fall 2003 was just over $200,000, with the most popular show, *Friends,* bringing in around $475,000 for a 30-second spot. Other popular shows commanded impressive numbers as well: *Survivor,* $390,000; *CSI,* $310,000, and *ER,* $404,000. [27] Remember this is prime time pricing. Off prime-time slots go for much more modest fees like $20,000 to $50,000 for 30 seconds. In addition, the average cost of producing a quality 30-second television spot is around $300,000 to $400,000. These costs make television advertising prohibitively expensive for many advertisers. Of course, large, national consumer products companies—for which television advertising is best suited anyway—find the absolute cost acceptable for the coverage, reach, and repetition advantages discussed earlier.

27.   Richard Linnett, "'Friends' Tops TV Price Chart," *Advertising Age,* September 15, 2003, 1, 46.

- *Poor geographic selectivity.* While programming can be developed to attract specific audiences, program transmission cannot target geographic areas nearly as well. For a national advertiser that wants to target a city market, the reach of a television broadcast is too broad. Similarly, for a local retailer that wants to use television for reaching local segments, the television transmission is likely to reach a several-hundred-mile radius—which will increase the advertiser's cost with little likelihood of drawing patrons.
- *Poor audience attitude and attentiveness.* Since the inception of television advertising, consumers have bemoaned the intrusive nature of the commercials. Just when a movie is reaching its thrilling conclusion—on come the ads. The involuntary and frequent intrusion of advertisements on television has made television advertising the most distrusted form of advertising among consumers. In a recent survey, only 17 percent of consumers surveys felt that television advertising affected them in their purchase of a new car compared with 48 percent who claimed that direct mail advertising was a factor in their decision.[28]

Along with—and perhaps as a result of—this generally bad attitude toward television advertising, consumers have developed ways of avoiding exposure. Making a trip to the refrigerator or conversing with fellow viewers are the preferred low-tech ways to avoid exposure. On the high-tech side, **channel grazing,** or using a remote control to monitor programming on other channels while an advertisement is being broadcast, is the favorite way to avoid commercials. When programs have been videotaped for later viewing, zapping and zipping are common avoidance techniques. **Zapping** is the process of eliminating ads altogether from videotaped programs. **Zipping** is the process of fast-forwarding through advertisements contained in videotaped programs.

New technology has created yet another potential method for avoiding advertising—and this development has advertisers greatly concerned. The problems centers on the so-called "V-chip." The **V-chip** is a device that can block television programming based on the program rating system. It was developed as a way for parents to block programming that they do not want their children to see. While that was the original and intended use for the

---

CREATIVITY

Cable and the Web: The Perfect Combination for High Selectivity

The discussion of cable broadcast in the chapter highlights that one of the key advantages of cable is the ability to reach narrowly defined target segments. There are several other advantages of cable related to such "narrowcasting," including combining cable with Web placement to achieve an integrated brand promotion effect. Overall, the key advantages of cable include the following:

- *The expanded reach of cable.* Cable's appeal is growing among key demographic groups such as teens, who spend more time watching cable than broadcast television. Overall, cable now reaches nearly 70 percent of all U.S. households. Cable networks like TBS Superstation and ESPN have over 85 million viewers. Consumers are highly favorable toward cable as a medium. In a recent survey of consumer perceptions of quality across major media (TV, radio, magazines, and newspapers), cable ranked first in 15 of 25 ratings while broadcast television ranked first in only two categories.
- *Highly selective markets/minimal waste.* Cable is much more efficient in reaching target markets than broadcast television is. Viewers have more choices and those more precisely defined choices attract a more well-defined demographic, psychographic, and geographic audience. One of the fastest growing categories for television spending is the kids' TV program. Cable networks like Nickelodeon and the Cartoon Network are experiencing so much demand that the cost of a 30-second spot on such networks has increased 20 percent over the last few years.
- *Integrated brand promotion.* For advertisers who want to add new media options to the media mix, cable offers an interesting combination with the Internet. Cable offers many branded Web sites. In fact, cable-branded Web sites attract more than 60 percent of the audience for media-affiliated Web sites.

Sources: Joe Ostrow, "Cable Exec. Cites Value in Tight Market," *Advertising Age,* April 16, 2001, S26; Wayne Friedman and Jon Lafayette, "Kids' Upfront Soars as Prices Rise 15% to 20%," *Advertising Age,* April 26, 2004.

---

28.   Jean Halliday, "Study Claims TV Advertising Doesn't Work on Car Buyers," *Advertising Age,* October 13, 2003, 8.

V-chip, the technology can be easily adapted to block advertisements as well. Two manufacturers, RCA and Panasonic, say they want to build television sets with this sort of technology. Advertisers and broadcasters, of course, are challenging the rights of these manufacturers to build such sets. The consequences of sets with V-chips that block ads could be devastating to advertising revenues.

And, of course, the biggest news and highest-tech way to avoid television advertising is with TiVo. **TiVo,** and similar devices, are digital video recorders (DVRs) that use computer hard drives to store up to 140 hours of television programming. Consumers can use the devices to skip commercials and only watch the programming itself. Indeed, the overwhelming reason consumers use DVRs *is* to skip commercials. A survey of DVR users revealed that 81 percent of them invested in a DVR primarily to skip commercials, and they claim to fast forward through 75 percent of the ads that appear in the programming that they watch. As of 2004, only 3.5 percent of U.S. households had DVRs, but that percentage is expected to rise rapidly as cable companies like Comcast and Time Warner will make built-in DVRs an option with set-top boxes.[29] Obviously, widespread use of DVRs has advertisers looking for ways to get exposure for their brands on television. Do you think it was a coincidence that the winner of NBC's *The Apprentice* drove off in a 2005 Chrysler Crossfire as a bonus prize? And have you noticed the little "plug" that is appearing more and more often at the bottom right of your screen while programming is going on? Again, a way for advertisers to communicate in an age of DVRs.

- *Clutter.* All the advantages of television as an advertising medium have created one significant disadvantage: clutter. The major television networks run about 15 minutes of advertising during each hour of prime-time programming, and cable broadcasts carry about 14 minutes of advertising per hour.[30] Research has found that 65 percent of a surveyed group of consumers felt that they were "constantly bombarded with too much" advertising.[31]

A communications environment cluttered with advertising can cause viewers to invoke various information overload defenses to avoid information, as we discussed in Chapter 5.

Buying Procedures for Television Advertising. Discussions in Chapter 13 as well as in this chapter have identified the costs associated with television advertising from both a production and a space standpoint. Here we will concentrate on the issue of buying time on television. Advertisers buy time for television advertising through sponsorship, participation, and spot advertising.

- *Sponsorship.* In a **sponsorship** arrangement, an advertiser agrees to pay for the production of a television program and for most (and often all) of the advertising that appears in the program. Sponsorship is not nearly as popular today as it was in the early days of network television. Contemporary sponsorship agreements have attracted big-name companies such as AT&T and IBM, who often sponsor sporting events, and Hallmark, known for its sponsorship of dramatic series.
- *Participation.* The vast majority of advertising time is purchased on a participation basis. **Participation** means that several different advertisers buy commercial time during a specific television program. No single advertiser has a responsibility for the production of the program or a commitment to the program beyond the time contracted for.
- *Spot advertising.* **Spot advertising** refers to all television advertising time purchased from and aired through local television stations. Spot advertising provides

29. Patrick Seitz, "DVRs Changing Rules of Advertising on TV," Investor's Business Daily, April 29, 2004, available at http//biz.yahoo.com, accessed May 1, 2004.
30. Andrew Green, "Clutter Crisis Countdown," *Advertising Age,* April 21, 2003, 22.
31. A 2004 Yankelovich Partners poll was cited in Gary Ruskin, "A 'Deal Spiral of Disrespect,'" *Advertising Age,* April 26, 2004, 18.

EXHIBIT 15.23

Television broadcast dayparts (in Eastern U.S. time zone segments)

Morning	7:00 A.M. to 9:00 A.M., Monday through Friday
Daytime	9:00 A.M. to 4:30 P.M., Monday through Friday
Early fringe	4:30 P.M. to 7:30 P.M., Monday through Friday
Prime-time access	7:30 P.M. to 8:00 P.M., Sunday through Saturday
Prime time	8:00 P.M. to 11:00 P.M., Monday through Saturday 7:00 P.M. to 11:00 P.M., Sunday
Late news	11:00 P.M. to 11:30 P.M., Monday through Friday
Late fringe	11:30 P.M. to 1:00 A.M., Monday through Friday

national advertisers the opportunity to either adjust advertising messages for different markets or intensify their media schedules in particularly competitive markets. Spot advertising is the primary manner in which local advertisers, such as car dealers, furniture stores, and restaurants, reach their target audiences with television.

A final issue with respect to buying television advertising has to do with the time periods and programs during which the advertising will run. Once an advertiser has determined that sponsorship, participation, or spot advertising (or, more likely, some combination of the last two) meets its needs, the time periods and specific programs must be chosen. Exhibit 15.23 shows the way in which television programming times are broken into **dayparts,** which represent segments of time during a television broadcast day.

Measuring Television Audiences. Television audience measurements identify the size and composition of audiences for different television programming. Advertisers choose where to buy time in television broadcasts based on these factors. These measures also set the cost for television time. The larger the audience or the more attractive the composition, the more costly the time will be.

The following are brief summaries of the information used to measure television audiences.

- *Television households.* **Television households** is an estimate of the number of households that are in a market and own a television. Since more than 98 percent of all households in the United States own a television, the number of total households and the number of television households are virtually the same, about 101 million. Markets around the world do not have the same level of television penetration.
- *Households using television.* **Households using television (HUT),** also referred to as sets in use, is a measure of the number of households tuned to a television program during a particular time period.
- *Program rating.* A **program rating** is the percentage of television households that are in a market and are tuned to a specific program during a specific time period. Expressed as a formula, program rating is

$$\text{program rating} = \frac{\text{TV households tuned to a program}}{\text{total TV households in the market}}$$

A **ratings point** indicates that 1 percent of all the television households in an area were tuned to the program measured. If an episode of *CSI* is watched by 19.5 million households, then the program rating would be calculated as follows:

$$CSI \text{ rating} = \frac{19,500,000}{95,900,000} = 20 \text{ rating}$$

The program rating is the best-known measure of television audience, and it is the basis for the rates television stations charge for advertising on different programs. Recall that it is also the way advertisers develop their media plans from the standpoint of calculating reach and frequency estimates, such as gross rating points.

- *Share of audience.* **Share of audience** provides a measure of the proportion of households that are using television during a specific time period and are tuned to a particular program. If 65 million households are using their televisions during the *CSI* time slot, the share of audience measure is:

$$CSI \text{ share } = \frac{\text{TV households tuned to a program}}{\text{total TV households using TV}} = \frac{19,500,000}{65,000,000} = 30 \text{ share}$$

Controversy in Television Measurement. At the outset of the chapter, we revealed that there was some controversy in the area of measuring television audiences in that advertisers have been disputing Nielsen Media ratings particularly with respect to the size and viewing habits of 18-to-34-year-old males. While the 18-to-34-year-old male market is a key source of the controversy, another related issue has to do with technological change in the industry, like the digital video recorders discussed earlier, and their effect on actual television viewing across all audience types.[32] Nielsen executives respond by saying that for the 18-to-34-year-old segment specifically and the overall market generally, their national sample and Nielsen National People Meter sample provides accurate data.[33]

The Future of Television. The future of television is exciting for several reasons. First, the emerging interactive era will undoubtedly affect television as an advertising medium. Prospects include viewer participation in mystery programs and game shows in which household viewers play right along with studio contestants. Equally as important, though, is that technology is creating the ability to transmit advertising to a wide range of new devices from cell phones to personal digital assistants to pagers. Estimates are that by the year 2005, global interactive advertising will represent an $83 billion industry.[34] And recall the discussion from Chapter 3 regarding the growth of broadband access. By the year 2004, about 25 percent of all adult Americans (about 48 million people) had broadband connections.[35] Advertisers will have to seriously consider the implications of this mode of communication and how well it will serve as a way to send persuasive communications. Most specifically, broadband connections will increase the prospect that television advertising will be transmitted via the Internet to either PCs or handheld devices.

Another major change that will affect the future of television is emerging transmission technology. **Direct broadcast by satellite (DBS)** is a program delivery system whereby television (and radio) programs are sent directly from a satellite to homes equipped with small receiving dishes. This transmission offers the prospect of hundreds of different channels. While advertisers will still be able to insert advertising in programs, the role of networks and cable stations in the advertising process will change dramatically. Recently, DBS technology has added a new capability. Rather than transmitting directly to homes, a Japanese company has developed a system to deliver programming to automobiles.

Television advertisers and their agencies also have to be prepared for high-definition television broadcasts. **High-definition television (HDTV)** promises to offer

---

32   David Bauder, "Network Execs Question Nielsen Accuracy," Yahoo! News, November 16, 2003, available at http://www.news.yahoo.com.

33.   Michele Greppi, "Nielsen Says Nothing Wrong with Ratings," *Advertising Age,* November 17, 2003, 3.

34.   Russ Banham, "Advertising's Future," *Critical Mass,* Fall 2000, 51–56.

35.   Anick Jesdanun, "2 in 5 Web Users Have Broadband at Home," Yahoo! News, April 24, 2004, available at http://www.news.yahoo.com.

consumers picture and audio clarity that is a vast improvement over current technology. While HDTV equipment will certainly have the capability to reproduce images and sound with extraordinary quality, the uncertainties of visual and audio transmission may compromise the ability of the new HDTV sets to do so.

Television advertising has a high probability of migrating to the Internet. Due in large part to a firm called Unicast, the quality and accessibility of video advertising on the Web is greatly increased. Unicast technology is able to provide 30 seconds of pure video and expanded interactivity shown perfectly to every consumer every time. The company uses full-screen, broadcast-quality video to bring advertising messages online. The two-megabyte Video Commercial plays without any "freezing" or "buffering" and up to eight times faster than most broadband video units.

Finally, consolidation in the industry cannot be ignored. In 2004, Comcast made a $51 billion bid for all the media owned by Disney. The offer was finally dropped after pressure from both Comcast and Disney shareholders. But Comcast still has acquired about $20 billion in cable companies.[36] Similarly, Rupert Murdock has been expanding the Direct TV empire of cable holdings and media holdings that generates $30 billion in revenue from literally every corner of the earth.[37] And let's not forget media giants GE, Time Warner, and Disney, all of which in their own right have great broadcast media power. The issue, of course, is the extent to which these big and powerful media companies can end up controlling programming content. It is not automatically the case that big media companies shape programming in a biased way, but that is the concern of media watchdogs.

While it is hard to predict what the future will hold, one thing seems sure—television will continue to grow as an entertainment and information medium for households. The convenience, low cost, and diversity of programming make television an ideal medium for consumers. Additionally, television's expansion around the world will generate access to huge new markets. Television, despite its limitations, will continue to be an important part of the integrated communications mix of many advertisers.

4   Radio. Radio may seem like the least glamorous and most inconspicuous of the major media. This perception does not jibe with reality. Radio plays an integral role in the media plans of some of the most astute advertisers. Because of the unique features of radio, advertisers invest about $3.5 billion annually in radio to reach national audiences and over $16.5 billion per year on local radio advertising.[38] There are good reasons why advertisers of all sorts invest in radio as a means to reach target audiences. Let's turn our attention to the different radio options available to advertisers.

Radio Categories. Radio offers an advertiser several options for reaching target audiences. The basic split of national and local radio broadcasts presents an obvious geographic choice. More specifically, though, advertisers can choose among the following categories, each with specific characteristics: networks, syndication, and AM versus FM.

•   *Networks.* **Radio networks** operate much like television networks in that they deliver programming via satellite to affiliate stations across the United States. Network radio programming concentrates on news, sports, business reports, and short features. Some of the more successful radio networks that draw large audiences are ABC, CNN, and AP News Network.

•   *Syndication.* **Radio syndication** provides complete programs to stations on a contract basis. Large syndicators offer stations complete 24-hour-a-day programming

---

36. Tom Lowery, Amy Barrett, and Ronald Grover, "A New Cable Giant," *BusinessWeek,* November 18, 2002, 108-118.

37. Catherine Young, et al., "Rupert's World," *BusinessWeek,* January 19, 2004, 53-61.

38. "100 Leading National Advertisers," *Advertising Age,* June 23, 2003, S14.

Satellite radio providers like Sirius are betting that consumers are willing to pay for commercial-free radio and get a greater variety of music and higher-quality sound.

packages that totally relieve a station of any programming effort. Aside from full-day programming, they also supply individual programs, such as talk shows. Large syndication organizations such as Westwood One and Satellite Music Network place advertising within programming, making syndication a good outlet for advertisers.

- *AM versus FM.* AM radio stations send signals that use amplitude modulation (AM) and operate on the AM radio dial at signal designations 540 to 1600. AM was the foundation of radio until the 1970s. Today, AM radio broadcasts, even the new stereo AM transmissions, cannot match the sound quality of FM. Thus, most AM stations focus on local community broadcasting or news and talk formats that do not require high-quality audio. Talk radio has, in many ways, been the salvation of AM radio. FM radio stations transmit using frequency modulation (FM). FM radio transmission is of a much higher quality. Because of this, FM radio has attracted the wide range of music formats that most listeners prefer. Radio is, of course, now available via the Web.

- *Satellite radio.* Of course the biggest news in radio is satellite radio, which is transmitted from satellites circling the earth. Currently, satellite radio costs a consumer anywhere from $99 to $200 to set up and then about $10 per month for a subscription. The advantages of satellite radio have to do with variety of program, more crisp and clear sound reproduction, and, of course, *no ads on the music channels*. But by 2004, the two leading satellite radio providers, XM Satellite Radio and Sirius Satellite Radio, only had 2 million subscribers combined and both were losing money (see Exhibit 15.24). It remains to be seen whether consumers like the variety and quality offered by satellite radio or whether they will prefer to keep "free" radio and listen to ads. (See the Controversy box.)

Types of Radio Advertising. Advertisers have three basic choices in radio advertising: local spot radio advertising, network radio advertising, or national spot radio advertising. Spot radio advertising attracts 80 percent of all radio advertising dollars in a year. In **local spot radio advertising,** an advertiser places advertisements directly with individual stations rather than with a network or syndicate. Local spot radio dominates the three classes of radio advertising because there are more than 9,000 individual radio stations in the United States, giving advertisers a wide range of choices. And local spot radio reaches well-defined geographic audiences, making it the ideal choice for local retailers.

Network radio advertising is advertising placed within national network programs. Since there are few network radio programs being broadcast, only about $600 million a year is invested by advertisers in this format.

The last option, **national spot radio advertising,** offers an advertiser the opportunity to place advertising in nationally syndicated radio programming. The leading national spot radio advertisers are listed in Exhibit 15.25. An advertiser can reach millions of listeners nationwide on over 400 radio stations by contracting with Clear Channel's Premier Radio Networks.

CONTROVERSY

The Death of Radio?

In 2001, Sirius Satellite Radio launched its third satellite into space from the Soviet Union's once-secret Baikonur Cosmodrome in Kasakhstan. This is the same site where the first earth satellite was launched in 1957 and where the first human in orbit blasted off in 1961. Will this site also be know as the place where the slow death of radio began?

Right now, Sirius delivers 65 streams of commercial-free music in every radio genre and over 50 streams of news, sports, weather, talk, comedy, public radio, and children's programming. Sirius's programming is not available on conventional radio in any market in the United States. The CD-quality sound broadcasts can be accessed only through subscription (about $10 per month) The company holds one of only two licenses issued by the Federal Communications Commission (FCC) to operate a national satellite radio system. The other is held by XM Satellite Radio.

If the advantages of subscription satellite radio are appealing to radio listeners, it could rattle the very foundation of the $20 billion-a-year broadcast radio industry. And there are some very high-profile believers. Corporations like General Motors, DaimlerChrysler, and Clear Channel Communications as well as venture capital investors like Prime 66 Partners, Apollo, and Blackstone have sunk over $3 billion into Sirius and XM. One industry analyst believes that satellite radio is the "next big consumer phenomenon" and that by 2007 it will be generating up to $10 billion a year.

While all this sounds very exciting and convincing, the reality is that no satellite company has made a profit—quite to the contrary. By the end of 2004, Sirius counted about 100,000 subscribers and nearly $100 million in revenue, but no profits. So the question remains. Will Sirius and XM grow dramatically and "kill" commercial radio as we have always known it? Or are consumers too accustomed to free radio and the death of radio is greatly exaggerated?

Sources: Bethany McLean, "Satellite Killed the Radio Star," *Fortune,* January 22, 2001, 95. Financial data taken from a Sirius company press release, "Sirius Satellite Radio Retail Market Share Increases in March," April 30, 2004, available at http://www.sirius.com.

Advantages of Radio. While radio may not be the most glamorous or sophisticated of the major media options, it has some distinct advantages over newspapers, magazines, and television.

- *Cost.* On both a per-contact and absolute basis, radio is often the most cost-effective medium available to an advertiser. A full minute of network radio time can cost between $5,000 and $10,000—an amazing bargain compared with the other media we've discussed. In addition, production costs for preparing radio ads are quite low; an ad often costs nothing to prepare if the spot is read live during a local broadcast.

- *Reach and frequency.* Radio has the widest exposure of any medium. It reaches consumers in their homes, cars, offices, and backyards, and even while they exercise. The wireless and portable features of radio provide an opportunity to reach consumers that exceeds all other media. The low cost of radio time gives advertisers the opportunity to frequently repeat messages at low absolute cost and cost per contact.

- *Target audience selectivity.* Radio can selectively target audiences on a geographic, demographic, and psychographic basis. The narrow transmission of local radio stations gives advertisers the best opportunity to reach narrowly defined geographic audiences. For a local merchant with one store, this is an ideal opportunity. Radio programming formats and different dayparts also allow target audience selectivity. CBS Radio made the decision several years ago to convert four of 13 stations to a rock 'n' roll oldies format to target 35-to-49-year-olds—in other words, the baby boomers.[39] Hard rock, new age, easy listening, country, classical, and talk radio formats all attract different audiences. Radio dayparts, shown in Exhibit 15.26, also attract different audiences. Morning and afternoon/evening drive times attract a male audience. Daytime attracts predominantly women; nighttime, teens.

- *Flexibility and timeliness.* Radio is the most flexible medium because of very short closing periods for submitting an ad. This means an advertiser can wait until close to an air date before submitting an ad. With this flexibility, advertisers can

---

39. Kevin Goldman, "CBS Radio Retunes to Music of the '70s," *Wall Street Journal,* December 30, 1993. B5.

Top 10 national spot radio advertisers (U.S. dollars in millions)

Rank	Advertiser	National Spot Radio Ad Spending		
		2003	**2002**	**% Change**
1	SBC Communications	$144.2	$108.7	32.7
2	Home Depot	102.5	62.8	63.2
3	Verizon	79.2	71.3	11.2
4	Time Warner	73.4	50.3	45.9
5	News Corp.	67.9	48.9	38.9
6	Safeway	50.9	15.4	229.6
7	ViaCom	45.6	47.9	−4.8
8	Walt Disney	40.5	31.8	27.6
9	ATT Wireless	38.5	43.8	−12.2
10	General Electric	36.6	22.3	64.7

Source: *Advertising Age,* June 24, 2004, S-20.

Radio dayparts used for advertising scheduling.

Morning drive time	6:00 A.M. to 10:00 A.M.
Daytime	10:00 A.M. to 3:00 P.M.
Afternoon/evening drive time	3:00 P.M. to 7:00 P.M.
Nighttime	7:00 P.M. to 12:00 A.M.
Late night	12:00 A.M. to 6:00 A.M.

take advantage of special events or unique competitive opportunities in a timely fashion.

- *Creative opportunities.* While radio may be unidimensional in sensory stimulation, it can still have powerful creative impact. Recall that radio has been described as the theater of the mind. Ads such as the folksy tales of Tom Bodett for Motel 6 or the eccentric humor of Stan Freberg are memorable and can have tremendous impact on the attitude toward a brand. In addition, the musical formats that attract audiences to radio stations can also attract attention to radio ads. Research has discovered that audiences who favor certain music may be more prone to listen to an ad that uses songs they recognize and like.[40]

Disadvantages of Radio. As good as radio can be, it also suffers from some severe limitations as an advertising medium. Advertising strategists must recognize these disadvantages when deciding what role radio can play in an integrated marketing communications program.

- *Poor audience attentiveness.* Just because radio reaches audiences almost everywhere doesn't mean that anyone is paying attention. Remember that radio has also been described as audio wallpaper. It provides a comfortable background distraction while a consumer does something else—hardly an ideal level of attentiveness for advertising communication. Consumers who are listening and traveling in a car often switch stations when an ad comes on and divide their attention between the radio and the road.

40. Kevin Goldman, "Hot Songs Are Wooing Younger Ears," *Wall Street Journal,* January 2, 1993, B1.

- *Creative limitations.* While the theater of the mind may be a wonderful creative opportunity, taking advantage of that opportunity can be difficult indeed. The audio-only nature of radio communication is a tremendous creative compromise. An advertiser whose product depends on demonstration or visual impact is at a loss when it comes to radio. And like its television counterpart, a radio message creates a fleeting impression that is often gone in an instant.
- *Fragmented audiences.* The large number of stations that try to attract the same audience in a market has created tremendous fragmentation. Think about your own local radio market. There are probably four or five different stations that play the kind of music you like. Or consider that in the past few years, more than 1,000 radio stations in the United States have adopted the talk-radio format. This fragmentation means that the percentage of listeners tuned to any one station is likely very small.
- *Chaotic buying procedures.* For an advertiser who wants to include radio as part of a national advertising program, the buying process can be sheer chaos. Since national networks and syndicated broadcasts do not reach every geographic market, an advertiser has to buy time in individual markets on a station-by-station basis. This could involve dozens of different negotiations and individual contracts.

Buying Procedures for Radio Advertising. While buying procedures to achieve national coverage may be chaotic, this does not mean they are completely without structure. Although the actual buying may be time-consuming and expensive if many stations are involved, the structure is actually quite straightforward. Advertising time can be purchased from networks, syndications, or local radio stations. Recall that among these options, advertisers invest most heavily in local placement. About 80 percent of annual radio advertising is placed locally. About 15 percent is allocated to national spot placement, and only 5 percent is invested in network broadcasts.

The other factor in buying radio time relates to the time period of purchase. Refer again to Exhibit 15.26. This shows the five basic daypart segments from which an advertiser can choose. The time period decision is based primarily on a demographic description of the advertiser's target audience. Recall that drive-time dayparts attract a mostly male audience, while daytime is primarily female, and nighttime is mostly teen. This information, combined with programming formats, guides an advertiser in a buying decision.

As with magazine buying, radio advertising time is purchased from rate cards issued by individual stations. Run-of-station ads—ads that the station chooses when to run—cost less than ads scheduled during a specific daypart. The price can also increase if an advertiser wants the ad read live on the air by a popular local radio personality hosting a show during a daypart.

The actual process of buying radio time is relatively simple. A media planner identifies the stations and the dayparts that will reach the target audience. Then the rates and daypart availabilities are checked to be sure they match the media-planning objectives. At this point, agreements are made regarding the number of spots to run in specified time frames.

Measuring Radio Audiences. There are two primary sources of information on radio audiences. Arbitron ratings cover 260 local radio markets. The ratings are developed through the use of diaries maintained by listeners who record when they listened to the radio and to what station they were tuned. The *Arbitron Ratings/Radio* book gives audience estimates by time period and selected demographic characteristics. Several specific measures are compiled from the Arbitron diaries:

- **Average quarter-hour persons:** The average number of listeners tuned to a station during a specified 15-minute segment of a daypart.

- **Average quarter-hour share:** The percentage of the total radio audience that was listening to a radio station during a specified quarter-hour daypart.
- **Average quarter-hour rating:** The audience during a quarter-hour daypart expressed as a percentage of the population of the measurement area. This provides an estimate of the popularity of each station in an area.
- **Cume:** The cumulative audience, which is the total number of different people who listen to a station for at least five minutes in a quarter-hour period within a specified daypart. Cume is the best estimate of the reach of a station.
- RADAR (Radio's All Dimension Audience Research) is the other major measure of radio audiences. Sponsored by the major radio networks, RADAR collects audience data twice a year based on interviews with radio listeners. Designated listeners are called daily for a one-week period and asked about their listening behavior. Estimates include measures of the overall audience for different network stations and audience estimates by market area. The results of the studies are reported in an annual publication, *Radio Usage and Network Radio Audiences*. Media planners can refer to published measures such as Arbitron and RADAR to identify which stations will reach target audiences at what times across various markets.

The Future of Radio. Three factors must be considered with respect to the future of radio. First, the prospects for subscription satellite radio should not be underestimated. Satellite radio does away with radio advertising clutter and offers listeners multiple, detailed choices to match their listening preferences.[41] This is a huge advantage along with the increased audio quality. The key issue, of course, is whether radio listeners will be willing to pay for an entertainment medium that has been free from its inception.

Second, radio will be affected by emerging technologies much in the same way that television will be affected. The potential for transmitting radio programming—and advertising—via the Internet is very real. As broadband technology grows, so too will the attractiveness of Internet transmission of radio programming and advertising, much like the prospects for this technology discussed earlier with respect to television.

Finally, there has been a large degree of consolidation going on in the traditional radio market. Led by Clear Channel Communications (see Exhibit 15.27), fewer big competitors are owning more and more radio stations. Through an aggressive period of acquisitions in the early 2000s, Clear Channel now owns approximately 1,200 radio stations in all regions of the United States. Consolidation provides both opportunities and liabilities for both consumers and advertisers. Opportunities for consumers relate to the consistency of quality in the radio programming available and advertisers will have an easier time buying and placing radio spots.

EXHIBIT 15.27

The radio industry is in a state of flux. While Sirius and XM are providing subscription-based satellite radio programming, Clear Channel Communications has continued to expand its ownership of traditional radio stations and now owns and operates about 1,200 stations throughout the United States.

41. Bethany McLean, "Satellite Killed the Radio Star," *Fortune,* January 22, 2001, 95.

SUMMARY

 Detail the pros and cons of newspapers as a media class, identify newspaper categories, and describe buying and audience measurement for newspapers.

Newspapers can be categorized by target audience, geographic coverage, and frequency of publication. As a media class, newspapers provide an excellent means for reaching local audiences with informative advertising messages. Precise timing of message delivery can be achieved at modest expenditure levels. But for products that demand creative and colorful executions, this medium simply cannot deliver. Newspaper costs are typically transmitted via rate cards and are primarily a function of a paper's readership levels.

 Detail the pros and cons of magazines as a media class, identify magazine categories, and describe buying and audience measurement for magazines.

Three important magazine categories are consumer, business, and farm publications. Because of their specific editorial content, magazines can be effective in attracting distinctive groups of readers with common interests. Thus, magazines can be superb tools for reaching specific market segments. Also, magazines facilitate a wide range of creative executions. Of course, the selectivity advantage turns into a disadvantage for advertisers trying to achieve high reach levels. Costs of magazine ad space can vary dramatically because of the wide array of circulation levels achieved by different types of magazines.

 Detail the pros and cons of television as a media class, identify television categories, and describe buying and audience measurement for television.

The four basic forms of television are network, cable, syndicated, and local television. Television's principal advantage is obvious: Because it allows for almost limitless possibilities in creative execution, it can be an extraordinary tool for affecting consumers' perceptions of a brand. Also, it can be an efficient device for reaching huge audiences; however, the absolute costs for reaching these audiences can be staggering. Lack of audience interest and involvement certainly limit the effectiveness of commercials in this medium, and digital devices like TiVo that allow the viewer to skip commercials make TV advertising nonexistent for many. The three ways that advertisers can buy time are through sponsorship, participation, and spot advertising. As with any medium, advertising rates will vary as a function of the size and composition of the audience that is watching—yet audience measurement for television is not an exact science and its methods are often disputed.

 Detail the pros and cons of radio as a media class, identify radio categories, and describe buying and audience measurement for radio.

Advertisers can choose from three basic types of radio advertising: local spot, network radio, or national spot advertising. Radio can be a cost-effective medium, and because of the wide diversity in radio programming, it can be an excellent tool for reaching well-defined audiences. Poor listener attentiveness is problematic with radio, and the audio-only format places obvious constraints on creative execution. Satellite radio, which is subscriber-based, does away with advertising entirely on its music stations. Radio ad rates are driven by considerations such as the average number of listeners tuned to a station at specific times throughout the day. Buying and placing ads for radio is becoming easier due to ever-increasing consolidation in the industry.

KEY TERMS

general-population newspapers
business newspapers
ethnic newspapers
gay and lesbian newspapers
alternative press newspapers
display advertising
co-op advertising
preprinted insert
free-standing insert (FSI)
classified advertising
rate card
column inch
standard advertising unit (SAU)
run-of-paper (ROP) or run-of-press
preferred position
full position
circulation
paid circulation
controlled circulation
readership
bleed page
gatefold ads
first cover page

second cover page
third cover page
fourth cover page
double-page spreads
space contract
space order
closing date
on-sale date
cover date
guaranteed circulation
pass-along readership
network television
cable television
off-network syndication
first-run syndication
barter syndication
local television
satellite and closed-circuit
narrowcasting
channel grazing
zapping
zipping
V-chip

TiVo
sponsorship
participation
spot advertising
dayparts
television households
households using television (HUT)
program rating
ratings point
share of audience
direct broadcast by satellite (DBS)
high-definition television (HDTV)
radio networks
radio syndication
local spot radio advertising
network radio advertising
national spot radio advertising
average quarter-hour persons
average quarter-hour share
average quarter-hour rating
cume

QUESTIONS

1.   According to the chapter opener, what demographic group is cable television aggressively targeting, and why? What is cable's strategy for reaching this group of potential viewers, and do you think it will be successful? Why or why not?

2.   Magazines certainly proved to be the right media class for selling Absolut vodka. Why are magazines a natural choice for vodka advertisements? What has Absolut done with its advertising to take full advantage of this medium?

3.   Why have "digizines" fallen out of favor with publishers after receiving so much enthusiasm during the 1990s? Does the digizine have a future, and what advantages does the medium offer versus traditional printed magazines?

4.   Peruse several recent editions of your town's newspaper and select three examples of co-op advertising. What objectives do you believe the manufacturers and retailers are attempting to achieve in each of the three ads you've selected?

5.   Place your local newspaper and an issue of your favorite magazine side by side and carefully review the content of each. From the standpoint of a prospective advertiser, which of the two publications has a more dramatic problem with clutter? Identify tactics being used by advertisers in each publication to break through the clutter and get their brands noticed.

6.   The costs involved in preparing and placing ads in television programming such as the Super Bowl broadcast can be simply incredible. How is it that advertisers such as Pepsi and Nissan can justify the incredible costs that come with this media vehicle?

7.   Think about the television viewing behavior you've observed in your household. Of the five means for avoiding TV ad exposure discussed in this chapter, which have you observed in your household? What other avoidance tactics do your friends and family use?

8.   The choice between print and broadcast media is often portrayed as a choice between high- and low-involvement media. What makes one medium inherently more involving than another? How will the characteristics of an ad's message affect the decision to employ an involving versus an uninvolving medium?

9.   For an advertiser that seeks to achieve nationwide reach, can radio be a good buy? What frustrations are likely to be encountered in using radio for this purpose?

10. What are the potential liabilities and risks to consumers and advertisers of the consolidation of radio station ownership by a few, large media companies?

EXPERIENTIAL EXERCISES

1.   Look up the following four sites on the Internet and evaluate which medium (radio, television, magazines, or newspaper) you think is best suited for advertising the brands. Justify your choices based on an evaluation of these brands, and based on the pros and cons of each medium discussed in the chapter.

K2 Snowboards: http://www.k2snowboards.com

Cover Girl: http://www.covergirl.com

Metro-Goldwyn-Mayer: http://www.mgm.com

Southgate House: http://www.southgatehouse.com

2.   This chapter discusses the cost and buying procedures of four different types of media. Select a favorite magazine, newspaper, radio station, or television station and look over its media cost and buying procedures. (You can obtain rate cards at the company's Internet site or by contacting someone in the sales department.) Using this chapter's cost and buying information as your guide, gather specific ad rate information from the publication or station you selected. How do the rates and specifications of your selection compare with what is listed in the text? If the rates or buying procedures for your selected medium seem different from the ones listed in the text, explain why you think they varied. Do you think the advertising costs are justified for the medium you selected? Explain.

EXPERIENCING THE INTERNET

15-1   Alternative Press

While newspapers across the United States have been suffering a decline in circulation and readership, alternative press weeklies such as the *Village Voice* and *L.A. Weekly* have been growing. In the past, national advertisers often avoided these smaller papers due to their relatively small circulation. In recent years, however, hundreds of alternative press papers formed a network to give advertisers opportunities to transact national advertising buys across the country. This network provides them with an affordable, national reach.

Alternative Weekly Network: http://www.awn.org

1. Do alternative press papers provide advertisers with useful segmentation? What kinds of advertisers are likely to be interested in reaching the audience that alternative weeklies provide? Explain.

2. Search around the Alternative Weekly Network site for its demographics information, and read over some of the facts and figures. How is the average alternative-weekly reader depicted? Name an advertiser you think might not wish to target an alternative press audience, and give your reason.

3. Explain the benefits the Alternative Weekly Network provides to national advertisers. How does the service work?

15-2   Making Media Decisions

All media have inherent capabilities and limitations that advertisers must take into account when building a media plan. Even the most creative ad can't achieve sales and communications objectives if placement misses the target audience. These sites represent four major media, each having its unique pros and cons. Visit the sites and rank the usefulness of the media companies to advertisers based on the criteria listed in the questions below.

Fox: http://www.fox.com

Chicago Tribune: http://www.chicagotribune.com

KROQ: http://www.kroq.com

Spin: http://www.spin.com

1. Which medium is normally considered the best in terms of audience selectivity? What attributes give it this advantage over other media?

2. Which medium is normally considered the most accessible to the widest range of advertisers? What attributes give it this advantage over other media?

3. Which medium is normally considered the best at providing creative opportunities for an advertiser to express a brand's value? What attributes give it this advantage over other media?

4. Which medium is normally considered to have the greatest frequency and reach? What attributes give it this advantage over other media?

CHAPTER 16

After reading and thinking about this chapter, you will be able to do the following:

1

Understand the basic components and operation of the Internet.

2

Identify the nature of the Internet as a medium available for communicating advertising and promotion messages

3

Describe the different types of search engines used to surf the Web.

4

Describe the different advertising options on the Web.

5

Discuss the issues involved in establishing a site on the World Wide Web.

SIMON KNOWS MUSIC.

When it comes to finding music on the Web, Simon knows the score. From CDs to changers, artists to audio speakers, Simon helps you to compare prices, products, and album reviews. Simon doesn't sell anything. He searches thousands of online stores and millions of products for the music and audio equipment you want to buy—all from one place. Simon is smart, free, and totally plugged in. And, he can help you get connected too, at mySimon.com.

mySimon.com
The best in comparison shopping.

Introductory Scenario: No Wires Means New Rules.

The Internet has been a wild ride since 1999. First a boom. Then the dot.bomb. Now we appear to be firmly into another boom—and it may be permanent. Despite terrorism, recession, and skepticism from the large list of high-profile Internet sites that went from dot.darlings to dot.nots—including eToys, Garden.com, and Pets.com—the Internet has grown at an astounding rate. By 2003, networked business-to-business Internet transactions stood at $2.4 trillion—fifty percent greater than estimates. Growth in consumer e-commerce was just as spectacular, reaching $95 billion in 2003—and that was before you and I started buying music online![1] And the rebound is just as strong with respect to advertising, with online ad revenues approaching $7.5 billion in 2003, up over 20 percent from 2002.[2]

But despite this strength and the value of the Internet as we know it today, there is a very good chance that we are really witnessing just the very beginning of the boom in the Internet. Why? One word—wireless. But not the wireless that is now commonly referred to as WiFi. **WiFi** became widely popular in 2004 because it allowed Internet access connections that reach out about 300 feet. So everyone from coffee drinkers at Starbucks to emergency workers at disaster sites could have wireless access to information through their laptops. No, the new wireless revolution makes WiFi look like child's play for all kinds of applications including the use of the Internet for advertising and promotion. Over the next few years WiFi will yield to three innovative technologies that will push wireless networking into every facet of life from cars to homes to offices to the beach. These technologies are[3]

FIND THE KID WITH GLASSES

Your search should be easy. That's why we created a search experience where the emphasis is on finding, not searching. We obviously can't read your mind, but by using Teoma technology and natural language, Jeeves is able to better understand your keyword, phrase or question. That means a more refined search so you'll get to the relevant results you need a whole lot quicker. Searching is good. Finding is better. Ask Jeeves to find it.

An easier, more intuitive search. **Ask Jeeves** TO FIND IT.

EXHIBIT 16.1

In the next decade, new technologies like WiMax will provide wireless access to the Net that extends up to 30 miles. This will open up more ways for consumers to tap into their favorite information sources, like AskJeeves, and more ways for advertisers to reach those surfers.

- **WiMax.** WiMax is similar to WiFi in that both create "hot spots" around a central antenna within which people can wirelessly tap into the Net with a properly equipped laptop. One major difference—while WiFi creates a hotspot of perhaps 300 feet, WiMax has a range of 25–30 miles!
- **Mobile-Fi.** Mobile-Fi is similar to WiMax in that it has a multi-mile access but adds the capability of accessing the Net while the user is moving in a car or a train.
- **Ultrabroadband.** Ultrabroadband is a technology that will allow people to move extremely large files quickly over short distances. On the road, a driver could download a large file from an on-board PC to a handheld computer. Or, at home, you could do a wireless upload of your favorite concert from your PC to your TV.

Scientists at Intel, Alcatel, and Motorola are working on these technologies primarily as modes of communications for the high-speed transmission of data. But, in the practical application, these technologies will allow advertisers to communicate with audiences as Net surfers access the Internet through WiMax or Mobile-Fi. We are all just now getting accustomed to WiFi and the convenience it provides. These new

---

1.   Timothy J. Mullaney et al, "The E-Biz Surprise," *BusinessWeek,* May 12, 2003, 60–68. Using a different methodology, the U.S. Department of Commerce (http://www.census.gov.estats) estimates a somewhat lower $54 billion for 2003.
2.   PriceWaterhouseCoopers, "IAB Internet Advertising Report," April 2004, 5.
3.   Heather Green, "No Wires. No Rules," *BusinessWeek,* April 26, 2004, 95–97.

technologies are going to make it that much easier to Ask Jeeves any questions you want from any place you want! (See Exhibit 16.1.)

The Role of the Internet in the Advertising Process.

As the Internet has developed as a legitimate option for advertisers, many firms like Pepsi (http://www.pepsiworld.com) and BMW (http://www.bmw.com) have been highly successful in folding the Internet into their integrated brand promotion strategies. A trip to these sites shows that the these firms funnel a lot of information and promotion through their Web sites. But what about the Internet *overall* as a medium? What can and what will likely be the role of the Internet in a promotional effort? A few "truths" have made themselves evident to this point.

First, the Internet will *not* be replacing all other forms of advertising. Nor is it even likely that many advertisers will use the Internet as the main method of communicating with a target audience. But, like Pepsi and BMW, advertisers are discovering ways to use the Internet as a key component of integrated brand promotions. The music company Arista, which represents artists like Pink, Dido, and Sarah McLaughlin, uses Internet access like AOL's Music Discovery Network to deliver digital music streams of popular artists. Exposure through the Web has become a primary method of promoting both new artists and new singles.[4]

Second, yes, things are changing dramatically regarding all aspects of the Internet. The introductory scenario highlighted the new opportunities that wireless will provide. And auction sites like eBay have provided huge opportunities for small business all over the world. As a signal of this rapid change, consider this fact. In the last edition of this book, published in 2003, this chapter on the Internet referred to and cited about 100 different Web sites. As we prepared this current discussion of the Internet and advertising, we found that over 60 percent of those links did not exist! Those were sites that were all prominent and useful to the role and purpose of the Internet and advertising!

In the current view of the Internet and advertising, we will spend most of our time in this chapter focusing on two fundamental issues: the structure of the Internet and the potential of the Internet as an advertising medium. Through these analyses, we will come to a better understanding of how to use the Internet as part of an effective overall advertising and integrated brand promotion effort. First, we will consider a short history of the evolution of the Internet. Then, we'll have an overview of cyberspace and some of the basics of the way the Internet works. Next, we will consider the different types of advertising that can be used and some of the technical aspects of the process. Finally, we will look at the issues involved in establishing a Web site and developing a brand in the "e-community."

The (R)evolution of the Internet.

Technology changes everything—or at least it has the power and potential to change everything. When it's communications technology, such as the Internet, it can change something very fundamental about human existence. The Internet-connected consumer is connected to other consumers in real time, and with connection comes community, empowerment, even liberation.

Is the proliferation of the Internet an evolution in communication or a revolution? While revolutions are more common than they used to be, we have witnessed the Internet go through some growing pains. Still, what can be truly revolutionary about the Internet is its ability to alter the basic nature of communication within a commercial channel. And, despite the recent and ongoing shakeout of Internet sites talked about earlier, if you want an e-evolutionary perspective on the Internet and advertising, consider the short history of communication in this channel.[5]

---

4.   Tobi Elkin, "Record Labels Turning to Web to Boost Sales," *Advertising Age,* June 9, 2003, 16.
5.   Gene Koprowski, "A Brief History of Web Advertising," *Critical Mass,* Fall 1999, 8–14.

In 1994, advertisers began working with Prodigy and CompuServe, which were the first Internet service providers (ISPs). These advertisers had the idea that they would send standard television commercials online. Well, the technology was not in place back then for that to work. That technological fact sent the advertisers and the ISPs back to the drawing board. With the emergence of more commercial ISPs such as America Online and Earthlink, the new Web browsers were worth exploring as a way to send commercial messages. The first Web browser was Mosaic, the precursor to Netscape 1.0, and the first ads began appearing in *HotWired* magazine (the online version of *Wired* magazine) in October 1994. The magazine boasted 12 advertisers including MCI, AT&T, Sprint, Volvo, and ClubMed, and each one paid $30,000 for a 12-week run of online banner ads with no guarantee of the number or profile of the viewers.

Well, things have certainly changed since those early days. Now, the Internet is being accessed worldwide by just under 1 billion users.[6] Advertising revenues on the Internet were estimated at about $7.5 billion in 2004 and estimated to grow to over $14 billion by 2007.[7] The medium is used by all forms of companies, large and small, bricks and mortar, virtual, e-commerce, not-for-profit, you name it. Further, the medium is home to tens of thousands of personal Web sites, and the value of the Internet to individual consumers is growing daily. Let's turn our attention to some of the technical aspects of the Internet and then we'll explore the Internet as a strategic advertising and IBP option for advertisers.

An Overview of Cyberspace.
We refer to the Internet casually because it has become so prominent in the technological landscape. But just what is this thing called the Internet? The **Internet** is a global collection of computer networks linking both public and private computer systems. It was originally designed by the U.S. military to be a decentralized, highly redundant, and thus reliable communications system in the event of a national emergency. Even if some of the military's computers crashed, the Internet would continue to perform. Today the Internet comprises a combination of computers from government, educational, military, and commercial sources. In the beginning, the number of computers connected to the Internet would nearly double every year, from 2 million in 1994 to 5 million in 1995 to about 10 million in 1996. But beginning in1998, Internet use accelerated with around 90 million people being connected in the United States and Canada and 155 million people worldwide. Exhibit 16.2 shows that Internet access around the world has continued its accelerated rate of increase with about 1.3 *billion* users estimated worldwide as of 2006—a tenfold increase in just an eight-year period.[8]

Do not overlook the potential that still remains for Internet communications. The 1.3 billion Internet users represent only about 20 percent of the world's population. Further, countries with large populations, such as Russia and China, have only recently begun to provide widespread access to the Internet. Like many communication technologies, the Internet started rather upscale, but is now broadening to middle- and lower-income consumers with the advent of more affordable PCs and Web TV. Wireless technology will spread the application even further and faster to poor countries that cannot afford the infrastructure needed for wired connections.

The Basic Parts.
While many of you are no doubt frequent and savvy Web users, you may never have had the chance to explore the foundations of the Internet. Let's take some time to look at the basic parts of the Internet that allow all of us to surf and

6.   ClickZ, "Population Explosion," May 10, 2004, available at http://www.clickz.com, accessed May 23, 2004.
7.   "2003 Marketing Fact Book," *Marketing News*, July 7, 2003, 21. Data provided by Jupitermedia Corp.
8.   Estimate provided by Computer Industry Almanac at http://www.clickz.com, accessed May 23, 2004.

EXHIBIT 16.2

Estimates of Internet users worldwide as of 2004.

Country	Number Online	Percent of Total Population
Europe		
Austria	4.6 million	56.7%
Belgium	5.0 million	48.5
Czech Republic	3.5 million	33.6
Denmark	3.7 million	68.5
France	26.3 million	43.7
Germany	41.8 million	50.7
Hungary	3.0 million	30.0
Italy	28.6 million	49.3
Netherlands	10.3 million	63.9
Norway	3.1 million	68.8
Spain	16.6 million	41.2
Brazil	23.1 million	12.6
Mexico	11.1 million	10.5
China	95.8 million	9.3
Japan	77.9 million	61.2
Russia	22.3 million	15.4
United Kingdom	34.1 million	56.8
United States	185.9 million	64.1
World Total	**945.0 million**	**6.7%**

Source: Clickz data, http://www.clickz.com/stats.

that give advertisers the opportunity to use the Web as another tool in the promotional mix. There are four main components of the Internet: electronic mail, IRC, Usenet, and the World Wide Web. **Electronic mail (e-mail)** allows people to send messages to one another. In 2000, more than 1.5 trillion e-mails were sent from within the United States, which may explain the proliferation of services, technologies, and devices that support electronic messaging and the advertising associated with them—an example of which is seen in Exhibit 16.3. **Internet Relay Chat (IRC)** makes it possible for people to "talk" electronically in real time with each other, despite their geographical separation. For people with common interests, **Usenet** provides a forum for sharing knowledge in a public "cyberspace" that is separate from their e-mail program. Finally, with the **World Wide Web (WWW),** people can access an immense "web" of information in a graphical environment through the use of programs called Web browsers (such as Netscape and Internet Explorer). Many Web sites are still listed with the prefix http://, which stands for *hypertext transfer protocol,* or rules of interaction between the Web browser and the Web server that are used to deal with hypertext. Currently, many Web browsers assume that the file will be in hypertext, so they don't require users to type out the prefix.

To use the Internet, the user's personal computer must be connected to the network in some way. The most common way to access the Internet is by using a modem to call a *host computer,* which then provides the *client computer* access to the Internet. The four most common access options are through a commercial online service, such as America Online or Earthlink; a corporate gateway, such as AT&T's WorldNet Service; a local Internet service provider; or an educational institution. In

E-MAIL FROM NEARLY ANY PHONE FOR ONLY $9.95/MONTH.
No more phone jacks. No more expensive wireless services. Now with a simple toll free call you can
send and retrieve unlimited e-mails for only $9.95/month. PocketMail devices by SHARP and JVC available
at Staples, OfficeMax and Office Depot. Call 1-877-EMAILHERE or visit us at www.pocketmail.com

EXHIBIT 16.3

The 24/7, come-as-you-are convenience of Internet access is being fostered by new technology and new devices.
http://www.pocketmail .com

addition to using one of these networks, a personal computer needs software to communicate and move around while online, such as a Web browser or an e-mail application. For example, if you're interested in the graphic-oriented World Wide Web, then software such as Netscape Navigator or Microsoft Internet Explorer is needed. Or, if you're interested only in e-mail, then a program such as Eudora (http://www.eudora.com) will suffice. A new option for novice users and those not in need of computing capability is Web TV. With a simple keyboard and Internet connection, the user's television provides access to the World Wide Web. The user can then surf Web sites and send and receive e-mail. It's not exactly computing, but it is a connection to the Web.

While much of the vocabulary of the Web is common knowledge or intuitive, some of the language of the Web is, well, a mystery. The short glossary in Exhibit 16.4 defines some of the terms you have heard dozens of times, but may not be exactly sure what they really meant.

2 **Internet Media.** Internet media for advertising consist of e-mail (including electronic mailing lists), Usenet, and the World Wide Web.

E-Mail. E-mail is frequently used by advertisers to reach potential and existing customers. A variety of companies collect e-mail addresses and profiles that allow advertisers to direct e-mail to a specific group. Widespread, targeted e-mail advertising is just now materializing through organizations like Advertising.com (http://www .advertising.com) due to significant consumer resistance to advertisers' direct mailing to personal e-mail addresses (see Exhibit 16.5). Advertising.com will target, prepare, and deliver e-mails to highly specific audiences for advertisers. As techniques and guidelines are better established for direct e-mail advertising, it may become more accepted in the future. Many believe it's only a matter of time, because, historically, advertisers have rarely worried about being too intrusive. A case in point is the emergence of opt-in e-mail, also referred to as permission based e-mail. **Opt-in e-mail** is a list of Web site visitors who have given their permission to receive commercial e-mail about topics and products that interest them. If you have purchased a product online, it is likely you were asked to check a box acknowledging that you would like to receive future information about the company and its products. Service providers like optininc.com (http://www.optininc.com) help firms like OfficeMax, American Express, and Exxon manage their opt-in e-mail promotions.

People who wish to discuss specific topics through the Internet often join **electronic mailing lists.** Thousands of mailing lists are available on an incredible variety of topics. A message sent to the list's e-mail address is then re-sent to everybody on the mailing list. Organizations such as L-Soft International (http://www.lsoft.com) offer software for managing electronic mailing lists; this software can be downloaded for a few thousand dollars (see Exhibit 16.6). It is currently considered in very bad taste to openly sell products via topical electronic mailing lists, particularly when there is no apparent connection between the mailing list's topic and the advertised product. Product information shared through these mailing lists is similar to traditional word-of-mouth communications and is, at the moment, still in the hands of users.

Usenet. As we saw earlier, Usenet is a collection of discussion groups in cyberspace. People can read messages pertaining to a given topic, post new messages, and answer messages. For advertisers, this is an important source of consumers who care about certain topics. For example, the Usenet group alt.beer is an excellent place for a new microbrewery to promote its product. Advertisers can also use Usenet as a

Term	Definition
applet	A Java program that can be inserted into an HTML page (see definition for HTML below).
banner ad	An advertisement, typically rectangular, used to catch a consumer's eye on a Web page. Banner ads serve as a gateway to send a consumer to an expanded Web page where more extensive information is provided for a firm or a product. Many include an electronic commerce capability whereby a product or service can be ordered through the banner itself.
bandwidth	The capacity for transmitting information through an Internet connection. Internet connections are available through phone lines, cable, or various wireless options.
baud	A measure of data transmission speed, typically referring to a modem.
button	Small clickable square or circle running down the side of a Web site leading to an ad.
clicks	Number of times users click on a banner ad.
click-through	The process of a Web site visitor clicking on a banner ad and being sent to a marketer's home page for further information. Ad banner click-through rates average about 1 percent.
cookie	A piece of information sent by a Web server to a Web browser that tracks Web page activity. Because they identify users and their browsing habits, cookies are at the center of Web privacy issues.
CPC	*Cost per click*, the price advertisers pay for a banner ad based on the number of clicks the ad registers from Web site visitors.
CPM	*Cost per thousand impressions*, the long-standing measure of advertising rates used in traditional media and now carried over as a standard for the Internet.
domain name	The unique name of a Web site chosen by a marketer. There are twelve designations for domain names after the unique name chosen by the marketer: .com and .net refer to business and commercial sites; .org refers to an institution or nonprofit organization; .gov identifies government Web sites; .edu refers to academic institutions; .aero for the air transport industry; .biz for businesses; .coop for cooperatives; .info, unrestricted by organizational type; .museum for museums; .name for individuals; .pro for accountants, lawyers, and other professionals.
e-mail	Text messages exchanged via computer, Web TV, and various wireless devices such as Palm Pilots and cell phones.
hit	Used to measure the "traffic" at a Web site. Hits are measured by each time a file server sends a file to a browser. Hits may represent multiple requests by the same visitor and do not provide a measure of the number of people who visit a site (see "unique users" below).
HTML	An acronym that stands for *hypertext markup language*, which is used to display and link documents to the Web.
interstitial	Pop-up ads that appear when a Web user clicks on a designated (or not designated) area of a Web page.
intranet	An online network *internal* to a company that can be used by employees. Intranets are even showing up in some households.
link	The clickable connection between two Web sites.
opt-in email	A list of Internet users who sign up for commercial e-mail and give permission to have messages relayed to them via their e-mail addresses.
page views	The number of times a Web site visitor requests a page containing an ad. This measure serves as an indication of the number of times the ad was potentially viewed. Page views is analogous to gross impressions in traditional media.
rich media	Special technology effects used in Internet ads that provide enhanced audio and visual presentation. An example is streaming video.
spam	"Junk" e-mail sent to consumers who haven't requested the information. Not an acronym, the Internet term is said to have derived from a Monty Python skit about a restaurant where everything comes with Spam— the Hormel lunch meat, that is.
sponsorship	Site content paid for by an advertiser.
unique visitors	The number of different individuals who visit a Web site in a specified period of time.
views	Number of times a banner ad is downloaded.

EXHIBIT 16.4

A glossary of basic Internet terminology.

EXHIBIT 16.5

Several new service firms have emerged to help marketers place highly targeted e-mail messages on the Internet that serve as customized one-on-one advertising. http://www.advertising.com

source of unobtrusive research, getting the latest opinions on their products and services. Television shows such as *American Idol* often monitor Usenet groups to find out what people think about the show. Usenet is also used as a publicity vehicle for goods and services. Usenet represents a relatively self-segmented word-of-mouth channel.

Uninvited commercial messages sent to electronic mailing lists, Usenet groups, or some other compilation of e-mail addresses is a notorious practice known as **spam.** Estimates showed that 10.4 million spam e-mails were being sent every *minute* worldwide before restrictive legislation was enacted.[9] As we saw in Chapter 4 in the discussion of social and legal issues, few promotional techniques have drawn as much wrath from consumers and regulators alike as spam. In December 2003, federal anti-spam legislation was signed into law and in May of 2004 the first spammer was convicted. A New York state man accused of stealing Internet accounts to send hundreds of millions of spam messages was sentenced to up to seven years in prison.[10] So spam is not only annoying, now it is illegal and punishable with prison time. But before we close the discussion on spam, here is an interesting note: As annoying as spam seems to be to Web users, it appears to be effective. Those mass e-mailings can get a 5 to 7 percent response compared with 1 to 3 percent for offline direct marketing efforts.[11] So before we write off mass e-mails, we had better consider the results, not just the public reaction.

The World Wide Web. Finally, the World Wide Web (WWW) is a "web" of information available to most Internet users, and its graphical environment makes navigation simple and exciting. Of all the options available for Internet advertisers, the WWW holds the greatest potential. It allows for detailed and full-color graphics, audio transmission, delivery of in-depth messages, 24-hour availability, and two-way information exchanges between the marketer and customer. For some people, spending time on the Web is replacing time spent viewing other media, such as print, radio, and television. There is one great difference between the Web and other cyberadvertising vehicles: The consumer actively searches for the marketer's home page. Of course, Web advertisers are attempting to make their pages much easier to find and, in reality, harder to avoid.

To learn how a firm can make highly effective use of all the Internet media, see the IBP box describing how RCA records put together a Web-based strategy to create a buzz around Christina Aguilera's debut album.

③ Surfing the World Wide Web.
Using software such as Netscape, consumers can simply input the addresses of Web sites they wish to visit and directly access the information available there. However, the Web is a library with no card

EXHIBIT 16.6

Similar to e-mail messaging, firms can buy complete listservs, lists of e-mail groups, from companies like L-Soft for a few thousand dollars.

9.   Stephen Baker, "The Taming of the Internet," *BusinessWeek,* December 15, 2003, 78; Tobi Elkin, "Spam: Annoying but Effective," *Advertising Age,* September 22, 2003, 40.

10.   "Buffalo Spammer Found Guilty," *TechWeb News,* May 28, 2004, available at http://www.informationweek.com, accessed May 31, 2004.

11.   Elkin, "Spam: Annoying but Effective," 40.

IBP

Chatting a Star up the Charts

When executives at RCA records started plotting the advertising strategy for Christina Aguilera's debut album, they knew the Internet would play a crucial role in the introductory campaign. They understood that the teen target audience was skeptical and not receptive to traditional media. Or, in the words of one Internet marketing strategist, "They have their B.S. detectors on 11." With that knowledge, RCA put into motion an Internet-based advertising/word-of-mouth strategy to create an Internet buzz around Aguilera and her new album. The strategy was executed in four stages by Electric Artists, an Internet marketing firm that specializes in music marketing.

- *Stage 1:* To monitor what teens already knew about Aguilera and what they were saying, Electric Artists began monitoring popular teen sites such as http://www.alloy.com and http://www.gurl.com as well as sites created for other teen stars such as the Backstreet Boys and Britney Spears. The firm compiled some important information about fans' reactions to Aguilera's single "Genie in a Bottle" and also learned that there was a budding rivalry between Aguilera fans and Spears fans.
- *Stage 2:* Electric sent a team of cybersurfers to popular sites to start chatting up Aguilera, her single, her past, and the rumor of her new album. The surfers posted messages on sites or e-mailed individual fans with comments like "Does anyone remember Christina Aguilera—she sang the song from *Mulan* called 'Reflection'? I heard she has a new song out called 'Genie in a Bottle' and a new album is supposed to be out this summer." Electric strategists point out, "It's kids marketing to each other."
- *Stage 3:* The promotional strategy ascended to a new level as Electric shifted the emphasis of its Internet communication from Aguilera's single to the album itself. One challenge included motivating fans to go from a $1.98 purchase to a $16.00 purchase. Another hurdle was to convince big music retailers such as Amazon.com and CDNow that Aguilera deserved prominent visibility on their Web sites. To complement these strategies, Electric ensured that the album cover and album name were highly memorable to parents who were shopping for their teenagers. This included lots of major magazine and entertainment television media coverage that parents, particularly mothers, would come in contact with.
- *Stage 4:* To retain the momentum gained from the initial Internet effort, Electric continued to strengthen and broaden Aguilera's fan base using a variety of additional Internet strategies. The continually updated Web site offers teen audiences access to concert and TV appearances, chats, fan club information, merchandise, and e-mail. Electric also continues to monitor teen interest in competitors such as Mariah Carey and Whitney Houston to stay connected to the broader teen music scene.

The result of this Internet-based campaign was a number one album and eventually the Best New Artist award at the 2000 Grammy Awards. The story of Christina Aguilera shows that the power of Internet advertising lies in its ability to specifically target and communicate in very specific language to an audience. That is the distinguishing feature of the Internet as an advertising media alternative. The Aguilera story demonstrates that Internet advertising is much more than just banner ads. Currently, major record labels still find the Internet, particularly with the ability to use rich media like streaming video, to be a powerful way to promote new artists and new material.

Sources: Erin White, "Chatting a Singer up the Pop Charts," *Wall Street Journal,* December 5, 1999, B1, B4; Christopher John Farley and David E. Thigpen, "Christina Aguilera: Building a 21st Century Star," *Time,* March 6, 2000, 70–71; Tobi Elkin, "Record Labels Turning to Web to Boost Sales," *Advertising Age,* June 9, 2003, 16.

catalog. There is no central authority that lists all possible sites accessible via the Internet. This condition leads to **surfing**—gliding from page to page. Users can seek and find different sites in a variety of ways: through search engines, through direct links with other sites, and by word of mouth.

A **search engine** allows an Internet user to type in a few keywords, and the search engine then finds all sites that contain the keywords. Search engines all have the same basic user interface but differ in how they perform the search and in the amount of the WWW accessed. There are four distinct styles of search engines: hierarchical, collection, concept, and robot. There are also the special cases of portals, Web community sites, and mega–search engines.

the new
YAHOO! search
Faster. Easier. Bingo.

yahoo.com

Big Internet sites like Yahoo! offer Internet users a hierarchical search engine to seek out information on the Internet. Notice also that sites like Yahoo! and Lycos provide all sorts of links for travel, games, chat, e-mail, and news and information.
http://www.yahoo.com;
http://www.lycos.com;
http://www.excite.com

Hierarchical Search Engines. Most of you are familiar with Yahoo!, which is an example of a search engine with a hierarchical, subject-oriented system (see Exhibit 16.7). In a **hierarchical search engine,** all sites fit into categories. For example, Nike is indexed as Business and Economy/Shopping and Services/Apparel/Footwear/Athletic Shoes/Brand Names. Users are thus able to find and select a category as well as all the relevant Yahoo! sites. Going to Business and Economy/Shopping and Services/Sports/Snowboarding/Snowboards, for instance, gives a list of nearly 60 companies that sell snowboards on the Web. By checking these sites, a person could find a snowboard company and buy a snowboard over the Web. Although hierarchical sites like Yahoo! are great for doing general searches, they do have some significant limitations. For example, Yahoo!'s database of Web sites contains only submissions. That is, Yahoo! does not actually perform a search of the Web for sites, but contains only sites that users tell it about. Because of this, Yahoo! omits a significant portion of the vast information available on the Web.

Collection Search Engines. A second type of search engine is exemplified by AltaVista. **Collection search engines** use a **spider,** which is an automated program that crawls around the Web and collects information. As of mid-2000, the collection of Web pages indexed by AltaVista stood at over 3 million. With AltaVista, a person can perform a text search on all of these sites, resulting in access to literally tens of billions of words.

Concept Search Engines. Excite is a concept search engine. With a **concept search engine,** a concept rather than a word or phrase is the basis for the search. Using the alpine skiing example, the top sites with the concept "alpine skiing" are listed in an Excite search. This is a very efficient way of searching, producing relatively focused results compared to AltaVista and with the added ability of using the results of a search to further modify the search. The downside is that concept search engines such as Excite lack the comprehensiveness of collection search engines. Ask Jeeves (http://www.ask.com), another concept search engine, allows users to conduct searches using natural-language questions such as, "Who was the fourteenth president of the United States?" (Answer: Franklin Pierce, 1853–1857.)

Robot Search Engines. The newest technique, **robot search engines,** employs **robots** ("bots") to do the work for the consumer by roaming the Internet in search of information fitting certain user-specified criteria. For example, shopping robots specialize in finding the best deals for your music needs (see Exhibit 16.8), insurance needs (http://www.insweb.com), or traveling needs (http://www.travelocity.com). Web retailers concerned that such robots will result in an electronic marketplace governed entirely by price rather than brand loyalty have designed their sites to either refuse the robot admission to the site or confuse the robot. Still, some analysts believe that future e-commerce will be governed by "shopbots" and that loyalty will shift to the shopbot sites rather than retail brand names. We will explore this issue in great detail in Chapter 19 on direct marketing and e-commerce.

EXHIBIT 16.8

One way to search the Internet is with "shopbots" or "bots." These automated Internet search engines take directions on what to search for and then deliver it automatically back to the user. http://www .mysimon.com

EXHIBIT 16.9

Community portals like Latina.com offer the opportunity to visit a site that matches surfers' interests for information on a variety of topics from politics to culture to entertainment. What is teen site Alloy (http:// www.alloy.com) doing to make sure it wins the community portal war? Are the search functions and navigational features of Alloy.com designed to direct surfers to particular sites? Does it offer search access to the World Wide Web?

Portals. Portal has assumed the position as the most overused, misused, abused, and confused term in Internet vocabulary. A **portal** is a starting point for Web access and search. Portals can be vertical (serving a specialized market or industries, such as Chemdex [http://www.chemdex.org] for the chemical industry), horizontal (providing access and links across industries, such as Verticalnet [http://www.vertical net.com] with its 53 different business trade communities), or ethnic (http://www .latina.com; see Exhibit 16.9) or community-based. Several of the large search engines, such as Yahoo! and Google, are focusing their attention on becoming portals for Internet exploring. In addition to providing its own content, AOL serves as a convenient and well-organized entrance to the Web. From AOL a Web surfer can jump to many locations highlighted by AOL, particularly commercial sites who are partnering with AOL and have paid a fee for preferred placement on the site.

The portal wars are already hot, with each portal trying to provide access and incentive for using their service as a gateway to the Internet or commerce. Each is trying to top the other in monthly traffic and advertising revenue. This battle is going to only get hotter in the near term as portals vie for superiority and dominance in the wireless Web, or WiFi as it is called. As we saw at the outset of the chapter, WiFi is a radio signal that beams Internet connections out about 300 feet from a transmitter. A WiFi-accessible area is called a **hot spot**. Any computer equipped with a WiFi receptor can log on to the Internet. In 2003, 18 million people had wireless Web browsing capability. In 2005, over 90 percent of new laptops sold were WiFi ready.[12] Recall the chapter introduction where the proposition was offered that that wireless Web access appears to be emerging as a key aspect of Web use and one that advertisers have to access for opportunity.

Paid Search. The biggest news in Internet searching is not how it gets done but how much it costs. **"Paid" search** is the process by which companies pay Web search engines and portals to place ads in or near relevant search results. Paid search has grown astronomically is expected to reach $8 billion by 2008.[13] The catalyst for growth in paid search has been the success of Google, which pushed the concept from its beginning. Google's search technology fine-tunes the Web user's search to more relevant and specific Web sites. For example, if an astronomy buff enters the word "saturn" in a search, results would be returned for the planet, not the car company. Google has jumped to the top of the search engine world, representing about 48 percent of all Internet inquiries and over $1 billion in sales.[14]

Paid search is extremely valued by firms as they try to improve the effectiveness and efficiency of their use of the Internet as a promotional tool. Steve St. Andre, president of Ford Direct, spends 25 percent of his media budget on paid search and says, "Our goal is to drive online transactions. We want keywords to convert into leads and then sales. . . . Search allows you to rethink the entire advertising model and immediately see which keyword buys are successful and which aren't." [15] And paid search is considered relatively cheap—about 35 cents per verified click achieved through the search, compared with $1 or more for other direct marketing techniques.[16] But, strategy in paid search is complicated and competitive. Keep your eye out for **search engine optimization (SEO)** courses as consultants and more and more firms join in on paid search.

Personal Web Sites and Blogs. Many people have created their own Web pages that list their favorite sites. This is a fabulous way of finding new and interesting sites—as well as feeding a person's narcissism. For example, the Web site for this book, http://oguinn.swcollege.com, is a resource for information about advertising, including links to a wide range of industry resources. Since this page is maintained, updated, and checked regularly, it is a good resource for someone interested in advertising. Although most people find Web pages via Internet resources (over 80 percent of respondents in one survey found Web pages through search engines or other Web pages), sites can also be discovered through traditional word-of-mouth communications. Internet enthusiasts tend to share their experiences on the Web through discussions in coffeehouses, by reading and writing articles, and via other non-Web venues. There are also mega–search engines that combine several search engines at once (for example, http://www.dogpile.com).

The newest personal use of the Web is the blog. On a Web site, a **blog,** a short form for Weblog, is a personal journal that is frequently updated and intended for public access. Blogs generally represent the personality of the author or the Web site and its purpose. Topics include brief philosophical musings, favorite hobbies and music, political leanings, commentary on Internet and other social issues, and links to other sites the author favors. The essential characteristics of the blog are its journal form, typically a new entry each day, and its informal style. The author of a blog is often referred to as a **blogger.** People who post new journal entries to their blog may often say they blogged today, they blogged it to their site, or that they still have to blog.

12.   Heather Green et al., "WiFi World," *BusinessWeek,* April 28, 2003, 86–92.
13.   Tobi Elkin, "Paid Search's Appeal Escalates," *Advertising Age,* October 13, 2003, 62.
14.   Melanie Warner, "What Can Your Company Learn from Google?" *Business 2.0,* June 2004, 100–106.
15.   Tobi Elkin, "Paid Search's Appeal Escalates," *Advertising Age,* October 13, 2003, 62.
16.   Ben Elgin and Timothy J. Mullaney, "Search Engines are Picking Up Steam," *BusinessWeek,* March 24, 2003, 86–87.

While blogs may sound all underground and grassroots-y, nothing could be further from the truth. Search engines Google and Yahoo! are battling for the favor of bloggers and their blogs. Google's Blogger.com is designed to make it easier for novices to create and update their personal blogs for free. Estimates put users of Blogger.com at about 1 million members, 200,000 active blogs and growing rapidly.[17] And big corporations like Procter & Gamble are finding that some of their brands, like Swiffer (a long plastic stick with a swatch of dust-attracting cloth attached to the end), are featured on customer blogs.[18]

4 Advertising on the Internet.

A brief history of advertising on the Internet defines the volatility of the Internet industry. In 1995, $54.7 million was spent advertising on the Internet. Spending in 1996 was around $300 million. In 1997 it jumped to just around $1 billion, in 1998 it was somewhere around $2 billion, and the year 2000 logged in at just over $8 billion. Then the boom to turned to bust and the dot.bomb hit. In 2001 advertising revenues dropped to just over $7.1 billion and in 2002 another billion went out of the ad market and revenues came in at just over $6 billion (see Exhibit 16.10). By 2003, a recovery was in process and revenues spiked back to $7.25 billion and are estimated to grow to about $14 billion by 2007.[19] It is somewhat humorous to note that at the height of the dot.com "bubble" it was estimated that Internet advertising would reach $30 billion by 2004—an astronomical growth rate that was never achieved.[20] It remains to be seen whether the upward trend begun in 2003 can be sustained.

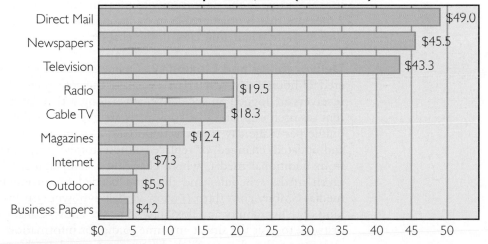

Overall U.S. Advertising Market-Media Comparisons, 2003 ($ in billions)

Medium	$ in billions
Direct Mail	$49.0
Newspapers	$45.5
Television	$43.3
Radio	$19.5
Cable TV	$18.3
Magazines	$12.4
Internet	$7.3
Outdoor	$5.5
Business Papers	$4.2

EXHIBIT 16.10

Internet advertising revenues grew dramatically through the year 2000 and then made an abrupt downturn. By 2003, a recovery was taking place with spending reaching $7.3 billion. Here is a comparison of advertising spending for the Internet and other major media.

17. Michael Liedtke, "Google's Blog Feature Steps Up Yahoo Fight," Associated Press, May 10, 2004, available at http://www.biz.yahoo.com/ap/, accessed May 10, 2004.

18. Nancy Einhart, "Clean Sweep of the Market," *Business 2.0,* March 2003, 56.

19. PriceWaterhouseCoopers, "IAB Internet Advertising Report," April 2004, 5; "2003 Marketing Fact Book," *Advertising Age,* July 7, 2003, 21.

20   This estimate was made by the Internet Advertising Bureau, "Total Ad Spend for 2000 Reached USD8.2 bn," April 22, 2001.

A wide range of issues are associated with using the Internet for advertising purposes. This section begins by exploring the advantages of Internet advertising. Then we'll look at who is advertising on the Internet, the costs associated with Internet advertising, and the different types of Internet advertising.

The Advantages of Internet Advertising.

Internet advertising has emerged as a legitimate advertising option for advertisers—and it is not just because the Web represents a new and different technological option. Several unique characteristics of Internet advertising offer advantages over traditional forms.

Target Market Selectivity.

The Web offers advertisers a new and precise way to target market segments. Not only are the segments precisely defined (you can place an ad on the numismatist [coin collecting] society page, for example), but the Internet allows forms of targeting that truly enhance traditional segmentation schemes such as demographics, geographics, and psychographics. Advertisers can focus on specific interest areas, but they can also target based on geographic regions (including global), time of day, computer platform, or browser. A great example of a highly targeted site is e.Harmony.com (http://www.eharmony.com), an electronic matchmaking/dating service. The site claims to be the fastest growing relationship site on the Web and offers free personality profiles to visitors. When American Airlines enlisted the help of TM Advertising to track the Web behavior of the readers of *Wall Street Journal* (http://www.wsj.com) online travel columns and then "follow" those surfers around with American Airlines ads at various other sections, response to the online advertising increased 115 percent.[21]

Tracking.

The Internet allows advertisers to track how users interact with their brands and learn what interests current and potential customers. Banner ads and Web sites also provide the opportunity to measure the response to an ad by means of hits, a measure that is unattainable in traditional media. We'll discuss tracking and measure in more detail a bit later in the chapter.

Deliverability and Flexibility.

Online advertising and Web site content is delivered 24 hours a day, seven days a week, at the convenience of the receiver. Whenever receivers are logged on and active, advertising is there and ready to greet them. Current research estimates that consumers are exposed to about 800 marketing messages online per usage day.[22] Just as important, a campaign can be tracked on a daily basis and updated, changed, or replaced almost immediately. This is a dramatic difference from traditional media, where changing a campaign might be delayed for weeks, given media schedules and the time needed for production of ads in traditional media. GMbuy.com (http://www.globalbuypower.com) is a perfect example of this kind of deliverability and flexibility. The site allows consumers considering a GM car or truck to visit the site at any time to dig for information about GM vehicles. And, as mentioned earlier, as Web delivery goes wireless, there will be even more flexibility and deliverability for Web communications.

Interactivity.

A lofty and often unattainable goal for a marketer is to engage a prospective customer with the brand and the firm. This can be done with Internet advertising in a way that just cannot be accomplished in traditional media. A consumer can go to a company Web site or click through from a banner ad and take a tour of the brand's features and values. A **click-through** is a measure of the number of page elements (hyperlinks) that have actually been requested (that is, "clicked

---

21.   Kris Oser, "Targeting Web Behavior Pays, America Airlines Study Finds," *Advertising Age,* May 17, 2004, 8.
22.   "2003 Marketing Fact Book," *Marketing News,* July 7, 2003, 21. Data provided by Jupitermedia Corp.

through" from the banner ad to the link). Software is a perfect example of this sort of advantage of the Web. Let's say you are looking for software to do your taxes. You can log on to H&R Block tax consulting (http://www.hrblock.com) and you will find all the software, tax forms, and online information you need to prepare your taxes. Then you can actually file your taxes with both the IRS and your state tax agency! And this sort of interactivity is not reserved for big national companies. Try this as an exercise. Find a sign company in your local phone directory. It is likely that one will have a Web site where you can design your own sign, order it, and ask for it to be delivered. You have complete interaction with the firm and its product without ever leaving your computer.

Cost. While the cost-per-thousand numbers on reaching audiences through the Web are still relatively high (see the next section) compared with radio or television, they compare very favorably with magazines, newspapers, and direct marketing. And the cost for producing a Web ad, including both banner ads and Web sites, is relatively low. Banner ads are very cheap at a few hundred or few thousand dollars to produce and place. Web sites can be expensive, tens or even hundreds of thousands of dollars to develop, but the cost may be fixed for a long period of time. We will cover more on the cost of Web advertising shortly.

Integration. Web advertising is easily integrated and coordinated with other forms of promotion. In the most basic sense, all traditional media advertising being used by a marketer can carry the Web site URL. Web banner ads can highlight themes and images from television or print campaigns. Special events or contests can be featured in banner ads and on Web sites. Overall, the integration of Web activities with other components of the marketing mix is one of the easiest integration tasks in the IBP process. This is due to the flexibility and deliverability of Web advertising discussed earlier. A great example of integrating consumer Web behavior with another part of the promotional process, personal selling, is the strategy used by Mazda Corp. It used to be that the salespeople hated the Web because shoppers would come to the showrooms armed with "cost" data on every vehicle obtained from various Web sites. Rather than battle consumers, Mazda embraced the fact that car shoppers surf the Web and search out pricing information. Now, visitors to Mazda showrooms can access Web data from onsite Internet kiosks. Rather than interfering with the personal selling process, one dealership owner claims that the Internet access right at the dealership "helps build trust and close sales faster."[23]

Who Advertises on the Internet?
Exhibit 16.11 demonstrates that advertising on the Web, compared with television and magazines, for example, is highly concentrated among a very few advertisers with similar business-model profiles. You can see that the big users of the Web are Internet companies themselves. This will have to change if the WWW is to really challenge traditional media.

The Cost of Internet Advertising.
On a cost-per-thousand (CPM) basis, the cost of Web ads for the most part compares favorably with ads placed in traditional media. Exhibit 16.12 shows the comparison of absolute cost and CPM for ads placed in traditional media and on the Web. The real attraction of the Internet is not found in raw numbers and CPMs, but rather in terms of highly desirable, highly segmentable, and highly motivated audiences (see Exhibit 16.13). The Internet is ideally suited for niche marketing—that is, for reaching only those consumers most likely to buy what the marketer is selling. This aspect of the Internet as an advertising option has always been

23. Bob Parks, "Let's Remake a Dealership," *Business 2.0,* June 2004, 65–67.

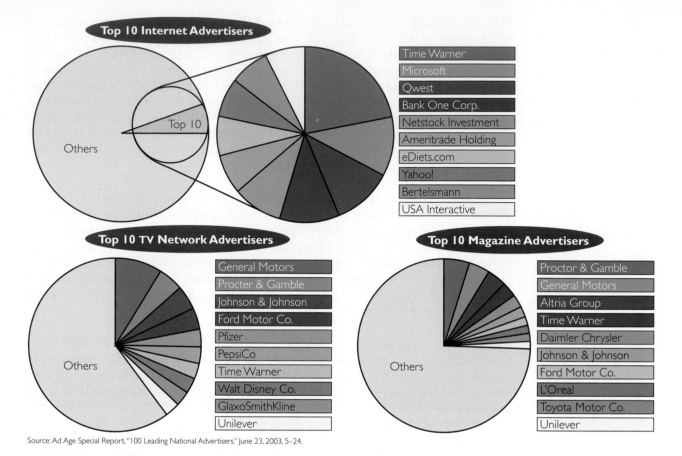

Top 10 Internet Advertisers

Time Warner
Microsoft
Qwest
Bank One Corp.
Netstock Investment
Ameritrade Holding
eDiets.com
Yahoo!
Bertelsmann
USA Interactive

Top 10 TV Network Advertisers

General Motors
Procter & Gamble
Johnson & Johnson
Ford Motor Co.
Pfizer
PepsiCo
Time Warner
Walt Disney Co.
GlaxoSmithKline
Unilever

Top 10 Magazine Advertisers

Proctor & Gamble
General Motors
Altria Group
Time Warner
Daimler Chrysler
Johnson & Johnson
Ford Motor Co.
L'Oreal
Toyota Motor Co.
Unilever

Source: Ad Age Special Report, "100 Leading National Advertisers." June 23, 2003, 5–24.

EXHIBIT 16.11

A comparison of top advertisers on the Web, on television, and in magazines.

EXHIBIT 16.12

The cost per thousand (CPM) for banner ads has been falling steadily over the past several years. However, compared with television or radio broadcasts, banner ad CPM is still relatively high. Notice, however, that the absolute cost in dollars of placing banner ads and other Internet-based communications can be much lower than traditional media.

	Absolute Cost	Cost per Thousand (CPM)
Traditional Media		
Local TV (30-second spot)	$4,000 to $45,000	$12 to $15
National TV (30-second spot)	80,000 to 600,000	10 to 20
Cable TV (30-second spot)	5,000 to 10,000	3 to 8
Radio (30-second spot)	200 to 1,000	1 to 5
Newspaper (top-10 markets)	40,000 to 80,000	80 to 120
Magazines (regional coverage)	40,000 to 100,000	50 to 120
Direct mail (inserts)	10,000 to 20,000	15 to 40
Billboards	5,000 to 25,000	—
Internet Media		
Banner ads	$1,000 to $5,000	$5 to $50
Rich media	1,000 to 10,000	40 to 50
E-mail newsletters	1,000 to 5,000	25 to 200
Sponsorship	Variable based on duration	30 to 75
Pop-up/pop-under	500 to 2,000	2 to 50

Sources: Forrester Research, http://www.forrester.com; Jennifer Rewick, "Choices, Choices," *Wall Street Journal*, April 23, 2001, R12.

TAKE YOUR FRIENDS' ADVICE ON MEN.
NOT DOCTORS.

CASE# 8779

The first place you turn for a doctor referral is your friends. But what makes you think they know any better than you do? Ask an expert. Visit HealthGrades.com, a free, objective source for ratings on doctors, hospitals and health plans nationwide. Now you can make your medical decisions informed ones.

✓ health grades .com
The Healthcare Rating Experts

EXHIBIT 16.13

One of the key advantages of the Internet is that Web sites can be targeted to the very specific information needs of narrowly defined segments.
http://www.healthgrades
.com

its great attraction: the ability to identify segments and deliver almost-customized (or in the case of e-mail, actually customized) messages directly to them—one by one.

The current Internet audience is relatively affluent, so they do have the means to buy. In cases where there is an active search for product or service information on the Internet, there is also a predisposed and motivated audience. This makes the Internet fairly special among advertising-supported vehicles. On the other hand, there are enormous audience measurement problems; we don't really know with much certainty who sees or notices Internet advertising. So advertisers don't know exactly what they are buying. This bothers them. Further, there is some evidence that audience tolerance for Web advertising is actually declining. Recent studies find that Web surfers are even less tolerant of advertising than are average consumers. The number of Web users who say they actively avoid the ads is up, and the number who say they notice ads is down.[24] This is consistent with the experience of advertising history in general: As advertising becomes more common, fewer ads are noticed, fewer are accepted, and fewer make any impact at all. Each ad thus becomes less powerful as ads become more common, familiar, and annoying. Advertising has always had a way of being a victim of its own success. What's more, Internet advertising comes into an already crowded and highly cluttered media and information environment.

Regardless of the lack of effective measurement and evaluation of reach, the narrow audience composition, and the unknown impact of Web advertising, companies seem to be afraid of being left behind. Apparently, there is some prestige attached to advertising on the WWW, or at least a feeling of inadequacy to not be there. In addition, most advertisers want to have a well-established Web image in the future, so getting involved now makes sense, even if the best strategy for doing so is unclear. Keeping on eye on the future seems like a good idea, too. By 2005, it is expected that there will be 77 million Internet users under age 18. This means that a new generation of Net surfers and users will be emerging and will be searching the Web with ease.[25]

Types of Internet Advertising.

There are several ways for advertisers to place advertising messages on the Web. The most widely known of these options is the banner ad, which includes several variations. But more complex and elaborate variations on Internet advertising include pop-up ads, e-mail communication, streaming video and audio, corporate Web sites, and virtual malls. We will consider the features and advantages of each of these types of Internet advertising options.

Banner Ads.   Banner ads, which account for about 50 percent of all online advertising revenue, are paid placements of advertising on other sites that contain editorial material.[26] A variation on the banner that you may encounter is the **skyscraper,** a

24. Stephen Baker, "Pop up Ads Better Start Pleasing," *BusinessWeek,* December 8, 2003, 40.
25. Bernadette Burke, "Meeting Generation Y," nua Internet Surveys, July 19, 1999, available at http://www.nua.net/surveys/.
26. Heather Green and Ben Elgin, "Do E-Ads Have a Future?" *BusinessWeek e.biz,* January 22, 2001, 46–49.

tall, skinny banner ad that is a variation on the traditional top-of-the-screen rectangle. A feature of banner ads is that consumers not only see the ad but also can make a quick trip to the marketer's home page by clicking on the ad (this is the "click-through" defined earlier). Thus, the challenge of creating and placing banner ads is not only to catch people's attention but also to entice them to visit the marketer's home page and stay for a while. Many high-traffic Web sites that provide information content have started to rely on advertisers to support their services. General consumer sites such as Yahoo! and HotWired have banner advertisements as part of their revenue-generation scheme.

A more targeted option is to place banner ads on sites that attract specific market niches. For example, a banner ad for running shoes would be placed on a site that offers information related to running. This option is emerging as a way for advertisers to focus more tightly on their target audiences. Currently, advertisers consider WWW users to be a focused segment of their own. However, as the Web continues to blossom, advertisers will begin to realize that, even across the entire Web, there are sites that draw specific subgroups of Web users. These niche users have particular interests that may represent important opportunities for the right marketer.

A pricing evaluation service for banner ads is offered by Interactive Traffic. The I-Traffic Index computes a site's advertising value based on traffic, placement and size of ads, ad rates, and evaluations of the site's quality.[27] Firms such as Forrester Research (see Exhibit 16.14) assess the costs of banner ads on a variety of sites and provide an estimate to advertisers of the audience delivered. Complicating the matter now is the fact that consumer resistance to banner ads is increasing. First, most online consumers do not click on Web banner ads. For example, one survey found that only 1 percent of surfers click on banner ads.[28] Second, many consumers resent banner ads, which they see as intrusive and annoying; banner ads increase Web page load times due to their complex graphics and animation. (Thus, banner advertisements should be designed with downloading time in mind.) Supporting this trend are fixes called *ad blockers,* which allow consumers to screen out banner ads. And recall the discussion of paid search. Many firms are diverting money from banner ads, with poor hit and click-through rates, to paid search investments with Google and Overture where tracking the effect of the paid search is much more precise.

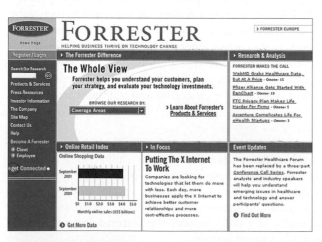

EXHIBIT 16.14

New service and research organizations can track advertising cost and audience delivered for various Web sites. http://www.forrester .com

There is currently wide debate about the value and even the future of banner ads. On the plus side, banner ads now account for a large percentage of online spending by companies trying to use the Web as part of their integrated brand promotion strategy. In addition, a study of recall for banner ads shows that recall for a single ad banner exposure is about 12 percent, which compares favorably with the 10 percent recall for a single exposure to a television ad.

On the negative side of the argument, eMarketer estimates that 99.9 percent of all banner ads don't get clicked. In addition, eMarketer's data suggests that 49 percent of Web surfers don't even look at a banner ad while they surf, and that in order to develop any brand recognition a consumer would have to be exposed to a banner ad 27 times—not a good combination of statistics. The current thinking is that most users of banner advertising will shift their Web spending from banners to strategic partnerships and sponsorships.[29]

27. K. Cleland, "SRDS, I Join Interactive Frenzy," *Advertising Age,* October 16, 1995, 22.

28. *The Economist,* September 26, 1998.

29. "Consumer Attitudes toward Web Marketing," eMarketing Report, July 7, 1999, available at http://www.emarketing.com, accessed March 22, 2000.

Sponsorship. Sponsorship occurs when a firm pays to maintain a section of a site. In some instances a firm may also provide content for a site along with sponsorship. If you go to Yahoo!'s home page (http://www.yahoo.com) you'll find that the Yahoo! Movies section and Yahoo! Marketplace section are almost always "sponsored by" a major movie studio and a brokerage house respectively. The Weather Channel Web site (http://www.weather.com) is also a site that attracts sponsors. Public service or not-for-profit Web sites often try to recruit local sponsors. In the context of more animated banner ads and paid search, it appears that sponsorships are becoming less and less popular.

Pop-Up/Pop-Under Ads. The only thing surfers hate more than banner ads is pop-up Internet ads. The idea is borrowed from TV. A **pop-up ad** is an Internet advertisement that opens in a separate window while a Web page is loading. The more times people click on these ads, the more money can be charged for the privilege of advertising. If the future of banner ads is uncertain, then the future of pop-ups must be doomed—a recent study found that 62 percent of surfers said that pop-ups interfered with their use of a Web page.[30] But, like spam, pop-ups are relatively effective with 2 percent of Web visitors clicking on the pop-up—that's double the click-through rate for banner ads.[31] But many service providers are offering "blockers" that greatly reduce an advertiser's ability to get a pop-up onto a user's screen.

A subcategory of pop-up ads is the *interstitial,* also called "splash screen." These appear on a site after a page has been requested but before it has loaded, and stay onscreen long enough for the message to be registered. So a surfer who wants to go to a certain site has to wade through an ad page first, just as a television viewer must watch a commercial before seeing a favorite show. It is often not merely a word from a sponsor, but an invitation to link to another related site.

Pop-under ads are ads that are present "under" the Web user's active window and are visible only once the surfer closes that window. It is debatable as to whether pop-ups or pop-unders are the greater nuisance. Regardless, if the click-through rate is not identifiable or if paid search begins to completely dominate online advertising investment (as it appears it may), then the pop-up and pop-under ad may end up being a bit of curious Internet history (please!).

E-Mail Communication. As mentioned earlier, e-mail communication may be the Internet's most advantageous application. Through e-mail, the Internet is the only mass medium capable of customizing a message for thousands or even millions of receivers. The message is delivered in a unique way, one at a time, which no other medium is capable of doing. The growth estimates for e-mail advertising have been greatly reduced given the attitude toward unwanted e-mail and the anti-spam legislation. E-mail advertising does have some promise though. As discussed earlier, when Web users agree to receive e-mails from organizations, this is called opt-in e-mail or **permission marketing**. Some Web firms, such as Inetgiant.com (see Exhibit 16.15), specialize in

E-mail as an advertising alternative can meet with some heavy resistance from Web users. One way to avoid the resistance is to use a permission marketing firm. These firms have lists of consumers who "opt in," or agree to have e-mail sent to them by commercial sources. http://www.inetgiant.com

30.   nua Internet Surveys, May 3, 2001, http://www.nua.ie, accessed May 28, 2001.

31.   Stephen Baker, "Pop-Up Ads Had Better Start Pleasing," *BusinessWeek,* December 8, 2003, 40.

developing what are called "opt-in" lists of Web users who have agreed to accept commercial e-mails.

The data on permission-based e-mailing versus spamming are compelling. Sixty-six percent of Web users who give their permission to have e-mail sent to them indicate that they are either eager or curious to read the e-mail. This compares with only 15 percent of Web users who receive e-mail through spamming.[32] And e-mail advertisers are turning to some traditional message strategies such as humor to make the e-mail messages more palatable and interesting. BitMagic, an Amsterdam-based Web advertising specialty firm, has Web users download software containing a joke, cartoon, or game along with the e-mail message.[33]

Through e-mail and electronic mailing lists, advertisers can encourage viral marketing. **Viral marketing** is the process of consumers marketing to consumers over the Internet through word of mouth transmitted through e-mails and electronic mailing lists. Hotmail (http://www.hotmail.com) is the king of viral marketing. Every e-mail by every Hotmail subscriber used to conclude with the tagline "Get your private, free e-mail at http://www.hotmail.com." That viral marketing program helped sign up 12 million subscribers, with 150,000 being added every day.[34]

Streaming Video and Audio. **Streaming video and audio** is merely the process of inserting TV- and radio-like ads into music and video clips that marketers send to Web users as they visit content networks. Firms such as RealNetworks, NetRadio, and MusicVision insert ads for advertisers. The future of such ads will depend on the ability to deliver bandwidth to accommodate the transmission and consumer access to high-speed Internet connections. The advantage, aside from being more interesting than a banner or a pop-up, is that streaming audio and video can realize click-through rates of 3.5 percent—hundreds of times greater than banner click-throughs.[35] There is also academic literature that supports the proposition that adding animation to Internet ads increases click-through rates, recall, and favorable attitudes toward Web ads.[36] One firm that experienced great success with streaming video over the Net is Adidas. When Adidas launched an online version of its television ad "Impossible is Nothing," which featured a fantasy bout between Muhammad Ali and his daughter Laila, the two-week Net placement attracted 5 million streams, or viewings. More importantly, the streams drew a large part of its audience from the 12–24-year-old consumer that is highly prized by sport-shoe sellers.[37] Similarly, when American Express launched its Superman and Jerry Seinfeld "Webisodes," the firm found much greater receptivity to the four-minute Web video than to its typical 30-second television spot.[38]

Corporate Home Pages. A **corporate home page** is simply the Web site where a business provides current and potential customers with information about the firm and usually its brands in great detail. The best corporate home pages not only provide corporate and brand information but also offer other content of interest to site visitors. The Saturn site (http://www.saturn.com) in Exhibit 16.16 allows people to find out about the line of Saturn cars, pricing, specifications, and the closest dealers. This product-oriented site also allows consumers to request brochures, communicate their comments and questions to the Saturn corporation, and find a dealer when they are ready to make a purchase. A corporate site that falls toward the lifestyle end of the spectrum is the Crayola site (http://www.crayola.com) displayed

32.   Ibid.

33.   Kathryn Kranhold, "Internet Advertisers Use Humor in Effort to Entice Web Surfers," *Wall Street Journal,* August 17, 1999, B9.

34.   Steve Jurvetson, "Turning Customers into a Sales Force," *Business 2.0,* March 2000, 231.

35.   Green and Elgin, "Do E-Ads Have a Future?" 48.

36.   S. Shyam Sundar and Sriram Kalyanaraman, "Arousal, Memory, and Impression Formation Effects of Animation Speed in Web Advertising," *Journal of Advertising,* vol. 33, no.1 (Spring 2004), 7–17.

37.   Kris Oser, "Adidas Mines Possibilities with Web Effort," *Advertising Age,* May 3, 2004, 79.

38.   Brian Steinberg, "Have You Ever Noticed How Web Ads Are More Creative?" *Wall Street Journal,* March 30, 2004, B3.

Some corporate Web sites are developed to be purely information sites. The Saturn site provides extensive product information for the full line of Saturn vehicles. http://www .saturn.com

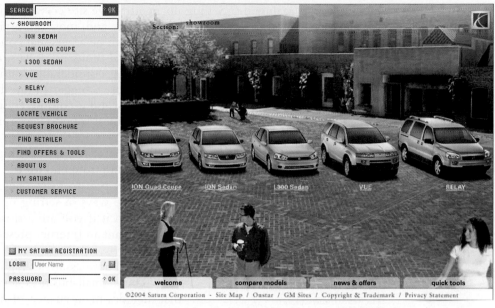

in Exhibit 16.17. Rather than focusing on its rather famous product, the company decided to focus on the needs of the parents and children who use Crayola crayons. Visitors can do such things as read bedtime stories, search for local child-care providers, discover hints on getting kids to help with housework, and browse movie reviews for family-oriented flicks. And, of course, there is a link to areas where kids can create art with computerized Crayolas (the crayons on the left side of the page).

Virtual Malls. A variation on the corporate Web site is a Web site placed inside a virtual mall. A **virtual mall** is a gateway to a group of Internet storefronts that provide access to mall sites by simply clicking on a category of store, as shown on the Mall Internet site (http://www.mall-internet.com). Notice that this site is set up to lead shoppers to product categories. Also notice that when a click is made to a product category, Mall Internet offers "featured store" click-throughs that lead to corporate Web sites and home pages. Having this additional presence gives stores such as the Shaper Image, Shoes.com, and Target more exposure.

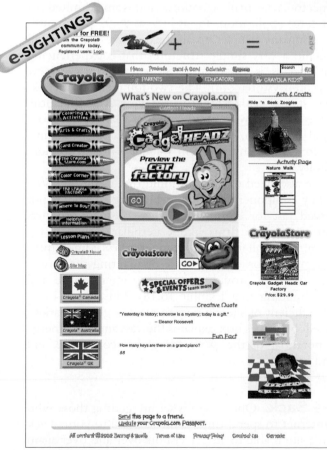

In contrast to purely information sites, other Web sites are more "lifestyle" sites. The Crayola site (http://www.crayola.com) *offers parents, educators, and kids all sorts of interesting, entertaining, and educational options. Compare the Crayola site to the Good Humor–Breyer's Popsicle site* (http://www.popsicle.com), *and evaluate which one does a better job of focusing on the needs of parents and children.*

⑤ Establishing a Site on the World Wide Web. While setting up a Web site can be done fairly easily, setting up a commercially viable one is a lot harder and a lot more expensive. The top commercial sites can cost $1 million to develop, about $4.9 million for the initial launch, and about $500,000 to over a million dollars a year to maintain.[39] Setting up an attractive site costs so much because of the need for specialized designers to create the site and, most important, to constantly update the site. The basic hardware for a site can be a personal computer, and the software to run the site ranges from free to several thousand dollars, depending on the number of extras needed. A site anticipating considerable traffic will need to plan for higher-capacity connections—and hence, a bigger phone bill. And, many analysts warn that setting up and running a Web and e-commerce site can have several hidden costs like transaction fees and technical support fees that can drive up the cost of running and maintaining a site.[40]

EXHIBIT 16.18

The Web is not just effective in serving household consumers. Business product and service firms of all sorts can use the Web to provide customer service and build brand awareness. From large multinational corporations like Caterpillar (http://www .cat.com) to smaller firms like PrintingForLess.com (http://www.printingfor less.com), the Web is highly effective in providing customer contact, customer service, and brand building.

But what if you're not a big IPO Internet firm with several million to spend for the first year of operating of a Web site? Not to fear. There are actually some very inexpensive ways of setting up a site and finding hosts to maintain it if you are a small or medium-size business and want an Internet presence. Companies like 1&1 (http:// www.1and1.com) offer a wide range of services to the small business including hosting at extremely low cost. These small-business service firms offer hosting that includes maintenance of domain names, Web site connectivity, e-mail accounts, and some limited e-commerce applications for as little as $9.99 per month. One company that set up an inexpensive site (and still maintains a very simple structure) that is experiencing great success is BackcountryStore.com (http://www .backcountrystore.com). The two founders, former ski bums, started with $2,000 in the year 2000 and now run the second-largest online outdoor gear organization, behind REI.[41] So, while there are ways to spend millions to develop and maintain a site, it is not an absolute necessity.

We also need to keep in mind that using the Web as a key component of a brand-building strategy is not reserved just for consumer brands. Business products advertisers—large firms like Caterpillar (http://www .cat.com) or small firms like PrintingForLess.com (http:// www.printingforless.com)—are discovering the power of the Web in providing both customer service and brand building (see Exhibit 16.18). Plus, there is no more efficient or speedy way to reach a global market. The Global Issues box explains the vast and still emerging potential of the Web for global commerce and brand building.

Getting Surfers to Come Back. Once a site is set up, getting those who spend considerable time on the Internet to spend time at the site and to come back often is a primary concern. When a site is able to attract visitors over and over again and keep them for a long time, it is said to be a **sticky site** or have features that are "sticky." A site with pages and pages showing the product and its specifications may have no appeal beyond attracting a single visit. Even a quick tour of various home

39.   Beth Snyder Bulik, "Procter & Gamble's Great Web Experiment," *Business 2.0,* November 28, 2000, 48–50.
40.   Lynn Ward, "Hidden Costs of Building an E-Commerce Site," available at http://www.ecommercetimes.com, accessed April 28, 2003.
41.   Duff McDonald, "A Website as Big (and Cheap) as the Great Outdoors," *Business 2.0,* October 2003, 70–71.

EXHIBIT 16.19

One of the biggest challenges facing Web marketers is making a site "sticky." A sticky site gets consumers to stay a long time and come back often. Notice that at the iwon.com site, you not only have a chance to win big money on a daily basis and bigger money on a monthly basis, but you also have access to all sorts of options such as checking sports scores, sending greeting cards, or visiting a chat room. http://www.iwon.com

pages reveals countless, boring corporate Web pages. Often Web sites merely include rich product descriptions that simply mimic printed brochures. Although such Web sites might satisfy the needs of consumers searching for specific product information, they are unlikely to attract and capture the interest of surfers long enough to get them to come back. The whole idea is to satisfy visitors and get them to come back.

To make a site sticky, a marketer should incorporate engaging, interactive features into the site. For the major hosting sites and portals, recurring information such as the weather, late-breaking news, sports scores, and stock quotes are key to attracting visitors daily or even several times a day. In an effort to break into the world of portals, iwon.com (http://www.iwon.com) offers all sorts of links to current information—as well as the chance to win $10,000 a day or $1 million each month for using the site—pretty much an all-out assault on trying to get surfers to come back (see Exhibit 16.19). For home pages or Web sites, entertaining features such as online games or videos can also get surfers to stay at a site and get them to come back. One site that does a good job of using devices such as these is the U.S. Army. Its Web site, http://www.goarmy.com, has 1.3 million people registered to play the Army's Web-based computer game.[42]

A well-developed site can keep customers coming back for more. A good example is the New Jersey Devils Web page (http://www.newjerseydevils.com). Visitors can do more than just read about how their favorite NHL team did the night before. They can read in-depth interviews with players, coaches, and even team trainers. Visitors compete for fan-of-the-month awards, while younger fans get a chance to be sportswriters. Tickets, schedules, and team merchandise are readily available as well as a direct link to the NHL's main Web site. These features give people multiple reasons to continue to visit the site. Such an approach to Web-presence design has been referred to as **rational branding** and stresses the need for a brand's Web site to provide some unique informational resource to justify visiting it. Some firms provide advertisers with all the tools they need to develop a sticky site. One such firm is Ingenux (http://www.ingenux.com), which provides design and features for Web sites to attract visitors and keep them coming back. And as Web design technology has become widely known, many, many firms are available locally to serve firms.

One crucial Web site feature (regardless of whether consumers are searching for specific information or browsing the Web) is the presence of multiple navigational tools; the more navigational tools available, the more the visitor will like the site. Navigational tools help guide the visitor around the site; examples include home and section icons, a search engine that is specific to the site, and a site index. Just as consumers need a cable guide to help them enjoy their cable services, so too do consumers need resources to help them realize and enjoy all the possibilities of the site.

Success in getting repeat visitors depends on substance, ease of use, and entertainment value. Web users are discriminating in that while pretty pictures are interesting, sites that have high user loyalty offer something more. This can be brand information and ongoing technical support, or it can be general news about a brand category, original writing, or the latest information about just about anything. That's

42.   Thomas Mucha, "Operation Sign 'Em Up," *Business 2.0,* April 2003, 44.

precisely what King Arthur Flour company did when it made the most mundane of commodities, baking flour, the feature of an energized Web site called the Baking Circle (http://www.bakingcircle.com). At this site, members swap recipes, post messages, and upload pictures of baked goods (honest). Is the site popular? Even in our carb-conscious society, the Baking Circle has 100,000 online members. [43]

GLOBAL ISSUES

The Next Net Wave

It's no secret that the instant you establish a Web site, you have become a "global" company. Any computer user from any part of the globe can access your site and navigate through all the features and information opportunities you care to provide. But as much as we know about the Web as a global medium, it is still hard to appreciate the vast potential that is still available for cultivating a global customer base.

When Internet global opportunities are considered, there is no great opportunity than China. Currently about 100 million Chinese users have piled on to the Net. That makes China second only to the United States as the county with the most Internet subscribers. But it is expected that China will not be No. 2 for very long: Piper Jaffery and Co. estimates that China will pass the United States by 2006. Since 100 million subscribers represent only 10 percent of the Chinese population, whereas nearly 70 percent of the U.S. population is already online, China has huge opportunity for future growth.

The growth is being fueled by several factors. First, Chinese consumers like the Internet for the same reasons Americans do—there is a lot of information and entertainment available. Second, a strong economy is letting more Chinese households buy PCs for access to the Internet. And third, the Internet offers the opportunity for the average Chinese citizen to skirt the Chinese government's tight censorship rules.

Here's a look at the firms currently serving the Chinese market with specific Internet services:

- Sina is the most popular portal in the country with 95 million registered visitors. It has links to online gaming and Yahoo! Auctions.
- Soho sends Internet content to its customers' cellular phones in the form of short text messages.
- Netease is a traditional portal earning revenue through online advertising, text messages, and games.
- Shanda is China's first indigenous online gaming company.
- Tom Online is a new portal that is a spinoff of China's largest traditional media group and will focus on cutting-edge wireless services.

Source: Bruce Einhorn, "The Net's Second Superpower," *BusinessWeek*, March 15, 2004, 54–56.

Purchasing Keywords and Developing a Domain Name.

Online search engines such as Yahoo! sell keywords. A marketer can purchase a keyword such that its banner appears whenever users select that word for a search. For example, when a user searches for a keyword such as "inn" on the search engine Google, he or she will see an ad from a directory for bed-and-breakfast inns. Keyword sponsorship on Google, for example, costs around five cents per impression ($50 CPM), but has been dropping recently due to competitive pressures. These search engines let advertisers pay a flat monthly fee or a per-impression fee (based on how many people see the ad). Thus, getting a popular word may result in a considerable number of impressions and a higher bill.

Purchasing keywords helps consumers find your site while they search for information. But before purchasing a keyword, a marketer must decide on a domain name first, which establishes the basis for a keyword. A **domain name** is the unique URL through which a Web location is established. If you are The Gap or Sony, your domain name is your corporate name and consumers know how to search for your location. But for thousands of Web startups that provide specialized Web products and services, the domain name issue is a dilemma. You want the name to be descriptive but unique, and intuitive but distinctive. That was the strategy used by Dennis Scheyer, a consultant, when he recommended that GoToTix.com, a ticketing and entertainment site, stick with its original name. The name was intuitive and easy to remember. But the firm insisted on running a consumer contest to rename the company. Scheyer said of the names

43.   Vicki Powers, "Flour Power," *Business 2.0*, June 2004, 80–81.

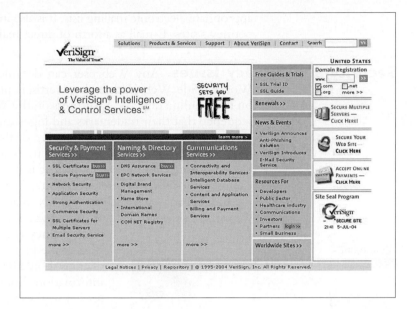

*Firms like VeriSign (http://
www.verisign.com) are
in the business of registering
names so surfers have direct
access to company Web sites—
a process made considerably
more complicated by the
introduction of TLDs (top-
level domains) such as .biz
and .name.*

that made the final cut, "One sounded like a breakfast cereal you wouldn't eat. One sounded like a cough medicine. And one sounded like a prophylactic." In the end, the firm chose Acteva.com (we suspect this is Scheyer's cough medicine entry) because "Act conveys activity. E signifies E-commerce and 'va' has that international flavor." The company has morphed beyond just tickets and now provides online registration and tracking for all sorts of events from fundraisers to corporate meetings (http://www.acteva.com). [44] Companies like VeriSign help companies identify, register, and manage Internet names and keywords in both domestic and global markets (see Exhibit 16.20).

The newest issue in domain names is the issuance of new top-level domains. The **top-level domain (TLD)** is the suffix that follows the Web site name. Until late 2000, there were only five TLDs—.com, .edu, .org, .gov, and .net. The Internet Corporation for Assigned Names and Numbers (ICANN) is a nonprofit formed in 1998 to coordinate technical management of the domain name system. You can visit their Web site http://www.icann.org and learn about the TLD extensions available and the new country-specific TLDs (e.g., .us and .uk).

The whole idea behind releasing new TLDs, like .tv and .us, is, of course, to relieve the pressure on the original five top-level domains. But there is the prospect of a degree of confusion among consumers as similar or identical prefixes are paired with the new suffixes.

Promoting Web Sites. Building a Web site is only the first step; the next is promoting it. Throughout the text, you have seen advertising by companies promoting their Web sites. Several agencies, including BBDO, Wieden & Kennedy, and Ogilvy One, specialize in promoting Web sites. The quickest and lowest cost way to promote a Web site is to notify Usenet groups. The other key method is to register the site with search engines such as Yahoo! and AltaVista. With Yahoo!, because it is a hierarchical search engine, it is important to pick keywords that are commonly chosen, yet describe and differentiate that site. Other places to register are with the growing Yellow Pages on the Internet (for example, Verizon's SuperPages, http://www.bigyellow.com) and with

---

44. Laurie Freeman, "Domain-Name Dilemma Worsens," *Advertising Age,* November 8, 1999, 100.

appropriate electronic mailing lists. It is also important to send out press releases to Internet news sites. E-mail as a form of direct mail is another method to promote the site.

Security and Privacy Issues. Any Web user can download text, images, and graphics from the World Wide Web. Although advertisers place trademark and copyright disclaimers on their online displays, advertisers on the Web have to be willing to accept the consequence that their trademarks and logos can easily be copied without authorization. Currently, there is no viable policing of this practice by users. Thus far, advertisers have taken legal action only against users who have taken proprietary materials and blatantly used them in a fashion that is detrimental to the brand or infringes on the exclusivity of the marketer's own site. This may change.

In Chapter 4 we discussed privacy as an ethical and regulatory issue. At this point, we can consider privacy from a strategic-management standpoint. As we saw in Chapter 4, privacy is a very complex and sensitive topic. Discussions at the highest levels focus on the extent to which regulations should be mandated for gathering and disseminating information about Web use. The concern among advertisers is not just the regulatory aspects of the issue. In addition, consumers are expressing concerns about using the Internet for fear of invasion of privacy—clearly a strategic-management issue. A recent survey found that a whopping 78 percent of consumers surveyed were either very or somewhat concerned that a company would use their personal information to send them unwanted information. This is up from 65 percent two years earlier.[45]

At the center of this debate was the marketing services company DoubleClick (http://www.doubleclick.net). DoubleClick is in the business of helping companies, like FedEx, MTV, and Digitas, identify and understand customer groups to better develop and target marketing, advertising, and promotional efforts (see Exhibit 16.21). Using DoubleClick's proprietary services like DARTmail and ClearEDGE, a company such as 3Com can keep track of the buying habits and traffic patterns of the 30 million people who visit the 3Com Web site each week. But as we learned in Chapter 4, this sort of profiling has come under intense scrutiny. In response, firms such as Double Click and Avenue A have issued extensive and detailed privacy statements and even appointed chief privacy officers as a way to assure consumers (and regulators) that consumer profile information is used strictly to improve customer service and not to dig into (or sell) information about consumers' private affairs.[46] This would seem to be the right approach, because consumers claim that with some assurance of privacy, their concerns about surfing or shopping the Web are greatly diminished.[47] With respect to consumer privacy, the Coalition for Advertising Supported Information and Entertainment (CASIE) has suggested five goals for advertisers, which we've reproduced in Exhibit 16.22. Striving for these goals will certainly contribute to the loyalty and confidence that consumers possess for a brand. Privacy is a legitimate concern for Internet users, and will likely continue to be one for civil libertarians and regulators as well. But one analyst assessed the privacy issue as a situation where, with the exception of DoubleClick, there have been

EXHIBIT 16.21

One firm deeply involved in the Internet privacy controversy was DoubleClick. Double Click has adopted an extensive privacy policy and appointed a chief privacy officer. http://www.doubleclick.net

---

45.   Heather Green et al., "It's Time for Rules in Wonderland," *BusinessWeek,* March 20, 2000, 82–96.

46.   "DoubleClick Appoints Chief Privacy Officer and Privacy Advisory Board Chairman," company press release, March 8, 2000, available at http://biz.yahoo.com, accessed March 17, 2000.

47.   Green et al., "It's Time for Rules in Wonderland," 84.

CASIE—the Coalition for Advertising Supported Information and Entertainment—has issued a set of goals for advertisers on the Internet.

1. We believe it is important to educate consumers about how they can use interactive technology to save time and customize product and service information to meet their individual needs. By choosing to share pertinent data about themselves, consumers can be provided the product information most relevant to them and can help marketers service them more economically and effectively.

2. We believe any interactive electronic communication from a marketer ought to disclose the marketer's identity.

3. We believe that marketers need to respect privacy in the use of "personal information" about individual consumers collected via interactive technology. "Personal information" is data not otherwise available via public sources. In our view, personal information ought to be used by a marketer to determine how it can effectively respond to a consumer's needs.

4. We believe that if the marketer seeks personal information via interactive electronic communication, it ought to inform the consumer whether the information will be shared with others. We also believe that before a marketer shares such personal information with others, the consumer ought to be offered an option to request that personal information not be shared. Upon receiving such a request, the marketer ought to keep such personal information confidential and not share it.

5. We believe consumers ought to have the ability to obtain a summary of what personal information about them is on record with a marketer that has solicited them via interactive electronic communication. In addition, a consumer ought to be offered the opportunity to correct personal information, request that such information be removed from the marketer's database (unless the marketer needs to retain it for generally accepted and customary accounting and business purposes), or request that the marketer no longer solicit the customer.

Source: Coalition for Advertising Supported Information and Entertainment, http://www.casie.com/guide1/priv.html, accessed June 6, 2004.

almost no instances where a company has suffered financial loss from a privacy controversy. "A lot of companies take a PR hit, but it is uncertain if that seriously damages their reputation or their customers' good will," said the founder of a consumer advocacy firm.[48] And it is not clear that consumers themselves (as opposed to critics or watchdog groups) really do care much about privacy. A survey of consumers found that only 6 percent of consumers always read a site's privacy policy and only another 15 percent "sometimes" read the policy.[49]

But a whole new level of concern and controversy may be finding its way into the privacy discussions. As more and more consumers access the Internet through WiFi and in the near future through WiMax, these methods of accessing the Internet are often subject to easy monitoring. In addition, in-home or in-firm wireless systems are easy to hack without the proper security hardware that creates restrictions. It's as easy as sitting in a car with a laptop with an antenna. That's how thieves allegedly snatched credit-card numbers of customers shopping at a Lowe's home improvement store. To protect WiFi systems, firms need to install encryption software know as WiFi Protected Access or develop a "virtual private network" that creates a secure pathway by requiring passwords for access.[50]

Measuring the Effectiveness of Internet Advertising. The information a Web site typically gets when a user connects with a site is the IP address of

48.   Ann Harrison, "Privacy? Who Cares," *Business 2.0,* June 12, 2001, 48–49.
49.   "Business 2.0 Snapshot," *Business 2.0,* January 23, 2001, 17.
50.   Roger O. Crockett, "For Now, Wi-Fi Is a Hacker's Delight," *BusinessWeek,* January 19, 2004, 79.

the Internet site that is requesting the page, what page is requested, and the time of the request. This is the minimum amount of information available to a Web site. If a site is an opt-in site and requires registration, then additional information (for example, e-mail address, zip code, gender, age, or household income) is typically requested directly from the user. Attempts at registration (and easy audience assessment) have been largely rejected by consumers because of the privacy concern, but plenty of service providers, such Nielsen//NetRatings (http://www.nielsen-netratings.com), are available to guide marketers through Web measurement options (see Exhibit 16.23).

Several terms are used in Web audience measurement. We will consider the most meaningful of these measurement factors. **Hits** represent the number of elements requested from a given page and consequently provide almost no indication of actual Web traffic. For instance, when a user requests a page with four graphical images, it counts as five hits. Thus by inflating the number of images, a site can quickly pull up its hit count. Consider what might happen at the *Seventeen* magazine site (http://www.seventeen.com). The *Seventeen* site may get three million hits a day, placing it among the top Web sites. However, this total of three million hits translates into perhaps only 80,000 people daily. Thus, hits do not translate into the number of people visiting a site. Another measure of site effectiveness is the extent to which a site will motivate visitors to **click through** and request information from the ad as we have discussed before. Most analysts feel that the click-through number (and percentage) is the best measure of the effectiveness Web advertising. If an ad is good enough to motivate a visitor to click on it and follow the link to more information, then that is verification that the ad was viewed and was motivating (more on this later).

Pages (or page views) are defined as the pages (actually the number of HTML files) sent to the requesting site. However, if a downloaded page occupies several screens, there is no indication that the requester examined the entire page. Also, it "doesn't tell you much about how many visitors it has: 100,000 page views in a week could be 10 people reading 10,000 pages, or 100,000 people reading one page, or any variation in between."[51] **Visits** are the number of occasions in which a user X interacted with site Y after time Z has elapsed. Usually Z is set to some standard time such as 30 minutes. If the user has not interacted with the site until after 30 minutes has passed, this would be counted as a new visit. **Users** (also known as unique visitors) are the number of different "people" visiting a site (a new user is determined from the user's registration with the site) during a specified period of time. Besides the address, page, and time, a Web site can find out the referring link address. This allows a Web site to discover what links people are taking to the site. Thus, a site can analyze which links do in fact bring people to the site. This can be helpful in Internet advertising planning. The problem is that what is really counted are similar unique IP numbers. Many Internet service providers use a dynamic IP number, which is different every time a

EXHIBIT 16.23

Because of the technology of the Web, tracking the behavior of Web site visitors is relatively easy. Firms like Nielsen//NetRatings help marketers measure the behavior of Web visitors. http://www.nielsen-netratings.com

---

51.   Scott Rosenberg, "Reach for the Hits," Salon.com, February 5, 1999, http://archive.salon.com/21st/rose/1999/02/05straight.html. This article focuses exclusively on measurement issues. See also Alan L. Baldinger, "Integrated Communication and Measurement: The Case for Multiple Measures," in Esther Thorson and Jeri Moore, eds., *Integrated Communications* (Mahwah, N.J.: Lawrence Erlbaum Associates, 1996), 271–283.

given user logs in through the service, so "you might show up as 30 different unique visitors to a site you visited daily for a month."[52]

Log analysis software is measurement software that not only provides information on hits, pages, visits, and users, but also lets a site track audience traffic within the site. A site could determine which pages are popular and expand on them. It is also possible to track the behavior of people as they go through the site, thus providing inferential information on what people find appealing and unappealing. An example of this software is MaxInfo's WebC, which allows marketers to track what information is viewed, when it is viewed, how often it is viewed, and where users go within a site. An advertiser can then modify the content and structure accordingly. It can also help marketers understand how buyers make purchase decisions in general. It still isn't possible, however, to know what people actually do with Web site information.[53]

Plenty of companies offer measurement services for interactive media. Yet there is no industry standard for measuring the effectiveness of one interactive ad placement over another. There also is no standard for comparing Internet with traditional media placements. Moreover, demographic information on who is using the WWW is severely limited to consumers who have signed up for opt-in programs and, for example, allow targeted e-mails to be sent to them. Until these limitations are overcome, many marketers will remain hesitant about spending substantial dollars for advertising on the World Wide Web. Here is a list of companies providing measurement and evaluation services:

- *Arbitron* (http://www.arbitron.com). One of the oldest advertising measurement firms and better know for its traditional media (especially radio and television) measures, Arbitron provides usage and lifestyle data on Internet usage but specializes in providing data on Internet broadcasting.

- *Audit Bureau of Circulations* (http://www.abcinteractiveaudits.com). The Audit Bureau has been for many years the main print circulation auditing organization. Recently, the firm has established ABC Interactive (ABCi), which offers independent measurement of online activity to ensure that Web site traffic and ad delivery metrics are accurately reported.

- *eMarketer* (http://www.emarketer.com). One of the newer entrants in the advertising measurement area, eMarketer accumulates data from various research sources and provides summary statistics.

- *Jupiter Research* (http://www.jupiterresearch.com). This firm provides a wide range of data analysis, research, and advice for firms using the Internet for both promotion and e-commerce.

- *Nielsen//NetRatings* (http://www.nielsenetratings.com). Probably the highest profile of the data providers, Nielsen has ruled the ratings game for many years. Nielsen relies on its traditional method of finding consumers who are willing to have their media behavior (in this case Internet use) monitored by a device attached to the consumers' computers.

- *Ranking.com* (http://www.ranking.com). Performs market research upon a statistically, geographically, and demographically significant number of Internet surfers. By recording these surfers' Web site visits, the company calculates the ranking for the top 900,000 (and growing every month) most visited Web sites. This is one of the very few free Web-data-research sites.

- *Simmons Market Research Bureau–SMRB* (http://www.smrb.com). Simmons measures the media and purchase behaviors of consumers and offers data on more than 8,000 brands across over 460 product categories. Included in these analyses is information on Web use and product purchase.

---

52. Rosenberg, "Reach for the Hits."
53. Ibid.

The Caching Complication in Internet Measurement. To conserve resources on the Web, computers employ a system known as caching. **Caching** is a memory function in Web and computer technology. Once a page is downloaded, the cache on the computer saves that page so it can be immediately accessed later. Suppose a person first goes to a Web site's home page. After clicking on a link to go somewhere else, the user decides to go back to the home page. Instead of asking the Web site again for that home page, the user's computer will have stored it in anticipation of the user wanting it again. And commercial online services such as America Online cache heavily trafficked sites on their computers so users get quicker response times when they request that page. Caching, whether on the user's computer or on the site's, conserves Internet resources, commonly called **bandwidth,** because the user is not needlessly requesting the same material twice. However, this complicates matters in measuring activity at the site because once a computer has cached a page, the Web site has no idea whether the user spent considerable time at the page in one visit, returned to the page several times, or immediately moved on.

Caching may result in fewer apparent page requests to a Web site than have actually occurred. Moreover, if a person hits the reload button, a Web site will register more traffic than there actually is. Technological solutions can reduce the amount of caching, thus allowing sites better data on how often a page is viewed, but it comes with the cost of additional bandwidth for the site and a slower response time for the person viewing the site. While cache-busting technology (technology that allows sites to look inside users' computer caches to determine the true number of pages) does exist, its widespread use seems unlikely in the near future. What is possible is that because caching allows a look at whether the site is handling traffic effectively or not, firms can measure the performance of their sites in terms of capacity and expandability.

Internet Measurement and Payment. Internet marketers pay for ads in several ways but they all, in one way or another, depend on the measurement of activity related to Web site visits where banner ads or sponsorships appear. Many pay in terms of impressions. It's supposed to mean the number of times a page with your ad on it is viewed; in reality these are roughly equivalent to hits, or opportunities to view. Often these are priced as flat fees—so many dollars for so many impressions. Others price with pay-per-click, which is in all reality the same as impressions. Others pay in click-throughs. "The overall average for click-throughs for all Web advertising, as we have seen, is an astoundingly low 0.1 percent."[54] That's one person out of a thousand who bothers to click on a banner ad to seek more information! These rates, down from about 2 percent, are driving down prices on banner ad placement costs— as you might expect. Others will buy on cost per lead (documented business leads) or cost per actual sale (very rare). A net rate refers to the 15 percent discounted rate given to advertising agencies, although direct deals with portals and browsers are very common. Also recall the discussion earlier in the chapter about paid search. Paid search is a completely different way of paying for and tracking the behavior of Web site visitors.

Managing the Brand in an E-Community.
A final strategic issue to be considered is the concept of creating a brand community, or e-community, for a brand by using the Internet. The Internet, in addition to providing a new means for advertisers to communicate to consumers, also provides consumers a new and efficient way to communicate with one another. In fact, the social aspect of the Internet is

54.   Gary Khermouch and Tom Lowry, "The Future of Advertising," *BusinessWeek*, March 26, 2001.

one of the most important reasons for its success. Via Usenet newsgroups, e-mail, IRC, blogs, and even Web pages, consumers have a new way to interact and form communities. Sometimes communities are formed online among users of a particular brand. These online brand communities behave much like a community in the traditional sense, such as a small town or ethnic neighborhood. They have their own cultures, rituals, and traditions. Members create detailed Web pages devoted to the brand. Members even feel a sense of duty or moral responsibility to other members of the community. For example, among many Volkswagen drivers, it is a common courtesy to pull over to help another VW broken down on the side of the road. Harley-Davidson riders feel a similar sense of affinity and desire to help others who use the same brand when they are in trouble.

In most respects, such communities are a good thing. One of the reasons members of these communities like to get together is to share their experiences in using the brand. They can share what they like about the brand and what it means to them, or suggest places to go to buy replacement parts or have the product serviced. However, advertisers need to be careful not to alienate members or turn them off to the brand. These consumers can also share their dislikes about recent changes in the brand and its advertising, rejecting them if severe enough. Since the Internet makes it easier for members of these communities to interact, brand communities are likely to proliferate in coming years. Consequently, dealing effectively with these communities will be one of the challenges facing advertisers. Several firms, such as Collabrio Technologies' MyEvents.com (http://www.myevents.com), have emerged to facilitate the community interaction process by providing shared access to a site that promotes communication between members. (See Exhibit 16.24.) Harley Davidson is a company whose site tries to accomplish e-community interaction. Notice at the Harley Web site, http://www.harleydavidson.com, that the events around the country are a highlight for riders. Another technique is to create a community around the brand in a portal-like manner—that is, drawing consumers to a brand site with content and features that include lifestyle and entertainment information much like what the big portals provide. One firm that has always tried to develop community with its Web site is teen apparel seller Candie's. Visit http://www.candies.com and read the Creativity box to see how the Candie's site is as community oriented as it is sales oriented.

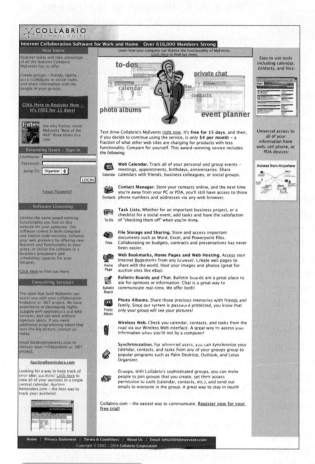

EXHIBIT 16.24

Building an e-community with great loyalty to a site is a tall task. Today's typical computer users have islands of disparate information located everywhere, from on their computer and home bulletin board to in their electronic organizer. Collabrio Corporation provides these users with a free, central place to manage and organize their lives and to share information with any group of people—their friends or family, their investment or book club, or even their co-workers.

The Future of Advertising and IBP and the Internet.

When it comes to the Internet, talking about the future is usually futile. The future seems to come with every new issue of *BusinessWeek, Fortune, Wired,* or *Business 2.0*. But the future of the Internet and advertising and IBP seems unavoidably linked to two influences: technology and strategic IBP.

From a technological standpoint, two technologies—wireless communication and Web-launched video—will have the biggest impact. (See Exhibit 16.25.) The AOL/Time Warner merger in 2001 signaled the future direction for the Web and

Web advertising. Time Warner brought to this merger all of its movie studio properties as well as an emerging Internet movie business and digital delivery of Warner Bros. movies on demand. Time Warner also has Time Warner cable television. What AOL brought to the merger, of course, was AOL's online services, including Netscape, CompuServe, MovieFone, and Instant Messenger. Now another media giant, InterActive-Corp, is putting together a conglomerate of Internet companies that can promote and sell each other's products. The collection of Web sellers now included in IAC/InterActiveCorp (http://www.usainteractive.com) consists of IAC Travel, which includes Expedia, Hotels.com, Hotwire, Interval International, and TV Travel Shop; HSN; Ticketmaster, which oversees ReserveAmerica; Match.com; LendingTree; Precision Response Corporation; and IAC Local and Media Services, which includes Citysearch, Evite, Entertainment Publications, and TripAdvisor.[55] The collection of sites attracts about 50 million visitors a month (small compared to Yahoo!'s 250 million visitors a month), but visitors to IAC sites are there to buy, not just browse. This Internet promotion empire reached over $10 billion in sales in 2003.[56]

Mergers and partnerships of broadcast and Internet firms is one side of the story. On the other side, advertisers and advertising agencies are preparing for new opportunities with "broadcast Web." For example, *Forbes* and Sears, Roebuck have tested new technology that can instantly connect TV sets to specific Internet sites. With this technology, TV watchers can click on an icon during a television program and be connected to Web sites pertaining to the nature of the programming—sports, entertainment, news, and so

CREATIVITY

Skipping Sales in Favor of Community

Candie's, a teen-focused, hip shoe and apparel maker, knew that the world was going online and it felt that it needed to keep up. But the New York–based company faced a problem. As a wholesaler, Candie's was hesitant to bypass retailers and go direct to consumers with online sales. First, such a strategy could damage relationships in the supply chain. Second, the firm was ill-equipped to even handle a direct-to-consumer selling effort.

Instead of establishing a sales site, the firm decided to establish a brand community portal. Candies.com was designed to be a site for teenage girls with a host of e-community features—free e-mail, online chat, Web page hosting, entertainment news, and the like. But it wanted to go further than traditional e-community options. To do so, Candie's also became a publisher of sorts. In a deal with *Rolling Stone* magazine, the site also publishes music news and CD reviews. The original agreement with Rolling Stone has now been extended to include television and film entertainment reviews.

Of course, the whole idea behind the content-based, rather than sales-based, focus of the site is to keep girls coming back. David Conn, vice president of marketing for Candie's, explains, "We felt if we could build a site that became a prime gather point for our customer, that gave them a platform and entertained them, we could data-mine and learn a lot about our market, which is really important when marketing to fickle teenage girls."

Aside from being primarily community oriented, another interesting feature of the Candie's Web strategy is that it flies in the face of the lessons learned by the ill-fated Levi's online strategy. Levi's began its online effort with what was described at the time as an attempt to create "a platform for kids to see what other kids are doing." But, after a short time, Levi's abandoned the "no sales" strategy in favor of a more e-commerce-oriented site. It would seem that Candie's is heading down the same path. But the Candie's site is more broad-based and elaborate and includes partnership content that Levi's did not. So it remains to be seen whether the Candie's strategy will survive. So far, so good, but go to http://www.candies.com and see if the strategy is still working!

Sources: Joe Ashbrook Nickell, "501 Blues," *Business 2.0*, January 2000, 53; Joe Ashbrook Nickell, "Teen Scene Maker," *Business 2.0*, March 2000, 108–110.

forth.[57] Not only does this technology merge the Net with television programming, but it can also provide advertisers with general demographic and preference data to its registered users without resorting to names or e-mail addresses—the crux of the privacy concerns we have discussed. In the words of one agency executive, "This will

55.   Ronald Grover et al., "From Media Mogul to Web Warlord," *BusinessWeek*, May 19, 2003, 46.
56.   Timothy J. Mullaney and Ronald Grover, "The Web Mogul," *BusinessWeek*, October 13, 2003, 62–70.
57.   Diane Mermigas, "Net Technology Connects Data with Marketers," *Advertising Age*, January 17, 2000, 2.

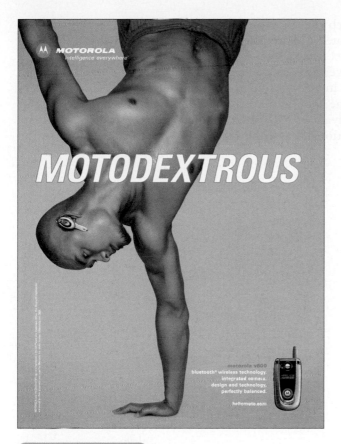

EXHIBIT 16.25

Whatever direction the dynamic nature of Web advertising and IBP takes, it will no doubt be influenced by wireless technology and high speed (broadband) access. As more consumers access the Web through their laptops or cell phones, advertisers have more and more ways of sending messages and communicating about their brands.

revolutionize advertising on the Web because it establishes accountability and connection. I know that every one of our clients that has been shown this technology has been blown away."[58] And there may be some good reasons to get excited. In an Arbitron Internet Information Services/Edison Media research study, "streamies" (the nickname for Webcast viewers and online radio listeners) were twice as likely as general online users to click on banner ads or buy from a Web site, with 40 percent reporting that they had made a purchase online.[59]

Does this mean that in the near future every television ad is really a Web ad? Well, maybe it won't be that extreme, but the technology is available to provide direct links to Web sites for information and purchasing through television ads—a huge opportunity and potential for advertisers. And, as more Web users have access to broadband, that number in the United States is now 40 percent, and more complex data can be streamed to users.[60] The possibilities are attracting all the big players—Microsoft, ABC, CBS, and Warner Brothers Online, to name just a few. They all see video streaming as another piece of this Web broadcast puzzle.[61] Of course, this next step in the evolution of the Internet and its potential as an advertising alternative depends on the consumer's willingness to allow the communication to occur. Some things never change.

With respect to the strategic use of the Internet, we are seeing some very clever and effective integrated brand promotions that rely on the Web, but are not dominated by it. For example, when Mazda wanted to reposition its brand and appeal more broadly to a younger market, understanding the Web behavior of 24-to-36-year-old males was critical. But it wasn't just the knowledge that this target segment was Web savvy when it came to buying cars. The dealership itself and the salespeople had to be changed as well. Mazda's strategy—drive traffic to the dealership through the Web, redesign the dealerships' physical appearance (coffeeshops and hip waiting rooms), make sure the salespeople are as Web-savvy as the shopper. The resulting of combining the promotional tools of the Web and salespeople has been impressive—sales at Web-savvy Mazda dealerships are up 32 percent and profits are up 50 percent.[62]

A less elaborate but equally effective IBP that features the Web is using television advertising to drive traffic to the Web site. Mitsubishi had enormous success with its "seewhathappensnext.com" campaign. The firm ran action-packed television ads that ended just before the climax of the scene. As the scene came to a stop, the television screen went black except for the words "seewhathappensnext.com." When

58.   Ibid.
59.   Amanda Beeler, "Marketers Find Lucrative Audience in 'Streamies,'" *Advertising Age,* February 21, 2000, 48.
60.   Anick Jesdanun, "2 in 5 Web Users Have Broadband at Home," AP Internet News, April 18, 2004, available at http://www.news.yahoo.com, accessed April 18, 2004.
61.   Dana Blankenhorn, "Where TV, Net Link," *Advertising Age,* January 17, 2000, S20.
62.   Parks, "Let's Remake a Dealership."

TV viewers arrive at the Web site, they can watch the conclusion of the scene in streaming video. Mazda debuted the campaign during the SuperBowl and the Web site drew 11 million hits in six hours.[63]

It seems likely that as advertisers try to "engage" consumers in brand messages that the Internet will play an increasing role in IBP campaigns. Will Internet advertising and promotion become the "lead" tool in IBP campaigns? Not likely. But expect that as technology advances and consumers become accustomed to accessing information in nontraditional ways, the Internet will be a valued tool in the IBP kit.

63.   Jean Halliday, "Bowl Ads Spark Web Upticks," *Advertising Age,* February 9, 2004, 48.

SUMMARY

Understand the basic components and operation of the Internet.

There are four main components of the Internet: electronic mail, IRC, Usenet, and the World Wide Web. Electronic mail (e-mail) allows people to send messages to one another using the Internet. Internet Relay Chat (IRC) makes it possible for people to "talk" electronically in real time with each other, despite their geographical separation. For people with common interests, Usenet provides a forum for people with common interests to share knowledge in a public "cyberspace" that is separate from their e-mail program. The World Wide Web (WWW) allows people to access an immense "web" of information in a graphical environment through the use of programs called Web browsers (such as Netscape and Internet Explorer).

Identify the nature of the Internet as a medium available for communicating advertising and promotion messages.

E-mail allows users to communicate much as they do using standard mail. People who wish to discuss specific topics through the Internet often join electronic mailing lists. Thousands of mailing lists are available on an incredible variety of topics. A message sent to the list's e-mail address is then re-sent to everybody on the mailing list. Usenet is a collection of discussion groups in cyberspace. People can read messages pertaining to a given topic, post new messages, and answer messages. The World Wide Web (WWW) is the "web" of information available to most Internet users, and its graphical environment makes navigation simple and exciting. Of all the options available for Internet marketers, the WWW holds the greatest potential as an advertising medium.

Describe the different types of search engines used to surf the Web.

In a hierarchical search engine, such as Yahoo!, all sites fit into categories. Collection search engines, such as AltaVista, use a spider, which is an automated program that crawls around the Web and collects information.

With a concept search engine, a concept rather than a word or phrase is the basis for the search. The top sites that match the concept are listed in order after a search. The newest technique, robot search engines, employs robots ("bots") to do the "legwork" for the consumer by roaming the Internet in search of information fitting certain user-specified criteria. A portal is a starting point or gateway for Web access and search. Companies like Google and Yahoo! seek to become the most popular gateways to the Web, especially as trends such as WiFi, paid search, and blogs stimulate higher Internet usage and make the medium more profitable for advertising.

Describe the different advertising options on the Web.

The Internet's unique advantages and abilities make it an attractive option for advertisers, and there are several ways to place advertising messages on the Web. Banner ads are paid placements of advertising on other sites that contain editorial material. Sponsorship allows advertisers to have their brands associated with popular Web sites. A pop-up/pop-under ad is an Internet advertisement that appears as a Web site page is loading or after a page has loaded. E-mail can be used to customize a message for thousands or even millions of receivers. Streaming video and audio enables advertisers to insert TV- and radio-like ads into highly interactive content. A corporate home page is a Web site where a marketer provides current and potential customers information about the firm in great detail. A variation on the corporate Web site is the virtual mall, which is a gateway to a group of Internet storefronts that provide access to mall sites by simply clicking on a category of store.

Discuss the issues involved in establishing a site on the World Wide Web.

There are three key issues to successfully establishing and maintaining a site on the World Wide Web: getting surfers to come back by creating a "sticky" site; purchasing keywords and developing a domain name; and promoting the Web site.

KEY TERMS

WiFi
WiMax
Mobile-Fi
Ultrabroadband
Internet
electronic mail (e-mail)
Internet Relay Chat (IRC)
Usenet
World Wide Web (WWW)
opt-in e-mail
electronic mailing lists
spam
surfing
search engine
hierarchical search engine
collection search engine

spider
concept search engine
robot search engine
robots
portal
hot spot
paid search
search engine optimization (SEO)
blog
blogger
click-through
banner ads
skyscraper
sponsorship
pop-up/pop-under ad
permission marketing

viral marketing
streaming video and audio
corporate home page
virtual mall
sticky site
rational branding
domain name
top-level domain (TLD)
hits
pages
visits
users
log analysis software
caching
bandwidth

QUESTIONS

1. Despite its ups and downs over the past decade, the Internet is experiencing a strong recovery. Why is there reason to believe that the current Internet boom could be permanent?

2. What may have driven advertisers to embrace the Internet early on in its development despite considerable uncertainty about audience size, audience composition, and cost-effectiveness?

3. Since it no longer appears that the Internet will replace all other forms of advertising as some analysts had once hastily predicted, what is likely to be its role in the advertising process?

4. How can an understanding of search engines and how they operate benefit an organization initiating an ad campaign on the WWW?

5. What unique characteristics of Internet advertising offer advantages over traditional forms?

6. Explain the two basic strategies for developing corporate home pages, exemplified in this chapter by Saturn and Crayola.

7. Niche marketing will certainly be facilitated by the WWW. What is it about the WWW that makes it such a powerful tool for niche marketing?

8. Visit some of the corporate home pages described in this chapter, or think about corporate home pages you have visited previously. Of those you have encountered, which would you single out as being most effective in giving the visitor a reason to come back? What conclusions would you draw regarding the best ways to motivate repeat visits to a Web site?

9. The Internet was obviously not conceived or designed to be an advertising medium. Thus, some of its characteristics have proven perplexing to advertisers. If advertising professionals had the chance to redesign the Internet, what single change would you expect they would want to make to enhance its value from an advertising perspective?

10. What are *blogs*, and what are some of their personal and commercial uses?

EXPERIENTIAL EXERCISES

1.   Pick one of your favorite hobbies, pastimes, or areas of interest—music, sports, literature, investing—you decide. Travel to three or four prominent Web sites featuring your interest area. What similarities and differences can you detect between sites with respect to the advertising or sponsorship at the site? What site features are designed to keep surfers coming back? Do you think they are effective? Explain.

2.   Visit portal sites like Google, Yahoo, or Ask Jeeves that use *paid search* for sponsored links and banner advertising. Search for items related to popular products or personal interests. What sponsored links or banner ads appeared along side of your search results? How do those sponsored links or banner ads correlate to your search topic, if at all? Next, click on some of the sponsored links or banner ads that were produced along with your search results, and describe what happens. Did you get transferred to a product Web site? Were you taken to an online promotion such as a sweepstakes? What purpose did the company have in prompting your click-throughs, and what incentives were you given to oblige the advertiser with your time and effort? Finally, describe the different experiences you had clicking through different banner ads and rate their effectiveness from a consumer perspective.

EXPERIENCING THE INTERNET

16-1   Establishing a Site on the World Wide Web

When CBS needed to establish a Web site to help build the brand of its wildly popular *Survivor* series, it turned to Xceed, a strategic consulting and digital solutions firm known for its expertise with highly interactive e-business solutions. CBS aimed to capitalize on the suspense and interest associated with the program and to capture it in an interactive format that would keep fans coming back to the site.

Survivor: http://www.cbs.com

Xceed: http://www.xceed.com

1.   Visit the CBS site and search for the *Survivor* Web page. What makes this site "sticky," and how does it capitalize on the program's interesting features?

2.   What is *rational branding*? Does the *Survivor* site make full use of this concept? Have you ever visited the *Survivor* site before? If so, how did you use it?

3.   Visit Xceed's site and research its list of clients. Visit one of the Web sites it has produced for another client, and compare and contrast that site's features with those of the *Survivor* site. Do you think this site is as effective as the *Survivor* site? Why?

16-2   E-Mail Advertising and Marketing

Advertising and marketing through e-mail is one of the most promising and useful Internet developments in recent years. The popularity of electronic messaging has led to the proliferation of e-mail-based tools that help advertisers reach extremely targeted audiences around the globe at a very low cost. XactMail is one of many Internet firms leading the way in harnessing the power of messaging-based advertising.

XactMail—Permission E-Mail:
http://www.xactmail.com

Coalition Against Unsolicited Commercial E-Mail:
http://www.cauce.org

1.   What services does XactMail offer, and what is *opt-in e-mail*?

2.   How does the text define *spam,* and how does spam relate to XactMail? Does XactMail run the risk of being blacklisted by the Coalition Against Unsolicited Commercial E-mail? Why or why not?

3.   What are the benefits of e-mail–based advertising to advertisers? How do most businesses allow consumers to avoid getting electronic junk mail?

4.   Do you ever receive electronic ads or promotions in your mailbox? How do you respond to them?

INTEGRATED BRAND PROMOTION

PART 4

Cincinnati Bell℠

Cincinnati Bell Wireless: The Launch Campaign

As noted in Part 2 of this case history, one of the most laudable aspects of the launch campaign designed and executed by Northlich was the skillful mix of persuasion tools deployed on behalf of Cincinnati Bell Wireless in the spring of 1998. As you will see, it is reasonable to conclude that these tools worked in harmony from both the standpoint of communicating a multifaceted value proposition and creating awareness, credibility, and excitement for the CBW brand, which culminated in a desire to purchase this service.

From Part 2 you should also recall the launch strategy that guided the preparation of the campaign: MOPEs (managers, owners, professionals, entrepreneurs) using other wireless services were targeted for conversion to digital PCS from Cincinnati Bell. The value proposition communicated through a diversified IBP campaign advanced this package of benefits:

- *Simple pricing, better value.* Subscribers sign no contracts; they choose a simple pricing plan, such as 500 minutes for $49.95 per month or 1,600 minutes for $99.95 per month.
- *The coolest phone on the planet.* CBW launched its service with the feature-laden Nokia 6160 phone.
- *Member of the AT&T wireless network.* As a member of AT&T's network, CBW offered customers wireless access in over 400 cities at one "hometown rate."
- *Worry-free security.* Business transactions that may be compromised over analog cellular are secure over digital PCS.

As you will see in the sample communication materials that follow, the critical points advanced throughout the launch campaign were superiority over cellular, simplification, and hey, it's a cool phone! Various ads played different parts to yield precisely the kind of beautiful music that Jack Cassidy and others at CBW were waiting to hear: These ads made the cash register sing!

An Overview of the CBW Launch Campaign.
Here we will describe and provide examples of many of the different persuasion tools deployed in this multimillion-dollar launch. You will see that this was a multilayered campaign with different elements called on to contribute the best of what each has to offer, as represented in Chapters 14 through 20. We will discuss TV, print, radio, and outdoor ads; special events and promotions; direct mail; and point-of-purchase advertising. Each built on the other to advance the CBW brand. But we begin at the beginning, with public relations.

Public Relations. As you will learn in Chapter 20, there can be at least six different objectives for public relations activities. Two of these six were very clearly being pursued by public relations staff on behalf of CBW: the use of press releases and staged events to develop

Launch Highlights

WATCH for CBW on **tv** in:

The **season finales** of NYPD Blue, Spin City, Dharma & Greg, Promised Land, Chicago Hope, Mad About You, Frasier, 3rd Rock, Party of Five, Ally McBeal, Simpsons, and the X-Files.

Sporting events like Reds and NBA Playoffs. Other popular prime time programs such as: Movies, Home Improvement, The Practice, Drew Carey, Cosby, George & Leo, Pretender, Law & Order and Millennium.

Primetime news programs such as: 20/20, 48 Hours, 60 Minutes, Primetime Live & Dateline.

Daily episodes of Wheel of Fortune, Jeopardy, Oprah, News, David Letterman, Nightline, The Tonight Show, and the 7o'clock edition of Seinfeld/Frasier.

LISTEN for huge on-air **radio** exposure:

Big advertising schedules on WLW, WEBN, WOFX, WUBE, WYGY, WGRR, WIZF, WRRM, WVMX, WKRQ, WBOB and WVAE. **On air contests** like: CBW as "official remote phones" of WEBN, WOFX, WAQZ, and WYGY WVMX's Impossible Trivia, WRRM's Wireless Wednesday, WKRQ's Wireless Olympics, WAVE's Father's Day

Two to three **on site remotes** every weekend at CBW stores and retail chains from stations like WVAE, WKRQ, WOFX, WEBN, WGRR, WRRM, WBOB, WIZF and WVMX.

WATCH for lots of **print ads** in:

The Cincinnati Enquirer. We're here almost every day. **In the first week, you'll see 4 and 5 page consecutive ads.** National magazines. Full Page color ads will be in the June issues of **Newsweek, Business Week, Money, Time, U.S. News Report, Nation's Business and Financial World**

DRIVE BY outdoor boards:

In high traffic locations on I-75, I-71, Norwood Lateral, Colerain Avenue, Ridge Avenue, Montgomery Rd. and Rt. 747. On TANK buses in N. Kentucky driving on I-75, Dixie Highway, on I-275 and near Florence Mall.

Come **VISIT** CBW at events like Party at the Point and concerts at The Beach Waterpark

EXHIBIT IBP 4.1

CBW internal newsletter: Launch preview.

awareness for CBW, and active development and direct dissemination of information to employees of Cincinnati Bell to turn them into knowledgeable spokespeople for the company's newest offering. Public relations efforts often are initiated in advance of more conventional advertising. In this case, press releases were created and circulated as early as February 1998 to announce newsworthy developments such as the signing of the partnership agreement between Cincinnati Bell and AT&T, which established the infrastructure to support CBW. One could think of this activity as preparatory awareness building.

Another excellent example of the PR function at work is illustrated through Exhibit IBP 4.1. This "Launch Highlights" document was part of a corporate newsletter distributed to Cincinnati Bell employees to advise them of the forthcoming launch. It provides a wonderful synopsis of the complete launch campaign in an effort to create interest and enthusiasm for the new service from within the company. Other internal corporate communications included a special invitation to attend an employees-only sneak preview for CBW on May 5, 1998. Hundreds of Cincinnati Bell employees turned out to watch the official count down and blastoff for the new service. But guess who else got a special invitation to this "employees only" event? That's right, the press! All the Cincinnati media were in attendance to make sure the whole scene was reported that evening on the local news and in the next day's newspapers. So here again, we see the two PR objectives of awareness building and internal selling working for CBW.

Television. May 11, 1998, was the official start of the advertising support for CBW. Three television advertisements were at the center of the advertising barrage. One of these, "Classroom," was described briefly in Part 3 (see Exhibit IBP 3.1). The other two were titled "The Big Easy" (see the storyboard in Exhibit IBP 4.2) and "X-Ray: Cool Phone." These two ads advanced different aspects of the CBW value proposition. Many of the programs where these ads were initially aired are listed in Exhibit IBP 4.1.

Throughout this text we have emphasized that good advertising must be based on an understanding of the customer's wants and needs. Northlich lives by this principle, and we see it brought to life very vividly in the two spots "Classroom" and "The Big Easy." Northlich's consumer research repeatedly identified that consumers were frustrated by the complexity of the wireless category. Their complaints were that the deals were confusing; they got locked in by a contract; and it was hard, even after the fact, to understand the pricing plan that applied to them. CBW's service tackled these concerns with its simple pricing plan and no-contracts offer. "The Big Easy" presents CBW as a breakthrough service that eliminates all the hassles people associate with cellular. What's more, this is a service from "people you know you can rely on." "The Big Easy" set the stage for all that would follow.

Print, Radio, and Outdoor. Television is the ultimate medium for achieving broad reach for an appeal almost instantly. However, when repetition of the basic message is called for, the high absolute cost of this medium makes it an expensive option to rely on exclusively. It is

The Big Easy :30 (launch)

(We open on our spokesman in a clean, minimalist room.)

Spokesman: If a cell phone is supposed to make life easier, then why am I so un-easy about getting one?

(We see a rapid-fire montage of all the things that make buying a mobile phone so frustrating:

A confusing array of phones.

Numerous peak and off-peak calling hours.

Lengthy contracts you have to commit to.

"No service" areas where you don't have access.)

(Music abruptly stops and changes tone)
Spokesman: But now there's Cincinnati Bell Wireless.

The only phone with the clarity of digital around town,

and thanks to AT&T, virtually everywhere else.

Plus one low rate that's more affordable than cellular.

Stop by the Store at Cincinnati Bell and see if wireless is right for you.

I don't know about you, but I feel better already.

EXHIBIT IBP 4.2

Bell Wireless storyboard: "The Big Easy."

common to use other, more economical media as a complement to television to achieve frequency or repetition of the basic message(s). For the CBW launch, Northlich made heavy use of both print and radio ads to complement the messages being advanced in the television campaign. Actual spending levels for TV, radio, print, and outdoor are detailed in Exhibit IBP 4.3.

As reflected in Exhibit IBP 4.3, there was a consistent commitment to print ads as a means to keep the CBW offer on the table on almost a daily basis. Print ads like the one in Exhibit IBP 4.4 hammered away at the point that CBW is simply a better deal than cellular and that the world's most advanced digital phone is part of the package. Additionally, the actor shown in Exhibit IBP 4.4 appeared in all CBW TV ads, which again reinforced the integrated look of the campaign. Per Exhibit IBP 4.1, print ads ran both in local newspapers and in regional editions of several major magazines.

As you learned in Chapter 15, radio is a very cost-effective medium for executing high levels of message repetition in a targeted geography. Northlich deployed radio ads to achieve frequency of exposure of the campaign's basic themes. Using several different executions, the radio ads reinforced the claims that with CBW you get the best coverage, a great phone, no contracts, and much better prices than cellular. One sample of the radio ad copy is featured in Exhibit IBP 4.5. This particular ad emphasizes the point that with CBW, you can roam far and wide and still stay in touch. The main actor in the radio ad is the same actor who appeared in the TV and print ads. Are you starting to get the picture that the folks at Northlich took this "one look," "one voice" integration thing pretty seriously?

From the spending levels in Exhibit IBP 4.3, it should be clear that outdoor advertising was not a major emphasis but instead served its traditional role as a sup-

Description	January	February	March	April	May	June	July
TV					$142,982	$ 95,887	$ 0
Radio					49,904	22,844	27,536
Print					153,977	65,265	63,374
Outdoor					8,339	8,339	6,589
Production Totals	$19,179	$50,053	$281,165	$314,835	246,118	202,306	169,507
Media Totals	0	0	0	0	355,202	192,335	97,499
Total Spending	$19,179	$50,053	$281,165	$344,835	$601,320	$394,641	$267,006

EXHIBIT IBP 4.3

CBW launch: Media billing summary for the first half of 1998.

EXHIBIT IBP 4.4

Sample print ad from the CBW launch.

(Sound effects: outdoor, nature sounds.)

Scott: This truly is a modern way to travel, Roy.

Roy: Yeah, the largest mobile home ever made. Theater-style seating. Sleeps 52. So big, it beeps when I back up . . . and when I'm going forward.

Scott: Wow! Now where have you been, what have you seen?

Roy: The world's largest talking cow in Georgia. A bicycle-eating tree in Washington. And pretty much everything in between.

Scott: Oh, that's great . . . now, you know, if you had a Cincinnati Bell Wireless phone, you could talk to virtually anyone, anywhere you went.

Roy: Oh yeah, is that right, even at the sand sculpture of the Last Supper?

Scott: Oh, the sand sculpture of the Last Supper . . .

Roy: All right, how about the lickable house of salt?

Scott: Oh . . . yeah, wherever that is. You know . . . plus home-rate roaming in AT&T cities across the U.S.

Roy: Well, what are we waiting for?!

(Sound effects: engine starts, then the familiar beeping sound a truck makes when it's backing up, continues under Scott.)

Scott: Get the nationwide coverage and simple more affordable rates than cellular: 100 minutes for 25 bucks or 500 minutes for $50. Stop by the Store@Cincinnati Bell or call 565-1CBW for details.

NOTE: This ad was voted *Best of Show* by the 1998–99 Addy Awards, Cincinnati Advertising Club.

EXHIBIT IBP 4.5

Radio copy: Roadside America (:60).

port medium. Billboard and transit ads bolstered the basic proposition that CBW is clearer, smarter, and better than cellular. As we pointed out in Part 3 of this case, the billboard design supported the uniform look of the campaign.

Promotions and Events.
Northlich and CBW also made adept use of promotions and special events for a variety of purposes. The schedule of launch events and promotions for May and June 1998 is listed in Exhibit IBP 4.6. Several points are evident here. First, there was participation in citywide spring outdoor events, such as Taste of Cincinnati, Day in Eden (Park), and Kid Fest, that provided exposure and lead generation for CBW at virtually no cost. Note as well that with an event like Kid Fest, CBW was also probing customers who were not part of the primary launch target. This gave CBW an opportunity to gauge the appeal of their service with a broader base of potential users, without diluting the focus of their primary advertising campaign.

Second, from Exhibit IBP 4.6 we see that CBW offered price promotions around traditional gift-giving occasions such as Mother's Day, Father's Day, and graduation. These promotions were supported by special radio and print ads and direct mail. One advantage CBW has over any local competitor is that its parent company, Cincinnati Bell Telephone, makes regular mailings to nearly every household in the city in the form of monthly phone bills. For CBW, the bill insert is a very cost-effective way to announce promotions.

Finally, Exhibit IBP 4.6 also notes CBW's participation as a sponsor of professional baseball and the women's professional golf tour. Through their "businessmen's special" promotions at Cincinnati Reds games, CBW was afforded an awareness-building opportunity with its primary target segment—MOPEs. An affiliation with the Ladies' Professional Golf Association facilitated outreach to the primary target segment and beyond.

Direct Marketing.
The set of communication tools previously described—from PR, to various forms of mass-media advertising, to event participation—set the stage for the success of CBW by building awareness, excitement, and credibility for the brand. At this point, a MOPE may have been convinced to walk into a Store@Cincinnati Bell to purchase a cool phone and activate this new service; however, Northlich was clearly leaving no stone unturned. To build on the broad base of awareness created by the communication tools described thus far, direct marketing specialists on the account team prepared a coordinated and extensive direct mail campaign.

The goal for this campaign was to prompt action in one of several ways. Recipients of the direct mail brochure were invited to either sign up immediately for wireless service by calling an 800 number or get more details at the CBW Web site. Or, as the brochure explained, they could sign up by visiting any Store@Cincinnati Bell or another CBW-authorized dealer. As part of this mailing, MOPEs also received a letter from Mike Vanderwoude, CBW's marketing director, detailing the benefits of CBW for the sophisticated business user. Attached to Mike's letter was a $10 coupon redeemable on any CBW purchase. Again, the goal of this direct marketing effort was to sway hesitant MOPEs to close the deal.

With the help of a list broker that specialized in geodemographic segmentation (remember Chapter 6?), Northlich identified nearly 100,000 households in greater Cincinnati that contained a MOPE. Simultaneously, they were planning a campaign that included a built-in experiment. As you will see in Chapter 19, the mind-set of the direct marketing specialist always includes experimentation to benefit future programs. For the CBW launch, four groups were created to facilitate this research:

1. 46,000 MOPE households were designated to receive the complete mailing package plus outbound telemarketing follow-up *and* an extra offer of a free leather case for their Nokia 6160 phone.

EXHIBIT IBP 4.6

CBW launch: Promotion and events schedule.

May	June
Taste of Cincinnati	**Day in Eden**
Target: Adults 25–54	Target: Adults 25–54
Objective: Introduce CBW and build awareness; generate leads (database)	Objective: Introduce CBW and build awareness; generate leads (database)
Vehicles: Event only	Vehicles: Event only
Promo: Booth at event; free trial (phone calls); contest entry	Promo: Booth at event; free trial (phone calls); contest entry
Mother's Day	**Kid Fest**
Target: Users and nonusers	Target: Users and nonusers
Objective: Drive response; store traffic	Objective: Build awareness; drive response
Message: Safety; multiple phones per household	Message: Safety
Vehicles: Radio and print; bill inserts	Vehicles: Event only
Promo: Special price package; radio contest (best mother; mother in most need of wireless)	Promo: Booth at event giving away safety-related item (windshield distress sign; emergency flag) logo'd CBW; special offer to sign up for service and receive family pass to local amusements
Graduate Program (high school and college)	
Target: Nonusers (soon-to-be young professionals); users (families)	**Father's Day**
Objectives: Drive response	Target: Users and nonusers
Message: Safety and productivity benefits	Objective: Drive response; traffic in stores
Vehicles: Radio and print; bill inserts	Message: Productivity benefits
Promo: Special price package	Vehicles: Radio and print; bill inserts
Baseball	Promo: Special price package; radio contest (best father; father in most need of wireless)
Target: Businessmen (Businessmen's Special)	**LPGA**
Objective: Build awareness; drive response	Target: Nonusers and users
Message: Productivity benefits	Objective: Drive response
Vehicles: Event only	Message: Safety and convenience
Promo: Coupon on back of ticket for discount; raffle free phone/service	Vehicles: Event only
	Promo: Coupon on back of ticket for discount; raffle free phone/service

2. 46,000 MOPE households were designated to receive the complete mailing package plus outbound telemarketing follow-up, but no offer for the free leather case.
3. 5,000 MOPE households were designated to receive the complete mailing package with follow-up by a second direct mail contact in place of telemarketing.
4. 1,500 MOPE households were designated to receive outbound telemarketing only.

It should be apparent that Northlich's direct marketing department expected direct mail followed by outbound telemarketing to be the best combination to drive response. The overwhelming majority of the targeted MOPEs received this combination. Groups 3 and 4 were used to assess the relative effectiveness of other combinations for future campaigns. In addition, the comparison of responses from group

1 versus group 2 showed Northlich the value of the leather case offer, again for future reference. As it turned out, the incremental responses generated by the leather case offer were not enough to justify the extra costs associated with that offer. Looking to the future, there would be no more leather freebies, and direct mail followed by outbound telemarketing was established as the most effective tactical combination.

P-O-P Advertising, Collateral, and Sales Support. The final layer that must be addressed as part of any multilayered IBP campaign is point-of-purchase. At P-O-P, everything the customer hears, sees, touches, tastes, and smells must support the promises that were made by other communication tools. While there isn't much tasting or smelling to worry about in activating a new mobile phone, there are plenty of other details.

At P-O-P, and particularly in the Stores@Cincinnati Bell, the prospective customer was reminded of the larger IBP campaign in many ways. As you saw in Part 3 of this case history (see especially Exhibit IBP 3.3), the numerous informational brochures developed by Northlich shared many design features with other materials from the campaign, as did the interior design of the Stores@Cincinnati Bell. Northlich also used the same design features for the package sleeve that slid over the protective packaging of the Nokia 6160 phone.

In-store salespeople were also well versed in the messages and details of the larger IBP campaign. As already mentioned, the details of the campaign were communicated to all employees throughout the CBW system by newsletter announcements (see Exhibit IBP 4.1). Additionally, the multiple benefits of CBW's value proposition were recast as a list of the top 10 reasons why one should become a CBW subscriber (for example, reason number one was "No contracts to sign!"). This top 10 list was featured on in-store placards and window posters to reinforce the benefit promises that customers may have heard in other campaign executions.

An IBP plan should also anticipate brand contacts. Brand contacts are all the ways in which prospective customers come in contact with the organization—through packaging, employees, in-store displays, and sales literature, as well as media or event exposure. Each contact must be evaluated for consistency with the overall IBP program. We see this drive for consistency at every level of the CBW launch campaign.

Gauging the Impact of the CBW Launch Campaign.
Hopefully, this overview has given you an appreciation for the breadth of the IBP campaign that Northlich orchestrated on behalf of its client and partner, Cincinnati Bell Wireless. But were the campaign's objectives achieved? Did the client consider the campaign a success? Looking back now, we are able to accurately assess the outcomes from this launch campaign, and this assessment must start with the issue of objectives. You may recall from Part 2 that the client's primary objective targeted new subscribers. Success for CBW begins with service activations. The campaign's goal was 16,868 subscribers by the end of the calendar year, a conservative and attainable goal that both the client and agency hoped to surpass. But no one really anticipated how much was possible.

It didn't take long for all parties to realize that they needed to think bigger. After just one week into the launch campaign, they had 10,500 activations. While this pace could not continue, the new-subscriber goal for the campaign was easily surpassed in the first 90 days. By the end of 1998, CBW had more than 60,000 subscribers, nearly four times the original goal. And the profile of these subscribers was truly remarkable. About half of these activations came from MOPEs who were converting to CBW from another mobile phone service. As you know by now, these MOPEs were the primary target segment. The other 30,000 activations came from young professionals who hadn't previously subscribed to a mobile phone service. To explain the outcome, Jack Cassidy, president of CBW, surmised that the launch campaign had been exceptionally effective in communicating the *no hassles, great pricing,* and *cool phone* elements of the CBW value proposition. Users and nonusers alike were persuaded that CBW was different and better than anything available previously.

Users switched carriers, and nonusers signed on in about equal numbers. As you might expect, Cassidy was very pleased with this outcome.

There are other concrete indicators of the campaign's success. One has to do with CBW's realized churn rate. *Churn rates* are expressed as a percentage and indicate the percent of current customers that a company is losing each month. Average monthly churn in the wireless business is about 4 percent. If a company is losing 4 percent of its customers every month, then after just a year, it will have lost nearly half its customers. Obviously, high churn rates are an indication of customer dissatisfaction. In 1998, CBW's churn rate was less than 1.5 percent per month, indicating that CBW customers were considerably more satisfied than the industry average. It also indicates that there was a good balance between the benefits promised in CBW advertising and the actual benefits realized in the use of the service. Striking this balance is one mark of great advertising.

You probably also will recall that the primary reason MOPEs were targeted had to do with their usage potential. The thinking was that MOPEs (that is, business users) make heavier use of their mobile phones each month than do household users. Thus, if Northlich targeted their advertising efforts properly, they would attract heavy (more profitable) users. Here again, Northlich delivered the goods. Industry averages provide the critical point of reference: Average revenue per customer per month for analog cellular companies is $29, and for other digital PCS companies it is $45. In 1998, CBW's average revenue per customer per month was just over $60, which means that Northlich's communication tools were delivering the high-value mobile phone customers to Jack Cassidy's door, again making him very happy.

Finally, in the spring of 1998, CBW had intended to spend about $3 million on its launch campaign. But astute marketers monitor their own successes carefully and make budget adjustments to support programs that clearly are working. Strong programs get budget increases and weak programs get budget cuts. Given that this campaign clearly was working, which became obvious to all just one week into the campaign, what do you suppose Jack Cassidy did with his advertising and IBP budget? Well, he effectively doubled it. By the end of 1998, CBW had spent $6 million to support its aggressive launch. This spending is yet another indicator of the campaign's unprecedented success. As 1998 came to a close, investment analysts, AT&T executives, business journalists, and Jack Cassidy were all drawing the same conclusion about the CBW campaign: By any measure, this was the most successful digital PCS launch in North America.

IBP EXERCISES

1. Compare this CBW launch campaign with the iMac campaign described at the beginning of Chapter 8. How are they similar? How are they different? What aspects of the iMac campaign would have made it a more complex undertaking than the CBW launch?

2. In this CBW example we see that direct marketing people are most prone to learning through trial and error. Why is this type of learning so important to direct marketers? What is it about direct marketing that makes learning in this way more feasible? What did the direct marketers on Northlich's account team learn in the CBW launch?

3. Make a list of at least five different communication tools that were used as part of the IBP campaign for CBW. Now critique each tool with respect to how well it supported or reinforced key aspects of the CBW value proposition.

4. Visit the CBW Web site at http://www.cbwireless.com. Obviously, the launch campaign described was just the beginning for CBW. From the Web site, can you infer any changes in marketing strategy? Has the value proposition changed? What about the primary target segment? Given the effectiveness of their launch campaign, how could CBW justify any changes in their marketing strategy, on the Web or elsewhere?

Paul Ghiz
Co-Founder and Creative Director, Global Cloud, Ltd.

The National Underground Railroad Freedom Center serves as a tribute to the path to freedom journeyed by thousands of escaped American slaves, and to those who have worked to end racism and secure liberty for all people. When organizers for the newly completed Freedom Center recognized the need to develop an online strategy to promote the museum and communicate its message of freedom and justice, they turned to an experienced interactive agency co-led by talented Creative Director Paul Ghiz. In partnership with the museum's representatives, Mr. Ghiz created a strategic planning and development effort that resulted in the creation of freedomcenter.org, the center's official Web site.

Ghiz's successful career as an interactive designer and creative director developed in tandem with the world of new media in the late 1990s. As a graphic design student entering his final year at Miami University of Oxford, Ohio, Ghiz felt the usual jitters about life in the "real world" beyond graduation and wondered what path to take. Following a gut instinct that a new high-tech medium called the Internet could be the next big thing, the young art student began looking for opportunities to tackle his first interactive project, and was hired to design a Web site for Miami University's School of Fine Arts. "That," recalls Ghiz, "is when I got the Internet itch."

After graduating with a BFA in graphic design, Ghiz began freelancing, and was commissioned to paint a mural commemorating the 160th Anniversary of the Campbell Hausfeld Company, a leading tool manufacturer founded in the early 1800s. After providing some additional advertising and package-design work for the manufacturer, Ghiz pursued his desire to stake a claim on the World Wide Web and began hounding a new interactive agency for a job. Ghiz was soon awarded a position as creative director at Access Point Interactive. "This was my big break," said Ghiz. "That tenure was essentially my graduate work in Web design and development. I had made up my mind during that period that this career was dynamic and creative enough to keep me satisfied." That "graduate work" paid off, for within one year the young designer met up with a seasoned marketing and advertising professional and co-founded Global Cloud, Ltd., a full-service interactive agency that develops Internet-based sites and business solutions for regional and international clients.

Ghiz immediately began pouring his creative talents and managerial abilities into the new firm and has since established himself as an accomplished director and business pioneer in the realm of interactive media. His company serves a range of business and non-profit organizations, and Paul's interactive designs have been essential to the branding- and corporate-advertising strategies of clients like Wild Flavors, Inc., the E.W. Scripps Company, the Juvenile Diabetes Research Foundation International, and the National Underground Railroad Freedom Center.

Creative directors wear many hats and must exhibit strong management and interpersonal skills. Ghiz's professionalism proved essential to achieving project goals with client E.W. Scripps. "I was responsible for visually and verbally communicating every detail and interaction of this enormous informational Web site throughout the entire project lifecycle," Ghiz recalls. "Having strong communication and work processes allowed me to keep the project moving forward to meet their deadline." The Scripps site, which features real-time newsroom stories, Doppler weather radar, and a sky-cam video, served as the rollout model for multiple Scripps TV stations. Ghiz emphasizes the importance of developing a collaborative relationship with clients from the early planning and strategy stages to the completed execution of the project. In discussing his work with the Juvenile Diabetes Research Foundation, he says, "Taking the necessary time in the planning stage paid off for everyone. I believe 30 to 50 percent of an allocated project time should be spent on planning—documenting, story boarding, scheduling. If the planning and scoping-out phase is clearly defined, the execution will go smoothly and your customers will be happy."

Ghiz enjoys seeing the "light bulb go on" as clients begin to grasp the potential of his firm's interactive media solutions, and each new client relationship brings new adventures. Paul's work with the NFL Alumni Association landed him in a charity golf classic the year Bengal Offensive Lineman Anthony Muñoz was inducted into the Pro Football Hall of Fame. "I met all of the big names: Forrest Gregg, Boomer Esiason—you name it," said Ghiz. On one of the holes, Ghiz sent a clump of earth along with the club head soaring into a pond. "I was surrounded by NFL players that fell down laughing. That was a long day," remembers Ghiz, "but I enjoyed every minute."

Whether it's the client outings, job challenges, or forward-looking developments related to his industry, Ghiz has many reasons to love his work. The co-founder enjoys the company parties, luncheons, and Friday after-work imported-beer runs, but he gets just as excited about creating new interactive solutions for wireless devices or integrating Flash technology with databases.

Through hard work and a gutsy desire to navigate the uncharted waters of the Internet, Ghiz turned his education and design skills into a successful career in the world of new media. To students considering his line of work, Ghiz offers, "Read as much as you can and experiment on your own. Collaborate. Select a product or service you like and develop a fictitious online storefront. . . . Dive in and have fun doing it. If you aren't having fun, you either aren't doing it right or you are in the wrong profession." He adds, "Be open and flexible to a job role you may not ideally want at first. It may be your 'foot in the door' to the ideal job."

Integrated Brand Promotion

Part Five of the text brings us to the end of our journey in the study of advertising.

This part highlights the full range of communications tools a firm can use in creating

an integrated brand promotion campaign. Throughout the text, we have been

emphasizing that IBP is a key to effective brand development. You will find that the

variety and breadth of communications options discussed here represent a

tremendous opportunity for marketers to be creative and break through the clutter

in today's marketplace. Each of the tools discussed in Part Five has unique capability

to influence the audience's perception of and desire to own a brand.

PART FIVE

Support Media, Event Sponsorship, and Branded Entertainment. Chapter 17, "Support Media, Event Sponsorship, and Branded Entertainment," reflects the extraordinary range of options available to today's advertiser, from billboards and transit advertising to event sponsorship and product placements in TV shows and movies. The examples in this chapter highlight how creative marketers and their IBP agencies must be in finding compelling ways to reach target markets. Having all these possibilities amplifies the need for integration in effectively building and sustaining brands.

Sales Promotion and Point-of-Purchase Advertising. Chapter 18, "Sales Promotion and Point-of-Purchase Advertising," describes the ways that contests, sweepstakes, price incentives, and point-of-purchase materials attract the attention of customers. The impact of many sales promotion techniques is much easier to measure than the impact of advertising, thus prompting many marketers to shift spending from advertising to sales promotion in their integrated brand promotion campaigns. Highlighted in this chapter are the fundamental differences between the purpose of advertising and the purpose of sales promotion. This chapter also features discussion for use with trade and business market buyers. The risks of relying on sales promotional tools are revealed in this chapter. Finally, there is extensive discussion of point-of-purchase advertising materials. Many experts refer to this form of promotion as the "last three feet" of the promotional effort.

Direct Marketing. Consumers' desire for greater convenience and marketers' never-ending search for competitive advantage have spawned growth in direct marketing. Chapter 19, "Direct Marketing," considers this area, which is a combination of both marketing and promotion. With direct marketing, advertisers communicate to a target audience, but they also seek an immediate response. You will learn why direct marketing continues to grow in popularity, what media are used by direct marketers to deliver their messages, and how direct marketing creates special challenges for achieving integrated brand promotion.

Public Relations and Corporate Advertising. Chapter 20, "Public Relations and Corporate Advertising," concludes the discussion of integrated brand promotion. Public relations offers the opportunity for positive communication but also provides damage control when negative events affect an organization. Corporate advertising is image-, cause-, or advocacy-focused and can serve a useful role in supporting an advertiser's broader brand advertising programs. These important areas can be key aspects of an organization's overall integrated brand promotion effort—particularly in the context of negative publicity. Each has the potential to make a distinct and important contribution to the unified message and image of an organization, which is the ultimate goal of IBP.

CHAPTER 17

After reading and thinking about this chapter, you will be able to do the following:

1

Describe the role of support media in a comprehensive media plan.

2

Justify the growing popularity of event sponsorship as another supporting component of a media plan.

3

Explain the benefits and limitations of connecting with entertainment properties in building a brand.

4

Discuss the challenges presented by the ever-increasing variety of communication and branding tools for achieving integrated brand promotion.

Introductory Scenario: The Brave New World of IBP. It's a no-brainer when you have the choice. One side of the street was lined with the typically smelly porta-potties that are common eyesores at public sporting events, concerts, and street fairs. Across the street were squeaky-clean, tractor-trailer-mounted bathrooms, complete with running water, wallpaper, faux wood floors, and plenty of Charmin toilet tissue, Safeguard hand soap, Pampers changing tables, and Bounty paper towels. Exhibit 17.1 will help you envision the scene. The 30 Charmin-sponsored bathrooms had people lined up for 15 to 20 minutes, while the porta-potties across the street sat empty. The choice comes natural, but raises the question: When is a clean potty the ultimate brand-building tool? Answer: When you're Procter & Gamble, maker of Charmin, Safeguard, Pampers, and Bounty.

The scenario described above has become typical for the Charmin Pottypalooza tour. P&G takes the rig on the road to 20 or more major events each year, attracting on the order of 2 million party and potty goers. Add in a related brand-building program that delivers clean restrooms at state fairs across the United States, and the number of satisfied potty goers skyrockets. P&G executives estimate that they are

EXHIBIT 17.1

Associating your brands with a pleasing experience is a great way to connect with consumers. The Charmin Pottypalooza tour has been both a great brand builder and revenue generator. It is hard to imagine a "cleaner" example of integrated brand promotion.

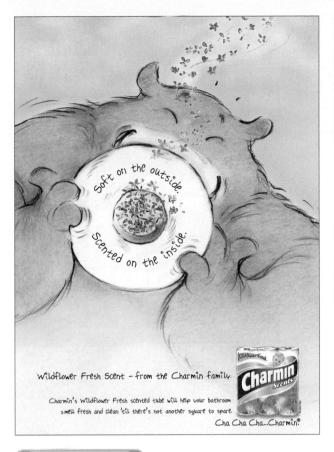

EXHIBIT 17.2

No more Mr. Whipple. The Charmin family committed to the bear mascot in a 2004 Super Bowl ad. Their tagline that day: "Soft and Strong for Your Endzone."

reaching 30 million consumers with their restroom enrichment program, which in its first year on tour delivered a 14 percent increase in Charmin sales. As one P&G marketing director put it, "Pottypalooza is definitely paying out."[1]

Pottypalooza also provides P&G with a great opportunity for integrated brand promotion. People waiting gratefully in line are entertained by the strolling Charmin bear mascot. Once inside their bathroom, the see a continuous loop of Charmin ads starring that playful bear. Seldom are consumers more completely immersed in a brand-building experience, and given the alternative (remember that smelly porta-potty), seldom are they happier about it. Of course, all this great exposure for Charmin and the other P&G brands on board is further supported by advertising in more conventional media, like that shown in Exhibit 17.2, in a fully integrated campaign.

The Pottypalooza example is the perfect starter for this fifth and final part of the book because it exemplifies the creative ways that marketers are now using to create meaningful connections to consumers. Additionally, it reminds us that the unconventional is becoming conventional, and that traditional mass media are no longer enough. As you no doubt have already recognized, perhaps in a restroom near you, advertisers are always on the lookout for new venues to advance their messages. And this can lead them to many different places. Often these efforts are directed at hard-to-reach niche markets, particularly in urban locations, where new market trends often originate. Other examples include trucks that drive endlessly through city streets as mobile billboards; ads beamed onto the sides of office buildings; racks of postcard ads placed in trendy restaurants and nightspots; ads printed on coffee cups with coordinated signage attached to coffee carts; and even small signs attached to the backs of messenger bikes that patrol the canyons of downtown corporate America.

Although print and broadcast media continue to draw big advertising dollars, many other options exist for communicating with consumers. This chapter will first examine a set of options commonly referred to as support media. Traditional support media such as signs and billboards have been around for many years, but with technological advancements are enjoying renewed interest from advertisers. Next we look at event sponsorship, which continues to produce impressive results and thus is receiving more and more funding from many marketers. Related to event sponsorship is the latest rage in advertising circles—branded entertainment. We'll examine this "new" form of brand building and assess what's new about it. When it comes to building brands—as with the Charmin Pottypalooza tour—there are very few limits on what one can try. Indeed, quirky/edgy/off-the-wall may be just what the doctor ordered.

❶ Traditional Support Media. This section will feature traditional support media: outdoor signage and billboard advertising, transit and aerial advertising, and directory advertising. **Support media** are used to reinforce or supplement a message

1.   Jack Neff, "P&G Brings Potty to Parties," *Advertising Age,* February 17, 2003, 22.

EXHIBIT 17.3

Brands like Adidas need to be in constant contact with the sports fan. In this case Adidas delivers its "forever sport" mantra through a print ad that appeared in the college football preview issue of Sports Illustrated. Hence the first line of copy: "Leaves that let you know it's football season."

EXHIBIT 17.4

Here we see the Adidas logo providing the backdrop for everyday life. But always affirming "forever sport."

being delivered via some other media vehicle; hence the name *support media*. Exhibits 17.3 and 17.4 show a pair of ads for Adidas, with the outdoor signage supporting the print campaign. Support media are especially productive when used to deliver a message near the time or place where consumers are actually contemplating product selections (e.g., imagine that building in Exhibit 17.4 as a Foot Locker store). Since these media can be tailored to local markets, they can have value to any organization that wants to reach consumers in a particular venue, neighborhood, or metropolitan area.

Outdoor Signage and Billboard Advertising. Billboards, posters, and outdoor signs are perhaps the oldest advertising form. Posters first appeared in North America when they were used during the Revolutionary War to keep the civilian population informed about the war's status. In the 1800s they became a promotional tool, with circuses and politicians being among the first to adopt this new medium. Exhibit 17.5 shows a classic ad execution for "The Greatest Show on Earth." With the onset of World War I, the U.S. government turned to posters and billboards to call for recruits, encourage the purchase of war bonds, and cultivate patriotism. By the 1920s outdoor advertising also enjoyed widespread commercial applications and, until the invention of television, was the medium of choice when an advertiser wanted to communicate with visual imagery.

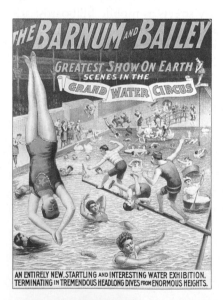

EXHIBIT 17.5

Advertising in the United States began with posters and billboards. Circuses were the early pioneers in this medium. http://www.ringling .com

While the rise of television stifled the growth of outdoor advertising, the federal highway system that was laid across the nation in the 1960s pumped new life into billboards. The 40-foot-high burgers and cigarette packs were inevitable, but throughout the 1970s and '80s billboards became an outlet for creative expression in advertising. One exceptional example of using the medium to its fullest was a Nike campaign run in the mid-'80s featuring high-profile athletes, such as Olympian Carl Lewis, performing their special artistry. Today, the creative challenge posed by outdoor advertising is as it has always been—to grab attention and communicate with minimal verbiage and striking imagery, as do the billboards in Exhibits 17.6 and 17.7.

In recent years total spending on outdoor advertising in the United States has held steady at just over $5.2 billion.[2] Outdoor advertising offers several distinct advantages.[3] This medium provides an excellent means to achieve wide exposure of a message in specific local markets. Size is, of course, a powerful attraction of this medium, and when combined with special lighting and moving features, billboards can be captivating. Billboards created for Dayton Hudson in Minneapolis have even wafted a mint scent throughout the city as part of a candy promotion for Valentine's Day.[4] Billboards also offer around-the-clock exposure for an advertiser's message and are well suited to showing off a brand's distinctive packaging or logo.

Billboards are especially effective when they reach viewers with a message that speaks to a need or desire that is immediately relevant. For instance, they are commonly deployed by fast-food restaurants along major freeways to help hungry travelers know

EXHIBIT 17.6

Minimal verbiage is one key to success with billboard advertising. This example easily satisfies the minimal-verbiage rule. http://www.horst-salons.com

EXHIBIT 17.7

As with all media, creativity is a must in making effective use of billboards. This dramatic ad was created by Northlich, one of the stars in our ongoing IBP case study.

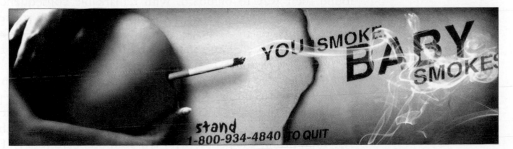

2.   "Outdoor," *Advertising Age,* June 9, 2003, C1.

3.   Jack Z. Sissors and Lincoln Bumba, *Advertising Media Planning* (Lincolnwood, IL: NTC Business Books, 1993).

4.   Ronald Grover, "Billboards Aren't Boring Anymore," *BusinessWeek,* September 21, 1998, 88–89.

This sign uses the perfect slogan for a sports venue. Has there ever been a referee who didn't need glasses?

where to exit to enjoy a Whopper or Big Mac. Exhibit 17.8 features a clever example of putting one's outdoor signage in the right place at the right time to maximize its appeal.

Billboards have obvious drawbacks. Long and complex messages simply make no sense on billboards; some experts suggest that billboard copy should be limited to no more than six words. Additionally, the impact of billboards can vary dramatically depending on their location, and assessing locations is tedious and time-consuming. To assess locations, companies may have to send individuals to the site to see if the location is desirable. This activity, known in the industry as **riding the boards,** can be a major investment of time and money. Moreover, the Institute of Outdoor Advertising has rated billboards as expensive in comparison to several other media alternatives.[5] Considering that billboards are constrained to short messages, are often in the background, and are certainly not the primary focus of anyone's attention, their costs may be prohibitive for many advertisers.

Despite the cost issue, and frequent criticism by environmentalists that billboards represent a form of visual pollution, there are advocates for this medium who contend that important technological advances will make outdoor advertising an increasingly attractive alternative in the future. The first of these advances offers the prospect of changing what has largely been a static medium to a dynamic medium with heretofore-unimagined possibilities.[6] Digital and wireless technologies have found their way to billboards with remarkable consequences. In one application, wireless technology and digital displays let advertisers rotate their messages on the board at different times during the day. This capability is especially appealing to local marketers—like television stations and food sellers—whose businesses are very time sensitive. For example, FreshDirect uses this technology to change the messaging for its food-delivery service—morning, noon, and night—on the billboard outside NYC's Queens Midtown Tunnel. Ultimately, billboard time may be sold in day-parts like radio or television, making them more appealing to time-sensitive advertisers.

Another key development that also features amazing technology entails a testing system to profile the people who saw your billboard today.[7] For the past 70 years the

5.   Sissors and Bumba, *Advertising Media Planning.*
6.   Kimberly Palmer, "Highway Ads Take High-Tech Turn," *Wall Street Journal,* September 12, 2003, B5.
7.   Lisa Sanders, "Nielsen Outdoor Tracks Demo Data," *Advertising Age,* May 31, 2004, 14.

only information available to assess the impact of billboard advertising came from raw traffic counts. Now, Nielsen Outdoor, part of the company known for rating television viewer-ship, has developed a system using GPS satellites to track minute-by-minute movements in the "impact zone" of a billboard. Drivers in the Nielsen panel are paid a small stipend to have their latitude and longitude recorded by GPS every 20 seconds. Nielsen also knows the demographic characteristics of its panel, so they can advise advertisers about the characteristics of persons who viewed a billboard at any given time. Sounds pretty wild, but when a similar system was deployed in the U.K., revenues from outdoor ads grew dramatically.[8] Advertisers are more willing to invest when they can track results. The lesson here is simply that advertisers want to know who is viewing their billboards. Renewed creativity and new technologies should lead to more advertising dollars moving "outdoors" in many markets around the world.

Transit and Aerial Advertising. **Transit advertising** is a close cousin to billboard advertising, and in many instances it is used in tandem with billboards. The phrase **out-of-home media** is commonly used to refer to the combination of transit and billboard advertising; this is a popular advertising form around the world with global revenues approaching $20 billion.[9] As illustrated in Exhibits 17.9, 17.10, and 17.11, out-of-home ads appear in many venues, including on backs of buildings, in subway tunnels, and throughout sports stadiums. Transit ads may also appear as signage on terminal and station platforms, or actually envelop mass transit vehicles, as exemplified in Exhibit 17.12. One of the latest innovations in out-of-home media is taxi-top electronic billboards that deliver customized messages by neighborhood using wireless Internet technology.[10] We've come a long way from the circus poster.

EXHIBIT 17.9

This wonderful old building has a big, flat backside, facing a major interstate freeway. No wonder the Gap wants to keep it in jeans. Does the Gap site (http://www.gap .com) show signs of integrated brand promotion?

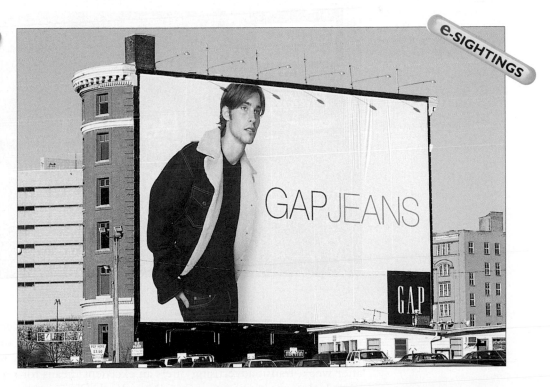

8. Elizabeth Boston, "New Outdoor Rating Systems Ready for Battle," from AdAge.com, article dated 6/11/03 available at http://www.adage.com/news, accessed July 3, 2003.
9. Alastair Ray, "A Market on the Move," *adageglobal,* April 2001, 36.
10. Stephen Freitas, "Evolutionary Changes in the Great Outdoors," *Advertising Age,* June 9, 2003, C4.

EXHIBIT 17.10

Happy Berliners enjoy their Cokes at 3 degrees Celsius while waiting on the U-bahn (subway).

EXHIBIT 17.11

As this Fenway Park scoreboard shows, signage and advertiser slogans are standard fare at the ballpark. Why do you think each advertiser chose to pick this particular place to advertise?

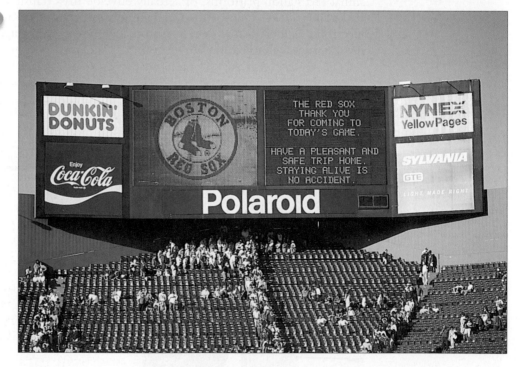

Transit advertising is especially valuable when an advertiser wishes to target adults who live and work in major metropolitan areas. The medium reaches people as they travel to and from work, and because it taps into daily routines repeated week after week, transit advertising offers an excellent means for repetitive message exposure. In large metro areas such as New York City—with its 200 miles of subways and 3 million subway riders—transit ads can reach large numbers of individuals in a cost-efficient manner. The once utilitarian bus stop has also become big business, with all the usual complications, as outlined in the Controversy box on page 618.

The story is the same all over the world. Mass transit has become an advertising vehicle too. Can you identify this European city? http://www.converse.com

When working with this medium, an advertiser may find it most appropriate to buy space on just those trains or bus lines that consistently haul people belonging to the demographic segment being targeted. This type of demographic matching of vehicle with target audience derives more value from limited ad budgets. Transit advertising can also be appealing to local merchants because their messages may reach a passenger as he or she is traveling to a store to shop. For some consumers, transit ads are the last medium they are exposed to before making their final product selection.

Transit advertising works best for building or maintaining brand awareness; as with outdoor billboards, lengthy or complex messages simply cannot be worked into this medium. Also, transit ads can easily go unnoticed in the hustle and bustle of daily life. People traveling to and from work via a mass transit system are certainly one of the hardest audiences to engage with an advertising message. They can be bored, exhausted, absorbed by their thoughts about the day, or occupied by some other medium. Given the static nature of a transit poster, breaking through to a harried commuter can be a tremendous challenge.

When advertisers can't break through on the ground or under the ground, they can always look to the sky. **Aerial advertising** can involve airplanes pulling signs or banners, skywriting, or those majestic blimps. For several decades, Goodyear had blimps all to itself; now, the availability of smaller, less-expensive blimps has made this medium more popular to advertisers. For example, Virgin Lightships created a fleet of small blimps that measure 70,000 cubic feet in size and can be rented for advertising purposes for around $200,000 per month. Aerial billboards, pulled by small planes or jet helicopters equipped with screeching loudspeakers, have also proliferated in recent years, as advertisers look for new ways to connect with consumers.[11]

Sanyo, Fuji Photo, MetLife, Outback Steakhouse, and Anheuser-Busch have clearly bought into the appeal of an airborne brand presence. The Family Channel has also been a frequent user of Virgin Lightships' mini-blimps at sporting events such as the Daytona 500 NASCAR race. A recall study done after one such event

11.   Barry Newman, "Sky-Borne Signs Are on the Rise as Most Ad Budgets Take a Dive," *Wall Street Journal,* August 27, 2002, B3.

showed that 70 percent of target consumers remembered the Family Channel as a result of the blimp flyovers.[12] Blimps carrying television cameras at sporting events also provide unique video that can result in the blimp's sponsor getting several on-air mentions. This brand-name exposure comes at a fraction of the cost of similar exposure through television advertising.

When a medium proves itself, more and more marketers will want it in their media mix. Of course, the irony is that as a medium becomes more attractive and hence cluttered, its original appeal begins to be diluted. We already see this occurring with aerial advertising. With more and more blimps showing up at sporting events, networks can be choosy about which one gets the coveted on-air mention. Besides carrying an overhead camera for them, networks now demand that blimp sponsors purchase advertising time during the event if they want an on-air mention. Additionally, the sportscasters' casual banter about the beautiful overhead shots from so-and-so's wonderful blimp have now been replaced by scripted commentary that is written out in advance as part of the advertising contract.[13] As we've noted before, this cycle of uniqueness and effectiveness, followed by clutter and dilution of effectiveness, repeats itself over and over again. Hence, the never-ending search for something fresh.

CONTROVERSY

"Street Furniture" Means Big Bucks for Someone

The idea of "street furniture" started in Europe, but is catching on fast in North America. San Francisco, Los Angeles, and Chicago all have street furniture deals. But the biggest prize is New York City. The city has called for proposals to redesign all the city's street furniture to make it a more productive venue for selling ad space. The request for proposals called for the winning bidder to redesign, install, and maintain 3,300 bus-stop shelters, 20 self-cleaning automatic public toilets, 330 newsstands, and a variety of other "public-service structures" like trash cans and information kiosks. New York City is looking for a 20-year deal. Why would anyone want to take on such a task? Well, those in the know estimate that the city's street furniture will generate a billion dollars in ad revenue over the life of the contract.

The opportunity has attracted all the big players in outdoor ad media. There is JCDecaux, the French firm that first conceived the premise of street furniture in 1964. Clear Channel Communications of San Antonio is also a player with big plans for customizing the look of each structure to reflect the unique architecture of New York City's many neighborhoods. And Viacom, which has previously controlled transit ad space in New York City, definitely knows the value of reaching its legion of commuters. Each hired well-connected lobbyists to help pitch their proposals to City Hall.

For overseeing this street furniture project, one of these media companies stands to gain a major new source of advertising revenue. The City of New York is a winner as well, because around 30 percent of the revenue will be the city's take. But not everyone will profit from the new arrangement. In particular, the Newsstand Operators Association isn't pleased and has threatened to sue the city to thwart the deal. Independent newsstand owners basically will be put out of business if the program isn't amended with them in mind. As their lawyer noted, "We are not too pleased with the scheme. It will transfer ownership of newsstands from private mom-and-pop operations to large corporations with no compensation to us." Until the matter is settled, probably in the courts, New York City's commuters will just have to wait for their bus at a bus stop, perhaps unaware that one day they'll have "street furniture."

Sources: Lisa Sanders, "Gimme Shelter: NYC Seeks Ad Sites," *Advertising Age*, April 5, 2004, 3; Erin White, "Companies to Bid for Bus-Stop Ads," *Wall Street Journal*, April 7, 2004, B3.

Directory Advertising.

The last time you reached for a phone directory to appraise the local options for Chinese or Mexican food, you probably didn't think about it as a traditional support medium. However, Yellow Pages advertising plays an important role in the media mix for many types of organizations, as evidenced by the $14 billion spent in this medium annually.[14] A wealth of current facts and figures about this media option are available from the Yellow Pages Integrated Media Association's Web site, http://www.yppa.org.

A phone directory can play a unique and important role in consumers' decision-making processes. While most support media keep the brand name or key product

---

12. Fara Warner, "More Companies Turn to Skies as Medium to Promote Products," *Wall Street Journal*, January 5, 1995, B6.

13. Bill Richards, "Bright Idea Has Business Looking Up for Ad Blimps," *Wall Street Journal*, October 14, 1997, B1.

14. Almar Latour, "Yellow Book USA Grabs Business From Baby Bells with Cheap Ads," *Wall Street Journal*, April 13, 2004, A1, A16.

information in front of a consumer, Yellow Pages advertising helps people follow through on their decision to buy. By providing the information that consumers need to actually find a particular product or service, the Yellow Pages can serve as the final link in a buying decision. Because of their availability and consumers' familiarity with this advertising tool, Yellow Pages directories provide an excellent means to supplement awareness-building and interest-generating campaigns that an advertiser might be pursuing through other media.

On the downside, the proliferation and fragmentation of phone directories can make this a challenging medium to work in.[15] Many metropolitan areas are covered by multiple directories, some of which are specialty directories designed to serve specific neighborhoods, ethnic groups, or interest groups. Selecting the right set of directories to get full coverage of large sections of the country can be a daunting task. Thus, of the $14 billion spent in this medium annually, less than $2 billion is from advertisers looking for national coverage.[16] Additionally, working in this medium requires long lead times; and over the course of a year, information in a Yellow Pages ad can easily become dated. There is also limited flexibility for creative execution in the traditional paper format.

Growth of the Internet was once viewed as a major threat to providers of paper directories.[17] Many Web sites such as http://www.switchboard.com and http://www.superpages.com provide online access to Yellow Pages–style databases that allow individualized searches at one's desktop. Other high-profile players such as Yahoo and AOL have also developed online directories as components of their service offerings for Web surfers. But as it turns out, consumers still want their old-style Yellow Pages; market research has established that people who spend the most time on the Internet searching for addresses and phone numbers are also the same people who make heavy use of paper directories.[18] When people are in an information-gathering mode, they commonly use multiple media. So, thus far the Internet has been more of an opportunity than a threat for Yellow Pages publishers, and "old-fashioned" Yellow Pages directories continue to produce something that has been hard to find on the Web—profitability!

When Support Media Are More Than Support Media. There will be times when the capabilities and economies of support media lead them to be featured in one's media plan. Obviously, in such instances, it would be a misnomer to label them as merely "supportive." Out-of-home media used creatively and focused in major metropolitan markets are especially effective in this regard. A couple of examples should make this point clear.

Altoids, "the curiously strong mints" made in England since 1780, used out-of-home media to invigorate its brand in 12 major U.S. cities. Turns out that Altoids' target segment of young, socially active adults living in urban neighborhoods are very hard to reach with conventional broadcast or print advertising. Perhaps they are just too busy being socially active. But, using geodemographic segmentation systems like those described in Chapter 6, it is not hard to identify their neighborhoods. So Altoids and its ad agency, Leo Burnett, set out to plaster those neighborhoods with quirky advertising signage on telephone kiosks, bus shelters, and the backs of buses. Once again, quirky rules! In each of the 12 targeted metro areas, sales of Altoids increased by more than 50 percent.[19] Now that's invigorating!

15. *Yellow Pages and the Media Mix* (Troy, MI: Yellow Pages Publishers Association, 1990).
16. Lisa Sanders, "Major Marketers Turn to Yellow Pages," *Advertising Age,* March 8, 2004, 4, 52.
17. *Yellow Pages: Facts & Media Guide 1998* (Troy, MI: Yellow Pages Publishers Association, 1998), 4, 5.
18. Rachel E. Silverman, "Print Yellow Pages Are Still Profitable," *Wall Street Journal,* May 22, 2000, B16; Bradley Johnson, "Yellow Pages Deals Red Hot as Telecom Industry Regroups," *Advertising Age,* January 6, 2003, 4, 20.
19. Brad Edmondson, "The Drive/Buy Equation," *Marketing Tools,* May 1998, 28–31.

Edgy, often inexpensive, promotional initiatives executed in major urban markets have become so popular that they now have their own name—**guerrilla marketing.** And many firms have adopted guerilla marketing as their primary promotional style, tailoring different executions market by market. A great exemplar of guerrilla marketing gone global is provided by Ikea, the Swedish furniture maker.[20] For instance, Ikea China, focusing on low-income customers in Beijing, transformed the elevators of 20 apartment buildings into furnished "rooms" with small cabinets, teapots, and an elevator operator handing out Ikea catalogs. The intent was to illustrate that Ikea offers many things for dressing up small spaces. Ikea Germany went a slightly different route, taking over train stations in Berlin. The walls of the dingy train stations were decorated with brightly colored fabrics and hanging lamps to make the point that any room can be brightened with a little help from Ikea. The Ikea philosophy is to use nontraditional approaches to make a big splash. That's the essence of guerilla marketing and obviously raises out-of-home media from support to a central role in the media mix.

② Event Sponsorship.

As indicated by the Charmin Pottypalooza example and Ikea's elevator makeovers, marketers around the world are receptive to many possibilities, and the list of possibilities continues to grow. An important issue propelling this search for new ways to reach consumers is the slow but steady erosion in the effectiveness of traditional broadcast media. By now you have been sensitized to the many forces that are working to undermine broadcast media. One is simply a question of options. In today's world, people have an ever-expanding set of options to fill their leisure time, from video games to Web surfing to watching DVDs. Does anyone actually watch television any more? And if they do, there is growing concern among advertisers that soon we will all have set-top technology that will make watching TV ads truly obsolete.[21] As noted in Exhibit 17.13, TiVo Central offers an array of features but, TiVo makes TV better in the minds of many because it lets you skip the advertising.

One of the time-tested means for reaching targeted groups of consumers on their terms is event sponsorship; this tool will only become more popular as advertisers continue their retreat from the broadcast media. General Motors, one of the world's biggest ad spenders, typifies the trend. GM has experimented with a number of ways to "get closer" to its prospective customers. Most entail sponsoring events that get consumers in direct contact with its vehicles, or sponsoring events that associate the GM name with causes or activities that are of interest to its target customers. For example, GM has sponsored a traveling slave-ship exhibition, a scholarship program for the Future Farmers of America, and Seventh Avenue's week of fashion shows in New York City. GM has also

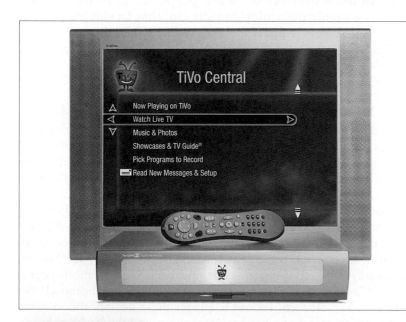

EXHIBIT 17.13

A TiVo® DVR automatically finds and records your favorite shows without video tape and allows you to pause live TV, watch in slow motion, and create your own instant replays. You can also fast forward quickly through any pre-recorded content.

20.   Emma Hall, "Ikea Courts Buyers with Offbeat Ideas," *Advertising Age,* April 12, 2004, 10.
21.   Jack Neff and Lisa Sanders, "It's Broken," *Advertising Age,* February, 16, 2004, 1, 30; Julia Angwin, "In Embracing Digital Recorders, Cable Companies Take Big Risk," *Wall Street Journal,* April 26, 2004, A1, A11; Ronald Grover, "Can Mad Ave. Make Zap-Proof Ads?" *BusinessWeek,* February 2, 2004, 36–37.

launched a movie theater on wheels that travels to state fairs, fishing contests, and auto races to show its 15-minute "movie" about the Silverado pickup truck. Like many marketers large and small, GM has been shifting more of its advertising budget into event sponsorships.[22]

Event sponsorship has some similarities with the other advertising and promotional options discussed thus far in this chapter. Event sponsorship often is used to support or supplement other ongoing advertising efforts. Thus, while it is not quite accurate to think of event sponsorship as a support *medium,* there will be times when it plays a supportive role in the media plan akin to that of out-of-home advertising. Additionally, event sponsorship can provide a base for wonderful synergies with other tactical options such as sales promotions and public relations. Some of these synergies will be made apparent in this chapter, and are elaborated on in Chapters 18 and 20. As always, the challenge is to get multiple tactical alternatives working together to break through the clutter of the marketplace and register the message with the target customer. That's the essence of integrated brand promotion.

EXHIBIT 17.14

While there are no gold medals at the Flying Pig Marathon in Cincinnati (a.k.a. Porkopolis), crossing the "finish swine" at the head of the pack is still cause for a bit of snorting.

Who Else Uses Event Sponsorship?

Event sponsorship is a special and increasingly popular way to reach consumers. **Event sponsorship** involves a marketer providing financial support to help fund an event, such as a rock concert or golf tournament. In return, that marketer acquires the rights to display a brand name, logo, or advertising message on-site at the event. If the event is covered on TV, the marketer's brand and logo may also receive exposure with the television audience. In 2003, marketers around the world spent approximately $26 billion for sponsorship rights, with the majority of this going for sports sponsorships.[23]

Event sponsorship can take many forms. The events can be international in scope, as in the Olympics, with big name sponsors like Kodak, Swatch, John Hancock, and Visa. Or they may have a distinctive local flavor, like the Flying Pig Marathon. As shown in Exhibit 17.14, local events provide sponsorship opportunities for organizations like Mercy Health Partners and a regional office of Ernst & Young. Marketers may offer funding to an existing event, or they may create an event they can sponsor in hopes of engaging a specific segment of their customers. Events provide a captive audience, may receive live coverage by radio and television, and often are reported in the print media. Hence, event sponsorship can both yield face-to-face contact with real consumers and receive simultaneous and follow-up publicity.

The list of companies participating in event sponsorships seems to grow every year. Best Buy, Reebok, Atlantic Records, Heineken, Citibank, and a host of other companies have sponsored tours and special appearances for recording artists such as Brandy, Jewel, Jay-Z, Sting, Britney Spears, Elton John, and 50 Cent. If you have ever hit the beaches for spring break,

22.   Fara Warner, "Under Pressure, GM Takes Its Sales Show on the Road," *Wall Street Journal,* November 4, 1998, B1.
23.   "Marketing Fact Book," *Marketing News,* July 7, 2003, 22.

PUMA is a proud sponsor of the Jamaican Athletics Federation

PUMA®
puma.com

EXHIBIT 17.15

It's hard to compete with the Nikes and the Reeboks of the world when it comes to sports sponsorship. The dollars that get thrown around in this regard are simply prohibitive for some companies. But rather than abandoning sport, here we see Puma choose a different path. If all sports fans have a place in their hearts for the underdog, then perhaps it makes perfect sense to be on the sideline with all teams from Jamaica. Find out more about the Puma strategy at http://www .puma.com.

you already know that companies such as Coca-Cola, MCI, and Sega will be there to greet you. Research conducted by Intercollegiate Communications has established that 65 percent of college students on break not only accept corporate events on the beach, they expect and look forward to them.[24] And, of course, the world is absolutely crazy about football—no, not that kind of football. English professional soccer has become one of the darlings of the sports business because of the valuable marketing opportunities it supports. For example, Manchester United of the English Premier Soccer League surpasses the New York Yankees in its ability to generate revenues. In this world of big-time sports, global companies like Pepsi, Nike, and Vodafone pay huge amounts to have their names linked to the top players and teams.[25] Sports sponsorships also come in all shapes and sizes, providing advertisers diverse opportunities to associate their brands with the distinctive images of various players and teams. Reflect on Exhibit 17.15. What benefit might Puma be looking for as a proud sponsor of the Jamaican Athletics Federation?

The Appeal of Event Sponsorship. In the early days of event sponsorship, it often wasn't clear what an organization was receiving in return for its sponsor's fee. Even today, many critics contend that sponsorships, especially those of the sporting kind, can be ego-driven and thus a waste of money.[26] Company presidents are human, and they like to associate with sports stars and celebrities. This is fine, but when sponsorship of a golf tournament, for example, is motivated mainly by a CEO's desire to play in the same foursome as Annika Sorenstam or Tiger Woods, the company is really just throwing away advertising dollars.

One of the things fueling the growing interest in event sponsorship is that many companies have found ways to make a case for the effectiveness of their sponsorship dollars. Boston-based John Hancock has been a pioneer in developing detailed estimates of the advertising equivalencies of its sponsorships. John Hancock began sponsoring a college football bowl game in 1986 and soon after had a means to judge the value of its sponsor's fee.[27] Hancock employees scoured magazine and newspaper articles about their bowl game to determine name exposure in print media. Next they'd factor in the exact number of times that the John Hancock name was mentioned during television broadcast of the game, along with the name exposure in pre-game promos. In 1991, Hancock executives estimated that they received the equivalent of $5.1 million in advertising exposure for their $1.6 million sponsorship fee. One John Hancock executive called this result "an extraordinarily efficient media buy."[28] However, as the television audience for the John Hancock bowl dwindled in subsequent years, Hancock's estimates of the bowl's value also

24.   Dan Hanover, "School's Out!" *PROMO Magazine,* February 1998, 42–46.
25.   Charles Goldsmith, "Join the Club: Thai Wants In on U.K. Soccer," *Wall Street Journal,* May 12, 2004, B1, B2.
26.   Amy Hernandez, "Research Studies Gauge Sponsorship ROI," *Marketing News,* May 12, 2003, 16; Ian Mount, "Exploding the Myths of Stadium Naming," *Business 2.0,* April 2004, 82, 83.
27.   Michael J. McCarthy, "Keeping Careful Score on Sports Tie-Ins," *Wall Street Journal,* April 24, 1991, B1.
28.   Ibid.

plunged.[29] Subsequently, Hancock moved its sports sponsorship dollars into other events, such as the Olympics, the Boston Marathon, and Major League Baseball.

IBP

Stop, Look, and Listen

Sponsorships yield their greatest benefit when they foster a relationship or deep connection between the target consumer and the sponsoring company or brand. This connection is created when the consumer's passion for the event in question (say, World Cup soccer) becomes associated with a sponsoring brand (such as Adidas, Fujifilm, or MasterCard). There is no guarantee that all brands will realize an emotional connection to the events they sponsor. Indeed, most won't. And while traditional evaluation tools like telephone interviewing or media analysis are important in assessing the value of sponsorships, they cannot reveal deep connections. Careful listening is key to uncovering these connections.

When we know the right questions to ask, listening to the consumer can prove very rewarding. Three areas of questioning can provide important insights for evaluating the relationship-building benefits of event sponsorship. This qualitative research process should begin by exploring eventgoers' subjective experience of an event. Do they have strong feelings about the events they attend? What is it that ignites their passion for an event? Next, it is critical to explore whether fans really understand the role of the sponsor. Most fans know little about the benefits that sponsors provide; research has shown that the more they know, the more the sponsor benefits. Auto-racing fans have the greatest understanding of the role of the sponsor, which helps explain the eagerness of companies to get involved as sponsors of this sport. Finally, one needs to probe the issue of connection: What specific brands do people connect with specific events and how have their opinions of those brands been affected, if at all?

Tapping emotional connections will require sophisticated listening. Listen for fans' descriptions of their emotional experiences, their understanding of the role of the sponsor, and the connections they take away regarding what brands stood out as contributors to what events. Keen listening in these areas will help reveal whether sponsorships are deepening a brand's relevance and meaning in the lives of eventgoers.

Source: Julie Zdziarski, "Evaluating Sponsorships," *PROMO Magazine*, March 2001, 92, 93.

Improving one's ability to gauge the effectiveness of ad dollars spent will generally drive more spending on any IBP tool. Enter a familiar player—Nielsen Media Research—and a service they are offering advertisers called the Sponsorship Scorecard. Nielsen is testing this new service, which will, among other things, give advertisers a read on the impact of their signage in sports stadiums. In one assessment for Fleet Bank in Boston's Fenway Park, Nielsen calculated that Fleet signage received 84 impressions of at least five seconds each during a telecast of the Red Sox/Yankees baseball game. Each impression was time stamped as to when it appeared during the game. Factoring in the size of the viewing audience, Nielsen determined that the 84 impressions for Fleet resulted in a total of 418 million impressions among adults age 18 and up.[30] That's an impressive-sounding number and will become easier to interpret as Nielsen gains more experience with the Sponsorship Scorecard. But again, the key point is that as advertisers and research companies get more proficient in tracking the impact of sponsorships, they will only become a more attractive option as a brand-building tool.

Adding to their appeal, event sponsorships can furnish a unique opportunity to foster brand loyalty. When marketers connect their brand with the potent emotional experiences often found at rock concerts, in soccer stadiums, or on Fort Lauderdale beaches in late March, positive feelings may be attached to that brand that linger well beyond the duration of the event. As part of its spring break promotion, Coca-Cola sponsors dance contests on the beach, where it hands out hundreds of Coca-Cola T-shirts and thousands of cups of Coke each day. The goal is to build brand loyalty with those 18-to-24-year-old students who've come to the beach for fun and sun. As assessed by one of Coke's senior brand managers, "This is one of the best tools in our portfolio."[31] Judging whether your brand is receiving this loyalty dividend is another important aspect of sponsorship assessment, and as discussed in the IBP box, will require a more qualitative

29. William M. Bulkeley, "Sponsoring Sports Gains in Popularity; John Hancock Learns How to Play to Win," *Wall Street Journal*, June 24, 1994, B1.
30. Rich Thomaselli, "Nielsen to Measure Sports Sponsorship," *Advertising Age*, May 3, 2004, 14.
31. Bruce Horovitz, "Students Get Commercial Crash Course," *USA Today*, March 22, 1995, B1–B2.

EXHIBIT 17.16

One of the best uses of events is in reaching well-defined audiences that may be hard to reach through other channels. JBL and TREK have teamed up to support events that reach a target segment that interests them both. Visit the TREK site (http://www.trekbikes .com) and look for examples of tie-ins to events such as the Tour de France. How many examples of sponsorship can you find at the TREK site? While the relationship between TREK and biking events is obvious, why does JBL (http://www.jbl.com) think racing fans will respond to its sponsorship of such events?

approach featuring careful listening and observation on the scene with event participants.

Since various types of events attract well-defined target audiences, marketers can and should choose to sponsor just those events that help them reach their desired target. Such is the case for the sponsors featured in Exhibit 17.16. Notice that JBL Electronics is teaming up with TREK to sponsor nationwide mountain biking events. These so-called "gravity" sports are particularly attractive to skeptical teens, who reject traditional broadcast advertising and are even starting to reject other forms of promotion. Their support of these sports at least puts JBL and TREK on the radar screen of this demanding target audience.[32]

Seeking a Synergy around Event Sponsorship. As we have seen, one way to justify event sponsorship is to calculate the number of viewers who will be exposed to a brand either at the event or through media coverage of the event, and then assess whether the sponsorship provides a cost-effective way of reaching the target segment. This approach assesses sponsorship benefits in direct comparison with traditional advertising media. Some experts now maintain, however, that the benefits of sponsorship can be fundamentally different from anything that traditional media might provide. These additional benefits can take many forms.

Events can be leveraged as ways to entertain important clients, recruit new customers, motivate the firm's salespeople, and generally enhance employee morale. Events provide unique opportunities for face-to-face contact with key customers. Marketers commonly use this point of contact to distribute specialty-advertising items so that attendees will have a branded memento to remind them of the rock concert or soccer match. Marketers may also use this opportunity to sell premiums such as T-shirts and hats, administer consumer surveys as part of their marketing research efforts, or distribute product samples. As you will see in Chapter 20, a firm's event participation may also be the basis for public relations activities that then generate additional media coverage. A comprehensive set of guidelines for selecting the right events and maximizing their benefits for the brand are outlined in Exhibit 17.17.

③ Branded Entertainment. For a stock-car racing fan, there is nothing quite like being at the Lowe's Motor Speedway on the evening of the Coca-Cola 600. It's NASCAR's longest night. But being there live is a rare treat, and so the NASCAR Nextel Cup Series gets plenty of coverage on television, making it among the most popular televised sporting events in North America (second only to the National Football League).[33] If you've never watched a NASCAR race, you owe it to yourself to do so, because while NASCAR is all about the drivers and the race, every race is also a colossal celebration of brands. There are the cars themselves—as in Exhibit 17.18—carrying the logo large and small of something like 800

32.   Laura Petrecca, "Defying Gravity: NBC, Peterson Connect with Cynical Teens via Sports Fest," *Advertising Age*, October 11, 1999, 36.
33.   Tom Lowry, "The Prince of NASCAR," *Business Week*, February 23, 2004, 91–98.

EXHIBIT 17.17

Guidelines for event sponsorship.

Guidelines for Event Sponsorship

1. **Match the brand to the event.** Be sure that the event matches the brand personality. Stihl stages competitions at Mountain Man events featuring its lumbering equipment. Would the Stihl brand fare as well sponsoring a boat race or a triathalon? Probably not.

2. **Tightly define the target audience.** Closely related to point number one is the fact that the best event in the world won't create impact for a brand if it's the wrong target audience. Too often the only barometer of success is the number of bodies in attendance. Far more important is the fact that the brand is getting exposure to the right audience. This is what JBL and TREK accomplished with the mountain bike tour sponsorship.

3. **Stick to a few key messages.** Most events try to accomplish too much. People are there to experience the event and can accommodate only a limited amount of persuasion. Don't overwhelm them. Stick to a few key messages and repeat them often.

4. **Develop a plot line.** An event is most effective when it is like great theater or a great novel. Try to develop a beginning, a middle, and an exciting ending. Sporting events are naturals in this regard, which explains much of their popularity. In nonsporting events, the plot line needs to be developed and delivered in small increments so the attendees can digest both the event and the brand information.

5. **Deliver exclusivity.** If you are staging a special event, make it by invitation only. Or, if you are a featured sponsor, invite only the most important customers, clients, or suppliers. The target audience wants to know that this event is special. The exclusivity provides a positive aura for the brand.

6. **Deliver relevance.** Events should build reputation, awareness, and relationships. Trying to judge the success of an event in terms of sales is misleading and shortsighted. Don't make the event product-centric; make it a brand-building experience for the attendees.

7. **Use the Internet.** The Internet is a great way to promote the event, maintain continuous communication with the target audience, and follow up with the audience after an event. Plus, it's a good way to reach all the people who can't attend the event in person. For golf fans, pga.com gets viewers involved with each event on the PGA tour and gives sponsors another chance to reach the target audience.

8. **Plan for the before and after.** Moving prospects from brand awareness to trial to brand loyalty doesn't happen overnight. The audience needs to see the event as part of a broad exposure to the brand. This is the synergy that needs to be part of the event planning process. The event must be integrated with advertising, sales promotions, and advertising specialty items.

Source: Laura Shuler, "Make Sure to Deliver When Staging Events," *Marketing News*, September 13, 1999, 12.

NASCAR sponsors. The announcers keep you informed throughout via the Old Spice Lap Leaders update and the Visa Race Break. We are told that Home Depot is the Official Home Improvement Warehouse of NASCAR and UPS is The Official Delivery Service of NASCAR. At commercial breaks there's the ever-present beer ads with Budweiser and Miller shouting at each other, and we rejoin the race following the Budweiser or Miller Lite car around the track. None of this comes as any surprise, because NASCAR openly and aggressively bills itself as the best marketing opportunity in sports. Said another way, a NASCAR race is a fantastic example of branded entertainment.

NASCAR is truly a unique brand building "vehicle," but we use it here as an exemplar of something bigger, something more pervasive, and something that is growing in popularity as a way to support and build brands across diverse entertainment venues. Although it has been called many things, we have settled on the label branded entertainment. **Branded entertainment** entails embedding one's brand or brand icons as part of any entertainment property (e.g., a sporting event, TV show, theme

There is something special i n the relationship between fans and their brands at a NASCAR event. Each race is truly a celebration, with brands as co-stars of the show. View the galaxy of stars at http://www.nascar .com.

park, short film, movie, or videogame) in an effort to impress and connect with your consumer in a unique and compelling way. If you have the sense that brands are showing up in more and more places these days, you're right. This new visibility for brands is being driven by a desire in the marketing community to participate in the development of all forms of entertainment. When Paula Abdul reaches for the big red Coca-Cola cup to quench her thirst during the TV show *American Idol,* it is not a coincidence. Coca-Cola was embedded as part of this entertainment property in cooperation with the shows producers, after paying a $20 million placement fee.[34]

It's not hard to understand why NAPA Auto Parts or Budweiser, the King of Beers, would be willing to shell out millions of dollars to be a featured brand in the NASCAR Nextel Cup Series. But how is it conceivable that a company such as Procter & Gamble could justify sponsorship of the Tide Car, which you see whizzing by in Exhibit 17.19? Well, first of all, lots of women are NASCAR fans and lots of women buy Tide. Additionally, general industry research indicates that NASCAR fans are unusually loyal to the brands that sponsor cars and have absolutely no problem with marketers plastering their logos all over their cars and their drivers. Indeed, many NASCAR fans often wear those logos proudly. Moreover, the data say that race fans are three times more likely to purchase a product promoted by their favorite NASCAR driver, relative to the fans of all other sports.[35] One NASCAR marketing executive put it this way: "Our teams and drivers have done a wonderful job communicating to fans that the more Tide they buy, the faster Ricky Cravens is going to go."[36] Obviously, this entails impressing and connecting with consumers in a most compelling way, making the Tide car or the Bud car or the Viagra car or the Lowe's car all great symbols of branded entertainment.

Product Placements. In more and more instances brands are showing up as costars of the show, no matter what the show. This is obvious and accepted as part of the NASCAR circuit, but

34. Ronald Grover, "Can Mad Ave. Make Zap-Proof Ads?" *Business Week,* February 2, 2004, 36–37.
35. Rich Thomaselli, "Nextel Link Takes NASCAR to New Level," *Advertising Age,* October 27, 2003, S-7.
36. Lisa Napoli, "A New Era in Stock-Car Racing," *The New York Times,* July 14, 2003, accessed at www.nytimes.com, 7/14/03.

Automobile racing attracts loyal fans with lots of devotion to their favorite brands. Is it any surprise that advertisers want to be part of this unique venue? http://www.pg.com

in other venues the presence of brands is less familiar and sometimes controversial. Some writers, producers, and entertainers resent the infusion of commercialization in their art form, but many are simply accepting of brands as the new reality of doing business. Branded entertainment has come a long way since E.T. nibbled on Reese's Pieces in the movie *E.T. the Extra-Terrestrial*. But that product (or brand) placement foreshadowed much that has followed.

Product placement is the practice of placing any branded product into the content and execution of any entertainment product. In today's world, product-placement agencies work with marketers to build bridges to the entertainment industry. Working collaboratively, agents, marketers, producers, and writers find ways to incorporate the marketer's brand as part of the show. The show can be of almost any kind. Movies, short films on the Internet, and reality TV are great venues for branded entertainment. Videogames, novels, and magazines (or mag-a-logs) offer great potential. Anywhere and any time people are being entertained, there is opportunity for branded entertainment.

Television viewers have become accustomed to product placements on the tube. Soap operas and reality shows have helped make product placements seem the norm on TV, and the tactic is spreading like wildfire. On Time Warner's WB network, a shiny orange Volkswagen Beetle convertible played an important role in the teen superhero drama *Smallville*. Ray Romano chased his wife around the grocery store, knocking over a display of Ragu products, in an episode of the CBS sitcom *Everybody Loves Raymond*. *Queer Eye for the Straight Guy*, on the Bravo network, has provided a bonanza of placement opportunities with brands like Amaretto, Redken, and Diesel. The final episode of NBC's long-running comedy *Frasier* included a special moment where Niles gave his brother a little gift to cheer him up. That gift? Pepperidge Farm Mint Milano cookies. The branded "special moment," like that one on *Frasier*, is likely to become more common in the years ahead.[37]

The "car chase" is a classic component of many action/adventure movies, and in recent years has been seized as a frequent platform for launching new automotive brands. If you'd like to immerse yourself in a superb example of branded entertainment,

37.   Brian Steinberg and Suzanne Vranica, "Prime-Time TV's New Guest Stars: Products," *Wall Street Journal*, January 12, 2004, B1, B4; Brian Steinberg, "Frasier Finale: Amid Nostalgia, A Product Plug," *Wall Street Journal*, May 12, 2004, B1, B2.

EXHIBIT 17.20

The Mini Cooper launch campaign featured many innovative examples of integrated brand promotion, including a starring role in the film The Italian Job. *Let's motor!*

rent the DVD of *The Italian Job,* a movie released in 2003 starring the lovable Mini Cooper, like the one on display in Exhibit 17.20. The Mini proves to be the perfect getaway car, as it deftly maneuvers in and out of tight spots throughout the movie. BMW has been a pioneer in the product-placement genre, starting with its Z3 placement in the 1995 James Bond thriller *Goldeneye* and more recently with its original Web-distributed short films like *Beat the Devil,* starring James Brown, Marilyn Manson, and most especially, the BMW Z4. Pontiac re-launched its GTO brand in the 2004 made-for-TV movie *The Last Ride,* costarring Dennis Hopper and Chris Carmack; Toyota tried to rev up sales of its boxy Scion brand through a featured role in the made-for-the-Internet film *On the D.L.* And Audi touted its futuristic RSQ concept car in a science fiction feature film, *I, Robot.* As they say, birds of a feather flock together.

But of course it is not just automakers that have discovered product placements in movies and films. White Castle, American Express, Nokia, and the Weather Channel—to name a few—have joined the party as well. All this activity is supported by research indicating that persons under 25 years old are most likely to notice product placements in films, and are also willing to try products they see in movies and films.[38] As we have noted previously, young consumers are increasingly difficult to reach via traditional broadcast media. While they are likely to soon get their fill of product placements at the movies, in the near term this looks like a good tactic for reaching an age cohort that can be hard to reach.

Speaking of reaching the unreachable, consider these numbers: According to Jupiter Research, in 2004 there were something like 36 million people in the United States playing personal-computer or console videogames at least five hours per week. Jupiter projects that number to soar to 63 million by 2009.[39] Add in these elements: Most analysts conclude that around 40 percent of these players are from the 18-to-34 age cohort—highly sought after by advertisers because of their discretionary spending but expensive to reach via conventional media. Now factor in that

38.   Emma Hall, "Young Consumers Receptive to Movie Product Placements," *Advertising Age,* March 29, 2004, 8.
39.   Suzanne Vranica, "Y&R Bets on Videogame Industry," *Wall Street Journal,* May 11, 2004, B4.

videogames are not only an attractive entertainment option but are also a form of entertainment where players rarely wander off during a commercial break. With all those focused eyeballs in play, is it any wonder that marketers want to be involved? Billboard ads and virtual products have become standard fare in games like "True Crime: Streets of L.A.," starring Puma-wearing Nick Kang. This practice is bound to proliferate as ad agencies like WPP Group's Young & Rubicam and Publicis Group's Starcom launch new videogame divisions to service their clients' interest in "game-vertising" or "adver-gaming." (Take your pick, but remember it's all branded entertainment.) If you're a gamer, expect to see more of brands like these in your virtual world: LG Mobile, Coca-Cola, BMW, Sony, Levi Strauss, Nokia, Callaway Golf, Ritz Bits, Target, Radio Shack, the U.S. Army, and oodles more.[40]

Where Is Branded Entertainment Headed? It is easy to understand the surging popularity of branded entertainment. Reaching the unreachable through a means that allows your brand to stand out and connect with the consumer can only mean more interest from marketers. But there are always complicating and countervailing forces. No one can really say how rapidly advertising dollars will flow into branded entertainment in the next decade. Several forces could work to undermine that flow.

One of the obvious countervailing forces is instant oversaturation. Like any other faddishly popular promotional tactic, if advertisers pile on too quickly, a jaded consumer and a cluttered environment will be the result. As stated by a former marketing vice president at General Motors, "Any reasonable observer today has to see most of the marketing world is chasing a handful of product-placement deals. This is problematic and limiting. There just aren't enough bona fide hits to go around."[41] Some will argue that creative collaboration can always yield new opportunities for branded entertainment, but you have to acknowledge at some point that yet another motion picture featuring yet another hot automobile will start to feel a little stale. Indeed, we may already be there.

A related problem involves the processes and systems that currently exist for matching brands with entertainment properties. Traditional media provide a well-established path for reaching consumers. Marketers like that predictability. Branded entertainment is a new and often unpredictable path. As noted by a senior executive at Fallon, Minneapolis, a pioneer in branded entertainment with BMW Films, "For every success you have several failures, because you're basically using a machete to cut through the jungle . . . with branded entertainment, every time out, it's new."[42] Lack of predictability causes the process to break down. A soured relationship between General Motors and Warner Bros. over the promotion of the film *Matrix Reloaded* illustrates that marketers and filmmakers don't always appreciate the needs of the other. In this instance GM's Cadillac division abandoned a big-budget TV campaign associated with the sequel when it couldn't get the talent cooperation or film footage it wanted. Samsung, Heineken, and Coke also complained in public about poor treatment from Warner Bros. These kinds of high-profile squabbles make big news and leave the people with the money to spend wondering whether the branded entertainment path is really worth all the aggravation.[43]

Finally, there is a concern about playing it straight with consumers. More specifically, Ralph Nader's Commercial Alert consumer advocacy group has filed a complaint with the Federal Trade Commission and the Federal Communication Commission alleging that TV networks deceive the public by failing to disclose the details of product-placement deals.[44] The group's basic argument seems to be that since

40.   T. L. Stanley, "Joystick Nation," *Advertising Age,* March 22, 2004, 1, 29.
41.   Phil Guarascio, "Decision Time at Mad + Vine," *Advertising Age,* September 1, 2003, 15.
42.   Kate MacArthur, "Branded Entertainment, Marketing Tradition Tussle," *Advertising Age,* May 10, 2004, 6.
43.   T. L. Stanley, "Sponsors Flee Matrix Sequel," *Advertising Age,* October 13, 2003, 1, 71.
44.   Claire Atkinson, "Watchdog Group Hits TV Product Placements," *Advertising Age,* October 6, 2003, 12.

most product placements are in fact "paid advertisements," consumers should be advised as such. It is conceivable that a federal agency will call for some form of disclosure when fees have been paid to place brands in U.S. TV shows, although now that the practice has become so prevalent, we expect that consumers already perceive that there is money changing hands behind the scenes. Consumers are generally pretty savvy about this sort of thing. On the global front, this can be one of those issues where you find great differences of opinion from country to country. For example, as described in the Global Issues box, the Chinese approach product placements much like we in the United States do, whereas the Brits see things very differently.

GLOBAL ISSUES

Regulators Run Hot and Cold on Product Placements

H. J. Heinz will tell you that the world is a very complicated place when it comes to the use of product placements. All you need to know about the United Kingdom is that when reruns of *American Idol* ran there, the U.K.'s Independent Television Commission made producers disguise the logo on those big red cola cups. But when Heinz launched a cooking show called *Dinner Doctors* in the U.K., they of course had in mind featuring many of their foods products as part of the show's normal fare. The regulator's response: No way. No products could be mentioned in any part of the programming. When one executive from the home office in Pittsburgh asked, "How many times is the product shown?" he was told bluntly by Heinz general manager of corporate affairs in Europe, "It's not shown." Why bother with such programming? Heinz does get sponsorship mentions as part of the credits, and in Britain's sparse product-placement environment, apparently that's enough to generate positive feedback from consumers. Perhaps this is just another example of the "law of advertising relativity." In a sparse environment, a little bit of credit can seem like a lot.

Conversely, Chinese media seem happy to deal with producers like Ford, Nike, Sony, and Heinz. In this situation, Chinese stations get new programming and advertisers get direct access to the consumers they want to impress. So in China H. J. Heinz sponsors *Mommy & Baby—Healthy World*, broadcast in Shanghai, Wuhan, and Guangdong. The plot: Cameras follow moms focusing on their day-to-day challenges in raising kids under three years of age. Nutrition is a central topic in the show, and guess whose baby foods are the featured costar. Sure thing. It's an H. J. Heinz love fest!

In China product placements are seen as mutually beneficial. New laws there have actually helped promote the practice. For marketers the development of programming provides a critical alternative to the high cost of television advertising. For broadcasters the deals offer the prospect of higher ratings, with many marketers picking up on proven reality TV formats like the talent contest, the travelogue, or the *Survivor* knock-off. Media executives in China welcome brands as costars. It's just good business: "Since we are not rich in our production team, if other companies could bring some sponsorship and fresh ideas, we could share the revenues with them—and we get better programs." There is one caveat. The model works in China or anywhere else only if the brand helps or at least doesn't get in the way of the entertainment. Consumers around the world know an infomercial when they see one, and when they do most will simply change the channel.

Sources: Erin White, "U.K. TV Can Pose Tricky Hurdles," *Wall Street Journal*, June 27, 2003, B7; Geoffrey A. Fowler, "New Star on Chinese TV: Product Placements," *Wall Street Journal*, June 2, 2004, B1, B3.

What's Old Is New Again.

Some hate to admit it, but marketers, media moguls, advertisers, and entertainers have much in common. They do what they do for business reasons. And they have and will continue to do business together. That's reality. It's been reality for decades. Smart advertisers have always recognized this, and then go about their business of trying to reach consumers with a positive message on behalf of their brands. No firm has managed this collaboration better over the years than Procter & Gamble, and to close this section on branded entertainment, we take a then-and-now look at P&G initiatives to acknowledge that, while it is enjoying a huge surge of popularity recently, branded entertainment has been around for decades.

In 1923 P&G was on the cutting edge of branded entertainment in the then new medium of radio. (Try if you dare to imagine a world without television or the Internet—how did people survive?) To promote their shortening product Crisco, they helped create a new radio program called *Crisco Cooking Talks*. This was a fifteen-minute program that featured recipes and advice to encourage cooks, like the one in

Exhibit 17.21, to find more uses for Crisco. While it was a good start, P&G's market research soon told them that listeners wanted something more entertaining than just a recipe show. So a new form of entertainment was created just for radio that

In the 1920's P&G was an innovator in the new medium of radio, trying to reach consumers on behalf of brands like Crisco, Ivory and Oxydol.

Today P&G markets something like 250 brands, including Pantene, Tide, Old Spice, Swiffer, and Pringles. Branded entertainment remains an important part of the P&G model for connecting with consumers, decades after their invention of the soap opera.

would come to be known as the soap opera. These dramatic series used a storyline that encouraged listeners to tune in day after day. *Guiding Light,* P&G's most enduring "soap," was started on the radio in 1937. In 1952 *Guiding Light* made the successful transition to television. It thus holds the distinction of being the longest-running show in the history of electronic media.[45] And one more thing . . . P&G has done all right selling soap.

Fast forward to the new millennium. P&G's consumer has changed. The soap opera has lost much of its traditional appeal and new forms of integrated brand promotion are necessary. Today P&G works with its media partner Viacom International Inc. to modernize its offerings of branded entertainment. For example, to support the Pantene hair care brand, a music competition for young women was launched using a format that *American Idol* made commonplace. *Pantene Pro-Voice* (see Exhibit 17.22) airs on Viacom's MTV network, and of course you can check out the competitors and download their music online (http://www.pro-voice.com). If you participate in the voting process, there's also a chance to win a trip to New York City to hear the contest winner and other popular performers. Although it's not likely to have the longevity of a *Guiding Light, Pro-Voice* represents the right entertainment option for today's consumer. As a world-class brand builder, you can bet

45.   Davis Dyer, Frederick Dalzell, and Rowena Olegario, *Rising Tide: Lessons from 165 Years of Brand Building at Procter & Gamble* (Boston, MA: Harvard Business School Publishing, 2004).

that P&G will find more opportunities to entertain the consumer, with its brands always as costars in the show.

④ The Coordination Challenge.

When we add various support media to the many options that exist in print and broadcast media and on the Internet, there is just an incredible assortment of choices for delivering messages to a target audience. And it doesn't stop there. As you have seen, marketers and advertisers are constantly searching for new, cost-effective ways to break through the clutter and connect with consumers. Today, everything from advertising in restrooms to adver-gaming to street furniture to sponsoring a marathon is part of the portfolio.

In concluding this chapter, a critical point about the explosion of advertising and IBP tools needs to be reinforced. Advertisers have a vast and ever-expanding array of options for delivering messages to their potential customers. From cable TV to national newspapers, from high-tech billboards to online contests and giveaways, the variety of options is staggering. The keys to success for any campaign are choosing the right set of options to engage a target segment and then coordinating the placement of messages to ensure coherent and timely communication.

Many factors work against coordination. As advertising and IBP have become more complex, organizations often become reliant on diverse functional specialists. For example, an organization might have separate managers for advertising, event sponsorship, branded entertainment, and Web development. Specialists, by definition, focus on their specialty and can lose sight of what others in the organization are doing.[46] Specialists also want their own budgets and typically argue for more funding for their particular area. This competition for budget dollars often yields rivalries and animosities that work against coordination. Never underestimate the power of competition for the budget. It is exceedingly rare to find anyone who will volunteer to take less of the budget so someone else can have more.

Coordination is further complicated by the fact that there can be an incredible lack of alignment around who is responsible for achieving the integration.[47] Should the client accept this responsibility, or should integration be the responsibility of a "lead" agency? Ad agencies often see themselves in this lead role, but have not played it to anyone's satisfaction.[48] One vision of how things should work has the lead agency playing the role of an architect and general contractor.[49] The campaign architect is charged with drawing up a plan that is media neutral and then hiring subcontractors to deliver those aspects of the project that the agency per se is ill suited to handle. The plan must also be profit-neutral. That is, the budget must go to the subcontractors who can deliver the work called for in the master plan. Here again the question becomes, Will the "architect/general contractor" really spread the wealth, if by doing so it forfeits wealth? Life usually doesn't work that way. But one thing is for sure: When it is not clear who is accountable for delivering an integrated campaign, there is little chance that synergy or integration will be achieved.

Remember finally that the objective underlying the need for coordination is to achieve a synergistic effect. Individual media can work in isolation, but advertisers get more for their dollars if various media and IBP tools build on one another and work together. Even savvy marketers like American Express are challenged by the need for coordination, and especially so as they cut back on their use of the 30-second TV spot and venture into diverse IBP tools. For instance, to launch its Blue card,

46.   Don E. Schultz, Stanley I. Tannenbaum, and Robert F. Lauterborn, *Integrated Marketing Communications* (Lincolnwood, IL: NTC Business Books, 1993); Daniel Klein, "Disintegrated Marketing," *Harvard Business Review,* March 2003, 18–19.

47.   Laura Q. Hughes and Kate MacArthur, "Soft Boiled: Clients Want Integrated Marketing at Their Disposal, but Agencies Are (Still) Struggling to Put the Structure Together," *Advertising Age,* May 28, 2001, 3, 54; Claire Atkinson, "Integration Still a Pipe Dream for Many," *Advertising Age,* March 10, 2003, 1, 47.

48.   Joe Cappo, *The Future of Advertising* (Chicago, IL: McGraw-Hill Publishing, 2003), ch. 8.

49.   Ibid, 153, 154.

AmEx employed an innovative mix, starting with Blue-labeled water bottles given away at health clubs and Blue ads printed on millions of popcorn bags. The company sponsored a Sheryl Crow concert in New York's Central Park and transformed L.A.'s House of Blues jazz club into the "House of Blue," with performances by Elvis Costello, Stevie Wonder, and Counting Crows. Print ads and TV have also been used to back the Blue, but AmEx's spending in these traditional media is down by over 50 percent relative to previous campaigns. Making diverse components like these work together and speak to the targeted consumer with a "single voice" is the essence of advertising and integrated brand promotion. AmEx appears to have found a good formula: The Blue card was the most successful new-product launch in the company's history.[50]

The coordination challenge does not end here. Chapters that follow will add more layers of complexity to this challenge. Topics to come include sales promotion, point-of-purchase advertising, direct marketing, and public relations. These activities entail additional contacts with a target audience that should reinforce the messages being delivered through broadcast, print, and support media. Integrating these efforts to speak with one voice represents a marketer's best and maybe only hope for breaking through the clutter of competitive advertising to engage with a target segment in today's crowded marketplace.

50.   Suzanne Vranica, "For Big Marketers Like AmEx, TV Ads Lose Starring Role," *Wall Street Journal*, May 17, 2004, B1, B3.

SUMMARY

 1 Describe the role of support media in a comprehensive media plan.

The traditional support media include out-of-home media and directory advertising. Billboards and transit advertising are excellent means for carrying simple messages into specific metropolitan markets. Street furniture is becoming increasingly popular as a placard for brand builders around the world. Aerial advertising can also be a great way to break through the clutter. Finally, directory advertising can be a sound investment because it helps a committed customer locate an advertiser's product.

 2 Justify the growing popularity of event sponsorship as another supporting component of a media plan.

The list of companies sponsoring events grows with each passing year, and the events include a wide variety of activities. Of these various activities, sports attract the most sponsorship dollars. Sponsorship can help in building brand familiarity; it can promote brand loyalty by connecting a brand with powerful emotional experiences; and in most instances it allows a marketer to reach a well-defined target audience. Events can also facilitate face-to-face contacts with key customers and present opportunities to distribute product samples, sell premiums, and conduct consumer surveys.

 3 Explain the benefits and limitations of connecting with entertainment properties in building a brand.

Brand builders want to connect with consumers, and to do so they are connecting with the entertainment business. While not everyone can afford a NASCAR sponsorship, in many ways NASCAR sets the standard for celebrating brands in an entertaining setting. Product placements in films, TV shows, and videogames are becoming more common. However, the rush to participate in branded entertainment ventures raises the risk of oversaturation and consumer backlash, or at least consumer apathy. As with any tool, while it is new and fresh, good things happen. When it gets old and stale, advertisers will turn to the next "big thing."

 4 Discuss the challenges presented by the ever-increasing variety of media for achieving integrated brand promotion.

The tremendous variety of media options we have seen thus far represents a monumental challenge for an advertiser who wishes to speak to a customer with a single voice. Achieving this single voice is critical for breaking through the clutter of the modern advertising environment. However, the functional specialists required for working in the various media have their own biases and subgoals that can get in the way of integration. We will return to this issue in subsequent chapters as we explore other options available to marketers in their quest to win customers.

KEY TERMS

support media   out-of-home media   event sponsorship
riding the boards   aerial advertising   branded entertainment
transit advertising   guerrilla marketing   product placement

QUESTIONS

1. Read the opening section of this chapter and briefly describe the Charmin Pottypalooza tour. In what ways does Pottypalooza exemplify the brave new world of integrated brand promotion?

2. Explain the important advances in technology that are likely to contribute to the appeal of billboards as an advertising medium.

3. Critique the out-of-home media as tools for achieving reach-versus-frequency objectives in a media plan.

4. Explain the unique role for directory advertising in a media plan. Given what you see happening on the Internet, what kind of future do you predict for traditional Yellow Pages advertising?

5. When would it be appropriate to conclude that out-of-home media are serving more than just a supportive role in one's media plan? Give an example of out-of-home media being used as the principal element in the advertising plan, either from your own experience or from examples that were offered in this chapter.

6. Present statistics to document the claim that the television viewing audience is becoming fragmented. What are the causes of this fragmentation? Develop an argument that links this fragmentation to the growing popularity of event sponsorship and branded entertainment.

7. Event sponsorship can be valuable for building brand loyalty. Search through your closets, drawers, or cupboards and find a premium or memento that you acquired at a sponsored event. Does this memento bring back fond memories? Would you consider yourself loyal to the brand that sponsored this event? If not, why not?

8. Why is NASCAR a good placement for the Tide brand?

9. Explain the need for functional specialists in developing IBP campaigns. Who are they and what skills do they offer? What problems do these functional specialists create for the achievement of integrated brand promotion?

EXPERIENTIAL EXERCISES

1.   Product placement is the practice of placing or embedding a branded product into the content of any entertainment vehicle. Examples of product placement include Reese's Pieces in the movie *E.T. the Extra-Terrestrial,* Coca-Cola cups at the judges' table on *American Idol,* and Craftsman tools on *Extreme Makeover: Home Edition.* As a creative exercise, select a favorite brand for placement in a popular TV series, movie, or video game. List three ways the brand could be incorporated ("embedded") naturally into the show or game as a form of branded entertainment. Finally, explain why you think this product placement would be an appropriate, effective method for promoting your brand.

2.   Event sponsorship is becoming more important to advertisers, as the effectiveness of traditional broadcast media continues to erode with increasing fragmentation. Event sponsorship can be international, like the Olympics, or have local color, such as a chili cook-off. Find an example of event sponsorship and describe the relationship between the advertiser and the event. What role does the advertiser perform during the event? Why do companies think sponsoring this event is an effective means to reaching target audiences? As a consumer, do you think event sponsorships have influenced your decision to use a product?

EXPERIENCING THE INTERNET

17-1 Out-of-Home Media

Advertising media such as outdoor signage, billboard advertising, transit ads, and aerial advertising are commonly known as *support media* or *out-of-home media.* Advertisers rely on support media to reinforce brand messages communicated through primary media such as television, print, or radio. To coordinate out-of-home components with their broader campaign efforts, advertisers hire firms that specialize in the development and execution of outdoor advertising. Mobile Ad Group and Mobile Airships are two such firms that have become popular with big advertisers like Coca-Cola, Nestle Waters, and Red Hat for delivering innovative outdoor-advertising solutions to high-traffic target zones.

Mobile Ad Group: http://www.mobileadgroup.com

Mobile Airships: http://www.blimpguys.com

1.   Visit the Web sites of these out-of-home media companies and provide a brief summary of the services each offers to advertisers.

2.   Browse the testimonials and ad galleries that appear at these sites, and identify a popular brand that has used out-of-home media as part of its advertising campaign. Do you think out-of-home media is an effective promotion vehicle for this particular brand? Why or why not?

3.   What are the advantages of using these types of traditional support media, and where would you expect to see these ads in operation?

17-2 Billboards

Billboards, posters, and outdoor signs are considered by some to be the oldest forms of advertising. From the time of the Revolutionary War, when posters were used for propaganda, outdoor signage has been used to promote events such as circuses, political campaigns, and military recruiting. Although the advent of television put the future of outdoor signage in question, the establishment of a federal highway system in the 1960s brought new promise, and billboards and other creative outdoor displays were revitalized by new opportunity.

Beach 'N Billboard: http://www.beachnbillboard.com

1.   What types of markets are best suited for outdoor signage?

2.   Describe how Beach 'N Billboard has seized upon a unique market opportunity, as outdoor signage such as posters and billboards did in advertising's history.

3.   Explain how Beach 'N Billboard represents an environmentalist response to the notion that billboards represent a form of visual pollution.

CHAPTER 18

After reading and thinking about this chapter, you will be able to do the following:

1

Explain the importance and growth of different types of sales promotion.

2

Describe the main sales promotion techniques used in the consumer, trade channel, and business markets.

3

Identify the risks to the brand of using sales promotion.

4

Understand the role and techniques of point-of-purchase advertising.

5

Explain the coordination issues for integrated brand promotion associated with using sales promotion and point-of-purchase advertising.

All-New!
1099 HOURS FREE!
FOR 50 DAYS –
see details inside
No Credit Card Required!
Get
Connected
in your
new home!
Try
AOL 9.0
OPTIMIZED

Introductory Scenario: Power Struggles and Sales Promotion.

How important is sales promotion in the household-products market? Well, no matter how important it has been historically, it's even more important now. Big brand marketers like Procter & Gamble, Johnson & Johnson, and Clorox are realizing that unless they support their household product brands, like Tide and Glad, with a heavy sales promotion effort, big retailers like Wal-Mart, Albertson's, and Target will hold the power position and dictate which brands get store shelf space and which ones do not. When the big brand names—Tide, Pledge, Pampers—lack sales promotions like couponing, contests, or point-of-purchase displays, two things can happen. First, any competitive brands—like All, Old English, and Huggies—that are being supported with sales promotions *will* get retailer's attention and shelf space preference. Second, the private label or "house" brands can make inroads on the big names.

How big a problem do manufacturers of consumer packaged goods face? Well, for starters, the top ten retailers in the United States control the sale of 43 percent of the consumer packaged goods sold.[1] With this sort of power, they can dictate what products appear on store shelves, how much shelf space each brand gets, and how those brands get promoted in store advertising. And, if manufacturers are not willing to support their brands with sales promotions, the big retailers will gladly sell consumers the retailer's own house brand. So, the big brand name manufacturers offer coupons or run a sweepstakes; then consumers feel like they are getting something a little extra and will bypass the house brand.

So the big manufacturers have bellied up to the sales promotion and point-of-purchase bar and are spending big on techniques that will both promote their brands and at least keep a balance of power with the retailers (see Exhibit 18.1). How big an investment are manufacturers making in sales promotion and point of purchase? About $30 billion a year.[2] The reason manufacturers spend so much is that their view of what "consumer loyalty" needs to be is different from the retailers' view. Retailers want consumers to come to their *store* and once inside, they are (in the retailer's

EXHIBIT 18.1

Consumer-goods manufacturers need to support their brands with strong sales promotion and point-of-purchase programs to maintain a balance of power with the big retailers who control the distribution of their brands.

1.   Kelly Shermach, "Power Struggle," *Marketing News,* November 10, 2003, 13, 16.
2.   PROMO 2004 Industry Trends Report, http://www.promomagazine.com/mag/marketing_upward_bound/.

view of the world) welcome to choose *any* brand that suits them. Of course, that's not going to work for the Procter & Gambles and General Millses of the world. In the words of Don Stuart, a marketing consultant who works with the big consumer-product marketers, "Retailers develop loyalty programs that are not necessarily consistent with building manufacturer loyalty. That can create a conflict between retailers and manufacturers."[3]

An example of how one manufacturer discovered the power of sales promotion and point-of-purchase advertising is Clorox. When Clorox acquired the Glad brand (plastic bags and wraps) from First Brands, it applied its standard turnaround strategy to the brand—cut retailer and consumer promotion and revive the brand through media advertising. Well, the brand immediately went on a downhill slide and Clorox strategists had to rethink their decision. Without trade and consumer sales promotion support, Glad sales were down overall about 15 percent the first year after the acquisition. So to help sagging market share, Clorox increased trade promotion dollars to be used for in-store display and merchandising assistance. Simultaneously, more coupons were distributed to consumers. Check out the Glad display next time you're in the supermarket and see how Clorox is doing.[4]

Sales Promotion Defined.
Sales promotion is often a key component within an integrated brand promotion campaign. As the Glad example highlights, sales promotions like dealer incentives and coupons can attract attention and give new energy to the advertising and the IBP effort. While mass media advertising is designed to build a brand image over time, sales promotion is immediate and conspicuous and designed to make things happen in a hurry. Used properly, sales promotion is capable of almost instant demand stimulation, like the kind that contests and sweepstakes can create. The "message" in a sales promotion features price reduction (or free sample), a prize, or some other incentive for consumers to try a brand or for a retailer to feature the brand in the store. Sales promotion has proven to be a popular complement to mass media advertising because it accomplishes things advertising cannot.

Formally defined, **sales promotion** is the use of incentive techniques that create a perception of greater brand value among consumers, the trade, and business buyers. The intent is to create a short-term increase in sales by motivating trial use, encouraging larger purchases, or stimulating repeat purchases. **Consumer-market sales promotion** includes coupons, price-off deals, premiums, contests and sweepstakes, sampling and trial offers, rebates, loyalty/frequency programs, and phone and gift cards. All are ways of inducing household consumers to purchase a firm's brand rather than a competitor's brand. Notice that some incentives reduce price, offer a reward, or encourage a trip to the retailer. **Trade-market sales promotion** uses point-of-purchase displays, incentives, allowances, or cooperative advertising as ways of motivating distributors, wholesalers, and retailers to stock and feature a firm's brand in their store merchandising programs. **Business-market promotion** is designed to cultivate buyers in large corporations who are making purchase decisions about a wide range of products including computers, office supplies, and consulting services. Techniques used for business buyers are similar to the trade-market techniques and include trade shows, premiums, incentives, and loyalty/frequency programs.

The Importance and Growth of Sales Promotion.
Sales promotion is designed to affect demand differently than advertising does. As we have learned throughout the text, most advertising is designed to have awareness-, image-, and preference-building effects for a brand over the long run. The role of sales

---

3.   Shermach, "Power Struggle," 13.
4.   Jack Neff, "Clorox Gives In on Glad, Hikes Trade Promotion," *Advertising Age,* November 27, 2000, 22.

*Marketers use a wide range
of incentives to attract
attention to a brand. Here,
David Oreck offers new
buyers a free iron for trying
the Oreck lightweight
vacuum.*

promotion, on the other hand, is primarily to elicit an immediate purchase from a customer. Coupons, samples, rebates, contests and sweepstakes, and similar techniques offer a consumer an immediate incentive to chose one brand over another, as exemplified in Exhibit 18.2. Notice that Oreck is offering a free product (referred to as a premium offer) just for trying the Oreck vacuum cleaner.

Other sales promotions, such as frequency programs (for example, frequent-flyer programs), provide an affiliation value with a brand, which increases a consumer's ability and desire to identify with a particular brand. Sales promotions featuring price reductions, such as coupons, are effective in the convenience goods category, where frequent purchases, brand switching, and a perceived homogeneity (similarity) among brands characterize consumer behavior.

Sales promotions are used across all consumer goods categories and in the trade and business markets as well. When a firm determines that a more immediate response is called for—whether the target customer is a household, business buyer, distributor, or retailer—sales promotions are designed to provide that incentive. The goals for sales promotion versus those of advertising are compared in Exhibit 18.3. Notice the key differences in the goals for these different forms of promotion. Sales promotion encourages more immediate and short-term responses while the purpose of advertising is to cultivate an image, loyalty, and repeat purchases over the long term.

The Importance of Sales Promotion. The importance of sales promotion in the United States should not be underestimated. Sales promotion may not seem as stylish and sophisticated as mass media advertising, but expenditures on this tool are impressive. In recent years, sales promotion expenditures have grown at an annual rate of about 4 to 8 percent, compared to about a 3 to 5 percent rate for advertising. By 2003, the investment by advertisers in sales promotions reached over $107 billion representing 28.5 percent of all marketing dollars spent on consumer promotions.[5] Add to that figure consumer savings by redeeming coupons and rebates and the figure exceeds $150 billion.[6] Exhibit 18.4 shows 2003 and 2002 spending for promotion and point-of-purchase advertising.

It is important to realize that full-service advertising agencies specializing in advertising planning, creative preparation, and media placement typically do not prepare sales promotion materials for clients. These activities are normally assigned to sales promotion agencies (spending on such agencies is also listed in Exhibit 18.4) that specialize in coupons, premiums, displays, or other forms of sales promotion and point of purchase that require specific skills and creative preparation.

The development and management of an effective sales promotion program requires a major commitment by a firm. During any given year, it is typical that as much as 30 percent of brand management time is spent on designing, implement-

5.   PROMO 2004 Industry Trends Report, http://www.promomagazine.com/mag/marketing_upward_bound/.
6.   Betsy Spethmann, "So Much for Targeting," *PROMO Magazine,* April 2000, 69.

Sales promotion and advertising serve very different purposes in the promotional mix. What would you describe as the key difference between the two based on the features listed here?

Purpose of Sales Promotion	Purpose of Advertising
Stimulate short-term demand	Cultivate long-term demand
Encourage brand switching	Encourage brand loyalty
Induce trial use	Encourage repeat purchases
Promote price orientation	Promote image/feature orientation
Obtain immediate, often measurable results	Obtain long-term effects, often difficult to measure

Marketers rely on several different sales promotion techniques to complement and support the advertising effort. This list shows spending on those techniques as well as the amount spent on promotion agency services and research.

Segments	2003	2002	% Change	% of total
Premiums	$45.9	$44.1	4.1%	42.8
P-O-P	17.5	17.3	1.2	16.3
Specialty Printing	5.9	5.7	5.0	5.5
Sponsorships	9.8	9.3	6.2	9.1
Coupons	7.0	6.8	3.5	6.5
Licensing	6.1	6.0	2.0	5.7
Fulfillment	4.1	3.6	11.0	3.8
Agency Revenues	3.7	3.2	17.9	3.4
Interactive	2.0	1.7	15.5	1.9
Games, Contests, Sweeps	1.8	1.8	0.0	1.7
Loyalty	1.9	1.8	1.5	1.8
Sampling	1.5	1.3	10.0	1.4
Total (in billions)	**$107.2**	**$102.6**	**4.5%**	**100.0%**

Source: *PROMO* 2004 Industry Trends Report.

ing, and overseeing sales promotions. The rise in the use of sales promotion and the enormous amount of money being spent on various programs makes it one of the most prominent forms of marketing activity. But again, sales promotion must be undertaken only under certain conditions and then carefully executed for specific reasons.

Growth in the Use of Sales Promotion.

Marketers have shifted the emphasis of their promotional spending over the past decade. Most of the shift has been away from mass media advertising and toward consumer and trade sales promotions. Currently, the budget allocation on average stands at about 17.5 percent for advertising, 54 percent for trade and business promotions, and 28.5 percent for consumer promotions.[7] (Note: These percentages differ from the data in Exhibit 14.7 because a "bigger pie" that includes all incentives to the trade is being used in the calculation of total dollars spent.) There are several reasons why many marketers have been shifting funds from mass media advertising to sales promotions. The reasons include managers' demand for greater accountability for promotional spending; an increasingly short-term

7.   PROMO 2004 Industry Trends Report.

orientation among managers; consumers' positive response to sales promotions; the proliferation of brands in many product categories; the increased power of retailers; and advertising clutter in mass media.

Demand for Greater Accountability. In an era of cost cutting and downsizing, companies are demanding greater accountability across all functions, including marketing, advertising, and promotions. When activities are evaluated for their contribution to sales and profits, it is often difficult to draw specific conclusions regarding the effects of advertising. In addition, the immediate effects of sales promotions are typically easier to document. Various studies are now showing that only 18 percent of TV advertising campaigns (the traditional promotional tool relied on for consumer goods) produced a short-term positive return on investment (ROI) on promotional dollars.[8] Conversely, point-of-purchase in-store displays have been shown to positively affect sales by as much as 35 percent in some product categories.[9]

Short-Term Orientation. Several factors have created a short-term orientation among managers. Pressures from stockholders to produce better quarter-by-quarter revenue and profit per share is one factor. A bottom-line mentality is another factor. Many organizations are developing marketing plans—with rewards and punishments for performance—based on short-term revenue generation. This being the case, companies are seeking tactics that can have short-term effects. Nabisco found that a contest directed at kids had just the sort of short-term effect the firm was looking for. McDonalds credits its "Plan to Win" game with boosting store sales anywhere from 8.4 percent to 15 percent while the game promotion was being run.[10]

Consumer Response to Promotions. The precision shopper in the contemporary marketplace is demanding greater value across all purchase situations, and the trend is battering overpriced brands.[11] These precision shoppers search for extra value in every product purchase. Coupons, premiums, price-off deals, and other sales promotions increase the value of a brand in these shoppers' minds. The positive response to sales promotion goes beyond value-oriented consumers, though. For consumers who are not well informed about the average price in a product category, a brand featuring a coupon or price-off promotion is sensed to be a good deal and will likely be chosen over competitive brands—this is a basic tenet of consumer behavior analysis.[12] Historically, consumers report that coupons, price, and good value for their money influence 75 to 85 percent of their brand choice decisions.[13] (Be careful here—coupons, price, and value, in particular, do not necessarily mean consumers are choosing the *lowest*-priced item. The analysis suggests that these sales promotion techniques act as an incentive to purchase the brand *using* a promotion.)

Proliferation of Brands. Each year, thousands of new brands are introduced into the consumer market. The drive by marketers to design products for specific market segments to satisfy ever more narrowly defined needs has caused a proliferation of brands that creates a mind-dulling maze for consumers. At any point in time, consumers are typically able to choose from about 60 spaghetti sauces, 100 snack chips, 50 laundry detergents, 90 cold remedies, and 60 disposable-diaper varieties. As you can see in Exhibit 18.5, gaining attention in this blizzard of brands is no easy task. Because of this proliferation and "clutter" of brands, marketers turn to sales promotions—contests, coupons, premiums, loyalty programs, point-of-purchase displays—

8. Jack Neff, "TV Doesn't Sell Packaged Goods," *Advertising Age,* May 24, 2004, 1, 30.
9. Cara Beardi, "POP Ups Sales Results," *Advertising Age,* July 23, 2001, 27.
10. Kate MacArthur, "McD's Sees Growth, but Are Ads a Factor?" *Advertising Age,* November 24, 2003, 3, 24.
11. Jack Neff, "Black Eye in Store for Big Brands," *Advertising Age,* April 30, 2001, 1, 34.
12. Leigh McAlister, "A Model of Consumer Behavior," *Marketing Communications,* April 1987, 26–28.
13. Cox Direct 20th Annual Survey of Promotional Practices, Chart 22, 1998, 37.

As you can see by this shelf of spaghetti sauces, getting the consumer to pay attention to any one brand is quite a challenge. This proliferation of brands in the marketplace has made marketers search for ways to attract attention to their brands, and sales promotion techniques often provide an answer. Notice the point-of-purchase promotion attached to the shelves.

to gain some recognition in a consumer's mind and maintain loyalty or stimulate a trial purchase.

Increased Power of Retailers. As the introductory scenario highlighted, retailers such as Target, Home Depot, Gap, Toys "R" Us, and the most powerful of all, Wal-Mart, now dominate retailing in the United States. These powerful retailers have responded quickly and accurately to the new environment for retailing, where consumers are demanding more and better products and services at lower prices. Because of the lower-price component of the retailing environment, these retailers are demanding more deals from manufacturers. Many of the deals are delivered in terms of trade-oriented sales promotions: point-of-purchase displays, slotting fees (payment for shelf space), case allowances, and cooperative advertising allowances. In the end, manufacturers use more and more sales promotion devices to gain and maintain good relations with the new, powerful retailers—a critical link to the consumer. And retailers use the tools of sales promotion as competitive strategies against each other. Manufacturers are coming up with clever ways to provide value to retailers and thus maintain the balance of power. But some of these tools may be just another intrusion on privacy, as the Controversy box highlights.

Media Clutter. A nagging and traditional problem in the advertising process is clutter. Many advertisers target the same customers because their research has led them to the same conclusion about whom to target. The result is that advertising media are cluttered with ads all seeking the attention of the same people. One way to break through the clutter is to feature a sales promotion. In print ads, the featured deal is often a coupon. In television and radio advertising, sweepstakes, premium, and rebate offers can attract listeners' and viewers' attention. The combination of advertising and creative sales promotions has proven to be a good way to break through the clutter.

2 Sales Promotion Directed at Consumers.
It is clear that U.S. consumer-product firms have made a tremendous commitment to sales promotion in their overall marketing plans. During the 1970s, consumer goods marketers allocated

only about 30 percent of their budgets to sales promotion, with about 70 percent allocated to mass media advertising. Now we see that for many consumer-goods firms, the percentages are just the opposite, with nearly 75 percent of promotional budgets being spent on various forms of promotion and point-of-purchase materials. With this sort of investment in sales promotion and point of purchase as part of the integrated brand promotion process, let's examine in detail the objectives for sales promotion in the consumer market and the wide range of techniques that can be used.

CONTROVERSY

Big Brother Has a New Toy

In the constant battle to provide big retailers with reasons to feature one brand over another, manufacturers work hard to come up with new ways to gain favors for their brands versus competitors. As one manufacturer put it, "One Wal-Mart is worth 101 other companies." A new weapon in this battle is the successor to bar codes called Radio Frequency Identification (RFID) tags. These tags can potentially provide an instant assessment of inventory and stock on the shelf.

RFID tags work by combining tiny information chips with an antenna. When a tag is placed on an item, it starts to radio its location. Receivers can be placed in management offices, storerooms, and even consumer shopping carts. And herein lies the problems. Critics of RFID argue that this is just another instance of "Big Brother" Corporation intruding on consumers' privacy by tracking consumers' behavior. This is how it would work. When you get to your favorite grocery store, you will grab a shopping cart just like you always do. But this is not your typical shopping cart. With this cart, you swipe your store loyalty card (a different version of being tracked) through an RFID reader attached to the cart. Now that you are officially "checked in" (i.e., being tracked), the store can offer you special deals based on the items you put in your cart on this day or, since your purchase history is tracked through your loyalty card, offer you deals on items you have purchased in the past. Eventually, you'll be able to ring up your purchases as you put them in your specially equipped RFID cart and just walk straight out the door when you are done shopping.

Are there real benefits to RFID? Absolutely. The efficiency gained from inventory control, restocking alerts, and automated checkout would no doubt result in significant cost savings. But is this just another way that corporation can track and monitor our behavior? And if they can track our behavior in the store, what's keeping them from tracking our behavior after we leave the store?

Source: Gerry Khermouch and Heather Green, "Bar Codes Better Watch Their Backs," *BusinessWeek*, July 14, 2003, 42.

Objectives for Consumer-Market Sales Promotion.

To help ensure the proper application of sales promotion, specific strategic objectives should be set. The following basic objectives can be pursued with sales promotion in the consumer market.

Stimulate Trial Purchase. When a firm wants to attract new users, sales promotion tools can reduce the consumer's risk of trying something new. A reduced price, offer of a rebate, or a free sample may stimulate trial purchase. Exhibit 18.6 illustrates an attempt to stimulate trial use. Note that this promotion is trying to get consumers to try a *brand* for the first time. Recall the discussions from Chapters 2 and 4 that highlighted the fact that advertising and promotion *cannot* stimulate product use initiation in mature product categories—like coffee. For innovations new to the market, like an MP3 player, advertising and promotion can play a role in product category use initiation. It is important to recognize this key distinction.

Stimulate Repeat Purchases. In-package coupons good for the next purchase, or the accumulation of points with repeated purchases, can keep consumers loyal to a particular brand. The most prominent frequency programs are found in the airline industry, where competitors such as Delta, American, and United try to retain their most lucrative customers by enrolling them in frequency programs. Frequent flyers can earn free travel, hotel stays, gifts, and numerous other perks through the programs.

Stimulate Larger Purchases. Price reductions or two-for-one sales can motivate consumers to stock up on a brand, thus allowing firms to reduce inventory or increase cash flow. Shampoo is often double-packaged to offer a value to consumers. Exhibit 18.7 is a sales promotion aimed at stimulating a larger purchase.

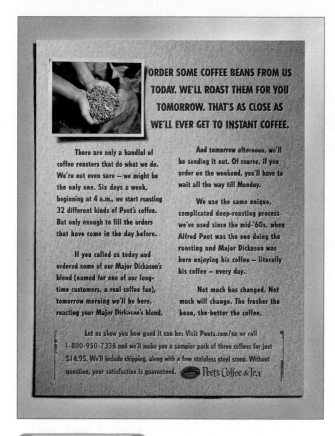

EXHIBIT 18.6

One objective for sales promotion in the consumer market is to stimulate trial use of a brand. Here, Peet's Coffee and Tea is offering consumers a sample pack they can request either online or by calling a toll-free number.

EXHIBIT 18.7

Sales promotions are often used to encourage larger purchases. This coupon for Spaghettios offers consumers the opportunity to stock up on three cans.

Introduce a New Brand. Because sales promotion can attract attention and motivate trial purchase, it is commonly used for new brand introduction. One of the most successful uses of sales promotions to introduce a new brand was when the makers of Curad bandages wanted to introduce their new kid-size bandage. 7.5 million sample packs were distributed in McDonald's Happy Meal sacks. The promotion was a huge success, with initial sales exceeding estimates by 30 percent.[14]

Combat or Disrupt Competitors' Strategies. Because sales promotions often motivate consumers to buy in larger quantities or try new brands, they can be used to disrupt competitors' marketing strategies. If a firm knows that one of its competitors is launching a new brand or initiating a new advertising campaign, a well-timed sales promotion offering deep discounts or extra quantity can disrupt the competitors' strategy. Add to the original discount an in-package coupon for future purchases, and a marketer can severely compromise competitors' efforts. *TV Guide* magazine used a sweepstakes promotion to combat competition. In an effort to address increasing competition from newspaper TV supplements and cable-guide magazines, *TV Guide* ran a Shopping Spree Sweepstakes in several regional markets. Winners won $200 shopping sprees in grocery stores—precisely the location where 65 percent of *TV Guide* sales are realized.[15]

14. Glen Heitsmith, "Still Bullish on Promotion," *PROMO Magazine,* July 1994, 40.
15. "*TV Guide* Tunes in Sweepstakes," *PROMO Magazine,* November 1995, 1, 50.

Contribute to Integrated Brand Promotion. In conjunction with advertising, direct marketing, public relations, and other programs being carried out by a firm, sales promotion can add yet another type of communication to the mix. Sales promotions suggest an additional value, with price reductions, premiums, or the chance to win a prize. This is an additional and different message within the overall communications effort a firm can use in its integrated brand promotion effort.

Consumer-Market Sales Promotion Techniques.

Several techniques are used to stimulate demand and attract attention in the consumer market. Some of these are coupons, price-off deals, premiums, contests and sweepstakes, samples and trial offers, phone and gift cards, rebates, and frequency (continuity) programs.

Coupons. A **coupon** entitles a buyer to a designated reduction in price for a product or service. Coupons are the oldest and most widely used form of sales promotion. The first use of a coupon is traced to around 1895, when the C. W. Post Company used a penny-off coupon as a way to get people to try its Grape-Nuts cereal. Annually, about 350 billion coupons are distributed to American consumers, with redemption rates ranging from 2 percent for gum purchases to nearly 45 percent for disposable diaper purchases. Exhibit 18.8 shows coupon-redemption rates for several product categories. In 2003, marketers invested $7 billion in coupons as a sales promotion technique.

There are five advantages to the coupon as a sales promotion tool:

- The use of a coupon makes it possible to give a discount to a price-sensitive consumer while still selling the product at full price to other consumers.
- The coupon-redeeming customer may be a competitive-brand user, so the coupon can induce brand switching.
- A manufacturer can control the timing and distribution of coupons. This way a retailer is not implementing price discounts in a way that can damage brand image.

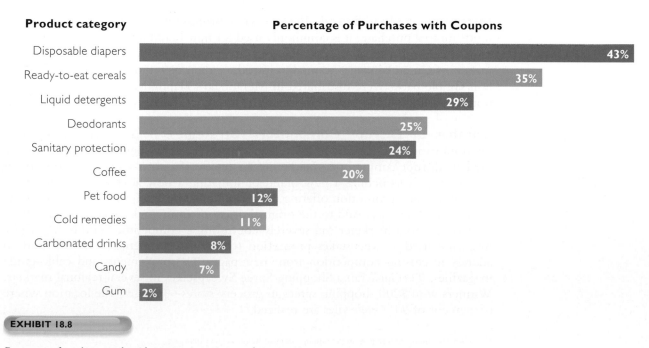

EXHIBIT 18.8

Percentage of purchases made with coupons in various product categories.

- A coupon is an excellent method of stimulating repeat purchases. Once a consumer has been attracted to a brand, with or without a coupon, an in-package coupon can induce repeat purchase. While an in-package coupon is designed to encourage repeat purchase and brand loyalty, retailers believe that coupons attached to the store shelf and distributed at the point of purchase are the most effective for stimulating brand switching/trial use of a brand.

- Coupons can get regular users to trade up within a brand array. For example, users of low-priced disposable diapers may be willing to try the premium version of a brand with a coupon.

The use of coupons is not without its problems. There are administrative burdens and risks with coupon use:

- While coupon price incentives and the timing of distribution can be controlled by a marketer, the timing of redemption cannot. Some consumers redeem coupons immediately; others hold them for months.

- Coupons do attract competitors' users and some nonusers, but there is no way to prevent current users from redeeming coupons with their regular purchases. Heavy redemption by regular buyers merely reduces a firm's profitability.

- Couponing entails careful administration. Coupon programs include much more than the cost of the face value of the coupon. There are costs for production and distribution and for retailer and manufacturer handling. In fact, the cost for handling, processing, and distribution of coupons is typically equal to about two-thirds of the face value of the coupon. Historically, Procter & Gamble has distributed as many as 700 million coupons for its Folgers coffee brand with administrative costs totaling more than $14 million.[16] Marketers need to track these costs against the amount of product sold with and without coupon redemption.

- Fraud is a chronic and serious problem in the couponing process. The problem relates directly to misredemption practices. There are three types of misredemption that cost firms money: redemption of coupons by consumers who do not purchase the couponed brand; redemption of coupons by salesclerks and store managers without consumer purchases; and illegal collection or copying of coupons by individuals who sell them to unethical store merchants, who in turn redeem the coupons without the accompanying consumer purchases.

Price-Off Deals. The price-off deal is another straightforward technique. A **price-off deal** offers a consumer cents or even dollars off merchandise at the point of purchase through specially marked packages. The typical price-off deal is a 10 to 25 percent price reduction. The reduction is taken from the manufacturer's profit margin rather than the retailer's (another point of contention in the power struggle). Manufacturers like the price-off technique because it is controllable. Plus, the price off, judged at the point of purchase, can effect a positive price comparison against competitors. Consumers like a price-off deal because it is straightforward and automatically increases the value of a known brand. Regular users tend to stock up on an item during a price-off deal. Retailers are less enthusiastic about this technique. Price-off promotions can create inventory and pricing problems for retailers. Also, most price-off deals are snapped up by regular customers, so the retailer often doesn't benefit from new business.

Premiums and Advertising Specialties. **Premiums** are items offered free, or at a reduced price, with the purchase of another item. Many firms offer a related product free, such as a free granola bar packed inside a box of granola cereal. Service firms, such as a car wash or dry cleaner, may use a two-for-one offer to persuade

---

16.   "Coffee's On," *PROMO Magazine*, February 1996, 48–49.

consumers to try the service. Premiums represent the single largest category of investment by firms in sales promotion with over $45 billion spent on premiums during 2003.

There are two options available for the use of premiums. A **free premium** provides consumers with an item at no cost; the item is either included in the package of a purchased item or mailed to the consumer after proof of purchase is verified. The most frequently used free premium is an additional package of the original item or a free related item placed in the package. Some firms do offer unrelated free premiums, such as balls, toys, and trading cards. These types of premiums are particularly popular with cereal manufacturers.

A **self-liquidating premium** requires a consumer to pay most of the cost of the item received as a premium. For example, Snapple can offer a "Snapple Cooler" with the purchase of six bottles of Snapple for $6.99—the cost of the cooler to Snapple. Self-liquidating premiums are particularly effective with loyal customers. However, these types of premiums must be used cautiously. Unless the premium is related to a value-building strategy for a brand, it can, like other sales promotions, serve to focus consumer attention on the premium rather than on the benefits of the brand. Focusing on the premium rather than the brand erodes brand equity. For example, if consumers buy a brand just to get a really great looking T-shirt at $4.99, then they won't purchase the brand again until there is another great premium available at a low price.

Advertising specialties have three key elements: a message, placed on a useful item, and given to consumers with no obligation. Popular advertising specialties are baseball caps, T-shirts, coffee mugs, computer mouse pads, pens, and calendars. Sales of promotional products in 2003 increased 4.57 percent over the previous year to $16 billion.[17] The Promotional Products Association International (http://www.promotion-clinic.ppa.org) puts promotional products into 17 different categories ranging from buttons/badges/bumper stickers to apparel to jewelry and watches.[18] Advertising specialties allow a firm to tout its company or brand name with a target customer in an ongoing fashion. Many of us have ball caps or coffee mugs that carry brand names (see Exhibit 18.9).

Contests and Sweepstakes. Contests and sweepstakes can draw attention to a brand like no other sales promotion technique. Technically, there are important differences between contests and sweepstakes. In a **contest,** consumers compete for prizes based on skill or ability. Winners in a contest are determined by a panel of judges or based on which contestant comes closest to a predetermined criterion for winning, such as picking the total points scored in the SuperBowl. Contests tend to be somewhat expensive to administer because each entry must be judged against winning criteria.

A **sweepstakes** is a promotion in which winners are determined purely by chance. Consumers need only to enter their names in the sweepstakes as a criterion

EXHIBIT 18.9

Advertising specialty items, like these ball caps, allow a firm to regularly remind target customers of the brand name and logo. While a sales promotion item like this will never be the main strategic tool in an IBP campaign, it does serve to create a regular brand presence and conversation piece with consumers.

17. Data obtained from Promotional Products Association International at the association's Web site, http://www.promotion-clinic.ppa.org, accessed June 25, 2004.

18. Dan S. Bagley III, *Understanding and Using Promotional Products* (Irving, TX: Promotional Products Association International, 1999), 6.

for winning. Sweepstakes often use official entry forms as a way for consumers to enter the sweepstakes. Other popular types of sweepstakes use scratch-off cards. Instant-winner scratch-off cards tend to attract customers. Gasoline retailers, grocery stores, and fast-food chains commonly use scratch-off card sweepstakes as a way of building and maintaining store traffic. Sweepstakes can also be designed so that repeated trips to the retail outlet are necessary to gather a complete set of winning cards. In order for contests and sweepstakes to be effective, advertisers must design them in such a way that consumers perceive value in the prizes and find playing the games intrinsically interesting.

Contests and sweepstakes can span the globe. British Airways ran a contest with the theme "The World's Greatest Offer," in which it gave away thousands of free airline tickets to London and other European destinations. While the contest increased awareness of the airline, there was definitely another benefit. Contests like these create a database of interested customers and potential customers. All the people who didn't win can be mailed information on future programs and other premium offers.

Contests and sweepstakes often create excitement and generate interest for a brand, but the problems of administering these promotions are substantial. Consider these challenges to effectively using contest and sweepstakes in the IBP effort.

*   There will always be regulations and restrictions on contests and sweepstakes. Advertisers must be sure that the design and administration of a contest or sweepstakes complies with both federal and state laws. Each state may have slightly different regulations. The legal problems are complex enough that most firms hire agencies that specialize in contests and sweepstakes to administer the programs.
*   The game itself may become the consumer's primary focus, while the brand becomes secondary. Like other sales promotion tools, this technique thus fails to build long-term consumer affinity for a brand.
*   It is hard to get any meaningful message across in the context of a game. The consumer's interest is focused on the game, rather than on any feature of the brand.
*   Administration of a contest or sweepstakes is sufficiently complex that the risk of errors in administration is fairly high and can create negative publicity.[19]
*   If a firm is trying to develop a quality or prestige image for a brand, contests and sweepstakes may contradict this goal.

Sampling and Trial Offers. Getting consumers to simply try a brand can have a powerful effect on future decision making. **Sampling** is a sales promotion technique designed to provide a consumer with an opportunity to use a brand on a trial basis with little or no risk. To say that sampling is a popular technique is an understatement. Most consumer-product companies use sampling in some manner, and invest approximately $1.5 billion a year on the technique. A recent survey shows that consumers are very favorable toward sampling with 43 percent indicating that they would consider switching brands if they liked a free sample that was being offered.[20]

Sampling is particularly useful for new products, but should not be reserved for new products alone. It can be used successfully for established brands with weak market share in specific geographic areas. Ben and Jerry's "Stop & Taste the Ice Cream" tour gave away more than a million scoops of ice cream in high-traffic urban areas in an attempt to reestablish a presence for the brand in weak markets.[21] Six techniques are used in sampling:

*   **In-store sampling** is popular for food products and cosmetics. This is a preferred technique for many marketers because the consumer is at the point of purchase

19.   Barry M. Benjamin, "Plan Ahead to Limit Potential Disasters," *Marketing News*, November 10, 2003, 15.
20.   Cox Direct 20th Annual Survey of Promotional Practices, 1998, 28.
21.   Betsy Spethmann, "Branded Moments," *PROMO Magazine*, September 2000, 84.

and may be swayed by a direct encounter with the brand. Increasingly, in-store demonstrators are handing out coupons as well as samples.

- **Door-to-door sampling** is extremely expensive because of labor costs, but it can be effective if the marketer has information that locates the target segment in a well-defined geographic area. Some firms enlist the services of newspaper delivery people, who package the sample with daily or Sunday newspapers as a way of reducing distribution costs.

- **Mail sampling** allows samples to be delivered through the postal service (see Exhibit 18.10). Again, the value here is that certain zip-code markets can be targeted. A drawback is that the sample must be small enough to be economically feasible to mail. Specialty sampling firms, such as Alternative Postal Delivery, provide targeted geodemographic door-to-door distribution as an alternative to the postal service. Cox Target Media has developed a mailer that contains multiple samples related to a specific industry—like car-care products—and that can reach highly targeted market segments.[22]

- **Newspaper sampling** has become very popular in recent years and 42 percent of consumers report having received samples of health and beauty products in this manner.[23] Much like mail sampling, newspaper samples allow very specific geographic and geodemographic targeting. Big drug companies like Eli Lilly and Bristol-Myers Squibb are using newspaper distribution of coupons to target new users for antidepressant and diabetes drugs.[24]

- **On-package sampling,** a technique in which the sample item is attached to another product package, is useful for brands targeted to current customers. Attaching a small bottle of Ivory conditioner to a regular-sized container of Ivory shampoo is a logical sampling strategy.

- **Mobile sampling** is carried out by logo-emblazoned vehicles that dispense samples, coupons, and premiums to consumers at malls, shopping centers, fairgrounds, and recreational areas. Strategists at Iomega, makers of the popular computer Zip drive, used a mobile display to introduce its new product, the

EXHIBIT 18.10

Sampling is a sales promotion technique designed to provide a consumer with an opportunity to use a brand on a trial basis with little or no risk. Glad used mail sampling to introduce consumers to its new "Odor Shield" trash bag.

22.   Cara Beardi, "Cox's Introz Mailer Bundles Samples in Industry," *Advertising Age,* November 2000, 88.
23.   Cox Direct 20th Annual Survey of Promotional Practices, 1998, 27.
24.   Susan Warner, "Drug Makers Print Coupons to Boost Sales," Knight Ridder Newspapers, June 4, 2001.

HipZip portable digital audio player, to target consumers on college campuses. Personal contact with the new product was used to increase awareness.[25]

CREATIVITY

Building a Market $3 at a Time

There are few success stories as spectacular as Starbucks'. The specialty coffee retailer has grown to more than 7,000 stores and over $5 billion in annual revenue. Not bad for a company that has had to build a market $3 at a time. But despite the enormous number of customers shelling out $3 an average of 17 times per week to create such huge revenue, Starbucks was plagued with knowing very little about its customers. The reason? Starbucks' customers always paid cash for their purchases—no checks, no credit cards though which the firm could develop a database.

Well, that problem was solved by the launch of the Starbucks prepaid gift card, which customers use instead of cash. The card is serving many purposes. First, it is a way to save customers time in line, since swiping the card speeds the transaction process. Second, it allows customers to give a small gift to friends and family—it makes a great holiday gift. And finally, it does allow Starbucks to get to know its customers better by tracking the frequency and nature of their transactions.

Currently, there are about 20 million cards outstanding generating over $150 million in revenue for the initial card purchase. One in every 10 transactions at Starbucks' stores is now accounted for by a card. And, to the company's surprise, over a third of the cards are being "reloaded" for reuse—a clear indication that the convenience factor is important to customers.

While phone and gift cards can seem pretty insignificant to the average consumer, the impact on brand loyalty and customer service can be significant, as Starbucks, Barnes & Noble, Home Depot, and other marketers have discovered.

Source: John Clark, "At Starbucks, the Future Is in Plastic," *Business 2.0*, August 2003, 56.

Of course, sampling has its critics. Unless the product has a clear value and benefit over the competition, a simple trial of the product is unlikely to persuade a consumer to switch brands. This is especially true for convenience goods because consumers perceive a high degree of similarity among brands, even after trying them. The perception of benefit and superiority may have to be developed through advertising in combination with sampling. In addition, sampling is expensive. This is especially true in cases where a sufficient quantity of a product, such as shampoo or laundry detergent, must be given away for a consumer to truly appreciate a brand's value. In-store sampling techniques are being devised to reduce the cost of traditional sampling methods.[26] Finally, sampling can be a very imprecise process. Despite the emergence of special agencies to handle sampling programs, a firm can never completely ensure that the product is reaching the targeted audience.

Trial offers have the same goal as sampling—to induce consumer trial use of a brand—but they are used for more expensive items. Exercise equipment, appliances, watches, hand tools, and consumer electronics are typical of items offered on a trial basis. Trials offers can be free for low-priced products, as we saw in Exhibit 18.6. Or trials can be offered for as little as a day to as long as 90 days for more expensive items like vacuum cleaners or computer software. The expense to the firm, of course, can be formidable. Segments chosen for this sales promotion technique must have high sales potential.

Phone and Gift Cards. Phone and gift cards represent a new and increasingly popular form of sales promotion. This technique could be classified as a premium offer, but it has enough unique features to warrant separate classification as a sales promotion technique. The use of phone and gift cards is fairly straightforward. Manufacturers or retailers offer either free or for-purchase debit cards that provide the holder with a pre-set spending limit or minutes of phone time. The cards are designed to be colorful and memorable. A wide range of marketers, including luxury car manufacturers like Lexus and retailers like the Gap, have made effective use of phone and gift cards. Starbucks has made particularly effective use of gift cards, as the Creativity box describes. Exhibit 18.11 shows a Starbucks gift card as a promotional tool.

25. Kate Fitzgerald, "Iomega Makes Music," *Advertising Age*, October 30, 2000, 42.
26. Debbie Usery, "What's In-Store," *PROMO Magazine*, May 2000, 54.

EXHIBIT 18.11

Firms use gift cards as a way to draw attention to the brand and as a way for loyal customers to introduce their friends and family to the brand.

Rebates. A **rebate** is a money-back offer requiring a buyer to mail in a form requesting the money back from the manufacturer, rather than the retailer (as in couponing). The rebate technique has been refined over the years and is now used by a wide variety of marketers. Rebates are particularly well suited to increasing the quantity purchased by consumers, so rebates are commonly tied to multiple purchases. For example, if you buy a ten-pack of Kodak film you can mail in a rebate coupon worth $2.

Another reason for the popularity of rebates is that few consumers take advantage of the rebate offer after buying a brand. The best estimate of consumer redemption of rebate offers by the research firm Market Growth Resources is that only 5 to 10 percent of buyers ever bother to fill out and then mail in the rebate request. This may signal a waning popularity of the rebate with consumers.

Frequency (Continuity) Programs. In recent years, one of the most popular sales promotion techniques among consumers has been frequency programs. **Frequency programs,** also referred to as continuity programs, offer consumers discounts or free product rewards for repeat purchase or patronage of the same brand or company. These programs were pioneered by airline companies. Frequent-flyer programs such as Delta Air Lines' SkyMiles, frequent-stay programs such as Marriott's Honored Guest Award Rewards program, and frequent-renter programs such as Hertz's #1 Club are examples of such loyalty-building activities. But frequency programs are not reserved for big national airline and auto-rental chains. Chart House Enterprises, a chain of 65 upscale restaurants, successfully launched a frequency program for diners, who earned points for every dollar spent. Frequent diners were issued "passports," which were stamped with each visit. Within two years, the program had more than 300,000 members.[27] Exhibit 18.12 features Marriott's frequency program.

③ Sales Promotion Directed at the Trade Channel and Business Markets.
Sales promotions can also be directed at members of the trade—wholesalers, distributors, and retailers—and business markets. For example, Hewlett-Packard designs sales promotion programs for its retailers, like Circuit City, in order to ensure that the H-P line gets proper attention and display. But H-P will also have sales promotion campaigns aimed at business buyers like Accenture (formerly Andersen Consulting) or IHC HealthCare. The purpose of sales promotion as a tool does not change from the consumer market to the trade or business markets. It is still intended to stimulate demand in the short term and help *push* the product through the distribution channel or cause business buyers to act more immediately and positively toward the marketer's brand.

Effective trade- and business-market promotions can generate enthusiasm for a product and contribute positively to the loyalty distributors show for a brand. In the business market, sales promotions can mean the difference between landing a very large order and missing out entirely on a revenue opportunity. With the massive

27. Kerry J. Smith, "Building a Winning Frequency Program—The Hard Way," *PROMO* Magazine, December 1995, 36.

"WHY IS OUR AWARD PROGRAM SO POPULAR WITH FREQUENT TRAVELERS? WE'RE IN EVERY CITY THEY FREQUENT."

Bill Marriott

As a business traveler you earn free vacations faster with Marriott's Honored Guest Award program. With over 250 locations worldwide, we're doing business wherever you're doing business. To join the program call 1-800-648-8024. For reservations, call your travel agent or 1-800-228-9290.

Marriott
HOTELS · RESORTS · SUITES

WE MAKE IT HAPPEN FOR YOU

EXHIBIT 18.12

Frequency (continuity) programs build customer loyalty and offer opportunities for building a large, targeted database for other promotions.

proliferation of new brands and brand extensions, manufacturers need to stimulate enthusiasm and loyalty among members of the trade and also need a way to get the attention of business buyers suffering from information overload.

Objectives for Promotions in the Trade Market.
As in the consumer market, trade-market sales promotions should be undertaken with specific objectives in mind. Generally speaking, when marketers devise incentives for the trade market they are executing a **push strategy;** that is, sales promotions directed at the trade help push a brand into the distribution channel until it ultimately reaches the consumer. Four primary objectives can be identified for these promotions.

Obtain Initial Distribution. Because of the proliferation of brands in the consumer market, there is fierce competition for shelf space. Sales promotion incentives can help a firm gain initial distribution and shelf placement. Like consumers, members of the trade need a reason to choose one brand over another when it comes to allocating shelf space. A well-conceived promotion incentive may sway them.

Bob's Candies, a small family-owned business in Albany, Georgia, is the largest candy cane manufacturer in the United States. But Bob's old-fashioned candy was having trouble keeping distributors. To reverse the trend, Bob's designed a new name, logo, and packaging for the candy canes. Then, each scheduled attendee at the All-Candy Expo trade show in Chicago was mailed three strategically timed postcards with the teaser question "Wanna Be Striped?" The mailing got a 25 percent response rate, and booth visitations at the trade show were a huge success.[28]

Increase Order Size. One of the struggles in the channel of distribution is over the location of inventory. Manufacturers prefer that members of the trade maintain large inventories so the manufacturer can reduce inventory-carrying costs. Conversely, members of the trade would rather make frequent, small orders and carry little inventory. Sales promotion techniques can encourage wholesalers and retailers to order in larger quantities, thus shifting the inventory burden to the channel.

Encourage Cooperation with Consumer-Market Sales Promotions. It does a manufacturer little good to initiate a sales promotion in the consumer market if there is little cooperation in the channel. Wholesalers may need to maintain larger inventories, and retailers may need to provide special displays or handling during consumer-market sales promotions. To achieve synergy, marketers often run trade promotions simultaneously with consumer promotions. When Toys "R" Us ran a "scan and win" promotion, the retailer actually ran out of several very popular toy items during the critical holiday buying season because distributors (and Toys "R" Us) were unprepared for the magnitude of the response to the promotion.

28.   Lee Duffey, "Sweet Talk: Promotions Position Candy Company," *Marketing News,* March 30, 1998, 11.

Increase Store Traffic. Retailers can increase store traffic through special promotions or events. Door-prize drawings, parking-lot sales, or live radio broadcasts from the store are common sales promotion traffic builders. Burger King has become a leader in building traffic at its 6,500 outlets with special promotions tied to Disney movie debuts. Beginning in 1991 with a *Beauty and the Beast* tie-in promotion, Burger King has set records for generating store traffic with premium giveaways. The *Pocahontas* campaign distributed 55 million toys and glasses. A promotion tie-in with Disney's enormously successful film *Toy Story* resulted in 50 million toys, based on the film's characters, being given away in $1.99 Kid Meals.[29] Manufacturers can also design sales promotions that increase store traffic for retailers. A promotion that generates a lot of interest within a target audience can drive consumers to retail outlets.

Trade-Market Sales Promotion Techniques.

The sales promotion techniques used with the trade are incentives, allowances, trade shows, sales training programs, and cooperative advertising.

Incentives. Incentives to members of the trade include a variety of tactics not unlike those used in the consumer market. Awards in the form of travel, gifts, or cash bonuses for reaching targeted sales levels can induce retailers and wholesalers to give a firm's brand added attention. Consider this incentive ploy. The Volvo national sales manager put together an incentive program for dealerships. The leading dealership in the nation won a trip to the Super Bowl including dinner with Hall of Fame footballer Lynn Swann (Swann alone added 20 large to the cost of the incentive package).[30] But the incentive does not have to be large or expensive to be effective. Weiser Lock offered its dealers a Swiss Army knife with every dozen cases of locks ordered. The program was a huge success. A follow-up promotion featuring a Swiss Army watch was an even bigger hit. And firms are finding that Web-based incentive programs can be highly effective as well. When the sales manager at Netopia, a manufacturer of broadband equipment, wanted to offer an incentive to dealers, he did *not* want to manage the whole process. The solution? Implement innergE, an online incentive-management program that features a Web site where salespeople can track their progress and claim their rewards.[31]

Another form of trade incentive is referred to as push money. **Push money** is carried out through a program in which retail salespeople are offered a monetary reward for featuring a marketer's brand with shoppers. The program is quite simple. If a salesperson sells a particular brand of refrigerator for a manufacturer as opposed to a competitor's brand, the salesperson will be paid an extra $50 or $75 "bonus" as part of the push money program.

One risk with incentive programs for the trade is that salespeople can be so motivated to win an award or extra push money that they may try to sell the brand to every customer, whether it fits that customer's needs or not. Also, a firm must carefully manage such programs to minimize ethical dilemmas. An incentive technique can look like a bribe unless it is carried out in a highly structured and open fashion.

Allowances. Various forms of allowances are offered to retailers and wholesalers with the purpose of increasing the attention given to a firm's brands. Allowances are typically made available to wholesalers and retailers about every four weeks during a quarter. **Merchandise allowances,** in the form of free products packed with regular shipments, are payments to the trade for setting up and maintaining displays. The payments are typically far less than manufacturers would have to spend to maintain the displays themselves.

29.   Editors' Special Report, "Having It Their Way," *PROMO Magazine,* December 1995, 79–80.
30.   Ron Donoho, "It's Up! It's Good!" *Sales and Marketing Management,* April 2003, 43–47.
31.   Michelle Gillan, "E-Motivation," *Sales and Marketing Management,* April 2003, 50.

In recent years, shelf space has become so highly demanded, especially in supermarkets, that manufacturers are making direct cash payments, known as **slotting fees,** to induce food chains to stock an item. The proliferation of new products has made shelf space such a precious commodity that these fees now run in the hundreds of thousands of dollars per product. Another form of allowance is called a bill-back allowance. **Bill-back allowances** provide retailers a monetary incentive for featuring a marketer's brand in either advertising or in-store displays. If a retailer chooses to participate in either an advertising campaign or a display bill-back program, the marketer requires the retailer to verify the services performed and provide a bill for the services. A similar program is the **off-invoice allowance,** in which advertisers allow wholesalers and retailers to deduct a set amount from the invoice they receive for merchandise. This program is really just a price reduction offered to the trade on a particular marketer's brand. The incentive for the trade with this program is that the price reduction increases the margin (and profits) a wholesaler or retailer realizes on the off-invoiced brand.

EXHIBIT 18.13

Here is a classic example of co-op advertising between manufacturer and retailer. Omega is being featured by this Hawaiian retailer in a magazine ad. Is there another form of sales promotion going on here as well?

Sales-Training Programs. An increasingly popular trade promotion is to provide training for retail store personnel. This method is used for consumer durables and specialty goods, such as personal computers, home theater systems, heating and cooling systems, security systems, and exercise equipment. The increased complexity of these products has made it important for manufacturers to ensure that the proper factual information and persuasive themes are reaching consumers at the point of purchase. For personnel at large retail stores, manufacturers can hold special classes that feature product information, demonstrations, and training about sales techniques.

Another popular method for getting sales-training information to retailers is the use of videotapes and brochures. Manufacturers can also send sales trainers into retail stores to work side by side with store personnel. This is a costly method, but it can be very effective because of the one-on-one attention it provides.

Cooperative (Co-op) Advertising. Cooperative advertising as a trade promotion technique is referred to as vertical cooperative advertising. (Such efforts are also called vendor co-op programs.) Manufacturers try to control the content of this co-op advertising in two ways. They may set strict specifications for the size and content of the ad and then ask for verification that such specifications have been met. Alternatively, manufacturers may send the template for an ad, into which retailers merely insert the names and locations of their stores. Just such an ad is featured in Exhibit 18.13. Notice that the James Bond and Omega watch components are national with the co-op sponsorship of the Hawaiian retailer highlighted in the lower right.

Business-Market Sales Promotion Techniques. Often the discussion of sales promotion focuses only on consumer and trade techniques. It is major oversight to leave the business market out of the discussion. The Promotional Product Association estimates that several billion dollars a year in sales promotion is targeted to the business buyer.[32]

Can You Really Do a Trade Show over the Web?

In an odd combination of promotional tools, firms are creating "virtual" booths for the Web much like those used at trade shows to get even more exposure to the business market for their brands. One compelling motivation for the virtual booth is the time and expense of sending people to "real" trade shows. Online shows are similar to those "Webinars" you hear about that bring together multiple participants, including those outside the United States. These virtual booths and trade shows feature presentations, product displays, demonstrations, and downloadable brochures—just like the ones that take place live.

There is some question, though, whether the virtual version of the trade show will be sustained beyond the "fad" stage. Although the technology is there and the cost-saving incentive is there, analysts are skeptical as to whether this technique will flourish at any substantial level. One analyst summed it up this way: "Salespeople will still want to sit down and talk to people one-on-one. This [the virtual booth] may be a good way to generate leads, but you probably won't close any sales this way."

Despite some of the drawbacks, experts suggest that if you want to give the virtual route a try, there are ways to increase your "presence" at an online trade show:

- Design an attractive virtual booth that attracts and holds the Web visitors' attention.
- Have someone available at all times to communicate with attendees. This can be done with instant messaging or toll-free telephone access.
- Ensure technical quality and reliability. The Internet connection is the only way to communicate with virtual attendees during the trade show. Companies that are not technically savvy should not try to go the virtual route.

Source: Ned Shaw, "Building a Virtual Booth," *Sales and Marketing Management*, July 2003, 14.

Trade Shows. **Trade shows** are events where several related products from many manufacturers are displayed and demonstrated to members of the trade. Literally every industry has trade shows, from gourmet products to the granddaddy of them all, Comdex. Comdex is the annual computer and electronics industry trade show held in Las Vegas that attracts over a quarter of a million business buyers.

At a typical trade show, company representatives are on hand staffing a booth that displays a company's products or service programs. The representatives are there to explain the products and services and perhaps make an important contact for the sales force. The use of trade shows must be carefully coordinated and can be an important part of the business-market promotional program. Trade shows can be critically important to a small firm that cannot afford advertising and has a sales staff too small to reach all its potential customers. Through the trade-show route, salespeople can make far more contacts than would be possible with direct sales calls. And speaking of making more contacts, the trade show has gone high-tech and global, as the IBP box explains.

Trade shows are also an important route for reaching potential wholesalers and distributors for a company's brand. But the proliferation of trade shows has been so extensive in recent years that the technique is really more oriented to business buyers these days.

Business Gifts. Estimates are that nearly half of corporate America gives business gifts.[33] These gifts are given as part of building and maintaining a close working relationship with suppliers. Business gifts that are part of a promotional program may include small items like logo golf balls, jackets, or small items of jewelry. Extravagant gifts or expensive trips that might be construed as "buying business" are not included in this category of business-market sales promotion.

Premiums and Advertising Specialties. As mentioned earlier, the key chain, ball cap, T-shirt, mouse pad, or calendar that reminds a buyer of a brand name and

32.   PROMO 2004 Industry Trends Report.
33.   Ibid.

slogan can be an inexpensive but useful form of sales promotion. A significant portion of the $14 billion premium and advertising specialty market is directed to business buyers. While business buyers are professionals, they are not immune to the value perceptions that an advertising specialty can create. In other words, getting something for nothing appeals to business buyers as much as it does to household consumers. Will a business buyer choose one consulting firm over another to get a sleeve of golf balls? Probably not. But advertising specialties can create awareness and add to the satisfaction of a transaction nonetheless.

Trial Offers. Trial offers are particularly well suited to the business market. First, since many business products and services are high cost and often result in a significant time commitment to a brand (i.e., many business products and services have long life), trial offers provide a way for buyers to lower the risk of making a commitment to one brand over another. Second, a trial offer is a good way to attract new customers who need a good reason to try something new. The chance to try a new product for 30 days with no financial risk can be a compelling offer.

Frequency Programs. The high degree of travel associated with many business professions makes frequency programs an ideal form of sales promotion for the business market. Airline, hotel, and restaurant frequency programs are dominated by the business market traveler. But frequency programs for the business market are not restricted to travel-related purchases. Retailers of business products like Staples, OfficeMax, and CostCo have programs designed to reward the loyalty of the business buyer. CostCo has teamed with American Express to offer business buyers an exclusive CostCo/American Express credit card. Among the many advantages of the card is a rebate at the end of the year based on the level of buying—the greater the dollar amount of purchases, the greater the percentage rebate.

Sales Promotion, the Internet, and New Media.
Sales promotion has entered the era of new media as well. Marketers are expanding their use of sales promotion techniques in the consumer, trade, and business markets by using the Internet and other new media options. In a recent survey, 49 percent of advertisers said they used Internet-based promotions.[34] There are two parts to the issue of sales promotion in new media applications. First, there is the use *by* Internet and new media companies of sales promotion techniques. Second, there is the use *of* the Internet and new media to implement various sales promotion techniques.

The Use of Sales Promotion by Internet and New Media Organizations.
The new titans of technology—AOL, Earthlink, Linux—have discovered a new way to generate revenue fast: They give their products away. More specifically, they have discovered the power of sales promotion in the form of distributing free samples. These fast-growing, highly successful companies have discovered an alternative to advertising—sales promotion.

Of course, giving away free samples, as we have seen, is not a new sales promotion technique. But giving away intellectual property, such as software, is new and America Online is the king of giveaways (see Exhibits 18.14 and 18.15). With each new release AOL blankets the United States with diskettes and CD-ROMs offering consumers a free trial of its Internet services. No distribution channel is left untapped in trying to reach consumers with the free diskettes. They have been stashed in boxes of Rice Chex cereal, in United Airlines in-flight meals, and in packages of

---

34.   "Proceed With Caution," report introduction, 2001 Annual Report of the Promotion Industry, May 2001, compiled by *PROMO Magazine*, available at http://www.industryclick.com, accessed June 5, 2001.

EXHIBITS 18.14 AND 18.15

AOL has discovered the power of sales promotion in the form of giving its product away free for a trial period. Here we can see the combined use of a tradition media print ad with the mass distribution of free access CD-ROMs.

Omaha Steaks—not to mention inside the plastic sack along with your local Sunday paper that the neighborhood kid delivers.

What makes sampling so attractive for AOL is that it helps takes all the risk away from consumer trial. Consumers with computers can give AOL a try without investing a penny or making a long-term commitment to a piece of software. If they like what they see, they can sign up for a longer period of time. The technology companies have embraced the concept and accepted the main liabilities of sampling—cost and time.[35]

But sampling is not the only sales promotion tool discovered by the dot.coms. In their desire to create "sticky" Web sites, Internet firms have relied heavily on incentives as a way to attract and retain Web surfers. Many of them are offering loyalty programs, and others have devised offers to make members out of visitors. In an attempt to make the incentive programs more interesting, many of the Web companies allow participants to review their standings in contests and then take a virtual tour of prizes—including the classic grand prize, an exotic travel destination.[36]

These technology companies have discovered that sales promotion can be a valuable component of the overall promotional program—and that the potential impact of sales promotion is quite different from advertising. Internet and new media com-

35.   Patricia Nakache, "Secrets of the New Brand Builders," *Fortune*, June 22, 1998, 167–170.
36.   "Motivating Matters," Promotion Trends 2000, Annual Report of the Promotions Industry, compiled by *PROMO Magazine*, May 2000, A13.

panies have invested heavily in advertising as a way to develop brand recognition. Now they have discovered sales promotion as a way to help drive revenues.

The Use of the Internet and New Media to Implement Sales Promotions.

It is interesting to see Internet and new media companies rely on traditional sales promotions. But it is also interesting to see how companies of all types are learning to use the Internet and new media to implement sales promotion techniques. In a survey of firms using various promotional techniques, over half responded that the Internet and new media were having a large impact on their promotional planning. In 2000, marketers invested an estimated $1 billion in Web-based promotions including online sweepstakes, couponing, and loyalty and sampling programs.[37]

There are a variety of ways in which the Internet is being used to implement sales promotions. First, companies like Sweeps Advantage (www.sweepsadvantage .com) are emerging to provide widespread visibility and access to company sweepstakes (see Exhibit 18.16). Second, the Internet is being used as a distribution system for couponing. In the packaged goods area, Internet "triggered" coupons (either printed from the site or requested online for mail delivery) have become so popular that a printable-coupon Web site, coolsavings.com, now boasts over 11 million members.[38] Sites like coolsavings.com (www.coolsavings.com) allow you to print coupons for savings on pet products, beauty items, and baby products. Rebates are also being distributed through the Internet as a way to expand access to this sales promotion option. And sweepstakes are simply highly popular on the Web. A General Motors game for the Chevy Tracker drew 1.3 million Web-based entries.

While the Internet attracts most of the attention for sales promotion implementation, new media applications are also taking hold. The CD-ROMs distributed by AOL represent one form of new media application. In-store coupon dispensers are

EXHIBIT 18.16

Web-based games and sweepstakes are highly popular with consumers. Several sweepstakes and context directories have emerged with provide visibility and access for firms using these sales promotion techniques delivered over the Web.

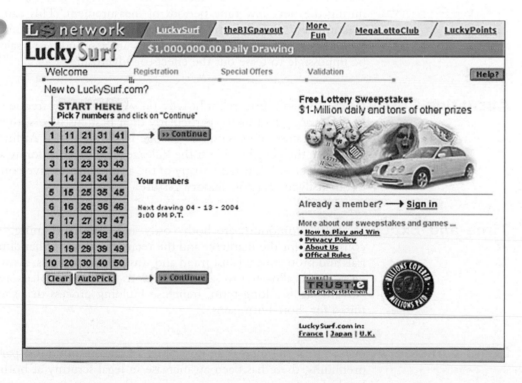

37. "Internet Invasion," Promotion Trends 2000, Annual Report of the Promotions Industry, compiled by *PROMO Magazine*, May 2000, A30.
38. Roger O. Crockett, "Penny Pinchers' Paradise," *BusinessWeek E-Biz*, January 22, 2000, 12.

another. Finally, interactive kiosks are being developed that provide both information and incentives in retail locations.

❹ The Risks of Sales Promotion. Sales promotion can be used to pursue important sales objectives. As we have seen, there are a wide range of sales promotion options for both the consumer and trade markets. But there are also significant risks associated with sales promotion, and these risks must be carefully considered.

Creating a Price Orientation. Since most sales promotions rely on some sort of price incentive or giveaway, a firm runs the risk of having its brand perceived as cheap, with no real value or benefits beyond low price. Creating this perception in the market contradicts the concept of integrated marketing communication. If advertising messages highlight the value and benefit of a brand only to be contradicted by a price emphasis in sales promotions, then a confusing signal is being sent to the market. This was a risk run by Schick and Gillette as their "razor wars" continue to escalate. At one point, both firms were giving away razors that cost $10 and including a $2 coupon to try to stimulate repeat purchase. The cost of this one "skirmish" in the ongoing war was $40 million to Gillette and somewhere between $40 million and $70 million for Schick.[39] Clearly the ongoing risk here is that men will simply take both free razors and wait to see which firm offers the next deal.

Borrowing from Future Sales. Management must admit that sales promotions are typically short-term tactics designed to reduce inventories, increase cash flow, or show periodic boosts in market share. The downside is that a firm may simply be borrowing from future sales. Consumers or trade buyers who would have purchased the brand anyway may be motivated to stock up at the lower price. This results in reduced sales during the next few time periods of measurement. This can play havoc with the measurement and evaluation of the effect of advertising campaigns or other image-building communications. If consumers are responding to sales promotions, it may be impossible to tease out the effects of advertising.

Alienating Customers. When a firm relies heavily on sweepstakes or frequency programs to build loyalty among customers, particularly their best customers, there is the risk of alienating these customers with any change in the program. Airlines suffered just such a fate when they tried to adjust the mileage levels needed for awards in their frequent-flyer programs. Ultimately, many of the airlines had to give concessions to their most frequent flyers as a conciliatory gesture.

Time and Expense. Sales promotions are both costly and time-consuming. The process is time-consuming for the marketer and the retailer in terms of handling promotional materials and protecting against fraud and waste in the process. As we have seen in recent years, funds allocated to sales promotions are taking dollars away from advertising. Advertising is a long-term, franchise-building process that should not be compromised for short-term gains.

Legal Considerations. With the increasing popularity of sales promotions, particularly contests and premiums, there has been an increase in legal scrutiny at both the federal and state levels. Legal experts recommend that before initiating promotions that use coupons,

---

39. Jack Neff, "Gillette, Schick Fight with Free Razors," *Advertising Age,* December 1, 2003, 8.

games, sweepstakes, and contests, a firm check into lottery laws, copyright laws, state and federal trademark laws, prize notification laws, right of privacy laws, tax laws, and FTC and FCC regulations.[40] The best advice for staying out of legal trouble with sales promotions is to carefully and clearly state the rules and conditions related to the program so that consumers are fully informed.

Point-of-Purchase Advertising.

From 1981 to 2003, marketers' annual expenditures on point-of-purchase (P-O-P) advertising rose from $5.1 billion to over $17 billion per year.[41] Why this dramatic growth? First, consider that P-O-P is the only medium that places advertising, products, and a consumer together in the same place at the same time. Then, think about these results. Research conducted by the trade association Point-of-Purchase Advertising International (http://www.popai.com) indicates that 70 percent of all product selections involve some final deliberation by consumers at the point of purchase. Additionally, a joint study sponsored by Kmart and Procter & Gamble found that P-O-P advertising boosted the sales of coffee, paper towels, and toothpaste by 567 percent, 773 percent, and 119 percent, respectively.[42] With results like these, it is plain to see why P-O-P advertising is one of the fastest-growing categories in today's marketplace.

Point-of-Purchase Advertising Defined.

Point-of-purchase (P-O-P) advertising refers to materials used in the retail setting to attract shoppers' attention to one's product, convey primary product benefits, or highlight pricing information. P-O-P displays may also feature price-off deals or other consumer sales promotions. A corrugated-cardboard dump bin and an attached header card featuring the brand logo or related brand information can be produced for pennies per unit. When the bin is filled with a brand and placed as a freestanding display at retail, sales gains usually follow. Marketers clearly believe in the power of P-O-P; spending on P-O-P is second only to event and premiums/incentives spending.

As an example of the kind of impact P-O-P advertising can have, a dump bin with tower display was designed for Nabisco's Barnum's Animals crackers. This colorful 76-inch-tall cardboard tower spent 14 weeks in design before being mass-produced and rolled out across the country. The gorilla towers, along with their tiger and elephant predecessors, hold small boxes of animal crackers and are the cornerstone of the advertising strategy for Barnum's.[43] While other Nabisco brands such as Oreo, Chips Ahoy, and Nilla Wafers are supported by more comprehensive advertising programs, they too benefit from P-O-P displays.

Effective deployment of P-O-P advertising requires careful coordination with the marketer's sales force. Gillette found this out when it realized it was wasting money on lots of P-O-P materials and displays that retailers simply ignored.[44] Gillette sales reps visit about 20,000 stores per month, and are in a position to know what retailers will and will not use. Gillette's marketing executives finally woke up to this fact when their sales reps told them, for example, that 50 percent of the shelf signs being shipped to retailers from three separate suppliers were going directly to retailers' garbage bins. Reps helped redesign new display cards that megaretailers such as Wal-Mart approved for their stores and immediately put into use. Now any time Gillette launches a new P-O-P program, it tracks its success through the eyes and ears of 20 of its sales reps who have been designated as monitors for the new program. Having

40.   Maxine S. Lans, "Legal Hurdles Big Part of Promotions Game," *Marketing News,* October 24, 1994, 15.
41.   Data cited in Lisa Z. Eccles, "P-O-P Scores with Marketers," *Advertising Age,* September 26, 1994, 1–4; Leah Haran, "Point of Purchase: Marketers Getting with the Program," *Advertising Age,* October 23, 1995, 33; PROMO 2004 Industry Trends Report.
42.   Eccles, "P-O-P Scores with Marketers"; Haran, "Point of Purchase: Marketers Getting with the Program."
43.   Yumiko Ono, "'Wobblers' and 'Sidekicks' Clutter Stores, Irk Retailers," *Wall Street Journal,* September 8, 1998, B1.
44.   Nicole Crawford, "Keeping P-O-P Sharp," *PROMO Magazine,* January 1998, 52, 53.

a sales force that can work with retailers to develop and deliver effective P–O–P programs is a critical element for achieving integrated brand promotion.

Objectives for Point-of-Purchase Advertising.

The objectives of point–of–purchase advertising are similar to those for sales promotion. The goal is to create a short–term impact on sales while preserving the long–term image of the brand being developed and maintained by advertising for the brand. Specifically, the objects for sales promotion are as follows:

- Draw consumers' attention to a brand in the retail setting.
- Maintain purchase loyalty among brand loyal users.
- Stimulate increased or varied usage of the brand.
- Stimulate trial use by users of competitive brands.

These objectives are self-explanatory and follow closely on the objects of sales promotion. Key to the effective use of P–O–P is to maintain the brand image being developed by advertising.

Types of Point-of-Purchase Advertising and Displays.

A myriad of displays and presentations are available to marketers. P–O–P materials generally fall into two categories: **short-term promotional displays,** which are used for six months or less, and **permanent long-term displays,** which are intended to provide point-of-purchase presentation for more than six months. Within these two categories, marketers have a wide range of choices:[45]

- *Window and door signage:* Any sign that identifies and/or advertises a company or brand or gives directions to the consumer.
- *Counter/shelf unit:* A smaller display designed to fit on counters or shelves.
- *Floor stand:* Any P–O–P unit that stands independently on the floor.
- *Shelf talker:* A printed card or sign designed to mount on or under a shelf.
- *Mobile/banner:* An advertising sign suspended from the ceiling of a store or hung across a large wall area.
- *Cash register:* P–O–P signage or small display mounted near a cash register designed to sell impulse items such as gum, lip balm, or candy, as in Exhibit 18.17.
- *Full line merchandiser:* A unit that provides the only selling area for a manufacturer's line. Often located as an end-of-aisle display.
- *End-of-aisle display/gondola:* Usually a large display of products placed at the end of an aisle, as in Exhibit 18.18.
- *Dump bin:* A large bin with graphics or other signage attached.
- *Illuminated sign:* Lighted signage used outside or in-store to promote a brand or the store.
- *Motion display:* Any P–O–P unit that has moving elements to attract attention.
- *Interactive unit:* A computer-based kiosk where shoppers get information such as tips on recipes or how to use the brand. Can also be a unit that flashes and dispenses coupons.
- *Overhead merchandiser:* A display rack that stocks product and is placed above the cash register. The cashier can reach the product for the consumer. The front of an overhead merchandiser usually carries signage.
- *Cart advertising:* Any advertising message adhered to a shopping cart, as in Exhibit 18.19.
- *Aisle directory:* Used to delineate contents of a store aisle; also provides space for an advertising message.

This array of in-store options gives marketers the opportunity to attract shoppers' attention, induce purchase, and provide reinforcement for key messages that are

---

45. *Retailer Guide to Maximizing In-Store Advertising Effectiveness* (Washington, D.C.: Point-of-Purchase Advertising International, 1999), 5–7.

Displays in a cash register checkout lane are designed to sell impulse items such as candy, or easily forgotten items such as batteries.

End-of-aisle displays provide space to draw attention to a large display of product.

A shopping-cart ad carries an immediate message to shoppers.

being conveyed through other components of the advertising plan. Retailers are increasingly looking to P-O-P displays as ways to differentiate and provide ambience for their individual stores, which means that the kind of displays valued by Wal-Mart versus Walgreens versus Albertson's versus Target (to name just a few) will often vary considerably. Once again, it is the marketer's field sales force that will be critical in developing the right P-O-P alternative for each retailer stocking that marketer's products. Without the retailers' cooperation, P-O-P advertising has virtually no chance to work its magic.

P-O-P Advertising and the Trade and Business Markets. While we have focused our discussion of the use of point-of-purchase advertising as a technique to attract consumers, this promotional tool is also strategically valuable to the trade and business markets. Product displays and information sheets often encourage retailers to support one distributor or manufacturer's brand over another. P-O-P promotions can help win precious shelf space and exposure in a retail setting. From a retailer's perspective, a

P-O-P display should be designed to draw attention to a brand, increase turnover, and possibly distribute coupons or sweepstakes entry forms. But brand manufacturers and distributors obviously share that interest. When the retailer is able to move a particular brand off the shelf, that, in turn, positively affects the manufacturer and distributor's sales. Over $17 billion was invested in on P-O-P materials in 2003—an 18.1 percent increase over the prior year. This is more than was spent on either magazine or radio advertising.[46]

In an attempt to combat the threat of losing business to online shopping, retailers are trying to enliven the retail environment, and point-of-purchase displays are part of the strategy. Distributors and retailers are trying to create a better and more satisfying shopping experience. The president of a large display company says, "We're trying to bring more of an entertainment factor to our P-O-P programs."[47]

5 The Coordination Challenge: Sales Promotion, Point-of-Purchase Advertising, and IBP.

There is an allure to sales promotion that must be put into perspective. Sales promotions can make things happen—quickly. While managers often find the immediacy of sales promotion valuable, particularly in meeting quarterly sales goals, sales promotions are rarely a viable means of long-term success. But when used properly, sales promotions can be an important element in a well-conceived IBP campaign. Key to their proper use is coordinating the message emphasis in advertising with the placement and emphasis of sales promotions. When advertising and sales promotion are well coordinated, the impact of each is enhanced—a classic case of synergy. When advertisers were surveyed about their perspective on sales promotion, 57 percent said that they employed a mix of brand building and sales incentives in the promotional process. Similarly, the majority of respondents indicated that sales promotion was an ancillary part of their IBP campaigns rather than a core component or the key component.[48] The effectiveness of coordination was demonstrated dramatically by *Jane* magazine. The magazine ran a contest designed to prove to advertisers that the magazine's readers do buy advertisers' brands. Readers who wanted to participate in the contest collected the UPC codes of specified brands from their purchases and entered them on the magazine's Web site, http://www.janemag.com. This coordinated effort was a huge success, attracting 51,543 Web contest entries and 37 new ad pages from advertisers.[49]

Message Coordination.

The typical sales promotion should either attract attention to a brand or offer the target market greater value: reduced price, more product, or the chance to win a prize or an award. In turn, this focused attention and extra value acts as an incentive for the target market to choose the promoted brand over other brands. One of the coordination problems this presents is that advertising messages, designed to build long-term loyalty, may not seem totally consistent with the extra-value signal of the sales promotion.

This is the classic problem that marketers face in coordinating sales promotion with an advertising campaign. First, advertising messages tout brand features or emotional attractions. Then, the next contact a consumer may have with the brand is an insert in the Sunday paper offering a cents-off coupon. These mixed signals can be damaging for a brand.

Increasing the coordination between advertising and various sales promotion efforts requires only the most basic planning. First, when different agencies are involved in preparing sales promotion materials and advertising materials, those

---

46.   PROMO 2004 Industry Trends Report.
47.   Ibid.
48.   Ibid.
49.   Brian Steinberg, "*Jane* Links Promotions to Purchases," *Wall Street Journal,* May 14, 2003, B5.

agencies need to be kept informed by the advertiser regarding the maintenance of a desired theme. Second, simple techniques can be used to carry a coordinated theme between promotional tools. The use of logos, slogans, visual imagery, or spokespersons can create a consistent presentation. As illustrated in Exhibits 18.14 and 18.15, even if advertising and sales promotion pursue different purposes, the look and feel of both efforts may be coordinated. The more the theme of a promotion can be tied directly to the advertising campaign, the more impact these messages will generally have on the consumer. A good example of coordinating the message across all forms of communication is the M&M "Great Color Quest" promotion. Masterfoods USA introduced bold new colors for the old M&M brand but first turned all the candies black and white for a period. The release of the new colors was coordinated with print ads, billboards, coupons, and a new package.[50]

Media Coordination.   Another key in coordination involves timing. Remember that the success of a sales promotion depends on the consumer believing that the chance to save money or receive more of a product represents enhanced value. If the consumer is not aware of a brand and its features and benefits, and does not perceive the brand as a worthy item, then there will be no basis for perceiving value—discounted or not. This means that appropriate advertising should precede price-oriented sales promotions for the promotions to be effective. The right advertising can create an image for a brand that is appropriate for a promotional offer. Then, when consumers are presented with a sales promotion, the offer will impress the consumer as an opportunity to acquire superior value. This is precisely why Internet firms began investing so heavily in advertising before turning to sales promotions as a way of attracting visitors. In coordinating online with offline media, the chief marketing officer of a high-tech promotions shop makes the observation, "Online promotions used to be ugly stepchildren. But brands are now starting to use the Web smartly. They're combining the media and no longer treating online and offline separately."[51]

Conclusions from Research.   The synergy theme prominent in the preceding discussion is not just a matter of speculation. Research using single-source data generated by A. C. Nielsen reaffirms many of the primary points of this chapter.[52] The major conclusions of this research are

- The short-term productivity of promotions working alone is much more dramatic than that of advertising. Promotions that involve price incentives on average yield a 1.8 percent increase in sales for each 1 percent price reduction. A 1 percent increase in advertising yields just a 0.2 percent sales increase on average.
- The average cost of a 1 percent reduction in price is always far greater than the cost of a 1 percent increase in advertising. Thus, more often than not, sales promotions featuring price incentives are actually unprofitable in the short term.
- It is rare that a sales promotion generates a long-term effect. Hence, there are no long-term revenues to offset the high cost of promotions in the short run. Successful advertising is much more likely to yield a profitable return over the long run, even though its impact on short-run sales may be modest.
- While both advertising and sales promotions may be expected to affect sales in the short run, the evidence suggests that the most powerful effects come from a combination of the two. The impact of advertising and promotions working together is dramatically greater than the sum of each sales stimulus working by itself.

50.   Stephanie Thompson, "M&M's Wraps Up Promo with Color," *Advertising Age,* March 8, 2004, 4, 51.
51.   "Internet Invasion," Promotion Trends 2000.
52.   John Philip Jones, *When Ads Work* (New York: Lexington Books, 1995).

SUMMARY

 Explain the importance and growth of sales promotion.

Sales promotions use diverse incentives to motivate action on the part of consumers, members of the trade channel, and business buyers. They serve different purposes than does mass media advertising, and for some companies, sales promotions receive substantially more funding. The growing reliance on these promotions can be attributed to the heavy pressures placed on marketing managers to account for their spending and meet sales objectives in short time frames. Deal-prone shoppers, brand proliferation, the increasing power of large retailers, and media clutter have also contributed to the rising popularity of sales promotion.

 Describe the main sales promotion techniques used in the consumer market, trade channel, and business markets.

Sales promotions directed at consumers can serve various goals. For example, they can be employed as means to stimulate trial, repeat, or large-quantity purchases. They are especially important tools for introducing new brands or for reacting to a competitor's advances. Coupons, price-off deals, phone and gift cards, and premiums provide obvious incentives for purchase. Contests, sweepstakes, and product placements can be excellent devices for stimulating brand interest. A variety of sampling techniques are available to get a product into the hands of the target audience. Rebates and frequency programs provide rewards for repeat purchase.

Sales promotions directed at the trade can also serve multiple objectives. They are a necessity in obtaining initial distribution of a new brand. For established brands, they can be a means to increase distributors' order quantities or obtain retailers' cooperation in implementing a consumer-directed promotion. Incentives and allowances can be offered to distributors to motivate support for a brand. Sales training programs and cooperative advertising programs are additional devices for effecting retailer support.

In the business market, professional buyers are attracted by various sales promotion techniques. Fre-

quency (continuity) programs are very valuable in the travel industry and have spread to business-product advertisers. Trade shows are an efficient way to reach a large number of highly targeted business buyers. Gifts to business buyers are a form of sales promotion that is unique to this market. Finally, premiums, advertising specialties, and trial offers have proven to be successful in the business market.

 Identify the risks to the brand of using sales promotion.

There are important risks associated with heavy reliance on sales promotion. Offering constant deals for a brand can erode brand equity, and it may simply be borrowing sales from a future time period. Constant deals can also create a customer mindset that leads consumers to abandon a brand as soon as a deal is retracted. Sales promotions are expensive to administer and fraught with legal complications. Sales promotions yield their most positive results when carefully integrated with the overall advertising plan.

 Understand the role and techniques of point-of-purchase advertising.

Point-of-purchase advertising (P-O-P) refers to materials used in the retail setting to attract shoppers' attention to a firm's brand, convey primary brand benefits, or highlight pricing information. The effect of P-O-P can be to reinforce a consumer's brand preference or change a consumer's brand choice in the retail setting. P-O-P displays may also feature price-off deals or other consumer and business sales promotions. A myriad of displays and presentations are available to marketers. P-O-P materials generally fall into two categories: short-term promotional displays, which are used for six months or less, and permanent long-term displays, which are intended to provide point-of-purchase presentation for more than six months. In trade and business markets, P-O-P displays encourage retailers to support one manufacturer's brand over another; they can also be used to gain preferred shelf space and exposure in a retail setting.

Explain the coordination issues for integrated brand promotion associated with using sales promotion and point-of-purchase advertising.

One of the coordination problems is message coordination. Advertising messages, designed to build long-term loyalty, may not seem to consumers to be totally consistent with the extra-value message of the sales promotion. This is the classic problem that marketers face in coordinating sales promotion with an advertising campaign. First, advertising messages tout brand features or emotional attractions. Then, the next contact a consumer

may have with the brand is an insert in the Sunday paper that touts a price reduction or contest.

Another key in coordination involves media coordination. The success of a sales promotion depends on the consumer believing that the chance to save money or receive extra quantity of a product represents enhanced value. If the consumer is not aware of a brand and its features and benefits, and does not perceive the brand as a worthy item, then there will be no basis for perceiving value—discounted or not. This means that appropriate advertising should precede price-oriented sales promotions for them to be effective.

KEY TERMS

sales promotion
consumer-market sales promotion
trade-market sales promotion
business-market promotion
coupon
price-off deal
premiums
free premium
self-liquidating premium
advertising specialties
contest
sweepstakes

sampling
in-store sampling
door-to-door sampling
mail sampling
newspaper sampling
on-package sampling
mobile sampling
trial offers
rebate
frequency programs
push strategy
push money

merchandise allowances
slotting fees
bill-back allowances
off-invoice allowances
cooperative advertising
trade shows
point-of-purchase (P-O-P)
   advertising
short-term promotional displays
permanent long-term displays

QUESTIONS

1. Compare and contrast sales promotion and mass media advertising as promotional tools. In what ways do the strengths of one make up for the limitations of the other? What specific characteristics of sales promotions account for the high levels of expenditures that have been allocated to them in recent years?

2. What is brand proliferation and why is it occurring? Why do consumer sales promotions become more commonplace in the face of rampant brand proliferation? Why do trade sales promotions become more frequent when there is excessive brand proliferation?

3. Pull all the preprinted and free-standing inserts from the most recent edition of your Sunday newspaper. From them find an example of each of these consumer-market sales promotions: coupon, free premium, self-liquidating premium, contest, sweepstakes, and trial offer.

4. In developing an advertising plan, synergy may be achieved through careful coordination of individual elements. Give an example of how mass media advertising might be used with on-package sampling to effect a positive synergy.

5. Consumers often rationalize their purchase of a new product with a statement such as, "I bought it because I had a 50-cent coupon and our grocery was doubling all manufacturers' coupons this week." What are the prospects that such a consumer will emerge as a loyal user of the product? What must happen if he or she is to become loyal?

6. Early in the chapter, it was suggested that large retailers like Wal-Mart are assuming greater power in today's marketplace. What factors contribute to retailers' increasing power? Explain the connection between merchandise allowances and slotting fees and the growth in retailer power.

7. In your opinion, are ethical dilemmas more likely to arise with sales promotions directed at the consumer or at the business market? What specific forms of consumer or business promotions seem most likely to involve or create ethical dilemmas?

8. What role does point-of-purchase advertising play as a promotional tool? In what ways can a firm ensure coordination of its P-O-P with other promotional efforts?

EXPERIENTIAL EXERCISES

1. As an in-class exercise, debate the issue "Sales promotion erodes brand loyalty and creates a commodity perception of a brand." Does sales promotion make you switch brands or are you loyal to certain brands no matter what incentive a marketer might offer?

2. This chapter gives two general categories of P-O-P displays and lists over a dozen examples of in-store

options such as floorstands, shelf talkers, and the dump bin. Take that list and go to any retail store or grocer. Make a list of how many examples you can find to match the displays discussed in the text, and identify the advertisers that used each display you found. Briefly describe each and evaluate its usefulness based on what you learned in the chapter.

EXPERIENCING THE INTERNET

18-1 The Wonderful World of Disney

Integrated brand promotion involves a strategic coordination of multiple communication tools to promote products and services. Instead of viewing advertising, public relations, sales promotions, and other marketing functions as separate, the IBP approach aims to streamline them together to execute campaigns with a clear, consistent, and persuasive message. Large corporations such as Disney use the IBP approach for the promotion of their brands on a global level.

Disney.com: http://www.disney.com

Disney Store Affiliates: http://www.disneystoreaffiliates.com

Disney Store: http://www.disneystore.com

1.   From the Disney.com home page, list features of the site that suggest that integrated brand promotion is an important concept in Disney's advertising and marketing efforts.

2.   List a consumer-market sales promotion technique that you see on the Disney.com home page. Explain the strengths of that promotion technique and describe how visitors participate in the promotion via the Internet.

3.   What is the purpose of the Disney Store Affiliates program, and how does it work? What is a push strategy, and how does it relate to the Disney Store Affiliates program?

18-2 Millstone's Famous Coffee-Bean Bins

Entrepreneur Phil Johnson started selling 100-pound sacks of whole-bean arabicas to gourmet shops in the early 1980s. While shopping at his local supermarket, he had an idea that changed the way consumers think of coffee. Johnson designed a retail distribution and placement model that would soon put the Millstone Coffee Company front and center in supermarkets everywhere. With beans on display in clear bins in stores, consumers would have a strong visual incentive to bypass competing brands and purchase the numerous gourmet coffees that have made Millstone famous.

Millstone Coffee: http://www.millstone.com

1.   Define P-O-P advertising. In the case of Millstone Coffee, describe how the actual beans become part of the P-O-P display. Have you ever purchased Millstone coffee because of the attraction of the clear bins full of rich coffee beans?

2.   What research conclusions have to led the dramatic rise of annual expenditures on P-O-P advertising by large companies? Why do you think P-O-P advertising is so effective in persuading customers to buy Millstone coffee?

3.   Explain the role of the sales force in the successful deployment of P-O-P materials and displays. What can happen if sales reps aren't coordinating the deployment of P-O-P displays with retail managers?

CHAPTER 19

After reading and thinking about this chapter, you will be able to do the following:

1

Identify the three primary purposes served by direct marketing and explain its growing popularity.

2

Distinguish a mailing list from a marketing database and review the many applications of each.

3

Describe the prominent media used by direct marketers in delivering their messages to the consumer.

4

Articulate the added challenge created by direct marketing for achieving integrated brand promotion.

Introductory Scenario: Don't Mess with Les.
In 1958 Lester Wunderman launched a new services firm to help clients with a different style of marketing—a style he would label "direct marketing." It turned out to be a potent style and his firm prospered, changed names, and today is part of WPP Group, the global ad holding company based in London.[1] Over his career Les Wunderman worked with numerous clients to help them grow their businesses. One of his success stories involved Columbia House Music Club, and a brief look back at Wunderman's work with Columbia provides instant insights regarding the unique style of the direct marketer.[2]

Wunderman had worked with Columbia for a number of years when executives at Columbia had a notion to hire another ad agency to help with the job. The new agency was to be McCann Erickson, renowned for its creativity and sophistication in ad development. To put it mildly, Les was not thrilled about sharing the account with McCann, but Columbia wanted something different. So Les proposed a test. He said, give me 13 cities to work in, give McCann a comparable 13 cities, and the two of us will develop and run new campaigns—winner take all. Everyone agreed a test was in order.

McCann would take the classic approach of the traditional ad agency. They developed an awareness-building campaign featuring prime-time TV ads, designed to heighten familiarity with Columbia. Then, as consumers found the Columbia House offers in *TV Guide* and *Parade* magazines (you know, Buy One and Get 12 FREE), the more-aware consumer was expected to jump at the offer.

Wunderman used a different approach. Rather than glitzy, prime-time TV ads, he went late night, where air time is much less expensive (about one-quarter the cost of McCann's programming). However, the key to his plan would be a "treasure hunt." In every magazine ad, Wunderman's designers incorporated a little gold box. Then, in his series of TV commercials, a critical theme was the invitation to solve the secret of the Gold Box and win a prize. The gold box gave viewers a reason to look for the companion ads in *TV Guide* and *Parade* magazines. In Wunderman's words, "It made the readers/viewers part of an interactive advertising system. Viewers . . . became participants."[3] The little gold box served to "integrate" the different components of the overall campaign. That's the magic word, so you can already guess who wins this competition.

Both the McCann and Wunderman approaches improved results. Spending four times as much on prime-time media, McCann produced nearly a 20 percent increase in the sign-up rate for Columbia's Music Club. Using his, some might say, cheesy idea of the secret of the Gold Box, Wunderman and company generated an 80 percent increase in sign-ups. Needless to say, Les preempted the splitting of Columbia's business through this in-market competition, and the Gold Box tactic was unveiled as part of Columbia's national campaign.

There are several aspects of this story that illustrate the mindset of the direct marketer. First is simply the idea of staging a test. Direct marketers always seek to be in a position to judge results. Clients want results, and the Les Wundermans of the world first recommend going to the marketplace to see what works, and then spend the big dollars after you know the winner. Testing "in-market" is a hallmark of the direct marketer. Second, we see in the Wunderman gold box tactic keen insight about how to initiate a dialogue with the consumer. Use a little bit of mystery and throw in the prospect of winning something, and consumers get interested and send you back a response. This proclivity for promoting dialogue is another defining characteristic of the direct marketer's style. Getting in a dialogue with consumers leads to

1.   Alessandra Galloni, "WPP, Citing 'Madness,' Restores a Name," *Wall Street Journal,* June 1, 2001, B6.
2.   This account is adapted from Malcolm Gladwell, *The Tipping Point* (Boston, MA: Little, Brown and Company, 2002), 93–95.
3.   Ibid, 95.

relationships that can mean multiple purchases over time (as in a CD/DVD club like Columbia's). And that's where the real gold lies—in those multiple purchases.

① The Evolution of Direct Marketing.

In this chapter we will examine the growing field of direct marketing and explain how it may be used to both complement and supplant other forms of advertising. With the growing concern about fragmenting markets and the diminishing effectiveness of traditional media in reaching those markets, one can expect that more and more advertising dollars will be shifted to direct marketing programs.[4] Before we examine the evolution of direct marketing and look deeper at the reasons for its growing popularity, we need a clear appreciation for what people mean when they use the term *direct marketing*. The "official" definition from the Direct Marketing Association (DMA) provides a starting point:

Direct marketing is an interactive system of marketing, which uses one or more advertising media to effect a measurable response and/or transaction at any location.[5]

When examined piece by piece, this definition furnishes an excellent basis for understanding the scope of direct marketing.[6]

Direct marketing is interactive in that the marketer is attempting to develop an ongoing dialogue with the customer. Direct marketing programs are commonly planned with the notion that one contact will lead to another and then another so that the marketer's message can become more focused and refined with each interaction. The DMA's definition also notes that multiple media can be used in direct marketing programs. This is an important point for two reasons. First, we do not want to equate direct mail and direct marketing. Any media can be used in executing direct marketing programs, not just the mail. Second, as we have noted before, a combination of media is likely to be more effective than any one medium alone.

Another key aspect of direct marketing programs is that they almost always are designed to produce some form of immediate, measurable response. Direct marketing programs are often designed to produce an immediate sale. The customer might be asked to return an order form with check or money order for $189 to get a stylish Klaus Kobec Couture Sports Watch, or to call an 800 number with credit card handy to get 22 timeless hits on a CD called *The Very Best of Tony Bennett*. Because of this emphasis on immediate response, direct marketers are in a position to judge the effectiveness of a particular program. As in the Wunderman example, this ability to gauge the immediate impact of a program has great appeal to clients like Columbia House.

The final phrase of the DMA's definition notes that a direct marketing transaction can take place anywhere. The key idea here is that customers do not have to make a trip to a retail store for a direct marketing program to work. Follow-ups can be made by mail, over the telephone, or on the Internet. At one time the thinking was that Web-based direct marketers such as Amazon.com, pets.com, and eToys.com could ultimately provide so much convenience for shoppers that traditional retail stores might fall by the wayside.[7] Not! It now seems clear that consumers like the option of contacting companies in many ways. So smart retailers both large (see Exhibit 19.1) and small (see Exhibit 19.2) make themselves available in both the physical and virtual worlds.[8] Customers are then free to choose where and how they want to shop.

4.   Anthony Bianco, "The Vanishing Mass Market," *BusinessWeek*, July 12, 2004, 61–68.
5.   Bob Stone, *Successful Direct Marketing Methods* (Lincolnwood, IL: NTC Business Books, 1994), 5.
6.   The discussion to follow builds on that of Stone, *Successful Direct Marketing Methods*.
7.   Patrick M. Reilly, "In the Age of the Web, a Book Chain Flounders," *Wall Street Journal*, February 22, 1999, B1, B4.
8.   Allanna Sullivan, "From a Call to a Click," *Wall Street Journal*, July 17, 2000, R30.

Among other things, pure-play Internet retailers came to realize that when shoppers are dissatisfied with their purchases, many want a physical store where they can return the merchandise for a refund or a trade. In this ad BestBuy.com has some fun with this issue in the context of online CD shopping. At Best Buy, if "Folksongs from Rumania" is not what you thought it would be, you can always return it to one of their retail stores. http://www.bestbuy.com

How about a new moose rug or carved loon for your grandparent's cottage Up North? Well, you could visit the Adirondack Country Store in upstate New York, call them at 1-800-LOON-ADK for the catalog, or go online to pick out something nice. Check out the call of the loon at http://www.adirondackcountrystore.com.

Direct Marketing—A Look Back.

From Johannes Gutenberg and Benjamin Franklin to Richard Sears, Alvah Roebuck, Les Wunderman, and Lillian Vernon, the evolution of direct marketing has involved some of the great pioneers in business. As Exhibit 19.3 shows, the practice of direct marketing today is shaped by the successes of many notable mail-order companies and catalog merchandisers.[9] Among these, none is more exemplary than L. L. Bean. Bean founded his company in 1912 on his integrity and $400. His first product was a unique hunting shoe made from a leather top and rubber bottom sewn together. Other outdoor clothing and equipment soon followed in the Bean catalog.

A look at the L. L. Bean catalog of 1917 (black and white, just 12 pages) reveals the fundamental strategy underlying Bean's success. It featured the Maine Hunting Shoe and other outdoor clothing with descriptive copy that was informative, factual, and low-key. On the front page was Bean's commitment to quality. It read: "Maine Hunting Shoe—guarantee. We guarantee this pair of shoes to give perfect satisfaction

9. See Edward Nash, "The Roots of Direct Marketing," *Direct Marketing Magazine,* February 1995, 38–40; Cara Beardi, "Lillian Vernon Sets Sights on Second Half-Century," *Advertising Age,* March 19, 2001, 22.

EXHIBIT 19.3

Direct-marketing milestones.

c. 1450	Johannes Gutenberg invents movable type.
1667	The first gardening catalog is published by William Lucas, an English gardener.
1744	Benjamin Franklin publishes a catalog of books on science and industry and formulates the basic mail-order concept of customer satisfaction guaranteed.
1830s	A few mail-order companies began operating in New England, selling camping and fishing supplies.
1863	The introduction of penny postage facilitates direct mail.
1867	The invention of the typewriter gives a modern appearance to direct-mail materials.
1872	Montgomery Ward publishes his first "catalog," selling 163 items on a single sheet of paper. By 1884 his catalog grows to 240 pages, with thousands of items and a money-back guarantee.
1886	Richard Sears enters the mail-order business by selling gold watches and makes $5,000 in his first six months. He partners with Alvah Roebuck in 1887, and by 1893 they are marketing a wide range of merchandise in a 196-page catalog.
1912	L. L. Bean founds one of today's most admired mail-order companies on the strength of his Maine Hunting Shoe and a guarantee of total satisfaction for the life of the shoe.
1917	The Direct Mail Advertising Association is founded. In 1973 it becomes the Direct Mail/Direct Marketing Association.
1928	Third-class bulk mail becomes a reality, offering economies for the direct-mail industry.
1950	Credit cards first appear, led by the Diners' Club travel and entertainment card. American Express enters in 1958.
1951	Lillian Vernon places an ad for a monogrammed purse and belt and generates $16,000 in immediate business. She reinvests the money in what becomes the Lillian Vernon enterprise. Vernon recognizes early on that catalog shopping has great appeal to time-pressed consumers.
1953	Publishers Clearing House is founded and soon becomes a dominant force in magazine subscriptions.
1955	Columbia Record Club is established, and eventually becomes Columbia House—the music-marketing giant.
1967	The term *telemarketing* first appears in print, and AT&T introduces the first toll-free 800 service.
1983	The Direct Mail/Direct Marketing Association drops Direct Mail from its name to become the DMA, as a reflection of the multiple media being used by direct marketers.
1984	Apple introduces the Macintosh personal computer.
1992	The number of people who shop at home surpasses 100 million in the United States.
1998	The Direct Marketing Association, http://www.the-dma.org, eager to adapt its members' bulk mailing techniques for the Internet, announces it will merge with the Association for Interactive Media, http://www.interactivehq.org.
2003	U.S. consumers register over 10 million phone numbers in the first four days of the national Do Not Call Registry.

Sources: Adapted from the DMA's "Grassroots Advocacy Guide for Direct Marketers" (1993). Reprinted with permission of the Direct Marketing Association, Inc.; Rebecca Quick, "Direct Marketing Association to Merge with Association of Interactive Media," *Wall Street Journal,* October 12, 1998, B6.

in every way. If the rubber breaks or the tops grow hard, return them together with this guarantee tag and we will replace them, free of charge. Signed, L. L. Bean."[10] Bean realized that long-term relationships with customers must be based on trust, and his guarantee policy was aimed at developing and sustaining that trust.

As an astute direct marketer, Bean also showed a keen appreciation for the importance of building a good mailing list. For many years he used his profits to promote his free catalog via advertisements in hunting and fishing magazines. Those replying to the ads received a rapid response and typically became Bean customers. Bean's obsession with building mailing lists is nicely captured by this quote from his friend, Maine native John Gould: "If you drop in just to shake his hand, you get home to find his catalog in your mailbox."[11]

By 1967 Bean's sales approached $5 million, and by 1990 they had exploded to $600 million, as the product line was expanded to include more apparel and recreation equipment. Today, L. L. Bean is still a family-operated business that emphasizes the basic philosophies of its founder, which are carefully summarized at the company's Web site at http://www.llbean.com. Quality products, understated advertising, and sophisticated customer-contact and distribution systems still drive the business. Additionally, L. L.'s 100-percent-satisfaction guarantee can still be found in every Bean catalog, and it remains at the heart of the relationship between Bean and its customers.

Direct Marketing Today.

Direct marketing today is rooted in the legacy of mail-order giants and catalog merchandisers such as L. L. Bean, Lillian Vernon, Publishers Clearing House, and JCPenney. Today, however, direct marketing has broken free from its mail-order heritage to become a tool used by all types of organizations throughout the world. Although many types of businesses and not-for-profit organizations are using direct marketing, it is common to find that such direct-marketing programs are not carefully integrated with an organization's other advertising efforts. Integration should be the goal for advertising and direct marketing (remember the Gold Box!). Impressive evidence supports the thesis that integrated programs are more effective than the sum of their parts.[12]

Because the label "direct marketing" now encompasses many different types of activities, it is important to remember the defining characteristics spelled out in the DMA definition given earlier. Direct marketing involves an attempt to interact or create a dialogue with the customer; multiple media are often employed in the process, and direct marketing is characterized by the fact that a measurable response is immediately available for assessing a program's impact. With these defining features in mind, we can see that direct marketing programs are commonly used for three primary purposes.

As you might imagine, the most common use of direct marketing is as a tool to close the sale with a customer. This can be done as a stand-alone program, or it can be coordinated with a firm's other advertising. Telecommunications giants such as AT&T, Sprint, T-Mobile, and Verizon make extensive use of the advertising/direct marketing combination. High-profile mass media campaigns build awareness for their latest offer, followed by systematic direct marketing follow-ups to close the sale. A direct mail follow-up for Road Runner High Speed Online is featured in Exhibit 19.4.

A second purpose for direct marketing programs is to identify prospects for future contacts and, at the same time, provide in-depth information to selected customers. Any time you respond to an offer for more information or for a free sample, you've identified yourself as a prospect and can expect follow-up sales pitches

10.   Allison Cosmedy, *A History of Direct Marketing* (New York: Direct Marketing Association, 1992), 6.

11.   Ibid.

12.   Ernan Roman, *Integrated Direct Marketing* (Lincolnwood, IL: NTC Business Books, 1995); Daniel Klein, "Disintegrated Marketing," *Harvard Business Review,* March 2003, 18, 19.

EXHIBIT 19.4

Closing the sale typically involves an incentive for immediate action. Here the offer is free installation plus the first 3 months at $29.95 per month. Welcome to the fast lane!

from a direct marketer. The StairMaster ad in Exhibit 19.5 is a marketer's attempt to initiate a dialogue with prospective customers. Ordering the free catalog and video, whether through the 800 number or at the Web site, begins the process of interactive marketing designed to ultimately produce the sale of another Free-Climber 4600.

Direct marketing programs are also initiated as a means to engage customers, seek their advice, furnish helpful information about using a product, reward customers for using a brand, and in general foster brand loyalty. For instance, the manufacturer of Valvoline motor oil seeks to build loyalty for its brand by encouraging young car owners to join the Valvoline Performance Team.[13] To join the team, young drivers

13.   Nash, "The Roots of Direct Marketing."

EXHIBIT 19.5

*Most people are not going to
buy a major piece of exercise
equipment based on this or
any other magazine ad.
That's not the intent of this
ad. The purchase process could
start here, however, with the
simple act of ordering that free
video either through the 800
number or at* http://www
.stairmaster.com.

just fill out a questionnaire that enters them into the
Valvoline database. Team members receive posters,
special offers on racing-team apparel, news about
racing events that Valvoline has sponsored, and
promotional reminders at regular intervals that reinforce the virtues of Valvoline for the driver's next
oil change.

What's Driving the Growing Popularity of Direct Marketing?

The growth
in popularity of direct marketing is due to a number of factors. Some of these have to do with
changes in consumer lifestyles and technological
developments that in effect create a climate more
conducive to the practice of direct marketing. In
addition, direct marketing programs offer unique
advantages vis-à-vis conventional mass media
advertising, leading many organizations to shift
more of their marketing budgets to direct marketing activities.

From the consumer's standpoint, direct marketing's growing popularity might be summarized in a
single word—*convenience*. Dramatic growth in the
number of dual-income and single-person households has reduced the time people have to visit
retail stores. Direct marketers provide consumers
access to a growing range of products and services in their homes, thus saving many
households' most precious resource—time.

More liberal attitudes about the use of credit and the accumulation of debt have
also contributed to the growth of direct marketing. Credit cards are the primary
means of payment in most direct marketing transactions. The widespread availability of credit cards makes it ever more convenient to shop from the comfort of one's
home.

Developments in telecommunications have also facilitated the direct marketing
transaction. After getting off to a slow start in the late 1960s, toll-free telephone
numbers have exploded in popularity to the point where one can hardly find a product or a catalog that does not include an 800 or 888 number for interacting with the
seller. Whether one is requesting the StairMaster video, ordering a twill polo shirt
from Eddie Bauer, or planning that *Adventure* in Wyoming (see Exhibit 19.6), the
preferred mode of access for many consumers has been the 800 number.

Another obvious development having a huge impact on the growth of direct
marketing is the computer. (Did you know that your parents' new Buick has more
computer power than the Apollo spacecraft that took astronauts to the moon?) The
incredible diffusion of computer technology sweeping through all modern societies
has been a tremendous boon to direct marketers. The computer now allows firms to
track, keep records on, and interact with millions of customers with relative ease. As
we will see in an upcoming discussion, the computer power now available for modest dollar amounts is fueling the growth of direct marketing's most potent tool—the
marketing database.

And just as the computer has provided marketers with the tool they need to
handle massive databases of customer information (see also the IBP box on page
680), it too has provided convenience-oriented consumers with the tool they need
to comparison shop with the point and click of a mouse. What could be more convenient than logging on to the Internet and pulling up a shopping agent like

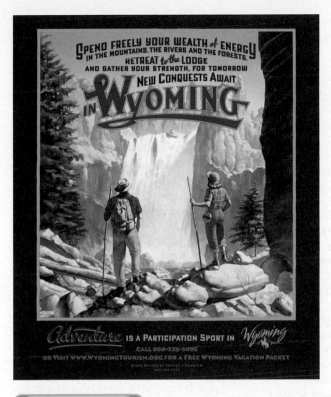

EXHIBIT 19.6

Finding that waterfall in Wyoming will take some planning, and Wyoming's Office of Travel & Tourism is happy to help. The adventure begins with a request for their vacation packet, and if the phone feels a little old fashioned, you know you can start the visit at http://www.wyoming tourism.org.

http://www.pricescan.com or http://www.my simon.com to check prices on everything from toaster ovens to snowboards? Why leave the apartment?

Direct marketing programs also offer some unique advantages that make them appealing compared with what might be described as conventional mass marketing. A general manager of marketing communications with AT&T's consumer services unit put it this way: "We want to segment our market more; we want to learn more about individual customers; we want to really serve our customers by giving them very specific products and services. Direct marketing is probably the most effective way in which we can reach customers and establish a relationship with them."[14] As you might expect, AT&T is one of those organizations that has shifted more and more of its marketing dollars into direct-marketing programs.

The appeal of direct marketing is enhanced further by the persistent emphasis on producing measurable effects. For instance, in direct marketing, it is common to find calculations such as **cost per inquiry (CPI)** or **cost per order (CPO)** being featured in program evaluation. These calculations simply divide the number of responses to a program by that program's cost. When calculated for every program an organization conducts over time, CPI and CPO data tell an organization what works and what doesn't work in its competitive arena.

This emphasis on producing and monitoring measurable effects is realized most effectively through an approach called *database marketing.*[15] Working with a database, direct marketers can target specific customers, track their actual purchase behavior over time, and experiment with different programs for affecting the purchasing patterns of these customers. Obviously, those programs that produce the best outcomes become the candidates for increased funding in the future. Let's look into database marketing.

② Database Marketing. If any ambiguity remains about what makes direct marketing different from marketing in general, that ambiguity can be erased by the database. The one characteristic of direct marketing that distinguishes it from marketing more generally is its emphasis on database development. Knowing who the best customers are along with what and how often they buy is a direct marketer's secret weapon.[16] This knowledge accumulates in the form of a marketing database.

Databases used as the centerpieces in direct marketing campaigns take many forms and can contain many different layers of information about customers. At one extreme is the simple mailing list that contains nothing more than the names and addresses of possible customers; at the other extreme is the customized marketing database that augments names and addresses with various additional information about customers' characteristics, past purchases, and product preferences. Understanding

14.   Gary Levin, "AT&T Exec: Customer Access Goal of Integration," *Advertising Age,* October 10, 1994, S1.

15.   Like many authors, Winer contends that direct marketing starts with the creation of a database. See Russell Winer, "A Framework for Customer Relationship Management," *California Management Review,* Summer 2001, 89–105.

16.   Ibid.

this distinction between mailing lists and marketing databases is important in appreciating the scope of database marketing.

It Takes a Warehouse . . .

Data warehousing refers to the use of huge databases filled with information about consumers and their shopping habits as a means to create marketing promotions and programs. How huge is huge, you ask. Well, Wal-Mart has a whopper. Wal-Mart uses NCR equipment to house the 100 terabytes of data that it has collected on shoppers thus far. That's 100 trillion bytes, which translates into about 16,000 bytes of data for every one of the world's six billion people. However, because Wal-Mart does most of its business in North America, most of these bytes are about shoppers in North America. The insights Wal-Mart executives glean from this massive data file help them decide what products to stock and where and how to shelve them. Store signage and the Wal-Mart in-store radio network are also programmed to take advantage of what is learned from the data warehouse. Since on the order of 100 million customers visit a Wal-Mart every week, and Wal-Mart knows a ton about these customers, it makes perfect sense for Wal-Mart to use its stores as its primary advertising medium.

By comparison, Fingerhut, a mail-order unit of Federated Department Stores, keeps a data warehouse of a mere six terabytes. But that's enough bytes to keep 30 analysts employed full-time just trying to ascertain key insights about shoppers from these data. Fingerhut mails on average 100 catalogs per year to each name in its customer file of six million people, so judging when and to whom to mail is something they have turned into a data-based science. What's next on Fingerhut's list of database applications? The direct marketer's other favorite tool: targeted e-mail.

So does it follow that he or she with the most data wins? Judging from Wal-Mart's success, maybe so.

Source: Dana Blankenhorn, "Marketers Hone Targeting," *Advertising Age*, June 18, 2001, T16.

Mailing Lists. A **mailing list** is simply a file of names and addresses that an organization might use for contacting prospective or prior customers. Mailing lists are plentiful, easy to access, and inexpensive. For example, CD-ROM phone directories available for a few hundred dollars provide a cheap and easy way to generate mailing lists. More-targeted mailing lists are available from a variety of suppliers. The range of possibilities is mind-boggling, including groupings like the 238,737 subscribers to *Mickey Mouse Magazine;* 102,961 kindergarten teachers; 4,145,194 physical fitness enthusiasts; 117,758 Lord & Taylor credit card purchasers, and a whopping 269 archaeologists.[17]

Each time you subscribe to a magazine, order from a catalog, register your automobile, fill out a warranty card, redeem a rebate offer, apply for credit, join a professional society, or log in at a Web site, the information you provided about yourself goes on another mailing list. These lists are freely bought and sold through many means, including over the Internet. Sites such as http://www.worldata.com, http://www.hdml.com, and http://www.dblink.com allow one to buy names and addresses, or e-mail address lists, for as little as 10 cents per record. What's out there is truly remarkable—go have a look.

Two broad categories of lists should be recognized: the internal, or house, list versus the external, or outside, list. **Internal lists** are simply an organization's records of its own customers, subscribers, donors, and inquirers. **External lists** are purchased from a list compiler or rented from a list broker. At the most basic level, internal and external lists facilitate the two fundamental activities of the direct marketer: Internal lists are the starting point for developing better relationships with current customers, whereas external lists help an organization cultivate new business.

List Enhancement. Name-and-address files, no matter what their source, are merely the starting point for database marketing. The next step in the evolution of a database is mailing-list enhancement. Typically this involves augmenting an internal list by combining it with other, externally supplied lists or databases. External lists can be appended or merged with a house list.

17. *The 2001 Mailing List Catalog* (New York: Hugo Dunhill Mailing Lists, 2001).

One of the most straightforward list enhancements entails simply adding or appending more names and addresses to an internal list. Proprietary name-and-address files may be purchased from other companies that operate in noncompetitive businesses. With today's computer capabilities, adding these additional households to an existing mailing list is simple. Many well-known companies such as Sharper Image, American Express, Bloomingdale's, and Hertz sell or rent their customer lists for this purpose.

A second type of list enhancement involves incorporating information from external databases into a house list. Here the number of names and addresses remains the same, but an organization ends up with a more complete description of who its customers are. Typically, this kind of enhancement includes any of four categories of information:

- *Demographic data*—the basic descriptors of individuals and households available from the Census Bureau.
- *Geodemographic data*—information that reveals the characteristics of the neighborhood in which a person resides.
- *Psychographic data*—data that allow for a more qualitative assessment of a customer's general lifestyle, interests, and opinions.
- *Behavioral data*—information about other products and services a customer has purchased; prior purchases can help reveal a customer's preferences.

List enhancements that entail merging existing records with new information rely on software that allows the database manager to match records based on some piece of information the two lists share. For example, matches might be achieved by sorting on zip codes and street addresses. Many suppliers gather and maintain databases that can be used for list enhancement. One of the biggest is InfoUSA of Omaha, Nebraska (see http://www.infousa.com). With over 200 million people in its database, and literally dozens of pieces of information about each person, InfoUSA offers exceptional capabilities for list enhancement. Because of the massive size of the InfoUSA database, it has a high match rate (60 to 80 percent) when it is merged with clients' internal lists. A more common match rate between internal and external lists is around 50 percent.

The Marketing Database. Mailing lists come in all shapes and sizes, and by enhancing internal lists they obviously can become rich sources of information about customers. But for a mailing list to qualify as a marketing database, one important additional type of information is required. Although a marketing database can be viewed as a natural extension of an internal mailing list, a **marketing database** also includes information collected directly from individual customers. Developing a marketing database involves pursuing dialogues with customers and learning about their individual preferences and behavioral patterns. This can be potent information for hatching marketing programs that will hit the mark with consumers.

Aided by the dramatic escalation in processing power that comes from every new generation of computer chip, marketers see the chance to gather and manage more information about every individual who buys, or could buy, from them. Their goal might be portrayed as an attempt to cultivate a kind of cybernetic intimacy with the customer. A marketing database represents an organization's collective memory, which allows the organization to make the kind of personalized offer that once was characteristic of the corner grocer in small-town America. For example, working in conjunction with The Ohio State University Alumni Association, Lands' End created a special autumn promotion to offer OSU football fans all their favorite gear just in time for the upcoming session. Prints ads in the September issue of the OSU alumni magazine set the stage for a special catalog of merchandise mailed to Buckeye faithful. Of course, Lands' End had similar arrangements with other major universities

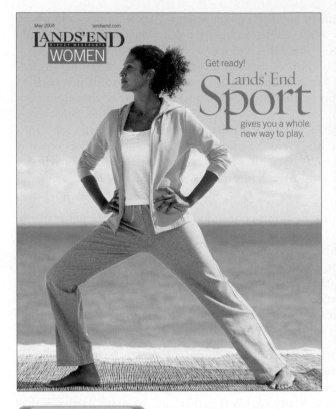

EXHIBIT 19.7

Lands' End for Women.

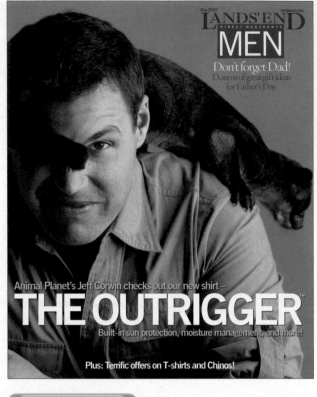

EXHIBIT 19.8

Lands' End for Men.

to tap into fall football frenzy. Database marketing at its best puts an offer in the hands of the consumer that is both relevant and timely. That's cybernetic intimacy.

Database marketing can also yield important efficiencies that contribute to the marketer's bottom line. As suggested in Exhibits 19.7 and 19.8, Lands' End found it useful to create separate "his" and "hers" versions of it base or core catalog. Why? The gender-specific catalogs runs about 50 pages in length, versus 108 for the core catalog. A customer qualifies to receive the "his" or "hers" version if he or she has purchased five or more men's only or women's only items in the past. The separate catalogs don't yield any new revenues, but they help control costs for things like postage, paper, and printing. Steady revenues with lowered costs can only mean one thing: more profits!

It certainly is the case that a marketing database can have many valuable applications. Before we look at more of these applications, let's review the terminology introduced thus far. We now have seen that direct marketers use mailing lists, enhanced mailing lists, and/or marketing databases as the starting points for developing many of their programs. The crucial distinction between a mailing list and a marketing database is that the latter includes direct input from customers. Building a marketing database entails pursuing an ongoing dialogue with customers and continuous updating of records with new information, as illustrated in the Creativity box. While mailing lists can be rich sources of information for program development, a marketing database has a dynamic quality that sets it apart.

Marketing Database Applications. Many different types of customer-communication programs are driven by marketing databases. One of the greatest benefits of a database is that it allows an organization to quantify how much business the organization is actually doing with its current best customers. A good way to isolate the best customers is with a recency, frequency, and monetary (RFM) analysis.[18] An **RFM analysis** asks how recently and how often a specific customer is buying from a company, and how much money he or she is spending per order and over time. With this transaction data, it is a simple matter to calculate the value of every customer to the organization and identify customers that have given the organization the most business in the past. Past behavior is an excellent predictor of future behavior, so yesterday's best customers are likely to be any organization's primary source of future business.

A marketing database can be a powerful tool for organizations that seek to create a genuine relationship with their best customers. The makers of Ben & Jerry's ice cream have used their database in two ways: to find out how customers react to potential new flavors and product ideas, and to involve their customers in social causes.[19] In one program, their goal was to find 100,000 people in their marketing database who would volunteer to work with Ben & Jerry's to support the Children's Defense Fund. Jerry Greenfield, cofounder of Ben & Jerry's, justifies the program as follows: "We are not some nameless conglomerate that only looks at how much money we make every year. I think the opportunity to use our business and particularly the power of our business as a force for progressive social change is exciting."[20] Of course, when customers feel genuine involvement with a brand like Ben & Jerry's, they also turn out to be very loyal customers.

CREATIVITY

Cybernetic Intimacy Meets the NASCAR Fan

When Josh Linkler was young, he bought a lot of Cracker Jacks in hopes of finding decoder rings as his sticky surprise. Always intrigued by the decoder mystic, he used it as the big idea in launching a new marketing service. His company, ePrize, uses decoder contests to drive curious customers to the Web, where they can play games online and in the process provide information about themselves and their interests. Just like that, we have the makings of a marketing database.

In one application Linkler worked with the Michigan International Speedway to build a database to unlock the secrets of NASCAR fans. It all starts with mass distribution of e-decoder game pieces, through ticket-order envelopes, movie theaters, and Pepsi retailers. The game pieces encourage NASCAR fans to go online to win prizes like a $10,000 garage makeover from Gladiator Garage Works (part of Whirlpool Corp. in Benton Harbor, Mich.). First-time players are required to give their name, address, e-mail, age, and gender. With each return visit, more questions must be answered to go deeper into the game. Ultimately, the database gets enriched with answers to something like 150 demographic and lifestyle questions. There are also specific questions dealing with leisure-time pursuits like camping and fishing, and specific questions like "Do you shop at Cabela's?"

Detailed insights about NASCAR fans help advertisers to connect with them via personalized offers that are timely and relevant. For example, Cabela's, a huge outdoor sports retailer in Dundee, Michigan, can target just the right offers to hunters versus campers versus boaters versus fisherman in the ePrize database. But in this age of privacy concerns, why are these NASCAR fans so willing to divulge their personal information? Well, not all are willing, but Josh Linkler sees it simply as an issue of value. According to Linkler, "If you want consumers to speak to you and provide information, you have to give them something to get them to react." Apparently, the combination of a decoder game and a $10,000 Grand Prize can be pretty hard to resist.

Source: Kris Oser, "Speedway Effort Decodes NASCAR Fans," *Advertising Age*, May 17, 2004, 150

Reinforcing and recognizing your best customers is an essential application of the marketing database. This application may be nothing more than a simple follow-up letter that thanks customers for their business or reminds them of the positive features of the brand to reassure them that they made the right choice. Since date of birth is a common piece of information in a marketing database, it naturally follows that another great time to contact customers is on their birthday. Sunglass Hut International uses a birthday card mailing as part of its program to stay in a dialogue with its best customers. Of course, everyone likes a little birthday present too, so along with the card Sunglass Hut includes a Customer Appreciation Check for $20 (shown in Exhibit 19.9) good at any Sunglass Hut store nationwide. Sunglass Hut executives

---

18. Rob Jackson and Paul Wang, *Strategic Database Marketing* (Lincolnwood, Ill.: NTC Business Books, 1994).

19. Murray Raphel, "What's the Scoop on Ben & Jerry?" *Direct Marketing Magazine*, August 1994, 23, 24.

20. Ibid.

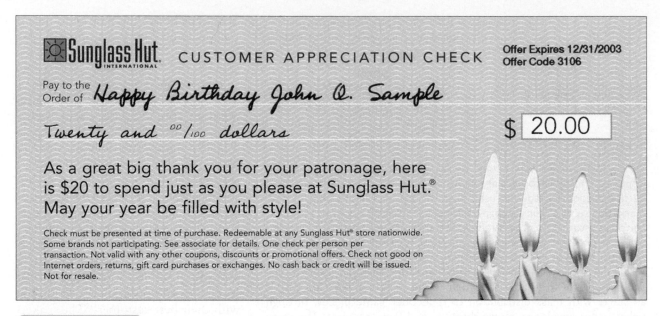

EXHIBIT 19.9

Think of your "best customer" as your most profitable customer. For most businesses, spending more advertising and promotional dollars to win more business from best customers is often money well spent. The real gold lies in not just one purchase, but in a continuous stream of purchases. Can a person ever have too many pairs of cool shades?

maintain that this birthday card promotion, targeted to current best customers identified from their marketing database, is one of their best investments of advertising dollars.

To recognize and reinforce the behaviors of preferred customers, marketers in many fields are offering frequency-marketing programs that provide concrete rewards to frequent customers. **Frequency-marketing programs** have three basic elements: a *database,* which is the collective memory for the program; a *benefit package,* which is designed to attract and retain customers; and a *communication strategy,* which emphasizes a regular dialogue with the organization's best customers.

The casino industry is renowned for its application of frequency-marketing principles, and Harrah's Entertainment has set the standard for program innovation.[21] Harrah's "Total Rewards" program started out as a way for its 27 million members to accumulate points that could be cashed in for free meals and other casino amenities. This is a good, simple approach, which was quickly copied by the competition. Harrah's subsequently upgraded its program on a number of dimensions. One involved the benefit package: Harrah's upped the ante. Now points can be used for Sony televisions and shopping sprees at Macy's. Harrah's also recognized that it needed separate reward packages for men and women, especially since women make up the majority of its customers. So for the men there are Big Bertha golf clubs and tickets to boxing matches; for the ladies, spa treatments and an evening with Chippendale dancers. That's innovation, Las Vegas style.

Another common application for the marketing database is **cross-selling.**[22] Since most organizations today have many different products or services they hope to sell, one of the best ways to build business is to identify customers who already purchase some of a firm's products and create marketing programs aimed at these customers but featuring other products. If they like our ice cream, perhaps we should also encourage them to try our frozen yogurt. If they have a checking account with

21.　Christina Binkley, "Harrah's Is Revamping Rewards Plan," *Wall Street Journal,* June 17, 2003, D4.
22.　Jackson and Wang, *Strategic Database Marketing.*

us, can we interest them in a credit card? If customers dine in our restaurants on Fridays and Saturdays, with the proper incentives perhaps we can get them to dine with us midweek, when we really need the extra business. A marketing database can provide a myriad of opportunities for cross-selling.

A final application for the marketing database is a natural extension of cross-selling. Once an organization gets to know who its current customers are and what they like about various products, it is in a much stronger position to go out and seek new customers. Knowledge about current customers is especially valuable when an organization is considering purchasing external mailing lists to append to its marketing database. If a firm knows the demographic characteristics of current customers—knows what they like about products, knows where they live, and has insights about their lifestyles and general interests—then the selection of external lists will be much more efficient. The basic premise here is simply to try to find prospects who share many of the same characteristics and interests with current customers. And what's the best vehicle for coming to know the current, best customers? Marketing-database development.

The Privacy Concern. One very large dark cloud looms on the horizon for database marketers: consumers' concerns about invasion of privacy. It is easy for marketers to gather a wide variety of information about consumers, and this is making the general public nervous. Many consumers are uneasy about the way their personal information is being gathered and exchanged by businesses and the government without their knowledge, participation, or consent. Of course, the Internet only amplifies these concerns because the Web makes it easier for all kinds of people and organizations to get access to personal information.

In response to public opinion, state and federal lawmakers have proposed and sometimes passed legislation to limit businesses' access to personal information. Additionally, consumers' desire for privacy was clearly the motivation for the launch of the Federal Trade Commission's Do Not Call Registry. It has proved to be a very popular idea with consumers, but has many opponents in business, including the Direct Marketing Association.[23] The DMA estimates that the list could cost telemarketers on the order of $50 billion in lost sales. How much the "do not call" list will ultimately mean to both sides remains to be seen. If you are one of those people who would like to do more to protect the privacy of your personal information, you can start with a visit to http://www.ftc.gov/privacy/protect.htm.

As suggested by Exhibit 19.10, many in business are keenly aware of consumers' concerns about the privacy of their personal information. Companies can address customers' concerns about privacy if they remember two fundamental premises of database marketing. First, a primary goal for developing a marketing database is to get to know customers in such a way that an organization can offer them products and services that better meet their needs. The whole point of a marketing database is to keep junk mail to a minimum by targeting only exciting and relevant programs to customers. If customers are offered something of value, they will welcome being in the database.

Second, developing a marketing database is about creating meaningful, long-term relationships with customers. If you want someone's trust and loyalty, would you collect personal information from them and then sell it to a third party behind their back? We hope not! When collecting information from customers, an organization must help them understand why it wants the information and how it will use it. If the organization is planning on selling this information to a third party, it must get customers' permission. If the organization pledges that the information will

23.   Yochi Dreazen, "'Do Not Call' Roster Debuts Today," *Wall Street Journal,* June 27, 2003, B2; David Ho, "Do-Not-Call List Grows to More Than 10M," http://www.apnews.excite.com, accessed July 1, 2003.

EXHIBIT 19.10

This Orwellian ad paints a dark picture of our future if database marketers go unchecked. There is definitely something about the Internet that has heightened people's concerns about who is in control of their personal information. Who controls your personal information? Does it matter to you? How might the Online Privacy Alliance (http://www.privacyalliance.org) keep database marketers from going too far with personal information?

remain confidential, it must honor that pledge. Integrity is fundamental to all meaningful relationships, including those involving direct marketers and their customers. Recall that it was his integrity as much as anything else that enabled L. L. Bean to launch his successful career as a direct marketer. It will work for you too.

3 Media Applications in Direct Marketing.
While mailing lists and marketing databases are the focal point for originating most direct marketing programs, information and arguments need to be communicated to customers in implementing these programs. As we saw in the definition of direct marketing offered earlier in this chapter, multiple media can be deployed in program implementation, and some form of immediate, measurable response is typically an overriding goal. The immediate response desired may be an actual order for services or merchandise, a request for more information, or the acceptance of a free trial offer. Because advertising conducted in direct marketing campaigns is typified by this emphasis on immediate response, it is commonly referred to as **direct response advertising.**

As you probably suspect, **direct mail** and **telemarketing** are the direct marketer's prime media. However, all conventional media, such as magazines, radio, and television, can be used to deliver direct response advertising; nowadays, a wide array of companies are also deploying e-mail as a most economical means of interacting with customers. In addition, a dramatic transformation of the television commercial—the infomercial—has become especially popular in direct marketing. Let's begin our examination of these media options by considering the advantages and disadvantages of the dominant devices—direct mail and telemarketing.

Direct Mail. Direct mail has some notable faults as an advertising medium, not the least of which is cost. It can cost 15 to 20 times more to reach a person with a direct mail piece than it would to reach that person with a television commercial or newspaper advertisement.[24] Additionally, in a society where people are constantly on the move, mailing lists are commonly plagued by bad addresses. Each bad address represents advertising dollars wasted. And direct mail delivery dates, especially for bulk, third-class mailings, can be unpredictable. When the timing of an advertising message is critical to its success, direct mail can be the wrong choice.

But as suggested by the ad from the U.S. Postal Service in Exhibit 19.11, there will be times when direct mail is the right choice. Direct mail's advantages stem from the selectivity of the medium. When an advertiser begins with a database of prospects, direct mail can be the perfect vehicle for reaching those prospects with little waste. Also, direct mail is a flexible medium that allows message adaptations on literally a household-by-household basis. For example, through surveys conducted with its 15 million U.S. subscribers, *Reader's Digest* amassed a huge marketing database detailing the health problems of specific subscribers.[25] In the database are 771,000 people with arthritis, 679,000 people with high blood pressure, 206,000 people with osteoporosis, 460,000 smokers, and so on. Using this information, *Reader's Digest* sends its subscribers disease-specific booklets containing advice on coping with their afflictions, wherein it sells advertising space to drug companies that have a tailored message that they want to communicate to those with a particular problem. This kind of precise targeting of tailored messages is the hallmark of direct marketing.

Direct mail as a medium also lends itself to testing and experimentation. With direct mail it is common to test two or more different appeal letters using a modest budget and a small sample of households. The goal is to establish which version yields the largest response. When a winner is decided, that form of the letter is backed by big-budget dollars in launching the organization's primary campaign.

Additionally, the array of formats an organization can send to customers is substantial with direct mail. It can mail large, expensive brochures; videotapes; computer disks; or CDs. It can use pop-ups, foldouts, scratch-and-sniff strips, or a simple, attractive postcard, as in Exhibit 19.12. If a product can be described in a limited space with minimal graphics, there really is no need to get fancy with the direct mail piece. The double postcard (DPC) format has an established track record of outperforming more expensive and elaborate direct mail packages.[26] Moreover, if an organization follows U.S. postal service guidelines carefully in mailing DPCs, the pieces can go out as first-class mail for reasonable rates. Since the Postal Service supplies address corrections on all first-class mail, using DPCs usually turns out to be a winner on either CPI or CPO measures, and DPCs can be an effective tool for cleaning up the bad addresses in a mailing list!

EXHIBIT 19.11

The U.S. postal service is saying, Use our services to drive consumers to your Web site. They make a great point: With millions of Web sites out there in cyberspace, you really must find economical ways to help people notice yours. For more help reaching qualified visitors, they suggest you visit—where else?—their Web site, http://www .uspsdirectmail.com.

24.   Stone, *Successful Direct Marketing Methods.*
25.   Sally Beatty, "Drug Companies Are Minding Your Business," *Wall Street Journal,* April 17, 1998, B1, B3.
26.   Michael Edmondson, "Postcards from the Edge," *Marketing Tools,* May 1995, 14.

This postcard for Fleece and Flannel announces the Grand Opening of its new store in Livingston, Montana. In that part of the world, it's perfectly natural to select a fly-fishing guide and guru to serve as your spokeswoman. Learn more about either at www.MontanaFleeceAnd Flannel.com *or* www .montana.org.

Telemarketing. Telemarketing is probably the direct marketer's most invasive tool. As with direct mail, contacts can be selectively targeted, the impact of programs is easy to track, and experimentation with different scripts and delivery formats is simple and practical. Because telemarketing involves real, live, person-to-person dialogue, no medium produces better response rates. Telemarketing shares many of direct mail's limitations. Telemarketing is very expensive on a cost-per-contact basis, and just as names and addresses go bad as people move, so do phone numbers. Further, telemarketing does not share direct mail's flexibility in terms of delivery options. When you reach people in their home or workplace, you have a limited amount of time to convey information and request some form of response.

If you have a telephone, you already know the biggest concern with telemarketing. It is a powerful yet highly intrusive medium that must be used with discretion. High-pressure telephone calls at inconvenient times can alienate customers. Telemarketing will give best results over the long run if it is used to maintain constructive dialogues with existing customers and qualified prospects.

E-Mail. Perhaps the most controversial tool deployed of late by direct marketers has been unsolicited or "bulk" e-mail. Commonly referred to as spam, this junk e-mail can get you in big trouble with consumers. In a worst-case scenario, careless use of the e-mail tool can earn one's company the label of a "spammer," and because of the community-oriented character of Internet communications, can then be a continuing source of negative buzz. But is this discouraging direct marketers from deploying this tool? Hardly. Consumers received something in the neighborhood of 833 billion e-mail messages from direct marketers in 2004, and that number was projected to pass a trillion in 2005.[27] It does make you wonder, with so much spam out there, and with so many who hate it, why is there more all the time? The Controversy box tackles this weighty question.

27. Kris Oser, "ISPs Band Together to Fight Spam," *Advertising Age,* June 28, 2004, 8.

There definitely is a school of thought that says some consumers are not averse to receiving targeted e-mail advertisements, and that as the Internet continues to evolve as an increasingly commercial medium, those companies that observe proper etiquette on the Net (dare we say "Netiquette"?) will be rewarded through customer loyalty.[28] The key premise of netiquette is to get the consumer's permission to send information about specific products or services, or, to use the current buzzword, they must "opt in." This opt-in premise has spawned a number of e-marketing service providers who claim to have constructed e-mail lists of consumers who have "opted in" for all manner of products and services. Exhibit 19.13 features an ad from one firm that worked diligently to make e-mail marketing a workable alternative for conscientious advertisers. Others now promise large lists of consumers who have agreed to receive commercial e-mails (e.g., see http://www.infousa.com or http://www.dblink.com). As noted in Exhibit 19.13, the future of direct marketing may be in reaching those people who have already said "Yes."

Our advice is to stay away from the low-cost temptations of bulk e-mail. The quickest way to get flamed and damage your brand name is to start sending out bulk e-mails to people who do not want to hear from you. Instead, through database development, ask your customers for permission to contact them via e-mail. Honor their requests. Don't abuse the privilege by selling their e-mail addresses to other companies, and when you do contact them, have something important to say. Seth Godin, whose 1999 book *Permission Marketing* really launched the "opt-in" mindset, puts it this way: "The best way to make your [customer] list worthless is to sell it. The future is, this list is mine and it's a secret."[29] Isn't it funny—you can imagine L. L. Bean feeling exactly the same way about his customer list 95 years ago.

CONTROVERSY

Meet a Spam Queen

Everybody hates spam. Which raises the question, why is there more all the time? Well, it is probably not accurate to say that everybody hates spam. Laura Betterly prefers to call it commercial or bulk e-mail, and she certainly doesn't hate it. After all, she makes her living by delivering bulk e-mail, direct from her home office to you. The company that Betterly founded with three of her friends, Data Resources Consulting, can send out as many as 60 million e-mail messages a month.

The crown jewel of DRC is its database of 100 million e-mail addresses. Betterly assembled it from a number of sources, including Excite, About.com, and Ms. Cleo's psychic Web site. Like most spammers, she also makes money by selling e-mail addresses to other bulk e-mailers, and she is always looking to add more names to her database when the price is right. While large companies too are in the business of sending unsolicited, bulk e-mail, a large part of this industry is small entrepreneurs like Laura Betterly and DRC. There's nothing hard about it.

Now here's the secret as to why there is more spam all the time—it's a profitable business. According to Betterly, depending on the commission she negotiates, it is possible to make money on a bulk e-mailing when as few as 100 people respond out of a mailing of 10 million. No doubt spammers are able to survive with response rates that could never work for the paper-junk mailer. For "snail mail" the direct marketer is typically looking for a response of 2 percent or better to turn a profit on the program. For bulk e-mail, profits kick in with a response rate of 0.001 percent. Sometimes you wonder how anyone would respond to the kinds of messages we all receive in our e-mail boxes, but the point is, if 1 out of 1,000 responds, Betterly is making money. Those are pretty good odds.

"I'm just trying to make a living like everyone else," is how Laura Betterly sees it. Because of Data Resources Consulting, she can raise her two children comfortably and spend lots of quality time with them. "You can call me a spam queen if you want," she says. "As long as I'm not breaking any laws, you don't have to love me or like what I do for a living."

Sources: Mylene Mangalindan, "Web Vigilantes Give Spammers a Big Dose of Their Medicine," *Wall Street Journal,* May 19, 2003, A1, A13; Mylene Mangalindan, "For Bulk E-Mailer, Pestering Millions Offers a Path to Profit," *Wall Street Journal,* November 13, 2002, A1, A17.

28.   Cara Beardi, "Opt-In Taken to Great Heights," *Advertising Age,* November 6, 2000, S54; Michael Battisto, "Preparation Yields Spam-Free E-mail Lists," *Marketing News,* February 17, 2003, 17.

29.   Jodi Mardesich, "Too Much of a Good Thing," *Industry Standard,* March 19, 2001, 85.

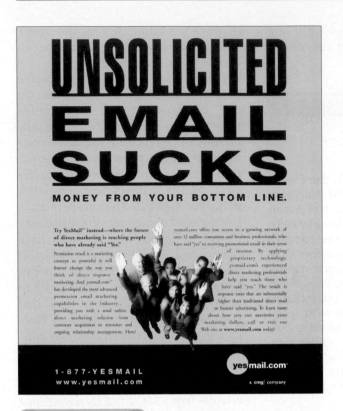

Purveyors of permission e-mail have sprung up like mushrooms in the forest after a rain. It is hard to argue with the premise that Unsolicited Email Sucks. Wouldn't you agree? http://www.yesmail.com

Direct Response Advertising in Other Media. Direct marketers have experimented with many other methods in trying to convey their appeals for a customer response. In magazines, a popular device for executing a direct marketer's agenda is the bind-in insert card. Thumb through a copy of any magazine and you will see how effective these light-cardboard inserts are in stopping the reader and calling attention to themselves. Insert cards not only promote their product, but also offer the reader an easy way to order things such as Murray's All-Natural Chicken Dinner Kit from http://www.epicurious.com, request a free sample of Skoal smokeless tobacco, or select those 12 CDs for the price of one that will make the reader a member of the BMG Music Club.

When AT&T introduced the first 800 number in 1967, it simply could not have known how important this service would become to direct marketing. Newspaper ads from the *Wall Street Journal* provide toll-free numbers for requesting everything from really cheap online trading services (800-619-SAVE) to leasing a Learjet 40 (800-FLEXJET). If you watch late-night TV, you may know the 800 number to call to order the Grammy-winning CD by Walter Ostanek and his polka band. Finally, magazine ads like the one shown in Exhibit 19.14 out of *Bon Appetit* are commonly used to provide an 800 number to initiate contact with customers. As these diverse examples indicate, toll-free numbers make it possible to use nearly any medium for direct response purposes.

Infomercials. The infomercial is a novel form of direct response advertising that merits special mention. An **infomercial** is fundamentally just a long television advertisement made possible by the lower cost of ad space on many cable and satellite channels. They range in length from 2 to 60 minutes, but the common length is 30 minutes. Although producing an infomercial is more like producing a television program than it is like producing a 30-second commercial, infomercials are all about selling. There appear to be several keys to successful use of this unique vehicle.

A critical factor is testimonials from satisfied users. Celebrity testimonials can help catch a viewer as he or she is channel surfing past the program, but celebrities aren't necessary, and, of course, they add to the production costs. Whether testimonials are from celebrities or from folks just like us, one expert summarizes matters this way: "Testimonials are so important that without them your chances of producing a profitable infomercial diminish hugely."[30]

Another key point to remember about infomercials is that viewers are not likely to stay tuned for the full 30 minutes. An infomercial is a 30-minute direct response sales pitch, not a classic episode of *South Park* or *The Simpsons*. The implication here is that the call to action should come not just at the end of the infomercial; most of the audience could be long gone by minute 28 into the show. A good rule of thumb in a 30-minute infomercial is to divide the program into 10-minute increments and close three times.[31] Each closing should feature the 800 number or Web address that

---

30. Herschell Gordon Lewis, "Information on Infomercials," *Direct Marketing Magazine,* March 1995, 30–32.
31. Ibid.

The World's Best Hotels use the 8-pound Oreck XL. What are you waiting for, a free $100 Iron?

Luxury Suite, Windsor Court, selected by Condé Nast Traveler as the best hotel in the world.

The $100 Cordless Oreck Speed Iron™ is yours free just for trying the Oreck XL risk free for 30 days.

Strong Enough To Pick Up A 16-lb. Bowling Ball.™ It's the perfect above-the-floor vacuum. This $165 value is yours free with purchase of the 8-lb. Oreck XL.

1-800-471-1891 ext. **BK458**

Visit oreck.com or mail in this coupon today BK458

☐ Yes, please call me to arrange a free 30-day home trial of the 8-lb. Oreck XL and send me a **free $100 Oreck Speed Iron™** just for taking our risk-free, 30-Day Oreck Challenge. I understand **I will receive the Super Compact Canister free with purchase.**
☐ Please send me a free information kit on the amazing Oreck XL.
☐ Also include details of Oreck's 12-month Interest Free Payment Plan.

Name_____
Address_____ City_____
State _____ Zip_____ Tel (____)_____

ORECK
Nothing gets by an Oreck.®   PNN5R
Oreck Direct, LLC 100 Plantation Road, New Orleans, LA 70123

EXHIBIT 19.14

Nothing fancy here. Just good, sound direct marketing.
http://www.oreck.com

allows the viewer to order the product or request more information. And an organization should not offer information to the customer unless it can deliver speedy follow-up; same-day response should be the goal in pursuing leads generated by an infomercial.

Many different types of products and services have been marketed using infomercials, and now via Internet extensions such as http://www.iqvc .com. CD players, self-help videos, home exercise equipment, kitchen appliances, and Annette Funicello Collectible Bears have all had success with the infomercial. While it is easy to associate the infomercial with things such as the Ronco Showtime Rotisserie & BBQ (yours for just four easy payments of $39.95!), many familiar brands have experimented with this medium. Brand marketers such as Quaker State, America Online, Primestar, Lexus, Monster.com, Hoover, Kal Kan, Pontiac, and yes, Mercedes-Benz, have all used infomercials to help inform consumers about their offerings.[32]

4 The Coordination Challenge Revisited.

As you have seen throughout this book, the wide variety of media available to an advertiser poses a tremendous challenge with respect to coordination and integration. Organizations are looking to achieve the synergy that can come when various media options reach the consumer with a common and compelling message. However, to work in various media, functional specialists both inside and outside an organization need to be employed. It then becomes a very real problem to get the advertising manager, special events manager, sales promotion manager, and Web designer to work in harmony.[33] And now we must add to the list of functional specialists the direct marketing or database manager.

The evolution and growing popularity of direct marketing raise the challenge of achieving integrated communication to new heights. In particular, the development of a marketing database commonly leads to interdepartmental rivalries and can create major conflicts between a company and its advertising agency. The marketing database is a powerful source of information about the customer; those who do not have direct access to this information will be envious of those who do. Additionally, the growing use of direct marketing campaigns

32. Kathy Haley, "Infomercials Score for Brand-Name Advertisers," *Advertising Age,* September 8, 1997, A1, A2; Evantheia Schibsted, "Ab Rockers, Ginsu Knives, E320s," *Business 2.0,* May 29, 2001, 46–49; Jean Halliday, "Pontiac Models Get Infomercial Push," *Advertising Age,* April 19, 2004, 12.

33. Laura Q. Hughes and Kate MacArthur, "Soft Boiled," *Advertising Age,* May 28, 2001, 3, 54; Klein, "Disintegrated Marketing," 18,19.

must mean that someone else's budget is being cut. Typically, direct marketing programs come at the expense of conventional advertising campaigns that might have been run on television, in magazines, or in other mass media.[34] Since direct marketing takes dollars from activities that have been the staples of the traditional ad agency business, it is easy to see why a pure advertising guru like Saatchi's Kevin Roberts views direct marketing with some disdain.[35]

There are no simple solutions for achieving integrated communication, but one recommended approach is the establishment of a marketing communications manager, or "marcom" manager for short.[36] A **marcom manager** plans an organization's overall communications program and oversees the various functional specialists inside and outside the organization to ensure that they are working together to deliver the desired brand-building message to the customer.

General Motors is one company that is learning how to pull the pieces together to make the right impression with consumers.[37] In 1992 General Motors launched the GM Card, and now maintains a database of about 4 million active cardholders. With this marketing database, special offers and incentives can be sent to persons who have given GM permission to contact them with information at specific times about specific models. One such mailing to more than a million cardholders leveraged a corporate advertising campaign developed by McCann Erickson, which had ads placed in national TV and print media. Cardholders used their savings that had accrued in using the GM card to complement the incentives offered in GM's nationwide "Overdrive" campaign. The results tell the story: Within two weeks of the mailing, General Motors recorded four of its top 10 new-vehicle sales days since the launch of the GM Card. More evidence to support the thesis that integrated programs are more effective than the sum of their parts.

The GM example amplifies a theme developed throughout this book. Perhaps the major challenge in the world of advertising today is to find ways to break through the clutter of competitors' ads—and really all advertising in general—to get customers' attention and make a point with them. If the various media and programs an organization employs are sending different messages or mixed signals, the organization is only hurting itself. To achieve the synergy that will allow it to overcome the clutter of today's marketplace, an organization has no choice but to pursue advertising and integrated brand promotion.

34.   Kate Fitzgerald, "Beyond Advertising," *Advertising Age,* August 3, 1998, 1, 14.
35.   Alessandra Galloni, "Is Saatchi Helping Publicis Bottom Line?" *Wall Street Journal,* June 22, 2001, B6.
36.   Don E. Schultz, Stanley I. Tannenbaum, and Robert F. Lauterborn, *Integrated Marketing Communications* (Lincolnwood, IL: NTC Business Books, 1993).
37.   Jean Halliday, "GM Plays Cards Right," *Advertising Age,* May 27, 2002, 45.

SUMMARY

 Identify the three primary purposes served by direct marketing and explain its growing popularity.

Many types of organizations are increasing their expenditures on direct marketing. These expenditures serve three primary purposes: direct marketing offers potent tools for closing sales with customers, for identifying prospects for future contacts, and for offering information and incentives that help foster brand loyalty. The growing popularity of direct marketing can be attributed to several factors. Direct marketers make consumption convenient: Credit cards, 800 numbers, and the Internet take the hassle out of shopping. Additionally, today's computing power, which allows marketers to build and mine large customer information files, has enhanced direct marketing's impact. The emphasis on producing and tracking measurable outcomes is also well received by marketers in an era when everyone is trying to do more with less.

 Distinguish a mailing list from a marketing database and review the many applications of each.

A mailing list is a file of names and addresses of current or potential customers, such as lists that might be generated by a credit card company or a catalog retailer. Internal lists are valuable for creating relationships with current customers, and external lists are useful in generating new customers. A marketing database is a natural extension of the internal list, but includes information about individual customers and their specific preferences and purchasing patterns. A marketing database allows organizations to identify and focus their efforts on their best customers. Recognizing and reinforcing preferred customers can be a potent strategy for building loyalty. Cross-selling opportunities also emerge once a database is in place. In addition, as one gains keener information about the motivations of current best customers, insights usually emerge about how to attract new customers.

 Describe the prominent media used by direct marketers in delivering their messages to the customer.

Direct marketing programs emanate from mailing lists and databases, but there is still a need to deliver a message to the customer. Direct mail and telemarketing are the most common means used in executing direct marketing programs. E-mail has recently emerged as a low-cost alternative. Because the advertising done as part of direct marketing programs typically requests an immediate response from the customer, it is known as direct response advertising. Conventional media such as television, newspapers, magazines, and radio can also be used to request a direct response by offering an 800 number or a Web address to facilitate customer contact.

 Articulate the added challenge created by direct marketing for achieving integrated brand promotion.

Developing a marketing database, selecting a direct mail format, or producing an infomercial are some of the tasks attributable to direct marketing. These and other related tasks require more functional specialists, who further complicate the challenge of presenting a coordinated face to the customer. Some organizations employ marcom managers, who are assigned the task of coordinating the efforts of various functional specialists working on different aspects of a marketing communications program. To achieve an integrated presence that will break through in a cluttered marketplace, this coordination is essential.

KEY TERMS

direct marketing
cost per inquiry (CPI)
cost per order (CPO)
mailing list
internal lists

external lists
marketing database
RFM analysis
frequency-marketing programs
cross-selling

direct response advertising
direct mail
telemarketing
infomercial
marcom manager

QUESTIONS

1. Who was Lester Wunderman, and in what ways does his historic campaign for Columbia House illustrate the mindset of direct marketing?

2. Direct marketing is defined as an interactive system of marketing. Explain the meaning of the term *interactive system* and give an example of a noninteractive system. How would an interactive system be helpful in the cultivation of brand loyalty?

3. Review the major forces that have promoted the growth in popularity of direct marketing. Can you come up with any reasons why its popularity might be peaking? What are the threats to its continuing popularity as a marketing approach?

4. Describe the various categories of information that a credit card company might use to enhance its internal mailing list. For each category, comment on the possible value of the information for improving the company's market segmentation strategy.

5. What is RFM analysis, and what is it generally used for? How would RFM analysis allow an organization to get more impact from a limited marketing budget? (Keep in mind that every organization views its marketing budget as too small to accomplish all that needs to be done.)

6. Compare and contrast frequency-marketing programs with the tools described in Chapter 18 under the heading "Sales Promotion Directed at Consumers." What common motivators do these two types of activities rely on? How are their purposes similar or different? What goal is a frequency-marketing program trying to achieve that would not be a prime concern with a sales promotion?

7. There's a paradox here, right? On the one hand, it is common to talk about building relationships and loyalty with the tools of direct marketing. On the other hand, direct-marketing tools such as junk e-mail and telephone interruptions at home during dinner are constant irritants. How does one build relationships by using irritants? In your opinion, when is it realistic to think that the tools of direct marketing could be used to build long-term relationships with customers?

8. What is it about direct marketing that makes its growing popularity a threat to the traditional advertising agency?

EXPERIENTIAL EXERCISES

1. This chapter discusses serious privacy concerns raised by database marketing. Today's marketers are gathering enormous amounts of information about individuals, and much of the database development occurs without the consent or awareness of consumers. Visit the following sites and explain the contribution of each to the issue of online privacy.

http://www.bbbonline.org

http://www.truste.com

2. Identify some of the recent direct mail and e-mail marketing items you have received. Did they target your relevant hobbies, interests, or work-related needs? If so, how did the marketer know of your specific interests? What previous consumer relationship have you had with these marketers, and do you react favorably to their direct marketing efforts? What convenience do consumers gain from today's direct marketing initiatives, and do you feel more loyalty to specific brands as a result of these efforts?

EXPERIENCING THE INTERNET

19-1 Don't Call Us, We'll Call You

The Federal Trade Commission's National Do Not Call Registry is one of the most popular and successful consumer-protection initiatives undertaken by the federal government. By signing up at the online registry, millions of American consumers have prohibited telemarketers from calling their personal phone numbers. Violators of the regulation face steep fines. Consumers' desire for privacy was the motivation for the launch of the FTC's "do not call" list, yet some groups angered by the initiative challenge its constitutionality. Visit the registry online and answer the following questions.

National Do Not Call Registry: http://www.donotcall .gov

1. Would you consider signing up at donotcall.gov to block telemarketers from calling your home phone number? Why or why not?

2. What groups might be opposed to the Do Not Call Registry, and why?

3. Do you think the National Do Not Call Registry violates the constitutional right to free speech? Explain.

19-2 Database Marketing

MyPoints.com is a leading provider of Internet direct marketing services. The company's service features a true "opt-in" database containing millions of members, and provides advertisers with an integrated suite of rewards-based media products that target, acquire, and retain customers. Web users can earn free rewards from name-brand merchants such as Target, Barnes & Noble Booksellers, and Blockbuster Video by regularly visiting Web sites, responding to targeted e-mail promotions, filling out surveys, shopping, or taking advantage of trial offers. The ultimate purpose of these rewards programs is to help marketers develop databases that track the shopping and surfing habits of Web consumers, resulting in more effective future marketing and advertising efforts.

MyPoints.com: http://www.mypoints.com

MyPoints.com Corporate Site: http://www.mypoints corp.com

1. Based on the definition in the text, is MyPoints.com an example of a frequency-marketing program? What are the three basic elements that constitute a frequency-marketing program?

2. Read over the company information on MyPoints.com and explain how members accumulate and redeem loyalty points. How can one spend and earn points?

3. Visit the MyPoint.com corporate site and read about its advertising solutions. Who are some clients that partner with MyPoints.com and what benefits do they receive? What are some of the ultimate benefits of database marketing?

CHAPTER 20

After reading and thinking about this chapter, you will be able to do the following:

1

Explain the role of public relations as part of an organization's overall integrated brand promotion strategy.

2

Detail the objectives and tools of public relations.

3

Describe how firms are using buzz and viral marketing in the public relations effort.

4

Describe two basic strategies motivating an organization's public relations activities.

5

Discuss the applications and objectives of corporate advertising.

Introductory Scenario: The Buzz Biz. Spin, buzz, hype, PR, word of mouth,

viral marketing—public relations goes by many names and has many variations and innuendoes. In the end, a good public relations campaign can have a powerful impact on a brand—positive or negative.

Consider the approach used by Handspring (now palmOne) when the firm introduced its new Treo 600 cell phone/PDA/digital camera combo to the market (see Exhibit 20.1). Typically, a feature-laden innovation like this would hit the market with a big ad campaign designed to attract widespread attention. But earlier models of the Treo were considered oversized and clumsy, and the firm needed new, positive "buzz" for the brand given the relatively negative buzz from previous launches.

To get the public relations machinery going, Jeff Hawkins, the Treo product designer and chairman of the firm, nonchalantly carried the Treo 600 into a corporate publicity shot months before its actual market release. Gear-heads went wild. Gadget Web sites like Treocentral.com latched on to this early glimpse of the device like the CIA to spy photos. From that point on, the buzz flames were fanned with high-tech reviews and blog flogging in full swing. To "manage" the publicity in the press, Handspring made only two dozen Treo 600s available, and those went to reviewers and journalists who had been favorably disposed to earlier models.[1] The buzz campaign unfolded this way:

- Week 1: The 600's release in Great Britain added to the mystique of the device and started a deafening chatter on gadget-freak Web sites like Gizmodo, which built huge anticipation in the United States. Bargainpda.com exclaimed, "At $500, it can't miss."
- Week 2: Handspring lifts its self-imposed press "embargo" in the United States and gives influential *Wall Street Journal* tech writer Walter S. Mossberg first crack at the product. Mossberg writes a glowing review: "Handspring has done it again. . . . I love it."
- Week 3: Coverage lags after the Mossberg review. The lull in national and local television coverage is a disappointment but tech Web sites are still talking up the 600 enough to keep the buzz alive.
- Week 5: The firm holds a press conference announcing narrower losses than expected by Wall Street. The launch of the new Treo is cited in every newscast and newspaper article. Typical of coverage is the CNET.com quote of Handspring CEO Donna Dubinsky: "Interest is tremendous and greater than we have seen in past launches."
- Week 6: Treo 600s are sent to celebrities for "trial" periods.

In the end, Biz360, a media analysis company, estimated that the PR campaign was worth the equivalent of $265,000 worth of advertising. That is likely a gross underestimation of impact, though, since it estimates only the "exposure" rather than the weight of a favorable review from an influential tech writer or a plug from a celebrity. Most importantly, the product introduction was a huge success. Over 100,000 Treo 600s were sold in the first month (despite a higher than originally anticipated $600 price tag); more than 250,000 were sold in the first nine months; and production was ramped up to turn out another 800,000 units.[2]

The launch of the Treo 600 shows that public relations—or buzz, hype, or spin, as it is often called—is a "behind the scenes" process. It does not "appear" to be controlled by the firm or its advertising and promotion agencies. Indeed, as we will see, much of the public relations process is uncontrollable—the reviewers, after all, could have hated the Treo 600 and killed the launch and the brand.

---

1.   Damon Darlin, "Anatomy of a Buzz Campaign," *Business 2.0,* December 2003, 70–71.
2.   Paul Keegan, "How Palm Got Cool Again," *Business 2.0,* June 2004, 92–98.

Before it employed widespread advertising, the Treo 600 launch relied heavily on public relations techniques to create a positive "buzz" in the market.

Throughout this chapter, we will discuss the many tools and a new, exciting era for public relations. Public relations has moved far beyond its traditional role of simply "dealing with" a firm's many "publics" or providing damage control for negative publicity.

Corporate advertising is the other major topic of this chapter. Corporate advertising uses major media to communicate a unique, broad-based message that is distinct from the typical brand advertising a firm might do. Corporate advertising contributes to the development of an overall image for a firm without touting an individual brand or the brand's unique features. While public relations and corporate advertising are rarely the foundation of an IBP program, they do represent key communications tools under certain conditions. We will explore the nature of these two specialized promotional tools and the conditions under which they are ideally suited for the IBP effort.

Public Relations. Public relations focuses on communication that can foster goodwill between a firm and its many constituent groups. These constituent groups include customers, stockholders, suppliers, employees, government entities, citizen action groups, and the general public. Public relations is used to highlight positive events in an organization like quarterly sales and profits or noteworthy community service programs carried out by the firm. Or, conversely, public relations is used strategically for "damage control" when adversity strikes an organization. In addition, new techniques in public relations have fostered a bolder, more aggressive role for PR in some IBP campaigns.

A New Era for Public Relations. A couple of corporate consultants have written a book, titled *The Fall of Advertising & The Rise of PR*, in which they try to argue that today's "major" brands are born with publicity, not advertising. And further, that advertising should be used only to *maintain* brands once they have been *established* through publicity. We all got a big laugh out of that! To say that you can base the entire foundational launch of a brand on an uncontrollable technique like publicity is indefensible. To say that public relations has entered a new era—that would be a very true statement.

The new era for public relations has pretty much been timed with the new century. As corporate strategists began to demand more "action" and visibility for their promotional dollars, advertising (primarily) bore the brunt of some pretty heavy criticism. At the top of the criticism list is the blast leveled by the head of General Motors marketing (remember, GM spends $3.5 billion a year on advertising alone), who said that traditional ad agencies are "soft and flabby" and that they no longer know how to "sell product by coming up with the big idea."[3] Before him, you had execs at PR agencies saying things like "I really do think that we're seeing the demise of advertising. What helps companies build their businesses is hard-working PR."[4]

3.   Betsy Streisand, "Why the Great American Brands Are Doing Lunch," *Business 2.0,* September 2003, 146.
4.   Laurie Freeman, "From the Basement to the Penthouse," *Advertising Age,* September 25, 2000, 40, 42.

But before we buy the proposition (especially from people who run PR agencies) that PR should be the centerpiece of every promotional effort, let's look at the current status of public relations in the array of promotional tools and get some perspective. First, in terms of perspective, let's consider the revenue stream of agencies who earn their money by providing services across the full array of promotional efforts. Only about 13 percent of all agency revenues are earned by providing PR services. The other 87 percent of revenue is generated by advertising and media, interactive, sales promotion, and direct marketing.[5] Second, growth in agency revenues was led by direct marketing and interactive media, not public relations services. Finally, as we saw in Chapters 1 and 2, firms are investing heavily in advertising and promotion as a way to both launch *and* maintain brands. Control of the message and its dissemination are key the brand building effort. Is public relations more important than it was five years ago? Absolutely. Will it replace advertising? Let's make sure we're clear on that point. No.

Public Relations and Damage Control. One reason public relations will always remain an important and unique component of integrated brand promotions is that PR serves a role that no other promotional tool can. Public relations is the one and only tool that can provide damage control from bad publicity. Such public relations problems can arise from either a firm's own activities or from external forces completely outside a firm's control. Let's consider two classic public relations incidents that occurred at highly visible companies—Intel and Pepsi—and the problems they faced. In one case, the firm caused its own public relations and publicity problems; in the other, an external, uncontrollable force created problems for the firm. Let's see how they handled these very different PR problems.

Intel is one of the great success stories of American industry. Intel has risen from relative techno-obscurity as an innovative computer technology company to one of the largest corporations in the world with one of the most visible brands (who doesn't know "Intel Inside?"). Sales have grown from $1.3 billion to more than $40 billion in just 25 years. But all this success did not prepare Intel for the one serious public relations challenge that the firm encountered. In early 1994, Intel introduced its new-generation chip, the now-well-known Pentium, as the successor to the widely used line of X86 chips. But in November 1994, Pentium users were discovering a flaw in the chip. During certain floating-point operations, some Pentium chips were actually producing erroneous calculations—and even though the error showed up in only the fifth or sixth decimal place, power users in scientific laboratories require absolute precision and accuracy in their calculations.

Having a defect in a high-performance technology product such as the Pentium chip was one thing; how Intel handled the problem was another. Intel's initial "official" response was that the flaw in the chip was so insignificant that it would produce an error in calculations only once in 27,000 years. But then IBM, which had shipped thousands of PCs with Pentium chips, challenged the assertion that the flaw was insignificant, claiming that processing errors could occur as often as every 24 days. IBM announced that it would stop shipment of all Pentium-based PCs immediately.[6]

From this point on, the Pentium situation became a runaway public relations disaster. Every major newspaper, network newscast, and magazine carried the story of the flawed Pentium chip. Even the cartoon series *Dilbert* got in on the act, running a whole series of cartoon strips that spoofed the Intel controversy (see Exhibit 20.2). One observer characterized it this way: "From a public relations standpoint, the train has left the station and is barreling out of Intel's control."[7] For weeks Intel did nothing but publicly argue that the flaw would not affect the vast majority of users.

5.   Kenneth Wylie, "Marketing Services Agencies—17th Annual Report," *Advertising Age,* May 17, 2004, S1.
6.   Barbara Grady, "Chastened Intel Steps Carefully with Introduction of New Chip," *Computerlink,* February 14, 1995, 11.
7.   James G. Kimball, "Can Intel Repair the Pentium PR?" *Advertising Age,* December 19, 1994, 35.

Source: Dilbert reprinted by permission of United Features Syndicate, Inc.

EXHIBIT 20.2

When Intel did not respond quickly and positively to problems with its Pentium chip, the press unloaded a barrage of negative publicity on the firm. Even Dilbert got into the act with this parody of Intel decision making.

Finally, in early 1995, Intel decided to provide a free replacement chip to any user who believed he or she was at risk. In announcing the $475 million program to replace customers' chips, Andy Grove, Intel's highly accomplished CEO, admitted publicly that "the Pentium processor divide problem has been a learning experience for Intel."[8]

Intel's public relations and publicity problems were mostly of its own doing. But in many cases, firms are faced with public relations crises that are totally beyond their control. One of these cases, which goes down in history as a classic, happened to PepsiCo. In 1993, Pepsi had a public relations nightmare on its hands. Complaints were coming in from all over the United States that cans of Pepsi, Diet Pepsi, and Caffeine Free Diet Pepsi had syringes inside them. Other callers claimed their cans of Pepsi contained such things as a screw, a crack vial, a sewing needle, and brown goo in the bottom. Unlike Intel, Pepsi immediately mobilized a management team to handle the crisis. The team considered a national recall of all Pepsi products—no matter what the cost. The Food and Drug Administration (FDA) told Pepsi there was no need for such action, since no one had been injured and there was no health risk. The Pepsi team was sure that this was not a case of tampering in the production facility. A can of Pepsi is filled with cola and then sealed in nine-tenths of a second—making it virtually impossible for anyone to get anything into a can during production.

The president of Pepsi went on national television to explain the situation and defend his firm and its products. Pepsi enlisted the aid of a powerful and influential constituent at this point—the Food and Drug Administration. The commissioner of the FDA, David Kessler, said publicly that many of the tampering claims could not be substantiated or verified. A video camera in Aurora, Colorado, caught a woman trying to insert a syringe into a Pepsi can. Pepsi was exonerated in the press, but the huge public relations problem had significantly challenged the firm to retain the stature and credibility of a truly global brand.

What happened to Intel and Pepsi highlights why public relations (and particularly publicity) is such a difficult form of communication to manage. In many cases, a firm's public relations program is called into action for damage control, as the Pepsi ad in Exhibit 20.3 illustrates. Intel and Pepsi had to be totally reactive to the situation rather than, as can be done with the other tools in the integrated communications process, strategically controlling it. But while many episodes of public relations must be reactive, a firm can be prepared with public relations materials to conduct an orderly and positive goodwill and image-building campaign among its many constituents. To fully appreciate the role and potential of public relations in the broad communications efforts of a firm, we will consider the objectives of public relations, the tools of public relations, and basic public relations strategies.

8.   Grady, "Chastened Intel Steps Carefully with Introduction of New Chip."

Pepsi is pleased
to announce...
...nothing.

As America now knows, those stories about Diet Pepsi were a hoax. Plain and simple, not true. Hundreds of investigators have found no evidence to support a single claim.

As for the many, many thousands of people who work at Pepsi-Cola, we feel great that it's over. And we're ready to get on with making and bringing you what we believe is the best-tasting diet cola in America.

There's not much more we can say. Except that most importantly, we won't let this hoax change our exciting plans for this summer.

We've set up special offers so you can enjoy our great quality products at prices that will save you money all summer long. It all starts on July 4th weekend and we hope you'll stock up with a little extra, just to make up for what you might have missed last week.

That's it. Just one last word of thanks to the millions of you who have stood with us.

**Drink All The Diet Pepsi You Want.
Uh Huh.**

DIET PEPSI and UH HUH are registered trademarks of PepsiCo Inc.

EXHIBIT 20.3

When the truth about the tampering with Pepsi cans was finally resolved, the firm took the opportunity for some positive public relations by running this ad. http://www.pepsi.com

2 Objectives for Public Relations.

Firms regularly encounter PR problems like Intel's and Pepsi's. Remember that a corporation is a complex business *and* social organization. As long as a firm has employees and operates facilities in a community, issues will arise. Recent examples of such issues are Nike and Boeing, very different kinds of companies but both encountering significant PR problems—Nike for its alleged "sweatshop" labor practices and Boeing for the ethical conduct of its now departed CEO Philip Condit.[9] But the key to dealing with events as they arise is to have a structured approach to public relations, including a clear understanding of objectives for PR. Within the broad guidelines of image building, damage control, and establishing relationships with constituents, it is possible to identify six primary objectives of public relations:

- *Promoting goodwill.* This is an image-building function of public relations. Industry events or community activities that reflect favorably on a firm are highlighted. When Pepsi launched a program to support school music programs—programs hard hit by funding decreases—the firm garnered widespread public relations goodwill.
- *Promoting a product or service.* Press releases, events, or brand "news" that increase public awareness of a firm's brands can be pursued through public relations. Large pharmaceutical firms such as Merck and GlaxoSmithKline issue press releases when new drugs are discovered or FDA approval is achieved. Or a great story about the brand like the Treo 600 can create widespread buzz as well. (See the Creativity box for another example of positive PR as a brand promotion effort.)
- *Preparing internal communications.* Disseminating information and correcting misinformation within a firm can reduce the impact of rumors and increase employee support. For events such as reductions in the labor force or mergers of firms, internal communications can do much to dispel rumors circulating among employees and in the local community.
- *Counteracting negative publicity.* This is the damage control function of public relations, as we discussed earlier. The attempt here is not to cover up negative events, but rather to prevent the negative publicity from damaging the image of a firm and its brands. When a lawsuit was filed against NEC alleging that one of its cellular phones had caused cancer, McCaw Cellular Communications used public relations activities to inform the public and especially cellular phone users of scientific knowledge that argued against the claims in the lawsuit. And one industry's public relations problems are another industry's golden opportunity, as the ad in Exhibit 20.4 shows.
- *Lobbying.* The public relations function can assist a firm in dealing with government officials and pending legislation. Microsoft reportedly spent $4.6 billion on such lobbying efforts when antitrust violations were leveled at the company. Industries maintain active and aggressive lobbying efforts at both the state and federal levels. As an example, the beer and wine industry has lobbyists monitoring legislation that could restrict beer and wine advertising.

9.   Stanley Holmes, "Free Speech or False Advertising," *BusinessWeek,* April 28, 2003, 69–70; Lorraine Woellert, "Why Boeing Is Suddenly Making So Much Noise," *BusinessWeek,* June 23, 2003, 35.

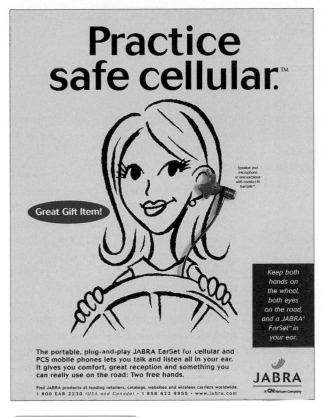

EXHIBIT 20.4

Public relations problems in one industry create opportunities in another. When medical research suggested that extensive cellular phone use could be linked to brain tumors, firms developed cell phone accessories to address the issue. Here, Jabra is alluding to the negative publicity and the medical research as the basis for its brand appeal. http://www.jabra.com

Tuesday, June 5, 6:30 A.M. Eastern Time
Press Release
SOURCE: Myriad Genetics, Inc.

Myriad Genetics Discovers High Cholesterol Gene
CHD2 Enzyme is in Novel Pathway, May Lead to New Class
of Cholesterol Lowering Drugs

Salt Lake City, June 5/PRNewswire/—Myriad Genetics, Inc. (NASDAQ: MYGN-news), has discovered a human gene responsible for high total cholesterol and low HDL (also known as "good cholesterol"), in individuals with early age myocardial infarction. The research shows that the gene's protein product is produced in abnormal amounts in these individuals and has enzymatic activity and other characteristics that suggest it will be readily amenable as a drug target. The CHD2 (Coronary Heart Disease 2) protein acts in a novel, previously unknown pathway, distinct from the cholesterol synthesis pathway that is acted upon by the statin class of drugs and other classes of drugs.

The CHD2 gene, and its function, was discovered by a combination of genetic analyses of families whose members had heart attacks at an early age and an analysis of biological pathways. In total, more than 5,000 individuals from 145 families were analyzed to identify the gene. The discovery in this population, made by Myriad in collaboration with scientists from the Cardiovascular Genetics Research Clinic at the University of Utah, means that abnormal levels of the CHD2 protein are critical to the development of disease. Because disorders of the CHD2 gene lead to high LDL cholesterol, low HDL cholesterol, and early-onset heart disease, inhibition of the gene with a small molecule drug is expected to lower cholesterol and reduce the risk of heart disease across the general population of individuals with high cholesterol. Current therapies, including the statins, are inadequate in lowering the total cholesterol to recommended levels in many patients. Heart disease remains the most common cause of death in the United States. Studies estimate that half of all men and one-third of women will develop heart disease during their lives.

"The discovery of this novel drug target for the treatment of heart disease points to the strengths of Myriad's integrated approach to drug development incorporating the best technologies of genomics and proteomics in a high-throughput, industrialized fashion," said Peter Meldrum, President and Chief Executive Officer of Myriad Genetics, Inc. "Myriad now has a full pipeline of earlier stage preclinical compounds to back up our lead prostate cancer drug, which has completed a Phase IIa human clinical trial, and we intend to aggressively advance these compounds toward commercialization."

EXHIBIT 20.5

A press release is good way to communicate positive information about a firm to a wide variety of constituents and stakeholders. Here, Myriad Genetics has issued a press release regarding a new drug designed to lower cholesterol. http://www.myriad.com

- *Giving advice and counsel.* Assisting management in determining what (if any) position to take on public issues, preparing employees for public appearances, and helping management anticipate public reactions are all part of the advice and counsel function of public relations.

The Tools of Public Relations. There are several vehicles through which a firm can make positive use of public relations and pursue the objectives just cited. The goal is to gain as much control over the process as possible. By using the methods discussed in the following sections, a firm can integrate its public relations effort with other brand communications.

Press Releases. Having a file of information that makes for good news stories puts the firm in a position to take advantage of free press coverage. Press releases allow a firm to pursue positive publicity from the news media. Exhibit 20.5 is a press release announcing Myriad Genetics' discovery of a gene related to high cholesterol. Items that make for good public relations include the following:

- New products
- New scientific discoveries
- New personnel
- New corporate facilities
- Innovative corporate practices, such as energy-saving programs or employee benefit programs
- Annual shareholder meetings
- Charitable and community service activities

CREATIVITY

The Cat's Meow for PR

"Meow, meow, meow, meow. Meow, meow, meow, meow. Meow, meow, meow, meow, meow, meow, meow, meow."

Every cat lover knows the Meow Mix "Meow, Meow" song (and even cat haters too, but they won't admit it). So when Meow Mix Company wanted to launch a new campaign that would challenge the big cat-food marketers—Procter & Gamble and Nestlé—they knew they needed a novel approach. The firm worked with its advertising and public relations agencies—Kirshenbaum Bond & Partners and Lime Public Relations & Promotion, respectively—to develop a multi-faceted and highly creative campaign using everything from TV programs for cats to a children's book, *Mr. Meow's Amazing ABC Adventure,* featuring an illustrated Mr. Meow.

Wait a minute—TV programs for cats!? That's right. When consumer researchers discovered that cat owners often leave their TVs on for their pets, Kirshenbaum and Lime execs had the idea to create an actual TV show for cats *and* their owners. So Kirshenbaum set out to create Meow TV—and take on the challenges of such a unique task. The show had to appeal to cat owners without being deathly dull or run out of content after one show. It also had to be something that would sell well to a cable or network channel and attract advertisers. And this all had to be accomplished for under $400,000.

The result: Meow TV, produced by Half-Baked productions, launched on May 30, 2003, on the Oh! Oxygen cable network. It is hosted by Annabelle Gurwitch and her cat Stinky. It takes a silly but serious programming approach that mocks home shopping channels and exercise shows along with cat-related content. But regardless of the success or failure of the show itself (it was still on the air as of this writing and had its own Web site, http://www.meowtv.com), the PR value of the effort was enormous. Over 153 million impressions were achieved in print and broadcast media leading up to the show's release. When the question, "What cat-food company is making the first TV show for cats?" was asked on *The Hollywood Squares* TV game show, Claudia Strauss, president of Lime, said, "I knew we had done it." You just can't buy exposure like that.

Source: Lisa Sanders, "Meow Mix TV Pulls off PR Coup," *Advertising Age,* June 23, 2003.

The only drawback to press releases is that a firm often doesn't know if or when the item will appear in the media. Also, the news media are free to edit or interpret a news release, which may alter its intended message. To help reduce these liabilities, consultants recommend carefully developing relationships with editors from publications the organization deems critical to its press release program. And editors prefer information from firms that focuses on technical or how-to features and more case studies about company successes.

Feature Stories. While a firm cannot write a feature story for a newspaper or televise a story over the local television networks, it can invite journalists to do an exclusive story on the firm when there is a particularly noteworthy event. A feature story is different from a press release in that it is more controllable. A feature story, as opposed to a news release, offers a single journalist the opportunity to do a fairly lengthy piece with exclusive rights to the information. Jupiter Communications, a leading research organization that tracks Internet usage and generates statistics about the Internet, has a simple philosophy when it comes to using feature stories as a public relations tool. Says Jupiter's CEO, "It is our goal to get every research project we do covered somewhere. We know this is the cheapest, and maybe most effective, way to market ourselves."[10]

Company Newsletters. In-house publications such as newsletters can disseminate positive information about

10. Andy Cohen, "The Jupiter Mission," *Sales and Marketing Management,* April 2000, 56.

Companies have discovered that electronic distribution of newsletters is an effective and efficient way to offer consumers information in a low-key way. Here, Procter & Gamble has created an electronic newsletter that not only gets information out about the Tide brand of laundry detergent, but also helps create a community around Tide. How does Cheer (http://www.cheer .com) use its electronic newsletter to reinforce the notion that hip, young people use the product? Is competing brand Purex (http://www .purex.com) finding a way to build positive, ongoing relations with its consumers through its product site? What real effect do you think these public relations initiatives have?

a firm through its employees. As members of the community, employees are proud of achievements by their firm. Newsletters can also be distributed to important constituents in the community, such as government officials, the chamber of commerce, or the tourism bureau. Suppliers often enjoy reading about an important customer, so newsletters can be mailed to this group as well. Firms are also discovering that the Internet is an excellent way to distribute information that traditionally has been the focus of newsletters. Procter & Gamble has done just that at http://www.tide.com/newsletter (see Exhibit 20.6).

Interviews and Press Conferences. As in the Pepsi tampering crisis, interviews and press conferences can be a highly effective public relations tool. Often, interviews and press conferences are warranted in a crisis management situation. But firms have also successfully called press conferences to announce important scientific breakthroughs or explain the details of a corporate expansion. The press conference has an air of importance and credibility because it uses a news format to present important corporate information. New technology is fostering the use of press conferences as a means of getting the word out.

Sponsored Events. Sponsored events were discussed as a form of support media in Chapter 17. Sponsoring events can also serve as an important public relations tool. Sponsorships run the gamut from supporting local community events to sponsoring global events such as the World Cup soccer competitions. At the local level, prominent display of the corporate name and logo offers local residents the chance to see that an organization is dedicated to the community.

Another form of sponsorship is the fund-raiser. Fund-raisers of all sorts for non-profit organizations give positive visibility to corporations (see Exhibit 20.7). For many years, Chevrolet has sponsored college scholarships through the NCAA by choosing the best offensive and defensive player in each game. The scholarships are announced weekly at the conclusion of televised games. This sort of notoriety for Chevrolet creates a favorable image for viewers.

One of the most difficult aspects of investing in sponsorships is determining the positive payoff the organization can expect from such an investment. Typically, corporations will try to assess the effect of sponsorships by (a) establishing an evaluation procedure that tracks awareness generated from sponsorships, (b) establishing an event-tracking model that can identify target audience attitudes and purchase behavior, and (c) identifying the components of the sponsorship that were most effective in achieving awareness and attitude goals. While these are general criteria for assessing the effects of sponsorship, there is an important image effect of the sponsorship. This is where the public relations role for sponsored events is manifested. Current research shows that there is a positive transfer of image from the event to the brand—precisely the effect a company seeks when using a public relations tool.[11]

Publicity. **Publicity** is unpaid-for media exposure about a firm's activities or its products and services, as we saw in the chapter-opening scenario about the Treo 600. Publicity is dealt with by the public relations function but cannot, with the exception of press releases, be strategically controlled like other public relations

---

11.   Kevin P. Gwinner and John Eaton, "Building Brand Image through Event Sponsorship: The Role of Image Transfer," *Journal of Advertising,* vol. 28, no. 4 (Winter 1999), 47–57.

IMAGINE, A GOLF TOURNAMENT ACTUALLY DESIGNED TO REDUCE STROKES.

Taking a few strokes off your game is any golfer's goal, but at the American Heart Association, we're looking to eliminate strokes and heart disease altogether. That's why we gratefully acknowledge Mercedes-Benz, USA and the 178 participating dealers across the country who hosted amateur golf tournaments this past year. As part of the Mercedes Dealer Championships, the tournaments raised over $1 million in cash and services to help fund American Heart Association-sponsored research and education, turning possibilities into realities – and saving lives.

American Heart Association。
Fighting Heart Disease and Stroke

Mercedes-Benz

EXHIBIT 20.7

Sponsoring an event, especially one that benefits a charity, is another form of public relations.

efforts. This lack of control was demonstrated earlier in the chapter with respect to the situations faced by Intel and Pepsi. In addition, publicity can turn into a global problem for a firm. Benetton, the Italian sportswear maker, is another classic case of a firm that regularly has had to deal with negative publicity. The firm has learned several times (or maybe not at all) the lesson that public information about a brand is not always controllable. Benetton has created much of this uncontrollable publicity with its controversial advertising. In one instance the firm ran an ad depicting a white child wearing angel's wings alongside a black child wearing devil's horns. In another campaign, the firm featured death-row inmates to promote its clothing line, although company officials argued they were merely trying to raise public consciousness of the death penalty. The reaction to such advertising was severe enough that at one point German retailers refused to carry the company's products. Public relations professionals can react swiftly to publicity, as the team from Pepsi did, but they cannot control the flow of information. Despite the lack of control, publicity can build an image and heighten consumer awareness of brands and organizations. An organization needs to be prepared to take advantage of events that make for good publicity and to counter events that are potentially damaging to a firm's reputation.

One major advantage of publicity—when the information is positive—is that it tends to carry heightened credibility. Publicity that appears in news stories on television and radio and in newspapers and magazines assumes an air of believability because of the credibility of the media context. Not-for-profit organizations often use publicity in the form of news stories and public interest stories as ways to gain widespread visibility at little or no cost.

And publicity is not always completely out of the companies' control. During the 2001 Academy Awards, a bracelet worn by Academy Award–winning actress Julia Roberts caused quite a publicity stir. After Roberts won the award for best actress, she stood smiling (which we all know she does so well) and waving to the cameras, and suddenly the whole world wanted to know about the snowflake-design Van Cleef & Arpels bracelet that adorned her right (waving) wrist. What a lucky break! Not. The whole episode was carefully planned by Van Cleef's PR agency, Ted, Inc. The agency lobbied hard to convince Roberts that the bracelet and matching earrings were stunning with her dress, knowing that if she won the Oscar, she would be highly photographed wearing (and waving) the bracelet.[12]

Buzz and "Viral" Marketing. The newest "tools" of public relations are buzz and viral marketing. Essentially, both of these efforts are attempts at stimulating word-of-mouth among key target markets that might otherwise be impervious to more traditional advertising and promotional tools. **Buzz** can be defined as "seeding" the media, particularly the Internet, with news and information about a brand in an attempt to create positive word of mouth. **Viral marketing** is the process of consumers marketing to consumers via the Web (blogs and e-newsgroups) or

12.   Beth Snyder Bulik, "Well-Heeled Heed the Need for PR," *Advertising Age*, June 11, 2001, S2.

through personal contact stimulated by a firm marketing a brand. The idea behind both buzz and viral marketing strategies is to target a handful of carefully chosen trendsetters in a target market and let their leadership act as a stimulus to demand for the brand.[13]

Some examples are in order here. Two firms that have tried to stimulate demand by using buzz to gain attention for their brands while shunning traditional media advertising are Vespa Scooters and Pabst Blue Ribbon beer. On a recent Saturday evening in Portland, Oregon, about a hundred serious bicyclists, many of whom were bike messengers and most of whom were tattooed, gathered near a fenced-off hard-top court and in teams of three began a "bike polo" contest. They played bike polo, drank beer, smoked cigarettes, and yelled at each other. The official sponsor for the event had no banners, no signs, and no on-site marketing rep. The sponsor was Pabst Blue Ribbon—PBR to the polo-bikers. Pabst has virtually shunned advertising and let the brand gravitate to being a symbol of the "lifestyle of dissent." It seems to be working. Sales of PBR, which had been falling steadily since the 1970s, were up about 10 percent in 2003. In some parts of the country the increase has been even more dramatic—sales in the Chicago area, for example, were up 134 percent.[14]

In a very different setting, consider this scene at the cafes on Third Street Promenade in and around Los Angeles. A gang of sleek, impossibly attractive motorbikers pulls up and, guess what, they seem *genuinely* interested in getting to know you over an iced latte—their treat, no less! Sooner or later the conversation turns to their Vespa scooters glinting in the sun, and they eagerly pull out a pad and jot down an address and phone number—for the nearest Vespa dealer. The scooter-riding, latte-drinking models are on the Vespa payroll, and they're paid to create buzz about the scooters by engaging hip café dwellers in conversation and camaraderie. [15]

Are buzz and viral marketing campaigns like these effective? Could be. All the information is still not in on what effect such campaigns can have or are having. We do know that public relations efforts like this can't reach many people very fast, so niche markets seem to be the only place to even try such an effort.

③ Public Relations and New Media. The fact that firms large and small are using the Internet to distribute newsletters reveals only one application of new media for public relations purposes. Firms are using the Internet for a variety of public relations activities. Procter & Gamble at one point had to create a special section at its main Web site to battle nagging rumors that the firm has some sort of connection to satanic cults. The site offered facts about P&G's moon-and-stars logo (the 13 stars represent the 13 original colonies, not a satanic symbol). The site also carried testimonials posted from the Billy Graham Evangelistic Association. The rumors were being spread through the Web, so P&G was fighting fire with fire by using the Web for a public relations counterattack.[16]

The issue was raised earlier that new media can create a "buzz" through word of mouth that with certain target segments is more effective than any other tactic. In a noisy and crowded competitive environment, mainstream promotional tools such as advertising, sales promotion, and sponsorships may get lost in the clutter. Public relations using new media, particularly Web sites, chat room posts, and Web press releases, can reach targeted audiences in a different way that carries more credibility than "in your face" company self-promotion. That was true for New Line Cinema. This is the studio that has released the *Lord of the Rings* films. At first, the studio thought that it needed to shut down or sanction the more than 400 fan sites that were posting information about the films. But after reviewing the sites and the

13. Gerry Khermouch and Jeff Green, "Buzz-z-z Marketing," *BusinessWeek,* July 30, 2001, 50–56.
14. Rob Walker, "The Marketing of No Marketing," *New York Times Magazine,* June 22, 2003, 42–45.
15. Gerry Khermouch and Jeff Green, "Buzz-z-z Marketing," *BusinessWeek,* July 30, 2001, 50–56.
16. Nicholas Kulish, "Still Bedeviled by Satan Rumors, P&G Battles Back on the Web," *Wall Street Journal,* September 21, 1999, B1.

enormous positive buzz they were creating, the studio realized it made more sense to just let them buzz away to the benefit of the films.[17]

CONTROVERSY

Where Is the Spin Control?

Throughout the text, we have seen that the Internet is a great place to create a buzz and spread the "word" at lightning speed. But the way "content" can be splashed across the Web, it is getting difficult to know what is real content and news versus what is corporate PR.

Here is the crux of the problem. The trend toward "dressing" public relations as "news" is being driven by economics. A standard press release on the Internet costs only a few hundred dollars to compose and distribute electronically, which makes the Web a bargain for information dissemination—but we knew that. Entering the scene, however, are content-hungry publishers. In an effort to provide their outlets with fresh text fast and cheap, they simply forward corporate news releases. Estimates are that a company that wants to create significant online presence with advertising would need to spend about $500,000 monthly on various advertising, paid search, content development, and placement. But the price to news sites for most of PR content is zero.

This issue is particularly relevant when you consider that of the dot.com failures in 2000, 30 percent of the shutdowns were content providers. Despite the shakeout, the need for content continues to grow. If you're a firm seeking a PR presence on the Internet, this is certainly good news, partly because the remaining number of sites featuring "news" areas (such as portals or special-interest sites) is nearly inestimable. But almost 100 million users currently visit the top 10 general news sites. The pressure within content providers to attract those eyeballs is huge. One analyst notes, "Online news outlets are not only competing against one another but against traditional media. The pressure to be the first or to scoop the others is immense. Rushed stories can mean less time for fact-checking and less time to interview subjects."

As a test, visit some of these sites and see whether the articles are "news" or a company PR press release:

- ABCnews.com: Go to the MoneyScope section, http://money.go.com.
- America Online: Go to the Channels and click "news." Locate the stories by selecting the "News Search" button at the top of the menu.
- CNET: Click "CNET Investor" or go directly to http://investor.cnet .com and check out the company press releases.
- Newsalert.com: Press releases are mixed in with news stories on the site from all the major wire organizations—CBS, Reuters, Business Wire, and UPI.

Source: Joanne R. Helperin, "Spinning Out of Control?," *Business 2.0,* May 1, 2001, 54–56.

But many new Web sites run by amateurs, like blogs, that purport to be providing "inside, confidential, or late-breaking news" about an issue or a brand are highly susceptible to bogus press releases. Even the big news organizations like ABCnews.com and specialty sites like ZDnet.com for investors have a hard time deciphering what is real news and what is spin-doctored PR hype.[18]

Finally, there is a major drawback to new media when it comes to public relations. Because of the speed with which information is disseminated, staying ahead of negative publicity is indeed challenging. While word of mouth can be used to create a positive buzz, it can also spread bad news or, even worse, misinformation just as fast. When a crisis hits the Internet, one PR expert says, "'Act quickly' becomes 'Act *even more* quickly.'"[19] Acting quickly and responding with the right facts is the topic of the next section. And new Web sites, in an effort to get recognized (and these days even survive), are less likely to scrutinize public relations press releases as carefully as perhaps they should (see the Controversy box for a detailed discussion).

4 Basic Public Relations Strategies. Given the breadth of possibilities for using public relations as part of a firm's overall integrated brand promotion effort, we need to identify basic public relations strategies. Public relations strategies can be categorized as either proactive or reactive. **Proactive public relations strategy** is guided by marketing objectives, seeks to publicize a company and its brands, and takes an offensive rather than defensive posture in the public relations process. **Reac-**

17. Marc Weingarten, "Get Your Buzz to Breed Like Hobbits," *Business 2.0,* January 2002, 96–97.
18. Joanne R. Helperin, "Spinning Out of Control?" *Business 2.0,* May 1, 2001, 54–56.
19. Kathryn Kranhold, "Handling the Aftermath of Cybersabotage," *Wall Street Journal,* February 10, 2000, B22.

Biotechnology
is helping him
protect the land
and preserve his
family's heritage.

"I'm raising a better soybean crop that
helps me conserve the topsoil, keep
my land productive and help this farm
support future generations of my family."
—Rod Gangwish, farmer

Biotechnology is helping Rod Gangwish
to grow a type of soybean that requires
less tilling of the soil. That helps him
preserve precious topsoil and produce
a crop with less impact on the land.
Preserving topsoil today means a
thriving farm for generations to come.
  Biotechnology allows farmers to
choose the best combination of ways to
help grow their crops. It helps cotton
farmers use fewer chemicals to protect
their crops against certain pests. And,
it's helping provide ways for developing
countries to better feed a growing
population. And, in the future, it can
help farmers grow better quality, more
nutritious food.
  Biotechnology is also enhancing lives
in other ways, helping to create more
effective treatments for diseases such
as leukemia and diabetes.
  Biotechnology is helping create solutions that are improving lives today,
and solutions that could improve our
world tomorrow. If you're interested in
learning more, visit our Web site or call
the number below for a free brochure
about biotechnology and agriculture.

COUNCIL FOR
BIOTECHNOLOGY
INFORMATION

good ideas are growing

1-800-980-8660
www.whybiotech.com

EXHIBIT 20.8

The biotechnology industry is taking a proactive approach to the controversies surrounding the industry and its processes. http://www.whybiotech.com

tive public relations strategy is dictated by influences outside the control of a company, focuses on problems to be solved rather than opportunities, and requires a company to take defensive measures. These two strategies involve different orientations to public relations.[20]

Proactive Public Relations Strategy. In developing a proactive public relations strategy, a firm acknowledges opportunities to use public relations efforts to accomplish something positive. Companies often rely heavily on their public relations firms to help them put together a proactive strategy. The biotechnology industry, for example, is subject to much controversy in the press regarding genetically altered food and seed products. The advertisement in Exhibit 20.8 from the biotechnology industry attempts to take a proactive approach to dealing with the controversies by presenting a positive image and information.

In many firms, the positive aspects of employee achievements, corporate contributions to the community, and the organization's social and environmental programs go unnoticed by important constituents. To implement a proactive public relations strategy, a firm needs to develop a comprehensive public relations program. The key components of such a program are as follows:

1. *A public relations audit.* A **public relations audit** identifies the characteristics of a firm or the aspects of the firm's activities that are positive and newsworthy. Information is gathered in much the same way as information related to advertising strategy is gathered. Corporate personnel and customers are questioned to provide information. The type of information gathered in an audit includes descriptions of company products and services, market performance of brands, profitability, goals for products, market trends, new product introductions, important suppliers, important customers, employee programs and facilities, community programs, and charitable activities.

2. *A public relations plan.* Once the firm is armed with information from a public relations audit, the next step is a structured public relations plan. A **public relations plan** identifies the objectives and activities related to the public relations communications issued by a firm. The components of a public relations plan include the following:

   a. *Current situation analysis.* This section of the public relations plan summarizes the information obtained from the public relations audit. Information contained here is often broken down by category, such as product performance or community activity.

   b. *Program objectives.* Objectives for a proactive public relations program stem from the current situation. Objectives should be set for both short-term and long-term opportunities. Public relations objectives can be as diverse and complex as advertising objectives. As with advertising, the focal point is not sales or profits. Rather, factors such as the credibility of product performance (that is, placing products in verified, independent tests) or the stature of the

20.   These definitions were developed from discussions offered by Jordan Goldman, *Public Relations in the Marketing Mix* (Lincolnwood, IL: NTC Business Books, 1992), xi–xii.

firm's research and development efforts (highlighted in a prestigious trade publication article) are legitimate statements of objective.

c. ***Program rationale.*** In this section, it is critical to identify the role the public relations program will play relative to all the other communication efforts—particularly advertising—being undertaken by a firm. This is the area where an integrated brand promotion perspective is clearly articulated for the public relations effort.

d. ***Communications vehicles.*** This section of the plan specifies precisely what means will be used to implement the public relations plan. The public relations tools discussed earlier in the chapter—press releases, interviews, newsletters—constitute the communications vehicles through which program objectives can be implemented. There will likely be discussion of precisely how press releases, interviews, and company newsletters can be used.[21]

e. ***Message content.*** Analysts suggest that public relations messages should be researched and developed in much the same way that advertising messages are researched and developed. Focus groups and in-depth interviews are being used to fine-tune PR communications. For example, a pharmaceutical firm learned that calling obesity a "disease" rather than a "condition" increased the overweight population's receptivity to the firm's press release messages regarding a new anti-obesity drug.[22]

A proactive public relations strategy has the potential for making an important supportive contribution to a firm's IBP effort. Carefully placing positive information targeted to important and potentially influential constituents—such as members of the community or stockholders—supports the overall goal of enhancing the image, reputation, and perception of a firm and its brands.

Reactive Public Relations Strategy. A reactive public relations strategy seems a contradiction in terms. As stated earlier, firms must implement a reactive public relations strategy when events outside the control of the firm create negative publicity. Coca-Cola was able to rein in the publicity and negative public reaction by acting swiftly after an unfortunate incident occurred in Europe. Seven days after a bottling glitch at a European plant caused teens in Belgium and France to become sick after drinking Coke, the firm acted quickly and pulled all Coca-Cola products from European shelves, and the CEO issued an apology.[23] But Coca-Cola's actions did not prevent negative consequences. Because of the incident, Coca-Cola went from being one of the most admired and trusted names in Europe to a company that ultimately had to start giving the product away to regain people's trust. The event was so catastrophic that Coke sales dropped 21 percent, and earnings were pummeled as well. But Coke's president of the Greater Europe Group said, "We reevaluated and retailored our marketing programs to meet the needs of consumers on a country-by-country basis and continue to reach out with marketing programs specifically designed to reconnect the brands with consumers."[24] The programs relied heavily on integrated brand promotion strategies including free samples; dealer incentive programs; and beach parties featuring sound and light shows, live music DJs, and cocktail bars with free Cokes to win back the critical teen segment.[25] By early 2000, Coca-Cola was well on its way to recapturing the lost sales and market share.

It is much more difficult to organize for and provide structure around reactive public relations. Since the events that trigger a reactive public relations effort are

21. Ibid., 4–14.
22. Geri Mazur, "Good PR Starts with Good Research," *Marketing News,* September 15, 1997, 16.
23. Kathleen V. Schmidt, "Coke's Crisis," *Marketing News,* September 27, 1999, 1, 11.
24. Amie Smith, "Coke's European Resurgence," *PROMO Magazine,* December 1999, 91.
25. Ibid.

unpredictable as well as uncontrollable, a firm must simply be prepared to act quickly and effectively. Two steps help firms implement a reactive public relations strategy:

1. *The public relations audit.* The public relations audit that was prepared for the proactive strategy helps a firm also prepare its reactive strategy. The information provided by the audit gives a firm what it needs to issue public statements based on current and accurate data. In the Pepsi situation, a current list of distributors, suppliers, and manufacturing sites allowed the firms to quickly determine that the problems were not related to the production process.

2. *The identification of vulnerabilities.* In addition to preparing current information, the other key step in a reactive public relations strategy is to recognize areas where the firm has weaknesses in its operations or products that can negatively affect its relationships with important constituents. From a public relations standpoint, these weaknesses are called *vulnerabilities.* If aspects of a firm's operations are vulnerable to criticism, such as environmental issues related to manufacturing processes, then the public relations function should be prepared to discuss the issues in a broad range of forums with many different constituents. Leaders at Pepsi, Quaker Oats, and Philip Morris were taken somewhat by surprise when shareholders challenged the firms on their practices with respect to genetically modified foods. While the concern was among a minority of shareholders, there were enough concerned constituents to warrant a proxy vote on the genetically modified foods issue.[26]

And, in an odd turn of events, we now see political figures firing up the public relations machinery to try to protect and enhance their image. When George W. Bush's popularity ratings started to wane due to the ongoing expense of conflict in Iraq and allegations of abuse of Iraqi prisoners, Bush hit the road with a campaign praising postwar developments (see Exhibit 20.9).[27] Tony Blair, the British Prime Minister, invokes the services of his spokesman, Alastair Campbell, to provide similar public relations service for the PM's positions.[28] Normally, organizations lobby the government or customers rather than the reverse.

Public relations is an prime example of how a firm (or an individual) can identify and then manage aspects of communication in an integrated and synergistic manner to diverse audiences. Without recognizing public relations activities as a component of the firm's overall communication effort, misinformation or disinformation could compromise more mainstream communications such as advertising. The coordination of public relations into an integrated program is a matter of recognizing and identifying the process as an information source in the overall IBP effort.

"HOW'S THAT PRO-AMERICAN FOREIGN-ADVERTISING P.R. BLITZ THINGY COMING ALONG?"

EXHIBIT 20.9

Politicians have discovered that public relations can be used to try to influence public perception.

A Final Word on Public Relations. And let's be clear: Public relations can be a positive contributor to the overall IBP effort. Whether that contribution comes from the damage

26.   James Cox, "Shareholders Get to Put Bio-Engineered Foods to Vote," *USA Today,* June 6, 2000, 1B.

27.   Scott Lindlaw, "Bush Launches PR Campaign for Iraq Policy," Associated Press Online, October 9, 2003, accessed at http://story.news.yahoo, October 9, 2003.

28.   James Blitz, "Tony Blair's Spin Doctor in War of Words with the BBC," *Financial Times,* June 28–29, 2003, 22.

control function of PR or the positive, proactive strategies firms can implement. But there is no defendable argument to forward the proposition that public relations and the publicity it can generate will be the lead strategy in launching or building a brand. Public relations is not controllable enough nor can it be implemented quickly enough to provide the impact a brand needs. As a support tool, PR plays a key role. As a lead strategy, it will fall flat. As an example of using public relations in a powerful and ideal way, consider how Guinness, the venerable Irish brewer, launched a PR effort that appealed to both long-time Guinness loyalists and a new generation of Guinness drinkers (see the Global Issues box).

GLOBAL ISSUES

Public Relations with Global Impact

Few brands generate as much cultural association as Guinness. The 250-year-old brand of stout beer has been attracting tourists to its St. James's Gate brewery in Dublin, Ireland, for more than a century. But executives at Guinness faced a tough challenge: The old reception area was totally inadequate to handle the thousands of tourists who flocked to the brewery each year. The task, however, was much larger than just building a new reception area. The brewery was the very pinnacle of the traditional image of the brand.

The task of building a new reception/visitor area was as much a public relations problem as it was a practical problem. The tradition of the brand image had to preserved while thousands of tourists had to be accommodated. Guinness strategists conceived the problem this way:

- How to accommodate the ever-growing flock of devotees who come to Dublin to connect with the brand's "spiritual home"
- How to modernize the conference and meeting room facilities for corporate use
- How to maintain its traditional relationships with Guinness loyalists while also appealing to younger consumers, many of whom have watched their fathers quaff many a pint of Guinness

The last point was of particular concern to marketing managers at Guinness. Stout beer has, over the past 10 years, been challenged in Ireland by a wide range of new, contemporary beers and other alcoholic drinks targeted to younger drinkers.

The solution chosen for all the public relations and promotion issues the firm felt it faced was a new seven-story structure called The Guinness Storehouse. The Storehouse preserved and incorporated the five-story Market Street Storehouse, which had served as a Guinness storage facility in the early 1900s. The solution was an expensive one, with a price tag of over $45 million. But the investment seems to be paying off. Within two years of its opening, the visitor center attracted its millionth visitor and the Storehouse is now the number one fee-paying tourist spot in all of Ireland. Most importantly, the Storehouse aims to evoke in visitors an affinity with the brand. With 10 million glasses of Guinness consumed every day around the world, it would appear this PR effort is an appropriate testimony to the brand.

Source: Arundhati Parmar, "Guinness Intoxicates," *Marketing News*, November 10, 2003, 4, 6.

5 Corporate Advertising.

As we learned in Chapter 1, **corporate advertising** is not designed to promote a specific brand but rather is intended to establish a favorable attitude toward a company as a whole. A variety of highly regarded and highly successful firms use corporate advertising to enhance the image of the firm and affect consumers' attitudes. This perspective on corporate advertising is gaining favor worldwide. Firms with the stature of General Electric, Toyota, and Hewlett-Packard have invested in corporate advertising campaigns. Exhibit 20.10 shows a corporate campaign for Elkay—a high-end manufacturer of sinks and plumbing hardware.

The Scope and Objectives of Corporate Advertising.

Corporate advertising is a significant force in the overall advertising carried out by organizations in the United States. Billions of dollars are invested annually in media for corporate advertising campaigns. Interestingly, most corporate campaigns run by consumer-goods manufacturers are undertaken by firms in the shopping-goods category, such as appliance and auto marketers. Studies have also found that larger firms (in terms of gross sales) are much more prevalent users of corporate advertising than are smaller firms. Presumably, these firms have broader communications programs and more money to invest in advertising, which allows the use of corporate campaigns. Apple is a firm that has historically relied on broad corporate campaigns rather than promoting individual brands in the product line (see Exhibit 20.11).

EXHIBIT 20.10

Firms often use corporate advertising as a way to generate name recognition and a positive image for the firm as a whole rather than for any one of its brands. Here ELKAY touts the company name rather than any specific feature of its brand. http://www.elkayusa.com

EXHIBIT 20.11

Corporate image advertising is meant to build a broad image for the company as a whole rather than tout the features of a brand. Does this ad qualify as a corporate image ad? http://www.apple.com

In terms of media use, firms have found both magazine and television media to be well suited to corporate advertising efforts.[29] Corporate advertising appearing in magazines has the advantage of being able to target particular constituent groups with image- or issue-related messages. Hewlett-Packard chose to use both television and magazine ads in its corporate campaign (see Exhibit 20.12).[30] The campaign was designed to unify the image of the firm after its new CEO, Carly Fiorina, determined that the firm's image had become fragmented in the market. Magazines also provide the space for lengthy copy, which is often needed to achieve corporate advertising objectives. Television is a popular choice for corporate campaigns, especially image-oriented campaigns, because the creative opportunities provided by television can deliver a powerful, emotional message.

The objectives for corporate advertising are well focused. In fact, corporate advertising shares similar purposes with proactive public relations when it comes to what firms hope to accomplish with the effort. While corporate managers can be

29.   David W. Schumann, Jan M. Hathcote, and Susan West, "Corporate Advertising in America: A Review of Published Studies on Use, Measurement and Effectiveness," *Journal of Advertising,* vol. 20, no. 3 (September 1991), 40.
30.   Greg Farrell, "And Then There Was One H-P," *USA Today,* June 1, 2000, 5B.

The DNA of Silicon Valley.

The original company of inventors started here. 367 Addison Avenue, the garage out back.
Two young inventors, radicals really, with a few simple tools and a passion to invent. In this garage
more than a company was born. The spirit that has launched hundreds of companies was born.
Today, this garage is still the workshop of the world's inventors, and it will be for years to come.

www.hp.com

EXHIBIT 20.12

Hewlett-Packard felt the company's image had become fragmented. This is one of the ads in a new corporate image campaign designed to unify the image of the firm.
http://www.hp.com

somewhat vague about the purposes for corporate ads, the following objectives are generally agreed upon:

- To build the image of the firm among customers, shareholders, the financial community, and the general public
- To boost employee morale or attract new employees
- To communicate an organization's views on social, political, or environmental issues
- To better position the firm's products against competition, particularly foreign competition, which is often perceived to be of higher quality
- To play a role in the overall integrated brand promotion of an organization as support for main product or service advertising

Notice that corporate advertising is not always targeted strictly at consumers. A broad range of constituents can be targeted with a corporate advertising effort. For example, when Glaxo Wellcome and SmithKline Beecham merged to form a $73 billion pharmaceutical behemoth, the newly created firm, known as GlaxoSmithKline, launched an international print campaign aimed at investors who had doubts about the viability of the new corporate structure. The campaign was broadly image-oriented and led with the theme "Disease does not wait. Neither will we."[31]

Types of Corporate Advertising. Three basic types of corporate advertising dominate the campaigns run by organizations: image advertising, advocacy advertising, and cause-related advertising. Each is discussed in the following sections.

Corporate Image Advertising. The majority of corporate advertising efforts focus on enhancing the overall image of a firm among important constituents—typically customers, employees, and the general public. When IBM promotes itself as the firm providing "Solutions for a small planet" or when Toyota uses the slogan "Investing in the things we all care about" to promote its five U.S. manufacturing plants, the goal is to enhance the broad image of the firm. Bolstering a firm's image may not result in immediate effects on sales, but as we saw in Chapter 5, attitude can play an important directive force in consumer decision making. When a firm can enhance its overall image, it may well affect consumer predisposition in brand choice.[32] Exhibit 20.13 is an example of an image-oriented corporate ad. In the ad, Bristol-Myers Squibb is touting the life-saving impact of its high-technology line of pharmaceuticals.

A distinguishing feature of corporate image advertising is that it is not designed to directly or immediately influence consumer brand choice. Energy giant BP developed a series of television and print ads that featured real people out on the street candidly answering questions about the environment, pollution, and the use of nat-

31. David Goetzl, "GlaxoSmithKline Launches Print Ads," *Advertising Age,* January 8, 2001, 30.
32. For an exhaustive assessment of the benefits of corporate advertising, see David M. Bender, Peter H. Farquhar, and Sanford C. Schulert, "Growing from the Top," *Marketing Management,* vol. 4, no. 4 (Winter–Spring 1996), 10–19, 24.

Two miracles. Three Bristol-Myers Squibb medicines.
And one very happy ending.

The little miracle above is Luke David Armstrong. The
big one is his dad, Lance. Winner of the 1999 and 2000
Tours de France. And of an even more grueling battle —
against testicular cancer. Using three Bristol-Myers Squibb
cancer drugs, doctors worked with Lance to beat his

illness. For over three decades, Bristol-Myers Squibb has
been at the forefront of developing cancer medicines.
Now, we're working with Lance to spread the word about
early detection, treatment, hope, and triumph. Learn
more by visiting our Web site: www.bms.com.

Bristol-Myers Squibb Company

Hope, Triumph, and the Miracle of Medicine

EXHIBIT 20.13

*This corporate image ad for
Bristol-Myers Squibb is
touting the beneficial, life-
enhancing effects of its high-
technology pharmaceuticals.*
http://www.bms.com

ural resources and saying things like "I'd rather have a cleaner environment, but I can't imagine me without my car." One critic's assessment is that the spots "don't convey a lot of information" and that the campaign is likely to be successful in "getting the name equated in people's minds with a progressive, forward-thinking company."[33] An appropriate and important goal for corporate image advertising.

While most image advertising intends to communicate a general, favorable image, several corporate image advertising campaigns have been quite specific. When PPG Industries undertook a corporate image campaign to promote its public identity, the firm found that over a five-year period the number of consumers who claimed to have heard of PPG increased from 39.1 percent to 79.5 percent. The perception of the firm's product quality, leadership in new products, and attention to environmental problems were all greatly enhanced over the same period.[34] Another organization that has decided that image advertising is worthwhile is the national newspaper *USA Today*.[35] The newspaper has spent $1 million on print and outdoor ads that highlight the four color-coded sections of the newspaper: National, Money, Sports, and Life.

Advocacy Advertising. Advocacy advertising attempts to establish an organization's position on important social, political, or environmental issues. Advocacy advertising is advertising that attempts to influence public opinion on issues of concern to a firm and the nature of its brands. For example, in a corporate advertising program begun in the early 1990s, Phillips Petroleum links its commitment to protect and restore bird populations and habitats to its efforts to reduce sulfur in gasoline. Some of the ads from this campaign can be viewed at http://www.phillips66.com/about/Flyway/Tradition-Advertising.htm. Typically, the issue in advocacy advertising is directly relevant to the business operations of the organization.

Cause-Related Advertising. Cause-related advertising features a firm's affiliation with an important social cause—reducing poverty, increasing literacy, and curbing drug abuse are examples—and takes place as part of the cause-related marketing efforts undertaken by a firm. The idea behind cause-related marketing and advertising is that a firm donates money to a nonprofit organization in exchange for using the company name in connection with a promotional campaign. The purpose of cause-related advertising is that a firm's association with a worthy cause enhances the image of the firm in the minds of consumers. The ad in Exhibit 20.14, in which Anheuser-Busch is promoting the control of teenage drinking, fits this definition perfectly. This campaign helps establish the firm as a responsible marketer of alcoholic beverages, its primary business, while also helping society deal with a widespread social problem.

33. "Campaign Close-up—BP," *Sales and Marketing Management,* February 2004, 13.
34. Schumann, Hathcote, and West, "Corporate Advertising in America," 43, 49.
35. Keith J. Kelly, "*USA Today* Unveils Image Ads," *Advertising Age,* February 6, 1996, 8.

TEENAGE DRINKING IS DOWN BECAUSE PARENTS ARE DOING THEIR

HOMEWORK.

Susan knows if Emily has all the facts, she'll make a better decision about any subject. Even underage drinking. So she took advantage of "Family Talk About Drinking," a free guide offered by Anheuser-Busch to help parents talk to their kids. In the past decade alone, Anheuser-Busch and its distributors have provided more than 5.2 million guides. It's people like Susan and programs like this that have made a difference in the fight against underage drinking.

For a free family guidebook, call 1-800-359-TALK, or download it at www.beeresponsible.com.

WE ALL MAKE A DIFFERENCE.®

Budweiser

www.beeresponsible.com

EXHIBIT 20.14

In this cause-related corporate campaign, Anheuser-Busch is promoting the control of teenage drinking. This campaign helps establish the firm as a responsible marketer of alcoholic beverages. http://www.beeresponsible.com

Cause-related advertising is thus advertising that identifies corporate sponsorship of philanthropic activities. Each year, *PROMO Magazine* provides an extensive list of charitable, philanthropic, and environmental organizations that have formal programs in which corporations may participate. Most of the programs suggest a minimum donation for corporate sponsorship and specify how the organization's resources will be mobilized in conjunction with the sponsor's other resources.

Some very high-profile cause-related marketing programs have made extensive use of cause-related advertising. The Dixie Chicks promoted the World Wildlife Fund during a summer tour and donated proceeds of album sales to the organization. Eddie Bauer and Crystal Geyser Spring Water are brands using cause-related marketing as they support American Forests' ReLeaf program.[36]

Firms are also finding that new media outlets such as the Internet offer opportunities to publicize their cause-related activities. This is especially true for environmental activities that firms are engaged in. The higher-education, upscale profile of many Web users matches the profile of consumers who are concerned about the natural environment. When firms engage in sound environmental practices, the Web is a good place for these firms to establish a "green" presence. "Green site" operators (http://www.greenmarketplace.com and http://www.envirolink.org are examples) give firms a forum to describe their environmental activities.[37]

While much good can come from cause-related marketing, there is some question as to whether consumers see this in a positive light. In a study by Roper Starch Worldwide, 58 percent of consumers surveyed believed that the only reason a firm was supporting a cause was to enhance the company's image.[38] The image of a firm as self-serving was much greater than the image of a firm as a philanthropic partner.

The belief among consumers that firms are involved with causes only for revenue benefits is truly unfortunate. Firms involved in causes do, indeed, give or raise millions of dollars for worthy causes. And the participation by U.S. firms in supporting worthy causes is broad based. About 92 percent of all U.S. companies contribute to a cause and spend over $770 million annually supporting causes.[39] While there is some suspicion among adult consumers, there is growing evidence that cause marketing and advertising may be much more effective with teenagers. Researchers have found that 67 percent of teens shop for clothing and other items with a "cause" in mind, and more than half said they would switch to brands or retailers that were associated with a good cause.[40] In the words of one teen, "I bought a lot of my clothes at the Gap because they support the environment."[41]

Corporate advertising will never replace brand-specific advertising as the main thrust of corporate communications. But it can serve an important supportive role

36.   Stephanie Thompson, "Good Humor's Good Deeds," *Advertising Age,* January 8, 2001, 6.

37.   Jacquelyn Ottman, "Stalking the Green Consumer on the Internet," *Marketing News,* February 26, 1996, 7.

38.   Geoffrey Smith and Ron Stodghill, "Are Good Causes Good Marketing?," *BusinessWeek,* March 21, 1994, 64–65.

39.   John Palmer, "We Are the Children," *PROMO Magazine,* February 2001, 55–57.

40.   Melinda Ligos, "Mall Rats with a Social Conscience," *Sales and Marketing Management,* November 1999, 115.

41.   Ibid.

ETHICS

McDonald's Markets Itself as a Good Corporate Citizen

In 2004 McDonald's held a day-long media event to try to show the public it is a good corporate citizen. This was an attempt to counteract negative publicity on food safety, nutrition, and workers' rights. Critics claim they contribute to the United States' obesity crisis.

As the world's largest hamburger chain, McDonald's has taken the burden of recent criticism of the U.S. fast-food industry. The company was the subject of the documentary film *Super Size Me*, in which the filmmaker ate only McDonald's food and tracked his weight gain and other health problems for a month. In addition, the company's chief executive, Jim Cantalupo, died in April 2004 at the age of 60, apparently from a heart attack. Then two teenagers filed a high-profile lawsuit that said McDonald's food made them overweight. With all of these negative things occurring it is critical that McDonald's use corporate advertising to build a positive image for the company. At the day-long media event at the company's headquarters in Oak Brook, Illinois, McDonald's executives discussed new healthier products, efforts to deal with its labor practices, and efforts to recycle.

Consider McDonald's actions in the marketplace and ask yourself these questions:

- Does McDonald's have any responsibility beyond its shareholders?
- What is the role of personal responsibility in all this?
- Does McDonald's advertising make people eat too much?
- Should fast food advertising be more carefully regulated?
- Does McDonald's use of cartoon characters and clowns unfairly target children?

for brand advertising, and it can offer more depth and breadth to an integrated brand promotion program. One fundamental criticism corporate managers have of corporate advertising is the difficulty of measuring its specific effects on sales. If the sales effects of brand-specific advertising are difficult to measure, those for corporate advertising campaigns may be close to impossible to gauge.

SUMMARY

 Explain the role of public relations as part of a firm's overall integrated brand promotion strategy.

Public relations focuses on communication that can foster goodwill between a firm and constituent groups such as customers, stockholders, employees, government entities, and the general public. Businesses utilize public relations activities to highlight positive events associated with the organization; PR strategies are also employed for "damage control" when adversity strikes. Public relations has entered a new era, as changing corporate demands and new techniques have fostered a bolder, more aggressive role for PR in IBP campaigns.

 Detail the objectives and tools of public relations.

An active public relations effort can serve many objectives, such as building goodwill and counteracting negative publicity. Public relations activities may also be orchestrated to support the launch of new products or communicate with employees on matters of interest to them. The public relations function may also be instrumental to the firm's lobbying efforts and in preparing executives to meet with the press. The primary tools of public relations experts are press releases, feature stories, company newsletters, interviews and press conferences, and participation in the firm's event sponsorship decisions and programs.

 Describe how firms are using buzz and viral marketing in the public relations effort.

Firms are using the Internet for a variety of public relations activities. In Chapter 18, we saw that new media can create "buzz" through word of mouth that with certain target segments is more effective than any other tactic. In a noisy and crowded competitive environment, mainstream promotional tools such as advertising, sales promotion, and sponsorships may get lost in the clutter. Public relations using new media, particularly Web sites, chat room posts, and Web press releases, can reach targeted audiences in a different way, and carry more credibility than "in your face" company self-promotion. Viral marketing is similar to buzz, although it will typically rely on direct contact between opinion leaders and influencers and a narrowly targeted market niche. Finally, there is a major drawback to new media when it comes to public relations. Because of the speed with which

information is disseminated, staying ahead of negative publicity is indeed challenging. While word of mouth can be used to create a positive buzz, it can also spread bad news or, even worse, misinformation just as fast.

 Describe two basic strategies motivating an organization's public relations activities.

When companies perceive public relations as a source of opportunity for shaping public opinion, they are likely to pursue a proactive public relations strategy. With a proactive strategy, a firm strives to build goodwill with key constituents via aggressive programs. The foundation for these proactive programs is a rigorous public relations audit and a comprehensive public relations plan. The plan should include an explicit statement of objectives to guide the overall effort. In many instances, however, public relations activities take the form of damage control, and in these instances the firm is obviously in a reactive public relations strategy mode. While a reactive strategy may seem a contradiction in terms, it certainly is the case that organizations can be prepared to react to bad news. Organizations that understand their inherent vulnerabilities in the eyes of important constituents will be able to react quickly and effectively in the face of hostile publicity.

 Discuss the applications and objectives of corporate advertising.

Corporate advertising is not undertaken to support an organization's specific brands, but rather to build the general reputation of the organization in the eyes of key constituents. This form of advertising uses various media—but primarily magazine and television ads—and serves goals such as enhancing the firm's image and building fundamental credibility for its line of products. Corporate advertising may also serve diverse objectives, such as improving employee morale, building shareholder confidence, or denouncing competitors. Corporate ad campaigns generally fall into one of three categories: image advertising, advocacy advertising, or cause-related advertising. Corporate advertising may also be orchestrated in such a way to be very newsworthy, and thus it needs to be carefully coordinated with the organization's ongoing public relations programs.

KEY TERMS

public relations

publicity

buzz

viral marketing

proactive public relations strategy

reactive public relations strategy

public relations audit

public relations plan

corporate advertising

advocacy advertising

cause-related advertising

QUESTIONS

1.   Explain how the release of Handspring's Treo 600 cell phone/PDA/digital camera combo discussed in the chapter opener serves to illustrate the effectiveness of buzz and viral marketing as new tools of public relations.

2.   In what ways has public relations entered a new era? Is it likely that continued momentum will drive public relations to become the centerpiece of promotional efforts in the future, as some experts predict? Explain.

3.   Review the criteria presented in this chapter and in Chapter 17 regarding the selection of events to sponsor. Obviously, some events will have more potential for generating favorable publicity than others. What particular criteria should be emphasized in event selection when a firm has the goal of gaining publicity that will build goodwill via event sponsorship?

4.   Would it be appropriate to conclude that the entire point of public relations activity is to generate favorable publicity and stifle unfavorable publicity? What is it about publicity that makes it such an opportunity and threat?

5.   There is an old saying to the effect that "there is no such thing as bad publicity." Can you think of a situation in which bad publicity would actually be good publicity?

6.   Most organizations have vulnerabilities they should be aware of to help them anticipate and prepare for unfavorable publicity. What vulnerabilities would you associate with each of the following companies?

R. J. Reynolds, makers of Camel cigarettes

Procter & Gamble, makers of Pampers disposable diapers

Kellogg's, makers of Kellogg's Frosted Flakes

ExxonMobil, worldwide oil and gasoline company

McDonald's, worldwide restaurateur

7.   Review the three basic types of corporate advertising and discuss how useful each would be as a device for boosting a firm's image. Is corporate advertising always an effective image builder?

EXPERIENTIAL EXERCISES

1.   Whether responding to claims of unfair labor practices, corporate censorship, or responsibility over the obesity crisis, businesses constantly use the tools of public relations to anticipate and react to negative publicity and bad events. Corporate scandals, environmental disasters, and other general mishaps quickly snowball into big controversies, and can damage a firm's reputation with consumers. Search news sources, business magazines, or the Internet to identify a recent corporate crisis that required "damage control" by a firm. Describe the extent of the crisis and who was involved. Identify tools and strategies of public relations that were employed to manage the crisis. How has the issue been resolved to date? Do you think the company could have avoided the controversy or done more to resolve the problem in the eyes of stakeholders? Explain.

2.   This chapter discusses the many ways new media contributes to the activities of public relations. After reading the section of this chapter on Public Relations and New Media, visit the following sites and explain how each contributes to online public relations.

Beeresponsible: http://www.beeresponsible.com

CSRwire: http://www.csrwire.com

eReleases: http://www.ereleases.com

Atomic: http://www.atomicpr.com

EXPERIENCING THE INTERNET

20-1   Objectives for Public Relations

The goal of the public relations function is to manage positive public relations efforts as well as to soften the impact of negative events that threaten the relationship between businesses and consumers. Agencies must set very specific objectives for promoting healthy public relations, and must use the right tools to maintain the good reputation of their clients. McSpotlight is a consumer-protection organization that directs its efforts to raise awareness among fast-food customers.

McSpotlight: http://www.mcspotlight.org

1.   What is the purpose of the McSpotlight organization?

2.   Of the primary objectives for public relations listed in the chapter, which is most likely to direct the McDonald's public relations effort in response to McSpotlight?

3.   What public relations tools is McSpotlight using to achieve its goals? What public relations tools do you suppose McDonald's uses most often to counteract negative publicity?

20-2   Public Relations Agencies

Carter Ryley Thomas ranks among the largest independent agencies in the nation. CRT boasts a values-based philosophy that guides the firm's employees in their everyday decisions. The agency is recognized as one of the best PR firms to work for in America, and has been named among the top mid-sized PR firms in the country.

Carter Ryley Thomas Public Relations:
http://www.crtpr.com

1.   Browse the site and describe one of the recent public relations campaigns CRT has conducted for its clients.

2.   What objectives and tools guided the campaign?

3.   Was the effort characteristic of a proactive public relations strategy or a reactive one?

4.   What direct benefits do you believe the client received as a result of this public relations strategy?

Cincinnati Bell℠

PART 5
Cincinnati Bell Wireless: Growing and Sustaining the Brand after Launch

There's a predictable aspect to advertising and marketing: Last year's results are last year's results. After a few bottles of champagne are popped to celebrate a good year, it's time to do it all again. And the new year will most certainly present opportunities and challenges that will need to be addressed in one's advertising and IBP planning, if a brand like Cincinnati Bell Wireless is to continue to thrive and grow. As we saw at the end of Part 4 of this case, 1998 was a very good year for Cincinnati Bell Wireless. Could CBW and its partner Northlich hope for a repeat performance in 1999? What were the prospects for continued growth of their wireless business? Jack Cassidy, then president of CBW, was proud of what CBW had been able to accomplish in its launch year, but by the fourth quarter of 1998, planning was already under way to make 1999 even better.

There were good reasons to be optimistic about CBW's prospects, heading into 1999. Consumers responded immediately to the superior features of digital PCS technology versus analog cellular, and CBW had emerged as the market leader for digital PCS in Cincinnati and surrounding communities. More generally, wireless phone service was evolving from a specialized technology adopted by a few to a mass-market product. The 30 percent annual growth rates in adoption of wireless phone services were projected to continue into 1999, making Cincinnati a marketplace with substantial, unfulfilled market potential.

Another thing that is predictable in advertising and marketing: If you have spotted a great opportunity for growing your business, rest assured that many of your competitors will have spotted it too. This would be CBW's biggest challenge heading into 1999. At least five wireless competitors envious of CBW's success in 1998 were preparing to do everything in their power to rob CBW of some of that success in 1999. These included Nextel, AirTouch Cellular, GTE Wireless, Ameritech, and Sprint PCS. Sprint represented an especially formidable foe because it offered the same state-of-the-art technology as CBW, and as a nationwide player was prepared to spend heavily behind its own brand-building campaign in 1999. No one expected that the Cincinnati market could support six wireless service providers. Only the strong would survive, and 1999 would prove to be a critical year in separating the weak from the strong.

Refining the CBW Advertising and IBP Plan for 1999.
The launch plan implemented by Northlich on behalf of Cincinnati Bell Wireless had produced outstanding results. But before moving forward to create new executions for 1999, Northlich reassessed the plan by reevaluating the key strategic issues from Thorson and Moore's strategic planning triangle (see Part 2 of this case if you need a refresher). Before selecting the mix of persuasion tools to be deployed in 1999, Northlich reassessed both the appropriate target segment(s) and the focal value proposition(s) for the brand. Direct feedback from the marketplace was essential in this reevaluation.

Target Segment Identification. You may recall that CBW and Northlich had initially targeted MOPES (managers, owners, professionals, and entrepreneurs) in the launch campaign. While the campaign was effective in reaching these high-value business users, it was also clear that a market existed beyond those who would use the phone for business purposes. Almost overnight, wireless phone service had moved from novelty to necessity in the lifestyles of affluent, time-starved consumers. So Northlich entered 1999 with two target segments clearly specified. One was young (25-plus), college-educated, working professionals who (much like the MOPES) represented a high-value segment that used their phones to enhance on-the-job productivity. The second was an older (45 to 54) group of well-educated professionals who appeared to be adopting wireless phone service as a convenient alternative to the wired phone for everyday communication. These two segments were labeled Charter 500 Customers and Charter 100 Customers, respectively, indicating the pool of monthly minutes (that is, 500 and 100) that was expected to be most attractive to each.

Consolidating the Value Proposition for the CBW Brand. Northlich and Cincinnati Bell launched the wireless brand with a value proposition featuring the functional benefits of this new service. To assess whether this proposed value was in fact being recognized by its customers, Northlich conducted a series of focus groups in January 1999 to hear directly from CBW customers what they liked most about this new service. In their customers' own words, CBW stood for *flexible, best choice, simple and affordable, no surprises, no contracts, reliable,* and *putting me in control.* Based on this qualitative research, the CBW value proposition for 1999 became a more focused version of what it had been in 1998. The goal for all advertising was to convince target audiences that CBW represented the "Simple Choice" for wireless communication. Additionally, to be in sync with Nokia's increasingly fashionable phones, CBW also aspired to be perceived as current and cool. The smart choice, cool enough to set current trends, was the brand equity that CBW set out to own in 1999.

Building the Brand and Growing the Business.
Here we will describe several of the various persuasion tools that were deployed to build the CBW brand in 1999. Much as it had done in the launch campaign, Northlich again called on its multidisciplinary teams to generate a sophisticated, multilayered advertising and IBP campaign to sustain and grow the CBW brand. The campaign in 1999 integrated nearly all the tools that you have learned about in the previous 20 chapters, but in the following discussion we will emphasize the IBP tools that were featured in Chapters 17 through 20.

Equity Building. As the foundation for continuing success, Northlich used several tools to reinforce what consumers knew about the CBW brand. Several television spots were developed with the goal of cultivating CBW's brand equity as the smart and cool choice. Like the "Classroom" and "Big Easy" spots described in Part 4, the emphasis of the new ads for 1999 was to position CBW as the simple, smart choice in wireless, and to portray signing contracts and complicated pricing schemes as an old-fashioned way of doing business. One particularly creative execution in 1999 was an ad that spoofed *Antiques Road Show,* PBS's most popular prime-time program at the time. In this ad a clunky analog cellular phone was written off as a worthless artifact of some bygone era, with of course a CBW phone being represented as the only appropriate choice for modern living. If imitation is the sincerest form of flattery, the creatives at Northlich must have been very flattered when Sprint PCS basically copied this ad execution as part of its national television campaign in 2001.[1]

1.   Suzanne Vranica, "Madison Avenue Plays on Antiques' Lure," *Wall Street Journal,* May 16, 2001, B7.

In 1999 the creatives at Northlich also generated several out-of-the-box outdoor ad executions to contribute to the equity-building effort. A sample is provided in Exhibit IBP 5.1. This "Carol & Ted" ad was designed for one of the city's most prominent billboards; this billboard is equipped with a special feature where it can support three rotating panels, which can be programmed to rotate on any sequence that a client wants. So panels A, B, and C were designed to be rotated in a methodical sequence, delivering the punch line that if contracts scare you, then CBW is definitely the right choice.

The special genius associated with this outdoor ad came in how it was deployed to create a public relations coup for Cincinnati Bell. Rather than rotate through all the panels initially, only panel A from Exhibit IBP 5.1 was displayed for the first week. This drove all the local TV news departments wild with curiosity, and became

EXHIBIT IBP 5.1

The "Carol & Ted" three-panel billboard.

a regular topic during the evening news. Why make your marriage proposal on the city's most visible billboard? Who was Ted? Carol? Did they live and work in Cincinnati? On and on it went. In week two, panel B was revealed. Carol said no! Poor Ted. He must be heartbroken. Would we ever hear from Ted again? By the time the third week came, when CBW was ready to reveal panel C, the local media had drummed up so much attention around this billboard that nearly everyone in the city would ultimately learn that the punch line was CBW's swipe against wireless service providers that make you sign contracts. This is a wonderful example of how a little creativity can pay big dividends in getting low-cost, mass exposure for a brand-building message.

Closing the Sale. As noted in Chapter 18, many diverse sales promotion tactics are employed by marketers to supplement their advertising for the purpose of closing the sale. The kind of tactics used and the frequency of use depend on one's industry and competitive field. Turns out that the telecommunications business is intensely competitive, and 1999 would be a year of wireless warfare in Cincinnati.[2] So, beyond the general brand-building ads, Northlich and CBW also worked fervently to create and advertise a series of sales promotions designed to persuade new customers to take that plunge and activate their wireless phone service with Cincinnati Bell.

The competitive intensity of the wireless phone business means that, ideally, one should have a fresh sales promotion ready to go each and every month. Northlich pretty much delivered on this demanding schedule. Sample print ads from the Valentine's Day promotion of February 1999 and the March Madness promotion of March 1999 appear in Exhibits IBP 5.2 and 5.3. Other sales promotions included a

EXHIBIT IBP 5.2

There's nothing like a $50 gift certificate for flowers to get people's attention in mid-February.

EXHIBIT IBP 5.3

March Madness is the perfect time to help sports fans show their true colors.

2.   Mike Boyer, "Wireless Wars," *Cincinnati Enquirer,* November 15, 1998, E1, E4.

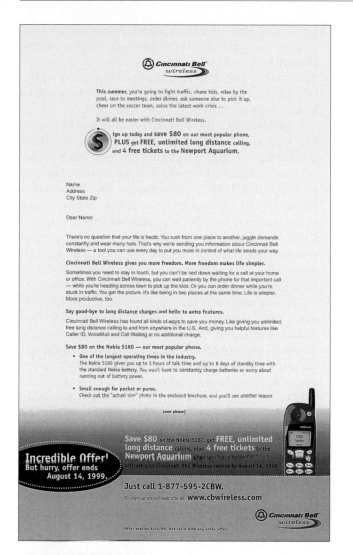

EXHIBIT IBP 5.4

This direct mail piece carried all the incredible news about Summer Splash.

Mother's Day event, a Summer Splash, Fall Football Faceplates, and a host of offers during the holiday season in late fall, where 40 percent of annual activations are typically generated. All of these events included a price deal on a Nokia phone, and/or a freebie such as a $50 floral gift certificate, to help close the sale.

Another tool for delivering news about an exciting sales promotion to carefully targeted households is direct mail. Northlich and CBW deployed this tool skillfully in 1999. An example of their collaboration from the Summer Splash promo is shown in Exhibit IBP 5.4. Examine this direct mail piece carefully and you'll find all the right elements for closing a sale. The piece features a great offer: a nice price on a spiffy Nokia phone plus four free tickets to the then newly opened Newport Aquarium—everyone's number one destination in the summer of 1999. Note as well the clear call to action: "Hurry, this incredible offer ends August 14!" How can I sign up? With CBW it's always easy. Take your pick: the toll-free number; the Web site, http://www.cbwireless.com; or any Cincinnati Bell Wireless retail outlet, including Best Buy, Circuit City, Office Depot, and Staples. This is great local sales execution, making the smart choice an obvious choice.

Nurturing Relationships with Customers.
Cincinnati Bell is an experienced database marketer. Working with Northlich, the company created a number of innovative programs in 1999 designed to reward, engage, and build a bond with existing CBW customers. Too often marketers make the mistake of spending all their advertising dollars trying to win new customers, and they take existing customers for granted. Then they wonder why their churn rates exceed industry averages. As we saw in Part 4 of this case, in its first year CBW had churn rates well below industry averages. No slippage would be acceptable in 1999.

Database marketing at its best is about building enduring relationships with customers, and CBW used its customer database in an attempt to do just that in 1999. Relationships depend on communication, and to foster that communication CBW launched its own branded newsletter—*The Talk*. The cover page of the summer 1999 issue is shown in Exhibit IBP 5.5. The communication goals for *The Talk* involved things such as keeping customers aware of changes taking place in the wireless industry, tips for making your phone more convenient to use and program, and details about special promotions designed exclusively for CBW customers. *The Talk* also encouraged customer comments and complaints by phone (877-CBW-8877) or e-mail (thetalk@cinbell.com).

Well, a newsletter like *The Talk* can be a great thing when you have something special to talk about. So, as part of its Summer Splash extravaganza, CBW decided to throw a party to celebrate the first anniversary of its launch. But what kind of party makes sense if your brand stands for *smart, current, and cool*? And whom should we invite? How about a rock 'n' roll concert for 10,000 of our closest friends—only CBW customers allowed. Perfect. Using *The Talk* to deliver its exclusive invitations,

EXHIBIT IBP 5.5

Newsletters are an increasingly common tool for would-be relationship builders.

CBW was able to attract about 10,000 of its customers to a free concert featuring Hootie & the Blowfish. In addition, Nokia got so caught up in the activity that they ended up footing most of the bill for the evening's entertainment, turning it into a huge win for CBW and CBW customers.

An event like this Hootie concert works in several ways to stir passion for a brand. First, the band put on a great show, leaving everyone with memories of a pleasant evening that are now connected to the CBW brand. Additionally, the local news media would of course create a big fuss over this event, making anyone who attended feel that, as a CBW customer, they really did get to be part of something special. Pity those poor souls who haven't gotten the message about which wireless brand in Cincinnati is *smart, current, and cool.*

It also turns out that every time someone activates a CBW phone, Cincinnati Bell sets aside two dollars for Boomer Esiason's foundation for the cure of cystic fibrosis. Esiason, former quarterback for the Cincinnati Bengals, is one of the city's mega-celebrities, and he was on hand for the Hootie concert to accept a check to his foundation for more than $200,000. It was an evening filled with passion and emotion. Passion and emotion drive brand loyalty and turn customers into brand advocates who then go out and tell two friends who tell two friends who tell two more friends, and all of a sudden you've touched a whole lot of customers and potential customers with a powerful brand-building message. You're probably starting to get the hint that 1999 turned out to be another very good year for Cincinnati Bell Wireless.

Measuring Up in 1999.

When a client understands its business and its customers like Cincinnati Bell, and an agency understands how to execute advertising and integrated brand promotion like Northlich, good things are going to happen in the marketplace. This certainly proved to be the case for CBW's launch in 1998, when more than 60,000 activations were achieved by year's end. But things turned out just as well or maybe even a little better for CBW in 1999. By December 1999 Cincinnati Bell had activated over 150,000 customers for its wireless business; CBW's market share had more than doubled versus one year earlier, with much of this gain coming from consumers who were abandoning the rapidly fading analog cellular format. With creative advertising, aggressive promotions like March Madness and Summer Splash, adept direct marketing, and a flair for public relations, CBW established itself as a feisty local brand ready to defend its home turf against telecommunication heavyweights such as Sprint and AT&T. Smart, current, and cool is right where they wanted to be.

Five Years in Review. . .

As the new century arrived, Cincinnati Bell Wireless remained on a steep growth curve. CBW rode that growth wave and captured more market share than any of the six competitors it faced. Through a focus on keeping things simple and having the coolest phones out there, CBW had become the wireless provider of choice in the Cincinnati metro area. Continued investment in advertising and integrated brand promotion kept the product in the forefront. By the end of

2001 CBW had best-in-class market share numbers of just over 40 percent and a churn rate at an industry low of 1.5 percent.

The growth of wireless began to slow in 2002. As a result, the advertising budget had to be cut and the mix of IBP tools in use was adjusted accordingly. CBW continued to have a weekly presence in newsprint and a steady presence on radio, but TV spending was confined to heavy promotional periods such as the back to school and holiday seasons. By 2002 the product itself was becoming more similar across all carriers. No longer was PCS the cool new technology; it was the same technology all were using. Also, no longer were Nokia phones available at only Cincinnati Bell. They were everywhere. This made the competitive environment much more challenging and a strong brand with a focused message even more important. Through it all CBW continued to have success, in fact winning the J. D. Power award for customer service. Through 2002, some growth continued for CBW and churn was kept at an industry-low level; however, more change was on the way in the world of wireless sales. By the end of the year there was a major threat to CBW—the threat of no longer having the most current or coolest wireless services.

By 2003, CBW management faced a daunting challenge. All major competitors were in the process of upgrading, or already had upgraded, their networks to next-generation technology. Code Division Multiple Access (CDMA) and Global System for Mobile Communications (GSM) were the new models for wireless, and they could now allow for better access to e-mail, picture taking and sending, and popular new features like custom ring tones and color screens. Because CBW was not in a position to upgrade its network and offer the newest services, it found itself in a battle to keep its status as the "smart, current, and cool" provider. In an effort to fend off competition until the new services would be available, CBW continued to rely on the essence of its brand: As we see in Exhibit IBP 5.6, this involved keeping things simple with no contracts and, as shown in Exhibit IBP 5.7, offering terrific deals on the latest and greatest new phones, like this one from Panasonic.

Five years is a long time to consider. We hope that along the way in learning about the wireless phone business, you have also learned a lot about advertising and integrated brand promotion. There are many lessons in this comprehensive case history that are typical of advertising and IBP in all walks of business life. As we come to the end, there is one last lesson to make note of, and there is none more important. Recall in 1998 that CBW launched with a product (i.e., digital PCS) that performed better, at a better price, than the existing competition. Five years later, with competitive challengers on all sides, things had changed dramatically. No longer did CBW have the superior performing service; in fact, they had fallen a little behind in the latest technologies. Without the best product to advertise in 2003, there is simply no way that their advertising could work as well as it did in 1998 and 1999. It is a simple and perhaps obvious truth that great advertising will always start with a great product. Without distinctive benefits to offer consumers, it's hard to know what to talk about. So, find great products to advertise, and you'll live happily ever after.

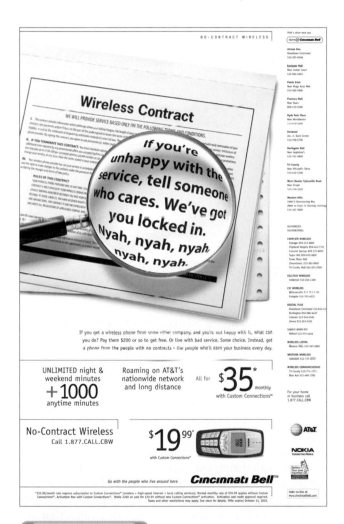

EXHIBIT IBP 5.6

Strong brands deliver a consistent message about what they do and do not stand for. Here we see CBW keeping its eye on the ball with yet another jab at those who want you to sign a contract.

EXHIBIT IBP 5.7

Five years after its offer of the Nokia 6160, CBW hadn't lost sight of the appeal of a cool phone.

IBP EXERCISES

1. Review Thorson and Moore's strategic planning triangle from Part 2 of this case study. What were the key strategic issues that Northlich had to reconsider as part of the planning process for 1999? What changes (if any) did this reconsideration lead to in the advertising and IBP campaign that Northlich would execute for CBW in 1999?

2. Using this CBW example, explain how equity-building advertising, sales promotions, and direct marketing programs can be used in combination to produce the kind of outcome that all clients are looking for. What makes the combination of these tools more potent than any one of the tools by itself?

3. Local brands need to be creative in capitalizing on their local roots if they are to stave off the attacks of powerful national brands. The folks at Northlich and CBW seem keenly aware of this point. Provide three examples from the 1999 campaign that illustrate CBW's willingness to connect to issues or events that are meaningful in its local community.

4. In 1999, Jack Cassidy launched a second wireless service under the brand name i-wireless, specifically targeted to consumers in the 16-to-24 age segment. Compare the Web sites for Cincinnati Bell Wireless (http://www.cbwireless.com) and i-wireless (http://www.i-ontheweb.com). What features or aspects of the two Web sites serve to differentiate these two brands? Based on what you find at these Web sites, how would you describe the similarities and differences in the value propositions for these two brands?

Douglas A. Zarkin
Director of Marketing and Creative
Services (Avon Future—mark),
Avon Products Inc.

When the world's leading direct seller of beauty and related products wanted to launch a new fashion and beauty experience for women by women, the company looked to an unlikely candidate to develop and launch its campaign—a guy. Douglas Zarkin, an up-and-coming brand-development professional and co-founder of Grey Global Group's youth-and-entertainment subsidiary G WHIZ, was hired by Avon Products, Inc. in early 2002 to develop the company's new Gen-Y targeted cosmetics brand: mark. Zarkin's background in youth-related advertising and marketing made him an ideal candidate to shape a direct-selling Avon business for a younger demographic, and, after some good-natured harassment from the all-female cosmetics team, the new director went to work on the firm's newest line of beauty products. Avon's appointment turned out to be an equal-opportunity success story: mere months after its launch, mark brought home $17 million and had enlisted over 25,000 enthusiastic young reps—entrepreneurial women pleased to "meet mark." The venture earned the cosmetics-and-accessories line top honors as *CosmoGIRL Magazine's* Best New Brand and gave Zarkin a seat among *Brandweek's* 2004 Top 10 Marketers of the Next Generation.

To anyone familiar with Douglas Zarkin's impressive resume of past clients, agencies, and brand successes, the thirty-something director's early achievement at Avon might not come as a surprise. What may strike some as unusual, however, is that Zarkin's ascendant career in advertising and marketing started out, as he puts it, "completely by accident." Recounting the progression from his days as a college student to his present day status as the envy of all *Queer Eye* fans, Zarkin humorously gibes, "I graduated from American University wanting to be the next Gordon Gecco from *Wall Street*. I had no idea I'd end up being Max Factor." The young graduate may have had Wall Street aspirations, but it didn't take him long to follow his creative muse, first to Saatchi & Saatchi, and later to Grey Worldwide where he got his break developing global youth-targeted product directives for M&M Mars, Konami Video Games, Reebok, and others. Each step along the way, Zarkin applied his brand-promotion philosophy to his own career advancement: "Think of yourself as a brand," invites the Avon director. "What is your point of difference? How do you differentiate yourself from the pack?" Zarkin's ability to see himself as the brand has been instrumental in scoring good positions with highly respected firms.

Being Doug Zarkin must be pretty good. He is the toast of thousands of young enterprising women from all over the states and around the world. Zarkin is perhaps stating the obvious when he claims that the greatest thing about his job is, "Meeting successful mark representatives and knowing that I have played a part in helping them to achieve their dreams." If the svelte models appearing in the "meet mark" TV spots are representative of the mark reps whose dreams he has helped to achieve, his point is well taken. Unfortunately for Zarkin, he does miss out on some of the fun at mark make-up parties: "With the exception of our skincare, there is not much of the product we produce that I can use or experience. It makes marketing just a bit more difficult versus working on something that I can better relate to as a man (i.e., sneakers, soda)!" It's a small price to pay.

Zarkin's interesting positions come with many attractive perks. Overseeing the creative process means going to TV and print shoots, and this places Zarkin in and around celebrities. "I am probably one the few people not having played college or pro sports that can actually say that they have tossed a touchdown pass to Jerry Rice and gotten an assist from Magic Johnson," says the Avon director. "There's often a lot of down time when you are doing a commercial or a program, and so we just started playing around on the set. Zarkin received his own fifteen minutes of advertising fame when a model failed to show up for an M&M

Mars photo shoot: "The next thing I knew I was in front of the camera as part of the national print campaign."

When one evaluates the creative ideas and marketing strategies behind Avon's new brand of beauty and accessory products, its no wonder that *Brandweek* named Zarkin one of the top 10 Marketers of the Next Generation. In an age of saturated media and increasing market fragmentation, Zarkin has created a hip, lifestyle platform that makes direct selling relevant to a whole new generation. "It is becoming increasingly more difficult to break through the clutter and find interesting ways to reach young people without seeming too overt," explains Zarkin. Beyond the make-up parties and socials that form the foundation of Avon's success, Zarkin finds creative ways to integrate mark across various media and even into branded entertainment. Millions of TV viewers saw mark billboard ads during the firing scenes of NBC's *The Apprentice,* and the brand made its way into a storyline of NBC's daytime drama *Passions.* Mark appeared in a three-minute MTV segment that highlighted the life of a young female mark representative. Zarkin's covert operations even extend to the mark "magalog," a blended retail catalog and magazine that contains feature stories about celebrities in addition to product information.

Douglas Zarkin has a blazing career, and the lifestyle appeal he has created for Avon's mark brand portends an even brighter future for the American University alum. To the casual observer, mark may seem like just another line of cosmetics. But in Zarkin's world, mark is a new beauty experience for young women. It's makeup you can buy or sell. It's about girls getting together, sharing tips, stories, and, yes, products—over 250 beauty products designed for today's young women. As the relaxed and sophisticated bathtub beauty asks at the close of one of Zarkin's TV spots, "Have you met mark?"

GLOSSARY

A

account planner A relatively recent addition to many advertising agencies; it is this person's job to synthesize all relevant consumer research and use it to design a coherent advertising strategy.

account planning A system by which, in contrast to traditional advertising research methods, an agency assigns a coequal account planner to work alongside the account executive and analyze research data. This method requires the account planner to stay with the same projects on a continuous basis.

account services A team of managers that identify the benefits a brand offers, its target audiences, and the best competitive positioning, and then develops a complete promotion plan.

Action for Children's Television (ACT) A group formed during the 1970s to lobby the government to limit the amount and content of advertising directed at children.

adaptors In reference to the *adaptation/innovation theory* generated by a study of creativity in employees, adaptors are the ones who, when faced with creative tasks, tend to work within the existing paradigm.

advertisement A specific message that an organization has placed to persuade an audience.

advertiser Business, not-for-profit, or government organization that uses advertising and other promotional techniques to communicate with target markets and to stimulate awareness and demand for its brands.

advertising A paid, mass-mediated attempt to persuade.

advertising agency An organization of professionals who provide creative and business services to clients related to planning, preparing, and placing advertisements.

advertising campaign A series of coordinated advertisements and other promotional efforts that communicate a single theme or idea.

advertising clutter An obstacle to advertising resulting from the large volume of similar ads for most products and services.

advertising plan A plan that specifies the thinking and tasks needed to conceive and implement an effective advertising effort.

advertising response function A mathematical relationship based on marginal analysis that associates dollars spent on advertising and sales generated; sometimes used to help establish an advertising budget.

advertising specialties A sales promotion having three key elements: a message, placed on a useful item, given to consumers with no obligation.

advertising substantiation program An FTC program initiated in 1971 to ensure that advertisers make available to consumers supporting evidence for claims made in ads.

advertorial A special advertising section designed to look like the print publication in which it appears.

advocacy advertising Advertising that attempts to influence public opinion on important social, political, or environmental issues of concern to the sponsoring organization.

aerial advertising Advertising that involves airplanes (pulling signs or banners), skywriting, or blimps.

affirmative disclosure An FTC action requiring that important material determined to be absent from prior ads must be included in subsequent advertisements.

agency of record The advertising agency chosen by the advertiser to purchase media time and space.

alternative press newspapers Newspapers geared toward a young, entertainment-oriented audience.

animation The use of drawn figures and scenes (like cartoons) to produce a television commercial.

appropriation The use of pictures or images owned by someone else without permission.

ARS Persuasion Method Testing service that offers true pre-post attitude testing through a theater-type test in which commercials are embedded in television shows and audience members indicate brand preference.

aspirational groups Groups made up of people an individual admires or uses as role models but is unlikely to ever interact with in any meaningful way.

association tests A type of projective technique that asks consumers to express their feelings or thoughts after hearing a brand name or seeing a logo.

assorted media mix A media mix option that employs multiple media alternatives to reach target audiences.

attitude An overall evaluation of any object, person, or issue that varies along a continuum, such as favorable to unfavorable or positive to negative.

attitude-change study A type of advertising research that uses a before-and-after ad exposure design.

audience A group of individuals who may receive and interpret messages sent from advertisers through mass media.

average quarter-hour persons The average number of listeners tuned to a radio station during a specified 15-minute segment of a daypart.

average quarter-hour rating The radio audience during a quarter-hour daypart expressed as a percentage of the population of the measurement area.

average quarter-hour share The percentage of the total radio audience that was listening to a radio station during a specified quarter-hour daypart.

axis A line, real or imagined, that runs through an advertisement and from which the elements in the ad flare out.

B

balance An orderliness and compatibility of presentation in an advertisement.

bandwidth A measure of the computer resources used by a Web site on the Internet.

banner ads Advertisements placed on World Wide Web sites that contain editorial material.

barter syndication A form of television syndication that takes both off-network and first-run syndication shows and offers them free or at a reduced rate to local television stations, with some national advertising presold within the programs.

beliefs The knowledge and feelings a person has accumulated about an object or issue.

benefit positioning A positioning option that features a distinctive customer benefit.

benefit segmentation A type of market segmenting in which target segments are delineated by the various benefit packages that different consumers want from the same product category.

between-vehicle duplication Exposure to the same advertisement in different media.

bill-back allowances A monetary incentive provided to retailers for featuring a marketer's brand in either advertising or in-store displays.

blackletter A style patterned after monastic hand-drawn letters characterized by the ornate design of the letters. Also called gothic.

bleed page A magazine page on which the background color of an ad runs to the edge of the page, replacing the standard white border.

blog (short for Weblog) A personal journal on a Web site that is frequently updated and intended for public access. Such sites are emerging as new and sophisticated sources of product and brand information.

blogger The author of a blog.

border The space surrounding an advertisement; it keeps the ad elements from spilling over into other ads or into the printed matter next to the ad.

brand A name, term, sign, symbol, or any other feature that identifies one seller's good or service as distinct from those of other sellers.

brand advertising Advertising that communicates the specific features, values, and benefits of a particular brand offered for sale by a particular organization.

brand attitudes Summary evaluations that reflect preferences for various products and brands.

brand communities Groups of consumers who feel a commonality and a shared purpose grounded or attached to a consumer good or service.

branded entertainment Embedding one's brand or brand icons as part of any entertainment property (e.g., a sporting event) in an effort to impress and connect with consumers in a unique and compelling way.

brand equity Developed by a firm that creates and maintains positive associations with the brand in the mind of consumers.

brand extension An adaptation of an existing brand to a new product area.

branding The strategy of developing brand names so that manufacturers can focus consumer attention on a clearly identified item.

brand loyalty A decision-making mode in which consumers repeatedly buy the same brand of a product as their choice to fulfill a specific need.

brand-loyal users A market segment made up of consumers who repeatedly buy the same brand of a product.

brand switching An advertising objective in which a campaign is designed to encourage customers to switch from their established brand.

build-up analysis A method of building up the expenditure levels of various tasks to help establish an advertising budget.

business buyer sales promotion Incentive techniques designed to cultivate buyers in large corporations who are making purchase decisions about a wide range of products.

business-market promotion Promotion designed to cultivate buyers from large corporations who are making purchase decisions.

business markets The institutional buyers who purchase items to be used in other products and services or to be resold to other businesses or households.

business newspapers Newspapers like the *Financial Times*, which serve a specialized business audience.

buzz "Seeding" the media, particularly the Internet, with news and information about a brand in an attempt to create positive word of mouth.

C

cable television A type of television that transmits a wide range of programming to subscribers through wires rather than over airwaves.

caching The use of a kind of active memory to conserve computer system resources.

cause-related advertising Advertising that identifies corporate sponsorship of philanthropic activities.

cease-and-desist order An FTC action requiring an advertiser to stop running an ad within 30 days so a hearing can be held to determine whether the advertising in question is deceptive or unfair.

celebrity A unique sociological category that matters a great deal to advertisers.

celebrity endorsements Advertisements that use an expert or celebrity as a spokesperson to endorse the use of a product or service.

channel grazing Using a television remote control to monitor programming on other channels while an advertisement is being broadcast.

channel power Power of setting prices in favor of the media.

circulation The number of newspapers distributed each day (for daily newspapers) or each week (for weekly publications).

classified advertising Newspaper advertising that appears as all-copy messages under categories such as sporting goods, employment, and automobiles.

click-throughs When Web users click on advertisements that take them to the homepages of those advertisers.

client The company or organization that pays for advertising. Also called the *sponsor*.

closing date The date when production-ready advertising materials must be delivered to a publisher for an ad to make a newspaper or magazine issue.

cognitive consistency The maintenance of a system of beliefs and attitudes over time; consumers' desire for cognitive consistency is an obstacle to advertising.

cognitive dissonance The anxiety or regret that lingers after a difficult decision.

cognitive responses The thoughts that occur to individuals at that exact moment in time when their beliefs and attitudes are being challenged by some form of persuasive communication.

collection search engine An automated program that crawls (a spider) around the Web and collects information.

column inch A unit of advertising space in a newspaper, equal to one inch deep by one column wide.

commission system A method of agency compensation based on the amount of money the advertiser spends on the media.

communication tests A type of pretest message research that simply seeks to see if a message is communicating something close to what is desired.

community A group of people loosely joined by some common characteristic or interest.

comp A polished version of an ad.

comparison advertisements Advertisements in which an advertiser makes a comparison between the firm's brand and competitors' brands.

competitive field The companies that compete for a segment's business.

competitive positioning A positioning option that uses an explicit reference to an existing competitor to help define precisely what the advertised brand can do.

competitor analysis In an advertising plan, the section that discusses who the competitors are, outlining their strengths, weaknesses, tendencies, and any threats they pose.

concentrated media mix A media mix option that focuses all the media placement dollars in one medium.

concept search engine A concept rather than a word or phrase is the basis for the search.

concept test A type of developmental research that seeks feedback designed to screen the quality of a new idea, using consumers as the final judge and jury.

consent order An FTC action asking an advertiser accused of running deceptive or unfair advertising to stop running the advertisement in question, without admitting guilt.

consideration set The subset of brands from a particular product category that becomes the focal point of a consumer's evaluation.

consultants Individuals that specialize in areas related to the promotional process.

consumer behavior Those activities directly involved in obtaining, consuming, and disposing of products and services, including the decision processes that precede and follow these actions.

consumer culture A way of life centered around consumption.

consumerism The actions of individual consumers to exert power over the marketplace activities of organizations.

consumer markets The markets for products and services purchased by individuals or households to satisfy their specific needs.

consumer-market sales promotion A type of sales promotion designed to induce household consumers to purchase a firm's brand rather than a competitor's brand.

consumer sales promotion A type of sales promotion aimed at consumers that focuses on price-off deals, coupons, sampling rebates, and premiums.

contest A sales promotion that has consumers compete for prizes based on skill or ability.

context effects How the context of the media through which an ad is presented affects consumers' impressions of the ad.

continuity The pattern of placement of advertisements in a media schedule.

continuous scheduling A pattern of placing ads at a steady rate over a period of time.

controlled circulation The number of copies of a newspaper that are given away free.

cookies Online tracking markers that advertisers place on a Web surfer's hard drive to track that person's online behavior.

coolhunts Researchers actually go to the site where they believe cool resides, stalk it, and bring it back to be used in the product and its advertising.

co-op advertising *See* **cooperative advertising.**

cooperative advertising The sharing of advertising expenses between national advertisers and local merchants. Also called *co-op advertising.*

copywriting The process of expressing the value and benefits a brand has to offer, via written or verbal descriptions.

corporate advertising Advertising intended to establish a favorable attitude toward a company as a whole, not just toward a specific brand.

corporate home page A site on the World Wide Web that focuses on a corporation and its products.

corrective advertising An FTC action requiring an advertiser to run additional advertisements to dispel false beliefs created by deceptive advertising.

cost per inquiry (CPI) The number of inquiries generated by a direct-marketing program divided by that program's cost.

cost per order (CPO) The number of orders generated by a direct-marketing program divided by that program's cost.

cost per rating point (CPRP) The cost of a spot on television divided by the program's rating; the resulting dollar figure can be used to compare the efficiency of advertising on various programs.

cost per thousand (CPM) The dollar cost of reaching 1,000 members of an audience using a particular medium.

cost per thousand–target market (CPM–TM) The cost per thousand for a particular segment of an audience.

coupon A type of sales promotion that entitles a buyer to a designated reduction in price for a product or service.

cover date The date of publication appearing on a magazine.

creative boutique An advertising agency that emphasizes copywriting and artistic services to its clients.

creative brief A document that outlines and channels an essential creative idea and objective.

creative concept The unique creative thought behind an advertising campaign.

creative plan A guideline used during the copywriting process to specify the message elements that must be coordinated during the preparation of copy.

creative revolution A revolution in the advertising industry during the 1960s, characterized by the "creatives" (art directors and copywriters) having a bigger say in the management of their agencies.

creative services A group that develops the message that will be delivered through advertising, sales promotion, direct marketing, event sponsorship, or public relations.

creative team The copywriters and art directors responsible for coming up with the creative concept for an advertising campaign.

cross-selling Marketing programs aimed at customers that already purchase other products.

culture What a people do—the way they eat, groom themselves, celebrate, mark their space and social position, and so forth.

cume The cumulative radio audience, which is the total number of different people who listen to a station for at least five minutes in a quarter-hour period within a specified daypart.

customer satisfaction Good feelings that come from a favorable postpurchase experience.

D

dailies Newspapers published every weekday; also, in television ad production, the scenes shot during the previous day's production.

database agency Agency that helps customers construct databases of target customers, merge databases, develop promotional materials, and then execute the campaign.

dayparts Segments of time during a television broadcast day.

deal-proneness The ease with which a consumer can get a deal, know what a good deal is, operate with knowledge of what a good price would be, and know a seller's cost.

deception Making false or misleading statements in an advertisement.

defamation When a communication occurs that damages the reputation of an individual because the information was untrue.

delayed response advertising Advertising that relies on imagery and message themes to emphasize the benefits and satisfying characteristics of a brand.

demographic dividend Situation in developing nations such as China, Brazil, and Mexico where falling labor costs, a younger and healthier population, and the entry of millions of women into the work force produce a favorable climate for economic expansion.

demographic segmentation Market segmenting based on basic descriptors like age, gender, race, marital status, income, education, and occupation.

design The structure (and the plan behind the structure) for the aesthetic and stylistic aspects of a print advertisement.

designers Specialists intimately involved with the execution of creative ideas and efforts.

developmental copy research A type of copy research that helps copywriters at the early stages of copy development by providing audience interpretations and reactions to the proposed copy.

dialogue Advertising copy that delivers the selling points of a message to the audience through a character or characters in the ad.

dialogue balloons A type of projective technique that offers consumers the chance to fill in the dialogue of cartoonlike stories, as a way of indirectly gathering brand information.

differentiation The process of creating a perceived difference, in the mind of the consumer, between an organization's brand and the competition's.

digital video (DV) A less expensive and less time-consuming alternative to film, it produces a better quality image than standard videotape.

direct broadcast by satellite (DBS) A program delivery system whereby television (and radio) programs are sent directly from a satellite to homes equipped with small receiving dishes.

direct mail A direct-marketing medium that involves using the postal service to deliver marketing materials.

direct marketing According to the Direct Marketing Association, "An interactive system of marketing which uses one or more advertising media to affect a measurable response and/or transaction at any location."

direct-marketing agency Agency that maintains large databases of mailing lists; some of these firms can also design direct-marketing campaigns either through the mail or by telemarketing.

direct response Copy research method measuring actual behavior of consumers.

direct response advertising Advertising that asks the receiver of the message to act immediately.

direct response agency Also called direct marketing agency.

direct response copy Advertising copy that highlights the urgency of acting immediately.

display advertising A newspaper ad that includes the standard components of a print ad—headline, body copy, and often an illustration—to set it off from the news content of the paper.

domain name The unique URL through which a Web location is established.

door-to-door sampling A type of sampling in which samples are brought directly to the homes of a target segment in a well-defined geographic area.

double-page spreads Advertisements that bridge two facing pages.

E

e-business A form of e-advertising and/or promotion in which companies selling to business customers rely on the Internet to send messages and close sales.

e-commerce agency Agency that handles a variety of planning and execution activities related to promotions using electronic commerce.

economies of scale The ability of a firm to lower the cost of each item produced because of high-volume production.

editing In television ad production, piecing together various scenes or shots of scenes to bring about the desired visual effect.

effective frequency The number of times a target audience needs to be exposed to a message before the objectives of the advertiser are met.

effective reach The number or percentage of consumers in the target audience that are exposed to an ad some minimum number of times.

elaboration likelihood model (ELM) A model that pertains to any situation where a persuasive communication is being sent and received.

electronic, laser, and inkjet printing A printing process that uses computers, electronics, electrostatics, and special toners and inks to produce images.

electronic mail (e-mail) An Internet function that allows users to communicate, much as they do using standard mail.

electronic mailing list A collection of e-mail addresses.

embedded Tightly connected to a context.

emergent consumers A market segment made up of the gradual but constant influx of first-time buyers.

emotional benefits Those benefits not typically found in some tangible feature or objective characteristic of a product or service.

ethics Moral standards and principles against which behavior is judged.

ethnic newspapers Newspapers that target a specific ethnic group.

ethnocentrism The tendency to view and value things from the perspective of one's own culture.

evaluative copy research A type of copy research used to judge an advertisement after the fact—the audience expresses its approval or disapproval of the copy used in the ad.

evaluative criteria The product attributes or performance characteristics on which consumers base their product evaluations.

event-planning agencies Experts in finding locations, securing dates, and putting together a "team" of people to pull off a promotional event.

event sponsorship Providing financial support to help fund an event, in return for the right to display a brand name, logo, or advertising message on-site at the event.

extended problem solving A decision-making mode in which consumers are inexperienced in a particular consumption setting but find the setting highly involving.

external facilitator An organization or individual that provides specialized services to advertisers and agencies.

external lists Mailing lists purchased from a list compiler or rented from a list broker and used to help an organization cultivate new business.

external position The competitive niche a brand pursues.

external search A search for product information that involves visiting retail stores to examine alternatives, seeking input from friends and relatives about their experiences with the products in question, or perusing professional product evaluations.

eye-tracking systems A type of physiological measure that monitors eye movements across print ads.

F

fact sheet radio ad A listing of important selling points that a radio announcer can use to ad-lib a radio spot.

Federal Trade Commission (FTC) The government regulatory agency that has the most power and is most directly involved in overseeing the advertising industry.

fee system A method of agency compensation whereby the advertiser and the agency agree on an hourly rate for different services provided.

field work Research conducted outside the agency, usually in the home or site of consumption.

film The most versatile and highest quality medium for television ad production.

first cover page The front cover of a magazine.

first-run syndication Television programs developed specifically for sale to individual stations.

flexography A printing technique similar to offset printing but that uses water-based ink, allowing printing to be done on any surface.

flighting A media-scheduling pattern of heavy advertising for a period of time, usually two weeks, followed by no advertising for a period, followed by another period of heavy advertising.

focus group A brainstorming session with a small group of target consumers and a professional moderator, used to gain new insights about consumer response to a brand.

"forgetting function" Idea that people's forgetting is fairly predictable and seems to obey a mathematical function.

formal balance A symmetrical presentation in an ad—every component on one side of an imaginary vertical line is repeated in approximate size and shape on the other side of the imaginary line.

fourth cover page The back cover of a magazine.

frame-by-frame test Copy research method that works by getting consumers to turn dials (like/dislike) while viewing television commercials in a theater setting.

free premium A sales promotion that provides consumers with an item at no cost; the item is either included in the package of a purchased item or mailed to the consumer after proof of purchase is verified.

free-standing insert (FSI) A newspaper insert ad that contains cents-off coupons for a variety of products and is typically delivered with Sunday newspapers.

frequency The average number of times an individual or household within a target audience is exposed to a media vehicle in a given period of time.

frequency-marketing programs Direct-marketing programs that provide concrete rewards to frequent customers.

frequency programs A type of sales promotion that offers consumers discounts or free product rewards for repeat purchase or patronage of the same brand or company.

fulfillment center Centers that ensure customers receive the product ordered through direct mail.

full position A basis of buying newspaper ad space, in which the ad is placed near the top of a page or in the middle of editorial material.

full-service agency An advertising agency that typically includes an array of advertising professionals to meet all the promotional needs of clients.

functional benefits Those benefits that come from the objective performance characteristics of a product or service.

G

gatefold ads Advertisements that fold out of a magazine to display an extra-wide ad.

gay and lesbian newspapers Newspapers targeting a gay and lesbian readership.

gender The social expression of sexual biology or choice.

general-population newspapers Newspapers that serve local communities and report news of interest to the local population.

geodemographic segmentation A form of market segmentation that identifies neighborhoods around the country that share common demographic characteristics.

geographic scope Scope of the geographic area to be covered by advertising media.

geo-targeting The placement of ads in geographic regions where higher purchase tendencies for a brand are evident.

global advertising Developing and placing advertisements with a common theme and presentation in all markets around the world where the firm's brands are sold.

global agencies Advertising agencies with a worldwide presence.

globalized campaigns Advertising campaigns that use the same message and creative execution across all (or most) international markets.

government officials and employees One of the five types of audiences for advertising; includes employees of government organizations, such as schools and road maintenance operations, at the federal, state, and local levels.

gravure A print production method that uses a plate or mat; it is excellent for reproducing pictures.

gross domestic product (GDP) A measure of the total value of goods and services produced within an economic system.

gross impressions The sum of exposures to all the media placement in a media plan.

gross rating points (GRP) The product of reach times frequency.

guaranteed circulation A stated minimum number of copies of a particular issue of a magazine that will be delivered to readers.

guerrilla marketing Edgy, inexpensive promotional initiatives executed in major urban markets.

H

habit A decision-making mode in which consumers buy a single brand repeatedly as a solution to a simple consumption problem.

headline The leading sentence or sentences, usually at the top or bottom of an ad, that attract attention, communicate a key selling point, or achieve brand identification.

heavy-up scheduling Placing advertising in media more heavily when consumers show buying tendencies.

heavy users Consumers who purchase a product or service much more frequently than others.

hierarchical search engine A database engine divided into categories for searching.

high-definition television (HDTV) Television that displays picture and produces sound from a satellite that sends a digital signal.

highly industrialized countries Countries with both a high GNP and a high standard of living.

hits The number of pages and graphical images requested from a Web site.

hot spot A WiFi-accessible area.

household consumers The most conspicuous of the five types of audiences for advertising; most mass media advertising is directed at them.

households using television (HUT) A measure of the number of households tuned to a television program during a particular time period.

I

illustration In the context of advertising, the drawing, painting, photography, or computer-generated art that forms the picture in an advertisement.

illustration format The way the product is displayed in a print advertisement.

impressions One way an advertiser can pay for space on a Web site page. In this case, a flat fee is charged for each time the advertisement is viewed.

Industrial Revolution A major change in Western society beginning in the mid-eighteenth century and marked by a rapid change from an agricultural to an industrial economy.

industry analysis In an advertising plan, the section that focuses on developments and trends within an industry and on any other factors that may make a difference in how an advertiser proceeds with an advertising plan.

inelasticity of demand Strong loyalty to a product, resulting in consumers being less sensitive to price increases.

infomercial A long advertisement that looks like a talk show or a half-hour product demonstration.

informal balance An asymmetrical presentation in an ad—nonsimilar sizes and shapes are optically weighed.

information intermediator An organization that collects customer purchase transaction histories, aggregates them across many firms that have sold merchandise to these customers, and then sells the customer names and addresses back to the firms that originally sold to these customers.

in-house agency The advertising department of a firm.

innovators In reference to the *adaptation/innovation theory* generated by a study of creativity in employees, innovators are the ones who, when faced with creative tasks, treat the existing paradigm as an obstacle.

inquiry/direct response measures A type of posttest message tracking in which a print or broadcast advertisement offers the audience the opportunity to place an inquiry or respond directly through a reply card or toll-free number.

in-store sampling A type of sampling that occurs at the point of purchase and is popular for food products and cosmetics.

integrated brand promotion (IBP) The use of various promotional tools, including advertising, in a coordinated manner to build and maintain brand awareness, identity, and preference.

integrated marketing communications (IMC) The process of using promotional tools in a unified way so that a synergistic communications effect is created.

interactive agencies Advertising agencies that help advertisers prepare communications for new media like the Internet, interactive kiosks, CD-ROMs, and interactive television.

interactive media Media that allow consumers to call up games, entertainment, shopping opportunities, and educational programs on a subscription or pay-per-view basis.

intergenerational effect When people choose products based on what was used in their childhood household.

internal lists An organization's records of its customers, subscribers, donors, and inquirers, used to develop better relationships with current customers.

internal position The niche a brand achieves with regard to the other similar brands a firm markets.

internal search A search for product information that draws on personal experience and prior knowledge.

international advertising The preparation and placement of advertising in different national and cultural markets.

international affiliates Foreign-market advertising agencies with which a local agency has established a relationship to handle clients' international advertising needs.

Internet A vast global network of scientific, military, and research computers that allows people inexpensive access to the largest storehouse of information in the world.

Internet Relay Chat (IRC) A component of the Internet that makes it possible for users to "talk" electronically with each other, despite their geographical separation.

involvement The degree of perceived relevance and personal importance accompanying the choice of a certain product or service within a particular context.

iri BehaviorScan Supplier of single-source data testing.

J, K, L

layout A drawing of a proposed print advertisement, showing where all the elements in the ad are positioned.

less-developed countries Countries whose economies lack almost all the resources necessary for development: capital, infrastructure, political stability, and trained workers.

letterpress The oldest and most versatile method of printing, in which text and images are printed from a plate or mat.

libel Defamation that occurs in print and would relate to magazine, newspaper, direct mail, or Internet reports.

life-stage A circumstantial variable, such as when a family's youngest child moves away from home, which changes the consumption patterns of the family.

lifestyle segmentation A form of market segmenting that focuses on consumers' activities, interests, and opinions.

limited problem solving A decision-making mode in which consumers' experience and involvement are both low.

live production The process of creating a live television commercial, which can result in realism and the capturing of spontaneous reactions and events but comes with a loss of control that can threaten the objectives of the commercial.

live script radio ad A detailed script read by an on-air radio personality.

local advertising Advertising directed at an audience in a single trading area, either a city or state.

local agency An advertising agency in a foreign market hired because of its knowledge of the culture and local market conditions.

localized campaigns Advertising campaigns that involve preparing different messages and creative executions for each foreign market a firm has entered.

local spot radio advertising Radio advertising placed directly with individual stations rather than with a network or syndicate.

local television Television programming other than the network broadcast that independent stations and network affiliates offer local audiences.

log analysis software Measurement software that allows a Web site to track hits, pages, visits, and users as well as audience traffic within the site.

logo A graphic mark that identifies a company and other visual representations that promote an identity for a firm.

M

mailing list A file of names and addresses that an organization might use for contacting prospective or prior customers.

mail sampling A type of sampling in which samples are delivered through the postal service.

marcom manager A marketing-communications manager who plans an organization's overall communications program and oversees the various functional specialists inside and outside the organization to ensure that they are working together to deliver the desired message to the customer.

market analysis In an advertising plan, the section that examines the factors that drive and determine the market for a firm's product or service.

marketing The process of conceiving, pricing, promoting, and distributing ideas, goods, and services to create exchanges that benefit consumers and organizations.

marketing database A mailing list that also includes information collected directly from individual customers.

marketing mix The blend of the four responsibilities of marketing—conception, pricing, promotion, and distribution—used for a particular idea, product, or service.

market niche A relatively small group of consumers who have a unique set of needs and who typically are willing to pay a premium price to a firm that specializes in meeting those needs.

market segmentation The breaking down of a large, heterogeneous market into submarkets or segments that are more homogeneous.

markup charge A method of agency compensation based on adding a percentage charge to a variety of services the agency purchases from outside suppliers.

meaning What an advertisement intends or conveys.

measured media Media that are closely measured to determine advertising costs and effectiveness: television, radio, newspapers, magazines, and outdoor media.

mechanical A carefully prepared pasteup of the exact components of an advertisement, prepared specifically for the printer.

media buying Securing the electronic media time and print media space specified in a given account's schedule.

media-buying service An independent organization that specializes in buying media time and space, particularly on radio and television, as a service to advertising agencies and advertisers.

media class A broad category of media, such as television, radio, or newspapers.

media mix The blend of different media that will be used to effectively reach the target audience.

media objectives The specific goals for a media placement: Reach the target audience, determine the geographic scope of placement, and identify the message weight, which determines the overall audience size.

media plan A plan specifying the media in which advertising messages will be placed to reach the desired target audience.

media planning and buying services Services related to media planning or buying that are provided by advertising agencies or specialized media-buying organizations.

media specialists Organizations that specialize in buying media time and space and offer media strategy consulting to advertising agencies and advertisers.

media vehicle A particular option for placement within a media class (e.g., *Newsweek* is a media vehicle within the magazine media class).

medium The means by which an illustration in a print advertisement is rendered: either drawing, photography, or computer graphics.

membership groups Groups an individual interacts with in person on some regular basis.

members of business organizations One of the five types of audiences for advertising; the focus of advertising for firms that produce business and industrial goods and services.

members of a trade channel One of the five types of audiences for advertising; the retailers, wholesalers, and distributors targeted by producers of both household and business goods and services.

merchandise allowances A type of trade-market sales promotion in which free products are packed with regular shipments as payment to the trade for setting up and maintaining displays.

message strategy A component of an advertising strategy, it defines the goals of the advertiser and how those goals will be achieved.

message weight A sum of the total audience size of all the media specified in a media plan.

miscellaneous In regard to font styles, a category that includes display fonts that are used not for their legibility, but for their ability to attract attention. Fonts like garage and novelty display belong in this category.

Mobile-Fi Wireless Internet technology having multi-mile access and the capability of accessing the Net while the user is moving in a car or train.

mobile sampling A type of sampling carried out by logo-emblazoned vehicles that dispense samples, coupons, and premiums to consumers at malls, shopping centers, fairgrounds, and recreational areas.

monopoly power The ability of a firm to make it impossible for rival firms to compete with it, either through advertising or in some other way.

multi-attribute attitude models (MAAMs) A framework and set of procedures for collecting information from consumers to assess their salient beliefs and attitudes about competitive brands.

N

narrative Advertising copy that simply displays a series of statements about a brand.

narrowcasting The development and delivery of specialized television programming to well-defined audiences.

national advertising Advertising that reaches all geographic areas of one nation.

National Advertising Review Board A body formed by the advertising industry to oversee its practice.

national spot radio advertising Radio advertising placed in nationally syndicated radio programming.

need state A psychological state arising when one's desired state of affairs differs from one's actual state of affairs.

network radio advertising Radio advertising placed within national network programs.

network television A type of television that broadcasts programming over airwaves to affiliate stations across the United States under a contract agreement.

newly industrialized countries Countries where traditional ways of life that have endured for centuries change into modern consumer cultures in a few short years.

newspaper sampling Samples distributed in newspapers to allow very specific geographic and geodemographic targeting.

nonusers A market segment made up of consumers who do not use a particular product or service.

normative test scores Scores that are determined by testing an ad and then comparing the scores to those of previously tested, average commercials of its type.

O

objective-and-task approach A method of advertising budgeting that focuses on the relationship between spending and advertising objectives by identifying the specific tasks necessary to achieve different aspects of the advertising objectives.

off-invoice allowance A program allowing wholesalers and retailers to deduct a set amount from the invoice they receive for merchandise.

off-network syndication Television programs that were previously run in network prime time.

offset lithography A printing process in which a flat, chemically treated surface attracts ink to the areas to be printed and repels ink from other areas; the inked image is then transferred to a rubber blanket on a roller, and from the roller the impression is carried to paper.

online editing The transferring of the finalized rough cut of a television ad onto one-inch videotape, which is of on-air quality suitable for media transmission.

on-package sampling A type of sampling in which a sample item is attached to another product package.

on-sale date The date on which a magazine is issued to subscribers and for newsstand distribution.

opt-in e-mail A list of Web site visitors who have given their permission to receive commercial e-mail about topics and products that interest them.

out-of-home media The combination of transit and billboard advertising.

P

pages The particular pages sent from a Web site to a requesting site.

paid circulation The number of copies of a newspaper sold through subscriptions and newsstand distribution.

paid search Process by which companies pay Web search engines and portals to place ads in or near relevant search results.

parallel layout structure A print ad design that employs art on the right-hand side of the page and repeats the art on the left-hand side.

participation A way of buying television advertising time in which several different advertisers buy commercial time during a specific television program.

pass-along readership An additional number of people, other than the original readers, who may see a magazine.

pay-for-results A compensation plan that results when a client and its agency agree to a set of results criteria on which the agency's fee will be based.

percentage-of-sales approach An advertising budgeting approach that calculates the advertising budget based on a percentage of the prior year's sales or the projected year's sales.

peripheral cues The features of an ad other than the actual arguments about the brand's performance.

permanent long-term displays P-O-P materials intended for presentation for more than six months.

permission marketing Web users agree to receive e-mails from organizations.

physiological measures A type of pretest message research that uses physiological measurement devices to detect how consumers react to messages, based on physical responses.

pica A measure of the width or depth of lines of type.

picturing Creating representations of things.

pilot testing A form of message evaluation consisting of experimentation in the marketplace.

point A measure of the size of type in height.

point-of-purchase (P-O-P) advertising Advertising that appears at the point of purchase.

pop-up/pop-under ad An Internet advertisement that appears as a Web site page is loading or after a page has loaded.

portal A starting point for Web access and search.

positioning The process of designing a product or service so that it can occupy a distinct and valued place in the target consumer's mind, and then communicating this distinctiveness through advertising.

positioning strategy The key themes or concepts an organization features for communicating the distinctiveness of its product or service to the target segment.

posttest message tracking Advertising research that assesses the performance of advertisements during or after the launch of an advertising campaign.

preferred position A basis of buying newspaper ad space, in which the ad is placed in a specific section of the paper.

premiums Items that feature the logo of a sponsor and that are offered free, or at a reduced price, with the purchase of another item.

preprinted insert An advertisement delivered to a newspaper fully printed and ready for insertion into the newspaper.

preproduction The stage in the television production process in which the advertiser and advertising agency (or in-house agency staff) carefully work out the precise details of how the creative planning behind an ad can best be brought to life with the opportunities offered by television.

price/cost transparency Ease with which consumers can find out the price of a product and the seller's cost.

price-off deal A type of sales promotion that offers a consumer cents or even dollars off merchandise at the point of purchase through specially marked packages.

primary demand The demand for an entire product category.

primary demand stimulation Using advertising to create demand for a product category in general.

principle of limited liability An economic principle that allows an investor to risk only his or her shares of a corporation, rather than personal wealth, in business ventures.

principles of design General rules governing the elements within a print advertisement and the arrangement of and relationship between these elements.

proactive public relations strategy A public relations strategy that is dictated by marketing objectives, seeks to publicize a company and its brands, and is offensive in spirit rather than defensive.

production facilitator An organization that offers essential services both during and after the production process.

production services A team that takes creative ideas and turns them into advertisements, direct mail pieces, or events materials.

production stage The point at which the storyboard and script for a television ad come to life and are filmed. Also called the *shoot*.

production timetable A realistic schedule for all the preproduction, production, and postproduction activities involved with making a television commercial.

product placement The sales promotion technique of getting a marketer's product featured in movies and television shows.

professionals One of the five types of audiences for advertising, defined as doctors, lawyers, accountants, teachers, or any other professionals who require special training or certification.

program rating The percentage of television households that are in a market and are tuned to a specific program during a specific time period.

projective techniques A type of developmental research designed to allow consumers to project thoughts and feelings (conscious or unconscious) in an indirect and unobtrusive way onto a theoretically neutral stimulus.

promotion agencies Specialized agencies that handle promotional efforts.

psychogalvanometer A type of physiological measure that detects galvanic skin response—minute changes in perspiration that suggest arousal related to some stimulus (such as an advertisement).

psychographics A form of market research that emphasizes the understanding of consumers' activities, interests, and opinions.

publicity Unpaid-for media exposure about a firm's activities or its products and services.

public relations A marketing and management function that focuses on communications that foster goodwill between a firm and its many constituent groups.

public relations audit An internal study that identifies the characteristics of a firm or the aspects of the firm's activities that are positive and newsworthy.

public relations firms Firms that handle the needs of organizations regarding relationships with the local community, competitors, industry associations, and government organizations.

public relations plan A plan that identifies the objectives and activities related to the public relations communications issued by a firm.

puffery The use of absolute superlatives like "Number One" and "Best in the World" in advertisements.

pulsing A media-scheduling strategy that combines elements from continuous and flighting techniques; advertisements are scheduled continuously in media over a period of time, but with periods of much heavier scheduling.

purchase intent A measure of whether or not a consumer intends to buy a product or service in the near future.

Pure Food and Drug Act A 1906 act of Congress requiring manufacturers to list the active ingredients of their products on their labels.

push money A form of trade incentive in which retail salespeople are offered monetary reward for featuring a marketer's brand with shoppers.

push strategy A sales promotion strategy in which marketers devise incentives to encourage purchases by members of the trade to help push a product into the distribution channel.

Q, R

radio networks A type of radio that delivers programming via satellite to affiliate stations across the United States.

radio syndication A type of radio that provides complete programs to stations on a contract basis.

rate card A form given to advertisers by a newspaper and containing information on costs, closing times, specifications for submitting an ad, and special pages or features available in the newspaper.

ratings point A measure indicating that 1 percent of all the television households in an area were tuned to the program measured.

rational branding A Web-presence design that gives people multiple reasons to continue to visit the site.

reach The number of people or households in a target audience that will be exposed to a media vehicle or schedule at least one time during a given period of time. It is often expressed as a percentage.

reactive public relations strategy A public relations strategy that is dictated by influences outside the control of a company, focuses on problems to be solved rather than opportunities, and requires defensive rather than offensive measures.

readership A measure of a newspaper's circulation multiplied by the number of readers of a copy.

rebate A money-back offer requiring a buyer to mail in a form requesting the money back from the manufacturer.

recall tests Tests of how much the viewer of an ad remembers of the message; they are used to measure the cognitive residue of the ad. These are the most commonly employed tests in advertising.

recognition In a test, when the audience members indicate that they have seen an ad before.

recognition tests Tests in which audience members are asked if they recognize an ad or something in an ad. These are the standard cognitive residue test for print ads and promotion.

reference group Any configuration of other persons that a particular individual uses as a point of reference in making his or her own consumption decisions.

regional advertising Advertising carried out by producers, wholesalers, distributors, and retailers that concentrate their efforts in a particular geographic region.

repeat purchase A second purchase of a new product after trying it for the first time.

repositioning Returning to the process of segmenting, targeting, and positioning a product or service to arrive at a revised positioning strategy.

resonance test A type of message assessment in which the goal is to determine to what extent the message resonates or rings true with target audience members.

RFM analysis An analysis of how recently and how frequently a customer is buying from an organization, and of how much that customer is spending per order and over time.

riding the boards Assessing possible locations for billboard advertising.

rituals Repeated behaviors that affirm, express, and maintain cultural values.

robots A software that roams the Internet through a user-specified criteria.

robot search engine Employs the use of "bots" to roam the Internet in search of information fitting certain user-specified criteria.

roman The most popular category of type because of its legibility.

rough cut An assembly of the best scenes from a television ad shoot edited together using digital technology.

rough layout The second stage of the ad layout process, in which the headline is lettered in and the elements of the ad are further refined.

run-of-paper or **run-of-press (ROP)** A basis of buying newspaper or magazine ad space, in which an ad may appear anywhere, on any page in the paper or magazine.

S

sales promotion The use of incentive techniques that create a perception of greater brand value among consumers or distributors.

salient beliefs A small number of beliefs that are the critical determinants of an attitude.

sampling A sales promotion technique designed to provide a consumer with a trial opportunity.

sans serif A category of type that includes typefaces with no small lines crossing the ends of the main strokes.

satellite and closed-circuit A method of transmitting programming to highly segmented audiences.

scratch track A rough approximation of the musical score of a television ad, using only a piano and vocalists.

script The written version of an ad; it specifies the coordination of the copy elements with the video scenes.

search engine A software tool used to find Web sites on the Internet by searching for keywords typed in by the user.

search engine optimization (SEO) Utilizing a search engine to a company's best advantage.

secondary data Information obtained from existing sources.

second cover page The inside front cover of a magazine.

selective attention The processing of only a few advertisements among the many encountered.

selective demand stimulation Using advertising to stimulate demand for a specific brand within a product category.

self-expressive benefits What consumers gain by using products that they perceive will send a set of signals identifying them with their desired reference group.

self-liquidating premium A sales promotion that requires a consumer to pay most of the cost of the item received as a premium.

self-reference criterion (SRC) The unconscious reference to one's own cultural values, experiences, and knowledge as a basis for decisions.

self-regulation The advertising industry's attempt to police itself.

sentence and picture completion A type of projective technique in which a researcher presents consumers with part of a picture or a sentence with words deleted and then asks that the stimulus be completed; the picture or sentence relates to one or several brands.

serif The small lines that cross the ends of the main strokes in type; also the name for the category of type that has this characteristic.

share of audience A measure of the proportion of households that are using television during a specific time period and are tuned to a particular program.

share of voice A calculation of any advertiser's brand expenditures relative to the overall spending in a category.

shoot *See* **production stage.**

short-term promotional displays P-O-P materials that are used for six months or less.

single-source data Information provided from individual households about brand purchases, coupon use, and television advertising exposure by combining grocery store scanner data with TV-viewing data from monitoring devices attached to the households' televisions.

single-source tracking measures A type of posttest message tracking that provides information about brand purchases, coupon use, and television advertising exposure by combining grocery store scanner data and devices that monitor household television-viewing behavior.

single-source tracking services Research services that offer information not just on demographics but also on brands, purchase size, prices paid, and media exposure.

situation analysis In an advertising plan, the section in which the advertiser lays out the most important factors that define the situation, and then explains the importance of each factor.

skyscraper A tall, skinny banner ad that is a variation on the traditional top-of-the-screen rectangle.

slander Oral defamation that in the context of promotion would occur during television or radio broadcast of an event involving a company and its employees.

slogan A short phrase used in part to help establish an image, identity, or position for a brand or an organization, but mostly used to increase memorability.

slotting fees A type of trade-market sales promotion in which manufacturers make direct cash payments to retailers to ensure shelf space.

social meaning What a product or service means in a societal context.

society A group of people living in a particular area who share a common culture and consider themselves a distinct and unified entity.

space contract A contract that establishes a rate for all advertising placed in a magazine by an advertiser over a specified period.

space order A commitment by an advertiser to advertising space in a particular issue of a magazine. Also called an *insertion order*.

spam To post messages to many unrelated newsgroups on Usenet.

specialty-advertising items Items used for advertising purposes and that have three defining elements: (1) they contain the sponsor's logo and perhaps a related promotional message; (2) this logo and message appear on a useful or decorative item; and (3) the item is given freely, as a gift from the sponsor.

spider An automated program used in collection search engines.

split-cable transmission A type of pilot testing in which two different versions of an advertisement are transmitted to two separate samples of similar households within a single, well-defined market area; the ads are then compared on measures of exposure, recall, and persuasion.

split-list experiment A type of pilot testing in which multiple versions of a direct mail piece are prepared and sent to various segments of a mailing list; the version that pulls the best is deemed superior.

split-run distribution A type of pilot testing in which two different versions of an advertisement are placed in every other issue of a magazine; the ads are then compared on the basis of direct response.

sponsor *See* **client.**

sponsorship A way of buying television advertising time in which an advertiser agrees to pay for the production of a television program and for most (and often all) of the advertising that appears in the program.

spot advertising A way of buying television advertising time in which airtime is purchased through local television stations.

square root law The recognition of print ads increases with the square of the illustration.

standard advertising unit (SAU) One of 57 defined sizes of newspaper advertisements.

Starch Readership Services An example of a company that performs recognition tests.

sticky site A site that is able to attract visitors over and over again and keep them for a long time.

still production A technique of television ad production whereby a series of photographs or slides is filmed and edited so that the resulting ad appears to have movement and action.

storyboard A frame-by-frame sketch or photo sequence depicting, in sequence, the visual scenes and copy that will be used in an advertisement.

story construction A type of projective technique that asks consumers to tell a story about people depicted in a scene or picture, as a way of gathering information about a brand.

STP marketing (**S**egmenting, **T**argeting, **P**ositioning) A marketing strategy employed when advertisers focus their efforts on one subgroup of a product's total market.

straight-line copy Advertising copy that explains in straightforward terms why a reader will benefit from use of a product or service.

stratification (social class) A person's relative standing in a social system as produced by systematic inequalities in things such as wealth, income, education, power, and status. Also referred to as social class.

streaming video and audio The process of inserting TV and radio-like ads into music and video clips.

subhead In an advertisement, a few words or a short sentence that usually appears above or below the headline and includes important brand information not included in the headline.

subliminal advertising Advertising alleged to work on a subconscious level.

support media Media used to reinforce a message being delivered via some other media vehicle.

surfing Gliding from Web site to Web site using a search engine, direct links, or word of mouth.

sweepstakes A sales promotion in which winners are determined purely by chance.

switchers A market segment made up of consumers who often buy what is on sale or choose brands that offer discount coupons or other price incentives. Also called *variety* seekers.

symbolic value What a product or service means to consumers in a nonliteral way.

T

target audience A particular group of consumers singled out for an advertisement or advertising campaign.

target segment The subgroup (of the larger market) chosen as the focal point for the marketing program and advertising campaign.

taste A generalized set or orientation to consumer preferences.

telemarketing A direct-marketing medium that involves using the telephone to deliver a spoken appeal.

television households An estimate of the number of households that are in a market and own a television.

testimonial An advertisement in which an advocacy position is taken by a spokesperson.

third cover page The inside back cover of a magazine.

thought listing A type of pretest message research that tries to identify specific thoughts that may be generated by an advertisement.

three-point layout structure A print ad design that establishes three elements in an ad as dominant forces.

thumbnails, or **thumbnail sketches** The rough first drafts of an ad layout, about one-quarter the size of the finished ad.

TiVo A service that automatically records a consumer's favorite television shows every time they air and allows consumers to skip commercials.

top-level domain (TLD) The suffix that follows the Web site name.

top-of-the-mind awareness Keen consumer awareness of a certain brand, indicated by listing that brand first when asked to name a number of brands.

tracking studies Studies that document the apparent effect of advertising over time, assessing attitude change, knowledge, behavioral intent, and self-reported behavior. They are one of the most commonly used advertising and promotion research methods.

trade journals Magazines published specifically for members of a trade that carry highly technical articles.

trade-market sales promotion A type of sales promotion designed to motivate distributors, wholesalers, and retailers to stock and feature a firm's brand in their merchandising programs.

trade reseller Organizations in the marketing channel of distribution that buy products to resell to customers.

trade shows Events where several related products from many manufacturers are displayed and demonstrated to members of the trade.

transit advertising Advertising that appears as both interior and exterior displays on mass transit vehicles and at terminal and station platforms.

trial offers A type of sales promotion in which expensive items are offered on a trial basis to induce consumer trial of a brand.

trial usage An advertising objective to get consumers to use a product new to them on a trial basis.

type font A basic set of typeface letters.

U

ultrabroadband Wireless Internet technology allowing people to move extremely large files quickly over short distances.

unfair advertising Defined by Congress as "acts or practices that cause or are likely to cause substantial injury to consumers, which is not reasonably avoidable by consumers themselves and not outweighed by the countervailing benefits to consumers or competition."

unique selling proposition (USP) A promise contained in an advertisement in which the advertised brand offers a specific, unique, and relevant benefit to the consumer.

unit-of-sales approach An approach to advertising budgeting that allocates a specified dollar amount of advertising for each unit of a brand sold (or expected to be sold).

unmeasured media Media less-formally measured for advertising costs and effectiveness (as compared to the measured media): direct mail, catalogs, special events, and other ways to reach business and household consumers.

Usenet A collection of more than 13,000 discussion groups on the Internet.

user positioning A positioning option that focuses on a specific profile of the target user.

users The number of different people visiting X Web site during Y time.

V

value A perception by consumers that a product or service provides satisfaction beyond the cost incurred to acquire the product or service.

value proposition A statement of the functional, emotional, and self-expressive benefits delivered by the brand, which provide value to customers in the target segment.

values The defining expressions of culture, demonstrating in words and deeds what is important to a culture.

variety seekers *See* **switchers.**

variety seeking A decision-making mode in which consumers switch their selection among various brands in a given category in a random pattern.

V-chip A device that can block television programming based on the recently developed program rating system.

vertical cooperative advertising An advertising technique whereby a manufacturer and dealer (either a wholesaler or retailer) share the expense of advertising.

videotape An option for television ad production that is less expensive than film but also of lower quality.

viral marketing The process of consumers marketing to consumers over the Internet through word of mouth transmitted through e-mails and electronic mailing lists.

virtual mall A gateway to a group of Internet storefronts that provides access to mall sites by simply clicking on a storefront.

visits The number of occasions on which a user X looked up Y Web site during Z period of time.

W

white space In a print advertisement, space not filled with a headline, subhead, body copy, or illustration. White space is not just empty space: it is typically used to mark qualities that include luxury, elegance and simplicity.

WiFi Wireless technology allowing Internet access connections to reach out about 300 feet.

WiMax A wireless Internet technology similar to WiFi but capable of creating a hot spot with a range of 25-30 miles.

within-vehicle duplication Exposure to the same advertisement in the same media at different times.

World Wide Web (WWW) A universal database of information available to Internet users; its graphical environment makes navigation simple and exciting.

X, Y, Z

Zaltman Metaphor Elicitation Technique (ZMET) A research technique to draw out people's buried thoughts and feelings about products and brands by encouraging participants to think in terms of metaphors.

zapping The process of eliminating advertisements altogether from videotaped programs.

zipping The process of fast-forwarding through advertisements contained in videotaped programs.

NAME/BRAND/COMPANY INDEX

Page references in **bold** print indicate ads or photos. Page references in *italics* indicate tables, charts, or graphs. Page references followed by "n" indicate footnotes.

SUBJECT INDEX

Page references in **bold** print indicate ads or photos. Page references in *italics* indicate tables, charts, or graphs. Page references followed by "n" indicate footnotes.

CREDITS

Chapter 1

1.00 Courtesy of Taramax S.A. Switzerland
1.01 Courtesy, Evian Waters. Photo by Guzman; Model: Doug Mullins/Ford Agency LA
1.02 Courtesy of General Motors Corporation
1.03 Courtesy, Volkswagen of America
1.04 ©2001 American Advertising Federation. The Intel logo is used with the express written permission of Intel and is a trademark of Intel Corporation. The AAF thanks Intel Corporation for their support and participation. **1.05** Courtesy, Medpointe, Inc. **1.06** Health Education Authority **1.07** ©The Procter & Gamble Company. Used by permission. **1.08** ©EPA/Mark Lyons/Landov **1.09** ©Geof Kern **1.10** ©Geof Kern **1.11** ©Geof Kern **1.12** ©Geof Kern **1.14** Courtesy of The Coca-Cola Company. **1.15** ©2001, Blue Martini Software, Inc. **1.16** Courtesy of Rolex Watch U.S.A., Inc. **1.17** Courtesy of Rolex Watch U.S.A., Inc. **1.18** Courtesy of Daffy's. **1.19** Courtesy of Shapiro Luggage, Gifts, Leather **1.22** ©Disney Enterprises, Inc. & Sherwin Williams Paints **1.23** Weider Nutrition International ©1995. **1.24** Courtesy of Bayer HealthCare LLC, Consumer Care Division. **1.25** Courtesy of Taramax S.A. Switzerland **1.26** Courtesy, Hunter Fan Company **1.27** Courtesy of Ben & Jerry's® **1.28** ©The Procter & Gamble Company. Used by permission. **1.29** Matsushita Electric Corporation of America. **1.30** ©1996 National Fluid Milk Processor Promotion Board. Reprinted by permission of Bozell Worldwide, Inc. **1.31** Courtesy of State of Florida, Department of Citrus 1994/95. **1.32** Foote, Cone & Belding **1.33** Courtesy of Toshiba America Consumer Products, Inc. **1.34** Permission granted by The Franklin Mint and Sheffield Enterprises. **1.35** ©1995 Lever Brothers Company "All" Laundry Detergent, Courtesy of The Lever Brothers Company. **1.36** Reprinted by permission of American Plastic Council. **1.38** Ray-Ban Sunglasses by Bausch & Lomb. ©1995 Bausch & Lomb Incorporated. **1.39** United Airlines **1.40** Waterford Wedgwood USA, Inc. **1.41** Courtesy of Gucci.

Chapter 2

2.00 Courtesy, Porter Richter7, formerly FJC&N **2.01** WENN/Landov **2.02** Courtesy of DoubleClick. **2.06** Courtesy, Rocky Mt. Choppers **2.07** Used with permission of the American Red Cross **2.09** Bluestreak **2.10** The Xactmail Opt-in E-mail Network is a service of VentureDirect Worldwide, a Manhattan based Integrated Media Agency. **2.12** Courtesy, Porter Richter7, formerly FJC&N **2.14** Courtesy, Business Objects

SA **2.15** Courtesy, Hyperion **2.17** Starband Communications, Inc.

Chapter 3

3.00 Courtesy, General Mills Archives
3.01 Courtesy of Lever Brothers Company.
3.04 Courtesy, Unilever USA, Inc. **3.05** Reproduced with permission of Chevron U.S.A. Inc.
3.06 The Dial Corporation **3.07** Courtesy, Sonatron Radio Tubes **3.08** International Multifoods Corp. **3.09** Used with Permission of Eastman Kodak Company. **3.10** Courtesy, American Standard Companies **3.11** Courtesy, American Standard Companies **3.12** ©The Procter & Gamble Company. Used by permission. **3.13** Courtesy, General Mills Archives **3.14** Borden Foods Holdings **3.16** Reproduced from the Collections of the Library of Congress **3.19** "Coca-Cola"® is a registered trademark of The Coca-Cola Company. **3.20** Courtesy, Pennsylvania Railroad **3.21** Archive Photos, Inc. **3.22** Retrofile.com **3.23** Courtesy, Wyeth Consumer Healthcare **3.24** Courtesy, Ford Motor Company **3.25** Courtesy of IBM Corporation **3.27** Serta, Inc., Des Plains, IL **3.29** KELLOGG'S® and SPECIAL K® are trademarks of Kellogg Company. All rights reserved. Used with permission. **3.30** Courtesy, Ogilvy & Mather **3.31** Volkswagen of America, Inc. **3.32** History of Aviation Collection. Special Collections Department, McDermott Library, The University of Texas at Dallas **3.33** Courtesy of Goodyear Tire & Rubber Company **3.34** Pepsi-Cola Company **3.35** ©The Procter & Gamble Company. Used by permission. **3.36** Courtesy, Audiovox Corporation **3.37** Courtesy of Pfizer Inc. **3.38** Courtesy, Republican National Committee **3.39** Courtesy of MasterCard. **3.40** MTV advertisements used with permission by MTV. ©2004 MTV Networks. All Rights Reserved. MTV: MUSIC TELEVISION and all related titles, logos and characters are trademarks owned by Viacom International Inc. **3.41** Reproduced by kind permission of Red Card Immersion Marketing. **3.42** ©1998 MTV Networks. All rights reserved. MTV, MUSIC TELEVISION and all related titles, characters and logos are trademarks owned by MTV Networks, a division of Viacom International Inc. **3.43** Courtesy of NIKE **3.44** Courtesy, Patrick Cox & Wannabe **3.45** Photo courtesy of Target Stores, Minneapolis **3.46** Courtesy, Phoenix Footwear Group, Inc. **3.47** ©The Procter & Gamble Company. Used by permission.

3.48 Courtesy, The Steak 'N Shake Company **3.49** Pets.com **3.50** ©The Procter & Gamble Company. Used by permission. **3.51** Hugo Philpott/Reuters/Landov

Chapter 4

4.00 Courtesy, Miller Brewing Company
4.01 Buystream Inc. **4.02** Courtesy, Miller Brewing Company **4.03** Courtesy of Toyota Motor Sales, U.S.A., Inc; Advertising Agency, Saatchi & Saatchi. **4.04** Courtesy American Honda, Inc.
4.05 CLOROX®WIPES, Courtesy of The Clorox Company; Advertising Agency, DDB SF; Photographer: Leigh Beisch **4.06** Courtesy, Lachman Imports Inc. **4.07** Richard Avedon for Gianni Versace. **4.08** Courtesy, ©Unilever USA, Inc. **4.09** Extract used with kind permission of The Body Shop Int'l PLC UK. **4.10** ©The Procter & Gamble Company. Used by Permission.
4.11 ©Darlene Hammond/Archive Photos.
4.12 Partnership for a Drug Free America
4.13 Courtesy, S.C. Johnson & Son, Inc.
4.18 Courtesy, E-bay, Inc. **4.19** Courtesy of Luckysurf.com **4.20** www.donotcall.gov
IBP1.02a Courtesy of Northlich
IBP1.02b Courtesy of Northlich
IBP1.02c Courtesy of Northlich
IBP1.02d Courtesy of Northlich
IBP1.04a Courtesy of Northlich
IBP1.04b Courtesy of Northlich
IBP1.04c Courtesy of Northlich

Chapter 5

5.00 ©Christopher T. Allen **5.01** ©The Procter & Gamble Company. Used by Permission.
5.02 ®/™ STARBURST is a registered trademark of Mars, Incorporated and its affiliates. It is used with permission. Mars, Incorporated is not associated with South-Western Publishing. Advertisement printed with permission of Mars, Incorporated. ©Mars, Inc. 2005 **5.03** Courtesy, Johnson & Johnson **5.04** Courtesy of Colgate-Palmolive Company **5.05** ©The Procter & Gamble Company. Used by Permission. **5.06** Courtesy of Campbell Soup Company. **5.07** Courtesy of Northwest Airlines. **5.08** Casio, Inc. **5.09** The IAMS Company **5.11** Diamond Information Center **5.12** Courtesy, McDonald's. Inc.
5.14 ©Christopher T. Allen **5.15** Reprinted by arrangement with Sears, Roebuck and Co.
5.16 Used with permission of Unilever USA, Inc.
5.18 Convention & Visitors Bureau of Greater Cleveland **5.19** Singapore Tourism Board

5.20 ©Thomas O'Guinn **5.22** Paul Wakefield/B&A **5.23** ©Thomas O'Guinn **5.24** KRAFT® is a registered trademark. Used with permission of Kraft Foods. **5.25** Courtesy of SPLENDA® No Calorie Sweetner. **5.26** ©The Procter & Gamble Company. Used by Permission. **5.27** HORMEL® & CURE 81® are registered trademarks of Hormel Foods, LLC and are used with Permission of Hormel Foods. **5.28** ™/®"M&M's". "M" and the "M&M's" Characters are registered trademarks of Mars Incorporated and its affiliates. All are used with permission. Mars Incorporated is not associated with the Advertising and Integrated Brand Promotion or O'Guinn, Allen & Semenik, the authors. **5.29** G-Unit Clothing Company **5.30** AP/Topic Gallery **5.31** Chivas Regal and Chivas Brothers are trademarks of Chivas Brothers Limited. **5.32** Courtesy, Miller Brewing Company **5.33** Courtesy, Mastercard **5.34** ©Gonalco Productions, Inc./CBS **5.36** AP/Topic Gallery **5.37** Cramer-Krasselt/ Phoenix **5.38** ©Sesame Workshop. Sesame Street Tickles and their logos are trademarks and or service marks of Sesame Workshop. All rights reserved. **5.39** ©2004 Trimspa **5.40** AP/Topic Gallery **5.42** Reprinted with permission from the April 5, 2004 issue of ADVERTISING AGE. Copyright, ©Crain Communications Inc. 2004 **5.43** Reprinted with permission from the December 1, 2003 issue of ADVERTISING AGE. Copyright, ©Crain Communications Inc. 2003 **5.44** Courtesy of Wal-Mart, Inc. **5.45** ©1997 American Express Financial Division. **5.46** Ad concept by Mad Dogs & Englishmen; Illustration by Stuart Patterson **5.47** Commercial Closet Association **5.48** Courtesy of Saturn Corporation. **5.49** ©John McMurtrie/RETNA **5.51** Courtesy, Johnston & Murphy, Nashville, TN **5.52** ©Thomas O'Guinn

Chapter 6

6.00 ©2004 Hoyu Co., Ltd. **6.01** Courtesy of The Gillette Company **6.02** Courtesy of The Gillette Company **6.03** Courtesy, Energizer Holdings, Inc. **6.05** Neither the United States Marine Corp nor any other component of the Department of Defense has approved, endorsed, or authorized this product. USMC advertising creative by J. Walter Thompson **6.06** Courtesy of Hard Candy **6.07** Courtesy of Wells Fargo **6.08** Reprinted with permission of Simmons Market Research Bureau. **6.09** Reprinted with permission of Simmons Market Research Bureau.

6.10 Courtesy of Pillsbury Company; created by Foote, Cone & Belding **6.11** Courtesy of Pillsbury Company; created by Leo Burnett (Chicago) **6.13** Courtesy of TIGI Bed Head **6.14** Courtesy of TIGI Catwalk **6.15** Xerox Developing Markets Operations **6.16** ®2003 FedEx. Used with Permission. **6.17** Created in house by Svetlana Electron Devices. Creative Director: Terri Bates; Photographer: Jared Cassidy. **6.18** Copyright State Farm Mutual Automobile Insurance Company, 2003. Used by Permission. **6.19** Courtesy of Pontiac Division, General Motors Corporation **6.20** Courtesy, Colgate Palmolive Company **6.21** Courtesy of UNICEF; Ad Agency: Loyalty Partner GmbH, München **6.22** ©2004 Hoyu Co., Ltd. **6.23** ©Experimental & Applied Sciences, Inc. **6.24** Saatchi & Saatchi, New York **6.25** Courtesy of Nova Cruz Products & Lunar Design

Chapter 7

7.00 ©2004 and the TABASCO® marks, bottle and label designs are registered trademarks and serevice marks exclusively of McIlhenny Company, Avery Island, LA 70513. **7.01** Courtesy of Volkswagen of America Inc. **7.02** Used with Permission of General Motors Corporation. **7.03** ©Warner Brothers Entertainment, Inc. **7.05** S.C. Johnson—A Family Company **7.06** ©The Procter & Gamble Company. Used with permission **7.07** AP/Topic Gallery **7.09** U.S. Census Bureau **7.10a** Courtesy, Claritas **7.10b** Courtesy, Claritas **7.10c** Courtesy, Claritas **7.10d** Courtesy, Claritas **7.12** Courtesy, Google.com **7.14** Courtesy of The Coca-Cola Company **7.15** Client: Converse; Agency: Pyro, Dallas; Art Directors: Andy Mahr, Shannon; Copywriter: Todd Tilford, Gail Barlow, Josh Cannon. Photographer: Cheryl Dunn. **7.16** ©2004 and the TABASCO® marks, bottle and label designs are registered trademarks and serevice marks exclusively of McIlhenny Company, Avery Island, LA 70513. **7.17** Diamond Information Center **7.18** Reproduced Courtesy of Lever Bros. Co. **7.19** Reproduced Courtesy of Altoids; Ad Agency: Leo Burdett, Chicago. **7.20** Client: Mars. Agency: D'Arcy, London Art Director: Susan Byrne, Michelle Power. Copyrighter: Michelle Power, Susan Byrne. Photographer: Julie Fisher. **7.22** Courtesy, Bruzzone Research Company **7.23** Reprinted with Permission of General Motors Corporation. **7.24** Courtesy of Ford Motor Company **7.25** Used with Permission of General Motors Corporation

Group **11.20h** Courtesy, Azzuré Denim **11.20i** Volvo Cars of North America, LLC **11.21** Reprinted with permission from the April 5, 2004 issue of ADVERTISING AGE. Copyright ©Crain Communications Inc. 2004. **11.23** Courtesy of Electrolux **11.24** Center for Advanced Dental Studies, Las Vegas, NV **11.25** Courtesy of Wm. Wrigley Jr. Company **11.26** Courtesy, Miller Brewing Company **11.27** ©Disney Enterprises, Inc. **11.28** Cheryl Heller Design; Art Direction, copy Heller Communications **11.29** Redken For Men **11.30** Courtesy, Verizon Communications Inc. **11.31** Courtesy of Skyy Spirits. LLC, San Francisco, CA **11.32** Courtesy, Prada; Photographer: Norbert Schoerner **11.33a** Courtesy, Messner, Vetere, Berger, McNamee, Scjmettere/Euro RSCG; Photographer, Guzzman; Model: Jennifer Williams for T Models. **11.33b** Courtesy of Pernod-Ricard USA **11.33c** Sony Computer Entertainment America **11.34d** Courtesy, Diesel-StyleLab **11.33e** Image Courtesy of Kohler Co.

Chapter 12

12.00 Courtesy of The Cattlemen's Beef Board **12.01** Thomson Learning **12.02** Courtesy of Bartle, Bogle Hogarty LLC. By Rolling Stone LLC ©2002. All Rights Reserved. Reprinted by Permission. **12.03** Advertising Agency:TBWA/Paris for Nissan Europe. Used by Permission. **12.04** Courtesy, AVIS **12.05** Courtesy, Ogilvy & Mather **12.06** ©2001 MasterCard International Incorporated. **12.07** ©2001 MasterCard International Incorporated. **12.08** ©2001 MasterCard International Incorporated. **12.09** Societe Bic. Used by Permission. Advertising Agency: TBWA/Paris **12.10** Manolo Moran **12.11** Courtesy of Tangueray **12.12** ©2004 General Motors Corporation. Used by permission of HUMMER and General Motors. **12.13** Courtesy of Roxio, Inc. **12.14** Women.com was acquired by iVilliage in 2001. Used by permission of iVillage.com **12.15** Courtesy of the Dairy Council **12.16** Reprinted with permission of AT&T **12.17** Permission to reprint granted by Land Rover North America, Inc. **12.18** Courtesy of Oregon Food Bank **12.19** Courtesy of The Cattlemen's Beef Board **12.20** Courtesy of The Clorox Company **12.21** Courtesy of The American Cancer Society **12.22** Registered Trademark ®GarageBand.com **12.23** ©2004 Johnsonville Sausage, LLC **12.24** ©2004 Columbia Sportswear **12.25** John Michael Linck—toymaker—

www.woodcntoy.com **12.26** Goodby, Silverstein & Partners/San Francisco **12.26** Southwest Airlines **12.28** Cliff Freeman & Partners, New York **12.29** Stephen Frisch/Stock Boston **12.30** Courtesy of Honda **12.31** Courtesy of John Hancock Insurance Company **12.34** DILBERT©UFS. Reprinted by Permission.

Chapter 13

13.00 ©MINI, a division of BMW NA, LLC **13.01** Reprinted by permission of Homestore.com, Inc. **13.02** Ad created for Oddbins Ltd. By TBWA London; Illustrator: Andy Smith; Copywriter: Nigel Roberts; Art Director: Paul Bedford **13.03** Courtesy Ubachs Wisbrun **13.04** Courtesy of Volkswagen of America; Ad Agency: Arnold Worldwide, Boston **13.05** Kai Zastrow, Amsterdam **13.06** Courtesy of Beck & Co. **13.07** ©2004, Motorola, Inc. **13.08** ©2004, Motorola, Inc. **13.09** Oralabs, Inc. **13.10** Art Director: Mary Rich; Copy: Steven Meitelski; Photo: Craig Orsini. **13.11** ©MINI, a division of BMW NA, LLC **13.12** Courtesy, ESPN; Ad Agency: Wieden & Kennedy; Photographer: Collier Schorr/Art & Commerce; Model: Matthew Seife/Lifestyles **13.13** Courtesy of Parmalat **13.14** Land Rover North America **13.15** Courtesy of Volkswagen of America, Inc. **13.16** Courtesy of Volkswagen of America, Inc. **13.17** Client: Dockers®/Levi Strauss & Co.; Agency: Foote, Cone & Belding SF; Photographer: Tim Walker **13.18** Reprinted with permission from Hidesign **13.19** Client: The Epiphone Company, a division of Gibson Guitar Corp.; Agency: CORE, St. Louis; Creative Director: Eric Tilford; Art Director: Eric Tilford; Copy Writer: Wade Paschall; Strategy: Jeff Graham; Photographer: James Schwartz. **13.25** Pepsi-Cola North America **13.26** Courtesy of Kohler, Inc. **13.27** Reprinted by permission of Krispy Kreme Doughnut Corporation **13.28** 7UP and SEVEN UP© are registered trademarks of ©Dr. Pepper/Seven Up, Inc. 2000 **13.29** ©Kobal Collection **13.30** ©Paramount (Courtesy of Kobal Collection) **13.32** Used with permission of the Public Broadcasting Service. **13.33** Client: Balsen; Agency: Leo Burnett, Warsaw; Artists: Darek Zaorski, KC Ariwong; Copywriter: Kerry Keenan; Production Company: Stink; Photographer: Pep Bosch **13.34** Courtesy, Democratic National Committee **13.35** Courtesy of Miller Brewing Company. "Donut" television commercial. Jeff Williams: Art Director; Jeff Kling:

Writer; Susan Hoffman: Creative Director; Jeff Sels: Producer; Errol Morris: Director: @radical.media: Production Company; Wieden & Kennedy (Portland, OR); Ad Agency.
13.36 Courtesy of Hewlett Packard. **13.38** Courtesy of Miller Brewing Company **13.39** Courtesy of Miller Brewing Company **13.40a** ©Apple Computer, Inc. Used with permission. All rights reserved. Apple® and the Apple logo are register trademarks of Apple Computer. **13.40b** ©Universal (Courtesy Kobal Collection) **13.41a** ©Ladd Co. (Courtesy of Kobal Collection) **13.41b** 40 Acres and a Mule Filmworks
IBP3.01 Courtesy of Northlich
IBP3.02 Courtesy of Northlich
IBP3.03 Courtesy of Northlich
IBP3.04 Courtesy of Northlich

Chapter 14

14.00 GSN. The Network for Games/Seininger Advertising **14.01b** ©Bettmann/CORBIS **14.01c** EPA/Rhona Wise/Landov
14.03 Reprinted with permission from the November 10, 2004 issue of ADVERTISING AGE. Copyright ©Crain Communications Inc. 2004. **14.04** The Wall Street Journal **14.06** Shopping.com Ltd.—www.shopping.com **14.07** Ad courtesy of Telemundo Network, The NBC Agency and Red Tettemer. Photo Courtesy of Juan Manuel Garcia **14.12** ©2004 World Wrestling Entertainment, Inc. All Rights Reserved. **14.14** Courtesy, Saatchi & Saatchi: Michael Rausche, David Lebon, John Early **14.15** MTV advertisements used with permission by MTV. ©2004 MTV Networks. All Rights Reserved. MTV: MUSIC TELEVISION and all related titles, logos and characters are trademarks owned by Viacom International Inc.
14.17 ConAgra Foods, Inc. **14.20** Courtesy Shape Magazine Photography by Steve Shaw, Icon International; Model: Cari Rivador, LA Models **14.21** GSN. The Network for Games/Seiniger Advertising **14.22** Mens Health, Rodale, Inc. Photographer: Deborah Jaffe **14.23** Courtesy, Donner Advertising: Photos: ©Rausser/GETTY IMAGES; ©Photodisc/Getty Images **14.28** Word Entertainment, Inc.
14.29 Courtesy, Christie's, Inc. **14.30** Courtesy of Sunglasses Hut & Universal Studios

Chapter 15

15.00 Sirius Satellite Radio. Crative by Crispin, Porter & Bogusky, Miami. **15.01** ©MTVN. Used

by Permission. **15.03** Courtesy, Tire America **15.04** Reuters/Landov **15.05** Photography by Joe Higgins **15.06** Courtesy, Zale Corporation **15.07** Photo Courtesy of Pizza Hut **15.08** Reprinted by permission of Newspaper National Network. **15.09** Courtesy, Schwinn Corporation **15.12** Cover Photo by James McLaughlin/FPG From Men's Journal. March 1998. From Men's Journal LLC 1998. All rights reserved. Reprinted by Permission. **15.13** Courtesy, Ogilvy & Mather for Wilson **15.14** Clarins S.A. **15.15** AP/Topic Gallery **15.18** Company: Lenox Brands 1998; Agency: Grey Advertising NY **15.19** Courtesy, Fujitsu Computer Systems Corporation **15.22** ©2003 Speed Channel, Inc. **15.24** ©Sirius Satellite Radio. Crative by Crispin, Porter & Bogusky, Miami. **15.27** Courtesy, Clear Channel Worldwide

Chapter 16

16.00 Used with permission of CNET Networks, Inc. Copyright©1995–2004 CNET Networks, Inc. All rights reserved. **16.01** Copyright ©2003–2004 Ask Jeeves, Inc. All Rights Reserved. Ask Jeeves and Ask.com are registered trademarks of Ask Jeeves, Inc. **16.03** Reprinted by permission of PocketMail **16.05** Courtesy of Advertising.com **16.06** L-SoFT International, developers of LISTSERV® **16.07** Reproduced with permission of Yahoo! Inc. ©2004 by Yahoo! Inc. YAHOO! And the YAHOO! Logo are trademarks of Yahoo! Inc. **16.08** Used with permission of CNET Networks, Inc. Copyright ©1995–2004 CNET Networks, Inc. All Rights Reserved.
16.09 Latina.com 2002 **16.13** ©Health Grades, Inc. **16.14** Courtesy of Forrester. **16.15** Courtesy, InetGiant. Inc. **16.16** ©Saturn Corporation. Used with Permission **16.17** Permission granted by Binney & Smith **16.18** Copyright ©1998–2004 PrintingForLess.com **16.19** Copyright ©1999–2004 iWon.com. All Rights Reserved. iWon is a registered trademark of The Excite Network, Inc. **16.20** Courtesy, VeriSign Inc. **16.21** Courtesy DoubleClick **16.23** Nielsen Media Research **16.24** Courtesy of Broadworld, LLC; www.broadworld.com **16.25** ©2004, Motorola, Inc.
IBP4.01 Courtesy of Northlich
IBP4.02 Courtesy of Northlich
IBP4.03 Courtesy of Northlich
IBP4.04 Courtesy of Northlich
IBP4.05 Courtesy of Northlich
Career Profile Courtesy of Northlich

Chapter 17

17.00 Cincinnati Flying Pig Marathon; Photographer: Mark Bowen **17.01a** The Procter & Gamble Company. Used by Permission. **17.01b** The Procter & Gamble Company. Used by Permission. **17.01c** The Procter & Gamble Company. Used by Permission. **17.01d** The Procter & Gamble Company. Used by Permission. **17.02** ©The Procter & Gamble Company. Used by permission. **17.03** ©Susan Van Etten **17.04** ©Christopher T. Allen **17.05** ©Bettmann/ CORBIS **17.06** Courtesy of Horst Salons **17.07** ©Northlich **17.08** Courtesy, David Auerbach Opticians **17.09** ©Christopher T. Allen **17.10** ©Christopher T. Allen **17.11** ©Bob Kramer/Stock Boston **17.12** ©Christopher T. Allen **17.13** Reprinted by permission of TiVo **17.14** Cincinnati Flying Pig Marathon; Photographer: Mark Bowen **17.15** Courtesy of PUMA, INC.; Photographer: Warwick Saint. Used by Permission. **17.16** Courtesy of JBL Harman International **17.18** Chad Cameron/UPI/Landov **17.19** Robert Padgett/Reuters/Landov **17.20** BMW of North America, LLC **17.21** ©The Procter & Gamble Company. Used by permission. **17.22** ©The Procter & Gamble Company. Used by permission.

Chapter 18

18.00 AOL 9.0 Optimized ad ©2004 America Online, Inc. Used with permission. **18.01** Courtesy of The Gillette Company **18.02** Courtesy of Oreck Corporation, **18.05** Photo by Jeff Greenberg/Thomson Learning **18.06** Vitro Robertson **18.07** Courtesy, Campbell Soup Company **18.09** ©Susan Van Etten **18.10** GLAD® and ODOR SHIELD® are registered trademarks of The Glad Products Company. Used with Permission. **18.11** ©Susan Van Etten **18.12** Reprinted by permission of Marriott International, Inc. **18.13** Photo courtesy of Omega Ltd. **18.14** AOL 9.0 Optimized ad ©2004 America Online, Inc. Used with permission. **18.15** AOL 9.0 Optimized ad ©2004 America Online, Inc. Used with permission. **18.16** Courtesy, LuckySurf.com **18.17** ©Rachel Epstein/PhotoEdit **18.18** ©Bonnie Kamin/PhotoEdit **18.19** ©Novastock/Index Stock Imagery

Chapter 19

19.00 Courtesy, Wyoming Travel & Tourism **19.01** Courtesy of Best Buy Co., Inc. Minneapolis, MN **19.02** Adirondack Country Store www.adirondackcountrystore.com **19.04** TM & ©Road Runner ad courtesy of Warner Bros. Entertainment Inc. and ©Road Runner High Speed Internet **19.05** Courtesy, Stairmaster, Inc. Kirkland, Washington **19.06** Courtesy, Wyoming Travel & Tourism **19.07** ©Lands' End. Used with Permission. **19.08** ©Lands' End. Used with Permission. **19.09** Courtesy, Sunglass Hut International **19.10** Courtesy, Zero Knowledge Systems, Inc. **19.11** United States Postal Service **19.12** Courtesy of Colette Stewart, Owner of Montana Fleece & Flannel, Livingston, MT **19.13** Courtesy, Yesmail.com. Used with permission. **19.14** Courtesy of Oreck Corporation, New Orleans, Louisiana

Chapter 20

20.00 Courtesy, Elkay Corporation **20.01** Photography: Susan Van Etten **20.02** DILBERT Reprinted by Permission of United Feature Syndicate, Inc. **20.03** Pepsi-Cola North America **20.04** ©2000 JABRA Corporation **20.05** Myriad Genetics, Inc. **20.06** ©The Procter & Gamble Company. Used by permission. **20.07** Reprinted with Permission ©2002 The American Heart Association and Mercedes Benz; Ad Agency: Merkley & Partners; Photographer: Andy Bennett **20.08** Courtesy of Council for Biotechnology Information **20.09** Reprinted with special permission of King Features Syndicate. **20.10** Courtesy, Elkay Corporation **20.11** ©Michael Newman/ PhotoEdit **20.12** Permission granted by IIP through Creative Advertising **20.13** Bristol-Myers Squibb **20.14** Courtesy Anheuser Busch Companies, Inc.

IBP5.01 Courtesy of Northlich
IBP5.02 Courtesy of Northlich
IBP5.03 Courtesy of Northlich
IBP5.04 Courtesy of Northlich
IPB5.05 Courtesy of Northlich
IPB5.06 Courtesy of Northlich
IBP5.07 Courtesy of Northlich